New to the Fourth Edition

 **Chapter opening vignettes** from *Business Week* illustrate how chapter topics affect managers in the business world. End-of-chapter questions tied to the vignettes help students make the connections. In Chapter 4, for example, the *Business Week* article "Justice's Cartel Crackdown" underscores the importance of global managers' ethical and socially responsible behavior, while also pointing out that what is considered unethical in some countries may not be viewed as unethical in others.

Internet Exercises encourage students to explore the World Wide Web to answer relevant chapter questions. In Chapter 3's exercise, "Going World Wide With Wal-Mart," for example, students are directed to visit the Wal-Mart Web site and answer several questions, including, "What has Wal-Mart been doing over the last couple of years to increase its international presence?"

An **Internet Appendix**, following Chapter 1, examines the internet as a global information source, offers advice on the best way to conduct Web research, and provides an internet directory for international management.

Integrative Case Studies, now at the end of each part, are designed for strategic analysis and in-depth class discussion. The cases—such as Part 1's "Brazil and Argentina," "Israel: A Unique Member of the Global Community," "Colgate's Distasteful Toothpaste," and "Levi's Takes Its Ethical Aspirations International"—feature a variety of countries, organizations, and situations, helping students further relate text material to the real world of international management.

International Manager Skill-Building Exercises at the end of the text represent the three key topics covered in the text—culture, strategy, and behavior—and give students hands-on experience at international management. Try your hand at: "The Culture Quiz," "Using Gung Ho to Understand Cultural Differences," "When in Bogota," "The International Cola Alliance," and "Who to Hire."

International Management

Culture, Strategy, and Behavior

International Management

Culture, Strategy, and Behavior

Fourth Edition

Richard M. Hodgetts
Florida International University

Fred Luthans
University of Nebraska

Boston   Burr Ridge, IL   Dubuque, IA   Madison, WI
New York   San Francisco   St. Louis
Bangkok   Bogotá   Caracas   Lisbon   London
Madrid   Mexico City   Milan   New Delhi   Seoul
Singapore   Sydney   Taipei   Toronto

McGraw-Hill Higher Education ⚛

*A Division of The **McGraw-Hill** Companies*

INTERNATIONAL MANAGEMENT: CULTURE, STATEGY, AND BEHAVIOR

This book is printed on acid-free paper.

domestic   1 2 3 4 5 6 7 8 9 0 VNH/VNH 9 0 9 8 7 6 5 4 3 2 1 0 9
international 1 2 3 4 5 6 7 8 9 0 VNH/VNH 9 0 9 8 7 6 5 4 3 2 1 0 9

ISBN   0-07-228282-7

Vice president/Editor-in-chief: Michael W. Junior
Publisher: Craig S. Beytien
Senior sponsoring editor: Jennifer Roche
Senior developmental editor: Laura Hurst Spell
Marketing manager: Kenyetta Giles Haynes
Project manager: Pat Frederickson
Production supervisor: Kari Geltemeyer
Designer: Ellen Pettengell
Cover photo: P. Crowthers/S. Carter © Tony Stone Images
Photo research coordinator: Sharon Miller
Supplement coordinator: Cathy L. Tepper
Compositor: Precision Graphics
Typeface: 10/12 Times Roman
Printer: Von Hoffmann Press, Inc.

Library of Congress Cataloging-in-Publication Data

Hodgetts, Richard M.
        International management : culture, strategy and behavior /
    Richard M. Hodgetts, Fred Luthans. : 4th ed.
        p.   cm.
     ISBN   0-07-228282-7
     Includes index.
      1. International business enterprises -- Management.
     2. International business enterprises -- Management -- Case studies.
    I. Luthans, Fred.   II. Title.
    HD63.4.H63   2000
    658´.049 dc–21   9929270

INTERNATIONAL EDITION   ISBN 0-07-116958-X
Copyright © 2000. Exclusive rights by The McGraw-Hill Companies, Inc. for manufacture and
export.
This book cannot be re-exported from the country to which it is cosigned by McGraw-Hill.
The International Edition is not available in North America.

http://www.mhhe.com

Dedicated to

Henry H. Albers
Scholar, Mentor, and Friend

Preface

Along with the new millennium, the global economy, the borderless world, has finally arrived. The first three editions of this text were still trying to convince and prepare for the emerging global economy. Just as sure as the year 2000 is now upon us, so is the global economy. Fortunately, just like effective organizational learning, we feel that the development of this text over the years has not just reacted to the global environment, but instead has anticipated and proactively established a conceptual framework and content for international management. The previous edition introduced a number of new chapters and cases, while this edition can best be described by the Japanese term *kaizen* or "continuous improvement."

Along with information technology, international management is the major challenge facing organizations in the new millennium. All countries and companies now are part of the hypercompetitive global marketplace, which is sometimes referred to as the "3 Any's" environment—anyone, anywhere, anytime. Such an environment points to one incontestable fact: Students of management must now be knowledgeable about the international dimensions of management. Although much of this book and most of the examples are from the perspective of the United States, because most of the student readers will be Americans, it is recognized that a global perspective is needed and has become a reality. This is why a conscious effort is made to include as many different parts of the world as possible in the text discussion and cases.

We continue to take a *balanced approach* to this fourth edition of *International Management: Culture, Strategy, and Behavior.* We now emphasize this balanced approach in the new subtitle. Whereas other texts stress one of these, we feel that balance and the resulting synergy is needed for a true international management text and course. Thus, we have the following chapter distribution: Environment (4 chapters), Culture (4 chapters), Strategy (4 chapters), and organizational behavior/human resource management (5 chapters). The only change in conceptual framework from the previous edition is that the ethics chapter is moved from the back of the text to the front as part of the environmental foundation, Intercultural Communication is moved up to Part Two on Culture, and the Strategic Planning chapter now precedes the chapter on Managing Political Risk and Negotiations within the Strategic Management part. Obviously, since international management is such a dramatically changing field, all the chapters have been completely updated and improved. For example, there are about 10–15 new references (and thus real-world examples and research results) in each of the chapters.

The new and exciting dimension of this edition is the addition of a chapter opening article from *Business Week.* These are very recent, relevant, short news stories to get the readers' interest and attention before going into the chapter topic. A transition paragraph for the chapter follows these opening stories and at the end of each chapter, there is a new pedagogical feature titled *The World of Business Week Revisited.* This has a few discussion questions based on the opening news article that requires drawing from the chapter material in order to answer. As a teaching tool, suggested answers to these discussion questions are placed in the Instructor's Manual and also some multiple choice and true–false questions directly from the story are in the test bank for instructors who want to include this material in their tests.

Another new end-of-chapter feature is an *Internet Exercise.* The purpose of these exercises is to use the Internet to find information from web sites on prominent MNCs needed to answer relevant questions about the chapter topic. A new end-of-book feature is *International Manager Skill Building.* These in-class exercises represent the various parts of the text (culture, strategy, and behavior) and give hands-on experience and actual skill building. Finally, the use of cases is expanded. The two short end-of-chapter cases remain (and are updated). However, the intermediate length (3–4 pages) end-of-book cases are now positioned at the end of each part. About half of these cases are new to this edition. These cases were retained or newly selected for high-interest discussion and strategic analysis. Unlike the shorter end-of-chapter cases on a specific country (In the International Spotlight) and cases covering specific topics in the preceding chapter (You Be the International Consultant), which can be read and discussed in class, these longer, end-of-part cases normally would be read outside of class and then discussed in depth. Along with the boxed application examples within each chapter and other pedagogical features at the end of each chapter (e.g., Key Terms, Review and Discussion Questions, The World of *Business Week* Revisited, and Internet Exercise), the longer end-of-part cases provide the complete package for relating text material to the real world of international management.

To help instructors teach international management, this text is accompanied by a revised and expanded Instructor's Resource Manual and Test Bank. New to this edition are power-point presentation slides for each chapter and a set of videos complementing many of the key concepts and examples from the text.

International Management is generally recognized to be the first "mainline" text of its kind (strategy case books and specialized books in organizational behavior, human resources, and, of course, international business, finance, marketing, and economics preceded it, but there were no international management texts before this one) and is the market leader. We have had sustainability because of the effort and care put into the revisions. We hope you agree this Fourth Edition continues the tradition and remains the best "world-class" text for the study of international management.

We would like to acknowledge those who have helped to make this book a reality. Special thanks go to our growing number of colleagues throughout the world who have given us many ideas and inspired us to think internationally. Closer to home, we would like to give special recognition to two international management scholars who have had a direct influence on both of us. First is Henry H. Albers, former Chair of the Management Department at the University of Nebraska and former Dean at the University of Petroleum and Minerals, Saudi Arabia, to whom we have dedicated this book. He had a significant influence on our early careers and stimulated us to research and write in the field of management but, most importantly, to think internationally. More recently, we would like to acknowledge the influence of Sang M. Lee, currently Chair of the Management Department at Nebraska and President of the Pan Pacific Business Association. He is a true "Global-Academic," and we appreciate his stimulation, advice, and support. Also, we would like to thank Suzanne Peterson and Cathy Watson for their work on various stages of the manuscript.

In addition, we would like to acknowledge the help that we received from the many reviewers from around the globe, whose feedback guided us in preparing the fourth edition of the text.

Gunther S. Boroschek
  University of Massachusetts-Boston
Val Finnigan
  Leeds Metropolitan University
Richard C. Hoffman
  Salisbury State University
Johan Hough
  University of South Africa
Mohd Nazari Ismail
  University of Malaya
Douglas M. McCabe
  Georgetown University
Jeanne M. McNett
  Assumption College

Rebecca J. Morris
 University of Nebraska-Omaha
Ernst W. Neuland
 University of Pretoria
Richard B. Peterson
 University of Washington
Suzanne J. Peterson
 University of Nebraska-Lincoln
Joseph A. Petrick
 Wright State University
Dale V. Steinmann
 San Francisco State University
Aimee Wheaton
 Regis College
Corinne Young
 University of Tampa
Anatoly Zhuplev
 Loyola Marymount University

Our thanks, too, to the reviewers of previous editions of the text: Yohannan T. Abraham, Southwest Missouri State University; Kibok Baik, James Madison University; R.B. Barton, Murray State University; Mauritz Blonder, Hofstra University; Charles M. Byles, Virginia Commonwealth University; Helen Deresky, SUNY Plattsburgh; David M. Flynn, Hofstra University; Robert T. Green, University of Texas at Austin; Jean M. Hanebury, Salisbury State University; Robert Kuhne, Hofstra University; Robert C. Maddox, University of Tennessee; Ray Montagno, Ball State University; Yongsun Paik, Loyola Marymount University; Richard David Ramsey, Southeastern Louisiana University; Mansour Sharif-Zadeh, California State Polytechnic University, Pomona; Jane H. Standford, Texas A&M-Kingsville University; Randall Stross, San Jose State University; George Sutija, Florida International University; David Turnipseed, Georgia Southern College; Katheryn H. Ward, Chicago State University; and Marion M. White, James Madison University.

Thanks to the people at McGraw-Hill who worked on this book: Craig Beytien, Publisher; Jennifer Roche, Senior Sponsoring Editor; Kenyetta Giles Haynes, Marketing Manager; Pat Frederickson, Project Manager; and Michael Warrell, Designer.

Last, but by no means least, we greatly appreciate the love and support provided by our families—Sally, Steven, and Jennifer; and Kay, Kristin, Todd, Brett, Angie, Kyle, Dina, Paige, Kourtney, and Taylor.

Richard M. Hodgetts
Fred Luthans

About the Authors

RICHARD M. HODGETTS is a professor at Florida International University in the Department of Management and International Business. He is a Fellow of the Academy of Management and in 1999 he received the Academy's Distinguished Educator Award. In recent years, he has also been actively involved in international activity. He has lectured in Chile, Colombia, Denmark, Jamaica, Kuwait, Mexico, Peru, Taiwan, Uruguay, and Venezuela. In addition, he has worked with, among others, AT&T Technologies, Carrier Corporation, Digital Equipment, Exxon International, General Motors, Hewlett-Packard, Motorola, and Polaroid. He is the author of numerous texts, many of which have been translated and are used in countries around the world. Some of his latest articles include "Sustaining Competitive Advantage into the 21st Century: The Role of Human Resource Management," which appeared in the *National Productivity Review,* "Management in North America," which appeared in the *Concise International Encyclopedia of Business and Management,* and "The Use of High Performance Work Practices in Eastern European Organizations" that was published in the Pan Pacific Proceedings. In addition, he is the editor of the *Journal of Leadership Studies* and is the author of the "business" section of the latest editions of both Microsoft's *Encarta Encyclopedia* as well as the *World Book Encyclopedia.* He is also on the editorial boards of *Organizational Dynamics,* the *Journal of Business Research,* and the *Journal of Economics and Business.* His current international research focuses on developing international strategies for competing in the new millennium.

FRED LUTHANS is the George Holmes Distinguished Professor of Management at the University of Nebraska-Lincoln. He is also a senior research scientist with Gallup, Inc. He has been a visiting scholar at a number of colleges and universities and has lectured in most European and Pacific Rim countries. He has taught international management courses as a visiting faculty member at the Universities of Hawaii, Henley in England, Norwegian Management School, Monash in Australia, Macau, Chemnitz in the former East Germany, and Tirana in Albania. A past president of the Academy of Management, in 1997 he received the Academy's Distinguished Educator Award. Currently, he is editor-in-chief of the *Journal of World Business,* editor of *Organizational Dynamics,* and the author of numerous books. His book *Organizational Behavior* (Irwin/McGraw-Hill) is now in its eighth edition. He is one of very few management scholars who is a Fellow of the Academy of Management, the Decision Sciences Institute, and the Pan Pacific Business Association, and he has been a member of the Executive Committee for the Pan Pacific Conference since its beginning 16 years ago. This committee helps to organize the annual meeting held in Pacific Rim countries. He has been involved with some of the first empirical studies on motivation and behavioral management techniques and the analysis of managerial activities in Russia; these articles have been published in the *Academy of Management Journal, Journal of International Business Studies, Journal of World Business,* and *European Management Journal.* Since the very beginning of the transition to a market economy after the fall of communism in Eastern Europe, he continues to be actively involved in management education programs sponsored by the U.S. Agency for International Development in Albania and Macedonia, and U.S. Information Agency programs involving the Central Asian countries of Kazakhstan, Kyrgyzstan, and Tajikistan. Professor Luthans' most recent international research involves the relationship between psychological variables and attitudes and performance of managers and entrepreneurs across cultures.

Brief Contents

Contents

Part Four   **Organizational Behavior and Human Resource Management**

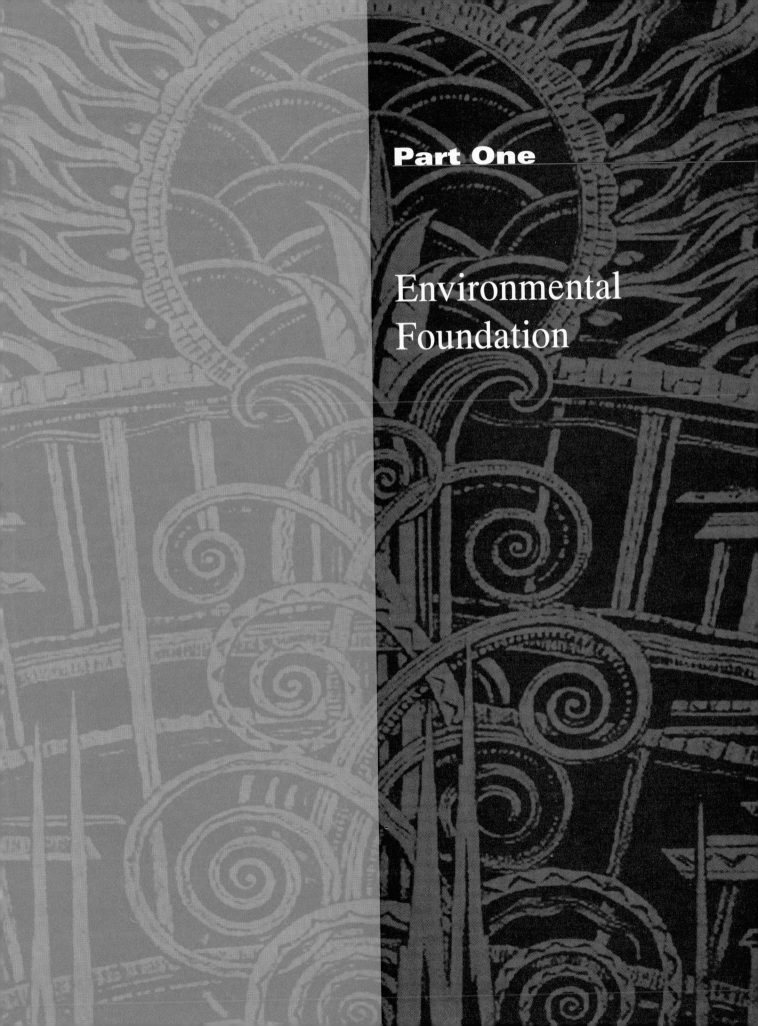

Part One

Environmental Foundation

Chapter 1

Worldwide Developments

Objectives of the Chapter

The global economy has arrived. In the United States, a dramatically increasing number of not only large corporations, but medium and small firms, are going international, and a growing percentage of overall revenue is coming from overseas markets. The same is true throughout Europe, Asia, and the rest of the world. As a result, international management, the process of applying management concepts and techniques in a multinational environment, is rapidly gaining importance.

Although there has been considerable historical evolution, the overriding focus of this opening chapter is to examine the worldwide developments of the last few years. The end of the cold war and the onset of the Information Age has created a new world and true global competition. These developments both create and influence the opportunities, challenges, and problems that managers in the international arena will face during the years ahead. Since the environment facing international management is so all encompassing, this chapter is mostly concerned with the economic dimensions and the next chapter is focused more on the political, legal and technological dimensions. The specific objectives of this chapter are:

1. REVIEW current trends in international investment and trade.

2. EXAMINE the present economic status in the major regions of the global community.

3. ANALYZE some of the major developments and issues in the various regions of the world.

BusinessWeek

The World of Business Week:

The Year of the Deal

The market is applauding the turnaround at France's Alcatel, but its hard-driving chief executive, Serge Tchuruk, isn't about to sit back yet. Investors are so pleased with Tchuruk's efforts to restructure the once troubled telecom equipment maker that they have nearly doubled its market value—to $34.9 billion—in the past year. Tchuruk's goal, though, is to make Alcatel a world leader in new technology and equipment for Internet communications. So, in early June, he took a big step, using his fat share price to buy Texas-based DSC Communications Corp. in a $4.4 billion stock deal.

Expect to see many more moves such as Tchuruk's in the coming age of the global deal. Alcatel's absorption of the U.S. company places it among a growing list of deals in the global consolidation sweepstakes. Others include Daimler Benz and Chrysler, Citicorp and Travelers, Northern Telecom and Bay Networks. This year's Global 1000 has more significance than ever. In the past, market value was considered a measure of corporate success or just plain bigness. But this year, the Global 1000 also is a measure of the merger power among the world's corporate elite. It wasn't too long ago that pundits were asking: "Is your company too big?" Now it is: "Is your company big enough?"

This year's list shows clearly that the Americans and Europeans are the ones with the clout. The Global 1000, using data compiled by Geneva-based

Morgan Stanley Capital International, ranks some 2,700 companies in 22 countries by market capitalization as of May 29. U.S. companies, as a group, have seen their stock prices rise some 37%. The U.S. now accounts for nearly half of the world's leading companies—a stunning 480—up 33 from last year. General Electric Co. is No. 1, with a market value of $271.6 billion. Meanwhile, European companies make up more than a third of the list—350 companies, up by 54. The stock prices of German companies have climbed 42%, while French shares are up 60%.

Continental Shifts

If the trend of European and U.S. dominance continues to play out, it's the Asians—particularly the Japanese—who stand to lose. Reflecting the seemingly never-ending travail in the region, Japanese companies saw their share prices shrink by 23% in U.S. dollar terms, and some 8% in yen terms. Some 66 Japanese companies have dropped off the Global 1000 altogether. Combined, the 116 survivors now account for just 8.5% of total market value of all 1,000 tallied.

Since the Global 1000 ranks market value in dollar terms, currency plays a role in who's up and who's down. But this year's shifts are driven largely by surging markets in Europe and the U.S., by investors' approval of industrial restructuring on the Continent, and by merger mania everywhere.

All three forces powered the historic merger of Daimler and Chrysler Corp. With its market value up 31% since last year, to $52.1 billion, Daimler had the

wherewithal to approach No. 3 U.S. automaker Chrysler as a serious buyer. By paying stock, Daimler CEO Jürgen Schrempp was able to finance the $39.5 billion deal without taking on debt. The result: a global giant offering everything from luxury autos to sport utility vehicles geared for drivers of the 21st century.

In industries ranging from autos to telecoms, analysts predict the merger craze will continue. Finance is sizzling. Towering above all finance megamergers, of course, is the Travelers-Citicorp deal, for $72.6 billion in stock. Banking consolidation is gathering pace in Europe as financial institutions prepare for monetary union in January. And smaller but important deals are happening in Japan, where barriers to foreign investors are tumbling under its Big Bang liberalization. Merrill Lynch & Co., for example, is reopening, under its own name, 33 branch offices of Yamaichi Securities Co., which collapsed last year.

Antitrust Angst

In telecommunications, meanwhile, the M&A action is wilder. From L. M. Ericsson in Sweden to Northern Telecom in Canada, telecom companies are in a race for partners that will help them create digital systems capable of carrying voice and data via mobile phones, satellites, or cable. The decision of AT&T and cable provider Tele-Communications Inc. to team up—in a pact worth $48 billion—is likely to spur further consolidation.

Of course, as the global deal engine roars along, there's no saying that all cross-border mergers—or even those in single markets—will work out. Last

International management
Process of applying management concepts and techniques in a multinational environment.

winter's failed $100 billion tieup of Glaxo Wellcome PLC and SmithKline Beecham PLC is a case in point. Antitrust worries also are delaying some pending agreements. European Union officials held up WorldCom Inc.'s $37 billion purchase of MCI Communications Corp. until MCI agreed to sell its major Internet businesses.

Still, it seems likely that corporations attuned to the forces of global competition will continue to look for new partners or acquisitions.

By Joseph Weber in Toronto, with bureau reports

www.alcatel.com

Source: Reprinted from July 13, 1998, pp. 52–53 issue of *Business Week* by special permission, copyright © 1998 by the McGraw-Hill Companies, Inc.

The news story that opens this chapter highlights one of the major trends associated with global competition. As barriers between nations are being removed and markets continue to surge, multinational corporations (MNCs) are turning to partnerships and acquisitions to become world leaders. From the automobile to telecommunications to banking industries, members of the Global 1000 are using their rising market values to pursue consolidation deals. As the article points out, it is not unusual for traditional corporate competitors to become fast friends. Evidence in point is the recent global dealings between Texas-based DSC Communications Corporation and France's Alcatel Telecom, Bay Networks and Northern Telecom, and Citicorp and Travelers. Such "merger mania" is allowing companies to not only flex their corporate muscles on the world stage, but also to increase their product lines. One of the year's biggest deals is Daimler Benz's purchase of U.S. automaker, Chrysler, which can now offer its drivers a wide array of vehicle choices. As you read this chapter, keep in mind how internationalization and worldwide developments will affect future global consolidation deals.

Introduction

The world of international management is changing rapidly, and one primary reason is because increased foreign investment and trade are bringing managers from one country into ongoing contact with those in others. For example, General Motors has been investing heavily in China over the last couple of years. The huge automaker recently announced that it was putting $100 million into a joint venture with a Chinese company to make pickup trucks and sport utility vehicles in northeast China. According to the terms of the agreement, the new venture will make Chevrolet Blazer sport utility vehicles and a revamped Chevrolet S-1 crew-cab pickup. Production will begin with 4,000 vehicles the first year and eventually increase to 50,000 vehicles annually. At the same time, GM has just completed a $1.5 billion plant in Shanghai, where Buicks will be manufactured.[1]

MNC
A firm having operations in more than one country, international sales, and a nationality mix of managers and owners.

GM is not alone in this new transnational environment. Increasingly, firms are finding that they must develop international management expertise. Managers from today's multinational firms must learn to work effectively with those from many different countries. MNCs can be defined as firms having operations in more than one country, international sales, and a nationality mix of managers and owners. For example, MNCs such as Ford Motor have operations in Mexico, Latin America, Europe, and Asia, as do Volkswagen and Toyota. International computer, electronics, and consumer-goods firms also fit the definition of MNCs. Examples include IBM, General Electric, Coca-Cola, Unilever, and PepsiCo. In fact, some MNCs depend on the international market for a large percentage of their total revenue. Table 1–1 reports the 20 American MNCs that garner the greatest amount of income from the international arena. As seen in the table, Exxon, General Motors, Mobil, Ford Motor, and IBM all have made in excess of $40 billion annually in recent years from their international operations. In addition, there are some American MNCs that earn well over 50 percent of their income from the international market.

Rank	Firm	Foreign Revenues (Millions of U.S. $)	Foreign Sales as % of Total Sales	Foreign Net Profits (Millions of U.S. $)	Foreign Net Profits as % Total
	Table 1–1				
	U.S. Firms with the Largest Foreign Revenue				
1	Exxon	92,540	76.9	5,072	60.0
2	General Motors	51,046	28.6	2,884	43.4
3	Ford Motor	46,991	32.3	2,232	24.4
4	IBM	45,845	58.4	3,717	61.0
5	Mobil	35,606	59.4	2,169	59.6
6	Texaco	33,292	55.6	1,313	50.4
7	General Electric	26,981	29.7	1,702	20.7
8	Hewlett-Packard	23,819	55.5	2,005	64.3
9	Chevron	23,055	47.2	2,009	61.7
10	Citicorp	21,566	62.2	2,498	69.6
11	Phillip Morris	19,797	35.3	1,188	18.8
12	Procter & Gamble	17,457	48.8	1,239	36.3
13	American Intl Group	16,461	53.8	2,292	68.8
14	E.I. du Pont de Nemours	16,283	41.0	1,240	51.6
15	Intel	14,017	55.9	2,256	32.5
16	Motorola	13,480	45.2	1,108	93.9
17	Xerox	12,371	57.4	810	55.8
18	Coca-Cola	12,357	65.5	3,100	75.1
19	Dow Chemical	11,271	56.3	773	40.5
20	Compaq Computer	11,153	45.4	722	38.9

Source: Reported in *Forbes,* July 27, 1998, pp. 163–164.

Examples include Digital Equipment, Eastman Kodak, the 3M Company, Colgate-Palmolive, Gillette, McDonald's, Crown, Cork & Seal, Avon Products, and Ralston Purina. In fact, of the 100 largest American MNCs, in recent years approximately one-third earn more annual income in the international market than in the domestic market.

The data in Table 1-1 point out two important findings. First, MNCs now must rely heavily on the international market for sales growth. Second, as the breadth and scope of their operations increase, small and medium sized firms will also need to address the impact of this development. Competitors will have to respond by going international and fighting harder for their local market share; suppliers and vendors will have to offer higher quality and competitive prices if they hope to get and hold business with these multinationals. The result has been an increasing internationalization of business.

Increasing Internationalization

International business is not a new phenomenon; however, the volume of international trade has increased dramatically over the last decade. Today, every nation and an increasing number of companies buy and sell goods in the international marketplace. A number of developments in regions around the world have helped to fuel this activity.

Regional Developments Impacting Internationalization

Although the status and issues facing major regions of the global economy are given detailed attention in the last part of this chapter, several important developments have had a direct impact on internationalization and should be noted. Some of the most important have been:

North American Free Trade Agreement (NAFTA)
A free trade agreement between the United States, Canada, and Mexico which has in essence removed all barriers to trade.

1. The United States, Canada, and Mexico make up the **North American Free Trade Agreement (NAFTA),** which in essence has removed all barriers to trade between these countries and created a huge North American market. This market eventually will be expanded to include Latin American countries as well. Chile will probably join NAFTA in the near future, and others, such as Argentina and Brazil, are likely to follow. The result may be a giant "American Market" that would parallel similar developments in Europe and Asia.

2. The European Union (EU) is now well on its way to creating a unified market that many have described as the United States of Europe. This group consists of 15 nations including Austria, Belgium, Denmark, Finland, France, Germany, Great Britain, Greece, Holland, Ireland, Italy, Luxembourg, Portugal, Spain, and Sweden. Not only have most trade barriers between the members been removed, but the group has adopted a unified currency called the "euro." In 1998, eleven of these countries agreed to the exchange rate between their respective currencies and the euro. Table 1–2 provides these data. It should be pointed out that the nonparticipating countries will trade in the euro so they are in essence participating by default. As a result of this agreement, it will now be possible for customers to compare prices between countries because everything can be done in a uniform currency. In other words, most of the business done in the EU will be in euros.[2] Of even more importance is that the EU is better integrated as a single market than either NAFTA or the allied Asian countries. Additionally, other nations such as Turkey have applied for membership. In the near future, the former communist bloc countries of Central and Eastern Europe undoubtedly also will become part of the EU. For example, Poland, Hungary, and the Czech Republic are already taking steps toward membership, and others such as Albania, Romania, Slovakia, Lithuania, Latvia, Estonia, and Bulgaria have the goal to become members. Once East and West join together, the result will be a giant economic market that no major MNC can afford to ignore.

World Trade Organization
Started in 1995 to replace GATT, the WTO has power to enforce rulings in trade disputes and monitor trade practices.

3. The most recent changes of the General Agreement on Tariffs and Trade (GATT) are stimulating increased world trade. Under the new agreement, tariffs will be reduced worldwide by 38 percent, and in some cases eliminated completely. The percentage of products entering the United States duty free will rise from the current 10 percent to 40 percent, and for industrialized countries worldwide, the percentage will rise from 20 to 44. Under the new agreement, GATT itself has been replaced by the **World Trade Organization (WTO),** which came into existence on January 1, 1995.[3] The WTO has more power to enforce rulings on trade disputes and create a more efficient system for monitoring trade policies. Perhaps most important, however, is that the vast majority of former GATT

Table 1–2
Exchange Rates and the Euro

Country	Currency	Dollar Rate	Euro Rate
Austria	Schilling	0.08	13.91
Belgium	Franc	0.271	40.78
Finland	Mark	0.1842	6.01
France	Franc	0.1666	6.35
Germany	Mark	0.558	1.98
Ireland	Punt	1.4058	0.80
Italy	Lira	0.000566	1958.0
Luxembourg	Guilder	0.496	2.23
Portugal	Escudo	0.00545	202.70
Spain	Pesata	0.00658	168.20

Source: Reported in the *Wall Street Journal,* May 4, 1998, p. A17.

members have agreed to join the WTO. World economic powers such as the EU, United States, Canada, and Japan are now part of the WTO. Collectively, 126 nations who have joined so far account for about 90 percent of world trade.

4. Although Japan has experienced economic problems throughout the 1990s, it continues to be the primary economic force in the Pacific Rim. Japan recently has invested relatively more in its own backyard of Asia than in any other part of the world. Japanese MNCs want to take advantage of the underdeveloped and, until recently, the rapidly growing Asian markets. At the same time, China is proving to be a major economic force (some experts forecast that China eventually will be the biggest economy in the world). Although all of the economies in Asia are now feeling the impact of the economic downturn starting in the middle of 1997, the Four Tigers (Hong Kong, Taiwan, South Korea, and Singapore) have arrived as developed economies and the Southeast Asia countries of Malaysia, Thailand, Indonesia, and most recently, Vietnam, should bounce back to become major export-driven economies. As in other parts of the world, an economic bloc called ASEAN (Association of Southeast Asian Nations) made up of Indonesia, Malaysia, the Philippines, Singapore, Brunei, Thailand, and in recent years Cambodia, Myanmar, and Vietnam, promotes exports to other countries.

5. Central and Eastern Europe, Russia, and the other republics of the former Soviet Union currently are still trying to make the transition to market economies. Although the Czech Republic, Slovenia, Poland, and Hungary have basically completed the process, the others (the Balkan countries, Russia, and the other republics of the former Soviet Union), still have a long way to go. However, all are a target for MNCs looking for expansion opportunities. For example, after the fall of the Berlin Wall in 1989, Coca-Cola quickly began to sever its relations with most of the state-run bottling companies in the former communist bloc countries. The soft drink giant began investing heavily to import its own manufacturing, distribution, and marketing techniques. To date, Coca-Cola has pumped billions into Central and Eastern Europe—and this investment is beginning to pay off. Its business in Central and Eastern Europe has been expanding at twice the rate of its other foreign operations. For example, in Romania, which Coca-Cola entered in 1992, Coke is the dominant soft drink, outselling competitor Pepsi, which has been there for years, by a ratio of 2:1.[4]

6. Economic activity in Latin America continues to increase. Despite the political and economic setbacks these countries periodically experience, economic growth and exports continue in Argentina, Chile, Venezuela, and Mexico. Additionally, while outside MNCs continually target this geographic area, there also is a great deal of cross-border investments between Latin American countries. A number of regional trade agreements are helping in this cross-border process, including Mercosur, a common market created by Argentina, Brazil, Paraguay, and Uruguay, and the Andean Common Market, a subregional free trade compact that is designed to promote economic and social integration and cooperation between Bolivia, Colombia, Ecuador, Peru, and Venezuela.[5]

7. There also is recent economic progress among less developed nations. A good example is India, which for years has had a love–hate relationship with multinational businesses. The Indian government has been known for its slow-moving bureaucracy and this has been a major stumbling block in attracting foreign capital. Over the last few years, however, there has been a dramatic turnaround in government policy, and a growing number of multinationals recently have been attracted to India. Much of this spurt has resulted from the current Indian government's willingness to reduce the bureaucratic red tape that accompanies the necessary approvals to move forward with investments.[6]

These are specific, geographic examples of emerging internationalism. Equally important to this new climate of globalization, however, are the recent developments in both international investment and trade.

International Investment and Trade

Approximately 80 percent of all international investments come from developed countries. For example, foreign direct investment (FDI), the term used to indicate the amount invested in another country, in the United States currently stands at over $600 billion, while U.S. FDI is almost $800 billion. The largest investors in the United States in recent years have been Great Britain, Japan, the Netherlands, Germany, and Canada. Conversely, the major stake for U.S. investors has been the EU, followed by Canada, and then Japan. Tables 1–3 and 1–4 provide additional information on FDI in the United States and by U.S. investors.

Research reveals that as nations have become more affluent, they have pursued FDI in geographic areas that have economic growth potential. Because of their economic prob-

Table 1–3
Foreign Direct Investment in the United States

Country/Region	Millions of U.S. $	Percent of All Countries
All countries	630,045	100.0
Canada	53,845	8.5
Europe	410,425	65.1
France	49,307	7.8
Germany	62,242	9.9
Netherlands	73,803	11.7
United Kingdom	142,607	22.6
Latin America and other		
Western Hemisphere	24,627	3.9
Brazil	591	0.1
Mexico	1,078	0.2
Africa	717	0.1
Middle East	6,177	1.0
Asia and Pacific Rim	134,255	21.3
Australia	9,747	1.5
Japan	118,116	18.7

Source: U.S. Department of Commerce, *Survey of Current Business,* March 1998.

Table 1–4
Foreign Direct Investment by the United States

Country/Region	Millions of U.S. $	Percent of All Countries
All countries	796,494	100.0
Canada	91,487	11.5
Europe	399,632	50.2
France	34,000	4.3
Germany	44,259	5.6
Netherlands	44,667	5.6
United Kingdom	142,560	17.9
Latin America and other		
Western Hemisphere	144,209	18.1
Brazil	26,166	3.3
Mexico	18,747	2.4
Africa	7,568	1.0
Middle East	8,743	1.1
Asia and Pacific Rim	140,402	17.6
Australia	28,769	3.6
Japan	39,593	5.0

Source: U.S. Department of Commerce, *Survey of Current Business,* March 1998.

lems in the 1990s, Japanese FDI has leveled off, but they still have a heavy commitment to the EU. Since 1985 they have more than tripled the percentage of their FDI there. A large percentage of these funds are in manufacturing, but there are also substantial holdings in the banking and insurance sectors. One reason for this strategy has been the projected growth for the EU in the coming years. Another reason is the increasing barriers to entry into the EU market, making it more profitable to be on the inside than on the outside. U.S. and Canadian MNCs have been investing in the EU for similar reasons.

Japanese and European MNCs have substantial investment in the United States. However, for a number of years Japanese firms have reduced their investment in the U.S. market and instead are putting it into emerging economies. With the downturn of the Asian economies, this decision may seem unwise, but now some MNCs throughout the world see the downturn of Asian economies as an opportunity to gain a foothold at reduced prices. For example, GE Capital has recently carried out a host of deals in Asia. In Thailand, the company agreed to acquire a majority stake in a charge-card issuer, boosted to 100 percent its ownership of an auto financing business, and purchased a 49 percent stake in a consumer finance company. GE Capital has also entered Japan's insurance market for the first time with a $575 million investment in a new joint venture with Toho Mutual Life Insurance Company.[7] GE Capital is not alone. Merrill Lynch is taking over 33 branches of the Japanese Yamaichi Securities firm, and Coca-Cola has bought a 50 percent interest in a Thai bottler. Other examples are provided in Table 1–5.

U.S. investment goes to Canada, Latin America, and Europe, and a much smaller relative amount goes to Asia. However, Asia, in spite of recent problems, cannot be overlooked because of its market potential. China alone has 1.2 billion people, and more and more of them are becoming consumers of MNC products and services. On the other hand, European MNCs have been targeting Eastern Europe in recent years as well as Asia.

Besides international investment, trade has increased substantially over the last decade as well. For example, in 1983, the United States exported slightly over $200 billion of goods and services and imported $269 billion of goods and services. By 1996 exports were in the range of $580 billion annually, and imports were over $770 billion. In other words, during this 13-year period, the United States almost tripled its trade with the rest of the world.

Table 1–5
Recent Asian Acquisitions by American Investors

Investor	Company Being Purchased	Purchase Price
Travelers and Salomon Smith Barney	Nikko Securities (25% stake in Japanese operation)	$1.6 billion
Associates First Capital	DIC Finance, 90% stake (Japan)	$995 million
AES	Hanwha Energy power plant (South Korea)	$870 million
Adaptec	Symbios (South Korea)	$775 million
Investment group including George Soros, Enron, and Steel Dynamics	Nakornthal Strill Mill (Thailand)	$650 million
Goldman Sachs	Office building/Yamato Mutual Life (Japan)	$455 million
Coca-Cola	Doosan Beverage facility (South Korea)	$441 million
NCR Corporation	NCR Japan, 30% stake	$304 million
American Skiing	Steamboat and Heavenly ski resorts (Japan)	$288 million

Source: Reported in *USA Today,* June 10, 1998, p. 4B.

The EU countries, mainly because of within-EU trading, had even more dramatic activity. In 1983, they exported almost $600 billion of goods and services while importing just over $625 billion of goods and services. By 1996 their exports were $1911 billion, and imports were $1902 billion.

Japan's increased trade has also been vigorous. In 1983, Japanese exports and imports were $147 and $126 billion, respectively. By 1996 exports had risen to $443 billion, and imports stood at $336 billion.

What is particularly interesting about these data is that the *percentage* of world trade that is accounted for by the three major trading blocs of the United States, the EU, and Japan, has remained fairly consistent. Between 1983 and 1996, this group's share of world exports rose from 56.5 percent to 59.2 percent. During this same period, its share of world imports rose slightly, from 59.4 percent to 59.8 percent. Simply stated, this triad accounts for most of the world's international trade, and the United States is the major economic power among the three. As seen in Table 1–6, the United States sells over $600 billion of goods and services to its top 10 trading partners and, in turn, buys over $800 billion of goods and services from them. In other words, the U.S. imports more than it exports. This trade deficit soared to $168.8 billion in 1998, breaking the old record of $153.3 billion set in 1987.[8]

Trade barriers continue to fall (as discussed earlier with the new GATT agreement and creation of the WTO), so the amount of trade undoubtedly will continue to rise. Moreover, recent statistics show that most developed countries now export a growing share of their output.

At the beginning of the new century, exports are projected to rise, even though there was a slight decline in 1998 in the U.S. and the nature of the trade flows is likely to change. For example, the percentage of exports that the United States sells to Japan, public perception to the contrary, has begun to shrink. U.S. sales to Japan are still enormous, but exports to Japan are at a lower rate than to other countries. U.S. MNCs are finding more lucrative markets—and the same is true for Japan. Both are turning their attention to emerging markets. Additionally, as nations become more economically interdependent and national currencies better adjusted to reflect both strengths and weaknesses, trade flow will adjust accordingly.

Finally, it is important to note that foreign investment and trade do not rely exclusively on MNCs exporting or setting up operations locally. In some cases, it is far easier to buy a domestic firm. Beer companies, for example, are finding that customers like local products, so rather than trying to sell them an imported beer, the MNC will invest in or buy a local brewery. Moreover, the name of the local company may remain the same, so

Table 1–6				
The Top 10 Trading Partners of the United States				
Rank	Importing Country	U.S. Exports (in Millions of Dollars)	Exporting Country	U.S. Imports (Millions of Dollars)
1	Canada	132,584	Canada	159,746
2	Japan	67,536	Japan	117,963
3	Mexico	56,761	Mexico	74,111
4	United Kingdom	30,916	China	54,409
5	Germany	23,474	Germany	39,989
6	Korea	23,297	Taiwan	31,023
7	Taiwan	18,413	United Kingdom	29,700
8	Singapore	16,686	Korea	23,297
9	Netherlands	16,614	Singapore	20,648
10	France	14,413	Malaysia	18,331
	Other	222,251	Other	248,568
	Total exports	622,945	Total imports	817,785

Source: Adapted from the International Monetary Fund, 1997 Directory of Trade Statistics.

that many local residents are unaware that the firm has changed hands. To illustrate this point, answer the following questions about well-known products sold in the United States, then check your answers at the end of the chapter:

1. Where is the parent company of Braun household appliances (electric shavers, coffee markers, etc.) located?
   a. Switzerland   *b.* Germany   *c.* the United States   *d.* Japan

2. The BIC pen company is
   a. Japanese   *b.* British   *c.* American   *d.* French

3. The company that owns Häagen-Dazs ice cream is in:
   a. Germany   *b.* Great Britain   *c.* Sweden   *d.* Japan

4. RCA television sets are produced by a company based in:
   a. France   *b.* the United States   *c.* Malaysia   *d.* Taiwan

5. The firm that owns Green Giant vegetables is:
   a. American   *b.* Canadian   *c.* British   *d.* Italian

6. The owners of Godiva chocolate are:
   a. American   *b.* Swiss   *c.* Dutch   *d.* Swedish

7. The company that produces Vaseline is:
   a. French   *b.* Anglo-Dutch   *c.* German   *d.* American

8. Wrangler jeans are made by a company that is:
   a. Japanese   *b.* Taiwanese   *c.* British   *d.* American

9. The company that owns Holiday Inn is headquartered in:
   a. Saudi Arabia   *b.* France   *c.* the United States   *d.* Britain

10. Tropicana orange juice is owned by a company that is headquartered in:
    a. Mexico   *b.* Canada   *c.* the United States   *d.* Japan

This quiz helps to illustrate how transnational today's MNCs have become. This trend is not restricted to firms in North America, Europe, or Asia. An emerging global community is becoming increasingly interdependent economically. Although there may be a true, totally integrated global market in the near future, at present regionalization, as represented by North America, Europe, Asia, and the less developed countries, is most descriptive of the world economy.

The Economic Status and Issues of the Major Regions

International investment and trade are more likely to occur between nations in close geographic proximity; for example, in North America, Mexico and Canada are two of the United States' largest trading partners. However, there also is a growing trend toward expanding these horizons and doing business with nations thousands of miles away. For example, Japan is a major trading partner of the United States, and China does more business with the United States than with most other nations. The following sections examine trends that are occurring in each major region of the world and the impact of these developments on international management.

North America

As noted earlier, North America constitutes one of the three largest trading blocs in the world. The combined purchasing power of the United States, Canada, and Mexico is close to $9 trillion. In 1989, the United States and Canada signed a free trade agreement, and in 1994, Mexico officially joined, thereby creating the North American Free Trade Agreement

(NAFTA). A number of economic developments have occurred because of this agreement, and all are designed to remove trade barriers and promote commerce between these three countries. Some of the more important include: (1) the elimination of tariffs as well as import and export quotas; (2) the opening of government procurement markets to companies in the other two nations; (3) an increase in the opportunity to make investments in each others' country; (4) an increase in the ease of travel between countries; and (5) the removal of restrictions on agricultural products, auto parts, and energy goods.[9]

The NAFTA provisions will take place over time. For example, in the case of Mexico, the most recent country to join, quotas on Mexican products in the textile and apparel sectors will be phased out, and customs duties on all textile and apparel products will be completely eliminated by the year 2004. At the same time, investment in Mexico will be easier for Canadian and U.S. businesses. In the automotive sector, Mexico will allow 51 percent ownership of auto and truck companies by 2001, and 100 percent by 2004. Steps such as these will go far toward creating a unified trading bloc. Even though there will be more integration both globally and regionally, effective international management still requires knowledge of individual countries.

United States   U.S. MNCs have holdings throughout the world. In Europe, General Motors and Ford command dominant market positions, and they are finally beginning to make inroads in Japan as well. U.S. MNCs also do extremely well in the European computer market and are becoming a major force in this industry throughout the Pacific Rim. Telecommunications is another high-tech area where the United States has been garnering international market share. U.S. firms compete with each other in the international arena as well. For example, AT&T now finds itself getting international competition from the U.S. "Baby Bells" (the regional firms that used to be part of AT&T). These firms are becoming more interested in expanding their market coverage and meeting the growing worldwide demand for higher-quality telephone services.[10]

U.S. consumer-goods companies also are finding overseas markets to be very attractive. For example, Coca-Cola has a soft drink plant and distribution operation in Moscow and, as stated earlier, is vigorously targeting Eastern Europe. Toys "R" Us has expanded in Germany and Japan, and it is gaining market share in both locales. U.S. airline companies, such as Delta, United, and American, also are vigorously expanding into Europe.

At the same time, foreign MNCs are finding the United States to be a lucrative market for expansion. BMW has set up operations in South Carolina, and Mercedes produces a lower-priced car ($20,000 range) in Alabama designed to help it gain U.S. market share. Additionally, the United States has again become an attractive target for acquisitions. In 1994, the United States replaced China as the country in which the greatest annual foreign direct investment was made. As pointed out in the chapter-opening *Business Week* story, besides the highly visible Daimler Benz and Chrysler merger, other examples of outside investment in the United States include SmithKline Beecham PLC of Britain, which paid almost $3 billion to acquire the over-the-counter drug business of Sterling Winthrop, Inc., an Eastman Kodak unit.[11] Hoechst AG of Germany paid over $7 billion for Marion Merrell Dow, Inc., a Dow Chemical subsidiary.[12] France Telecom and Deutsche Telecom combined to pay over $4 billion for a 20 percent stake in the Sprint Corporation.[13]

Even though Japanese firms are going to Asia more than in the past, they now are turning to the United States to find suppliers who can help increase the quality of their products while keeping down costs. Ricoh, for example, is purchasing customized microcontrollers from Motorola that allow a digital office copier to double as a high-quality printer or fax machine. Toyota, Isuzu, and Suzuki all are buying antilock brake systems from General Motors. IBM is selling computers to Mitsubishi Electric, and Sun Microsystems Inc. is selling workstations to Japanese firms. Understanding these developments in the United States contributes to the field of international management.[14]

Canada   Canada is the United States' largest trading partner, a position it has held for many years. The United States also has considerable foreign direct investment in Canada, more than in any other country except the United Kingdom (see Table 1–4). This helps to explain why most of the largest foreign-owned companies in Canada are totally, or heavily, U.S.-owned.

The legal and business environment in Canada is similar to that in the United States, and this similarity helps to promote trade between the two countries. Geography, language, and culture also help, as does NAFTA, which will help Canadian firms become more competitive worldwide. They will have to be able to go head-to-head with their U.S. and Mexican competitors as trade barriers are removed. This should result in greater efficiency and market prowess on the part of the Canadian firms, which must compete successfully or go out of business.

In recent years, Canadian firms have begun investing heavily in the United States. For example, Canadian Pacific has purchased the Delaware & Hudson Railway, and Bombardier, Inc., has bought the Learjet Corporation of Wichita, Kansas. Meanwhile, Bronfman, Inc., best known for its Canadian whiskeys, sold its large stake in Du Pont for $1.4 billion (less than market value) to buy 80 percent of MCA[15] (now called Universal) and recently purchased Polygram, the largest music company in the world.[16] Canadian firms also do business in many other countries, including Mexico, Great Britain, Germany, and Japan, where they find ready markets for Canada's vast natural resources, including lumber, natural gas, crude petroleum, and agriproducts.

At the same time, Canada is becoming a target for increased international investment, especially by firms from the United States. American, Delta, and Northwest airlines all have expanded their Canadian routes. Chrysler, Ford, and General Motors all have plants in Canada, and so do other major U.S. MNCs, including IBM, Kodak, and Xerox. Again, a major reason for this outside investment is to tap Canada's vast natural resources, which offer a potential bonanza to enterprising firms. Another reason is the growing population and increasing purchasing power of the country. Still another is the chance to take advantage of the opportunities provided under the NAFTA provisions.

Mexico   By the early 1990s, Mexico had recovered from its economic problems of the previous decade and become the strongest economy in Latin America. In 1994, Mexico became part of NAFTA, and it appeared to be on the verge of becoming the major economic power in Central and South America. The country's economic optimism proved to be short-lived, however. By late 1994, the value of the peso collapsed, and the economy took a nose-dive. By early 1995, the United States, the International Monetary Fund, and the Bank for International Settlements were teaming up to create a $50 billion assistance package.[17] At the same time, the government of Mexico was instituting a number of important economic changes, which included cutting the federal budget (thus holding down the country's spiraling deficit), instituting wage and price controls to limit growing inflation, and privatizing more state-held businesses to raise money and stimulate economic growth.[18] These moves helped to bring the Mexican economy back on its course, and the loans were paid back before they were due. Since 1996 the Mexican economy has generally been doing well, but dependence on oil prices and other cyclical impacts still make for a volatile situation.

At the same time, there have been some very positive developments that bode well for the future. For example, Mexico has built a very strong **maquiladora industry.** Long before NAFTA, this was an arrangement by the Mexican government that permitted foreign manufacturers to send materials to their Mexican-based plants, process or assemble the products, and then ship them back out of Mexico with only the value added being taxed. Ford Motor, for example, took advantage of this opportunity and annually exports over 250,000 engines from its Chihuahua plant to the United States. General Motors assembles 3 million car radios a year in its Matamoros plant for shipment north. Hundreds of other large firms have followed suit, taking advantage of the low-cost, but quality conscious, Mexican workforce.

U.S. labor unions argue that this arrangement has cost many jobs in the United States, but the U.S. Department of Labor reports that *maquiladora* operations actually support jobs by helping U.S. firms maintain their international competitiveness. For example, Packard Electric has noted that without *maquiladora* operations, it would have closed its Warren, Ohio, plant and moved everything to Southeast Asia. The argument that the close

Maquiladora industry
Derived from the Spanish word for the fee that a miller collected for processing grain that now represents the arrangement created by the Mexican government that permits the flow of materials and products in and out of Mexico with only the value added being taxed.

economic relationship with Mexico is mutually rewarding, such as in the U.S. auto industry, has been summarized by one analyst as follows:

> In a larger sense, both countries have a lot to gain from the continued development of the Mexican industry. The U.S. wants a prosperous, stable Mexico, and the automobile industry is a magnificent engine for raising unskilled workers into the middle class. It creates not only better-paying jobs but also a class of skilled workers and managers, and demand for roads, services, gas stations, drive-ins, repairs. Perhaps, most important, it creates mobility and enables people to look about for the best job, the best price, the best place to live. Yes, growth of the Mexican industry will cost U.S. autoworkers jobs, but these jobs may be doomed anyway. As David Hendrickson, manager of GM's Deltronics in Matamoros, puts it: "I'd rather see a job go to Mexico than to Taiwan."[19]

At the same time U.S. firms are going to Mexico, Mexican businesses are finding themselves able to exploit the U.S. market by replacing goods that were previously purchased from Asia. Mexican firms are now able to produce products at highly competitive prices thanks to lower cost labor and proximity to the American market. Location has helped hold down transportation costs and allows for fast delivery. As a result, Hewlett-Packard has increased by 25 percent its imports of copier products from Mexican manufacturers; and IBM is pushing its Asian suppliers to set up joint ventures in Mexico, so that its own costs and inventories can be reduced.[20] Overseas auto producers are also turning their attention to this market location opportunity. Volkswagen, for example, manufactures in Mexico the new Beetle that it is currently selling in the United States. The company now produces almost 500,000 units annually at its Puebla plant by sourcing more than 50 percent of the auto's components from nearby Mexican suppliers. Nissan and Daimler-Benz also have production facilities in Mexico. As a result, when coupled with the American auto firms that have operations there, almost 1 million cars and trucks for the U.S. market are now being made in Mexico.[21]

These developments have helped Mexico build a positive trade balance with the United States. However, the country is not depending just on the United States for its economic future. Mexico currently is increasing exports to Canada and to countries outside North America. In particular, Mexico is turning more and more to South American countries, where trade pacts recently have been signed. Although this economic activity is still small compared with their big neighbor to the north, Mexico is increasingly becoming a major player in the global economy.

South America

In the 1980s and early 1990s, many countries in South America had difficult economic problems. The major countries of Argentina, Brazil, Chile, and Venezuela accumulated heavy foreign debt obligations, and along with the other countries in the region they were devastated by severe inflation. For example, both Argentina's and Brazil's inflation rates ran up to four digits in the late 1980s and into the 1990s.

Most South American countries underwent the necessary economic reforms, such as reducing their debt. For example, in 1989 Argentina's consumer prices rose by 5,000 percent; in 1990, they rose by another 1,500 percent. From 1991 to 1994, however, under the administration of Carlos Menem, inflation in Argentina dropped sharply, and the gross domestic product rose by over 5 percent annually. By 1998 annual GDP in Argentina was increasing at an 8 percent rate, industrial production was rising 7 percent, and inflation was a mere one-half of 1 percent.

Brazil, until very recently, had similar success. From 1992 to 1995, the country's GDP rose by 5 percent annually, and inflation, which was running as high as 50 percent in some months, had dropped to 5 percent by mid-1998. Most important, like Argentina, Brazil attracted outside investors. Examples include Compaq Computer, which opened a factory capable of producing 400,000 personal computers annually. Anheuser-Busch spent $105 million on a brewery to market Budweiser to Brazilians, and General Electric constructed $9 billion worth of coal-fired power electricity plants in the southern part of the country. At the same time, many other well-known companies have set up operations in Brazil, including Arby's, J.C. Penney, Kentucky Fried Chicken, McDonald's, and Wal-Mart.[22] All of this international business activity should spell success. However, by the beginning of 1999, Brazil was experiencing difficulties in the volatile world economy.

Chile has been an economic success story in South America. Annual average growth of GDP in 1997 was 8.1 percent, which was higher than that for any other country in South America except Argentina.[23] In addition, Chile's export volume has increased dramatically more than double that of Brazil, Venezuela, or Mexico. At the same time, the amount of foreign direct investment has been increasing, and the nation is being targeted by multinationals that believe Chile will eventually enter NAFTA. If the long-run objective is to have a free trade zone throughout the Western Hemisphere, then Chile is in an enviable position.

Another major development in South America is the growth of intercountry trade, spurred on by the progress toward free market policies.[24] For example, beginning in 1995, 90 percent of trade among Mercosur members was duty free. Also, members of the Andean Pact formed a customs union by adopting common external tariffs and eliminating most duties between the members. Currently, negotiations are under way for merging Mercosur and the Andean Pact into a South American Free Trade Association. Because of such developments, intercountry trade is increasing sharply.

At the same time, South American countries are increasingly looking to do business with the United States. In fact, a recent survey of businesspeople from Argentina, Brazil, Chile, Colombia, and Venezuela found that the U.S. market, on average, was more important for them than any other. Some of these countries, however, also are looking outside of the Americas for growth opportunities. Mercosur has begun talks with the EU to create free trade between the two blocs, and Chile has joined the Asia-Pacific Economic Cooperation group. These developments help to illustrate the economic dynamism of South America and, especially in light of Asia's recent economic problems, explain why so many multinationals are interested in doing business within this part of the world.

Europe

Although often in the past overshadowed because of Asia's spectacular growth, major economic developments have occurred in Europe over the past decade. One interesting development has been the privatization of traditionally nationalized industries (see the accompanying box, "Privatization in Great Britain"). Another has been the full emergence of the EU as an operational economic union, and yet another the close economic linkages established between the EU and newly emerging Central and Eastern European countries. Including the former communist bloc, by the year 2000, Greater Europe will be a trading area of about 550 million, mostly middle-class consumers in at least 25 countries.

The EU The ultimate objective of the EU is to eliminate all trade barriers among member countries (like between the states in the United States). This economic community eventually will have common custom duties as well as unified industrial and commercial policies regarding countries outside the union. Another goal that has finally become a reality is a single currency and a regional central bank.

Such developments will allow companies based in EU nations that are able to manufacture high-quality, low-cost goods to ship them anywhere within the EU without paying duties or being subjected to quotas or even exchange rate fluctuations with the single currency now in use. This helps to explain why many North American and Pacific Rim firms have established operations in Europe; however, all these outside firms are finding their success tempered by the necessity to address local needs. This need for local differentiation in Europe has been explained by a marketing expert as follows:

> The fact is that dissimilarities exist in the way products are viewed within countries in the [EU]. The Renault 11, for example, may be a good economy car in the U.K., but in Spain it is still perceived as a luxury item. These ways of thinking, desires, needs, and consumer habits are not going to change considerably, and this cannot be ignored in a positioning strategy.

International Management in Action
Privatization in Great Britain   www.cgtd.com/global/europe/gbritain.htm

Many people think that privatization is a strategy confined to former communist governments that now are transforming to free enterprise. In fact, a number of Western countries have been selling off their state-owned properties, and they are finding that this economic strategy can be extremely profitable. Great Britain is an excellent example.

By the late 1970s, the British government had nationalized a sizable number of industries, including steel, coal, electricity generation, trucking, and railways. The government also owned most of the telecommunications industry, as well as aircraft, shipbuilding, car manufacture, silicon-chip production, and North Sea oil holdings. The borrowings and losses of these operations were running 3 billion pounds annually. A number of reasons can be cited for these results, including high cost, low productivity, poor labor relations, inefficient use of resources, and unsatisfactory customer service. It was at this time the government embarked on a new strategy: Sell these industries and businesses to private buyers, and let them operate the companies based on market economy principles.

By the early 1990s, many of the national firms had been privatized, and the results were astounding. In virtually all cases, the operations were profitable, and productivity, labor relations, and customer service had improved. For example, at British Airways and British Gas, productivity per employee was up 20 percent. At Associated British Ports, there were virtually no labor disputes, in sharp contrast to the major disruptions of earlier years. At British Telecom, the call failure rate (a quality service measure) had declined from 4 percent to one-half of 1 percent, and the long waiting list for telephone installation, so common before privatization, had all but disappeared. Moreover, while under government ownership, the company reported that three-quarters of its public telephones were operational (a statistic vigorously denied as overinflated by most members of the general public). In contrast, today, with many more public telephones in existence, 96 percent of them work.

The transition of Great Britain from government-owned enterprises to privatization has greatly improved the nation's economic performance. No wonder so many other countries, both in the EU and outside, are currently following a similar strategy. As one ex-government minister who was part of Britain's privatization effort put it, "The worldwide collapse of state socialism has created a new inevitability—the rise of free economic institutions."

Of course, this is not to say that all privatization efforts have dramatically increased productivity, and not everyone agrees that all state-owned businesses should be sold. For example, recent research shows that only 16 percent of the British population believe the railway system should be privatized, while 64 percent oppose such action. Nevertheless, the question facing nations—"is no longer whether to introduce or expand the practice of capitalism but only how to do it." For many privatization will be an important part of how to accomplish the transition to a market economy; and this is a goal that the recently elected Labor government supports. The Laborites have announced that they also plan to sell off $1.63 billion of state assets each year for the next three years.

Toothpaste and oral care are another example of products which cannot be marketed in the same way across Europe. In Spain and Greece, toothpaste is regarded as cosmetic, so their commercials look glamorous, like soft drink ads. In the U.K. and in Holland toothpaste is seen as a therapeutic product and its consumption is three times as high as in Spain and Greece.[25]

As a result of differing local tastes, EU-based firms follow the international strategy adage, "plan globally, act locally." Although this strategy also applies to other parts of the world and will be covered in subsequent chapters, it must be given special consideration if unity in Europe is to become a reality. For example, EU appliance makers will add a self-cleaning option to those ovens for the French market, but leave this option out of units for the German market, where food generally is cooked at lower temperatures. Another interesting strategy is to draw heavily on a network of factories in the EU that can produce both components and finished goods. For example, the Philips television factory in Brugge, Belgium, uses tubes that are supplied from a factory in Germany, transistors that come from France, plastics that are produced in Italy, and electronic components that come from another factory in Belgium.

The most common way that foreign MNCs have gained a foothold in the EU is by using two strategy approaches: acquisitions and alliances. The opening *Business Week* news story provides a number of examples. Also, co-operative research and development (R&D) programs are becoming increasingly common as firms team up to share expenses. Siemens and Philips have used this approach to develop computer chips, and IBM has a number of agreements with European firms for developing advanced computer technology. EU-based firms also are able to obtain financial assistance through the **European Research Cooperation Agency (Eureka),** which funds projects in the fields of energy, medical technology, biotechnology, communications, information technology, transportation, new materials, robotics, production automation, lasers, and the environment.[26] The objective of Eureka is to make Europe more productive and competitive in the world market. In the years ahead, the EU will continue to be a major focal point for international investment; U.S. firms in particular have been buying businesses in the EU, joining in strategic alliances with EU firms, and exporting into the European market.

The challenge for the future of the EU is to absorb their Eastern neighbors, the former communist bloc countries. This could result in a giant, single European market. In fact, a unified Europe could become the largest economic market in terms of purchasing power in the world. Such a development is not lost on U.S. firms, which are working to gain a stronger foothold in Eastern European countries as well as the existing EU. In recent years, the U.S. government has been very active in helping to stimulate and develop the market economies of Central and Eastern Europe to enhance U.S. economic growth as well as world peace.

Central and Eastern Europe   In December 1989, the Berlin Wall came down, and about 2 years later, on December 8, 1991, the Soviet Union ceased to exist. Each of the individual republics that made up the U.S.S.R. in turn declared its independence. The Russian Republic has the most population, territory, and influence, but others, such as Ukraine, also are industrialized and potentially can be important in the global economy. Of the ideas promoted by former Soviet president Mikhail Gorbachev, *glasnost* (openness) has been achieved, but *perestroika* (economic and political restructuring) is still having major problems. A brief overview of the historical developments in Russia is shown in Table 1-7. Of most importance to the study of international management are the Russian

European Research Cooperation Agency (Eureka)
An EU agency that funds projects in a number of fields with the objective of making Europe more productive and competitive in the world market.

Table 1–7
The Three Eras of the Soviet Union

Traditional Russian Society (Pre-1917)	Red Executive Managers (1917–1987)	Market-Oriented (1987–present)
Centralization of authority and responsibility	Centralized leadership	Sharing of power with numerous stakeholders in state enterprises
Collective action	Communist domination	Responsibility for private enterprise success
Dual ethical standards (honesty in personal relationships, deception in business relationships)	Party service	Effective delegation of responsibility to employees
Feelings ranging from helplessness (only a religious savior will deliver people from their plight) to bravado (belief in one's ability to outsmart others)	Rise of collective enterprises	Use of informal influence to obtain favors
	Dual ethical standards (honesty in personal conduct with employees, dishonesty in business dealings)	Bipolar extremes of cynicism in problem solving
	Use of informal influence to obtain favors	Use of overpromising to both clients and business partners
	Feelings of helplessness due to producing inferior products and bravado in operating some of the world's largest organizations	A high degree of achievement motivation regarding quality service and products but social contempt for success

Source: Adapted from Sheila Puffer, "Understanding the Bear: A Portrait of Russian Business Leaders," *Academy of Management Executive,* February 1994, pp. 41–61. Used with permission.

economic reforms, the dismantling of Russian price controls (allowing supply and demand to determine prices), and privatization (converting the old communist-style public enterprises to private ownership).

Clearly, Russia still has tremendous problems. In fact, in the late 1990s, once-mighty Russia's economy was not nearly as strong as those of its once-dominated neighbors, the Czech Republic, Hungary, and Poland. Even with rapid economic progress, closing the gap with their Western European neighbors will take many more years.

One of the ways that Russia is attempting to get its economy going is by removing many administered prices and subsidies and letting free market forces take over. The problem with this strategy is that it results in very high inflation (demand is much greater than supply). Hyperinflation is very hard on the people, and for political expediency, this slows down price reforms.

On the positive side, many efforts are under way to help stimulate the Russian economy. Russia has been given membership in the International Monetary Fund (IMF), which pledged $1 billion in development loans to help the country make the transition to a free market economy and, in 1998, put together a $22.6 billion loan package to help keep the economy from collapsing.[27] In addition, the Group of Seven (the United States, Germany, France, England, Canada, Japan, and Italy) has pledged billions for humanitarian and other types of assistance. So, while the Russian economy likely will have a number of years of painfully slow economic recovery and many current problems, most economic experts predict that if the Russians can hold things together politically and maintain social order, things should get better in the long run.[28]

Besides freeing up prices, the other major development that is needed for Russia to transform into a market economy is privatization. Russian enterprises no longer are fully subsidized, and they no longer can automatically sell all their output to the state. Enterprises are increasingly becoming more self-sustaining and are operating in more of a market-based environment.[29] Privatization is taking a number of different forms, including turning a large number (25 to 35 percent) of state-run businesses over to the workers and managers, letting them set up a board of directors and run the operation. In addition, an increasing number of public enterprises are being allowed to issue stock, and both employees and outside investors can purchase ownership. Shareholders not only get equity but also a vote in how the company will be run.

Although these economic reforms are being implemented slowly, there are significant problems in Russia associated with growing crime of all kinds as well as political uncertainty. Many foreign investors feel that the risk is too high. Russia is such a large market, however, and has so much potential for the future, many MNCs feel they must get involved. For example, IBM is providing 40,000 personal computers for Russian schools. Daimler-Benz of Germany has a contract for a $140 million plant to build buses. The Carroll Group of Britain is constructing a $250 million hotel-trade center. Alcatel, the giant French telecommunications company, has a $2.8 billion contract to supply advanced digital telephone equipment switches. McDonald's opened a restaurant in Moscow several years ago and now operates 20 additional restaurants throughout the country. United Technologies installed the first-ever data communications switching center to handle fax and electronic mail. Overall, however, Russia still has a long way to go in becoming like its Western neighbors. The *Economist* Intelligence Unit (EIU) has reported that Russia was one of the least successful countries in Central and Eastern Europe in making the transition to a market economy, and it also was ranked as one of the most politically risky countries in the world.[30]

Former communist countries that have become most visible in the international arena include the Czech Republic, Hungary, and Poland.[31] All three initially were battered by inflation, unemployment, and slow economic growth during their transition efforts. All three made significant progress, and they have been successful in attracting Western capital. Although recently they have been experiencing economic problems as will be discussed in the next chapter, they have been able to attract outside investors, including: (1) Volkswagen taking a $6.6 billion take in the Skoda Auto Works; (2) Japan's Fravalex purchasing the glass manufacturer Sklo-Union Teplice for $1 billion; (3) Linde of Germany investing $106 million in Technoplyn, a natural gas company; (4) US West and Bell Atlantic entering into an $80 million telecommunications joint venture with the Czech government to produce telephone switches; (5) Swedish furniture maker Ikea investing $60 million in a furniture production plant in Trnava; and (6) Siemens of Germany investing $35 million for an interest in Electromagnetica, a medical equipment company, and $15 million in Tesla Karin, a telecommunications firm. There also has been a movement toward teaching Western-style business courses, as well as MBA programs in all the Central European countries.

In Hungary, state-owned hotels have been privatized, and Western firms, attracted by the low cost of highly skilled, professional labor, have been entering into joint ventures with local companies. MNCs also have been making direct investments, as in the case of General Electric's purchase of Tungsram, the giant Hungarian electric company. Another example is Britain's Telfos Holdings, which paid $19 million for 51 percent of Ganz, a Hungarian locomotive and rolling stock manufacturer. Still others include Suzuki's investment of $110 million in a partnership arrangement to produce cars with local manufacturer Autokonzern, Ford Motor's construction of a new $80 million car component plant, and Italy's Ilwa $25 million purchase of the Salgotarjau Iron Works.

Poland had a head start on the other former communist bloc countries. General political elections were held in June 1989, and the first noncommunist government was established, well before the fall of the Berlin Wall. In 1990, the Communist Polish United Workers Party dissolved, and Lech Walesa was elected President. Earlier than its neighbors, Poland instituted radical economic reforms (characterized as the so-called "shock therapy"). Although the relatively swift transition to a market economy has been very difficult for the Polish people, with very high inflation initially, continuing unemployment, and the decline of public services, Poland's economy has done relatively well. However, political instability and risk, large external debts, a still-deteriorating infrastructure, and only modest education levels may bode poorly for the future.

Despite some continuing problems, the international business climate in Poland remains optimistic. Western businesses continue to bring in capital and technology, and they are looking for opportunities to participate in the Polish economy. For example, Pilkington, the internationally known British glass manufacturer, has invested in HSO Sandomierz, a local firm in the same industry. Asea Brown Boveri (ABB), the giant Swiss conglomerate, purchased Zamech, a turbine manufacturer. At the same time, the Polish economy is being spurred forward by the rapid growth of new, small, private businesses. There are now over 500,000 entrepreneurially driven firms in Poland, accounting for most of the economic growth in recent years.

Although Russia, the Czech Republic, Hungary, and Poland are the largest and receive the most media coverage, the other former communist countries also are struggling to right their economic ships. A small but particularly interesting example is Albania. Ruled ruthlessly by the Stalinist dictator Enver Hoxha for over four decades following World War II, Albania was the last, but most devastated, Eastern European country to abandon communism and institute radical economic reforms.[32] At the beginning of the 1990s, Albania started from zero. Industrial output initially fell over 60 percent, and inflation reached 40 percent monthly. Today, Albania remains the poorest country in Europe.

After making some progress in the mid-1990s,[33] Albania was set back in 1997 when armed civil disorder erupted when pyramid-like investment schemes collapsed. Added to this severe problem, the violent conflict in the Yugoslavian province of Kosovo has spilled over into Albania with thousands of ethnic Albanian refugees. Despite these obstacles and resulting frustrations, legislation has been enacted relating to private property, joint stock companies, and individual rights. Agriculture and housing have been privatized, and most small shops and services have been bought by their former operators. The key for Albania and the other Eastern European countries, however, is to rebuild the collapsed infrastructure and get factories and other value-added, job-producing firms up and running. Foreign investment must be forthcoming for these countries to join the global economy. A key challenge for Albania and the other "have-not" Eastern European countries will be to make themselves less risky and more attractive for international business.

Asia

Despite the severe economic downturn starting in 1997, Asia promises to continue being one of the major players in the world economy. Because there are far too many nations to allow for comprehensive coverage here, the following provides insights into the current economic status and international management challenges of selected Asian countries.

Japan During the 1970s and 1980s, Japan's economic success had been without precedent. The country had a huge positive trade balance, the yen was strong, and in manufacturing and consumer goods the Japanese became recognized as a world leader.

Analysts ascribe Japan's phenomenal success to a number of factors. Some areas that have received a lot of attention are the Japanese cultural values supporting a strong work ethic and group/team effort, consensus decision making, the motivational effects of guaranteed lifetime employment, and the overall commitment that Japanese workers have to their organizations. However, as seen in "International Management in Action: Separating Myths from Reality," at least some of these assumptions about the Japanese workforce have turned out to be more myth than reality.

Ministry of International Trade and Industry (MITI)
A Japanese government agency that identifies and ranks national commercial pursuits and guides the distribution of national resources to meet these goals.

Keiretsus
An organizational arrangement in Japan in which a large group of vertically integrated companies bound together by cross-ownership, interlocking directorates, and social ties provide goods and services to end users.

Some of the early success of the Japanese economy can be attributed to the **Ministry of International Trade and Industry (MITI).** This is a governmental agency that identifies and ranks national commercial pursuits and guides the distribution of national resources to meet these goals. In recent years, MITI has given primary attention to the so-called ABCD industries: automation, biotechnology, computers, and data processing.

Another major reason for Japanese success was the use of **keiretsus.** This Japanese term stands for the large, vertically integrated corporations whose holdings provide much of the assistance needed in providing goods and services to end users. Being able to draw from the resources of the other parts of the keiretsu, a Japanese MNC often can get things done more quickly and profitably than its international competitors.

Over the last decade, Japanese multinationals have invested billions of dollars abroad. In both the United States and the EU, Japanese auto firms have built new assembly plants. Japanese MNCs have made controversial acquisitions as well, including such well-known U.S. landmarks as Rockefeller Center, the Pebble Beach golf course, and Columbia Pictures. Beginning in the 1990s, however, there was a marked slowdown in overseas investment, and Japan's international holdings declined. This decline was mostly attributable to the slowing of the Japanese economy; however, poor management decisions also played an important role. For example, in the case of Rockefeller Center, Mitsubishi found that it was unable to generate sufficient revenue to pay the huge interest on its mortgage. As a result, it sought protection under American bankruptcy laws, causing a furor among the investors who held the mortgage and demanded the company dip into its corporate coffers and make the payments.[34]

Throughout the 1990s, the Japanese economy has endured a serious recession. The government has had great difficulty correcting the situation. During the 1980s many major Japanese banks made large loans to local businesses. Some of these loans were backed up with real estate, while others were based on projected revenues. In the early 1990s when the Japanese real estate market collapsed, these loans were no longer fully collateralized and the borrowers, in most cases, could not afford to pay the debt. At the same time, the economy began slowing up and many businesses found that with reduced profits they could not meet their loan obligations to the banks. By 1999 the situation was so bad that most of the major banks had billions of dollars in uncollectible loans on their books and lacked the financial resources to make additional loans that could help turn around the economy. The Finance Ministry estimated that there were over $548 billion of problem loans, while other sources put the figure over $700 billion and climbing.[35] At the same time the government began insisting that the banks write off their bad loans and straighten out their portfolios. Coupled with these problems, international competition increased and small and medium-sized Japanese firms found themselves scurrying to stay afloat.[36] Yet, despite these setbacks, Japan remains a formidable international competitor and is well poised in all three major economic regions: the Pacific Rim, North America, and Europe.

One objective of multicultural research is to learn more about the customs, cultures, and work habits of people in other countries. After all, a business can hardly expect to capture an overseas market without knowledge of the types of goods and services the people there want to buy. Equally important is the need to know the management styles that will be effective in running a foreign operation. Sometimes this information can be quite surprising. For example, recent analysis of Japanese management styles and techniques reveals that much of what Americans "know" about the Japanese may not always be true. Here are some examples that provide food for thought about Japanese management:

1. Many people believe that the Japanese are hardworking by nature. However, recent research shows that there is little difference in productivity among workers in Japanese plants throughout the world. Moreover, many of the differences that do exist are a result of factors such as subcontracting, vendors, and labor regulation. In addition, research among workers at Japanese municipal offices and the national railways shows that many of these workers are not industrious at all.

2. Most Japanese do not have lifelong employment. In fact, about the one-third that did in the past no longer have this security in recent years of the economic downturn. In addition, because of compulsory retirement, many workers must leave their jobs between the ages of 55 and 60. If they do not have a good retirement program

or have not saved enough for their later years, they may have to get another job at a greatly reduced salary.

3. Many Japanese managers are not participative managers; they tend to be autocratic. A recent study found that almost half of all Japanese executives indicated that they autocratically set annual goals for their division; in contrast, only 32 percent of U.S. managers follow this practice.

4. Young Japanese college graduates entering the workforce express a desire to stay with their firm for a lifetime and say they are willing to work hard to get ahead. After only a few years on the job, however, these attitudes change, and only about one-third feel this way. In short, company loyalty among many Japanese may not be as high as commonly believed.

5. Most Japanese do not work long hours because they enjoy work. The most common reason is that their family needs the money for living expenses. A second common reason is that the boss works long hours, and the staff are afraid to leave the office until the manager does. As a result, many employees end up staying at the office until late in the evening.

These examples show the importance of studying international management and learning via systematic analysis and firsthand information how managers in other countries really do behave toward their employees and their work. Such analysis is critical in separating international management myths from reality.

Japan also has been the target of foreign investment. Automakers such as BMW and Mercedes annually dominate foreign auto sales in the Japanese market. Meanwhile, Ford has been improving its sales in Japan each year, and General Motors has created a sales network that will allow the company greater access to the Japanese market. IBM, Coca-Cola, Dow, McDonald's, and Toys "R" Us also do extremely well in Japan, collectively accounting for annual sales of over $100 billion. Moreover, the future likely will see even greater progress as the U.S. government continues its efforts to force Japan into opening its markets to American firms. Other MNCs, particularly those from the EU and newly industrialized Pacific Rim countries, are targeting the Japanese market as well. Given that Japan relies heavily on exporting to sustain its economic growth, the years ahead should prove to be interesting as international managers from around the world continue to compete against the down but not out Japan, Inc.

China During the 1980s, China's average annual real economic growth was about 10 percent. From 1990 to 1995 GDP maintained this spectacular rate of growth and by 1998, despite a severe economic downturn by its Asian neighbors, its annual GDP growth was about 7 percent. On the surface this appears relatively good, but it is the lowest since 1991 and because of cheap goods flooding China's markets from cash-strapped neighbors in Southeast Asia, Chinese export growth in 1998 dropped to 7.6 percent from 22 percent a year earlier. Many of the economic initiatives such as eliminating housing subsidies and firing unneeded workers at state enterprises have been put on hold. Analysts believe that if the economic growth slows below 6 percent, because of the growing number of unemployed Chinese workers, social stability of the country would be a risk.[37]

Despite being caught up in the economic problems facing all of Asia starting in 1997, since 1990 GDP per capita on a purchasing-power basis has risen dramatically. In addition, China's exports have become formidable in the world economy. Between 1980 and 1998, China's exports increased by more than 500 percent. In recent years, trade with the United States has been so strong that as of 1998 China had a $45 billion surplus.

In spite of the setback from its bloody crackdown on protesters in Beijing's Tiananmen Square in June 1989 and its recent economic slowdown, China has arrived as an economic power in Asia. At current growth rates, China is projected to be one of, if not, the biggest economy in the world. One pragmatic reason for China's growth is its low wage rates, which make it extremely attractive to manufacturers looking to control their production costs. As these wages rise, however, as they have throughout Asia, then the Chinese will be challenged to increase the productivity of their workers and leverage technology to sustain economic growth and compete internationally. Southeast China already is a modern hub of economic activity, and many companies, especially those in Hong Kong, which China peacefully absorbed in 1997, use China as a major manufacturing source. In fact, southeast China has become such an industrial powerhouse that it is already bigger than the economy of countries such as France and some observers predict this area of China alone will soon enjoy a GDP that is larger than that of every other nation except Japan and the United States.

Many multinationals are making investments in China to tap this country's resources. U.S. energy firm Wig-Merrill built power plants for $2 billion. Motorola has put $120 million into facilities producing semiconductors and mobile phones. General Motors has a $100 million investment in a truck assembly plant, and Procter & Gamble has invested $10 million in a joint-venture factory to produce laundry and personal care products. Although the current communist government still requires local partners, this has not deterred MNCs from targeting China as a major market for the years ahead.

At the same time, however, China remains a major political risk for investors, and as the recent downturn indicates, it has many problems to overcome. For example, product pirating is still common, and while the government has promised to prosecute companies that engage in this illegal and unethical practice, still much remains to be done about it.[38] In fact, many Chinese admire counterfeiting and believe it should be allowed.[39] Perhaps more disconcerting for outside firms is that contractual agreements often prove to be worthless. For example, McDonald's received a long-run lease on property in Beijing and built a large restaurant there; since then the government has told the company that it must move because the entire area was to be razed and turned into a huge office and retail complex. This is not an isolated incident. Outside chemical producers have found themselves facing $10,000-per-product "registration fees," and U.S. law firms operating in Shanghai recently were forced to close until the government granted them new licenses. German and Japanese banks have found that collecting loans from the government can be extremely difficult as well. In addition, some securities firms have learned that Chinese clients sometimes refuse to pay for trades that turn out to be losers, and there is no government protection for such actions.[40] Simply put, China remains a complicated and high-risk venture. Even so, effective MNCs know that China with its 1.2 billion people is and will be a major world market and that they must have a presence there.

The Four Tigers   In addition to Japan and China, there are four other widely recognized economic powerhouses in Asia. Note that the traditionally used term "newly industrialized countries" (NICs) is not used, because they are not really new anymore.

South Korea, Hong Kong, Singapore, and Taiwan have arrived as major economic powers and probably now should be referred to more accurately as the "Four Tigers." The GDP of all four had grown rapidly up until the problems starting in the Southeast Asian countries of Thailand, Indonesia, and Malaysia in 1997 began to affect them also.

In South Korea, the major conglomerates, called chaebols, include such internationally known firms as Samsung, Daewoo, Hyundai, and the LG Group. Many key managers in these huge firms have attended universities in the West, where in addition to their academic programs, they learned the culture, customs, and language. Now they are able to use this information to help formulate competitive international strategies for their firms. This will be very helpful for South Korea, which among the Four Tigers has been most hard hit by the recent Southeast Asian economic crisis. Its GDP declined in the late 1990s and the value of its currency dropped almost 50 percent against the dollar.[41] This led the government to announce plans for privatizing a wide range of industries and to withdraw some of the restrictions on overall foreign ownership.[42] Going into the 21st century, many Korean businesses are struggling. For example, Samsung had become the number one computer chip maker in the world, but by 1998 it was encountering its third year of minimal net income and was retrenching operations in a wide number of areas from insurance to chemicals to auto production.[43]

Bordering southeast China and now part of the PRC (People's Republic of China), Hong Kong has been the headquarters for some of the most successful multinational operations in Asia. Hong Kong has had some recent economic problems like its neighbors but is in a good situation to bounce back. Although it can rely heavily on southeast China for manufacturing, and the Chinese have so far kept its hands-off pledge to maintain political and social stability, there is still uncertainty about the future. However, the former British colony should continue to play a strong international role in the Pacific Rim.

Singapore is a major success story. It has been hurt least by the recent economic downturn because of its solid foundation. A major problem Singapore now faces is how to continue expanding this economic foundation in the face of increasing international competition. To date, however, Singapore has emerged as the leader and financial center of Southeast Asia. As shown in Table 1–8, the World Economic Forum using a variety of criteria has named Singapore the most competitive nation in the world three years run-

Chaebols
The very large, family-held Korean conglomerates that have considerable political and economic power.

Table 1–8 The World's Most Competitive Nations			
Country	1998 Rank	1997 Rank	1996 Rank
Singapore	1	1	1
Hong Kong	2	2	2
United States	3	3	4
United Kingdom	4	7	15
Canada	5	4	8
Taiwan	6	8	9
Netherlands	7	12	17
Switzerland	8	6	6
Norway	9	10	7
Luxembourg	10	11	5
Ireland	11	16	26
Japan	12	14	13
New Zealand	13	5	3
Australia	14	17	12
Finland	15	19	16
Denmark	16	20	11
Malaysia	17	9	10
Chile	18	13	18
Korea	19	21	20

Source: World Economic Forum, 1998.

ning. Although other such rankings put the United States first, Singapore is consistently ranked close behind.

The fourth Tiger, Taiwan, has been moving from a labor-intensive economy to one that is dominated by more technologically sophisticated industries, including banking, electricity generation, petroleum refining, and computers. Although its economy has also been recently hit by the downturn in Asia and its currency has significantly dropped against the dollar, at the same time, Taiwan remains a major economic power in the Pacific Rim. China still considers Taiwan to be a breakaway province, but Taiwan's government continues to work out its relationship with the mainland to become an even bigger force in the future.

Each of the Four Tigers has been the target of foreign MNCs. For example, IBM and Hewlett-Packard, determined to build their local shares of the computer market, have invested in laboratories and factories within these countries. Motorola has followed the same strategy in enlarging its telecommunications market. Other major MNCs in "Tiger Country" range from the Japanese (Matsushita, Nissan, and Sharp) to the Europeans (Volkswagen, Philips, and Nestlé). As a result, the amount of trade and investment occurring between the Four Tigers and the rest of the world continues to expand.

Southeast Asian Countries   Besides Singapore, other countries of Southeast Asia also should be recognized. Although not yet having the economic prowess of the Four Tigers and suffering severe economic problems starting in 1997, Thailand, Malaysia, Indonesia (sometimes called the "Baby Tigers"), and now Vietnam[44] have economically developed along the lines of the Four Tigers. All have a relatively large population base, inexpensive labor, and natural resources. These countries were also known to have social stability, but in the aftermath of the economic crisis there has been considerable turmoil in this part of the world. Nevertheless, as Japan and the Four Tigers have begun to level off and mature, these export-driven Southeast Asian countries remain attractive to outside investors. MNCs from Japan, the Four Tigers, North America, and the EU all want to have a presence in these countries.

Less Developed Countries

In contrast to the fully developed countries of North America, Europe, and Asia are the less developed countries (LDCs) around the world. An LDC typically is characterized by two or more of the following: low GDP, slow (or negative) GDP growth per capita, high unemployment, high international debt, a large population, and a workforce that is either unskilled or semiskilled. In some cases, such as in the Middle East, there also is considerable government intervention in economic affairs. In recent years, some of these LDCs have shown improvement, but they still have a long way to go to fully compete in the world marketplace. Although complete coverage of all LDCs is beyond the scope of this chapter, the following focuses on representative LDCs and regions.

India   With a population of about 900 million and growing, India has traditionally had more than its share of political and economic problems. Per-capita GDP remains low, but there is still a large middle- and upper-class market for goods and services. Although India's economic growth does not compare with that of countries such as China, there has been a steady growth in recent years. The government continues its attempt to attract investors and further stimulate economic growth.

For a number of reasons, India is attractive to multinationals, and especially to U.S. and British firms. Many Indian people speak English and are well educated. Also, the Indian government is providing funds for economic development. For example, India intends to spend $30 billion by the year 2000 to expand its telecommunication systems and increase the number of phone lines fivefold, a market that AT&T is vigorously pursuing. Many frustrations remain in doing business in India (see "In the International

Spotlight" at the end of this chapter), but there is little question that the country will receive increased attention in the years ahead. Recent foreign direct investments in India include $1.1 billion by Enron, which is engaged in offshore oil and gas exploration; $400 million by Mission Energy, which is building a power plant; and $100 million by US West Inc. to provide a pilot project for the nation's first privately operated telecommunications service.[45]

Middle East and Central Asia   Israel, the Arab countries, Iran, Turkey, and the Central Asian countries of the former Soviet Union are considered by the World Bank to be LDCs. Because of their oil, however, some people would consider these countries to be economically rich.[46] In recent years, Israel has been the target of terrorists. It has also been hard hit by inflation, and although the GDP per capita is well over $6,000, there are balance-of-payment problems. Despite the tragedies and economic problems, the Israelis continue to be active in the international arena, and students of international management should have a working knowledge of the country's customs, culture, and management practices.[47]

The same is true for Arab nations, which rely almost exclusively on oil production. The price of oil, which reached almost $40 per barrel by the late 1970s, fell below $15 a barrel in the mid-1980s as the Organization of Petroleum Exporting Countries (OPEC) had trouble holding together its cartel. During the Persian Gulf war, the price of oil again rose to almost $40 a barrel, but by 1999, it had fallen dramatically.

Because most industrial nations rely, at least to some degree, on imported oil, an understanding of this part of the world is important to the study of international management. So, too, is the fact that Arab countries have invested billions of dollars in U.S. property and businesses, and many people around the world, including those in the West, work for Arab employers. For example, the bankrupt United Press International was purchased by the Middle East Broadcasting Centre, a London-based MNC owned by the Saudis.

Africa   Even though they have considerable natural resources, on the whole African nations remain very poor and undeveloped, and international trade is not a major source of income. Although African countries do business with developed countries, it is on a limited scale. One major problem of doing business in the African continent is the overwhelming diversity of about 700 million people divided into 3,000 tribes that speak 1,000 languages and dialects. Also, there is political instability in many countries with the associated risks, especially as far as direct foreign investment is concerned.

In recent years, Africa, especially sub-Saharan Africa, has had tremendous problems. In addition to tragic tribal wars, there has been the spread of terrible diseases such as AIDS and Ebola. Other severe problems include poverty, starvation, illiteracy, corruption, social breakdown, vanishing resources, overcrowded cities, drought, and homeless refugees. There is still hope in the future for Africa despite this bleak situation, however, because African countries remain virtually untapped. Not only are there considerable natural resources, but the diversity can also be used to advantage. For example, many African people are familiar with the European cultures and languages of the former colonial powers (e.g., English, French, Dutch, and Portugese), which can serve them well in international business. Also, the spirit of these emerging countries has not been broken. There are continuing efforts to stimulate economic growth. Examples of what can be done include Togo, which has sold off many of its state-owned operations and leased a steel-rolling mill to a U.S. investor, and Guinea, which has sold off some of its state-owned enterprises and cut its civil service force by 30 percent. A special case is South Africa, where apartheid, the former white government's policies of racial segregation and oppression, has been dismantled and the healing process began. Long-jailed black president Nelson Mandela is recognized as a world leader. These significant developments have led to an increasing number of the world's MNCs returning to South Africa; however, there continue to be both social and economic problems which, despite Mandela's best efforts, signal uncertain times for the years ahead.

World of Business Week—Revisited

Having read this chapter you should now be more cognizant of developments occurring around the world. According to "The Year of the Deal," corporate leaders are being evaluated on the basis of their merger power like never before. It seems that in today's competitive environment, the phrase "bigger is better" is a truism. This is especially true in the case of the United States and Europe, as these regions account for more than 80 percent of the world's leading companies. More and more European and U.S. multinationals are combining their clout by sharing core competencies. In contrast, nations such as Japan are seeing their MNC's market share shrinking and are therefore not attractive targets for mergers. In light of what you read in the chapter, answer the following questions: (1) Reflecting on the continual economic uncertainty in Asia, what should these nations do to make their economies more conducive to global consolidation? (2) What potential problems can you foresee with cross-border mergers and acquisitions? (3) What are some potential problems associated with creating a few large companies instead of many small ones?

Summary of Key Points

1. International trade and investment have increased dramatically over the last decade. Major multinational corporations (MNCs) have holdings throughout the world, from North America to Europe to the Pacific Rim to Africa. Some of these holdings are a result of direct investment; others are partnership arrangements with local firms. Small firms also are finding that they must seek out international markets to survive in the future. There definitely is a trend toward the internationalization of all business.

2. International economic activity is most pronounced in the triad of North America, Europe, and the Pacific Rim. In North America, the United States, Canada, and Mexico have signed a North American Free Trade Agreement (NAFTA) that is well on the way to turning the region into one giant market. In South America, there is an increasing amount of intercountry trade, sparked by Mercosur and the Andean Pact nations. Additionally, Chile has been projected to join NAFTA, and other South American countries may in the future follow suit. In Europe, the 15 countries of the European Union (EU) form a major economic power, and the former communist countries to the east are seeking membership in the EU. The Central European countries of the Czech Republic, Poland, and Hungary already are becoming trading partners, and if Russia and the other Eastern European countries make progress in their transformation efforts, then Greater Europe will be an even more formidable market in the future. Although having recent economic problems, Asia is another major regional power, as shown not only by Japan but also the economies of China and the Four Tigers (Singapore, South Korea, Hong Kong, and Taiwan). Other areas of the world, including India, the Middle East and Central Asia, and Africa, continue to have complex problems, but still hold economic promise for the future.

Key Terms

international management
European Research Corporation
  Agency (Eureka)
MNC

North American Free Trade
  Agreement (NAFTA)
Ministry of International Trade and
  Industry (MITI)

World Trade Organization (WTO)
keiretsus
maquiladora industry
chaebols

Review and Discussion Questions

1. How does NAFTA have an impact on the economies of North America? What importance does this economic pact have for international managers in Europe and Asia?

2. How has the formation of the EU created new opportunities for member countries? Of what importance are these opportunities to international managers in other geographic regions such as North America or Asia?

3. Why are Russia and Eastern Europe of interest to international managers? Identify and describe some reasons for such interest.

4. Many MNCs have secured a foothold in Asia, and many more are looking to develop business relations there. Why does this region of the world hold such interest for international management? Identify and describe some reasons for such interest.

5. Why would MNCs be interested in South America, India, the Middle East and Central Asia, Africa, the LDCs of the world? Would MNCs be better off focusing their efforts on more industrialized regions? Explain.

Answers to the In-Chapter Quiz

1. **c.** Gillette, a U.S.-based MNC, owns the Braun company.
2. **d.** Bic SA is a French company.
3. **b.** The British MNC Grand Metropolitan PLC owns Häagen-Dazs.
4. **a.** Thomson SA of France produces RCA televisions.
5. **c.** Britain's Grand Metropolitan PLC owns Green Giant.
6. **a.** Godiva chocolate is owned by Campbell Soup, an American firm.
7. **b.** Vaseline is manufactured by the Anglo-Dutch MNC Unilever PLC.
8. **d.** Wrangler jeans are made by the VF Corporation based in the United States.
9. **d.** Holiday Inn is owned by Britain's Bass PLC.
10. **c.** Tropicana orange juice was recently purchased by U.S.-based PepsiCo.

Internet Exercise: Franchise Opportunities at McDonald's

One of the best-known franchise operations in the world is McDonald's; and in recent years the company has been working to expand its international presence. Why? Because the U.S. market is becoming saturated and the major growth opportunities lie in the international arena. Visit the McDonald's web site **www.mcdonalds.com** and find out what is going on in the company. Begin by perusing their latest annual report and see how well they are doing both domestically and internationally. Then turn to the franchise information that is provided and find out how much it would cost to set up a franchise in the following countries: Belgium, Brazil, Korea, Mexico, Slovenia, and Turkey. Which seems like the most attractive international investment? In addition to this group, in what other countries is the firm seeking franchisees? Would any of these seem particularly attractive to you as investor? Which ones? Why?

Then, based on the this assignment and the chapter material, answer these last two questions: (1) Will the fact the euro has become the standard currency in the EU over the next decade help or hinder a new McDonald's franchisee in Europe? (2) If there are exciting worldwide opportunities, why does McDonald's not exploit these itself instead of looking for franchisees? (3) What is the logic in McDonald's expansion strategy?

India

India is located in southern Asia, with the Bay of Bengal on the east and the Arabian Sea on the west. One-sixth of the world's population (approximately 900 million people) lives within the country's 1.27 million square miles. Over 80 percent of the population are Hindus, and the official language is Hindi, although many people also speak English. Because the literacy rate is less than 40 percent, radio and television are the most influential media. The country operates as a democratic republic, and for the most part, one party has dominated the government since independence in 1947. At that time, India was born of the partition of the former British Indian empire into the new countries of India and Pakistan. This division has been a source of many problems through the years. For example, much to the dismay of the world community, both countries had nuclear tests in a cold war atmosphere. Also, many millions of Indians still live at the lowest level of subsistence, and the per-capita income is very low.

In the past, doing business in India has been quite difficult. For example, it took PepsiCo 3 years just to set up a soft drink concentrate factory, and Gillette, the U.S. razor blade company, had to wait 8 years for its application to enter the market to be accepted. Additionally, many MNCs have complained that there are too many barriers to effective operations. In the mid-1970s, the country changed its rules and required that foreign partners hold no more than 40 percent ownership in any business. As a result, some MNCs left India.

In recent years, the government has been relaxing its bureaucratic rules, particularly those relating to foreign investments. From 1981 to 1991, total foreign direct investment in India increased by $250 million, and between 1991 and 1993, it jumped by an additional $2.5 billion, and the pace continues. Most of this new investment has come from the United States and nonresident Indians. One reason for this change in the nation's policies toward business is that the government realizes many MNCs are making a critical choice: India or China? Any monies not invested in India may be lost to China forever. Additionally, it can be seen that foreign investments are having a very positive effect on the Indian economy. After the first big year of new investments (1991), India's annual GDP jumped to over 4 percent and has remained at this level.

The relaxation of rules definitely has encouraged more foreign investment. Coca-Cola was able to get permission for a 100-percent-owned unit in India in 8 weeks, and Motorola received clearance in 2 days to add a new product line—and did all of this via fax. Other companies that have reported rapid progress include Daimler-Benz, Enron, Procter & Gamble, and Whirlpool. At the same time, however, not everything is roses. Enron is finding that while it received permission in record time to build a power plant, there were a great many political roadblocks that still had to be overcome in pushing the project through to completion.

Nevertheless, the Indian government's new approach is helping a great deal. In addition, there are other attractions that entice MNCs to India. These include: (1) a large number of highly educated people, especially in critically short supply areas such as in medicine, engineering and computer science; (2) widespread use of English, long accepted as the international language of business; and (3) low wages and salaries, which often are 10 to 30 percent of those in the world's economic superpowers.

www.ib-net.com

Questions

1. What is the climate for doing business in India? Is it supportive of foreign investment?

2. How important is a highly educated human resource pool for MNCs wanting to invest in India? Is it more important for some businesses than for others?

3. Given the low per-capita income of the country, why would you still argue for India to be an excellent place to do business in the coming years?

Here Comes the Competition

The Wadson Company is a management research firm headquartered in New Jersey. The company was recently hired by a large conglomerate with a wide range of products, ranging from toys to electronics and financial services. This conglomerate wants Wadson to help identify an acquisition target. The conglomerate is willing to spend up to $2.5 billion to buy a major company anywhere in the world.

One of the things the research firm did was to identify the amount of foreign direct investment in the United States by overseas companies. The research group also compiled a list of major acquisitions by non-U.S. companies. It gathered these data to show the conglomerate the types of industries and companies that are currently attractive to the international buyers. "If we know what outside firms are buying," the head of the research firm noted, "this can help us identify similar overseas businesses that may also have strong growth potential. In this way, we will not confine our list of recommendations to U.S. firms only." In terms of direct foreign investment by industry, the researchers found that the greatest investment was being made in manufacturing (almost $100 billion). Then,

in descending order, came wholesale trade, petroleum, real estate, and insurance.

On the basis of this information, the conglomerate has decided to purchase a European firm. "The best acquisitions in the United States have already been picked," the president told the board of directors. "However, I'm convinced that there are highly profitable enterprises in Europe that are ripe for the taking. I'd particularly like to focus my attention on France and Germany." The board gave the president its full support, and the research firm will begin focusing on potential European targets within the next 30 days.

Questions

1. Is Europe likely to be a good area for direct investment during the years ahead?

2. Why is so much foreign money being invested in U.S. manufacturing? Based on your conclusions, what advice would be in order for the conglomerate?

3. If the conglomerate currently does not do business in Europe, what types of problems is it likely to face?

Chapter 2

The Political, Legal, and Technological Environment

Objectives of the Chapter

The environment that international managers face is changing rapidly. The past is proving to be a poor indicator of what will happen in the future. Changes are not only more common now but also more significant than ever before, and these dramatic forces of change are creating new challenges. Although there are many dimensions in this new environment, most relevant to international management would be the economic environment that was covered in the last chapter and the cultural environment covered in the chapters of Part 2. Also important are the political, legal and regulatory, and technological dimensions of the environment. The objective of this chapter is to examine how the political, legal and regulatory, and technological environments have changed in recent years. Some major trends in each that will help dictate the world in which international managers will compete also are presented. The specific objectives of this chapter are:

1. EXAMINE some of the major changes that are currently taking place in the political environment of China, Europe, Russia, and Central and Eastern Europe.

2. PRESENT an overview of the legal and regulatory environment in which MNCs operate worldwide.

3. REVIEW key technological developments as well as their impact on MNCs now and in the future.

BusinessWeek

The World of Business Week:

Startups to the Rescue

Leopoldo Fernández Pujals has a tempting recipe for a continent that craves jobs. A decade ago, as more Spanish women began entering the workforce, the Cuban-American marketer sensed Spain's growing appetite for fast food. So he invested $80,000 to start a pizza-delivery service in Madrid. Now, TelePizza boasts $260 million in sales and employs 6,000 workers. Since going public on the Spanish Bolsa in late 1996, TelePizza's shares have soared from 14 to 123, and its market cap now tops $1.3 billion. Says Pujals, a 50-year-old Vietnam war veteran: "More and more people are asking me: 'What's our secret?'"

No wonder. At a time when Europe's industrial giants continue to shed workers, a raft of small, dynamic companies such as Pujals' are emerging. They are creating jobs and spurring economic regeneration—despite obstacles such as heavy taxes and red tape that have discouraged the Continent's entrepreneurs. Indeed, Europe's hot growth companies are showing a remarkable ability to take advantage of the Continent's growing trend toward deregulation, its nascent secondary stock markets, and the spread of the Internet, which puts companies in instant touch with new customers. Says Juan Roure, a professor at IESE Business School in Barcelona: "These are the companies that are most effectively creating value and jobs. They are changing the rules of how to compete in their markets."

Smaller growth companies have gone largely unnoticed among Europe's political elite until recently. But their continued success is vital if the Continent is to reduce the ranks of its 19 million unemployed. A new study by Europe's 500 association, a nonprofit group linked to the European Foundation of Entrepreneurship Research, identified 500 small and midsize companies whose sales—and employment ranks—are soaring. Conducted by IP Strategies, an independent consultant, the study found that both service companies and small-scale manufacturers are providing the entry-level jobs needed to combat Europe's 11% jobless rate. Moreover, they aren't just clustered around tech zones such as Munich but are dotted across the Continent.

The No. 1 job creator is Pujals' TelePizza. It increased its payroll by 62% annually from 1991 to 1996, creating 5,787 jobs over five years as its sales jumped 1,364%. And it's not only low-skilled jobs that are sprouting among Europe's flourishing small and midsize players. Technology companies have also been among the leading job creators in Europe. France's Gemplus—a maker of plastic cards containing an embedded microprocessor and memory chip used in phone booths and bank cards—saw its sales leap 48%, to $569 million, last year alone as it hired 1,092 new staffers. Now, the company may go public. Although there are disadvantages to starting a company in France, concedes CEO Daniel LeGal, Gemplus owes its success to "being in a market growing 25% to 30% a year."

The surge in jobs at tech companies is expected to accelerate as Internet use continues to spread. "Growth in the Internet has helped fuel our business," observes Christopher Horn, CEO of Ireland's IONA Technologies PLC, which sells products that help diverse software packages work together. Founded in 1991, IONA now employs 470 people. Sales more than doubled last year, to $48 million in 1997, and some analysts see revenues hitting $85 million this year.

In industries such as aviation and telecommunications, meanwhile, small growth companies are taking advantage of market openings in the European Union. Regional airlines such as Britain's Cityflyer Express Ltd. are taking off now that Europe is allowing full-fledged competition in air travel across the Continent. In telecom, Finland's Elcoteq Network has benefited from the boom in mobile phones. Once a struggling flat-panel-display maker, Elcoteq now supplies mobile phones to Nokia Corp. and L. M. Ericsson.

Many European growth companies are scoring simply by answering consumers' demands for better service. Four years ago, Euro-Med opened a hotel, fitness center, beauty spa, and medical clinic near Nüremberg aimed at Europeans who want first-class health facilities at prices not much higher than those of conventional hospitals. Euro-Med plans to double its staff of doctors to 100 by 2000, says President and co-founder Wolf-Michael Wunsche.

Such success stories offer a glimmer of hope for the Continent. It will take lower taxes and more relaxed work rules to really create an environment where entrepreneurs thrive and unemployment dwindles. But Europe may be finally waking up to the fact that small companies are key to growth and prosperity.

By Julia Flynn, with Heidi Dawley, in London, Stephen Baker in Madrid, Gail Edmondson in Paris, and bureau reports
www.telepizza.es

This opening news article illustrates the changes occurring in the political, regulatory, and technological environments around the world. Despite the typical obstacles associated with bureaucratic red tape, high taxation, and strict work rules, success stories such as Spain's TelePizza company illustrate how small, nimble start-ups can overcome such impediments to create jobs and spur economic growth. As the article indicates, the nature and structure of employment is changing throughout the European continent. A blend of deregulation and rapid technological change combined with the emergence of service and knowledge-based economies has allowed the rise of entrepreneurial firms. Technology companies are leading the way, creating thousands of new jobs as the Internet has helped to fuel new business by putting companies and people in touch with their customers instantaneously. In addition, other new companies are able to take advantage of market openings in telecommunications and aviation as full-fledged competition is now allowed in these industries. Overall, Europe's recent success demonstrates a valuable lesson from which others can learn—in order for an economy to flourish, political leaders must foster an environment conducive to entrepreneurial growth.

Political Environment

The domestic and international political environment has a major impact on MNCs. As government policies change, MNCs must adjust their strategies and practices to accommodate the new perspectives and actual requirements. Moreover, in a growing number of geographic regions and countries, governments appear to be less stable; therefore, these areas carry more risk than they have in the past. The assessment of political risk will be given specific attention in Chapter 10, but the following examines political developments in selected areas and countries that are particularly relevant to today's international management.

China

As discussed in Chapter 1, China is such an emerging economic power that it cannot be ignored by international business. The Chinese political environment, however, is very complex and risky because of the government's desire to balance national, immediate needs with the challenge of modernization. For example, at the present time the Chinese government is trying to sustain its economic growth. If growth is slower than the 1998 7 percent, the economy will likely not be able to generate enough jobs to take in the 6 million Chinese that enter the workforce each year, as well as the 12 million being laid off by restructured state enterprises.[1] In the past, economic growth was not a problem. In 1992, for example, the country's GDP increased by 14 percent. However, since then this rate has been continually declining.[2]

In order to ensure that the economy does not fall into the economic malaise that has been sweeping the rest of Asia, the Chinese government stepped up efforts to encourage foreign investment. Yet, by 1998–1999 there were indications that the country's economic strength was showing signs of fatigue. For example, foreign investment was slowing up because cash-starved Asian companies could no longer afford to build in China; and Chinese exporters were seeing overseas business customers shift to less expensive factories in Thailand and Malaysia. At the same time, local unemployment was starting to rise and bad loans were piling up in the state-owned banks.

In response, the government began giving the green light to projects that had been bogged down in bureaucratic red tape. For example, after years of negotiation the Royal Dutch/Shell Group received permission for a $4.5 billion chemical complex, the largest foreign investment in China to date. At the same time the government announced a series of steps to open up the economy.[3] Some of these included: (1) speeding up a program to convert state enterprises, which as of 1998 still account for one-third of industrial output, into corporations owned by shareholders; (2) dramatically expanding the size of capital markets by authorizing hundreds of new stock listings annually in Shanghai and Shenzhen; (3) allowing government bodies to sell off all but 1,000 of the country's 305,000 state enterprises and letting those that could not be sold go bankrupt; (4) accelerating worker retraining, building low-cost housing, and creating other social services to relieve burdens on state enterprises and care for millions of workers who would lose their jobs; and (5) reducing tariffs to 15 percent.[4]

As all of this is happening, the Chinese people are facing what is called the "four fears." The first is the average Chinese consumer's fear of being robbed by inflation, and the second is the workers' fear of growing underemployment. The third is the anger of farmers, whose land is being encroached on by industrialization and who prefer to sell their output to local entities and black markets rather than Beijing's state purchasers. The fourth is the general fear and disgust of the increasing corruption that exists throughout the political system.[5]

Despite this bad news, several developments currently reshaping China also may prove to be effective in helping the country get back on track of being a major economic power.[6] For example, the first group of students after the Cultural Revolution to gain entry to universities based on competitive exams rather than political connections now are coming into influential positions. Commonly referred to as the "Class of '77," many of these graduates have risen largely on merit rather than political or family ties, and they represent some of the country's brightest minds. This new generation has built extensive personal networks based on friendships during the Cultural Revolution, and they are more open to Western ideas and less bound by communist ideology than the older leaders. Here is how one close observer describes them:

> They are by no means a monolithic group. Highly independent, they hold varying opinions on such issues as political and economic reforms. But most want a China that is more open to the outside world, tolerates greater debate, is driven by the private sector, and is run by modern institutions and the rule of law. While a more liberal China is a long-term goal, some support a government run by pragmatic technocrats. Above all, members of the Class of '77 believe they are the most qualified to lead China, by virtue of their experience with rural poverty and Western society. With Deng Xiaoping now dead and doddering Communist Party career men fading from the scene, members of the Class of '77 are preparing to take the reins.[7]

If the Class of '77 end up in charge, the political environment in China will be markedly different than if cronyism and corruption continues and the old-line communists continue running the country.

Europe

Far away from Chinese politics, the political situation in Europe also continues to change. One reason is that leaders in major countries, as well as the EU itself, are finding it difficult to firmly establish a foothold of power.[8] As a result, international managers must remain alert as to how political changes may impact their business. For example, in France, the 12-year reign of the Socialists under François Mitterand ended in mid-1995. Mitterand was replaced by Jacques Chirac, a more conservative Gaullist, and this heralded a host of political changes impacting on doing business in France.

The same kind of changes are occurring in the other major European countries. In Germany, Helmut Kohl was re-elected in late 1994 but soon was having troubles. Three months into his new term, he was forced to consider forming a coalition with the opposition Social Democrats, who already controlled the upper house of Parliament. More recently, Gerald Schröder, subsequent to his 1998 election as Chancellor succeeding Kohl, faced a similar situation involving the Green Party. In Great Britain, political change has been even more pronounced. The Labor Party swept into power in 1997 with a strong majority. Since then, under the leadership of Tony Blair, Britain's economy has continued to improve and the government has moved into the middle of the political continuum as seen by one of its recent programs designed to reduce the welfare roles by offering work incentives to the unemployed.[9] This strategy is a strong reversal of earlier Labor party philosophy and shows that the winds of political change can alter very quickly.

That the nations of Western Europe, with the exception of Norway and Switzerland, now are part of the EU only adds to the complexity of the political environment. MNCs cannot avoid political risks even when doing business with individual countries because of what the EU may dictate. It is important to realize that there are vast cultural differences, as will be pointed out in Chapter 5, but also that the fate of the EU members is interdependent. Now, what happens to one can often influence the others. A good example is provided by France and Germany. Today, Franco-German relations are the cornerstone of a united Europe.[10] The two are tied closely together in a number of ways. For example, each is the other's major trading partner; each has a vested interest in the other doing well. MNCs doing business in either country find that they must focus on developments in both nations, as well as in the EU at large. Simply put, Europe is no longer a series of fragmented countries; it is a giant, interwoven region in which international management must be aware of what is happening politically both in the immediate area of operations as well as throughout the continent.[11]

Russia

Russia presents the most extreme example of how the political environment impacts on international management. For almost a decade, Boris Yeltsin has governed Russia by barely holding together a number of broad-based coalitions. The war in Chechnya a few years ago badly hurt his standing both at home and in the world community, but the 1998 economic plunge that sent the ruble into a tailspin may be the biggest crisis to date.

Importantly, in recent years the political situation in Russia has become irrevocably intertwined with the economic situation. As noted in Chapter 1, Russia has needed International Monetary Fund (IMF) assistance, and this assistance is closely tied to economic changes in the country. These changes, however, cannot be made without political support and there are many factions in the country that would like to ignore, or at least heavily modify, the IMF conditions that accompany the assistance. A good example is provided by the tax situation in Russia.

Many companies refuse to pay their taxes. Analysts estimate that 40–50 percent of all taxes are uncollected at a time when the government is running at a deficit. The government is trying to crack down on this situation. Some of the steps include forcing the big utilities and raw materials producers to pay up or face sanctions such as denying oil companies export permits. However, this strategy is not going to be easy to implement. Russia's lower house of parliament, the Duma, with its large minority of communists and nationalists, are unlikely to go along with such efforts.[12]

Another problem confronting the government is that in recent years the price of oil has declined sharply, and Russia depends on this export to earn foreign currency. Additionally, every month the government has to redeem $5 billion in treasury bills and interest rates are in the range of 60 percent. Meanwhile, large numbers of Russians have not been paid their wages and barter has become a way of life for many people. The Russian European Centre for Economic Policy has estimated that between 1992–1997 the share of barter in industrial sales rose from less than 5 percent to approximately 40 percent.[13]

Another major problem confronting the government is unemployment. By the late 1990s over 10 percent of the workforce was unemployed and 20 percent of the population was living well below subsistence level. Commenting on the backlog of wage and other payments, an economist at the Center for Strategic and International Studies in Washington noted that:

> The government has not been paying its employees, the armed services, doctors, teachers, and scientists. The Ministry of Finance has simply sequestered budgetary payments to keep the deficit within manageable limits. Enterprise directors, confronted with tighter money, have merely stopped paying their suppliers and their employees; in turn, their customers have stopped paying them. To complete the vicious circle, increasingly . . . enterprises stopped paying their taxes…Overdue payables, such as wage and tax arrears and arrears to suppliers and banks, rose to an estimated 21% of GDP. . . . The . . . salaries, wages, and transfer payments of 65–67 million people were in arrears.[14]

These grim statistics show how difficult it is to govern in Russia—and why so many MNCs are reluctant to do business there. What will the future hold? It is unlikely that a communist will replace Yeltsin, but that party does have a substantial number of voters (about 20 percent in 1998). So the communists are in a good position to delay and sidetrack economic reforms; and as the *Economist* recently noted, "Reforming Russia remains a risky business. And the fight isn't over yet."[15]

Central and Eastern Europe

Besides Russia, the political situation in the rest of Central and Eastern Europe is also in a state of flux as these nations work to make the transition to a market economy. As shown in Table 2–1, since the days of communism most of these countries first moved to the political right, then the left, and now back to the right. The "right" in these countries largely represents a commitment to reforms such as market prices privatization/elimination of subsidies, while the "left" generally represents socialists (largely former communists) who want to slow down the reforms and maintain subsidies for social services. Yet, whether left or right, progress toward a market economy varies from country to country and some are finding that the changes that helped get them to where they are today are also resulting in political problems that can prevent them from moving more vigorously toward a market economy. A good example is Poland.

In late 1997 Polish voters replaced a government of former communists and brought in a coalition of trade unionists, nationalists, and free marketeers. Since then the

Table 2–1
Political Leanings of Post-Communist Central and Eastern Europe Since the Beginning of the Transformation

Country	First Post-Communist Government	Next Government	Most Recent Government
Bulgaria	Right	Left	Right
Czech Republic	Right	Right	Right
Estonia	Right	Mixed	Right
Hungary	Right	Left	Right
Latvia	Right	Mixed	Mixed
Lithuania	Right	Left	Right
Poland	Right	Left	Right
Romania	Left	Left	Right
Slovakia	Right	Left	Left
Slovenia	Left	Left	Mixed

Note: Right refers to a government climate of generally pushing hard for reforms such as privatization, market price determination and elimination of subsidies and left refers to socialists who generally may want to slow down the transformation process and give more priority to social welfare programs.

government's plan to streamline the economy and get the country ready to enter the EU has been fraught with problems. One of these is a result of a restructuring plan to cut around 250,000 mining jobs and close approximately 35 percent of the mines. This action will save the government billions of dollars each year because of the coal industry's losses. However, the largest share of seats in the national parliament are held by Solidarity, which promised before the election that there would be no mass firings in the mining industry.[16] So even though the economic growth has been the best since the transition process began in Central and Eastern Europe (about 5 percent in 1998) government economic policy and political decisions are not on the same track and this may spell trouble for the Polish economy in the future.

In Hungary, another of the stronger economies in Central Europe (over 5 percent in 1998) that is on track to join the EU, there has been a political movement similar to that in Poland. In the latest elections the government led by ex-communists was turned out of office and replaced with a coalition of the right. The previous government had pulled the country back from a debt crisis, reformed pensions, and engineered an impressive export- and investment-led recovery. However, the voters felt that the pain of reform was too great and voted for a new government. The current ruling party is now trying to maintain the positive investment image, which will be important given that foreign investors have put more money per capita into Hungary than anywhere else in post-communist Europe. In fact, the future success of the nation will depend heavily on the ability of the government to maintain this momentum.[17]

The Czech Republic privatized very quickly, gambling that private owners could reorganize and manage firms more effectively than the state. The government also allowed citizens to bid for shares in newly privatized firms—and for a time the country was pointed to as one of the success stories in Central Europe. More recently, however, the economy has been having trouble. The nation's trade deficit has ballooned and there was a negative economic growth of almost 3 percent in 1998. As a result, the government is now wrestling with the need to boost competitiveness and stop the banks from propping up industrial firms that would otherwise go bankrupt. There is also concern over the fact that many Czechs turned their shares over to investment funds which are controlled by the major banks and these institutions remain largely in the hands of the state. As a result, noted the *Wall Street Journal,* "The invisible hand of the state—and indirect subsidies in the form of overdue bank loans— still helps support most large Czech companies."[18] So the Czech government still has a ways to go in keeping the economy strong and on the road to a free market.

More severe problems face the governments of the Balkan countries (e.g., Bulgaria, Romania, and Albania) and, with the possible exception of the Baltic states (Estonia, Latvia, and Lithuania), the republics of the former Soviet Union. The governments of these former communist countries all went at the necessary economic reforms (freeing up prices, privatization, elimination of subsidies, and building the needed financial and legal systems and supporting infrastructure) at a much slower pace. Now, they are paying the price (literally in the case of increasing inflation) with generally depressed economies and lack of foreign investment. They are lagging behind the Central European countries in the transformation process and only time will tell what will happen in the future.

Legal and Regulatory Environment

Islamic law
Law that is derived from interpretation of the *Qur'an* and the teachings of the Prophet Mohammed and is found in most Islamic countries.

Socialist law
Law that comes from the Marxist socialist system and continues to influence regulations in countries formerly associated with the Soviet Union as well as China.

One reason that today's international environment is so confusing and challenging for MNCs is because there are so many different laws and regulations. There are four foundations on which laws are based around the world. Briefly summarized, these are:

1. **Islamic law.** This is law derived from interpretation of the *Qur'an* and the teachings of the Prophet Mohammed. It is found in most Islamic countries in the Middle East and Central Asia.

2. **Socialist law.** This law comes from the Marxist socialist system and continues to influence regulations in former communist countries, especially those from the former Soviet Union, as well as present-day China, Vietnam, North Korea, and Cuba.

3. **Common law.** This comes from English law, and it is the foundation of the legal system in the United States, Canada, England, Australia, New Zealand, and others.

4. **Civil or code law.** This law is derived from Roman law and is found in the non-Islamic and nonsocialist countries such as France, some countries in Latin America, and even Louisiana in the United States.[19]

With these broad statements serving as points of departure, the following sections discuss basic principles and examples of the international legal environment facing MNCs today.

Basic Principles of International Law

When compared with domestic law, international law is less coherent, because its sources embody not only the laws of individual countries concerned with any dispute but also treaties (universal, multilateral, or bilateral) and conventions (such as the Geneva Convention on Human Rights or the Vienna Convention of Diplomatic Security). In addition, international law contains unwritten understandings that arise from repeated interactions among nations. Conforming to all the different rules and regulations can create a major problem for MNCs. Fortunately, much of what they need to know can be subsumed under several broad and related principles that govern the conduct of international law.[20]

Sovereignty and Sovereign Immunity The **principle of sovereignty** holds that governments have the right to rule themselves as they see fit. In turn, this implies that one country's court system cannot be used to rectify injustices or impose penalties on another unless that country agrees. So, while U.S. laws require equality in the workplace for all employees, U.S. citizens who take a job in Japan cannot sue their Japanese employer under the provisions of U.S. law for failure to provide equal opportunity for them.

International Jurisdiction International law provides for three types of jurisdictional principles. The first is the **nationality principle,** which holds that every country has jurisdiction (authority or power) over its citizens no matter where they are located. Therefore, a U.S. manager who violates the American Foreign Corrupt Practices Act while traveling abroad can be found guilty in the United States. The second is the **territoriality principle,** which holds that every nation has the right of jurisdiction within its legal territory. Therefore, a German firm that sells a defective product in England can be sued under English law even though the company is headquartered outside of England. The third is the **protective principle,** which holds that every country has jurisdiction over behavior that adversely affects its national security, even if that conduct occurred outside the country. Therefore, a French firm that sells secret U.S. government blueprints for a satellite system can be subjected to U.S. laws.

Doctrine of Comity The **doctrine of comity** holds that there must be mutual respect for the laws, institutions, and government of other countries in the matter of jurisdiction over their own citizens. Although this doctrine is not part of international law, it is part of international custom and tradition.

Act of State Doctrine Under the **act of state doctrine,** all acts of other governments are considered to be valid by U.S. courts, even if such acts are inappropriate in the United States. As a result, for example, foreign governments have the right to set limits on the repatriation of MNC profits and to forbid companies from sending more than this amount out of the host country.

Treatment and Rights of Aliens Countries have the legal right to refuse admission of foreign citizens and to impose special restrictions on their conduct, right of travel, where they can stay, and what business they may conduct. Nations also can deport aliens.

Common law
Law that derives from English law and is the foundation of legislation in the United States, Canada, and England, among other nations.

Civil or code law
Law that is derived from Roman law and is found in the non-Islamic and nonsocialist countries.

Principle of sovereignty
An international principle of law which holds that governments have the right to rule themselves as they see fit.

Nationality principle
A jurisdictional principle of international law which holds that every country has jurisdiction over its citizens no matter where they are located.

Territoriality principle
A jurisdictional principle of international law which holds that every nation has the right of jurisdiction within its legal territory.

Protective principle
A jurisdictional principle of international law which holds that every country has jurisdiction over behavior that adversely affects its national security, even if the conduct occurred outside that country.

Doctrine of comity
A jurisdictional principle of international law which holds that there must be mutual respect for the laws, institutions, and government of other countries in the matter of jurisdiction over their own citizens.

Act of state doctrine
A jurisdictional principle of international law which holds that all acts of other governments are considered to be valid by U.S. courts, even if such acts are illegal or inappropriate under U.S. law.

For example, the United States has the right to limit the travel of Iranian or Chinese scientists coming into the U.S. to attend a scientific convention and can insist they remain within 5 miles of the hotel.

Forum for Hearing and Settling Disputes   This is a principle of U.S. justice as it applies to international law. At their discretion, U.S. courts can dismiss cases brought before them by foreigners; however, they are bound to examine issues such as where the plaintiffs are located, where the evidence must be gathered, and where property to be used in restitution is located. One of the best examples of this principle is the Union Carbide pesticide plant disaster in Bhopal, India. Over 2,000 people were killed and thousands left permanently injured when a toxic gas enveloped 40 square kilometers around the plant. The New York Court of Appeals sent the case back to India for resolution.

Examples of Legal and Regulatory Issues

The principles described earlier help to form the international legal and regulatory framework within which MNCs must operate. The following examines some examples of specific laws and situations that can have a direct impact on international business.

Foreign Corrupt Practices Act (FCPA)
Made into U.S. law in 1977 because of concerns over bribes in the international business arena, this act makes it illegal to influence foreign officials through personal payment or political contributions.

Foreign Corrupt Practices Act   During the special prosecutor's investigation of the Watergate scandal in the early 1970s, a number of questionable payments made by U.S. corporations to public officials abroad were uncovered. These bribes became the focal point of investigations by the U.S. Internal Revenue Service, Securities and Exchange Commission (SEC), and Justice Department. This concern over bribes in the international arena eventually culminated in the 1977 passage of the **Foreign Corrupt Practices Act (FCPA),** which makes it illegal to influence foreign officials through personal payment or political contributions. The objectives of the FCPA were to stop U.S. MNCs from initiating or perpetuating corruption in foreign governments and to upgrade the image of both the United States and its businesses abroad.[21]

Critics of the FCPA fear the loss of sales to foreign competitors, especially in those countries where bribery is an accepted way of doing business. Nevertheless, the U.S. government pushed ahead and attempted to enforce the act. Some of the countries that were named in early bribery cases under the law included Algeria, Kuwait, Saudi Arabia, and Turkey. The U.S. State Department tried to convince the SEC and Justice Department not to reveal countries or foreign officials who were involved in its investigations for fear of creating internal political problems for U.S. allies. Although this political sensitivity was justified, for the most part, several interesting developments occurred: (1) MNCs found that they could live within the guidelines set down by the FCPA; and (2) many foreign governments actually applauded these investigations under the FCPA, because it helped them to crack down on corruption in their own country.

One analysis has reported that since passage of the FCPA, U.S. exports to "bribe prone" countries actually increased.[22] Investigations reveal that once bribes were removed as a key competitive tool, more MNCs were willing to do business in that country. This proved to be true even in the Middle East, where many U.S. MNCs always assumed that bribes were required to ensure contracts. Data show this no longer is true. Additionally, Gillespie has noted:

> Multinational managers should be wary of believing the comforting writers . . . who assured them that bribing in developing countries was an accepted cultural norm. . . . The fact is that revolutionary new social orders *are* changing the patterns of centuries. Revolutionary forces swept away the Pahlavi dynasty in Iran and the Marcos regime in the Philippines. In the Middle East alone, numerous heads of state are scrambling to somehow deal with issues of corruption before revolutionary movements affect them. If multinational managers wish to remain cynical in the face of these evolving social changes, they may; but, in the meantime, they should be careful whom they bribe.[23]

Bureaucratization   Very restrictive foreign bureaucracies are one of the biggest problems facing MNCs. This is particularly true when bureaucratic government controls are inefficient and not corrected. A good example is Japan, whose political parties feel more beholden to their local interests than to those in the rest of the country.[24] As a result, it is extremely difficult to reorganize the Japanese bureaucracy and streamline the ways things are done, because so many politicians are more interested in the well-being of their own districts than in the long-run well-being of the nation as a whole.[25] In turn, parochial actions create problems for MNCs trying to do business there. The election of Keizo Obuchi as the new prime minister of Japan may help reduce some of this bureaucracy. Certainly the long-running recessionary economy of the country is leading to the beginning of change in the nation's antiquated banking system and is likely to make the markets there more open to competition. However, the fact that the bad debts held by Japanese banks was recently estimated to be near $1 trillion helps highlight some of the challenges that will be faced by Prime Minister Obuchi.[26]

Japanese businesses are also becoming more aware of the fact that they are dependent on the world market for many goods and services and when bureaucratic red tape drives up the costs of these purchases, local consumers pay the price. These businesses are also beginning to realize that government bureaucracy can create a false sense of security and leave them unprepared to face the harsh competitive realities of the international marketplace.

A good example was provided during the mid-1990s when the value of the yen rose sharply and resulted in a decline in international sales by local businesses. Foreign purchasers were unwilling to buy Japanese products that cost 30–40 percent more than they did just a few years earlier. At the same time, foreign firms exporting goods into the Japanese market found that they could easily compete because their prices were lower than those of Japanese producers whose costs were pegged to the high-value yen. As a result, Chrysler cut the price of its Jeep Cherokee by 10 percent and sales rose; and American computer manufacturers such as Compaq and IBM, largely on the basis of price, were able to double their share of the Japanese market. Since this time the yen has declined in market value and local businesses have been able to recapture some lost market share. However, local firms still face greater international competition than ever before.

Additionally, Japan now faces new problems. One of these is that the cost of doing business in Japan is often higher than in other Asian countries. As a result, there has been a recent trend by MNCs toward buying from these less expensive sources. In an effort to deal with this new challenge, the Japanese will have to continue to cut bureaucratic red tape and open their markets to foreign competition. The accompanying "International Management in Action: The United States Goes to the Mat" shows the pressure that has been put on Japan to open its markets. Only in this way in the long run will they drive down their own costs of doing business and remain competitive against world-class organizations.

Japan is not alone in terms of competitive regulations that reduce the ability of outsiders to do business locally. Figure 2–1 ranks a host of countries based on the fairness of competitive laws. As can be seen, Indonesia ranked last, primarily because the government dominates the economy and controls competition. At the other extreme, Australia has been found to have the best legislation for preventing unfair competition. A close look at the chart shows that Japan is well down in the bottom half of the list.

Privatization   Another example of the changing international regulatory environment is the current move toward privatization by an increasing number of countries. The German government, for example, has decided to speed up deregulation of the $66 billion telecommunications market. This has opened a host of opportunities for MNCs looking to create joint ventures with local German firms. Additionally, as noted in Chapter 1, the British government, even though they have moved from the conservative to the liberal Labour Party, continues selling off state-run operations; and in France the government is putting some of its businesses on the sale block. Meanwhile, in China the government has ordered the military to close or sell off between 10,000 and 20,000 companies that earn an estimated $9.5 billion annually. Known collectively as PLA Inc., the Chinese Army's business interests stretch from Hong Kong to the United States and include five-star hotels, paging

International Management in Action

The U.S. Goes to the Mat

www.fugi.stanford.edu/jguide

For a number of years, the United States has demanded that Japan open its markets and provide the same access that Japanese MNCs are accorded. One of the strategies used by the U.S. government has been to negotiate purchasing targets. For example, in the case of automobiles, the Japanese government several years ago agreed to buy a specific amount of U.S.-made auto parts. This strategy now seems to be a thing of the past, however. Japanese negotiators believe it was a mistake and say they will hold fast in future negotiations.

For their part, the current U.S. administration is pushing hard to level the playing field for trading with Japan. In 1995, the United States threatened to impose a major import tax on luxury Japanese cars coming into America. Some observers noted, however, that the U.S. government immediately tempered its hard line with a willingness to set an early date for talks with the Japanese about the trade impasse. The administration countered that this concession was quite minor and used simply to meet a condition set forth by the World Trade Organization (WTO). According to WTO rules, in the absence of a mutual agreement on a date to meet, the parties are required to get together before new sanctions are instituted. This does not mean that there will be a settlement, however, only that the two parties will discuss their differences.

One major roadblock to an early resolution of U.S. demands is that EU countries want to be included in these negotiations. They argue that any arrangement between the United States and Japan will result in their being denied market access. After all, if the Japanese agree to buy $6 billion of U.S.-made auto parts, this is market share that cannot be captured by EU MNCs. The EU wants Japan to open its markets to all countries and let each compete on the level playing field.

How far will Japan go in giving concessions? How determined is the United States to wrestle additional agreements from the Japanese? These questions are yet unanswered. One thing is certain, however: Japan is a major world market, and its citizens have enormous purchasing power. Therefore, all nations will continue efforts to break down trade walls and get into the lucrative Japanese market. For example, General Motors sells its Saturn line in Japan through a network of stand-alone dealerships. The cost of distributing and retailing vehicles in Japan is extremely high, but GM feels that the strong market there is worth this risk. Additionally, GM has been selling Saturns in Taiwan and believes this experience has helped reduce the risk in the Japanese market.

The steps being taken by the U.S. government and some of the major MNCs, such as GM, are important in opening up the Japanese market. Much needs to be done, however, and the U.S. government believes that success in this area will require it to "go to the mat" with Japan. The outcome promises to be not only interesting, but vital to the success of world trade.

Figure 2–1

National Competitive Laws Based on Fairness

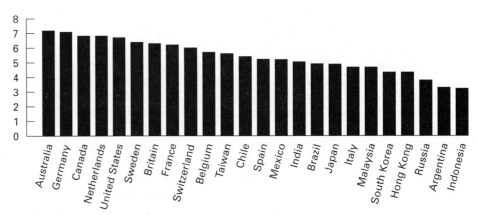

Source: Reported in the *Economist,* May 16, 1998, p. 113.

services to golf courses, and Baskin-Robbins ice cream franchises. When the government cut the military budget during the early 1990s, it allowed the Army to make up this short-fall by earning commercial revenue. However, now the government has decided that the Army must get out of this end of the business and let the free market take over.[27]

Other good examples of privatization can be found in Latin America. In this decade Mexico has sold almost $20 billion of government assets, while Argentina and Brazil have collectively earned almost $30 billion through such sales. Moreover, in the case of Brazil, which has proceeded very quietly with its privatization efforts, total sales are expected to top the $50 billion mark before the program is complete.[28] One of its largest recent privatization transactions involved the auction of the telephone system for $19 billion. Telefonica of Spain, Portugal Telecom, and the MCI Communications Corporation, partners in a loose global alliance, spent $11.6 billion for a large portion of this system, and the total raised by the auction was 64 percent more than the advertised minimum bids.[29]

Technological Environment

The technological environment is moving at lightning speed. Computers, telephones, televisions, and wireless forms of communication now are merging into telecommunications both to create multimedia products and to allow individuals anywhere in the world to communicate with each other. In addition, a growing number of people now have access to the Internet, allowing them to obtain information from literally millions of sources, and the number of web sites is rising sharply. In recent years the worldwide number has increased by more than 300 percent.[30] In addition, more and more non-English speaking people are turning to the Internet for information. Estimates are that by 2002 there will be 250 million English speaking people accessing the Net and 400 million accessing the Net in languages other than English, the most common of these being Japanese and German.[31] In addition to Internet access, other specific ways in which technology will affect international management in the next decade include:

1. Rapid advances in biotechnology that are built on the precise manipulation of organisms, which will revolutionize the fields of agriculture, medicine, and industry.

2. The emergence of nanotechnology, in which nanomachines will possess the ability to remake the whole physical universe.

3. Satellites that will play a role in learning. For example, communication firms will place tiny satellites into low orbit, thus making it possible for millions of people, even in remote or sparsely populated regions like Siberia, the Chinese desert, and the African interior, to send and receive voice, data, and digitized images through handheld telephones.

4. Automatic translation telephones, which will allow people to communicate naturally in their own language with anyone in the world who has access to a telephone.

5. Artificial intelligence and embedded learning technology, which will allow thinking that formerly was felt to be only the domain of humans to occur in machines.

6. Silicon chips containing up to 100 million transistors, allowing computing power that now rests only in the hands of supercomputer users to be available on every desktop.

7. Supercomputers that are capable of 1 trillion calculations per second, which will allow advances such as simulations of the human body for testing new drugs and computers that respond easily to spoken commands.[32]

Although all these technological wonders will affect international management, more specific technologies also will have an even more direct impact. The following discussion highlights some specific dimensions of the technological environment currently facing international management.

E-Commerce

As the Internet becomes increasingly common, it is having a dramatic effect on international commerce. Customers can now use their computers to travel through electronic shops, view products, and read descriptions of merchandise. Not as common, however, is use of their keyboard to pay by credit card. However, as the security issues are being solved, the day is fast approaching when electronic cash (e-cash) will be common. When this happens, there will be a convergence of money, commerce, and personal computers. Here is a brief description of how e-cash might work:

> To see how e-cash might evolve on the Internet, start with the rudimentary transaction scheme run by Mr. Stein's First Virtual Holdings. Both buyer and seller must have accounts at the "bank." In the case of the buyer, this amounts to an authority for First Virtual to make charges against his credit card. When the buyer, having investigated the seller's wares on the Internet and found something that he likes, makes a purchase, he gives his account number to the seller, who ships the product. Each day or each week the merchant sends his list of who-bought-what to First Virtual, which sends e-mail messages to buyers asking them to confirm the transactions. Once a buyer confirms, his (conventional) credit card is charged and the money is transferred to the seller's account. If the buyer withholds confirmation, First Virtual withholds settlement.[33]

This scenario already occurs in a number of not-as-sophisticated forms. A good example is prepaid smart cards, which are being used mostly for telephone calls and public transportation. An individual can purchase one of these cards and use it in lieu of cash. This idea will blend into the Internet, allowing individuals to buy and sell merchandise and transfer funds electronically. The result will be global digital cash, which will take advantage of existing worldwide markets that allow buying and selling on a 24-hour basis.[34]

This technological development also will have a major impact on financial institutions. After all, who will need the local corner ATM when they can tap into their funds through the Internet? Similarly, companies will not have to wait for their money from buyers, thus eliminating (or at least substantially reducing) bad debts while increasing their working capital. Therefore, if General Electric shipped $12 million of merchandise to Wal-Mart in Hong Kong with payment due on delivery, the typical 7- to 10-day waiting period between payment and collection of international transactions would, for all intents and purposes, be eliminated.[35]

Of course, e-cash will create many problems, and it will take some time for these to be resolved. For example, if a Mexican firm pays for its merchandise in pesos, there must be some system for converting these pesos into U.S. dollars. At present, such transactions are handled through regulated foreign exchange markets. In the near future, these transactions likely will be denominated in a single, conventional currency and exchanged at conventional market rates. It is equally likely, however, that the entire system of transactions eventually will become seamless and require no processing through foreign exchange markets. One expert explained it this way:

> Ideally, the ultimate e-cash will be a currency without a country (or a currency of all countries), infinitely exchangeable without the expense and inconvenience of conversion between local denominations. It may constitute itself as a wholly new currency with its own denomination—the "cyber dollar," perhaps. Or, it may continue to fix itself by reference to a traditional currency, in which case the American dollar would seem to be the likeliest possibility. Either way, it is hard to imagine that the existence of an international, easy-to-use, cheap-to-process, hard-to-tax electronic money will not then force freer convertibility on traditional currencies.[36]

Telecommunications

The most obvious dimension of the technological environment facing international management today is telecommunications. To begin with, it no longer is necessary to hardwire a city to provide residents with telephone service. This can be done wirelessly, thus allowing people to use cellular phones, beepers, and other telecommunications services. As a result, growth in the wireless technology business worldwide has been rapid, and the future promises even more. In South America and Eastern Europe, customers once waited years to get a telephone installed. Now, thanks to cellular phones, a form of technologic leapfrogging is occurring, in which the populace is moving from a situation where phones were unavailable to one where cellular is available throughout the country, including rural areas, because the infrastructure needed to support this development can be installed both quickly and easily.[37]

One reason for this rapid increase in telecommunications services is many countries believe that without an efficient telephone system, their economic growth may stall. Additionally, governments are accepting the belief that the only way to attract foreign investment and know-how in telecommunications is to give up control to private industry. As a result, while most telecommunications operators in the Asia-Pacific region were state-run in 1990, approximately 30 percent were in private hands by 1995. Singapore Telecommunications, Pakistan Telecom, Thailand's Telecom Asia, and Globe Telecom in the Philippines all have been privatized, and MNCs have helped in this process by providing investment funds. Today, NYNEX holds a stake in Telecom Asia; US West owns 20 percent of Binariang, which is building a digital cell-phone system in Malaysia; Bell Atlantic and Ameritech each own 25 percent of Telecom New Zealand; and Bell South has an ownership position in Australia's Optus. At the same time, Australia's Telstra is moving into Vietnam; Japan's NTT is investing in Thailand, and Korea Telecommunications is in the Philippines and Indonesia.[38]

Many governments are reluctant to allow so much private and foreign ownership of such a vital industry; however, they also are aware that foreign investors will go elsewhere if the deal is not satisfactory. The Hong Kong office of Salomon Brothers, a U.S. investment bank, estimates that to meet the expanding demand for telephone service in Asia, companies will need to increase the number of telephone lines by 17 percent annually. This will require raising $90 billion in capital, most of which will have to come from overseas. MNCs are unwilling to put up this much money unless they are assured of operating control and a sufficiently high return on their investment.

A good example occurred in China, where in 1994 the government announced that foreign investors who were interested in building and operating power plants would have their annual rate of return (ROI) capped at 12 percent. Investors immediately began looking for more lucrative opportunities in other power-hungry Asian nations, and now China has increased the ROI cap to continue attracting deals. China presently is facing a similar backlash from telecommunications firms as well, which are only allowed to provide advice and to supply and manufacture telecommunication equipment for the Chinese market and are banned from the potentially more lucrative business of owning and/or operating these services.

Unlike China, however, other developing countries are eager to attract telecommunication firms and offer liberal terms. Cable & Wireless of Great Britain has opened an office in Hanoi. In India, MNCs from around the world are bidding to become part of a joint venture with Indian firms that will compete against state monopolies in 21 regions. In Hong Kong, while the local telephone monopoly will not lose its grip on international services until 2006, its monopoly on local services recently ended, and private groups are competing to provide service.

The Employment Fallout from Technology

In international management, technology also impacts the number of employees who are needed to carry out operations effectively. As MNCs use advanced technology to help them communicate, produce, and deliver their goods and services internationally, they face a new challenge: how technology will affect the nature and number of their employees. Some informed observers note that technology already has eliminated much, and in the future will eliminate even more of the work now being done by middle management and white-collar staff. In this century, machines have replaced millions of manual laborers, but those who worked with their minds were able to thrive and survive.

During the past two decades in particular, blue-collar, smoke-stack industries such as steel and autos have been downsized by technology, and the result has been a permanent restructuring of the number of employees needed to run factories efficiently. In the 1990s, the same thing was happening in the white-collar service industries (insurance, banks, and even government).

Some experts predict that in the future technology will be so all-pervasive that it has the potential to largely displace employees in all industries, from those doing low-skilled jobs to those holding positions traditionally reserved for human thinking. For example, voice recognition is helping to replace telephone operators; the demand for postal workers has been reduced severely by address-reading devices; and cash-dispensing machines can do 10 times more transactions in a day than bank tellers, so the number of tellers can be reduced, or even eliminated entirely, in the future. Also, expert (sometimes called "smart") systems can eliminate human thinking completely. For example, American Express has an expert system that performs the credit analysis formerly done by college-graduate financial analysts. In the medical field, expert systems can diagnose some illnesses as well as doctors, and robots capable of performing hip replacements are under development.

Emerging information technology also makes work more portable. This is especially true for work that can be easily contracted with overseas locations. For example, low-paid workers in India and Asian countries now are being given subcontracted work such as labor-intensive software development and data-entry jobs. A restructuring of the nature of work and of employment is resulting from such information technology; Figure 2–2 provides some specific, projected winners and losers in the workforce of the future.

The new technological environment has both positives and negatives for MNCs and societies as a whole. On the positive side, the cost of doing business worldwide should go down thanks to the opportunities that technology offers in substituting lower-cost machines for higher-priced labor. Productivity should go up, and prices should go down. On the negative side, many employees will find either their jobs eliminated or their wages and salaries reduced because they have been replaced by machines and their skills are no longer in high demand. This job loss from technology can be especially devastating in developing countries. However, it doesn't have to be this way. A case in point is South Africa's showcase for automotive productivity, the Delta Motor Corporation's Opel Corsa plant in Port Elizabeth. To provide as many jobs as possible, this world-class operation automated only 23 percent compared to more than 85 percent of European and North American auto assembly.[39] Also, some industries can add jobs. For example, in the computer and information technology industry, the negative has been offset by the positive. For example, over the last decade, employment in the U.S. computer-software industry has tripled, and the Bureau of Labor Statistics forecasts even more rapid growth in the next decade. Additionally, even though developed countries such as Japan and the United States are most affected by technological displacement of workers, both nations still lead the world in creating new jobs and shifting their traditional industrial structure toward a high-tech, knowledge-based economy.

The precise impact that the advanced technological environment will have on international management over the next decade is difficult to forecast. One thing is certain, however; there is no turning back the technological clock. MNCs and nations alike must evaluate the impact of these changes carefully and realize that their economic performance is closely tied to keeping up, or ahead, of advancing technology.

World of Business Week—Revisited

As the *Business Week* article presented in the beginning of this chapter illustrated, traditional political and regulatory barriers that prohibited the growth of the small business sector are rapidly being dismantled worldwide. Nowhere is this more

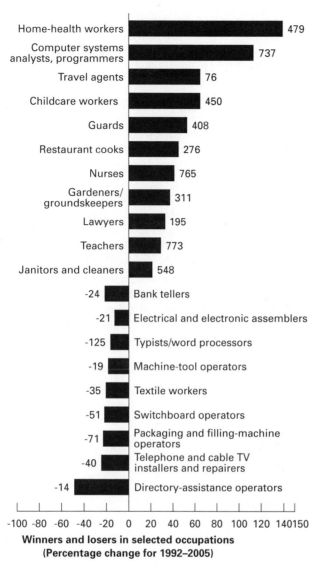

Figure 2–2

Winners and Losers in Selected Occupations (Percentage Change Forecasts for 1992–2005)

**Winners and losers in selected occupations
(Percentage change for 1992–2005)**

Source: U.S. Bureau of Labor Statistics.

apparent than in Europe where the deregulation and restructuring of industrial giants have sent a myriad of workers to the ranks of unemployment. As the article notes, many are turning to entrepreneurism as an alternative. Entrepreneurs, such as TelePizza's Leopoldo Fernández Pujals, who in the past could only dream of starting their own business given the rates of taxation, inflexible labor laws, and political red tape, are now experiencing a more entrepreneurial friendly climate and seeing their companies grow at phenomenal rates. In addition, companies such as France's Gemplus are utilizing sophisticated new technologies as they become more readily available to help their businesses grow. Now that you have read this chapter, you should have a better understanding of how the political, regulatory, and technological environments affect companies around the world. In light of this, answer the following questions: (1) What role can the Internet play in the growth of the entrepreneurial sector? (2) What can governments do to help pave the way for new start-ups that they aren't already doing? (3) What implications are there for sending a mixed message to businesses by encouraging large corporate mergers on the one hand and small start-ups on the other?

Summary of Key Points

1. Today's political environment presents a myriad of challenges for MNCs. China is going through a transition as the old guard passes from the scene. The political situation in Europe also continues to change. Russia is facing economic problems and social upheaval, and the rest of Central and Eastern Europe has had varying degrees of success with their newfound freedom and continue to struggle with their past.

2. The current legal and regulatory environment is both complex and confusing. There are many different laws and regulations to which MNCs doing business internationally must conform, and each nation is unique. Also, MNCs must abide by the laws of their own country. For example, U.S. MNCs must obey the rules set down by the Foreign Corrupt Practices Act. MNCs doing business in Japan face a wide range of bureaucratic rules and regulations that often are both time-wasting and inefficient, and MNCs in

Europe have to adopt to the ever-changing guidelines accompanying the respective government's privatization programs.

3. The technological environment is changing quickly and is having a major impact on international business. This will continue in the future. For example, money transfers and exchange are changing dramatically. Also, areas such as telecommunications offer developing countries new opportunities to leapfrog into the twenty-first century. New markets are being created for high-tech MNCs that are eager to provide telecommunications service. Technological developments also impact on both the nature and the structure of employment, shifting the industrial structure toward a more high-tech, knowledge-based economy. MNCs who understand and take advantage of this high-tech environment should prosper, but they also must keep up, or ahead, to survive the highly competitive years ahead.

Key Terms

Islamic law	principle of sovereignty	doctrine of comity
socialist law	nationality principle	act of state doctrine
common law	territoriality principle	Foreign Corrupt Practices Act
civil or code law	protective principle	(FCPA)

Review and Discussion Questions

1. In what way does the new political environment around the world create challenges for MNCs? Would these challenges be less for those operating in the EU than for those in Russia or China? Why or why not?

2. How do the following legal principles impact on MNC operations: the principle of sovereignty, the nationality principle, the territoriality principle, the protective principle, and principle of comity?

3. How could the national and local government bureaucracy in Japan impede the operations of a U.S. MNC doing business there? What are some Japanese laws or regulations that would reduce the MNC's effectiveness?

4. Why are developing countries interested in privatizing their telecommunications industries? What opportunities does this privatization have for telecommunication MNCs?

Internet Exercise: Hitachi Goes Worldwide

Hitachi products are well-known in the United States, as well as in Europe and Asia. However, in an effort to continue maintaining its international momentum, the Japanese MNC is continuing to push forward into new markets, while also developing new products. Visit the MNC at its web site **www.hitachi.com** and examine some of the latest developments that are taking place. Begin by reviewing the firm's current activities in Asia, specifically Hong Kong and Singapore. Then look at how it is doing business in North America. Finally, read about

its European operations. All of these are available at this web site. Then answer these three questions: (1) What kinds of products does the firm offer? What are its primary areas of emphasis? (2) In what types of environments does it operate? Is Hitachi primarily interested in developed markets or is it also pushing into newly emerging markets? (3) Based on what it has been doing over the last 2–3 years, what do you think Hitachi's future strategy will be in competing in the environment of international business during the first decade of the new millenium?

Vietnam

Located in Southeast Asia, the Socialist Republic of Vietnam is bordered to the north by the People's Republic of China, to the west by Laos and Cambodia, and to the east and south by the South China Sea. The country is a mere 127,000 square miles but has a population of almost 76 million. The language is Vietnamese and the principal religion Buddhism, although there are a number of small minorities, including Confucian, Christian (mainly Catholic), Caodist, Daoist, and Hoa Hao. In recent years, the country's economy has been improving dramatically, but average per-capita income still is in the hundreds of dollars as the peasants still remain very poor.

One of the reasons that Vietnam has lagged behind its fast-developing neighbors in Southeast Asia, such as Thailand, Malaysia, and Indonesia, is its isolation from the industrial west, and the United States in particular, because of the Vietnam war. From the mid-1970s, the country had close relations with the U.S.S.R., but the collapse of communism there forced the still-communist Vietnamese government to work on establishing stronger economic ties with other countries. The nation recently has worked out many of its problems with China, and today, the Chinese have become a useful economic ally. Vietnam would most like to establish a vigorous trade relationship with the United States, however. Efforts toward this end began over a decade ago, but because of lack of information concerning the many U.S. soldiers still unaccounted for after the war, it was not until 1993 that the United States permitted U.S. companies to take part in ventures in Vietnam that were financed by international aid agencies. Then, in 1994, the U.S. trade embargo was lifted, and a growing number of American firms began doing business in Vietnam.

Caterpillar began supplying equipment for a $2 billion highway project. Mobil teamed with three Japanese partners to begin drilling offshore. Exxon, Amoco, Conoco, Unocal, and Arco negotiated production-sharing contracts with Petro Vietnam. General Electric opened a trade office and developed plans to use electric products throughout the country. AT&T began working to provide long-distance service both in and out of the country. Coca-Cola began bottling operations. Within the first 12 months, 70 U.S. companies obtained licenses to do business in Vietnam. Mobil and Occidental Petroleum are actively exploring for offshore oil, and U.S. consumer products from Pepsi to Motorola are big sellers. Convenience stores carry Heinz ketchup and Kraft salad dressing, and Baskin-Robbins has opened an ice-cream parlor in Ho Chi Minh City. If relations between the two countries continue on their present course, more and more opportunities will open up for U.S. MNCs.

www.vietnamacces.com

Questions

1. In what way does the political environment in Vietnam pose both an opportunity and a threat for American MNCs seeking to do business there?

2. Why are U.S. multinationals so interested in going into Vietnam? How much potential does the country offer? Conversely, how much benefit can Vietnam derive from a business relationship with U.S. MNCs?

3. Would there be any opportunities in Vietnam for high-tech American firms? Why or why not?

A Chinese Venture

The Darby Company is a medium-size communications technology company headquartered on the west coast of the United States. Among other things, Darby holds a patent on a portable telephone that can operate effectively within a 5-mile radius. The phone does not contain state-of-the-art technology, but it can be produced extremely cheaply. As a result, the Chinese government has expressed interest in manufacturing and selling this phone throughout their country.

Preliminary discussions with the Chinese government reveal that some major terms of the agreement that it would like include: (1) Darby will enter into a joint venture with a local Chinese firm to manufacture the phones to Darby's specifications; (2) these phones would be sold throughout China at a 100 percent markup, and Darby will receive 10 percent of the profits; (3) Darby will invest $35 million in building the manufacturing facility, and these costs will be recovered over a 5-year period; and (4) the government in Beijing will guarantee that at least 100,000 phones are sold every year, or it will purchase the difference.

The Darby management is not sure whether this is a good deal. In particular, Darby executives have heard all sorts of horror stories regarding agreements that the Chinese government has made and then broken. The company also is concerned that once its technology is understood, the Chinese will walk away from the agreement and start making these phones on their own. Because the technology is not state-of-the-art, the real benefit is in the low production costs, and this knowledge is more difficult to protect.

For its part, the Chinese government has promised to sign a written contract with Darby, and it has agreed that any disputes regarding enforcement of this contract can be brought, by either side, to the World Court at the Hague for resolution. Should this course of action be taken, each side would be responsible for its own legal fees, but the Chinese have promised to accept the decision of the court as binding.

Darby has 30 days to decide whether to sign the contract with the Chinese. After this time, the Chinese intend to pursue negotiations with a large telecommunications firm in Europe and try cutting a deal with them. Darby is more attractive to the Chinese, however, because of the low cost of producing its telephone. In any event, the Chinese are determined to begin mass producing cellular phones in their country. "Our future is tied to high-tech communication," the Chinese Minister of Finance recently told Darby's president. "That is why we are so anxious to do business with your company; you have quality phones at low cost." Darby management is flattered by these kind words but still not sure if this is the type of business deal in which it wants to get involved.

Questions

1. How important is the political environment in China for the Darby Company? Explain.

2. If a disagreement arises between the two joint-venture partners and the government of China reneges on its promises, how well protected is Darby's position? Explain.

3. Are the economic and technological environments in China favorable for Darby? Why or why not?

Chapter 3

Global Competitiveness

Objectives of the Chapter

As MNCs continue to expand their operations and begin to do business in every part of the globe, the competitive pressures will mount. In competitive battles, MNCs will try to gain an advantage (i.e., gain a competitive advantage) over rivals in attracting and maintaining targeted customers and obtaining a larger share of the global market. In the type of environment outlined in Chapters 1 and 2, all MNCs must become increasingly competitive. They must be able to compete with anybody, anywhere, anytime (the "Three Any's"). Being third or fourth in an industry or the world market in this competitive environment is not sufficient in the long run. Organizations must strive to be the best: a world-class organization (WCO).

The overriding objective of this chapter is to examine how MNCs are trying to become WCOs. First, attention is given to the issues of quality and why MNCs must strive to develop the highest-quality goods and services anywhere. Next, the discussion shifts beyond quality to learning organizations and their major characteristics. Finally, the characteristics of WCOs and some specific, real-world examples of how some MNCs are becoming WCOs are considered. These MNCs are able to compete with anybody, anywhere, anytime. The specific objectives of this chapter are:

1. DESCRIBE The importance of quality in helping multinational organizations in Three Any's competitiveness.

2. DEFINE learning organizations and their key characteristics.

3. DESCRIBE the major pillars of world-class organizations (WCOs) and how these pillars are critical in Three Any's competitiveness.

BusinessWeek

The World of Business Week:

Make Way for GE Capital

Not far from the center of Leeds in northeastern England is Burton Business Park, an industrial complex that dates from the 1930s. With loading bays that look like row houses and other antiquated flourishes, it seems a relic. But the 1,000 or so people working on the site for General Electric Capital Services Inc. are doing their bit to reshape Europe's economy.

At the beginning of the decade, GE Capital Services was a nonentity in Europe. Now, it is hard to avoid. If you apply for a Harrods store card in London, the Leeds operation will approve it. If you buy a Peugeot car in France, your purchase will likely be financed through Sovac, a lending company that GE Capital bought in 1995 for $1.5 billion. GE Capital can sell you health insurance for your dog through Pet Protect, a 1996 British acquisition. And it can provide a company with everything from a fleet of cars to shipping containers, modular office space, and time on a communications satellite.

Outflanked?

Stealthily, General Electric Co.'s financial wing has become one of Europe's biggest nonbank finance players. With footholds in some 20 business lines and in 21 European countries, it is already a leader in fleet and aircraft leasing and in consumer finance. So far, GE Capital Europe has grown through acquisitions, buying up more than 100 European compa-

nies or units with more than $30 billion in assets in the last few years.

That may have been the easy part. With the single currency, the company is under pressure to integrate its businesses into an efficient, Europewide empire. If it succeeds, Europe's big banks could find themselves seriously outflanked. "We need to figure out the appropriate level of consolidation," says Daniel W. Porter, the new managing director of GE Capital Europe.

GE Capital is already hugely profitable. But as Europe becomes integrated economically and shifts more toward services, the platforms GE Capital has established could become foundations for even more power. A few businesses, including equipment leasing and reinsurance, are already run on a Europewide basis. Others, such as auto and consumer finance, are likely to benefit from broad consolidation in the future. And GE Capital could realize big gains from merging back-office operations across Europe, perhaps across business lines.

Strategically, Capital has taken the same course in Europe that has brought it success in the U.S.—snapping up unglamorous businesses in leasing, insurance, or consumer credit. The company puts in new management, if needed, and introduces more efficient technology and work methods. It combines companies in similar business lines to gain economies of scale, and it sets tough targets for its managers.

And in the mid-1990s, Europe was a natural hunting ground for GE Capital. Prices were lower than in the U.S., and European finance was much more frag-

mented. There were big gains to be made by reorganizing businesses on a Europewide scale. It was a bet, says CEO Gary C. Wendt, that "Europe would follow the U.S. and consolidate economically." That bet turned out to be right on the money.

Like Europe's banks, GE Capital is looking for ways to cut costs and position itself for the euro. In Ireland, it is setting up a Europewide multilingual center at Shannon to handle collections for all European consumer finance—thus combining the work now being done in several locations. But it is just as interested in boosting revenues. On a tour of the Leeds facility, Andrew K. Haste, who runs the business, points to a group of telemarketers selling home loans or insurance to people who have lost their credit cards or moved. "We are introducing more and more common packages across consumer businesses," he says.

A setback was the May departure of Porter's predecessor, Christopher Mackenzie, a British investment banker who had spearheaded the acquisition drive in Europe since 1994. Mackenzie was offered a promotion to head GE Capital's global acquisitions but left to join the New York buyout firm of Clayton, Dubilier & Rice Inc. Sources familiar with the situation say Mackenzie had argued with Wendt that a Europe-based head was needed to integrate the business lines. At present, most unit chiefs report to executives in the U.S. Mackenzie also tangled with headquarters in Stamford, Conn., over who should get credit for GE Capital's European successes. Wendt says that Mackenzie left to cut his travel schedule. Mackenzie declined to comment.

Now, Porter, a Californian, leads a team of 30 young merger specialists working in a nondescript office building in London. He acknowledges that the pace of acquisitions in Western Europe is likely to slow. But he sees big opportunities in Eastern Europe and in Greece, Italy, Portugal, and Spain, which are not as well covered by investment bankers.

By Stanley Reed in London

www.ge.com/capital

Source: **Reprinted from July 20, 1998, pp. 50–51 issue of** *Business Week* **by special permission, copyright ©1998 by the McGraw-Hill Companies, Inc.**

The opening news story focuses on the growing realization of what is required to succeed and even survive in today's global market. Companies that once served a specific geographic area or serviced a specific need have learned to compete with Anybody, Anywhere, Anytime. Needing to diversify in order to compete in the new millennium, more and more multinationals are finding it essential to be proactive—seizing opportunities, recognizing obstacles, and anticipating (not just responding to) change if they want to be not only a total quality organization, but a world-class organization (WCO). GE is one company that was able to do just that. By being one of the first to recognize the potential of the European market, GE Capital, a subsidiary offering everything from financing, health insurance, autos, and office space, to fleet and aircraft leasing, became a potent competitor on the continent. By anticipating their markets, creating economies of scale, and employing innovative human resource management techniques, GE Capital represents the type of competitive MNC vying for global market dominance in the 21st century.

The Total Quality Issue

Total quality is a major issue for MNCs in the new millennium. One major reason is because in the international marketplace customers do not care who provides the goods and services they want; they simply want their expectations to be met or exceeded. This is why auto consumers across the world now pay little attention to where the company is headquartered. International consumers are more concerned that the autos perform well, have few (if any) mechanical defects, last a long time, and are competitively priced, than whether the firm is Japanese, Korean, U.S. or German based. The same is true for many other products, from cameras and televisions to computers and video laser disks. To meet or exceed customer expectations, at minimum the MNC must give attention to quality as well as cost. Accordingly, a technology paradox is inherent in this total quality emphasis, and, of course, innovation takes on new importance.

The Technology Paradox Facing MNCs

Paradox
A statement that appears to be contradictory but is not, such as "increases in product quality often result in a decline of the cost of producing the goods."

A **paradox** is a statement that appears to be contradictory but is not. For example, when Motorola began developing a worldwide strategy for its cellular telephones and pagers, it faced the "quality versus cost" dilemma. If the firm increased the quality of its products to unprecedented levels, would their price not become prohibitive? For years, engineers contended that it would, and they explained this idea in terms of a "bath tub" diagram, an example of which is provided in Figure 3-1. As the number of failures is reduced, the cost of achieving these quality levels goes up dramatically. As a result, the company at first attempted to balance quality and cost by producing products that offered "sufficient" quality and fairly low price.

By the 1980s, however, Motorola began to challenge this thinking by asking: How much will it cost to increase quality to ever-higher levels? In particular, the MNC decided to reduce the number of errors to as low a level as possible and compute the cost of producing these quality products. In doing so, Motorola engineers began measuring quality in terms of defective parts per million. This answer can be expressed in terms of sigma, and the higher the sigma, the lower the number of defects per million parts. Here are four examples:

Sigma	Errors per million
3	66,810.0
4	6,210.0
5	233.0
6	3.4

Now Motorola began to examine the costs associated with these various levels of sigma. As the error rate fell, so did the cost of producing the product. For example, the cost of rework and the amount of scrap decreases, and of course there is an indirect but very significant impact on customer satisfaction and demand/loyalty. Figure 3-2 shows this graphically. Clearly, what this amazingly showed was that quality and cost are inversely related! In other words, MNCs that produce quality products can do so at a lower cost per unit than for products with higher error rates. The reason that so many MNCs did not see this relationship earlier is that they were blindsided by the old quality/cost paradox. Now the idea is becoming widespread. For example, General Electric recently committed $200 million to a quality program designed to sharply reduce the number of product defects. The cost of such defects in a typical firm runs 10–15 percent of revenues. GE estimates that if it can reach 6 sigma, it will cut costs by around $10 billion annually.[1]

Technology also presents MNCs with a paradox, but this one is far more significant. For many years, multinational firms believed that new technology could be exploited best

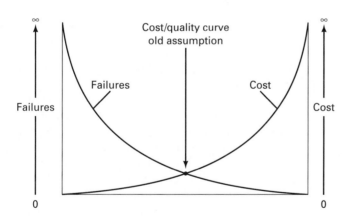

Figure 3–1

The Quality/Cost Curve as Initially Perceived

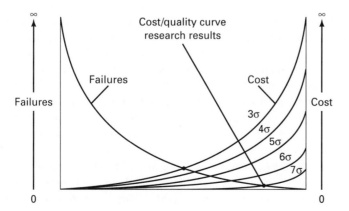

Figure 3–2

Quality/Cost Curve as Determined Through Research

by getting to the market first and charging premium prices. Now, however, they are learning that perhaps the best way to exploit their advantage is to lower prices as quickly as possible. The lower price helps them to grow international market share and substantially increase their revenues and profits. In fact, in many cases, MNCs now are even giving away their technology or selling it at a very low price, because the follow-on market is where the most profits are generated. For example, the Japanese MNC Toshiba will not earn back the investment poured into its digital-movie player through sales of this piece of equipment; however, it likely will more than recover its money by selling spinoff products, such as high-capacity audio players, storage devices for laptop computers, and other products that use related technology.[2] Similarly, Teleport Communications Group Inc. will install a dozen optical fibers with 1 million times more capacity than a customer needs, at no extra charge, because this MNC realizes optical fibers are so inexpensive that it makes sense to install enough capacity to last a lifetime. Sooner or later, the customer will begin using this added capacity.

Technology paradox
That high-tech businesses can thrive at the very moment that their prices are falling the fastest.

The Toshiba and Teleport examples illustrate the **technology paradox:** high-tech MNCs can thrive at the very moment their prices are falling the fastest. As George Fisher, past CEO of Motorola and now head of Eastman Kodak, puts it, "The only thing that matters is if the exponential growth of your market is faster than the exponential decline of your prices."[3] Today, successful MNCs are less interested in developing a single product than they are in creating a technology allowing them to develop a series of interrelated products that provide them with entry into an increasing number of markets around the world. This new development can be explained as follows:

> Successful strategists soak out costs, cut prices, and then wait for business to roll in. Step 1 is a price decline—say, in DRAM chips. At first it causes chaos, as in the early 1980s, when American producers fled the DRAM market amid cries of Japanese dumping. In Step 2, the market finds a new use for the cheap resource. Case in point: Windows software, which is ubiquitous and gobbles megabytes of DRAMs. Unit prices of the chips may fall, but gross revenue soars—a point that is lost on those who once again predict doom for commodity chip-makers. The next wave of chip demand will come from the likes of computers that obey spoken commands and communicate in 3-D images. After that? Believable virtual reality and intelligent artificial intelligence.[4]

And even among WCOs, this can be a major challenge. For example, Intel has long held a near-monopoly in providing the microprocessors that are the brains of personal computers (PCs). However, competitors have now succeeded in creating less expensive microprocessors for use in non-PC applications. As a result, these competitors are dominating the market for devices such as smart identification cards, Internet-ready telephones, handheld computers, and digital cameras. Since this market is likely to offer far more growth than PCs, Intel is now working to gain a competitive foothold here.[5]

Another example is Motorola, which stumbled in recent years when it failed to anticipate the industry's switch to digital cell phones from its long-dominant analog devices, and then overestimated its capability to get digital equipment to market. So while Motorola still held the greatest share of the U.S. wireless phone market in the late 1990s, its share of the worldwide wireless network system had dropped sharply to below one-third. Clearly the company faces a major challenge in the millennium.[6]

Successful MNCs understand the impact of the technology paradox, and they are prepared to pursue international market share by competing anytime and anywhere through creating total quality products. These products' "technology architecture" allows for the development or integration of many other products. For example, personal computer makers know their success would be greatly limited if all they did was sell these machines; however, by combining other value-added features, such as software, troubleshooting, and training, they can add to their initial package and keep their product from becoming a generic offering sold strictly on price. Additionally, in the case of firms such as Dell Computer, these machines can be tailor-made to meet the expectations of international customers. This strategy, commonly referred to as **mass customization,** helps maintain product uniqueness and prevents the machine from being viewed as a generic offer-

Mass customization
Tailor-making mass-production products to meet the expectations of the customer.

ing. A major part of the success equation remains the MNC's ability to develop and maintain its innovative capacity.

The Innovation Challenge Facing MNCs

Michael Porter has emphasized that the key to successful multinational efforts in global competitive battles is the ability to innovate continually.[7] This has been especially true for the most successful MNCs. For example, 3M generates 30 percent of its annual revenues from products that were brought to market in the last four years, and the number of patents issued to the MNC annually continues to increase. At the same time, 3M has managed to accelerate the product cycle by reducing cost and waste and bringing their products to fruition in record time. One way in which this is accomplished is through vast databases that allow employees bureaucracy-free access to company experts in each of its diverse technologies; in this way, one good idea is more likely to team up with another. The company also brings in outside experts, and it encourages scientists to present innovations to their peers, thus increasing the opportunities for cross-fertilization. Despite this drive for innovation, 3M also never loses sight of its customers, and this is noted in one report as follows:

> At the same time, 3M's inventors are getting closer to its customers, whose needs and preferences have sometimes taken second place to the firm's obsessive quest for innovation. Now customer preferences are constantly reassessed at each stage of a new product's development. Marketing folk have been moved closer to scientists: R&D staff are now more closely involved in overall product strategy. "Cross-functional" teams abound. To squeeze every last product out of each innovation, says Mr. Coyne [head of R&D], the company must empower every employee. "Managers must set goals, then get out of the way."[8]

The Importance of Vision   The approaches of other successful MNCs in developing quality products often are quite similar. One such approach to stimulate innovation involves having a vision. The MNC will develop an idea of how the market will look in the future, then create products or services based on this vision. For example, Canon of Japan envisioned a world in which photocopiers were small, cheap, and ubiquitous, then used this vision to drive its developmental and production strategies. Harley-Davidson has its senior-level executives spend time in the field with bikers, visiting rallies, and discussing with customers what they like about their bikes and what changes they would like to see. Epson, which is world famous for its small printers, has its young engineers spend 6 months as salespeople, and then 6 months in the service department, so they can learn directly what the customer wants and expects.

The Need to Benchmark   Another approach commonly used by MNCs in their relentless effort to develop innovative products is the effective use of **benchmarking.** This is the process of identifying what leading-edge competitors are doing, then using information to produce improved products or services. Among the best MNCs, benchmarking often entails competing against oneself and producing products that outmode those the MNC sells currently.

Benchmarking
The process of identifying what leading-edge competitors are doing and then using this information to produce improved products or services.

New Versions of Products   Still another innovative approach is **product proliferation,** which involves the creation of a wide array of products that the competition cannot copy quickly enough. Additionally, as the firm begins offering different versions of a product, the customer often becomes confused and is not sure which is the best buy. As a result, the company offering the large number of products often succeeds, because it gains market share at the expense of its competitors, which offer far fewer products. Moreover, this process of creating new versions of current products is ongoing; for example, Canon started planning its second-generation personal copier before the first had even come off the assembly line.[9]

Product proliferation
The creation of a wide array of products that the competition cannot copy quickly enough.

Importantly, product development need not come just from in-house research and development (R&D). IBM, for example, recently slashed $1 billion from its R&D budget.[10] Today, the trend is toward acquiring more and more needed knowledge from other

Figure 3–3

Direct and Acquired Research and Development as a Percentage of Gross Output in Select Countries

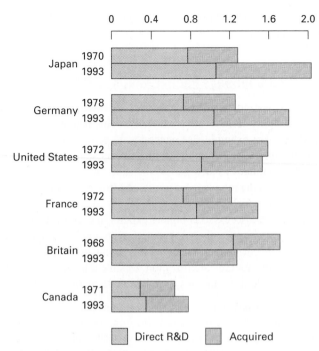

Source: Organization for Economic Cooperation and Development, 1997.

firms. This is particularly true for companies in services industries, which use high technology developed by computer and equipment manufacturers to increase their own efficiency. Figure 3-3 shows that over the last quarter century acquired R&D has increased much more rapidly than direct R&D in economically advanced countries.

Quality Pays Off for MNCs

Besides recognizing the technology paradox and creating a climate of innovation, quality goods and services simply pay off. The following sections examine some specific examples of the importance of quality.

Auto Manufacturing   Auto firms that produce quality products appeal to customers throughout the world, and quality products can lead to increased market share and profits. In the United States, the big automakers (General Motors, Ford, and Chrysler) all increased quality in the 1990s, and this helped them to hold off imports, especially from Japan, in world markets. According to the J.D. Power ratings, well-known for their independent research on auto quality, American manufacturers have continued to reduce their defects per car in recent years. However, Japanese and German automakers such as Honda, Toyota, and BMW have still been doing even better.[11]

It will be difficult for American manufacturers to continue to meet these outstanding quality levels, but they must try in this competitive market. One strategy has been to start from scratch and do it right, as in the case of Saturn, which has done well. Another has been to replace old car lines with new ones. GM emphasized the completely redesigned Chevrolet Lumina and Chevrolet Cavalier, both of which had far fewer defects than the previous versions they replaced, and this helped to drive up GM's average overall quality.

Aircraft Manufacturing   Another example that quality pays is Boeing, the giant commercial aircraft manufacturer. Boeing has been known for its quality aircraft and this is paying off in international sales. The MNC recently had a combined sale from five Asian airlines, including Cathay Pacific Airlines, Japan Air Lines, Korean Airlines, All Nippon Airways, and Thai International Airways, for more than 30 of the company's 777 stretch jet. These sales officially launched the firm's new 368-passenger plane, the 777-300X, which is a larger-capacity variant of Boeing's two-engine 777 airliner. In addition, Boeing also sold to Eva Airways and China Airways of Taiwan, United Parcel Service, Lauda Air, Eurobelgian, Air Europa, and Saudia, the Saudi Arabian state-run carrier. At the same time the company, having merged with McDonnell Douglas, the other large American aircraft manufacturer, is focusing on the production of smaller single-aisle, super-efficient jetliners such as the 737 twinjet. Boeing has forecasted that by 2007 there will be a 40 percent increase in the world's fleet of single-aisle passenger jets, and it hopes to dominate this market by producing state-of-the-art, highly efficient craft.[12]

High-quality airplane builders from other parts of the world are becoming more competitive with Boeing. Airbus Industrie of Europe, which now holds approximately the same worldwide market share as Boeing, recently announced that it had landed a 76-plane, $2.6 billion order from Iberia Airlines, as well as orders for 124 planes from US Airway Group, 50 from Northwest Airlines, and 36 from Belgium's Sabena Airlines.[13]

In all of these cases, orders were based on proven track records that showed the MNCs were able to deliver a high-quality, cost-effective product. Quite clearly, quality pays off in the worldwide aircraft manufacturing business.

Emerging Chinese High Tech Many MNCs have entered the Chinese market in hopes of selling high-tech equipment. To their chagrin, they are finding that local Chinese firms are producing quality that is often superior and more cost effective than that offered by them. As a result, local Chinese firms are beginning to win back market share. An example is the PC market. By the mid-1990s western PC makers had captured more than 50 percent of this market, but by 1998 Chinese firms held a 55 percent share and were continuing to gain ground. Moreover, noted the *Economist:*

> The same is true in medical technology, where Chinese firms are now beating foreigners in sales of CAT scanners and radiation therapy machines. In power generation, the state company no longer buys foreign equipment below 600 MW now that Chinese firms can make it themselves. Even Chinese car makers are improving. Sales of the Alto are growing more rapidly than those of any other care in China; it is designed by Suzuki, but made efficiently by an all-Chinese company, Norinco.[14]

How are the Chinese managing to compete effectively with international WCOs? One way is by learning how to drive down costs. A second, and complementary, way is by hiring young engineers who are willing to work around the clock in exchange for a promise of stock options. A third is by partnering with high-tech WCOs and using the joint venture to share costs and information useful for penetrating the local market.

At present, Chinese high-tech firms are focusing exclusively on the domestic market. However, as they continue to increase their market share they are likely to begin moving into the international arena and competing with such well-known giants as Motorola, Ericcson, and Sony.

Asian Services Still another good example of how quality pays off is Asia's service industry, which has become internationally competitive. When most people think of Asia, they picture countries that produce competitive manufactured products; however, these countries also are becoming very competitive in the services area. For example, the national airlines of Malaysia, Singapore, and Thailand regularly top the quality-service rankings in polls of international businesspeople. For example, Singapore's Changi International Airport has been ranked number one in the world in recent years. So, too, do Asian hotel groups such as the Shangri-La and Mandarin Oriental chains. Now an increasing number of Asian governments and businesses hope to build on such successes and create a service sector that is just as competitive as their manufacturing sector.

Because of such activity throughout Asia, the total trade in services of the 10 largest Asian economies increased almost 300 percent in the last 10 years. Much of this was accounted for by small firms, and many Asian governments have been slow to open up their service industries to foreign competition. This is slowly beginning to change, however, because governments realize that if they are going to have other industries such as manufacturing compete worldwide, they must withstand international competition for their service industry as well. As a result, Thailand has granted a number of banking licenses to foreign firms, the Philippine government has concluded that it cannot revamp its domestic telex phone system without outside help and allowed a number of foreign firms into this marketplace, and India has opened cellular and basic telephone service to foreign investors.

These developments all point to the fact that if countries close themselves to outside competition, they will be unable to compete worldwide. This is because they become isolated and fail to develop state-of-the-art goods and services. By opening their markets to the outside world, Asian nations are able to attract MNCs that place a premium on knowledge, technology, and capital. Additionally, while these MNCs are anxious to sell things such as environmental services, computer software, and health care, these outputs also help Asian nations to develop low-tech services industries, such as retailing. One recent report notes that:

> In retailing, for example, the ties made by Goldlion, a firm based in Hong Kong, are as hot in China as those produced by any Paris fashion house. Five Hong Kong firms—Lane Crawford, a department store; two supermarket chains, Dairy Farm and A.S. Watson; and two clothing chains, Esprit Asia and Giordano—have with varying degrees of success opened stores in other parts of the region. Giordano has stressed customer service. The firm encourages its staff to be friendly (in Hong Kong they even smile), and it accepts returns, something almost unheard of in Asia retailing. Esprit Asia's chairman, Michael Ying, originally worked as a supply scout for Esprit's San Francisco headquarters before acquiring marketing rights for the brand in Asia.[15]

Service is becoming as important as manufacturing as economies grow around the world. If this does not happen, both developed and developing countries eventually will find their growth severely limited. "International Management in Action: Where's the Quality Service in Deutschland?" examines the traditionally ignored, but now recognized, importance of customer service in Germany.

What are MNCs doing to develop and sustain a competitive edge? They employ a number of strategies that best can be summarized in terms of three stages or paradigm shifts through which organizations must progress to compete in today's Three Any's environment. Although there is a fine line of distinction and some obvious overlap between total quality, learning, and world-class organizations, there are some longitudinal differences, and Figure 3-4 illustrates these: from total quality, adaptive organizations to anticipative learning organizations to being simply the best, world-class organizations (WCOs). So far attention has been given to total quality organizations, and the rest of the chapter is devoted to the emerging learning and world-class organizations in the global economy.

Figure 3–4

New Paradigm Organizations

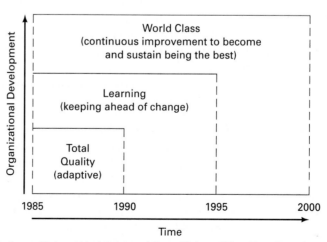

Source: Fred Luthans, Richard Hodgetts, and Sang M. Lee, "New Paradigm Organizations: From Total Quality to Learning to World-Class," *Organizational Dynamics,* Winter 1994, p. 10. Used with permission of the publisher, © 1994, American Management Association, New York. All rights reserved.

International Management in Action

Where's the Quality Service in Deutschland?

http://www.dtag.de

Service productivity is on the rise in a number of regions, most notably the United States and Asia, and one of the major issues this raises deals with the loss of employment. For example, many who are employed in the traditionally labor-intensive service sector now are being let go in the name of efficiency and increased service productivity. Will this downsizing become a worldwide development, resulting in massive unemployment? This is unlikely, but one thing is certain: Among those countries where service productivity does not increase, there likely will be an influx of outside competition. A good example is Germany (Deutschland).

Conventional wisdom holds that the Germans are industrious, efficient, and hardworking people. This does not always seem to carry over into their service sector, however. Consider the case of Deutsche Telekom (DT), the nation's phone monopoly. Everyone in the country seems to have their own story about poor telephone service. One favorite is the woman who waited 23 years to get a phone in old East Germany and, after unification, is now in her second year of waiting for one from DT. This contrasts sharply with the United States, where most people can get a new line installed in a few days at most, and they pay much lower rates than those charged by the German phone company.

While DT is a very visible example, it is by no means the only firm that has poor service in Germany. Many German retail establishments also provide notoriously bad service: Customers who walk in near closing time often are greeted by rude stares from the clerks. Some restaurants still refuse to take credit cards as well.

Even so, the phone company still probably deserves the vocal criticism. Here are some of the facts. In terms of productivity, NTT of Japan has 42.4

employees per 10,000 phone lines, and the U.S. Baby Bells average 43.2 per 10,000. Deutsche Telekom has 62.6 employees per 10,000 phones lines, a number higher than that in any other major EU power. Additionally, over 20 years ago, France launched a massive digitalization effort and significantly increased its productivity. British Telecom PLC, the former phone monopoly, also began modernizing and has cut its workforce by almost 50 percent since 1988.

What can German customers do about this? One step that many German businesses are taking is to find alternative sources. The giant German chemical firm BASF AG has switched to British Telecom for all of its international service, and it saves between 15 and 60 percent on each call. On the other hand, individual customers have no alternative but to use the German service. This undoubtedly helps to explain why the average German makes only 600 calls a year, compared with the average U.S. citizen who makes over three times this number.

The good news for Germans is that the telephone monopoly is coming to an end. Deregulation sweeping Europe is affecting Germany. There are now privatization options in the telecommunication industry. Also, DT is undertaking a massive TQM effort. As new competitors enter the market, quality of service undoubtedly will increase sharply. The bad news is that these new entrants likely will pick the most lucrative market niches and ignore the rest. This means that large German businesses, which spend thousands of dollars on telephone calls, will be targeted; the average customer will be far down the list.

At least in the short run, German customers may still be asking, "Where's the quality service?" In the long run, however, DT's quality efforts should begin to pay off.

MNCs as Learning Organizations

Increasingly common are MNCs that achieve quality and excellence but then slip back either because they were too slow in keeping up with needed changes or did not anticipate changes.[16] These MNCs typically are referred to as **adaptive organizations,** which are characterized by reaction to required changes but a failure to anticipate and stay on or ahead of the cutting edge. Those MNCs such as General Electric or Sony that do succeed in keeping ahead are learning organizations.

A **learning organization** is able to transform itself by anticipating change and discovering new ways of creating products and services; it has learned how to learn. Kodak is a good example. Under George Fisher, this MNC is changing direction and engaging in large-scale implementation with new technologies that move across the boundaries of tra-

Adaptive organizations
Organizations that are characterized by reaction to required changes but failure to anticipate them and stay on or ahead of the cutting edge.

Learning organizations
Organizations that are able to transform themselves by anticipating change and discovering new ways of creating products and services; they have learned how to learn.

ditional silver-based film and into the area of electronic photography, now possible by high-resolution imaging. Importantly, Kodak also is focusing on digital technology, which it anticipates will be the wave of the future.

Another example of an MNC that is a learning organization is Gruppo GFT, the world's largest manufacturer of designer clothing. Unlike its competitors, who tend to view the world market in terms of standardized apparel with universal appeal, GFT focuses on designing products in response to a host of local differences in key markets. This MNC learned the needs of those markets and anticipated appropriately—redefining the way it did business in the process. In other words, GFT learned how to learn; and they anticipated the needed changes.

Three common characteristics of learning organizations are openness, creativity, and self-efficacy.[17] The following discussion examines each of these, and Table 3-1 provides additional comparisons between MNCs that are traditional adaptive and generative learning organizations.[18]

Openness

Learning organizations not only are prepared to accept new trends, they encourage and anticipate changes. Rather than fight change, they learn how to accommodate, create, and profit from it. Although the chapters in Part II on the cultural context will point out the need to understand and apply concepts such as openness differently across cultures, MNCs that are learning organizations will in general try to suspend their need to control all aspects of operations as well as the people who run the place and interact with customers. Their managers empow-

---

Table 3–1

Characteristics of Traditional Adaptive and Generative Learning Organizations

Characteristics	Adaptive	Generative
Strategic		
Core competence	Better sameness	Meaningful difference
Source of strength	Stability	Change
Output	Market share	Market creation
Organizational perspective	Compartmentalization (SBU)	Systemic
Developmental dynamic	Change	Transformation
Structural		
Structure	Bureaucratic	Network
Control systems	Formal rules	Values, self-control
Power bases	Hierarchic position	Knowledge
Integrating mechanisms	Hierarchy	Teams
Networks	Disconnected	Strong
Communications flow	Hierarchic	Lateral
Human resource practices		
Performance appraisal system	Rewards stability	Flexibility
Reward basis	Short-term financial	Long-term financial and human resource development
Focus of rewards	Distribution of scarcity	Determination of synergy
Status symbols	Rank and title	Making a difference
Mobility patterns	Within division or function	Across divisions or functions
Mentoring	Not rewarded	Integral part of performance appraisal process
Culture	Market	Clan
Managers' behaviors		
Perspective	Controlling	Openness
Problem-solving orientation	Narrow	Systemic thinking
Response style	Conforming	Creative
Personal control	Blame and acceptance	Efficacious
Commitment	Ethnocentric	Empathetic

Source: Michael E. McGill, John W. Slocum, Jr., and David Lei, "Management Practices in Learning Organizations," *Organizational Dynamics,* Summer 1992, p. 14. Used with permission of the publisher, © 1992. American Management Association, New York. All rights reserved.

er associates, flatten the structure, and allow flexibility on everything; they examine their core values and try to identify how these must change for the MNC to grow and prosper.

Whirlpool is an example of a firm that reinvented itself. Several years ago, this MNC analyzed its markets and structure, and it concluded that the U.S. market no longer would be the largest, nor would it provide enough business for them to grow and prosper. They found that growth would come from untapped markets, such as in Central and Eastern Europe, Mexico, and Asia. Here is how the company reacted to this future world market:

> Today, Whirlpool has oriented itself to a new vision: growing a transnational company and creating value for stakeholders. To translate vision into action, the company has indicated that all its senior managers will have global experience by the year 2000. In addition, it created a joint venture with N.V. Philips to capture the European market and started joint ventures in India and Mexico. To build shared cross-cultural values, in June of 1990 Whirlpool staged a worldwide leadership conference in Montreux, Switzerland. One hundred forty managers got to know each other and understand each others' cultural backgrounds. To achieve a "one company" culture, it established fifteen cross-national-functional teams to establish and implement specific plans of action.[19]

Creativity

Of all the requisite skills and abilities for learning, creativity is the most widely and readily acknowledged, and two of the most important aspects of creativity are critical to effective learning: personal flexibility and a willingness to take risks. MNCs that are learning organizations nurture and promote both of these dimensions.

In the case of flexibility, MNCs such as Emerson and RCA missed the boat in their analysis of changes in the radio market. They believed that sales would follow a natural growth curve, eventually reach maturity and decline. In contrast, learning organizations such as Sony were highly flexible and saw a variety of different alternative possibilities for the radio. Sony believed that it could alter the product life cycle through creative innovation; the result was the Sony Walkman, which changed how, where, and when people listened to radios. MNCs lacking the flexibility to anticipate and make such changes end up losing out. Examples are provided in the accompanying "International Management in Action: Bit Players Bite the Dust."

In the case of risk-taking, many MNCs are losing out because they remain overly conservative. Japanese automakers conducted market research in the United States and found no support from U.S. customers for minivans. As a result, they decided not to enter this market. Chrysler also conducted market research and received the same results, but this MNC was convinced there was a market for these vehicles and decided to take the risk. This decision proved to be one of the most profitable in Chrysler's history, helping the firm to attain record annual profits.

Self-Efficacy

Drawn from well-known psychologist Albert Bandura's social cognitive theory, **self-efficacy** is a person's belief or confidence in his or her abilities to marshall the motivation, resources, and courses of action needed to successfully accomplish a specific task.[20] In the workplace, here is a description of how this self-efficacy applies to employees:

> Before they select their choices and initiate their effort, employees tend to weigh, evaluate, and integrate information about their perceived capabilities. Expectations of personal efficacy determine whether an employee's coping behavior will be initiated, how much task-related effort will be expended, and how long that effort will be sustained despite disconfirming evidence.[21]

Stajkovic and Luthans in a recent meta-analysis of 114 empirical studies found a strong positive correlation (.38) between this self-efficacy and work-related performance.[22] Importantly, learning organizations can and do promote and develop such self-efficacy to take advantage of the positive impact on human performance and thus competitive advantage through people. There are a number of specific ways that self-efficacy can be

Self-efficacy
A person's belief or confidence in his or her abilities to marshall the motivation, resources, and courses of action needed to successfully accomplish a specific task.

Keeping up with the competition can be difficult, especially for small MNCs that lack the resources and flexibility to change quickly. Small Japanese exporters that in recent years have found their competitiveness being slowly eroded provide a good example.

For many of these small MNCs the downhill slide began when the Japanese yen started rising against the U.S. dollar. As exports to the United States and other countries that were tied to the dollar became more expensive for buyers, Japanese MNCs, large and small, quickly realized they needed to control costs. Many of Japan's small manufacturing firms are suppliers to large MNCs such as Toyota, Nissan, and Sony, and they soon found these giant MNCs beginning to demand that products be produced at a lower price.

In the last decade, thousands of small Japanese enterprises have been driven out of business. One primary reason is that these small companies borrowed large sums of money during the early 1990s to upgrade their equipment and remain state-of-the-art for their big domestic customers. This strategy appeared to be very effective, because it meant these firms would be able to design, develop, and manufacture all sorts of output, from specialized machine parts to high-tech components. However, this strategy was premised on the companies continuing to garner orders from their giant customers. As the yen's value increased sharply and the large Japanese

MNCs saw that the only way to protect their overseas markets was by remaining price competitive, these giant customers began demanding that their suppliers cut prices or lose their business—and this is exactly what happened to many of them. As an example, one small firm that made lenses and other camera parts found that when it could no longer drive down prices, the orders stopped coming. At its peak, this company made 5,000 lenses a month, but this eventually dropped to under 2,000 and the firm had trouble surviving. In the case of run-of-the-mill parts, many Japanese MNCs found they could easily replace their domestic producers by outsourcing to cheaper, offshore resources. As a result, Ricoh, the big Japanese office-equipment MNC, now imports 10 percent of its parts from China and other low-cost world locations, in contrast to the 2 percent the MNC used to purchase just a few years ago.

Those small Japanese manufacturers that have survived and prospered have market niches where more sophisticated parts and components are needed and face very limited competition. In these markets, the small firms are not bit players. They are mainstream competitors, and this makes all the difference for their present survival. However, they also must anticipate future changes and learn how to learn. In other words, they must become learning organizations.

developed (e.g., making sure employees experience success, verbal persuasion, or training through vicarious learning/modeling),[23] but practicing learning organizations can also use a more general approach of creating a climate or culture that teaches and promotes associated self-awareness and active problem solving.

Self-awareness is fostered by a clear organizational vision that gives direction regarding critical choices and provides feedback about results. In particular, associates are taught to actively seek information about the impact of their behavior on others, and on issues that are important to others, as a means of maximizing their own efficacy. In other words, "information seeking" is turning out to be an important characteristic of effective employees in learning organizations. At Whirlpool, for example, the assessment of managerial talent is multiple and conducted on a worldwide basis. They conduct what are termed "360 (degree) evaluations," which include self-assessments as well as assessments from peers, subordinates, direct supervisors, and managers a level above one's own supervisor. These 360 assessments are not performance reviews per se. Instead, they focus on people's potential and capability, and they help individuals to understand themselves better. Most often, only the target individual, not his or her boss, receives the feedback.[24]

Proactive problem solving is used to teach managers in learning organizations how to anticipate and become more efficacious with issues before they become serious. Managers also learn how to prevent these problems from recurring. For example, IBM used to rely on customer feedback to help identify service problems. The MNC eventual-ly discovered, however, that most customers who are dissatisfied with service do not fill out questionnaire surveys—they simply stop doing business with the firm. Now, IBM han-dles customer problems proactively by contacting customers who have stopped doing business with them and finding out what went wrong and how they can win back this cus-tomer. This proactivity is characteristic of a learning organization.

World-Class Organizations

Today, the very best MNCs are going beyond even the learning organization and have become what can be called "world-class organizations." **World-class organizations (WCOs)** are enterprises that are able to compete with anybody, anywhere, anytime. In most cases, WCOs have operations throughout the globe. IBM and Sony, discussed so far as total quality and learning organizations, are also WCOs, but so are MNCs such as Hewlett-Packard, General Electric, Honda, and Xerox. In a few cases, WCOs may focus heavily on only one geographic locale and have only limited worldwide operations; examples here include the Ritz-Carlton Hotel chain, Wainwright Industries, and Wal-Mart. In either case, WCOs are able to compete effectively against all comers, whether foreign or domestic.

> **World-class organizations (WCOs)**
> Enterprises that are able to compete with anybody, anywhere, anytime.

To become a WCO, an organization must excel in a number of dimensions that in both an additive and synergistic way create a new level of competitive excellence that goes beyond the total quality and learning organizations. As shown in Figure 3-5, some major pillars forming the basis of WCOs include: (1) a customer-based focus; (2) continuous improvement; (3) fluid, flexible or "virtual organizations"; (4) creative human resources; (5) egalitarian climate; and (6) technological support. The details of each of these charac-teristics of the world-class organization will be discussed in the remainder of the chapter.

Customer-Based Focus

WCOs are customer-driven. They have identified their internal and external customers and have determined how to serve them effectively. In doing so, WCOs tend to have flat struc-tures, so that everyone can be closer to the customer. Additionally, WCOs go beyond just sat-isfying their customers; they work very hard to delight their customers and have a bond with them. In the process, they also create new demands for their goods and services. A good example again is Sony's Walkman. The buyers were impressed not only with the innovative-ness of the product but also with the CD version, and how much value they were receiving.

Another example is Wal-Mart, which has dominated the U.S. retail market and now is beginning to make in-roads in Mexico and China, among other international markets. Focusing heavily on the customer, this firm has helped to break the old retailing model in which manufacturers would "push" their goods to retail stores and the latter in turn would

Figure 3–5   **Some Major Pillars of World-Class Organizations**

Source: Fred Luthans, Richard M. Hodgetts, and Sang M. Lee, "New Paradigm Organizations: From Total Quality to Learning to World-Class," *Organizational Dynamics,* Winter 1994, p. 15. Used with permission of the publisher, © 1994, American Management Association, New York. All rights reserved.

push them onto customers. Wal-Mart, relying heavily on its ability to identify customer needs and negotiate competitive prices from suppliers, has created a "pull" system, in which customers buy things they need and thus pull the goods from the store. This strategy is not unique to Wal-Mart. Successful retailers in others parts of the world such as Metro International of Germany, Ito-Yokado of Japan, and Carrefour of France also employ customers-driven, market-pull strategies.

Continuous Improvement

A second distinctive characteristic of WCOs is their commitment to continuous improvement (CI). In contrast to their competitors, WCOs can improve faster, more efficiently, and more effectively. A good example is Ford Motor, which found that it took weeks to process vendor receipts because so many people had to approve the payment. By carefully studying this process, Ford was able to reduce sharply the number of individuals who needed to sign off on payments and cut the processing time by 90 percent.

Microsoft, although recently undergoing scrutiny for being a monopoly in the computer services and software industry, feels it must continually improve in order to compete with the likes of Netscape, IBM, Novell, Oracle, and UNIX. To counter the antitrust argument, chairman and CEO (and richest person in the world) Bill Gates points out that Windows continuously, dramatically improves. For example, he notes that Windows 98 includes a new Web-like user interface, a more efficient file system, faster launching of applications, multiple-monitor support, faster 3D graphics, easier connection to peripherals (such as digital cameras), and more—all for the same low price as Windows 95.[25]

Use of Flexible or Virtual Organizations

Virtual organization
An organization that is able to conduct business as if it were a very large enterprise when, in fact, it is much smaller, made up of core business competencies and the rest outsourced or partnered.

Global sourcing
The use of worldwide suppliers, regardless of where they are located geographically, who are best able to provide the needed output.

Another characteristic of WCOs is their use of flexible or virtual organizations. A **virtual organization** is one that is able to conduct business as if it were a very large enterprise with major facilities while in fact it is much smaller, made up of core business competencies with the rest outsourced or partnered. How is this possible? One major way when taken into the international arena is global sourcing.

Global sourcing is the use of worldwide suppliers, regardless of where they are located geographically, who are best able to provide the needed output.[26] For example, Japanese automakers today rely increasingly on U.S. suppliers for their cars. Similarly, U.S. laptop computer firms rely on Japanese sources to provide screen technology. Where possible, however, MNCs prefer home-based suppliers because of the benefit this provides them in maintaining their worldwide competitive advantage. Widely recognized strategy guru Michael Porter explains it this way:

> Perhaps the most important benefit of home-based suppliers . . . is the *process of innovation and upgrading.* Competitive advantage emerges from close working relationships between world-class suppliers and the industry. Suppliers help firms perceive new methods and opportunities to apply new technology. Firms gain quick access to information to new ideas and insights and to supplier innovations. They have the opportunity to influence suppliers' technical efforts as well as to serve as test sites for development work. The exchange of R&D and joint problem solving lead to faster and more efficient solutions. Suppliers also tend to be a conduit for transmitting information and innovations from firm to firm. Through this process the pace of innovation within the entire national industry is accelerated. All these benefits are enhanced if suppliers are located in proximity to firms, shortening the communication lines.[27]

This also helps to explain why suppliers often locate near their major customers. When Ford Motor decides to set up new facilities in Europe, its U.S.-based suppliers will locate nearby so that they can continue to work closely with the giant automaker. This strategy helps Ford to become, essentially, a virtual organization because it does not have to produce these supplies in-house but derives the same benefits as if it did. Other firms have taken this concept further. For example in Argentina, Metalurgica Romet SA makes and assembles doors at Volkswagen's new plant. In fact, VW workers at the factory are responsible for building only the chassis, powertrain, and a few other parts. The rest of the car is produced and assembled by suppliers working in the factory. These suppliers buy the equipment they need to do their jobs and are responsible for their own inventory and carrying costs. As a result, VW is now able to manufacture a car in half the time it took at its old plant in Argentina, and the firm has reduced total costs in the factory by 50 percent.[28] In the coming years, an increasing number of MNCs will rely on global sourcing to provide materials and products that once were produced in-house. As a result, these companies can act like larger enterprises when in fact they are smaller and depend on partnering and global sourcing to take care of many of their needs.

Creative Human Resource Management

Human resources generally are given lip service to be the most important asset for any organization. Yet, as Pfeffer recently pointed out, "Rather than putting their people first, numerous firms have sought solutions to competitive challenges in places and means that have not been very productive—treating their businesses as portfolios of assets to be bought and sold in an effort to find the right competitive niche, downsizing and outsourcing in a futile attempt to shrink or transact their way to profit, and doing myriad other things that weaken or destroy their organizational culture in efforts to minimize labor costs—even as they repeatedly proclaim, 'people are our most important asset.'"[29] Yet, there is growing research evidence that human resources and how they are managed do make the difference. In Pfeffer's recent book *The Human Equation,* he summarizes these substantial findings: The returns from managing people in ways that build high commitment, involvement, and learning and organizational competence are typically on the order of 30 to 50 percent.[30]

World-class organizations such as Southwest Airlines, Virgin Airlines, Rubbermaid, ABB, and Gallup, Inc. do recognize the importance of their people. The relative value of human resources is becoming increasingly important as knowledge-based organizations are replacing traditional asset-based MNCs. WCOs know they must compete based on what their human resources are capable of doing rather than on mere physical assets, such as buildings, machinery, and equipment. WCOs have state-of-the-art, creative approaches to managing their human resources, and they effectively stimulate and have a supportive climate for employee creativity. More specifically, their human resource management (HRM) programs are designed to help their people share ownership of problems and solutions, achieve a strong commitment and involvement by top management, communicate consistent goals and objectives to all levels and functions in the organization, and help develop an effective use of recognition and reward programs.

There are many examples of creative HRM practices. One is the use of empowered teams with the authority to make all decisions in their own work area. For example, at the world-class Ritz-Carlton Hotels, employees can spend up to $1,000 on customer service-related matters. Another example is the creation of suggestion systems that generate new, useful ideas for better serving clients. Wainwright Industries, a small but world-class U.S. manufacturer, has a suggestion system so effective that it annually generates 55 suggestions per employee, which is sharply higher than the 12 generated by typical Japanese MNCs and the 0.3 by the typical U.S. firm.[31]

Another important aspect of WCO HRM strategy is effective recognition and monetary reward systems. In particular, WCOs ensure that rewards are positive, given openly, and highly publicized. At the Ritz-Carlton chain any employee can send a "First Class" card—a 3″ × 5″ card designed with the company logo, to express his or her appreciation to anyone else in the organization for a job well done. The company also uses "Lightning Strikes"—monetary rewards granted by a member of the Executive Committee to any employee for outstanding service. In addition, individuals who submit the best ideas for improvement are listed on a bulletin board and given a dinner for two, and those who generate the greatest number of useful ideas are honored at quarterly receptions.

Egalitarian Climate

WCOs create an egalitarian climate in which all stakeholders—employees, customers, owners, suppliers, and the community—are treated with dignity and respect. This is done in a number of ways. At Wal-Mart, everyone is referred to as an "associate," there are no subordinates or employees. Another common approach is the way in which customers are treated. At the Ritz-Carlton chain, when a guest asks for directions to a particular locale in the hotel, the associate will stop whatever he or she is doing and become a personal escort to that location.

Another sign of an egalitarian approach is the way in which WCOs treat their suppliers. In the past, companies would negotiate with vendors and pit one against the other to get the lowest possible price. Under an egalitarian approach, this strategy is abandoned in favor of a team approach, in which the supplier is regarded as an integral part of the in-house team. For example, at IBM, suppliers participate in new product design, learn the company's needs, and work with the firm to provide materials and parts at the highest quality levels and most competitive prices. In the process, suppliers learn their customer's culture and how the organization operates. Suppliers then are in a better position to integrate their own approach with that of their partner company. Japanese WCOs such as Sony and Mitsubishi take this idea a step further, getting suppliers involved in helping cost the product and continually working together to drive down expenses. Figure 3-6 provides an example.

Figure 3–6

Cost Reduction Approaches: The United States versus Japan

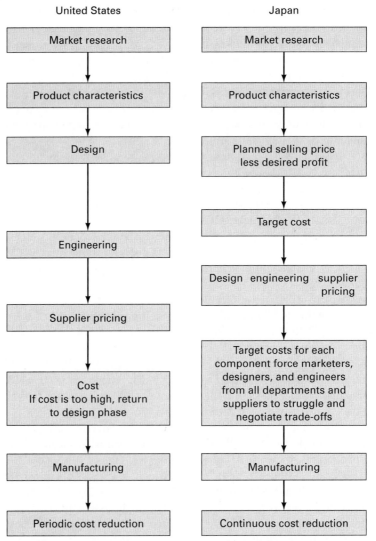

Source: Adapted from Ford S. Worthy, "Japan's Smart Secret Weapon," *Fortune,* August 12, 1991, p. 73.

Technological Support

Most of the creative, innovative, and effective approaches of WCOs are supported by advanced, cutting-edge technological support. Examples of such technology include computer-aided design and computer-aided manufacturing (CAD/CAM), telecommunications networks, expert or "smart" systems, distributed information systems, multimedia systems, and executive or management information systems. One good example is found in the retailing industry, where competition is fierce and profit margins are typically low.

Information technology (IT) is critical to the operations of retailing WCOs. Thanks to IT, retailers can tell instantly what they are selling in each of their hundreds of stores, how much money they are making on each sale, and increasingly, who their customers are. Additionally, an effective IT system can help a company to minimize its inventory but still reduce the likelihood of stockouts. Wal-Mart uses such a just-in-time (JIT) inventory system to reduce costs and increase revenue-producing sales space in their stores.

Computers also have helped world-class retailers to exercise closer control over their international units and thus transform themselves into truly global firms. Again, the best example is Wal-Mart, which has been the leader in blending IT with operations. More recently, other big retailers have followed suit. Tesco, the giant British supermarket chain, has used IT to cut the amount of stock in its distribution chain to a mere 2 weeks' supply.[32] Tesco is using automated picking and sorting systems to break down deliveries into smaller units and believes that within 5 years, it will be operating with only 1 week's supply. Like Wal-Mart, Tesco also is using computer modeling derived from electronic point-of-sale data to predict future demand.

Thanks to inexpensive yet powerful PC-based computer systems, WCO retailers now can identify small suppliers that offer special niche products. For example, a small, local cheese producer now can supply a single Tesco supermarket in York, England. Five years ago, it would not have been economically feasible to identify such a small supplier and negotiate a contract; Tesco would have opted for a larger supplier who could provide a wider range of products to a greater number of stores. Because of effective technological support, WCOs are able to increase their market coverage while simultaneously reducing price and improving customer service.

In the years ahead, all MNCs will begin to recognize and attempt to adopt the types of WCO characteristics discussed in this chapter. If MNCs do not become world class, they may not survive in the long run. If they take on the characteristics of WCOs, however, they increasingly should be able to compete with anybody, anywhere, anytime.

World of Business Week Revisited

The *Business Week* article that opened this chapter illustrated that world-class organizations (WCOs) can indeed compete with anybody, anywhere, anytime. Having read this chapter you should now be aware of some of the innovative techniques used by WCOs to gain a competitive advantage. This is particularly apparent in the case of GE Capital, a multinational that has transformed itself from an inefficient company into a WCO by making acquisitions, utilizing new technologies, diversifying product lines, and developing an efficient worldwide empire of integrated profitable businesses. More importantly, from a human resources perspective, GE Capital has focused on gaining a competitive advantage through people by using new training methods and setting challenging goals for managers. Reflecting on what you have read in the chapter and imagining yourself as a manager of a multinational ready to enter the European market, answer the following questions: What benefits will WCOs find as Europe becomes more integrated economically? What are some potential drawbacks to employing a strategy based on creating economies of scale in Europe? In your opinion should GE Capital, which owns hundreds of diversified businesses, continue to acquire more companies or focus on improving its current ones?

Summary of Key Points

1. Quality is having a major impact on international operations. One reason is because it transcends national boundaries and allows firms to compete in a borderless world. Another is because, paradoxically, as technology increases, costs tend to be driven down, and only the most effective MNCs succeed. This emphasis on quality is leading MNCs to become increasingly more competitive in terms of both products and services.

2. One way in which successful MNCs are going beyond total quality to sustain, and even increase, their world competitiveness is through learning. Total quality has become just the cost of entry into today's highly competitive world economy. Now, MNCs not only must adapt, they must anticipate and even create change. They must transform themselves into learning organizations. Three of the major characteristics of learning organizations are openness, creativity, and self-efficacy.

3. World-class organizations (WCOs) are able to compete with anybody, anywhere, anytime. There are several major pillars that form the basis for WCOs: customer-based focus, continuous improvement, flexible or virtual organizations, creative human resource management practices, an egalitarian climate, and technological support. Today, more and more firms are adopting the characteristics of WCOs, because they realize this is the only way of ensuring that they can compete, and in the long run even survive, in today's Three Any's environment.

Key Terms

adaptive organizations
benchmarking
global sourcing
learning organizations

mass customization
paradox
product proliferation
self-efficacy

technology paradox
world-class organizations (WCOs)
virtual organizations

Review and Discussion Questions

1. What is the relationship between quality and cost? Why is this relationship important to MNCs that want to develop products for the international market?

2. Why would an understanding of the technology paradox be valuable to high-tech MNCs? What practical value would it offer these firms regarding how to price and market their products?

3. How do learning organizations differ from traditional adaptive organizations? Why would MNCs be interested in developing the characteristics of learning organizations? What value would it have for stakeholders? In your answer, be sure to identify and incorporate the three characteristics of learning organizations.

4. As MNCs try to become world-class organizations, what are some of the steps that they should take? In your answer, be sure to identify and incorporate the six pillars.

Internet Exercise: Going Worldwide with Wal-Mart

When it comes to competing with anybody, anywhere, anytime, there are few companies that can surpass Wal-Mart, the world's largest discount retailer. In recent years the company has continued to expand its coverage of the U.S. market. At the same time it has begun moving into the international arena and has plans to become the world's leading discount retailer. How will it accomplish this feat? Visit the company at **www.wal-mart.com** and read about their expansion plans. Then answer these three questions: (1) What has Wal-Mart been doing over the last couple of years to increase its international presence? In particular, concentrate your attention on Argentina, Brazil, Canada, Mexico, China, and the United Kingdom. How well is the company doing in these countries? (2) Is its sales in these international locations increasing faster or slower than in the U.S. market? (3) Will the fact that Wal-Mart has been able to meet the criteria of a world-class organization be of value to it in these expansion activities? Why or why not?

France

The French Republic is situated in Western Europe. It is bounded on the north by the English Channel; to the east by Belgium, Luxembourg, Germany, Switzerland, and Italy; to the south by the Mediterranean Sea and Spain; and to the west by the Atlantic Ocean. The island of Corsica is part of metropolitan France, while four overseas departments, two overseas *collectivites territoriales,* and four overseas territories also form an integral part of the Republic. The principal language is French, which has numerous regional dialects; small minorities speak Breton and Basque. There were approximately 57 million residents in France during the latest census.

France is one of the most economically powerful countries in Europe, and it is one of the G-7 nations. According to United Nations estimates, the country currently has a GDP of over $1 trillion and a per-capita GDP of about $20,000. During recent years, the GDP has continued to grow at an annual rate of 3.0 to 3.5 percent.

Mining, manufacturing, construction, and power provide around 30 percent of French GDP, and industrial production in this decade grew at a 3.3 to 3.5 percent annual rate. Manufacturing in particular accounts for a sizable portion of economic activity, and the country is a net exporter. In 1997, France had a trade surplus of over $11 billion, and the nation typically has a favorable balance of trade with the United States. Its major trading partner is Germany, however, which buys 18 percent of all France's exports and accounts for about 19 percent of French imports. Most of the rest of the country's import and export activity occurs between other EU nations.

Because of France's recent steady economic growth, the country has been the target of much MNC activity. The purchasing power of an average French family is far higher than that in many other EU nations, including Spain, Portugal, Greece, and Finland. Additionally, MNCs from around the world doing business in Germany have found that the French economy is so interrelated that France becomes a second market. France also is a target for new expansion, as in the case of the big German auto firm Mercedes-Benz, which has recently built a new factory in France because of its faith in the workers' productivity and work ethic.

On the negative side, the near future likely will see more difficult times for this country. French GDP has not grown as fast as that in Germany, and the gap continues to widen. At the same time, government spending as a percentage of GDP remains higher than that of Germany or the United States. Additionally, the unemployment rate in France is higher than that in other economic powers, and in fact, by mid-1998, it was twice that of the United States.

To get the French economy moving, President Jacques Chirac, the first conservative president in 14 years, promised to give tax breaks, speed up privatization, and institute pension reform. Recently there have been demonstrations against these reforms and many French businesspeople still complain that the government has too much control and prevents them from making needed changes to ensure the efficiency of their operations. For example, when Perrier, the world-famous French bottling MNC, wanted to cut 600 jobs to boost efficiency, the government turned down its request. When Michelin, the tire maker, tried to increase productivity by running its plants 24 hours a day, the government delayed a long time before giving the MNC permission to run one of its five plants continuously. The other four must still close on weekends, conforming to the current rules requiring French businesses to operate only 5 days a week These bureaucratic rules have a negative effect on productivity and could begin to weaken France's competitive position in the world economy.
www.france.com/index.html

Questions

1. Why would MNCs be interested in doing business in France?

2. How would French customers be likely to measure quality in products such as cars? Computers? Televisions? What would they be looking for?

3. Why would MNCs need to have a total quality commitment if they hoped to succeed in the French market?

4. Would successful MNCs in France need to be learning organizations? Why or why not?

5. If a WCO were successful in France, might it also do well throughout the EU? Why or why not?

It's a Price and Quality Issue

A German high-tech firm has just achieved a major breakthrough in cellular technology that likely will drive down the cost of such phones. The company estimates that it can manufacture a phone for less than $4 that will retail for approximately $15, and these units will have higher quality and more features than any others on the market. The company intends to have a prototype completed within 60 days and is planning a worldwide launch within 4 months.

The initial market will be Germany and then the European Union; however, the company also intends to begin selling these phones in the United States and Japan within 6 months. At present, the firm is focusing on three key areas. First are the distribution channels that will be needed to successfully market the product in Europe, North America, and Japan. Second is continuing research and development (R&D) efforts to increase the quality of the product even further. Third are the manufacturing processes that will be used to build the units, because the company wants to continue driving down the cost. To senior-level management, these three areas constitute the major opportunities and threats for the firm. The head of R&D put it this way:

> When we first release this product, there will be a wave of initial demand that will sustain us through the first 90 days. However, we will not be able to rest on this initial success. We must continue improving our technology. Ideally, we would like to come out with a new version of the phone within 6 months, and we have to continue this improvement for the indefinite future. At the same time, we must work to drive down our costs, so that it becomes less and less expensive for people to purchase our prod-

uct. If we don't do this, the competition will be able to reverse engineer our product and soon have a similar offering on the market that will be just as good as ours, but at a lower price. To achieve these goals, we must be flexible and prepared to change and rethink everything we are doing. We are in a fast-moving industry, and if we cannot keep up, we are going to fall behind and not even survive. This new product should thrust us into the lead, but the real challenge will be sustainability and, hopefully, growth.

The head of manufacturing agreed with this statement but also believes that the firm can meet the challenge. "We have been carefully designing the production processes that will be needed to produce this product," he recently told the board of directors, "and if we continue to improvise and modify our manufacturing approaches, we will be able to drive down costs by 40 percent within 12 months while maintaining a sigma level of close to six." The board members agree that if this can be done, the company likely will do very well indeed. As one board member put it, "it's all a matter of controlling price and quality."

Questions

1. How would the technology paradox help to shape the strategy of this German firm?

2. Why would the company need to become a learning organization if it hopes to dominate the cellular phone market?

3. If the firm wanted to become a WCO, what are some steps it would need to take? Identify and describe four of the most important.

Chapter 4

Ethics and Social Responsibility

Objectives of the Chapter

The current concern that all businesses and the general public have for ethical behavior and social responsibility is not restricted to the domestic situation. In this era of a global economy, MNCs must be concerned with how they carry out their business and their social role in host countries. This chapter examines business ethics and social responsibility in the international arena, and it looks at some of the critical social issues that will be confronting MNCs in the years ahead. The discussion includes ethical decision making in various countries, regulation of foreign investment, and current responses to social responsibility by today's multinationals. The specific objectives of this chapter are:

1. **EXAMINE** some of the major ethical issues and problems confronting MNCs in selected countries.

2. **EXPLAIN** some of the ways that host countries are attempting to regulate foreign investments and why reciprocity is such an important trade issue.

3. **DISCUSS** some of the action being taken by selected industrialized countries to be more socially responsive to world problems.

BusinessWeek

The World of Business Week:

Justice's Cartel Crackdown

It sounds like the plot of a paperback thriller. Top executives from competing companies in the United States, Germany, and Japan jet around the world holding clandestine price-fixing meetings at glittering world capitals. Carving up the world market in a key industrial commodity, they agree to limit production and avoid unnecessary competition. Keeping their activities secret, even from fellow employees, the execs use code names when talking to each other on the phone.

This isn't fiction, though. The Justice Dept. charges that leading manufacturers of graphite electrodes, an important component in steel-mill machinery, followed this script for several years. After a multiyear investigation, the agency joined European authorities in a simultaneous raid on the conspirators' facilities in three countries in June 1997, and succeeded in breaking up the cartel. In April, UCAR International Inc. in Danbury, Conn., agreed to pay $110 million—the largest fine in antitrust history—for its role in the conspiracy. Japan's Showa Denko K.K. has also admitted participating in the cartel, and Carbon/Graphite Group in Pittsburgh was granted immunity from prosecution in return for helping the Justice probe. At least five other manufacturers are under investigation by U.S., Japanese, and European Commission antitrust authorities.

The case is just the latest of a recent spate of big-time global price-fixing prosecutions. On July

9, Justice launched a criminal suit against former Archer Daniels Midland Co. executives Michael D. Andreas, Mark E. Whitacre, and Terrance S. Wilson in the highest-profile price-fixing case yet. The ADM lawsuit may be getting the headlines, but it's just part of a much broader crackdown. At the behest of the Justice Dept., a record 25 grand juries are investigating international price-fixing in industries as diverse as vitamins, glass, and marine equipment. The agency is also pushing for new cooperation agreements with other countries, boosting the number of Federal Bureau of Investigation agents investigating suspect companies, and conducting special border watches aimed at catching conspirators.

U.S. Damage

Driving the Justice campaign is a conviction that international price-fixing is on the rise—and hurting the U.S. economy. Although there's no hard data on the subject, complaints about the problem have been increasing, according to the agency. Assistant U.S. Attorney General for Antitrust Joel I. Klein believes that as trade barriers fall, companies that once had national markets to themselves may look to cross-border cartels to fend off competitors that are grabbing market share and forcing down prices. "We're looking at cartels that are doing a billion dollars in business," Klein says. "If you assume that they are inflating prices by 15% to 20%, we're looking at hundreds of million of dollars sucked right out of the economy."

The new wave of price-fixing may not be igniting inflation, but it is increasing costs in discrete markets, Klein contends. In the ADM case, prosecutors say, the U.S. price for lysine, a livestock-feed additive, doubled in the first three months of the conspiracy.

Frequently, the cartels are composed of foreign companies specifically attempting to hike prices in the U.S. The Justice Dept. recently won guilty pleas from several Japanese companies for conspiring to raise prices of fax paper here by about 10% (though a mistrial was declared in a case against another manufacturer on July 14th).

Despite its recent successes, Justice can't fight price cartels alone. And winning cooperation from other countries gets complicated in a hurry. Foreign governments have long tolerated price-fixing cartels, believing that they protect local companies and maintain employment levels. When the United States asks for permission to interview witnesses and review documents, authorities are often reluctant to help. International cooperation is slowly improving, but federal antitrust cops are frustrated. "In most countries, price-fixing is not a crime," says U.S. Deputy Assistant Attorney General for Antitrust Gary R. Spratling. "It's not seen as very serious, and their procedures for pursuing it are more restrictive."

The price-fixing conspiracies that Justice has prosecuted take a wide variety of forms, says Spratling. Conspirators may set a single worldwide price, or one company will be allowed to set the rate that others must follow in its particular region, as is alleged in the graphic-electrode case. Other times, executives will simply divide up the map, charging whatever they want in their assigned countries without fear of competition.

Stunning Development

Slowly but surely, international reluctance to come down hard on price-fixing conspiracies is changing. Antitrust authorities in Europe played key roles in both the lysine and graphite-electrode price-fixing investigations. On May 27, the Japan Fair Trade Commission raided the offices of four graphite-electrode producers. 'It's truly a stunning development," says James R. Loftis III, a Washington antitrust attorney with the firm of Collier, Shannon & Rill. "Historically, Japanese competition authorities had been insular about these issues, rebuffing any requests by the United States for forced access to Japanese companies."

Still, huge barriers to cooperation remain. But if Justice can bring some of its current price-fixing investigations to fruition, the agency believes it can make a strong case that cartels are a serious global problem, especially in an era of rising global trade. And that might well force other countries to get on the U.S. bandwagon.

By Susan B. Garland in Washington, with Emily Thornton in Tokyo
www.admworld.com

The news article that opens this chapter underscores the importance of ethical and socially responsible behavior by multinationals. However, as the article noted, what is considered unethical in some countries may not be viewed as unethical in others. Practices such as bribery, dumping, and piracy are but some of the issues which MNCs must be concerned with when operating abroad, as regulations regarding these practices may differ from nation to nation. In the case of Archer Daniels Midland Co. (ADM), charges of international price-fixing have gained the ethical issue worldwide attention. Getting together to determine prices drains millions of dollars out of economies each year. However, while the United States is interested in cracking down on such unethical practices, other nations are not so eager. Both the Japanese and European countries have been chastised by the United States for failing to cooperate and come down hard on cartels and their price-fixing conspiracies. As the following chapter will indicate, differences in levels of acceptance for such practices between nations leave MNCs in a difficult position when trying to maintain their own ethical behavior.

Ethics Around the World

The ethical behavior of business has become a major issue. Not only in the United States but all countries around the world have received considerable media attention and aroused the public's concern about ethics in international business.

Ethics
The study of morality and standards of conduct

Ethics is the study of morality and standards of conduct. In recent years a growing number of MNCs have formulated codes of ethics to guide their behavior and ensure that their operations conform to these standards worldwide. The big MNC Johnson & Johnson's code is a good example.

> We are responsible to our employees, the men and women who work with us throughout the world. Everyone must be considered as an individual. We must respect their dignity and recognize their merit. They must have a sense of security in their jobs. Compensation must be fair and adequate, and working conditions clean, orderly and safe. We must be mindful of ways to help our employees fulfill their family responsibilities. Employees must feel free to make suggestions and complaints. There must be equal opportunity for employment, development and advancement for those qualified. We must provide competent management, and their actions must be just and ethical.
>
> We are responsible to the communities in which we will live and work and to the world community as well. We must be good citizens—support good works and charities and bear

our fair share of taxes. We must encourage civic improvements and better health and education. We must maintain in good order the property we are privileged to use, protecting the
environment and natural resources.[1]

Ethics is important in the study of international management, because ethical behavior in
one country sometimes is viewed as unethical behavior in other countries. Considerable
attention has been given in the management literature to ethical problems in the United
States; not so well-known are the ethical issues in other parts of the world.[2] The following
sections examine some of the ethical problems that occur in international business in
selected countries.

Ethical Problems and Concerns in Japan

In terms of both internal and external business relations, Japan, like the United States, has
had more than its share of ethical problems in recent years.[3] Some of the most devastating
and widely publicized have occurred in both the political and business arenas.

Political and Business Scandals Several years ago, Japan was rocked by a
bribery scandal involving the Recruit Company. In an effort to curry favor, this firm had
been giving politicians and influential businesspeople an opportunity to buy cut-rate stock
in a Recruit real estate subsidiary. The shares eventually were listed on the public stock
exchange, and the early stockholders, many of whom were these targeted people, made
large returns on their investment. When this information became public, some members of
the cabinet, including the prime minister, were forced to resign.[4]

Since the widely publicized Recruit case, there have been additional scandals. One of
the most recent began with the arrest of a career bureaucrat, the finance director for the
Japanese Public Highway Corporation, who was accused of accepting lavish entertainment, a
common occurrence in pre-recession Japan, from a stock brokerage firm. Tokyo prosecutors
charged this official with being influenced by this largesse and, in turn, selecting the brokerage as the chief underwriter of $800 million worth of bonds issued by the Highway
Corporation. This resulted in prosecutors raiding the office of Japan's highway authority and
those of Nomura Securities, as part of the investigation, and carting off boxes of materials.
When questioned about the matter, the Japanese prime minister said, "Bureaucrats are already
subject to a moral code. I expect employees of public corporations to follow this code."[5]

As a result of the highway bonds investigation, more than 30 executives of financial
institutions were arrested. Additionally, four officials of the Finance Ministry and one from
the Bank of Japan were taken into custody on charges of having accepted bribes in the
form of entertainment. However, very little happened as a result. Within a few months, the
chief prosecutor in Tokyo was transferred to a remote coastal city and the investigation
drew to a halt. About the only change that took place was that Finance Ministry personnel
and other government bureaucrats began refusing meals and entertainment from business
executives. One news reporter summed up the final outcome by noting:

> For the Finance Ministry mandarins, though, probably the worst part of the punishment was
> that their names were published in the newspapers, along with the punishments received.
> "Even if they don't indict a single person, the question is whether these people have been pun-
> ished socially," said [a university law professor] "For those who quit the Finance Ministry or
> received other punishments announced by the Finance Ministry, that is considered to have
> been punished enough." Ministry officials say that morale is low, and that attitudes are indeed
> changing. The Finance Ministry and the central bank are not attracting the elite graduates the
> way they used to. The best students are taking jobs elsewhere.[6]

Another scandal that has rocked Japan in recent years has been the failure of its
banking system to take corrective action and prevent a deepening of the country's drawn
out recession. This problem seems to have been caused by both the government and business. The government failed to institute strong procedures designed to prevent the banks
from taking large, dangerous risks and the banks failed to adjust their loan policies, write
off bad loans, and accept the responsibility for their errors. As a result, by the late-1990s

the total amount of uncollectible loans by major Japanese banks was greater than their total equity. Simply put, many of them were technically bankrupt![7]

Changing Social Climate in Japan

The growing sensitivity to global ethics has helped to focus the attention of many MNCs on the changing social environment in Japan. The role of business ethics in the coming years likely will differ sharply from what it has been in the past. Previously, Japanese politicians and businesspeople thought nothing of giving favors to each other and looking for reciprocity, but this behavior is changing. Influence peddling (trying to influence others through reciprocal favors) in Japan now is serious business, and everyone from the president of a foreign MNC to the head of huge domestic corporations such as NTT are now being held to the same high standard of ethical behavior.

Hostile Work Environment Issues in Japan

An area where Japan and most other countries have recently faced up to is sexual harassment in the workplace, an issue on which more and more Japanese women are fighting back. Several years ago, a Japanese woman won a judgment of $12,500 from her company. This was the first lawsuit ever filed in Japan charging sexual harassment, and it set off a wave of concern.[8] Within 48 hours of the verdict, the government had issued 10,000 copies of a booklet on sexual harassment, and all were quickly snapped up.

Despite a heightened sensitivity in recent years, sexual harassment remains a major social issue in Japan. A good example is provided by a Japanese saleswoman for a large bank, who was visiting clients with a male deputy branch manager. This manager made improper advances toward her, but when she reported the incident the only thing the company did was to give her a new work partner. Soon afterwards the branch manager approached the woman and told her that her previous partner had been having work problems and he would like the two of them to again become job partners. The woman refused, quit her job, and filed a sexual harassment law against the firm. The case is now pending.

One of the major reasons why sexual harassment remains a problem in Japan is that traditionally many male managers regard female employees as mere assistants and, following a stereotype, feel that women employees will soon marry and leave the firm. So women are often not given the opportunity for promotion and are not considered for management positions. Additionally, sexual harassment is a new concept to many Japanese managers. One labor economist recently tried to put the issue into perspective by noting that most Japanese managers do not consider it a moral issue or think about why it happens or of improving the work environment. In fact, while many Japanese know that there are sexual harassment lawsuits filed in the United States, they fail to grasp why it is such an important issue for Americans. One analyst recently conveyed this idea by noting that in Japan, "There is no specific law against sexual harassment, so those suing must use general civil law. Suits can take years in the courts, and awards are typically only a few thousand dollars. And victory can be difficult."[9] In the United States, however, Japanese firms have met more resistance and successful lawsuits. For example, Mitsubishi was the target of picketing and a boycott by the U.S. National Organization for Women and other activist groups. The action began when the Equal Employment Opportunity Commission (EEOC) filed a lawsuit charging the company with sexual harassment of more than 300 women. The firm eventually settled the suit agreeing, among other things, to donate $100,000 to women's causes as well as making substantial cash payments to some of the women who had brought suits of their own.[10]

Equal Opportunity Issues in Japan

Besides sex discrimination, some Japanese firms also are having problems dealing with minority workers. Comments made by Japanese political figures about African-Americans and Hispanics, for example, have been criticized for their discriminatory meaning.[11] Japanese businesses also have been known to engage in insensitive racial stereotypes.[12]

The biggest furor, however, has been created by Japanese firms' attempts to keep minority hiring to a minimum. For example, evidence shows Japanese firms that set up operations in the United States tend to favor areas where minorities in general, and

African-Americans in particular, are not situated. Most people live within 30 miles of their job site, and national census data show that the propensity to commute declines rapidly once one goes beyond this limit. One analysis found that Japanese assembly plants and supplier plants in North America are less likely to set up operations within 30 miles of areas inhabited by minorities. The researchers made observation such as the following:

> In the course of our research, we heard Japanese managers specifically explain their decisions on plant siting in such terms. . . . Des Rosiers, who has carried out several site studies for Japanese auto companies, added: "They ask for profiles of the community by ethnic background, by religious background, by professional make-up. . . . There are demographic aspects that they like. They like a high German content. . . . [The Japanese] probably don't like other types of profiles."[13]

This study provided further evidence for discrimination in the workplace when the percentage of African-Americans in the local area was compared with the percentage that were employed by Japanese firms. The results showed that African-Americans were consistently underrepresented in the Japanese plants. Legal action stemming from discriminatory employment practices has been successful against some Japanese firms in the United States. For example, several years ago, Honda of America Manufacturing, Inc., agreed to give 370 African-Americans and women a total of $6 million in back pay to resolve a federal discrimination complaint.

These examples and empirical evidence indicate that at least in the recent past Japanese firms in the United States have had more than their share of problems in dealing with the hiring and treatment of minorities and women. Importantly, equality in the workplace continues to be a central social issue and indicator for social responsibility of business in the United States. It should be noted that the Japanese are currently making an effort to improve equality in employment, and their concern for the safety and health of workers may be unmatched anywhere in the world.[14]

Social Responsibility Implication from Lobbying   Another area of ethical concern has been the Japanese lobbying effort in the United States.[15] Japan, more than other countries, spends millions of dollars every year for lobbying in Washington. For this money, Japanese firms have been able to hire very savvy, effective lobbyists. Is this ethical for Japanese firms to hire bank-rolled, well-connected, talented lobbyists to argue their case in Washington? Is it ethical for former U.S. cabinet officers and elected officials to become lobbyists for Japan? Certainly, these activities are legal. Many Americans feel that the interests of the United States and Japan are not the same when it comes to business dealings, however, and that Americans are being shortchanged in the process. To the extent that these feelings persist, Japanese lobbying will continue to be an area of ethical concern during the years ahead.

Ethical Problems and Concerns in Europe

Ethical behavior in European countries is an important area of interest in international management, because in some respects, these countries differ sharply from Japan and the United States.[16] Although ethical issues are a concern throughout the world and all European countries, France and Germany seem to get most of the attention in the literature.

One study surveyed 124 U.S., 72 French, and 70 German managers.[17] Each was asked to respond to a series of five vignettes that examined ethical situations related to coercion and control, conflict of interest, the physical environment, paternalism, and personal integrity. In most cases, the U.S. managers' responses were quite different from those of their European counterparts. The following is an example of one of the vignettes:

> Rollfast Bicycle Company has been barred from entering the market in a large Asian country by collusive efforts of the local bicycle manufacturers. Rollfast could expect to net 5 million dollars per year from sales if it could penetrate the market. Last week a businessman from the country contacted the management of Rollfast and stated that he could smooth the way for the company to sell in his country for a price of $500,000.[18]

The executives from the three countries were asked how they would respond to the request for payment. The Americans were opposed to paying the money; 39 percent of them said that a bribe was unethical or illegal under the Foreign Corrupt Practices Act. Only 12 percent of the French managers felt that way, and none of the Germans agreed. However, 55 percent of the French and 29 percent of the Germans said that paying the money was not unethical but merely the price to be paid for doing business.

Part of the reason for these answers is that to date, neither France nor Germany has laws that make it a crime to bribe or corrupt a public or private official of another country.[19] Legal restrictions are not the only reasons for the differences in managerial views of ethical behavior, however. Here is the conflict-of-interest vignette that was presented to the managers:

> Jack Brown is vice president of marketing for Tangy Spices, a large spice manufacturer. Jack recently joined a business venture with Tangy's director of purchasing to import black pepper from India. Jack's new company is about to sign a five year contract with Tangy to supply their black pepper needs. The contract is set at a price 3 cents per pound above the current market price for comparable black pepper imports.[20]

Should Brown sign the contract? Once again, the managers were divided regarding what should be done and why. Most U.S. managers felt that signing the contract would be dishonest or a conflict of interest. Many of the French managers agreed, but only one-third of the Germans indicated that they would not sign the agreement.

Summing up the responses of the managers to all five vignettes, the researchers concluded:

> If one were to generalize, the U.S. managers were noticeably more concerned with ethical and legal questions. Their French and German counterparts appeared to worry more about maintaining a successful business posture. To be sure, there was some overlapping of responses; however, the differences remained.[21]

This cross-national research on ethical behavior shows that MNCs must be aware that the ethical practices of their home country may be quite different from those of countries where they do business. A number of reasons account for these differences, including culture, personal values, incentives, and the obvious legal restrictions.

The Status of Women Managers in Europe

Because most European countries have experienced only limited population growth in recent years, integration of women into the workforce has become a critical goal. Similar to the United States and Japan, however, European women have encountered equal opportunity problems and a "glass ceiling" in the managerial ranks. The following discussion examines the current status of women managers in three of the largest European nations: France, Germany, and Great Britain.

France   The proportion of French women in the labor force from 1900 until 1970 remained at about 35 percent. Since then, however, more than 2 million women have entered the workforce, compared with less than 200,000 men. This trend would seem to indicate that women now should be gaining a greater foothold in the managerial ranks—and to a degree, this is true. Over the last 35 years, the number of women managers has increased almost twice the number of managerial position has increased. The greatest gains have been in product promotion and sales, import-export, sales administration, real estate, urban planning and architecture, socioeconomic studies, and chemistry.

Although French women are making strides in the management ranks, they still are underrepresented in corporate management. Women still are far behind men in terms of corporate management and the traditional functions of manufacturing and sales. A number of reasons are given for this underrepresentation. One is that promotion into top management depends on more than diplomas, abilities, and ambitions.[22] As in the United States and Japan, French women face many obstacles when trying to break the glass ceiling. As one analysis of women managers in France notes:

Being a manager includes having to work long hours, travel, make difficult decisions, motivate people, and achieve high objectives—most often with limited resources and strong business competitors. For women managers, it also often means fighting within their own company to establish a reputation as a leader—since women are rarely spontaneously seen as leaders, avoiding or responding appropriately to sexist criticisms, motivating employees to accept and execute their decisions, and sometimes hiding their family problems. Women frequently have more difficulty than men getting access to information necessary to make wise career decisions. Although it is important for women to understand the organization's career criteria, few companies in France provide such information through either equal opportunity managers or assertiveness courses.[23]

From a legal standpoint, French law guarantees equal treatment and equal professional opportunities. Enforcement of these guarantees is fairly weak, however, and organization that could be valuable to women generally are uninvolved. For example, unions have generally resisted taking on women's issues, and there are no organizations in France comparable to the Coalition of Labor Union Women in the United States that could promote equal opportunity issues. Even French associations of women managers are limited in their efforts and, for the most part, focus primarily on social networking. So, while some French companies have promoted women into higher-level position and have affirmative action programs in place, these firms unfortunately still are the exception rather than the rule. As one analyst recently put it, "Companies' needs for the best possible managers will favor highly qualified women; but to succeed, these women will most likely have to accept even more difficult working conditions."[24]

Germany Before unification, 47 percent of working-age women in West Germany and 91 percent of those in East Germany were in the workforce. In both West and East, however, women held few top management positions. Studies of large West German firms found that 5.9 percent of top managers and 7.8 percent of managers at the next level were women, but only 0.7 percent were members of managing boards of public companies. In East Germany, one-third of all management positions were held by women, but these primarily were low-level jobs. With the unification of Germany, the status of women in management does not look any more promising. One reason is that professional qualifications appear to relate inversely to hierarchical position. Antal and Krebsbach-Gnath explained this seeming paradox as follows:

> The higher the position, the less significance the organization attaches to . . . "objective" criteria. The factors that receive more weight in promotion decisions for senior management positions are both less objective and more often based on traditional male career patterns. In effect, therefore, they discriminate against women. Among the factors listed in one study for promotion into upper-level management were professional competence, effectiveness, professional experience, length of experience, time with the company, commitment to the job, and professional and regional mobility. To the extent that "objective" factors and qualifications, such as education and training that women can consciously acquire, play a lesser role in decision making, other sociopsychological and systemic factors assume increasing importance and create less easily surmountable barriers to career development for women.[25]

Unlike some other countries, Germany in the last decade has introduced laws that mandate equal opportunity and the creation of equal opportunity positions throughout the public sector. Today, all German states must ensure that their legislation provides for equal treatment of men and women in the workplace. On the other hand, use of quotas is unacceptable, and this makes the legislation difficult to enforce. Additionally, those individuals who are designated as equal opportunity officers typically have difficulty carrying out their tasks, because they often lack the needed authority to enforce their decisions.

In the private sector, there has been some progress toward increasing the number of women in upper-level management position through the introduction of voluntary equal opportunity programs. Some German firms also have nominated individuals or groups and assigned them the responsibility of ensuring equal opportunity for all personnel. Another, and more recent, development is the conclusion of company-level, work-family agreements between employers and workers' representatives regarding parental leave and return plans. These plans allow employees to take a longer parental leave than is granted by law, and to attract these employees back, these plans guarantee an equivalent job on returning from the extended leave.

Some analysts indicate that Germany's growing need for competent managers likely will increase the number of women in management and the opportunity for them to achieve higher-level positions. On the other side, critics argue this is wishful thinking and that what is needed is stronger legislation. Still others contend that until there is a fundamental change in the way that male managers view the role and status of women, nothing significant will happen. These arguments all point to one conclusion: Opportunities for women managers in Germany remain limited and do not seem likely to improve significantly in the near future.

Great Britain   By the end of the 1990s, approximately 13 million women were in the British workforce, which was about 45 percent of the country's total workforce. The number of women in management and related occupation has been steadily increasing over the last two decades. Once again, however, as in other countries, British women are not well represented at the highest levels of most organizations.[26]

Most women managers in Britain are employed in retail distribution, hotel and catering, banking, finance, medical and other health services, and food, drink, and tobacco. Almost all of these women managers are at the lowest levels, and they have a long way to go if they hope to reach the top. Legislation designed to prevent discrimination in the workplace is proving to be of limited value; however, a number of steps are being taken to help British women attain equal opportunity in employment.

In recent years, British women have been setting up their own associations, such as the Women's Engineering Society, to develop sources for networking and to increase their political lobbying power. There also is a national association, known as The 300 Group, that campaigns for women seeking election to Parliament. In addition, women have become very active in joining management and professional associations, such as the Hotel, Catering and Institutional Management Association; the Institute of Personnel Management; and the Institute of Health Service Management. Women now constitute 50 percent or more of the membership in these professional associations.

At the same time, a growing number of British companies are proactively trying to recruit and promote women into the management ranks. They are introducing career development programs specifically for women and are prepared to take whatever steps are necessary to ensure that outstanding women remain with the company. For example, the National Westminster Bank allows women managers to leave for up to 5 years to raise their children and then return to a management position at their previous level. Firms also are designing strategies to ensure that equal opportunities are, in fact, being implemented. Chief executives and directors of leading companies recently have formed a group known as Opportunity 2000. One of the group's goals is to provide a wide range of assistance to women who are interested in business careers; in particular, the focus is on helping firms to demonstrate a commitment to these goals, change their old ways of doing business, communicate their desires to potential women managers, and make the necessary financial and time commitments that are needed to ensure success. While it is still too early to say how successful Opportunity 2000 will be, these efforts do appear to be on the right track. One analysis summed up the current status and future direction as follows:

> Recent forecasts of the economy in Britain have highlighted the increased dependence that companies will have on women in the twenty-first century. It forecasts that there will be greater need for managers, professionals, and associated staff and that women will generally represent an increasing proportion of that workforce. It remains to be seen whether initiatives such as Opportunity 2000 will enable the number of women managers to reach a self-sustaining critical mass. Women managers have made strides forward in the last decade. Perhaps with many companies waking up to the necessity of retaining all good employees, more will also learn to use the full potential of their women as managers in order to benefit both the corporate and the national economies.[27]

Ethical Problems and Concerns in China

Along with the tremendous market opportunities in China are some ethical problems for MNCs doing business there. After the violent, June 1989 crackdown on the student protestors in Beijing's Tiananmen Square, many questioned whether any business should be conducted there until more freedom and human rights were restored.

Despite continuing ethical issues such as piracy of intellectual property and human rights violations such as the use of prisoner and child labor, many MNCs were, and still are, attracted to the competitive advances offered by China. One of these advantages is the low cost of labor. Countries as nearby as Hong Kong, now part of China itself, and as far away as the United States have found this cheap labor attractive. In the case of Hong Kong, a severe labor shortage and strict labor laws have made it difficult to meet mounting work demands in industries such as clothing and toy making. In the case of U.S. manufacturers, many toy makers have subcontracted their work to the mainland Chinese, because labor is such a large percentage of their overall costs.

Factory workers in China are not well paid, and to meet the demand for output, they often are forced to work 12 hours a day, 7 days a week. In some cases, children are used for this work and are paid very little, usually only one-half of an adult's wages. The government also has been using prison labor to produce goods for the export market.[28] In addition, with China now open to the outside world, there has been a rush to get rich under the market economy reforms and a dramatic increase in crime and illegal business activities.[29]

These developments have led to friction between the U.S. Congress and China, and they have resulted in continual efforts by the Senate to impose conditions on the renewal of China's favorable trade status with the United States.[30] A closer look at the existing piracy, industrial spying and counterfeit problems, and the status of women in employment shows why there is still controversy surrounding China.

Piracy, Industrial Spying, and Counterfeit Problems In recent years the U.S. government has been taking a hard line on Chinese piracy of intellectual property (e.g., patent, copyright, and trademark) and demanding that China crack down on those who are copying illegally. Software is a good example. In recent years worldwide piracy in this industry has exceeded $10 billion annually. Figure 4-1 shows that all countries have problems, but China is the second largest violator of software property rights—and it does not end here. The accompanying sidebar, "Get Tough . . . or Else," gives some specific examples of the huge pirating problem in China.

Fortune magazine recently reported that over the past several years Chinese-backed industry spying has increased dramatically against U.S. business. In fact, a recently released survey of 1,300 major American firms found that U.S. companies now sees China as its major foreign economic-espionage threat. Some recent examples include:

- Amgen discovered that a Chinese spy had infiltrated its organization and was trying to steal a vial of cell cultures for Epogen, now a $1.2-billion-a-year anemia drug.
- A Chinese spy in Hong Kong was recently caught using sophisticated telecommunications software to secretly listen in on sensitive phone conversations between American executives.
- A Chinese engineer working at a Boulder, Colorado, software company allegedly stole proprietary source code and peddled it to a PRC company. As a result, the company went out of business.[31]

Chinese firms also illegally produce counterfeit CD-ROMs, music-CDs, and video-CDs in factories throughout the country. In an effort to deal with this problem, the U.S. government has been putting pressure on the Chinese government to shutter these factories, and there has been some progress to date. In addition to taking direct action, the Chinese government has been offering rewards to those who provide information that leads to the closing of an illegal operation.[32] However, the problem is not so easily resolved. Recent reports reveal that Hong Kong and Macau have also become hot beds for piracy.[33]

Figure 4–1

**Software Piracy
Rates 1994 vs.
1997**

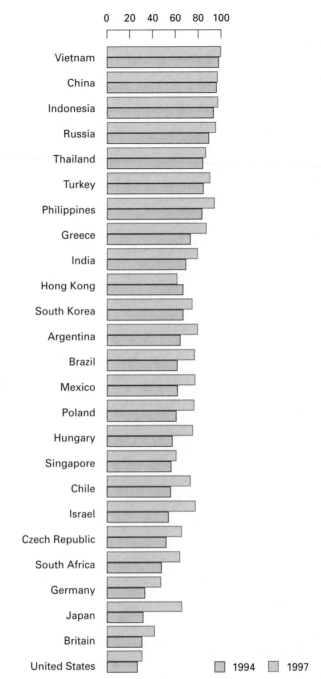

Source: International Planning and Research Corporation.

A related problem is joint ventures in which Chinese partners break the agreement and walk off with patents and/or capital or simply start an operation that is in direct competition with the venture. Kimberly-Clark is a good example.

Its plant in Handan, which is 97% owned by [Kimberly-Clark] produces around $10 million annually of feminine-care pads. Located in the northeastern province of Hebei, it is one of 12 company factories in China. The operation seemed to be running smoothly until last spring, when plant officials noticed a nearby factory was making a similar product. Worse, the Americans discovered that the head of the rival operation was Li Hongzhi, who was picked by Kimberly-Clark's Chinese partner, Xingha Factory Co., to be the manager of the joint venture. Li was "stealing" and "diverting materials" such as spare parts and pulp from the venture to the new factory, alleged . . . Kimberly-Clark's vice-president for corporate communications.[34]

International Management in Action

Get Tough . . . or Else

A growing number of multinationals are very concerned about doing business in China, and they have good reason to be. Within hours of the time their goods are on the street, many find that counterfeiters are already working on developing their own version of the product—and in many cases, these clones look just like the original. Today, there are fake cans of Coca-Cola, fake McDonald's hamburger restaurants, fake versions of the Jeeps that Chrysler manufactures with a joint-venture partner in Beijing, and fake Gillette razor blades.

One of the most disconcerting things for foreign MNCs in China is that counterfeiters often are blatantly obvious in their efforts. One good example is a fast-food restaurant in downtown Shanghai about 100 yards from a McDonald's outlet. This restaurant uses a sign with golden arches on a red background in a way that makes it look like a McDonald's. Lawyers for McDonald's say they are looking into taking legal action.

Even more disconcerting is that when counterfeiters are caught, the Chinese government often does very little about it. The Gillette Razor Blade Company is a good example of this. The Huaxing Razor Blade Factory was producing Gillette look-alike blades and packaging them in the same blue package as that used by Gillette. After Chinese authorities raided the factory, they fined the company $3,500 and told management that it was illegal to produce counterfeit blades and they were to stop. Five months later, when it became evident that the company was still manufacturing the blades, there was a second raid, followed by a fine of $3,300. At that time, the manager was asked why he not only kept producing the blades but also used the same

packaging as before. He remarked that he did not want to throw away packaging that had already been printed. "We didn't want to waste it," he said.

Will such a "slap on the wrist" type of enforcement stop the counterfeiting? This is unlikely, because the fines are small compared with the revenues being generated. The Chinese government also does not seem to be very interested in taking sterner measures. In fact, in some cases when MNCs have complained that counterfeiters have gone back to their old ways, inspectors have refused to take any additional action, arguing that "we already addressed that issue and we are now moving on to other matters." Such an attitude worries MNCs, because they feel there is no protection for their intellectual properties. A lawyer who has represented several U.S. companies in trademark disputes in China put it this way:

> In most countries, if you have 10 pirates, you can go after one, expect seven to stop, and then figure out how to get the remaining two. But in China, when you go after one the other nine see exactly what you're doing. Not only do they keep pirating, but you invite 10 more to join in.

Unless the government of China takes more stringent steps to do something about pirating and counterfeiting, MNCs likely will take action of their own. One of the most commonly mentioned steps is to demand that Chinese exports to the United States be limited and that levies be assessed on these goods to offset the loss of revenues being sustained by the U.S. MNCs. In the final analysis, it appears that China will have to get tough on pirates and counterfeiters . . . or else.

Kimberly-Clark went to the American Embassy to complain and eventually the situation was satisfactorily resolved. The same was not true for Chicago-based Borg-Warner Automotive, Inc. Soon after this company signed a joint venture agreement, the firm realized that its Chinese partner had no intention of making the deal work. In fact, the partner intended to set up a rival operation. So Borg-Warner filed a request with the requisite Chinese agency to end the joint venture, pointing out that its partner had not fulfilled its obligation to provide utilities such as water and electricity and so the company was unable to accept the factory site that had been given to it. The Chinese regulatory agency rejected Borg-Warner's request, and in the interim the Chinese partner filed a lawsuit against the firm for rejecting the plant site. In the judgment that ensued, a Chinese court awarded all of the joint venture assets of $2.2 million, 60 percent of which came from Borg-Warner, to the Chinese partner. By the time the American MNC found out about the judgment, it was too late to appeal the decision at the local level. So the company filed a petition with China's supreme court and asked the U.S. embassy for help.

The above story is only one of many that are coming out of China and the rest of the world. And they all reinforce the same point: Doing international business can be very risky and even joint ventures with in-country partners do not ensure that the MNC will be protected from the adverse effects of unethical and illegal actions.[35]

The Status of Women Managers in China   As in other countries, women managers in China confront a "glass ceiling" when trying to reach top management ranks. There are a number of reasons for this, including cultural stereotypes, restricted opportunities, and of course, discrimination.

Cultural stereotypes are deep-rooted and very prevalent in China, and they go a long way toward hindering women's preparation for managerial roles as well as their more direct opportunities for promotion. Women have been socialized to be shy and unassertive. As a result, they often are viewed as being unprepared to assume leadership positions. A common stereotype is that Chinese women are disorganized, narrow-minded, and hard to work with compared to men.[36] Such widespread thinking greatly inhibits the advancement of women in management.

Coupled with this are restricted opportunities. For example, Chinese women are not well represented in the Communist party, which is one of the fastest ways to gain upward mobility. Additionally, Chinese women are less likely to be chosen for education and training programs, again restricting their opportunity to enter the upper-managerial ranks. In particular, women typically are required to have higher test scores on university entrance exams to ensure their admission. They also face segregation on the job and, as a result, often end up with the less meaningful tasks. For example, men typically operate the high-tech equipment and processes, while women do the routine work.

Discrimination in the workplace is both blatant and subtle. For example, women often are given additional workplace favors, such as extra rest periods, but in turn, these serve as the basis for bypassing them for promotions, which go instead to men who work longer hours. Additionally, women are required to retire at the age of 60, while men can work until 65. This inhibits their career advancement and helps to prevent them from reaching senior management positions. Drawing together many of these perception and stereotypes, Korabik has summed up the series of interviews that she conducted with women managers in the People's Republic of China by noting:

> Stereotypes in China are particularly insidious because no research exists to show them to be inaccurate. Many Chinese therefore believe them to represent the "true" nature of women and men. Government campaigns to eradicate such stereotypes have been largely ineffective, and their consequences are often not redressed because they are not viewed as discriminatory. Thus, despite many laws intended to insure equality in the workplace, Chinese women managers are still at a disadvantage compared to men.[37]

Regulating Foreign Investment

The regulation of foreign investment is another area of international business that has at least indirect implications for ethics and social responsibility. Many countries have a growing concern regarding the ethics of an MNC's gaining an economic foothold and then taking the resources and profits back home. This concern focuses on reciprocity between the home country of MNCs and the host country. The United States again provides a good example. The latest available data reveal that foreigners have invested triple-digit billions in the United States, and U.S. investments abroad also are in triple-digit billions. Moreover, foreign investors have put more money into this country than U.S. investors have put overseas.

The rapid increase of foreign investment in the United States has raised ethical concerns among many Americans, who believe that such foreign investment needs to be regulated more closely. In addition, some are concerned that countries like Japan seem much more interested in selling to the United States than in buying from U.S. firms. These concerns have ethical and social responsibility implications, and they have led to regulation of acquisitions and reciprocal trade agreements in the United States. Other countries are following the U.S. lead by also looking more closely at these two areas and how they affect their own country.

Regulation of Acquisitions

In the United States, under preliminary regulations published by the Treasury Department, most foreign investors now must obtain formal approval before acquiring a U.S. company. The primary exceptions, are industries such as toys and games, food products, hotels and restaurants, and legal services. Acquisition requests are reviewed by the interagency Committee on Foreign Investment, which is made up of eight agencies and headed by the Treasury Department. The stated objective of the regulation is to prevent foreign firms from gaining control of U.S. businesses that are important to U.S. security.

Although at first glance this regulation might appear to be a major barrier to acquisition by overseas investors, its scope is really quite restricted, and it applies to only a small number of deals. The Treasury Department estimates that fewer than 170 acquisition a year are covered by this regulation; however, as noted in the following analysis, there can be far-reaching consequences:

> The proposed regulations subject acquisitions, including those that have already been completed since the bill was passed, to divestiture over an indefinite period. They provide that a transaction could be dissolved any time should a foreign investor fail to notify the Government, provide false and misleading information or omit material information. Foreign investors could also become subject to the law if under an acquisition loan agreement, a default would allow them to step in and control the company.[38]

Other countries are following the U.S. lead and implementing similar regulatory practices. For example, many Third World nations now refuse to allow MNCs to establish new operations or purchase ongoing businesses unless they first obtain governmental clearance. This ensures that the government remains in control of the economy and is not overly reliant on foreign companies. In practice, however, many of these countries need MNC operation and are willing to accede to most requests for setting up, acquiring, or expanding local operations.

The countries in the European Union also are beginning to limit the business dealings of foreign multinationals. In particular, in the EU new regulations are making it more difficult for MNCs not located in Europe to do business there. The EU, except for England, is particularly sensitive to the rise of Japanese industrialism and the likelihood that Japanese auto manufacturers will dominate the world market. The EU also is trying to support local companies by mandating that certain parts and equipment, such as computer chips, that are to be sold in Europe also be built there by firms from the EU.

These regulatory developments show that countries around the globe are concerned about the increasingly large amount of foreign investment being made in their economies. This is particularly true in the case of those nations that are viewed as **nonreciprocal trade partners,** or those which sell goods to others but do not buy from them.

Nonreciprocal trade partners
Nations that sell (export) goods to other countries but do not buy (import) from them.

The Implications of Reciprocity

Is there an ethical and social responsibility to engage in reciprocal trade? This question is at the forefront of current trade talks between many countries, but especially between the United States and Japan. How much of an obligation does Japan have to import U.S. goods and services in light of its tremendous volume of exports to the United States? Every year, the Japanese have massive trade surpluses with the United States. The 1990s provided an excellent example. Despite some success in reducing barriers in areas such as tobacco and telecommunications and the weakening of the dollar against the yen for most of the decade, the annual trade deficit remained in the $50 to $60 billion range.

In recent years, the executive branch has undertaken a review of U.S.-Japanese trade relations. One primary source of information for the analysis was a voluminous report prepared by a special task force consisting of members from both government and business. The group recommended a 1-year trial period during which trade negotiations would be conducted with Japan. If no substantive results were achieved, the group suggested using Super 301, which is a provision of the Omnibus Trade and Competitiveness Act of 1988 that allows for sanctions against "unfair traders."

In the past few years, the United States has targeted Japan and Brazil, among others, for retaliatory action. Whether or not retaliatory action will work, the important thing to remember is that the United States feels it is unethical and irresponsible for countries such as Japan and Brazil to behave in trade relations as they do.[39] Most European countries disagree with the United States and believe there are more effective ways of negotiating trade problems than the use of sanctions. However, as long as the U.S. administration believes that the United States is not being treated ethically in the international trade arena, retaliation will continue to be a means to obtain reciprocity in international trade.

Remember that many critics of Japan point to the fact that Japan deserves such retaliation, that Japan refuses to do business with many outside companies, and that Japan stacks the deck so that all the cards are favorable to its self-interests. A second argument in favor of a retaliatory stance against Japan focuses on the fact that the Japanese often buy foreign businesses such as hotels. Then, when the Japanese travel abroad, they stay at these hotels and Japan recaptures funds that otherwise would flow into the international community. One report describes this process as follows:

> Japan's well-heeled travelers . . . prefer neatly wrapped package tours when they go abroad. The Tokyu group, another retailing conglomerate, provides such services by funneling vacationers through an affiliated travel agency to Tokyu's 15 Pacific Basin resorts, hotels, and condominiums. An airline partially owned by Tokyu flies vacationers to the holiday complexes. Joining the retailers in going global are Japan's airlines. In addition to managing 23 Nikko hotels, JAL uses its reservations network to book passengers into 90 other affiliated Nikko hotels. The airline is also developing five overseas resorts. Rival All Nippon Airways manages seven overseas hotels, from China to California, and is scouting for more. . . . And a hefty chunk of profits will end up in Japanese coffers.[40]

Another reason to support retaliation against Japan is that many countries already have sought and reached joint trade agreements with the United States. The argument goes that if Japan were serious in its efforts, it would have done so as well. For example, as early as 1987, South Korea had reached an agreement with the United States to increase imports from the United States by $2.6 billion and to buy a wide range of products, from supercomputers to grain. South Korea also allowed the import of U.S. computers a year ahead of schedule, cut financing to exporters to restrain exports, and pledged to create a service network for imported U.S. machinery. Similarly, Taiwan cut tariffs on a wide variety of products, from farm goods to footwear. Taiwan also allowed U.S. insurance companies to enter its market, liberalized restrictions on foreign banks, and gave some U.S. firms contracts for building the Taipei subway. By offering concessions, countries are more likely to placate the United States, which often is their largest international market, and to ensure there is no trade backlash. There is recent evidence that the years of U.S. pressure on Japan are beginning to pay off. By the mid-1990s, with only a few exceptions, such as rice imports, foreign companies no longer are hampered by law, regulation, or cultural issues from doing business in Japan.

Response to Social Obligations

So far, the discussion has focused on differences in ethical standards between countries and why nations such as the United States are concerned about trade reciprocity. However, many countries are responsive to their international social obligations. For example, the United States is pushing for higher ethical codes, and others, such as Italy, which has had a tradition of corruption, are putting forth considerable effort to clean things up. Japan is also trying to help less developed countries deal with their problems.

Foreign Corrupt Practices Act Revisited

As noted in the previous chapter, the Foreign Corrupt Practices Act (FCPA) makes it illegal for U.S. companies and their managers to attempt to influence foreign officials through personal payments or political contributions. Prior to passage of the FCPA, some American multinationals had engaged in this practice, but realizing that their stockholders were unlikely to approve of these tactics the firms typically disguised the payments in the form of entertainment expenses, consulting fees, etc. The FCPA not only prohibits these activities but the Internal Revenue Service audited the books of MNCs found to have made such payments, disallowed the deductions, and penalized the firms for these activities. As a result, American MNCs clearly understand that such practices are illegal and any attempt to hide these expenses can result in high financial penalties as well as prison sentences for those involved.

These developments have been applauded by many people. At the same time some critics wonder if such a strong social responsibility stance has not hurt the competitive ability of American MNCs. On the positive side, research shows that many U.S. multinationals have now increased the amount of business in countries where they used to pay bribes.[41] Additionally, many institutional investors in the United States have made it clear that they will not buy stock in companies that engage in unethical practices; and if they hold stock in these firms, they will sell their holdings. Given that these institutions have hundred of billions of dollars invested, senior-level management must be responsive to their needs.

Looking at the effect of the FCPA on U.S. multinationals, it appears that the law has had far more of a positive effect than a negative one. In fact, some observers wonder if companies did not overstate the importance of such covert activities. And given the growth of American MNCs in recent years, it seems fair to conclude that bribes are not a basic part of business in many countries as seen by the fact that when they stopped this activity, these multinationals were still able to sell in that particular market.

On the other hand, this does not mean that bribery is a thing of the past. A recent report issued by the U.S. Commerce Department contends that since 1994, foreign companies have used bribes to edge out U.S. MNCs on some $45 billion of international business deals. The report describes a case of bribery involving the contract for a power-generating plant in Central Europe as follows:

> A European company was awarded the multimillion-dollar contract even though the Central European government's own review board had recommended the contract be awarded to a U.S. firm. The report says there was clear evidence that a power-company official had been given a cash bribe by the European company that won the contract. The company used the same practice to win other contracts in Eastern and Central Europe, according to the report.[42]

These recent experiences reveal that bribery continues to be a problem for U.S. MNCs. At the same time, to comply with the provisions of the FCPA, U.S. firms must be careful not to follow suit and resort to bribery themselves. This advice also is useful for multinational managers doing business in the United States. The U.S. government has been vigorous in its prosecution of bribery and kickback schemes, and one example would be the case of Honda employees who were officials of American Honda. They were involved in an illegal program to solicit bribes from Honda auto dealers in exchange for ensuring that the dealers had a steady supply of cars. The scheme, which lasted from the late 1970s until 1992, involved American Honda executives who received cash, Rolex watches, and swimming pools in exchange for their awarding franchises or larger allotments of hot-selling Accords and other cars. The highest-ranking executive in the scheme was given 5 years in federal prison and fined $364,000; other convicted employees received lesser, but still significant, sentences.[43]

Another development that promises to give teeth to "anti-bribing" is the recent formal agreement by a host of industrialized nation that have agreed to outlaw the practice of bribing foreign government officials. The treaty, signed in Paris by 29 nations that belong to the Organization for Economic Cooperation and Development, marked a victory for the United States, which outlawed foreign bribery two decades previously, but had not been able to persuade other countries to follow its lead. As a result, American firms had long complained that they lost billions of dollars in contracts each year to rivals that bribed their way to success.[44]

This new treaty does not outlaw most payments to political party leaders. In fact, the treaty provisions are much narrower than U.S. negotiators wanted, and there will be undoubtedly ongoing pressure from the American government to expand the scope and coverage of the agreement. For the moment, however, it is a step in the right direction. Additionally, in summing up the impact and value of the treaty, one observer noted that:

> For their part, business executives say the treaty . . . reflects growing support for anti-bribery initiatives among corporations in Europe and Japan that have openly opposed the idea. Some of Europe's leading industrial corporations, including a few that have been embroiled in recent allegations of bribery, have spoken out in favor of tougher measures and on the increasingly corrosive effect of corruption.[45]

International Assistance

Besides fighting corruption, another way to meet social responsibilities has been to provide assistance to underdeveloped countries. For many years, this foreign aid has taken the form of food, machinery, and equipment to help feed the people of less developed countries and stimulate their economies. Traditionally, many less-developed countries have attempted to improve their conditions by borrowing large sums of money for economic development. In most cases, the monies were not wisely spent, and the countries now are having difficulty meeting their debt obligations. Poland, for example, has foreign debts in double-digit billions and very little hope of paying back this money. Mexico and South American countries such as Peru, Argentina, and Brazil are no better off. As a result, some of the economic superpowers recently have been calling for assistance to these countries. Two primary avenues are under investigation: (1) debt reduction or renegotiation; and (2) direct grants.

The United States and Japan are the two leading proponents of international aid. Some Americans have called for a Third World debt reduction plan, and the Japanese government has proposed a package worth $43 billion designed to improve the global environment and spur economic growth in countries suffering under the burden of poverty and indebtedness. Some specific parts of the Japanese package include: (1) low-interest loans to other countries; (2) grants to specific nations in sub-Saharan Africa; and (3) a 3-year program of grants and credits for environmental needs, including tree planting and helping poor people to find alternatives to cutting down trees for fuel and fodder. These decisions will affect MNCs, because they will help to stimulate world economies and open up markets for more goods and services.

Another form of aid is being carried out by MNCs themselves. Multinationals are beginning to realize that they must take steps to ingratiate themselves in the countries where they do business. A philanthropic role can pragmatically help protect their investments, improve their corporate image, and help meet their social responsibilities. The Japanese are a good example. When former Prime Minister Nakasone made derogatory remarks about U.S. African-Americans and Hispanics, Japanese foundations and companies in the United States tried to minimize the damage by increasing their donations to funds that help to promote African-American college students and similar groups. Honda, which was the target of a racial discrimination suit over hiring practices in Ohio, became a big donor to organizations such as the Clara Hale House in Harlem and has provided a scholarship for minority students at Duke University. Mazda has been giving $70,000 annually to the United Way, and Hitachi America has given $30,000 to a local library. Quite clearly, these Japanese MNCs understand the long-run benefits of philanthropy. As one observer pointed out, "In coming years, Japan's role as philanthropist in the U.S. is destined to grow, perhaps even to explode. Clearly, the tracks needed to roll out major fundraising drives and manage large projects have been laid down. American institutions are certain to benefit, and Corporate Japan should, too."[46]

U.S. and European multinationals follow similar philanthropy patterns. Quite clearly, MNC assistance directed at host countries is a two-way street. Each side stands to benefit economically through MNCs' meeting their social responsibilities.

World of Business Week Revisited

The *Business Week* article that initiated this chapter scrutinized some of the unethical behaviors performed by multinationals. As trade barriers continue to fall between nations, companies which once felt very secure in their domestic markets are turning to international cartels and global price-fixing practices to fend off competitors. Having read this chapter, you should now be more conscious of the differences between how companies of various nations regard standards of conduct. What may be right or wrong, proper or improper, or moral or immoral in one country may not be perceived this way in another. However, if the United States has its way, more and more countries will demonstrate concern about ethical behavior in the future. As is stressed in the article, by prosecuting large companies such as ADM, the United States is sending a message that this type of behavior is detrimental to fair play and eventually the economy and should not be tolerated. Currently, the U.S. Justice Department is optimistic that price-fixing around the world is weakening and the Agency is pushing for new cooperation agreements with other countries so that the crackdown on unethical practices will continue. Given this and what you have read in the chapter, answer the following questions: (1) Why is it so important that the United States worry about what other nations consider ethical or unethical? Shouldn't the United States worry about itself? (2) Why do you think the United States is facing so much resistance from other nations to get global standards for ethical conduct? (3) What do you think is causing the shift in those countries traditionally tolerant of unethical practices to change their approach?

Summary of Key Points

1. Ethics is the study of morality and standards of conduct. It is important in the study of international management because ethical behavior often varies from one country to another. For example, in recent years in Japan, political and business scandals and apparent cases of avoiding minority hiring have drawn attention to the need for another look at ethical and socially responsible behavior. Japan's lobbying efforts in Washington also have been questioned from an ethical standpoint.

2. Research in France and Germany reveals that European and U.S. MNCs seem to have different standards of ethics that result in different types of decisions and business practices. For example, U.S. MNCs do not believe in bribing businesspeople or politicians to gain favors, while some studies find that more respondents in samples of both German and French managers were

not as concerned with bribes as being unethical and instead felt payoffs were merely a cost of doing business. In the area of equal opportunity for women, the Europeans have goals for fully integrating women into the workforce and even recent EU legislation to ensure equal pay and equal treatment in employment. However, similar to U.S. women, European women are still being deprived of equal opportunities and are underrepresented in the managerial ranks of European firms, although some progress is being made.

3. Ethics also is a problem in countries such as China. Since the violent crackdown at Tiananmen Square and continued ethical and human rights violations, many MNCs have questioned whether they should do business with the Chinese. Those that found the low labor cost attractive too often overlooked the fact that the Chinese factory employees work long hours for

very low pay and that some of these workers are underaged or prisoners. These types of exploitive practices have ethical implications. So, too, does the status of women managers. As in many other countries, women managers in China face a "glass ceiling" blocking their advancement into top management. Three of the main reasons are cultural stereotypes, restricted opportunities, and discrimination.

4. A more indirect area of ethics and social responsibility deals with the regulation of foreign investment. In the United States, for example, the interagency Committee on Foreign Investment, which involves eight agencies headed by the Treasury Department, was set up to curb the indiscriminant buying of U.S. firms by foreign investors. The committee regulates the acquisi-

tion of U.S. companies by foreign multinationals. A similar, indirect area of ethics and social responsibility is reciprocal trade and the desire of countries such as the United States to get trading partners such as Japan to open their markets to U.S. goods.

5. During the years ahead, multinationals likely will become more concerned about being socially responsive, and legislation such as the U.S. Foreign Corrupt Practices Act is forcing the issue. Other countries also are passing laws to regulate the ethical practices of their MNCs. MNCs are being more proactive (often because they realize it makes good business sense) in providing international assistance in the form of philanthropy and direct community involvement as well.

Key Terms

ethics

nonreciprocal trade partners

Review and Discussion Questions

1. What lessons can U.S. multinationals learn from the political and bribery scandals in Japan that can be of value to them in doing business in this country? Discuss two.

2. In recent years, some prominent spokespeople have argued that those who work for the U.S. government in trade negotiations should be prohibited for a period of 5 years from accepting jobs as lobbyists for foreign firms. Is this a good idea? Why?

3. How do ethical practices differ among the United States and European countries such as France and Germany? What implications does your answer have for U.S. multinationals operating in Europe?

4. Why are many MNCs reluctant to produce or sell their goods in China? What role can the Chinese government play in helping to resolve this problem?

5. In what way is trade reciprocity an ethics or social responsibility issue? How important is this issue likely to become during the current decade?

6. Why are MNCs getting involved in philanthropy and local communities? Are they displaying a sense of social responsibility, or is this merely a matter of good business? Defend your answer.

Internet Exercise: Mitsubishi's Philanthropy

In this chapter some of the social responsibility problems that Mitsubishi has had in recent years were discussed. However, on the other side of the coin, the huge Japanese MNC has been trying very hard to improve its image and to address its social responsibility shortcomings. Visit the company's web site at **www.mitsubishi.com** and learn some of the latest social-type of activities in which the firm has been engaged. In particular, look closely at the "philanthropy" and "environment" sections of the web site. Then answer these questions: (1) What are some of

the most recent things that Mitsubishi is doing in terms of philanthropy? Do you think these actions represent sincere concern for the community or do you think that Mitsubishi is simply trying to create a positive image for itself to offset past bad coverage by the press? (2) What steps is the MNC taking in its environmental efforts and of what value are these actions? (3) Based on your responses to these questions, what conclusions can you draw regarding the current social responsibility stance of Mitsubishi?

Saudi Arabia

Saudi Arabia is a large Middle Eastern country covering 865,000 square miles. Part of its east coast rests on the Persian Gulf, and much of the west coast rests along the Red Sea. One of the countries on its borders is Iraq. After Iraq's military takeover of Kuwait in August 1990, Iraq next threatened to invade Saudi Arabia. This, of course, did not happen, but only time will tell what will happen next in this explosive part of the world.

There are approximately 20 million people in Saudi Arabia, and the per-capita income is around $10,000. This apparent prosperity is misleading, because most Saudis are poor farmers and herders who tend their camels, goats, and sheep. In recent years, however, more and more have moved to the cities and have jobs connected to the oil industry. Nearly all are Arab Muslims. The country has the two holiest cities of Islam: Mecca and Medina. The country depends almost exclusively on the sale of oil (it is the largest exporter of oil in the world) and has no public debt. The government is a monarchy, and the king makes all important decisions but is advised by ministers and other government officials. Royal and ministerial decrees account for most of the promulgated legislation. There are no political parties.

Earlier this week, Robert Auger, the executive vice president of Skyblue, a large commercial aircraft firm based in Kansas City, had a visit with a Saudi minister. The Saudi official explained to Auger that the government planned to purchase 10 aircraft over the next 2 years. A number of competitive firms were bidding for the job. The minister went on to explain that despite the competitiveness of the situation, several members of the royal family were impressed with Auger's company. The firm's reputation for high-quality performance aircraft and state-of-the-art technology gave it the inside track. A number of people are involved in the decision, however, and in the minister's words, "anything can happen when a committee decision is being made."

The Saudi official went on to explain that some people who would be involved in the decision had recently suffered large losses in some stock market speculations on the London Stock Exchange. "One relative of the King,

who will be a key person in the decision regarding the purchase of the aircraft, I have heard, lost over $200,000 last week alone. Some of the competitive firms have decided to put together a pool of money to help ease his burden. Three of them have given me $100,000 each. If you were to do the same, I know that it would put you on a par with them, and I believe it would be in your best interests when the decision is made." Auger was stunned by the suggestion and told the minister that he would check with his people and get back with the minister as soon as possible.

As soon as he got back to his temporary office, Auger sent a coded message to headquarters asking management what he should do. He expects to have an answer within the next 48 hours. In the interim, he has had a call from the minister's office, but Auger's secretary told the caller that Auger had been called away from the office and would not be returning for at least 2 days. The individual said he would place the call again at the beginning of this coming week. In the interim, Auger has talked to a Saudi friend whom he had known back in the United States who was currently an insider in the Saudi government. Over dinner, Auger hinted at what he had been told by the minister. The friend seemed somewhat puzzled about what Auger was saying and indicated that he had heard nothing about any stock market losses by the royal family or pool of money being put together for certain members of the decision-making committee. He asked Auger, "Are you sure you got the story straight, or as you Americans say, is someone pulling your leg?"

Questions

1. What are some current issues facing Saudi Arabia? What is the climate for doing business in Saudi Arabia today?

2. Is it legal for Auger's firm to make a payment of $100,000 to help ensure this contract?

3. Do you think other firms are making these payments, or is Auger's firm being singled out? What conclusion can you draw from your answer?

4. What would you recommend that Skyblue do?

It Sounds a Little Fishy

For the past 2 years, the Chicago-based Brattle Company has been thinking about going international. Two months ago, Brattle entered into negotiations with a large company based in Paris to buy one of its branches in Lyon, France. This would give Brattle a foreign subsidiary. Final arrangements on the deal should be completed within a month, although a few developments have occurred that concern the CEO of Brattle, Angela Scherer.

The most serious concern resulted from a conversation that Scherer had with one of the Lyon firm's largest customers. This customer had been introduced to Scherer during a dinner that the Paris headquarters gave in her honor last month. After the dinner, Scherer struck up a conversation with the customer to assure him that when Brattle took over the Lyon operation, they would provide the same high-quality service as their predecessor. The customer seemed interested in Scherer's comments and then said, "Will I also continue to receive $10,000 monthly for directing my business to you?" Scherer was floored; she did not know what to say. Finally she stammered, "That's something I think you and I will have to talk about further." With that, the two shook hands and the customer left. Scherer has not been back in touch with the customer since the dinner and is unsure of what to do next.

The other matter that has Scherer somewhat upset is a phone call from the head of the Lyon operation last week. This manager explained that his firm was very active in local affairs and donated approximately $5,000 a month to charitable organizations and philanthropic activities. Scherer is impressed with the firm's social involvement but wonders whether Brattle will be expected to assume these obligations. She then told her chief financial officer, "We're buying this subsidiary as an investment and we are willing to continue employing all the local people and paying their benefits. However, I wonder if we're going to have any profits from this operation after we get done with all the side payments for nonoperating matters. We have to cut back a lot of extraneous expenses. For example, I think we have to cut back much of the contribution to the local community, at least for the first couple of years. Also, I can't find any evidence of payment of this said $10,000 a month to that large customer. I wonder if we're being sold a bill of goods, or have they been paying him under the table? In any event, I think we need to look into this situation more closely before we make a final decision on whether to buy this operation."

Questions

1. If Scherer finds out that the French company has been paying its largest customer $10,000 a month, should Brattle back out of the deal? If Brattle goes ahead with the deal, should it continue to make these payments?

2. If Scherer finds out that the customer has been making up the story and no such payments were actually made, what should she do? What if this best customer says he will take his business elsewhere?

3. If Brattle buys the French subsidiary, should Scherer continue to give $5,000 monthly to the local community? Defend your answer.

Brazil and Argentina

If there are two nations that are bursting with economic activity today, they are Brazil and Argentina. In the red-hot investment region of Latin America, these two countries are well into unprecedented programs of government, economic and monetary reforms that began this decade and dwarf anything they have attempted in the past 30 years.

It is as though these nations have distilled textbook turnaround advice and put it into practice. Certainly, not everything is smooth; high levels of unemployment, crime, and poverty persist in both countries, along with stark divisions between rich and poor. Inflation also endures, more critically in Brazil. But even in light of the Asian financial crisis that is currently deflecting international interest and investment to other parts of the world, including Latin America, the efforts of Brazil and Argentina would be impressive at any time:

- Inflation is being wrestled under control, albeit with spotty success because of the Asian and Russian turmoil. Argentina brought its 3,100 percent inflation in 1989 to zero in 1994. The real, Brazil's currency introduced in 1994, supplants a long line of paper money.

- Privatization of state-owned industries since 1990 continues apace. Argentina has sold 55 companies for a total of $23.1 billion. During the same period, Brazil sold off 102 enterprises for a total of $32.3 billion. This does not include the recent sale of Brazil's telephone system, Telecomunicações Brasileiras S.A., known as Telebrás, for $19 billion in one of the largest privatizations ever.

- Argentina has been growing at 6 percent to 7 percent a year for the past 10 years. In 1997, it posted economic growth of 8.6 percent. In the second quarter of this year, the country's economic output grew 5.5 percent—virtually without inflation. Economists predict that 1998 GDP will be more than 6 percent.

- Mercosur (Mercosul in Portuguese), a regional trade bloc, was inaugurated in 1988 with member-states Brazil, Argentina, Paraguay, and Uruguay and new members Chile and Bolivia. The four original members represent a market of more than 200 million consumers.

- In line with liberalized trade, foreign companies are finding it easier to repatriate profits. Governments in the region, including those of Argentina and Brazil, are offering generous incentives such as tax breaks and land for development. Since American companies aren't part of free-trade pacts and must pay various duties, many key U.S. players are considering moving operations to the region.

- Argentina and Brazil are prime examples of leapfrogging—when advanced technology in a developing country supersedes older technologies that were never introduced in the region. Brazilians, for example, can wait years to obtain a conventional telephone. But the country is one of the world's fastest-growing users of cellular phones. This market in Brazil is expected to grow at a compound annual rate of 40 percent between 1997 and 2001. Sales of U.S. computer hardware and peripherals in Brazil are predicted to grow 20 percent this year.

Some international companies have entered Latin America slowly during this decade, preferring limited-risk strategies such as service and distribution centers or joint ventures with local companies. Others, including BellSouth, Wal-Mart, Tenneco, and Pizza Hut International, have been more aggressive. Companies are understandably wary about a return of hyperinflation and roiling stock markets in the region. Earlier this year, this reporter talked with Argentine and Brazilian executives, asking them these questions: What are important recent changes in your business? What are the implications for foreign companies that want to enter your market? And, most importantly, what is your advice to them?

Brazil

This colossus of Latin America, whose economic output and consumption overshadow all other countries in the region, is having a hard time bringing its economy in line. The Russian crisis—the latest turmoil to send shocks throughout emerging economies—has shaken Brazil's stock market. Moreover, economists are forecasting an enormous budget deficit for Brazil this year—in the neighborhood of 7 percent of GDP. Antônio Márcio Buainain, assistant professor at the State University of Campinas Economic Institute, cited Brazil's record unemployment levels and its overvalued currency, the real.

Yet Brazilian experts predict that at least $100 billion—40 percent of it from overseas investors—will be introduced into the nation's economy as direct investment just in the period from mid-1997 to the end of 1999. (Brazil will attract $17 billion in such investments this year alone, the highest of any emerging market.) Experts predict that $70 billion of it will be invested in the equities of government-owned companies being privatized. As Buainain put it, "Brazil is in the game again."

In discussions with executives in many industries, a key factor emerged: Brazil has radically changed its business climate from paternalistic and protected to one of free enterprise. Brazilian President Fernando Henrique Cardoso, a former sociologist and leftist political exile, has introduced an aura of honesty and competency, even as some Brazilians grumble that he is selling off their country to foreigners. Cardoso is expected to be reelected to his second term this month.

Privatization has its detractors and its supporters. Marco A. Oliveira, a consultant and trainer, said that the differences in Brazil's economy and culture before and after privatization are too big for many to perceive. "But privatization takes a company from the state and puts it into the hands of clever, even brilliant executives," said Oliveira. "Those who stay will be managed by those who will teach them."

The modernization has produced a class of executives skilled in managing change—so much so, that Brazilian managers are sought after for overseas postings by non-Brazilian companies. After all, if you made money during the years when inflation was in the triple digits and monetary policy was haphazard, you could certainly make money in healthy circumstances.

Fernando B. Pinheiro, a leading São Paulo attorney, advised foreign companies to do business for two years with a distributor to get to know the country intimately. Send a senior person to absorb the business culture of Brazil, he said, even as the executive imparts the corporate culture. Above all, he exhorted investors to think of Brazil as a New York taxi: "Be prepared for short stops."

"In Brazil, there is improvisation, creativity," agreed Dirk Blaesing, president of Fairway Filamentos S.A., a new maker of filament yarns formed by a joint venture between the French Rhône-Poulenc and the German Hoechst, known locally as Rhodia S.A. and Hoechst do Brasil S.A. Anyone who has business here must learn the culture—"how things move," as Blaesing put it.

How things move these days is via the emerging Brazilian entrepreneur class, one at ease with change. "We've always had to adjust our business activity from one month to the next," Blaesing explained. To cite just one circumstance, he noted that the prime borrowing rate earlier this year was a hefty 28 percent, something outside managers would surely find hard to deal with. To accommodate such uncertainties, Brazilian strategic corporate plans usually span one year, not five, and quarterly reports must be constantly adjusted to reflect ongoing realities.

"Brazilian managers are welcome worldwide because we are flexible," Blaesing said. "We act and react much faster than any part of the world. Brazil is a tremendous university—better than MIT or Stanford." Blaesing ticked off a litany of absolutes for doing business in today's Brazil: state-of-the-art systems and technology, lean structures, and a well-trained and flexible workforce.

Ronald Jean Degen, director general of a leading Brazilian privatized utility, finds himself in an interesting atmosphere of change. "This company was one of the 10 best energy companies in Brazil," said Degen, director and president of Companhia Paulista de Força e Luz (CPFL). The company was started by Americans earlier this century and later was nationalized. Typical of state-owned enterprises, the workforce was 100 percent unionized, there was no evaluation or promotion on merit, and employees were rarely fired. "The managers confused social responsibility with the company business," Degen commented.

Degen, a Swiss who has lived and worked in Brazil for 19 years, had joined the company only the previous month. He was not an experienced utilities executive because CPFL's owners wanted an outside turnaround expert. "We went from a politically appointed board and managers and a paternalistic, protected culture to a free-enterprise system," said Degen. "It was a completely regulated industry."

Uncharted waters notwithstanding, the consortium of new owners paid 70 percent above the minimum asking price for CPFL. It recognized the utility's major asset: the potential to serve the 2.5 million households and businesses that are likely customers for the Internet, fiber-optic services, and cable TV. Degen has moved quickly, offering substantial buyouts to 900 workers. He hoped to align the remaining workforce with a new strategy of technological change and improved communication, controls, and procedures. "Now I can invest in technology," he said.

Degen's advice echoed that of Blaesing. "Managers have to manage in fuzzy conditions here. Speed decision making," he said.

Human Resources

Many local companies are wrestling with low worker productivity—called "Brazil costs"—as fallout from privatization. Brazilian workers operate at a 27 percent productivity rate compared with their American counterparts. "How did we improve productivity, making our workers more involved and motivated?" asked Leonardo Nogueira Diniz, an executive at Construtora Lider, a big land development and construction company. Lider's solution was to offer free food baskets (as do its competitors) each month to employees who were not absent. The average wage is 400 to 800 reals, so the baskets containing cooking oil, sugar, beans, and other staples are valuable.

Lider also runs a voluntary on-site school four days a week to teach illiterate employees reading, writing, and basic math. Perfect attendance here means another food basket, and each worker-student is paid double wages for the first hour. "Workers can't read work orders, signs, schedules, and containers," Diniz pointed out, adding that the company is developing a complementary project in which reading improvement could lead to job promotion.

Operating the school for the first year cost Lider 30,000 reals, and Diniz said the company was already seeing benefits—fewer site accidents, reduced waste and, most importantly, employees asking for additional training to rise higher in the company. "Already there is an improvement in the poverty-homelessness-unemployability [cycle]," said Diniz. "Companies must do something now. This can help the economy change the concentration of money between the very rich and the very poor." Indeed, in Brazil today, companies are increasingly taking on elementary teaching roles to compensate for the nation's troubled educational system.

"Basic education in Brazil is low and could be a problem for foreign companies," remarked Firmin António, president of Accor Brasil, a leading hotel, restaurant, and service voucher company. He went on to list other chronic problems: social inequities, crumbling or nonexistent infrastructure, and taxes. "But the size of the future markets in Brazil means their potential is very important. European and American markets will be saturated in 10 years. You have to come here."

António said he created the $3 billion company—a subsidiary of a French hotelier—22 years ago and that he and his people lived through the inflationary crises. "Now, without inflation, competition is about price and quality. The future of this country is the dynamism of the business and the entrepreneur." To those who would do business in Brazil, he said, "Be confident in Brazil's potential. Fight hard and be competitive, as in your own country. Find a partner that has had other successful foreign partnerships, and don't depend on banks for your capital."

Accor is known for its human resources practices, in which its 17,000 employees are treated as equal partners in the corporate strategy. The company offers employee "synergy clubs" to brainstorm improvement ideas, profit sharing for all, team rewards, and corporate training. According to Luiz Edmundo Prestes Rosa, corporate HR director, Accor has embarked on an extensive project to motivate employees to be capable of working at any of Accor's facilities. "We do not intend to invest in people and have them leave," he said.

Argentina

Carlos Saúl Menem, Argentina's flamboyant president since 1989, has worked miracles out of an economy burdened with hyperinflation, bloated public expenditures, and a tax system out of control. Menem, a Peronist from the province of La Rioja, heads a successful but unpopular neoliberal government. This year he has flip-flopped on whether he will seek reelection (he now says no), having urged his party to push to overturn a constitutional ban on his seeking a third consecutive term in 1999.

Nevertheless, under Menem, Argentina turned its face to the world. It adopted the International Monetary Fund reform program and, to the chagrin of many Argentines, became a major non-NATO ally. Today, Argentina is near the end of its decade-long privatization program. The country's currency, the peso, is strictly pegged to the U.S. dollar—some say artificially so—and the $23 billion in central bank reserves more than backs every peso in circulation.

But problems persist. The cost of living remains high—$1,600 a month for a family of four, according to government estimates—while the average monthly factory wage is $700. Yet this wage is too high for many Argentine companies to compete with the low-wage workforces in other parts of the developing world. Rigorous domestic economic controls and privatization have produced an underclass of Argentine workers who may be permanently out of the job market. Labor unions, their traditional bargaining force, have seen their collective bargaining power wane because companies want more flexibility to hire and fire. Finally, the Asian and Russian crises have hit, causing a 25 percent fall in the Argentine stock market.

"Back in 1989, it was almost impossible to sell [state-owned] enterprises without arrangements with the unions," said Hector Armando Domeniconi, superintendent of a private network of pension funds in Buenos Aires. "Now, the idea is smaller, well-paid workforces—fewer people with better salaries." Domeniconi is adamant that more attention needs to be paid to worker education and training. "Argentina is a leading case of mixing the old system with a new one," he said, adding that companies beginning operations in the country for the first time would be well-advised to understand this.

Basic Training

One enterprise that pays attention to training is 103-year-old Banco de la Nacion Argentina, a leading public bank that holds 15 percent of total deposits in the Argentine banking system. According to Roberto L. Esteso, coordinator of the bank-owned training arm, called Instituto de Capacitacion Daniel E. Cash, half of the bank's 15,500 employees will be computer-literate by the end of this year. The rest will be trained next year.

"We are training people to be promoted, engaging [the training] with the person's career," Esteso said. "Up to now, people reached upper levels of management because of friendship." He said that the training includes a selection system—individuals must pass a series of tests and demonstrate the ability to run a branch. Recently, for instance, only 58 individuals out of a proposed 200 were selected for promotion.

Esteso added that the bank's training budget has increased tenfold over the past four years. According to Esteso, the new emphasis on technical and professional bank management is linked to a new operating stance throughout the nation's banking system. Loans to clients, for example, have become less dependent on relationships and more on sound financial criteria.

Even small companies are changing the way they conduct business in light of the new realities. In 1994, Caro Cuore, a small ($18 million) upscale lingerie maker in

Buenos Aires, shifted its emphasis from mere production to customer-focused manufacturing. "We realized important changes would happen in the Argentine market," said Fernando Andrés Fresco, finance and administration officer. "We started changing things inside the factory." For Caro Cuore, the changes meant more concentration on customized, just-in-time goods, better branding, marketing and distribution, and a steady supply of seasonal merchandise to compete with international producers. The company devises sales and production plans; previously "it was just stock-filling," said Fresco. "Now, the image—the creative area of the business—is important."

Accordingly, Caro Cuore is looking more carefully at where it advertises and where it places franchises. "Globalization allows us to position ourselves in a segment of upper-class locations worldwide," Fresco said. The company's manufacturing and assembly plant in Buenos Aires now has a quality area where incoming raw materials and finished products are examined. Above the sewing room is a sign, the English translation of which reads, "The quality depends on us and on us, the quality depends."

Fresco's advice to those wanting to do business in the new Argentina? "Adapt to permanent change. It is absolutely necessary for management. Your permanent objective should be training in mid- and upper-management."

Another enterprise that puts great stock in training is General Motors de Argentina S.A. Workers at its new $350 million, state-of-the-art plant in Rosario underwent 450 paid hours of training before they set foot in the facility. "They are trained in interpersonal skills, teamwork, consensus building, and lean manufacturing," said Basil N. Drossos, president.

The training goes along with Drossos' insistence that the 34 foreign nationals working at GM in Argentina have prior work experience outside the United States. "We have a sophisticated recruitment, assessment and hiring process in place," he said, adding that training at all levels is designed to "cascade information" throughout the organization. Many classes are taught by non-GM managers, and workers are encouraged to take outside courses.

"'Openness and forthrightness' is the best advice I could give to new managers here," Drossos asserted. He noted that GM renewed operations in Argentina in 1994. The corporation had begun operations there in 1925 but pulled out in 1978 because of political and social conditions—by implication, the widespread militarism and corruption that gripped Argentina for years.

Privatization as Impetus

For Hewlett-Packard Argentina, the aggressive privatization has, logically, meant considerable new business. "We are selling computers to privatized companies because they have a different mind-set," said Hugo Ricardo Strachan, president and director general. "We introduced UNIX, a color printer, here in 1986. But no one was thinking of changing to it. Because the [state-owned] business community was not so competitive, it didn't need it."

All this has changed. Strachan noted that the new, lean companies are in line with H-P's strong entrepreneurial culture. He offered a lesson learned for prospective new managers doing business in Argentina: "The change is coming very fast. Be ready to be very competitive."

Another company that has found itself with considerable privatized business is Techint, a $10 billion multinational producer of steel, engineering services and infrastructures. "Ten years ago, our biggest customer was the state; now our biggest customers are privatized companies," said Hector Masoero, director general of communications and services. "Stability in the economy changed the focus of management."

Before reforms, Masoero explained, Argentine managers were concerned with hyperinflation, regulatory problems, and inflationary interest rates. Now, they are focusing on worker productivity, HR issues, and customer service. He advised prospective investors to form a good local partnership for the first few years when operating in Argentina. "Look at the history of each prospective local partner—its culture, its business principles." He noted that some American companies during the past 10 years lent their name without serious engagement in Argentina, while companies from France, Spain, Italy, and Germany worked seriously in the region. "Now, they [Americans] have changed their attitudes 10 years later."

1. How great is the economic potential in Brazil and Argentina? Are these markets that would be attractive to MNCs? Why or why not?

2. How cold an MNC go about evaluating the political environment in Brazil? Argentina?

3. What are some of the characteristics that one would expect in world class organizations in Brazil and Argentina? Are these the same as those found in world class American MNCs? Explain.

4. What are some of the likely social responsibility differences between Brazil and Argentina and the United States which could result in problems for American MNCs? Explain.

Source: Barbara Ettorre, "Brazil and Argentina,"reprinted from *Management Review,* October 1998, pp. 10–15. Reprinted by permission of American Management Association International, New York. All rights reserved. **www.amanet.org**

Israel: A Unique Member of the Global Community

Israel frequently finds itself in the world news. Despite playing an active role in modern history, its economy is relatively small, and the size of its consumer market is considered to be small and unattractive for many Western MNCs. Still, the Israeli economy has been growing rapidly in recent years, and after reaching more than 400 percent in the mid-1980s, inflation has been brought under control.

Human, Not Natural Resources

Being short of natural resources, the greatest asset that Israel possesses is an educated and skilled pool of scientific and technically trained human resources. The country has the highest per-capita ratio of research scientists in the workforce worldwide. This wealth of human resources has been cited by many foreign companies as the primary reason for investing in Israel. The recent mass immigration from the former Soviet Union has further enhanced the quality of Israel's labor force.

Even though Israel has a quality workforce, wages are relatively low compared with other industrialized economies such as the United States, Japan, and most European countries. The average gross salary of an electrical engineer in Israel amounts to about $18,000 per year, while counterparts in the United States and other industrialized countries earn between $28,600 and $53,600 annually.

Trade Agreements Provide a Competitive Advantage

Israel has signed free trade agreements (FTAs) with the United States and the European Union (EU). These FTAs eliminate most of the customs, duties, and other trade barriers. Israel also has signed reciprocal trade agreements with Canada, Japan, Australia, and New Zealand, which provide Israel with a preferred status. Although Israel is always in the political "hotseat," since the end of the Persian Gulf war in mid-1991, it has gained full diplomatic relations with emerging markets such as China and India and obtained most-favored-nation status with the republics of Eastern Europe (except Russia). More important, relations have thawed between Israel and the Pacific Rim countries.

These trade agreements are very beneficial to Israel. For example, the European FTA potentially may provide a significant competitive advantage to Israeli manufacturers and exporters. U.S. businesses trying to penetrate "Fortress Europe" face significant trade barriers and may find it beneficial to use Israel as an exporting bridge to bypass them. Outside MNCs placing production facilities in Israel may take advantage of Israel's inexpensive skilled labor as well as compete successfully in Europe by exploiting the advantages provided by these FTAs. Currently, Israel is the only country that has FTAs with both the United States and the EU. The fact that Israel is a geographic bridge and crossroads connecting Africa, Asia, and Europe increases the country's attractiveness to foreign investors.

Investment Incentives

The Israeli government has adopted a set of goals to create more jobs and increase exports. To achieve these goals, the government offers a wide range of incentive programs that include grants, government-backed loan guarantees, subsidies, free trade zones, and tax benefits. These incentives are offered to enterprises that create more jobs (especially in the nation's less populated and industrialized areas), increase exports, and contribute to research and development (R&D) as well as new product development. In fact, the Israeli government will help any venture that will have an overall effect of improving the nation's economy.

The government has created Yozma Venture Capital Ltd., a state-owned investment company that offers investors opportunities to form joint-venture funds or invest directly in high-tech companies on favorable terms. Another funding source is the Israel–U.S. Bi-National Research and Development Foundation (Bird-F), which funds joint ventures that engage in R&D and product development.

Strategies for Doing Business

Israel's strategy is that the operational benefits of international diversification will be higher for firms possessing intangible, firm-specific assets (e.g., R&D technology) that they want to exploit in other national markets. Indeed, most corporations that engage in business with Israel possess at least one intangible asset, usually technological innovation capacity. Intel was a pioneer in this regard, opening a semiconductor-design center in Israel over 20 years ago. Since then, Israel has witnessed a flood of foreign hardware, software, and telecommunication companies using the Israeli skilled, technical workforce.

Typical Israeli companies have a well-defined niche market. Their technological expertise generally is strong enough to offset their lack of capital resources, marketing skills, and distance from major markets. In the classic form of strategic alliance, the Israeli side typically develops the products while the foreign investor supplies product identification and marketing skills. This formula combines the strengths of both parties to reduce the product's cycle time, thus providing the customer with a better and/or cheaper product much faster. Not only does this approach allow foreign companies to tap Israeli resources without building facilities or hiring employees, it also fits Israel's own economic goals.

In contrast to many other developing countries, the main reason for investing in Israel, according to U.S. executives, is to gain access to its quality technical talent. The influx of immigrants that escaped the Nazi regime in Europe during the 1940s and, more recently, from the former Soviet Union has provided Israel with a large pool of talents that are of particular interest to electronic companies. These include expertise in digital signal processes, communication theory, electro-optics, and software designs. In the 1980s, the Israelis developed great products that they did not know how to sell. Today, most local companies combine innovative technology with low cost, ease of installation, and excellent service. Foreign venture capital can give these companies the management and marketing expertise they lack.

Another form of investment in Israel is wholly owned development and manufacturing centers. This strategy was used by prominent MNCs such as Intel, IBM, Motorola, and DEC. The strategy is consistent with recent trends in international trading markets. The global marketplace consists of large numbers of small-scale ventures that are very focused in scope and a relatively small number of widely known, large multinational manufacturers of consumer goods, such as Sony, Volkswagen, GM, DEC, and so on. These large, multinational manufacturers are the major customers of the small-scale ventures that typically concentrate on the development and production of a limited number of components and parts and possess little, if any, marketing skills. Similarly, MNCs expanding to Israel have enormous resources to spend on designing and customizing their products. More important, they have the market knowledge and the muscle in distribution channels. No Israeli company has this kind of marketing advantage, no matter how great its end product.

U.S. MNCs in Israel

Semiconductor giants such as Intel and Motorola have made major investments in Israel during recent years, thus giving local engineers the chance to develop leading-edge components and parts that are driving the entire computer and communication industry. Soft-drink giants Coca-Cola and Pepsi also have a presence in Israel.

Intel

Dov Fruman, Intel's CEO, believes that the Israeli workforce is the primary reason the company decided to enter this country. He is quoted as calling the Israelis "improvisors and networkers." Another reason for Intel's investment is that overall costs run 10 percent below U.S. operations.

Intel has designed coprocessors in Haifa for 21 years and also has produced microprocessors, including the 386 and 486, at its $300 million Jerusalem lab since 1986. The expansion of the Har Hahotzevim industrial zone in Jerusalem is the largest single investment ever made in Israel. Recently, the Israeli government approved a $380 million grant to support a major upgrading of the Jerusalem plant. Spread over 7 years, this money was approved under the law authorizing state grants covering 38 percent of high-technology business ventures in the city.

Motorola

Motorola Israel is a wholly owned subsidiary of Motorola, Inc. Like Intel, Motorola expanded to Israel to take advantage of its highly skilled workforce and to exploit its R&D capabilities. Motorola, Inc., provides funding and marketing expertise to develop its products, while the Israeli subsidiary concentrates on bringing out new and improved products.

Originally, Motorola only had design centers in Israel but later built production facilities to exploit the economic benefits of having these facilities close to design centers located in Tel Aviv and the southern city of Arad. The company develops and exports digital signal processors, radio-communication, remote systems, cellular radio telephones, and data transmission devices. It also develops, manufactures, markets, and exports communications, water control and irrigation, and paging systems.

Motorola Israel won the Prize for Quality from Motorola, Inc., for a communications process that it developed for UPS. In 1994, Motorola Israel received Motorola, Inc.'s, "International Mandate" to be the exclusive developer, manufacturer, and marketer of the international company's wireless transmitters.

Pepsi and Coca-Cola

Coca-Cola was the first soft drink firm to enter the Israeli market (in 1968). As a pioneer in this market, Coca-Cola created entry barriers, mainly brand identity and access to distribution channels, that provided it with a competitive advantage.

Initially, Coca-Cola had to make a strategic choice: whether to enter the Israeli or the Arab market. Having chosen Israel, the company was placed on the Arab League's "blacklist" of international companies doing business with the Jewish state and therefore was barred from most of these Arab markets.

Coca-Cola brought in the most recent and advanced manufacturing technology and built a fully automated plant in Tel Aviv. All operations, production, and support functions are entirely computerized. Coke also employed its famous marketing competencies to secure market share. This strategy is consistent with Coke's highly touted global marketing philosophy, which involves aggressive advertising and promotion campaigns to maintain existing brand loyalty. For example, passengers arriving in Israel are served Coca-Cola products on board El Al (the Israeli government-owned airline) and are exposed to heavy advertising at the airport and on all major highways leading to the big cities. At present, Coca-Cola controls approximately two-thirds of the Israeli soft-drink market.

While Coca-Cola was setting up operations in Israel, Pepsi was targeting the Arab markets, which are more lucrative in terms of market potential. Recently, Pepsi expanded into Israel and is trying to obtain shelf space in supermarkets, which sell over one-half of Israel's beverages. With its "first-in-the-market" advantage, Coca-Cola possesses solid shelf space in virtually every retail chain in the country. To meet its goal of getting into the stores, Pepsi has developed a tracing and tracking system to convince supermarket owners to allocate space shelf for its products. Another strategy that Pepsi is pursuing is to distribute products through "mom-and-pop" outlets, which also sell a large amount of Israel's soft drinks.

Soon after entering the Israeli market, Pepsi faced a major crisis that forced the company to re-evaluate its marketing strategy. Ultraorthodox religious groups objected to Pepsi's advertisement campaign that included a billboard poster of an ape dragging its fists on the ground and the caption "Ten million years before the choice." The religious objection was not only the implication that man evolved from the ape, which runs counter to their belief in God's creation of man, but also to the reference of "10 million years," which contradicts the Jewish tradition holding that creation occurred only 5755 years ago. The influential religious group threatened to withdraw the kosher seal from Pepsi's products, which could have meant a significant blow to sales. In addition, the ultraorthodox claimed that Pepsi was violating traditional Jewish values by sponsoring rock concerts on Saturday evenings (Shabat), a sacred day in the Jewish religion. In response, Pepsi decided to modify the advertising campaign, removing the reference to "10 million years" and the ape, leaving only a Neanderthal man to hint at evolution. Despite this, the ultraorthodox group declared that the attitude behind Pepsi's advertising campaign contradicted their beliefs. Regarding the Pepsi-sponsored concerts, Reuven Avital, general manager of Pepsi Israel, said: "They came and said of our marketing campaign, 'Gentlemen, this is unacceptable,' and we said 'We can't do without it, the young generation wants concerts, wants this music, and it is our target market.' This was a macro issue, a philosophical issue, a conceptual issue." As it stands now, the conflict between Pepsi and the orthodox religious group is unresolved.

1. What important issues should MNCs take into consideration when investing and operating in Israel?

2. What are the major challenges that Pepsi is facing in Israel? What would you recommend that Pepsi do to solve its problems?

Source: This case was written specially for this book with the assistance of Erez Hasdai and Elizabeth Novick.

Colgate's Distasteful Toothpaste

Colgate is a well-known consumer products company based in New York. Its present products are in the areas of household and personal care, which include laundry detergents such as Ajax and Fab, health-care products manufactured for home health care, and specialty products such as Hill pet food. The household products segment represents approximately 75 percent of company revenues, while the specialty segment accounts for less than 7 percent. Colgate's value has been set in excess of $5.6 billion. Through both recessionary and recovery periods in the United States, Colgate has always been advocated by investment analysts as a good long-term stock.

Colgate's lagging domestic market share has been present for several years. In the 1970s, when diversification seemed to be the tool to hedge against risk and sustain profits, Colgate bought companies in various industries, including Kosher hot dogs, tennis and golf equipment, and jewelry. However, such extreme diversification diverted the company's attention away from its key money-making products: soap, laundry detergents, toothpaste, and other household products. The product diversification strategy ended in 1984 when Reuben Mark became CEO. At the young age of 45, he ordered the sale of parts of the organization that deviated too far from Colgate's core competency of personal and household products. He followed consultant Tom Peters's prescription for excellence of "stick to the knitting."

Colgate's International Presence

Colgate traditionally has had a strong presence overseas. The company has operations in Australia, Latin America, Canada, France, and Germany. International sales presently represent one-half of Colgate's total revenue. In the past, Colgate always made a detailed analysis of each international market for demand. For instance, its entry into South America required an analysis of the type of product that would be most successful based on the dental hygiene needs of South American consumers. Because of this commitment to local cultural differences, the company has the number-one brand of toothpaste worldwide, Total.

To create a strong share of the Asian market without having to build its own production plant, Colgate bought a 50 percent partnership in the Hawley and Hazel group in August 1985 for $50 million. One stipulation of this agreement was that Colgate had no management prerogatives; Hawley and Hazel maintained the right to make the major decisions in the organization. This partnership turned out to be very lucrative for Colgate, with double-digit millions in annual sales.

Enter the Distasteful Toothpaste

Hawley and Hazel is a chemical products company based in Hong Kong. The company was formed in the early part of the twentieth century, and its only product of note, believe it or not, was called "Darkie" toothpaste. Over the years, this had been one of the popular brands in Asia and had a dominant presence in markets such as Taiwan, Hong Kong, Singapore, Malaysia, and Thailand.

"Darkie" toothpaste goes back to the 1920s. The founder of this product, on a visit to the United States, loved Al Jolson, then a very popular black-faced entertainer (i.e., a white person with black make-up on his face). The founder decided to re-create the spirit of this character in the form of a trademark logo for his toothpaste because of the character's big smile and white teeth. When the founder returned to Asia, he copyrighted the name "Darkie" to go along with the logo. Since the 1920s, there has been strong brand loyalty among Asians for this product. One housewife in Taipei whose family used the product for years remarked, "The toothpaste featuring a Black man with a toothy smile is an excellent advertisement."

The Backlash against Colgate

"Darkie" toothpaste had been sold in Asia for about 65 years. After Colgate became partners with Hawley and Hazel and its distasteful product, however, there was a wave of dissatisfaction with the logo and name from U.S. minorities and civil rights groups. There really has been no definite source on how this issue was passed to U.S. action groups and the media; however, a book entitled *Soap Opera: The Inside Story of Procter and Gamble* places responsibility in the hands of Procter and Gamble in an effort to tarnish Colgate's image and lower its market share.

The Americans' irate response to "Darkie" was a surprise to the Hawley and Hazel group. They reasoned that the product had always been successful in their Asian markets, and there had been no complaints. In fact, the success of "Darkie" had led the firm to market a new product in Japan called "Mouth Jazz," which had a similar logo. A spokesperson for Hawley and Hazel remarked, "There had been no problem before, you can tell by the market share that it is quite well received in Asia."

ICCR, the Interfaith Center on Corporate Responsibility, started the fight against Colgate about 10 years ago when it received a package of "Darkie" toothpaste from a consumer in Thailand. ICCR is composed of institutional investors that influence corporations through stock ownership. At the time the movement against Colgate's racially offensive product started, three members of ICCR already owned a small amount of stock in the company, and they filed a shareholder petition against Colgate requesting a change in the logo and name.

In a letter to Colgate, the ICCR Executive Director summarized the position against the distasteful toothpaste as follows:

> "Darkie" toothpaste is a 60-year-old product sold widely in Hong Kong, Malaysia, Taiwan and other places in the Far East. Its packaging includes a top-hatted and gleaming-toothed smiling likeness of Al Jolson under the words "Darkie" toothpaste. As you know the term "Darkie" is deeply offensive. We would hope that in this new association with the Hawley and Hazel Chemical Company, that immediate action will be taken to stop this product's name so that a U.S. company will not be associated with promoting racial stereotypes in the Third World.

In response to this letter, R.G.S. Anderson, Colgate's director of corporate development, replied, "No plans exist or are being contemplated that would extend marketing and sales efforts for the product in Colgate subsidiaries elsewhere or beyond this Far East area." Anderson then went on to explain that Darkie's founder was imitating Al Jolson and that in the Chinese view, imitation was the "highest form of flattery." The ICCR then informed Colgate that if the logo was not changed, the organization would create a media frenzy and help various civil rights action groups in a possible boycott.

Because Colgate still refused to remove the logo, ICCR did form a coalition with civil rights groups such as the NAACP and National Urban League to start protest campaigns. The protest took all forms, including lobbying at both the state and local levels. At one point, after heavy lobbying by the ICCR, the House of Representatives in Pennsylvania passed a resolution urging Colgate to change the name and logo. Also, similar resolutions had been proposed in the U.S. Congress.

The pressures at home placed Colgate in a difficult position, especially as it had no management rights in its agreement with Hawley and Hazel. In the Asian market, neither Colgate nor Hawley and Hazel had any knowledge of consumer dissatisfaction because of racial offensiveness, despite the fact that the local Chinese name for "Darkie" (pronounced *hak ye nga goh*) can be translated as "The Black Man" toothpaste. The logo seemed to enhance brand loyalty. One Asian customer stated, "I buy it because of the Black man's white teeth."

The demographics of the Asian market may help to explain the product's apparent acceptance. There are a relatively small number of Africans, Indians, Pakistanis, and Bangladeshis in the region; therefore, the number of people who might be offended by the logo is low. Also, some people of color did not seem disturbed by the name. For

example, when asked about the implications of "Darkie" toothpaste, the secretary of the Indian Chamber of Commerce noted, "It doesn't offend me, and I'm sort of dark-skinned."

Initially, Colgate had no intentions of forcing Hawley and Hazel to change the product. R.G.S. Anderson issued another formal statement to the ICCR as follows: "Our position . . . would be different if the product were sold in the United States or in any Western English-speaking country; which, as I have stated several times, will not happen." Hawley and Hazel concurred with the stance. The alliance was very fearful of a loss of market share and did not believe that the complaints were issues relevant to Pacific Rim countries. A spokesperson for the alliance referred to the protest campaign as "a U.S. issue." The trade-off for revamping a successful product was deemed to be too risky and costly.

Colgate's Change of Heart

The issue did not go away. As U.S. leaders in Congress began to learn about this very offensive logo and name, the pressure on Colgate mounted. Interestingly, however, the value of Colgate's stock increased throughout this period of controversy. Wall Street seemed oblivious to the charges against Colgate, and this was another reason why Colgate took no action. Colgate management believed that an issue about overseas products should not have a negative effect on the company's domestic image. However, pressures continued from groups such as the Congressional Black Caucus, a strong political force. Colgate finally began to waver, but because of its agreement with Hawley and Hazel, it felt helpless. As one Colgate executive remarked, "One hates to let exogenous things drive your business, but you sometimes have to be aware of them."

Colgate CEO Reuben Mark eventually became very distressed over the situation. He was adamantly against racism of any kind and had taken actions to exhibit his beliefs. For instance, he and his wife had received recognition for their involvement in a special program for disadvantaged teenagers. He commented publicly about the situation as follows: "It's just offensive. The morally right thing dictates that we must change. What we have to do is find a way to change that is least damaging to the economic interests of our partners." He also publicly stated that Colgate had been trying to change the package since 1985, when it bought into the partnership.

Colgate's Plan of Action to Repair the Damage

The protest campaign initiated by ICCR and carried further by others definitely caused Colgate's image to be tarnished badly in the eyes of not only African-Americans but of all Americans. To get action, some members of the Congressional Black Caucus (including Rep. John Conyers, D-Mich.) even bypassed Colgate and tried to negotiate directly with Hawley and Hazel. To try to repair the damage, Colgate, in cooperation with Hawley and Hazel, finally developed, although two years after ICCR's initial inquiry, a plan to change the product. In a letter to ICCR, CEO Mark stated, "I and Colgate share your concern that the caricature of a minstrel in black-face on the package and the name 'Darkie' itself could be considered racially offensive." Colgate and Hawley and Hazel then proposed some specific changes for the name and logo. Names considered included Darlie, Darbie, Hawley, and Dakkie. The logo options included a dark, nondescript silhouette and a well-dressed Black man. The alliances decided to test market the options among their Asian consumers; however, they refused to change the Chinese name ("Black Man Toothpaste"), which is more used by their customers.

They decided that changes would be implemented over the course of a year to maintain brand loyalty and avoid advertising confusion with their customers. There was the risk that loyal customers would not know if the modified name/logo was still the same toothpaste that had proven itself through the years. Altogether, the process would take approximately 3 years, test marketing included. Colgate also decided to pay for the entire change process, abandoning their initial suggestion that the change be paid for by Hawley and Hazel.

Colgate and Hawley and Hazel then made a worldwide apology to all insulted groups. Although Hawley and Hazel was slow to agree with the plan, a spokesperson for the group emphasized that racial stereotyping was against its policy. It also helped that Hawley and Hazel would pay no money to make the needed changes. They felt that the product was too strong to change quickly; thus, three years was not too long to implement the new logo and name fully into all Asian markets. Further, they insisted that as part of the marketing campaign, the product advertising use the following statement in Chinese, "Only the English name is being changed. Black Man Toothpaste is still Black Man Toothpaste."

Response Worldwide

Colgate and Hawley and Hazel still suffer from the effects of their racially offensive product. In 1992, while dealing with its own civil rights issues, the Chinese government placed a ban on Darlie toothpaste because of the product's violation of China's trademark laws. Although the English name change was implemented across all markets, the retained Chinese name and logo still were deemed derogatory by the Chinese, and the government banned the product. Also, Eric Molobi, an African National Congress representative, was outraged at the toothpaste's logo on a recent visit to the Pacific Rim. When asked if Darlie toothpaste would be marketed in his country, the South African representative replied, "If this company found itself in South Africa it would not be used. There would be a permanent boycott."

Today, the name of Colgate cannot be found anywhere on the packaging of what is now called Darlie toothpaste. In a strategic move, Colgate has distanced itself completely away from the controversial product. In the Thailand and Indonesia health-products markets, Colgate even competes against Darlie toothpaste with its own brand.

1. Identify the major strategic and ethical issues faced by Colgate in its partnership with Hawley and Hazel.

2. What do you think Colgate should have done to handle the situation?

3. Is it possible for Colgate and Hawley and Hazel to change the toothpaste's advertising without sacrificing consumer brand loyalty? Is that a possible reason for Colgate's not responding quickly to domestic complaints?

4. In the end, was a "no management rights" clause good for Colgate? What could have happened during the negotiations process to get around this problem?

Source: This case was written specially for this book by Alisa L. Mosley, University of Nebraska.

Levi's Takes Its Ethical Aspirations International

In 1993, Levi's decided to terminate most of its business relations with Chinese contractors. (It had no foreign direct investment in China.) As a reason, it gave what it termed China's "pervasive violation of human rights." At the time, some commented that neither Levi's nor China would be much affected by the action—Levi's because it only had small contracts with Chinese sewing and laundry firms, and China because Levi's trade amounted to only about $50 million annually of some $13.5 billion in total U.S. purchases. Nevertheless, Levi's withdrawal from China was recognized as having serious implications for its ability to do business there in the future. On the one hand, its competitors would be well established in the China apparel market. Furthermore, the Chinese government would be expected to hold Levi's in permanent disfavor, thus making it difficult for the company to either open manufacturing facilities there or win a change to China's policy of stiff tariffs on imported clothing.

Background on Levi's

The history of Levi Strauss & Company is almost an archetype of the American dream, including twenty-first century updates. The company was founded in the 1850s by a European immigrant who found success by listening to the customer. Levi Strauss tailored the first jeans from tent canvas in response to California gold miners' complaints that trousers just could not take the abuse of panning nuggets and staking claims. Furthermore Strauss accepted incremental improvement ideas from suppliers; the copper rivets at stress points were suggested by a tailor who was part of Levi's downstream network. The company is private, having been taken through a leveraged buyout in the 1980s by its current chairman and CEO, Robert Haas, great-grandnephew of the founder.

Levi's enjoyed a stream of record sales and earnings from 1989 through 1993. Several milestones also were reached in 1993: a 36 percent increase in profits, to $492 million on sales of $5.9 billion. Its 1993 sales earned Levi's the number-90 position in the *Fortune* 500. The following year, however, the company dropped to number 193. Its 1994 revenues rose only 3.1 percent over 1993, to $6 billion, and its profits dropped by 34.8 percent to $321 million. Levi's profit margin of 5.3% ranked only 222nd within the *Fortune* 500, although its rankings were considerably better for profits as a percentage of assets (8.2 percent, rank 82) and for profits as a percentage of stockholder's equity (21.8 percent, rank 80). Within the apparel industry, Levi's sales ranked first of seven competitors; its revenues of $6,074 million compared favorably to the $4,972 million for VF and to the industry median of $2,163 million. Levi's sales increase of 3 percent from 1993, however, was well below the industry median of 12 percent. The profit comparison is similar. Levi's $321 million profit compared with $270 million for VF and was well above the industry median of $79 million, but Levi's 35 percent loss in profits compared with 1993 was considerably below the industry median of 12 percent. Levi's profits as a percentage of revenue and of assets were both right on the industry median, at 5 percent and 8 percent, respectively.

Analysts explained Levi's slowdown in 1994 by the company's problems in new product development and distribution. For example, the company estimates it lost at least $200 million in sales by its delay in developing wrinkle-free slacks (the fastest-growing segment of the men's-pants business). Likewise, it may take Levi's two or three times as long to replenish its supply of pants for major retailers compared with the 10 days achieved by competitors.

Levi's Reputation

Despite recent problems, Levi's remains a strong company with a reputation for high-quality clothes and an impressive brand name. The company also has other valuable assets that bring it recognition within its industry. In *Fortune* magazine's annual poll to determine the "most admired" corporations, Levi's repeatedly earns top place in the 10-company apparel group. Companies are rated on attributes such as quality of management, quality of products, innovativeness, long-term investment value, financial soundness, human resources practices, and responsibility to the community and environment. Levi's 1995 score of 7.82 compares with 7.30 for Berkshire Hathaway (second place in the apparel group) and 8.65 for the most admired company overall, Rubbermaid, Inc.

Part of Levi's reputation rests on its organizational culture, its mission and vision. As articulated by chairman and CEO Bob Haas, this involves "responsible commercial success." In other words, the company should not just be profitable but ethical; it should not only make a profit but make the world a better place in which to live. To guide this twofold endeavor, company executives crafted what they call an "Aspiration Statement" spelling out the kind of firm that Levi Strauss & Company intends to become together with the kind of leadership that will be needed to make these aspirations reality. Not just words on paper, management and employees together incorporate the mission and aspiration statement into daily decisions and actions. Applications range from open and direct communication, commitment to diversity, recognition and related compensation and reward systems, empowerment, and ethical management practices to expectations for ethical behavior by suppliers. In today's business environment, cynics might attribute such principles to a public relations ploy or a proactive defense against employee litigation, but Levi's chairman Haas insists, "We are doing this because we believe in the interconnection between liberating the talents of our people and business success"—in other words, responsible commercial success.

The Application of Levi's Ethical Values in the International Arena

Levi's aspiration statement has been applied specifically to international contracting. In the 1980s, Levi's management felt that it was lax in keeping informed about conditions for employees at its overseas factories. A little-publicized incident involving the working conditions of its Saipan contractor caused Levi's management to re-examine its monitoring, and a committee of top executives was named to review the company's dealings with its suppliers. In 1992, following 3 years of work, the committee's guidelines for contractors were adopted, covering employee working conditions, labor relations, environmental impact, and regular inspection for compliance—the first such code adopted by any MNC. Following its code, the company has terminated business relations with 30 businesses and demanded changes from 120 others around the world. Two outcomes made headlines. When it was found that a contractor in Malaysia employed underage children, Levi's and the contractor found a solution that allowed the children to continue to contribute to their families' support: The contractor pays the children to attend school, Levi's pays for the school (tuition, texts, uniforms), and the contractor will hire the children back at the legal age of 14. The second outcome was Levi's withdrawal from China in response to what it considered "systemic labor inequities." Conditions in China's garment industry are bleak. For example, a recent article by William Beaver in *Business Horizons* reports that in Shenzhen, the work schedule requires 12-hour days plus overtime, with only 2 days off each month, for pay below the legal minimum of 12 cents an hour. Poor safety conditions in China's apparel factories also have resulted in dozens of employee deaths.

Responsible commercial success applies not just to the ethical position of Levi's international operations but also to its profitability. The international division contributed significantly to Levi's strong profit picture throughout the late 1980s and into the 1990s. In 1992, sales outside the United States accounted for 38 percent of company revenues—but 53 percent of profits. In part, this reflects the connection that consumers make to Levi's as an icon of U.S. styles and attitudes; in part, it also reflects Levi's pricing strategy, which is leveraged on that brand position.

Levi's sell for a higher price overseas than in the United States. Internationally, they are regarded as a premium product, in contrast to their commodity position domestically. Therefore, international profit margins are higher (e.g., for 501 jeans, 45 percent vs. 30 percent), and sales are strong.

Another element in the success of Levi's international division is its management practices. The president of Levi Strauss International, Lee C. Smith, says, "We seek out the best ideas [among our worldwide operations] and trade them." This internal benchmarking only is possible because local units are encouraged to innovate. By encouraging foreign managers to adapt to local tastes as they change, Levi's achieves responsiveness, and at the same time, headquarters has globally integrated the form of organization (subsidiaries rather than licensing to assure quality and brand identity) as well as information systems (e.g., the Levi Link system to track sales and manufacturing).

Conclusion

The international division has not always been successful. In 1984, it posted a loss, but by 1990, when Levi's U.S. sales were up only 6 percent over the previous year, foreign sales were booming: up 19 percent in Asia, up 27 percent in Latin America, and up 47 percent in Europe. Nearly 40 percent of the company's total revenues and 60 percent of its pretax profit before interest and corporate expenses came from abroad.

Plans for the future of Levi's international operations are truly global in scope. Corporate president Thomas Tusher recently indicated, "We're starting up in India. We're looking at Russia, South Africa, China, Southeast Asia. And there are places where we've just started: Hungary and Poland, Korea and Taiwan, Turkey. The Czech Republic is next." Therefore, although Levi's withdrew from doing business in 1993 for ethical reasons, it now is looking once again at China, among other sites, for global expansion. The questions are whether the company can ethically reopen operations in China or, practically speaking, will China's government allow the company back?

1. Why did Levi's leave China? Is this decision part of the firm's overall social responsibility philosophy or did the company overreact to the situation?

2. If you were advising the company, what conditions would you set as prerequisites for it to reenter the Chinese market?

3. Overall, what is your evaluation of Levi's decision? Do you agree or disagree? Explain.

Source: This case was written specially for this book by Jan Hansen, Bellevue University.

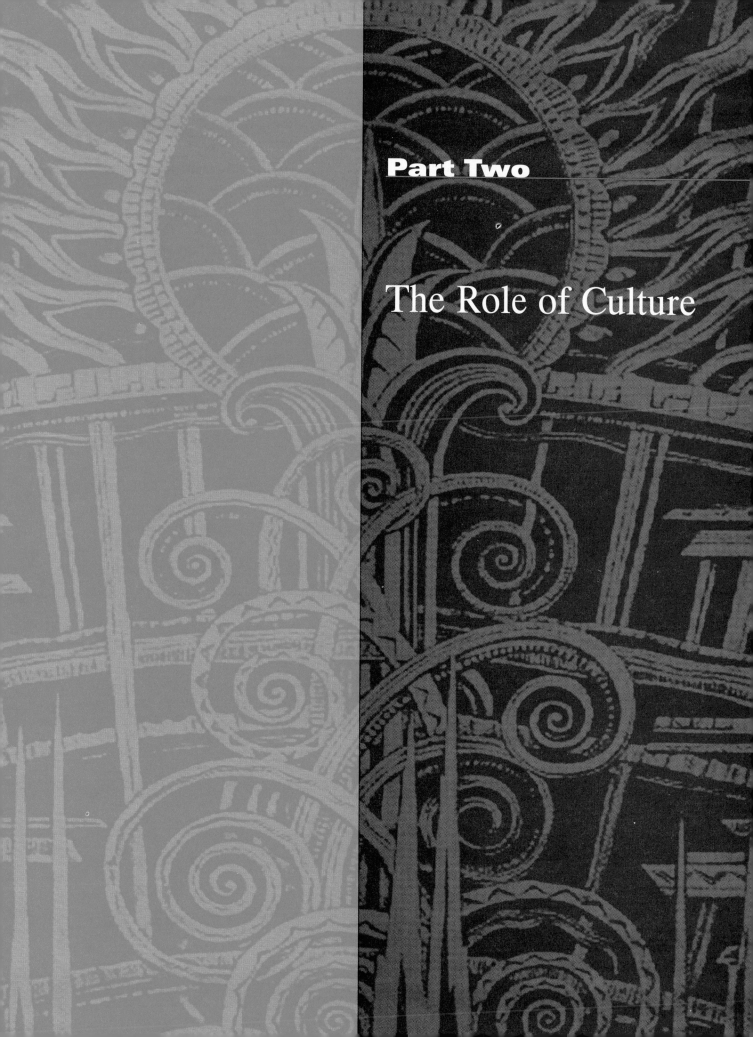

Part Two

The Role of Culture

Chapter 5

The Meanings and Dimensions of Culture

Objectives of the Chapter

A major challenge of doing business internationally is to adapt effectively to different cultures. Such adaptation requires an understanding of cultural diversity, perceptions, stereotypes, and values. In recent years, a great deal of research has been conducted on cultural dimensions and attitudes, and the findings have proved useful in providing integrative profiles of international cultures. However, a word of caution must be given when discussing these country profiles. It must be remembered that stereotypes and overgeneralizations should be avoided; there are always individual differences and even subcultures within every country.

This chapter examines the meaning of culture as it applies to international management, reviews some of the value differences and similarities of various national groups, studies important dimensions of culture and their impact on behavior, and finally, examines attitudinal dimensions and country clusters. The specific objectives of this chapter are:

1. **DEFINE** the term "culture," and discuss some of the comparative ways of differentiating cultures.

2. **DESCRIBE** the concept of cultural values, and relate some of the international differences, similarities, and changes occurring in terms of both work and managerial values.

3. **IDENTIFY** the major dimensions of culture relevant to work settings, and discuss their effect on behavior in an international environment.

4. **DISCUSS** the value of country cluster analysis and relational orientations in developing effective international management practices.

BusinessWeek

The World of Business Week:

Korea Inc. Balks

For years, no industry seemed too crowded and no market too far-flung to escape the tendrils of South Korea's expansion-minded *chaebol*. Conglomerates such as the $47.6 billion Hyundai Group boasted of making everything from "chips to ships" from Europe to Latin America. The omnivore strategy seemed to work—until the Korean economy almost collapsed under the weight of $150 billion in foreign debt.

Now, with Korea's debt restructuring still in doubt, investors are looking for signs that the *chaebol* are slimming down into focused companies that can produce steady profits. Investors especially want to see the top four—Hyundai, Daewoo, Lucky Goldstar, and Samsung, who account for more than half of Korean corporate debt—set the course for Korea's new economy.

Yet as the crisis drags on, it looks increasingly unlikely that any changes the big *chaebol* make will go far enough. Certainly, they will back away from some marginal businesses. But analysts worry they will simply try to muddle along for now, then revert to old practices once the crisis calms down. "Basically, no *chaebol* chiefs want to lose control over their empires," figures Lee Chae Kwang, head of research at Daiwa Securities in Seoul. "Their tendency is to lie flat on the ground, tough it out, and then resume business as usual."

New Liabilities

Already, some chieftains are declaring defiance. Kim Woo Choong, chairman of Daewoo Group, gave his employees surprising news in his New Year's address. He pledged more "expansion-looking management" rather than "shrinking in the face of difficulties."

Other executives are sounding less sanguine and have acknowledged that they must lay off workers and sell off parts of their businesses. Samsung Group, the No. 2 *chaebol* with assets of $45 billion, will slash investment this year by 25%, or $1.3 billion, and cut production of electronic goods in Asia by up to 40%. It vows that the growth-at-any-cost ethos is history. "We will consider big deals with other *chaebol* and spinning out businesses to foreigners," says Hung Young Key, a Samsung senior managing director. Analysts say the group may sell AST Research Inc., a money-losing computer maker based in Irvine, Calif.

Korea's biggest *chaebol,* Hyundai Group, has also announced investment cuts of 30% and is delaying a $1.4 billion microchip plant in Scotland. Bankrupt carmaker Kia Motors Corp., and failed shipbuilder Halla Group are sacking workers and selling off assets. But with the top *chaebol* expected to post losses for 1997, just tapping on the brakes won't be enough. What's needed is a healthy shakeout of the overbuilt auto, steel, petrochemical, and semiconductor industries. Analysts figure investment needs to be cut 30%, as Samsung and Hyundai have announced.

Exit Aerospace

Many analysts believe the *chaebol* will have to give up lines of business altogether, rather than just suspend them temporarily. Samsung may need to exit shipbuilding, heavy machinery, aerospace, and petrochemicals and concentrate on four of their more profitable areas: semiconductors, liquid-crystal display panels, computer monitors, and financial services.

Hyundai, analysts say, could fashion a stronger group if it stuck with core manufacturing in autos, ships, machinery, and construction and gave up its costly forays into aerospace, petrochemicals, and chipmaking. Daewoo should also concentrate on those industries. LG—which was the least aggressive in expanding and therefore has fewer units to shed—should focus on chemicals, refining, and electronics, where its operations are strong enough to withstand gluts in those industries.

Many expect the *chaebol* to resist international accounting standards and to continue their stealthy cross-lending among subsidiaries, despite a ban as part of the International Monetary Fund's bailout package. They will also probably avoid the hostile takeovers that would get them focused on bottom-line growth.

Until that becomes a reality, few see *chaebol* chieftains cleaning up their acts. "Hostile takeovers should be allowed immediately," insists Yoo Seong Min, a fellow at the Korea Development Institute, a government think tank. Yet although a ban on foreign companies taking majority stakes in Korean companies was lifted in December as part of the IMF loan package, it is unlikely to result in huge sell-offs. Family-dominated *chaebol* boards still have the ultimate veto power on acquisitions and are likely to allow only less-important sales of assets to raise cash.

Cronies

The new government of left-leaning Kim Dae Jung, due to take office on Feb. 25, has pledged to push the *chaebol* to restructure and pass laws allowing layoffs. Yet some doubt whether the President-elect's economic advisers will push hard on the key issues. Chung Un Chan, economics professor at Seoul National University, points out that a 12-member panel in charge of generating reform ideas has not presented any concrete proposals to improve business transparency and corporate governance. Perhaps one reason is that the panel is led by Kim Yong Hwan, a former Finance Minister under autocratic President Park Chung Hee. "They are the ones who put in place the command-and-control economy," says Chung. "You need infusion of new blood for reforms."

By Moon Ihlwan in Seoul, with Brian Bremner in Tokyo
www.hdcorp.co.kr

Source: **Reprinted from January 19, 1998, pp. 44–45 issue of *Business Week* by special permission, copyright © 1998 by the McGraw-Hill Companies, Inc.**

The opening news article examines the far-reaching effects of culture as it affects MNCs. In the wake of the recent Asian currency crisis, more eyes than ever are focused on the large Korean conglomerates (*chaebols*). Their problems have not only contributed to an economic downturn, but have also challenged a traditional value system and threatened a conservative and rigid way of doing business. Since the Korean culture, as well as many of the other Asian cultures, tend to be somewhat averse to risk-taking and are accustomed to following rules and procedures within a well-defined hierarchy, this often presents an immense challenge for MNCs trying to conduct business there. As the title of the article reads, "Korea Inc. Balks," the *chaebols'* refusal to make any real changes to their business practices is hindering their economic recovery and growth and is discouraging much needed foreign investment. By failing to comply with international accounting standards, refusing to pass laws allowing layoffs, and continuing with nepotistic decision making, the *chaebols* have thus far been unsuccessful in setting the course for the new Korean economy.

Nature of Culture

The world "culture" comes from the Latin *cultura*, which is related to cult or worship. In its broadest sense, the term refers to the result of human interaction.[1] For the purposes of the study of international management, then **culture** is acquired knowledge that people use to interpret experience and generate social behavior.[2] This knowledge forms values, creates attitudes, and influences behavior. Most scholars of culture would agree on the following characteristics of culture:

Culture
The acquired knowledge that people use to interpret experience and generate social behavior. This knowledge forms values, creates attitudes, and influences behavior.

1. *Learned.* Culture is not inherited or biologically based; it is acquired by learning and experience.
2. *Shared.* People as members of a group, organization, or society share culture; it is not specific to single individuals.
3. *Transgenerational.* Culture is cumulative, passed down from one generation to the next.
4. *Symbolic.* Culture is based on the human capacity to symbolize or use one thing to represent another.

5. *Patterned.* Culture has structure and is integrated; a change in one part will bring changes in another.

6. *Adaptive.* Culture is based on the human capacity to change or adapt, as opposed to the more genetically driven adaptive process of animals.[3]

Because different cultures exist in the world, an understanding of the impact of culture on behavior is critical to the study of international management.[4] If international managers do not know something about the cultures of the countries they deal with, the results can be quite disastrous.[5] For example, a partner in one of New York's leading private banking firms tells the following story:

> I traveled nine thousand miles to meet a client and arrived with my foot in my mouth. Determined to do things right, I'd memorized the names of the key men I was to see in Singapore. No easy job, inasmuch as the names all came in threes. So, of course, I couldn't resist showing off that I'd done my homework. I began by addressing top man Lo Win Hao with plenty of well-placed Mr. Hao's—sprinkled the rest of my remarks with a Mr. Chee this and a Mr. Woon that. Great show. Until a note was passed to me from one man I'd met before, in New York. Bad news. "Too friendly too soon, Mr. Long," it said. Where diffidence is next to godliness, there I was, calling a room of VIPs, in effect, Mr. Ed and Mr. Charlie. I'd remembered everybody's name—but forgot that in Chinese the surname comes *first* and the given name *last.*[6]

Cultural Diversity

There are many ways of examining cultural differences and their impact on international management. Culture can affect technology transfer, managerial attitudes, managerial ideology, and even business–government relations. Perhaps most important, culture affects how people think and behave.[7] Table 5-1, for example, compares the most important cultural values of the United States, Japan, and Arab countries. A close look at this table shows a great deal of difference among these three cultures. Culture affects a host of business-related activities, even including the common handshake. Here are some contrasting examples:

Culture	Type of Handshake
United States	Firm
Asian	Gentle (shaking hands is unfamiliar and uncomfortable for some; the exception is the Korean, who usually has a firm handshake)
British	Soft
French	Light and quick (not offered to superiors); repeated on arrival and departure
German	Brusk and firm; repeated on arrival and departure
Latin American	Moderate grasp; repeated frequently
Middle Eastern	Gentle; repeated frequently[8]

In overall terms, the cultural impact on international management is reflected by these basic beliefs and behaviors. Here are some specific examples where the culture of a society can directly affect management approaches:

- *Centralized vs. decentralized decision making.* In some societies, all important organizational decisions are made by top managers. In others, these decisions are diffused throughout the enterprise, and middle- and lower-level managers actively participate in, and make, key decisions.
- *Safety vs. risk.* In some societies, organizational decision makers are risk-aversive and have great difficulty with conditions of uncertainty. In others, risk-taking is encouraged, and decision making under uncertainty is common.
- *Individual vs. group rewards.* In some countries, personnel who do outstanding work are given individual rewards in the form of bonuses and commissions. In others, cultural norms require group rewards, and individual rewards are frowned on.

Table 5–1
Priorities of Cultural Values: United States, Japan, and Arab Countries

United States	Japan	Arab Countries
1. Freedom	1. Belonging	1. Family security
2. Independence	2. Group harmony	2. Family harmony
3. Self-reliance	3. Collectiveness	3. Parental guidance
4. Equality	4. Age/seniority	4. Age
5. Individualism	5. Group consensus	5. Authority
6. Competition	6. Cooperation	6. Compromise
7. Efficiency	7. Quality	7. Devotion
8. Time	8. Patience	8. Patience
9. Directness	9. Indirectness	9. Indirectness
10. Openness	10. Go-between	10. Hospitality

Note: "1" represents the most important cultural value, "10" the least.

Source: Adapted from information found in F. Elashmawi and Philip R. Harris, *Multicultural Management* (Houston: Gulf Publishing, 1993), p. 63.

- *Informal vs. formal procedures.* In some societies, much is accomplished through informal means. In others, formal procedures are set forth and followed rigidly.
- *High vs. low organizational loyalty.* In some societies, people identify very strongly with their organization or employer. In others, people identify with their occupational group, such as engineer or mechanic.
- *Cooperation vs. competition.* Some societies encourage cooperation between their people. Others encourage competition between their people.
- *Short-term vs. long-term horizons.* Some nations focus most heavily on short-term horizons, such as short-range goals of profit and efficiency. Others are more interested in long-range goals, such as market share and technologic development.
- *Stability vs. innovation.* The culture of some countries encourages stability and resistance to change. The culture of others puts high value on innovation and change.

These cultural differences influence the way that international management should be conducted. The accompanying box, "Business Customs in Japan," provides some examples in a country where many international managers are unfamiliar with day-to-day business protocol.

Another way of depicting cultural diversity is through concentric circles. Figure 5-1 provides an example. The outer layer consists of the explicit artifacts and products of the culture. This level is observable and consists of such things as language, food, buildings, and art. The middle layer contains the norms and values of the society. These can be both formal and informal, and they are designed to help people understand how they should behave. The inner layer contains the basic, implicit assumptions that govern behavior. By understanding these assumptions, members of a culture are able to organize themselves in a way that helps them increase the effectiveness of their problem-solving processes and interact well with each other. In explaining the nature of this inner layer, Trompenaars and Hampden-Turner have noted that:

> The best way to test if something is a basic assumption is when the [situation] provokes confusion or irritation. You might, for example, observe that some Japanese bow deeper than others . . . . if you ask why they do it the answer might be that they don't know but that the other person does it too (norm) or that they want to show respect for authority (value). A typical Dutch question that might follow is: "Why do you respect authority?" The most likely Japanese reaction would be either puzzlement or a smile (which might be hiding their irritation). When you question basic assumptions you are asking questions that have never been asked before. It might lead others to deeper insights, but it also might provoke annoyance. Try in the USA or the Netherlands to raise the question of why people are equal and you will see what we mean.[9]

International Management in Action

Business Customs in Japan

When doing business in Japan, foreign business-people should follow certain customs if they wish to be as effective as possible. Experts have put together the following guidelines:

1. Always try to arrange for a formal introduction to any person or company with which you want to do business. These introductions should come from someone whose position is at least as high as that of the person whom you want to meet or from someone who has done a favor for this person. Let the host pick the subjects to discuss. One topic to be avoided is World War II.

2. If in doubt, bring a translator along with you. For example, the head of Osaka's $7 billion international airport project tells the story of a U.S. construction company president who became indignant when he discovered that the Japanese project head could not speak English. By the same token, you should not bring along your lawyer, because this implies a lack of trust.

3. Try for a thorough personalization of all business relationships. The Japanese trust those with whom they socialize and come to know more than they do those who simply are looking to do business. Accept afterhours invita-

tions. However, a rollicking night out on the town will not necessarily lead to signing the contract to your advantage the next morning.

4. Do not deliver bad news in front of others, and if possible, have your second-in-command handle this chore. Never cause Japanese managers to lose face by putting them in a position of having to admit failure or say they do not know something that they should know professionally.

5. How business is done often is as important as the results. Concern for tradition, for example, is sometimes more important than concern for profit. Do not appeal solely to logic, because in Japan, emotional considerations often are more important than facts.

6. The Japanese often express themselves in a vague and ambiguous manner, in contrast to the specific language typically used in the United States. A Japanese who is too specific runs the risk of being viewed as rudely displaying superior knowledge. The Japanese avoid independent or individual action, and they prefer to make decisions based on group discussions and past precedent. The Japanese do not say no in public, which is why foreign business-people often take away the wrong impression.

A supplemental way of understanding cultural differences is to compare culture as a normal distribution, as in Figure 5-2, and then to examine it in terms of stereotyping, as in Figure 5-3. French and American culture, for example, have quite different norms and values. So the normal distribution curves for the two cultures have only limited overlap. However, when one looks at the tail ends of the two curves, it is possible to identify stereotypical views held by members of one culture about the other. The stereotypes are often exaggerated and used by members of one culture in describing the other, thus helping reinforce the differences between the two while reducing the likelihood of achieving cooperation and communication. This is one reason why an understanding of national culture is so important in the study of international management.

Values in Culture

A major dimension in the study of culture is values. **Values** are basic convictions that people have regarding what is right and wrong, good and bad, important or unimportant. These values are learned from the culture in which the individual is reared, and they help to direct the person's behavior. Differences in cultural values often result in varying management practices. Table 5-2 provides an example. Note that U.S. values can result in one set of business responses, and alternative values can bring about different responses.

Values
Basic convictions that people have regarding what is right and wrong, good and bad, important or unimportant.

Value Differences and Similarities across Cultures   Personal values have been the focus of numerous intercultural studies. In general, the findings show both differences and similarities between the work values and managerial values of different cultural groups.

Figure 5–1

A Model of Culture

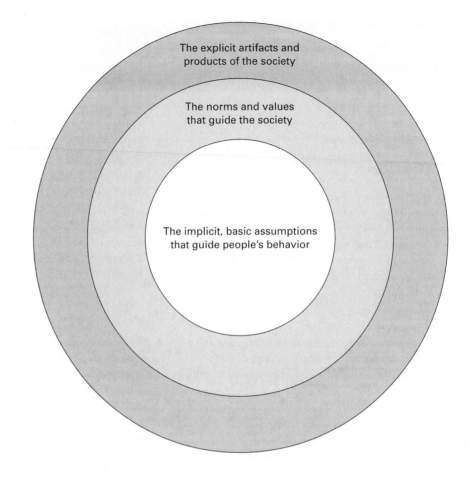

Figure 5–2

Comparing Cultures as Overlapping Normal Distributions

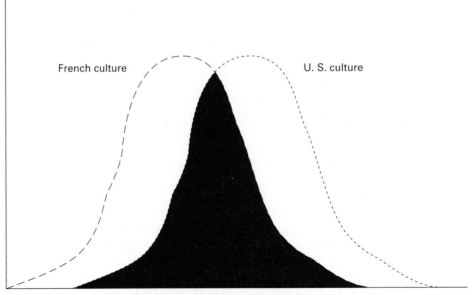

Source: Adapted from Fons Trompenaars and Charles Hampden-Turner, *Riding the Waves of Culture: Understanding Diversity in Global Business,* 2nd ed. (New York: McGraw-Hill, 1998), p. 25.

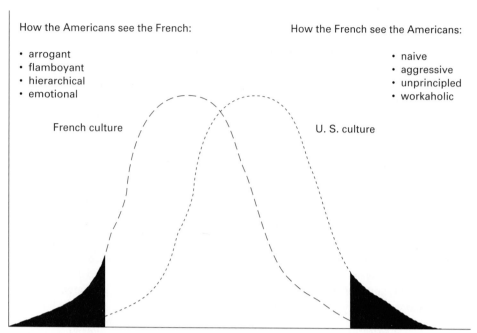

How the Americans see the French:

- arrogant
- flamboyant
- hierarchical
- emotional

French culture

How the French see the Americans:

- naive
- aggressive
- unprincipled
- workaholic

U. S. culture

Figure 5–3

Stereotyping from the Cultural Extremes

Source: Adapted from Fons Trompenaars and Charles Hampden-Turner, *Riding the Waves of Culture: Understanding Diversity in Global Business,* 2nd ed. (New York: McGraw-Hill, 1998), p. 23.

Table 5–2

U.S. Values and Possible Alternatives

U.S. Cultural Values	Alternative Values	Examples of Management Function Affected
Individuals can influence the future (when there is a will there is a way).	Life follows a preordained course, and human action is determined by the will of God.	Planning and scheduling.
Individuals should be realistic in their aspirations.	Ideals are to be pursued regardless of what is "reasonable."	Goal-setting and career development.
We must work hard to accomplish our objectives (Puritan ethic).	Hard work is not the only prerequisite for success. Wisdom, luck, and time also are required.	Motivation and reward system.
A primary obligation of an employee is to the organization.	Individual employees have a primary obligation to their family and friends.	Loyalty, commitment, and motivation.
Employees can be removed if they do not perform well.	The removal of an employee from a position involves a great loss of prestige and will rarely be done.	Promotion.
Company information should be available to anyone who needs it within the organization.	Withholding information to gain or maintain power is acceptable.	Organization, communication, and managerial style.
Competition stimulates high performance.	Competition leads to unbalances and disharmony.	Career development and marketing.
What works is important.	Symbols and the process are more important than the end point.	Communication, planning, and quality control.

Source: Adapted from information found in Philip R. Harris and Robert T. Moran, *Managing Cultural Differences* (Houston: Gulf Publishing, 1991), pp. 79–80.

For example, one study found differences in work values between Western-oriented and tribal-oriented black employees in South Africa.[10] The Western-oriented group accepted most of the tenets of the Protestant work epic, but the tribal-oriented group did not. The results were explained in terms of the differences of the cultural backgrounds of the two groups.

Differences in work values also have been found to reflect culture and industrialization. Researchers gave a personal-values questionnaire (PVQ) to over 2,000 managers in five countries: Australia ($n = 281$), India ($n = 485$), Japan ($n = 301$), South Korea ($n = 161$), and the United States ($n = 833$).[11] The PVQ consisted of 66 concepts related to business goals, personal goals, ideas associated with people and groups of people, and ideas about general topics. Ideologic and philosophic concepts were included to represent major value systems of all groups. The results showed some significant differences between the managers in each group. U.S. managers placed high value on the tactful acquisition of influence and regard for others. Japanese managers placed high value on deference to superiors, on company commitment, and on the cautious use of aggressiveness and control. Korean managers placed high value on personal forcefulness and aggressiveness and low value on recognition of others. Indian managers put high value on the nonaggressive pursuit of objectives. Australian managers placed major importance on values reflecting a low-keyed approach to management and a high concern for others.[12] In short, value systems across national boundaries often are different.

At the same time, value similarities exist between cultures. In fact, research shows that managers from different countries often have similar personal values that relate to success. England and Lee examined the managerial values of a diverse sample of U.S. ($n = 878$), Japanese ($n = 312$), Australian ($n = 301$), and Indian managers ($n = 500$). They found that:

1. There is a reasonably strong relationship between the level of success achieved by managers and their personal values.

2. It is evident that value patterns predict managerial success and could be used in selection and placement decisions.

3. Although there are country differences in the relationships between values and success, findings across the four countries are quite similar.

4. The general pattern indicates that more successful managers appear to favor pragmatic, dynamic, achievement-oriented values, while less successful managers prefer more static and passive values. More successful managers favor an achievement orientation and prefer an active role in interaction with other individuals who are instrumental to achieving the managers' organizational goals. Less successful managers have values associated with a static and protected environment in which they take relatively passive roles.[13]

"International Management in Action: Common Personal Values" discusses these findings in more depth.

Values in Transition   Do values change over time? George England found that personal value systems are relatively stable and do not change rapidly.[14] However, changes are taking place in managerial values as a result of both culture and technology. A good example is the Japanese. Reichel and Flynn examined the effects of the U.S. environment on the cultural values of Japanese managers working for Japanese firms in the United States. In particular, they focused attention on such key organizational values as lifetime employment, formal authority, group orientation, seniority, and paternalism. Here is what they found:

1. Lifetime employment is widely accepted in Japanese culture, but the stateside Japanese managers did not believe that unconditional tenure in one organization was of major importance. They did believe, however, that job security was important.

2. Formal authority, obedience, and conformance to hierarchic position are very important in Japan, but the stateside managers did not perceive obedience and conformity to be very important and rejected the idea that one should not question a superior. However, they did support the concept of formal authority.

International Management in Action

Common Personal Values

One of the most interesting findings about successful managers around the world is that while they come from different cultures, many have similar personal values. Of course, there are large differences in values within each national group. For example, some managers are very pragmatic and judge ideas in terms of whether they will work; others are highly ethical-moral and view ideas in terms of right or wrong; still others have a "feeling" orientation and judge ideas in terms of whether they are pleasant. Some managers have a very small set of values; others have a large set. Some have values that are related heavily to organization life; others include a wide range of personal values; others have highly group-oriented values. There are many different value patterns; however, overall value profiles have been found within successful managers in each group. Here are some of the most significant:

U.S. managers

- Highly pragmatic
- High achievement and competence orientation
- Emphasis on profit maximization, organizational efficiency, and high productivity

Japanese managers

- Highly pragmatic
- Strong emphasis on size and growth
- High value on competence and achievement

Korean managers

- Highly pragmatic
- Highly individualistic
- Strong achievement and competence orientation

Australian managers

- High moral orientation
- High humanistic orientation
- Low value on achievement, success, competition, and risk

Indian managers

- High moral orientation
- Highly individualistic
- Strong focus on organization compliance and competence

The findings listed here show important similarities and differences. Most of the profiles are similar in nature; however, note that successful Indian and Australian managers have values that are distinctly different. In short, although values of successful managers within countries often are similar, there are intercountry differences. This is why the successful managerial value systems of one country often are not ideal in another country.

3. Group orientation, cooperation, conformity, and compromise are important organizational values in Japan. The stateside managers supported these values but also believed it was important to be an individual, thus maintaining a balance between a group and a personal orientation.

4. In Japan, organizational personnel often are rewarded based on seniority, not merit. Support for this value was directly influenced by the length of time the Japanese managers had been in the United States. The longer they had been there, the lower their support for this value.

5. Paternalism, often measured by a manager's involvement in both personal and off-the-job problems of subordinates, is very important in Japan. Stateside Japanese managers disagreed, and this resistance was positively associated with the number of years they had been in the United States.[15]

Other researchers have found supporting evidence that Japanese values are changing—and not just among managers outside the country. One study examined value systems among three groups of managers in Japan: (1) a group of Japanese managers who had graduated from the Japanese Institute for International Studies and Training at least 10 years previously; (2) a group of Japanese management trainees who currently were enrolled in the institute; and (3) a group of U.S. M.B.A. students who were taking M.B.A. courses at the institute[16] The results showed that the Japanese managers were greatly concerned with job security, whereas the U.S. M.B.A. students valued achievement. The Japanese managers put great importance on group success; the U.S. M.B.A. students highly valued personal success. Although there were some exceptions, the two groups had contrasting values. The profiles of the Japanese students, meanwhile, fell between these two extremes. Two-thirds of responses were in this middle range. The researchers therefore concluded that "the data seem to indicate a significant difference in values between Japanese respondents who have already attained responsible managerial positions in their organization and the Japanese management trainees, who have held lower positions and been employed less long with their present company or government agency."[17]

Cultural Dimensions

Some researchers have attempted to provide a composite picture of culture by examining its subparts, or dimensions. In particular, Dutch researcher Geert Hofstede found there are four dimensions of culture that help to explain how and why people from various cultures behave as they do.[18] His initial data were gathered from two questionnaire surveys with over 116,000 respondents from over 70 different countries around the world—making it the largest organizationally based study ever conducted.[18] The individuals in these studies all worked in the local subsidiaries of IBM. As a result, Hofstede's research has been criticized because of its focus on just one company; however, he has recently countered this criticism. Hofstede is well aware of

> The amazement of some people about how employees of a very specific corporation like IBM can serve as a sample for discovering something about the culture of their countries at large. "We know IBMers," they say, "they are very special people, always in a white shirt and tie, and not at all representative of our country." The people who say this are quite right. IBMers do not form representative samples from national populations. . . . However, samples for cross-national comparison need not be representative, as long as they are functionally equivalent. IBM employees are a narrow sample, but very well matched. Employees of multinational companies in general and of IBM in particular form attractive sources of information for comparing national traits, because they are so similar in respects other than nationality: their employers . . . , their kind of work, and—for matched occupations—their level of education. The only thing that can account for systematic and consistent differences between national groups *within* such a homogenous multinational population is nationality itself. The national environment in which people were brought up *before* they joined this employer. Comparing IBM subsidiaries therefore shows national culture differences with unusual clarity.[19]

Hofstede's massive study continues to be a focal point for additional research. The four now-well-known dimensions that Hofstede examined were: (1) power distance, (2) uncertainty avoidance, (3) individualism, and (4) masculinity.

Power Distance

Power distance

The extent to which less powerful members of institutions and organizations accept that power is distributed unequally.

Power distance is "the extent to which less powerful members of institutions and organizations accept that power is distributed unequally."[20] Countries in which people blindly obey the orders of their superiors have high power distance. In many societies, lower-level employees tend to follow orders as a matter of procedure. In societies with high power distance, however, strict obedience is found even at the upper levels; examples include Mexico, South Korea, and India. For example, a senior Indian executive with a Ph.D. from a prestigious U.S. university related the following story:

> What is most important for me and my department is not what I do or achieve for the company, but whether the [owner's] favor is bestowed on me. . . . This I have achieved by saying "yes" to everything [the owner] says or does. . . . To contradict him is to look for another job. . . . I left my freedom of thought in Boston.[21]

The effect of this dimension can be measured in a number of ways. For example, organizations in low power-distance countries generally will be decentralized and have flatter organization structures. These organizations also will have a smaller proportion of supervisory personnel, and the lower strata of the works force often will consist of highly qualified people. By contrast, organizations in high power-distance countries will tend to be centralized and have tall organization structures. Organizations in high power-distance countries will have a large proportion of supervisory personnel, and the people at the lower levels of the structure often will have low job qualifications. This latter structure encourages and promotes inequality between people at different levels.[22]

Uncertainty Avoidance

Uncertainty avoidance is "the extent to which people feel threatened by ambiguous situations, and have created beliefs and institutions that try to avoid these."[23] Countries populated with people who do not like uncertainty tend to have a high need for security and a strong belief in experts and their knowledge: examples include Germany, Japan, and Spain. Cultures with low uncertainty avoidance have people who are more willing to accept that risks are associated with the unknown, that life must go on in spite of this. Examples here include Denmark and Great Britain.

The effect of this dimension can be measured in a number of ways. Countries with high uncertainty-avoidance cultures have a great deal of structuring of organizational activities, more written rules, less risk-taking by managers, lower labor turnover, and less ambitious employees.

Low uncertainty-avoidance societies have organization settings with less structuring of activities, fewer written rules, more risk-taking by managers, higher labor turnover, and more ambitious employees. The organization encourages personnel to use their own initiative and assume responsibility for their actions.

Uncertainty avoidance
The extent to which people feel threatened by ambiguous situations and have created beliefs and institutions that try to avoid these.

Individualism

Individualism is the tendency of people to look after themselves and their immediate family only.[24] Hofstede measured this cultural difference on a bipolar continuum, with individualism on one end and collectivism on the other. **Collectivism** is the tendency of people to belong to groups or collectives and to look after each other in exchange for loyalty.[25]

Similar to those of the other cultural dimensions, the effects of individualism and collectivism can be measured in a number of different ways.[26] Hofstede has found that wealthy countries have higher individualism scores and poorer countries higher collectivism scores (see Table 5-3 for the country abbreviations used in Figure 5-4 and subsequent figures). Note that in Figure 5-4, the United States, Canada, Australia, Denmark, and Sweden, among others, have high individualism and high GNP. Conversely, Guam, Pakistan, and a number of South American countries have low individualism (high collectivism) and low GNP. Countries with high individualism also tend to have greater support for the Protestant work ethic, greater individual initiative, and promotions based on market value. Countries with low individualism tend to have less support for the Protestant work ethic, less individual initiative, and promotions based on seniority.

Individualism
The tendency of people to look after themselves and their immediate family only.

Collectivism
The tendency of people to belong to groups or collectives and to look after each other in exchange for loyalty.

Masculinity

Masculinity is defined by Hofstede as "a situation in which the dominant values in society are success, money, and things."[27] Hofstede measured this dimension on a continuum ranging from masculinity to femininity. Contrary to some stereotypes and connotations, **femininity** is the term used by Hofstede to describe "a situation in which the dominant values in society are caring for others and the quality of life."[28] Countries with a high masculinity index, such as Japan, place great importance on earnings, recognition, advancement, and challenge. Individuals are encouraged to be independent decision makers, and achievement is defined in terms of recognition and wealth. The workplace is often characterized by high

Masculinity
A culture in which the dominant values in society are success, money, and things.

Femininity
A situation in which the dominant values in society are caring for others and quality of life.

Table 5–3
Countries and Regions Used in Hofstede's Research

ARA	Arab countries (Egypt, Lebanon, Libya, Kuwait, Iraq, Saudi Arabia, U.A.E.)	JPN	Japan
		KOR	South Korea
ARG	Argentina	MAL	Malaysia
AUL	Australia	MEX	Mexico
AUT	Austria	NET	Netherlands
BEL	Belgium	NOR	Norway
BRA	Brazil	NZL	New Zealand
CAN	Canada	PAK	Pakistan
CHL	Chile	PAN	Panama
COL	Colombia	PER	Peru
COS	Costa Rica	PHI	Philippines
DEN	Denmark	POR	Portugal
EAF	East Africa (Kenya, Ethiopia, Zambia)	SAF	South Africa
EQA	Equador	SAL	Salvador
FIN	Finland	SIN	Singapore
FRA	France	SPA	Spain
GBR	Great Britain	SWE	Sweden
GER	Germany	SWI	Switzerland
GRE	Greece	TAI	Taiwan
GUA	Guatemala	THA	Thailand
HOK	Hong Kong	TUR	Turkey
IDO	Indonesia	URU	Uruguay
IND	India	USA	United States
IRA	Iran	VEN	Venezuela
IRE	Ireland	WAF	West Africa (Nigeria, Ghana, Sierra Leone)
ISR	Israel		
ITA	Italy		
JAM	Jamaica	YUG	Former Yugoslavia

Source: Adapted from Geert Hofstede, *Cultures and Organizations: Software of the Mind* (London: McGraw-Hill U.K., Ltd., 1991), p. 55. Used with permission.

job stress, and many managers believe that their employees dislike work and must be kept under some degree of control.

Countries with a low masculinity index (Hofstede's femininity dimension), such as Norway, tend to place great importance on cooperation, a friendly atmosphere, and employment security. Individuals are encouraged to be group decision makers, and achievement is defined in terms of layman contacts and the living environment. The workplace tends to be characterized by low stress, and managers give their employees more credit for being responsible and allow them more freedom.

Cultures with a high masculinity index tend to favor large-scale enterprises, and economic growth is seen as more important than conservation of the environment. The school system is geared toward encouraging high performance. Young men expect to have careers, and those who do not often view themselves as failures. Fewer women hold higher-level jobs, and these individuals often find it necessary to be assertive. There is high job stress in the workplace, and industrial conflict is common.

Cultures with a low masculinity index (high femininity) tend to favor small-scale enterprises, and they place great importance on conservation of the environment. The school system is designed to teach social adaptation. Some young men and women want careers; others do not. Many women hold higher-level jobs, and they do not find it necessary to be assertive. Less job stress is found in the workplace, and there is not much industrial conflict.

Integrating the Dimensions

A description of the four dimensions of culture is useful in helping to explain the differences between various countries, and Hofstede's research has extended beyond this focus

Figure 5–4

Individualism Index vs. Per Capita GNP

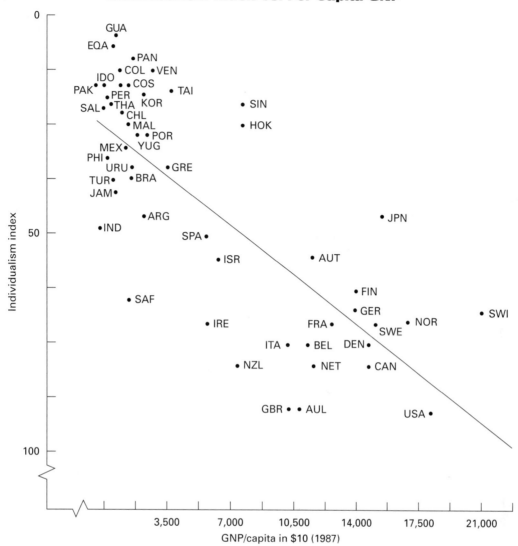

Source: Geert Hofstede, *Cultures and Organizations: Software of the Mind* (London: McGraw-Hill U.K., Ltd., 1991), p. 75. Used with permission.

and showed how countries can be described in terms of pairs of dimensions. Figure 5-5, which incorporates power distance and individualism, provides an example.

In Figure 5-5, the United States is located in the lower left-hand quadrant. Americans have very high individualism and relatively low power distance. They prefer to do things for themselves and are not upset when others have more power than they do. In fact, Americans are taught to believe that everyone is equal, so they are not overly impressed by individuals with important titles or jobs. Australians, Canadians, British, Dutch, and New Zealanders have the same basic values. Conversely, many of the underdeveloped or newly industrialized countries, such as Colombia, Hong Kong, Portugal, and Singapore, are characterized by large power distance and low individualism. These nations tend to be collectivist in their approach.

Figure 5-6 plots the uncertainty avoidance index for the 53 countries against the power-distance index. Once again, there are clusters of countries. Many of the Anglo nations tend to be in the upper left-hand quadrant, which is characterized by small power distance and weak uncertainty avoidance (they do not try to avoid uncertainty). These countries tend to be moderately unconcerned with power distance, and they are able to

Figure 5–5   **A Power Distance and Individualism-Collectivism Plot**

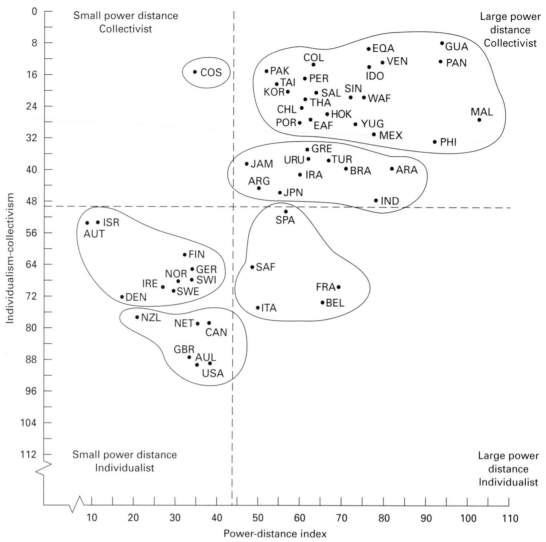

Source: Geert Hofstede, *Cultures and Organizations: Software of the Mind* (London: McGraw-Hill U.K., Ltd., 1991), p. 54. Used with permission.

accept conditions of uncertainty. In contrast, many Latin countries (both in Europe and the Western hemisphere), Mediterranean countries, and Asian nations (e.g., Japan and Korea) are characterized by high power distance and strong uncertainty avoidance. Most other Asian countries are characterized by large power distance and weak uncertainty avoidance.

Figure 5-7 plots the position of 53 countries in terms of uncertainty avoidance and masculinity-femininity. The most masculine country is Japan, followed by the Germanic countries (Austria, Switzerland, Germany) and Latin countries (Venezuela, Mexico, Italy). Many countries in the Anglo cluster, including Ireland, Australia, Great Britain, and the United States, have moderate degrees of masculinity. So do some of the former colonies of Anglo nations, including India, South Africa, and the Philippines. The Northern European cluster (Denmark, Sweden, Norway, the Netherlands) has low masculinity, indicating that these countries place high value on factors such as quality of life, preservation of the environment, and the importance of relationships with people over money.

The integration of these cultural factors into two-dimensional plots helps to illustrate the complexity of understanding culture's effect on behavior. A number of dimensions are at work, and sometimes, they do not all move in the anticipated direction. For

Figure 5–6

A Power Distance and Uncertainty Avoidance Plot

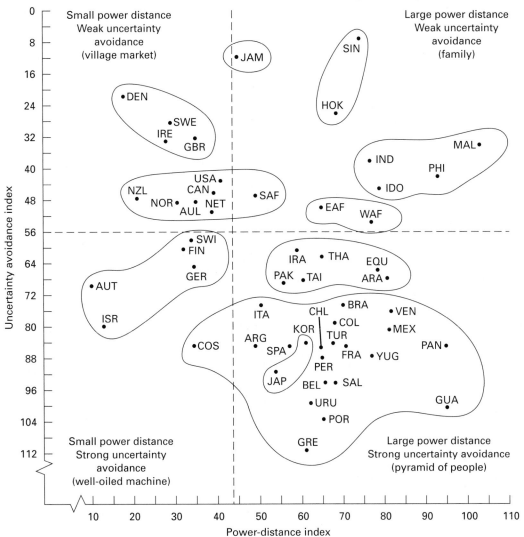

Source: Geert Hofstede, *Cultures and Organizations: Software of the Mind* (London: McGraw-Hill U.K., Ltd., 1991), p. 141. Used with permission.

example, at first glance, a nation with high power distance would appear to be low in individualism, and vice versa, and Hofstede found exactly that (see Figure 5-5). However, low uncertainty avoidance does not always go hand-in-hand with high masculinity, even though those who are willing to live with uncertainty will want rewards such as money and power and accord low value to the quality of work life and caring for others (see Figure 5-7). Simply put, empirical evidence on the impact of cultural dimensions may differ from commonly held beliefs or stereotypes. Research-based data are needed to determine the full impact of differing cultures. However, some interesting attempts have been made to classify countries in uniform clusters on variables such as attitudes and deal with cultures on a more structured basis. These efforts are described in the next section.

Attitudinal Dimensions of Culture

For over a decade, researchers have attempted to cluster countries into similar cultural groupings for the purpose of studying similarities and differences. Such research also helps us to learn the reasons for cultural differences and how they can be transcended.

Figure 5–7

A Masculinity-Femininity and Uncertainty Avoidance Plot

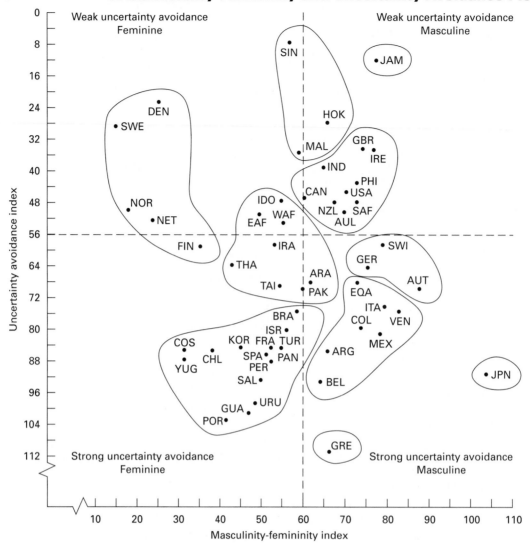

Source: Geert Hofstede, *Cultures and Organizations: Software of the Mind* (London: McGraw-Hill U.K., Ltd., 1991), p. 123. Used with permission.

Much of the initial research in this area examined similarities among countries based on employee work values and attitudes.

Work Value and Attitude Similarities

Smallest space analysis (SSA)

A nonparametric multivariate analysis. This mathematic tool maps the relationship among the countries by showing the distance between each. By looking at this two-dimensional map, it is possible to see those countries that are similar to each other and those that are not.

Drawing on his extensive data, Hofstede was able to use the four cultural dimensions discussed in the last section to compile a series of country clusters, as shown in Figures 5-5, 5-6, and 5-7. His work was only preliminary, but it served as a point of departure for other multicultural research, which revealed many similarities in both work values and attitudes among certain countries. For example, early research by Ronen and Kraut reported that "countries could be clustered into more or less homogeneous groups based on intercorrelations of standard scores obtained for each country from scales measuring leadership, role descriptions, and motivation."[29] These researchers then attempted to cluster the countries by use of the mathematic technique of nonparametric multivariate analysis, known as **smallest space analysis (SSA)**. Simply put, this approach maps the relationships of various culture dimensions among the countries by showing the distance between each. By looking at the resulting two-dimensional map, one can see those countries that are similar to each other and those that are not.

Drawing on the work of many earlier researchers as well as that of 4,000 technical employees in 15 countries, Ronen and Kraut were able to construct SSA maps of various countries, including the United States, France, India, Sweden, and Japan. These maps showed five country clusters: (l) Anglo-American (United States, United Kingdom, Australia); (2) Nordic (Norway, Finland, Denmark); (3) South American (Venezuela, Mexico, Chile); (4) Latin European (France and Belgium); and (5) Central European (Germany, Austria, and Switzerland). Commenting on the overall value of their research, Ronen and Kraut concluded:

> An important aspect of this study is the potential for practical application by multinational organizations. For example, knowledge of relative similarities among countries can guide the smooth placement of international assignees the establishment of compatible regional units, and predict the ease of implementing various policies and practices across national boundaries.[30]

Since Ronen and Kraut, additional multicultural studies have been conducted, and the number of countries and clusters has increased. These country clusters are particularly important in providing an overall picture of international cultures.

Country Clusters

To date, perhaps the most integrative analysis of all available findings has been provided by Ronen and Shenkar.[31] After conducting a thorough review of the literature, they found that eight major cluster studies had been conducted over the previous 15 years. These studies examined variables in four categories: (1) the importance of work goals; (2) need deficiency, fulfillment, and job satisfaction; (3) managerial and organizational variables; and (4) work role and interpersonal orientation. Each of the eight country cluster studies had produced different results. Some had focused only on one part of the world, such as the Far East or Arabia; others had been more international in focus but arrived at different cluster groupings. Based on careful analysis of these research efforts, Ronen and Shenkar identified eight country clusters and four countries that are independent and do not fit into any of the clusters (see Figure 5-8).

Each country in Figure 5-8 that has been placed in a cluster is culturally similar to the others in that cluster. In addition, the closer a country is to the center of the overall circle, the greater its per-capita gross national product (GNP). Those countries with similar GNPs will not necessarily have intercluster similarity, but to the extent that GNP influences values and culture, these countries will have converging cultural values.

Not everyone agrees with the synthesis presented in Figure 5-8. Some researchers place India and Israel in the Anglo culture because of the strong Anglo ties of these countries. Others combine the Nordic and Germanic clusters into one. Still others believe that some of the Latin European countries, such as Italy, Portugal, and Spain, are culturally much closer to those of the South American culture and cluster them there. Nevertheless, Figure 5-8 does provide a useful model and point of departure for examining international culture. The concept of country clusters is useful to those studying multinational management as well. Ronen and Shenkar note:

> As multinational companies increase their direct investment overseas, especially in less developed and consequently less studied areas, they will require more information concerning their local employees in order to implement effective types of interactions between the organization and the host country. The knowledge acquired thus far can help one to understand better the work values and attitudes of employees throughout the world. American theories work very well for Western nations. Are they equally applicable in non-Western countries? Clearly, more cluster research is called for, including research in countries from all parts of the globe.[32]

Empirical evidence shows that international managers share a common international culture, so there may well be much more convergence than previously has been believed. There also may be much more recent adaptation to the local culture by national firms than many outside observers realize. In short, although recognizing cultural diversity still is vital, convergence and flexibility in the international arena are gaining momentum.

Figure 5–8

A Synthesis of Country Clusters

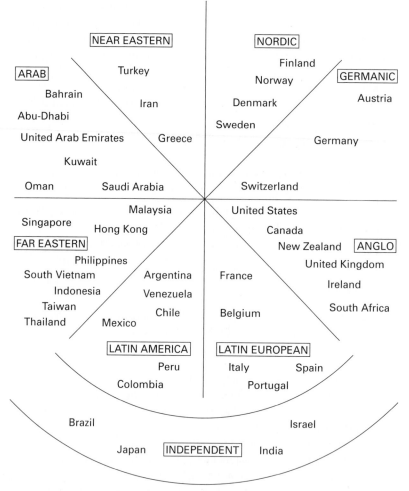

Source: Simcha Ronen and Oded Shenkar, "Clustering Countries on Attitudinal Dimensions: A Review and Synthesis," *Academy of Management Journal,* September, 1985, p. 449. Used with permission.

Trompenaars' Cultural Dimensions

Both the Hofstede cultural dimensions and the Ronen and Shenkar country clusters are widely recognized and accepted in the study of international management. A more recent description of how cultures differ, by another Dutch researcher, Fons Trompenaars, is receiving increasing attention as well. Trompenaars' research was conducted over a 10-year period and published in 1994.[33] He administered research questionnaires to over 15,000 managers from 28 countries and received usable responses from at least 500 in each nation; the 23 countries in his research are presented in Table 5-4. Building heavily on value orientations and the relational orientations of well-known sociologist Talcott Parsons,[34] Trompenaars derived five relationship orientations that address the ways in which people deal with each other; these can be considered to be cultural dimensions that are analogous to Hofstede's dimensions. Trompenaars also looked at attitudes toward both time and the environment, and the result of his research is a wealth of information helping to explain how cultures differ and offering practical ways in which MNCs can do business in various countries. The following discussion examines each of the five relationship orientations as well as attitudes toward time and the environment.[35]

Table 5–4	
Trompenaars' Country Abbreviations	
Abbreviation	**Country**
ARG	Argentina
AUS	Austria
BEL	Belgium
BRZ	Brazil
CHI	China
CIS	Former Soviet Union
CZH	Former Czechoslovakia
FRA	France
GER	Germany (excluding former East Germany)
HK	Hong Kong
IDO	Indonesia
ITA	Italy
JPN	Japan
MEX	Mexico
NL	Netherlands
SIN	Singapore
SPA	Spain
SWE	Sweden
SWI	Switzerland
THA	Thailand
UK	United Kingdom
USA	United States
VEN	Venezuela

Universalism vs. Particularism

Universalism is the belief that ideas and practices can be applied everywhere without modification. **Particularism** is the belief that circumstances dictate how ideas and practices should be applied. In cultures with high universalism, the focus is more on formal rules than on relationships, business contracts are adhered to very closely, and people believe that "a deal is a deal." In cultures with high particularism, the focus is more on relationships and trust than on formal rules. In a particularist culture, legal contracts often are modified, and as people get to know each other better, they often change the way in which deals are executed. In his early research, Trompenaars found that in countries such as the United States, Australia, Germany, Sweden, and the United Kingdom, there was high universalism, while countries such as Venezuela, the former Soviet Union, Indonesia, and China were high on particularism. Figure 5-9 shows the continuum.

In follow-up research Trompenaars and Hampden-Turner uncovered additional insights regarding national orientations on this universalism-particularism continuum. They did this by presenting the respondents with a dilemma and asking them to make a decision. Here is one of these dilemmas along with the national scores of the respondents:[36]

> You are riding in a car driven by a close friend. He hits a pedestrian. You know he was going at least 35 miles per hour in an area of the city where the maximum allowed speed is 20 miles per hour. There are no witnesses. His lawyer says that if you testify under oath that he was driving 20 miles per hour it may save him from serious consequences. What right has your friend to expect you to protect him?
>
> (*a*) My friend has a definite right as a friend to expect me to testify to the lower figure.
>
> (*b*) He has some right as a friend to expect me to testify to the lower figure.
>
> (*c*) He has no right as a friend to expect me to testify to the lower figure.

Universalism
The belief that ideas and practices can be applied everywhere in the world without modification.

Particularism
The belief that circumstances dictate how ideas and practices should be applied and something cannot be done the same everywhere.

Figure 5–9

**Trompenaars'
Relationship
Orientations on
Cultural
Dimensions**

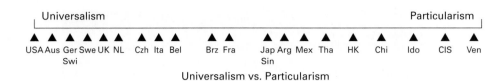

Universalism vs. Particularism

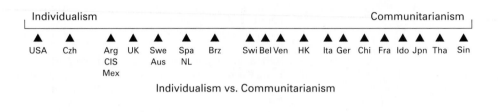

Individualism vs. Communitarianism

Neutral vs. Emotional

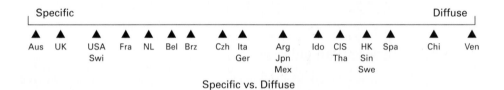

Specific vs. Diffuse

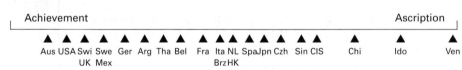

Achievement vs. Ascription

Source: Adapted from information found in Fons Trompenaars, *Riding the Waves of Culture* (New York: Irwin, 1994) and Charles M. Hampden-Turner and Fons Trompenaars, "A World Turned Upside Down: Doing Business in Asia," in Pat Joynt and Malcolm Warner (eds.), *Managing across Cultures: Issues and Perspectives* (London: International Thomson Business Press, 1996), pp. 275–305.

With a high score indicating strong universalism (choice *c*) and a low score indicating strong particularism (choice *a*), here is how the different nations scored:

Universalism (no right)

Canada	96
United States	95
Germany	90
United Kingdom	90
Netherlands	88
France	68
Japan	67
Singapore	67
Thailand	63
Hong Kong	56

Particularism (some or definite right)

China	48
South Korea	26

As noted earlier, respondents from universalism cultures (e.g., North America and Western Europe) felt that the rules applied regardless of the situation, while respondents from particularism cultures were much more willing to bend the rules and help their friend.

Based on these types of findings, Trompenaars recommends that when individuals from particularist cultures do business in a universalist culture, they should be prepared for rational, professional arguments and a "let's get down to business" attitude. Conversely, when individuals from universalist cultures do business in a particularist environment, they should be prepared for personal meandering or irrelevancies that seem to go nowhere and should not regard personal, get-to know-you attitudes as mere small talk.

Individualism vs. Communitarianism

Individualism and communitarianism are key dimensions in Hofstede's earlier research. Although Trompenaars derived these two relationships differently than Hofstede, they still have the same basic meaning, although in his most recent work Trompenaars has used the word "communitarianism" rather than "collectivism." For him, individualism refers to people regarding themselves as individuals, while **communitarianism** refers to people regarding themselves as part of a group. As shown in Figure 5-9, the United States, Czechoslovakia, Argentina, the former Soviet Union, and Mexico have high individualism. These findings of Trompenaars are particularly interesting, because they differ somewhat from those of Hofstede, as reported in Figure 5-5. Although the definitions are not exactly the same, the fact that there are differences (e.g., Mexico and Argentina are communitarianistic in Hofstede's findings but individualistic in Trompenaars' research) points out that cultural values may be changing (i.e., Hofstede's findings may be dated). For example, with Mexico now part of NAFTA and the global economy, this country may have moved from dominant collectivistic or communitarianistic cultural values to more individualist values. Trompenaars also found that the former communist countries of Czechoslovakia and the Soviet Union now appear to be quite individualistic, which of course is contrary to assumptions and conventional wisdom about the former communist bloc. In other words, Trompenaars points out the complex, dynamic nature of culture and the danger of overgeneralization.

In his most recent research, and again using the technique of presenting respondents with a dilemma and asking them to make a decision, Trompenaars posed the following situation. If you were to be promoted, which of the two following issues would you emphasize most: (a) the new group of people with whom you will be working; or (b) the greater responsibility of the work you are undertaking and the higher income you will be earning. The following reports the latest scores associated with the individualism of option b—greater responsibility and more money.[37]

Communitarianism
Refers to people regarding themselves as part of a group.

Individualism (emphasis on larger responsibilities and more income)

Canada	77
Thailand	71
United Kingdom	69
United States	67
Netherlands	64
France	61
Japan	61
China	54
Singapore	50
Hong Kong	47

Communitarianism (emphasis on the new group of people)

Malaysia	38
Korea	32

These findings are somewhat different from those presented in Figure 5-9 and show that cultural changes may be occurring more rapidly than many people realize. For example, the latest findings show Thailand very high on individualism (possibly indicating an increasing entrepreneurial spirit/cultural value) whereas the Thais were found to be low on individualism a few years before as shown in Figure 5-9. At the same time, it is important to remember that there are major differences between people in high individualism societies and those in high communitarianism societies. The former stress personal and individual matters; the latter value group-related issues. Negotiations in cultures with high individualism typically are made on the spot by a representative, people ideally achieve things alone, and they assume a great deal of personal responsibility. In cultures with high communitarianism, decisions typically are referred to committees, people ideally achieve things in groups, and they jointly assume responsibility.

Trormpenaars recommends that when people from cultures with high individualism deal with those from communitarianism cultures, they should have patience for the time taken to consent and to consult, and they should aim to build lasting relationships. When people from cultures with high communitarianism deal with those from individualist cultures, they should be prepared to make quick decisions and commit their organization to these decisions. Also, communitarianistics dealing with individualists should realize that the reason they are dealing with only one negotiator (as opposed to a group) is that this person is respected by his or her organization and has its authority and esteem.

Neutral vs. Emotional

Neutral culture
A culture in which emotions are held in check.

Emotional culture
A culture in which emotions are expressed openly and naturally.

A **neutral culture** is one in which emotions are held in check. As seen in Figure 5-9, both Japan and the United Kingdom are high neutral cultures. People in these countries try not to show their feelings; they act stoically and maintain their composure. An **emotional culture** is one in which emotions are openly and naturally expressed. People in emotional cultures often smile a great deal, talk loudly when they are excited, and greet each other with a great deal of enthusiasm. Mexico, the Netherlands, and Switzerland are examples of high emotional cultures.

Trompenaars recommends that when individuals from emotional cultures do business in neutral cultures, they should put as much as they can on paper and submit it to the other side. They should realize that lack of emotion does not mean disinterest or boredom, but rather that people from neutral cultures do not like to show their hand. Conversely, when those from neutral cultures do business in emotional cultures, they should not be put off stride when the other side creates scenes or grows animated and boisterous, and they should try to respond warmly to the emotional affections of the other group.

Specific vs. Diffuse

Specific culture
A culture in which individuals have a large public space they readily share with others and a small private space they guard closely and share with only close friends and associates.

Diffuse culture
A culture in which both public and private space are similar in size and individuals guard their public space carefully, because entry into public space affords entry into private space as well.

A **specific culture** is one in which individuals have a large public space they readily let others enter and share and a small private space they guard closely and share with only close friends and associates. A **diffuse culture** is one in which both public and private space are similar in size and individuals guard their public space carefully, because entry into public space affords entry into private space as well. As shown in Figure 5-9, Austria, the United Kingdom, the United States, and Switzerland all are specific cultures, while

Venezuela, China, and Spain are diffuse cultures. In specific cultures, people often are invited into a person's open, public space; individuals in these cultures often are open and extroverted; and there is a strong separation of work and private life. In diffuse cultures, people are not quickly invited into a person's open, public space, because once they are in, there is easy entry into the private space as well. Individuals in these cultures often appear to be indirect and introverted, and work and private life often are closely linked.

An example of these specific and diffuse cultural dimensions is provided by the United States and Germany. A U.S. professor, such as Robert Smith, Ph.D., generally would be called Dr. Smith by students when at his U.S. university. When shopping, however, he might be referred to by the store clerk as Bob, and he might even ask the clerk's advice regarding some of his intended purchases. When bowling, Bob might just be one of the guys, even to a team member who happens to be a graduate student in his department. The reason for these changes in status is that, with the specific U.S. cultural values, people have large public spaces and often conduct themselves differently depending on their public role. At the same time, however, Bob has private space that is off-limits to the students who must call him Doctor in class. In high diffuse cultures, on the other hand, a person's public and private life often are similar. Therefore, in Germany, Herr Professor Doktor Halls Schmidt would be referred to this way at the university, local market, and bowling alley—and even his wife might address him formally in public. A great deal of formality is maintained, often giving the impression that Germans are stuffy or aloof.

Trompenaars recommends that when those from specific cultures do business in diffuse cultures, they should respect a person's title, age, and background connections, and they should not get impatient when people are being indirect or circuitous. Conversely, when individuals from diffuse cultures do business in specific cultures, they should try to get to the point and be efficient, learn to structure meetings with the judicious use of agendas, and not use their titles or acknowledge achievements or skills that are irrelevant to the issues being discussed.

Achievement vs. Ascription

An **achievement culture** is one in which people are accorded status based on how well they perform their functions. An **ascription culture** is one in which status is attributed based on who or what a person is. Achievement cultures give high status to high achievers, such as the company's number one salesperson or the medical researcher who has found a cure for a rare form of bone cancer. Ascription cultures accord status based on age, gender, or social connections. For example, in an ascription culture, a person who has been with the company for 40 years may be listened to carefully because of the respect that others have for the individual's age and longevity with the firm, and an individual who has friends in high places may be afforded status because of whom she knows. As shown in Figure 5-9, Austria, the United States, Switzerland, and the United Kingdom are achievement cultures, while Venezuela, Indonesia, and China are ascription cultures.

Trompenaars recommends that when individuals from achievement cultures do business in ascription cultures, they should make sure that their group has older, senior, and formal position-holders who can impress the other side, and they should respect the status and influence of their counterparts in the other group. Conversely, he recommends that when individuals from ascription cultures do business in achievement cultures, they should make sure that their group has sufficient data, technical advisers, and knowledgeable people to convince the other that they are proficient, and they should respect the knowledge and information of their counterparts on the other team.

Achievement culture
A culture in which people are accorded status based on how well they perform their functions.

Ascription culture
A culture in which status is attributed based on who or what a person is.

Time

Aside from the five relationship orientations, another major cultural difference is the way in which people deal with the concept of time. Trompenaars has identified two different approaches: sequential and synchronous. In cultures where sequential approaches are prevalent, people tend to do only one activity at a time, keep appointments strictly, and show a strong preference for following plans as they are laid out and not deviating from them. In cultures where synchronous approaches are common, people tend to do more than one activity at a time, appointments are approximate and may be changed at a moment's notice, and schedules generally are subordinate to relationships. People in synchronous-time cultures often will stop what they are doing to meet and greet individuals coming into their office.

A good contrast is provided by the United States, Mexico, and France. In the United States, people tend to be guided by sequential-time orientation and thus set a schedule and stick to it. Mexicans operate under more of a synchronous-time orientation and thus tend to be much more flexible, often building slack into their schedules to allow for interruptions. The French are similar to the Mexicans and, when making plans, often determine the objectives they want to accomplish but leave open the timing and other factors that are beyond their control; this way, they can adjust and modify their approach as they go along. As Trompenaars noted, "For the French and Mexicans, what was important was that they get to the end, not the particular path or sequence by which that end was reached."[38]

Another interesting time-related contrast is the degree to which cultures are past- or present-oriented as opposed to future-oriented. In countries such as the United States, Italy, and Germany, the future is more important than the past or the present. In countries such as Venezuela, Indonesia, and Spain, the present is most important. In France and Belgium, all three time periods are of approximately equal importance. Because different emphases are given to different time periods, adjusting to these cultural differences can create challenges.

Trompenaars recommends that when doing business with future-oriented cultures, effective international managers should emphasize the opportunities and limitless scope that any agreement can have, agree to specific deadlines for getting things done, and be aware of the core competence or continuity that the other party intends to carry with it into the future. When doing business with past- or present-oriented cultures, he recommends that managers emphasize the history and tradition of the culture, find out whether internal relationships will sanction the types of changes that need to be made, and agree to future meetings in principle but fix no deadlines for completions.

The Environment

Trompenaars also examined the ways in which people deal with their environment. Specific attention should be given to whether they believe in controlling outcomes (inner-directed) or letting things take their own course (outer-directed). One of the things he asked managers to do was choose between the following statements:

1. What happens to me is my own doing.
2. Sometimes I feel that I do not have enough control over the directions my life is taking.

Managers who believe in controlling their own environment would opt for the first choice; those who believe that they are controlled by their environment and cannot do much about it would opt for the second. Here is an example by country of the sample respondents who believe that what happens to them is their own doing:[39]

United States	89%
Switzerland	84%
Australia	81%
Belgium	76%
Indonesia	73%
Hong Kong	69%
Greece	63%
Singapore	58%
Japan	56%
China	35%

In the United States, managers feel strongly that they are masters of their own fate. This helps to account for their dominant attitude (sometimes bordering on aggressiveness) toward the environment and discomfort when things seem to get out of control. Many Asian cultures do not share these views. They believe that things move in waves or natural shifts and one must "go with the flow," so a flexible attitude, characterized by a willingness to compromise and maintain harmony with nature, is important.

Trompenaars recommends that when dealing with those from cultures that believe in dominating the environment, it is important to play hard ball, test the resilience of the opponent, win some objectives, and always lose from time to time. When dealing with those from cultures that believe in letting things take their natural course, it is important to be persistent and polite, maintain good relationships with the other party, and try to win together and lose apart.

Cultural Patterns or Clusters

Like Hofstede's and the earlier work of Ronen and Shenkar, Trompenaars' research lends itself to cultural patterns or clusters. Table 5-5 relates his findings to the five relational orientations, categorized into the same types of clusters that Ronen and Shenkar used (see Figure 5-5). There is a great deal of similarity between the Trompenaars and the Ronen and Shenkar clusters. Both the United States and United Kingdom profiles are the same, except for the neutral (U.K.) and emotional (U.S.) dimension. So are those in most of the Asian countries, including Japan, which was left out of the Ronen and Shenkar clusters and labeled an independent. Brazil, which also was left out of the Ronen and Shenkar clusters, continues to be sufficiently different from other members of the Latin American group in the Trompenaars-derived Table 5-5. In other words, Brazil still appears to be independent. Additionally, while France and Belgium, in the Latin European Trompenaars group, have identical profiles, Spain is significantly different from both of them as well as from Italy. This shows that earlier cluster groups, such as that of Ronen and Shenkar, may need to be revised in light of more recent data.

Overall, Table 5-5 shows that a case can be made for cultural similarities between clusters of countries. With only small differences, Trompenaars' research helps to support, and more importantly, to extend, the work of Hofstede as well as Ronen and Shenkar. Such research provides a useful point of departure for recognizing cultural differences, and it provides guidelines for doing business effectively around the world.

World of Business Week Revisited

As the article that opened this chapter suggested, cultural change can be a very slow yet necessary process. Having read this chapter you are now familiar with the mayor dimensions of culture relevant to work settings and understand the effects they can have on various behaviors. This is particularly true in the case of

Table 5–5
Cultural Groups Based on Trompenaars' Research

Anglo cluster

Relationship	United States	United Kingdom
Individualism	X	X
Communitarianism		
Specific relationship	X	X
Diffuse relationship		
Universalism	X	X
Particularism		
Neutral relationship		X
Emotional relationship	X	
Achievement	X	X
Ascription		

Asian cluster

Relationship	Japan	China	Indonesia	Hong Kong	Singapore
Individualism					
Communitarianism	X	X	X	X	X
Specific relationship					
Diffuse relationship	X	X	X	X	X
Universalism					
Particularism	X	X	X	X	X
Neutral relationship	X		X	X	
Emotional relationship		X			
Achievement					
Ascription	X	X	X	X	X

Latin American cluster

Relationship	Argentina	Mexico	Venezuela	Brazil
Individualism	X	X		X
Communitarianism			X	
Specific relationship				X
Diffuse relationship	X	X	X	
Universalism				X
Particularism	X	X	X	
Neutral relationship	X	X	X	
Emotional relationship				X
Achievement	X	X		
Ascription			X	X

Latin European cluster

Relationship	France	Belgium	Spain	Italy
Individualism			X	
Communitarianism	X	X		X
Specific relationship	X	X		
Diffuse relationship			X	X
Universalism	X	X		X
Particularism			X	
Neutral relationship			X	
Emotional relationship	X	X		X
Achievement			X	
Ascription	X	X		X

Table 5–5 *(continued)*
Cultural Groups Based on Trompenaars' Research

Relationship	Germanic cluster			
	Austria	Germany	Switzerland	Czechoslovakia
Individualism	X			
Communitarianism		X	X	X
Specific relationship	X		X	X
Diffuse relationship		X		
Universalism	X	X	X	X
Particularism				
Neutral relationship	X			X
Emotional relationship		X	X	
Achievement	X	X		X
Ascription			X	

Source: Adapted from information in Fons Trompenaars, *Riding the Waves of Culture* (New York: Irwin, 1994).

Korea where the *chaebols* are clinging to their old practices by refusing to divest businesses, adopt standard accounting and financial practices, allow layoffs, and cease family-dominated board membership. While some Korean companies may make a few of the needed corrections to ward off immediate economic pressures, it is doubtful that this change will last long or be effective enough to aid a full recovery into the next decade. The values and priorities of these Korean MNCs are too ingrained to shift more than marginally. Reflecting on what you have read about the Asian/Korean culture and Hofstede and Trompenaars' work on cultural dimensions, answer the following questions: (1) What cultural dimensions best describe why the Korean culture appears so resistant to change? Why? (2) Why do you think that Korean companies have generally been opposed to takeovers by foreign companies even though it might be in their best economic interest? (3) How would cutting investment and divesting various businesses help a *chaebol's* recovery ?

Summary of Key Points

1. Culture is acquired knowledge that people use to interpret experience and generate social behavior. Culture also has the characteristics of being learned, shared, transgenerational, symbolic, patterned, and adaptive. There are many dimensions of cultural diversity, including centralized vs. decentralized decision making, safety vs. risk, individual vs. group rewards, informal vs. formal procedures, high vs. low organizational loyalty, cooperation vs. competition, short-term vs. long-term horizons, and stability vs. innovation.

2. Values are basic convictions that people have regarding what is right and wrong, good and bad, important and unimportant. Research shows that there are both differences and similarities between the work values and managerial values of different cultural groups. Work values often reflect culture and industrialization, and managerial values are highly related to success. Research shows that values tend to change over time and often reflect age and experience.

3. Hofstede has identified and researched four major dimensions of culture: power distance, uncertainty avoidance, individualism, and masculinity. Each will affect a country's political and social system. The integration of these factors into two-dimensional figures can illustrate the complexity of culture's effect on behavior.

4. In recent years, researchers have attempted to cluster countries into similar cultural groupings to study

similarities and differences. Through use of smallest space analysis, they have constructed two-dimensional maps that illustrate the similarities in work values and attitudes between countries. These syntheses, one of which is provided in Figure 5-8, help us to understand intercultural similarities.

5. Recent research by Trompenaars has examined five relationship orientations: universalism-particularism, individualism-communitarianism, affective-neutral, specific-diffuse and achievement-ascription.

Trompenaars also looked at attitudes toward time and the environment. The result is a wealth of information helping to explain how cultures differ as well as practical ways in which MNCs can do business effectively in these environments. In particular, his findings update those of Hofstede while at the same time help to support the previous work by both Hofstede and Ronen and Shenkar on clustering countries.

Key Terms

achievement culture	emotional culture	power distance
ascription culture	femininity	smallest space analysis (SSA)
collectivism	individualism	specific culture
communitarianism	masculinity	uncertainty avoidance
culture	neutral culture	universalism
diffuse culture	particularism	values

Review and Discussion Questions

1. What is meant by the term "culture"? In what way can measuring attitudes about the following help to differentiate between cultures: centralized or decentralized decision making, safety or risk, individual or group rewards, high or low organizational loyalty, cooperation or competition? Use these attitudes to compare the United States, Germany, and Japan. Based on your comparisons, what conclusions can you draw regarding the impact of culture on behavior?

2. What is meant by the term "value"? Are cultural values the same worldwide, or are there marked differences? Are these values changing over time, or are they fairly constant? How does your answer relate to the role of values in a culture?

3. What are the four dimensions of culture studied by Geert Hofstede? Identify and describe each. What is the cultural profile of the United States? Of Asian countries? Of Latin American countries? Of Latin European countries? Based on your comparisons of these four profiles, what conclusions can you draw

regarding cultural challenges facing individuals in one group when they interact with individuals in one of the other groups?

4. Of what value is Figure 5-8 to the study of international management? Offer at least three advantages or benefits of the figure.

5. As people engage in more international travel and become more familiar with other countries, will cultural differences decline as a roadblock to international understanding, or will they continue to be a major barrier? Defend your answer.

6. What are the characteristics of each of the following pairs of cultural characteristics derived from Trompenaars' research: universalism vs. particularism, neutral vs. emotional, specific vs. diffuse, achievement vs. ascription? Compare and contrast each pair.

7. In what way is time a cultural factor? In what way is the need to control the environment a cultural factor? Give an example for each.

Internet Exercise: BMW Goes National and International

BMW is an internationally known auto firm. However, in recent years the company has been finding that its success in Europe does not necessarily translate into the American market, the largest, richest target for overseas sales. Visit both BMW sites, the one in Europe and the one in the United States. The addresses for these are **www.bmw.com** and **www.bmw-usa.com** and carefully examine what the big automaker is doing in both markets.

Compare and contrast both the similarities and the differences. Then answer these three questions: (1) How do you think cultural differences affect the way the firm operates in Europe vis-à-vis the United States? (2) In what way is culture a factor in auto sales? (3) Is it possible for a car company to transcend national culture and produce a global automobile that is accepted by people in every culture? Why or why not?

Taiwan

Taiwan is an island located 100 miles off the southeast coast of the China mainland. The island is only 13,900 square miles, but its population is approximately 23 million, one of the highest population densities in the world. In 1949, the government of the Republic of China (ROC) moved to Taiwan after establishment of the communist government on the mainland. China still considers Taiwan to be a breakaway province. Taiwan has been controlled by the Nationalists through the years, but Lee Teng-hui was chosen in the first democratic election on March 23, 1996. The literacy rate is 90 percent, and many people speak English. Taiwan is known as one of the four Tigers of Asia (along with South Korea, Singapore, and Hong Kong). The gross national product is approximately $315 billion, and per-capita income is around $15,000. This is relatively low by U.S., Japanese, and Western European standards, but much higher than that in mainland China. This so-called Other China has moved its export-oriented economy into high gear: A good example is the computer industry, which is growing by leaps and bounds.

A few years ago, many people would have scoffed at a consumer who was buying computer equipment made in Taiwan. The country's computer equipment, in the eyes of the world, consisted of rip-offs or copycat machines clearly inferior to the name brands. However, Taiwan's computer industry now has a very different reputation. In recent years, Sun Microsystems, Microsoft, and Intel, to name but three computer firms, have gone to Taiwan and cut deals to have hardware built there; Sun Microsystems, for example, has entered into a deal with the Taiwanese to build versions of SPARCstation. Aware that this development could greatly affect their own ability to produce chips for PC clones, Microsoft and Intel immediately started their own search for Taiwanese suppliers. All three

MNCs have come to realize not only that Taiwan manufacturers are less expensive but also have highly developed technology and likely will be a major source of PCs during the years ahead.

In 1987, Taiwan shipped 2 million personal computers. By the early 1990s, this number was up to 3 million and still is growing today. In fact, Taiwan has now leapfrogged South Korea in the production of PCs and entered into a series of private-label contracts with U.S. importers. Not only were Taiwanese firms able to offer state-of-the-art technology, but because they could obtain more of their components locally, they offered lower prices than even the Japanese.

Taiwan does not intend to rest on its laurels. As one knowledgeable observer has noted, "Ultimately, Taiwan's PC makers will have to shift to more sophisticated machines. They'll also have to time the move right—before the market takes off, but not way before." Many international experts believe that because of its previous successes, Taiwan will be able to meet this new challenge.
www.asiapages.com.sg/vgt/welcome.htm

Questions

1. What are some current issues facing Taiwan? What is the climate for doing business in Taiwan today?

2. In terms of cultural dimensions, is Taiwan much different from the United States? (Use Figure 5-8 in your answer.) Why or why not?

3. In what way might culture be a stumbling block for firms seeking to set up businesses in Taiwan?

4. How are the three firms in this case managing to sidestep or overcome the cultural barriers?

A Jumping-Off Place

A successful, medium-sized U.S. manufacturing firm in Ohio has decided to open a plant near Madrid, Spain. The company was attracted to this location for three reasons. First, the firm's current licensing agreement with a German firm is scheduled to come to an end within 6 months, and the U.S. manufacturer feels that it can do a better job of building and selling heavy machinery in the EU than the German firm. Second, the U.S. manufacturer has invested almost $300 million in R&D over the last 3 years. The result is a host of new patents and other technological breakthroughs that now make this company a worldwide leader in the production of specialized heavy equipment. Third, labor costs in Spain are lower than in most other EU countries, and the company feels that this will prove extremely helpful in its efforts to capture market share in Greater Europe.

Because this is the manufacturer's first direct venture into the EU, it has decided to take on a Spanish partner. The latter will provide much of the on-site support, such as local contracts, personnel hiring, legal assistance, and governmental negotiations. In turn, the U.S. manufacturer will provide the capital for renovating the manufacturing plant, the R&D technology, and the technical training.

If the venture works out as planned, the partners will expand operations into Italy and use this location as a jumping-off point for tapping the Central and Eastern European markets. Additionally, because the cultures of Spain and Italy are similar, the U.S. manufacturer feels that staying within the Latin European cultural cluster can be synergistic. Plans for later in the decade call for establishing operations in northern France, which will serve as a jumping-off point for both Northern Europe and other major EU countries, such as Germany, the Netherlands, and Belgium. However, the company first wants to establish a foothold in Spain and get this operation working successfully; then it will look into expansion plans.

Questions

1. In what way will the culture of Spain be different from that of the United States? In answering this question, refer to Figures 5-5, 5-6, 5-7, and 5-8.

2. If the company expands operations into Italy, will its experience in Spain be valuable, or will the culture be so different that the manufacturer will have to begin anew in determining how to address cultural challenges and opportunities? Explain.

3. If the firm expands into France, will its previous experiences in Spain and Italy be valuable in helping the company address cultural challenges? Be complete in your answer.

Chapter 6

Managing across Cultures

Objectives of the Chapter

Traditionally, both scholars and practitioners have assumed the universality of management. There was a tendency to take those management concepts and techniques that worked at home into other countries and cultures. It is now clear, both from practice and cross-cultural research, that this universality assumption of management, at least across cultures, does not hold up. Although there is a tendency in a borderless economy and with global integration strategies of MNCs to promote a universalist approach, there is enough evidence from cross-cultural researchers such as Nancy Adler and others to conclude that the universalist assumption that may have held for U.S. organizations and employees is not generally true in other cultures.[1]

The overriding purpose of this chapter is to examine how MNCs can and should manage across cultures. This chapter puts into practice the previous Chapter 5 on the meaning and dimensions of culture and serves as a foundation and point of departure for subsequent Chapters 9 and 10 on strategic management. The first part addresses the traditional tendency to attempt to replicate successful home country operations overseas without addressing cultural differences. Next, attention is given to cross-cultural challenges, focusing on how differences can impact on multinational management strategies. Finally, the cultures in specific countries and geographic regions are examined. The specific objectives of this chapter are:

1. **EXAMINE** the impact of globalization and national responsiveness on international strategic management.

2. **DISCUSS** cross-cultural differences and similarities.

3. **REVIEW** cultural differences in select countries and regions, and note some of the important strategic guidelines for doing business in each.

BusinessWeek

World of Business Week:

The Big Cleanup Begins

It's a salvage operation extending from Jakarta's Jalan Sudriman financial strip to the concrete canyons of Tokyo's Ohtemachi banking quarter. The goal: To move almost $1 trillion in bad loans off the books of the regions' banks and create a smaller and sounder bank sector that can start lending again. The cost: easily in the hundreds of billions of dollars. The chance of success: probably not better than 50-50 given the enormity of the problem, the weakening state of Asia's economies, and the likelihood of political backlash. The cost of failure: huge, since the banking crisis is starving Asia of essential credit.

Policymakers should have tackled the bank mess months or even years ago. Yet financial technocrats are finally starting to talk a serious game across the region—in Japan, South Korea, Thailand, Indonesia, and Malaysia. While the details may vary, all five have or will set up rough versions of the U.S. Resolution Trust Corp. that played a critical role in ending the savings and loan crisis of the 1980s. The RTC conducted audits, shut down thrifts, and sold off their loans and underlying collateral as repackaged securities or via public auctions, usually at discounts to their face value. None of the Asian workouts will probably match the RTC in ruthlessness. But if they can tackle the worst problems, it will be a giant step forward.

Most important, of course, is the "Total Plan" announced by Japan to fix the country's banks. The plan would shake up failed institutions, remove

managers, and even close some banks' doors. And in Seoul, where authorities shut down five smaller lenders on June 29, the government will impose mergers on the major commercial banks if need be.

Favored Deadbeats

Accountability and shotgun mergers? You wouldn't have heard such talk a year ago. Now, Japan, Korea, and the Tigers of Southeast Asia are under intense pressure by the markets to clean up the mess left by reckless lending to overextended real estate developers, coddled state-run enterprises, and politically favored corporate deadbeats. If they don't clean up the banks, fresh capital may not flow into the region for years to come.

The Japanese plan gives a good idea of what these workout vehicles are like. A new Financial Supervisory Agency, staffed mostly by former MOF (Ministry of Finance) officials, will conduct audits of banks' books and have the power to close problem banks and appoint financial receivers. At banks earmarked for shutdown, regulators will transfer deposits and loans to one of several new "bridge banks" funded by state-owned Heisei Financial Rehabilitation Corp. The bridge banks will keep credit flowing to sound borrowers but cut off unsound customers and force them into bankruptcy. The bridge bank will look for merger partners for up to five years before shutting down failed bank operations for good.

That's the theory. The rub is that any real cleanup would have to cut off new loans to the overextended construction and real estate companies that bankroll

Prime Minister Ryutaro Hashimoto's ruling Liberal Democratic Party. So politics may enter into the decision on which banks get a lifeline. A tough plan will also throw thousands of bank employees out into the streets. ING Barings Ltd. analyst James Fiorillo figures seven major banks—including Nippon Credit Bank, Yasuda Trust & Banking, and Daiwa Bank—could be candidates for such restructuring. The burning question is whether the government has the will to flush out the bad debts and pull the trigger on chronically ill banks.

Although the common assumption is that the banks can only sell their problem loans for a third of their face value, that may be too low. In Thailand, ground zero of the regional crisis, public auctions of autos and auto loans have fetched 50% to 60% of their book value, thanks to bids by companies like GE Capital Services Inc., which has snapped up $500 million worth. Most thought these assets would fetch only 40% of book value. Some property-backed loans, to be sold off later this month, may recoup half their value, too, reckons Salomon Smith Barney Vice President James Mitchell. "The foreigners are ready to buy."

Not all the workout plans are as tough as they could be. Malaysia will launch a gentler version of the RTC to take on problem loans, work out repayment plans with debts, and broker mergers. Yet it has also slashed reserve requirements to prevent outright failures. In China, home to $200 billion in dud loans, a workout vehicle isn't even on the table. Instead, Beijing is shutting down poorly managed local bank branches, nudging loan-classification standards closer to international levels, and training bankers to assess risk.

As the Asian crisis grinds on, global investors can easily avoid the countries that keep propping up their sickest banks. Sloppy lending triggered the meltdown. Fixing the banks, credibly and quickly, is the best way out.

By Brian Bremner in Tokyo, with Moon Ihlwan in Seoul, Bruce Einhorn in Hong Kong, and Michael Shari in Jakarta.

Source: July 20, 1998, pp. 46–47 issue of *Business Week* by special permission, copyright © 1998 by the McGraw-Hill Companies, Inc.

The news story that opens this chapter highlights the importance of finding a global solution to Asia's economic problems. From Thailand, Indonesia, and Malaysia in emerging economies in Southeast Asia to more developed countries in Japan and South Korea, the cultural resistance that has delayed a workable solution to the banking crisis of recent years appears to be slowly coming to an end. Faced with hundreds of billions of dollars in bad loans, weakened economies, and a lack of fresh capital, Asian policy makers have finally conceded that they are ready to face their problems and accept the necessary, albeit painful, solutions. Massive layoffs, bank closings, and radical changes to bankruptcy laws have created cultural and political resistance in the form of labor demonstrations and political cronyism, adding to investors' lack of confidence in the region. As you read through the chapter, keep in mind the difficulties foreign companies might have when managing in an environment such as that described in this article. Moreover, consider why cultural change might go hand in hand with economic change when competing in this type of environment.

The Strategy for Managing across Cultures

Awareness of cultural similarities and differences is becoming increasingly important to the successful strategies of MNCs as they become more transnational.[2] A good example is Asea Brown Boveri (ABB), the giant multinational conglomerate formed by the merger of Swedish, German, and Swiss firms. Although headquartered in Zurich, Switzerland, it has operations throughout the world.[3] Over the past two decades, this MNC has bought or taken minority positions in more than 60 firms, including U.S. companies such as Combustion Engineering, well-known for its manufacture of power generation and process automation equipment, and Westinghouse's transmission and distribution operations. In addition to making locomotives in Sweden, ABB has a diverse product line, including robots, electric power equipment, thermonuclear reaction equipment, and hospital instruments. Because of its global business, this MNC is forced to balance a concern for globalization with a need to address local or regional needs.

How does ABB accomplish this feat? Obviously, the MNC must develop state-of-the-art quality products and services; however, it also needs to learn about the differing cultural contexts of the far-flung operations and unique needs of its customers. For example, when ABB won a $420 million contract to build locomotives for moving freight through the Alps, part of this success resulted from realizing the deep concern that the Swiss have for the environment. Realizing this cultural value resulted in the company's designing trains that would be strong enough to get the job done but not pollute the environment. Recently, ABB also won a contract to manufacture locomotives for India. The Indian government needed credit to pay for these imports, and the two countries most willing to grant such credit were Germany and Italy. Because ABB had operations in both of these nations and was building locomotive components there, it was able to persuade the German and Italian governments to give India the credit that it needed. In short, ABB has learned to balance a concern for selling its products worldwide with a need to address local concerns. As the chairman of ABB noted, "We can't have people abdicating their nationalities, saying 'I am no longer German, I am international.' The world doesn't work like that. If you are selling products and services in Germany, you better be German!"[4]

The ABB examples helps to illustrate one of the major problems facing MNCs as they attempt to manage across cultures: a natural tendency to do things abroad the way they are done at home. This commonly is referred to in strategic international management as the "globalization vs. national responsiveness conflict." As used here, **globalization** is the production and distribution of products and services of a homogeneous type and quality on a worldwide basis. To a growing extent, the customers of MNCs have homogenized tastes, and this has helped to spread international consumerism. For example, throughout North America, the EU, and Japan, there has been a growing acceptance of standardized consumer electronic goods, automobiles, computers, calculators, and similar products. This goal of efficient economic performance through a universal globalization strategy, however, has left MNCs open to the charge that they are overlooking the need to address national responsiveness.

National responsiveness is the need to understand the different consumer tastes in segmented regional markets and respond to different national standards and regulations imposed by autonomous governments and agencies. National responsiveness also relates to the need to adapt tools and techniques for managing the local workforce. Sometimes what works well in one country does not work in another, as seen by the following example:

> An American computer company introduced pay-for-performance in both the USA and the Middle East. It worked well in the USA and increased sales briefly in the Middle East before a serious slump occurred. Inquiries showed that indeed the winners among salesmen in the Middle East had done better, but the vast majority had done worse. The wish for their fellows to succeed had been seriously eroded by the contest. Overall morale and sales were down. Ill-will was contagious. When the bosses discovered that certain sales people were earning more than they did, high individual performances also ceased. But the principal reason for eventually abandoning the system was the discovery that customers were being loaded up with products they could not sell. As A tried to beat B to the bonus, the care of customers began to slip, with serious, if delayed, results.[5]

Globalization vs. National Responsiveness Matrix

The issue of globalization vs. national responsiveness can be analyzed conceptually via a two-dimensional matrix. Figure 6–1 provides an example.

The vertical axis in the figure measures the need for economic integration, frequently referred to as globalization. Movement up the axis results in a greater degree of economic integration. Globalization generates economies of scale (takes advantage of large size) and also capital on further lower unit costs (through experience curve benefits) as a firm moves into worldwide markets selling its products or services. These economies are captured through centralizing specific activities in the value-added chain. They also occur by reaping the benefits of increased coordination and control of geographically dispersed activities.

The horizontal axis measures the need for multinationals to respond to national responsiveness or differentiation. This suggests that MNCs must address local tastes and government regulations. The result may be a geographic dispersion of activities or a decentralization of coordination and control for individual MNCs.

Figure 6–1 depicts four basic situations in relation to the degrees of globalization vs. national responsiveness. Quadrants 1 and 4 are the simplest cases. In quadrant 1, the need for integration is high and for awareness of differentiation low. In terms of economies of scale, this situation leads to globalization strategies based on price competition. In this quadrant 1-type of environment, mergers and acquisitions often occur. The opposite situation is represented by quadrant 4, where the need for differentiation is high but the concern for integration low. Besides the term "national responsiveness," this quadrant is also referred to as "multi-domestic" strategies. In this case, niche companies adapt products to satisfy the high demands of differentiation and ignore economies of scale because integration is not very important.

Globalization
The production and distribution of products and services of a homogeneous type and quality on a worldwide basis.

National responsiveness
The need to understand the different consumer tastes in segmented regional markets and respond to different national standards and regulations imposed by autonomous governments and agencies.

Figure 6–1

**Globalization vs.
National
Responsiveness**

National responsiveness (differentiation)

	Low	High
High	1 Globalization strategy	3 Mixed strategy (Transnational strategy)
Low	2 Mixed strategy (International strategy)	4 National responsiveness (Multi-domestic) strategy

Globalization (intergration)

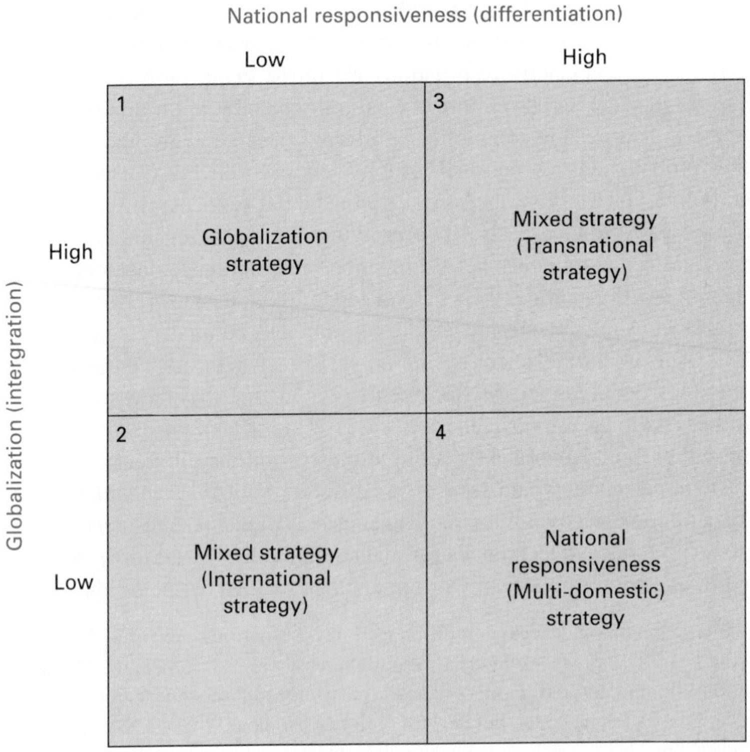

Source: Adapted from information in Christopher A. Bartlett and Sumantra Ghoshal, *Managing across Borders: The Transnational Solution 2nd ed.* (Boston: Harvard Business School Press, 1998).

Quadrants 2 and 3 reflect more complex environmental situations. Quadrant 2 incorporates those cases in which both the need for integration and awareness of differentiation are low. Both the potential to obtain economies of scale and the benefits of being sensitive to differentiation are of little value. Typical strategies in quadrant 2 are characterized by increased international standardization of products and services. This mixed approach is often referred to as just international strategies. This situation can lead to lower needs for centralized quality control and centralized strategic decision making, while simultaneously eliminating requirements to adapt activities to individual countries.

In quadrant 3, the needs for integration and differentiation are high. There is a strong need for integration in production along with higher requirements for regional differentiation in marketing. MNCs trying to simultaneously achieve these objectives often refer to them as their transnational strategies. Quadrant 3 is the most challenging quadrant and one where successful MNCs seek to operate. The problem for many MNCs, however, is the cultural challenges associated with "localizing" a global focus.

Meeting the Challenge

Globalization imperative
A belief that one worldwide approach to doing business is the key to both efficiency and effectiveness.

Research reveals that far from addressing regional differentiation issues, many MNCs are committed to a **globalization imperative,** which is a belief that one worldwide approach to doing business is the key to both efficiency and effectiveness. One study, involving extensive examination of 115 medium and large MNCs and 103 affiliated subsidiaries in the United States, Canada, France, Germany, Japan, and the United Kingdom, found an overwhelming preponderance to use the same strategies abroad as at home.[6]

Despite these tendencies to use home strategies, effective MNCs are continuing their efforts to address local needs. A number of factors are helping to facilitate this need to develop unique strategies for different cultures, including:

1. The diversity of worldwide industry standards such as those in broadcasting, where television sets must be manufactured on a country-by-country basis.

2. A continual demand by local customers for differentiated products, as in the case of consumer goods that must meet local tastes.

3. The importance of being an insider, as in the case of customers who prefer to "buy local."

4. The difficulty of managing global organizations, as in the case of some local subsidiaries that want more decentralization and others that want less.

5. The need to allow subsidiaries to use their own abilities and talents and not be restrained by headquarters, as in the case of local units that know how to customize products for their market and generate high returns on investment with limited production output.

By responding to the cultural needs of local operations and customers, MNCs find that regional strategies can be used effectively in capturing and maintaining worldwide market niches. One of the best examples is Thomson Consumer Electronics, which has factories in four European countries: France, Germany, Spain, and the United Kingdom. Each factory assembles specific types of television sets for the European market. The German plant, for example, makes high-feature, large TV sets; the Spanish plant focuses on low-cost, small-screen sets. At the same time, Thomson has operations in North America, where it makes TV sets under the RCA and GE nameplates, drawing on suppliers and subassemblers, mostly in Mexico, to produce units for the regional market. Another example is Warner-Lambert, which has manufacturing facilities in Belgium, France, Germany, Italy, Ireland, Spain, and the United Kingdom. Each plant is specialized and produces a small number of products for the entire European market; in this way, each can focus on tailoring products for the unique demands of the various markets.

The globalization vs. national responsiveness challenge is even more acute when marketing cosmetics and other products that vary greatly in consumer use. For example, marketers sell toothpaste as a cosmetic product in Spain and Greece but as a cavity-fighter in the Netherlands and United States. Soap manufacturers market their product as a cosmetic item in Spain but as a functional commodity in Germany. Moreover, the way in which the marketing message is delivered also is important. For example:

- Germans want advertising that is factual and rational; they fear being manipulated by "the hidden persuader." The typical German spot features the standards family of two parents, two children, and grandmother.
- The French avoid reasoning or logic. Their advertising is predominantly emotional, dramatic, and symbolic. Spots are viewed as cultural events—art for the sake of money—and are reviewed as if they were literature or films.
- The British value laughter above all else. The typical broad, self-deprecating British commercial amuses by mocking both the advertiser and consumer.[7]

Meanwhile, in China McDonald's has worked hard to befriend young children and make them feel special. One way is by recording their names and birthdates in a special list called "The Book of Little Honorary Guests," and then sending them cards and urging them to drop by their local McDonald's.

> The burger joints are all run by locals. And far from accepting the same McDonald's that Americans do, Asian consumers gradually twist McDonald's to their own purposes. Rather than being fast, efficient take-out joints, many McDonald's restaurants are more akin to Seattle coffee houses—places to hang out for the young. In several places, McDonald's has gone so native that many of its customers do not realize it is American. In China, one of its appeals is the fact that its menu is so limited; there is no danger of losing face because the table next door orders a more expensive dish. As [one observer] concludes, people come for the experience, not the product; and they make sure that it is their experience—not one foisted upon them by an American juggernaut.[8]

In some cases, however, both the product and the marketing message are similar worldwide. This is particularly true for high-end products, where the lifestyles and expectations of the market niche are similar regardless of the country. Heineken beer, Hennessey brandy, Porsche cars, and the *Financial Times* all appeal to consumer niches that are fairly homogeneous, regardless of geographic locale. The same is true at the lower end of the market for goods that are impulse purchases, novel products, or fast foods, such as Coca-Cola's soft drinks, Levi's jeans, pop music, and ice-cream bars. In most cases, however, it is necessary to modify products as well as the market approach for the regional or local market. One analysis noted that the more marketers understand about the way in which a particular culture tends to view emotion, enjoyment, friendship, humor, rules, status, and other culturally based behaviors, the more control they have over creating marketing messages that will be interpreted in the desired way.

Figure 6–2 provides an example of the role that culture should play in advertising by recapping the five relationship orientations identified through Trompenaars' research (see Chapter 5). Figure 6–2 shows how value can be added to the marketing approach by carefully tailoring the advertising message to the particular culture. For example, advertising in the United States should target individual achievement, be expressive and direct, and appeal to U.S. values of success through personal hard work. On the other hand, the focus in China and other Asian countries should be much more indirect and subtle, emphasizing group references, shared responsibility, and interpersonal trust.

The need to adjust global strategies for regional markets presents three major challenges for most MNCs. First, the MNC must stay abreast of local market conditions and sidestep the temptation to assume that all markets are basically the same. Second, the MNC must know the strengths and weaknesses of its subsidiaries so that it can provide these units with the assistance needed in addressing local demands. Third, the multinational must give the subsidiary more autonomy so that it can respond to changes in local demands. "International Management in Action: Ten Key Factors for MNC Success" provides additional insights into the ways that successful MNCs address these challenges.

Cross-Cultural Differences and Similarities

As shown in Chapter 5, culture can be similar or quite different across countries. The challenge for MNCs is to recognize and effectively manage these similarities and differences. For instance, the way in which MNCs manage their home businesses often should be different from the way they manage their overseas operations. After recognizing the danger for MNCs to drift toward parochialism and simplification because of cultural differences, the discussion shifts to some examples of both cultural similarities and differences and how to effectively manage across cultures by a contingency approach.

Parochialism and Simplification

Parochialism
The tendency to view the world through one's own eyes and perspectives.

Parochialism is the tendency to view the world through one's own eyes and perspectives. This can be a difficult problem for many international managers, who often come from advanced economies and believe that their state-of-the-art knowledge is more than adequate to handle the challenges of doing business in lesser-developed countries. In addition, many of these managers have had a parochial point of view fostered by their background. A good example is provided by Randall and Coakley, who studied the impact of culture on successful partnerships in the former Soviet Union. Initially after the breakup of the Soviet Union, the republics called themselves the Commonwealth of Independent States or CIS. This term will be used to refer to the former Soviet Union. They found that while outside MNC managers typically entered into partnerships with CIS enterprises with a view

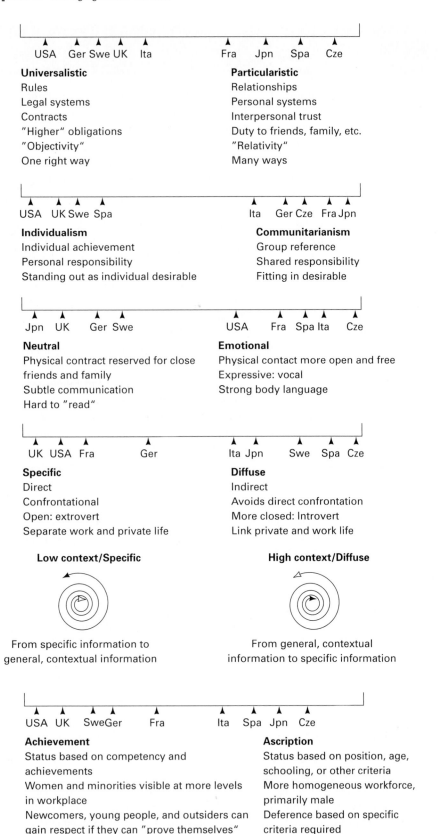

Figure 6–2

Trompenaars' Cultural Dimensions and Advertising: Adjusting the Message for Local Meaning

Universalistic
Rules
Legal systems
Contracts
"Higher" obligations
"Objectivity"
One right way

Particularistic
Relationships
Personal systems
Interpersonal trust
Duty to friends, family, etc.
"Relativity"
Many ways

Individualism
Individual achievement
Personal responsibility
Standing out as individual desirable

Communitarianism
Group reference
Shared responsibility
Fitting in desirable

Neutral
Physical contract reserved for close
friends and family
Subtle communication
Hard to "read"

Emotional
Physical contact more open and free
Expressive: vocal
Strong body language

Specific
Direct
Confrontational
Open: extrovert
Separate work and private life

Diffuse
Indirect
Avoids direct confrontation
More closed: Introvert
Link private and work life

Low context/Specific

From specific information to
general, contextual information

High context/Diffuse

From general, contextual
information to specific information

Achievement
Status based on competency and
achievements
Women and minorities visible at more levels
in workplace
Newcomers, young people, and outsiders can
gain respect if they can "prove themselves"

Ascription
Status based on position, age,
schooling, or other criteria
More homogeneous workforce,
primarily male
Deference based on specific
criteria required

Source: Lisa Hoecklin, *Managing Cultural Differences* (Workingham, England: Addison-Wesley, 1995), p. 107, which is drawn from information found in Fons Trompenaars, *Riding the Waves of Culture* (New York: Irwin, 1994).

International Management in Action

Ten Key Factors for MNC Success   www.url.com

Why are some international firms successful while others are not? Some of the main reasons are that successful multinational firms take a worldwide view of operations, support their overseas activities, pay close attention to political winds, and use local nationals whenever possible. These are the overall findings of a report that looked into the development of customized executive education programs. Specifically, there are 10 factors or guidelines that successful global firms seem to employ. Successful global competitors:

1. See themselves as multinational enterprises and are led by a management team that is comfortable in the world arena.

2. Develop integrated and innovative strategies that make it difficult and costly for other firms to compete.

3. Aggressively and effectively implement their worldwide strategy and back it with large investments.

4. Understand that technologic innovation no longer is confined to the United States and

develop systems for tapping technologic innovation abroad.

5. Operate as if the world is one large market rather than a series of individual, small markets.

6. Have organization structures that are designed to handle their unique problems and challenges and thus provide them the greatest efficiency.

7. Develop a system that keeps them informed about political changes around the world and the implications of these changes on the firm.

8. Have management teams that are international in composition and thus better able to respond to the various demands of their respective markets.

9. Allow their outside directors to play an active role in the operation of the enterprise.

10. Are well managed and tend to follow such important guidelines as sticking close to the customer, having lean organization structures, and encouraging autonomy and entrepreneurial activity among the personnel.

---

toward making them efficient and profitable, the CIS managers often brought a different set of priorities to the table. As a result, some of the practices that were implemented by the CIS mangers did not generate profit—but they were culturally acceptable in the CIS. These included:

1. Some managers laid off as much as 30–40 percent of their workforces in order to reduce overemployment. While this was a good start, many more needed to be let go, but the managers kept them on because they felt a social obligation to help provide employment and services for the workers and their families.

2. Many high-tech CIS managers and their scientists wanted to produce and sell products in the international arena, but they downplayed the need for making a systematic analysis of the competition and evaluating the needs of customers. They believed that if they could simply build a technologically superior product they would be able to succeed in the world marketplace.

3. Most CIS managers believed that the first responsibility of the partnership was to provide jobs to people. So even when it came to maximizing core competencies and remaining competitive in this area, the company was viewed as a vehicle for providing health care, education, social goods and services, and basic full-time employment to the personnel. In fact, CIS managers were adamant regarding the fact that profits were not as important in achieving a successful partnership arrangement.[9]

Commenting on their research, Randall and Coakley noted that the way CIS managers do business is sharply different from that of their American counterparts. In particular, there is an inconsistency between CIS cultural norms, their past training, and their work experiences, and the emerging economic structure and way in which they must do business if they hope to succeed in the international arena. This led the researchers to conclude:

> As behavioral change continues to lag behind structural change, it becomes imperative to understand that this inconsistency between what economic demands and cultural norms require manifests problems and complexities far beyond mere structural change. In short, the implications of the different perspectives on technology, labor, and production . . . for potential partnerships between U.S. and CIS companies need to be fully grasped by all parties entering into any form of relationship.[10]

Simplification is the process of exhibiting the same orientation toward different cultural groups. For example, the way in which a U.S. manager interacts with a British manager is the same way in which he or she behaves when doing business with an Asian executive. Moreover, this orientation reflects one's basic culture. Table 6–1 provides an example, showing several widely agreed-on, basic cultural orientations and the range of variations for each. Asterisks indicate the dominant U.S. orientation. Quite obviously, U.S. cultural values are not the same as those of managers from other cultures; as a result, a U.S. manager's attempt to simplify things can result in erroneous behavior. Here is an example of a member of the purchasing department of a large European oil company who was negotiating an order with a Korean supplier.

> At the first meeting, the Korean partner offered a silver pen to the European manager. The latter, however, politely refused the present for fear of being bribed (even though he knew about the Korean custom of giving presents). Much to our manager's surprise, the second meeting began with the offer of a stereo system. Again the manager refused, his fear of being bribed probably heightened. When he gazed at a piece of Korean china on the third meeting, he finally realized what was going on. His refusal had not been taken to mean: "let's get on with business right away," but rather: "If you want to get into business with me, you had better come up with something bigger."[11]

Understanding the culture in which they do business can make international managers more effective. Unfortunately, when placed in a culture with which they are unfamiliar,

Simplification
The process of exhibiting the same orientation toward different culture groups.

Table 6–1
Six Basic Cultural Variations

Orientations	Range of Variations
What is the nature of people?	Good (changeable/unchangeable) A mixture of good and evil* Evil (changeable/unchangeable)
What is the person's relationship to nature?	Dominant* In harmony with nature Subjugation
What is the person's relationship to other people?	Lineal (hierarchic) Collateral (collectivist) Individualist*
What is the modality of human activity?	Doing* Being and becoming Being
What is the temporal focus of human activity?	Future* Present Past
What is the conception of space?	Private* Mixed Public

Note: *Indicates the dominant U.S. orientation.

Source: Adapted from information found in Florence Rockwood Kluckhohn and Fred L. Stodtbeck, *Variations in Value Orientations* (New York: Peterson Publishing, 1961).

most international managers are not culturally knowledgeable, so they often misinterpret what is happening. This is particularly true when the environment is markedly different from the one in which they live. Consider, for example, the difference between the cultures in Japan and the United States. Japan has what could be called a high-context culture, which possesses characteristics such as:

1. Relationships between people are relatively long-lasting, and individuals feel deep personal involvement with each other.

2. Communication often is implicit, and individuals are taught from an early age to interpret these messages accurately.

3. People in authority are personally responsible for the actions of their subordinates, and this places a premium on loyalty to both superiors and subordinates.

4. Agreements tend to be spoken rather than written.

5. Insiders and outsiders are easily distinguishable, and outsiders typically do not gain entrance to the inner group.

These Japanese cultural characteristics are markedly different from those of low-context cultures such as the United States, which possess the following characteristics:

1. Relationships between individuals are relatively short in duration, and in general, deep personal involvement with others is not valued greatly.

2. Messages are explicit, and individuals are taught from a very early age to say exactly what they mean.

3. Authority is diffused throughout the bureaucratic system, and personal responsibility is hard to pin down.

4. Agreements tend to be in writing rather than spoken.

5. Insiders and outsiders are not readily distinguished, and the latter are encouraged to join the inner circle.[12]

These differences help to explain why Japanese managers in the United States often have trouble managing local operations, and vice versa. At the same time, it is important to realize that while there are cultural differences, there also are similarities. Therefore, in managing across cultures, not everything is totally different. Some approaches that work at home also work well in other cultural settings.

Similarities across Cultures

When internationalization began to take off in the 1970s, many companies quickly admitted that it would not be possible to do business in the same way in every corner of the globe. There was a secret hope, however, that many of the procedures and strategies that worked so well at home could be adopted overseas without modification. This has proved to be a false hope. At the same time, some similarities across cultures have been uncovered by researchers. For example, the co-author of this text (Luthans) and his associates studied through direct observation a sample of managers ($n = 66$) in the largest textile factory in Russia to determine their activities.[13] Similar to U.S. managers studied earlier, Russian managers carried out traditional management, communication, human resources, and networking activities. The study also found that again similar to U.S. managers, the relative attention given to the networking activity increased the Russian managers' opportunities for promotion, and communication activity was a significant predictor of effective performance in both Russia and the United States.[14]

Besides the similarities of managerial activities, another study at the same Russian factory tested whether organizational behavior modification (O.B. Mod.) interventions that led to performance improvements in U.S. organizations would hold true in Russia.[15] As with the applications of O.B. Mod. in the United States, Russian supervisors were trained to administer contingently social rewards (attention and recognition) and positive feedback when they observed workers engaging in behaviors that contributed to the production of quality fabric. In addition, Russian supervisors were taught to give corrective feedback for behaviors that reduced product quality. The researchers found that this O.B. Mod. approach, which had worked so well in the United States, also produced positive results in the Russian factory, and they concluded that "the class of interventions associated with organizational behavior modification are likely to be useful in meeting the challenges faced by Russian workers and managers is given initial support by the results of this study.[16]

In another cross-cultural study, this time using a large Korean sample (1,192 employees in 27 large Korean firms), Luthans and colleagues analyzed whether demographic and situational factors identified in the U.S.-based literature had the same antecedent influence on the commitment of Korean employees.[17] As in the U.S. studies, Korean employees' position in the hierarchy, tenure in their current position, and age all related to organizational commitment. Other similarities with U.S. firms included: (1) as organizational size increased, commitment declined; (2) as structure became more employee-focused, commitment increased; and (3) the more positive the perceptions of organizational climate, the greater the employee commitment. The following conclusion was drawn:

> This study provides beginning evidence that popular constructs in the U.S. management and organizational behavior literature should not be automatically dismissed as culture bound. Whereas some organizational behavior concepts and techniques do indeed seem to be culture specific . . . a growing body of literature is demonstrating the ability to cross-culturally validate other concepts and techniques, such as behavior management. . . . This study contributed to this cross-cultural evidence for the antecedents to organizational commitment. The antecedents for Korean employees' organizational commitment was found to be similar to their American counterparts.[18]

Many Differences across Cultures

Despite similarities between cultures in some studies, far more differences than similarities have been found. In particularly, MNCs are discovering that they must carefully investigate and understand the culture where they intend to do business and modify their approaches appropriately.

Sometimes these cultures are quite different from the United States—as well as from each other! One human resource management (HRM) example has been offered by Trompenaars, who examined the ways in which personnel in international subsidiaries were appraised by their managers. The head office had established the criteria to be used in these evaluations, but left the prioritization of the criteria to the national operating company. As a result, the outcome of the evaluations could be quite different from country to country because what was regarded as the most important criterion in one subsidiary might be ranked much lower on the evaluation list of another subsidiary. In the case of Shell Oil, for example, Trompenaars found that the firm was using a HAIRL system of appraisal. The five criteria in this acronym stood for: (a) Helicopter—the capacity to take a broad view from above; (b) Analysis—the ability to evaluate situations logically and completely; (c) Imagination—the ability to be creative and think outside the box; (d) Reality—the ability to use information realistically; and (e) Leadership—the ability to effectively galvanize and inspire personnel. When Shell's operating companies were asked to prioritize these five criteria, the results were as follows:

Netherlands	France	Germany	Britain
Reality	Imagination	Leadership	Helicopter
Analysis	Analysis	Analysis	Imagination
Helicopter	Leadership	Reality	Reality
Leadership	Helicopter	Imagination	Analysis
Imagination	Reality	Helicopter	Leadership

Quite obviously, personnel in different operating companies were being evaluated differently. In fact, none of the operating companies in the above four countries had the same criteria at the top of their list. Moreover, the criterion that was at the top of the list for operating companies in the Netherlands—reality—was at the bottom of the list for those in France; and the one at the top of the list in French operating companies—imagination—was at the bottom of that of the Dutch firms. Similarly, the German operating companies put leadership at the top of their list and helicopter at the bottom, while the British companies did just the opposite! In fact, the whole list for the Germans are in the exact reverse order from the British.[19]

Other HRM differences can be found in areas such as wages, compensation, pay equity, and maternity leave. Here are some representative examples.

1. The concept of an hourly wage plays a minor role in Mexico. Labor law requires that employees receive full pay 365 days a year.

2. In Austria and Brazil, employees with 1 year of service are automatically given 30 days of paid vacation.

3. Some jurisdictions in Canada have legislated pay equity—known in the United States as comparable worth—between male- and female-intensive jobs.

4. In Japan, compensation levels are determined using the objective factors of age, length of service, and educational background rather than skill, ability, and performance. Performance does not count until after an employee reaches age 45.

5. In the United Kingdom, employees are allowed up to 40 weeks of maternity leave, and employers must provide a government-mandated amount of pay for 18 of those weeks.

6. In 87% of large Swedish companies, the head of human resources is on the board of directors.[20]

These HRM practices certainly are quite different from those in the United States, and U.S. MNCs need to modify their approaches when they go into these countries if they hope to be successful. Compensation plans in particular provide an interesting area of contrast across different cultures.

Drawing on the work of Hofstede (see Chapter 5), it is possible to link cultural clusters and compensation strategies. Table 6–2 shows a host of different cultural groupings, including some in Asia, the EU, and Anglo countries. Each cluster requires a different approach to formulating an effective compensation strategy, and after analyzing each such cluster, we suggest that:

1. In Pacific Rim countries, incentive plans should be group-based. In high masculinity cultures (Japan, Hong Kong, Malaysia, the Philippines, Singapore), high salaries should be paid to senior-level managers.

2. In EU nations such as France, Spain, Italy, and Belgium, compensation strategies should be similar. In the latter two nations, however, significantly higher salaries should be paid to local senior-level managers because of the high masculinity index. In Portugal and Greece, both of which have a low individualism index, profit-sharing plans would be more effective than individual incentive plans, while in Denmark, the Netherlands, and Germany, personal-incentive plans would be highly useful because of the high individualism in these cultures.

3. In Great Britain, Ireland, and the United States, managers value their individualism and are motivated by the opportunity for earnings, recognitions, advancement, and challenge. Compensation plans should reflect these needs.[21]

Additionally, some MNCs have found that compensation plans that are very attractive to their local workforce have no value for members of their international workforce.[22]

For example, when the Gillette Company decided to offer stock to its 33,000 employees worldwide, the firm discovered that its plan was not global in terms of worker interest.[23] Other companies have had similar experiences. Some of the reasons are provided in Table 6–3; others include low employee disposable income and a feeling that stocks are risky investments. Simply put, workers in other cultures often do not have the same view

Table 6–2
Cultural Clusters in the Pacific Rim, EU, and United States

	Power Distance	Individualism	Masculinity	Uncertainty Avoidance
Pacific Rim				
Hong Kong, Malaysia, Philippines, Singapore	+	–	+	–
Japan	+	–	+	+
South Korea, Taiwan	+	–	–	+
EU and United States				
France, Spain	+	+	–	+
Italy, Belgium	+	+	+	+
Portugal	+	–		+
Greece	+	–	+	+
Denmark, Netherlands	–	+	+	–
Germany	–	+	+	+
Great Britain, Ireland, United States	–	+	+	–

Note: + indicates high or strong; – indicates low or weak.

Source: Based on research by Hofstede and put together in Richard M. Hodgetts and Fred Luthans, "U.S. Multinationals' Compensation Strategies for Local Management: Cross-Cultural Implications," *Compensation & Benefits Review,* March–April 1993, p. 47. Used with permission of the publisher, © 1993. American Management Association, New York. All rights reserved.

Table 6–3
Problems with Employee Stock Plans in Select Countries

Country	Reasons for Lack of Success
Belgium	Problematic. Some stock plans conflict with a government-imposed wage freeze.
Brazil	Impossible. Foreign-exchange controls prohibit out-of-country stock investment; phantom stock plans are a headache.
Britain	Easy. But sometimes labor unions can get in the way.
Eastern Europe	Forget it. Even if you get government permission, chances are you talked to the wrong bureaucrat.
Germany	Can I get that in deutsche marks? U.S. plans suffer when the dollar is weak.
Israel	Difficult. Exchange controls forced National Semiconductor to a third-party system, but the plan has only scant participation.
Luxembourg	Tax haven. Great place to set up a trust to administer stock plans.
Mexico	May regret it. Labor laws can force a one-time stock grant into an annual event.
Netherlands	No thanks. Employees may like the stock options, but they will not appreciate a hefty tax bill upfront.
Philippines	Time-consuming. Requires government approval and lots of worker education.

Source: Adapted from information found in Tara Parker-Pope, "Culture Clash," *Wall Street Journal,* April 12, 1995, p. R7.

of compensation plans as U.S. workers do. This is why many MNCs now are developing their own contingency-based compensation strategies that are geared toward meeting the needs of the local workers.

Figure 6–3 shows how specific HRM areas can be analyzed contingently on a country-by-country basis. Take, for example, the information on Japan. When contrasted with U.S. approaches, a significant number of differences are found. Recruitment and selection in Japanese firms often are designed to help identify those individuals who will do the best job over the long run. In the United States, people often are hired based on what they can do for the firm in the short run, because many of them eventually will quit or be downsized. Similarly, the Japanese use a great deal of cross-training, while the Americans tend to favor specialized training. The Japanese use group performance appraisal and reward people as a group; at least traditionally, Americans use manager–subordinate performance appraisal and reward people as individuals. In Japan, unions are regarded as partners; in the United States, both management and unions view each other in a much more adversarial way. Only in the area of job design, where the Japanese use a great deal of

Figure 6–3

A Partially-Completed Contingency Matrix for International Human Resources Management

	Japan	Germany	Mexico	China
Recruitment and selection	• Prepare for long process • Ensure that your firm is "here to stay" • Develop trusting relationship with recruit	• Obtain skilled labor from government subsidized apprenticeship program	• Use expatriates sparingly • Recruit Mexican nationals at U.S. colleges	• Recent public policy shifts encourage use of sophisticated selection procedures
Training	• Make substantial investment in training • Use general training and cross-training • Training as everyone's responsibility	• Reorganize and utilize apprenticeship programs • Be aware of government regulations on training	• Use bilingual trainers	• Careful observations of existing training programs • Utilize team training
Compensation	• Use recognition and praise as motivator • Avoid pay for performance	• Note high labor costs for manufacturing	• Consider all aspects of labor cost	• Use technical training as reward • Recognize egalitarian values • Use "more work more pay" with caution
Labor relations	• Treat unions as partners • Allow time for negotiations	• Be prepared for high wages and short work week • Expect high productivity from unionized workers	• Understand changing Mexican labor law • Prepare for increasing unionization of labor	• Tap large pool of labor cities • Lax labor laws may become more stringent
Job design	• Include participation • Incorporate group goal setting • Use autonomous work teams • Use uniform, formal approaches • Encourage co-worker input • Empower teams to make decision	• Utilize works councils to enhance worker participation	• Approach participation cautiously	• Determine employee's motives before implementing participation

Source: Fred Luthans, Paul A. Marsnik, and Kyle W. Luthans, "A Contingency Matrix Approach to IHRM," *Human Resource Management Journal,* © 1997. Reprinted with permission of John Wiley & Sons, Inc.

participative management and autonomous work teams, are the Americans beginning to employ a similar approach. The same types of differences can be seen in the matrix of Figure 6–3 among the United States, Germany, Mexico, and China.

These differences should not be interpreted to mean that one set of HRM practices are superior to another. In fact, recent research from Japan and Europe shows these firms often have a higher incidence of personnel-related problems than U.S. companies. For example, one study found that Japanese MNCs ($n = 34$) and European MNCs ($n = 23$) had more problems than U.S. MNCs ($n = 24$) in areas such as: (1) home-country personnel who possessed sufficient international management skills; (2) home-country personnel who wanted to work abroad; (3) difficulty in attracting high-caliber local nationals; and (4) high turnover of local employees. Additionally, when compared with Japanese MNCs, U.S. multinationals had less friction and better communication between their home-country expatriates and local employees, and there were fewer complaints by local employees regarding their ability to advance in the company.[24]

Figure 6–3 clearly indicates the importance of MNCs using a contingency approach to HRM across cultures. Not only are there different HRM practices in different cultures, there also are different practices within the same cultures. For instance, one study involving 249 U.S. affiliates of foreign-based MNCs found that in general, affiliate HRM practices closely follow local practices when dealing with the rank-and-file but even more closely approximate parent-company practices when dealing with upper-level management.[25] In other words, this study found that a hybrid approach to HRM was being used by these MNCs.

Aside from the different approaches used in different countries, it is becoming clear that common assumptions and conventional wisdom about HRM practices in certain countries no longer are valid. For example, for many years, it has been assumed that Japanese employees do not leave their jobs for work with other firms. They are loyal to their first employer, and it would be virtually impossible for MNCs operating in Japan to recruit talent from Japanese firms. Recent evidence, however, reveals that job-hopping among Japanese employees is increasingly common. One report concluded:

> While American workers, both the laid-off and the survivors, grapple with cutbacks, one in three Japanese workers willingly walks away from his job within the first 10 years of his career, according to the Japanese Institute of Labor, a private research organization. And many more are thinking about it. More than half of salaried Japanese workers say they would switch jobs or start their own business if a favorable opportunity arose, according to a survey by the Recruit Research Corporation.[26]

These findings clearly illustrate one important point: managing across cultures requires careful understanding of the local environment, because common assumptions and stereotypes may not be valid. Cultural differences must be addressed, and this is why cross-cultural research will continue to be critical in helping firms learn how to manage across cultures.[27]

Cultural Differences in Selected Countries and Regions

Chapter 5 introduced the concept of country clusters, which is the idea that certain regions of the world have similar cultures. For example, the way that Americans do business in the United States is very similar to the way that British do business in England. Even in this Anglo culture, however, there are pronounced differences, and in other clusters, such as in Asia, these differences become even more pronounced. The accompanying box, "Managing in Hong Kong," depicts such differences. Chapter 1 examined some important worldwide developments, and the following sections focus on cultural highlights and differences in selected countries and regions that provide the necessary understanding and perspective for effective management across cultures.

Managing across cultures has long been recognized as a potential problem for multinationals. To help expatriates who are posted overseas deal with a new culture, many MNCs offer special training and coaching. Often, however, little is done to change expatriates' basic cultural values or specific managerial behaviors. Simply put, this traditional approach could be called the *practical school of management thought,* which holds that effective managerial behavior is universal and a good manager in the United States also will be effective in Hong Kong or any other location around the world. In recent years, it generally has been recognized that such an approach no longer is sufficient, and there is growing support for what is called the *cross-cultural school of management thought,* which holds that effective managerial behavior is a function of the specific culture. As Black and Porter point out in a recent article, successful managerial action in Los Angeles may not be effective in Hong Kong.

Black and Porter investigated the validity of these two schools of thought by surveying U.S. managers working in Hong Kong, U.S. managers working in the United States, and Hong Kong managers working in Hong Kong. Their findings revealed some interesting differences. The U.S. managers in Hong Kong exhibited managerial behaviors similar to those of their counterparts back in the United States; however, Hong Kong managers had managerial behaviors different from either group of U.S. managers. Commenting on these results, the researchers noted:

> This study...points to some important practical implications. It suggests that American firms and the practical school of thought may be mistaken in the assumption that a good manager in Los Angeles will necessarily do fine in Hong Kong or some other foreign country. It may be that because firms do not include in their selection criteria individual characteristics such as cognitive flexibility, cultural flexibility, degree of ethnocentricity, etc., they end up sending a number of individuals on international assignments who have a tendency to keep the same set of managerial behaviors they used in the U.S. and not adjust or adapt to the local norms and practices. Including the measurement of these characteristics in the selection process, as well as providing cross-cultural training before departure, may be a means of obtaining more effective adaptation of managerial behaviors and more effective performance in overseas assignments.

Certainly the study shows that simplistic assumptions about culture are erroneous and that what works in one country will not necessarily produce the desired results in another. If MNCs are going to manage effectively throughout the world, they are going to have to give more attention to training their people about intercultural differences.

Doing Business in China

The People's Republic of China (PRC or China, for short) has had a long tradition of isolation. In 1979, Deng Xiaoping opened his country to the world. Although his bloody 1989 put-down of protestors in Tiananmen Square was a definite setback for progress, China is rapidly trying to close the gap between itself and economically advanced nations and to establish itself as a power in the world economy. As noted in Chapter 1, southeast China in particular has become a hotbed of business activity. Presently, China is actively trading in world markets, and it is a major trading partner of the United States. Despite this global presence, many U.S. and European multinationals still find that doing business in the PRC can be a long, grueling process that often results in failure. Very few outside firms have yet to make a profit in China. One primary reason is that Western-based MNCs do not appreciate the important role and impact of Chinese culture.

Experienced travelers report that the primary criterion for doing business in China is technical competence. For example, in the case of MNCs selling machinery, the Chinese want to know exactly how the machine works, what its capabilities are, and how repairs and maintenance must be handled. Sellers must be prepared to answer these questions in precise detail. This is why successful multinationals send only seasoned engineers and technical people to the PRC. They know that the questions to be answered will require both knowledge and experience, and young, fresh-out-of-school engineers will not be able to answer them.

A major cultural difference between the PRC and many Western countries is the issue of time. The Chinese tend to be punctual, so it is important that those who do business with them arrive on time. During meetings, such as those held when negotiating a contract, the Chinese may ask many questions and nod their assent at the answers. This nodding usually means that they understand or are being polite; it seldom means that they like what they are hearing and want to enter into a contract. For this reason, when dealing with the Chinese, one must keep in mind that patience is critically important. The Chinese will make a decision in their own good time, and it is common for outside businesspeople to make several trips to China before a deal is finally concluded. Moreover, not only are there numerous meetings, sometimes these are unilaterally canceled at the last minute and rescheduled. This often tries the patience of outsiders and is inconvenient in terms of rearranging travel plans and other problems.

Another important dimension of Chinese culture is **guanxi**, which means "good connections."[28] However, the term means more than just effective networking. In practice, *guanxi.* resembles nepotism where individuals in authority make decisions on the basis of family ties or social connections rather than objective indices. Tung has reported that:

Guanxi
In China, it means good connections.

> In a survey of 2,000 Chinese from Shanghai and its surrounding rural community, 92% of the respondents confirmed that *guanxi* played a significant role in their daily lives. Furthermore, the younger generation tended to place greater emphasis on *guanxi*. In fact, *guanxi* has become more widespread in the recent past. . . . Most business practitioners who have experience in doing business with East Asians will readily agree that in order to succeed in these countries "who you know is more important than what you know." In other words, having connections with the appropriate individuals and authorities is often more crucial than having the right product and/or price.[29]

Additionally, outsiders doing business in China must be aware that Chinese people will typically argue that they have the *guanxi* to get a job done, when in reality they may or may not have the necessary connections.

In China, it is important to be a good listener. This may mean having to listen to the same stories about the great progress that has been made by the PRC over the past decade. The Chinese are very proud of their economic accomplishments and want to share these feelings with outsiders.

When dealing with the Chinese, one must realize they are a collective society in which people pride themselves on being members of a group. This is in sharp contrast to the situation in the United States and other Western countries, where individualism is highly prized. For this reason, one must never single out a Chinese and praise him or her for a particular quality, such as intelligence or kindness, because this may well embarrass the individual in the face of his or her peers. It is equally important to avoid using self-centered conversation, such as excessive use of the word "I," because it appears that the speaker is trying to single him- or herself out for special consideration.

The Chinese also are much less animated than Westerners. They avoid open displays of affection, do not slap each other on the back, and are more reticent, retiring, and reserved than North or South Americans. They do not appreciate loud, boisterous behavior, and when speaking to each other, they maintain a greater physical distance than is typical in the West.

Cultural highlights that affect doing business in China can be summarized and put into some specific guidelines as follows:

1. The Chinese place a great deal of emphasis on trust and mutual connections, and they are true to their word.

2. Business meetings typically start with pleasantries such as tea and general conversation about the guest's trip to the country, local accommodations, and family. In most cases, the host already has been briefed on the background of the visitor.

3. When a meeting is ready to begin, the Chinese host will give the appropriate indication. Similarly, when the meeting is over, the host will indicate that it is time for the guest to leave.

4. Once the Chinese decide who and what is best, they tend to stick with these decisions. Therefore, they may be slow in formulating a plan of action, but once they get started, they make fairly good progress.

5. In negotiations, reciprocity is important. If the Chinese give concessions, they expect some in return. Additionally, it is common to find them slowing down negotiations to take advantage of Westerners desiring to conclude arrangements as quickly as possible. The objective of this tactic is to extract further concessions. Another common ploy used by the Chinese is to pressure the other party during final arrangements by suggesting that this counterpart has broken the spirit of friendship in which the business relationship originally was established. Again, through this ploy, the Chinese are trying to gain additional concessions.

6. Because negotiating can involve a loss of face, it is common to find Chinese carrying out the whole process through intermediaries. This allows them to convey their ideas without fear of embarrassment.[30]

Doing Business in Russia

The Russian economy has experienced severe problems.[31] At the same time, however, by following certain guidelines, MNCs can begin to tap the potential opportunities. Here are some suggestions for being successful in Russia:

1. Build personal relationships with partners. Business laws and contracts do not mean as much in Russia as they do in the West. When there are contract disputes, there is little protection for the aggrieved party because of the time and effort needed to legally enforce the agreement. Detailed contracts can be hammered out later on; in the beginning, all that counts is friendship.

2. Use local consultants. Because the rules of business have changed so much in recent years, it pays to have a local Russian consultant working with the company. Russian expatriates often are not up-to-date on what is going on and, quite often, are not trusted by local businesspeople who have stayed in the country. So the consultant should be someone who has been in Russia all the time and understands the local business climate.

3. Consider business ethics. Ethical behavior in the United States is not always the same as in Russia. For example, it is tradition in Russia to give gifts to those with whom one wants to transact business, an approach that is often regarded as bribery in the United States.

4. Be patient. In order to get something done in Russia, it often takes months of waiting. Those who are in a hurry to make a quick deal are often sorely disappointed.

5. Stress exclusivity. Russians like exclusive arrangements and often negotiate with just one firm at a time. This is in contrast to Western businesspeople who often "shop" their deals and may negotiate with a half dozen firms at the same time before settling on one.

6. Remember that personal relations are important. Russians like to do business face-to-face. So when they receive letters or faxes, they often put them on their desk but do not respond to them. They are waiting for the businessperson to contact them and set up a personal meeting.

7. Keep financial information personal. When Westerners enter into business dealings with partners, it is common for them to share financial information with these individuals and to expect the same from the latter. However,

Russians wait until they know their partner well enough to feel comfortable before sharing financial data. Once trust is established, then this information is provided.

8. Research the company. In dealing effectively with Russian partners, it is helpful to get information about this company, its management hierarchy, and how it typically does business. This information helps ensure the chances for good relations because it gives the Western partner a basis for establishing a meaningful relationship.

9. Stress mutual gain. The Western idea of "win-win" in negotiations also works well in Russia. Potential partners want to know what they stand to gain from entering into the venture.

10. Clarify terminology. For-profit business deals are new in Russia, so the language of business is just getting transplanted there. As a result, it is important to double-check and make sure that the other party clearly understands the proposal, knows what is expected and when, and is agreeable to the deal.[32]

These 10 steps can be critical to the success of a business venture in Russia. They require careful consideration of cultural factors and it often takes a lot longer than initially anticipated. However, the benefits may be worth the wait. And when everything is completed, there is a final cultural tradition that should be observed: Fix and reinforce the final agreements with a nice dinner together and an invitation to the Russians to visit your country and see your facilities.[33]

Doing Business in India

Foreign trade is critical to India's economy. In recent years, the country has been particularly interested in promoting exports and creating import substitutions. The government plays an important role in this process, and approval for investment is selective and typically granted only on a case-by-case basis.[34] In addition, although most Indian businesspeople speak English, many of their values and beliefs are markedly different from those in the West. Thus, understanding Indian culture is critical to doing business in India.

Shaking hands with male business associates is almost always an acceptable practice. U.S. businesspeople in India are considered equals, however, and the universal method of greeting an equal is to press one's palms together in front of the chest and say *namaste,* which means "greetings to you." Therefore, if a handshake appears to be improper, it always is safe to use *namaste.*

Western food typically is available in all good hotels. Most Indians do not drink alcoholic beverages, however, and many are vegetarians or eat chicken but not beef. Therefore, when foreign businesspeople entertain in India, the menu often is quite different from that back home. Moreover, when a local businessperson invites an expatriate for dinner at home, it is not necessary to bring a gift, although it is acceptable to do so. The host's wife and children usually will provide help from the kitchen to ensure that the guest is well treated, but they will not be at the table. If they are, it is common to wait until everyone has been seated and the host begins to eat or asks everyone to begin. During the meal, the host will ask the guest to have more food. This is done to ensure that the person does not go away hungry; however, once one has eaten enough, it is acceptable to politely refuse more food.

For Western businesspeople in India, shirt, trousers, tie, and suit are proper attire. In the southern part of India, where the climate is very hot, a light suit is preferable. In the north during the winter, a light sweater and jacket are a good choice. Indian businesspeople, on the other hand, often will wear local dress. In many cases, this includes a *dhoti,* which is a single piece of white cloth (about 5 yards long and 3 feet wide) which is passed around the waist up to half its length, then the other half is drawn between the legs and tucked at the waist. Long shirts are worn on the upper part of the body. In some locales, such as Punjab, Sikhs will wear turbans, and well-to-do Hindus sometimes will wear long coats like the Rajahs. This coat, known as a *sherwani,* is the dress recognized by the government for official and ceremonial wear. Foreign businesspeople are not expected to dress like locals, and in fact, many Indian businesspeople will dress like Europeans. Therefore, it is unnecessary to adopt local dress codes.

When doing business in India, one will find a number of other customs useful to know. Some of the most useful include:

1. It is important to be on time for meetings.
2. Personal questions should not be asked unless the other individual is a friend or close associate.
3. Titles are important, so people who are doctors or professors should be addressed accordingly.
4. Public displays of affection are considered to be inappropriate, so one should refrain from backslapping or touching others.
5. Beckoning is done with the palm turned down, while pointing often is done with the chin.
6. When eating or accepting things, use the right hand, because the left is considered to be unclean.
7. The *namaste* gesture can be used to greet people; it also is used to convey other messages, including a signal that one has had enough food.
8. Bargaining for goods and services is common; this contrasts with Western traditions, where bargaining might be considered rude or abrasive.[35]

Finally, it is important to remember that Indians are very tolerant of outsiders and understand that many are unfamiliar with local customs and procedures. Therefore, there is no need to make a phony attempt to conform to Indian cultural traditions. Making an effort to be polite and courteous is sufficient.

Doing Business in France

Many in the United States believe that it is more difficult to get along with the French than with other Europeans. This feeling probably reflects the French culture, which is markedly different from that in the United States. In France, one's social class is very important, and these classes include the aristocracy, the upper bourgeoisie, the upper-middle bourgeoisie, the middle, the lower-middle, and the lower. Social interactions are affected by class stereotypes, and during their lifetime, most French people do not encounter much change in social status. Unlike an American, who through hard work and success can move from the lowest economic strata to the highest, a successful French person might, at best, climb one or two rungs of the social ladder. Additionally, the French are very status conscious, and they like to provide signs of this status, such as a knowledge of literature and the arts; a well-designed, tastefully decorated house; and a high level of education.

The French also tend to be friendly, humorous, and sardonic (sarcastic), in contrast to Americans, for example, who seldom are sardonic. The French may admire or be fascinated with people who disagree with them; in contrast, Americans are more attracted to those who agree with them. As a result, the French are accustomed to conflict and during negotiations accept that some positions are irreconcilable and must be accepted as such. Americans, on the other hand, believe that conflicts can be resolved and that if both parties make an extra effort and have a spirit of compromise, there will be no irreconcilable differences. Moreover, the French often determine a person's trustworthiness based on their firsthand evaluation of the individual's character. This is in marked contrast to Americans, who tend to evaluate a person's trustworthiness based on past achievements and other people's evaluations of this person.

In the workplace, many French people are not motivated by competition or the desire to emulate fellow workers. They often are accused of not having as intense a worth ethic as, for example, Americans or Asians. Many French workers frown on overtime, and statistics show that on average, they have the longest vacations in the world (4 to 5 weeks annually). On the other hand, few would argue that they work extremely hard in their regularly scheduled time and have a reputation for high productivity. Part of this reputation results from the French tradition of craftsmanship. Part of it also is accounted for by a large percentage of the workforce being employed in small, independent businesses, where there is widespread respect for a job well done.

Most French organizations tend to be highly centralized and have rigid structures. As a result, it usually takes longer to carry out decisions. Because this arrangement is quite different from the more decentralized, flattened organizations in the United States, both middle- and lower-level U.S. expatriate managers who work in French subsidiaries often find bureaucratic red tape a source of considerable frustration. There also are marked differences at the upper levels of management. In French companies, top managers have far more authority than their U.S. counterparts, and they are less accountable for their actions. While top-level U.S. executives must continually defend their decision to the CEO or board of directors, French executives are challenged only if the company has poor performance. As a result, those who have studied French management find them to take a more autocratic approach.[36]

In countries such as the United States, a great deal of motivation is derived from professional accomplishment. Americans realize there is limited job and social security in the their country, so it is up to them to work hard and ensure their future. The French do not have the same view. While they admire Americans' industriousness and devotion to work, they believe that quality of life is what really matters. As a result, they attach a great deal of importance to leisure time, and many are unwilling to sacrifice the enjoyment of life for a dedication to work.

The values and beliefs discussed here help to explain why French culture is so different from that in other countries. Some of the sharp contrasts with the United States, for example, provide insights regarding the difficulties of doing business in France. Additional cultural characteristics, such as the following, also help to explain the difficulties that outsiders may encounter in France:

1. When shaking hands with a French person, use a quick shake with some pressure in the grip. A firm, pumping handshake, which is so common in the United States, is considered to be uncultured.

2. It is extremely important to be on time for meetings and social occasions. Being "fashionably late" is frowned on.

3. During a meal, it is acceptable to engage in pleasant conversation, but personal questions and the subject of money are never brought up.

4. Great importance is placed on neatness and taste. Therefore, visiting businesspeople should try very hard to be cultured and sophisticated.[37]

Doing Business in Arab Countries

The media attention given to continuing conflicts in the Middle East have pointed out that Arab cultures are distinctly different from Anglo cultures. Americans often find it extremely hard to do business in Arab countries, and a number of Arab cultural characteristics can be cited for this difficulty.

One is the Arabian view of time. In the United States, it is common to use the cliche "time is money." In Arab countries, a favorite expression is *Bukra insha Allah,* which means "tomorrow if God wills," an expression that explains the Arabs' fatalistic approach to time. Arabs believe that Allah controls time, in contrast to Westerners, who believe that they control their own time. As a result, if Arabs commit themselves to a date in the future and fail to show up, there is no guilt or concern on their part, because they have no control over time in the first place.

A word of caution on overgeneralizing is needed here and in all of the examples used throughout this chapter's discussion of cultural characteristics. There are many Arabs that are very particular about promises and appointments. There are also many Arabs that are very proactive and not fatalistic. The point is that there are always exceptions and stereotyping in cross cultural dealings can be dangerous.

Another Arab cultural belief that generally holds is that destiny depends more on the will of a supreme being than on the behavior of individuals. A higher power dictates the outcome of important events, so individual action is of little consequence. This thinking affects not only Arabs' aspirations but also their motivation. Also of importance is that the status of Arabs largely is determined by family position and social contact and connections, not necessarily by their own accomplishments. This view helps to explain why some Middle Easterners take great satisfaction in appearing to be helpless. In fact, helplessness can be used as a source of power, for in this area of the world, the strong are resented and the weak compensated. Here is an example:

> In one Arab country, several public administrators of equal rank would take turns meeting in each other's offices for their weekly conferences, and the host would serve as chairman. After several months, one of these men had a mild heart attack. Upon his recovery, it was decided to hold the meetings only in his office, in order not to inconvenience him. From then on, the man who had the heart attack became the permanent chairman of the conference. This individual appeared more helpless than the others, and his helplessness enabled him to increase his power.[38]

This approach is quite different from that in the United States, where the strong tend to be compensated and rewarded. If a person were ill, such as in this example, the individual would be relieved of this responsibility until he or she had regained full health. In the interim, the rest of the group would go on without the sick person, and he or she may have lost power.

Another important cultural contrast between Arabs and Americans is that of emotion and logic. Arabs often act based on emotion; in contrast, those in an Anglo culture are taught to act on logic. Many Arabs live in unstable environments where things change constantly, so they do not develop trusting relationships with others. Americans, on the other hand, live in a much more predictable environment and develop trusting relationships with others.

Arabs also make wide use of elaborate and ritualized forms of greetings and leave-takings. A businessperson may wait for past the assigned meeting time before being admitted to an Arab's office. Once there, the individual may find a host of others present; this situation is unlike the typical one-on-one meetings that are so common in the United States. Moreover, during the meeting, there may be continuous interruptions, visitors may arrive and begin talking to the host, and messengers may come in and go out on a regular basis. The businessperson is expected to take all this activity as perfectly normal and remain composed and ready to continue discussions as soon as the host is prepared to do so.

Business meetings typically conclude with an offer of coffee or tea. This is a sign that the meeting is over and that future meetings, if there are to be any, should now be arranged.

Unlike the case in many other countries, titles are not in general use on the Arabian Peninsula, except in the case of royal families, ministers, and high-level military officers. Additionally, initial meetings typically are used to get to know the other party. Business-related discussions may not occur until the third or four meeting. Also, in contrast to the common perception among many Western businesspeople who have never been to an Arab country, it is not necessary to bring the other party a gift. If this is done, however, it should be a modest gift. A good example is a novelty or souvenir item from the visitor's home country.

Arabs attach a great deal of importance to status and rank. When meeting with them, one should pay deference to the senior person first. It also is important never to criticize or berate anyone publicly. This causes the individual to lose face, and the same is true for the person who makes these comments. Mutual respect is required at all times.

Other useful guidelines for doing business in Arab cultures include:

1. It is important never to display feelings of superiority, because this makes the other party feel inferior. No matter how well someone does something, the individual should let the action speak for itself and not brag or put on a show of self-importance.

2. One should not take credit for joint efforts. A great deal of what is accomplished is a result of group work, and to indicate that one accomplished something alone is a mistake.

3. Much of what gets done is a result of going through administrative channels in the country. It often is difficult to sidestep a lot of this red tape, and efforts to do so can be regarded as disrespect for legal and governmental institutions.

4. Connections are extremely important in conducting business. Well-connected businesspeople can get things done much faster than their counterparts who do not know the ins and outs of the system.

5. Patience is critical to the success of business transactions. This time consideration should be built into all negotiations, thus preventing one from giving away too much in an effort to reach a quick settlement.

6. Important decisions usually are made in person, not by correspondence or telephone. This is why an MNC's personal presence often is a prerequisite for success in the Arab world. Additionally, while there may be many people who provide input on the final decision, the ultimate power rests with the person at the top, and this individual will rely heavily on personal impressions, trust, and rapport.[39]

World of Business Week Revisited

As the *Business Week* article at the beginning of the chapter indicated, doing business in different cultures presents multinationals with a variety of challenges. Nowhere is this more apparent than in Asia where years of reckless lending, protecting of state-run industries, and propping up of politically corrupt dealings, has led to an economic crisis. However, as global investors assert more and more pressure, change is finally emerging. The shutting down or consolidating of inefficient banks and the removal of ineffective management are just some of the necessary steps being taken to ensure Asia's economic recovery. Now that you have read this chapter, you should have a better understanding of the difficulties of managing in uncertain business environments. Using this knowledge as a platform, answer the following questions: (1) Why will investors avoid Asian economies if they continue to prop up unhealthy banks? (2) Why are the Asian people resistant to bank closings and other changes in the banking industry? (3) In your opinion what are some of the largest cultural differences between doing business in the United States and one of the Asian nations?

Summary of Key Points

1. One major problem facing MNCs is that they attempt to manage across cultures just the way they do in their home country. Globalization is given greater attention than national responsiveness or sovereignty; however, in recent years, under strategic international management, this globalization imperative has begun to be de-emphasized and the need for local focus has gained in importance. A number of factors help to account for this new strategy: (1) the need to address diverse worldwide standards; (2) the importance of differentiating products for local markets; (3) the need to become an insider rather than relying solely on export policies; and (4) the need to give subsidiaries more authority to respond to local conditions.

2. One major challenge when dealing with cross-cultural problems is that of overcoming parochialism and simplification. Parochialism is the tendency to view the world through one's own eyes and perspectives. Simplification is the process of exhibiting the same orientation toward different cultural groups. Another problem is that of doing things the same way in for-eign markets as they are done in domestic markets. Research shows that in some cases, this approach can be effective; however, effective cross-cultural management more commonly requires approaches different than those used at home. One area where this is particularly evident is human resource man-agement. Recruitment, selection, training, and com-pensation often are carried out in different ways in different countries, and what works in the United States may have limited value in other countries and geographic regions.

3. Doing business in various parts of the world requires the recognition and understanding of cultural differ-ences. Some of these differences revolve around the importance the society assigns to time, status, control of decision making, personal accomplishment, and work itself. These types of cultural differences help to explain why effective managers in China or Russia often are quite different from those in France, and why a successful style in the United States will not be ideal in Arab countries.

Key Terms

globalization

globalization imperative

guanxi

national responsiveness

parochialism

simplification

Review and Discussion Questions

1. Define "globalization" as used in strategic interna-tional management. In what way might globalization be a problem for a successful national organization that is intent on going international? In your answer, provide an example of the problem.

2. Some international management experts contend that globalization and national responsiveness are diamet-rically opposed forces, and that to accommodate one, a multinational must relax its efforts in the other. In what way is this an accurate statement? In what way is it incomplete or inaccurate?

3. In what way are parochialism and simplification bar-riers to effective cross-cultural management? In each case, give an example.

4. Many MNCs would like to do business overseas in the same way that they do business domestically. Do research findings show that any approaches that work well in the United States also work well in other cul-tures? If so, identify and describe two.

5. In most cases, local managerial approaches must be modified when doing business overseas. What are three specific examples that support this statement? Be complete in your answer.

6. What are some categories of cultural differences that help make one country or region of the world differ-ent from another? In each case, describe the value or norm and explain how it would result in different behavior in two or more countries. If you like, use the countries discussed in this chapter as your point of reference.

Internet Exercise: Sony's Approach

Sony is a multinational corporation that sells a wide variety of goods in the international marketplace. These range from electronics to on-line games to music—and the Japanese MNC is even in the entertainment business (Sony Pictures Entertainment), producing offerings for both the big screen as well as for television. Visit the MNC's web site at **www.sony.com** and read about some of the latest developments in which the company is engaged. Pay close attention to its new offerings in the areas of electronics, television shows, movies, music, and on-line games. Then answer these three questions: (1) What type of cultural challenges does Sony face when it attempts to market its products worldwide? Is demand universal for all of these offerings or is there a "national responsiveness/ globalization" challenge, as discussed in the chapter, that must be addressed? (2) Investigate the Sony credit card that the company is now offering on-line. Is this a product that will have worldwide appeal, or is it more likely to be restricted to more economically advanced countries? (3) In managing its far-flung enterprise, what are two cultural challenges that the company is likely to face and what will it need to do to respond to these?

Mexico

Located directly south of the United States, Mexico covers an area of 756,000 square miles. It is the third-largest country in Latin America and the thirteenth-largest in the world. The 1997 census placed the population at 97.6 million, and this number is increasing at a rate of approximately 1.84 percent annually because of a traditionally high birthrate and a sharply reduced death rate. Today, Mexico is one of the "youngest" countries in the world. Approximately 55 percent of the population is under the age of 20, while a mere 4 percent is 65 years of age or older.

During the 1980s, Mexico encountered severe economic crises. From 1982 to 1988, the economy was basically stagnant, the average annual growth of GDP was less than 0.1 percent, and for most of this period, inflation was above 60 percent a year. Beginning in 1988, however, the economy started to improve. By 1991, inflation was under 20 percent, and the federal deficit, which was 16 percent of GDP in 1988, had shrunk to 1.3 percent. During this same period, GDP rose from less than 1 percent annually to over 4 percent.

In 1994, however, the economy began to falter again. National savings as a percentage of gross domestic product fell to 14 percent, the lowest in well over a decade. In the same year the peso was sharply devalued and economic growth began to contract. The next year was worse yet as the economy shrunk by more than 6 percent. Then beginning in 1996 things started to turn around and the economy grew by 6 percent that year and another 5 percent in 1997. At the same time, the country's trade balance with the United States shifted and Mexico began running trade surpluses.

Today, even though the economy is still somewhat volatile and has political risk, Mexico has made itself attractive for foreign investment. In particular, foreign investors like the fact that they now can hold 100 percent ownership in many firms without having to get government approval. Included in this list are cement, computers, electronics, most manufacturing, pharmaceuticals, and tourism, among others. The only restrictions on new majority-owned foreign investment projects in areas not reserved to the state or to Mexican nationals are: (1) the investment not exceed $100 million; (2) the funding be external; (3) investments in industrial facilities be located outside the country's three largest metropolitan areas (Mexico City, Guadalajara, and Monterrey); (4) the investment create permanent jobs and establish job training and personnel development programs; and (5) the project use adequate technologies and comply with basic environmental requirements. If the project does not meet with these requirements, the investors must file an application with the National Commission on Foreign Investment, which has 45 business days to rule on the application or it is automatically approved.

Before and after the collapse of the peso in 1994, there has been considerable foreign investment in Mexico. The largest investor by far is the United States, which accounts for over 60 percent of all outside investment. The largest investments are in the manufacturing and industrial sector (around 60 percent of the total) and services (around 30 percent).

One major benefit of locating in Mexico is a highly skilled labor force that can be hired at fairly low wages when compared with those paid elsewhere. Additionally, manufacturing firms that have located there report high productivity growth rates and quality performance. A study by the Massachusetts Institute of Technology on auto assembly plants in Canada, the United States, and Mexico reported that Mexican plants performed well. Another by J. D. Power and Associates noted that Ford Motor's Hermisillo plant was the best in North America. Computer and electronics firms also are finding Mexico to be an excellent choice for new expansion plants.
www.mexicool.com

Questions

1. Why would multinationals be interested in setting up operations in Mexico? Give two reasons.

2. In what way would national responsiveness be a strategic issue that these firms would have to face?

3. Would cultural differences be a major stumbling block for U.S. firms doing business in Mexico? For European firms? For Japanese firms? Explain your answer.

4. Why might MNCs be interested in studying the organizational culture in Mexican firms before deciding whether to locate there? Explain your logic.

Beijing, Here We Come!

A large toy company located in Canada is considering a business arrangement with the government of China. Although company representatives have not yet visited the PRC, the president of the firm recently met with Chinese representatives in Ottawa and discussed the business proposition. The Canadian CEO learned that the Chinese government would be quite happy to study the proposal, and the company's plan would be given a final decision within 90 days of receipt. The toy company now is putting together a detailed proposal and scheduling an on-site visit.

The Canadian firm would like to have the Chinese manufacture a wide variety of toys for sale in Asia as well as in Europe and North America. Production of these toys requires a large amount of labor time, and because China is reputed to have one of the largest and least expensive workforces in the world, the company believes that it can maximize profit by having the work done there. For the past 5 years, the company has had its toys produced in Taiwan. Costs there have been escalating recently, however, and because 45 percent of the production expense goes for labor, the company is convinced that it will soon be priced out of the market if it does not find another source.

The company president and three officers plan on going to Beijing next month to talk with government officials. They would like to sign a 5-year agreement with a price that will not increase by more than 2 percent annually. Production operations then will be turned over to the Chinese, who will have a free hand in manufacturing the goods.

The contract with the Taiwanese firm runs out in 90 days. The company already has contacted this firm, and the latter understands that its Canadian partner plans to terminate the arrangement. One major problem is that if it cannot find another supplier soon, it will have to go back to the Taiwanese firm for at least 2 more years. The contract stipulates that the agreement can be extended for another 24 months if the Canadian firm makes such a request; however, this must be done within 30 days of expiration of the contract. This is not an alternative that appeals to the Canadians, but they feel they will have to take it if they cannot reach an agreement with the Chinese.

Questions

1. What is the likelihood that the Canadians will be able to reach an agreement with the Chinese and not have to go back to their Taiwanese supplier? Explain.

2. Are the Canadians making a strategically wise decision in letting the Chinese handle all the manufacturing, or should they insist on getting more actively involved in the production process? Defend your answer.

3. What specific cultural suggestions would you make to the Canadians regarding how to do business with the Chinese?

Chapter 7

Organizational Cultures and Diversity

Objectives of the Chapter

Objectives of the Chapter

The previous two chapters focused on national cultures. The overriding objective of this chapter is to examine the interaction issues of national culture (diversity) versus organizational cultures and to discuss ways in which MNCs can manage the often inherent conflicts between national and organizational cultures. Many times, the cultural values and resulting behaviors that are common in a particular country are not the same as those needed for a successful MNC; therefore MNCs must learn to deal with this diversity/challenge. Although the field of international management has long recognized the impact of national cultures, only recently has attention been given to the importance of managing organizational cultures and diversity. This chapter first examines common organizational cultures that exist in MNCs, then presents and analyzes ways in which multiculturalism and diversity are being addressed by the best, world-class multinationals. The specific objectives of this chapter are:

1. DEFINE exactly what is meant by "organizational culture," and discuss the interaction between national and MNC culture.

2. IDENTIFY the four most common categories of organizational culture that have been found through research, and discuss the characteristics of each.

3. PROVIDE an overview of the nature and degree of multiculturalism and diversity in today's MNCs.

4. DISCUSS common guidelines and principles that are used in building multicultural effectiveness at the team and the organizational levels.

BusinessWeek

The World of Business Week:

A Quiet Revolution

The deal was a mold-breaker. In May, French Defense Minister Alain Richard for the first time awarded a naval ship-repair contract to a private company rather than the state-owned shipyard in Toulon. The $2 million winning bid was half that of the state shipyard, and the company promised to do the job in a third of the time. Toulon workers struck for eight weeks in protest, to no avail.

A quiet revolution is sweeping tradition-bound France, whose government-dominated economy looks increasingly outmoded. Until now, efforts to modernize its distinctive welfare state amounted mainly to privatizing the biggest companies. Now, the forces of globalization, technology, and deregulated markets are encouraging reform-minded French people to change the system itself.

A small but growing army of citizens want to shrink the state's role, reverse a pervasive hostility toward entrepreneurs, and erase the handout mentality that is intoned in French society. The fighting forces come from every walk of life, from entrepreneurs and shareholder activists to government officials and labor leaders. They have little in common except the belief that France must rethink the centuries-old economic model it has held so dear. "France is the only country that still has its head in the 1970s," says Christian Saint-Etienne, a Paris-based economist.

Even Prime Minister Lionel Jospin has begun injecting the concept of "modernizing France" into

his Socialist government. It has sold off more state companies, begun reversing laws that hobble new businesses, called for education reforms, made the Internet a national priority, and slashed the number of jobs public officials can hold at one time.

A new generation of executives wants to replace the worker-vs.-capitalist enmity in France with a more democratic, motivating relationship that spreads wealth through employee shareholding. During a recent public offering of shares in industrial giant Saint-Gobain, a surprising 40% of the company's blue-collar workers bought stock. "The model that makes Microsoft's employees so happy could be transplanted to France," says CEO Jean-Louis Beffa.

The reformers face daunting resistance. Nearly 26% of French workers are employed by the state, receiving generous pay, benefits, and early-retirement packages. Politicians push taxes ever higher to fund the country's bankrupt social security system, rather than reform it. Unionized civil servants in the transportation sector regularly shut France down with nationwide strikes, demanding pay hikes and resisting any benefit cuts. Unemployment compensation is so high that taking a minimum-wage job is uneconomical. Overall, only 38% of the French population works, vs. a weighted average of 48% in the U.S., Japan, and Germany.

But the forces of globalization promise to erode the state's stubborn monolith, slowly but surely. The European Union's evolution into a single market, in which each member must compete with the others for capital and jobs, is exposing France's sclerosis.

Union leaders, too, quietly admit that monetary union will change work rules by making countries compete for investment with attractive labor markets. A watershed of sorts was reached on June 9 when Air France's striking pilots accepted a deal that gives them a choice between a seven-year wage freeze and a 15% pay cut offset by share ownership. The pact, which will save Air France $6 billion in personnel costs over seven years, was proof that France's labor traditions are giving way to economic reality.

Even some government enterprises are bucking the system behind closed doors. In the early 1990s, state-owned Company X needed massive restructuring and layoffs to survive. At a meeting at its Paris headquarters, union leaders said they would negotiate, on the condition that management keep their agreement secret. Not a word was leaked to the press. Over the next several years, Company X shed nearly half its 40,000 workers without a strike. It has expanded internationally and gets 70% of sales from exports. To this day, few outsiders know about the layoffs.

At private French companies, management is brainstorming to find ways around barriers to growth. Take the example of a new law that shortens the French workweek to 35 hours starting in 2000, from 39 now. Global software companies, whose programmers often log 60 to 70 hours a week, would have to flee France to remain competitive. So some CEOs will bypass the law with technology, giving employees personal computers, e-mail software, and remote access to the company's network. "Our people will be able to work 35 hours in the building and around the clock from home," says the CEO of one technology company.

Indeed, the need to nurture French technology start-ups to create jobs could become one of the most powerful tools for dismantling the old state-dominant French model. Faced with a chronic unemployment rate hovering around 12%, government officials have little choice but to pay closer attention to entrepreneurs' needs. That's encouraging young companies to fight for change.

The wrenching restructuring the private sector has already gone through in the name of global competitiveness is likely to put the public sector through an equally jolting shake-up. "We are at the end of the first wave of transformation and the beginning of the second wave," says Bruno Roger, a partner at Lazard Frères in Paris. For the troops toiling for change in France, that's the battle cry of the future.

By Gail Edmondson in Paris
www.france.com/index.html

Source: **Reprinted from June 29, 1998, pp. 46–48 issue of** *Business Week* **by special permission, copyright © 1998 by the McGraw-Hill Companies, Inc.**

The opening news article highlights the problems that may arise when national cultures interact with organizational cultures. As is evident from the article, the cultural values necessary to be a successful organization in today's global economy often differ from traditional national values practiced for decades. The result is resistance to change from the mass public, politicians, and companies. The conflict between national and organizational culture is extremely apparent in France where the old and the new generations are clashing over the restructuring process necessary for European unity. France is traditionally described as having high taxes, rigid labor markets, and technological inferiority, making success in the global economy difficult. In today's environment where workers are working 60 to 70 hours a week, France's 35-hour workweek, and generous pay and benefits shows how national culture can dominate organizational culture. However, as the news story describes, French government policy makers as well as the unions and people themselves are slowly realizing the need to eliminate the characteristics associated with the welfare state so that French companies can grow and compete in the twenty-first century. As you read through the chapter, consider how MNCs might respond when faced with having to conduct business in organizational and national cultures like in France that are so dissimilar to their own.

The Nature of Organizational Culture

The chapters in Part One provided the background on the external environment, and the chapters so far in this part have been concerned with the external culture. Regardless of this environment or cultural context impacting on the MNC, when individuals join an MNC, they not only bring their national culture, which greatly affects their learned beliefs, attitudes, values, and behaviors, with them, but at the same time, they enter into an organizational culture. Employees of MNCs are expected to "fit in." For example, at PepsiCo, personnel are expected to be cheerful, positive, enthusiastic, and have committed optimism; at Ford, they are expected to show self-confidence, assertiveness, and machismo.[1] Regardless of the external environment or their national culture, managers and employees must understand and follow their organization's culture to be successful. After first defining organizational culture, the interaction between national and organizational culture is analyzed. An understanding of this interaction has become recognized as vital to effective international management.

Definition and Characteristics

Organizational culture has been defined in several different ways. Widely recognized organizational cultural theorist Edgar Schein defines it as a

> pattern of basic assumptions—invented, discovered, or developed by a given group as it learns to cope with its problems of external adaptation and internal integration—that has worked well enough to be considered valuable and, therefore, to be taught to new members as the correct way to perceive, think, and feel in relation to those problems.[2]

Regardless of how the term is defined, a number of important characteristics are associated with an organization's culture. These have been summarized as:

1. Observed behavioral regularities, as typified by common language, terminology, and rituals;

2. Norms, as reflected by things such as the amount of work to be done and the degree of cooperation between management and employees;

3. Dominant values that the organization advocates and expects participants to share, such as high product and service quality, low absenteeism, and high efficiency;

4. A philosophy that is set forth in the MNC's beliefs regarding how employees and customers should be treated;

5. Rules that dictate the do's and don'ts of employee behavior relating to areas such as productivity, customer relations, and intergroup cooperation; and

6. Organizational climate, or the overall atmosphere of the enterprise as reflected by the way that participants interact with each other, conduct themselves with customers, and feel about the way they are treated by higher-level management.[3]

These characteristics are not intended to be all-inclusive, but they do help to illustrate the nature of organizational culture.[4] The major problem is that sometimes, an MNC's organizational culture in one country's facility differs sharply from those in other countries. For example, managers who do well in England may be ineffective in Germany, despite the fact that they work for the same MNC. In addition, the cultures of the English and German subsidiaries may differ sharply from those of the home U.S. location. Effectively dealing with this multiculturalism within the various locations of an MNC is a major challenge for international management.

A good example is provided by the German MNC Hoechst AG, the world's largest chemical company that employs more people on the other side of the Atlantic than in Germany. As its chairman has noted, "We are not merely a German company with foreign interests. One could almost say we are a nonnational company." And because of the high labor costs in Germany, the firm has been expanding its operations to lower-cost regions. It has also been selling some of its German operations, while purchasing businesses in other countries. In the process, Hoechst has also made its top management less German. For example, a Brazilian and an American are now members of the firm's nine-member board. The company is also trying to change its culture through new performance-based pay programs. However, getting people to buy into the new culture has proven a challenge. For example:

> After Hoechst integrated its German, French, and American drug operations, German workers feared the American side would have the upper hand. A group of scientists in Frankfurt tried to block a conference to decide which of the company's 55 research projects to eliminate. "For the German employees, it was difficult to hear that what they were doing was not good enough," says research chief Frank Douglas. . . . "There were only a lot of suspicions." As it turned out, only three American projects were given high priority while German projects fared well. Now, Mr. Douglas says, "the German scientists welcome the scrutiny." But the German scientists remain wary of the emphasis on marketing, fearing that it will stifle innovative research. "Everything has to be backed up by 5,000 market studies," one researcher says. But he conceded that Hoechst thought too little about sales in the past.[5]

Organizational culture
A pattern of basic assumptions that are developed by a group as it learns to cope with problems of external adaptation and internal integration and that are taught to new members as the correct way to perceive, think, and feel in relation to these problems.

Interaction between National and Organizational Cultures

There is a widely held belief that organizational culture tends to moderate or erase the impact of national culture. The logic of such conventional wisdom is that if a U.S. MNC set up operations in France, it would not be long before the French employees began to "think like Americans." In fact, evidence is accumulating that just the opposite may be true. Hofstede's research found that the national cultural values of employees have a significant impact on their organizational performance, and that the cultural values employees bring to the workplace with them are not easily changed by the organization. So, for example, while some French employees would have a higher power distance than Swedes and some a lower power distance, chances are "that if a company hired locals in Paris, they would, on the whole, be less likely to challenge hierarchical power than would the same number of locals hired in Stockholm."[6]

Andre Laurent's research supports Hofstede's conclusions.[7] He found that cultural differences actually are more pronounced among foreign employees working within the same multinational organization than among personnel working for firms in their native lands. Nancy Adler summarized these research findings as follows:

> When they work for a multinational corporation, it appears that Germans become more German, Americans become more American, Swedes become more Swedish, and so on. Surprised by these results, Laurent replicated the research in two other multinational corporations, each with subsidiaries in the same nine Western European countries and the United States. Similar to the first company, corporate culture did not reduce or eliminate national differences in the second and third corporations. Far from reducing national differences, organization culture maintains and enhances them.[8]

There often are substantial differences between the organizational cultures of different subsidiaries, and of course, this can cause coordination problems. For example, when the Upjohn Company of Kalamazoo, Michigan merged with Pharmacia AB of Sweden, which also has operations in Italy, the Americans failed to realize some of the cultural differences between themselves and their new European partners. As was reported in the *Wall Street Journal,* "Swedes take off the entire month of July for vacation, virtually en masse, and Italians take off August. Everyone in *Europe* knows, that is, but apparently hardly anyone in Kalamazoo, Mich., does."[9] As a result, a linkup that was supposed to give a quick boost to the two companies, solving problems such as aging product lines and pressure from giant competitors, never got off the ground. Things had to be rescheduled and both partners ended up having to meet and talk about their cultural differences, so that each side better understood the "dos and don'ts" of doing business with the other.

When the two firms first got together, they never expected these types of problems. Upjohn, with household names such as Rogaine and Motrin, had no likely breakthroughs in its product pipeline, so it was happy to merge with Pharmacia. The latter had developed a solid roster of allergy medicines, human-growth hormone, and other drugs, but its distribution in the United States was weak and its product line was aging. So a merger seemed ideal for both firms. The big question was how to bring the two companies together. Given that Pharmacia had recently acquired an Italian firm, there was a proposal by the European group that there be three major centers—Kalamazoo, Stockholm, and Milan—as well as a new headquarters in London. However, this arrangement had a number of built-in problems. For one, the executives in Italy and Sweden were accustomed to reporting to local bosses. Second, the people in London did not know a great deal about how to coordinate operations in Sweden and Italy. American cultural values added even more problems in that at Upjohn workers were tested for drug and alcohol abuse, but in Italy waiters pour wine freely every afternoon in the company dining room and Pharmacia's boardrooms were stocked with humidors for executives who liked to light a cigar during long meetings. Quite obviously, there were cultural differences that had to be resolved by the companies. In the end, Pharmacia & Upjohn said, it would meld the different cultures and attitudes and get on with its growth plans. However, one thing is certain: The different cultures of the merged firms created a major challenge.

In examining and addressing the differences between organizational cultures, Hofstede has provided the early database of a set of proprietary cultural-analysis techniques and programs known as DOCSA (Diagnosing Organizational Culture for Strategic Application). This approach has identified the dimensions of organizational culture summarized in Table 7-1. It was found that when cultural comparisons were made between different subsidiaries of an MNC, different cultures often existed in each one. Such cultural differences within an MNC could reduce the ability of units to work well together; an example is provided in Figure 7-1, which shows the cultural dimensions of a California-based MNC and its European subsidiary as perceived by the Europeans. A close comparison of these perceptions reveals some startling differences.

The Europeans viewed the culture in the U.S. facilities as only slightly activities-oriented (see Table 7-1 for a description of these dimensions), but they saw their own European operations much more heavily activities-oriented. The U.S. operation was viewed as moderately people-oriented, but their own relationships were viewed as very job-oriented. The Americans were seen as having a slight identification with their own organization, while the Europeans had a much stronger identification. The Americans were perceived as being very open in their communications; the Europeans saw themselves as moderately closed. The Americans were viewed as preferring very loose control, while the Europeans felt they preferred somewhat tight control. The Americans were seen as somewhat conventional in their conduct, while the Europeans saw themselves as somewhat pragmatic. If these perceptions are accurate, then it obviously would be necessary for both groups to discuss their cultural differences and carefully coordinate their activities to work well together.

Table 7–1
Dimensions of Corporate Culture

Motivation

Activities	Outputs
To be consistent and precise. To strive for accuracy and attention to detail. To refine and perfect. Get it right.	To be pioneers. To pursue clear aims and objectives. To innovate and progress. Go for it.

Relationship

Job	Person
To put the demands of the job before the needs of the individual.	To put the needs of the individual before the needs of the job.

Identity

Corporate	Professional
To identify with and uphold the expectations of the employing organizations.	To pursue the aims and ideals of each professional practice.

Communication

Open	Closed
To stimulate and encourage a full and free exchange of information and opinion.	To monitor and control the exchange and accessibility of information and opinion.

Control

Tight	Loose
To comply with clear and definite systems and procedures.	To work flexibly and adaptively according to the needs of the situation.

Conduct

Conventional	Pragmatic
To put the expertise and standards of the employing organization first. To do what we know is right.	To put the demands and expectations of customers first. To do what they ask.

Source: Reported in Lisa Hoecklin, *Managing Cultural Differences: Strategies for Competitive Advantage* (Workingham, England: Addison-Wesley, 1995), p. 146.

Figure 7–1

**Europeans'
Perception of the
Cultural
Dimensions of
U.S. Operations
(A) and European
Operations (B) of
the Same MNC**

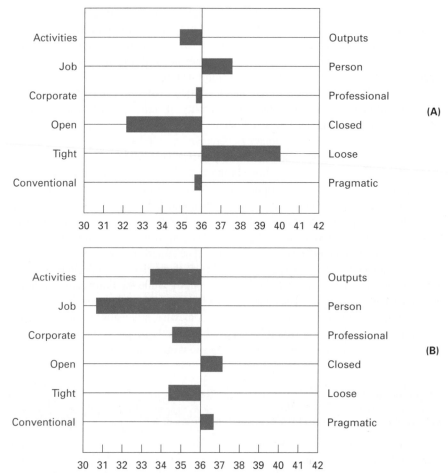

Source: Reported in Lisa Hoecklin, *Managing Cultural Differences: Strategies for Competitive Advantage* (Workingham, England: Addison-Wesley, 1995), pp. 147–148.

This analysis is relevant to multinational alliances. It shows that even though an alliance may exist, the partners will bring different organizational cultures with them. Lessem and Neubauer, who have portrayed Europe as offering four distinct ways of dealing with multiculturalism (based on the United Kingdom, French, German, and Italian characteristics), provide an example, and Table 7-2 briefly describes each of these sets of cultural characteristics. A close examination of the differences highlights how difficult it can be to do business with two or more of these groups, because each perceives things differently from the others. Another example is the way in which negotiations occur between groups; here are some contrasts between French and Spanish negotiators[10]:

French	Spanish
Look for a meeting of minds.	Look for a meeting of people.
Intellectual competence is very important.	Social competence is very important.
Persuasion through carefully prepared and skilled rhetoric is employed.	Persuasion through emotional appeal is employed.
Strong emphasis is given to a logical presentation of one's position coupled with well-reasoned, detailed solutions.	Socialization always precedes negotiations, which are characterized by an exchange of grand ideas and general principles.
A contract is viewed as a well-reasoned transaction.	A contract is viewed as a long-lasting relationship.
Trust emerges slowly and is based on the evaluation of perceived status and intellect.	Trust is developed on the basis of frequent and warm interpersonal contact and transaction.

Table 7–2
European Management Characteristics

	Characteristic			
Dimension	**Western (United Kingdom)**	**Northern (France)**	**Eastern (Germany)**	**Southern (Italy)**
Corporate	Commercial	Administrative	Industrial	Familial
Management attributes				
Behavior	Experiential	Professional	Developmental	Convivial
Attitude	Sensation	Thought	Intuition	Feeling
Institutional models				
Function	Salesmanship	Control	Production	Personnel
Structure	Transaction	Hierarchy	System	Network
Societal ideas				
Economics	Free market	Dirigiste	Social market	Communal
Philosophy	Pragmatic	Rational	Holistic	Humanistic
Cultural images				
Art	Theatre	Architecture	Music	Dance
Culture	(Anglo-Saxon)	(Gallic)	(Germanic)	(Latin)

Source: Reported in Lisa Hoecklin, *Managing Cultural Differences: Strategies for Competitive Advantage* (Workingham, England: Addison-Wesley, 1995), p. 149.

Such comparisons also help to explain why it can be difficult for an MNC to break into foreign markets where there is only local competition. The accompanying box "McDonald's Tackles Eating Habits in Brazil," provides an illustration. When dealing with these challenges, MNCs must work hard to understand the varying nature of the organizational cultures in their worldwide network and to both moderate and adapt their operations in a way that accommodates these individual units. A large part of this process calls for carefully understanding the nature of the various organizational cultures, and the next section examines the different types in detail.

Organizational Cultures in MNCs

Organizational cultures of MNCs are shaped by a number of factors, including the cultural preferences of the leaders and employees. In the international arena, some MNCs have subsidiaries that, except for the company logo and reporting procedures, would not be easily recognizable as belonging to the same multinational.[11]

Given that many recent international expansions are a result of mergers or acquisition, the integration of these organizational cultures is a critical concern in international management. Numeroff and Abrahams have suggested that there are four steps that are critical in this process: (1) The two groups have to establish the purpose, goal, and focus of their merger; (2) Then they have to develop mechanisms to identify the most important organizational structures and management roles; (3) They have to determine who has authority over the resources needed for getting things done; and (4) They have to identify the expectations of all involved parties and facilitate communication between both departments and individuals in the structure.

> Companies all over the world are finding out firsthand that there is more to an international merger or acquisition than just sharing resources and capturing greater market share. Differences in workplace cultures sometimes temporarily overshadow the overall goal of long-term success of the newly formed entity. With the proper management framework and execution, successful integration of cultures is not only possible, but the most preferable paradigm in which to operate. It is the role of the sponsors and managers to keep sight of the necessity to create, maintain, and support the notion of a united front. It is only when this assimilation has occurred that an international merger or acquisition can truly be labeled a success.[12]

International Management in Action

McDonald's Tackles Eating Habits in Brazil   www.mcdonalds.com

People in Brazil like to buy American goods. This is one reason why McDonald's, with perhaps the strongest organizational culture representing American values, is rapidly expanding its investment in this country. Over the last three years the firm has spent almost $500 million to nearly double the number of restaurants in Brazil. At the same time, sales growth has been slow and when the inflation rate is factored into the investment equation, McDonald's is not taking home a great deal of profit. Nor have things been helped along by the fact that the firm has had to discount its prices in order to increase demand. This Brazilian experience by McDonald's is an example where organizational culture, no matter how strong, is affected by national culture.

A challenge is how to get more Brazilians to eat at their local McDonald's. Over the last 36 months the company's Brazilian revenues have more than doubled to about $800 million. However, much of this demand has come from upper- and middle-class customers. As the company begins to further penetrate the market, it will have to begin making inroads among those consumers for whom a milkshake and a hamburger seem exotic. An accompanying challenge is that of changing the culture and getting people to eat breakfast at a local unit. In Brazil people have breakfast at home, thus making it next to impossible to market offerings such as Egg McMuffins. And even getting people to come to the unit for lunch can be difficult. Most workers are accustomed to going home for lunch—and then taking a nap.

The company is currently facing a big gamble that the economy will remain sufficiently strong and it can change the eating habits of millions of people and get them to come to Mickey D's on a regular basis. Unfortunately, some of this may be wishful thinking. As one observer recently noted:

> Especially in the lower-income areas, McDonald's finds that old habits die hard. Just a couple of blocks from a McDonald's in a working-class Rio neighborhood, delivery man Manoel Ribeiro stands at the counter of a typical Brazilian greasy spoon feasting on a baked ham-and-cheese wrap and a boiled egg—a meal that costs half the $2.80 or so that he would pay for a Big Mac. "I work too hard for my money to experiment on American food," he says, between bites. His attitude isn't uncommon in a country where per-capita income runs about $3,500 a year.[14]

The challenge for McDonald's is going to be to keep its prices low and to convince a growing number of people that a Big Mac and a milkshake can be a meal for everybody—not just for North Americans. The firm also hopes that by lowering its prices, it will be able to break down some of these cultural barriers. Recent research, however, shows that even with these lower prices, annual sales have been flat in dollar terms. Moreover, while the company continues to open more and more new stores, current unit owners believe that this strategy is simply drawing business away from them. As one of them explained it, "There is a definite limit as to how much fast food in this market is ready to consume now."[15] Obviously Mickey D, regardless of its strong organizational culture, has work cut out for it to penetrate the Brazilian market (culture).

In addition, there are three aspects of organizational functioning that seem to be especially important in determining MNC organizational culture: (1) the general relationship between the employees and their organization; (2) the hierarchical system of authority that defines the roles of managers and subordinates; and (3) the general views that employees hold about the MNC's purpose, destiny, goals, and their places in them.[13] When examining these dimensions of organizational culture, Trompenaars has suggested the use of two continua. One distinguishes between equity and hierarchy; the other examines orientation to the person and the task. Along these continua, which are shown in Figure 7-2, he identifies and describes four different types of organizational cultures: family, Eiffel Tower, guided missile, and incubator.

In practice, of course, organizational cultures do not fit neatly into any of these four, but the groupings can be useful in helping to examine the bases of how individuals relate to each other, think, learn, change, are motivated, and resolve conflict. The following discussion examines each of these cultural types.

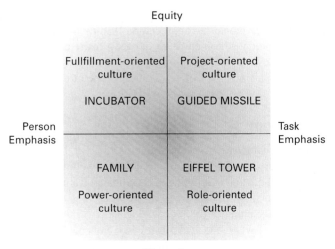

Equity

Fullfillment-oriented culture

INCUBATOR

Project-oriented culture

GUIDED MISSILE

Person Emphasis

Task Emphasis

FAMILY

Power-oriented culture

EIFFEL TOWER

Role-oriented culture

Hierarchy

Source: Adapted from Fons Trompenaars, *Riding the Waves of Culture: Understanding Diversity in Global Business* (Burr Ridge, IL: Irwin, 1994), p. 154.

Figure 7–2

Organizational Cultures

Family Culture

Family culture is characterized by a strong emphasis on the hierarchy and orientation to the person. The result is a family-type environment that is power-oriented and headed by a leader who is regarded as a caring parent and one who knows what is best for the personnel. Trompenaars has found that this organizational culture is common in countries such as Turkey, Pakistan, Venezuela, China, Hong Kong, and Singapore.

In this culture, personnel not only respect the individuals who are in charge but look to them for both guidance and approval as well. In turn, management assumes a paternal relationship regarding their personnel, looks after them, and tries to ensure that they are treated well and have continued employment. These cultures also are characterized by traditions, customs, and associations that bind together the personnel and make it difficult for outsiders to become members.

When it works well, the family culture can catalyze and multiply the energies of the personnel and appeal to their deepest feelings and aspirations. When it works poorly, members of the organization end up supporting a leader who is ineffective and drains their energies and loyalties.

This type of culture is foreign to most in the United States, who believe in valuing people based on their abilities and achievements, not on their age or position in the hierarchy. As a result, many managers in U.S.-based MNCs fail to understand why senior-level managers in overseas subsidiaries might appoint a relative to a high-level, sensitive position even though that individual might not appear to be the best qualified for the job. They fail to realize that family ties are so strong that the appointed relative would never do anything to embarrass or let down the family member who made the appointment. Here is an example:

> A Dutch delegation was shocked and surprised when the Brazilian owner of a large manufacturing company introduced his relatively junior accountant as the key coordinator of a $15 million joint venture. The Dutch were puzzled as to why a recently qualified accountant had been given such weighty responsibilities, including the receipt of their own money. The Brazilians pointed out that the young man was the best possible choice among 1,200 employees since he was the nephew of the owner. Who could be more trustworthy than that? Instead of complaining, the Dutch should consider themselves lucky that he was available.[16]

Other characteristics of family culture include the emphasis given to intuitive rather than rational knowledge. More concern is given to the development of people rather than their deployment or use. Personal knowledge of others is more important than empirical knowledge about them. Conversations are more important than research questionnaires,

Family culture
A culture that is characterized by a strong emphasis on hierarchy and orientation to the person.

and subjective data are superior to objective data. In addition, people in family cultures tend to be motivated more by praise and appreciation than by money. They tend to socialize risk by spreading it among the members, and they resist motivation programs that threaten family bonds. These cultural values suggest that human-resource approaches such as pay-for-performance plans may be ineffective in this type of culture.

Eiffel Tower Culture

Eiffel Tower culture
A culture that is characterized by strong emphasis on hierarchy and orientation to the task.

Eiffel Tower culture is characterized by a strong emphasis on the hierarchy and orientation to the task. Under this organizational culture, jobs are well defined, employees know what they are supposed to do, and everything is coordinated from the top. As a result, this culture is steep, narrow at the top, and broad at the base, thus the term "Eiffel Tower," which is constructed in this manner.

Unlike family culture, where the leader is revered and considered to be the source of all power, the person holding the top position in the Eiffel Tower culture could be replaced at any time, and this would have no effect on the work that organization members are doing or on the organization's reasons for existence. In this culture, relationships are specific, and status remains with the job. Therefore, if the boss of an Eiffel Tower subsidiary were playing golf with a subordinate, the subordinate would not feel any pressure to let the boss win. In addition, these managers seldom create off-the-job relationships with their people, because they believe this could affect their rational judgment. In fact, this culture operates very much like a formal hierarchy—impersonal and efficient.

> Each role at each level of the hierarchy is described, rated for its difficulty, complexity, and responsibility, and has a salary attached to it. There then follows a search for a person to fill it. In considering applicants for the role, the personnel department will treat everyone equally and neutrally, match the person's skills and aptitudes with the job requirements, and award the job to the best fit between role and person. The same procedure is followed in evaluations and promotions.[17]

Eiffel Tower cultures most commonly are found in North American and Northwest European countries. Examples include Canada, Denmark, France, Norway, and the United Kingdom. The way that people in this culture learn and change differs sharply from that in the family culture. Learning involves the accumulation of skills necessary to fit a role, and organizations will use qualifications in deciding how to schedule, deploy, and reshuffle personnel to meet their needs. The organization also will employ such rational procedures as assessment centers, appraisal systems, training and development programs, and job rotation in managing its human resources. All these procedures help to ensure that a formal hierarchic or bureaucracy-like approach works well. When changes need to be made, however, the Eiffel Tower culture often is ill-equipped to handle things. Manuals must be rewritten, procedures changed, job descriptions altered, promotions reconsidered, and qualifications reassessed.

This same, methodic approach is used in motivating and rewarding people and in resolving conflict. Carefully designed rules and policies are relied on, and things are done "by the book." Conflicts are viewed as irrational and offenses against efficiency; criticisms and complaints are handled through channels. The organizational participants carry out these tasks by viewing them as obligations to their jobs, not as responsibilities to specific individuals. Because the Eiffel Tower culture does not rely on values that are similar to those in most U.S. MNCs, U.S. expatriate managers often have difficulty initiating change in these cultures. As Trompenaars notes:

> An American manager responsible for initiating change in a German company described to me the difficulties he had in making progress, although the German managers had discussed the new strategy in depth and made significant contributions to its formulation. Through informal channels, he had eventually discovered that his mistake was not having formalized the changes to structure or job descriptions. In the absence of a new organization chart, this Eiffel Tower company was unable to change.[18]

Guided Missile Culture

Guided missile culture is characterized by a strong emphasis on equality in the workplace and orientation to the task. This organizational culture is oriented to work, which typically is undertaken by teams or project groups. Unlike the Eiffel Tower culture, where job assignments are fixed and limited, personnel in the guided missile culture do whatever it takes to get the job done. This culture derived its name from high-tech organizations such as the National Aeronautics and Space Administration (NASA), which pioneered the use of project groups working on space probes that resembled guided missiles. In these large project teams, more than a hundred different types of engineers often were responsible for building, say, a lunar landing module. The team member whose contribution would be crucial at any given time in the project typically could not be known in advance. Therefore, all types of engineers had to work in close harmony and cooperate with everyone on the team.

To be successful, the best form of synthesis must be used in the course of working on the project. For example, in a guided missile project, formal hierarchical considerations are given low priority, and individual expertise is of greatest importance. Additionally, everyone in the team is equal (or at least potentially equal), because their relative contributions to the project are not yet known. All teams treat each other with respect, because they may need the other for assistance. This egalitarian and task-driven organizational culture fits well with the national cultures of the United States and United Kingdom, which helps to explain why high-tech MNCs commonly locate their operations in these countries.

Guided missile organizational cultures generally are made up of professionals who are formed into cross-disciplinary teams. Moreover, the objectives of project teams are time bound; once objectives are accomplished, the team members move to other groups. An interesting situation sometimes develops in MNCs where an operation with a guided missile culture is combined (superimposed) with another unit having a more traditional, Eiffel Tower culture into what is called a "matrix structure." Of course, given the nature of both organizations, there can be a culture clash, because the bureaucratic design of the Eiffel Tower arrangement contrasts sharply with the flexible, changing design of the guided missile group.

The way in which members of a guided missile organizational culture learn and change differs sharply from that of either family or Eiffel Tower cultures. The missile structure could be called "cybernetic," meaning that the focus is on a particular objective and there is direct feedback to measure progress. Additionally, changes typically are corrective and conservative, because the overall goal remains constant. Learning involves finding out how to get along with people; playing the role of an active, contributing team member; being practical rather than theoretic; and focusing on problem solving. Moreover, in these missile cultures, performance appraisal often is carried out by peers and subordinates rather than just the boss. When bosses, peers, and subordinates all have an input into the evaluation, this is called "360-degree feedback," which is becoming increasingly popular in these organizations.

Unlike the family and Eiffel Tower cultures, change in the guided missile culture comes quickly. Goals are accomplished, and teams are reconfigured and assigned new objectives. People move from group to group, and loyalties to one's profession and project often are greater than those to the organization per se.

Trompenaars found that the motivation of those in guided missile cultures tends to be more intrinsic than just concern for money and benefits. Team members become enthusiastic about, and identify with, the struggle toward attaining their goal. For example, a project team that is designing and building a new computer for the Asian market may be highly motivated to create a machine that is at the leading edge of technology, user friendly, and will sweep the market. Everything else is secondary to this overriding objective. Thus, both intragroup and intergroup conflicts are minimized and petty problems between team members set aside; everyone is so committed to the project's main goal that they do not have time for petty disagreements. As Trompenaars notes:

> This culture tends to be individualistic since it allows for a wide variety of differently specialized persons to work with each other on a temporary basis. The scenery of faces keeps changing. Only the pursuit of chosen lines of personal development is constant. The team is

Guided missile culture
A culture that is characterized by a strong emphasis on equality in the workplace and orientation to the task.

a vehicle for the shared enthusiasm of its members, but is itself disposable and will be discarded when the project ends. Members are garrulous, idiosyncratic, and intelligent, but their mutuality is a means, not an end. It is a way of enjoying the journey. They do not need to know each other intimately, and may avoid doing so. Management by objectives is the language spoken, and people are paid for performance.[19]

Incubator Culture

Incubator culture
A culture that is characterized by a strong emphasis on equality and orientation to the person.

Incubator culture is the fourth major type of organizational culture that Trompenaars identified, and it is characterized by a strong emphasis on equality and personal orientation. This culture is based heavily on the existential idea that organizations per se are secondary to the fulfillment of the individuals within them. This culture is based on the premise that the role of organizations is to serve as incubators for the self-expression and self-fulfillment of their members; as a result, this culture often has little formal structure. Participants in an incubator culture are there primarily to perform roles such as confirming, criticizing, developing, finding resources for, and/or helping to complete the development of an innovative product or service. These cultures often are found among start-up firms in Silicon Valley, California, or Silicon Glen, Scotland. These incubator-type organizations typically are entrepreneurial and often founded and made up by a creative team who left larger, Eiffel-Tower-type employers. They want to be part of an organization where their creative talents will not be stifled.

Incubator cultures often create environments where participants thrive in an intense, emotional commitment to the nature of the work. For example, the group may be in the process of gene splitting that could lead to radical medical breakthroughs and extend life. Often, personnel in such cultures are overworked, and the enterprise typically is underfunded. As breakthroughs occur and the company gains stability, however, it starts moving down the road toward commercialization and profit. In turn, this engenders the need to hire more people and develop formalized procedures for ensuring the smooth flow of operations. In this process of growth and maturity, the unique characteristics of the incubator culture begin to wane and disappear, and the culture is replaced by one of the other types (family, Eiffel Tower, or guided missile).

As noted, change in the incubator culture often is fast and spontaneous. All participants are working toward the same objective. Because there may not yet be a customer who is using the final output, however, the problem itself often is open to redefinition, and the solution typically is generic in that it is aimed at a universe of applications. Meanwhile, motivation of the personnel remains highly intrinsic and intense, and it is common to find them working 70 hours a week—and loving it. The participants are more concerned with the unfolding creative process than they are in gathering power or ensuring personal monetary gain. In sharp contrast to the family culture, leadership in this incubator culture is achieved, not gained by position.

Organizational Cultures and Country Preferences

The four organizational cultures described by Trompenaars are "pure" types and seldom exist in practice. Rather the types are mixed and, as shown in Table 7-3, overlaid with one of the four major types of culture dominating the corporate scene.

Recently, Trompenaars and his associates have created a questionnaire designed to identify national patterns of corporate culture as shown in Figure 7-3. Commenting on the instrument and the results of the analysis, he has explained that:

> Sixteen questions were devised which deal with general concepts of egalitarianism versus hierarchy, degrees of formality, different forms of conflict resolution, learning, and so on. Respondents are asked to choose between four possible descriptions of their company, which are geared respectively to the power-priority of the family, the role-dominance of the Eiffel Tower, the task-orientation of the guided missile and the person-orientation of the incubator. This work is fairly new; the database currently totals 13,000 and we have significant samples

Table 7–3
Summary Characteristics of the Four Corporate Cultures

	Corporate Culture			
Characteristic	**Family**	**Eiffel Tower**	**Guided Missile**	**Incubator**
Relationships between employees	Diffuse relationships to organic whole to which one is bonded	Specific role in mechanical system of required interaction	Specific tasks in cybernetic system targeted on shared objectives	Diffuse, spontaneous relationships growing out of shared creative process
Attitude toward authority	Status is ascribed to parent figures who are close and powerful	Status is ascribed to superior roles that are distant yet powerful	Status is achieved by project group members who contribute to targeted goal	Status is achieved by individuals exemplifying creativity and growth
Ways of thinking and learning	Intuitive, holistic, lateral and error-correcting	Logical, analytical, vertical, and rationally efficient	Problem centered, professional, practical, cross-disciplinary	Process oriented, creative, ad hoc, inspirational
Attitudes toward people	Family members	Human resources	Specialists and experts	Co-creators
Ways of changing	"Father" changes course	Change rules and procedures	Shift aim as target moves	Improvise and attune
Ways of motivating and rewarding	Intrinsic satisfaction in being loved and respected	Promotion to greater position, larger role	Pay or credit for performance and problems solved	Participation in the process of creating new realities
	Management by subjectives	Management by job description	Management by objectives	Management by enthusiasm
Criticism and conflict resolution	Turn other cheek, save other's face, do not lose power game	Criticism is accusation of irrationalism unless there are procedures to arbitrate conflicts	Constructive task-related only, then admit error and correct fast	Improve creative idea, not negate it

Source: Adapted from Fons Trompenaars and Charles Hampden-Turner, *Riding the Waves of Culture: Understanding Diversity in Global Business,* 2nd ed. (Burr Ridge, IL: Irwin, 1998), p. 183.

Figure 7–3

National Patterns of Corporate Culture

Source: Adapted from Fons Trompenaars and Charles Hampden-Turner, *Riding the Waves of Culture: Understanding Diversity in Global Business,* 2nd ed. (New York: McGraw-Hill, 1998), p. 184.

for 42 countries. These show very marked distinctions. . . . [They show] the highest scores for guided missile companies in the USA and the UK, and the highest for family companies in France and Spain. Sweden scores highest for incubators and Germany for Eiffel Towers.[20]

This analysis would suggest that MNCs who have operations in a number of different countries should adjust their local organizational cultures to fit that country's culture. At the same time, however, these subsidiaries must be able to coordinate their local operations with other organizational groups in the MNC so that all units operate in harmony and unity of purpose. A good example is provided by the accompanying "International Management in Action: Matsushita Goes Global."

Managing Multiculturalism and Diversity

As the "International Management in Action" box on Matsushita indicates, success in the international arena often is greatly determined by an MNC's ability to manage both multiculturalism and diversity. Both domestically and internationally, organizations find themselves leading workforces that have a variety of cultures (and subcultures) and consist of a largely diverse population of women, men, young and old people, blacks, whites, Latins, Asians, Arabs, Indians, and many others.

Phases of Multicultural Development

The effect of multiculturalism and diversity will vary depending on the stage of the firm in its international evolution. Table 7-4 depicts the characteristics of the major phases in this evolution. For example, Adler has noted that international cultural diversity has minimal impact on domestic organizations, although domestic multiculturalism has a highly significant impact. As firms begin exporting to foreign clients, however, and become what she calls "international organizations" (Phase II in Table 7-4), they must adapt their approach and products to those of the local market. For these international firms, the impact of multiculturalism is highly significant. As companies become what she calls "multinational firms" (Phase III), they often find that price tends to dominate all other considerations, and the direct impact of culture may lessen slightly. For those who continue this international evolution, however, and become full-blown "global companies" (Phase IV), the impact of culture again becomes extremely important. Notes Adler:

> Global firms need an understanding of cultural dynamics to plan their strategy, to locate production facilities and suppliers worldwide, to design and market culturally appropriate products and services, as well as to manage cross-cultural interaction throughout the organization—from senior executive committees to the shop floor. As more firms today move from domestic, international, and multinational organizations to operating as truly global organizations and alliances, the importance of cultural diversity increases markedly. What once was "nice to understand" becomes imperative for survival, let alone success.[21]

As shown in Figure 7-4, international culture diversity traditionally affects neither the domestic firm's organizational culture nor its relationship with its customers or clients. These firms work domestically, and only domestic multiculturalism has a direct impact on their dynamics as well as their relationship to the external environment.

Conversely, among international firms, which focus on exporting and producing abroad, cultural diversity has a strong impact on their external relationships with potential buyers and foreign employees. In particular, these firms rely heavily on expatriate managers to help manage operations; as a result, the diversity focus is from the inside out. This is the reverse of what happens in multinational firms, where there is less emphasis on managing cultural differences outside the firm and more on managing cultural diversity within the company. This is because multinational firms hire personnel from all over the world. Adler notes that these multinational firms need to develop cross-cultural management skills up the levels of the hierarchy. As shown in Figure 7-4, this results in a diversity focus that is primarily internal.

In recent years, a growing number of multinationals have begun to expand their operations, realizing that if they do not increase their worldwide presence now, they likely will be left behind in the near future. In turn, this has created a number of different challenges for these MNCs, including making a fit between their home organizational culture and those at local levels in the different countries where the MNC operates. Matsushita provides an excellent example in how they have handled this challenge with their macro/micro approach. This huge, Japanese MNC has developed a number of guidelines that it uses in setting up and operating its more than 150 industrial units. At the same time, the company complements these macro guidelines with on-site micro techniques that help to create the most appropriate organizational culture in the subsidiary.

At the macro level, Matsushita employs six overall guidelines that are followed in all locales. They include: (1) be a good corporate citizen in every country, among other things, by respecting cultures, customs, and languages; (2) give overseas operations the best manufacturing technology the company has available; (3) keep the expatriate head count down, and groom local management to take over; (4) let operating plants set their own rules, fine-tuning manufacturing processes to match the skills of the workers; (5) create local research and development to tailor products to markets; and (6) encourage competition between overseas outposts and with plants back home.

Working within these macro guidelines, Matsushita then allows each local unit to create its own culture. The Malaysian operations are a good example. Since 1987, Matsushita has set up 13 new subsidiaries in Malaysia, and employment there has more than quadrupled, to approximately 25,000 people. Only 230 of these employees, however, are Japanese. From these Malaysian operations, Matsushita currently produces 1.3 million televisions and 1.8 million air conditioners annually, and 90 percent of these units are shipped overseas. To produce this output, local plants reflect Malaysia's cultural mosaic of Muslim Malays, ethnic Chinese, and Indians. To accommodate this diversity, Matsushita cafeterias offer Malaysian, Chinese, and Indian food, and to accommodate Muslim religious customs, Matsushita provides special prayer rooms at each plant and allows two prayer sessions per shift.

How well does this Malaysian workforce perform for the Japanese MNC? In the past, the Malaysian plants' slogan was "Let's catch up with Japan." Today, however, these plants frequently outperform their Japanese counterparts in both quality and efficiency. The comparison with Japan no longer is used. Additionally, Matsushita has found that the Malaysian culture is very flexible, and the locals are able to work well with almost any employer. Commenting on Malaysia's multiculturalism, Matsushita's managing director notes, "They are used to accommodating other cultures, and so they think of us Japanese as just another culture. That makes it much easier for us to manage them than some other nationalities."

Today, Matsushita faces a number of important challenges, including remaining profitable in a slow-growth, high-cost Japanese economy. Fortunately, this MNC is doing extremely well overseas, which is buying it time to get its house in order back home. A great amount of this success results from the MNC's ability to nurture and manage overseas organizational cultures (such as in Malaysia) that are both diverse and highly productive.

Global firms need both an internal and an external diversity focus (again see Figure 7-4). To be effective, everyone in the global organization needs to develop cross-cultural skills that allow them to work effectively with internal personnel as well as external customers, clients, and suppliers.

Types of Multiculturalism

For the international management arena, there are several ways of examining multiculturalism and diversity. One is to focus on the domestic multicultural and diverse workforce that operates in the MNC's home country. In addition to domestic multiculturalism, there is the diverse workforce in other geographic locales, and increasingly common are the mix of domestic and overseas personnel found in today's MNCs. The following discussion examines both domestic and group multiculturalism and the potential problems and strengths.

Table 7–4
The Evolution of International Corporations

Characteristics/ Activities	Phase I (Domestic Corporations)	Phase II (International Corporations)	Phase III (Multinational Corporations)	Phase IV (Global Corporations)
Primary orientation	Product/service	Market	Price	Strategy
Competitive strategy	Domestic	Multidomestic	Multinational	Global
Importance of world business	Marginal	Important	Extremely important	Dominant
Product/service	New, unique	More standardized	Completely standard-ized (commodity)	Mass-customized
	Product engineering emphasized	Process engineering emphasized	Engineering not emphasized	Product and process engineering
Technology	Proprietary	Shared	Widely shared	Instantly and extensively shared
R&D/sales	High	Decreasing	Very low	Very high
Profit margin	High	Decreasing	Very low	High, yet immediately decreasing
Competitors	None	Few	Many	Significant (few or many)
Market	Small, domestic	Large, multidomestic	Larger, multinational	Largest, global
Production location	Domestic	Domestic and primary markets	Multinational, least cost	Imports and exports
Exports	None	Growing, high potential	Large, saturated	Imports and exports
Structure	Functional divisions	Functional with international division	Multinational lines of business	Global alliances, hierarchy
	Centralized	Decentralized	Centralized	Coordinated, decentralized
Primary orientation	Product/service	Market	Price	Strategy
Strategy	Domestic	Multidomestic	Multinational	Global
Perspective	Ethnocentric	Polycentric/ regiocentric	Multinational	Global/multicentric
Cultural sensitivity	Marginally important	Very important	Somewhat important	Critically important
With whom	No one	Clients	Employees	Employees and clients
Level	No one	Workers and clients	Managers	Executives
Strategic assumption	"One way"/ "one best way"	"Many good ways," equifinality	"One least-cost way"	"Many good ways," simultaneously

Source: Nancy J. Adler, *International Dimensions of Organizational Behavior,* 2nd ed. (Boston: PWS-Kent Publishing, 1991), pp. 7–8.

Figure 7–4

Location of International Cross-Cultural Interaction

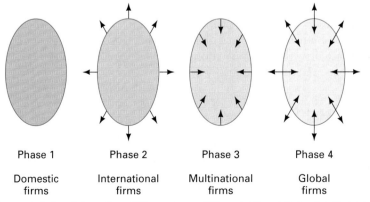

Phase 1   Phase 2   Phase 3   Phase 4

Domestic   International   Multinational   Global
firms   firms   firms   firms

Source: Nancy J. Adler, *International Dimensions of Organizational Behavior,* 2nd ed. (Boston: PWS-Kent Publishing, 1991), p. 123.

Domestic Multiculturalism It is not necessary for today's organizations to do business in another country to encounter people with diverse cultural backgrounds. Culturally distinct populations can be found within organizations almost everywhere in the world. In Singapore, for example, there are four distinct cultural and linguistic groups: Chinese, Eurasian, Indian, and Malay. In Switzerland, there are four distinct ethnic communities: French, German, Italian, and Romansch. In Belgium, there are two linguistic groups: French and Flemish. In the United States, millions of first-generation immigrants have brought both their language and their culture. In Los Angeles, for example, there are more Samoans than on the island of Samoa, more Israelis than in any other city outside Israel, and more first- and second-generation Mexicans than in any other city except Mexico City. In Miami, over one-half the population is Latin, and most residents speak Spanish fluently. More Puerto Ricans live in New York City than in Puerto Rico.

It is even possible to examine domestic multiculturalism within the same ethnic groups. For example, Lee, after conducting research in Singapore among small Chinese family businesses, found that the viewpoints of the old generation differ sharply from those of the younger generation. Table 7-5 provides specific contrasts between the old and young generations of Chinese.

Table 7–5

Perspectives of Older and Younger Generations in Small Chinese Family Businesses in Singapore

Older Generation	Younger Generation
Claim that they have more experiences.	Claim that they have more education.
Perceive that their role is to intervene for the workers and help them.	Perceive that their role is to hire competent workers and expect them to perform.
Believe that it is the boss's responsibility to solve problems.	Believe that it is the individual's responsibility to solve problems.
Stress that a boss has the obligation to take care of the workers.	Stress that workers have responsibility to perform the job well.
Emphasize that individuals should conform to the majority.	Emphasize that individuals should maximize his/her talents and potentials.
Believe that work cannot be divided clearly and like to be involved in everything.	Believe that a boss should mind his own work and leave the workers to do their jobs.
Perceive that work is more important than designation and organizational structure.	Perceive that designation and organizational structure are important in order to get the work done.
Believe that managers should help the workers to solve their problems.	Believe that managers should set objectives and achieve them.
Complain that the younger generation likes to use complicated management methods.	Complain that the old generation does things on an ad hoc basis.
Perceive that the younger generation likes to change and expects immediate results.	Perceive that the old generation is static and resistant to change.
Worry that the young generation is not experienced in running the business.	Frustrated that the old generation still holds on strongly to their power.
Emphasize that they have to take care of the old workers in the process of the company's growth.	Emphasize that they have to gain acceptance from their customers in order to enhance its image as a modern company.
Emphasize that ethics are important in business.	Emphasize that strategy is important in business.
Anticipate that the young generation is going to have many difficulties if they adopt Western concepts of management.	Frustrated that the old generation does not let them test out their concepts of management.
Believe that one's ability is limited and one should be contented with what one has.	Believe that there are a lot of opportunities for achievement and growth.

Source: Adapted from Jean Lee, "Culture and Management—A Study of Small Chinese Family Business in Singapore," *Journal of Small Business Management,* July 1996, p. 65.

In short, there is considerable multicultural diversity domestically in organizations throughout the world, and this trend will continue. For example, the U.S. civilian labor force of the next decade will change dramatically in ethnic composition.

In particular, there will be a significantly lower percentage of white males in the workforce and a growing percentage of women, African-Americans, Hispanics, and Asians.

Group Multiculturalism   There are a number of ways that diverse groups can be categorized. Four of the most common include:

Homogeneous group
A group that is characterized by members who share similar backgrounds and generally perceive, interpret, and evaluate events in similar ways.

Token group
A group in which all members but one have the same background, such as a group of Japanese retailers and a British attorney.

Bicultural group
A group in which two or more members represent each of two distinct cultures, such as four Mexicans and four Taiwanese who have formed a team to investigate the possibility of investing in a venture.

Multicultural group
A group in which there are individuals from three or more different ethnic backgrounds, such as three U.S., three German, three Uruguayan, and three Chinese managers who are looking into mining operations in South Africa.

1. **Homogeneous groups,** which are characterized by members who share similar backgrounds and generally perceive, interpret, and evaluate events in similar ways. An example would be a group of male German bankers who are forecasting the economic outlook for a foreign investment.
2. **Token groups,** in which all members but one have the same background. An example would be a group of Japanese retailers and a British attorney who are looking into the benefits and shortcomings of setting up operations in Bermuda.
3. **Bicultural groups,** which have two or more members of a group represent each of two distinct cultures. An example would be a group of four Mexicans and four Canadians who have formed a team to investigate the possibility of investing in Russia.
4. **Multicultural groups,** in which there are individuals from three or more different ethnic backgrounds. An example is a group of three American, three German, three Uruguayan, and three Chinese managers who are looking into mining operations in Chile.

As the diversity of a group increases, the likelihood of all members perceiving things in the same way decreases sharply. Attitudes, perceptions, and communication in general may be a problem. On the other hand, there also are significant advantages associated with the effective use of multicultural, diverse groups. The following sections examine the potential problems and the advantages.

Potential Problems Associated with Diversity

Overall, diversity may cause a lack of cohesion that results in the unit's inability to take concerted action, be productive, and create a work environment that is conducive to both efficiency and effectiveness. These potential problems are rooted in people's attitudes.

An example of an attitudinal problem in a diverse group may be the mistrust of others. For example, many U.S. managers who work for Japanese operations in the United States complain that Japanese managers often huddle together and discuss matters in their native language. The U.S. managers wonder aloud why the Japanese do not speak English. What are they talking about that they do not want anyone else to hear? In fact, the Japanese often find it easier to communicate among themselves in their native language, and because no Americans are present, the Japanese managers ask why they should speak English. If there is no reason for anyone else to be privy to our conversation, why should we not opt for our own language? Nevertheless, such practices do tend to promote an attitude of mistrust.

Another potential problem may be perceptual. Unfortunately, when culturally diverse groups come together, they often bring preconceived stereotypes with them. In initial meetings, for example, engineers from economically advanced countries often are perceived as more knowledgeable than those from less advanced countries. In turn, this can result in status-related problems, because some of the group initially are regarded as more competent than others and likely are accorded status on this basis. As the diverse group works together, erroneous perceptions often are corrected, but this takes time. In one diverse group consisting of engineers from a major Japanese firm and a world-class U.S. firm, a Japanese engineer was assigned a technical task because of his stereotyped technical educational background. The group soon realized that this particular Japanese engineer was not capable of doing this job, however, because for the last 4 years, he had been responsible for coordinating routine quality and no longer was on the technologic cutting edge. His engineering degree from the University of Tokyo had resulted in the other members perceiving him as technically competent and able to carry out the task; this perception proved to be incorrect.

A related problem is inaccurate biases. For example, it is well-known that Japanese companies depend on groups to make decisions. Entrepreneurial behavior, individualism, and originality are typically downplayed.[22] However, in a growing number of Japanese firms this stereotype is proving to be incorrect.[23] Here is an example.

> Mr. Uchida, a 28-year-old executive in a small software company, dyes his hair brown, keeps a sleeping bag by his desk for late nights in the office and occasionally takes the day off to go windsurfing. "Sometimes I listen to soft music to soothe my feelings, and sometimes I listen to hard music to build my energy," said Mr. Uchida, who manages the technology-development division of the Rimnet Corporation, an Internet access provider. "It's important that we always keep in touch with our sensibilities when we want to generate ideas." The creative whiz kid, a business personality often prized by corporate America, has come to Japan Inc. Unlikely as it might seem in a country renowned for its deference to authority and its devotion to group solidarity, freethinkers like Mr. Uchida are popping up all over the workplace. Nonconformity is suddenly in.[24]

Still another potential problem with diverse groups is inaccurate communication, which could occur for a number of reasons. One is misunderstandings caused by words used by a speaker that are not clear to other members. For example, in a diverse group in which one of the authors was working, a British manager told her U.S. colleagues, "I will fax you this report in a fortnight." When the author asked the Americans when they would be getting the report, most of them believed it would be arriving in 4 days. They did not know that the common British word "fortnight" (14 nights) means 2 weeks.

Another contribution to miscommunication may be the way in which situations are interpreted. Many Japanese nod their heads when others talk, but this does not mean that they agree with what is being said. They merely are being polite and attentive. In many societies, it is impolite to say no, and if the listener believes that the other person wants a positive answer, the listener will say yes even though this is incorrect. As a result, many U.S. managers find out that promises made by individuals from other cultures cannot be taken at face value—and in many instances, the other individual assumes that the American realizes this!

Diversity also may lead to communication problems because of the different uses of time. For example, many Japanese will not agree to a course of action on-the-spot. They will not act until they have discussed the matter with their own people, because they do not feel empowered to act alone. Many Latin managers refuse to be held to a strict timetable, because they do not have the same time-urgency that U.S. managers do. Here is another example, as described by a European manager:

> In attempting to plan a new project, a three-person team composed of managers from Britain, France, and Switzerland failed to reach agreement. To the others, the British representative appeared unable to accept any systematic approach; he wanted to discuss all potential problems before making a decision. The French and Swiss representatives agreed to examine everything before making a decision, but then disagreed on the sequence and scheduling of operations. The Swiss, being more pessimistic in their planning, allocated more time for each suboperation than did the French. As a result, although everybody agreed on its validity, we never started the project. If the project had been discussed by three Frenchmen, three Swiss, or three Britons, a decision, good or bad, would have been made. The project would not have been stalled for lack of agreement.[25]

Advantages of Diversity

While there are some potential problems to overcome when using culturally diverse groups in today's MNCs, there also are a host of benefits to be gained. In particular, there is growing evidence that culturally diverse groups can enhance creativity, lead to better decisions, and result in more effective and productive performance.

One main benefit of diversity is the generation of more and better ideas. Because group members come from a host of different cultures, they often are able to create a greater number of unique (and thus creative) solutions and recommendations. For example, a U.S. MNC recently was preparing to launch a new software package aimed at the mass consumer market. The company hoped to capitalize on the upcoming Christmas season with a strong advertising campaign in each of its international markets. A meeting of the sales managers from these markets in Spain, the Middle East, and Japan helped the company to revise and better target its marketing effort. The Spanish manager suggested that the company focus its campaign around the coming of the Magi (January 6) and not Christmas (December 25), because in Latin cultures, gifts typically are exchanged on the date that the Magi brought their gifts. The Middle East manager pointed out that most of his customers were not Christians, so a Christmas campaign would not have much meaning in this area. Instead, he suggested the company focus its sales campaign around the value of the software and how it could be useful to customers and not worry about getting the product shipped by early December. The Japanese manager concurred with his Middle East colleague, but additionally suggested that some of the colors being proposed for the sales brochure be changed to better fit with Japanese culture. Thanks to these ideas, the sales campaign proved to be one of the most effective in the company's history.

Groupthink
Social conformity and pressures on individual members of a group to conform and reach consensus.

A second major benefit is that culturally diverse groups can prevent **groupthink**, which is social conformity and pressures on individual members of a group to conform and reach consensus. When this occurs, group participants believe that their ideas and actions are correct and that those who disagree with them are either uninformed or deliberately trying to sabotage their efforts. Multicultural diverse groups often are able to avoid this problem, because the members do not think similarly or feel pressure to conform. As a result, they typically question each other, offer opinions and suggestions that are contrary to those held by others, and must be persuaded to change their minds. Therefore, unanimity is achieved only through a careful process of deliberation. Unlike homogeneous groups, where everyone can be "of one mind," diverse groups may be slower in reaching a general consensus; however, the decision may be more effective.

Building Multicultural Team Effectiveness

Multiculturally diverse teams have a great deal of potential to be either very effective or very ineffective. As shown in Figure 7-5, Kovach reports that if cross-cultural groups are led properly, they can indeed be highly effective; unfortunately, she also found that if they are not managed properly, they can be highly ineffective. In other words, diverse groups are more powerful than single-culture groups. They can hurt the organization, but if managed effectively, they can be the best. The following sections provide the conditions and guidelines for managing diverse groups in today's organizations effectively.

Understanding the Conditions for Effectiveness   Multicultural teams are most effective when they face tasks requiring innovativeness. They are far less effective when they are assigned to routine tasks. As Adler explained:

> Cultural diversity provides the biggest asset for teams with difficult, discretionary tasks requiring innovation. Diversity becomes less helpful when employees are working on simple tasks involving repetitive or routine procedures. Therefore, diversity generally

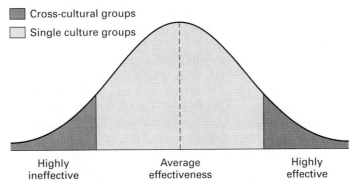

Source: Based on Dr. Carol Kovach's research, conducted at the Graduate School of Management, University of California at Los Angeles (UCLA), and reported in Nancy J. Adler, *International Dimensions of Organizational Behavior,* 2nd ed. (Boston: PWS-Kent Publishing, 1991), p. 135.

Figure 7–5

Group Effectiveness and Culture

becomes more valuable during the planning and development of projects (the "work" stage) and less helpful during their implementation (the "action" stage). The more senior the team members, the more likely they are to be working on projects that can benefit from diversity. Diversity is therefore extremely valuable to senior executive teams, both within and across countries.[26]

In achieving the greatest amount of effectiveness from diverse teams, activities must be determined by the stage of team development (e.g., entry, working, and action). For example, in the entry stage, the focus should be on building trust and developing team cohesion. This can be a difficult task for diverse teams, whose members are accustomed to working in different ways. For example, Americans, Germans, and Swiss typically spend little time getting to know each other; they find out the nature of the task and set about pursuing it on their own without first building trust and cohesion. This contrasts sharply with individuals from Latin America, Southern Europe, and the Middle East, where a great deal of initial time is spent getting to know each other. This contrast between task-oriented and relationship-oriented members of a diverse team may cause difficulty in creating cohesion. To counteract this problem, it is common in the entry stage of development to find experienced multicultural managers focusing attention on the team members' equivalent professional qualifications and status. Once this professional similarity and respect are established, the group can begin forming itself into a cohesive team.

In the work stage of development, attention may be directed more toward describing and analyzing the problem or task that has been assigned. This stage often is fairly easy for managers of multicultural teams, because they can draw on the diversity of the members in generating ideas. As noted earlier, diverse groups tend to be most effective when dealing with situations that require innovative approaches.

In the action stage, the focus shifts to decision making and implementation. This can be a difficult phase, because it often requires consensus building among the members. In achieving this objective, experienced managers work to help the diverse group recognize and facilitate the creation of ideas with which everyone can agree. In doing so, it is common to find strong emphasis on problem-solving techniques such as the nominal group technique (NGT), where the group members individually make contributions before group interaction and consensus is reached.

Using the Proper Guidelines   Besides some overall conditions, a number of specific guidelines for effectively managing culturally diverse groups have been identified. Here are some of the most useful:

1. Team members must be selected for their task-related abilities and not solely based on ethnicity. If the task is routine, homogeneous membership often is preferable; if the task is innovative, multicultural membership typically is best.

2. Team members must recognize and be prepared to deal with their differences. The goal is to facilitate a better understanding of cross-cultural differences and generate a higher level of performance and rapport. In doing so, members need to become aware of their own stereotypes, as well as those of the others, and use this information to better understand the real differences that exist between them. This can then serve as a basis for determining how each individual member can contribute to the overall effectiveness of the team.

3. Because members of diverse teams tend to have more difficulty agreeing on their purpose and task than members of homogeneous groups, the team leader must help the group to identify and define its overall goal. This goal is most useful when it requires members to cooperate and develop mutual respect in carrying out their tasks.

4. Members must have equal power so that everyone can participate in the process; cultural dominance always is counterproductive. As a result, managers of culturally diverse teams distribute power according to each person's ability to contribute to the task, not according to ethnicity.

5. It is important that all members have mutual respect for each other. This often is accomplished by managers choosing members of equal ability, making prior accomplishments and task-related skills known to the group, and minimizing early judgments based on ethnic stereotypes.

6. Because teams often have difficulty determining what is a good or a bad idea or decision, managers must give teams positive feedback on their process and output. This feedback helps the members to see themselves as a team, and it teaches them to value and celebrate their diversity, recognize contributions made by the individual members, and trust the collective judgment of the group.

These guidelines can be useful in helping leaders to manage culturally diverse teams effectively. World-class organizations use such an approach, and one good example is NUMMI (New United Motor Manufacturing), a joint venture between General Motors and Toyota that transformed an out-of-date GM plant in Fremont, California, into a world-class organization. This joint-venture partnership, formed over 10 years ago, continues to be a success story of how a culturally diverse workforce can produce state-of-the-art automobiles. The successful approach to culturally diverse work teams at NUMMI was built around four principles:

1. Both management and labor recognized that their futures were interdependent, thus committing them to a mutual vision.

2. Employees felt secure and trusted assurances that they would be treated fairly, thus enabling them to become contributors.

3. The production system formed interdependent relationships throughout the plant, thus helping to create a healthy work environment.

4. The production system was managed to transform the stress and conflict of everyday life into trust and mutual respect.[27]

In achieving success at NUMMI, Toyota sent trainers from Japan to work with its U.S. counterparts and teach the production system that would be used throughout the plant. During this period, both groups searched for points of agreement, establishing valuable relationships in the process. In addition, the Japanese taught the Americans some useful techniques for increasing productivity, including how to focus on streamlining operations, reduce waste, and learn how to blame mistakes on the situation or themselves (not on team members).

In overcoming multicultural differences at NUMMI, several changes were introduced, including: (1) reserved dining rooms were eliminated, and all managers now eat in a communal cafeteria; (2) all reserved parking spaces were eliminated; and (3) GM's 80 job classifications were collapsed into only 3 to equalize work and rewards and ensure fairness. Commenting on the overall success of the joint venture, it was noted that

> Toyota managers resisted temptations to forge ahead with a pure version of the system. Both the Japanese and Americans learned as they went. By adopting a "go slow" attitude, the Japanese and Americans remained open to points of resistance as they arose and navigated around them. By tolerating ambiguity and by searching for consensus, Toyota managers established the beginnings of mutual respect and trust with the American workers and managers.[28]

NUMMI is only one example of the many successful multicultural workforces producing world-class goods and services. In each case, however, effective multinationals rely on the types of guidelines that have been highlighted in this discussion.

World of Business Week Revisited

The *Business Week* article that opened this chapter offered an excellent example of how the conflict between national culture and organizational culture can create problems for multinationals. Now that you have read this chapter, you should have a better understanding of how national culture can potentially inhibit or enhance the effects of organizational culture. Using France as the example, it is easy to see how the forces of globalization, technology, and deregulation can overpower ingrained national values to affect organizational cultures. With the exception of unionized workers and hard-core conservatives, a new generation of French workers and companies want to shrink the role of the state, encourage entrepreneurship, focus on Internet technology, and erase the welfare mentality so typical of traditional French society. Realizing that a modernized French society will result in a strong and maybe new organizational culture, answer the following questions: (1) With the newly arrived European Monetary Union (EMU), what effect might this have on both national and organizational cultures? (2) Why is there so often resistance to change in organizations that can be traced to national culture? (3) What is it about France that makes the clash between national and organizational culture seem probable?

Summary of Key Points

1. Organizational culture is a pattern of basic assumptions that are developed by a group as it learns to cope with its problems of external adaptation and internal integration and that are taught to new members as the correct way to perceive, think, and feel in relation to these problems. Some important characteristics of organizational culture include observed behavioral regularities, norms, dominant values, philosophy, rules, and organizational climate.

2. Organizational cultures are shaped by a number of factors. These include the general relationship between employees and their organization, the hierarchic system of authority that defines the roles of managers and subordinates, and the general views that employees hold about the organization's purpose, destiny, goals, and their place in them. When examining these differences, Trompenaars has suggested the use of two continua: equity/hierarchy, and person/task orientation, resulting in four basic types of organizational cultures: family, Eiffel Tower, guided missile, and incubator.

3. The family culture is characterized by a strong emphasis on hierarchic authority and orientation to the person. The Eiffel Tower culture is characterized by a strong emphasis on hierarchy and orientation to the task. The guided missile culture is characterized by a strong emphasis on equality in the workplace and orientation to the task. The incubator culture is

characterized by a strong emphasis on equality and orientation to the person.

4. Success in the international arena often is heavily determined by a company's ability to manage multiculturalism and diversity. There are four phases through which firms progress in their international evolution: (1) domestic corporation; (2) international corporation; (3) multinational corporation; and (4) global corporation.

5. There are a number of ways to examine multiculturalism and diversity. One is by looking at the domestic multicultural and diverse workforce that operates in the MNC's home country. Another is by examining the variety of diverse groups that

exist in MNCs, including homogeneous groups, token groups, bicultural groups, and multicultural groups. Several potential problems as well as advantages are associated with multicultural, diverse teams.

6. A number of guidelines have proved to be particularly effective in managing culturally diverse groups. These include careful selection of the members, identification of the group's goals, establishment of equal power and mutual respect among the participants, and delivering positive feedback on performance. A good example of how these guidelines have been used is the NUMMI joint venture created by General Motors and Toyota.

Key Terms

bicultural group
Eiffel Tower culture
family culture
groupthink

guided missile culture
homogeneous group
incubator culture
multinational group

organizational culture
token group

Review and Discussion Questions

1. Some researchers have found that when Germans work for a U.S. MNC, they become even more German, and when Americans work for a German MNC, they become even more American. Why would this knowledge be important to these MNCs?

2. When comparing the negotiating styles and strategies of French versus Spanish negotiators, a number of sharp contrasts are evident. What are three of these, and what could MNCs do to improve their position when negotiating with either group?

3. In which of the four types of organizational cultures—family, Eiffel Tower, guided missile, incubator—would most people in the United States feel comfortable? In which would most Japanese feel comfortable? Based on your answers, what conclusions could you draw regarding the importance of understanding organizational culture for international management?

4. Most MNCs need not enter foreign markets to face the challenge of dealing with multiculturalism. Do you agree or disagree with this statement? Explain your answer.

5. What are some potential problems that must be overcome when using multicultural, diverse teams in today's organizations? What are some recognized advantages? Identify and discuss two of each.

6. A number of guidelines can be valuable in helping MNCs to make diverse teams more effective. What are five of these? Additionally, what underlying principles guided NUMMI in its effective use of multicultural teams? Were the principles used by NUMMI similar to the general guidelines identified in this chapter, or were they significantly different? Explain your answer.

Internet Exercise: Hewlett-Packard's International Focus

Mention the name Hewlett-Packard, or HP for short, and people are likely to think of printers—an area where the MNC has managed to excel worldwide in recent years. However, HP has many other offerings besides printers and has rapidly expanded its product line into the international arena over the last decade. Visit its Web site at **www.hp.com** and review some of the latest developments. In particular, pay close attention to its product line and international expansion. Then choose three different countries where the firm is doing business: one from the Americas, one from Europe, and one from Southeast Asia or India. (Since the sites are all presented in the local language, you might want to make India your choice, since this one is in English.) Compare and contrast the product offerings and ways in which HP goes about marketing itself over the Web in these locations. What do you see as some of the major differences? Second, using Figure 7-2 and Table 7-3 as your guide, in what way are national cultures likely to present significant challenges to HP's efforts to create a smooth-running international enterprise? What would you see as two of the critical issues with which the management will have to deal? Third, what are two steps that you think HP will have to take in order to build multicultural team effectiveness? What are two guidelines that can help them do this?

Japan

Japan is located in eastern Asia, and it comprises a curved chain of more than 3,000 islands. Four of these—Hokkaido, Honshu, Shikoku, and Kyushi—account for 98 percent of the country's land area. The population of Japan was approximately 127 million in the late 1990s, with over 8 million people living in the nation's capital, Tokyo. According to the World Bank, Japan's gross domestic product (GDP) during this time, approximately, was $23,000 per capita. At the same time, the country was in the throes of an economic recession, and growth has slowed considerably from that of the 1980s when an average annual increase of 6 percent in GDP was common. Most forecasts, however, indicate that by the end of this century, Japan's economy should be turning around.

This optimistic outlook is shared by two multinationals, one from the United States and the other from Germany. These two MNCs recently joined forces with a large Japanese MNC to create a new retailing chain throughout Japan. The joint venture will limit its merchandise selection to clothing and toys, which are two product areas where Japanese prices are relatively higher than those paid by consumers in other countries. The U.S. and German partners will design the clothing and toys, but they will be produced in Japan by local labor and sold there. The U.S. and German partners will contribute most of the capital needed for the venture and they also will help design the production and distribution system as well as the retail store layout. The Japanese partner will be responsible for choosing the type of merchandise to be produced, manage and/or coordinate (for subcontractors) the production facilities, and handle the marketing.

To provide a managerial presence in Japan, the two foreign partners will share a new headquarters building with their local partner. Located approximately 60 miles outside of Tokyo, this building will house the senior-level management from all three MNCs as well as key finance, production, and marketing personnel. The plan is to have strategy and major decisions made at this headquarters, then disseminated to the production facilities and retail stores. The joint venture hopes to have 6 stores operating within 24 months, and 20 more within 5 years.
www.japanlink.com

Questions

1. What type of organizational culture is each of the three partners likely to have? (Use Figure 7-3 as a guide in answering this question.)

2. Which of the organizational cultures will be most different from that of the other two? Explain.

3. What types of problems might the culturally diverse top-management team at headquarters create for the joint venture? Give some specific examples. How could these problems be overcome?

4. In terms of organizational culture, what is your estimate of success for this joint venture?

A Good Faith Effort Is Needed

Excelsior Manufacturing is a medium-sized firm located in the northeast part of the United States. Excelsior has long been known as a high-quality, world-class producer of precision tools. Recently, however, this MNC has been slowly losing market share in Europe, because many EU companies are turning to other European firms to save on taxes and transportation costs. Realizing that it needed a European partner if it hoped to recapture this lost ground, Excelsior began looking to buy a firm that could provide it a strong foothold in this market. After a brief search, the MNC made contact with Quality Instrumentation, a Madrid-based firm that was founded 5 years ago and has been growing at 25 percent annually. Excelsior currently is discussing a buyout with Quality Instrumentation, and the Spanish firm appears to be interested in the arrangement as it will provide them with increased technology, a quality reputation, and more funding for European expansion.

Next week, owners of the two companies are scheduled to meet in Madrid to discuss purchase price and potential plans for integrating their overall operations. The biggest sticking point appears to be a concern for meshing the organizational cultures and the work values and habits of the two enterprises. Each is afraid that the other's way of doing business might impede overall progress and lead to wasted productivity and lost profit. To deal with this issue, the president of Excelsior has asked his management team to draft a plan that could serve as a guide in determining how both groups could coordinate their efforts.

On a personal level, the head of Excelsior believes that it will be important for the Spanish management team to understand that if the Spaniards sell the business, they must be prepared to let U.S. managers have final decision-making power on major issues, such as research and development efforts, expansion plans, and customer segmentation. At the same time, the Americans are concerned that their potential European partners will feel they are being told what to do and resist these efforts. "We're going to have to make them understand that we must work as a unified team," the president explained to his planning committee, "and create a culture that will support this idea. We may not know a lot about working with Spaniards and they may not understand a great deal about how Americans do things, but I believe that we can resolve these differences if we put forth a good faith effort."

Questions

1. What do you think some of the main organizational culture differences between the two companies would be?

2. Why might the cultural diversity in the Spanish firm not be as great as that in the U.S. firm, and what potential problems could this create?

3. What would you recommend be done to effectively merge the two organizational cultures and ensure they cooperate harmoniously? Offer some specific recommendations.

Chapter 8

Intercultural Communication

Objectives of the Chapter

Communication takes on special importance in international management because of the difficulties in conveying meanings between parties from different cultures. The problems of misinterpretation and error are compounded in the international context. Chapter 8 examines how the communication process in general works, and it looks at the downward and upward communication flows that commonly are used in international communication. Then, the chapter examines the major barriers to effective international communication and reviews ways of dealing with these communication problems. The specific objectives of this chapter are:

1. DEFINE the term "communication," and examine some examples of external and internal communication.

2. REVIEW examples of verbal communication styles and explain the importance of message interpretation.

3. ANALYZE the common downward and upward communication flows used in international communication.

4. EXAMINE the language, perception, culture, and nonverbal barriers to effective international communications.

5. PRESENT the steps that can be taken to overcome international communication problems.

BusinessWeek

The World of Business Week:

Does Samsung Control Se Ri Pak?

Hand-made sign spotted at a recent LPGA golf tournament: "Tiger Out, Pak In." The hottest golfer on the planet this season isn't the guy who dresses like he's been dipped in a bucket of Swooshes. Tiger Woods, despite the hype, has but one win in 1998. Now it's 20-year-old Se Ri Pak of South Korea who is suddenly setting records and pushing up TV ratings.

After sweeping to three victories—including the prized U.S. Women's Open—in a torrid stretch during July, Pak went from unheralded to practically unbeatable. Her four wins this year, including two major titles, are the most by an LPGA rookie in 20 years.

For any other pro golfer, that performance would mean an avalanche of big-money endorsement contracts. But Pak has problems: She's a woman golfer, her English is a work in progress, and she seems tethered to Korean conglomerate Samsung Group.

Corporate America has long overlooked Ladies Professional Golf Assn. players, preferring to hire the stars of the PGA Tour. Says Rick Burton of the Warsaw Sports Marketing Center at the University of Oregon: "In all the years the LPGA has existed, no one has broken out" as a product endorser.

Still, Pak is off to a promising start. During last month's U.S. Open, Pak, her parents, and her business manager, Sung Yong "Steven" Kil, held meetings with

several major golf manufacturers, among them Callaway Golf and golf ball maker Maxfli. But negotiations have moved slowly, in part, because of confusion over who speaks for Pak. Kil, who also acts as driver, scheduler, and travel agent, is Pak's second representative this year. A third, said to be IMG, the Cleveland-based sports-management giant, appears to be on the way.

Whomever Pak chooses can expect to be on the phone daily to Seoul, headquarters of Samsung. "The position of manager of the professional golfer is quite important, not only for the player but also for the sponsoring company," says Raymond Yoon, director of corporate strategy for Samsung America. Pak's relationship with Samsung is close and complex. She wears its logo on her hats and slacks. And she is about to debut as spokeswoman and model for Samsung's golf clothing line, Astra, expected in U.S. stores next spring.

Samsung is paying millions to Pak, but how many millions over how many years isn't clear. Recently published reports say Samsung renegotiated Pak's deal after her string of victories and now is paying her $3 million a year for three years. Not so, says Yoon. He maintains that Pak's basic contract—estimated to be as high as $1 million a year for 10 years—"cannot be changed." Yoon adds, however, that Samsung is discussing ways to compensate Pak for her remarkable play.

Samsung's ties to Pak go way back. According to Yoon, Samsung Chairman Kun Hee Lee watched Pak develop her game at a Samsung-owned course near Seoul. Later, company officials arranged for her to go to Florida where, at Samsung's expense, she trained under famed golf instructor David Leadbetter.

Few doubt Samsung's major role in bringing out the best golf in Pak. But some LPGA observers wonder whether she would be better served by making more of her own decisions. Two weeks ago, a weary Pak competed in her sixth consecutive tournament, the du Maurier Classic in Windsor, Ont. She finished a disappointing 13 shots behind the winner and headed home to Orlando for what she thought would be a week of relaxation. But Samsung had scheduled a three-day photo shoot in Orlando. In a flash, Pak's week off vanished. "That was a shame. She was exhausted and really looking forward to a break," says former LPGA star Jane Blalock, who worked as a TV commentator at the du Maurier. "If she continues to be dominated by outside forces, things will be very difficult for her."

For now, however, Pak seems to be bearing up under the pressure. She is popular with her fellow players. And she has charmed the media with her honesty and memorable quotes, delivered in improving, yet halting, English. (Commenting on a cheering gallery, Pak observed: "They make big loud.") Perhaps Pak's greatest impact so far has been in stoking interest in women's golf. Last month, three tournaments in which Pak played set attendance records. "She clearly enjoys playing, and our fans clearly enjoy watching her play," says LPGA Commissioner Jim Ritts. There's no question that Pak, as the sign says, is "in." What's less certain is when she'll be in the really big money.

www.samsung.com

Source: Reprinted from August 17, 1998, p. 68 issue of *Business Week* by special permission, copyright © 1998 by McGraw-Hill Companies, Inc.

This opening news story represents perhaps the biggest and most common challenge facing multinationals in the international arena—communicating effectively with those from other cultures. As more and more companies expand operations into different countries, managers and executives working abroad are confronted with a variety of communication barriers. Most obvious are those associated with language differences, but differences in perception, interpretation, and cultural values are equally common barriers. In the case of South Korean golf sensation, Se Ri Pak, her lack of English speaking skills combined with her obligation to native conglomerate, Samsung Group, has resulted in her being overlooked by U.S. corporate sponsors. Thus, despite Pak's increasing U.S. popularity, confusion regarding Korean cultural values and style of communication has hindered business dealings between Pak and U.S. corporations. Overall, as the article suggests, it is difficult to succeed in international business or management if parties cannot communicate effectively. Thus, as you read the following chapter, consider how you might go about ensuring or improving effective communication between yourself, the MNC you might work for in the future, and those of other cultures.

The Overall Communication Process

Communication
The process of transferring meanings from sender to receiver.

Communication is the process of transferring meanings from sender to receiver. On the surface, this appears to be a fairly straightforward process. On analysis, however, there are a great many problems in the international arena that can result in the failure to transfer meanings correctly. One of these is the inability to effectively establish rapport with the other side. For example, many expatriates who have not been adequately trained will bring up conversation topics that more experienced international managers know should be avoided. Table 8–1 provides a brief list of some of the "dos" and the "don'ts." When an inappropriate topic arises, communication breakdown likely will result, because the other party interprets the message differently from what was intended.[1]

Table 8–1		
Topics of Conversation in Select Countries		
Country	**Appropriate Topic**	**Inappropriate Topic**
Austria	Cars, skiing, music	Money, religion, divorce/separation
France	Music, books, sports, theater	Prices of items, person's work, income, age
Germany	Travel abroad, hobbies, soccer, international politics	World War II, questions about personal life
Great Britain	History, architecture, gardening	Politics, money, prices
Japan	History, culture, art	World War II, government policies that help to exclude foreign competition
Mexico	Family, social concerns	Politics, debt or inflation problems, border violations

Source: Lillian H. Chaney and Jeanette S. Martin, *Intercultural Business Communication* © 1995, p. 102. Reprinted by permission of Prentice-Hall, Inc., Englewood Cliffs, New Jersey.

In gaining some insights to this communication process, it is helpful to examine Figure 8–1. As shown, the sender of a message will determine what he or she wants to say and then encode the message to convey his or her meanings. The communiqué then is transmitted using some medium, such as telephone, letter, or face-to-face verbal interaction. Finally, the message is decoded and interpreted by the receiver. If the message is unclear or the receiver feels that a response is required, the process then is reversed: The receiver now becomes the sender, and the sender becomes the receiver. This reverse flow of information is achieved through feedback, which creates a two-way process. In practice, this back-and-forth flow of meanings is used to clarify, elaborate, and monitor actions by one or more parties to the communication. Unfortunately, this process often is interrupted by what is called "noise," which is the deliberate or nondeliberate distortion of the communication process. (This so-called noise problem is discussed later.)

External and Internal Communications

Organizational communication involves both the external and internal flow of information. In international management, this flow becomes particularly important, because parties to messages often are located in different geographic areas and/or have been born and raised in different cultures. This international context can create communication problems that are quite different from those faced by companies operating within one country.

Examples of External Communication   One major form of external communication during the years ahead will be government attempts to secure agreements with other nations regarding international trade. For example, the United States has been engaged in prolonged discussions with China regarding reciprocal trade agreements. The United States feels that China is not opening up for imports, is lagging behind in doing business with foreign firms, and is exporting goods to virtually every corner of the globe.

This perception of the problem greatly influences the way that the U.S. government communicates with China during trade negotiations. There are other interpretations of international trade strategy, however, and the Chinese have their own version. They believe that Americans are overrating the danger to their own economy and are failing to see that many of the steps being taken by U.S. business will make the United States a dominant economic power in China for the indefinite future.

Other external communication is more one-way in that it does not directly involve all the parties affected by the message. A good example is the EU's rules designed to ensure that member firms are not forced out of their home markets. The EU's Competition Directorate has been empowered to approve mergers between large European firms. This action will help to ensure that U.S. and Japanese companies do not dominate the European market.

Examples of Internal Communication   Although the communication process is the same worldwide, its internal use often is influenced by cultural differences. How U.S. managers communicate may be quite different from how European or Asian managers do, and these differences are important to recognize. For example, a Harvard research team made a comparative study of the management of Russian and U.S. factories, and they found that Russian managers make greater use than U.S. managers of direct, face-to-face communications. U.S. managers rely more heavily on informal, written communication and the telephone.[2] On the other hand, a more recent observational study found both Russian and U.S. managers spend approximately one-third of their time carrying out communication activities.[3]

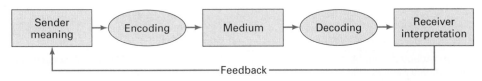

Figure 8–1

The Communication Process

In another study, Pascale investigated communication techniques used by U.S. and Japanese managers operating both at home and in each other's country. He found that in some ways, the two national groups used similar communication techniques. For example, U.S. managers in the United States made an average of 37 phone calls daily, and U.S. managers in Japan averaged 34 calls a day. Japanese managers in Japan made 35 calls a day, and the Japanese managers in the United States averaged 30 calls daily. Therefore, use of the telephone to convey information really did not vary between the two groups; however, Pascale did find some important differences. For example, Japanese managers in Japan made much greater use of face-to-face contacts than U.S. or Japanese managers in the United States. Pascale's study also found greater use of upward and lateral communication in Japanese-based Japanese firms, but managers in U.S.-based Japanese firms used communication patterns similar to those used in U.S. firms.[4] Were there any perceived differences in the quality of decision making among the various groups of managers? Pascale found none. Each group gave itself a high score on decision quality; however, the Japanese-based Japanese firms perceived the quality of decision implementation as higher than that of the other three groups.[5]

Verbal Communication Styles

Context
Information that surrounds a communication and helps to convey the message.

Another way of examining the ways in which individuals convey information is by looking at their communication styles. In particular, as has been noted by Hall, context plays a key role in explaining many communication differences.[6] **Context** is the information that surrounds a communication and helps convey the message. In high-context societies, such as Japan and many Arab countries, messages are often highly coded and implicit. As a result, the sender's job is to interpret what the message means by correctly filtering through what is being said and the way in which the message is being conveyed. This approach is in sharp contrast to low-context societies such as the United States and Canada where the message is explicit and the speaker says precisely what he or she means. Figure 8–2 provides an international comparison of high context/implicit and low context/explicit societies. In addition, Table 8–2 presents some of the major characteristics of communication styles.

Indirect and Direct Styles   In high-context cultures, messages are implicit and direct. One reason is because those who are communicating—family, friends, coworkers, clients—tend to have both close personal relationships and large information networks. As a result, each knows a lot about others in their communication network; they do not have to rely on language alone to communicate. Voice intonation, timing, and facial expressions can all play roles in conveying information.

Figure 8–2

Explicit/Implicit Communication: An International Comparison

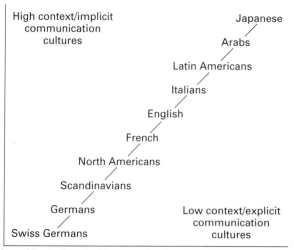

Source: Adapted from Martin Rosch, "Communications: Focal Point of Culture," *Management International Review,* vol. 27, no. 4, 1987, p. 60. Used with permission.

Table 8-2
Major Characteristics of Verbal Styles

Verbal Style	Variation	Major Characteristic	Cultures in Which It Is Found
Indirect vs. direct	Indirect	Implicit messages	Collective, high context
	Direct	Explicit messages	Individualistic, low context
Succinct vs. elaborate	Elaborate	High quantity of talk	Moderate uncertainty avoidance, high context
	Exacting	Moderate amount of talk	Low uncertainty avoidance, low context
	Succinct	Low amount of talk	High uncertainty avoidance, high context
Contextual vs. personal	Contextual	The focus is on the speaker and role relationships	High power distance, collective, high context
	Personal	The focus is on the speaker personal relationships	Low power distance, individualistic, low context
Affective vs. instrumental	Affective	Language is process oriented and receiver focused	Collective, high context
	Instrumental	Language is goal oriented and sender focused	Individualistic, low context

In low-context cultures, people often meet only to accomplish objectives. Since they do not know each other very well, they tend to be direct and focused in their communications.

A good example comparing these two kinds of culture—high context and low context—is the types of questions that are typically asked when someone is contacted and told to attend a meeting. In a high-context culture it is common for the person to ask, "Who will be at this meeting?" The individual wants to be prepared to interact correctly. This is in contrast to low-context cultures where the individual is likely to ask, "What is the meeting going to be about?" In the high-context society, the person focuses on the environment in which the meeting will take place; in the low context, the individuals is most interested in the objectives that are to be accomplished at the meeting.

Elaborate and Succinct Styles   There are three degrees of communication quantity—elaborate, exacting, and succinct. In high-context societies the elaborate style is often very common. There is a great deal of talking, description includes much detail, and people often repeat themselves. This elaborate style is widely used in Arabic countries.

The exacting style is more common in nations such as England, Germany, and Sweden, to name three. This style focuses on precision and the use of the right amount of words to convey the message. If a person uses too many words, this is considered exaggeration; if the individual relies on too few, the result is an ambiguous message.

The succinct style is most common in Asia where people tend to say few words and allow understatements, pauses, and silence to convey meaning. In particular, in unfamiliar situations communicators are succinct in order to avoid risking a loss of face.

Researchers have found that the elaborating style is more popular in high-context cultures that have a moderate degree of uncertainty avoidance. The exacting style is more common in low-context, low uncertainty avoidance cultures. The succinct style is more common in high-context cultures with considerable uncertainty avoidance.

Contextual and Personal Styles   A contextual style is one that focuses on the speaker and relationship of the parties. For example, in Asian cultures people use words that reflect the role and hierarchical relationship of those in the conversation. As a result, in an organizational setting speakers will choose words that indicate their status relative to those of the others. Commenting on this idea, Yoshimura and Anderson have noted that white collar, middle management employees in Japan, commonly known as salarymen, quickly learn how to communicate with others in the organization by understanding the context and reference group of the other party.

> A salaryman can hardly say a word to another person without implicitly defining the reference groups to which he thinks both of them belong. . . . [This is because] failing to use proper language is socially embarrassing, and the correct form of Japanese to use with someone else depends not only on the relationship between the two people, but also on the relationship between their reference groups. Juniors defer to seniors in Japan, but even this relationship is complicated when the junior person works for a much more prestigious organization (for example, a government bureau) than the senior. [As a result, it is] likely that both will use the polite form to avoid social embarrassment.[7]

A personal style focuses on the speaker and the reduction of barriers between the parties. In the United States, for example, it is common to use first names and to address others informally and directly on an equal basis.

Researchers have found that the contextual style is often associated with high power distance, collective, high-context cultures. Examples include Japan, India, and Ghana. In contrast, the personal style is more popular in low power distance, individualistic, low-context cultures. Examples include the United States, Australia, and Canada.

Affective and Instrumental Styles   The affective style is characterized by language which requires the listener to carefully note what is being said and to observe how the sender is presenting the message. Quite often the meaning that is being conveyed is nonverbal and requires the receiver to use his or her intuitive skills in deciphering what is being said. The part of the message that is being left out may be just as important as the part that is being included. In contrast, the instrumental style is goal-oriented and focuses on the sender. The individual clearly lets the other party know what he or she wants them to know.

The affective style is common in collective, high-context cultures such as the Middle East, Latin America, and Asia. The instrumental style is more commonly found in individualistic, low-context cultures such as Switzerland, Denmark, and the United States.

Table 8–3 provides a brief description of the four verbal styles that are used in select countries. A close look at the table helps explain why managers in Japan can have great difficulty communicating with their counterparts in the United States and vice versa. The verbal styles are completely opposite.

Table 8–3
Verbal Styles Used in 10 Select Countries

Country	Indirect vs. Direct	Elaborate vs. Succinct	Contextual vs. Personal	Affective vs. Instrumental
Australia	Direct	Exacting	Personal	Instrumental
Canada	Direct	Exacting	Personal	Instrumental
Denmark	Direct	Exacting	Personal	Instrumental
Egypt	Indirect	Elaborate	Contextual	Affective
England	Direct	Exacting	Personal	Instrumental
Japan	Indirect	Succinct	Contextual	Affective
Korea	Indirect	Succinct	Contextual	Affective
Saudi Arabia	Indirect	Elaborate	Contextual	Affective
Sweden	Direct	Exacting	Personal	Instrumental
United States	Direct	Exacting	Personal	Instrumental

Source: Reported in Anne Marie Francesco and Barry Allen Gold, *International Organizational Behavior* (Upper Saddle River, NJ: Prentice-Hall, 1998), p. 60.

Interpretation of Communications

The effectiveness of communication in the international context often is determined by how closely the sender and receiver have the same meaning for the same message.[8] If this meaning is different, effective communication will not occur. A good example was the U.S. firm that wanted to increase worker output among its Japanese personnel. This firm put an individual incentive plan into effect, whereby workers would be given extra pay based on their work output. The plan, which had worked well in the United States, was a total flop. The Japanese were accustomed to working in groups and to being rewarded as a group. In another case, a U.S. firm offered a bonus to anyone who would provide suggestions that resulted in increased productivity. The Japanese workers rejected this idea, because they felt that no one working alone is responsible for increased productivity. It is always a group effort. When the company changed the system and began rewarding group productivity, it was successful in gaining support for the program.

A related case is when both parties agree on the content of the message, but one party believes it is necessary to persuade the other to accept the message. Here is an example:

> Motorola University recently prepared carefully for a presentation in China. After considerable thought, the presenters entitled it "Relationships do not retire." The gist of the presentation was that Motorola had come to China in order to stay and help the economy to create wealth. Relationships with Chinese suppliers, subcontractors and employees would constitute a permanent commitment to building Chinese economic infrastructure and earning hard currency through exports. The Chinese audience listened politely to this presentation but was quiet when invited to ask questions. Finally one manager put up his hand and said: "Can you tell us about pay for performance?"[9]

Quite obviously, the Motorola presenter believed that it was necessary to convince the audience that the company was in China for the long run. Those in attendance, however, had already accepted this idea and wanted to move on to other issues.

Still another example has been provided by Adler, who has pointed out that people doing business in a foreign culture often misinterpret the meaning of messages. As a result, they arrive at erroneous conclusions as seen by the following story of a Canadian doing business in the Middle East. The Canadian was surprised when his meeting with a high-ranking official was not held in a closed office and was constantly interrupted.

> Using the Canadian-based cultural assumptions that (a) important people have large private offices with secretaries to monitor the flow of people into the office, and (b) important business takes precedence over less important business and is therefore not interrupted, the Canadian interprets the ...open office and constant interruptions to mean that the official is neither as high ranking nor as interested in conducting the business at hand as he had previously thought.[10]

Communication Flows

Communication flows in international organizations move both down and up. However, as Figure 8–3 humorously, but in many ways accurately, portrays, there are some unique differences in organizations around the world.

Downward Communication

Downward communication is the transmission of information from manager to subordinate. The primary purpose of the manager-initiated communication flow is to convey orders and information. Managers use this channel to let their people know what is to be done and how well they are doing. The channel facilitates the flow of information to those who need it for operational purposes.

In Asian countries, as noted earlier, downward communication is less direct than in the United States. Orders tend to be implicit in nature. Conversely, in some European countries, downward communication is not only direct but extends beyond business matters. For example, one early study surveyed 299 U.S. and French managers regarding the nature of

Downward communication
The transmission of information from superior to subordinate

Figure 8–3

Communication Epigrams

There are a number of different "organization charts" that have been constructed to depict international organizations. An epigram is a poem or line of verse that is witty or satirical in nature. The following organization designs are epigrams that show how communication occurs in different countries. In examining them, remember that each contains considerable exaggeration and humor, but also some degree of truth.

In America, everyone thinks he or she has a communication pipeline directly to the top.

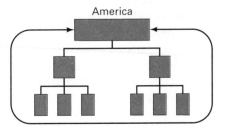

America

There are so many people in China that organizations are monolithic structures characterized by copious levels of bureaucracy. All information flows through channels.

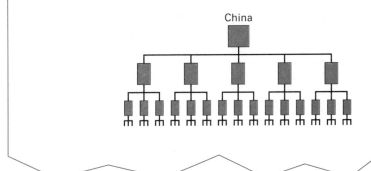

China

downward communication and the managerial authority they perceived themselves as having. This study found that U.S. managers basically used downward communication for work-related matters. A follow-up study investigated matters that U.S. and French managers felt were within the purview of their authority.[11] The major differences involved work-related and nonwork-related activities: U.S. managers felt that it was within their authority to communicate or attempt to influence their people's social behavior only if it occurred on the job or it directly affected their work. For example, U.S. managers felt that it was proper to look into matters such as how much an individual drinks at lunch, whether the person uses profanity in the workplace, and how active the individual is in recruiting others to join the company. The French managers were not as supportive of these activities. The researcher concluded that "the Americans find it as difficult [as] or more difficult than the French to accept the legitimacy of managerial authority in areas unrelated to work."[12]

Harris and Moran have noted that when communicating with nonnative speakers, it is extremely important to use language that is easy to understand and allows the other person to ask questions. Here are 10 of the suggestions that not only apply for downward, but for all types of communication:

1. Use the most common words with their most common meanings.
2. Select words that have few alternative meanings.
3. Strictly follow the basic rules of grammar—more so than would be the case with native speakers.
4. Speak with clear breaks between the words so that it is easier for the person to follow.
5. Avoid using words that are esoteric or culturally biased such as "he struck out" or "the whole idea is Mickey Mouse" because these cliches often have no meaning for the listener.

At the United Nations everyone is arranged in a circle so that no one is more powerful than anyone else. Those directly in front or behind are philosophically aligned, and those nearby form part of an international bloc.

United Nations

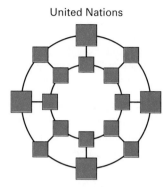

In France some people in the hierarchy are not linked to anyone, indicating how haphazard the structure can be.

France

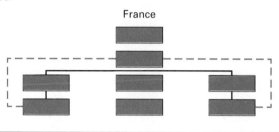

Source: Adapted from Simcha Ronen, *Comparative and Multinational Management* (New York: Wiley, 1986), pp. 318–319. The epigrams in turn were derived from a variety of sources, including Robert M. Worchester of the U.K.-based Market and Opinion Research International (MORI), Ole Jacob Raad of Norway's PM Systems, and anonymous managers.

6. Avoid the use of slang.

7. Do not use words or expressions that require the other person to create a mental image such as "we were knee deep in the Big Muddy."

8. Mimic the cultural flavor of the nonnative speaker's language, for example, by using more flowery communication with Spanish-speaking listeners than with Germans.

9. Continually paraphrase and repeat the basic ideas.

10. At the end, test how well the other person understands by asking the individual to paraphrase what has been said.[13]

Upward Communication

Upward communication is the transfer of information from subordinate to superior. The primary purpose of this subordinate-initiated upward communication is to provide feedback, ask questions, or obtain assistance from higher-level management. In recent years, there has been a call for and a concerted effort to promote more upward communication in the United States. In other countries, such as in Japan, Hong Kong, and Singapore, upward communication has long been a fact of life. Managers in these countries have extensively used suggestion systems and quality circles to get employee input and always are available to listen to their people's concerns. For example, here are some observations from the approach the Japanese firm Matsushita uses in dealing with employee suggestions:

Upward communication
The transfer of meaning from subordinate to superior.

Matsushita views employee recommendations as instrumental to making improvements on the shop floor and in the marketplace. [It believes] that a great many little people, paying attention each day to how to improve their jobs, can accomplish more than a whole headquarters full of production engineers and planners.

Praise and positive reinforcement are an important part of the Matsushita philosophy. . . . Approximately 90 percent of . . . suggestions receive rewards; most only a few dollars per month, but the message is reinforced constantly: "Thank about your job; develop yourself and help us improve the company." The best suggestions receive company-wide recognition and can earn substantial monetary rewards. Each year, many special awards are also given, including presidential prizes and various divisional honors.[14]

This company has used the same approach wherever it has established plants worldwide, and the approach has proved very successful. The company has all its employees begin the day by reciting its basic principles, beliefs, and values, which are summarized in Table 8–4, to reinforce in all employees the reason for the company's existence and to provide a form of spiritual fabric to energize and sustain them. All employees see themselves as important members of a successful team, and they are willing to do whatever is necessary to ensure the success of the group.

Outside these Asian countries, upward communication is not as popular. For example, in South America, many managers believe that employees should follow orders and not ask a lot of questions. German managers also make much less use of this form of communication. In most cases, however, evidence shows that employees prefer to have downward communication at least supplemented by upward channels. Unfortunately, such upward communication does not always occur because of a number of communication barriers.

Communication Barriers

A number of common communication barriers are relevant to international management. The more important include language, perception, culture, and nonverbal communication.

Language Barriers

Knowledge of the home country's language (the language used at the headquarters of the MNC) is important for personnel placed in a foreign assignment. If managers do not understand the language that is used at headquarters, they likely will make a wide

---

Table 8–4
Matsushita's Philosophy

Basic Business Principles
To recognize our responsibilities as industrialists, to foster progress, to promote the general welfare of society, and to devote ourselves to the further development of world culture.

Employees Creed
Progress and development can be realized only through the combined efforts and cooperation of each member of the Company. Each of us, therefore, shall keep this idea constantly in mind as we devote ourselves to the continuous improvement of our Company.

The Seven Spiritual Values
1. National service through industry
2. Fairness
3. Harmony and cooperation
4. Struggle for betterment
5. Courtesy and humility
6. Adjustment and assimilation
7. Gratitude

Table 8–5 Multilingualism in the EU Classroom	Percentage of pupils in general secondary education learning English, French, or German as a foreign language, 1991–1992		
	English	**French**	**German**
Holland	96	65	53
Germany	93	23	—
Denmark	92	8	58
Spain	92	10	0.3
France	84	—	27
Belgium (Flemish)	68	98	22
Belgium (French)	58	1	6
Italy	61	33	3
Portugal	55	25	0.4
Britain	—	59	20
Ireland	—	69	24
Source: Eurostat, 1995.			

assortment of errors. Additionally, many MNCs now prescribe English as the common language for internal communication, so that managers can more easily convey information to their counterparts in other geographically dispersed locales.[15] Despite such progress, however, language training continues to lag in many areas, although in an increasing number of European countries, more and more young people are becoming multilingual.[16] Table 8–5 shows the percentage of European students who are studying the major languages.

Language education is a good beginning, but it is also important to realize that just the ability to speak the language used at MNC headquarters is often not enough to ensure that the personnel are capable of doing the work. Stout recently noted that many MNCs worldwide place a great deal of attention on the applicant's ability to speak English without considering if the person has other necessary skills such as the ability to interact well with others and the technical knowledge demanded by the job.[17] Additionally, in interviewing people for jobs he has noted that many interviewers fail to take into account the applicant's culture. As a result, interviewers misinterpret behaviors such as quietness or shyness and use them to conclude that the applicant is not sufficiently confident or self-assured. Still another problem is that nonnative speakers may know the language but not be fully fluent. So they end up asking questions or making statements that convey the wrong message. After studying Japanese for only one year, Stout reports that he began interviewing candidates in their local language and made a number of mistakes. In one case, he reports, "a young woman admitted to having an adulterous affair—even though this was not even close to the topic I was inquiring about—because of my unskilled use of the language."[18]

More recently, written communication has been getting increased attention, because poor writing is proving to be a greater barrier than poor talking. For example, Hildebrandt has found that among U.S. subsidiaries studied in Germany, language was a major problem when subsidiaries were sending written communications to the home office. The process often involved elaborate procedures associated with translating and reworking the report. Typical steps included: (1) holding a staff conference to determine what was to be included in the written message; (2) writing the initial draft in German; (3) rewriting the draft in German; (4) translating the material into English; (5) consulting with bilingual staff members regarding the translation; and (6) rewriting the English draft a series of additional times until the paper was judged to be acceptable for transmission. The German managers admitted that they felt uncomfortable with writing, because their command of written English was poor. As Hildebrandt noted:

All German managers commanding oral English stated that their grammatical competence was not sufficiently honed to produce a written English report of top quality. Even when professional translators from outside the company rewrote the German into English, German middle managers were unable to verify whether the report captured the substantive intent or included editorial alterations.[19]

Problems associated with the translation of information from one language to another have been made even clearer by Schermerhorn, who conducted research among 153 Hong Kong Chinese bilinguals who were enrolled in an undergraduate management course at a major Hong Kong university. The students were given two scenarios written in either English or Chinese. One scenario involved a manager who was providing some form of personal support or praise for a subordinate. The research used the following procedures:

> [A] careful translation and back-translation method was followed to create the Chinese language versions of the research instruments. Two bilingual Hong Kong Chinese, both highly fluent in English and having expertise in the field of management, shared roles in the process. Each first translated one scenario and the evaluation questions into Chinese. Next they translated each other's Chinese versions back into English, and discussed and resolved translation differences in group consultation with the author. Finally, a Hong Kong professor read and interpreted the translations correctly as a final check of equivalency.[20]

The participants were asked to answer eight evaluation questions about these scenarios. A significant difference between the two sets of responses was found. Those who were queried in Chinese gave different answers from those who were queried in English. This led Schermerhorn to conclude that language plays a key role in conveying information between cultures, and that in cross-cultural management research, bilingual individuals should not be queried in their second language.

Cultural Barriers

Closely related to the language barriers are cultural barriers. For example, research by Sims and Guice compared 214 letters of inquiry written by native and nonnative speakers of English to test the assumption that cultural factors affect business communication. Among other things, the researchers found that nonnative speakers used exaggerated politeness, provided unnecessary professional and personal information, and made inappropriate requests of the other party. Commenting on the results and implications of their study, the researchers note that their investigation

> indicates that the deviations from standard U.S. business communication practices were not specific to one or more nationalities. The deviations did not occur among specific nationalities but were spread throughout the sample of nonnative letters used for the study. Therefore, we can speculate that U.S. native speakers of English might have similar difficulties in international settings. In other words, a significant number of native speakers in the U.S. might deviate from the standard business communication practices of other cultures. Therefore, these native speakers need specific training in the business communication practices of the major cultures of the world so they can communicate successfully and acceptably with readers in those cultures.[21]

Research by Scott and Green has extended these findings, showing that even in English-speaking countries, there are different approaches to writing letters. In the United States, for example, it is common practice when constructing a bad-news letter to start out "with a pleasant, relevant, neutral, and transitional buffer statement; give the reasons for the unfavorable news before presenting the bad news; present the refusal in a positive manner; imply the bad news whenever possible; explain how the refusal is in the reader's best interest; and suggest positive alternatives that build goodwill."[22] In Great Britain, however, it is common to start out by referring to the situation, discussing the reasons for the bad news, conveying the bad news (often quite bluntly), and concluding with an apology or statement of regret (something that is frowned on by business-letter experts in the United States) designed to keep the reader's goodwill. Here is an example:

Lord Hanson has asked me to reply to your letter and questionnaire of February 12 which we received today.

As you may imagine, we receive numerous requests to complete questionnaires or to participate in a survey, and this poses problems for us. You will appreciate that the time it would take to complete these requests would represent a full-time job, so we decided some while ago to decline such requests unless there was some obvious benefit to Hanson PLC and our stockholders. As I am sure you will understand, our prime responsibility is to look after our stockholders' interests.

I apologize that this will not have been the response that you were hoping for, but I wish you success with your research study.[23]

U.S. MNC managers would seldom, if ever, send this type of letter; it would be viewed as blunt and tactless. However, the indirect approach that Americans use would be viewed by their British counterparts as overly indirect and obviously insincere.

On the other hand, when compared to Asians, many American writers are far more blunt and direct. For example, Park, Dillon, and Mitchell recently reported that there are pronounced differences between the ways in which Americans and Asians write business letters of complaint. They compared the approach used by American managers, for whom English is a first language, who wrote international business letters of complaint, with that of Korean managers, for whom English is a second language, who wrote the same types of letters. They found that American writers used a direct organizational pattern and tended to state the main idea or problem first before sharing explanatory details that clearly related to the stated problem. In contrast, the standard Korean pattern was indirect and tended to delay the reader's discovery of the main point. This led the researchers to conclude that the U.S.-generated letter could well be regarded as rude by Asian readers, while American readers might regard the letter from the Korean writer as vague, emotional, and accusatory.[24]

Perceptual Barriers

Perception is a person's view of reality. How people see reality can vary and will influence their judgment and decision making. One example involves Japanese stockbrokers who now perceive that the chances of improving their career are better with U.S. firms, so they have changed jobs. Another involves Hong Kong hoteliers who have begun buying U.S. properties, because they have the perception that if they can offer the same top-quality hotel service as back home, they can dominate their U.S. markets. These are examples of how perceptions can play an important role in international management. Unfortunately, misperceptions also can become a barrier to effective communication. For example, when the Clinton administration decided to allow Taiwan President Lee Tenghui to visit the United States, the Chinese (PRC) government perceived this as a threatening gesture and took actions of its own.[25] Besides conducting dangerous war games very near Taiwan's border as a warning not to become too bold in its quest for recognition as a sovereign nation, the PRC also snubbed U.S. car manufacturers and gave a much-coveted, $1 billion contract to Mercedes-Benz of Germany.[26] The following sections provide examples of such perception barriers in the international arena.

Perception
A person's view of reality.

Advertising Messages   One way that perception can prove to be a problem in international management communication is when one person uses words that are misinterpreted by the other. Many firms have found to their dismay that a failure to understand home-country perceptions can result in disastrous advertising programs. Here are two examples:

Ford…introduced a low cost truck, the "Fiera," into some Spanish-speaking countries. Unfortunately, the name meant "ugly old woman" in Spanish. Needless to say, this name did not encourage sales. Ford also experienced slow sales when it introduced a top-of-the-line automobile, the "Comet," in Mexico under the name "Caliente." The puzzling low sales were finally understood when Ford discovered that "caliente" is slang for a street walker.[27]

One laundry detergent company certainly wishes now that it had contacted a few locals before it initiated its promotional campaign in the Middle East. All of the company's advertisements pictured soiled clothes on the left, its box of soap in the middle, and clean clothes on the right. But, because in that area of the world people tend to read from the right to the left, many potential customers interpreted the message to indicate the soap actually soiled the clothes.[28]

View of Others   Perception influences communication when it deals with how individuals "see" others. A good example is provided by the perception of foreigners who reside in the United states. Most Americans see themselves as extremely friendly, outgoing, and kind, and they believe that others also see them in this way. At the same time, many are not aware of what negative impressions they give to others. Another example is the way in which people act, or should act, when initially meeting others. "International Management in Action: Doing It Right the First Time" provides some insights regarding how to conduct oneself when doing business in Japan.

Another example of how the perceptions of others affect communication occurs in the way that some international managers perceive their subordinates. For example, a study examined the perceptions that German and U.S. managers had of the qualifications of their peers (those on the same level and status), managers, and subordinates in Europe and Latin America.[29] The findings showed that both the German and U.S. respondents perceived their subordinates to be less qualified than their peers. However, although the Germans perceived their managers to have more managerial ability than their peers, the Americans felt that their South American peers in many instances had equal or better qualifications than their own managers. Quite obviously, this perception will affect how U.S. expatriates communicate with their South American peers as well as how the expatriates communicate with their bosses.

Another study found that Western managers have more favorable attitudes toward women as managers than Asian or Saudi managers do.[30] This perception obviously affects the way these managers interact and communicate with their female counterparts. The same is true in the case of many Japanese managers, who according to one recent survey still regard women as superfluous to the effective running of their organizations and generally continue to not treat women as equals.[31]

The Impact of Culture

Besides language and perception, another major barrier to communication is culture, a topic that was given detailed attention in Chapter 5. Culture can affect communication in a number of ways, and one way is through the impact of cultural values.

Cultural Values   One expert on Middle Eastern countries notes that people there do not relate to and communicate with each other in a loose, general way as do those in the United States. Relationships are more intense and binding in the Middle East, and a wide variety of work-related values influence what people in the Middle East will and will not do.

> In North American society, the generally professed prevalent pattern is one of nonclass-consciousness, as far as work is concerned. Students, for example, make extra pocket money by taking all sorts of part-time jobs—manual and otherwise—regardless of the socioecnomic stratum to which the individual belongs. The attitude is uninhibited. In the Middle East, the overruling obsession is how the money is made and via what kind of job.[32]

These types of values indirectly, and in many cases directly, affect communication between people from different cultures. For example, one would communicate differently with a "rich college student" from the United States than with one from Saudi Arabia.

Another example is the way that people use time. In the United States, people believe that time is an asset and is not to be wasted, which is an idea that often has limited meaning in other cultures. Various values are reinforced and reflected through the use of proverbs that Americans are taught from an early age. These proverbs help to guide people's behavior. Table 8–6 lists some examples.

International Management in Action

Doing It Right the First Time

Like other countries of the world, Japan has its own business customs and culture. And when someone fails to adhere to these traditions, the individual runs the risk of being perceived as ineffective or uncaring. The following addresses three areas that are important in being correctly perceived by one's Japanese counterparts.

Business Cards

The exchange of business cards is an integral part of Japanese business etiquette, and Japanese businesspeople exchange these cards when meeting someone for the first time. Additionally, those who are most likely to interface with non-Japanese are supplied with business cards printed in Japanese on one side and a foreign language, usually English, on the reverse side. This is aimed at enhancing recognition and pronunciation of Japanese names, which are often unfamiliar to foreign businesspeople. Conversely, it is advisable for foreign businesspeople to carry and exchange with their Japanese counterparts a similar type of card printed in Japanese and in their native language. These cards can often be obtained through business centers in major hotels.

When receiving a card, it is considered common courtesy to offer one in return. In fact, not returning a card might convey the impression that the manager is not committed to a meaningful business relationship in the future.

Business cards should be presented and received with both hands. When presenting one's card, the presentor's name should be facing the person who is receiving the card so the receiver can easily read it. When receiving a business card, it should be handled with care and if the receiver is sitting a conference or other type of table, the card should be placed in front of the individual for the duration of the meeting. It is considered rude to put a prospective business partner's card in one's pocket before sitting down to discuss business matters.

Bowing

Although the handshake is increasingly common in Japan, bowing remains the most prevalent formal method of greeting, saying goodbye, expressing gratitude, or apologizing to another person. When meeting foreign businesspeople, however, Japanese will often use the handshake or a combination of both a handshake and a bow. even though there are different forms and styles of bowing, depending on the relationship of the parties involved, foreign businesspeople are not expected to be familiar with these intricacies, and therefore a deep nod of the head or a slight bow will suffice in most cases. Many foreign businesspeople are unsure whether to use a handshake or to bow. In these situations, it is best to wait and see if one's Japanese counterpart offers a hand or prefers to bow and then to follow suit.

Attire

Most Japanese businessmen dress in conservative dark or navy blue suits, although slight variations in style and color have come to be accepted in recent years. As a general rule, what is acceptable business attire in virtually any industrialized country is usually regarded as good business attire in Japan as well. Although there is no need to conform precisely to the style of dress of the Japanese, good judgment should be exercised when selecting attire for a business meeting. If unsure about what constitutes appropriate attire for a particular situation, it is best to err on the conservative side.

Sources: **www.jetro.go.jp/JETROINFO/DOING/4.html**; Alan M. Rugman and Richard M. Hodgetts, *International Business* (New York: McGraw-Hill Book Company, 1995); and Philip R. Harris and Robert T. Moran, *Managing Cultural Differences*, 3rd ed. (Houston: Gulf Publishing, 1991), pp. 393–406.

Misinterpretation   Cultural differences can cause misinterpretations both in how others see expatriate managers and in how the latter see themselves. For example, U.S. managers doing business in Austria often misinterpret the fact that local businesspeople always address them in formal terms. They may view this as meaning that they are not friends or are not liked, but in fact, this formalism is the way that Austrians always conduct business. The informal, first-name approach used in the United States is not the style of the Austrians.

Table 8–6	
U.S. Proverbs Representing Cultural Values	
Proverb	**Cultural Value**
A penny saved is a penny earned	Thriftiness
Time is money	Time thriftiness
Don't cry over spilt milk	Practicality
Waste not, want not	Frugality
Early to bed, early to rise, makes one healthy, wealthy, and wise	Diligence; work ethic
A stitch in time saves nine	Timeliness of action
If at first you don't succeed, try, try again	Persistence; work ethic
Take care of today, and tomorrow will take care of itself	Preparation for future

Source: Drawn from Nancy J. Adler, *International Dimensions of Organizational Behavior,* 2nd ed. (Boston: PWS-Kent Publishing, 1991), pp. 79–80.

Culture even affects day-to-day activities of corporate communications. For example, when sending messages to international clients, American managers have to keep in mind that there are many things that are uniquely American and overseas managers may not be aware of them. As an example, Daylight Savings Time is known to all Americans, but many Asian managers have no idea what the term means. Similarly, it is common for American managers to address memos to their "international office" without realizing that the managers who work in this office regard the American location as the "international" one! Other suggestions that can be of value to American managers who are engaged in international communications include:

- Be careful not to use generalized statements about benefits, compensation, pay cycles, holidays, or policies in your worldwide communications. Work hours, vacation accrual, general business practices, and human resource issues vary widely from country to country.
- Since most of the world uses the metric system, be sure to include converted weights and measures in all internal and external communications.
- Keep in mind that even in English-speaking countries, words may have different meanings. Not everyone knows what is meant by "counterclockwise," or "quite good."
- Remember that letterhead and paper sizes differ worldwide. The 8 1/2 by 11-inch page is a U.S. standard, but most countries use an A4 (8 1/4 × 11 1/2-inch) size for their letterhead, with envelopes to match.
- Dollars are not unique to the United States. There are Australian, Bermudian, Canadian, Hong Kong, Taiwanese, and New Zealand dollars, among others. So in referring to American dollars it is important to use "US$."

Many Americans also have difficulty interpreting the effect of national values on work behavior. For example, why do French and German workers drink alcoholic beverages at lunch time? Why are many European workers unwilling to work the night shift? Why do overseas affiliates contribute to the support of the employees' work council or donate money to the support of kindergarten teachers in local schools? These types of actions are viewed by some people as wasteful, but to those who know the culture of these countries, such actions promote the long-run good of the company. It is the outsider who is misinterpreting why these culturally specific actions are happening, and such misperceptions can become a barrier to effective communication.

Nonverbal communication
The transfer of meaning through means such as body language and the use of physical space.

Nonverbal Communication

Another major reason for perception problems is accounted for by **nonverbal communication,** which is the transfer of meaning through means such as body language and use of physical space. Table 8–7 summarizes a number of dimensions of nonverbal communication.

> **Table 8–7**
> **Common Forms of Nonverbal Communication**
>
> 1. Hand gestures, both intended and self-directed (autistic), such as the nervous rubbing of hands
> 2. Facial expressions, such as smiles, frowns, and yawns
> 3. Posture and stance
> 4. Clothing and hair styles (hair being more like clothes than like skin, both subject to the fashion of the day)
> 5. Interpersonal distance (proxemics)
> 6. Eye contact and direction of gaze, particularly in "listening behavior"
> 7. "Artifacts" and nonverbal symbols, such as lapel pins, walking sticks, and jewelry
> 8. Paralanguage (though often in language, just as often treated as part of nonverbal behavior—speech rate, pitch, inflections, volume)
> 9. Taste, including symbolism of food and the communication function of chatting over coffee or tea, and oral gratification such as smoking or gum chewing
> 10. Cosmetics: temporary—powder; permanent—tattoos
> 11. Time symbolism: what is too late or too early to telephone or visit a friend, or too long or too short to make a speech or stay for dinner
> 12. Timing and pauses within verbal behavior
>
> *Source:* This information is found in J. C. Condon and F. S. Yousef, *An Introduction to Intercultural Communication* (Indianapolis, IN: Bobbs-Merrill, 1975), pp. 123–124.

The general categories that are especially important to communication in international management are kinesics, proxemics, chronemics, and chromatics.

Kinesics Kinesics is the study of communication through body movement and facial expression. Primary areas of concern include eye contact, posture, and gestures. For example, when one communicates verbally with someone in the United States, it is good manners to look the other person in the eye. This area of communicating through the use of eye contact and gaze is known as **oculesics.** In some areas of the world oculesics is an important consideration because of what people should *not* do such as stare at others or maintain continuous eye contact because it is considered impolite to do these things.

Kenesics
The study of communication through body movement and facial expressions.

Oculesics
The area of communication that deals with conveying messages through the use of eye contact and gaze.

Another area of kinesics is posture which can also cause problems. For example, when Americans are engaged in prolonged negotiations or meetings, it is not uncommon for them to relax and put their feet up on a chair or desk, but this is insulting behavior in the Middle East. Here is just such an example from a classroom situation:

> In the midst of a discussion of a poem in the sophomore class of the English Department, the professor, who was British, took up the argument, started to explain the subtleties of the poem, and was carried away by the situation. He leaned back in his chair, put his feet up on the desk, and went on with the explanation. The class was furious. Before the end of the day, a demonstration by the University's full student body had taken place. Petitions were submitted to the deans of the various facilities. The next day, the situation even made the newspaper headlines. The consequences of the act, that was innocently done, might seem ridiculous, funny, baffling, incomprehensible, or even incredible to a stranger. Yet, to the native, the students' behavior was logical and in context. The students and their supporters were outraged because of the implications of the breach of the native behavioral pattern. In the Middle East, it is extremely insulting to have to sit facing two soles of the shoes of somebody.[33]

Gestures are also widely used and take many different forms. For example, Canadians shake hands, Japanese bow, Middle Easterners of the same sex kiss on the cheek. Communicating through the use of bodily contact is known as **haptics,** and it is a widely used form of nonverbal communication.

Haptics
Communicating through the use of bodily contact.

Sometimes gestures present problems for expatriate managers because these behaviors have different meanings depending on the country. For example, in the United States, putting the thumb and index finger together to form an "O" is the sign for "okay." In Japan, this is the sign for money; in southern France, the gesture means "zero" or "worthless"; and in Brazil, it is regarded as a vulgar or obscene sign. In France and Belgium, snapping the fingers of both hands is considered vulgar; in Brazil, this gesture is used to indicate that something has been done for a long time. In Britain, the "V for victory" sign is given with the palm out; if the palm is in, this roughly means "shove it"; in non-British countries, the gesture means two of something and often is used when placing an order at a restaurant.[34] Gibson, Hodgetts, and Blackwell found that many foreign students attending school in the United States have trouble communicating, because they are unable to interpret some of the most common nonverbal gestures.[35] A survey group of 44 Jamaican, Venezuelan, Colombian, Peruvian, Thai, Indian, and Japanese students at two major universities were given pictures of 20 universal cultural gestures, and each was asked to describe the nonverbal gestures illustrated. In 56 percent of the choices the respondents either gave an interpretation that was markedly different from that of Americans or reported that the nonverbal gesture had no meaning in their culture. These findings help to reinforce the need to teach expatriates about local nonverbal communication.

Proxemics
The study of the way people use physical space to convey messages.

Intimate distance
Distance between people that is used for very confidential communications.

Personal distance
In communicating, the physical distance used for talking with family and close friends.

Social distance
In communicating, the distance used to handle most business transactions.

Public distance
In communicating, the distance used when calling across the room or giving a talk to a group.

Proxemics   Proxemics is the study of the way that people use physical space to convey messages. For example, in the United States, there are four "distances" people use in communicating on a face-to-face basis (see Figure 8–4.) **Intimate distance** is used for very confidential communications. **Personal distance** is used for talking with family and close friends. **Social distance** is used to handle most business transactions. **Public distance** is used when calling across the room or giving a talk to a group.

One major problem for Americans communicating with those from the Middle East or South America is that the intimate or personal distance zones are violated. Americans often tend to be moving away in interpersonal communication with their Middle Eastern or Latin counterparts, while the latter are trying to physically close the gap. The American cannot understand why the other is standing so close; the latter cannot understand why the American is being so reserved and standing so far away. The result is a breakdown in communication.

Office layout is another good example of proxemics. In the United States, the more important the manager, the larger the office, and often a secretary screens visitors and keeps away those whom the manager does not wish to see. In Japan, most managers do not have large offices, and even if they do, they spend a great deal of time out of it and with the employees. Thus, the Japanese have no trouble communicating directly with their superiors. A Japanese manager's staying in his office would be viewed as a sign of distrust or anger toward the group.

Another way that office proxemics can affect communication is that in many European companies, there is no wall between the space allocated to the senior-level manager and that of the subordinates. Everyone works in the same large room. These working conditions often are disconcerting to Americans, who tend to prefer more privacy.[36]

Figure 8–4

Personal Space Categories for Those in the United States

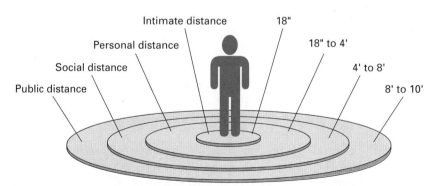

Source: Adapted from Richard M. Hodgetts and Donald F. Kuratko, *Management,* 2nd ed. (San Diego, CA: Harcourt Brace Jovanovich, 1991), p. 384.

Chronemics Chronemics refers to the way in which time is used in a culture. When examined in terms of extremes, there are two types of time schedules: monochronic and polychronic. A **monochronic time schedule** is one in which things are done in a linear fashion. A manager will address Issue A first and then move on to Issue B. In these societies, time schedules are very important and time is viewed as something that can be controlled and should be used wisely. In individualistic cultures such as the United States, Great Britain, Canada, and Australia, as well as many of the cultures in Northern Europe, managers adhere to monochronic time schedules.

This is sharp contrast to **polychronic time schedules** which are characterized by people tending to do several things at the same time and placing higher value on personal involvement than on getting things done on time. In these cultures, schedules are subordinated to personal relationships. Regions of the world where polychronic time schedules are common include Latin America and the Middle East.

When doing business in countries that adhere to monochronic time schedules, it is important to be on time for meetings. Additionally, these meetings typically end at the appointed time so that participants can be on time for their next meeting. When doing business in countries that adhere to polychronic time schedules, it is common to find business meetings starting late and finishing late.

Chromatics Chromatics is the use of color to communicate messages. Every society uses chromatics, but colors that mean one thing in the United States may mean something entirely different in Asia. For example, in the United States it is common to wear black when one is in mourning, while in some locations in India people where white when they are in mourning. In Hong Kong red is used to signify happiness or luck and traditional bridal dresses are red; in the United States it is common for the bride to wear white. In many Asian countries shampoos are dark in color because users want the soap to be the same color as their hair and if it were a light color, they believe it would remove color from their hair. In the United States shampoos tend to be light colored because people see this as a sign of cleanliness and hygiene. In Chile a gift of yellow roses conveys the message "I don't like you," while in the United States just the opposite message would be conveyed by this gift.

Knowing the importance of chromatics can be very helpful because, among other things, it can avoid embarrassing situations. A good example is the American manager in Peru who upon finishing a one-week visit to the Lima subsidiary decided to thank the assistant who was assigned to him. He sent her a dozen red roses. The lady understood the faux pas, but the American manager was somewhat embarrassed when his Peruvian counterpart smilingly told him, "It was really nice of you to buy her a present. However, red roses indicate a romantic interest!"

Achieving Communication Effectiveness

A number of steps can be taken to improve communication effectiveness in the international arena. These include providing feedback systems, providing language and cultural training, and increasing flexibility and cooperation.

Improve Feedback Systems

One of the most important ways of improving communication effectiveness in the international context is to open up feedback systems. Such feedback is particularly important between parent companies and their affiliates. There are two basic types of feedback systems: personal (e.g., face-to-face meetings, telephone conversations and personalized e-mail) and impersonal (e.g., reports, budgets, and plans). Both of these

Chronemics
The way in which time is used in a culture.

Monochronic time schedule
A time schedule in which things are done in a linear fashion.

Polychronic time schedule
A time schedule in which people tend to do several things at the same time and place higher value on personal involvement than on getting things done on time.

Chromatics
The use of color to communicate messages.

systems help affiliates to keep their home office aware of progress and, in turn, help the home office to monitor and control affiliate performance as well as set goals and standards.

At present, there seem to be varying degrees of feedback between the home offices of MNCs and their affiliates. For example, one study evaluated the communication feedback between subsidiaries and home offices of 63 MNCs headquartered in Europe, Japan, and North America.[37] A marked difference was found between the way that U.S. companies communicated with their subsidiaries and the way that European and Japanese firms did. Over one-half of the U.S. subsidiaries responded that they received monthly feedback from their reports, in contrast to less than 10 percent of the European and Japanese subsidiaries. In addition, the Americans were much more inclined to hold regular management meetings on a regional or worldwide basis. Seventy-five percent of the U.S. companies had annual meetings for their affiliate top managers, compared with less than 50 percent for the Europeans and Japanese. These findings may help to explain why many international subsidiaries and affiliates are not operating as efficiently as they should. The units may not have sufficient contact with the home office. They do not seem to be getting continuous assistance and feedback that are critical to effective communication.

Based on his research among U.S. and German managers in Europe, Hildebrandt echoes such conclusions about the need for improved feedback systems. Some of his specific recommendations include holding more face-to-face meetings between parent and staff personnel and assigning someone as a liaison between the two groups.[38]

Provide Language Training

Besides improving feedback systems, another way to make communication more effective in the international arena is through language training. Many host-country managers cannot communicate well with their counterparts at headquarters. Because English has become the international language of business, those who are not native speakers of English should learn the language well enough so that face-to-face and telephone conversations and e-mail are possible. If the language of the home office is not English, this other language also should be learned. As a U.S. manager working for a Japanese MNC recently told one of the authors, "The official international language of this company is English. However, whenever the home office people show up they tend to cluster together with their countrymen and speak Japanese. That's why I'm trying to learn Japanese. Let's face it. They say all you need to know is English, but if you want to really know what's going on you have to talk *their* language."

Written communication also is extremely important in achieving effectiveness. As noted earlier, when reports, letters, and e-mail messages are translated from one language to another, preventing a loss of meaning is virtually impossible. Moreover, if the communications are not written properly, they may not be given the attention they deserve. The reader will allow poor grammar and syntax to influence his or her interpretation and subsequent actions. Moreover, if readers cannot communicate in the language of those who will be receiving their comments or questions about the report, their messages also must be translated and likely will lose further meaning. Therefore, the process can continue on and on, each party failing to achieve full communication with the other. Hildebrandt has described the problems in this two-way process when an employee in a foreign subsidiary writes a report and then sends it to his or her boss for forwarding to the home office:

> The general manager or vice president cannot be asked to be an editor. Yet they often send statements along, knowingly, which are poorly written, grammatically imperfect, or generally unclear. The time pressures do not permit otherwise. Predictably, questions issued from the States to the subsidiary and the complicated bilingual process now goes in reverse, ultimately reaching the original…staff member, who receives the English questions retranslated.[39]

Language training would help to alleviate such complicated communication problems.

Provide Cultural Training

It is very difficult to communicate effectively with someone from another culture unless at least one party has some understanding of the other's culture. Otherwise, communication likely will break down. This is particularly important for multinational companies that have operations throughout the world. Although there always are important differences between countries, and even between subcultures of the same country, firms that operate in South America find that the cultures of these countries have certain commonalities. These common factors also apply to Spain and Portugal. Therefore, a basic understanding of Latin cultures can prove to be useful throughout a large region of the world. The same is true of Anglo cultures, where norms and values tend to be somewhat similar from one country to another. When a multinational has operations in South America, Europe, and Asia, however, multicultural training becomes necessary. The box "Communicating in Europe" provides some specific examples of cultural differences.

As Chapter 5 pointed out, it is erroneous to generalize about an "international" culture, because the various nations and regions of the globe are too different. Training must be conducted on a region or country-specific basis. Failure to do so can result in continuous communication breakdown.[40] Chapters 15 and 16 will give considerable attention to cultural training as part of selection for overseas assignments and human resource development.

Increase Flexibility and Cooperation

Effective international communications require increased flexibility and cooperation by all parties. To improve understanding and cooperation, each party must be prepared to give a little. Take the case of International Computers Ltd., a mainframe computer firm that does a great deal of business in Japan. This firm urges its people to strive for successful collaboration in their international partnerships and ventures. To drive home the point of flexibility and cooperation, the company gives all its people who are involved in a joint partnership with an overseas firm a list of "dos" that are designed to make the arrangement work. These guidelines, listed in Table 8–8, are designed to ensure the req-

---

Table 8–8
International Computer Ltd.'s Guidelines for Successful Collaboration

1. Treat the collaboration as a personal commitment. It's people that make partnerships work.
2. Anticipate that it will take up management time. If you can't spare the time, don't start it.
3. Mutual respect and trust are essential. If you don't trust the people you are negotiating with, forget it.
4. Remember that both partners must get something out of it (money, eventually). Mutual benefits is vital. This will probably mean you've got to give something up. Recognize this from the outset.
5. Make sure you tie up a tight legal contract. Don't put off resolving unpleasant or contentious issues until "later." Once signed, however, the contract should be put away. If you refer to it, something is wrong with the relationship.
6. Recognize that during the course of a collaboration, circumstances and markets change. Recognize your partner's problems and be flexible.
7. Make sure you and your partner have mutual expectations of the collaboration and its time scale. One happy and one unhappy partner is a formula for failure.
8. Get to know your opposite numbers at all levels socially. Friends take longer to fall out.
9. Appreciate that cultures—both geographic and corporate—are different. Don't expect a partner to act or respond identically to you. Find out the true reason for a particular response.
10. Recognize your partner's interests and independence.
11. Even if the arrangement is tactical in your eyes, make sure you have corporate approval. Your tactical activity may be a key piece in an overall strategic jigsaw puzzle. With corporate commitment to the partnership, you can act with the positive authority needed in these relationships.
12. Celebrate achievement together. It's a shared elation, and you'll have earned it!

Source: This information is found in Kenichi Ohmae, "The Global Logic of Strategic Alliances," *Harvard Business Review,* March–April 1989, p. 149.

In Europe, many countries are within easy commuting distance of their neighbors, so an expatriate who does business in France on Monday may be in Germany on Tuesday, Great Britain on Wednesday, Italy on Thursday, and Spain on Friday. Each country has its own etiquette regarding how to greet others and conduct oneself during social and business meetings. The following sections examine some of the things that expatriate managers need to know to communicate effectively.

France When one is meeting with businesspeople in France, promptness is expected, although tardiness of 5 to 10 minutes is not considered a major gaffe. The French prefer to shake hands when introduced, and it is correct to address them by title plus last name. When the meeting is over, a handshake again is proper manners.

French executives try to keep their personal and professional lives separate. As a result, most business entertaining is done at restaurants or clubs. When gifts are given to business associates, they should appeal to intellectual or aesthetic pursuits as opposed to being something that one's company produces for sale on the world market. In conversational discussions, topics such as politics and money should be avoided. Also, humor should be used carefully during business meetings.

Germany German executives like to be greeted by their title, and one should never refer to someone on a first-name basis unless invited to do so. Business appointments should be made well in advance, and punctuality is important. Like the French, the Germans often entertain clients outside their house, so an invitation to a German manager's home is a special privilege and always should be followed with a thank-you note. Additionally, as is the case in France, one should avoid using humor during business meetings.

Great Britain In Britain, it is common to shake hands on the first meeting, and first names are always used in introductions. Unlike the custom in France and Germany, it is common practice in Britain to arrive a little late for business and social occasions, and invitations to British homes are more likely than in some other European cultures. A typical gift for the host is flowers or chocolates.

During business meetings, suits and ties are common dress; however, striped ties should be avoided if they appear to be a copy of those worn by alumni of British universities and schools or by members of military or social clubs. Additionally, during social gatherings it is a good idea not to discuss politics, religion, or gossip about the monarchy unless the British person brings the topic up first.

Italy In traditional companies, executives are referred to by title plus last name. It is common to shake hands when being introduced, and if the individual is a university graduate, the professional title *dottore* should be used.

Business appointments should be made well in advance, although punctuality is not essential. In most cases, business is done at the office, and when someone is invited to a restaurant, this invitation is usually done to socialize and not to continue business discussions. If an expatriate is invited to an Italian home, it is common to bring a gift for the host, such as a bottle of wine or a box of chocolates. During the dinner conversation, there is a wide variety of acceptable topics, including business, family matters, and soccer.

Spain It is common to use first names when introducing or talking to people in Spain, and close friends typically greet each other with an embrace. Appointments should be made in advance, but punctuality is not essential.

If one is invited to the home of a Spanish executive, flowers or chocolates for the host are acceptable gifts. If the invitation includes dinner, any business discussions should be delayed until after coffee is served. During the social gathering, some topics that should be avoided include religion, family, and work. Additionally, humor rarely is used during formal occasions.

uisite amount of flexibility and cooperation in intercompany interaction and negotiation. At the heart of this process is effective communication. As put by Kenichi Ohmae:

> We must recognize and accept the inescapable subtleties and difficulties of intercompany relationships. This is the essential starting point. Then we must focus not on contractual or equity-related issues but on the quality of the people at the interface between organizations. Finally, we must understand that success requires frequent, rapport-building meetings by at least three organizational levels: top management, staff, and line management at the working level.[41]

The World of Business Week Revisited

The *Business Week* article that opened this chapter presented a number of intercultural communication challenges. As the article emphasized, her advisors literally become Korean golfer, Se Ri Pak's, voice, given her lack of English speaking skills. Also, her loyalty to Samsung Group back in her native Korea, which has paid for much of her golf training, has left the golfing sensation little decisional freedom to manage her own career. Having read this chapter, you can now clearly see how language barriers, the Koreans' preference for a downward communication style, and mutual limited tolerance for differences in cultural communication values, has made Pak's partnerships with U.S. sponsors difficult. In linking communication concepts from the chapter with the obstacles facing Pak, answer these questions: (1) If Pak is once able to form a partnership with a U.S. company(s), what other communication barriers might arise in future dealings? (2) What type of training would you recommend for Pak or corporate liaisons to bridge current intercultural communication gaps? (3) What are some specific ways in which a corporate sponsor might be able to capitalize on communication differences?

Summary of Key Points

1. Communication is the transfer of meaning from sender to receiver. This process can involve both the external and internal flow of information as well as verbal communication styles. The key to the effectiveness of communication is how accurately the receiver interprets the intended meaning.

2. Communicating in the international business context involves both downward and upward flows. Downward flows convey information from superior to subordinate; these flows vary considerably from country to country. For example, the downward system of organizational communication is much more prevalent in France than in Japan. Upward communication conveys information from subordinate to superior. In the United States and Japan, the upward system is more common than in South America or some European countries.

3. The international arena contains a number of communication barriers. Some of the most important are

language, perception, culture, and nonverbal communication. Language, particularly in written communications, often loses considerable meaning during interpretation. Perception and culture can result in people's seeing and interpreting things differently, and as a result, communication can break down. Nonverbal communication such as body language, facial expressions, and use of physical space time and even color often varies from country to country and, if improper, often results in communication problems.

4. A number of steps can be taken to improve communication effectiveness. Some of the most important include improving feedback, providing language and cultural training, and encouraging flexibility and cooperation. These steps can be particularly helpful in overcoming communication barriers in the international context and can lead to more effective international management.

Key Terms

chromatics
chronemics
communication
context
downward communication
haptics

intimate distance
kinesics
monochronic time schedule
nonverbal communication
oculesics
perception

personal distance
polychronic time schedule
proxemics
public distance
social distance
upward communication

Review and Discussion Questions

1. How does explicit communication differ from implicit communication? What is one culture that makes wide use of explicit communication? Implicit communication? Describe how one would go about conveying the following message in each of the two cultures you identified: "You are trying very hard, but you are still making too many mistakes."

2. One of the major reasons that foreign expatriates have difficulty doing business in the United States is that they do not understand American slang. A business executive recently gave the authors the following three examples of statements that had no direct meaning for her because she was unfamiliar with slang: He was laughing like hell. Don't worry; it's a piece of cake. Let's throw these ideas up against the wall and see if any of them stick. Why did the foreign expat have trouble understanding these statements, and what could be said instead?

3. Yamamoto Iron & Steel is considering setting up a minimill outside Atlanta, Georgia. At present, the company is planning to send a group of executives to the area to talk with local and state officials regarding this plant. In what way might misperception be a barrier to effective communication between the representatives for both sides? Identify and discuss two examples.

4. Diaz Brothers is a winery in Barcelona. The company would like to expand operations to the United States and begin distributing its products in the Chicago area. If things work out well, the company then will expand to both coasts. In its business dealings in the Midwest, how might culture prove to be a communication barrier for the company's representatives from Barcelona? Identify and discuss two examples.

5. Why is nonverbal communication a barrier to effective communication? Would this barrier be greater for Yamamoto Steel & Iron (question 3) or the Diaz Brothers (question 4)? Defend your answer.

6. For U.S companies going abroad for the first time, which form of nonverbal communication barrier would be the greatest, kinesics or proxemics? Why? Defend your answer.

Internet Exercise: Working Effectively at Toyota

By the late 1990s Toyota's Camry had become the best-selling car in the United States and the firm's share of the American automobile market was solid. However, the company is not resting on its laurels. Toyota has expanded worldwide and is now doing business in scores of countries. Visit the firm's web site and find out what it has been up to lately. The address is: **www.toyota.com.** In particular, choose five of the worldwide sites where it does business and read about what is going on in each location. (Since these are written in the local language, you will want to choose your sites carefully.) Then take a tour of the company's products and services including cars, air services, and sports vehicles. Next, go to the jobs section site and see what types of career opportunities there are at Toyota. Finally, find out what Toyota is doing in your particular locale and those in the immediate area. Then, drawing upon this information and the material you read in the chapter, answer these three questions: (1) What type of communication challenges do you think you would face if you worked for Toyota and were in constant communication with their home office personnel in Japan? (2) What type of communication training do you think the firm would need to provide to you to ensure that you were effective in dealing with senior-level Japanese managers in the hierarchy? (3) Using Table 8–2 as your guide, what conclusions can you draw regarding communicating with the Japanese managers and what guidelines would you offer to a non-Japanese employee who just entered the firm and is looking for advice and guidance regarding how to communicate more effectively?

Gulf States

The Gulf States comprise Bahrain, Kuwait, Oman, Qatar, and the United Arab Emirates (U.A.E.). These countries lie along the eastern coast of the Arabian Peninsula, with Saudi Arabia bordering on the west and Iran on the east across the Arabian Gulf (called the Persian Gulf by Westerners). Each of the Gulf States countries is very small, but their desert land is strategically located in one of the largest oil-producing regions of the world.

Oil has made these nations some of the richest in the world, with very high per-capita income. They generally have free education, free health and social services, and no income tax. Because of the heat, business hours from May to October tend to be from 7 to 1 and from 4 to 7. During the rest of the year, the hours are from 8 to 2 and from 4 to 6. The largely government-owned oil industry dominates the economies but does not provide many jobs. The governments are trying to promote economic activities other than oil production to get their people off welfare.

Herman Kerdling's firm has had a very profitable business supplying the Gulf countries with oil-production machinery. Last month, Kerdling learned that he would be going to Oman for a 1-year assignment servicing the firm's contract. He was delighted, because he knows that all the top managers at headquarters have had similar international assignments. Moreover, Oman is one of the company's most important accounts. Kerdling was determined to be successful in this assignment.

Unfortunately, after several weeks in Oman, things have not worked out quite as he expected. Specifically, Kerdling is finding that doing business with the Arabs is difficult, because their approach is so different from that of Americans. One of the most disconcerting things is the fact that people stand so close when they talk. He often tries to back away and put some room between them, but the other person usually follows and closes the distance again.

Another problem is the way that meetings are conducted. Last week, Kerdling went to talk to an Arab customer about some new equipment that was to be delivered and installed within the next few weeks. He and the customer talked for about 5 minutes when someone in the next office suddenly barged in and interrupted the conversation. The customer talked to this individual for almost 5 minutes and then turned back to Kerdling and picked up the conversation where he had left off. Within a few minutes, however, someone else came in, and another interruption ensued. The meeting, which should have taken approximately 30 minutes, took over 2 hours to complete. As Kerdling left, he turned and saw another person start a conversation with the customer only to be interrupted by a third party. "How does anyone get anything done around here?" he wondered to himself.

A third problem are the letters and e-mails that Kerdling receives from his customers. These messages are translated by company-paid Arabic interpreters, and the interpreted copy is attached to the original. Herman sometimes has trouble with the interpretation, because the interpreters are not very good. Unfortunately, no one on the company's staff is fluent in Arabic, and no better interpreters can be found. There seems to be no way around this problem. Kerdling is convinced that there are many communication breakdowns caused by this lack of language fluency, but he is unsure of how to resolve the matter.

www.arab.net/kuwait/geography/kt_geointro.html

Questions

1. What are some current issues facing the Gulf States? What is the climate for doing business in the Gulf States today?

2. Why is Kerdling upset that his Arab hosts stand so close when they talk to him? What can he do about this?

3. Should Kerdling feel insulted when his conversation is interrupted by outsiders?

4. Is Kerdling right regarding communication breakdowns caused by a lack of language fluency? Can anything be done about the problem?

Foreign or Domestic?

Connie Hatley is a very successful businesswoman who has holdings in a wide variety of industries. Hatley recently was approached by one of the Big Three automakers and offered a multidealership arrangement. In return for investing $50 million in facilities, the auto manufacturer would be willing to give her five dealerships spread throughout the United States. These locations, for the most part, are in rural areas, but over the next decade, these locales likely will become much more populated. In addition, the company pointed out that a large percentage of new cars are purchased by individuals who prefer to buy in rural locations, because prices at these dealerships tend to be lower. Hatley has been seriously considering the offer, although she now has a competitive alternative.

A South Korean auto manufacturer has approached Hatley and offered her the same basic deal. Hatley indicated that she was wary of doing business with a foreign firm so far away, but the Korean manufacturer presented her with some interesting auto sales data, including: (1) between 1981 and 1996, the South Korean share of the U.S. auto market went from 0 to 2.4 percent; (2) South Korean automakers are capturing market share in the United States at a faster rate than any other competitor; (3) new technology is being incorporated into these Korean-built cars at an unprecedented rate, and the quality is among the highest in the industry; (4) although the Big Three (GM, Ford, and Daimler-Chrysler) hold a large share of the U.S. auto market, their market among those 45 years of age or younger is declining and being captured by foreign competitors; and (5) the South Korean firm intends to increase its share of the U.S. market by 20 percent annually.

Hatley is very impressed with these data and forecasts. Recently, however, the Korean auto company's sales and market share are declining; she is uneasy about having to deal with someone located halfway around the world. "If I don't receive scheduled deliveries, whom do I call?" she asked one of her vice presidents. "Also, we don't speak their language. If there is a major problem, how are we going to really communicate with each other? I like the proposal, and I'd take it if I were sure that we wouldn't have communication problems. However, $50 million is a lot of money to invest. If a mistake is made, I'm going to lose a fortune. They did experience some problems last year, and their sales were off that year. Of course, if the South Koreans are right in their long-range forecasts and I have no major problems dealing with them, my return on investment is going to be almost 50 percent higher than it will be with the U.S. manufacturer."

Questions

1. What specific types of communication problems might Hatley encounter in dealing with the South Koreans?

2. Can these communication problems be resolved, or are they insurmountable and will simply have to be tolerated?

3. Based on communication problems alone, should Hatley back away from the deal or proceed? Give your recommendation, then defend it.

Integrative Case 1

IKEA: Managing Cultural Diversity

After firmly attaining leadership within Sweden, where it holds more than 20 percent of the overall market, IKEA has succeeded over the last 25 years in doing what no furniture distributor has ever attempted: to become a global player in an industry formerly considered by nature to be local.

Today IKEA delivers low-priced quality furniture to key markets throughout the world. It is the only distributor in its field to have successfully established itself in all parts of Europe, including southern and eastern Europe, and more notably in North America, including the USA. It has stores today in the Middle East, Singapore, and Hong Kong and is preparing to enter the Chinese market some time in the early part of the next century. Recently Ingvar Kamprad, the company's founder, secured his position in Europe with the acquisition of British-based Habitat, IKEA's chief rival in the UK and France.

To provide some idea of its worldwide presence, IKEA receives annually over 120 million visitors in its 125 stores, and distributes 35 million catalogs. Its sales revenues increased steadily over the last 10 years by an average of 12 percent annually, in spite of the flattening out of

its business in Western Europe which still represents nearly 80 percent of its annual volume (see Exhibit 1).

Ingvar Kamprad's stubborn insistence that people would buy more furniture if the price was low enough and the furniture was of decent quality, with no delays in delivery has gradually revolutionized the conservative national furniture markets in Europe and beyond. Kamprad intuitively anticipated the rise of consumerism in the 1950s and 1960s and virtually invented the practices of cash and carry, self-service, and volume buying in Europe.

IKEA was to invent many other concepts and new ways of dealing with logistics sourcing and retailing. Many of these innovations have become industry standards: knock-down furniture that can be stored and shipped in flat boxes; the involvement of customers in the value-adding process of handling the transportation and doing home-assembly themselves; and turning shopping into a family event by creating attractive open store environments that contain IKEA trademarks like the children's areas with brightly colored plastic balls and the buffet style restaurants where you can eat Swedish meatballs.

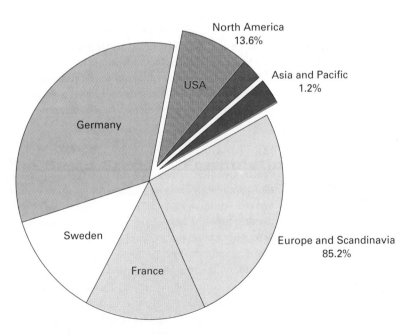

Exhibit 1

IKEA's Sales by Region, 1995–1996

North America 13.6%

USA

Germany

Asia and Pacific 1.2%

Sweden

France

Europe and Scandinavia 85.2%

Number of active articles: 11,400
Number of suppliers: 2,353 in 65 countries
Number of distribution centers: 14

IKEA has affected the way furniture is sold and distributed in every country where it is doing business, inspiring imitation and drawing respect, sometimes begrudgingly, from traditional furniture dealers.

One aspect of IKEA's success has been the development of unique product design capabilities, based on an almost religious dedication to the simple yet graceful design of contemporary Swedish furniture. In so doing, it has introduced millions of households around the world to the Swedish style that it, more than others, has come to typify.

IKEA's strength today comes from its mastery of three key aspects of the value chain: unique design capabilities, unique sourcing, and tightly controlled logistics. This means the company is able to produce products that are distinctive enough to provide market recognition, secure sourcing for long runs at profitable levels, and reduce inventory costs through regional warehouses which work very closely with stores. In this way it has been able to buck industry trends and steadily increase its share of slow growth, sometimes shrinking, markets.

IKEA has become a household name as much in Warsaw as in Los Angeles, attracting customers who just want to come to a store, look around, and have some fun. Something universally irresistible about IKEA makes it very difficult for people to come away from one of its stores without making a purchase and instills unprecedented loyalty among its customers and employees.

IKEA's successful development, particular organizational capacities, and the bold and inspired leadership of its entrepreneur-founder have all been largely written up and commented. Its organization, communication, marketing, product range, and store layouts, all tell the same story—the story of the "IKEA Way." A way strongly rooted in the personality of founder Ingvar Kamprad and the Swedish (regional) culture that he grew up in.

The "IKEA Way": Doing Things Differently

What is it that makes IKEA so different? Is it just a matter of "quality goods at affordable prices"? Or is there a deeper explanation? When asked these questions, IKEA managers and personnel become mystical and somewhat vague. "It is really a winning combination of price and merry feeling, a feeling of delight," a Dutch marketing manager answers. This feeling and a conscious awareness that, in addition to the competitive advantage, there is something strong and intangible at IKEA that drives and motivates its success, is shared by Ikeans throughout the organization. Could it be that the "IKEA Way's" combination of vision, charismatic leadership, sound business principles is subtly reinforced by the influence of Swedish culture? Could it be that Swedish, or Scandinavian, culture contains elements that facilitate international expansion?

Can a company's national culture in this case be a competitive advantage? Throughout our investigation of IKEA

we have kept these questions in the back of our minds, and we invite you to consider them as we explore the "IKEA Way" more closely.

How It All Started

IKEA's name is derived from the initials of the company's founder, architect, and driving force, Ingvar Kamprad, those of the farm where he was raised, Elmtaryd, and those of his native village Agunnaryd, located in Smaland, a poor farming region in the south-east of Sweden. Coming from a modest background, Kamprad began as a trader in everything from matches to Christmas cards. He got into the furniture business almost accidentally after buying out a furniture plant which had to close down in the early 1950s. He demonstrated from the very beginning a combination of strong salesmanship, practical business acumen, thrift, an identity with ordinary people, and an unconventional perseverance in the face of adversity. Always modest he was nonetheless a true entrepreneur and, more significantly, a nonconformist who was not the least bit restrained by the conventions and traditions of the contemporary Swedish furniture trade.

His habit of staying close to his customers and his reluctance to own manufacturing furniture plants gave him the freedom to focus and innovate on all the facets of distribution. With nearby furniture producers he codesigned furniture to meet very specific requirements for quality products that average customers could afford, and then printed them up in catalogs, which he had discovered as an economical and effective way of marketing to a growing customer base in his early days as a trader.

In 1953 he opened his first showroom at the furniture plant he had bought earlier in Almhult which has become the heart of his furniture empire. The only transportation link to the factory was by road but, at a time when more and more working class Swedes were purchasing their first automobiles, what was originally a problem would become a solution.

Kamprad was obsessed with low prices and the only way to offer them was to keep costs as low as possible—this conviction became a driving force of his business development. He would constantly seek new ways to lower prices. For example, he bought fabrics for his furniture directly from textile mills, placing large orders and then supplying the material himself to his network of small furniture manufacturers. In this way at the same time he was able to cut costs a bit more, and ensure that his customers would have a wider selection of upholstery to choose from in the catalog. Unwittingly he had introduced the notion of vertical integration, which provided IKEA even then with a strong competitive advantage compared to traditional distributors who only displayed and sold furniture.

Such practices enabled him to maintain close contact with his suppliers, and eventually to learn intimately the parameters of furniture production. The relationship between Kamprad and his suppliers was so good that to obtain their commitment he needed only to draw rough sketches of the furniture he wanted and discuss with them how to adapt production to their capabilities. In so doing, he established over the years another cornerstone of his business philosophy: marrying the customers' need for low prices with the suppliers' need for profit through efficiency and long production runs. This was a strong departure from the kind of relationship that distributors traditionally maintained with their suppliers, buying furniture as it was ordered piece by piece at high prices with long waiting periods for delivery.

Balancing customers' requirements and producers' needs, which enabled him to sell furniture at prices 30 to 50 percent below traditional distributors, is now the foundation of the "IKEA Way." This notion is so basic and imperative that a store manager in Germany told me, when walking through the accessories department where some Chinese gadgets were displayed, that this balancing of optimal product design with the supplier with the needs of the customer is the "Yin and Yang" of the IKEA strategy. It was already present in the way Ingvar Kamprad developed his business through the 1950s when his innovative ways provoked stubborn counterattacks from his more established Swedish competitors.

A legendary showdown took place at the Sankt Erik's Fair in Stockholm where, for the first time, IKEA introduced its products. Feeling threatened by Kamprad's unexpected success and many new customers, the Swedish furniture cartel tried to block IKEA's entry at the fair. They failed, but soon thereafter managed a successful boycott of IKEA by Swedish furniture manufacturers, accusing Kamprad of unfair practices. Undaunted by this seemingly insurmountable obstacle, Kamprad looked for and found new suppliers in Poland at the height of the Cold War.

Although Polish manufacturers were willing to sell at prices well below their counterparts in Sweden, the cost of transportation offset this advantage. This new obstacle was at the origin of yet another IKEA invention, as Kamprad discovered that by "knocking down" furniture into disassembled parts it could be packed and shipped in flat cardboard cartons, reducing by more than 80 percent the cost of transportation. To further save on costs, the furniture could be sold directly to customers in these same flat boxes. To help customers participate in the distribution cycle, IKEA offered to rent roof racks and invented the simple assembly tool which has become another of its trademarks.

To reach the largest possible market and benefit fully from volume sales, in 1964 IKEA opened Europe's first large "warehouse scale" store in Stockholm. Unexpectedly large crowds of people attended the grand opening causing yet another problem. Seemingly endless queues formed at the checkout stands as employees scurried to the storage areas to fetch the purchased furniture. Instead of hiring more employees, Kamprad simply opened the storage area to customers and invited them to fetch the furniture themselves. Such practices were unheard of then, but understanding that this would lead to lower prices, customers willingly complied. In just a few years IKEA had invented the concept of "prosumers," whereby customers actively participate in the distribution cycle.

Suddenly the whole system was in place: Customers were able to purchase attractive quality furniture at low prices; furniture suppliers benefited from long production runs; and IKEA, through volume sales, was able to make a considerable profit from small margins.

IKEA's business strategy did not evolve from "strategic planning," which is still scorned today in the company as "too sophisticated." It evolved from creative responses to difficult problems, turning them into solutions pragmatically and often with considerable risk. Not going by the book, or adopting conventional solutions, and learning by doing appears to be a distinguishing trait of Ingvar Kamprad's and IKEA's intuitive way of doing business.

The IKEA Mission

As IKEA grew, Ingvar Kamprad found ways to explain his unique way of doing business, always using simple language and metaphors He has consistently maintained that IKEA's mission is to offer "a wide range of home furnishing items of good design and function, at prices so low that the majority of people can afford to buy them." This statement is at the heart of the IKEA's philosophy and has shaped all the phases of its business, particularly product range. The concept is protected through numerous guidelines and special legal entities. Changes in the criteria for product range can only be made by joint decisions of INGKA Holding BV and Inter IKEA Systems BV, both of which are outside the sphere of management.

The essential guidelines appear in a 1976 publication, *Testament of a Furniture Dealer*, in which Kamprad emphasizes the company's ambition to cover the furnishing and decorative needs of the total home area with a distinctive style that reflects "our thoughts and is as simple and straightforward as ourselves." The guidelines also express such modern ideals as furniture that is durable and easy to live with, reflects a natural and free life style, and appeals to youthfulness with color and joy. Most of IKEA's products are designed by Swedes in Almhult, who consciously reproduce designs that reflect these values—values which are very consistent with Swedish culture. At the same time there is something in that specific design which has universal appeal throughout the markets of the world.

Business Principles

IKEA has developed unique competencies and an ability to deliver products which are distinctly Swedish, attractively presented in warm value-adding environments, and at prices consistently lower than its competitors.

What has made IKEA so different from other distributors is the balanced focus it has maintained on product range, sourcing, vertical integration, mass marketing, cost leadership, and a distinctive image. As such, the company is not market driven, and tends to react rather slowly to new consumer trends, studying them to see how they can be fitted into its operating systems and what value IKEA can add within its proven framework before adopting them into the company's range. The issue of range is vital for IKEA as, when it introduces new products, it must insure that the volumes it produces are leveraged from within: sourcing—logistics—store layouts.

The Yin/Yang metaphor, mentioned earlier, illustrates the imperative balance of strategic sourcing and marketing mix.

In the area of strategic sourcing, IKEA has established a long-standing competitive advantage. The durable partnerships that it has developed with furniture producers and other suppliers is based on the producers' capacity to provide long runs of parts, and their willingness to comply with IKEA's quality standards, and IKEA's guaranteed purchase of all parts produced. IKEA considers its producers as key stakeholders and provides them with technical assistance to increase their productivity, sometimes under-

writing investments in new technology. Together they actively contribute to both cost reduction and quality enhancement, which in turn optimizes the marketing mix.

Through such partnerships IKEA has virtually integrated production into its value-added chain without the heavy investments of actually owning and running its own furniture plants.

Management Style and Practices

IKEA's management style is described by non-Swedish members as informal, open, and caring. Hierarchy is not emphasized and in a typical store there are only three levels of responsibility between the store manager and coworkers (which is what employees are called).

A pragmatic approach to problem solving and consensus-based decision making are also strongly imbedded in IKEA management practice.

Coworkers at all levels are encouraged to take initiatives, and making mistakes is considered a necessary part of "learning by doing." Managers are expected not only to share information with coworkers but also their knowledge and skills. IKEA wants its coworkers to feel important: They can express their ideas, and should feel responsible for improving the way things are done.

An entrepreneurial zeal for getting the job done in the most direct way and a distaste for bureaucratic procedures are basic managerial attitudes that have long been promoted within IKEA. Managers are expected to be close to their coworkers, with few if any status barriers, and not to take themselves seriously. This egalitarian approach to management has also made it easy for motivated employees to work their way up the organization with little formal training. It is significant that Swedish managers' titles do not

The balance and complementariness of:

Strategic Sourcing and the Marketing Mix

Exhibit 2

**Distribution of
IKEA's Coworkers**

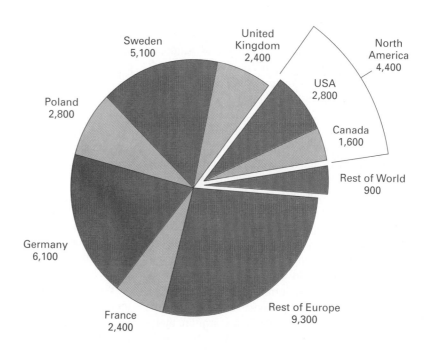

appear on their business cards, and that company cars are the same economy models for all of those who need them for work or business regardless of their position.

Rather than establish extensive training programs and detailed rules and procedures to propagate its unique culture, IKEA prefers a softer approach through discussion and explanation. The IKEA way has been spelled out through wide distribution of Kamprad's *Testament* which has been translated into a dozen languages. Kamprad himself explains that IKEA has "a strong and living culture" based on doing things differently. "It has grown step by step," and together with its business principles is the "cornerstone of our operations . . . which helps us retain the spirit and vitality of the early years . . . and create a feeling of belonging in a large international organization. Our corporate culture binds us together." To ensure that the IKEA Way is understood, the organization relies heavily on managers to act as "missionaries" carrying all that it embodies through their example and willingness to explain to new and senior employees why things are done the way they are. This, as much as anything else, provides the reason for the extensive presence of Swedish managers in IKEA's international units, as their knowledge stems from their direct exposure to Ingvar Kamprad and IKEA's subtle way of doing business and managing people. For those managers who do not have this exposure, week-long "IKEA Way" seminars are organized periodically in Almhult, the IKEA equivalent of Mecca and the heart of its culture.

IKEA's Strategy of International Expansion: Flexibility within Establishment Parameters

Patterns of International Expansion

IKEA's international expansion has taken place progressively over years with a focus on markets in countries with growth potential (see Exhibit 3). Expansion outside of Scandinavia was driven by Ingvar Kamprad's intuitive quest for new opportunities and his previous successful search for suppliers outside of Sweden more than any for-

mal development strategy. Some insights are provided by one of IKEA's Swedish executives, an early companion of Ingvar Kamprad. "When we opened our first store outside Scandinavia, in Switzerland, people asked why there? It was a difficult market. Ingvar said that if we could succeed there, we should succeed anywhere. He had intuitions, he spoke to people on the streets to learn what they were looking for." Such an empirical experiential approach goes against the orthodox rules of international retailing, which preach extensive market studies before entering a new market, catering to local tastes, and gaining expertise through acquisitions and joint ventures.

When IKEA expanded into Germany, competition was strong and German distributors didn't take them seriously. "They called us 'those crazy Swedes,' but we didn't mind; we even used this label in our advertising. It took them five years to really react, but by then we had eight stores and were setting the standards."

Charting its own course, IKEA has developed internationally by finding cheap land for stores, checking sourcing possibilities and proximity to central warehouses, or lowering marketing costs. When, in the late 1970s, the company decided to go into Belgium because it was cost effective to serve that country from its central warehouse in Germany, it ran into problems with building permits and so decided to develop in France instead. The preference has been for leveraging market costs by concentrating several stores in the same area. This explains why IKEA opened four stores in the Philadelphia/Washington DC/New Jersey area, sometimes in locations that were rather isolated. Similarly, the company also preferred to concentrate four stores in the Paris area, even if this could dilute individual store sales and create potential competition between stores.

Typically development has been done on a store-by-store basis. IKEA opens a beachhead in a given country with a group of trusted and experienced Swedish "Missionaries." Together they form a tight-knit group which can solve problems and make decisions quickly. They supervise the building work, lead operational teams who open the store, and run the store until local management has learned how the system

Exhibit 3   **The IKEA Expansion**

	No. of Outlets	No. of Countries	No. of Coworkers	Turnover (NLG)[d]
1954	1	1	15	2,200,000
1964	2	2	250	55,500,000
1974	10	5	1,500	372,900,000
1984	66	17	8,300	2,678,700,000
1994	120(125[a])	25 (26[a])	26,600[b]	8,350,000,000
1996	129(136[a])	27 (28[a])	33,400[b]	9,626,000,000[c]

Note: [a]Including stores opening after September 1, 1996.

[b]20% of coworkers are part time.

[c]Corresponding to net sales of the IKEA Group of companies.

[d]The holding company is in the Netherlands which explains the use of NLG.

works. After a short time, store management is turned over to local managers, while most of the key national positions remain in the hands of Swedes until the operation and market have reached maturity.

Adapting to National Markets

Adapting to new markets in western Europe throughout the 1970s and early 1980s was fairly simple. Catalog offerings were virtually the same. However, concessions had to be made, particularly in bedroom furnishings since bedding could be substantially different from country to country.

"When we entered a new country we did things our way. The ideas was to be IKEA everywhere: After all, our furniture is a cultural statement. But as the years went by we learned to be more flexible, particularly when demand in Sweden declined and we became more dependent on our non-Scandinavian markets," recalls one IKEA manager.

Adapting to the U.S. market was a real learning experience for IKEA, since many standards were different. Few product managers from IKEA of Sweden had traveled to North America because the price of air travel was prohibitive in terms of IKEA's cost-conscious policies. They expected their European range to sell just as easily in the United States, but this did not turn out to be the case. As a former U.S. country manager explains: "IKEA ran into problems in the United States so we had to ask ourselves what we could offer to Americans. Should we become an American company, or merely adapt our merchandising to American customers? We finally decided on a solution: merchandising to the American customer by speaking English with a Swedish accent; capitalizing on our strengths as an outsider."

Development of the range is now closely monitored by IKEA of Sweden (IOS) and the board of directors of INGKA Holding. The issue of range is vital for them as, when they introduce new products, they must insure that the volumes they produce are balanced from within (sourcing—logistics—store layout). It took IKEA of Sweden several years to introduce "futons" in Europe, and American store managers had to work hard to convince the company that a "Home Entertainment" line was feasible in North America.

As a former French country manager described, obtaining concessions from product managers to take into account specific national preferences was a consensual process that required many negotiation skills. "Some room is allowed for national considerations in our catalog range. But, since changes mean that it will be more expensive for the country manager, only limited numbers are allowed. Still, 90 percent of our range is the same all over the world: only 5 to 10 percent is country specific. The product manager has the final word, but he usually listens to the country manager. There is a healthy tension between the two and this enables us to adapt but not to over-adapt and weaken our cost effectiveness."

Although IKEA's stated mission is to provide home furnishing for the "greatest number" and its business is conducted on a volume basis, outside of Scandinavia it is in reality a niche player, appealing to the educated population with mid- to upper-level incomes. This segment is looking for nontraditional lines of furniture, and finds the Swedish style of IKEA suited to its modern taste.

"In spite of our image as the 'common man's store,' the majority of our customers have a university degree,"

Exhibit 4

The Organization of the IKEA Group

Supervisory Board,
Ingka Holding B.V.
Ingvar Kamprad,
Chairman
Jan I. Carlsson
Jan Ekman
Per Lindblad
Steffan Persson
Hans-Göran Stennert

Group
Management
Anders Moberg,
Group President
Lars Bråberg
Göran Carstedt
Hans Gydell
Mikael Ohlsson

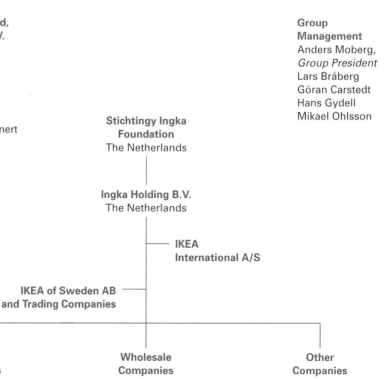

Stichtingy Ingka
Foundation
The Netherlands

Ingka Holding B.V.
The Netherlands

IKEA
International A/S

IKEA of Sweden AB
and Trading Companies

Retail
Companies

Wholesale
Companies

Other
Companies

admits a French store manager. This may appear paradoxical considering IKEA's avowed mission statement, but the paradox has proven successful as it keeps IKEA, at the same time, close to its roots and still makes it highly distinctive in foreign marketplaces. It also plays neatly into its strengths of sourcing, volume, long runs, and cost-efficient distribution.

Human Resource Management

Management of international operations has largely followed the IKEA Way and its strong Swedish flavor. The belief of those in IKEA is that their way of managing people has universal appeal. "People like to participate in making decisions. They like to feel respected, and that they can take responsibility," one Swedish expatriate states.

When recruiting, IKEA looks for people who have good communication skills, open minds, positive work attitudes, and good potential without necessarily having diplomas. It attracts people with its pleasant working environment, job security, and the caring attitude it shows towards the individual. IKEA employees, regardless of nationality, are more than likely to have strong preferences for cooperative informal relations, with a high degree of independence, and have tolerant approach to others. "We look for people who know how to listen, and who are able to transmit their knowledge to others. They should not feel they are better than others and be curious about what is going on around them."

Being an IKEA manager overseas isn't solely about running the stores and distribution systems smoothly. He or she must be able to explain to employees and managers why things are done in the way they are and win people's hearts and minds to the "IKEA Way." They are expected to be ambassadors and must educate their non-Swedish coworkers through patience, common understanding, and example. It is not always easy to transmit IKEA's egalitarian management style. While it goes down easily in the Netherlands, it is less acceptable in Germany or France, and for different reasons. In the United States, long-term employees generally feel more comfortable with Scandinavian managers than with Americans—younger American managers don't seem to know how to show "equalness."

The challenge IKEA may be facing is that, with its extended international network, it is becoming more difficult to find enough Swedish IKEA managers who are willing to work overseas for long periods. IKEA has had to hire Swedes from outside the company. Also in the past the company has not systematically searched out and developed at an early stage its international "high potentials," although it does send its most loyal and successful foreign managers to week-long seminars in Sweden and encourage its coworkers to learn something about the culture.

It is still very difficult for non-Scandinavians to work their way up the corporate ladder. To do so they need to have learned all of IKEA's key trades: retailing, logistics, product design, and purchasing. Non-Swedes can work their way up in retailing through the national organizations and sometimes in the logistical organizations which are run regionally, but very few have gone into product management because this function is part of IKEA of Sweden in Almhult, where IKEA's product managers and furniture schools are located. It is a very remote area and only Swedish is spoken. So, speaking the language as well and knowing the culture become prerequisites that very few managers from foreign branches have been able to fulfill.

There are no formal career paths, as a long-term Swedish expatriate executive admits. "To get ahead in IKEA you first have to know the range intimately, then you have to know and use the informal internal network, and then you have to understand the subtleties of the 'IKEA Way,' its cultural roots. It is really difficult for outsiders to know their way around. In reality it is a difficult company to understand. Humbleness is not a sign of weakness. It comes from Ingvar. People are expected to learn from their experience, and this takes time and patience. You can't be in a hurry to move up the ladder."

Dealing with the Europeans

Germany Germany is the largest national organization in the IKEA group, accounting for ±30 percent of the total group sales through more than 20 stores, including the newly opened stores in former East Germany.

Although IKEA has been established in Germany for more than two decades (its first store was opened in Munich in 1974), Swedish management is still perceived by German IKEA members as peculiar. As described by Thomas Larson, the store manager in Cologne: "Some senior coworkers still have problems addressing me by my first name, or using the German *du* (the informal equivalent for you, like *tu* in French). *"Dutzen,"* using the informal you, is often felt as undermining the respect and prestige of the boss. As Heike Oestreich, the personnel manager said: "There are two different *du's,* the IKEA *du* and the *du* which is used between friends."

The Germans are very disciplined and precise. They do exactly what the boss asks them to do and what is agreed or put down in writing. A problem is that the Swedish notion of "taking on responsibilities for yourself," the cornerstone of their work policy, is not perceived in the same way by the Germans, who have a tendency to adhere very closely to precisely defined rules and instructions. When IKEA translated the corporate brochure *The IKEA Way* into German, a need was felt to sharpen and make more explicit the original Swedish text which presented key IKEA concepts in sometimes vague terms in order to give freedom to people to adapt them and take personal responsibility for carrying them out. Once, Anders Moberg, Kamprad's successor, suggested in a letter that certain merchandising displays could be used in a variety of places. In Germany, department managers interpreted this as an order, and systematically set up the displays in every part of their stores.

In general, German employees feel that the Swedes are more result-oriented and treat every problem as a challenge that should be met. However, they believe that Swedish management does not sufficiently assess risks before taking action. According to Heike Oestreich: "The Swedes, to reduce bureaucracy, would like to dump all our office desks in the back yard." The lack of formality is also dismaying to Germans. To implement a decision "some notes on the back of a cigarette packet are often sufficient" for the Swedes. In contrast, Germans are more comfortable adhering to formal procedures: "We need procedures and forms. Germans love administration because it provides us with security."

France Development in France, which has fewer than half the number of stores in Germany, was always considered problematic because of the numerous administrative regulations on the retail trade, and a hostile attitude towards discounters that prevailed in the late 1970s and early 1980s. By carefully avoiding too much public attention and with only a limited number of store openings IKEA managed to secure a safe place for itself in the market and develop an 8 percent share.

The main challenge for IKEA management in France is the French tendency to judge informality as a sign of weakness, or indecisiveness. French people are accustomed to formal rules and strong hierarchy. In the words of a former Swedish country manager, when IKEA first started in France: "Some French managers felt that the Swedish informality meant they could do whatever they wanted. When we told them that they should inform their subordinates they did not take us seriously." Some aspects of the informality can even be irritating to the French, such as the lack of formal job descriptions and written procedures. Whereas Swedish managers will justify this by saying that they don't like to limit responsibility, and that they get more out of people with an informal approach, the French tend to be suspicious of informality for the same reasons.

In the view of IKEA's French human resource manager: "Working here isn't for everyone. It is particularly difficult for people over 35 because IKEA is different from all other workplaces in France. When you join IKEA, you enter another world—we do not behave like a normal French company. Status is not recognized, which can cause an identity problem: Everyone is put on the same level—no one stands out, and you can get lost in the crowd. It is hard to explain what IKEA is, everyone will give a different answer. One shouldn't freeze the system, it is flexible, and it should stay that way."

Two of the main reasons given for IKEA's appeal to French candidates are:

1. The esthetics of the stores—they look nice and are pleasant to work in.

2. The intelligent way in which IKEA works—it makes sense.

To make things clearer to employees, a formal communication platform has been developed in France to spell things out in facts and figures by comparing IKEA's benefits with those of competitors. Also, more formal training programs are being developed because in France "learning by doing" is not perceived as a credible way of developing competency. Typically, a boss would not be trusted to develop one's skills in France, and more faith is placed in "off-site programs." In France tolerance has its limits and when IKEA hired "too many" people of non-French origin, the company received complaints from customers, so now it makes a point of keeping non-French workers to a minimum.

Some years ago, relations with unions were hostile. There was a bitter strike and widespread discontent. French labor unions did not trust or understand IKEA's Swedish management style, with its tendency to seek consensus. More recently, IKEA's management has taken a more affirmative attitude, and relations have improved notably. They may continue to improve now that IKEA France is run by a Frenchman, Jean Louis Baillot, whose wife is Swedish and who has worked in Almhult.

Doing Things Differently in the United States

Expanding into the U.S. market was certainly the boldest developmental decision that IKEA had made up to that time. From an historical perspective the venture seemed unlikely to succeed. First, the culturally specific requirements for home furnishing in the United States are considerably different than the European markets, particularly in terms of the size and functions of furniture. Second, the American market had come to be known as the "graveyard" of European retailers with a long list of unfortunate ventures by such successful firms as Casino, Carrefour, and Marks & Spencer. But somehow, IKEA seemed confident that going about it in their own way would prove an exception to the laws of failure that seemed to doom European entrants to the U.S. market.

Initially, development in the United States was quite consistent with IKEA's pattern in Europe: Identify prime markets with volume potential; purchase cheap land on the periphery of big cities; use mass advertising with a unique message emphasizing IKEA's Swedishness; focus on range and price through the catalog, establishing a beachhead from which to launch and develop the organization. Also, its approach was empirical and pragmatic. It did not set out to take the United States by storm, but merely to test its existing formula and learn through experience how success could be achieved. In fact, from the mid-1970s to the early 1980s IKEA opened a series of franchised stores in Canada, developing during this time its logistics capabilities and demonstrating that its European range could sell in America's backyard, before it finally entered the U.S. market in 1985.

Its first stage of development in the United States began on the East Coast with the opening of Plymouth Meeting in Philadelphia's northwest suburbs, followed by a cluster of four other stores. "Development was initially based on the potato field approach. Find some place where there is cheap land, build, and the people will follow." This approach ignored the rule of American retailing based on fine-tuned segmentation and targeting. The choice of locations, driven by cost-consciousness, led IKEA to establish its stores in shopping centers that had no prestige "anchor stores" to draw the high-income customers that IKEA appeals to. This should have been a relative disadvantage, since competitors like Home Depot locate their stores in prime centers with "anchor stores" like Nordstroms and Macy's. But by maintaining the profile of a "different kind of store," very Swedish, with a wide range of products, it apparently has overcome this obstacle. Here, the catalog has served them well, as people can plan their purchases before they come and thus optimize their time investment.

Up until the late 1980s IKEA enjoyed a honeymoon of sorts. The American public was attracted by the novelty of Scandinavian style and IKEA's unique merchandising, which resembles in many ways a European village marketplace. Its advertising was a success. People drove six to eight hours to come to the stores and they initially came in large numbers. Riding on a high dollar, IKEA had appeared to have gotten off to as fast a start as they had in Germany and other European markets. The honeymoon ended suddenly when the dollar went down, revealing multiple weaknesses.

First and foremost, even though Americans were initially attracted by IKEA's advertising and novelty, the company's range of furniture was unsuited to American standards and sold poorly. One often told anecdote illustrates just how far from those standards they really were: Customers would purchase flower vases thinking they were American-size drinking glasses. Americans furnish their master bedrooms with king size beds, whereas IKEA's largest beds were five inches narrower. Also, Americans are harder on sitting room furniture, and IKEA's sofa and armchair offerings proved too lightly designed Additionally, IKEA did not offer furniture suitable for the "home entertainment centers" that blossomed throughout the 1980s and into the 1990s in American households with the proliferation of widescreen televisions, VCRs, and hi-fi equipment. With declining sales revenues and shrinking profits, by 1989 the "graveyard effect" seemed to have caught up with IKEA.

A courageous decision was then made by Anders Moberg and a new management team was brought in to head the organization. Faced with the alternatives of holding on and waiting for better times, withdrawing humbly, or fighting back, the latter course of action was chosen. In 1990, the American retail management group, under the leadership of Göran Carstedt, recently hired from Volvo, convinced the product managers at IKEA of Sweden that the IKEA European range had to be adapted and American-based sourcing stepped up. At the same time, he reassured them that IKEA would not prostitute itself. In the

words of Carstedt: "The IKEA strategy in North America will still be blue and yellow, but we will put more stars and stripes and more maple leaves in it."

It was not easy but they succeeded in changing the design of many household products. To make the point, one U.S. manager brought a plastic American-size turkey with him to Almhult and before a surprised group of product managers placed it on one of the best-selling dining tables in the European range. Given the size of the bird there was only room for two table settings instead of the normal six. He had made his point.

However there was a condition attached to adapting the range, and that condition was volume. Lines of furniture specifically designed for the American market would have to be produced in long enough runs to meet IKEA's commitment to suppliers and be priced at the lowest levels possible.

A combination of luck and bold counterattacking led to an unexpected expansion on the West Coast that was to ease pressure on its pricing and provide much needed growth in its retail business. An imitator, "Stor," inspired by IKEA's success, had illicitly acquired intimate knowledge of IKEA's floor plan and merchandising schemes and successfully opened four stores primarily around Los Angeles, far from IKEA's base on the East Coast. Responding as much to the threat to the company's image as to the opportunity to capitalize on Stor's advertising of Swedish style furniture, IKEA decided to counterattack. It opened a store in Los Angeles and eventually, through its price and sourcing advantage, drove Stor to the brink of bankruptcy. It then bought out its imitator at a bargain price and established a solid base in a prime market on the West Coast. If IKEA's low-profile stance stressed its humble origins and culture, it definitely did not mean that the company was a weakling. IKEA showed that it could be tough and decisive in that toughest of tough markets. The current U.S. country manager, Jan Kjellman, in comparing the U.S. market to his previous European experience used the following words: "The biggest difference is competition. Competitors are everywhere, and they are strong. The market is crowded, but still there always seem to be new competitors. Even with a million and a half customers, we are small. It is a total struggle for us, and it is tough to survive." Could IKEA adapt to such competition and still remain faithful to the "IKEA Way"?

Swedish managers are impressed with the professionalism of American salesmanship. "Over here, retailing is a profession. Salespersons are subjected to a lot of pressure for short-term results because large retailers are publicly owned and shareholders measure quarterly results. So they are very time-efficient and masters of the hard sell," relates Kjellman. IKEA has always maintained a soft approach believing that people know what they want, so that sales personnel are there to help them find it. Moreover, the strategy is that most of the selling is done by the catalog so that people arrive with specific purchases in mind. Impulse buying takes place for smaller items like candle holders, or accessories which are sought for as bargains. On this point IKEA has stood firm, and sales personnel from competitors such as Macy's or Bloomingdale's have to unlearn the hard sell approach.

Americans are always looking for convenience, which means more space, more information, anything that reduces effort and saves time. To respond to these demands, IKEA had to redesign its store layouts, providing more directions, and short cuts for people who don't want to just wander through the store. "Customers were screaming 'let us out' before we remodeled our layout," reported one store manager. "They couldn't find their way out of our maze of displays, there were no windows or signs, they felt lost and panicky." While making these adjustments in store layout, which have been criticized by IKEA International headquarters, IKEA has maintained its policy of minimal service. Customers who want home delivery or someone to assemble their furniture must pay the full add-on cost. In fact, IKEA stores carefully outsource these services to local providers and they never promote such services in their advertising. Instead, they encourage their customers to do it the "IKEA Way," which means renting a roof rack and assembling it yourself.

Adapting IKEA's floor plans and furniture to American dimensions paid off, and sales increased by 25 to 30 percent in comparison with the late 1980s. By 1994 IKEA had turned around the situation in the United States. Through its acquisition of Stor and by adapting its range to U.S. requirements, sales have increased steadily by about 10 percent annually, providing IKEA with the volume base necessary to sustain long production run and to keep prices low. Whereas at first only 15 percent of the furniture in American stores was produced locally, the figure is now about 50 percent.

In the view of several IKEA senior U.S. managers, the key to this successful turnaround was the granting of more autonomy to the American country management than their European counterparts had enjoyed. "You can't steer America from Europe," admitted Anders Moberg in 1994. "When we went in we hadn't planned a clear strategy of how to supply the American market at a low cost." Learning how to succeed in the United States through its own painful expense took more than five years. Although its U.S. operation showed a profit over the subsequent three years it still has not recovered its initial investment. With flat growth in Europe, and heavy investment in longer term expansion into eastern Europe and China putting pressure on IKEA's capital reserves, the focus in the United States is now on developing sales and profit from its existing stores before expanding into new regions. Following its bold actions in the early 1990s, IKEA has entered a more conservative phase of consolidation. Perhaps it has also learned that the price of being different means that you also have to be more careful about where you invest.

Unresolved Issues: Management and Human Resource Development

From an American perspective, Swedish managers don't show emotion in the workplace. "Praise is given for looking calm in all situations. They do not feel comfortable in conflictual situations. Also, they tend not to set themselves apart, and self-promotion is frowned upon. They don't like drum beating or cheerleading in a culture where both are common ways of motivating workers."

"The biggest conflicts here stem from the Americans who need to know who's in charge. People expect their managers to tell them what to do here." However, at IKEA the manager's role is more subtle and they tend to have a long-term approach to management. "It takes longer to do things our way but we want to train people to know how to do things the right way." Since there are few written procedures, the golden rule for managers is to help people understand why things are done in a particular way. This can be viewed as indecision by American employees new to IKEA who are more used to rules and procedures spelled out clearly and managers who take responsibility for quick decision making.

American employees perceive IKEA as being more employee-oriented than average American employers. IKEA attracts and selects people who value security, job enrichment, and benefits which are more generous than typical American employers (like five weeks of paid holiday) more than career advancement. However, with full employment in the United States it is becoming more difficult to find candidates, particularly for management positions, who have the necessary job qualifications and whose values match IKEA's.

Although IKEA has recently initiated an American style performance review procedure, which requires documenting employees' individual performance strengths and weaknesses, Swedish managers feel uncomfortable with the formality of the system and the need to provide negative feedback. Since they hold the more senior positions, their ambivalence has resulted in little real discrimination in pay increases which are directly linked to the reviews. Although turnover at IKEA is lower than the industry average, and coworkers generally appreciate IKEA's caring environment, there is some latent discontent with the way pay increases are distributed, even among long-term employees who feel that their individual achievements are not always rewarded.

In the opinion of one American manager, "A lot of people have left IKEA because they can't move up fast enough here. Some left the store to go to the Service Center (IKEA's national headquarters) then left because it was too hard for them to adjust, there was no clear frame of reference in terms of policies and procedures. We have lost some key American managers because they didn't have a clear idea of their role or future in the organization."

Acknowledging that there are not enough American managers in senior positions, IKEA is trying to attract management trainees through presentations at business schools. However, its low-key image and lack of structured career paths are not easy to sell to "high potentials" more attuned to the packages offered by retailers such as Home Depot which forcefully push rapid promotion and individualize pay incentives. There is a general consensus that IKEA needs to develop young American managers who can play a bigger role in the organization than at present. However, there is no agreement yet on how critical the need is, nor on how to solve the problem.

Two differing views that could be overheard in a fictitious debate between two long-term Ikeans illustrate the unresolved issues facing IKEA USA at the end of 1996.

The View of a Young American Manager "There is a glass ceiling here. I am at a level at which my growth will stop because I'm not Swedish. IKEA should be made less complicated for Americans, easier for us to adapt to, and develop in. Our management needs to be much more professional in managing human resources. We need to bring new people into the organization, and reward individual accountability for results. This requires a better balance between the IKEA Way and American management. Becoming a successful manager at IKEA requires a lot of time and effort to understand how everything fits together. Yet not everyone can go to Sweden or learn Swedish, and today too many talented Americans choose to go to competitors. Competition is catching up on us in terms of benefits, and with full employment we should be much more competitive than we are on the American job market."

The Swedish View "Being the underdog, not doing things the traditional way over here is vital to IKEA's success in the United States. We must keep a unique image and work better at getting our message across to employees and customers so that they understand why we are successful. Pride in being a part of IKEA must be built locally and since our system is unique, this takes time. The real danger is assimilation. We are becoming too American. Giving people bonuses and pay incentives doesn't make them more intelligent; people are motivated by learning and improving in an organization that provides them with room to grow. Rewards should be more on a give and take basis—when the company makes more, it can give more—but we must remain flexible. Although we must seek a balance between adapting and sticking to our proven ways, we must protect our unique concepts and way of doing things. This means that we will always need a strong Swedish presence in the United States. They are our 'on-site missionaries' who can develop loyalty to an understanding of our uniqueness."

Clouds on the Horizon

By the mid-1990s, in spite of its undisputed international success and expansion over the past 25 years, signs appeared that the pattern of growth and steady profit was slowing down. Costs were rising, complaints on quality were more frequent, and unaccustomed delays appeared in product delivery. External factors had changed from the early times in Europe. Economic growth slowed as baby boomers moved into middle age, with new tastes and demands, and fewer new homes were being sold. Competitors had also learned from IKEA's pioneering distribution and were offering better furniture at lower prices, seeking low-cost furniture suppliers in eastern Europe, which put pressure on IKEA's unique sourcing.

IKEA had become a large international organization and, in an effort to adapt to the requirements of its many domestic markets, its product range had grown from 10,000 to 14,000 items, thus weakening returns from long production runs and overburdening logistic supply lines. Increasingly greater attention had to be given to bringing costs down, often through productivity gains which put unprecedented pressure on retail staffs to improve sales to staff ratios. During the years of rapid growth, many recruits were brought in from outside the company, and were therefore not steeped in IKEA culture. Its extended network made it difficult to provide employees and mid-level managers with a clear perception of how their local business impacted on the corporation as a whole. Local initiatives were taken without regard to their impact on the whole system. Was this the price of diversity or was IKEA suffering in many ways from too much decentralization?

In 1993, to cope with this situation, Andreas Mober and IKEA's senior management launched a company-wide operation *"Nytt Läge"* (New Situation), with the formation of task forces and project teams to suggest ways of improving communication and eliminating snags in distribution. Many suggestions were implemented, including the creation of new regional divisions in Europe for closer coordination of country operations and the hiring of more professionals at headquarters to provide guidelines and more efficient corporate control systems. Although the *Nytt Läge* program met with a lot of enthusiasm and did achieve improvements in some areas it soon became clear to Ingvar Kamprad that a more radical change in the organization was needed.

In early 1996, a major organizational change was introduced to "shorten the value chain" between customers and suppliers. Regional organizations were eliminated to bring stores in more direct contact with IKEA of Sweden. New emphasis was given to the importance of a living corporate culture based on the IKEA values of simplicity and self-discipline, rather than relying on formal policies and procedures. At the same time, IKEA's expansion plans in Europe and the United States were delayed. The fear at corporate headquarters was that IKEA had drifted too far away from the basic principles that were behind its legendary success.

Back to the Roots

In May, Ingvar Kamprad gathered IKEA's 250 worldwide store mangers and senior managers at an important meeting in Poland to plan IKEA's need to refocus and redirect its efforts. He actually used the word "rejuvenate."

Our product range and purchasing people often have an unequal battle with retailers and their far too many interests. Many of our suppliers got stuck in the middle. Our IKEA idea as one of the world's few production-oriented companies is under threat.

Perhaps we were blinded by the booming years of the 1980s which increased the geographical spread of our operations to new markets, both on the retail and trading sides. Internal communication also became difficult, our administration expanded and our overheads became increasingly heavy. Our costs rose, and our customers and suppliers felt lost many of them got in touch with me directly.

Decision making took longer and longer, and endless discussions took place. It became more difficult to see the company as a whole. Far too much of our product development had too little to do with the tastes and wallets of the majority of people. Our product range expanded in every direction and could not be handled in a reasonable way on our sales floors. Our price advantage compared to competitors began to shrink. Even IKEA's soul, our fine corporate culture, was in danger. Have we forgotten to explain to our new workers about the IKEA Way? Have our desks prevented us from being involved enough in the commercial activity? Have we lost our way?

The managers who attended that meeting felt galvanized by the founder's strong message, and their confi- dence and belief in the IKEA Way had been doubtlessly reinforced. In an increasingly complex world environment, simplicity indeed appeared to be a true virtue that had guided the company in the past. Several wondered, as they left, how Kamprad's intuitive ability to see through the complexity of a worldwide organization and reignite the dynamics of IKEA's success could be transmitted throughout the organization? Others wondered if they would have as much autonomy as they had previously enjoyed in adapting to very different markets. Some wondered if the company could regain its developmental thrust through the late 1990s?

1. What type of organizational culture is most representative of IKEA: family, Eiffel Tower, guided missile, or incubator? Explain.

2. In what way has international culture proved to be a challenge for IKEA?

3. What are three things that IKEA had to learn in order to do business effectively in the United States?

4. How well has the company been able to deal with the diversity issue? What else does it still need to do?

Euro Disneyland

On January 18, 1993, Euro Disneyland chairperson Robert Fitzpatrick announced he would leave that post on April 12 to begin his own consulting company. Quitting his position exactly one year after the grand opening of Euro Disneyland, Fitzpatrick's resignation removed U.S. management from the helm of the French theme park and resort.

Fitzpatrick's position was taken by a Frenchman, Philippe Bourguignon, who had been Euro Disneyland's senior vice president for real estate. Bourguignon, 45 years old, faced a net loss of FFr 188 million for Euro Disneyland's fiscal year, which ended September 1992. Also, between April and September 1992, only 29 percent of the park's total visitors were French. Expectations were that closer to half of all visitors would be French.

It was hoped that the promotion of Philippe Bourguignon would have a public relations benefit for Euro Disneyland—a project that has been a publicist's nightmare from the beginning. One of the low points was at a news conference prior to the park's opening when protesters pelted Michael Eisner, CEO of the Walt Disney Company, with rotten eggs. Within the first year of operation, Disney had to compromise its "squeaky clean" image and lift the alcohol ban at the park. Wine is now served at all major restaurants.

Euro Disneyland, 49 percent owned by Walt Disney Company, Burbank, California, originally forecasted 11 million visitors in the first year of operation. In January 1993 it appeared attendance would be closer to 10 million. In response, management temporarily slashed prices at the park for local residents to FFr 150 ($27.27) from FFr 225 ($40.91) for adults, and to FFr 100 from FFr 150 for children in order to lure more French during the slow, wet winter months. The company also reduced prices at its restaurants and hotels, which registered occupancy rates of just 37 percent.

Bourguignon also faced other problems, such as the second phase of development at Euro Disneyland, which was expected to start in September 1993. It was unclear how the company planned to finance its FFr 8–10 billion cost. The company had steadily drained its cash reserves (FFr 1.9 billion in May 1993) while piling up debt (FFr 21 billion in May 1993). Euro Disneyland admitted that it and the Walt Disney Company were "exploring potential sources of financing for Euro Disneyland." The company was also talking to banks about restructuring its debts.

Despite the frustrations, Eisner was tirelessly upbeat about the project. "Instant hits are things that go away quickly, and things that grow slowly and are part of the culture are what we look for" he said. "What we created in France is the biggest private investment in a foreign country by an American company ever. And it's gonna pay off."

In the Beginning

Disney's story is the classic American rags-to-riches story which started in a small Kansas City advertising office, where Mickey was a real mouse prowling the unknown Walt Disney floor. Originally, Mickey was named Mortimer, until a dissenting Mrs. Disney stepped in. How close Mickey was to Walt Disney is evidenced by the fact that when filming, Disney himself dubbed the mouse's voice. Only in later films did Mickey get a different voice. Disney made many sacrifices to promote his hero-mascot, including selling his first car, a beloved Moon Cabriolet, and humiliating himself in front of Louis B. Mayer. "Get that mouse off the screen!" was the movie mogul's reported response to the cartoon character. Then, in 1955, Disney had the brainstorm of sending his movie characters out into the "real" world to mix with their fans and he battled skeptics to build the very first Disneyland in Anaheim, California.

When Disney died in 1966, the company went into virtual suspended animation. Their last big hit of that era was 1969's *The Love Bug*, about a Volkswagen named Herbie. Today, Disney executives trace the problem to a tyrannical CEO named E. Cardon Walker who ruled the company from 1976 to 1983, and to his successor, Ronald W. Miller. Walker was quick to ridicule underlings in public and impervious to any point of view but his own. He made decisions according to what he thought Walt would have done. Executives clinched arguments by quoting Walt like the Scriptures or Marx, and the company eventually supplied a little book of the founder's sayings. Making the wholesome family movies Walt would have wanted formed a key article of Walker's creed. For example, a poster advertising the unremarkable *Condorman* featured actress Barbara Carrera in a slit skirt. Walker had the slit painted over. With this as the context, studio producers ground out a thin stream of tired, formulaic movies that fewer and fewer customers would pay to see. In mid-1983, a similar low-horsepower approach to television production led to CBS's cancellation of the hour-long program *Walt Disney*, leaving the company without a regular network show for the first time in 29 years. Like a reclusive hermit, the company lost touch with the contemporary world.

Ron Miller's brief reign was by contrast a model of decentralization and delegation. Many attributed Miller's ascent to his marrying the boss's daughter rather than to any special gift. To shore Miller up, the board installed Raymond L. Watson, former head of the Irvine Co., as part-time chairperson. He quickly became full time.

Miller sensed the studio needed rejuvenation and he managed to produce the hit film, *Splash,* featuring an apparently (but not actually) bare-breasted mermaid, under the newly devised Touchstone label. However, the reluctance of freelance Hollywood talent to accommodate Disney's narrow range and stingy compensation often kept his sound instincts from bearing fruit. "Card [Cardon Walker] would listen but not hear," said a former executive. "Ron [Ron Miller] would listen but not act."

Too many box office bombs contributed to a steady erosion of profit. Profits of $135 million on revenues of $915 million in 1980 dwindled to $93 million on revenues of $1.3 billion in 1983. More alarmingly, revenues from the company's theme parks, about three-quarters of the company's total revenues, were showing signs of leveling off. Disney's stock slid from $84.375 a share to $48.75 between April 1983 and February 1984.

Through these years, Roy Disney, Jr. simmered while he watched the downfall of the national institution that his uncle, Walt, and his father, Roy Disney, Sr., had built. He had long argued that the company's constituent parts all work together to enhance each other. If movie and television production weren't revitalized, not only would that source of revenue disappear but the company and its activities would also grow dim in the public eye. At the same time the stream of new ideas and characters that kept people pouring into the parks and buying toys, books, and records would dry up. Now his dire predictions were coming true. His own personal shareholding had already dropped from $96 million to $54 million. Walker's treatment of Ron Miller as the shining heir apparent and Roy Disney as the idiot nephew helped drive Roy to quit as Disney vice president in 1977, and to set up Shamrock Holdings, a broadcasting and investment company.

In 1984, Roy teamed up with Stanley Gold, a tough-talking lawyer and a brilliant strategist. Gold saw that the falling stock price was bound to flush out a raider and afford Roy Disney a chance to restore the company's fortunes. They asked Frank Wells, vice chairperson of Warner Bros., if he would take a top job in the company in the event they offered it. Wells, a lawyer and a Rhodes scholar, said yes. With that, Roy knew that what he would hear in Disney's boardroom would limit his freedom to trade in its stock, so he quit the board on March 9, 1984. "I knew that would hang a 'For Sale' sign over the company," said Gold.

By resigning, Roy pushed over the first of a train of dominoes that ultimately led to the result he most desired. The company was raided, almost dismantled, greenmailed,

raided again, and sued left and right. But it miraculously emerged with a skilled new top management with big plans for a bright future. Roy Disney proposed Michael Eisner as the CEO but the board came close to rejecting Eisner in favor of an older, more buttoned-down candidate. Gold stepped in and made an impassioned speech to the directors. "You see guys like Eisner as a little crazy . . but every studio in this country has been run by crazies. What do you think Walt Disney was? The guy was off the goddamned wall. This is a creative institution. It needs to be run by crazies again."*

Meanwhile Eisner and Wells staged an all-out lobbying campaign, calling on every board member except two, who were abroad, to explain their views about the company's future. "What was most important," said Eisner, "was that they saw I did not come in a tutu, and that I was a serious person, and I understood a P&L, and 1 knew the investment analysts, and I read *Fortune.*"

In September 1984, Michael Eisner was appointed CEO and Frank Wells became president. Jeffrey Katzenverg, the 33-year-old, maniacal production chief followed Fisher from Paramount Pictures. He took over Disney's movie and television studios. "The key," said Eisner "is to start off with a great idea."

Disneyland in Anaheim, California

For a long time, Walt Disney had been concerned about the lack of family-type entertainment available for his two daughters. The amusement parks he saw around him were mostly filthy traveling carnivals. They were often unsafe and allowed unruly conduct on the premises. Disney envisioned a place where people from all over the world would be able to go for clean and safe fun. His dream came true on July 17, 1955, when the gates first opened at Disneyland in Anaheim, California.

Disneyland strives to generate the perfect fantasy. But magic does not simply happen. The place is a marvel of modern technology. Literally dozens of computers, huge banks of tape machines, film projectors, and electronic controls lie behind the walls, beneath the floors, and above the ceilings of dozens of rides and attractions. The philosophy is that "Disneyland is the world's biggest stage, and the audience is right here on the stage," said Dick

Exhibit 1   How the Theme Parks Grew

1955	Disneyland
1966	Walt Disney's death
1971	Walt Disney World in Orlando
1982	Epcot Center
1983	Tokyo Disneyland
1992	Euro Disneyland

---

* Stephen Koepp, "Do You Believe in Magic?" Time (April 25, 1988): pp. 66–73.

Hollinger, chief industrial engineer at Disneyland. "It takes a tremendous amount of work to keep the stage clean and working properly."

Cleanliness is a primary concern. Before the park opens at 8 A.M., the cleaning crew will have mopped and hosed and dried every sidewalk, every street, and every floor and counter. More than 350 of the park's 7,400 employees come on duty at 1 A.M. to begin the daily cleanup routine. The thousands of feet that walk through the park each day and chewing gum do not mix, and gum has always presented major clean up problems. The park's janitors found long ago that fire hoses with 90 pounds of water pressure would not do the job. Now they use steam machines, razor scrapers, and mops towed by Cushman scooters to literally scour the streets and sidewalks daily.

It takes one person working a full eight-hour shift to polish the brass on the Fantasyland merry-go-round. The scrupulously manicured plantings throughout the park are treated with growth retarding hormones to keep the trees and bushes from spreading beyond their assigned spaces and destroying the carefully maintained five-eighths scale modeling that is utilized in the park. The maintenance supervisor of the Matterhorn bobsled ride personally walks every foot of track and inspects every link of tow chain every night, thus trusting his or her own eyes more than the $2 million in safety equipment that is built into the ride.

Eisner himself pays obsessive attention to detail. Walking through Disneyland one Sunday afternoon, he peered at the plastic leaves on the Swiss Family Robinson tree house noting that they periodically wear out and need to be replaced leaf by leaf at a cost of $500,000. As his family strolled through the park, he and his eldest son Breck stooped to pick up the rare piece of litter that the cleanup crew had somehow missed. This old-fashioned dedication has paid off. Since opening day in 1955. Disneyland has been a consistent money-maker.

Disney World in Orlando, Florida

By the time Eisner arrived, Disney World in Orlando was already on its way to becoming what it is today—the most popular vacation destination in the United States. But the company had neglected a rich niche in its business: hotels. Disney's three existing hotels, probably the most profitable in the United States, registered unheard-of occupancy rates of 92 percent to 96 percent versus 66 percent for the industry. Eisner promptly embarked on an ambitious $1 billion hotel expansion plan. Two major hotels, Disney's Grand Floridian Beach Resort and Disney's Caribbean Beach Resort, were opened during 1987–89. Disney's Yacht Club and Beach Resort along with the Dolphin and Swan Hotels, owned and operated by Tishman Realty & Construction, Metropolitan Life Insurance, and Aoki Corporation opened during 1989–90. Adding 3,400 hotel rooms and 250,000 square feet of convention space, this made it the largest convention center east of the Mississippi.

In October 1982, Disney made a new addition to the theme park—the Experimental Prototype Community of Tomorrow or EPCOT Center. E. Cardon Walker, then president of the company, announced that EPCOT would be a "permanent showcase, industrial park, and experimental housing center." This new park consists of two large complexes: Future World, a series of pavilions designed to show the technological advances of the next 25 years, and World Showcase, a collection of foreign "villages."

Tokyo Disneyland

It was Tokyo's nastiest winter day in four years. Arctic winds and eight inches of snow lashed the city. Roads were clogged and trains slowed down. But the bad weather didn't keep 13,200 hardy souls from Tokyo Disneyland. Mikki Mausu, better known outside Japan as Mickey Mouse, had taken the country by storm.

Located on a fringe of reclaimed shoreline in Urayasu City on the outskirts of Tokyo, the park opened to the public on April 15, 1983. In less than one year, over 10 million people had passed through its gates, an attendance figure that has been bettered every single year. On August 13, 1983, 93,000 people helped set a one-day attendance record that easily eclipsed the old records established at the two parent U.S. parks. Four years later, records again toppled as the turnstiles clicked. The total this time: 111,500. By 1988, approximately 50 million people, or nearly half of Japan's population, had visited Tokyo Disneyland since its opening. The steady cash flow pushed revenues for fiscal year 1989 to $768 million, up 17 percent from 1988.

The 204-acre Tokyo Disneyland is owned and operated by Oriental Land under license from the Walt Disney Co. The 45-year contract gives Disney 10 percent of admissions and 5 percent of food and merchandise sales, plus licensing fees. Disney opted to take no equity in the project and put no money down for construction.

Exhibit 2 Investor's Snapshot: The Walt Disney Company (December 1989)

Sales	
(latest four quarters)	$4.6 billion
Change from year earlier	Up 33.6%
Net profit	$703.3 million
Change	Up 34.7%
Return on common stockholders' equity	23.4%
Five year average	20.3%
Stock price average	
(last 12 months)	$60.50–$136.25
Recent share price	$122.75
Price/Earnings Multiple	27
Total return to investors	
(12 months to 11/3/89)	90.6%

Source: Fortune, December 4, 1989

"I never had the slightest doubt about the success of Disneyland in Japan," said Masatomo Takahashi, president of Oriental Land Company. Oriental Land was so confident of the success of Disney in Japan that it financed the park entirely with debt, borrowing ¥180 billion ($1.5 billion at February 1988 exchange rates). Takahashi added, "The debt means nothing to me," and with good reason. According to Fusahao Awata, who co-authored a book on Tokyo Disneyland: "The Japanese yearn for [American culture]."

Soon after Tokyo Disneyland opened in April 1983, five Shinto priests held a solemn dedication ceremony near Cinderella's castle. It is the only overtly Japanese ritual seen so far in this sprawling theme park. What visitors see is pure Americana. All signs are in English, with only small *katakana* (a phonetic Japanese alphabet) translations. Most of the food is American-style, and the attractions are cloned from Disney's U.S. parks. Disney also held firm on two fundamentals that strike the Japanese as strange—no alcohol is allowed and no food may be brought in from outside the park.

However, in Disney's enthusiasm to make Tokyo a brick-by-brick copy of Anaheim's Magic Kingdom, there were a few glitches. On opening day, the Tokyo park discovered that almost 100 public telephones were placed too high for Japanese guests to reach them comfortably. And many hungry customers found countertops above their reach at the park's snack stands.

"Everything we imported that worked in the United States works here," said Ronald D. Pogue, managing director of Walt Disney Attractions Japan Ltd. "American things like McDonald's hamburgers and Kentucky Fried Chicken are popular here with young people. We also wanted visitors from Japan and Southeast Asia to feel they were getting the real thing," said Toshiharu Akiba, a staff member of the Oriental Land publicity department.

Still, local sensibilities dictated a few changes. A Japanese restaurant was added to please older patrons. The Nautilus submarine is missing. More areas are covered to protect against rain and snow. Lines for attractions had to be redesigned so that people walking through the park did not cross in front of patrons waiting to ride an attraction. "It's very discourteous in Japan to have people cross in front of somebody else," explained James B. Cora, managing director of operations for the Tokyo project. The biggest differences between Japan and America have come in slogans and ad copy. Although English is often used, it's "Japanized" English–the sort that would have native speakers shaking their heads while the Japanese nod happily in recognition. "Let's Spring" was the motto for one of their highly successful ad campaigns.

Pogue, visiting frequently from his base in California, supervised seven resident American Disney managers who work side by side with Japanese counterparts from Oriental Land Co. to keep the park in tune with the Disney

doctrine. American it may be, but Tokyo Disneyland appeals to such deep-seated Japanese passions as cleanliness, order, outstanding service, and technological wizardry. Japanese executives are impressed by Disney's detailed training manuals, which teach employees how to make visitors feel like VIPs. Most worth emulating, say the Japanese, is Disney's ability to make even the lowliest job seem glamorous. "They have changed the image of dirty work," said Hakuhodo Institute's Sekizawa.

Disney Company did encounter a few unique cultural problems when developing Tokyo Disneyland:

The problem: how to dispose of some 250 tons of trash that would be generated weekly by Tokyo Disneyland visitors?

The standard Disney solution: trash compactors.

The Japanese proposal: pigs to eat the trash and be slaughtered and sold at a profit.

James B. Cora and his team of some 150 operations experts did a little calculating and pointed out that it would take 100,000 pigs to do the job. And then there would be the smell . . .

The Japanese relented.

The Japanese were also uneasy about a rustic-looking Westernland, Tokyo's version of Frontierland. "The Japanese like everything fresh and new when they put it in." said Cora. "They kept painting the wood and we kept saying, 'No it's got to look old.'" Finally the Disney crew took the Japanese to Anaheim to give them a firsthand look at the Old West.

Tokyo Disneyland opened just as the yen escalated in value against the dollar and the income level of the Japanese registered a phenomenal improvement. During this era of affluence, Tokyo Disneyland triggered an interest in leisure. Its great success spurred the construction of "leisurelands" throughout the country. This created an increase in the Japanese people's orientation towards leisure. But demographics are the real key to Tokyo Disneyland's success. Thirty million Japanese live within 30 miles of the park. There are three times more than the number of people in the same proximity to Anaheim's Disneyland. With the park proven such an unqualified hit, and nearing capacity, Oriental Land and Disney mapped out plans for a version of the Disney-MGM studio tour next door. This time, Disney talked about taking a 50 percent stake in the project.

Building Euro Disneyland

On March 24, 1987, Michael Eisner and Jacques Chirac, the French Prime Minister, signed a contract for the building of a Disney theme park at Marne-la-Vallee. Talks between Disney and the French government had dragged on for more than a year. At the signing, Robert Fitzpatrick, fluent in French, married to the former Sylvie Blondet and the recipient of two awards from the French government, was introduced as the president of Euro Disneyland. He was expected to be a key player in wooing support from the French establishment for the theme park. As one analyst put it, Disney selected him to set up the park because he is "more French than the French."

Disney had been courted extensively by Spain and France. The Prime Ministers of both countries ordered their governments to lend Disney a hand in its quest for a site. France set up a five-person team headed by a Special Advisor to Foreign Trade & Tourism Minister, Edith Cresson, and Spain's negotiators included Ignacio Vasallo, Director-General for the Promotion of Tourism. Disney pummeled both governments with requests for detailed information. "The only thing they haven't asked us for is the color of the tourists' eyes," moaned Vasallo.

The governments tried other enticements, too. Spain offered tax and labor incentives and possibly as much as 20,000 acres of land. The French package, although less generous, included spending of $53 million to improve highway access to the proposed site and perhaps speeding up a $75 million subway project. For a long time, all that smiling Disney officials would say was that Spain had better weather while France had a better population base.

Officials explained that they picked France over Spain because Marne-la-Vallee is advantageously close to one of the world's tourism capitals, while also being situated within a day's drive or train ride of some 30 million people in France, Belgium, England, and Germany. Another advantage mentioned was the availability of good transportation. A train line that serves as part of the Paris Metro subway system ran to Torcy, in the center of Marne-la-Vallee, and the French government promised to extend the line to the actual site of the park. The park would also be served by A-4, a modern highway that runs from Paris to the German border, as well as a freeway that runs to Charles de Gaulle airport.

Once a letter of intent had been signed, sensing that the French government was keen to not let the plan fail, Disney held out for one concession after another. For example, Disney negotiated for VAT (value added tax) on ticket sales to be cut from a normal 18.6 percent to 7 percent. A quarter of the investment in building the park would come from subsidized loans. Additionally, any disputes arising from the contract would be settled not in French courts but by a special international panel of arbitrators. But Disney did have to agree to a clause in the contract which would require it to respect and utilize French culture in its themes.

The park was built on 4,460 acres of farmland in Marne-la-Vallee, a rural corner of France 20 miles east of Paris known mostly for sugar beets and Brie cheese. Opening was planned for early 1992 and planners hoped to attract some 10 million visitors a year. Approximately $2.5

billion was needed to build the park making it the largest single foreign investment ever in France. A French "pivot" company was formed to build the park with starting capital of FFr 3 billion, split 60 percent French and 40 percent foreign, with Disney taking 16.67 percent. Euro Disneyland was expected to bring $600 million in foreign investment into France each year.

As soon as the contract had been signed, individuals and businesses began scurrying to somehow plug into the Mickey Mouse money machine—all were hoping to benefit from the American dream without leaving France. In fact, one Paris daily, *Liberation,* actually sprouted mouse ears over its front-page flag.

The $1.5 to $2 billion first phase investment would involve an amusement complex including hotels and restaurants, golf courses, and an aquatic park in addition to a European version of the Magic Kingdom. The second phase, scheduled to start after the gates opened in 1992, called for the construction of a community around the park, including a sports complex, technology park, conference center, theater, shopping mall, university campus, villas, and condominiums. No price tag had been put on the second phase, although it was expected to rival, if not surpass, the first phase investment. In November 1989, Fitzpatrick announced that the Disney-MGM Studios, Europe would also open at Euro Disneyland in 1996, resembling the enormously successful Disney-MGM Studios theme park at Disney World in Orlando. The new studios would greatly enhance the Walt Disney Company's strategy of increasing its production of live action and animated filmed entertainment in Europe for both the European and world markets.

"The phone's been ringing here ever since the announcement," said Marc Berthod of EpaMarne, the government body that oversees the Marne-la-Vallee region. "We've gotten calls from big companies as well as small—everything from hotel chains to language interpreters all asking for details on Euro Disneyland. And the individual mayors of the villages around here have been swamped with calls from people looking for jobs." he added.

Euro Disneyland was expected to generate up to 28 000 jobs, providing a measure of relief for an area that had suffered a 10 percent plus unemployment rate for the previous year. It was also expected to light a fire under France's construction industry which had been particularly hard hit by France's economic problems over the previous year. Moreover, Euro Disneyland was expected to attract many other investors to the depressed outskirts of Paris. International Business Machines (IBM) and *Banque National de Paris* were among those already building in the area. In addition one of the new buildings going up was a factory that would employ 400 outside workers to wash the 50 tons of laundry expected to be generated per day by Euro Disneyland's 14,000 employees.

Exhibit 3 Chronology of the Euro Disneyland Deal

1984–85   Disney negotiates with Spain and France to create a European theme park
           Chooses France as the site
1987   Disney signs letter of intent with the French government
1988   Selects lead commercial bank lenders for the senior portion of the project
           Forms the *Societe en Nom Collectif* {SNC}
           Begins planning for the equity offering of 51% of Euro
           Disneyland as required in the letter of intent
1989   European press and stock analysts visit Walt Disney World in Orlando
           Begin extensive news and television campaign
           Stock starts trading at 20–25 percent premium from the issue price

Source: From Geraldine E. Willigan, "The value-adding CFO: an interview with Disney's Gary Wilson," *Harvard Business Review,* January–February 1990, pp. 85–93.

The impact of Euro Disneyland was also felt in the real estate market. "Everyone who owns land around here is holding on to it for the time being, at least until they know what's going to happen," said Danny Theveno, a spokesman for the town of Villiers on the western edge of Marne-la-Vallee. Disney expected 11 million visitors in the first year. The break-even point was estimated to be between seven and eight million. One worry was that Euro Disneyland would cannibalize the flow of European visitors to Walt Disney World in Florida, but European travel agents said that their customers were still eagerly signing up for Florida lured by the cheap dollar and the promise of sunshine.

Protests of Cultural Imperialism

Disney faced French communists and intellectuals who protested the building of Euro Disneyland. Ariane Mnouchkine, a theater director, described it as a "cultural Chernobyl." "I wish with all my heart that the rebels would set fire to Disneyland," thundered a French intellectual in the newspaper *La Figaro*. "Mickey Mouse," sniffed another, "is stifling individualism and transforming children into consumers." The theme park was damned as an example of American "neoprovincialism."

Farmers in the Marne-la-Vallee region posted protest signs along the roadside featuring a mean looking Mickey Mouse and touting sentiments such as "Disney go home," "Stop the massacre," and "Don't gnaw away our national wealth." Farmers were upset partly because under the terms of the contract, the French government would expropriate the necessary land and sell it without profit to Euro Disneyland development company.

While local officials were sympathetic to the farmers' position, they were unwilling to let their predicament interfere with what some called "the deal of the century." "For many years these farmers have had the fortune to cultivate what is considered some of the richest land in France," said Berthod. "Now they'll have to find another occupation."

Also less than enchanted about the prospect of a magic kingdom rising among their midst was the communist dominated labor federation, the *Confédération Générale du Travail* (CGT). Despite the job-creating potential of Euro Disney, the CGT doubted its members would benefit. The union had been fighting hard to stop the passage of a bill which would give managers the right to establish flexible hours for their workers. Flexible hours were believed to be a prerequisite to the profitable operation of Euro Disneyland, especially considering seasonal variations.

However, Disney proved to be relatively immune to the anti-U.S. virus. In early 1985, one of the three state-owned television networks signed a contract to broadcast two hours of dubbed Disney programming every Saturday evening. Soon after, *Disney Channel* became one of the top-rated programs in France.

In 1987, the company launched an aggressive community relations program to calm the fears of politicians, farmers, villagers, and even bankers that the project would bring traffic congestion, noise, pollution, and other problems to their countryside. Such a public relations program was a rarity in France, where businesses make little effort to establish good relations with local residents. Disney invited 400 local children to a birthday party for Mickey Mouse, sent Mickey to area hospitals, and hosted free trips to Disney World in Florida for dozens of local officials and children.

"They're experts at seduction, and they don't hide the fact that they're trying to seduce you," said Vincent Guardiola, an official with *Banque Indosuez,* one of the 17 banks wined and dined at Orlando and subsequently one of the venture's financial participants. "The French aren't used to this kind of public relations—it was unbelievable." Observers said that the goodwill efforts helped dissipate initial objections to the project.

Financial Structuring at Euro Disneyland

Eisner was so keen on Euro Disneyland that Disney kept a 49 percent stake in the project, while the remaining 51 percent of stock was distributed through the London, Paris, and Brussels stock exchanges. Half the stock under the offer was going to the French, 25 percent to the English, and the remainder distributed in the rest of the European community. The initial offer price of FFr 72 was considerably higher than the pathfinder prospectus estimate because the capacity of the park had been slightly extended. Scarcity of stock was likely to push up the price, which was expected to reach FFr 166 by opening day in 1992. This would give a compound return of 21 percent.

Walt Disney maintained management control of the company. The U.S. company put up $160 million of its own capital to fund the project, an investment which soared in value to $2.4 billion after the popular stock offering in Europe. French national and local authorities, by comparison, were providing about $800 million in low-interest loans and poured at least that much again into infrastructure.

Other sources of funding were the park's 12 corporate sponsors, and Disney would pay them back in kind. The "autopolis" ride, where kids ride cars, features coupes emblazoned with the "Hot Wheels" logo. Mattel Inc., sponsor of the ride is grateful for the boost to one of its biggest toy lines.

The real payoff would begin once the park opened. The Walt Disney Company would receive 10 percent of admission fees and 5 percent of food and merchandise revenue, the same arrangement as in Japan. But in France, it would also receive management fees, incentive fees, and 49 percent of the profits.

A Saloman Brothers analyst estimated that the park would pull in three to four million more visitors than the 11 million the company expected in the first year. Other Wall Street analysts cautioned that stock prices of both Walt Disney Company and Euro Disney already contained all the Euro optimism they could absorb. "Europeans visit Disneyworld in Florida as part of an 'American experience,'" said Patrick P. Roper, marketing director of Alton Towers, a successful British theme park near Manchester. He doubted they would seek the suburbs of Paris as eagerly as America and predicted attendance would trail Disney projections.

The Layout of Euro Disneyland

Euro Disneyland is determinedly American in its theme. There was an alcohol ban in the park despite the attitude among the French that wine with a meal is a God-given right. Designers presented a plan for a Main Street USA based on scenes of America in the 1920s, because research indicated that Europeans loved the Prohibition era. Eisner decreed that images of gangsters and speak-easies were too negative. Though made more ornate and Victorian than Walt Disney's idealized Midwestern small town, Main Street remained Main Street. Steamships leave from Main Street through the Grand Canyon Diorama en route to Frontierland.

The familiar Disney Tomorrowland, with its dated images of the space age, was jettisoned entirely. It was replaced by a gleaming brass and wood complex called Discoverland, which was based on themes of Jules Verne and Leonardo da Vinci. Eisner ordered $8 or $10 million in extras to the "Visionarium" exhibit, a 360-degree movie

about French culture which was required by the French in their original contract. French and English are the official languages at the park, and multilingual guides are available to help Dutch, German, Spanish, and Italian visitors.

With the American Wild West being so frequently captured on film, Europeans have their own idea of what life was like back then. Frontier land reinforces those images. A runway mine train takes guests through the canyons and mines of Gold Rush country. There is a paddle wheel steamboat reminiscent of Mark Twain, Indian explorer canoes, and a phantom manor from the Gold Rush days.

In Fantasyland, designers strived to avoid competing with the nearby European reality of actual medieval towns, cathedrals, and chateaux. While Disneyland's castle is based on Germany's Neuschwanstein and Disney World's is based on a Loire Valley chateau, Euro Disney's *Le Château de la Belle au Bois Dormant,* as the French insisted Sleeping Beauty be called, is more cartoon-like with stained glass windows built by English craftsmakers and depicting Disney characters. Fanciful trees grow inside as well as a beanstalk.

The park is criss-crossed with covered walkways. Eisner personally ordered the installation of 35 fireplaces in hotels and restaurants. "People walk around Disney World in Florida with humidity and temperatures in the 90s and they walk into an air-conditioned ride and say, 'This is the greatest,'" said Eisner. "When its raining and miserable, I hope they will walk into one of these lobbies with the fireplace going and say the same thing."

Children all over Europe were primed to consume. Even one of the intellectuals who contributed to Le Figaro's Disney-bashing broadsheet was forced to admit with resignation that his ten-year-old son "swears by Michael Jackson." At Euro Disneyland, under the name "Captain EO," Disney just so happened to have a Michael Jackson attraction awaiting him.

Food Service and Accommodations at Euro Disneyland

Disney expected to serve 15,000 to 17,000 meals per hour, excluding snacks. Menus and service systems were developed so that they varied both in style and price. There is a 400-seat buffeteria, 6 table service restaurants, 12 counter service units, 10 snack bars, one Discovery food court

Exhibit 4   The Euro Disneyland Resort

5,000 acres in size
30 attractions
12,000 employees
6 hotels (with 5,184 rooms)
10 theme restaurants
414 cabins
181 camping sites

Source: Roger Cohen, "Threat of strikes in Euro Disney debut," *The New York Times,* April 10, 1992, p. 20.

seating 850, 9 popcorn wagons, 15 ice-cream carts, 14 specialty food carts, and 2 employee cafeterias. Restaurants were, in fact, to be a showcase for American foods. The only exception to this is Fantasyland which re-creates European fables. Here, food service will reflect the fable's country of origin: Pinocchio's facility having German food; Cinderella's, French; Bella Notte's, Italian; and so on.

Of course recipes were adapted for European tastes. Since many Europeans don't care much for very spicy food, Tex-Mex recipes were toned down. A special coffee blend had to be developed which would have universal appeal. Hot dog carts would reflect the regionalism of American tastes. There would be a ball park hot dog (mild, steamed, a mixture of beef and pork), a New York hot dog (all beef, and spicy), and a Chicago hot dog (Vienna-style, similar to bratwurst).

Euro Disneyland has six theme hotels which would offer nearly 5,200 rooms on opening day, a campground (444 rental trailers and 181 camping sites), and single family homes on the periphery of the 27 hole golf course.

Disney's Strict Appearance Code

Antoine Guervil stood at his post in front of the l,000 room Cheyenne Hotel at Euro Disneyland, practicing his "Howdy!" When Guervil, a political refugee from Haiti, said the word, it sounded more like "Audi." Native French speakers have trouble with the aspirated "h" sound in words like "hay" and "Hank" and "Howdy." Guervil had been given the job of wearing a cowboy costume and booming a happy, welcoming Howdy to guests as they entered the Cheyenne, styled after a Western movie set.

"Audi," said Guervil, the strain of linguistic effort showing on his face. This was clearly a struggle. Unless things got better, it was not hard to imagine objections from Renault, the French car company that was one of the corporate sponsors of the park. Picture the rage of a French auto executive arriving with his or her family at the Renault-sponsored Euro Disneyland, only to hear the doorman of a Disney hotel advertising a German car.

Such were the problems Disney faced while hiring some 12,000 people to maintain and populate its Euro Disneyland theme park. A handbook of detailed rules on acceptable clothing, hairstyles, and jewelry, among other things, embroiled the company in a legal and cultural dispute. Critics asked how the brash Americans could be so insensitive to French culture, individualism, and privacy. Disney officials insisted that a ruling that barred them from imposing a squeaky-clean employment standard could threaten the image and long-term success of the park.

"For us, the appearance code has a "real effect from a product identification standpoint," said Thor Degelmann, vice president for human resources for Euro Disneyland. "Without it we wouldn't be presenting the Disney product that people would be expecting."

The rules, spelled out in a video presentation and detailed in a guide handbook, went beyond height and weight standards. They required men's hair to be cut above the collar and ears with no beards or mustaches. Any tattoos must be covered. Women must keep their hair in one "natural color" with no frosting or streaking and they may make only limited use of make-up like mascara. False eyelashes, eyeliners, and eye pencil were completely off limits. Fingernails can't pass the end of the fingers. As for jewelry, women can wear only one earring in each ear, with the earring's diameter no more than three-quarters of an inch. Neither men nor women can wear more than one ring on each hand. Further, women were required to wear appropriate undergarments and only transparent pantyhose, not black or anything with fancy designs. Though a daily bath was not specified in the rules, the applicant's video depicted a shower scene and informed applicants that they were expected to show up for work "fresh and clean each day." Similar rules are in force at Disney's three other theme parks in the United States and Japan.

In the United States, some labor unions representing Disney employees have occasionally protested the company's strict appearance code, but with little success. French labor unions began protesting when Disneyland opened its "casting center" and invited applicants to "play the role of [their lives]" and to take a "unique opportunity to marry work and magic." The CGT handed out leaflets in front of the center to warn applicants of the appearance code which they believed represented "an attack on individual liberty." A more mainstream union, the *Confédération Française Démocratique du Travail* (CFDT) appealed to the Labor Ministry to halt Disney's violation of "human dignity."

Exhibit 5 **What Price Mickey?**

	Euro Disneyland	Disney World, Orlando
	Peak season hotel rates	
4-person room	$97 to $345	$104-$455
	Campground space	
	$48	$30-$49
	One-day pass	
Children	$26	$26
Adults	$40	$33

Source: Business Week, March 30, 1992.

French law prohibits employers from restricting individual and collective liberties unless the restrictions can be justified by the nature of the task to be accomplished and are proportional to that end.

Degelmann, however, said that the company was "well aware of the cultural differences" between the United States and France and as a result had "toned down" the wording in the original American version of the guidebook. He pointed out that many companies, particularly airlines, maintained appearance codes just as strict. "We happened to put ours in writing," he added. In any case, he said that he knew of no one who had refused to take the job because of the rules and that no more than 5 percent of the people showing up for interviews had decided not to proceed after watching the video which also detailed transportation and salary.

Fitzpatrick also defended the dress code, although he conceded that Disney might have been a little naive in presenting things so directly. He added, "Only in France is there still a communist party. There is not even one in Russia any more. The ironic thing is that I could fill the park with CGT requests for tickets."

Another big challenge lay in getting the mostly French "cast members," as Disney calls its employees, to break their ancient cultural aversions to smiling and being consistently polite to park guests. The individualistic French had to be molded into the squeaky-clean Disney image. Rival theme parks in the area, loosely modeled on the Disney system, had already encountered trouble keeping smiles on the faces of the staff, who sometimes took on the demeanor of subway ticket clerks.

The delicate matter of hiring French citizens as opposed to other nationals was examined in the more than two year long preagreement negotiations between the French government and Disney. The final agreement called for Disney to make a maximum effort to tap into the local labor market. At the same time, it was understood that for Euro Disneyland to work, its staff must mirror the multicountry make-up of its guests. "Casting centers" were set up in Paris, London, Amsterdam, and Frankfurt. "We are concentrating on the local labor market, but we are also looking for workers who are German, English, Italian, Spanish, or other nationalities and who have good communication skills, are outgoing, speak two European languages—French plus one other—and like being around people," said Degelmann.

Stephane Baudet, a 28-year-old trumpet player from Paris refused to audition for a job in a Disney brass band when he learned he would have to cut his ponytail. "Some people will turn themselves into a pumpkin to work at Euro Disneyland." he said. "But not me."

Opening Day at Euro Disneyland

A few days before the grand opening of Euro Disneyland, hundreds of French visitors were invited to a pre-opening party. They gazed perplexed at what was placed before them. It was a heaping plate of spare ribs. The visitors were at the Buffalo Bill Wild West Show, a cavernous theater featuring a panoply of "Le Far West," including 20 imported buffaloes. And Disney deliberately didn't provide silverware. "There was a moment of consternation," recalls Fitzpatrick. "Then they just kind of said, 'The hell with it,' and dug in." There was one problem. The guests couldn't master the art of gnawing ribs and applauding at the same time. So Disney planned to provide more napkins and teach visitors to stamp with their feet.

On April 12, 1992, the opening day of Euro Disneyland, *France-Soir* enthusiastically predicted Disney dementia. "Mickey! It's madness," read its front-page headline, warning of chaos on the roads and suggesting that people may have to be turned away. A French government survey indicated that half a million might turn up with 90,000 cars trying to get in. French radio warned traffic to avoid the area.

By lunch time on opening day, the Euro Disneyland car park was less than half full, suggesting an attendance of below 25,000, less than half the park's capacity and way below expectations. Many people may have heeded the advice to stay home or, more likely, were deterred by a one-day strike that cut the direct rail link to Euro Disneyland from the center of Paris. Queues for the main rides, such as Pirates of the Caribbean and Big Thunder Mountain railroad, were averaging around 15 minutes less than on an ordinary day at Disney World, Florida.

Disney executives put on a brave face, claiming that attendance was better than at first days for other Disney theme parks in Florida, California, and Japan. However, there was no disguising the fact that after spending thousands of dollars on the pre-opening celebrations, Euro Disney would have appreciated some impressively long traffic jams on the auto route.

Other Operating Problems

When the French government changed hands in 1986, work ground to a halt, as the negotiator appointed by the Conservative government threw out much of the ground work prepared by his Socialist predecessor. The legalistic approach taken by the Americans also bogged down talks, as it meant planning ahead for every conceivable contingency. At the same time, right-wing groups who saw the park as an invasion of "chewing-gum jobs" and U.S. pop-culture also fought hard for a greater "local cultural context."

On opening day, English visitors found the French reluctant to play the game of queuing. "The French seem to think that if God had meant them to queue, He wouldn't have given them elbows," they commented. Different cultures have different definitions of personal space, and Disney guests faced problems of people getting too close or pressing around those who left too much space between themselves and the person in front.

Disney placed its first ads for work bids in English, leaving smaller and medium-sized French firms feeling like foreigners in their own land. Eventually, Disney set up a data bank with information on over 20,000 French and European firms looking for work and the local Chamber of Commerce developed a video text information bank with Disney that small- and medium-sized companies through France and Europe would be able to tap into. "The work will come, but many local companies have got to learn that they don't simply have the right to a chunk of work without competing," said a Chamber official.

Efforts were made to ensure that sooner, rather than later, European nationals take over the day-to-day running of the park. Although there were only 23 U.S. expatriates amongst the employees, they controlled the show and held most of the top jobs. Each senior manager had the task of choosing his or her European successor.

Disney was also forced to bail out 40 subcontractors, who were working for the Gabot-Eremco construction contracting group which had been unable to honor all of its commitments. Some of the subcontractors said they faced bankruptcy if they were not paid for their work on Euro Disneyland. A Disney spokesperson said that the payments would be less than $20.3 million and the company had already paid Gabot-Eremco for work on the park. Gabot-Eremco and 15 other main contractors demanded $157 million in additional fees from Disney for work that they said was added to the project after the initial contracts were signed. Disney rejected the claim and sought government intervention. Disney said that under no circumstances would they pay Gabot-Eremco and accused its officers of incompetence.

As Bourguignon thought about these and other problems, the previous year's losses and the prospect of losses again in the current year, with their negative impact on the company's stock price, weighed heavily on his mind.

1. Using Hofstede's four cultural dimensions as a point of reference, what are some of the main cultural differences between the United States and France?

2. In what way has Trompenaars' research helped explain cultural differences between the United States and France?

3. In managing its Euro Disneyland operations, what are three mistakes that the company made? Explain.

4. Based on its experience, what are three lessons the company should have learned about how to deal with diversity? Describe each.

This case was prepared by Research Assistant Sonali Krishna under the direction of Professors J. Stewart Black and Hal B. Gregersen as the basis for class discussion. Reprinted by permission of the authors

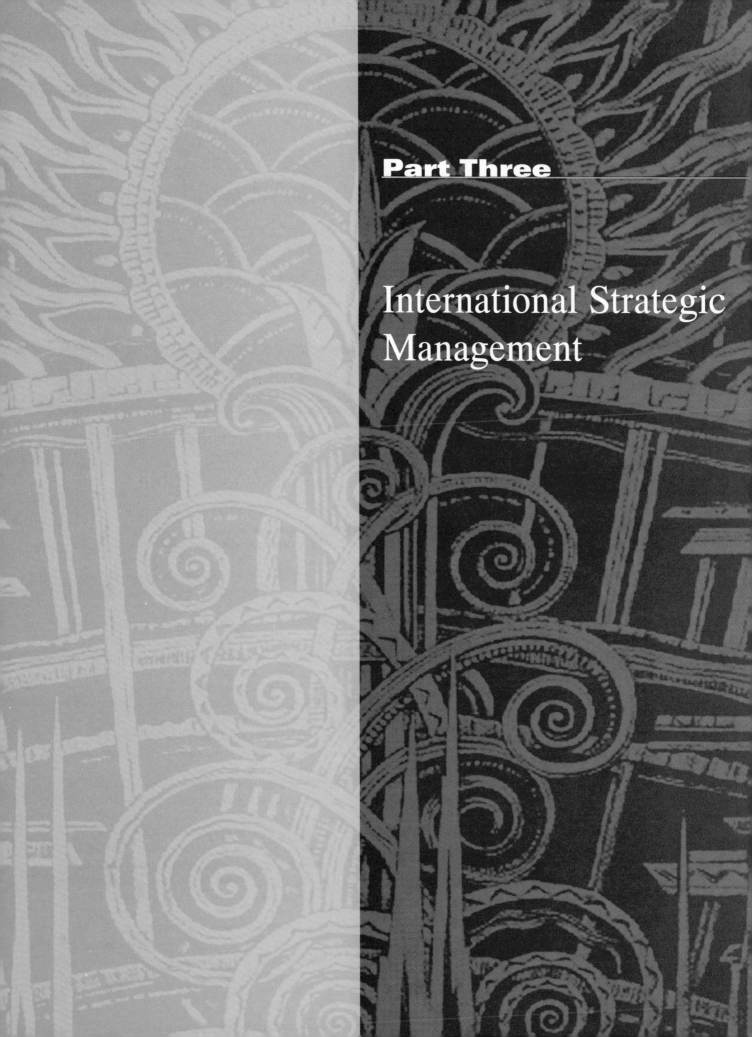

Part Three

International Strategic Management

Chapter 9

Strategic Planning

Objectives of the Chapter

All major MNCs employ strategic planning, a plan which results from a careful analysis of both the external and internal environments. In this process an MNC will identify the market environment for its goods and services and then evaluate its ability and competitive advantage to capture this market. The success of this strategic planning effort will largely depend on accurate forecasting of the external environment and a realistic appraisal of internal company strengths and weaknesses. In recent years, MNCs have relied on their strategic plans to help refocus their efforts by abandoning old domestic markets and entering new global markets. This strategic global planning process has been critical in their drive to gain market share, increase profitability, and in some cases, even survive.

Chapter 6 addressed overall strategic management across cultures. This chapter focuses on strategic planning in the international context, and the basic steps by which a strategic plan is formulated and implemented are examined. The specific objectives of this chapter are:

1. DISCUSS the meaning, needs, benefits, approaches, and predispositions of the strategic planning process for today's MNCs.

2. IDENTIFY the basic steps in strategic planning, including environmental scanning, internal resource analysis of the MNC's strengths and weaknesses, and goal formulation.

3. DESCRIBE how an MNC implements the strategic plan, such as how it chooses a site for overseas operations.

4. EXPLAIN how an MNC implements an ownership and/or entry strategy.

5. REVIEW the three major functions of marketing, production, and finance that are used in implementing a strategic plan.

BusinessWeek

The World of Business Week:

Rising from the Rubble

When Lothar Späth took the top post at the sprawling eastern German Kombinat VEB Carl Zeiss Jena in 1991, his job looked like mission impossible. The company's antiquated factories turned out a bewildering array of products, from leather telescope cases to computer chips. It was overburdened with 27,000 employees—3,000 of them working in the canteens alone. As the company's formerly captive markets in the East bloc dried up, one of Späth's main tasks was "to get rid of people as quietly as possible," he recalls.

Fast-forward to 1998, and the outlook seems rosier. The Jena-based company, now called Jenoptik, is a profitable maker of electronics, telecom gear, and cleanroom equipment. It earned $38.3 million on sales of $1.4 billion last year, and revenues are growing as Späth pushes into international markets. On June 16, he took Jenoptik public, selling $434 million worth of stock on Frankfurt's Neuer Markt—the largest new issue yet by an eastern German company.

Yet the tale of Jenoptik's rise from the rubble of communism isn't an entirely pretty one. Späth, 60, financed his corporate restructuring through $2 billion in government subsidies, including $492 million from the company's home state of Thuringia. He then bought up western German companies whose products could complement Jenoptik's. As a result, today just 20% of the company's 8,400-strong workforce is based in eastern Germany. The remainder are in western Germany or abroad.

Halfway There

Jenoptik's struggles show how tough it is for eastern German companies—and the region's economy—to revamp. Indeed, the east is unlikely to stand on its own feet for another decade. According to the Bundesbank, eastern German unemployment in May stood at 18.7%, vs. 9.4% in the west. Germany's federal government has poured $590 billion into the eastern sector since 1991, and the region will continue to need huge social transfers from the west. "At best, we have only the first half of our journey behind us," says Franz Schuster, Thuringia's minister of economics and infrastructure.

From the start, the deck seemed stacked against Jenoptik. Because Zeiss managers fled to Stuttgart in 1945 when the Russians occupied Thuringia, an eastern and a western company subsequently manufactured competing precision optical equipment under the same name for decades. After the wall fell, the western Carl Zeiss Group received most of the former Kombinat's traditional optics products—and exclusive rights to the Zeiss trademark. That left Späth with factories full of toxic waste, few marketable products, and a skilled workforce with almost nothing to do. On Dec. 31, 1991, he fired 17,500 people.

The government subsidies disappeared fast. Späth spent $560 million to retire the Kombinat's old debts. A further $500 million covered social costs for laid-off workers. In the end, Späth had about $645 million left for rebuilding the company. The sprawling plants in downtown Jena were in such miserable shape that Späth decided to rip most of them down.

In their place he constructed a glass-roofed shopping mall, offices, and the luxury Esplanade Hotel. Between 1992 and 1996, he sank an additional $175 million of precious capital into development projects.

Chance Encounter

Meanwhile, Jenoptik's technicians were scrambling to design high-technology products that could compete in tough global markets. The Kombinat had been a center for microprocessor manufacturing equipment for the entire East bloc. Using that knowhow, Jenoptik designed equipment to etch tiny circuits on computer chips. But selling it proved a huge challenge. When Jenoptik's marketers approached potential customers such as IBM, Fujitsu, and Motorola, they hit a stone wall. Jenoptik was a complete unknown in the West, and no one wanted to buy crucial equipment from a company with no track record. In 1993 and 1994, Späth laid off 1,200 more workers.

With time running out, Späth knew he needed a drastic strategy shift. The turning point came in 1994. During a fruitless sales trip to Asia, he had a chance encounter with celebrating salesmen for Meissner & Wurst, a Stuttgart supplier of equipment used in chip-factory cleanrooms. Späth realized Jenoptik's only chance at survival was to acquire other companies with solid international reputations in fields related to Jenoptik's products.

The resulting company, he figured, could supply complete chipmaking and other systems, rather than their parts. Späth persuaded Jenoptik's skeptical works council, which can veto takeovers, that the strategy meant survival. He also initiated talks with Meissner & Wurst. In October, 1994, Jenoptik reached an agreement to buy 97.8% of the company.

Späth has been on a buying binge ever since. he snapped up two small laser and optics companies in Hamburg and Munich, respectively. He made KRONE, a Berlin maker of telecom equipment, the core of a second division with $360 million in annual sales. He nabbed a maker of precision electronic controls for such products as aircraft to bolster Jenoptik's third division, which produces high-tech electronic gear. And last year, he agreed to acquire ZANDER Klimatechnik, a Nuremberg designer, builder, and manager of clean factories. This final move made Jenoptik a one-stop shop for chip manufacturers and biotechnology companies.

"Crafty Fellow"

Now, with more than a half-dozen western companies under his belt, Späth says the shopping spree is over. His job is to manage the company he has stitched together. Investors believe he'll do well. They bid up Jenoptik's shares from the offering price of $25 a share to $37 in late June. The company's diversified products and global reach put it in a good position to grow, says Christoph Bruns, fund manager at Frankfurt's Union Investments. "The most important thing at a company is the management," he says, "and Späth is a crafty fellow."

Is Jenoptik's restructuring a success? For Thuringia, the answer is a qualified yes. The state has nearly recouped its original investment. It pocketed $190 million in a 1997 private placement and June's stock offering. Its remaining 19% stake, which it plans to sell after two years, is worth $236 million. Moreover, through real estate development and the spin-off of noncore businesses, Jenoptik replaced several thousand of the jobs lost from the old Kombinat.

By David Woodruff in Jena, Germany
www.jenoptik.com

Source: **Reprinted from July 20, 1998, pp. 120 E4, E6 issue of *Business Week* by special permission, copyright © 1998 by the McGraw-Hill Companies, Inc.**

Strategic management is critical to international management. As seen in the opening vignette, in order to revamp Jenoptik and streamline its operations, senior-level management had to have a strategic plan of action that included downsizing, obtaining government subsidies, spinning off marginal businesses, purchasing high-tech firms, and going public in order to raise money. Without such planning, Jenoptik would have ended up like most of the government-owned enterprises in Eastern Europe under communist rule—out of business. The major question for the company now, of course, is whether it can continue on its road to success by learning to stand on its own. This will be greatly determined by how well the firm formulates and implements its strategic plan for the new millennium.

The beginning news article demonstrates the importance of sound strategic planning on multinational companies that are trying to make the transition to a market economy. As the article exemplifies, companies such as Jenoptik in the former East Germany have overcome economic and political obstacles by turning the once struggling electronics and telecom maker into a globally integrated and diversified giant. By employing a strategic plan based on acquisitions and joint ventures, as well as recruiting and training the best people, Jenoptik has solidified its international reputation as a global leader. As the following chapter will emphasize, multinationals intent on growth or even survival must have global strategic plans to help them push into international markets. Jenoptik provides an excellent example of a company that was able to rise from the "rubble" of communism, reform outdated facilities, and relieve an overburdened workforce, by rebuilding the company from the ground up. As you read the chapter, think of yourself as a manager in an MNC. How might you go about developing a strategic plan to capture a new market?

International Strategic Planning

Strategic planning is the process of determining an organization's basic mission and long-term objectives, and then implementing a plan of action for accomplishing this mission and attaining these objectives. As companies go international, this process takes on added dimensions. Toyota is a good example. This firm was recently described in *Fortune* magazine as "the world's most proficient auto company."[1] One of the reasons for this accolade is its high quality manufacturing processes that have helped it gain worldwide market acceptance. In Japan, for example, Toyota is the leading auto firm, holding almost 40 percent of the market; in Southeast Asia the company has garnered over 20 percent of the market, nearly double that of its nearest competitor; and in the United States the Toyota Camry sedan is the best-selling car on the market.

At the heart of the company's production strategy is its Toyota Production System (TPS) that includes a wide variety of tools and techniques ranging from just-in-time inventory to quality circles to employee empowerment. Collectively these types of tools allow Toyota to produce high quality cars and to generate larger profit margins than the competition. At the same time the company has been coordinating its worldwide activities for the purpose of both creating new products as well as introducing them quickly into the marketplace.

In recent years Toyota has also raised its product development another level by producing various models of the same car at the same time. In the auto industry it has always been the rule to develop similar models sequentially. First the sedan is designed, then the coupe. This approach lightens the engineering load and ensures that problems on one model will be resolved before the next one is started. But Toyota has begun developing similar models simultaneously, so that the engineering tasks overlap. This enables the suspension team to work on several different models at the same time, effectively cutting around 15 percent of the typical lead time for new models and 50 percent of the engineering hours. And the company's production strategy innovation has not stopped here.

> Toyota also caught the auto world napping by announcing a breakthrough in engine design. The 120-horsepower engine in the 1998 Corolla uses 25% fewer parts than its predecessor, making it 10% lighter, 10% more fuel-efficient, and significantly cheaper. Toyota isn't releasing all the details, but it eliminated several brackets by molding them into the engine block, and it consolidated several electronic sensors. The changes . . . helped Toyota slash the price of the '98 Corolla by an astounding $1,500 compared to the '97 model.[2]

As a result of its well-formulated worldwide strategic plan, Toyota is now able to produce more cars than ever outside of Japan. And while global sales still run behind those of General Motors and Ford, the firm's income per vehicle is higher than either of these two major international competitors.

The Growing Need for Strategic Planning

One of the primary reasons that MNCs need strategic planning is to keep track of their increasingly diversified operations in a continuously changing international environment. This need is particularly obvious when one considers the amount of foreign direct investment (FDI) that has occurred in recent years. Recent statistics reveal that FDI has grown three times faster than trade and four times faster than world gross domestic product (GDP).[3] These developments are resulting in a need to coordinate and integrate diverse operations with a unified and agreed-on focus. There are many examples of firms that are doing just this.

One is Ford Motor which has reentered the market in Thailand and, despite a shrinking demand for automobiles there, is beginning to build a strong sales force and to garner market share. The firm's strategic plan here is based on offering the right combination of price and financing to a carefully identified market segment. In particular, Ford is working to keep down the monthly payments so that customers can afford a new vehicle. This is the same approach that Ford used in Mexico, where the currency crises of 1994 resulted

Strategic planning
The process of determining an organization's basic mission and long-term objectives, then implementing a plan of action for attaining these goals.

in problems for many multinationals. However, this was not true for Ford which rolled out a carefully formulated strategy that allowed it to increase its vehicle market share in Mexico from 14 percent in 1994 to 20 percent three years later.[4]

Another example of the growing need for strategic planning is provided by Bertelsmann AG, the giant German book publisher that has now entered the Chinese market.[5] Bertelsmann has created a giant book club that could dramatically change the way Chinese buy books. In the past two years this club has signed up over 600,000 members, opened a handful of retail stores, and sold almost 5 million volumes. Moreover, Bertelsmann is now adding 2,000 new members every day, a growth rate that is easily sustainable given that approximately 180 million Chinese read books on a regular basis. The company's strategic plan calls for continual expansion well into the new millennium, driven by a wide assortment of books, low costs, and home delivery. In fact, things are going so well for Bertelsmann in China that the company has now sent salespeople to South Korea to lay the groundwork for a book club there and has plans for expanding to Japan, India, and Thailand.

A third example of the growing need for strategic planning is provided by Daimler-Chrysler, which has now expanded operations into Brazil, a rapidly growing market. The firm's plan involves minimum investment coupled with maximum production. This is being accomplished through the use of what are called "major modules." The idea behind modularity is that suppliers become responsible for assembling dozens of small parts into major components for a car or truck, while the main manufacturer is responsible for installing these modules into the vehicle. In the case of Daimler-Chrysler in Brazil, for example, the Dana Corporation provides these modules. The system works this way. First, Dana receives an order from a Daimler-Chrysler plant for a specific number of chassis for the firm's Dakota pickup vehicle. Then the supplier, which is located about two miles down the road from the Daimler-Chrysler plant, rapidly assembles the truck's frame, axles, brakes, and wheels. In all, there are 320 parts to be put together, along with fully inflated tires, and these are delivered to the plant within two hours of the time the order is received. The modular units roll into the plant just as the workers are bringing the engines, transmissions, and bodies across the factory floor from the interior line. Everything is then assembled and the vehicle is driven out of the production area. In addition to increasing the number of vehicles it can produce in an hour, Daimler-Chrysler has driven down the cost of each pickup truck by thousands of dollars. So for less than $100 million in investment, Daimler-Chrysler has been able to create a factory that will soon be able to produce 40,000 vehicles annually and account for sales in excess of $1 billion.[6]

Still another example of the growing need for strategic planning is offered by GE Capital, the focus of the opening *Business Week* story in Chapter 3, which has been expanding rapidly in Europe. Since the mid-1980s the company has amassed assets in excess of $50 billion, much of this since 1994. The firm began years ago by helping customers purchase General Electric products, but it has now expanded widely and provides diverse services from equipment financing for middle-market firms, to consumer finance, to reinsurance. Relying on a well-coordinated strategic plan, the company sets targets for each of its 28 stand-alone businesses. Overall, GE Capital looks for at least a 20 percent annual return on capital and strong growth. The approach flouts some time-honored traditions as seen by the fact that each business handles its customers independently. So one customer can have multiple relationships with GE Capital. And while this type of planning approach may seem questionable to some, the company's net income has increased by over 500 percent in the last five years and by the new millennium will be generating over $1 billion annually.[7] Obviously, strategic planning is proving critically important to the firm in these efforts.

Benefits of Strategic Planning

Now that the needs for strategic planning have been explored, what are some of the benefits? Many MNCs are convinced that strategic planning is critical to their success, and these efforts are being conducted both at the home office and in the subsidiaries. For example, one study found that 70 percent of the 56 U.S. MNC subsidiaries in Asia and Latin America had comprehensive 5- to 10-year plans.[8] Others found that U.S., European, and Japanese subsidiaries in Brazil were heavily planning-driven[9] and that Australian manufacturing companies use planning systems that are very similar to those of U.S. manufacturing firms.[10]

Do these strategic planning efforts really pay off? To date, the evidence is mixed. Certainly, that the strategic plan helps an MNC to coordinate and monitor its far-flung operations must be viewed as a benefit. Similarly, that the plan helps an MNC to deal with political risk problems (see Chapter 10), competition, and currency instability cannot be downplayed.

Despite some obvious benefits, there is no definitive evidence that strategic planning in the international arena always results in higher profitability. Most studies that report favorable results were conducted at least a decade ago.[11] More recent evidence tempers these findings with contingency-based recommendations. For example, one study found that when decisions were made mainly at the home office and close coordination between the subsidiary and home office was required, return on investment was negatively affected.[12] Simply put, the home office ends up interfering with the subsidiary, and profitability suffers.

A more recent study found that planning intensity (the degree to which a firm carries out strategic planning) is an important variable in determining performance.[13] Drawing on results from 22 German MNCs representing 71 percent of that country's multinational enterprises, one study found that companies with only a few foreign affiliates performed best with medium planning intensity. Those firms with high planning intensity tended to exaggerate the emphasis, and profitability suffered. Companies that earned a high percentage of their total sales in overseas markets, however, did best with a high-intensity planning process and poorly with a low-intensity process. Therefore, although strategic planning usually seems to pay off, as with most other aspects of international management, the specifics of the situation will dictate the success of the process.[14]

Approaches to Formulating and Implementing Strategy

Four common approaches to strategic planning are: (1) focusing on the economic imperative; (2) focusing on the political imperative; (3) addressing the quality imperative; and (4) implementing an administrative coordination strategy.

Economic Imperative MNCs that focus on the **economic imperative** employ a worldwide strategy based on cost leadership, differentiation, and segmentation. Many of these companies typically sell products for which a large portion of value is added in the upstream activities of the industry's value chain. By the time the product is ready to be sold, much of its value has already been created through research and development, manufacturing, and distribution. Some of the industries in this group include automobiles, chemicals, heavy electrical systems, motorcycles, and steel. Because the product is basically homogeneous and requires no alteration to fit the needs of the specific country, management uses a worldwide strategy that is consistent on a country-to-country basis.

The strategy also is used when the product is regarded as a generic good and therefore does not have to be sold based on name brand or support service. A good example is the European PC market. Until the early 1990s, this market was dominated by such well-known companies as IBM, Apple, and Compaq. However, more recently in Europe, clone manufacturers have begun to gain market share. This is because the most influential reasons for buying a PC have changed. A few years ago, the main reasons were brand name, service, and support. Today, price has emerged as a major input into the purchasing decision. Customers now are much more computer literate, and they realize that many PCs offer identical quality performance. Therefore, it does not pay to purchase a high-priced name brand when a lower-priced clone will do the same things. As a result, the economic imperative dominates the strategic plans of computer manufacturers.

Another economic imperative concept that has gained prominence over the last five years is global sourcing, which is proving very useful in formulating and implementing

Economic Imperative
A worldwide strategy based on cost leadership, differentiation, and segmentation.

strategy.[15] A good example is provided by the way in which manufacturers are reaching into the supply chain and shortening the buying circle. Li & Fung, Hong Kong's largest export trading company, is one of the world's leading innovators in the development of supply chain management and the company has managed to use its expertise to whittle costs to the bone. Instead of buying fabric and yarn from one company and letting that firm work on keeping its costs as low as possible, for example, Li & Fung gets actively involved in managing the entire process. In the case of how it keeps costs down for orders it receives from The Limited, for example, the chairman of the company has explained the firm's economic imperative strategy this way:

> We come in and look at the whole supply chain. We know The Limited is going to order 100,000 garments, but we don't know the style or the colors yet. The buyer will tell us that five weeks before delivery. The trust between us and our supply network means that we can reserve undyed yarn from the yarn supplier. I can lock up capacity at the mills for the weaving and dying with the promise that they'll get an order of a specified size; five weeks before delivery, we will let them know what colors we want. Then I say the same thing to the factories, "I don't know the product specs yet, but I have organized the colors and the fabric and the trim for you, and they'll be delivered to you on this date and you'll have three weeks to produce so many garments."
>
> I've certainly made life harder for myself now. It would be easier to let the factories worry about securing their own fabric and trim. But then the order would take three months, not five weeks. So to shrink the delivery cycle, I go upstream to organize production. And the shorter production time lets the retailer hold off before having to commit to a fashion trend. It's all about flexibility, response time, small production runs, small minimum-order quantities, and the ability to shift direction as the trends move.[16]

Political imperative
Strategic formulation and implementation utilizing strategies that are country-responsive and designed to protect local market niches.

Political Imperative   MNCs using the **political imperative** approach to strategic planning are country-responsive; their approach is designed to protect local market niches. "International Management in Action: Point/Counterpoint" demonstrates this political imperative. The products sold by MNCs often have a large portion of their value added in the downstream activities of the value chain. Industries such as insurance and consumer packaged goods are examples—the success of the product or service generally depends heavily on marketing, sales, and service. Typically, these industries use a country-centered or multidomestic strategy.

A good example of a country-centered strategy is provided by Thums Up, a local drink that Coca-Cola bought from an Indian bottler in 1993. This drink was created back in the 1970s, shortly after Coca-Cola pulled up stakes and left the country. In the ensuing two decades the drink, which is similar in taste to Coke, made major in-roads in the Indian market. But when Coca-Cola returned and bought the company it decided to put Thums Up on the back burner and began pushing its own soft drink. However, local buyers were not interested. They continued to buy Thums Up and Coca-Cola finally relented. Today Thums Up is the firm's biggest seller and fastest growing brand in India, and the company spends more money on this soft drink than it does on any of its other product offerings including Coke.[17] As one observer noted, "In India the 'Real Thing' for Coca-Cola is its Thums Up brand."

Quality imperative
Strategic formulation and implementation utilizing strategies of total quality management to meet or exceed customers' expectations and continuously improve products and/or services.

Quality Imperative   As Chapter 3 discussed, there has been a quality revolution among both domestic companies and MNCs. This **quality imperative** is taking two interdependent paths: (1) a change in attitudes and a raising of expectation for service quality; and (2) the implementation of management practices that are designed to make quality improvement an ongoing process.[18] Commonly called "total quality management," or simply TQM, the approach takes a wide number of forms, including cross-training personnel to do the jobs of all members in their work group, process re-engineering designed to help identify and eliminate redundant tasks and wasteful effort, and reward systems designed to reinforce quality performance.[19]

TQM covers the full gamut, from strategy formulation to implementation. Chapter 3 covered the environment of quality, but as an approach to strategy, TQM briefly can be summarized as follows:

International Management in Action

Point/Counterpoint

www.kodak.com

A good example of the political imperative in action is the recent Kodak/Fuji dispute. Kodak has accused Fuji of blocking its growth in the Japanese market. Fuji has responded by arguing that Kodak has long held a monopoly-type position in the United States. This debate began when Kodak complained to the U.S. government and asked for help in further opening the door to the Japanese market. Kodak's argument included the following points:

1. Unlike the United States, film manufacturers in Japan do not sell directly to retailers or photofinishers but to distributors, and Fuji has close ties with the four dominant distributors. Fuji holds an equity position in two of them and gives all four both rebates and cash payments.

2. Fuji controls 430 Japanese wholesale photofinishing labs through ownership, loans, rebates, and other forms of operational support. Additionally, the Japanese government has helped to establish the system to impede Kodak.

3. Kodak has invested $750 million in Japan and garnered less than 10 percent of the market.

4. Fuji uses profits from the Japanese market to subsidize the dumping of its products in other countries, thus effectively reducing Kodak's worldwide market share.

5. The Japanese government has not vigorously enforced antimonopoly legislation, and this has helped Fuji to establish distribution dominance.

These charges are answered by Fuji, which contends that Kodak uses many tactics that prevent Fuji from gaining U.S. market share. These include:

1. Kodak gives U.S. retailers rebates and upfront payments that effectively exclude competitors. For example, Kodak offered Genovese Drug Stores of Glen Cove, NY, $40,000 plus rebates if the company would carry no branded film but Kodak, use only Kodak paper and processing chemicals, and give Kodak 80 percent of the chain's shelfspace allotment for film.

2. Kodak holds 70 percent of the U.S. wholesale photofinishing market through ownership and by giving discounts, advertising dollars, and other investments to land exclusive accounts.

3. Fuji has invested $2 billion in the United States and holds less than 11 percent of the market.

4. Kodak's worldwide operating profit margin over the last two decades is 13 percent, close to Fuji's 15.5 percent.

5. The U.S. government has not vigorously enforced consent decrees that were created to limit Kodak's U.S. marketing practices and ensure that it did not gain an unfair advantage over competitors.

Will the U.S. government prevail in its efforts to help Kodak? Will Fuji be able to make further gains in the U.S. market? What role will political intervention play? These questions are yet to be answered. In the meantime, the two firms continue to compete—and cooperate. Together, they currently are developing a so-called "smart film," which is a new system that offers small cameras and film that can record information to improve the quality of processing. Whatever the outcome of their market-share argument, this strategic cooperative effort likely will continue.

---

1. Quality is operationalized by meeting or exceeding customer expectations. Customers include not only the buyer or external user of the product or service, but also the support personnel both inside and outside the organization who are associated with the good or service.

2. The quality strategy is formulated at the top management level and is diffused throughout the organization. From top executives to hourly employees, everyone operates under a TQM strategy of delivering quality products and/or services to internal and external customers.

3. The techniques range from traditional inspection and statistical quality control to cutting-edge human resource management techniques, such as self-managing teams and empowerment.[20]

Many MNCs make quality a major part of their overall strategy, because they have learned that this is the way to increase market share and profitability. For example, while the U.S. automakers have dramatically increased their overall quality in recent years to close the gap with Japanese auto quality, Japanese firms continue to have fewer safety recalls. On the other hand, many U.S. firms are world-class competitors thanks to their total quality imperative. For example, Stanley Works, which is known for its tools, was being hammered by Asian competition in the 1980s before incorporating a quality imperative into its strategic plan. Today, the firm's scrap rate is 20 percent of what it was 6 years ago, products are developed and improved for the world market based on the recommendation of engineers in each local area, and both profits and revenues have more than doubled in the last decade.[21] Another example is Monroe Auto Equipment, which has increased its productivity by 26 percent and profits by 70 percent in the last several years. Monroe's quality is so high that Toyota buys shock absorbers from the firm for assembly in its Toyoda City, Japan, plant. Moreover, a recent quality control check by Toyota of 60,000 shocks shipped to it by Monroe found a zero defect rate. Simply put, the quality imperative is becoming an integral part of strategic planning in international management.

At the same time a growing number of MNCs are finding that they must continually revise their strategies and make renewed commitment to the quality imperative because they are being bested by emerging market forces. One example is Nissan Motors which in recent years has seen its share of the U.S. auto market drop sharply. The company had done extremely well with its sporty car offerings, but as the market for sportsters declined, the company started dropping these lines. As a result, it soon had few offerings with which to compete in the North American market. Additionally, Nissan put all of its profits back into the Japanese market where it continued to develop products for that local market and did not pay much attention to the demands of the American market. Today the company is trying to turn things around.[22]

The same is true for Motorola, which has found that its failure to focus on quality has led to major problems. In particular, in the last few years the company has stumbled badly by failing to anticipate the industry's switch to digital cell phones from its long-dominant analog devices—and then Motorola overestimated its ability to get digital equipment to market. As a result, while the firm currently clings to the top spot in the U.S. market for wireless phones, its share has fallen by 30 percent in the last three years and its worldwide share of wireless network systems has dropped to less than one-third.[23] In other words, the quality imperative is never ending, and MNCs such as Motorola have a strategic challenge to sustain its quality efforts.

Administrative coordination
Strategic formulation and implementation in which the MNC makes strategic decision based on the merits of the individual situation rather than using a predetermined economically or politically driven strategy.

Administrative Coordination An **administrative coordination** approach to formulation and implementation is one in which the MNC makes strategic decisions based on the merits of the individual situation rather than using a predetermined economic or political strategy. A good example is provided by Wal-Mart, which has expanded rapidly into Latin America in recent years. While many of the ideas that worked well in the North American market served as the basis for operations in the southern hemisphere, the company soon realized that it was doing business in a market where local tastes were different and competition was strong.

Wal-Mart is counting on its international operations to grow 25–30 percent annually and South American operations are critical to this objective. For the moment, however, the company is reporting losses in Latin America, as it strives to adapt to the local market. The firm is learning, for example, that the timely delivery of merchandise in places such as Sao Paulo, where there are continual traffic snarls and the company uses contract truckers for delivery, is often far from ideal. Another challenge is finding suppliers who can produce products to Wal-Mart's specification for easy-to-handle packaging and quality control. A third challenge is learning to adapt to the culture. For example, in Brazil Wal-Mart brought in stock-handling equipment that did not work with standardized local pallets. It also installed a computerized bookkeeping system that failed to take into account Brazil's wildly complicated tax system. And the problems do not end here.

Wal-Mart has also been slow to adapt to Brazil's fast-changing credit culture. Not until last February did the company start accepting postdated checks, which have become the most common form of credit since Brazil stabilized its currency in 1995. Pao de Acucar, whose

Extra hypermarkets compete with Wal-Mart, has been taking postdated checks since they first became popular and has installed a sophisticated credit-checking system at its registers. Wal-Mart is hurrying to do so, too.

The six South American Sam's Club locations, the members-only warehouse stores that sell merchandise in bulk, got off to a slow start largely because shoppers weren't used to paying a membership and don't have enough room at home to store bulk purchases. In Argentina, the clubs have faced another barrier: Small business customers are reluctant to sign up for fear Wal-Mart could provide information to tax authorities on their purchases.[24]

Many large MNCs work to combine the economic, political, quality, and administrative approaches to strategic planning. For example, IBM relies on the economic imperative when it has strong market power (especially in less developed countries), the political and quality imperatives when the market requires a calculated response (European countries), and an administrative coordination strategy when rapid, flexible decision making is needed to close the sale. Of the four, however, the first three approaches are much more common because of the firm's desire to coordinate its strategy both regionally and globally.

Strategic Predispositions

In addition to the economic, political, quality, and administrative approaches, most MNCs also have a strategic predisposition toward doing things in a particular way. This orientation or predisposition helps to determine the specific steps the MNC will follow. Four distinct predispositions have been identified: ethnocentric, polycentric, regiocentric, and geocentric.

A company with an **ethnocentric predisposition** allows the values and interests of the parent company to guide the strategic decisions. Firms with a **polycentric predisposition** make strategic decision tailored to suit the cultures of the countries where the MNC operates. A **regiocentric predisposition** leads a firm to try to blend its own interests with those of its subsidiaries on a regional basis. A company with a **geocentric predisposition** tries to integrate a global systems approach to decision making.[25] Table 9-1 provides details of each of these orientations.

If an MNC relies on one of these profiles over an extended time, the approach may become institutionalized and greatly influence strategic planning. By the same token, a predisposition toward any of these profiles can provide problems for a firm if it is out of step with the economic or political environment. For example, a firm with an ethnocentric predisposition may find it difficult to implement a geocentric strategy, because it is unaccustomed to using global integration. Commonly, successful MNCs use a mix of these predispositions based on the demands of the current environment described in the chapters in Part One.

The Basic Steps in Formulating Strategy

The needs, benefits, approaches, and predispositions of strategic planning serve as a point of departure for the basic steps in formulating strategy. In international management, strategic planning can be broken into the following steps: (1) scanning the external environment for opportunities and threats; (2) conducting an internal resource analysis of company strengths and weaknesses; and (3) formulating goals in light of the external scanning and internal analysis. These steps are graphically summarized in Figure 9-1. The following sections discuss each step in detail.[26]

Environmental Scanning

Environmental scanning attempts to provide management with accurate forecasts of trends that relate to external changes in geographic areas where the firm is currently doing business and/or considering setting up operations. These changes relate to the economy, competition, political stability, technology, and demographic consumer data. Table 9-2

Ethnocentric predisposition
A nationalistic philosophy of management whereby the values and interests of the parent company guide the strategic decisions.

Polycentric predisposition
A philosophy of management whereby strategic decisions are tailored to suit the cultures of the countries where the MNC operates.

Regiocentric predisposition
A philosophy of management whereby the firm tries to blend its own interests with those of its subsidiaries on a regional basis.

Geocentric predisposition
A philosophy of management whereby the company tries to integrate a global systems approach to decision making.

Environmental scanning
The process of providing management with accurate forecasts of trends related to external changes in geographic areas where the firm currently is doing business and/or is considering setting up operations.

Table 9–1
Orientation of an MNC under Different Profiles

	Ethnocentric	Polycentric	Regiocentric	Geocentric
		Orientation of the Firm		
Mission	Profitability (viability)	Public acceptance (legitimacy)	Both profitability and public acceptance (viability and legitimacy)	Same as regiocentric
Governance	Top-down	Bottom-up (each subsidiary decides on local objectives)	Mutually negotiated between region and its subsidiaries	Mutually negotiated at all levels of the corporation
Strategy	Global integration	National responsiveness	Regional integration and national responsiveness	Global integration and national responsiveness
Structure	Hierarchical product divisions	Hierarchical area divisions, with autonomous national units	Product and regional organization tied through a matrix	A network of organizations (including some stakeholders and competitor organizations)
Culture	Home country	Host country	Regional	Global
Technology	Mass production	Batch production	Flexible manufacturing	Flexible manufacturing
Marketing	Product development determined primarily by the needs of home country customers	Local product development based on local needs	Standardize within region, but not across regions	Global product, with local variations
Finance	Repatriation of profits to home country	Retention of profits in host country	Redistribution within region	Redistribution globally
Personnel practices	People of home country developed for key positions everywhere in the world	People of local nationality developed for key positions in their own country	Regional people developed for key positions anywhere in the region	Best people everywhere in the world developed for key positions everywhere in the world

Source: Adapted from Balaji S. Chakravarthy and Howard V. Perlmutter, "Strategic Planning for a Global Business," *Columbia Journal of World Business,* Summer 1985, pp. 5–6. Copyright 1985, Columbia Journal of World Business. Used with permission.

Figure 9–1
Basic Elements of Strategic Planning for International Management

provides an example of gross national product growth rate data that would typically be included in this type of analysis.

Typically, the MNC will begin by conducting a forecast of macroeconomic and industry performance dealing with factors such as markets for specific products, per-capita income of the population, and availability of labor and raw materials. A second common forecast will predict likely trends in monetary exchange rates, exchange controls, balance of payments, and inflation rates. A third is the forecast of the company's potential market share in a particular geographic area as well as that of the competitors. Other considerations include political stability, government pressure, nationalism, and related areas of

Table 9–2
Gross National Product Growth Rates in Select Asian Nations

	Average Annual Percentage 1970–1996	Actual 1997	Forecast 1998	Forecast 1999
China	9.1	8.9	6.3	7.5
Hong Kong	7.5	5.1	1.8	3.8
Indonesia	6.8	5.4	−5.2	2.9
Korea	8.4	5.6	−2.5	1.7
Philippines	3.6	4.8	1.9	4.0
Singapore	8.2	7.6	2.7	5.0
Taiwan	8.3	6.3	5.0	5.7
Thailand	7.5	−0.7	−4.0	3.7

Source: Reported in *Management Review,* September 1998, p. 17.

political risk. These assessments are extremely important in determining the risk profile and profit potential of the region, which always is a major consideration when deciding where to set up international operations.

Mercedes is a good example of how this environmental scanning process is done.[27] Before the recent merger with Chrysler, this German firm was chosen by China to build minivans, and is the last major vehicle project that China will approve until the year 2000. What makes Mercedes' success so impressive is that initially, the company was not a leading contender for the contract. Now partner Chrysler had the lead in this bid to make vans as well as gas and diesel engines in China. Chrysler badly wanted this contract, because it would provide an important entry into the growing Chinese market. By mid-1994, Chrysler had agreed to invest over $1 billion to build vans, engines, and transmissions. At this point, however, negotiations turned sour. Chinese negotiators changed their tactics and introduced a host of new demands, including: (1) the right to export Chrysler vans and components without paying a licensee fee; (2) insistence that Chrysler invest the $1 billion up front rather than in phases, as was previously agreed; and (3) deletion of intellectual property protections from the contract, thus allowing the Chinese to copy Chrysler components freely. Chrysler refused to give such concessions, and the Chinese began looking at other bids, including one from Mercedes that gave them much of what they wanted. Mercedes agreed to eventually base all of its van production in China, set up technology centers, develop a components industry, and let the Chinese export 12,000 units annually. At the same time, Mercedes' parent company, Daimler Benz, has pledged to put China "on the map" in industries ranging from passenger aircraft to high-speed trains. By carefully scanning the environment and making the necessary concessions, Mercedes placed itself in an ideal position to gain a significant share of the rapidly expanding Chinese auto market. Interestingly, Chrysler through its merger strategy to form Daimler-Chrysler will also end up having a presence in China.

Many other firms also have profited from astute environmental scanning. For example, Alcatel Alsthom of France made a series of clever acquisition and alliances and now is the world's largest telephone equipment company. This has put Alcatel in an ideal position to garner market share in the rapidly growing telecommunications market. U.S. MNCs Ford and General Motors have been positioning themselves carefully in Europe and, thanks to their environmental scanning, now are two of the major automakers there.

Sometimes, companies will take the result of their environmental scanning and construct an evaluation matrix. Table 9-3 illustrates a matrix that was constructed for strategic analysis of the economic potential of countries transforming to market economies. As shown, these countries were divided into three groups based on a number of evaluative criteria. Similar matrixes can be constructed for many other areas of strategic analysis for MNCs, such as market entry or location sites.

Table 9–3 **An Evaluation Matrix for Transition Economies**			
Country	Economic Potential	Receptiveness to Foreign Investment	Speed of Reform
Most promising			
Czech Republic	B+	B	C–
Hungary	B	A	A
Promising			
Poland	C+	A	A
Least promising			
Bulgaria	C	B	C–
Romania	D+	C–	F

Source: Reported in David Pitt-Watson and Scott Frazer, "Eastern Europe: Commercial Opportunity or Illusion?" *Long Range Planning,* vol. 24, no. 5, 1991, p. 19. Used with permission.

Internal Resource Analysis

When formulating strategy, some firms wait until they have completed their environmental scanning before conducting an internal resource analysis. Others perform these two steps simultaneously. Internal resource analysis helps the firm to evaluate its current managerial, technical, material, and financial strengths and weaknesses. This assessment then is used by the MNC to determine its ability to take advantage of international market opportunities. The primary thrust of this analysis is to match external opportunities (gained through the environmental scan) with internal capabilities (gained through the internal resource analysis).

An internal analysis identifies the key factors for success that will dictate how well the firm is likely to do. A **key factor for success (KFS)** is a factor that is necessary for a firm to compete effectively in a market niche. For example, a KFS for an international airline is price. An airline that discounts its prices will gain market share vis-à-vis those that do not. A second KFS for the airline is safety, and a third is quality service in terms of on-time departures and arrivals, convenient schedules, and friendly, helpful personnel. In the automobile industry, quality of products has emerged as the number-one KFS in world markets. Japanese firms have been able to invade the U.S. auto market successfully, because they have been able to prove that the quality of their cars is better than the average domestically built U.S. car. Toyota and Honda have had such a quality edge over the competition in recent years in the eyes of U.S. car buyers. A second KFS is styling, The redesigned VW Beetle has been very successful because customers like its looks.

The key question for the management of an MNC is: Do we have the people and resources that can help us to develop and sustain the necessary KFSs, or can we acquire them? If the answer is yes, the recommendation would be to proceed. If the answer is no, management would begin looking at other markets where it has, or can develop, the necessary KFSs.

Key factor for success (KFS)
A factor necessary for a firm to effectively compete in a

Goal Setting for Strategy Formulation

In a sense, general goals concerning the philosophy of "going international" or growth actually precede the first two steps of environmental scanning and internal resource analysis. As used here, however, the more specific goals for the strategic plan come out of external scanning and internal analysis. MNCs pursue a variety of such goals; Table 9-4 provides a list of the most common ones. These goals typically serve as an umbrella beneath which the subsidiaries and other international groups operate.

Profitability and marketing goals almost always dominate the strategic plans of today's MNCs. Profitability, as show in Table 9-4, is so important because MNCs generally need higher profitability from their overseas operation than they do from their domestic operations. The reason is quite simple: Setting up overseas operations involves greater risk and effort. In addition, a firm that has done well domestically with a product or service usually

Table 9–4
Areas for Formulation of MNC Goals

Profitability

Level of profits
Return on assets, investment, equity, sales
Yearly profit growth
Yearly earnings per share growth

Marketing

Total sales volume
Market share—worldwide, region, country
Growth in sales volume
Growth in market share
Integration of country markets for marketing efficiency and effectiveness

Production

Ratio of foreign to domestic production volume
Economies of scale via international production integration
Quality and cost control
Introduction of cost-efficient production methods

Finance

Financing of foreign affiliates—retained earnings or local borrowing
Taxation—minimizing tax burden globally
Optimum capital structure
Foreign exchange management—minimizing losses from foreign fluctuations

Personnel/Human Resources

Development of managers with global orientation
Management development of host-country nationals

Source: Adapted from information found in Arvind V. Phatak, *International Dimensions of Management,* 2nd ed. (Boston: PWS-Kent Publishing, 1989), p. 72.

has done so because the competition is minimal or ineffective. Firms with this advantage often find additional lucrative opportunities outside their borders. Moreover, the more successful a firm is domestically, the more difficult it is to increase market share without strong competitive response. International markets, however, offer an ideal alternative to the desire for increased growth and profitability.

Another reason that profitability and marketing top the list is that these tend to be more externally environmentally responsive, whereas production, finance, and personnel functions tend to be more internally controlled. Thus, for strategic planning, profitability and marketing goals are given higher importance and warrant closer attention.

Once the strategic goals are set, the MNC will develop specific operational goals and controls, usually through a two-way process at the subsidiary or affiliate level (organization is covered in Chapter 12). Home office management will set certain parameters, and the overseas group will operate within these guidelines. For example, the MNC headquarters may require periodic financial reports, restrict on-site decisions to matters involving less than $100,000, and require that all client contracts be cleared through the home office. These guidelines are designed to ensure that the overseas group's activities support the goals in the strategic plan and that all units operate in a coordinated effort.

Strategy Implementation

Once formulated, the strategic plan next must be implemented. **Strategy implementation** provides goods and services in accord with a plan of action. Quite often, this plan will have an overall philosophy or series of guidelines that direct the process. In the case

Strategy implementation
The process of providing goods and services in accord with a plan of action.

of Japanese electronic-manufacturing firms entering the U.S. market, Chang has found a common approach:

> To reduce the risk of failure, these firms are entering their core businesses and those in which they have stronger competitive advantages over local firms first. The learning from early entry enables firms to launch further entry into areas in which they have the next strongest competitive advantages. As learning accumulates, firms may overcome the disadvantages intrinsic to foreignness. Although primary learning takes place within firms through learning by doing, they may also learn from other firms through the transfer or diffusion of experience. This process is not automatic, however, and it may be enhanced by membership in a corporate network: in firms associated with either horizontal or vertical business groups were more likely to initiate entries than independent firms. By learning from their own sequential entry experience as well as from other firms in corporated networks, firms build capabilities in foreign entry.[28]

International management must consider three general areas in strategy implementation. First, the MNC must decide where to locate operations. Second, the MNC must carry out entry and ownership strategies. Finally, management must implement functional strategies in areas such as marketing, production, and finance.

Location Considerations for Implementation

In choosing a location, today's MNC has two primary considerations: the country, and the specific locale within the chosen country. Quite often, the first choice is easier than the second, because there are many more alternatives from which to choose a specific locale.

The Country   Traditionally, MNCs have invested in highly industrialized countries and research reveals that annual investments have been increasing substantially. In 1993 over $325 billion was spent on mergers and acquisitions worldwide. By 1997 the annual total had jumped to $1.6 trillion.[29] Much of this investment, especially by American MNCs, has been in Europe and Canada, although Japan and Mexico have recently become major investment targets.

In the case of Japan, multinational banks and investors from around the world have been looking for properties that are being jettisoned by Japanese banks that are trying to unload some of their distressed loans. The Japanese commercial property market, as of 1998, has dropped by 80 percent, and land values in Tokyo plunged from $285,000 per square meter in 1990 to $57,000 in 1998. Thus there are many opportunities for investors. One has been U.S.-based MNC Bankers Trust which recently bought a large plot of properties of a failed affiliate of Nippon Credit Bank Ltd. Bankers Trust paid $220 million for properties that had a face value of $2.2 billion.[30] Nonbanking MNCs are also actively engaged in mergers and acquisitions in Japan. Intuit Inc. of Menlo Park, California recently purchased a financial software specialist in Japan for $52 million in stock and spent $30 million for the Nihon Mikon Company, which sells small business accounting software. These purchases point to a new trend in Japan—the acquisition of small firms. However, there are also many larger purchases being made, as seen in Table 9-5.

Foreign investors are also pouring into Mexico. One reason is because it is a gateway to the American and Canadian markets. A second reason is because Mexico is a very cost effective place in which to manufacture goods. A third is that the declining value of the peso in the late 1990s hit many Mexican businesses hard and left them vulnerable to mergers and acquisitions—an opportunity that was not lost on many large multinationals.

> Britain's B.A.T. Industries PLC took control of Cigarrera La Moderna, Mexico's tobacco giant, in a $1.5 billion deal. A few days earlier, Philip Morris Cos. increased its stake in the second-largest tobacco company, Cigarros La Tabacalera Mexicana SA, to 50% from about 29% for $400 million. In June, Wal-Mart Stores Inc., announced plans to acquire control of Mexico's largest retailer, Cifra SA, in a deal valued at more than $1 billion. In July, Procter & Gamble Co. acquired a consumer-products concern, Loreto y Pena Pobre, for $170 million. Bell Atlantic Co. has acquired full control of its cellular-phone partner, Grupo Iusacell SA, with total investments of more than $1 billion. The list goes on and on and is expected to keep growing.[31]

Table 9-5
Recent MNC Acquisitions in Japan

Glaxo Wellcome	Has purchased the remaining 50 percent of its Nippon Glaxo affiliate for $537 million.
Ford Motor	Has picked up an additional 9 percent of Mazda, bringing its stake to 33.4 percent, for $430 million.
BASF	The German drugmaker has purchased 51 percent of Hokuriku Seiyaku for $294 million.
Grande Group	The Singapore firm has acquired 70 percent of Nakamichi for $286 million.
GE Capital	Has bought 80 percent of Narubeni Car System, an auto-loan business, for $80 million.
Semi-Tech Group	The Hong Kong high-tech company has put out $167 million for an additional 11 percent of Akai Electric.
Boehringer Ingelheim	The German firm acquired 9 percent of SS Pharmaceutical for $71 million.
Amersham International	The British drug maker acquired 30 percent of Nihon Mediphysics for $76 million.

Source: Reported in *Business Week,* April 14, 1997, p. 57.

MNCs often invest in advanced industrialized countries because they offer the largest markets for goods and services. In addition, the established country or geographic locale may have legal restrictions related to imports, encouraging a local presence. Japanese firms, for example, in complying with their voluntary export quotas of cars to the United States as well as responding to dissatisfaction in Washington regarding the continuing trade imbalance with the United States, have established U.S.-based assembly plants. In Europe, because of EU regulations for outsiders, most U.S. and Japanese MNCs have operations in at least one European country, thus ensuring access to the European community at large. In fact, the huge U.S. MNC ITT now operates in each of the original 12 EU countries.

Another consideration in choosing a country is the amount of government control. Traditionally, MNCs from around the world refused to do business in Eastern European countries with central planning economies. The recent relaxing of the trade rules and move toward free market economies in the republics of the former Soviet Union and the other Eastern European nations, however, have encouraged MNCs to rethink their positions; more and more are making moves into this largely untapped part of the global market.[32] The same seems to be true in India as well, where the federal government now is considering private bids to build and operate 20-million telephone lines by the turn of the century. Only a very small percentage of India's population currently have telephones, so the market potential is huge. At the same time, the political climate is volatile, and MNCs must carefully weigh the risks of investing there.[33]

MNCs tend to avoid entering or expanding operations in countries where there is political turmoil or spillover effects caused by retaliation from other nations. For example, companies that did business in South Africa during the height of apartheid policies found retaliatory action from other African nations as well as politically active consumer groups in their own country.

Still another consideration in selecting a country is restrictions on foreign investment. Traditionally, countries such as China and India have required that control of the operation be in the hands of local partners. MNCs that are reluctant to accept such conditions will not establish operations there.

In addition to these considerations, MNCs will examine the specific benefits offered by host countries, including low tax rates, rent-free land and buildings, low-interest or no-interest loans, subsidized energy and transportation rates, and a well-developed infrastructure that provides many of the services found back home (good roads, communication systems, schools, health care, entertainment, and housing). These benefits will be weighed against any disincentives or performance requirements that must be met by the MNC, such as job-creation quotas, export minimums for generating foreign currency, limits on local market growth, labor regulations, wage and price controls, restrictions on profit repatriation, and controls on the transfer of technology.

Commenting on the overall effect of these potential gains and losses, Garland and Farmer noted:

> These incentives and disincentives often make operations abroad less amenable to integration on a global basis; essentially they may alter a company's strategy for the region. They affect, for example, a firm's make-or-buy decision, intracorporate transfer policies (e.g., between subsidiaries or between headquarters and the subsidiaries), both horizontal and vertical sourcing arrangements, and so on. In effect, they weaken the MNC's mandate for global efficiency by encouraging the firm to suboptimize.[34]

Local Issues Once the MNC has decided the country in which to locate the firm must choose the specific locale. A number of factors influence this choice. Common considerations include access to markets, proximity to competitors, availability of transportation and electric power, and desirability of the location for employees coming in from the outside.[35]

One study found that in selecting U.S. sites, both German and Japanese firms place more importance on accessibility and desirability and less importance on financial considerations.[36] However, financial matters remain important: Many countries attempt to lure MNCs to specific locales by offering special financial packages.

Another common consideration is the nature of the workforce. MNCs prefer to locate near sources of available labor that can be readily trained to do the work. A complementary consideration that often is unspoken is the presence and strength of organized labor (Chapter 17 covers this topic in detail). Japanese firms in particular tend to avoid heavily unionized areas.

Still another consideration is the cost of doing business. Manufacturers often set up operations in rural areas, commonly called "green field locations," which are much less expensive and do not have the problems of urban areas. Conversely, banks often choose metropolitan areas, because they feel they must have a presence in the business district.

Some MNCs opt for locales where the cost of running a small enterprise is significantly lower than that of running a large one. In this way, they spread their risk, setting up many small locations throughout the world rather than one or two large ones. Manufacturing firms are a good example. Some production firms feel that the economies of scale associated with a large-scale plant are more than offset by potential problems that can result should economic or political difficulties develop in the country. These firms' strategy is to spread the risk by opting for a series of small plants throughout a wide geographic region.

Ownership and Entry Considerations for Implementation

There are a number of common forms of ownership in international operations. Figure 9-2 reports some of the latest information regarding global expansion strategies in select world markets. Depending on the region of the world, some approaches are more popular than others. For example, as shown, in Australia and New Zealand alliances and the expansion of facilities are common approaches, while in China join ventures are widely used (although in recent years the Chinese have been reversing its trend toward more open markets and limiting joint ventures in some areas such as between foreign companies and Chinese telecom firms).[37] However, the most widely recognized are wholly owned subsidiaries acquired through acquisitions and alliances/mergers, joint ventures, licensing agreements, franchising, and basic export and import operations. Depending on the situation, any one of these can be a very effective way to implement an MNC's strategy.

Wholly owned subsidiary
An overseas operation that is totally owned and controlled by an MNC.

Wholly Owned Subsidiary A wholly owned subsidiary is an overseas operation that is totally owned and controlled by an MNC. In recent years a growing number of multinationals have acquired (fully own) their subsidiaries through alliances or mergers. The largest, in terms of acquisition price, was the British Petroleum (BP) Company's recent purchase of Amoco for $48.2 billion.[38] The merger made BP Amoco one of the biggest oil producers in the United States with operations in Alaska, the Gulf of Mexico,

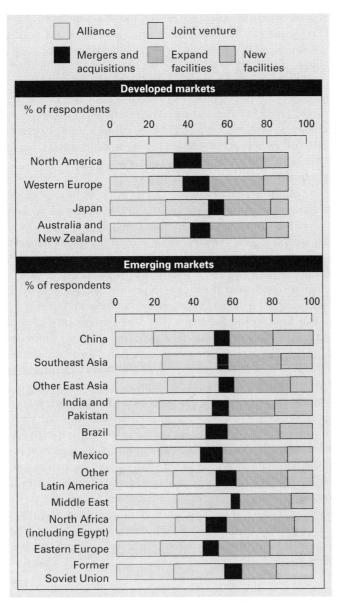

Figure 9–2

Preferred Strategies for Global Expansion

Source: Reported in the *Economist,* April 11, 1998, p. 82.

and parts of the 48 contiguous states. Additionally, both BP and Amoco have petrochemical operations which, when merged, will be among the largest in the world. The next few years should see the emergence of a strategic plan that will streamline BP Amoco operations and, if all goes well, make it one of the most profitable oil firms in the world.

Another recent example of a major acquisition mentioned earlier was that of Daimler-Benz and Chrysler, now called Daimler-Chrysler. In a deal valued at $39 billion, the German automaker bought Chrysler and, in the process, gained a lucrative North American market, while opening the door in Europe for a Chrysler expansion. The strategic plan of the merged companies calls for each to contribute a series of strengths toward making the firm a highly competitive operation. In particular, Daimler-Benz has luxury cars, heavy-duty trucks, modern V8 engines and diesel technology, and classic designs that are recognized worldwide. Chrysler has minivans, sports utility vehicles, pickup trucks, small cars, and niche vehicles such as the Dodge Viper sports car. Each also has complementary expertise that can be of value to the other. Daimler-Benz has advanced research into fuel cells, intelligent highway guidance systems, and a host of safety features that include skid control and protection of passengers in the case of a crash. Chrysler has new auto technologies, the ability to bring new models to market in under 24 months, and the ability to create new markets by developing innovative designs that exploit gaps in rival car offerings.[39] As Daimler-Chrysler begins rolling out its comprehensive strategic plan for the new millennium, it is likely to emphasize these strengths and areas of expertise and help ensure that it will be a major player in the worldwide auto market.

The primary reason for the use of fully owned subsidiaries is a desire by the MNC for total control and the belief that managerial efficiency will be better without outside partners. Host countries, however, often feel that the MNC is trying to gain economic control by setting up local operations but refusing to take in local partners. Some countries are concerned that the MNC will drive out local enterprises. In dealing with these concerns, many newly developing countries prohibit fully owned subsidiaries. A second drawback is that home country unions sometimes oppose the creation of foreign subsidiaries, which they see as an attempt to "export jobs," particularly when the MNC exports goods to another country and then decides to set up manufacturing operations there. As a result, today many MNCs opt for a joint venture rather than a fully owned subsidiary.[40]

Joint venture

An agreement in which two or more partners own and control an overseas business.

Joint Venture   As it relates to international operations, a **joint venture** is an agreement in which two or more partners own and control an overseas business. This business typically is located in the home country of one of the partners.

There are two types of joint ventures. The least common is the *nonequity venture*, which is characterized by one group's merely providing a service for another. The group providing the service typically is more active than the other. Examples include a consulting firm that is hired to provide analysis and evaluation and then make its recommendations to the other party, an engineering or construction firm that contracts to design or build a dam or series of apartment complexes in an undeveloped area of a partner's country, or a mining firm that has an agreement to extract a natural resource in the other party's country.

The more common arrangement is the *equity joint venture*, which involves a financial investment by the MNC in a business enterprise with a local partner. Many variations of this arrangement adjust the degree of control that each of the parties will have and the amount of money, technological expertise, and managerial expertise each will contribute.[41]

Most foreign firms are more interested in the amount of control they will have over the venture than in their share of the profits. Many local partners feel the same way, and this can result in problems. Nevertheless, joint ventures have become very popular in recent years because of the benefits they offer to both parties. Some of the most commonly cited advantages include:

1. *Improvement of efficiency.* The creation of a joint venture can help the partners achieve greater economies of scale and scope, something which can be difficult to accomplish by one firm operating alone. Additionally, the partners can spread the risks among themselves and profit from the synergies which arise from the complementarity of their resources.[42]

2. *Access to knowledge.* In joint ventures each partner has access to the knowledge and skills of the others. So one partner may bring financial and technological resources to the venture while another will bring a knowledge of the customer and market channels.

3. *Political factors.* A local partner can be very helpful in dealing with political risk factors such as a hostile government and/or restrictive legislation.

4. *Collusion or restriction in competition.* Joint ventures can help partners overcome the effects of local collusion or limits that are being put on foreign competition. By becoming part of an "insider" group, foreign partners manage to transcend these barriers.[43]

As noted above, joint venture partners often complement each other and can thus reduce the risks associated with their undertaking. A good example is European truck manufacturing and auto component industries. Firms in both groups have found that the high cost of developing and building their products can be offset through joint ventures. In particular, some partners to these ventures have contributed financial assistance while others provide the distribution networks needed to move the product through channels. Another example is the recent decision by Japanese semiconductor firms to consider banding together and jointly developing new chip production methods. The chip makers also have invited U.S. firms to join them in creating 12-inch wafer technology, but it appears likely that the Americans will form their own joint-venture group.[44]

Although much negotiation may be necessary before a joint-venture agreement is hammered out, the final result must be one that both sides can accept. Many successful examples of such agreements have emerged in recent years. One of the most complex was the General Motors–Toyota agreement, which involved scores of groups and thousands of individuals. Other examples include General Motors' venture with the Polish government to build Opels in that country, L. L. Bean's decision to sell clothing and equipment under a joint-venture agreement with two Japanese companies in Tokyo, and Occidental Petroleum's joint venture in a northern China coal mining project.

Joint ventures are proving to be particularly popular as a means for doing business in emerging market economies. For example, in the early 1990s, foreigners had signed more than 3,000 joint-venture agreements in Eastern Europe and the former republics of the Soviet Union, and interest remains high today. Careful analysis must be undertaken to ensure that the market for the desired goods and services is sufficiently large and that all parties understand their responsibilities, and that all parties agree regarding the overall operation of the venture. If these problems can be resolved, the venture stands a good chance of success. The accompanying box, "Joint Venturing in Russia," illustrates some of the problems that need to be overcome for a joint venture to be successful. Some of the other suggestions that have been offered by researchers regarding participation in strategic alliances include:

1. Know your partners well before an alliance is formed.

2. Expect differences in alliance objectives among potential partners headquartered in different countries.

3. Realize that having the desired resource profiles does not guarantee that they are complementary to your firm's resources.

4. Be sensitive to your alliance partner's needs.

5. After identifying the best partner, work on developing a relationship that is built on trust.[45]

Licensing   Another way to gain market entry to implement strategy is to acquire the right to a particular product by getting an exclusive license to make and/or sell the good in a particular geographic locale. A **license** is an agreement that allows one party to use an industrial property right in exchange for payment to the other party. In a typical arrangement, the party giving the license (the licensor) will allow the other (the licensee) to use a patent, trademark, or proprietary information in exchange for a fee. The fee usually is based on sales, such as 1 percent of all revenues earned from an industrial motor sold in Asia. The licensor typically restricts licensee sales to a particular geographic locale and limits the time period covered by the arrangement. Therefore, the firm in this example may have an exclusive right to sell this patented motor in Asia for the next 5 years. This allows the licensor to seek licensees for other major geographic locales, such as Europe, South America, and Australia.

Licensing is used under a number of common conditions. For example, the product typically is in the mature stage of the product life cycle, competition is strong, and profit margins are declining. Under these conditions, the licensor is unlikely to want to spend money to enter foreign markets. However, if the company can find an MNC that is already there and willing to add the product to its own current offerings, both sides can benefit from the arrangement. A second common instance of licensing is when foreign governments require newly entering firms to make a substantial direct investment in the country. By licensing to a firm already there, the licensee avoids entry costs. A third condition is

License
An agreement that allows one party to use an industrial property right in exchange for payment to the other party.

International Management in Action

Joint Venturing in Russia   www.russiatoday.com

Joint venturing is becoming an increasingly popular strategy for setting up international operations. Russia is particularly interested in these arrangements because of the benefits they offer for attracting foreign capital and helping the country tap its natural resource wealth. However, investors are finding that joint venturing in Russia and the other republics of the former Soviet Union can be fraught with problems. For example, Chevron, which has agreed to invest $10 billion over the next 25 years in developing the Tengiz oil field in Kazakhstan, recently found itself having to renegotiate the contract and drop its share of profits from 28 percent to under 20 percent. This became necessary because the original contract was negotiated with the Soviet Union under President Mikhail Gorbachev; after the breakup, the new government was unwilling to abide by the previous terms. Renegotiation is not the only problem facing joint-venture investors in Russia. Others include the following:

1. Many Russian partners view a joint venture as an opportunity to travel abroad and gain access to foreign currency; the business itself often is given secondary consideration.

2. Finding a suitable partner, negotiating the deal, and registering the joint venture often take up to a year, mainly because the Russians are unaccustomed to some of the basic steps in putting together business deals.

3. Russian partners typically try to expand joint ventures into unrelated activities, while foreign investors are more prone to minimizing risk and not overextending operations by getting into new areas.

4. Russians do not like to declare profits, because there is a 2-year tax holiday on profits that starts from the moment the first profits are declared. Foreign partners, on the other hand, are not influenced by this fact and often point out that because taxes must be paid in rubles, which have very little value, taxes are not a problem.

5. The government sometimes allows profits to be repatriated in the form of countertrade. However, much of what can be taken out of the country has limited value, because the government keeps control of those resources that are most salable in the world market.

These representative problems indicate why there is a growing reluctance on the part of some MNCs to enter into joint ventures in Russia. As one of them recently put it, "The country may well turn into an economic sink hole." As a result, many MNCs are very reluctant and are proceeding with caution.

that the licensor usually is a small firm that lacks financial and managerial resources. Finally, companies that spend a relatively large share of their revenues on research and development (R&D) are likely to be licensors, and those who spend very little on R&D are more likely to be licensees. In fact, some small R&D firms make a handsome profit every year by developing and licensing new products to large firms with diversified product lines.

Some licensors use their industrial property rights to develop and sell goods in certain areas of the world and license others to handle other geographic locales. This provides the licensor with a source of additional revenues, but the license usually is not good for much more than a decade. This is a major disadvantage of licensing. In particular, if the product is very good, the competition will develop improvement patents that allow it to sell similar goods or even new patents that make the current product obsolete. Nevertheless, for the period during which the agreement is in effect, a license can be a very low-cost way of gaining and exploiting foreign markets. Table 9-6 provides some comparisons between licensing and joint ventures and summarizes the major advantages and disadvantages of each.

Franchise

A business arrangement under which one party (the franchisor) allows another (the franchisee) to operate an enterprise using its trademark, logo, product line, and methods of operation in return for a fee.

Franchising   A **franchise** is a business arrangement under which one party (the franchisor) allows another (the franchisee) to operate an enterprise using its trademark, logo, product line, and methods of operation in return for a fee. Franchising is widely used in the fast-food and hotel/motel industries. The concept is very adaptable to the international arena, and with some minor adjustments for the local market, it can result in a highly profitable

Table 9-6
Partial Comparison of Global Strategic Alliances

Strategy	Organization Design	Advantages	Disadvantages	Critical Success Factors	Strategic Human Resources Management
Licensing—manufacturing industries	Technologies	Early standardization of design Ability to capitalize on innovations Access to new technologies Ability to control pace of industry evolution	New competitors created Possible eventual exit from industry Possible dependence on licensee	Selection of licensee unlikely to become a competitor Enforcement of patents and licensing agreements	Technical knowledge Training of local managers on-site
Licensing—servicing and franchises	Geography	Fast market entry Low capital cost	Quality control Trademark protection	Partners compatible in philosophies/values Tight performance standards	Socialization of franchisees and licensees with core values
Joint ventures—specialization across partners	Function	Learning a partner's skills Economics of scale Quasivertical integration Faster learning	Excessive dependence on partner for skills Deterrent to internal investment	Tight and specific performance criteria Entering a venture as "student" rather than "teacher" to learn skills from partner Recognizing that collaboration is another form of competition to learn new skills	Management development and training Negotiation skills Managerial rotation
Joint venture—shared value-adding	Product or line of business	Strengths of both partners pooled Faster learning along value chain Fast upgrading of technologic skills	High switching costs Inability to limit partner's access to information	Decentralization and autonomy from corporate parents Long "courtship" period Harmonization of management styles	Team-building Acculturation Flexible skills for implicit communication

Source: David Lei and John W. Slocum, Jr., "Global Strategic Alliances: Payoffs and Pitfalls," *Organizational Dynamics.* Winter 1991, p. 48. Used with permission.

business. In fast foods, McDonald's, Burger King, and Kentucky Fried Chicken have used franchise arrangements to expand their markets from Paris to Tokyo and from Cairo to Caracas. In the hotel business, Holiday Inn, among others, has been very successful in gaining worldwide presence through the effective use of franchisees.

Franchise agreements typically require payment of a fee up front and then a percentage of the revenues. In return, the franchisor provides assistance and, in some instances, may require the purchase of goods or supplies to ensure the same quality of goods or services worldwide. Franchising can be beneficial to both groups: It provides the franchisor with a new stream of income and the franchisee with a time-proven concept and products or services that can be quickly brought to market.

Export/Import Exporting or importing often are the only available choices for small firms wanting to go international. These choices also provide an avenue for larger firms that want to begin their international expansion with a minimum of investment. The paperwork associated with documentation and foreign-currency exchange can be turned over to an export management company to handle, or the firm can handle things itself by creating its own export department. The firm can turn to major banks or other specialists who, for a fee, will provide a variety of services, including letters of credit, currency conversion, and related financial assistance.

A number of potential problems face firms that plan to export. For example, if a foreign distributor does not work out well, some countries have strict rules about dropping that distributor. Therefore, an MNC with a contractual agreement with the distributor could be stuck with the distributor. If the firm decides to get more actively involved, it may make direct investments in marketing facilities, such as warehouses, sales offices, and transportation equipment, without making a direct investment in manufacturing facilities overseas.

When importing goods, many MNCs make deals with overseas suppliers who can provide a wide assortment. It is common to find U.S. firms purchasing supplies and components from Korea, Taiwan, and Hong Kong. In Europe, there is so much trade between EU countries that the entire process seldom is regarded as "international" in focus by the MNCs that are involved.

Exporting and importing can provide easy access to overseas markets; however, the strategy usually is transitional in nature. If the firm continues to do international business, it will get more actively involved in terms of investment.

The Role of the Functional Areas in Implementation

To implement strategies, MNCs must tap the primary functional areas of marketing, production, and finance. The following sections examine the roles of these functions in international strategy implementation.

Marketing The implementation of strategy from a marketing perspective must be determined on a country-by-country basis. What works from the standpoint of marketing in one locale may not necessarily succeed in another. In addition, the specific steps of a marketing approach often are dictated by the overall strategic plan, which in turn is based heavily on market analysis.

German auto firms in Japan are a good example of using marketing analysis to meet customer needs. Over the past 15 years, the Germans have spent millions of dollars to build dealer, supplier, and service-support networks in Japan, in addition to adapting their cars to Japanese customers' tastes. Volkswagen Audi Nippon has built a $320-million import facility on a deep-water port. This operation, which includes an inspection center and parts warehouse, can process 100,000 cars a year. Mercedes and BMW both have introduced lower-priced cars to attract a larger market segment, and BMW now offers a flat-fee, 3-year service contract on any new car, including parts. At the same time, German manufacturers work hard to offer first-class service in their dealerships. As a result, German automakers in recent years sell almost three times as many cars in Japan as their U.S. competitors do.[46]

The Japanese themselves also provide an excellent example of how the marketing process works. In many cases, Japanese firms have followed a strategy of first building up their market share at home and driving out imported goods. Then, the firms move into newly developed countries (e.g., Korea or Taiwan), honing their marketing skills as they go alone. Finally, the firms move into fully developed countries, ready to compete with the best available. This pattern of implementing strategy has been used in marketing autos, cameras, consumer electronics, home appliances, petrochemicals, steel, and watches. For some products, however, such as computers, the Japanese have moved from their home market directly into fully developed countries and then on to the newly developing nations. Finally, the Japanese have gone directly to developed countries to market products in some cases, because the market in Japan was too small. Such products include color TVs, videotape recorders, and sewing machines. In general, once a firm agrees on the goods it wants to sell in the international marketplace, then the specific marketing strategy is implemented.

The implementation of marketing strategy in the international arena is built around the well-known "four Ps" of marketing: product, price, promotion, and place. As noted in the example of the Japanese, firms often develop and sell a product in local or peripheral markets before expanding to major overseas targets. If the product is designed specifically to meet an overseas demand, however, the process is more direct. Price largely is a function of market demand. For example, the Japanese have found that the U.S. microcomputer market is price-sensitive; by introducing lower-priced clones, the Japanese have been able to make headway, especially in the portable laptop market. The last two Ps, promotion and place, are dictated by local conditions and often left in the hands of those running the subsidiary or affiliate. Local management may implement customer sales incentives, for example, or make arrangements with dealers and salespeople who are helping to move the product locally.

Production   Although marketing usually dominates strategy implementation, the production function also plays a role. If a company is going to export goods to a foreign market, the production process traditionally has been handled through domestic operations. In recent years, however, MNCs have found that whether they are exporting or producing the goods locally in the host country, consideration of worldwide production is important. For example, goods may be produced in foreign countries for export to other nations. Sometimes, a plant will specialize in a particular product and export it to all the MNC's markets; other times, a plant will produce goods only for a specific locale, such as Western Europe or South America. Still other facilities will produce one or more components that are shipped to a larger network of assembly plants. This latter option has been widely adopted by pharmaceutical firms and automakers such as Volkswagen and Honda.

If the firm operates production plants in different countries but makes no attempt to integrate its overall operations, the company is known as a **multidomestic.** A recent trend has been away from this scattered approach and toward global coordination of operations.

Finally, if the product is labor-intensive, as in the case of microcomputers, then the trend is to farm the product out to low-cost sites such as Mexico or Brazil, where the cost of labor is relatively low and the infrastructure (electric power, communications systems, transportation systems) is sufficient to support production. Sometimes, multiple sources of individual components are used; in other cases, only one or two are sufficient. In any event, careful coordination of the production function is needed when implementing the strategy, and the result is a product that is truly global in nature.

Multidomestic
A firm that operates production plants in different countries but makes no attempt to integrate overall operations.

Finance   Use of the finance function to implement strategy normally is developed at the home office and carried out by the overseas affiliate or branch. When a firm went international in the past, the overseas operation commonly relied on the local area for funds, but the rise of global financing has ended this practice. MNCs have learned that transferring funds from one place in the world to another, or borrowing funds in the international money markets, often is less expensive than relying on local sources. Unfortunately, there are problems in these transfers.

Such a problem is representative of those faced by MNCs using the finance function to implement their strategies. One of an MNC's biggest recent headaches when implementing strategies in the financial dimension has been the re-evaluation of currencies. For example, in the late 1990s the U.S. dollar increased in value against the Japanese yen. American overseas subsidiaries that held yen found their profits (in terms of dollars) declining. The same was true for those subsidiaries that held Mexican pesos when that government devalued the currency in the last few years. When this happens, a subsidiary's profit will decline.

When dealing with the inherent risk of volatile monetary exchange rates, some MNCs have bought currency options that (for a price) guarantee convertibility at a specified rate. Others have developed countertrade strategies, whereby they receive products in exchange for currency. For example, PepsiCo receives payment in vodka for its products sold in Russia. Countertrade continues to be a popular form of international business, especially in less developed countries and those with nonconvertible currencies.

World of Business Week Revisited

Thinking back to the *Business Week* article that began this chapter, it is easy to recognize the need for reliable and effective global strategic planning. Having read this chapter, you should now be aware of the need for multinationals to carefully and accurately conduct a strategic analysis when considering business dealings abroad. By assessing environmental opportunities and threats and recognizing internal strength and weaknesses, companies such as Jenoptik in the former East Germany are gaining world attention for their successful strategic planning skills. Through a restructuring process which included some necessary downsizing, acquisitions, and new management practices, Jenoptik has risen from the ranks of a distressed eastern-bloc company to a global powerhouse capable of gaining market share and increasing profitability. Realizing the growing need and benefits of strategic planning, answer these questions: (1) As managers from different nations come into contact with an MNC as customers or suppliers, what role does strategic planning play in this process? (2) What additional challenges might former communist nations face when formulating effective strategic plans that Western nations might not face?

Summary of Key Points

1. There is a growing need for strategic planning among MNCs. Some of the primary reasons include: foreign direct investment is increasing, planning is needed to coordinate and integrate increasingly diverse operations via an overall focus, and emerging international challenges require strategic planning.

2. A strategic plan can take on an economic focus, a political focus, a quality focus, an administrative coordination focus, or some variation of the four. In addition, an MNC typically is predisposed toward an ethnocentric, polycentric, regiocentric, or geocentric orientation. Companies may use a combination of these orientations in their strategic planning, but geocentric is the one employed most commonly by global companies.

3. Strategic planning is used by more MNCs every year, although no definitive evidence proves that this process always results in higher profitability. As with

other aspects of international management, the particular situation largely will dictate the success of a strategic plan.

4. Strategy formulation consists of several steps. First, the MNC carries out external environmental scanning to identify opportunities and threats. Next, the firm conducts an internal resource analysis of company strengths and weaknesses. Strategic goals then are formulated in light of the results of these external and internal analyses.

5. Strategy implementation is the process of providing goods and services in accord with the predetermined plan of action. This implementation typically involves such considerations as: deciding where to locate operations, carrying out an entry and ownership strategy, and using functional strategies to implement the plan. Functional strategies focus on marketing, production, and finance.

Key Terms

administrative coordination
economic imperative
environmental scanning
ethnocentric predisposition
franchise
geocentric predisposition

joint venture
key factor for success (KFS)
license
multidomestic
political imperative
polycentric predisposition

quality imperative
regiocentric predisposition
strategic planning
strategy implementation
wholly owned subsidiary

Review and Discussion Questions

1. Of the four imperatives discussed in this chapter—economic, political, quality, and administration—which would be most important to IBM in its efforts to make inroads in the Pacific Rim market? Would this emphasis be the same as that in the United States, or would IBM be giving primary attention to one of the other imperatives? Explain.

2. If a locally based manufacturing firm with sales of $350 million decided to enter the EU market by setting up operations in France, which orientation would be the most effective: ethnocentric, polycentric, regiocentric, or geocentric? Why? Explain your choice.

3. When a large MNC such as Ford Motor sets strategic goals, what areas are targeted for consideration? Incorporate the information from Table 9-4 in your answer. Would this list of strategic goals be very different from that formulated by the manufacturing firm in question 2? Why or why not?

4. One of the most common entry strategies for MNCs is the joint venture. Why are so many companies opting for this strategy? Would a fully owned subsidiary be a better choice?

5. In recent years McDonald's has found that its international franchise operation has been producing more revenue per unit than its domestic operations. What might account for this? Is it likely that the firm will continue its international expansion? Why?

6. Mercedes recently changed its U.S. strategy by announcing that it is developing cars for the $30,000 to $45,000 price range (as well as its typical upper-end cars). What might have accounted for this change in strategy? In your answer, include a discussion of the implications from the standpoints of marketing, production, and finance.

Internet Exercise: Dropping in on Dell Computer

One of the largest and fastest growing computer firms in the world is Dell Computer. Dell does not sell its products in retail stores. In order to purchase a Dell computer, it is necessary to go to the firm's web site, indicate the desired machine's configuration, and then arrange for the financing. Go to Dell's web site at www.dell.com and examine some of the background on the firm and the computers it is now offering. Then answer these questions: How do you think international strategic planning is reflected in what you see in the web site? What major strategic planning steps would Dell need to carry out in order to remain a world leader in this direct marketing niche? What potential threat, if it occurred, would prove most disastrous for Dell, and what could the company do to deal with the possibility of this negative development?

Poland

Poland is the sixth-largest country in Europe. It is bordered by Germany, the Czech Republic, and Slovakia in the west and south and by the former Soviet Union republics of the Ukraine in the south, Belarus in the east, and Lithuania in the northeast. The northwest section of the country is located on the Baltic Sea. Named after the Polane, a Slavic tribe that lived more than a thousand years ago, Poland has beautiful countryside and rapidly growing cities. Rolling hills and rugged mountains rise in southern Poland. There are approximately 40 million Poles, and GNP is around $250 billion. The country still is highly agricultural, and up to one-third of the population engages in farm work. The people have a rich heritage (at one point, the Poles ruled an empire that stretched across most of central Europe), many folk traditions (which the former communist government discouraged), and strong loyalty to the Roman Catholic church. The government is now dominated by former communists (socialists), and Lech Walesa, the democratic hero, was defeated in the 1993 presidential election. However, the socialists still are trying to establish a free-market system. Predictions are that the coming years will remain very difficult as Poland continues to undo some of the major mistakes made by the communists.

The Poles indeed have made considerable progress in establishing a viable economy for the years ahead. To take advantage of this economic outlook, a medium-sized Canadian manufacturing firm has begun thinking about renovating a plant near Warsaw and building small power tools for the expanding Central and Eastern European market. The company's logic is fairly straightforward. There appears to be no competition in this niche, because there has been little demand for power tools in this area. As these countries begin turning more and more toward a free-market model, however, they will have to increase their productivity if they hope to compete with Western European nations. Small power tools are one of the products they will need to accomplish this goal.

A second reason for the Canadian firm's interest in setting up operations in Poland is that the price of labor is fairly low. Other nearby countries have lower wage rates, but Warsaw, the company's specific choice, has a cadre of well-trained factory workers that could be transferred to this renovated factory. Product quality in the production of these tools is critical to success, so for this Canadian firm, Poland is an ideal location.

In addition, Poland likely will continue receiving economic and moral support from Western Europe as well as Canada and the United States. Exporting from Poland to Western Europe or the United States therefore should be easier than from more developed countries. Moreover, the manufacturing firm is convinced that its proximity to Russia will open up that market as well. Transportation costs to Russia will be low vis-à-vis competitors, and the Russians currently are looking for ways to increase their own worker productivity.

Finally, there likely will be little competition for the next couple of years, because small power tools do not carry a very large markup and no other manufacturer is attempting to tap what the Canadian firm views as "an emerging market for the twenty-first century." However, a final decision on this matter is going to have to wait until the company has made a thorough evaluation of the market and the competitive nature of the industry.
www.poland.pl

Questions

1. What are some current issues facing Poland? What is the climate for doing business in Poland today?

2. Is the Canadian manufacturing firm using an economic, political, or quality imperative approach to strategy?

3. How should the firm carry out the environmental scanning process? Would the process be of any practical value?

4. What are two key factors for success that will be important if this project is to succeed?

Go East, Young People, Go East

Amanda Brendhart, Jose Gutierrez, and Rhoda Schreiber founded and are partners in a small electronics firm, Electronic Visions, that has developed and patented some state-of-the-art computer components. Visions has had moderate success selling these components to large U.S.-based computer manufacturers. The biggest problem is that in recent months, the computer market has begun to turn soft, and many of the manufacturers are offering substantial discounts to generate sales. Therefore, although Visions has found an increasing demand for its product, it now is grossing less money than it was 4 months ago.

To increase both sales and profit, the partners have decided to expand into Asia. Although this region is known for its low-cost computer production, the group believes that countries such as China, South Korea, and Taiwan soon will become more lucrative markets, because the U.S. government will make these countries open their doors to imports more fully. If trade barriers are removed, the partners are convinced that they can export the goods at very competitive prices. In addition, the partners intend to find a partner in each market so that they have someone to help with the marketing and financing of the product.

Of course, if the components can be produced more cheaply with local labor, the partnership is willing to forgo exporting and have everything produced locally.

At present, the group is trying to answer three questions. First, what is the best entry strategy to use in reaching the Asian markets? Second, what type of marketing strategy will be most effective? Third, if production must be coordinated between the United States and an overseas country, what is the best way to handle this? The partners believe that over the next 2 months, they will have a very good idea of what is going to happen regarding the opening of Asian markets. In the interim, they intend to work up a preliminary strategic plan that they can use to guide them.

Questions

1. What type of entry and ownership approach would you recommend? Defend your choice.

2. How could the partners use the four Ps of marketing to help implement strategy?

3. If production must be globally coordinated, will Visions have a major problem? Why or why not?

Chapter 10

Managing Political Risk and Negotiations

Objectives of the Chapter

Firms go international to become more competitive and profitable. Unfortunately, many risks accompany this internationalization. One of the biggest involves the political situation of the countries in which the MNC does business, and MNCs must be able to assess political risk and conduct skillful negotiations. An overview of the political environment in selected areas of the world has already been provided, but this chapter specifically examines what political risk is all about and how MNCs try to manage this risk. One major way is through effective evaluation and risk reduction. This process extends from risk identification and quantification to the formulation of appropriate responses, such as integration and protective and defensive techniques. This chapter also examines how negotiations are managed and actually carried out, and it reviews some of the common tactics that are used. The specific objectives of this chapter are:

1. **EXAMINE** how MNCs evaluate political risk.

2. **PRESENT** some common methods used for managing and reducing political risk.

3. **DISCUSS** how the negotiation process works, and how cultural differences can affect this process.

4. **DESCRIBE** some common negotiation tactics.

BusinessWeek

The World of Business Week:

How to Reshape the World Financial System

It once was comforting to believe that the international financial system was a just and fair god. Countries that ran big budget deficits and borrowed from overseas to finance consumption, rather than investment, would be punished by capital flight and depreciating currencies. Nations pursuing prudent policies would be rewarded by strong growth and a steady stream of money from global investors.

But when the world's top finance ministers and bankers gather at the beginning of October in Washington for the annual meetings of the International Monetary Fund and the World Bank, they face a different reality. Despite being held up for years by the IMF as models of development for the rest of the world, countries such as South Korea, Thailand, Malaysia, and Indonesia have been ravaged by capital flight.

There is no perfect solution to the global mess—but *Business Week* believes there are ways to make things better. Some steps are easy: Everyone agrees that there needs to be better information and heightened regulation, both in developing and industrial countries. But the far bigger task is to tame the anarchic nature of the global financial markets.

The IMF Option

International finance is no longer the province of a relatively small number of large financial institutions. With the growth of rapid communications, investment banks, mutual funds, hedge funds, and multinational corporations all can jump in and out of markets at the click of a mouse. At the same time, financial wizards are creating swarms of new types of securities—ranging from derivatives to emerging-market debt—where the risks are hard to assess and price correctly.

Indeed, the current crisis stems, in part, from the breakdown of pricing discipline in global markets. Capital poured into emerging economies with little attention to the creditworthiness of the borrowers. As a result, countries like Thailand and Indonesia were able to borrow in dollars at far lower interest rates than they would be required to pay at home, encouraging them to take on far more foreign debt than they could handle.

When problems arose, everyone tried to get their money out as quickly as possible, making the crisis even worse. Complicating matters still more, there were no clear guidelines for which private-sector lenders had to share the cost of cleaning up the financial mess.

Incentives

Formally bringing the private sector into the rescue process would cut the likelihood of future financial crises. Because lenders know they would not be bailed out by the IMF, they would have an incentive to pay closer attention to the quality of their investments. They would also likely want higher returns on money invested in emerging countries. As a result, the existence of a bankruptcy option could moderate flows of destabilizing hot money to emerging markets.

When a financial crisis does occur, a borrowing country would be less likely to be crushed under the weight of its bad debts. Instead, the losses would be shared with institutions that made the loans originally, with the goal of getting the country back to economic health as soon as possible. This would reduce the chances of a spillover to other emerging countries. Moreover, if existing debt can be marked down or rolled over quickly, it becomes easier for a country that hit the skids to tap private capital markets again.

Of course, a global system modeled on Chapter 11 might not help every country with financial woes. Russia, for one, suffers from such severe internal problems that no fixes to the international system are likely to help. Japan, the linchpin of the Asian economy, is stuck in recession, unable to address its own enormous debt problems because of political paralysis.

Beyond that, some bankers object that allowing debtor countries to get out from under some of their obligations is a recipe for disaster. A Chapter 11 for nations is "the worst idea I've heard in my life," says Paulo Ferraz, CEO of Banco Bozano

Simonsen, one of Brazil's premier investment banks. "It would be the end of the global financial system."

History suggests that in times of crisis, demanding full repayment of debt can be an enormous mistake. After World War I, the victors' moves to collect war debts from each other and reparations from Germany helped create the conditions that bred the Great Depression and World War II. In the 1980s, Latin America struggled for years under debt problems until a deal was struck allowing capital to flow in and growth to resume. By contrast, the U.S. system doesn't require companies or people who fall on hard times to spend the rest of their life paying debts back. "Once your old mistakes get big enough, they drown your future," says Elizabeth Warren, a bankruptcy expert at the Harvard Law School. "Bankruptcy is a way to say to creditors, 'Get real. The money's not there.'"

Perhaps the hardest problem is how to decide when a debt standstill is appropriate. Clearly, it's important that a country not be able to unilaterally declare a debt moratorium—that's a sure route to chaos. Instead, the IMF should take the lead role in certifying when a country is in deep enough trouble to trigger the restructuring mechanism.

Both capital controls and a Chapter 11-type system have pluses and minuses. In the short run, capital controls are clearly an easier policy to adopt. Countries can implement them unilaterally, and they do not require new financing. By contrast, a formal debt-rescheduling scheme would be much harder to actually put into practice.

But capital controls do not solve the underlying problems of the world financial system. Rather, they are a temporary stopgap. A set of rules for global financial markets that codifies the now messy process of debt rescheduling may be difficult to achieve any time soon. But in the long run, moving in the direction of a system that prices risk appropriately and keeps capital markets open is the right thing to do.
www.imf.org

Source: **Reprinted from October 12, 1998, pp. 113–116 issue of *Business Week* by special permission, copyright © 1998 by McGraw-Hill Companies, Inc.**

This opening article helps explain why political risk is becoming an increasingly important area of consideration for international managers. When a nation's economy begins to falter, that government will take steps such as discussed in the vignette to right its economic ship. Other examples besides capital controls and bankruptcy laws include new regulations to protect local businesses from international competition, devaluation of the currency, and limits on profits being taken out of the country. These steps can have a negative effect on the profitability of multinationals doing business in this country. Although an individual MNC can do little to directly influence a government's policies, as the *Business Week* story and this chapter will show, MNCs can evaluate and manage such political risk and effectively negotiate for desired outcomes within a given political framework.

The Nature and Analysis of Political Risk

Political risk
The likelihood that a business's foreign investment will be constrained by a host government's policy.

Applied to international management, **political risk** is the likelihood that a multinational corporation's foreign investment will be constrained by a host government's policies. In the past, this risk was typified by the probability that the company's investment would be expropriated, as in the case of when Castro took over in Cuba, seizing the assets of private investors. However, over the past decade political risk has become a much more sophisticated and challenging area facing international management. Few governments today are interested in outright seizing the assets of multinational corporations. Rather, almost all countries are interested in attracting and sustaining MNC investment. The problem today facing MNCs is emerging economies, which are attractive markets for MNCs, may begin to falter. Then the governments of these struggling economies may make policy decisions that negatively impact on the MNCs. Examples include freezing the movement of assets out of the country, placing limits on remittance of profits or capital, devaluing of the currency, refusing to give import licenses needed for the acquisition of materials and equipment, and refusing to abide by the contractual terms of agreements that have been previously signed with the MNC. These forms of political risk are unfortunately becoming increasingly common for today's MNCs.

In the case of China, for example, the government had been very anxious to be admitted to the World Trade Organization (WTO). However, the United States and Japan, among others, opposed their admission until China opened its doors wider to foreign business. Now China has concluded that it is unlikely to gain WTO status any time soon, so it has decided, at least for the time being, to go its own way and make decisions that are in its own best short-run interests.[1] In the process, China has now started introducing changes that are creating new political risks for MNCs doing business there. One analysis recently noted:

> A series of recent moves by Chinese authorities—price controls, currency restrictions, limits on sale of state-owned companies—seem to reflect a slowdown in the nation's effort to shift from a planned to a market economy. Whether such steps are justifiably cautious or simply timid, economists and business executives agree that they are likely to further deter trade and investment in the near future. Today, China's central bank announced new restrictions on foreign exchange transactions, an attempt to control the flow of convertible currency out of the country. Officially described as a crackdown on illegal transactions, the moves will effectively make it more difficult for both domestic and international companies to move money in and out of China.[2]

These actions by the Chinese closely followed new restrictions on foreign investment in the telecommunications industry, one of the fastest growing industries in China and one that had attracted a great deal of attention from international investors.

These government policies cast a damper on the plans of MNCs that were considering going into China or expanding present operations there. In other words, there is greater political risk. For example, American MNCs must also consider the political risk of doing business in China, but Chinese MNCs must also assess the political risk inherent in doing business in the United States. The U.S. government has begun to review its trade policy with China. In particular, American trade officials claim that China has taken for granted its relationship with the United States and if markets there are not opened for American goods there will be reciprocal action against Chinese firms that are selling in the United States.[3] Given the enormous trade deficit that the Americans now have with China, this situation could end up creating major political risks for Chinese MNCs doing business in the politically stable, but very risky, United States.

Macro and Micro Analysis of Political Risk

Firms evaluate political risk in a number of ways. One is through **macro political risk analysis**, which reviews major political decisions that are likely to affect all business conducted in the country. For example, China's decision regarding restrictions on foreign exchange transactions is a macro political risk because it affects all MNCs. **Micro political risk analysis** is directed toward government policies and actions that influence selected sectors of the economy or specific foreign businesses. China's government policies regarding investment in the telecommunications industry fall into the micro political risk category. The following examines both of these areas—macro and micro political risk—in more depth.

Macro political risk analysis Analysis that reviews major political decisions likely to affect all enterprises in the country.

Micro political risk analysis Analysis directed toward government policies and actions that influence selected sectors of the economy or specific foreign businesses in the country.

Macro Risk Issues and Examples In recent years macro risk analysis has become of increasing concern to MNCs because of the growing number of countries that are finding their economies in trouble as in Southeast Asia, or, even worse, unable to make the transition to a market-driven economy. A good example of the latter is Russia, which has recently been tightening controls on the flow of foreign currencies. This represents a change in direction to the free market principles that the Russians had been following in order to insure that it continued to receive assistance from the International Monetary Fund. To date, the Russians do not totally ban foreign currencies, a step that would deeply anger many Russian nationals who protect themselves from inflation by holding their savings in U.S. dollars. However, the recent developments do limit access to foreign currency by the government setting the ruble exchange rate. The exchange rate would not only be based on free market principles of supply and demand, but also on the country's balance of payments, the size of the central bank's foreign-exchange and gold reserves, and the inflation rate. Additionally, this development in Russia would affect MNCs doing business there by allowing foreign currency transactions to be made only through the central bank.

As in the case of China discussed earlier, these developments not only affect outside MNCs doing business in Russia, but would put restrictions on Russian MNCs. For example, Russian MNCs would be required to sell 75 percent of their foreign currency export earnings at the state-set exchange rate. This is in addition to regulations that are already in place that require these businesses to sell their export earnings on licensed exchanges and let them purchase foreign currency only to fulfill contract obligations. Quite clearly, businesses that export goods from Russia would find themselves facing increased risk as these developments unfold.[4]

Other examples of developments that fall within the realm of macro political risk are provided by India, a country whose legal system is typified by a labyrinth of laws and bureaucratic red tape. In recent years, the Indian high courts have had a backlog of over 3 million cases. Moreover, approximately one-third of these cases have been winding their way through the legal system for more than 5 years. So while the government touts the fact that Indian law offers strong protection to foreign firms against counterfeiters, an MNC finding that it must rely on the Indian judicial system to enforce its proprietory rights is likely to be sadly disappointed. As a result, many MNCs accept this risk as a price of doing business in India and formulate strategies for managing the problem. A good example is provided by the Timken Company of Canton, Ohio, which makes bearings and alloy steel. When Timken found that the Indian market was rampant with fake Timken products, the MNC's initial reaction was to sue the counterfeiters. However, after realizing how long this would take, the MNC opted for a different strategy. Management switched the packaging of its products from cardboard boxes to heat-sealed plastic with eight-color printing and a hologram which could not be forged. Result: Within months the counterfeit market began drying up.

Timken is not alone, there are many counterfeit operations in India because the slow-moving judicial system encourages noncompliance. In fact, some counterfeiters have found that by filing counter suits they can tie up the case in court for years. For example, Ziff Davis Publishing, an American unit of Japan's Softbank Corporation, brought suit against a former Indian licensee for continuing to publish one of its computer magazines even though the license had expired. The defendant has now frivolously countersued, arguing that the magazine is generic and not proprietary. A similar brazen example recently hit Time Warner, owner of cable-television movie channel Home Box Office (HBO). This MNC won a temporary injunction preventing an Indian company from calling its movie channel Cable Box Office or CBO for short. So that firm has now changed its name to CVO standing for Cable Video Opera. Time Warner is pursuing damages for trademark infringement, but it will probably be years before there is a final settlement of the suit.[5]

Many other newly emerging economies besides the big countries of China, Russia and India also present macro political risks for MNCs. In Vietnam, for example, the government has earned a bad name among foreign investors because of all the pitfalls they have to face. In fact, until very recently the communist Vietnamese government required all foreign investors to establish joint ventures with local partners. And even with this arrangement, getting things done proved to be extremely slow and difficult because many levels of bureaucracy must be dealt with. One international manager described his MNCs experience this way, "The negotiations would follow a serpentine path, with breakthroughs in one session often being erased in the next."[6] To date, macro political risks in Vietnam remain high and investors find themselves proceeding with caution.

Another example of a macro consideration of political risk is an analysis of what would happen to a company's investment if opposition government leaders were to take control. Many U.S. companies in Iran failed to forecast the fall of the Shah and rise of Khomeini. As a result, they lost their investment. Because of this Iranian experience and the situation in Iraq under militant dictator Saddam Hussein, however, many multinationals now are very reluctant to invest very heavily in most Middle Eastern countries. In the late 1990s, the government of Iran appeared to be interested in attracting foreign investment, but there is still a great deal of concern that this region is too politically explosive. Eastern Europe appears to be a better bet, as seen by the millions of dollars that MNCs have poured into countries such as Hungary and Poland. This geographic region also is regarded as politically risky, however, as shown in the Bosnian conflict, the breakup of Czechoslovakia, and the political instability in the entire region. As a result, many multi-nationals have been tempering their expansion plans in Eastern Europe.

Still another area of consideration in macro political risk is that of government corruption. Common examples include bribery and the use of government rules and regulations that require the inclusion of certain locals in lucrative business deals. In fact, one of the most commonly cited reasons for the economic problems in Indonesia in recent years is the corrupt practices of the government. Because the family of former President Suharto was involved in virtually every big business deal that took place under his regime, many loans and major projects were approved by banks and government agencies simply because these family members were part of the process. However, when these loans or projects ran into trouble, more money was poured in to shore up things—and no one dared to challenge these unsound decisions. Many multinational firms became involved in this so-called "Asian-Way" of conducting business in this part of the world. Even U.S.–based MNCs, that by law are prohibited from offering bribes, were finding ways to circumvent these roadblocks. Notes one team of *Wall Street Journal* analysts:

> Aggressive European and Asian companies commonly use payoffs to gain access to new markets; some countries even consider bribes tax-deductible business expenses. Virtually alone among major economies, the U.S. forbids its companies from paying bribes to win international business, regardless of what rivals do. And so, to compete, U.S. companies have found new ways to make friends, influence people and win contracts. Some take foreign officials on junkets to Disney World. Others hire middlemen who—known to them or not—do the dirty work. And most multinationals do make small facilitation payments to hasten building inspections, telephone installations and customs clearances.[7]

What are the most and the least corrupt nations in the world? Table 10-1 provides the results of a recent survey of 85 nations that ranked the countries based on a wide variety of criteria. About half of the nations in the world were omitted from the survey because of the absence of reliable data. The United States ended up in 17th position. One reason for this apparent low ranking, in the view of analysts, is because the American press is very good at ferreting out stories about corruption; so in the United States practices that would go unnoticed in other countries ranked ahead of it, end up widely publicized in the local newspaper or reported on television and thus make the United States appear relatively worse than it may really be.

Micro Risk Issues and Examples Micro risk issues often take forms such as industry regulation, taxes on specific types of business activity, and various restrictive local laws. The essence of these micro risk issues is that some MNCs are treated differently from others. A good recent example was the Clinton administration's threat to implement trade sanctions against Japanese luxury cars in the United States. Faced with the loss of a major market, Japanese negotiators eventually agreed that their country's automakers would buy more U.S. parts, that their government would take steps to open its market for repair parts and encourage domestic auto dealers to sell more U.S. cars, and that Toyota, Honda, and Mitsubishi all would build more facilities in the United States.[8] These terms helped to reduce the U.S. trade imbalance with Japan. Such negotiations likely will not be the last, however, as the United States continues to seek greater access to the Japanese auto market. One reason is because the Europeans have been quite successful in negotiating a managed trade agreement with the Japanese, and the United States would like to do the same. For example, while Japanese firms dominate almost 30 percent of the U.S. market, their share of the European market is a mere 11 percent, and the Europeans have negotiated successfully for large quotas of European-made parts in Japanese cars built in Europe.[9]

Another more recent example of micro political risk is the situation faced by MNCs importing steel into the U.S. market. In 1992 American steelmakers filed more than 80

Table 10–1			
Corruption Rankings of Select Countries (Least to Most)			
Ranking	**Country**	**Ranking**	**Country**
1	Denmark	42	Uruguay
2	Finland	43	South Korea, Zimbabwe
3	Sweden	45	Malawi
4	New Zealand	46	Brazil
5	Iceland	47	Belarus
6	Canada	48	Slovak Republic
7	Singapore	49	Jamaica
8	Netherlands, Norway	50	Morocco
10	Switzerland	51	El Salvador
11	Australia, Britain, Luxembourg	52	China, Zambia
14	Ireland	54	Turkey
15	Germany	55	Ghana, Mexico, Philippines, Senegal
16	Hong Kong		
17	Austria, United States	59	Cote d'Ivoire, Guatemala
19	Israel	61	Argentina, Nicaragua, Romania, Thailand, Yugoslavia
20	Chile		
21	France		
22	Portugal	66	Bulgaria, Egypt, India
23	Botswana, Spain	69	Bolivia, Ukraine
25	Japan	71	Latvia, Pakistan
26	Estonia	73	Uganda
27	Costa Rica	74	Kenya, Vietnam
28	Belgium	76	Russia
29	Malaysia, Namibia, Taiwan	77	Ecuador, Venezuela
32	South Africa	79	Colombia
33	Hungary, Mauritius, Tunisia	80	Indonesia
36	Greece	81	Nigeria, Tanzania
37	Czech Republic	83	Honduras
38	Jordan	84	Paraguay
39	Italy, Poland	85	Cameroon
41	Peru		

Source: Reported in *Miami Herald,* September 23, 1998, p. 8A.

complaints against 20 nations on a single day. They charged that foreign steelmakers were dumping their products in the U.S. market at artificially low prices. By 1998, the industry again demanded action against foreign producers who, in the first six months of that year, doubled their imports into the American market. Domestic producers charged that Brazil, Japan, and Russia steelmakers were dumping steel in the United States at unfairly low prices. What was even more troubling was that the American producers were in the process of negotiating with big auto and appliance makers for the steel that is sold under long-term contracts. Since steel prices had dropped sharply because of the alleged "dumping," the American firms were concerned that they would end up getting locked into contracts that offered very little, if any, profit. The American steelmakers were insisting that their government force foreign producers to raise their prices.[10]

    Still another example of micro political risk is provided by countries in South America that face continued indebtedness and have introduced a variety of policies to promote exports and discourage imports. MNCs that feel they cannot abide by these policies will stay out; however, some that are looking for a location from which to produce and export goods will view these same government policies as very attractive. Table 10-2 lists criteria that MNCs could use to evaluate the degree of political risk.

Expropriation

The seizure of businesses by a host country with little, if any, compensation to the owners.

Analyzing the Expropriation Risk

Expropriation is the seizure of businesses with little, if any, compensation to the owners. Such seizures of foreign enterprises by developing countries were quite common in the old

Table 10–2
A Guide to Evaluation of Political Risk

External factors affecting subject country	*Other important groups:*
Prospects for foreign conflict	Unions and labor movements
Relations with border countries	Military, special groups within military
Regional instabilities	Families
Alliances with major and regional powers	Business and financial communities
Sources of key raw materials	Intelligentsia
Major foreign markets	Students
Policy toward United States	Religious groups
U.S. policy toward country	Media
Internal groupings (points of power)	Regional and local governments
Government in power:	Social and environmental activists
Key agencies and officials	Cultural, linguistic, and ethnic groups
Legislative entrenched bureaucracies	Separatist movements
Policies—economic, financial, social, labor, etc.	Foreign communities
Pending legislation	Potential competitors and customers
Attitude toward private sector	Internal factors
Power networks	Power struggles amongst elites
Political parties (in and out of power):	Ethnic confrontations
Policies	Regional struggles
Leading and emerging personalities	Economic factors affecting stability (consumer inflation, price and
Internal power struggles	wage controls, unemployment, supply shortages, taxation, etc.)
Sector and area strengths	Anti-establishment movements
Future prospects for retaining or gaining power	Factors affecting a specific project
	(Custom-designed for each project)

Note: Information in the table is an abridged version of Probe's Political Agenda Worksheet, which may serve as a guide for corporate executives initiating their own political evaluations. Probe International is located in Stamford, Conn.

Source: Benjamin Weinger, "What Executives Should Know about Political Risk," *Management Review,* January 1992, p. 20.

days. In addition, some takeovers were caused by **indigenization laws**, which required that nationals hold a majority interest in the operation. In the main, expropriation is more likely to occur in non-Western governments that are poor, relatively unstable, and suspicious of foreign multinationals.

> **Indigenization laws**
> Laws that require that nations hold a majority interest in the operation.

    Some firms are more vulnerable to expropriation than others. Those at greatest risk often are in extractive, agricultural, or infrastructural industries such as utilities and transportation because of the importance of these industries to the country. In addition, large firms often are more likely targets than small firms, because more is to be gained by expropriating from large firms.

    MNCs can take a wide variety of strategies to minimize their chances of expropriation. They can bring in local partners. They can limit the use of high technology so that if the firm is expropriated, the country cannot duplicate the technology. They also can acquire an affiliate that depends on the parent company for key areas of the operation, such as financing, research, and technology transfer, so that no practical value exists in seizing the affiliate.

The Role of Operational Profitability in Risk Analysis

Although expropriation is a major consideration, most MNCs are more directly concerned with operational profitability.[11] Will they be able to make the desired return on investment? A number of government regulations can have a negative impact on their profitability. Requiring MNCs to use domestic suppliers instead of bringing in components or raw materials from other company-owned facilities or purchasing them more cheaply in the world market is one such regulation. Another is a restriction on the amount of profit that can be taken out of the country. A third is the wages and salaries that must be paid to the employees. Despite these difficulties, MNCs have become very interested in designing models and frameworks for helping them to better understand and manage their political risk.

Managing Political Risk

For well over two decades, businesses have been looking for ways to manage their political risk. Quite often, the process begins with a detailed analysis of the various risks with which the MNC will be confronted, including development of a comprehensive framework that identifies the various risks and then assigns a quantitative risk or rating factor to them.

Developing a Comprehensive Framework

A comprehensive framework for managing political risk should consider all political risks and identify those that are most important. Schmidt has offered a three-dimensional framework that combines political risks, general investments, and special investments.[12] Figure 10-1 illustrates this framework, and the following sections examine each dimension in detail.

Transfer risks
Government policies that limit the transfer of capital, payments, production, people, and technology in and out of the country.

Operational risks
Government policies and procedures that directly constrain management and performance of local operations.

Ownership-control risks
Government policies or actions that inhibit ownership or control of local operations.

Conglomerate investment
A type of high-risk investment in which goods or services produced are not similar to those produced at home.

Political Risks   Political risks can be broken down into three basic categories: transfer risks, operational risks, and ownership-control risks. **Transfer risks** stem from government policies that limit the transfer of capital, payments, production, people, and technology in or out of the country. Examples include tariffs on exports and imports as well as restrictions on exports, dividend remittance, and capital repatriation. **Operational risks** result from government policies and procedures that directly constrain the management and performance of local operations. Examples include price controls, financing restrictions, export commitments, taxes, and local-sourcing requirements. **Ownership control risks** are brought about by government policies or actions that inhibit ownership or control of local operations. Examples include foreign ownership limitations, pressure for local participation, confiscation, expropriation, and abrogation of proprietary rights. For example, the Russian government recently cancelled an agreement with the Exxon Corporation that would have allowed the firm to tap huge oil deposits in the country's far north. The Russian minister for natural resources cited "legal irregularities" as the reason for the decision. As a result, the $1.5 billion project came to a grinding halt. Commenting on the government's action, one Western investment banker in Russia said that "it raises the question of whether a deal is a deal in Russia because Exxon is meticulous to a fault in following the letter of the law."[13] In any event, the decision provides a good example of ownership control risks. Still another is provided in "International Management in Action: Sometimes It's All Politics."

General Nature of Investment   The general nature of investment examines whether the company is making a conglomerate, vertical, or horizontal investment (see Figure 10-1). In a **conglomerate investment**, the goods or services produced are not simi-

Figure 10–1

A Three-Dimensional Framework for Assessing Political Risk

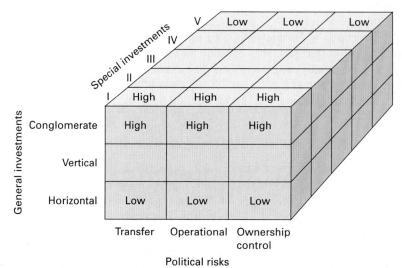

Source: David A. Schmidt, "Analyzing Political Risk," *Business Horizons,* July–August 1986, p. 50. Copyright 1986 by the Foundation for the School of Business at Indiana University. Used with permission.

International Management in Action

Sometimes It's All Politics   www. india-times.com/index.shtml

One of the biggest problems in doing business internationally is that yesterday's agreement with a government may be cancelled or delayed by today's politicians who disagree with that earlier decision. Enron, the Houston-based U.S. energy consortium, discovered this when its power project in Dabhol, India, became the focal point of political interest. India's economic nationalists began accelerating a campaign to scrap a high-profile, U.S.-backed power project despite warnings of potential damage to the confidence of foreign investors in the country. These politicians wanted to abandon the $28 billion deal as well as all other power projects in the country that had been approved under the government's "fast track" provisions. The contract for the two-stage, 2,000+ megawatt plant was signed before the current politicians came to power in Maharashtra, the state where Dabhol is located.

What effect would this political move have on foreign investment in India? A number of foreign investors indicated that if the Enron project were cancelled, they would review their investment plans for the country. A survey of international energy companies by the East-West Center in Hawaii found that of 13 Asian economies, India's investment climate ranked fifth from the bottom for power-sector investment. This seemed to have little effect on the politicians, who proceeded to cancel the project. Members of the political opposition, who supported the project, called it a mere political ploy designed to appeal to voters in the upcoming elections, and they urged foreign investors to sit tight and ride out the political storm. Many of these investors appeared to be apprehensive about taking such advice, and Enron announced plans for taking the case to international arbitration to reclaim the $300 million they have invested in the project—as well as $300 million in damages.

The political climate in India is not unique. Russia also offers its share of jitters to investors. In particu-lar, many joint ventures that were created during the Gorbachev era now are having problems. A good example is Moscow's Radisson-Slavjanskaya Hotel venture, in which American Business Centers of Irvine, California, owns a 40 percent stake. American Business Centers manages several floors of offices in the hotel, and now that the venture is making money, it appears that the Irvine firm's Russian partners and the Radisson hotel people are trying to oust them. The president of American Business Centers claims that his partners feel they do not need him any longer.

The dilemma faced by American Business Centers is becoming increasingly common in Russia. For example, the Seattle-based firm Radio Page entered into a joint venture with Moscow Public Telephone Network and another Russian company in 1992 to offer paging services. Together, they built a system of telephone pagers in the Moscow region. Radio Page held a 51 percent stake. When annual revenues hit $5 million and the venture was on the verge of making $1 million, however, the agreement began to unravel. The Russian partners demanded control of the operation and even threatened to pull the critical radio frequencies if they did not get their way.

There is little that foreign joint-venture firms doing business in high-risk countries can do except try to negotiate with their partners. For instance, the political situation in Russia is so unstable that support from one government ministry may be offset by opposition from another, or worse yet, the individuals supporting the foreign firm may be ousted from their jobs tomorrow. Economic considerations tend to be the main reason why firms seek international partners, but sometimes, it seems that everything boils down to politics and the risks associated with dealing in this political environment.

---

lar to those produced at home. These types of investments usually are rated as high risk, because foreign governments see them as providing fewer benefits to the country and greater benefits to the MNC than other investments. **Vertical investments** include the production of raw materials or intermediate goods that are to be processed into final products. These investments run the risk of being taken over by the government because they are export-oriented, and governments like a business that helps it to generate foreign capital. **Horizontal investments** involve the production of goods or services that are the same as those produced at home. These investments typically are made with an eye toward satisfying the host country's market demands. As a result, they are not very likely to be takeover targets.

Vertical investment
The production of raw materials or intermediate goods that are to be processed into final products.

Horizontal investment
An MNC investment in foreign operations to produce the same goods or services as those produced at home.

Special Nature of Investment The special nature of foreign direct investment relates to the sector of economic activity, technological sophistication, and pattern of ownership. There are three sectors of economic activity: (1) the primary sector, which consists of agriculture, forestry, and mineral exploration and extraction; (2) the industrial sector, consisting of manufacturing operations; and (3) the service sector, which includes transportation, finance, insurance, and related industries. Technological sophistication consists of science-based industry and non-science-based industry; the difference between the two is that science-based industry requires the continuous introduction of new products and/or processes. Patterns of ownership relate to whether the business is wholly or partially owned.

The special nature of foreign direct investments can be categorized as one of five types (see Figure 10-1). Type I is the highest-risk venture; type V is the lowest-risk venture. This risk factor is assigned based on sector, technology, and ownership. Primary sector industries usually have the highest risk factor, service sector industries have the next highest, and industrial sector industries have the lowest. Firms with technology that is not available to the government should the firm be taken over have lower risk than those with technology that is easily acquired. Wholly owned subsidiaries have higher risk than partially owned subsidiaries.

Using a framework similar to that provided in Figure 10-1 helps MNCs to manage their political risks. A way to complement this framework approach is to give specific risk ratings to various criteria.

Quantifying the Variables in Managing Political Risk

Some MNCs attempt to manage political risk through a quantification process that identifies important factors and then compares the results from different geographic locales. This comparison allows them, for example, to identify how risky a venture is in Argentina versus Russia.

Factors that typically are quantified reflect the political and economic environment, domestic economic conditions, and external economic conditions. Each factor is given a minimum and maximum score, and the person(s) responsible for making the evaluation will determine the score for each. When this process is complete, a total risk evaluation number is computed by simply adding the individual scores. Table 10-3 provides an example of a quantitative list of political risk criteria.

Formulating Appropriate Response

Once political risk has been analyzed by either the framework or quantitative approach, or both, the MNC then will attempt to manage the risk further by minimizing or limiting it through carefully formulated responses. Two such common approaches are the use of relative bargaining power and the use of integrative as well as protective and defensive techniques.

Relative Bargaining Power The theory behind relative bargaining power is quite simple. The MNC works to maintain a stronger bargaining power position than that of the host country. A good example is when the MNC has proprietary technology that will be unavailable to the host country if the operation is expropriated or the firm is forced to abide by government decisions that are unacceptable to it. Over time, of course, this technology may become common, and the firm will lose its bargaining power. To prevent this from happening, however, the firm will work to develop new technology that again establishes the balance of power in its favor. As long as the host country stands to lose more than it will gain by taking action against the company, the firm has successfully minimized its political risk by establishing an effective bargaining position. Figure 10-2 provides an example. As long as the MNC's bargaining power remains at or above the diagonal line, the government will not intervene. At point E in the figure, however, this power declines, and the host country will begin to intervene.[14]

Table 10–3
Criteria for Quantifying Political Risk

Major Area	Criteria	Scores	
		Minimum	Maximum
Political and economic environment	1. Stability of the political system	3	14
	2. Imminent internal conflicts	0	14
	3. Threats to stability emanating from the outside world	0	12
	4. Degree of control of the economic system	5	9
	5. Reliability of the country as a trading partner	4	12
	6. Constitutional guarantees	2	12
	7. Effectiveness of public administration	3	12
	8. Labor relations and social peace	3	15
Domestic economic conditions	9. Size of population	4	8
	10. Per capita income	2	10
	11. Economic growth during previous 5 years	2	7
	12. Prospective growth during next 3 years	3	10
	13. Inflation during previous 2 years	2	10
	14. Accessibility of domestic capital market to foreigners	3	7
	15. Availability of high-quality local labor	2	8
	16. Possibility of giving employment to foreign nationals	2	8
	17. Availability of energy resources	2	14
	18. Legal requirements concerning environmental protection	4	8
	19. Traffic system and communication	2	14
External economic relations	20. Restrictions imposed on imports	2	10
	21. Restrictions imposed on exports	2	10
	22. Restrictions imposed on foreign investments in the country	3	9
	23. Freedom to set up or engage in partnerships	3	9
	24. Legal protection for brands and products	3	9
	25. Restrictions imposed on monetary transfers	2	8
	26. Reevaluations against the DM during previous 5 years	2	7
	27. Development of the balance of payments	2	9
	28. Drain on foreign funds through oil and other energy imports	3	14
	29. International financial standing	3	8
	30. Restrictions imposed on the exchange of local money into foreign currencies	2	8

Source: Adapted from E. Dichtl and H. G. Koglmayr, "Country Risk Ratings," *Management International Review,* vol. 26, no. 4, 1986, p. 6. Used with permission.

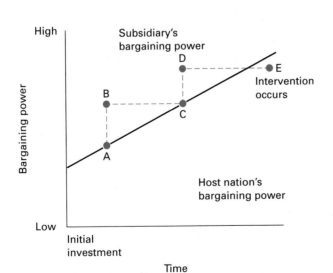

Figure 10–2

Relative Bargaining Power over Time

Source: Adapted from Thomas A. Pointer, "Political Risk: Managing Government Intervention," in Paul W. Beamish, J. Peter Killing, Donald J. LeCraw, and Harold Crookell, *International Management: Text and Cases* (Homewood, IL: Irwin, 1991), p. 125.

Integrative techniques
Techniques that help the overseas operation become a part of the host country's infrastructure.

Protective and defensive techniques
Techniques that discourage the host government from interfering in operations.

Integrative as well as Protective and Defensive Techniques   Another way that MNCs attempt to protect themselves from expropriation and/or minimize government interference in their operations is to use integration and the implementation of protective and defensive techniques. **Integrative techniques** are designed to help the overseas operation become part of the host country's infrastructure. The objective is to be perceived as "less foreign" and thus unlikely to be the target of government action. Some of the most integrative techniques include: (1) developing good relations with the host government and other local political groups; (2) producing as much of the product locally as possible with the use of in-country suppliers and subcontractors, thus making it a "domestic" product; (3) creating joint ventures and hiring local people to manage and run the operation; (4) doing as much local research and development as possible; and (5) developing effective labor-management relations.

Protective and defensive techniques are designed to discourage the host government from interfering in operations. In contrast to the integrative techniques, these actually encourage nonintegration of the enterprise in the local environment. Examples include: (1) doing as little local manufacturing as possible and conducting all research and development outside the country; (2) limiting the responsibility of local personnel and hiring only those who are vital to the operation; (3) raising capital from local banks and the host government as well as outside sources; and (4) diversifying production of the product among a number of countries.

When should a company use integrative techniques? Under what conditions should it employ protective and defensive techniques? Gregory has suggested that this choice will be heavily influenced by characteristics such as the MNC's technology, management skills, and logistics and labor transmission.[15] In all, four basic types of firms can be described using these characteristics.

The first type consists of dynamic, high-technology MNCs that have unique knowledge that the host country would like. Computer companies are a good example. As seen in Figure 10-3, these firms do not rely very much on integrative techniques. They attempt to keep their distance from the host country and rely heavily on protective and defensive strategies.

The second type consists of MNCs with low or stable technology. These MNCs make products that require little innovation or use relatively unsophisticated technology. Steel firms are an example. As seen in Figure 10-3, these firms typically use both high inte-

Figure 10–3

Use of Integrative and Protective and Defensive Techniques by Firms in Select Industries

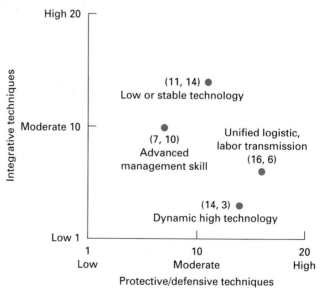

Source: Adapted from Ann Gregory, "Firm Characteristic and Political Risk Reduction in Overseas Ventures," *National Academy of Management Proceedings,* 1982, p. 77. Used with permission.

gration and high protective and defensive strategies, although they generally rely more on integration than the defensive approach.

The third type consists of MNCs whose managers need to be highly skilled. For example, food production firms require advanced marketing and management skills to be competitive. These MNCs typically use a balanced approach of integration and protective and defensive techniques, but they are less concerned with either than low or stable technology firms are.

The fourth type consists of MNCs characterized by highly labor-intensive products, high value in relation to weight and/or volume, and the need for a strong global marketing system for selling the product. Sewing machine companies are an example. Firms in this category tend to rely more heavily on protective and defensive measures than any of the other three groups and to employ only moderate concern for integrative techniques (again, see Figure 10-3).

The strategic response that a firm takes in managing its political risk will be influenced by a variety of factors besides the firm's technology, management skills, logistics, and labor transmission. Others include the nature of the industry, local conditions in the host country, and philosophy of the management. Whatever variables are considered, however, firms are going to use a combination of integrative and protective and defensive techniques.

Managing International Negotiations

Closely related to managing political risk, but deserving special attention, is managing negotiations. **Negotiation** is the process of bargaining with one or more parties to arrive at a solution that is acceptable to all. Negotiation often follows assessing political risk and can be used as an approach to conflict management. If the risk is worth it, then the MNC must negotiate with the host country to secure the best possible arrangements. The MNC and the host country will discuss the investment the MNC is prepared to make in return for certain guarantees and/or concessions. The initial range of topics typically includes critical areas such as hiring practices, direct financial investment, taxes, and ownership control. Negotiation also is used in creating joint ventures with local firms and in getting the operation off the ground. After the firm is operating, additional areas of negotiation often include expansion of facilities, use of more local managers, additional imports or exports of materials and finished goods, and recapture of profits.

On a more macro level of international trade are the negotiations conducted between countries. The current balance-of-trade problems between the United States and China are one example. The massive debt problems of Third World countries and the opening of trade doors with Eastern European countries are other current examples.[16]

Negotiation
The process of bargaining with one or more parties for the purpose of arriving at a solution that is acceptable to all.

The Negotiation Process

There are several basic steps that can be used in managing the negotiation process. Regardless of the issues or personalities of the parties involved, this process typically begins with planning.

Planning Planning starts with the negotiators' identifying those objectives they would like to attain. Then, they explore the possible options for reaching these objectives. Research shows that the greater the number of options, the greater the chances for successful negotiations. While this appears to be an obvious statement, research also reveals that many negotiators do not alter their strategy when negotiating across cultures.[17] Next, consideration is given to areas of common ground between the parties. Other major areas include: (1) the setting of limits on single-point objectives, such as deciding to pay no more than $10 million for the factory and $3 million for the land; (2) dividing issues into short- and long-term considerations and deciding how to handle each; and (3) determining the sequence in which to discuss the various issues.[18]

Impersonal Relationship Building

The second phase of the negotiation process involves getting to know the people on the other side. This "feeling out" period is characterized by the desire to identify those who are reasonable and those who are not. In contrast to negotiations in many other countries, those in the United States often give little attention to this phase; they want to get down to business immediately, which often is an ineffective approach. Adler notes:

> Effective negotiators must view luncheon, dinner, reception, ceremony, and tour invitations as times for interpersonal relationship building, and therefore as key to the negotiating process. When American negotiators, often frustrated by the seemingly endless formalities, ceremonies, and "small talk," ask how long they must wait before beginning to "do business," the answer is simple: wait until your opponents bring up business (and they will). Realize that the work of conducting a successful negotiation has already begun, even if business has yet to be mentioned.[19]

Exchanging Task-Related Information

In this part of the negotiation process, each group sets forth its position on the critical issues. These positions often will change later in the negotiations. At this point, the participants are trying to find out what the other party wants to attain and what it is willing to give up.

Persuasion

This step of negotiations is considered by many to be the most important. No side wants to give away more than it has to, but each knows that without giving some concessions, it is unlikely to reach a final agreement. The success of the persuasion step often depends on: (1) how well the parties understand each other's position; (2) the ability of each to identify areas of similarity and differences; (3) the ability to create new options; and (4) the willingness to work toward a solution that allows all parties to walk away feeling they have achieved their objectives.

Agreement

The final phase of negotiations is the granting of concessions and hammering out a final agreement. Sometimes, this phase is carried out piecemeal, and concessions and agreements are made on issues one at a time. This is the way those from the United States like to negotiate. As each issue is resolved, it is removed from the bargaining table and interest focused on the next. Asians and Russians, on the other hand, tend to negotiate a final agreement on everything, and few concessions are given until the end. Simply put, to negotiate effectively in the international arena, it is necessary to understand how cultural differences between the parties affect the process.[20]

Cultural Differences Affecting Negotiations

In negotiating effectively, it is important to have a sound understanding of the other side's culture.[21] This includes consideration of areas such as communication patterns, time orientation, and social behaviors.[22] A number of useful steps can help in this process.[23] One negotiation expert recommends the following:

1. Do not identify the counterpart's home culture too quickly. Common cues (e.g., name, physical appearance, language, accent, location) may be unreliable. The counterpart probably belongs to more than one culture.
2. Beware of the Western bias toward "doing." In Arab, Asian, and Latin groups, ways of being (e.g., comportment, smell), feeling, thinking, and talking can shape relationships more powerfully than doing.
3. Try to counteract the tendency to formulate simple, consistent, stable images.

4. Do not assume that all aspects of the culture are equally significant. In Japan, consulting all relevant parties to a decision is more important than presenting a gift.

5. Recognize that norms for interactions involving outsiders may differ from those for interactions between compatriots.

6. Do not overestimate your familiarity with your counterpart's culture. An American studying Japanese wrote New Year's wishes to Japanese contacts in basic Japanese characters, but omitted one character. As a result, the message became "Dead man, congratulations."[24]

Other useful examples have been offered by Trompenaars and Hampden-Turner, who note that a society's culture often plays a major role in determining the effectiveness of a negotiating approach. This is particularly true when the negotiating groups come from decidedly different cultures such as an ascription society and an achievement society. As noted in Chapter 5, in an ascription society status is attributed based on birth, kinship, gender, age, and personal connections. In an achievement society status is determined by accomplishments. As a result, each side's cultural perceptions can affect the outcome of the negotiation. Here is an example:

> sending whiz-kids to deal with people 10–20 years their senior often insults the ascriptive culture. The reaction may be: "Do these people think that they have reached our own level of experience in half the time? That a 30-year-old American is good enough to negotiate with a 50-year-old Greek or Italian?" Achievement cultures must understand that some ascriptive cultures, the Japanese especially, spend much on training and in-house education to ensure that older people actually are wiser for the years they have spent in the corporation and for the sheer number of subordinates briefing them. It insults an ascriptive culture to do anything which prevents the self-fulfilling nature of its beliefs. Older people are held to be important **so that** they will be nourished and sustained by others' respect. A stranger is expected to facilitate this scheme, not challenge it.[25]

U.S. negotiators have a style that often differs from that of negotiators in many other countries. Americans believe it is important to be factual and objective. In addition, they often make early concessions to show the other party that they are flexible and reasonable. Moreover, U.S. negotiators typically have authority to bind their party to an agreement, so if the right deal is struck, the matter can be resolved quickly. This is why deadlines are so important to Americans. They have come to do business, and they want to get things resolved immediately.

A comparative example would be the Arabs, who in contrast to Americans, with their logical approach, tend to use an emotional appeal in their negotiation style. They analyze things subjectively and treat deadlines as only general guidelines for wrapping up negotiations. They tend to open negotiations with an extreme initial position. However, the Arabs believe strongly in making concessions, do so throughout the bargaining process, and almost always reciprocate an opponent's concessions. They also seek to build a long-term relationship with their bargaining partners. For these reasons, Americans typically find it easier to negotiate with Arabs than with representatives from many other regions of the world.

Another interesting comparative example is provided by the Chinese. In initial negotiation meetings, it is common for these negotiators to seek agreement on the general focus of the meetings. The hammering out of specific details is postponed for later get-togethers. By achieving agreement on the general framework within which the negotiations will be conducted, the Chinese thus seek to limit and focus the discussions. Many Westerners misunderstand what is happening during these initial meetings and believe the dialogue consists mostly of rhetoric and general conversation. They are wrong and quite often are surprised later on when the Chinese negotiators use the agreement on the framework and principles as a basis for getting agreement on goals—and then insist that all discussions on concrete arrangements be in accord with these agreed upon goals. Simply put, what is viewed as general conversation by many

Western negotiators is regarded by the Chinese as a formulation of the rules of the game which must be adhered to throughout the negotiations. So in negotiating with the Chinese, it is important to come prepared to ensure that one's own agenda, framework, and principles are accepted by both parties.

Before beginning any negotiations, negotiators should review the negotiating style of the other parties. (Table 10-4 provides some insights regarding negotiation styles of the Americans, Japanese, Arabs, and Mexicans.) This review should help to answer certain questions: What can we expect the other side to say and do? How are they likely to respond to certain offers? When should the most important matters be introduced? How quickly should concessions be made, and what type of reciprocity should be expected? These types of questions help effectively prepare the negotiators. In addition, the team will work on formulating negotiation tactics. The accompanying sidebar, "Negotiating with the Japanese," demonstrates such tactics, and the following discussion gets into some of the specifics.[26]

Negotiation Tactics

A number of specific tactics are used in international negotiation. The following discussion examines some of the most common.

Table 10-4
Negotiation Styles from a Cross-Cultural Perspective

Element	United States	Japanese	Arabians	Mexicans
Group composition	Marketing oriented	Function oriented	Committee of specialists	Friendship oriented
Number involved	2–3	4–7	4–6	2–3
Space orientation	Confrontational; competitive	Display harmonious relationship	Status	Close, friendly
Establishing rapport	Short period; direct to task	Longer period; until harmony	Long period; until trusted	Longer period; discuss family
Exchange of information	Documented; step-by-step; multimedia	Extensive; concentrate on receiving side	Less emphasis on technology, more on relationship	Less emphasis on technology, more on relationship
Persuasion tools	Time pressure; loss of saving/making money	Maintain relationship references; intergroup connections	Go-between; hospitality	Emphasis on family and on social concerns; goodwill measured in generations
Use of language	Open, direct, sense of urgency	Indirect, appreciative, cooperative	Flattery, emotional, religious	Respectful, gracious
First offer	Fair ±5 to 10%	±10 to 20%	±20 to 50%	Fair
Second offer	Add to package; sweeten the deal	–5%	–10%	Add an incentive
Final offer package	Total package	Makes no further concessions	–25%	Total
Decision-making process	Top management team	Collective	Team makes recommendation	Senior manager and secretary
Decision maker	Top management team	Middle line with team consensus	Senior manager	Senior manager
Risk taking	Calculated personal responsibility	Low group responsibility	Religion based	Personally responsible

Source: Lillian H. Chaney and Jeanette S. Martin, *Intercultural Business Communication* © 1995, pp. 183–184. Reprinted by permission of Prentice Hall, Inc. Englewood Cliffs, New Jersey.

International Management in Action

Negotiating with the Japanese   www.jbc.gol.com/index/html

Some people believe that the most effective way of getting the Japanese to open up their markets to the United States is to use a form of strong-arm tactics, such as putting the country on a list of those to be targeted for retaliatory action. Others believe that this approach will not be effective, because the interests of the United States and Japan are intertwined and we would be hurting ourselves as much as them. Regardless of which group is right, one thing is certain: U.S. MNCs must learn how to negotiate more effectively with the Japanese. What can they do? Researchers have found that besides patience and a little table pounding, a number of important steps warrant consideration.

First, business firms need to prepare for their negotiations by learning more about Japanese culture and the "right" ways to conduct discussions. Those companies with experience in these matters report that the two best ways of doing this are to read books on Japanese business practices and social customs and to hire experts to train the negotiators. Other steps that are helpful include putting the team through simulated negotiations and hiring Japanese to assist in the negotiations.

Second, U.S. MNCs must learn patience and sincerity. Negotiations are a two-way street that require the mutual cooperation and efforts of both parties. The U.S. negotiators must understand that many times, Japanese negotiators do not have full authority to make on-the-spot decisions. Authority must be given by someone at the home office, and this failure to act quickly should not be interpreted as a lack of sincerity on the part of the Japanese negotiators.

Third, the MNC must have a unique good or service. So many things are offered for sale in Japan that unless the company has something that is truly different, persuading the other party to buy it is difficult.

Fourth, technical expertise often is viewed as a very important contribution, and this often helps to win concessions with the Japanese. The Japanese know that the Americans, for example, still dominate the world when it comes to certain types of technology and that Japan is unable to compete effectively in these areas. When such technical expertise is evident, it is very influential in persuading the Japanese to do business with the company.

These four criteria are critical to effective negotiations with the Japanese. MNCs that use them report more successful experiences than those who do not.

Location   Where should negotiations take place? If the matter is very important, most businesses will choose a neutral site. For example, U.S. firms negotiating with companies from the Far East will meet in Hawaii, South American companies negotiating with European firms will meet halfway, in New York City. A number of benefits derive from using a neutral site. One is that each party has limited access to its home office for receiving a great deal of negotiating information and advice and thus gaining an advantage on the other. A second is that the cost of staying at the site often is quite high, so both sides have an incentive to conclude their negotiations as quickly as possible. (Of course, if one side enjoys the facilities and would like to stay as long as possible, the negotiations could drag on.) A third is that most negotiators do not like to return home with nothing to show for their efforts, so they are motivated to reach some type of agreement.

Time Limits   Time limits are an important negotiation tactic when one party is under a time constraint. This is particularly true when this party has agreed to meet at the home site of the other party. For example, U.S. negotiators who go to London to discuss a joint venture with a British firm often will have a scheduled return flight. Once their hosts find out how long these individuals intend to stay, the British can plan their strategy accordingly. The "real" negotiations are unlikely to begin until close to the time that the Americans must leave. The British know that their guests will be anxious to strike some type of deal before returning home, so the Americans are at a disadvantage.

Time limits can be used tactically even if the negotiators meet at a neutral site. For example, most Americans like to be home with their families for Thanksgiving, Christmas, and the New Year holiday. Negotiations held right before these dates put Americans at a disadvantage, because the other party knows when the Americans would like to leave.

Buyer–Seller Relations   How should buyers and sellers act? As noted earlier, Americans believe in being objective and trading favors. When the negotiations are over, Americans walk away with what they have received from the other party, and they expect the other party to do the same. This is not the way negotiators in many other countries think, however.

The Japanese, for example, believe that the buyers should get most of what they want. On the other hand, they also believe that the seller should be taken care of through reciprocal favors. The buyer must ensure that the seller has not been "picked clean." For example, when many Japanese firms first started doing business with large U.S. firms, they were unaware of U.S. negotiating tactics. As a result, the Japanese thought the Americans were taking advantage of them, whereas the Americans believed they were driving a good, hard bargain.

The Brazilians are quite different from both the Americans and Japanese. Researchers have found that Brazilians do better when they are more deceptive and self-interested and their opponents more open and honest than they are.[27] Brazilians also tend to make fewer promises and commitments than their opponents, and they are much more prone to say no. However, Brazilians are more likely to make initial concessions. Overall, Brazilians are more like Americans than Japanese in that they try to maximize their advantage, but they are unlike Americans in that they do not feel obligated to be open and forthright in their approach. Whether they are buyer or seller, they want to come out on top.

Bargaining Behaviors

Closely related to the discussion of negotiation tactics are the different types of bargaining behaviors, including both verbal and nonverbal behaviors. Verbal behaviors are an important part of the negotiating process, because they can improve the final outcome. Research shows that the profits of the negotiators increase when they make high initial offers, ask a lot of questions, and do not make many verbal commitments until the end of the negotiating process. In short, verbal behaviors are critical to the success of negotiations.

Use of Extreme Behaviors   Some negotiators begin by making extreme offers or requests. The Chinese and Arabs are examples. Some negotiators, however, begin with an initial position that is close to the one they are seeking. The Americans and Swedes are examples here.

Is one approach any more effective than the other? Research shows that extreme positions tend to produce better results. Some of the reasons relate to the fact that an extreme bargaining position: (1) shows the other party that the bargainer will not be exploited; (2) extends the negotiation and gives the bargainer a better opportunity to gain information on the opponent; (3) allows more room for concessions; (4) modifies the opponents' beliefs about the bargainer's preferences; (5) shows the opponent that the bargainer is willing to play the game according to the usual norms; and (6) lets the bargainer gain more than would probably be possible if a less extreme initial position had been taken.[28]

Although the use of extreme position bargaining is considered to be "unAmerican," many U.S. firms have used it successfully against foreign competitors. When Peter Ueberroth managed the Olympic Games in the United States in 1984, he turned a profit of well over $100 million—and that was without the participation of Soviet bloc countries, which would have further increased the market potential of the games. In past Olympiads, sponsoring countries have lost hundreds of millions of dollars. How did Ueberroth do it? One way was by using extreme position bargaining. For example, the Olympic Committee felt that the Japanese should pay $10 million for the right to televise the games in the country, so when the Japanese offered $6 million for the rights, the Olympic Committee countered with $90 million. Eventually, the two sides agreed on $18.5 million. Through the effective use fo extreme position bargaining, Ueberroth got the Japanese to pay over three times their original offer, and amount well in excess of the committee's budget.

Promises, Threats, and Other Behaviors   Another approach to bargaining is the use of promises, threats, rewards, self-disclosures, and other behaviors that are designed to influence the other party. These behaviors often are greatly influenced by the culture. Graham conducted research using Japanese, U.S., and Brazilian businesspeople and found that they employed a variety of different behaviors during a buyer–seller negotiation simulation.[29] Table 10-5 presents the results.

Table 10–5
Cross-Cultural Differences in Verbal Behavior of Japanese, U.S., and Brazilian Negotiators

Behavior and Definition	Number of Times Tactic Was Used in a Half-Hour Bargaining Session		
	Japanese	United States	Brazilian
Promise. A statement in which the source indicated an intention to provide the target with a reinforcing consequence which source anticipates target will evaluate as pleasant, positive, or rewarding.	7	8	3
Threat. Same as promise, except that the reinforcing consequences are thought to be noxious, unpleasant, or punishing.	4	4	2
Recommendation. A statement in which the source predicts that a pleasant environmental consequence will occur to the target. Its occurrence is not under the source's control.	7	4	5
Warning. Same as recommendation except that the consequences are thought to be unpleasant.	2	1	1
Reward. A statement by the source that is thought to create pleasant consequences for the target.	1	2	2
Punishment. Same as reward, except that the consequences are thought to be unpleasant.	1	3	3
Positive normative appeal. A statement in which the source indicates that the target's past, present, or future behavior was or will be in conformity with social norms.	1	1	0
Negative normative appeal. Same as positive normative appeal, except that the target's behavior is in violation of social norms.	3	1	1
Commitment. A statement by the source to the effect that its future bids will not go below or above a certain level.	15	13	8
Self-disclosure. A statement in which the source reveals information about itself.	34	36	39
Question. A statement in which the source asks the target to reveal information about itself.	20	20	22
Command. A statement in which the source suggests that the target perform a certain behavior.	8	6	14
First offer. The profit level associated with each participant's first offer.	61.5	57.3	75.2
Initial concession. The differences in profit between the first and second offer.	6.5	7.1	9.4
Number of no's. Number of times the word "no" was used by bargainers per half-hour.	5.7	9.0	83.4

Source: Adapted from John L. Graham, "The Influence of Culture on the Process of Business Negotiations in an Exploratory Study," *Journal of International Business Studies,* Spring 1983, pp. 84, 88. Used with permission.

The table shows that Americans and Japanese make greater use of promises than Brazilians. The Japanese also rely heavily on recommendations and commitment. The Brazilians use a discussion of rewards, commands, and self-disclosure more than Americans and Japanese. The Brazilians also say no a great deal more and make first offers that have higher-level profits than those of the others. Americans tend to operate between these two groups, although they do make less use of commands than either of their opponents and make first offers that have lower profit levels than their opponents.

Nonverbal Behaviors   Nonverbal behaviors also are very common during negotiations. These behaviors refer to what people do rather than what they say. Nonverbal behaviors sometimes are called the "silent language." Typical examples include silent periods, facial gazing, touching, and conversational overlaps. As seen in Table 10-6, the Japanese tend to use silent periods much more often than either Americans or Brazilians during negotiations. In fact, in this study, the latter did not use them at all. The Brazilians did, however, make frequent use of other nonverbal behaviors. They employed facial gazing almost four times more often than the Japanese, and almost twice as often as the Americans. In addition, although the latter two groups did not touch their opponents, the Brazilians made wide use of this nonverbal tactic. They also relied heavily on conversational overlaps, employing them more than twice as often as the Japanese and almost three times as often as Americans. Quite obviously, the Brazilians rely very heavily on nonverbal behaviors in their negotiating.

The important thing to remember is that in international negotiations, people use a wide variety of tactics, and the other side must be prepared to counter or find a way of dealing with them. The response will depend on the situation. Managers from different cultures will give different answers. Table 10-7 provides some examples of the types of characteristics needed in effective negotiators. To the extent that international managers have these characteristics, their success as negotiators should increase.

The World of Business Week Revisited

There were a far-ranging number of political risks that were discussed in this chapter. However, as MNCs enter the new millennium, it is becoming evident that some of these risks are more common and more critical than others. Today, for

Table 10–6

Cross-Cultural Differences in Nonverbal Behavior of Japanese, U.S., and Brazilian Negotiators

Behavior and Definition	Number of Times Tactic Was Used in a Half-Hour Bargaining Session		
	Japanese	United States	Brazilian
Silent period. The number of conversational gaps of 10 seconds or more per 30 minutes.	5.5	3.5	0
Facial gazing. The number of minutes negotiators spend looking at their opponent's face per randomly selected 10-minute period.	1.3 minutes	3.3 minutes	5.2 minutes
Touching. Incidents of bargainers' touching one another per half-hour (not including handshakes).	0	0	4.7
Conversational overlaps. The number of times (per 10 minutes) that both parties to the negotiation would talk at the same time.	12.6	10.3	28.6

Source: Adapted from John L. Graham, "The Influence of Culture on the Process of Business Negotiations in an Exploratory Study," *Journal of International Business Studies,* Spring 1983, p. 84. Used with permission.

Table 10–7

Culture-Specific Characteristics Needed by International Managers for Effective Negotiations

U.S. managers	Preparation and planning skill
	Ability to think under pressure
	Judgment and intelligence
	Verbal expressiveness
	Product knowledge
	Ability to perceive and exploit power
	Integrity
Japanese managers	Dedication to job
	Ability to perceive and exploit power
	Ability to win respect and confidence
	Integrity
	Listening skill
	Broad perspective
	Verbal expressiveness
Chinese managers (Taiwan)	Persistence and determination
	Ability to win respect and confidence
	Preparation and planning skill
	Product knowledge
	Interesting
	Judgment and intelligence
Brazilian managers	Preparation and planning skill
	Ability to think under pressure
	Judgment and intelligence
	Verbal expressiveness
	Product knowledge
	Ability to perceive and exploit power
	Competitiveness

Source: Adapted from Nancy J. Adler, *International Dimensions of Organizational Behavior,* 2nd ed. (Boston: PWS-Kent Publishing, 1991), p. 187, and from material provided by Professor John Graham, School of Business Administration, University of Southern California, 1983.

example, there is less risk associated with the expropriation of an MNC's assets. On the other hand, there is increasing risk that an MNC will find itself imbedded in an emerging economy that is stagnant and cannot be easily jump-started. MNCs that are currently doing business in Malaysia or Indonesia are good examples. MNCs that have invested heavily in Brazil also fall into this category. In the foreseeable future, these emerging economies are going through some rough and uncertain times and government rules and regulations are going to be changing with resulting risk to the MNCs doing business there. For example, as the opening news story indicated, there may be limits placed on the free flow of capital. Up to a few years ago, China was an inviting market for MNC expansion. Then the recent economic slowdown resulted in the Chinese government actively intervening and increasing its control over financial and other business-related activities that previously were deregulated. Now that you have read the chapter and based on the opening news story, do you think political risk remains a major area of consideration for international business? Will effective negotiation be of growing importance for MNCs as they wind their way through the changing maze of international government rules, regulations, and red tape? How can this process be made as effective as possible?

Summary of Key Points

1. Political risk is the likelihood that the foreign investment of a business will be constrained by a host government's policies. In dealing with this risk, companies conduct both macro and micro political risk analyses. Specific consideration is given to changing host government policies, expropriation, and operational profitability risk.

2. MNCs attempt to manage their political risk in two basic ways. One is by developing a comprehensive framework for identifying and describing these risks. This includes consideration of political, operational, and ownership-control risks. A second is by quantifying the variables that help constitute the risk.

3. Two common risk formulation strategies are the use of relative bargaining power and of integrative as well as protective and defensive techniques. Figure 10-4 illustrates how firms in various industries use a combination of the integrative and the protective and defensive techniques in developing an overall response strategy.

4. Negotiation is the process of bargaining with one or more parties to arrive at a solution that is acceptable to all. This process involves five basic steps: planning, interpersonal relationship building, exchanging task-related information, persuasion, and agreement. The way in which the process is carried out often will vary because of cultural differences.

5. There are a wide variety of tactics used in international negotiating. These include location, time limits, buyer-seller relations, verbal behaviors, and nonverbal behaviors.

Key Terms

conglomerate investment

expropriation

horizontal investments

indigenization laws

integrative techniques

macro political risk analysis

micro political risk analysis

negotiation

operational risks

ownership-control risks

political risk

protective and defensive techniques

transfer risks

vertical investments

Review and Discussion Questions

1. What types of political risk would a company entering Russia face? Identify and describe three. What types of political risk would a company entering France face? Identify and describe three. How are these risks similar? How are they different?

2. Most firms attempt to quantify their political risk, although they do not assign specific weights to the respective criteria. Why is this approach so popular? Would the companies be better off assigning weights to each of the risks being assumed? Defend your answer.

3. If a high-tech firm wanted to set up operations in Iran, what steps might it take to ensure that the subsidiary would not be expropriated? Identify and describe three strategies that would be particularly helpful.

4. If a company new to the international arena was negotiating an agreement with a potential partner in an overseas country, what basic steps should it be prepared to implement? Identify and describe them.

5. Wilsten, Inc., has been approached by a Japanese firm that wants exclusive production and selling rights for one of Wilsten's new, high-tech products. What does Wilsten need to know about Japanese bargaining behaviors to strike the best possible deal with this company? Identify and describe five.

Internet Exercise: Motorola in China

Asia still offers great opportunities for multinational firms. However, given the slowdown that has occurred in this region in recent years, there are also great risks associated with doing business there. The large American-based MNC Motorola has determined that the opportunities are worth the risk and has staked a large claim in China and is determined to be a major player in the emerging Asian market. Visit Motorola's web site at **www.mot.com** and focus your attention on what this well-known MNC is now doing in Asia. Drawing from specific information obtained from the web site, this chapter, and your reading of the current news answer these questions: What political risks is Motorola facing in Asia, particularly China? How can Motorola manage these risks? How can effective international negotiating skills be of value to the firm in reducing its political risk and increasing its competitive advantage in this area of the world?

Peru

Peru is located on the west coast of South America. It is the third-largest nation on the continent (only Brazil and Argentina have more area), and it covers almost 500,000 square miles (about 14 percent of the size of the United States). The land has enormous contrasts, with a desert (drier than the Sahara), the towering snow-capped Andes Mountains, sparkling grass-covered plateaus, and thick rain forests. Peru has approximately 25 million people, of which about 20 percent live in Lima, the capital. More Indians (one-half of the population) live in Peru than any other country in the Western Hemisphere. The ancestors of Peru's Indians are the famous Incas, who built a great empire. The rest of the population is mixed, and a small percentage is white. The economy depends heavily on agriculture, fishing, mining, and services. GDP is approximately $90 billion and per-capita income in recent years has been around $3,600. In the early 1990s the country faced internal political turmoil. President Alberto Fujimori dissolved the National Congress, suspended parts of the constitution, and initiated press censorship. By the late 1990s, however, things had turned around, the economy was much stronger, and multinationals were beginning to again consider investing in the country.

One of these potential investors is a large New York bank that is considering a $25 million loan to the owner of a Peruvian fishing fleet. The owner wants to refurbish the fleet and add one more ship.

During the 1970s, the Peruvian government nationalized a number of industries and factories and began running them for the profit of the state. In most cases, these state-run ventures became disasters. In the late 1970s, the fishing fleet owner was given back his ships and allowed to operate his business as before. Since then, he has managed to remain profitable, but the biggest problem is that his ships are getting old and he needs an influx of capital to make repairs and add new technology. As he explained it to the New York banker: "Fishing is no longer just an art. There is a great deal of technology involved. And to keep costs low and be competitive on the world market, you have to have the latest equipment for both locating as well as catching and then loading and unloading the fish."

Having reviewed the fleet owner's operation, the large multinational bank believes that the loan is justified. The financial institution is concerned, however, that the Peruvian government might step in during the next couple of years and again take over the business. If this were to happen, it might take an additional decade for the loan to be repaid. If the government were to allow the fleet owner to operate the fleet the way he has over the last decade, the loan could be repaid within 7 years.

Right now, the bank is deciding the specific terms of the agreement. Once these have been worked out, either a loan officer will fly down to Lima and close the deal or the owner will be asked to come to New York for the signing. Whichever approach is used, the bank realizes that final adjustments in the agreement will have to be made on the spot. Therefore, if the bank sends a representative to Lima, the individual will have to have the authority to commit the bank to specific terms. These final matters should be worked out within the next 10 days.

www.peru-explorer.com

Questions

1. What are some current issues facing Peru? What is the climate for doing business in Peru today?

2. What type of political risks does this fishing company need to evaluate? Identify and describe them.

3. What types of integrative and protective and defensive techniques can the bank use?

4. Would the bank be better off negotiating the loan in New York or in Lima? Why?

Going to Gdansk

When Poland made the necessary reforms to move toward a market economy, Andrzej Jaworski from Chicago, Illinois, began thinking this might be an excellent place to set up an overseas operation. Andrzej and his two brothers own a firm that produces specialized computer chips. The company has a series of patents that provide legal protection and allow it to dominate a small but growing segment of the computer market. Their sales estimates reached $147 million within 3 years, but they believe that this could rise to $200 million if they were to expand internationally. They have thought about setting up a plant in Belgium so that they could take advantage of the European market growth. They would prefer Poland, however, because their parents grew up there before leaving for the United States in 1948. "We feel that we know the Poles because we have grown up in a Polish household here in the midwest," Andrzej explained to his banker. "We would like to see if the government would allow us to set up a small plant in Gdansk, train the necessary workers, and then export our product into the European Union."

One of the primary reasons that Andrzej believes that the Polish government would be agreeable to the plan is that not only is Poland moving to a market economy, but the country is still struggling with foreign debt, inflation, and outmoded technology. A state-of-the-art plant could help to reduce unemployment and provide an inflow of needed capital. However, the banker is concerned that because of the political risks and uncertainty in Central Europe in general and Poland in particular, the company may either lose its investment through government expropriation or find itself unable to get profits out of the country. Given that the company will have to invest approximately $20 million, the venture could seriously endanger the company's financial status.

Andrzej understands these risks but believes that with the help of an international management consultant, he can identify and minimize the problems. "I'm determined to push ahead, "he told the banker, "and if there is a good chance of making this project a success, I'm going to Gdansk."

Questions

1. What are some of the political risks that Andrzej's firm will face if he decides to go ahead with this venture? Identify and describe two or three.

2. Using Figure 10-1, what strategy would you recommend that the firm use? Why?

3. In his negotiations with the Polish government, what suggestions or guidelines would you offer to Andrzej? Identify and describe two or three.

Chapter 11

Organizing International Operations

Objectives of the Chapter

The success of an international firm can be greatly affected by the overall structure and design of operations. There are a wide variety of organizational structures and designs from which to choose. Selecting the most appropriate structure depends on a number of factors, such as the desire of the home office for control over its foreign operations and the demands placed on the overseas unit by both the local market and the personnel who work there.

This chapter first presents and analyzes traditional organizational structures for effective international operations. Then, it explores some of the new, nontraditional organizational arrangements stemming from mergers, joint ventures, and the Japanese concept of *keiretsu*. The specific objectives of this chapter are:

1. EXAMINE the major types of organizational structures used in handling international operations.

2. ANALYZE the advantages and disadvantages of each type of organizational structure, including the conditions that make one preferable to others.

3. DESCRIBE the recent, nontraditional organizational arrangements coming out of mergers, joint ventures, *keiretsus*, and other new designs including electronic networks and product development structures.

4. DISCUSS the value of subsidiary boards of directors in overseas operations.

5. EXPLAIN how organizational characteristics such as formalization, specialization, and centralization influence how the organization is structured and functions.

BusinessWeek

The World of Business Week:

P&G's Hottest New Product: P&G

At Washington State's Clark County Fair last month, coffee lovers got a front-row seat at a corporate revolution in the making. The local sales force for Procter & Gamble Co. was out in force at the Pancake Feed, distributing samples of of P&G's Millstone Coffee. To the amazement of the Fred Meyer supermarket employees running the pancake breakfast, the Procter reps worked the crowd, chatting with customers, even taking turns in the full-size coffee-maker costume with the cup-and-saucer hat. "You don't generally see them out there doing that kind of grassroots work with customers," says Jeanne Lawson, a Fred Meyer buyer.

But then, P&G has never needed ordinary customers quite so badly. Battered by disappointing revenue growth and demanding retail customers, Procter & Gamble is a company in a bind. Two years ago, its executives boldly declared that the consumer-products giant would double its net sales by 2006, to $70 billion. P&G has consistently missed its growth targets ever since.

Simplify, Simplify

In preparation for the task, top execs have been traversing the country, visiting the CEOs of a dozen major companies, including Kellogg Co. and 3M, in search of advice. The message from all was clear, says [P&G CEO] Pepper: "What thousands of people

298

have been telling us is that we need to be simpler and move faster."

The result of this unprecedented road trip is Organization 2005, a shuffling of the P&G hierarchy and a new product-development process designed to speed innovative offerings to the global market. The old bureaucracy, based on geography, will be reshaped into seven global business units organized by category, such as baby care, beauty care, and fabric-and-home care. The global business units will develop and sell products on a worldwide basis, erasing the old system that let Procter's country managers rule as colonial governors, setting prices and handling products as they saw fit.

Swift Rollout

This new global vision has already had an accidental test run. Last year, P&G introduced an extension of its Pantene shampoo line. The ad campaign for the product was almost entirely visual, with images of beautiful women and their lustrous hair, and had a very limited script. That meant the campaign was easily translated and shipped to P&G markets around the world without the usual months of testing and tinkering. The result: P&G was able to introduce the brand extension in 14 countries in six months, vs. the two years it took to get the original shampoo into stores abroad. "It's a success story that gets quite a big of talk internally," says Chris T. Allen, a marketing professor at the University of Cincinnati, who spent his sabbatical year working in the P&G new-products

department. "I see the reorganization as an attempt to do more Pantenes on a regular basis."

P&G didn't come to this global focus entirely on its own. Its biggest chain store customers, such as Wal-Mart Stores Inc. and French-owned Carrefour, have been agitating for just such a program to mirror their own global expansion. It has been Topic A at retail conventions for months, says Robin Lanier, senior vice-president for industry affairs at the International Mass Retail Assn. While P&G craves an international image for its products, retailers want something more tangible: a global price. As it stands, prices are negotiable on a country or regional basis. What an international retailer pays for Crest in the United States could be considerably less than what it costs the chain in Europe or Latin America. A consistent global price gives big chains more power to plan efficiently and save money. Wal-Mart Chief Executive David D. Glass describes his company's goal as "global sourcing," which includes worldwide relationships on pricing and distribution. Moving P&G products from regional to global management is "pointing somewhat in that direction," Glass says.

In addition to marketing and pricing, global business units will supervise new-product development. P&G will move away from its long-used "sequential" method, which tested products first in midsize U.S. cities and then gradually rolled them out to the world. An example: Swiffer, a new disposable mop designed by P&G, is being tested simultaneously in Cedar Rapids, Iowa; Pittsfield, Mass.; and Sens, France, in hopes of sculpting a globally popular product right out of the box.

Even if P&G could implement its strategy quickly, it would still run into the ugly realities of global economic markets. For its extra $35 billion in revenues through 2006, Procter is counting on about $8 billion from emerging markets in Eastern Europe, China, and Latin America, says Clayton C. Daley Jr., P&G's treasurer, who becomes chief financial officer in October. Yet Asian emerging markets are likely to remain mired in deep economic slumps for at least two more years. Recent turmoil in Russia, which was a bright prospect for Procter just a year ago, has gotten so bad that the company has temporarily halted shipments there. "Growing in underdeveloped geographies is clearly questionable," says Jay Freedman, an analyst at Lincoln Capital, a big institutional holder of Procter & Gamble stock. "Whatever they thought the purchasing power of those new customers was going to be is less now."

"A Lot of Ex-Chiefs"

Procter has additional obstacles closer to home. How, for example, will tradition-bound P&G managers react to the new hierarchy? "You're going from 144 chiefs to 8. That's a lot of ex-chiefs," says consultant Wacker. And everyone will be affected by the change in tone that is sure to come from the corner office. Gentlemanly Pepper, 60, will be succeeded by Jager, a Dutch-born P&G lifer with a reputation for aggressive moves and abrasiveness. In the 1980s, he turned around Procter's falling Japanese business with such a fury that his Japanese managers called him "Crazy Man Durk" behind his back.

Crazy or no, Jager is sticking to the 2006 target date. He's wasting no time stepping into his new role as champion of the global focus: Already, even before taking on the official title of CEO, he has started preaching the new structure to P&G managers. After all, the clock is ticking.

Source: **Reprinted from October 5, 1998, pp. 95–96 issue of** *Business Week* **by special permission, copyright © 1998 by McGraw-Hill Companies, Inc.**

The opening news story on P&G presents an interesting challenge that is facing most multinationals. How can they streamline and yet globalize their organization structures so that they are able to respond quickly and efficiently to their far-flung expanding markets? One way is by creating standardized worldwide pricing, marketing, and distribution networks that allow them to get their products and services to the market faster and less expensively. A key to the success of these efforts is going to be P&G's organizational structure, which is now being redesigned to increase needed global speed and focus. The term used for this strategy is "glocal" which means the application of a global organization that allows for accommodation of local needs. In this chapter the primary focus of attention is on the organizing approaches that MNCs such as P&G are now using to meet this emerging challenge.

Organizational Challenges

During the past decade, an increasing number of large and small MNCs have been rethinking their approach to organizing international operations. Motorola, Xerox, and Li & Fung, a well-known Hong Kong firm, are visible examples.

Recently, Motorola's share of the worldwide cellular market has been declining. In an effort to turn things around, the firm has now committed itself to an increased presence in Europe and in Asia. For example, the company recently decided to build a $150 million plant in Flensburg, Germany. While the labor costs here are quite high ($27 an hour) compared to the United States ($15 an hour) as well as other European locations ($20.40 an hour in the Netherlands and $21.35 an hour in Sweden, for example), Motorola believes that the European market is going to be a major one in the years to come and it wants to have a local presence.[1] The same is true for its recent decision to expand operations in Asia, most notably in China, Korea, the Philippines, and Taiwan. The company is currently building a $750 million high-tech semiconductor factory in the coastal city of Tianjin, China. This plant will be more advanced than any other Motorola facility, and it is structured to help the company regain the dominant position it once enjoyed in the region. Sales in Asia since 1995 have been stagnant, but Motorola estimates that by 2010 China will be the world's second largest semiconductor market and by establishing a strong presence there today, it will be in a good position to become the lead player in the new millennium.[2]

At the same time Motorola has been restructuring its overall worldwide operations in order to increase efficiency and drive down costs. The company recently merged a half-dozen separate businesses into two huge divisions. One focuses on consumers and the other on infrastructure equipment. The first is a separate division for handling the sales of devices such as cellular telephone handsets and pagers. The other is responsible for building infrastructure products for paging, two-way radio, and cellular telephones. Motorola hopes that this new organizational arrangement will help it better adapt to the global market, which is seeing rapid technological change that is forcing competitors to continually review their operations and their structures. In the case of Motorola, for example, the firm's wireless businesses such as police radios, cellular phones, and pagers for bike messengers were once distinct, separate businesses. Today, however, these product lines overlap, as seen by the fact that the company's land mobile-radio segment, which produces two-way radios, also makes a dispatch-style device that can handle cellular phone calls and accept alphanumeric and text messages similar to pagers.[3] So, in order to accommodate technology and its new product offerings, Motorola has found that it had to reorganize operations.

Another example of worldwide reorganizing is provided by Xerox which recently announced that it intends to cut 9,000 jobs by the year 2000. The main purpose of the reorganization is to trim costs. Until just a few years ago Xerox produced traditional copiers that were high-cost items but generated high profit as well. Today competitors are entering this market with streamlined units that are low price and carry razor thin profit margins. In order to meet this new threat, Xerox has to now roll out new, less expensive digital copiers. Over the last five years the company's overhead costs have stagnated in the range of 30 percent. If the MNC is to generate increased profit in a market where prices are falling, it must push down these overhead costs—and this is the objective of its reorganizing efforts.[4]

A third example of how firms are meeting international challenges through reorganization is provided by Li & Fung, Hong Kong's largest export trading company and an innovator in the development of supply chain management. The company has global suppliers worldwide who are responsible for providing the firm with a wide range of consumer goods ranging from toys to fashion accessories to luggage. In recent years Li & Fung has reorganized and now manages its day-to-day operations through a group of product managers who are responsible for their individual areas. This new organizational arrangement emerged in a series of steps. Beginning in the late 1970s the company was a regional sourcing agent. Big international buyers would come to Li & Fung for assistance in getting materials and products because the MNC was familiar with the producers throughout Southeast Asia and it knew the complex government regulations and how to successfully work through them. The MNC then moved into a more sophisticated stage in which it began developing the entire process for the buyer from concept to prototype to delivery of the goods. By the late 1980s, however, Hong Kong had become a very expensive place to manufacture products and Li & Fung changed its approach and began organizing around a new concept called "dispersed manufacturing," which draws heavily on dissection of the value chain and coordinating the operations of many suppliers in different geographic locations. For example, when the MNC receives an order from a European retailer to produce a large number of dresses, it has to decide where to buy the yarn in the world market, which companies should get the orders to weave and dye the cloth, where supplemental purchases such as buttons and zippers should be made, and how final shipment must be made to the customer. Commenting on this overall process, the company president recently noted:

This is a new type of value added, a truly global product that has never been seen before. The label may say "Made in Thailand," but it's not a Thai product. We dissect the manufacturing process and look for the best solution at each step. We're not asking which country can do the best job overall. Instead, we're pulling apart the value chain and optimizing each step—and we're doing it globally. Not only do the benefits outweigh the costs of logistics and transportation, but the higher value added also lets us charge more for our services. We deliver a sophisticated product and we deliver it fast. If you talk to the big global consumer products companies, they are all moving in this direction—toward being best on a global scale.[5]

Basic Organizational Structures

The above examples of Motorola, Xerox, and Li & Fung show how MNCs are dramatically reorganizing their operations to compete more effectively in the international arena. As with other MNCs following this strategic route, a number of basic organization structures need to be considered. In many cases, the designs are similar to those used domestically; however, significant differences may arise depending on the nature and scope of the overseas businesses and the home office's approach to controlling the operation. Ideally, an overseas affiliate or subsidiary will be designed to respond to specific concerns, such as production technology or the need for specialized personnel. The overall goal, however, is to meet the needs of both the local market and the home-office strategy of globalization.

Figure 11-1 illustrates how the pressures for globalization versus local responsiveness play out in a host of industries. As an MNC tries to balance these factors, an if–then contingency approach can be used. *If* the strategy needed to respond quickly to the local market changes, *then* there will be accompanying change in the organizational structure. Despite the need for such a flexible, fast-changing, contingency-based approach, most MNCs still slowly evolve through certain basic structural arrangements in international operations. The following sections examine these structures, beginning with initial, preinternational patterns.[6]

Initial Division Structure

Many firms make their initial entry into international markets by setting up a subsidiary or by exporting locally produced goods or services. A subsidiary is a common organizational

Figure 11–1

Organizational Consequences of Internationaliza-tion

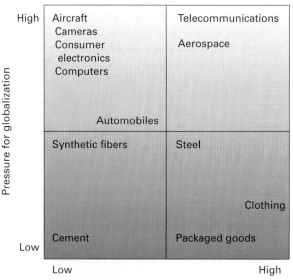

Source: Adapted from Paul W. Beamish, J. Peter Killing, Donald J. LeCraw, and Harold Crookell, *International Management: Text and Cases* (Homewood, IL: Irwin, 1991), p. 99.

arrangement for handling finance-related businesses or other operations that require an on-site presence from the start. In recent years, many service organization have begun exporting their expertise. Examples include architectural services, legal services, advertising, public relations, accounting, and management consulting. Research and development firms also fall into this category, exporting products that have been successfully developed and marketed locally.

An export arrangement is a common first choice among manufacturing firms, especially those with technologically advanced products. Because there is little, if any, competition, the firm can charge a premium price and handle sales through an export manager. If the company has a narrow product line, this export manager usually reports directly to the head of marketing, and international operations are coordinated by this department. If the firm has a broad product line and intends to export a number of different products into the international market, the export manager will head a separate department and often report directly to the president. These two arrangements work well as long as the company has little competition and is using international sales only to supplement domestic efforts.

If overseas sales continue to increase, local governments often exert pressure in these growing markets for setting up on-site manufacturing operations. A good example is the General Motors joint venture in China where between 30 and 40 percent of all parts are made locally. Additionally, many firms find themselves facing increased competition. Establishing foreign manufacturing subsidiaries can help the MNC to deal with both local government pressures and the competition. The overseas plants show the government that the firm wants to be a good local citizen. At the same time, these plants help the MNC greatly reduce transportation costs, thus making the product more competitive. This new structural arrangement often takes a form similar to that shown in Figure 11-2. Each foreign subsidiary is responsible for operations within its own geographic area, and the head of the subsidiary reports either to a senior executive who is coordinating international operations or directly to the home-office CEO.

International Division Structure

If international operations continue to grow, subsidiaries commonly are grouped into an **international division structure**, which handles all international operations out of a division that is created for this purpose. This structural arrangement is useful as it takes a great deal of the burden off the chief executive officer for monitoring the operations of a series of overseas subsidiaries as well as domestic operations. The head of the international division coordinates and monitors overseas activities and reports directly to the chief executive on these matters. Figure 11-3 provides an example. PepsiCo reorganized its international soft drink division into six such geographic business units covering 150 countries in which Pepsi does business. These geographic units each have self-sufficient operations and broad local authority.

International division structure
A structural arrangement that handles all international operations out of a division created for this purpose.

Home-office departments

Overseas subsidiaries

Figure 11–2

Use of Subsidiaries during the Early Stage of Internationalization

Figure 11–3

**An International
Division Structure**

(Partial Organization Chart)

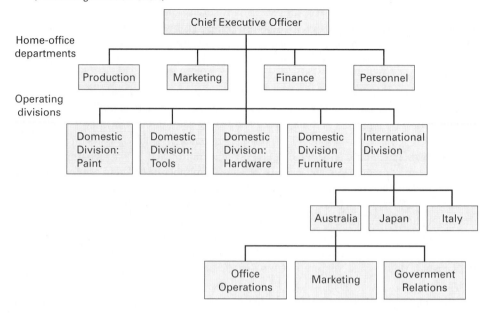

Companies still in the developmental stages of international business involvement are most likely to adopt the international division structure. Others that use this structural arrangement include those with small international sales, limited geographic diversity, or few executives with international expertise.

A number of advantages are associated with use of an international division structure. The grouping of international activities under one senior executive ensures that the international focus receives top management attention. The structural arrangement allows the company to develop an overall, unified approach to international operations, and the arrangement helps the firm to develop a cadre of internationally experienced managers.

Use of this structure does have a number of drawbacks, however. The structure separates the domestic and international managers, which can result in two different camps with divergent objectives. Also, as the international operation grows larger, the home office may find it difficult to think and act strategically and to allocate resources on a global basis; thus, the international division is penalized. Finally, most research and development efforts are domestically oriented, so ideas for new products or processes in the international market often are given low priority.

Global Structural Arrangements

MNCs typically turn to global structural arrangements when they begin acquiring and allocating their resources based on international opportunities and threats.[7] This international perspective signifies a major change in management strategy, and it is supported by the requisite changes in organization structure.[8] Global structures come in three common types: product, area, and functional.

Global product division
A structural arrangement in which domestic divisions are given worldwide responsibility for product groups.

Global Product Division   A **global product division** is a structural arrangement in which domestic divisions are given worldwide responsibility for product groups. Figure 11-4 provides an illustration. As shown, the manager who is in charge of product division C has authority for this product line on a global basis. This manager also has internal functional support related to the product line. For example, all marketing, production, and finance activities associated with product division C are under the control of this manager.

The global product divisions operate as profit centers. The products generally are in the growth stage of the product life cycle, so they need to be promoted and marketed care-

(Partial Organization Chart)

Figure 11–4

A Global Product Division Structure

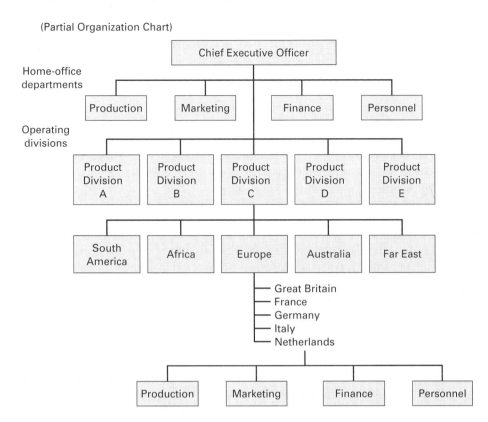

fully. In doing so, global product division managers generally run the operation with considerable autonomy; they have the authority to make many important decisions. However, corporate headquarters usually will maintain control in terms of budgetary constraints, home-office approval for certain decisions, and mainly "bottom-line" (i.e., profit) results.

A global product structure provides a number of benefits. If the firm is very diverse (e.g., it produces products using a variety of technologies or has a wide variety of customers), the need to tailor the product to specific demands of the buyer becomes important.[9] A global product arrangement can help to manage this diversity. Another benefit is the ability to cater to local needs. If many geographic areas must have the product modified to suit their particular desires (e.g., foods, toys, or electric shavers), a global product division structure can be extremely important. Still another benefit is that marketing, production, and finance can be coordinated on a product-by-product global basis. Firms also use a product division structure when a product has reached the maturity stage in the home country or similar markets but is in the growth stage in others, such as Third World countries. An example might be color televisions or VCRs. These differing life cycles require close technologic and marketing coordination between the home and foreign market, which is best done by a product division approach. Other advantages of a global product division structure can be summarized as follows:

> It preserves product emphasis and promotes product planning on a global basis; it provides a direct line of communication from the customer to those in the organization who have product knowledge and expertise, thus enabling research and development to work on development of products that serve the needs of the world customer; and it permits line and staff managers within the division to gain an expertise in the technical and marketing aspects of products assigned to them.[10]

Unfortunately, the approach also has some drawbacks. One is the necessity of duplicating facilities and staff personnel within each division. A second is that division managers may pursue currently attractive geographic prospects for their products and neglect other areas with better long-term potential. A third is that many division managers spend too much time trying to tap the local rather than the international market, because it is more convenient and they are more experienced in domestic operations.

Global area division
A structure under which global operations are organized on a geographic rather than a product basis.

Global Area Division   Instead of a global product division, some MNCs prefer to use a **global area division**. In this structure, global operations are organized based on a geographic rather than a product orientation. For example, the MNC may divide international operations into two groups; domestic and foreign, as shown in Figure 11-5. This approach often signals a major change in company strategy, because now international operations are put on the same level as domestic operations. In other words, European or Asian operations are just as important to the company as North American operations. For example, when British Petroleum purchased Standard Oil of Ohio, the firm revised its overall structure and adopted a global area division structure.

Under this arrangement, global division managers are responsible for all business operations in their designated geographic area. The chief executive officer and other members of top management are charged with formulating strategy that ensures the global divisions all work in harmony. For example, excess resources in one region are transferred to others that need them.

A global area division structure most often is used by companies that are in mature businesses and have narrow product lines. These product lines often are differentiated based on geographic area. For example, the product has a strong demand in Europe but not in South America, or the type of product that is offered in France differs from that sold in England. For example, the French want top-loading washing machines, but the British prefer front-loaders. Toys "R" Us stores in Japan feature a mix of roughly two-thirds Japanese toys and one-third imports.[11] In addition, the MNC usually seeks high economies of scale for production, marketing, and resource-purchase integration in that area. Thus, by manufacturing in this region rather than bringing the product in from somewhere else, the firm is able to reduce its cost per unit and bring the good to market at a very competitive price. Firms that produce autos, beverages, containers, cosmetics, food, or pharmaceuticals often use such a global area arrangement.

The geographic structure allows the division manager to cater to the tastes of the local market and make rapid decisions to accommodate environmental changes. A good example is food products. In the United States, soft drinks have less sugar than in South America, so the manufacturing process must be slightly different in these two locales. Similarly, in England, people prefer bland soups, but in France, the preference is for mildly spicy. In Turkey, Italy, Spain, and Portugal, people like dark, bitter coffee; in the United States, people prefer a milder, sweeter blend. In Europe, Canada, and the United States, people prefer less spicy food; in the Middle East and Asia, they like more heavily spiced food. A global area structure allows the geographic unit in a foods company to accommodate such local preferences.

Figure 11–5

A Global Area Division Structure

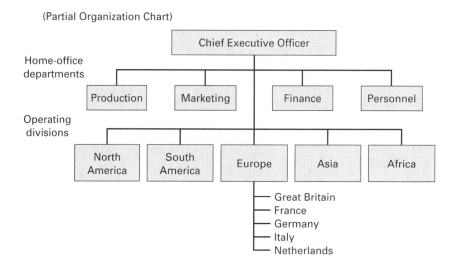

(Partial Organization Chart)

The primary disadvantage of the global area division structure is the difficulty encountered in reconciling a product emphasis with a geographic orientation. For example, if a product is sold worldwide, a number of different divisions are responsible for sales. This lack of centralized management and control, however, can result in increased costs and duplication of effort on a region-by-region basis. A second drawback is that new research and development efforts often are ignored by division groups, because they are selling goods that have reached the maturity stage. Their focus is not on the latest technologically superior goods that will win in the market in the long run but on those that are proven winners and now are being marketed conveniently worldwide.

Global Functional Division A **global functional division** organizes worldwide operations based primarily on function and secondarily on product. This approach is not widely used other than by extractive companies, such as oil and mining firms. Figure 11-6 provides an example.

A number of important advantages are associated with the global functional division structure. These include: (1) an emphasis on functional expertise; (2) tight centralized control; and (3) a relatively lean managerial staff. Some important disadvantages include: (1) coordination of manufacturing and marketing often is difficult; (2) managing multiple product lines can be difficult because of the separation of production and marketing into different departments; and (3) only the chief executive officer can be held accountable for the profits. As a result, the global functional process structure typically is favored only by those firms that need tight, centralized coordination and control of integrated production processes and those that are involved in transporting products and raw materials from one geographic area to another.

Mixed Organization Structures Some companies find that neither a global product, area, or functional arrangement is satisfactory. They opt for a **mixed organization structure,** which combines all three into an MNC that supplements its primary structure with a secondary one and, perhaps, a tertiary (third) one. For example, if a company uses a global area approach, committees of functional managers may provide assistance and support to the various geographic divisions. Conversely, if the firm uses a global functional approach, product committees may be responsible for coordinating transactions that cut across functional lines. In other cases, the organization will opt for a matrix structure that results in managers' having two or more bosses. Figure 11-7 illustrates this structure. In this arrangement, the MNC coordinates geographic and product lines through use of a matrix design.

In recent years, mixed organization structures have become increasingly popular. In one survey, more than one-third of responding firms indicated that they used this

Global functional division
A structure which organizes worldwide operations primarily based on function and secondarily on product.

Mixed organization structure
A structure that is a combination of a global product, area, or functional arrangement.

(Partial Organization Chart)

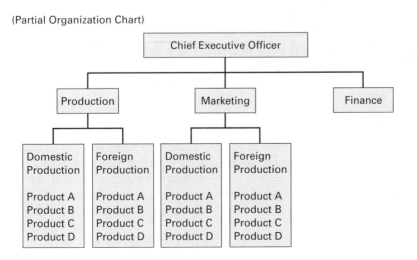

Figure 11–6

A Global Functional Structure

Figure 11–7

A Multinational Matrix Structure

(Partial Organization Chart)

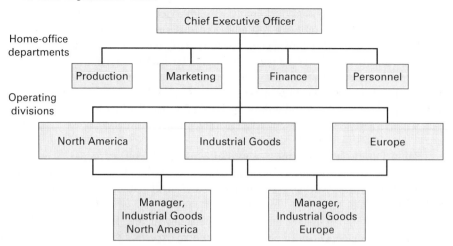

mixed organizational arrangement in contrast to others. In addition, respondents reported the following[12]:

International operations organized into national subsidiaries with local coordination for production/services, marketing, personnel, etc.	11.8%
International division structure with senior management reporting to the president or CEO of the company.	14.7%
One or more regional headquarters used to coordinate production/services, marketing, and personnel among national operations.	20.6%
World-production or world-matrix structure used for coordination of international operations.	17.6%
Mixed forms of structure.	35.3%

Many advantages can be gleaned from a mixed organization structure. In particular, it allows the organization to create the specific type of design that best meets its needs. However, there are shortcomings associated with matrix structures. The most important is that as the matrix design's complexity increases, coordinating the personnel and getting everyone to work toward common goals often become difficult. Too many groups are going their own way. Thus, many MNCs have not opted for a matrix structure; they are beginning to learn that simple, lean structures may be the best design.

Transnational Network Structures

Transnational network structure

A multinational structural arrangement that combines elements of function, product, and geographic designs, while relying on a network arrangement to link worldwide subsidiaries.

Besides matrix structures, another alternative international organizational design to recently emerge is the **transnational network structure.** This is designed to help MNCs take advantage of global economies of scale while also being responsive to local customer demands. The design combines elements of classic functional, product, and geographic elements, while relying on a network arrangement to link the various worldwide subsidiaries. At the center of the transnational network structure are nodes, which are units charged with coordinating product, functional, and geographic information. Different product line units and geographical area units have different structures depending on what is best for their particular operations. A good example of how the transnational network structure works is provided by N.V. Philips, which has operations in more than 60 countries and produces a diverse product line ranging from light bulbs to defense systems. In all, the company has eight product divisions with a varying number of subsidiaries in each—and the focus of these subsidiaries varies considerably. Some specialize in manufacturing, others in sales; some are closely controlled by headquarters, others are highly autonomous.

The basic structural framework of the transnational network consists of three components: dispersed subunits, specialized operations, and interdependent relationships. *Dispersed subunits* are subsidiaries that are located anywhere in the world where they can benefit the organization. Some are designed to take advantage of low factor costs, while others are responsible for providing information on new technologies or consumer trends. *Specialized operations* are activities carried out by subunits that focus on particular product lines, research areas, and marketing areas, and are designed to tap specialized expertise or other resources in the company's worldwide subsidiaries. *Interdependent relationships* are used to share information and resources throughout the dispersed and specialized subunits.

The transnational network structure is difficult to draw in the form of an organization chart because it is complex and continually changing. However, Figure 11-8 provides a view of N.V. Philips' network structure. These complex networks can be compared to some of the others that have been examined earlier in this chapter by looking at the ways in which the enterprise attempts to exercise control. Table 11-1 provides such a comparison.

Nontraditional Organizational Arrangements

In recent years, MNCs have increasingly expanded their operations in ways that differ from those used in the past. These include acquisitions, joint ventures, and *keiretsu*. These organizational arrangements do not use traditional hierarchical structures and therefore cannot be shown graphically. The following sections describe how they work.

Organizational Arrangements from Mergers

A recent development in the way that MNCs are organized stems from the acquisition of other firms. For example, in recent years British Petroleum acquired Amoco for $48.2 billion, Daimler-Benz bought the Chrysler Corporation for $40.5 billion, Northern Telecom acquired Bay Networks for $9 billion,[13] and Bayerische Vereinsbank and the Bayerische Hypotheken-und Wechsel-bank, both Munich-based banks, merged and created a German banking enterprise that is second in size only to Deutsche Bank.[14] Nippon Mining of Japan purchased Gould, the American semiconductor equipment firm; Hoechst, the German chemical and pharmaceutic giant, purchased Marion Merrell Dow[15]; and LG Electronics acquired Zenith.[16] In other cases, MNCs have taken an equity position but have not purchased the entire company. For example, Ford Motor owns 75 percent of Aston Martin Lagonda of Britain, 49 percent of Autolatina of Brazil, and 34 percent of Mazda of Japan.

In each of these examples, the purchasing MNCs have fashioned a structural arrangement that promotes synergy while encouraging local initiative by the acquired firm. The result is an organization design that draws on the more traditional structures that have been examined here but still has a unique structure specifically addressing the needs of the two firms.

Organizational Arrangements from Joint Ventures

Another good example of recent organizational developments is joint-venture agreements, in which each party contributes to the undertaking but all parties coordinate their efforts for the overall good of the enterprise.[17] Samsung, the giant Korean MNC, provides a good example. This company now is melding heavy investment, acquisitions, and alliances for multimedia gear, cellular phones, and personal digital assistants. The MNC is strong in the area of memory chips, but to become a broad-based technology giant, Samsung must rely on strategic alliances. Today, the company has an arrangement with Motorola to develop the next generation of personal digital assistants based on Motorola's DragonBall microprocessor. Samsung also has alliances with AT&T to create pen-based computers, with

Figure 11–8   **The Network Structure of N.V. Philips**

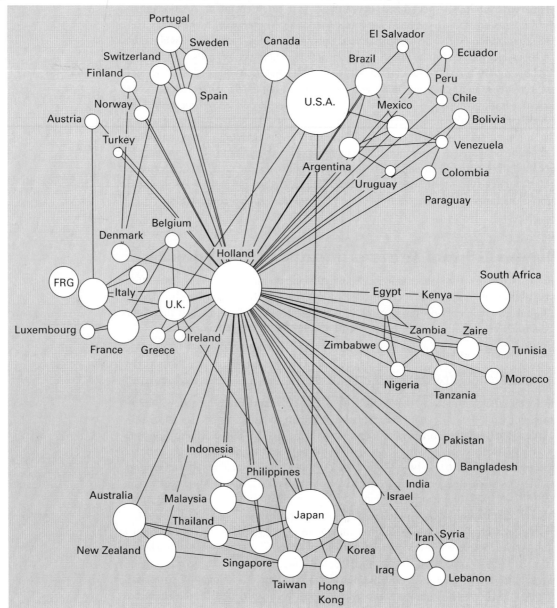

Source: See S. Ghoshal and C. A. Bartlett, "The Multinational Corporation as an Interorganizational Network," *Academy of Management Review,* October 1990, pp. 603–625.

Toshiba to make 64-megabyte flash memory chips, with USA Video to create video file servers, and with General Instrument to develop digital television.[18] Another recent example is the Morgan Stanley Group, which has entered a joint venture with the People's Construction Bank of China to create the China International Capital Corporation. Other partners in this venture include the Singapore government and a Hong Kong holding company. The objective is to help win deals involving project financing, direct investment, and both equity and bond offerings at a time when China needs to finance enormous infrastructure projects.[19]

Both of these joint ventures require carefully formulated structures that allow each partner to contribute what it does best and efficiently coordinate their efforts. In the case of Samsung, this calls for clearly spelling out the responsibilities of all parties and identifying the authority that each will have for meeting specific targets. In the case of China International Capital Corporation, the organizational structure will be used not only to raise capital but to network with the political structure.[20]

Table 11–1

Control Mechanisms Used in Select Multinational Organization Structures

Type of Multinational Structure	Output Control	Bureaucratic Control	Decision-Making Control	Cultural Control
International division structure	Profit control	Have to follow company policies	Typically there is some centralization	Treated like all other divisions
Global area division	Use of profit centers	Some policies and procedures are necessary	Local units are given autonomy	Local subsidiary culture is often the most important
Global product division	Unit output for supply; sales volume for sales	Tight process controls are used to maintain product quality and consistency	Centralized as the product-division headquarters level	Possible for some companies, but not always necessary
Matrix structure	Profit responsibility is shared with product and geographic units	Not very important	Balanced between the global area and product units	Culture must support the shared decision making
Transnational network structure	Used for supplier units and for some independent profit centers	Not very important	Few decision are centralized at headquarters; most are centralized in the key network nodes	Organization culture transcends national cultures, supports sharing and learning, and is the most important control mechanism

One of the main objectives in developing the structure for joint ventures is to help the partners address and effectively meld their different values, management styles, action orientation, and organization preferences. Figure 11-9 illustrates how Western and Asian firms differ in terms of these four areas; the figure also is useful in illustrating the types of considerations that need to be addressed by MNCs from the same area of the world. Consider, for example, two Asian MNCs such as Korea's Samsung, and Japan's NEC. Samsung has a joint-venture agreement with NEC for developing 256-megabyte DRAM chips. The two firms will need to structure their organizational interface carefully to ensure effective interaction, coordination, and cooperation. Simply put, in the case of both Samsung and its partners as well as the China International Capital Corporation and its partners, a mixed structure will be employed to ensure that the joint-venture partners are able to work both efficiently and harmoniously.[21]

Organizational Arrangements from *Keiretsus*

Still another type of newly emerging organizational arrangement is the **keiretsu**, which is a large, often vertically integrated group of companies that cooperate and work closely with each other. A good example is the Mitsubishi Group, which is shown in Figure 11-10. This figure simply shows the members of the Mitsubishi *keiretsu;* it is not intended to be a matrix structure showing authority relationships. This *keiretsu* consists of 28 core members who are bound together not by authority relationships but rather by cross-ownership, long-term business dealings, interlocking directorates, and social ties (many of the senior executives are college classmates). As shown in Figure 11-10, there are three flagship firms in the group: Mitsubishi Corporation, which is a trading company; Mitsubishi Bank, which finances the *keiretsu*'s operations; and Mitsubishi Heavy Industries, which is a leading worldwide manufacturer. In addition to the firms in Figure 11-10, hundreds of other Mitsubishi-related companies contribute to the power of the *keiretsu*.

Keiretsu

In Japan, a newly emerging organizational arrangement in which a large, often vertically integrated group of companies cooperate and work closely with each other to provide goods and services to end users; core members may be bound together by cross-ownership, long-term business dealings, interlocking directorates, and social ties.

Figure 11-9

A Comparison of Asian and Western Management Features

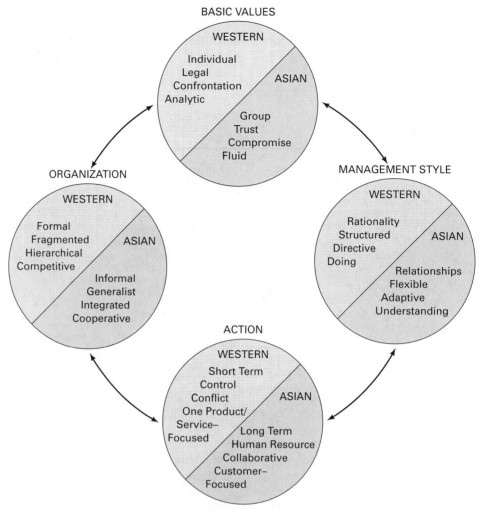

BASIC VALUES

WESTERN

Individual
Legal
Confrontation
Analytic

ASIAN

Group
Trust
Compromise
Fluid

ORGANIZATION

WESTERN

Formal
Fragmented
Hierarchical
Competitive

ASIAN

Informal
Generalist
Integrated
Cooperative

MANAGEMENT STYLE

WESTERN

Rationality
Structured
Directive
Doing

ASIAN

Relationships
Flexible
Adaptive
Understanding

ACTION

WESTERN

Short Term
Control
Conflict
One Product/
Service–
Focused

ASIAN

Long Term
Human Resource
Collaborative
Customer–
Focused

Source: Reprinted from *European Management Journal,* June, Frederic Swierczek and Georges Hirsch, "Joint Ventures in Asia and Multicultural Management," p. 203, © 1994, with kind permission from Elsevier Sciences Ltd., The Boulevard, Langford Lane, Kidlington, OX5 IGB, U.K.

This form of organizational arrangement has been cited by some international management analysts as the reason why Japanese MNCs are so successful. For example, before the Asian economic crisis that began a few years ago, *keiretsu* companies in Japan accounted for less than 1/10 of 1 percent of all Japanese firms, but over one-half of the value of all shares on the Tokyo Stock Exchange, as well as over 50 percent of all Japanese investments made in U.S. high-tech firms, and over 50 percent of all Japanese-affiliated manufacturing facilities in California.

The Japanese are not the only ones using this organizational arrangement, however. Even large U.S. MNCs are creating their own type of *keiretsus.* Ford Motor, for example, now focuses its attention only on automotive and financial services and has divested itself of most other businesses. In the process of reorganizing, Ford has created a giant, *keiretsu*-like arrangement that includes research and development (R&D), parts production, vehicle assembly, financial services, and marketing. For example, in R&D, Ford belongs to eight consortia that conduct research in areas such as improved engineering techniques, materials, and electric-car batteries. In parts production, Ford has equity stakes in Cummins (engines), Excel Industries (windows), and Decoma International (body parts, wheels), and it relies on these firms as major suppliers. In vehicle assembly, Ford has ownership interests in Europe, South America, and Asia and uses these arrangements to both manufacture

Figure 11–10   **The Mitsubishi *Keiretsu*** *

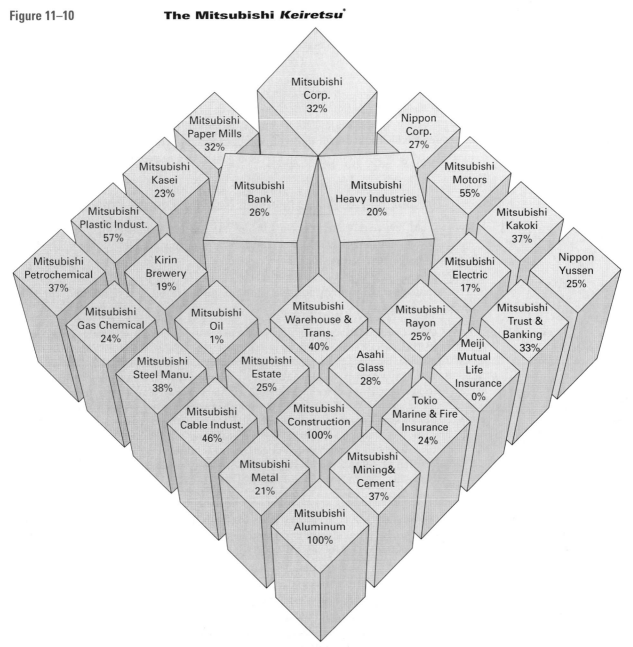

*Percentages refer to the shares of each company that are held by other members of the group.
Source: Adapted from William J. Holstein et al., "Mighty Mitsubishi Is on the Move," *Business Week,* Sept. 24, 1990, pp. 98–104.

and sell autos in these parts of the world. In financial services, Ford has seven wholly owned units that cover a wide gamut, from consumer credit to commercial lending.

    Ford is not alone. Today, more and more U.S. firms are cooperating to improve their competitiveness and offset the impact of foreign *keiretsus* that have been rapidly moving across the continuum of business activity, from upstream R&D to downstream marketing. For example, in the area of research, there now are more than 250 R&D consortia in the United States that are sharing both costs and information. The Big Three automakers are jointly working on new battery technology for electric cars. In design and production, manufacturers and suppliers are becoming partners; for example, at John Deere, workers now team up with their counterparts at suppliers such as McLaughlin Body Company to improve quality and cut costs. In the financing area, large companies such as Digital Equipment, IBM, and Novellus Systems are taking equity positions or lending money to their strategic suppliers to ensure high-quality parts and on-time delivery. In the marketing area, manufacturers and suppliers are selling and servicing each other's products. For example, Mazda buys vehicles from Ford for sale in the United States, and vice versa.

These new organizational arrangements are resulting in a need for flexible structures that are designed to promote cooperation between enterprises. As the positive effect of *keiretsu*-like arrangements begins to spread, more and more MNCs will find that their structures are interlinked with those of partners and suppliers. The result will be a design that is difficult to draw on paper but that is very effective in practice.

The Emergence of the Electronic Network Form of Organization

Over the last few years there has been a major increase in the number of "electronic free-lancers"—individuals who work on a project for a company, usually via the Internet, and when the assignment is done they move on to other employment. In a way, these individuals represent a new type of electronic network organization, "temporary companies" that serve a particular, short-term purpose and then go on to other assignments. There are numerous examples.

> Consider the way many manufacturers are today pursuing radical outsourcing strategies, letting external agents perform more of their traditional activities. The U.S. computer-display division of the Finnish company Nokia, for example, chose to enter the U.S. display market with only five employees. Technical support, logistics, sales, and marketing were all subcontracted to specialists around the country. The fashion accessories company Topsy Tail, which has revenues of $80 million but only three employees, never even touches its products through the entire supply chain. It contracts with various injection-molding companies to manufacture its goods; uses design agencies to create its packaging; and distributes and sells its products through a network of independent fulfillment houses, distributors, and sales reps. Nokia's and Topsy Tail's highly decentralized operations bear more resemblance to the network model of organization than to the traditional industrial model.[22]

Many multinationals are beginning to rely increasingly on electronic freelancers (e-lancers, for short) to perform key tasks for them. In the case of General Motors, for example, outsourcers via computers work very closely with the company in providing both design and engineering assistance. The rise of the multinational university is yet another example. A growing number of academic institutions from Europe to North America are now offering both undergraduate and graduate courses, and in some cases full-fledged degree programs, via the Internet. In staffing these courses, the universities rely heavily on e-lancers with PhD degrees who are responsible for delivering the course on-line. In most cases, the university has little face-to-face contact with these e-lancers. Everything is done via computers.

These electronic network organizations are now becoming increasingly prominent. MNCs are realizing that the outsourcing function can be delivered on-line. Examples include design specifications, analytical computations, and consulting reports. So, in a way, this new structure is a version of the matrix design discussed earlier in the chapter. The major difference, however, is that many of the people in the structure are not only temporary, contingent employees but often never see each other and communicate exclusively in an electronic environment.

The New Role of Organizational Synergy

As MNCs increase their globalization, they must meet the challenge of leveraging their knowledge and resources worldwide. The whole becomes greater than the sum of its parts, or there is a synergy effect. Such synergy can take a number of different forms. Some of the most common include the following:

1. Sharing know-how by having personnel in one geographic region pool their insights, knowledge, and information into a particular process or function with those in another region.

2. Sharing tangible resources such as by creating a research lab that serves the needs of all worldwide units.

3. Pooling purchases so that the company is able to achieve greater negotiating power and quantity discounts with its suppliers.

4. Coordinating strategies between units and divisions so that each is more efficient and profitable.

5. Using vertical integration to coordinate the flow of products or services from one unit to another, thus reducing inventory costs, speeding product development, increasing capacity utilization, and improving market access.

6. Creating new businesses by taking discrete activities from various units and combining them into new units or by establishing internal joint ventures or alliances.[23]

Unfortunately, many MNCs have found that the achievement of organizational synergy can be extremely difficult. Some companies, for example, have tried to attain this synergy by coordinating their main product lines and rolling out standardized offerings worldwide—and the outcomes have been very disappointing. In one case, pressured by the chief executive officer who wanted to promote collaboration and standardization across countries in order to leverage the firm's brands internationally, managers launched a succession of high-profile synergy initiatives that resulted in dismal results. Here are the specifics:

> A leading U.K. cookie brand was launched with considerable expense in the United States. It promptly flopped. A past promotion that had worked well in Germany was rolled out in Italy and Spain. It backfired, eroding both margins and market shares. An attempt was made to standardize ingredients across Europe for some confectionery products in order to achieve economies of scale in purchasing and manufacturing. Consumers balked at buying the reformulated products.[24]

Many MNCs have had similar experiences. As a result, there is now an increased movement toward making synergy work correctly. One of the emerging trends is that of conducting detailed analysis before deciding to pursue synergistic programs. This approach helps companies deal with the all-too-common belief that home-office personnel know that synergies can be achieved in the international market but local managers in these geographic regions do not want to make the changes that will be necessary in bringing about these synergies. In truth, many markets do not lend themselves to standardized, worldwide approaches. The culture of the local environment requires a specially designed program that works well here—but not necessarily anywhere else.

A second emerging trend is a focus on determining the types of skills needed in individuals who will be heading synergistic programs. Rather than simply assigning someone based on technical knowledge, MNCs are now looking very closely at the person's ability to create trust, empathize, listen, and achieve meaningful collaboration between all involved parties. The personal characteristics of these managers are now getting more attention than ever.

A third emerging trend is to focus on the downside of introducing synergy programs. In the past it was common for organizations to have an upside bias in which shortcomings were downplayed. Now MNCs are organizing the analysis of the program so that both the positive and negative effects are carefully examined.

A fourth approach that is gaining in popularity is the disaggregation of the various parts of synergy programs. For example, one manager who was charged with leveraging her firm's international brands found that the task had three separate components: (1) make the brand recognizable across borders; (2) reduce duplicated effort; and (3) increase the flow of marketing know-how. Each of these three components, in turn, could be further disaggregated. For example, to make the brand recognizable would involve a number of different efforts including brand positioning, pricing, packaging, ingredients, and advertising. And each of these could be broken down even farther. Packaging, for example, required attention to such things as material of the product, size, shape, and color of the unit, and size of the label. By carefully examining all of these disaggregated parts, the executive was able to create a synergistic program that was acceptable to the product managers worldwide and resulted in reduced cost and higher profits. As a result of such successes, many MNCs are now organizing their synergy efforts around disaggregation activities.

Organizing for Product Integration

Another recent organizing development is the emergence of designs that are tailored toward helping multinationals integrate product development into their worldwide operations. In the recent past the use of cross-functional coordination has been helpful in achieving this goal. However, MNCs have also found that this arrangement results in people spending less time within their functions and thus becoming less knowledgeable regarding developments that are occurring in their specialized areas. A second shortcoming of the cross-functional approach is that it has often led to product teams becoming autonomous and thus failing to integrate their overall efforts with the organization at large. Most recently Toyota has created a structure that combines a highly formalized system with new structural innovations which ensure that projects are flexibly managed and, at the same time, able to benefit from the learning and experiences of other projects. In accomplishing this, Toyota employs six organizational mechanisms.

One of these is called mutual adjustment. In most companies this is achieved by assigning people to a specific project and having them meet face-to-face and work out a plan of action for designing the new product. At Toyota, however, design engineers are not assigned to specific projects; rather they remain in their functional area and they typically communicate through written messages. This approach ensures that all members remain dedicated to their primary functional area and that they communicate succinctly and directly with each—thus saving time.

A second mechanism employed by Toyota is the use of direct, technically skilled supervisors. In a typical arrangement design engineers are led by individuals who are no longer doing engineering work; they are primarily responsible for seeing that others do this work. However, at Toyota supervisors remain highly skilled in the technical side of the work and are responsible for mentoring, training, and developing their engineers. So if anyone has a design-related problem, the supervisor is technically skilled and can provide this assistance.

A third mechanism is the use of integrative leadership. In typical product design structures, the manager in charge has full authority and relies on the engineering personnel to get the work done according to time, cost, and quality parameters. At Toyota, however, these managers are responsible for coordinating the work of the functional specialists and serving less as a manager than a lead designer on the entire project. In this way, they serve as the glue that binds together the whole process.

In typical design operations, engineers are hired from universities or from other companies where they have gained experience and they remain in their engineering position indefinitely. At Toyota most of the technical training is provided in-house and people are rotated within only one function such as body engineers who work on auto-body subsystems for most, if not all, of their careers. As a result, they are able to get more work done faster because they do not have to communicate and coordinate continually with their counterparts regarding what needs to be done. They are so familiar with their jobs that they know what needs to be done.

Another organizational difference is that in typical design work each new product calls for a new development process and there are complex forms and bureaucratic procedures for ensuring that everything is done correctly. At Toyota standard milestones are created by the project leader and simple forms and procedures are employed so that the work can be done simply and efficiently.

A final difference is that in many organizations design standards are obsolete and rigid. At Toyota these standards are maintained by the people who are doing the work and are continually changed to meet new design demands.

The organizational approach used at Toyota is now being carefully studied by other world-class auto manufacturers, who are coming to realize that the old way of organizing for product design is not sufficiently effective for dealing with the competitive challenges of the new millennium. In particular, a new organizational emphasis has to be placed on better blending the personnel and the work. Commenting on all of this, a group of experts who studied Toyota's approach recently wrote:

> the success of Toyota's system rides squarely on the shoulders of its people. Successful product development requires highly competent, highly skilled people with a lot of hands-on experience, deep technical knowledge, and an eye for the overall system. When we look at all the things that Toyota does well, we find two foundations for its product-development system: chief engineers using their expertise to gain leadership, and functional engineers using their expertise to reduce the amount of communication, supervision, trial and error, and confusion in the process. All the other coordinating mechanisms and practices serve to help highly skilled engineers do their job effectively. By contrast, many other companies seem to aspire to develop systems "designed by geniuses to be run by idiots." Toyota prefers to develop and rely on the skill of its personnel, and it shapes its product-development process around this central idea: people, not systems, design cars.[25]

The Changing Role of Information Technology in Organizing

Another major change that is taking place in the way multinationals organize themselves is related to the role of information technology (IT). After a slow start, Japanese firms, in particular, are now leading the way in redefining how IT will be used in the next decade. One of the major differences between IT in American multinationals and their Japanese counterparts is that in Japan IT is not seen as something special or different but, rather, is viewed as being part of a fully integrated picture. In the process, Japanese firms now carefully target how they are going to use information technology and try hard to neither overrate nor underrate its role and importance. A good contrast is provided by Seven-Eleven Japan and NSK, one of the world's leading bearings and auto component manufacturers.

In the case of Seven-Eleven Japan, the company has aggressively invested in IT and used this system to monitor and meet customer needs. For example, Japanese consumers place a high premium on product freshness. Many years ago the company began using its IT system to create a just-in-time arrangement that relied on multiple daily deliveries of products. Today, each store's fresh food changes over entirely three times a day, which allows managers to change their unit's physical layout throughout the day, as the flow of customers shifts from housewives to students to working people. Moreover, the company's just-in-time system allows the stores to be extraordinarily responsive to consumers' shifting tastes. For example, if a particular kind of take-out lunch sells out by noon, extra stock can be in the store within an hour. Conversely, if it is raining, the IT system will remind cash register operators to put umbrellas on sale next to the register. This level of responsiveness is made possible by a sophisticated point-of-sale data-collection system and an electronic ordering system that links individual stores to a central distribution center.

In the case of NSK, the company uses a combination of both highly integrated technology systems and low-tech systems. For example, for simulation and analysis in component design, engineers rely on the firm's flexible-engineering information control system and an array of databases and expert systems. Quality engineers use handheld terminals to monitor quality data, which are automatically recorded from in-line sensors and inspection machines. Salespeople can search sophisticated databases and narrow the range of products that they will suggest to a customer. At the same time, NSK has a number of low technology islands where the personnel use machinery and equipment that is over a decade old and rely on their own judgment in making decisions and processing information. By choosing the best mix of information technology, the company is able to maintain its competitiveness.[26]

Other contrasts between the ways in which IT issues are addressed by Western firms and Japanese companies are provided in Table 11-2. A close analysis of these contrasts shows that the integration of IT into the overall organizing process can have a dramatic effect on the performance of an organization.

Use of Subsidiary Boards of Directors

Organizing begins on the top, with boards of directors. These boards are responsible for overseeing the corporation and ensuring that senior managers are operating in accord with the overall policies and objectives established by the board. As firms increase their international focus, many are finding that subsidiary boards of directors are useful in helping to shape and guide the activities of global operations.

Subsidiary board of directors

A board that overseas and monitors the operations of a foreign subsidiary.

A **subsidiary board of directors** oversees and monitors the operations of a foreign subsidiary. In recent years, this organizational arrangement has become increasingly popular. Some of the best-known multinationals use this arrangement, including Dow Chemical; Hewlett-Packard; Pilkington Bros., Ltd.; Honda Motor; and Matsushita Electric.

There are a number of reasons for this trend toward subsidiary boards. The main one is that as the external environment in which MNCs operate becomes extremely complex, rapid decision making gains in importance. To meet this need for immediate response, subsidiaries must be given more authority for local operations. At the same time, however, the corporate board would like to ensure that the subsidiary does not become too autonomous. The solution to this dilemma is a local board, which can play an important

Table 11–2
Contrasting Approaches to Using Information Technology: Western and Japanese Views

Key Issue	How Western Firms Address the Matter	How Japanese Firms Address the Matter
How to decide the information systems needed by the business.	Develop an IT strategy that aligns with the company's business strategy.	Determine the basic way the firm competes, driven particularly by its operations goals, and use this to determine the IT investment.
How to determine if the investments in IT are worthwhile.	Adapt the capital budgeting process to manage and evaluate the IT investment.	Judge investments based on operational performance improvements.
When trying to improve a business process, how technology fits into management's thinking.	Assume that technology offers the smartest, cheapest way to improve performance.	Identify a performance goal and then select a technology that will help the firm achieve this goal in a way that supports the people doing the work.
How IT users and IT specialists should connect in the organization.	Teach specialists about business goals and develop technically adept, business-savvy Chief Information Officers.	Encourage integration by rotating managers through the IT function and giving IT oversight to executives who oversee other functions.
How systems to improve organization performance can be designed.	Design the most technically elegant system possible and ask employees to adapt to it.	Design a system that makes use of the tacit and explicit knowledge that employees already possess.

Source: Adapted from M. Bensaou and Michael Earl, "The Right Mind-set for Managing Information Technology," *Harvard Business Review,* September–October 1998, p. 121.

linking role between the two groups. The subsidiary board also can assist the unit in planning and controlling activities.

Four major areas in which MNCs use subsidiary boards have been identified. One is to advise, approve, and appraise local management. A second is to help the unit respond to local conditions. A third is to assist in strategic planning, and a fourth is to supervise the subsidiary's ethical conduct. These areas are spelled out in greater detail in Table 11-3, where survey responses from U.S., Canadian, Japanese, and European samples are provided. A close look at the table shows that the Japanese and the Swedes tend to place greater importance on these boards than Europeans and Americans, although all countries report important benefits from the use of these boards. Will the future see increasing use of this organizational arrangement? Very likely, the answer is yes.

Organizational Characteristics of MNCs

Although MNCs have similar organizational structures, they do not all operate the same way. A variety of factors have been identified that help to explain the differences. These include overall strategy, employee attitudes, and local conditions. Of particular significance to this discussion are the organizational characteristics of formalization, specialization, and centralization.

Table 11–3
Importance of Subsidiary Boards over the Next 5 to 10 Years
Mean Ratings (1 = Low; 5 = High)

	United States (n=31)	Canada (n=9)	Japan (n=14)	Europe, excluding Sweden (n=28)	Sweden (n=8)
Local management					
Advising local management	3.50	3.67	4.15	3.43	4.00
Approving budgets and short-term plans of the subsidiary	2.48	3.00	4.36	2.75	3.13
Monitoring operating performance and corrective measures in the subsidiary	2.81	3.00	4.00	2.71	3.38
Appraising the subsidiary's top management performance and top officers' compensation	2.10	2.33	3.64	2.46	2.63
Deciding the amount to remit as dividends	2.39	2.33	3.57	2.18	2.00
Local country contacts and conditions					
Facilitating the establishment of contacts with local leaders and institutions	2.90	3.56	3.62	3.32	3.88
Identifying and responding to concerned stakeholders (e.g., environmentalists and consumer groups)	2.10	1.44	3.50	1.68	1.00
Ensuring compliance with local legal requirements	3.50	2.67	4.23	3.00	3.75
Providing knowledge of local economic, political, and social conditions	3.48	3.44	4.00	3.39	4.25
Appraising and minimizing the subsidiary's political risk	3.00	2.89	3.79	2.57	2.57
Strategic plan					
Participating in drawing up the subsidiary's strategic plan	2.52	3.00	4.29	2.54	2.88
Ethical issues					
Supervising the subsidiary's ethical conduct	2.94	2.67	3.64	2.82	2.75

Source: Adapted from Mark P. Kriger and Patrick J. J. Rich, "Strategic Governance: Why and How MNCs Are Using Boards of Directors in Foreign Subsidiaries," *Columbia Journal of World Business,* Winter 1987, p. 43. Copyright 1987, reprinted with permission.

Formalization

Formalization

The use of defined structures and systems in decision making, communicating, and controlling.

Formalization is the use of defined structures and systems in decision making, communicating, and controlling. Some countries make greater use of formalization than others; in turn, this affects the day-to-day organizational functioning. One recent large research study of Korean firms found that unlike employees in the United States, Korean workers perceive more positive work environments when expectations for their jobs are set forth more strictly and formally. In short, Koreans respond very favorably to formalization.[27] Korean firms tend to be quite formal, but this may not hold throughout Asia. For example, a study that investigated whether Japanese organizations are more formalized than U.S. organizations found that although Japanese firms tend to use more labor-intensive approaches to areas such as bookkeeping and office-related work than their U.S. counterparts, no statistical data support the contention that Japanese firms are more formalized.[28]

Another study of U.S. and Japanese firms in Taiwan divided formalization into two categories: objective and subjective.[29] Objective formalization was measured by things such as the number of different documents given to employees, organizational charts, information booklets, operating instructions, written job descriptions, procedure manuals, written policies, and work-flow schedules and programs. Subjective formalization was measured by the extent to which goals were vague and unspecified, use of informal controls, and use of culturally induced values in getting things done. The findings of this study are reported in Table 11-4.

Commenting on differences in the use of formalization, the researchers concluded that

> American and Japanese firms appear to have almost the same level of written goals or objectives for subordinates, written standards of performance appraisals, written schedules, programs, and work specifications, written duties, authority and accountability. However, managers in Japanese firms perceive less formalization than do managers in American firms. Less reliance on formal rules and structure in Japanese firms is also revealed by the emphasis on face-to-face or behavioral mode of control indicated by the ratio of foreign expatriates to total employees in subsidiaries.[30]

Table 11–4
Organizational Characteristics of U.S. and Japanese Firms in Taiwan

Characteristics	U.S. Firms (n=38)	Japanese Firms (n=85)
Formalization (subjective)	3.54	3.47
Formalization (objective)	11.39	10.91
Horizontal specialization	12.89	10.02
Vertical specialization	7.04	7.75
Job routinization	2.25	2.86
Job autonomy	2.78	2.62
Foreign expatriates per 1,000 employees	4.2	16.6
Ratio of firms using quality circles (in percentages)	24	32

Note: The highest score for the subjective formalization index, job routinization index, and autonomy index is 6; the lowest score is 1. The highest score for the objective formalization index is 19; the lowest score is 0. The highest score for the horizontal specialization index is 16; the lowest score is 0. Ratios of foreign expatriates to total employees are calculated on the basis of firms with 50 or more employees.

Source: Adapted from Rhy-song Yeh and Tagi Sagafi-nejad, "Organizational Characteristics of American and Japanese Firms in Taiwan," *National Academy of Management Proceedings,* 1987, p. 113. Used with permission.

The study also found that U.S. MNCs tend to rely heavily on budgets, financial data, and other formalized tools in controlling their subsidiary operations. This contrasts with Japanese MNCs, in which wider use is made of face-to-face, informal controls. These findings reveal that although the outward structural design of overseas subsidiaries may appear to be similar, the internal functioning in characteristics such as formalization may be quite different.

In recent years, this formal/informal characteristic of organizations has become the focal point of increased attention.[31] One reason is because MNCs now realize there are two dimensions of formality/informality that must be considered: internal and external. Moreover, to a large degree, these formal/informal relationships require effective networking of a different type. As Yoshino and Rangan noted, there are

> two approaches that firms that must compete globally—and that includes most major firms— employ to achieve the layering of competitive advantages: (1) development of extensive *internal networks* of international subsidiaries in major national or regional markets and (2) forging *external networks* of strategic alliances with firms around the world. These approaches are not mutually exclusive, and increasingly firms are striving to build both types of networks.[32]

What is particularly interesting about these networking relationships is that each places a different set of demands on the MNC. In particular, external networking with joint-venture partners often involves ambiguous organizational mandates, less emphasis on systems and more on people, and ambiguous lines of authority. This is a marked difference from internal networking characteristics, where formality is much stronger than informality and the enterprise can rely on a shared vision, clear organizational mandates, and well-developed systems and lines of authority.[33] Table 11-5 summarizes the characteristics of these internal and external networks.

Specialization

As an organizational characteristic, **specialization** is the assigning of individuals to specific, well-defined tasks. Specialization in an international context can be classified into horizontal and vertical specialization.

Horizontal specialization assigns jobs so that individuals are given a particular function to perform, and people tend to stay within the confines of this area. Examples include jobs in areas such as customer service, sales, recruiting, training, purchasing, and marketing research. When there is a great deal of horizontal specialization, personnel will develop functional expertise in one particular area.

Vertical specialization assigns work to groups or departments where individuals are collectively responsible for performance. Vertical specialization also is characterized by distinct differences between levels in the hierarchy such that those higher up are accorded much more status than those further down, and the overall structure usually is quite tall.

Specialization
An organizational characteristic that assigns individuals to specific, well-defined tasks.

Horizontal specialization
The assignment of jobs so that individuals are given a particular function to perform and tend to stay within the confines of this area.

Vertical specialization
The assignment of work to groups or departments where individuals are collectively responsible for performance.

Table 11–5
Internal vs. External Networks

Managerial Dimensions	Internal Network	External Network
Shared vision	Yes	No
Animating mindset	Cooperation	Cooperation and competition
Organizational mandates	Clear	Ambiguous
Organizational objective	Global optimization	Develop win-win approaches
Emphasis on systems	More	Less
Emphasis on people	Less	More
Lines of authority	Clear	Ambiguous at best

Source: Information drawn from Michael Yoshino and N. S. Rangan, *Strategic Alliances* (Boston: Harvard Business School Press, 1995), p. 203.

In the earlier, comparative study of 55 U.S. and 51 Japanese manufacturing plants, Japanese organizations had lower functional specialization of employees. Specifically, three-quarters of the functions listed were assigned to specialists in the U.S. plants, but less than one-third were assigned in the Japanese plants.[34] Later studies with regard to formalization have echoed this finding on specialization. As shown in Table 11-4, U.S. subsidiaries have more specialists than Japanese firms do.

By contrast, studies find that the Japanese rely more heavily on vertical specialization. They have taller organization structures in contrast to the flatter designs of their U.S. counterparts. Japanese departments and units also are more differentiated than those in U.S. organizations. Vertical specialization can be measured by the amount of group activity as well, such as in quality circles. Table 11-4 shows that Japanese firms make much greater use of quality circles than the U.S. firms. Vertical specialization also can result in greater job routinization. Because one is collectively responsible for the work, strong emphasis is placed on everyone's doing the job in a predetermined way, refraining from improvising, and structuring the work so that everyone can do the job after a short training period. Again, Table 11-4 shows that the Japanese organizations make much wider use of job routinization than U.S. organizations.

Centralization

Centralization

A management system under which important decisions are made at the top.

Decentralization

Pushing decision making down the line and getting the lower-level personnel involved.

Centralization is a management system in which important decisions are made at the top. In an international context, the value of centralization will vary according to the local environment and the goals of the organization. Many U.S. firms tend toward **decentralization,** pushing decision making down the line and getting the lower-level personnel involved. German MNCs centralize strategic headquarter-specific decisions independent of the host country and decentralize operative decisions in accordance with the local situation in the host country. The accompanying sidebar, "Organizing in Germany," describes how relatively small German MNCs have been very successful with such a decentralization strategy. A comparative study found that Japanese organizations delegate less formal authority than their U.S. counterparts, but the Japanese permit greater involvement in decisions by employees lower in the hierarchy. At the same time, however, the Japanese manage to maintain strong control over their lower-level personnel by limiting the amount of authority given to the latter and carefully controlling and orchestrating worker involvement and participation in quality circles.[35] Other studies show similar findings.[36]

When evaluating the presence of centralization by examining the amount of autonomy that Japanese give to their subordinates, one study concluded:

> In terms of job autonomy, employees in American firms have greater freedom to make their decisions and their own rules than in Japanese firms. . . . Results show that managers in American firms perceive a higher degree of delegation than do managers in Japanese firms. Also, managers in American firms feel a much higher level of participation in the coordinating with other units, . . . in influencing the company's policy related to their work, and in influencing the company's policy in areas not related to their work.[37]

The finding related to influence is explained in more detail in Table 11-6; U.S. managers in Taiwanese subsidiaries felt that they had greater influence than did their Japanese counterparts. Moreover, when statistically analyzed, these data proved to be significant.

Putting Organizational Characteristics in Perspective

MNCs tend to organize their international operations in a manner similar to that used at home. If the MNC tends to have high formalization, specialization, and centralization at its home-based headquarters, these organizational characteristics probably will occur in the firm's international subsidiaries.[38] Japanese and U.S. firms are good examples. As the researchers of the comparative study in Taiwan concluded: "Almost 80 percent of Japanese firms and more than 80 percent of American firms in the sample have been oper-

International Management in Action
Organizing in Germany
www.stihlusa.com/chainsaws

In the mid-nineties Europe was well into an economic slump that gave every indication of being both deep and prolonged. German labor unions, the most powerful in Europe, were having to give ground, and major corporations were scaling back operations and reporting losses. At the same time, a number of medium- and small-sized German companies continued to be some of the most successful in the world. Part of this success resulted from their carefully designed decentralized organization structures, a result of company efforts to remain close to the customer. The goal of these German MNCs is to establish operations in overseas locales, where they can provide on-site assistance to buyers. Moreover, these subsidiaries in most cases are wholly owned by the company and have centralized controls on profits.

A common practice among German MNCs is to overserve the market by providing more than is needed. For example, when the auto firm BMW entered Japan in 1981, its initial investment was several times higher than that required to run a small operation; however, its high visibility and commitment to the market helped to create customer awareness and build local prestige.

Another strategy is to leave expatriate managers in their positions for extended periods of time. In this way, they become familiar with the local culture and thus the market, and they are better able to respond to customer needs as well as problems. As a result, customers get to know the firm's personnel and are more willing to do repeat business with them.

Still another strategy the German MNCs use is to closely mesh the talents of the people with the needs of the customers. For example, there is considerable evidence that most customers value product quality, closeness to the customer, service, economy, helpful employees, technologic leadership, and innovativeness. The German firms will overperform in the area that is most important and thus further bond themselves to the customer.

A final strategy is to develop strong self-reliance so that when problems arise, they can be handled with in-house personnel. This practice is a result of German companies' believing strongly in specialization and concentration of effort. They tend to do their own research and to master production and service problems so that if there is a problem, they can resolve it without having to rely on outsiders.

How well do these German organizing efforts pay off? Many of these relatively small companies hold world market shares in the 70 to 90 percent range. These are companies that no one has ever heard about, such as Booder (fish-processing machines), Gehring (honing machines), Korber/Hauni (cigarette machines), Marklin & Cle (model railways), Stihl (chain saws), and Webasto (sunroofs for cars). Even so, every one of these companies is the market leader not only in Europe but also in the world, and in some cases, its relative market strength is up to 10 times greater than that of the nearest competitor.

Table 11–6
Managers' Influence in U.S. and Japanese Firms in Taiwan

Managers' Work-Related Activity	U.S. Firm Average	Japanese Firm Average
Assigning work to subordinates	4.72	3.96
Disciplining subordinates	4.07	3.82
Controlling subordinates' work (quality and pace)	3.99	3.82
Controlling salary and promotion of subordinates	3.81	3.18
Hiring and placing subordinates	3.94	3.24
Setting the budget for own unit	3.45	3.16
Coordinating with other units	3.68	3.52
Influencing policy related to own work	3.22	2.85
Influencing policy not related to own work	2.29	1.94
Influencing superiors	3.02	3.00

Note: The highest score of means is 5 (very great influence); the lowest score is 1 (very little influence). The *T*-value for all scores is significant at the .01 level.

Source: Adapted from Rhy-song Yeh and Tagi Sagafi-nejad, "Organizational Characteristics of American and Japanese Firms in Taiwan," *National Academy of Management Proceedings,* 1987, p. 114. Used with permission.

ating in Taiwan for about ten years, but they maintain the traits of their distinct cultural origins even though they have been operating in the same (Taiwanese) environment for such a long time."[39]

These findings also reveal that many enterprises view their international operations as extensions of their domestic operations, thus disproving the widely held belief that convergence occurs between overseas operations, and local customs. In other words, there is far less of an "international management melting pot" than many people realize. European countries are finding that as they attempt to unify and do business with each other, differing cultures (languages, religions, and values) are very difficult to overcome.

One challenge for the years ahead will be bringing subsidiary organizational characteristics more into line with local customs and cultures. Besides the countries of the EU, the Japanese firms operating in the United States provide another excellent example. Their failure to accept U.S. social values sometimes has resulted in employment and promotion discrimination lawsuits as well as backlashes from workers who feel they are being overworked and forced to abide by rules and regulations that were designed for use in Japan. For example, Honda of America agreed to give 370 African-Americans and women a total of $6 million in back pay to resolve a federal discrimination complaint brought against the company.

The World of Business Week Revisited

In this chapter there were a number of different organizational arrangements discussed. Some of these were fairly standard approaches that have been traditionally used by MNCs. Others represent hybrid or flexible arrangements and emerging networks that are geared specifically to utilize advanced information technology and the needs of the new global marketplace. Which one of the organizational approaches that were described in this chapter do you think would be of most value to P&G as it tries to develop an enterprise that is moving away from a country-by-country setup and toward a handful of powerful departments that will supervise worldwide product areas such as hair care, diapers, and soap? How do you think this new arrangement will impact on the organizational characteristics of MNCs, specifically formalization, specialization, and centralization?

Summary of Key Points

1. A number of different organizational structures are used in international operations. Many MNCs begin by using an export manager or subsidiary to handle overseas business. As the operation grows or the company expands into more markets, the firm often will opt for an international division structure. Further growth may result in adoption of a global structural arrangement, such as a global production division, global area division structure, global functional division, or a mixture of these structures.

2. Although MNCs still use the various structural designs that can be drawn in a hierarchical manner, they recently have begun merging or acquiring other firms or parts of other firms, and the resulting organizational arrangements are quite different from those of the past. The same is true of the many joint ven-

tures now taking place across the world. Perhaps the biggest change, however, stems from the Japanese concept of *keiretsu*, which involves the vertical integration and cooperation of a group of companies. Although the Mitsubishi Group, with its 28 core member firms, is the best example of this organizational arrangement, U.S. MNCs also are moving in this direction. Other examples of new MNC organizational arrangements include the emergence of electronic networks, new roles for organizational synergy, new approaches to organizing for production development, and the more effective use of IT.

3. Some multinationals have subsidiary boards of directors that oversee and monitor the operations of a foreign subsidiary. As MNCs' worldwide operations increase, these boards likely will gain in popularity.

4. A variety of factors help to explain differences in the way that international firms operate. Three organizational characteristics that are of particular importance are formalization, specialization, and centralization. These characteristics often vary from country to country, so that Japanese firms will conduct operations differently from U.S. firms. When MNCs set up international subsidiaries, they often use the same organizational techniques they do at home without necessarily adjusting their approach to better match the local conditions.

Key Terms

centralization
decentralization
formalization
global area division
global functional division

global product division
horizontal specialization
international division structure
keiretsu
mixed organization structure

specialization
subsidiary board of directors
transnational network structure
vertical specialization

Review and Discussion Questions

1. A small manufacturing firm believes there is a market for handheld tools that are carefully crafted for local markets. After spending 2 months in Europe, the president of this firm believes that his company can create a popular line of these tools. What type of organization structure would be of most value to this firm in its initial efforts to go international?

2. If the company in question 1 finds a major market for its products in Europe and decides to expand into Asia, would you recommend any change in its organization structure? If yes, what would you suggest? If no, why not?

3. If this same company finds after 3 years of international effort it is selling 50 percent of its output overseas, what type of organizational structure would you suggest for the future?

4. Why are *keiretsus* becoming so popular? What benefits do they offer? How can small international firms profit from this development? Give an example.

5. In what way do formalization, specialization, and centralization have an impact on MNC organization structures? In your answer, use a well-known firm such as IBM or Ford to illustrate the effects of these three characteristics.

Internet Exercise: Organizing for Effectiveness

Every MNC tries to drive down costs by getting its goods and services to the market in the most efficient way. A good example are auto firms such as Ford Motor and Volkswagen which have worldwide operations. In recent years Ford has begun expanding into Europe and VW has begun setting up operations in Latin America. By building cars closer to the market, these companies hope to reduce their costs and be more responsible to local needs. At the same time this strategy requires a great deal of organization and coordination. Visit the web sites for both of these firms and examine the scope of their operations. The address for Ford Motor is **www2.ford.com** and for Volkswagen it is **www3.vw.com/index1/htm**. Then, based on your findings, answer these questions: What type of organizational arrangement(s) do you see the two firms are using in coordinating their worldwide operations? Which of the two companies has the more modern arrangement? Do you think this increases that firm's efficiency or does it hamper the company's efforts to contain costs and be more competitive? Why?

Australia

Australia is the smallest continent but the sixth-largest country in the world. It lies between the Indian and the Pacific Oceans in the southern hemisphere and has a land mass of almost 3 million square miles (around 85 percent the size of the United States). Referred to as being "down under" because it lies entirely within the southern hemisphere, it is a dry, thinly populated land. The outback is famous for its bright sunshine, enormous numbers of sheep and cattle, and unusual wildlife, such as kangaroos, koalas, platypuses, and wombats. Over 18 million people live in this former British colony, and 20 million are projected by the next couple of years. Although many British customs are retained, Australians have developed their own unique way of life. One of the world's most developed countries, Australia operates under a democratic form of government somewhat similar to that of Great Britain. Gross domestic product is over $400 billion, with the largest economic sectors being services, trade, and manufacturing.

A large financial-services MNC in the United States has been examining the demographic and economic data of Australia. This MNC has concluded that there will be increased demand for financial services in Australia during the next few years. As a result, the company is setting up an operation in the capital, Canberra, which is slightly inland from the two largest cities of Sydney and Melbourne.

This financial-service firm began in Chicago and now has offices in seven countries. Many of these foreign operations are closely controlled by the Chicago office. The overseas personnel are charged with carefully following instructions from headquarters and implementing centralized decisions. However, the Australian operation will be run differently. Because the country is so large and the population spread along the coast and to Perth in the west, and because of the "free spirit" cultural values of the Aussies, the home office feels compelled to give the manager of Australian operations full control over decision making. This manager will have a small number of senior-level managers brought from the United States, but the rest of the personnel will be hired locally. The office will be given sales and profit goals, but specific implementation of strategy will be left to the manager and his or her key subordinates on site.

The home office believes that in addition to providing direct banking and credit card services, the Australian operation should seek to gain a strong foothold in insurance and investment services. As the country continues to grow economically, this sector of the industry should increase relatively fast. Moreover, few multinational firms are trying to tap this market in Australia, and those that are doing so are from British Commonwealth countries. The CEO believes that the experience of the people being sent to Australia (the U.S. expatriates) will be particularly helpful in developing this market. He recently noted, "We know that the needs of the Australian market are not as sophisticated or complex as those in the United States, but we also know that they are moving in the same direction as we are. So we intend to tap our experience and knowledge and use it to garner a commanding share of this expanding market."

www.csu.edu.au/australia

Questions

1. What are some current issues facing Australia? What is the climate for doing business in Australia today?

2. What type of organizational structure arrangement is the MNC going to use in setting up its Australian operation?

3. Can this MNC benefit from any of the new organizational arrangements, such as a joint venture, the Japanese concept of *keiretsu,* or electronic networks?

4. Will this operation be basically centralized or decentralized?

Getting in on the Ground Floor

The EU currently is developing a strategy that will help member countries beat back the threat of U.S. and Japanese competition and develop a strong technological base for new product development. European multinational firms currently are strong in a number of different areas. For example, Germany's Hoechst and BASF and Switzerland's Sandoz and Hoffman-LaRoche are major companies in chemicals and pharmaceutics. Philips of the Netherlands invented compact discs and is dominant in the television market. Many strong European-based MNCs could provide a solid base for the EU to defend itself from outside economic invasion.

Ruehter Laboratories, a high-tech R&D firm located in New Jersey, holds a number of important pharmaceutic patents and would like to expand its operation worldwide. The company is considering buying a small, but highly profitable, Dutch insulin-maker. "This acquisition will help us enter the European market by getting in on the ground floor," noted the president.

Although the Dutch firm is quite small, it has strong R&D prowess and likely will play a major role in biotechnology research during the years ahead. Ruehter has talked to the Dutch firm, and the two have arrived at a mutually acceptable selling price. While waiting for the lawyers to work out the final arrangements, Ruehter intends to reorganize its overall operations so that the home-office management can work more closely with its new Dutch subsidiary. There are three areas that Ruehter intends to address in its reorganization efforts: (1) how the subsidiary will be structurally integrated into the current organization; (2) whether a subsidiary board will be an effective method of overseeing the Dutch operation; and (3) whether there can be any joint R&D efforts between the two groups.

Questions

1. What type of organization design would you recommend that Ruehter use?

2. Would a subsidiary board of directors be of any value in overseeing the Dutch operation?

3. If there were joint R&D efforts, would this be a problem?

Chapter 12

Decision Making and Controlling

Objectives of the Chapter

Although they are not directly related to internationalization, decision making and controlling are two management functions that play critical roles in international operations. In **decision making**, a manager chooses a course of action among alternatives. In **controlling**, the manager evaluates results in relation to plans or objectives and decides what action, if any, to take. How these functions are carried out is influenced by the international context. For example, the amount of decision-making authority given to subsidiaries is influenced by a number of international factors, such as the philosophy of the company and the amount of competition in the local environment. These factors may result in one international unit's having much more decision-making authority than another. Similarly, the tools and techniques that are used to control one subsidiary may differ from those used to control another.

This chapter examines the different decision-making and controlling management functions used by MNCs, notes some of the major factors that account for differences between these functions, and identifies the major challenges of the years ahead. The specific objectives of this chapter are:

1. **PROVIDE** comparative examples of decision making in different countries.

2. **PRESENT** some of the major factors affecting the degree of decision-making authority given to overseas units.

3. **COMPARE** and **CONTRAST** direct controls with indirect controls.

4. **DESCRIBE** some of the major differences in the ways that MNCs control operations.

5. **DISCUSS** some of the specific performance measures that are used to control international operations.

BusinessWeek

The World of Business Week:

SAP's Expanding Universe

For a couple of years now, success has come to Germany's SAP on a silver platter. The $3.5 billion software giant capitalized on fears that two looming events, the new millennium and the creation of a single European currency, would wreak havoc on multinationals' information-technology systems. Instead of combing through their computer systems looking for bugs, many of SAP's 8,000 customers just bought new software packages. This contributed to sales growth of 62% in 1997. Now SAP must figure out what to do for an encore.

Its executives have come up with an ambitious strategy. SAP already dominates the $12 billion market for so-called enterprise software, programs that can manage all of a corporation's internal operations in a single powerful network. Now, SAP plans to branch out beyond its customers' walls, building bridges to their suppliers and customers. In this scheme, a vast SAP-based network could track an entire industrial process, from mining iron ore in Minnesota to steelmaking in Indiana to car production in Detroit—all the way to selling autos in showrooms on the Web. The payoff, it is hoped, would be entire industries run as efficiently as a single plant, with razor-thin inventories and the leanest of workforces.

Friendlier Software

With time, if co-chairman Hasso Plattner has his way, SAP will grow from a faceless industrial supplier into

a global brand name. The plan is to push into consumer markets, from department stores to Internet malls. At a Los Angeles users' convention on Sept. 13, Plattner will unveil a strategy that could position the company virtually everywhere business takes place.

SAP is plowing ahead. All around its headquarters in rural Walldorf, in Germany's lush Rhine Valley, workers manning a forest of cranes are piecing together a vast complex of new SAP buildings. The company will hire 5,000 employees this year, expanding its workforce by 35%, and is expanding research labs from Palo Alto to Minsk.

The challenge for SAP, a company long known only to the techies in large companies, is to come up with a stream of snazzy, customer-friendly applications. Here, Plattner is looking for help. In the past year, SAP has begun placing pieces of its bread-and-butter enterprise software package, called R/3, on the Web.

The strategy has its risks, since those pieces include the computer code that forms the basis of SAP's success. But the idea is that by sharing the code with developers worldwide, SAP will encourage them to build a panoply of applications for its systems.

This spells a fundamental shift for the giant. Traditionally, SAP's systems have been carefully crafted, though often inflexible, marvels of German engineering. Installing these programs, sometimes at a price topping $100 million, has blossomed into a $30 billion industry. Now, Plattner wants to distribute his system far and wide, hoping to make SAP's code the lingua franca of global business. "For the first 25 years of our history, we provided data to people," he says. "For the next 25 years, we'll handle interactions between people."

While SAP embarks on its new path, it is also wrestling with generational change. Plattner's cofounders—the former IBMers who set up the company 26 years ago—are moving from executive into advisory roles. Dietmar Hopp, the technical whiz behind the enterprise software, last spring switched to a lower-profile post on the advisory board. And Plattner wants to hire young talent to guide the company in untried markets. In March, SAP raised its stake in a small German salesforce automation company, Kiefer & Veittinger, to 80%. That gives it a foothold in technology-aided sales, a market that is expected to grow from $1.4 billion to $3.8 billion in the next two years.

Indeed, it is in sales and marketing that SAP faces its biggest hurdles. First, the company has a reputation for torturous installations, despite a worldwide team of troubleshooters. It was a rocky installation that led Dell Computer Corp. to abandon SAP last year halfway through a multimillion-dollar enterprise project. And SAP faces a $500 million lawsuit from the trustee for bankrupt Fox Meyer Corp., charging that the failure of an SAP system led to the Carrolton (Tex.) drug distributor's collapse—a charge SAP executives hotly deny.

Gates at the Gate

Second, nimble competitors now occupy all the niches SAP plans to attack. In fact, many of SAP's biggest customers have already installed other systems for

Decision making
The process of choosing a
course of action among
alternatives.

Controlling
The process of evaluating
results in relation to plans or
objectives and deciding what
action, if any, to take.

sales and marketing applications. But like other industry leaders, SAP has the clout to bring products to market far later than its rivals. It can appropriate effective features from the pioneers, correct their mistakes, and try to wrest away market share by offering seamless integration with its massive installed base.

Eventually, SAP is likely to run head-on into that other software titan, Microsoft. For now they are partners, working together on loads of applications. Microsoft Chairman William H. Gates III, however, has declared an ambition to build the nervous system for business—the same goal as Plattner's. For the next few years, at least, the world looks big enough for both of them.

www.sap.com

Source: **Reprinted from September 14, 1998, pp. 168–169 issue of** *Business Week* **by special permission, copyright © 1998 by McGraw-Hill Companies, Inc.**

This opening news story describes the operations of an extremely successful, although for most of the general public, also basically unknown, German-based multinational technology firm. SAP provides comprehensive or what has become known as "enterprise" software for many companies around the world and, as seen in the story, SAP is not satisfied with its 62 percent growth in 1997 and then going downhill. The leadership is vigorously planning on expanding and entering new markets. As a result, decision making is going to be a key area of concern for SAP management. Even more important, because the market the company is going to be pursuing in the future has many both entrepreneurial upstart and sophisticated competitors such as Microsoft, careful control of expansion and operations will be critical to SAP's success. Simply put, decision making and controlling as discussed in this chapter are going to be two of the key factors in determining whether SAP can repeat its past successes and remain the leader in enterprise software and become a new leader in as yet untried markets.

The Decision-Making and Controlling Linkages

Decision making and controlling are two vital and often interlinked functions of international management. For example, in the mid-1990s Dell Computer's market share in Europe was a scant 2.5 percent and the company troubles on the continent helped produce the firm's first-ever loss. Five years later Dell was one of the fastest-growing PC makers in Western Europe, taking market share from such major rivals as IBM and Compaq Computer. How did the company accomplish this feat? By fine-tuning its U.S. approach for success and installing new managers to make the right decisions and better control its German and French operations. For example, Dell's managers made the decision to continue focusing on direct selling to European consumers. Many critics claimed the U.S. approach would never work with Europeans. Yet, this decision resulted in sales growth five times faster than that of the market. Now the challenge is to control this growth to maintain quality and profitability.

Another example is provided by Cemex SA of Mexico, the world's third-largest cement company. In recent years Cemex managers have made a number of important decisions, all designed to help the MNC gain worldwide market share. One of the latest has been the acquisition of the Rizal Cement Company in the Philippines. This decision was critical to Cemex's international expansion plans in Southeast Asia. Now that this part of the world is undergoing economic turmoil, the control function will become especially important. At the same time, Cemex has announced that it intends to buy other cement companies around the world. Under the current management:

> Cemex has transformed itself into a multinational powerhouse and taken on competitors in Mexico and in markets around the world. In the early 1990s, the company purchased cement properties in the U.S., Spain, Venezuela, Colombia, Trinidad, Panama, and the Dominican Republic. The company also holds minority stakes in Jamaica's Caribbean Cement Co. Ltd. and Peru's Cementos Lima SA.[1]

As a result of these international purchases and expansions, Cemex now grosses over $4 billion annually and has operations in the Far East, Spain, Venezuela, Colombia, Panama and the Caribbean, the United States, and, of course, Mexico. Will these decisions pay off for the firm? Cemex managers believe they will because as economies expand and build new structures, they are going to need cement—and with the proper controls in place Cemex intends to be a major player in this market for the indefinite future.

Still another example is provided by Boeing and General Motors, two well-known MNCs that recently signed major deals with the Chinese government. Boeing has agreed to sell the Chinese Civil Aviation Administration five 777-200 jetliners for approximately $685 million; and General Motors has finalized a $1.3 billion joint venture with a Shanghai automotive company to build Buick Century and Regal cars in China. The Boeing deal came after the giant aerospace MNC had been shut out of a number of recent contract bids in China and offers strong promise of even more business from the Chinese government. The GM deal is a 50/50 venture between the automotive MNC and the Shanghai Automotive Industry Corporation, a state-owned company. Both of these developments are viewed by the management decision makers of the respective American-based MNCs as opportunities to further open the China market and with proper controls increase their sales growth and profitability.[2]

The Decision-Making Process

As shown in the above examples, a number of decision-making areas currently are receiving attention in international management. MNCs manage the operation of their overseas subsidiaries or joint ventures through centralized or decentralized decision making. If centralized decision making is in place, most important decision are made at the top; if decentralized decision making is in place, decision are delegated to operating personnel. Another issue is how decision making is used to help the subsidiary respond to the economic and political demands of the country. Sometimes, these decisions are heavily economic in orientation and may concentrate on things such as return on investment for overseas operations. Other times, decisions are a result of cultural differences. For example, the performance evaluation decisions of local personnel by expatriate managers are greatly affected by the expatriate's cultural values. The best way to illustrate differences in decision-making styles in the international arena is to give some comparative examples.

Comparative Examples of Decision Making

Do decision-making philosophies and practices differ from country to country? Research shows that to some extent they do, although there also is evidence that many international operations, regardless of foreign or domestic ownership, use similar decision-making norms.

Most British organizations are highly decentralized. One major reason is that many upper-level managers do not understand the technical details of the business. Top-level managers depend heavily on middle managers to handle much of the decision making by decentralizing to their level.

The French use a different approach. One observer notes that many top French managers graduated from the Grand Écoles, and they often lack confidence in their middle managers.[3] As a result, decision making tends to be centralized.

In Germany, managers place a greater focus on productivity and quality of goods and services than they do on managing subordinates. In addition, management education is highly technical in focus, and a legal system called **codetermination** requires workers and their managers to discuss major decisions. As a result, German MNCs tend to be fairly centralized, autocratic, and hierarchical. Scandinavian countries also have codetermination, but the Swedes focus much more on quality of work life and the importance of the individual in the organization. As a result, decision making is heavily decentralized and participative.

Codetermination
A legal system that requires workers and their managers to discuss major decisions.

Ringisei
From Japan, decision making by consensus.

The Japanese are somewhat different from the Europeans. They make heavy use of a decision-making process called **ringisei**, or decision making by consensus. This approach can be described as follows:

> Under this system any changes in procedures and routines, tactics, and even strategies of a firm are organized by those directly concerned with those changes. The final decision is made at the top level after an elaborate examination of the proposal through successively higher levels in the management hierarchy, and results in acceptance or rejection of a decision only through consensus at every echelon of the management structure.[4]

Sometimes Japanese consensus decision making can be very time-consuming and is recently given as a reason why the Japanese have not responded well to the newly emerging "speed" requirement of the international marketplace. However, in practice most Japanese managers are beginning to learn how to respond to "suggestions" from the top and to act accordingly—thus saving a great deal of time. However, most outsiders misunderstand how Japanese managers make such decisions. In Japan, what should be done is called **tatemae**, while what one really feels, which may be quite different, is **honne**. Because it is vital to do what others expect in a given context, situations arise that often strike Westerners as the common game known as charades. However, it is very important in Japan to play out the situation according to what each person believes others expect to happen. To clarify this complicated but important Japanese decision-making process, here is a specific example offered by a Japanese scholar of a Mr. Seward, a Western employee of a Japanese firm.

Tatemae
A Japanese term which means "doing the right thing" according to norm.

Honne
A Japanese term which means "what one really wants to do."

> [Mr. Seward] joined a meeting as one of eight employees tasked with deciding where to go for a company trip. When the result of the vote was taken, it appeared that the group favored going to a place named Izu. At this point, one of the president's secretaries spoke up, saying, "The president wants to visit Suwa." In a tense atmosphere a second vote was taken, considering the president's opinion, and it turned out that the entire group, except Seward, voted for Suwa. Mr. Seward protested the procedure, insisting that, if members were forced to follow the president's opinion, there was no point in meeting and voting, but his objections were overridden and the company trip was set for Suwa.[5]

Many Westerners would ask why the president did not simply send out a memo announcing the destination of the meeting. The answer is that for the president having the meeting and taking a vote was *tatemae*—the right thing to do according to the normal models for reaching this kind of decision. At the same time, going to Suwa was *honne*— what the president wanted to do. Similarly, for the Japanese members of the committee, voting for Suwa was *tatemae* once the president's desires were made clear, while going to Izu was *honne*, what the employees really wanted to do. Obviously such culturally based subtleties make understanding whether decision making is centralized or decentralized across cultures very difficult.

MNCs based in the United States tend to use fairly centralized decision making in managing their overseas units. This approach provides the necessary control for developing a worldwide strategy, because it ensures that all units are operating according to the overall strategic plan.

As shown in these examples, a number of decision-making approaches are used around the world. Most evidence, however, indicates that the overall trend currently is toward centralization. For example, in terms of both delegation and decision-making authority of overseas subsidiaries, there is evidence of a fair degree of centralization in areas such as marketing policies, financial matters, use of expatriate personnel, and decisions on production capacity. The results of a comparative study are summarized as follows:

> The convergence in organizational practices in general, and decision making in particular, is taking place rapidly. This can be seen from the results of our recent study of United States, German, British, Japanese, and Swedish multinational companies. The results showed the United States management practices concerning decision making are the norms being followed by other nations. Other countries' practices correlated strongly with those of United States practices.[6]

A number of reasons help to account for this trend toward centralized decision making in international management areas. One is an advanced information technology as well as the desire to increase economies of scale and to attain higher operational efficiency. Such centralized decision making, however, can stifle the creativity and flexibility needed by the subsidiary. In resolving this dilemma, effective MNCs try to evaluate each overseas operation on its own merits.

Factors Affecting Decision-Making Authority

A number of factors will influence international managers' conclusions about retaining or delegating decision making to a subsidiary. Table 12-1 lists some of the most important situational factors, and the following discussion looks at each in detail.

Company size influences decision making in that large organizations have a greater need for coordination and integration of operations. To ensure that all subsidiaries are effectively managed, the MNC will centralize the authority for a number of critical decisions. This centralization is designed to increase the overall efficiency of operations, and to the extent that centralization creates the desired uniformity and coordination, this is precisely what happens.

The greater the MNC's capital investment, the more likely that decision making will be centralized. The home office wants to keep a tight rein on its investment and ensure that everything is running smoothly. The subsidiary manager will be required to submit periodic reports, and on-site visits from home-office personnel are quite common.

The more important the overseas operation is to the MNC, the closer the MNC will control it. Home-office management will monitor performance carefully, and the subsidiary manager usually will not be allowed to make any major decisions without first clearing them with the MNC senior management. In fact, in managing important overseas operations, the home office typically will appoint someone who they know will respond to their directives and will regard this individual as an extension of the central management staff.

In domestic situations, when competition increases, management will decentralize authority and give the local manager greater decision-making authority. This reduces the time that is needed for responding to competitive threats. In the international arena, however, just

---

Table 12–1
Factors That Influence Centralization or Decentralization of Decision Making in Subsidiary Operations

Encourage Centralization	Encourage Decentralization
Large size	Small size
Large capital investment	Small capital investment
Relatively high importance to MNC	Relatively low importance to MNC
Highly competitive environment	Stable environment
Strong volume-to-unit-cost relationship	Weak volume-to-unit-cost relationship
High degree of technology	Moderate to low degree of technology
Strong importance attached to brand name, patent rights, etc.	Little importance attached to brand name, patent rights, etc.
Low level of product diversification	High level of product diversification
Homogeneous product lines	Heterogeneous product lines
Small geographic distance between home office and subsidiary	Large geographic distance between home office and subsidiary
High interdependence between the units	Low interdependence between the units
Fewer highly competent managers in host country	More highly competent managers in host country
Much experience in international business	Little experience in international business

the opposite approach is used. As competition increases and profit margins are driven down, home-office management seeks to standardize product and marketing decisions to reduce cost and maintain profitability. More and more upper-level operating decisions are made by central management and merely implemented by the subsidiary.

If there is a strong volume-to-unit-cost relationship, firms that are able to produce large quantities will have lower cost per unit than those that produce smaller amounts. Under these conditions, home-office management typically will centralize decision making and assume authority over sourcing and marketing-related matters as well as overall strategy. This helps to ensure that the subsidiary's unit cost remains low.

The more sophisticated the level of technology, the greater the degree of centralized decision making. The MNC will attempt to protect these resources by making technology-related decisions at the home office. This is particularly true for high-tech, research-intensive firms such as computer and pharmaceutic companies, which do not want their technology controlled at the local level.

If strong importance is attached to brand name, patent rights, and so forth, decision making likely will be centralized. The MNC will want to protect its rights by making these types of decisions in the home office.

The greater the amount of product and service diversification, the greater the decentralization of the decision-making process, because the MNC typically will not have the staff or the resources for coordinating these diversified offerings on a worldwide basis. The home-office management will rely on the subsidiary management to handle this task. In addition, as the overseas unit becomes increasingly skilled in manufacturing and marketing products at the local level, the chance of the home management's recentralizing decision making becomes more remote.

If product and service lines are heterogeneous, differences often exist in the socio-economic, political, legal, and cultural environments in the various countries where the firm is operating. These differences typically result in the MNC's turning over operating control to the local subsidiaries. In addition, the greater the differences in the environment between the home country and the subsidiary, the more likely the MNC will decentralize the decision-making process.

If the subsidiary and home office are far apart, decentralization is more likely than if the subsidiary is located near the home office. There is evidence that U.S. subsidiaries in North America are more closely controlled than those in South America and that those in the Far East are least controlled of all. The farther away the subsidiary, the more likely the home office will give it increased autonomy.

The greater the degree of interdependence among the units, typically the greater the centralization of decision making. The home office will want to coordinate and integrate the units into an effective system, usually from headquarters.

If the subsidiary has highly competent local managers, the chances for decentralization are increased, because the home office has more confidence in delegating to the local level and less to gain by making all the important decisions. Conversely, if the local managers are inexperienced or not highly effective, the MNC likely will centralize decision making and make many of the major decisions at headquarters.

If the firm has had a great deal of international experience, its operations likely will be more centralized. This finding is in accord with the research cited earlier, which shows a convergence toward more centralization by multinational firms.

In some areas of operation, MNCs tend to retain decision making at the top (centralization); other areas fall within the domain of subsidiary management (decentralization). It is most common to find finance, research and development, and strategic planning decisions being made at MNC headquarters, and the subsidiaries must work within the parameters established by the home office. In addition, when the subsidiary is selling new products in growing markets, centralized decision making is more likely. As the product line matures and the subsidiary managers gain experience, however, the company will start to rely more on decentralized decision making. These decisions involve planning and budgeting systems, performance evaluations, assignment of managers to the subsidiary, and use of coordinating committees to mesh the operations of the subsidiary with the worldwide operations of the MNC. The right degree of centralized or decentralized decision making can be critical to the success of the MNC.

A good example is Germany's *Mittelstand*, which is a term used to describe the approximately 2.5 million small- and medium-sized firms that account for two-thirds of the nation's economy and 80 percent of employment in the private sector. In recent years, these firms have been hard hit by large wage increases won by the unions. As a result, they now are fighting back, determined to survive at all costs. The owners have begun centralizing authority, trimming their workforces, moving more and more production out of Germany and to lower-wage countries in Southern and Central Europe as well as Asia, and using technology to increase productivity. These decisions are helping these firms to weather this latest economic storm and may well affect decision-making styles in larger German firms that also are struggling to remain competitive internationally.[7]

Decision-Making Issues

There are a number of decision-making issues and challenges with which MNCs currently are being confronted. Three of the most prominent include total quality management decisions, use of joint ventures and other forms of cooperative agreements, and strategies for attacking competition in the international marketplace. The following examines some of the latest developments in each area.

Total Quality Management Decisions

To achieve world-class competitiveness as outlined in Chapter 3, MNCs are finding that a commitment to total quality management is critical. **Total quality management (TQM)** is an organizational strategy and accompanying techniques that result in delivery of high-quality products and/or services to customers.[8] The concept and techniques of TQM, which were introduced in Chapter 9 in relation to strategic planning, also are relevant to decision making and controlling.

One of the primary areas where TQM is having a big impact is in manufacturing.[9] For example, in recent years, U.S. automakers have greatly improved the quality of their cars, but the Japanese have continuous improvement of quality and thus still have the lead. A number of TQM techniques have been successfully applied to improve the quality of manufactured goods. One is the use of concurrent engineering/interfunctional teams in which designers, engineers, production specialists, and customers work together to develop new products. This approach involves all the necessary parties and overcomes what used to be an all-too-common procedure: The design people would tell the manufacturing group what to produce, and the latter would send the finished product to retail stores for sale to the customer. Today, MNCs taking a TQM approach are customer-driven. They use TQM techniques to tailor their output according to customer needs. As a Toshiba executive noted: "In the past few years, we have strengthened our design review method by implementing a more thorough analysis of customer requirements in the product development stage. We have developed checklists that help us monitor every step of product development from planning and design through manufacturing, marketing and after-sales service."[10] IBM followed a similar approach in developing its AS/400 computer systems. Customer advisory councils were created to provide input, test the product, and suggest refinements. The result was one of the most successful product launches in the company's history.

A particularly critical issue is how much decision making to delegate to subordinates. TQM uses employee **empowerment.** Individuals and teams are encouraged to generate and implement ideas for improving quality and given the decision-making authority and necessary resources and information to implement them. Many MNCs have had outstanding success with empowerment. For example, General Electric credits employee empowerment for cutting in half the time needed to change product-mix production of its dishwashers in response to market demand, and Kodak used the empowerment of its

Total quality management (TQM)
An organizational strategy and the accompanying techniques that result in the delivery of high-quality products and/or services to customers.

Empowerment
The process of giving individuals and teams the resources, information, and authority they need to develop ideas and effectively implement them.

workers to increase productivity by teaching workers how to inspect their own work, keep track of their own performance, and even fix their own machines.

Another TQM technique that MNCs are successfully employing to develop and maintain world-class competitiveness is rewards and recognition. These range from increases in pay and benefits to the use of merit pay, discretionary bonuses, pay-for-skills and knowledge plans, plaques, and public recognition. The important thing to realize is that the rewards and recognition approaches that work well in one country may be ineffective in another. For example, individual recognition in the United States may be appropriate and valued by workers, but in Japan, group rewards are more appropriate as Japanese do not like to be singled out for personal praise. Similarly, although putting a picture or plaque on the wall to honor an individual is common practice in the United States, these rewards are frowned on in Finland as they remind the workers of how their neighbor, the Russians, used this system to encourage people to increase output (but not necessarily quality) and now the Russian economy is in shambles.[11]

Still another technique associated with TQM is the use of ongoing training to achieve continual improvement. This training takes a wide variety of forms, ranging from statistical quality control techniques to team meetings designed to generate ideas for streamlining operation and eliminating waste. In all cases, the objective is to apply what the Japanese call **kaizen**, or continuous improvement. By adopting a TQM perspective and applying the techniques discussed earlier, MNCs find that they can both develop and maintain a worldwide competitive edge. A good example is Zytec, the world-class, Minnesota-based manufacturer of power supplies. The customer base for Zytec ranges from the United States to Japan to Europe. One way in which the firm ensures that it maintains a total quality perspective is to continually identify client demands and then work to exceed these expectations. Another is to totally revise the organization's philosophy and beliefs regarding what quality is all about and how it needs to be implemented. Table 12-2 provides some examples of the new thinking that is now emerging regarding quality.

Indirectly related to TQM is ISO 9000. This refers to the International Standards Organization (ISO) certification to ensure quality products and services. Areas that are examined by the ISO certification team include design (product or service specifications), process control (instruction for manufacturing or service functions), purchasing, service (e.g., instructions for conducting after-sales service), inspection and testing, and training. ISO 9000 certification is becoming a necessary prerequisite to doing business in the EU, but it also is increasingly used as a screening criterion for bidding on contracts or getting business in the United States and other parts of the world. For example, after a year of hard work, Foxboro Corporation, based in Massachusetts, obtained certification, and its business greatly increased.

Strategic Alliances

Besides TQM, another area where decision making has a particular impact on MNCs is creating and nurturing strategic alliances. One of the most common is **international joint ventures (IJVs)**, which are formal arrangements with foreign partners who typically, although not always, are located in the country where the business will be conducted. A good example is provided by Ford Motor and Mazda. For a number of years now the two have had a strategic alliance. In fact, Ford recently increased its stake in Mazda from 25 percent to 33.4 percent, a decision designed to help the Japanese automaker pull out of its sales skid. Now, with guidance from its American partner, Mazda is trimming costs and introducing a host of popular new models in Asia. At the same time the company is beginning to gain ground in both North America and Europe. Part of this success is accounted for by Ford executives who better controlled Mazda's freewheeling engineers and forced them to share auto platforms and to source more components overseas. Mazda also began following Ford's advice to use customer clinics, thus helping the company to develop low-priced, compact sport vehicles that are proving very popular in the Japanese market. Over the next few years Mazda intends to continue growing its market shares in North America

Kaizen
A Japanese term that means continuous improvement.

International joint ventures (IJVs)
Formal arrangements with foreign partners who typically, although not always, are located in the country where the business will be conducted.

Table 12–2
The Emergence of New Beliefs Regarding Quality

Old Myth	New Truth
Quality is the responsibility of the people in the Quality Control Department.	Quality is everyone's job.
Training is costly.	Training does not cost, it saves.
New quality programs have high initial costs.	The best quality programs do not have up-front costs.
Better quality will cost the company a lot of money.	As quality goes up, costs come down.
The measurement of data should be kept to a minimum.	An organization cannot have too much relevant data on hand.
It is human to make mistakes.	Perfection—total customer satisfaction—is a standard that should be vigorously pursued.
Some defects are major and should be addressed, but many are minor and can be ignored.	No defects are acceptable, regardless of whether they are major or minor.
Quality improvements are made in small, continuous steps.	In improving quality, both small and large improvements are necessary.
Quality improvement takes time.	Quality does not take time, it saves time.
Haste makes waste.	Thoughtful speed improves quality.
Quality programs are best oriented toward areas such as products and manufacturing.	Quality is important in all areas including administration and service.
After a number of quality improvements, customers are no longer able to see additional improvements.	Customers are able to see all improvements including those in price, delivery, and performance.
Good ideas can be found throughout the organization.	Good ideas can be found everywhere, including in the operations of competitors and organizations providing similar goods and services.
Suppliers need to be price competitive.	Suppliers need to be quality competitive.

Source: Reported in Richard M. Hodgetts, *Measures of Quality and High Performance* (New York: American Management Association, 1998), p. 14.

and Europe. At the same time the two firms are working closely together in Asia. Mazda recently closed its factory in Thailand and is making pickups there in a joint venture with Ford. Meanwhile, Ford is planning to build a next-generation car based on the Mazda 626. Clearly the IJV is providing benefits to both partners.[12]

IJVs and other strategic alliances are also becoming extremely popular because of the benefits they offer to both parties. In particular, they provide large firms with an opportunity to gain a foothold in new markets. Starbuck's Coffee International of Seattle, Washington, is a good example. This very successful MNC recently entered into a joint venture with the Beijing Mei Da Coffee Company to open coffee houses in China. Getting local consumers to switch from tea to coffee is likely to be a major challenge. However, for the moment the joint venture is focusing on the training of local managers who will run the coffee shops. Recruits are now being sent to Tacoma, Washington, to learn how to make the various types of Starbuck's coffee and to get a first-hand look at the company's culture. As one of the general managers for the Mei Da company put it, "People don't go to Starbucks for the coffee but for the experience. Focusing on the development of employees so that they can deliver that experience is our priority for now."[13] Part of Starbuck's strategy is also to show the new recruits that there are career and personal development opportunities in this new venture. This is an important area of emphasis for the firm because there is a major shortage of management personnel in China. As a result, many companies raid the management ranks of others, offering lucrative financial arrangements to those who are willing to change companies. One way that Starbuck's is trying to deal with this is by encouraging the trainees to take responsibility, question the system, take risks, and make changes that will keep the customers coming back. Many foreign MNCs in China want the employees to do as they are told. Starbuck's believes that its IJV emphasis on developing talent will give it an edge—and discourage people from leaving for higher financially attractive offers.

As shown in these examples, multinationals are and will be making a host of decisions related to IJVs. In Russia, the current trend is to renegotiate many of the old agreements and seek smaller deals that entail less bureaucratic red tape and are easier to bring to fruition. At the same time, the U.S. administration is trying to create a plan for providing assistance to the former Soviet republics, and this likely will generate increased interest in the use of IJVs.

Besides the former Soviet Union, other areas of the world that also were previously closed to foreign investment are beginning to open up. A good example is Vietnam. Japan's Idemitsu Oil Development Company signed a deal with the Vietnamese government that gave this company the rights to explore an offshore oil and gas field in the Gulf of Tonkin. U.S. firms are beginning to take advantage of opportunities in Vietnam as well. For example, Citibank and Bank of America both have been approved for branch status in Vietnam. The bulk of their business will be wholesale banking and, in the case of Bank of America, advising the government on financing the rebuilding of Vietnam's weak power sector.[14] Other U.S. firms with interest in Vietnam include AT&T, Coca-Cola, General Electric, Mobil, and Ralston Purina, to name but a few of the most visible. Over the next few years, more and more multinationals will seek to tap the economic potential of emerging economies that now are prepared to modify their political agendas to improve the standard of living for their people.

Decisions for Attacking the Competition

Another series of key decisions relates to MNC actions that are designed to attack the competition and gain a foothold in world markets. The accompanying box, International Management in Action: "Kodak Goes Digital, Making Film Obsolete" gives an example. Another is General Motors' decision to establish production operations on a worldwide basis and to be a major player throughout Asia, Australia, Europe, and South America, as well as select areas of Africa. As a result of this decision, the company is now closing U.S. factories and building new assembly plants abroad. Between 1995–1999 GM opened up a host of new facilities including a plant in Brazil that has an annual capacity of 120,000 units, and factories in Poland, India, Mexico, Thailand, and Shanghai, each of which has annual capacity of 100,000 units. By locating closer to the final customer and offering a well-designed and efficiently built car, the company has been able to increase its worldwide market share, thus more than offsetting the downturn it has encountered in the U.S. market where overall share has dropped below 30 percent. Between 1990–1996 the firm's annual sales more than doubled in Russia, China, India, Indonesia, Brazil, and Argentina, to mention just six major markets. Moreover in 10 of the markets that it entered since 1990, annual unit sales have been impressive, as seen by the results listed below in a recent year.[15]

Country	Units Sold
Thailand	128,365
China	54,602
Poland	30,384
Hungary	16,949
Czech Republic/Slovakia	15,780
Slovenia	3,900
Croatia	2,526
Russia	2,121
Baltic States	665
Ukraine	447

GM's expansion decisions, in many cases, have been designed to help it capture the lower end of the market with small, inexpensive cars. However, the company is also intent on appealing to the upper-level buyer as well, as seen by its recent decision to sell Cadillacs in Europe. This market is quite different from that in the United States. European luxury car buyers often settle for far less comfort and far more handling and performance. GM hopes to appeal to these buyers with many of the changes it has introduced into the

International Management in Action

Kodak Goes Digital, Making Film Obsolete

Kodak has been attacking the competition in a number of ways. One has been to file a complaint with the U.S. government accusing its main competitor, Fuji, of blocking Kodak growth in the Japanese market and asking the administration to take steps to correct this situation. This is only a short-term strategy designed to increase the growth of Kodak film in one country, however. Of far more future importance are technological developments such as the emergence of inexpensive cameras that use digital technology, which will make film obsolete.

Under its current CEO, George Fisher, who was hired away from Motorola, Kodak is in the throes of reorganizing and focusing its efforts on new growth areas while continuing to extract as much sales and profit as possible from its current product lines. For example, Fisher recently created a digital imaging unit, thus gathering most of the firm's digital talent into one division. Before this, efforts at digital product development were spread through the divisions. At the same time, Kodak is working to reignite overall growth by focusing on the Asian market. The company believes that it can double its growth rate in photography, a tough challenge given that the world market is growing very slowly.

The real focus of Fisher's effort is in digital technology, however, and the company's strategy in this area finally appears to be getting into focus. Still, this digital thrust will not be easy, because of both the difficulty in generating research and development breakthroughs and in marketing the new products. Some of Kodak's earlier efforts were anything but spectacular. For example, the photo-CD, which is a compact disk that Kodak developed to store photographs for viewing on TV screens or PC monitors, flopped as a consumer product. Buyers balked at paying $500 for a player that plugs into a TV plus $20 per disk. Fortunately, the company did find a ready market among small businesses such as desktop publishers and real-estate agents, which used the unit to display their offerings. The lesson is clear: Creating a new technologic product is not enough; it also is important to carefully identify the market where it can be sold successfully.

Kodak knows that the industry will go digital and the film business eventually will die out. Therefore the company must be prepared to meet the future with new products such as the digital camera. In the interim, the firm also must push ahead in the film business and with new camera offerings such as its single-use, throwaway cameras, which really is nothing more than an inexpensive cardboard-and-plastic box with a roll of film inside. Kodak also has extended this line to include telephoto, panoramic, portrait, and underwater versions of the camera. The firm hopes that all these efforts will help them to attack the competition successfully while continuing to develop and perfect digital products that will appeal to the masses.

Cadillac Sevilles that it has now begun selling in Europe. Examples of some of the differences between this car and the one marketed in the United States include: (a) right-hand-drive version for the United Kingdom; (b) less clutter inside the car including unobtrusive cup holders; (c) simpler, more elegant interiors; (d) a shorter auto length; (e) tighter suspension, wider wheel tracks, and better tires for driving at high speeds; and (f) floor-mounted shifts for automatic transmission.[16]

Will this decision result in greater sales for Cadillac in Europe? It is still too early to tell, but the company's decision certainly does not have firms such as BMW or Mercedes concerned. The luxury car market in Europe is highly competitive and Europeans take pride in placing performance over comfort. Buyers like tight steering, rear-wheel drive, and smaller cars that provide greater gas mileage. Cadillac is not known for any of these. Nor does the car have a reputation for high-speed performance, something that people on the continent like, given that on European freeways it is common to find the traffic moving at 80–100 miles per hour.

Another good example of decision making for attacking the competition is provided by Lucent Technologies that is very interested in buying or merging with companies that can help it offer better gear for data networking and participate more aggressively in overseas markets. The market for data networking is growing at about 25 percent annually, about double that of the traditional telecommunications equipment market. Some of the firms that Lucent has been looking at include Ascend Communications, a billion-dollar company that would give Lucent additional expertise in the fast-growing market for data networks; Nokia, the $10 billion Finnish telephone equipment maker that is very strong in wireless technology and that could give Lucent a big boost in Europe; Siemens Telecom, the German conglomerate that has a strong $16 billion telecommunication equipment business; and Alcatel, the $30 billion French firm that has operations in 130 countries and has been improving its digital capabilities. A decision to link operations with one or more of these firms would give Lucent the ability to become a major player in the international telecommunications business well into the new millennium.[17]

Another interesting way of attacking the competition is the decision by the Japanese government to help U.S. firms sell goods in Japan. The logic is simple: By increasing sales of U.S. MNCs, the Japanese hope to blunt criticism that their markets are closed to outsiders. To promote U.S. MNC success in Japan, the government has created an organization known as the Japan External Trade Organization, or "Jetro," for short. Jetro has advisors in the United States who are paid to help encourage and promote exports. These advisors serve as intermediaries, bringing together U.S. firms that want to sell with Japanese firms that are looking for suppliers and products. To date, a number of U.S. firms have done quite well thanks to Jetro. For example, Crane National Vendors of Bridgeton, Missouri, has sold $4 million of its computerized vending machines in Japan. Marlink, Inc., of Rocky Mount, North Carolina, has sold over $1.3 million of its log cabins in Japan. Andermac, Inc., of Yuba City, California, has designed hospital beds specifically for the Japan market and has sales of over $500,000 to the Japanese.

The Controlling Process

As indicated in the introduction to this chapter, controlling involves evaluating results in relation to plans or objectives and deciding what action to take. An excellent illustration is Mitsubishi's purchase of 80 percent of Rockefeller Center in the late 1980s. The Japanese firm paid $1.4 billion for this choice piece of Manhattan real estate, and it looked like a very wise decision. Over the next 6 years, however, depressed rental prices and rising maintenance costs resulted in Mitsubishi sinking an additional $500 million into the project. Finally, in late 1995, the company decided it had had enough and announced that it was walking away from the investment. Mitsubishi passed ownership to Rockefeller Center Properties Inc., the publicly traded, real-estate investment trust that holds the mortgage on the Center. The cost of keeping the properties was too great for the Japanese firm, which decided to cut its losses and focus efforts on more lucrative opportunities elsewhere.

Another example is provided by Dana Corporation, the giant auto parts-supply company, which in the last few years has been selling off some of its units, buying others, and refocusing its business. Some of the units that Dana has sold include its clutch and transmission operation and its heavy frame operations. In each case the company's control process concluded that the unit had low return on sales or investment, slow growth, operating losses, and/or eroding market share. At the same time, Dana has purchased a piston rings and cylinder liners unit, a transmission unit, and a couple of axle units. As a result, Dana is now able to build complete modular chassis assemblies that fit right into trucks and cars. Thanks to its control function and some good decisions, the firm can get more work done at a faster rate and increase its profitability at the same time.[18]

Another example of how the control process is being used by MNCs is in the personal computer (PC) business. Until about five years ago, PCs were built using the traditional model shown in Figure 12-1. However, today the direct sales model and the hybrid model are the most common. (See Figure 12-1.) PC firms are finding that they must keep on the cutting edge more than any other industry because of the relentless pace of technological change. This is where the control function becomes especially critical for success. For example, stringent controls keep the inventory in the system as low as possible. PCs are manufactured using a just-in-time approach (as in the case of a customer who orders the unit and has it made to specifications) or an almost just-in-time approach (as in the case

Figure 12–1   **Models of PC Manufacturing**

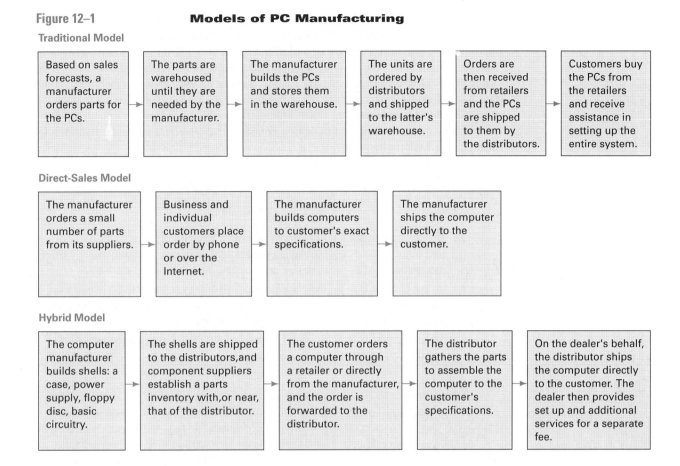

Traditional Model

| Based on sales forecasts, a manufacturer orders parts for the PCs. | → | The parts are warehoused until they are needed by the manufacturer. | → | The manufacturer builds the PCs and stores them in the warehouse. | → | The units are ordered by distributors and shipped to the latter's warehouse. | → | Orders are then received from retailers and the PCs are shipped to them by the distributors. | → | Customers buy the PCs from the retailers and receive assistance in setting up the entire system. |

Direct-Sales Model

| The manufacturer orders a small number of parts from its suppliers. | → | Business and individual customers place order by phone or over the Internet. | → | The manufacturer builds computers to customer's exact specifications. | → | The manufacturer ships the computer directly to the customer. |

Hybrid Model

| The computer manufacturer builds shells: a case, power supply, floppy disc, basic circuitry. | → | The shells are shipped to the distributors, and component suppliers establish a parts inventory with, or near, that of the distributor. | → | The customer orders a computer through a retailer or directly from the manufacturer, and the order is forwarded to the distributor. | → | The distributor gathers the parts to assemble the computer to the customer's specifications. | → | On the dealer's behalf, the distributor ships the computer directly to the customer. The dealer then provides set up and additional services for a separate fee. |

of a retailer who orders 30 units and sells them all within a few weeks). Because technology in the PC industry changes so quickly, any units that are not sold in retail outlets within 60 days may be outdated and must be severely discounted and sold for whatever the market will bear. In turn, these costs are often assumed by the manufacturer. As a result, PC manufacturers are very much inclined to build to order or to ship in quantities that can be sold quickly. In this way the firm's control system helps to ensure that inventory moves through the system and profitability does not suffer.[19]

In many ways, the control function is conceptually and practically similar to decision making. Like decision-making approaches, the approaches used by multinationals in controlling their operations have long been an area of interest. Of particular concern has been how companies attempt to control their overseas operations to become an integrated, coordinated unit. Unfortunately, a number of control problems arise. Examples include: (1) the objectives of the foreign operation and the corporate objectives conflict; (2) the objectives of joint-venture partners and corporate management conflict; (3) amount of experience and competence in planning are widely diverse among foreign CEOs; and (4) basic philosophic conflicts exist about objectives and policies of foreign operations, largely because of cultural differences between home- and host-country managers. The following discussion examines the various types of and approaches to control to help overcome such problems.

Types of Control

There are two common ways of looking at the ways in which MNCs control operations. These are not mutually exclusive approaches, but rather complementary ones. One way is by determining whether the enterprise chooses to use internal or external control in devising its overall strategy. The second is by looking at the ways in which the organization uses direct and indirect controls.

Internal and External Control   From an internal control standpoint, an MNC would focus on the things that it does best. At the same time, management wants to ensure that there is a market for the goods and services that it is offering. So the company first needs to find out what the customers want and be prepared to respond appropriately. This requires an external control focus. Of course, every MNC will give consideration to both internal and external perspectives of control. However, one is often given more attention than the other. In explaining this idea, Trompenaars and Hampden-Turner have set forth four management views regarding how a control strategy should be devised and implemented. The four are these:

1. No one dealing with customers is without a strategy of sorts. Our task is to find out which of these strategies work, which don't, and why. Devising our own strategy in the abstract and imposing it downwards only spreads confusion.

2. No one dealing with customers is without a strategy of sorts. Our task is to find out which of these strategies work and then create a master strategy from proven successful initiatives by encouraging and combining the best.

3. To be a leader is to be the chief devisor of strategy. Using all the experience, information and intelligence we can mobilize, we need to devise an innovative strategy and then cascade it down the hierarchy.

4. To be a leader is to be the chief devisor of strategy. Using all the experience, information and intelligence we can mobilize, we must create a broad thrust, while leaving it to subordinates to fit these to customer needs.

Trompenaars and Hampden-Turner ask managers to rank each of these four statements by placing a "1" next to the one they feel would most likely be used in their company, a "2" next to the second most likely, on down to a "4" next to the one that would be the last choice. This ranking helps managers better see whether they use an external or an internal control approach. Answer 1 above focuses most strongly on an external-direct approach and rejects the internal control option. Answer 3 represents just the opposite. Answer 2 affirms a connection between an external-directed strategy and an inner-directed one, whereas answer 4 does just the opposite.[20]

Cultures differ in the control approach they use. For example, among U.S. multinationals it is common to find managers using a more internal control approach. Among Asian firms an external control approach is more typical. Table 12-3 provides some contrasts between the two.

Direct controls
The use of face-to-face or personal meetings for the purpose of monitoring operations.

Direct Controls   Direct controls involve face-to-face or personal meetings to monitor operations. A good example is International Telephone and Telegraph (ITT), which holds monthly management meetings at its New York headquarters. These meetings are run by the CEO of the company, and reports are submitted by each ITT unit manager throughout the world. Problems are discussed, goals set, evaluations made, and actions taken that will help the unit to improve its effectiveness.

Another common form of direct control is visits by top executives to overseas affiliates or subsidiaries. During these visits, top managers, can learn firsthand the problems and challenges facing the unit and offer assistance.

A third form is the staffing practices of MNCs. By determining who to send overseas to run the unit, the corporation can directly control how the operation will be run. The company will want the manager to make operating decisions and handle day-to-day matters, but the individual also will know which decisions should be cleared with the home office. In fact, this approach to direct control sometimes results in a manager who is more responsive to central management than to the needs of the local unit.

A fourth form is the organizational structure itself. By designing a structure that makes the unit highly responsive to home-office requests and communications, the MNC ensures that all overseas operations are run in accord with central management's desires.

Table 12–3

The Impact of Internal and External-Oriented Cultures on the Control Process

Key Differences between	
Internal Control	**External Control**
Often dominating attitude bordering on aggressiveness towards the environment.	Often flexible attitude, willing to compromise and keep the peace.
Conflict and resistance means that a person has convictions.	Harmony, responsiveness, and sensibility are encouraged.
The focus is on self, function, one's own group, and one's own organization.	The focus is on others such as customers, partners, and colleagues.
There is discomfort when the environment seems "out of control" or changeable.	There is comfort with waves, shifts, and cycles, which are regarded as "natural."
Tips for Doing Business with	
Internally Controlled (for Externals)	**Externally Controlled (for Internals)**
Playing "hard ball" is legitimate to test the resilience of an opponent.	Softness, persistence, politeness, and long, long patience will get rewards.
It is most important to "win your objective."	It is most important to maintain one's relationships with others.
Win some, lose some.	Win together, lose apart.

Source: Adapted from Fons Trompenaars and Charles Hampden-Turner, *Riding the Waves of Culture: Understanding Diversity in Global Business,* 2nd ed. (New York: McGraw-Hill, 1998), pp. 160–161.

This structure can be established through formal reporting relationships and chain of command (who reports to whom).

Indirect Controls Indirect controls use reports and other written forms of communication to control operations. One of the most common examples is the use of monthly operating reports that are sent to the home office. Other examples, which typically are used to supplement the operating report, include financial statements, such as balance sheets, income statements, cash budgets, and financial ratios, that provide insights into the unit's financial health. An example of such data is shown in Table 12-4. The home office uses these operating and financial data to evaluate how well things are going and make decision regarding necessary changes. Three sets of financial statements usually are required from subsidiaries: (1) statements prepared to meet the national accounting standards and procedures prescribed by law and other professional organizations in the host country; (2) statements prepared to comply with the accounting principles and standards required by the home country; and (3) statements prepared to meet the financial consolidation requirements of the home country.

Indirect controls
The use of reports and other written forms of communication to control operations.

Indirect controls are particularly important in international management because of the great expense associated with direct methods. Typically, MNCs will use indirect controls to monitor performance on a monthly basis, whereas direct controls are used semiannually or annually. This dual approach best provides the company with effective control of its operations at a price that also is cost-effective.

Approaches to Control

International managers can employ many different approaches to control. These approaches typically are dictated by the MNC's philosophy of control, the economic environment in which the overseas unit is operating, and the needs and desires of the managerial personnel who staff the unit. Working within control parameters, MNCs will structure their processes so that they are as efficient and effective as possible. As one analysis notes, "selected tools must be used to manage data, to manage managers, and to manage conflicts; and . . . the

Table 12–4

A Comparison of Profit Margins as a Percentage of Sales among Select Auto Manufacturers

Year	General Motors		Ford Motor		Chrysler		Toyota	
	Operating	Net	Operating	Net	Operating	Net	Operating	Net
1994	4.1%	3.6%	5.4%	5.0%	11.5%	7.1%	3.1%	1.6%
1995	3.8%	4.2%	3.0%	3.7%	6.2%	3.8%	3.2%	2.4%
1996	2.2%	3.4%	2.1%	3.8%	9.9%	5.7%	5.4%	3.1%

1. Before discontinued operations and cumulative effects of accounting changes.
2. Automotive only.

Note: Operating margin is operating income—income before taxes, interest, and earnings from subsidiaries and affiliates—as a percentage of sales. Net margin is net income as a percentage of sales.

Source: Annual reports

successful companies blend an array of tools into a consistent management process."[21] Typically, these tools give the unit manager the autonomy needed to adapt to changes in the market and attract competent local personnel. The tools also provide for coordination of operations with the home office so that the overseas unit is in harmony with the MNC's strategic plan.

Some control tools are universal. For example, all MNCs use financial tools in monitoring overseas units. This was true as long as two decades ago, when the following was reported:

> The cross-cultural homogeneity in financial control is in marked contrast to the heterogeneity exercised over the areas of international operations. American subsidiaries of Italian and Scandinavian firms are virtually independent operationally from their parents in function pertaining to marketing, production, and research and development; whereas, the subsidiaries of German and British firms have limited freedom in these areas. Almost no autonomy on financial matters is given by any nationality to the subsidiaries.[22]

Some Major Differences   MNCs control operations in many different ways, and these often vary considerably from country to country. For example, how British firms control their overseas operations often is different from how German or French firms do. Similarly, U.S. MNCs tend to have their own approach to controlling that differs from both European and Japanese approaches. When Horovitz examined the key characteristics of top management control in Great Britain, Germany, and France, he found that British controls had four common characteristics: (1) financial records were sophisticated and heavily emphasized; (2) top management tended to focus its attention on major problem areas and did not get involved in specific, detailed matters of control; (3) control was used more for general guidance than for surveillance; and (4) operating units had a large amount of marketing autonomy.[23]

This model was in marked contrast to that of German managers, who employed very detailed control and focused attention on all variances large and small. These managers also placed heavy control on the production area and stressed operational efficiency. In achieving this centralized control, managers used a large central staff for measuring performance, analyzing variances, and compiling quantitative reports for senior executives. Overall, the control process in the German firms was used as a policing and surveillance instrument. French managers employed a control system that was closer to that of the Germans than to the British, however. Control was used more for surveillance than for guiding operations, and the process was centrally administered. Even so, the French system was less systematic and sophisticated.[24]

How do U.S. MNCs differ from their European counterparts? One comparative study found that a major difference is that U.S. firms tend to rely much more heavily on reports and other performance-related data. Americans make greater use of output control, and Europeans rely more heavily on behavioral control. Commenting on the differences between these two groups, the researcher noted: "This pattern appears to be quite robust and continues to exist even when a number of common factors that seem to influence control are taken into account."[25] Some specific findings from this study include:

1. Control in U.S. MNCs focuses more on the quantifiable, objective aspects of a foreign subsidiary, whereas control in European MNCs tends to be used to measure more qualitative aspects. The U.S. approach allows comparative analyses between other foreign operations as well as domestic units; the European measures are more flexible and allow control to be exercised on a unit-by-unit basis.

2. Control in U.S. MNCs requires more precise plans and budgets in generating suitable standards for comparison. Control in European MNCs requires a high level of companywide understanding and agreement regarding what constitutes appropriate behavior and how such behavior supports the goals of both the subsidiary and the parent firm.

3. Control in U.S. MNCs requires large central staffs and centralized information-processing capability. Control in European MNCs requires a larger cadre of capable expatriate mangers who are willing to spend long periods of time abroad. This control characteristic is reflected in the career approaches used in the various MNCs. Although U.S. multinationals do not encourage lengthy stays in foreign management positions, European MNCs often regard these positions as stepping stones to higher offices.

4. Control in European MNCs requires more decentralization of operating decision than control in U.S. MNCs.

5. Control in European MNCs favors short vertical spans or reporting channels from the foreign subsidiary to responsible positions in the parent.[26]

As noted earlier in the discussion of decision making, these differences help to explain why many researchers have found European subsidiaries to be more decentralized than U.S. subsidiaries. On the one hand, Europeans rely on the managerial personnel they assign from headquarters to run the unit properly. Americans tend to hire a greater percentage of local management people and control operations through reports and other objective, performance-related data. The difference results in Europeans' relying more on socioemotional control systems and Americans' opting for task-oriented, objective control systems.

Evaluating Approaches to Control   Is one control approach any better than the other? At present, each seems to work best for its respective group. Some studies predict that as MNCs increase in size, however, they likely will move toward the objective orientation of the U.S. MNCs. Commenting on the data gathered from large German and U.S. MNCs, the researchers concluded:

> Control mechanisms have to be harmonized with the main characteristics of management corporate structure to become an integrated part of the global organization concept and to meet situational needs. Trying to explain the differences in concepts of control we have to consider that the companies of the U.S. sample were much larger and more diversified. . . . Accordingly, they use different corporate structures, combining operational units into larger units and integrating these through primarily centralized, indirect, and task-oriented control. . . . The German companies have not (yet) reached this size and complexity, so a behavioral model of control seems to be fitting.[27]

Approaches to control also differ between U.S. and Japanese firms. For example, one study surveyed the attitudes of a large sample of Japanese and U.S. controllers and line managers. Respondents were drawn from the 500 largest industrial firms in both countries, and some of the results are presented in Table 12-5.

One overall finding of the research was that Japanese controllers and managers prefer less participation in the control process than their U.S. counterparts do. In addition, the

Table 12–5
Selected Beliefs Related to Planning and Control

| | Statement of Results—Average Responses[a] | | | |
| | Japan | | United States | |
	Managers	Controllers	Managers	Controllers
To be useful in performance evaluation of managers, a budget must be revised continuously throughout the year.	3.07	3.14	2.70	2.48
It is important that budgets be very detailed.	3.38	3.31	2.93	2.97
It is appropriate to charge other activities when budgeted funds are used up.	3.01	2.91	1.96	1.52
Budgets should be developed from the bottom up rather than from the top down.	3.13	3.01	3.68	3.96
Budgets are useful in communicating the goal and planned activities of the company.	4.54	4.68	4.11	4.23
Budgets are useful in coordinating activities of various departments.	4.24	4.46	3.78	4.02
A manager who fails to attain the budgets should be replaced.	2.56	2.67	2.00	1.92
Top management should judge a manager's performance mainly on the basis of attaining budget profit.	3.25	3.38	2.27	2.07
It is important that executive compensation depend on a comparison of actual and budgeted performance.	3.18	3.18	3.55	3.56
It is important that managers who perform exceptionally well receive more money than other managers in similar positions.	3.84	3.92	4.28	4.14
It is important for a manager to have quantitative or analytic skills as opposed to people skills.	3.12	3.15	2.04	1.96
The best way to determine the value of capital projects is through the use of quantitative analysis.	3.61	3.80	3.23	3.37

Note:[a]The response scale was as follows:

strongly disagree	1
disagree	2
neutral	3
agree	4
strongly agree	5

Source: Adapted from Lane Daley, James Jiambalvo, Gary L. Sundem, and Yasumasa Kondo, "Attitudes toward Financial Control Systems in the United States and Japan," *Journal of International Business Studies,* Fall 1985, pp. 100–102. Used with permission.

Japanese have longer-term planning horizons, view budgets as more of a communication device than a controlling tool, and prefer more slack in their budgets than the Americans. These results are extremely important in terms of adapting U.S. approaches to Japanese-owned subsidiaries. The study results suggest the following:

> U.S. managers who wish to design control systems for foreign divisions in Japan (or vice-versa) may wish to consider modifications to the typical domestic system, or they should at least be aware of the potential differences in responses to the system in the areas of budget development, evaluation against budgets, long-run/short-run orientation of budgets, the use of budget slack, and the use of analytic tools in developing inputs to the budget process to name a few.[28]

It is also important to understand why Japanese managers act as they do. Yoshimura and Anderson recently conducted a detailed analysis of white-collar middle managers in Japan in order to determine what foreign managers need to know about these "salarymen."

One thing that the researchers found was that Japanese managers place human relationships ahead of economic efficiency. As a result, when Western managers try to penetrate Japanese markets by offering superior technology or lower price as their levers, they often find that these strategies do not work. If a Japanese company has had a satisfactory relationship with a supplier, the company may continue doing business with this firm even if it means accepting higher costs. Second, when dealing with a Japanese company, nothing is more important than a supplier's ability to meet this customer's expectations. When salarymen complain about non-Japanese companies and the products or service they provide, they usually contend that consistency is missing.

> They want their suppliers to understand customer expectations without being told explicitly, and they want assurance that even "unreasonable" expectations, such as midnight service, will be met. They don't want their relationship manager changed frequently because of turnover; a new contact may not understand their expectations immediately. Japanese overseas subsidiaries do business with their traditional suppliers because they want to maintain continuity in relationships, even if lower-cost local firms are available. The Japanese believe that, in the long run, if both parties contribute to the relationship in good faith, results will take care of themselves.[29]

Another thing that the researchers discovered is that sometimes performance results are not as high as they could be because of the fear of embarrassing others in the organization. For example, even though some decisions might result in higher returns on investment for the company, if these decisions put others in a bad light, they will not be made. This means that if a bank has two groups that are charged with buying and selling foreign currency and one of the groups concludes that the U.S. dollar is going to decline against the Japanese yen, it would be wise for this group to sell those dollars and buy yen. On the other hand, if there is another group in the bank that has a large position in dollars and will be unable to unload this currency very quickly, the first group might refuse to sell its dollars because this would end up making the group that held dollars look foolish and this is something that Japanese salarymen try very hard to avoid.

In fact, the avoidance of embarrassment or saving "face" is one reason that many Japanese firms focus on long-term objectives rather than short-term ones. While their pronouncements seem to emphasize the long-term orientation of their company, in truth this approach is a way of deflecting embarrassment. After all, no one knows what will happen in the long run, so by pretending to be highly interested in 50-year goals, the management sidesteps any likelihood that its current performance will be criticized. After all, it can always argue that in the long run it will achieve high level performance, despite the fact that it is not doing very well at present. So in deciding which form of control to use, MNCs must determine whether they want a more bureaucratic or a more cultural control approach; and from the cultural perspective, it must be remembered that this control will vary across subsidiaries.

Control Techniques

A number of performance measures are used for control purposes. Three of the most common types are those related to financial performance, quality performance, and personnel performance.

Financial Performance

Financial performance evaluation of a foreign subsidiary or affiliate usually is based on profit and return on investment. **Profit** is the amount remaining after all expenses are deducted from total revenues. **Return on investment (ROI)** is measured through dividing profit by assets; some firms use profit divided by owners' equity (returns on owners' investment, or ROOI) in referring to the return-on-investment performance measure. In

Profit
The amount remaining after all expenses are deducted from total revenues.

Return on investment (ROI)
Return measured by dividing profit by assets.

any case, the most important part of the ROI calculation is profits, which often can be manipulated by management. Thus, the amount of profit directly relates to how well or how poorly a unit is judged to perform. For example, if an MNC has an operation in both country A and country B and taxes are lower in country A, the MNC may be able to benefit if the two units have occasion to do business with each other. This benefit can be accomplished by having the unit in country A charge higher prices than usual to the unit in country B, thus providing greater net profits to the MNC. Simply put, sometimes differences in tax rates can be used to maximize overall MNC profits. This same basic form of manipulation can be used in transferring money from one country to another, which can be explained as follows:

> Transfer prices are manipulated upward or downward depending on whether the parent company wishes to inject or remove cash into or from a subsidiary. Prices on imports by a subsidiary from a related subsidiary are raised if the multinational company wishes to move funds from the receiver to the seller, but they are lowered if the objective is to keep the funds in the importing subsidiary. . . . Multinational companies have been known to use transfer pricing for moving excess cash from subsidiaries located in countries with weak currencies to countries with strong currencies in order to protect the value of their current assets.[30]

The so-called bottom-line (i.e., profit) performance of subsidiaries also can be affected by a devaluation or revaluation of local currency. For example, if a country devalues its currency, then subsidiary export sales will increase, because the price of these goods will be lower for foreign buyers, whose currencies now have greater purchasing power. If the country revalues its currency, then export sales will decline because the price of goods for foreign buyers will rise, because their currencies now will have less purchasing power in the subsidiary's country. Likewise, a devaluation of the currency will increase the cost of imported materials and supplies for the subsidiary, and a revaluation will decrease these costs because of the relative changes in the purchasing power of local currency. Because devaluation and revaluation of local currency are outside the control of the overseas unit, bottom-line performance sometimes will be a result of external conditions that do not accurately reflect how well the operation actually is being run.

Of course, not all bottom-line financial performance is a result of manipulation or external environmental conditions. Comparing results from country to country sometimes is difficult, however, because the situations are not similar. For example, managers of South American subsidiaries would have been faced with inflation 100 times or more than inflation elsewhere during the late 1980s. The fluctuating value of the South American country's currency would have made it difficult to use profitability of the unit as a measure for evaluating management. Using financial performance alone when controlling a subsidiary for effective performance can be misleading.

Quality Performance

Just as quality has become a major focus in decision making, as discussed earlier under TQM, it also is a major dimension of the modern control process of MNCs. The term "quality control" (QC) has been around for a long time, and it is a major function of production and operations management. Besides the TQM techniques of concurrent engineering/interfunctional teams, employee empowerment, reward/recognition systems, and training, which were discussed under decision making, another technique more directly associated with the control function is the use of quality circles, which have been popularized by the Japanese. A **quality control circle (QCC)** is a group of workers who meet on a regular basis to discuss ways of improving the quality of work. This approach has helped many MNCs to improve the quality of their goods and services dramatically.

Why are Japanese-made goods of higher quality than those of many other countries? The answer cannot rest solely on technology, because many MNCs have the same or superior technology or the financial ability to purchase it. There must be other causal factors. The accompanying sidebar, "How the Japanese Do Things Differently," gives some details on these factors. One study attempted to answer the question by examining the differences between Japanese and U.S. manufacturers of air conditioners.[31] In this analysis, many of

Quality control circle (QCC)
A group of workers who meet on a regular basis to discuss ways of improving the quality of work.

How the Japanese Do Things Differently

There are a number of things that Japanese firms do extremely well. One is to train their people carefully, a strategy that many successful U.S. firms also employ. Another is to try and remain on the technological cutting edge. A third, and increasingly important because of its uniqueness to the Japanese, is to keep a keen focus on developing and bringing to market goods that are competitively priced.

In contrast to Western firms, many Japanese companies use what is called a "target cost" approach. Like other multinational firms, Japanese companies begin the new product development process by conducting marketing research and examining the characteristics of the product to be produced. At this point, however, the Japanese take a different approach. The traditional approach used by MNCs around the world is next to go into designing, engineering, and supplier pricing, then to determine if the cost is sufficiently competitive to move ahead with manufacturing. Japanese manufacturers, on the other hand, first determine the price that the consumer most likely will accept, and then they work with design, engineering, and supply people to ensure that the product can be produced at this price. The other major difference is that after most firms manufacture a product, they will engage in periodic cost reductions. The Japanese, however, use a *kaizen* approach, in which there are continuous cost-reduction efforts.

The critical difference between the two systems is that the Japanese get costs out of the product during the planning and design stage. Additionally, they look at profit in terms of product lines rather than just individual goods, so a consumer product that would be rejected for production by a U.S. or European firm because its projected profitability is too low may be accepted by a Japanese firm because the product will attract additional customers to other offerings in the line. A good example is Sony, which decided to build a smaller version of its compact personal stereo system and market it to older consumers. Sony knew that the profitability of the unit would not be as high as usual, but it went ahead because the product would provide another market niche for the firm and strengthen its reputation. Also, a side benefit is that once a product is out there, it may appeal to an unanticipated market. This was the case with Sony's compact personal stereo system. The unit caught on with young people, and Sony's sales are 50 percent greater than anticipated. Had Sony made its manufacturing decision solely on "stand alone" profitability, the unit never would have been produced.

These approaches are not unique to Japanese firms. Foreign companies operating in Japan are catching on and use them as well. A good example is Coca-Cola Japan. Coke is the leading company in the Japanese soft drink market, which sees the introduction of more than 1,000 new products each year. Most offerings do not last very long, and a cost accountant might well argue that it is not worth the effort to produce them. However, Coca-Cola introduces one new product a month. Most of these sodas, soft drinks, and cold coffees survive less than 90 days, but Coke does not let the short-term bottom line dictate the decision. The firm goes beyond quick profitability and looks at the overall picture. Result: Coca-Cola continues to be the leading soft drink firm in Japan despite competition that often is more vigorous than that in the United States.

the commonly cited reasons for superior Japanese quality were discovered to be inaccurate. One theory was that Japanese focus their production processes on a relatively limited set of tasks and narrow product lines, but this was not so. Nor was support found for the commonly held belief that single sourcing provided Japanese firms with cost advantages over those using multiple sourcing; the firms studied regularly relied on a number of different suppliers. So, what were the reasons for the quality differences?

One reason was the focus on keeping the workplace clean and ensuring that all machinery and equipment was properly maintained. The Japanese firms were more careful in handling incoming parts and materials, work-in-process, and finished products than their U.S. counterparts. Japanese companies also employed equipment fixtures to a greater extent than U.S. manufacturers in ensuring proper alignment of parts during final assembly.

The Japanese minimized worker error by assigning new employees to existing work teams or pairing them with supervisors. In this way, the new workers gained important experience under the watchful eye of someone who could correct their mistakes.

Another interesting finding was that the Japanese made effective use of QCCs. Quality targets were set, and responsibility for their attainment then fell on the circle while management provided support assistance. This was stated by the researcher as follows:

> In supporting the activities of their QCC's, the Japanese firms in this industry routinely collected extensive quality data. Information on defects was compiled daily, and analyzed for trends. Perhaps most important, the data were made easily accessible to line workers, often in the form of publicly posted charts. More detailed data were available to QCC's on request.[32]

This finding pointed out an important difference between Americans and Japanese. The Japanese pushed data on quality down to the operating employees in the quality circles, whereas Americans tended to aggregate the quality data into summary reports aimed at middle- and upper-level management.

Another important difference is that the Japanese tend to build in early warning systems so that they know when something is going wrong. A good example is that incoming field data are reviewed immediately by the quality department, and problems are assigned to one of two categories: routine or emergency. Special efforts then are made to resolve the emergency problems as quickly as possible. High failure rates attributable to a single persistent problem are identified and handled much faster than in U.S. firms.

Management attitudes toward quality also were quite different. The Japanese operate under the philosophy of "anything worth doing in the area of quality is worth overdoing." Workers are trained for all jobs on the line, even though they eventually are assigned to a single workstation. This method of "training overkill" ensures that everyone can perform every job perfectly and results in two important outcomes: (1) if someone is moved to another job, he or she can handle the work without any additional assistance; and (2) the workers realize that management puts an extremely high value on the need for quality. When questioned regarding whether their approach to quality resulted in spending more money than was necessary, the Japanese managers disagreed. They believed that quality improvement was technically possible and economically feasible. They did not accept the common U.S. strategy of building a product with quality that was "good enough."

These managers were speaking only for their own firms, however. Some evidence shows that at least in the short run, an overfocus on quality may become economically unwise. Even so, firms must remember that in the long run, quality goods and services lead to repeat business, which translates into profits and growth. From a control standpoint, however, the major issue is how to identify quality problems and resolve them as efficiently as possible. One approach that has gained acceptance in the United States is outlined by Genichi Taguchi, one of the world's foremost authorities on quality control. Taguchi's approach is to dispense with highly sophisticated statistical methods unless more fundamental ways do not work. Figure 12-2 provides an example of how his approach was used to identify the cause of defects in the paint on a minivan hood. This approach to solving quality control problems is proving to be so effective that any MNCs are adopting it. They also are realizing that the belief that Japanese firms will correct quality control problems regardless of the cost is not true. As Taguchi puts it, "the more efficient approach is to identify the things that can be controlled at a reasonable cost in an organized manner, and simply ignore those too expensive to control."[33] To the extent that U.S. MNCs can do this, they will be able to compete on the basis of quality.

Personnel Performance

Besides financial techniques and the emphasis on quality, another key area of control is personnel performance evaluation. This type of evaluation can take a number of different forms, although there is a great deal of agreement from firm to firm when looking at the overall criteria that are measured. Table 12-6 provides a list of the 25 most admired global companies. What makes these MNCs so successful? Consultants at the Hay Group made

Figure 12–2 **Solving a Quality Problem: Taguchi Method vs. Traditional Method**

Traditional Method Possible causes are studied one by one while holding the other factors constant.

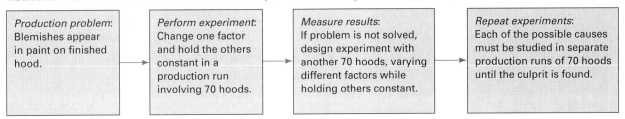

Production problem: Blemishes appear in paint on finished hood. → *Perform experiment*: Change one factor and hold the others constant in a production run involving 70 hoods. → *Measure results*: If problem is not solved, design experiment with another 70 hoods, varying different factors while holding others constant. → *Repeat experiments*: Each of the possible causes must be studied in separate production runs of 70 hoods until the culprit is found.

Taguchi Method Brainstorming and a few bold experiments seek to quickly find the problem.

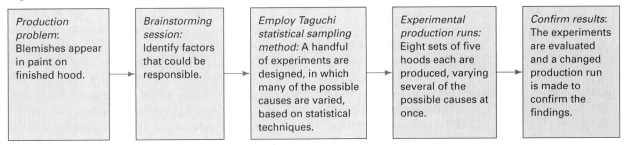

Production problem: Blemishes appear in paint on finished hood. → *Brainstorming session*: Identify factors that could be responsible. → *Employ Taguchi statistical sampling method*: A handful of experiments are designed, in which many of the possible causes are varied, based on statistical techniques. → *Experimental production runs*: Eight sets of five hoods each are produced, varying several of the possible causes at once. → *Confirm results*: The experiments are evaluated and a changed production run is made to confirm the findings.

Source: From information reported in John Holusha, "Improving Quality, the Japanese Way," *New York Times,* July 20, 1988, p. 35.

Table 12–6
The Most Admired Global Companies

Ranking	Company
1	General Electric (electronics, electrical equipment)
2	Coca-Cola (beverages)
3	Microsoft (computers)
4	Walt Disney (entertainment)
5	Intel (computers)
6	Hewlett-Packard (computers)
7	Berkshire Hathaway (securities/diversified financials)
8	Pfizer (pharmaceuticals)
9	Sony (electronics, electrical equipment)
10	Dell Computer (computers)
11	Toyota Motor (motor vehicles)
12	Merck (pharmaceuticals)
13	Southwest Airlines (airlines)
14	Johnson & Johnson (pharmaceuticals)
15	Procter & Gamble (soaps, cosmetics)
16	Gillette (soaps, cosmetics)
17	Citicorp (commercial banking)
18	Merrill Lynch (securities, diversified financials)
19	ABB Asea Brown Boveri (electronics, electrical equipment)
20	Daimler-Benz (motor vehicles)
21	Caterpillar (industrial and farm equipment)
22	AT&T (telecommunications)
23	British Airways (airlines)
24	IBM (computers)
25	Boeing (aerospace)

Source: Fortune, October 26, 1998, p. 214.

an analysis of the best global firms in a recent year and concluded that there were seven common themes that emerged.

1. Top managers at the most admired companies take their mission statements seriously and expect everyone else to do the same.
2. Success attracts the best people—and the best people sustain success.
3. The top companies know precisely what they are looking for.
4. These firms see career development as an investment, not a chore.
5. Whenever possible, these companies promote from within.
6. Performance is rewarded.
7. The firms are genuinely interested in what their employees think and they measure work satisfaction often and thoroughly.[34]

One of the most common approaches to personnel performance evaluation is the periodic appraisal of work performance. Although the objective is similar from country to country, how performance appraisals are done differs. For example, what is effective employee performance in one country is not always judged to be effective in another. This is particularly important when expatriate managers evaluate local managers based on home-country standards. A good example came out of a survey that found Japanese managers in U.S.-based manufacturing firms gave higher evaluations to Japanese personnel than to Americans. The results, which are provided in Table 12-7, led the researcher to conclude: "It seems that cultural differences and diversified approaches to management in MNCs of different nationalities will always create a situation where some bias in performance appraisal may exist."[35] Dealing with these biases is a big challenge facing MNCs.

Another important difference is how personnel performance control actually is conducted. A study that compared personnel control approaches used by Japanese managers in Japan with those employed by U.S. managers in the United States found marked differences.[36] For example, when Japanese work groups were successful because of the actions of a particular individual, the Japanese manager tended to give credit to the whole group. When the group was unsuccessful because of the actions of a particular individual, however, the Japanese manager tended to perceive this one employee as responsible. In addition, the more unexpected the poor performance, the greater the likelihood that the individual would be responsible. In contrast, individuals in the United States typically were given both the credit when things went well and the blame when performance was poor.

Other differences relate to how rewards and monitoring of personnel performance are handled. Both U.S. and Japanese managers offered greater rewards and more freedom from close monitoring to individuals when they were associated with successful performance, no matter what the influence of the group on the performance. The Americans carried this

Table 12–7
Performance Evaluations by Japanese and U.S. Managers in U.S.-Based Japanese Manufacturing Firms

Group	Average Score[a]	Frequency
U.S. rater's ratings of U.S. subordinates	5.10	139
U.S. rater's ratings of Japanese subordinates	5.04	27
Japanese rater's ratings of U.S. subordinates	4.71	65
Japanese rater's ratings of Japanese subordinates	5.53	30
Total sample	5.05	261

Note: [a]On a 7-point Likert scale.

Source: Adapted from Golpira Eshgi, "Nationality Bias and Performance Evaluation in Multinational Corporations," *National Academy of Management Proceedings,* 1985, p. 96. Used with permission.

tendency further than the Japanese in the case of rewards, however, including giving high rewards to a person who is a "lone wolf."[37]

A comparison of these two approaches to personnel evaluation shows that the Japanese tend to use a more social or group orientation, while the Americans are more individualistic. The researchers found that overall, however, the approaches were quite similar, and that the control of personnel performance by Japanese and U.S. managers is far more similar than different.

Such similarity also can be found in assessment centers used to evaluate employees. An **assessment center** is an evaluation tool that is used to identify individuals with the potential to be selected or promoted to higher-level positions. Used by large U.S. MNCs for many years, these centers also are employed around the world. A typical assessment center would involve simulation exercises such as: (1) in-basket exercises that require managerial attention; (2) a committee exercise in which the candidates must work as a team in making decisions; (3) business decision exercises in which participants compete in the same market; (4) preparation of a business plan; and (5) a letter-writing exercise. Table 12-8 provides an example of dimension used in an assessment center in the United Kingdom. These forms of evaluation are beginning to gain support, because they are more comprehensive than simple checklists or the use of a test to interview and thus better able to identify those managers who are most likely to succeed when hired or promoted.

Assessment center
An evaluation tool used to identify individuals with potential to be selected or promoted to higher-level positions.

The World of Business Week Revisited

This chapter focused very heavily on two areas that are going to be critical to tremendously growing MNCs such as SAP's future success: decision making and controlling. In particular, it will be interesting to see if SAP is able to carve out a major niche in its new markets, given that there is so much competition there already. Additionally, product quality is likely to remain a major issue and, as you saw in the news story, there are some companies that contend that SAP did not deliver the quality they needed. Another key issue raised by the news on SAP is whether it will have the same success in the future as it has in the past. In what way will quality remain an issue for SAP over the next decade? Specifically, what forms will this quality have to take? In monitoring performance and making control-related decisions, what type of control tools and techniques would you expect SAP to employ? In your answer be sure to focus on both financial and personnel-related areas.

Summary of Key Points

1. Decision making involves choosing from among alternatives. Some countries tend to use more centralized decision making than others, so that more decisions are made at the top of the MNC than are delegated to the subsidiaries and operating levels.

2. A number of factors help to influence whether decision making will be centralized or decentralized, including company size, amount of capital investment, relative importance of the overseas unit to the MNC, volume-to-unit-cost relationship, level of product diversification, distance between the home office and the subsidiary, and the competence of managers in the host country.

3. There are a number of decision-making issues with which MNCs currently are being confronted. Three of the most important include total quality management (TQM) decisions, use of joint ventures and other forms of cooperative agreements, and strategies for attacking the competition.

4. Controlling involves evaluating results in relation to plans or objectives, then taking action to correct deviations. MNCs control their overseas operations in a number of ways. Most combine direct and indirect controls. Some prefer heavily quantifiable methods, and others opt for more qualitative approaches. Some prefer decentralized approaches; others opt for greater centralization.

Table 12–8
Dimensions Assessed in a U.K. Assessment Center

Dimensions	In-Basket	Committee I (Presentation)	Committee II (Discussion)	Business Decisions (1)	Business Decisions (2–5)	Business Decisions (6–8)	Presentation (Business Plan)	Letter Writing
Analytic ability	*			*	*		*	
Administrative ability	*			*			*	
Business sense	*			*	*	*	*	
Written communication	*							*
Oral communication		*	*	*			*	*
Perceptive listening			*	*				
Vigor	*		*	*		*		
Emotional adjustment		*	*					
Social skill			*		*	*	*	*
Ascendancy		*	*		*	*	*	
Flexibility			*		*	*		
Relations with subordinates	*		*					*

Source: Adapted from Clive A. Fletcher and Victor Dulewicz, "An Empirical Study of a U.K.-Based Assessment Center," *Journal of Management Studies,* January 1984, pp. 84–97. Used with permission.

5. Three of the most common performance measures used to control subsidiaries are in the financial, quality, and personnel areas. Financial performance typically is measured by profit and return on investment.

Quality performance often is controlled through quality circles. Personnel performance typically is judged through performance evaluation techniques.

Key Terms

assessment center	*honne*	quality control circle (QCC)
codetermination	indirect controls	return on investment (ROI)
controlling	international joint ventures (IJVs)	*ringisei*
decision making	*kaizen*	*tatemae*
direct controls	profit	total quality management (TQM)

Review and Discussion Questions

1. A British computer firm is acquiring a smaller competitor located in Frankfurt. What are two likely differences in the way these two firms carry out the decision-making process? How could these differences create a problem for the acquiring firm? Give an example in each case.

2. Would the British firm in the question above find any differences between the way it typically controls operations and the way that its German acquisition carries out the control process?

3. How do U.S. and Japanese firms differ in the way they go about making decision and controlling operations? How are the two similar? In each case, provide an example.

4. How are U.S. multinationals trying to introduce total quality management (TQM) into their operations? Give two examples. Would a U.S. MNC doing business in Germany find it easier to introduce these concepts into German operations, or would there be more receptivity to them back in the United States? Why? What if the U.S. multinational were introducing these ideas into a Japanese subsidiary?

5. What are some common control approaches used by U.S. firms at home that may not work well in Europe? Identify and describe three. In your answer, be sure to explain how U.S. multinationals must change their approach in each of these examples.

6. Why are Japanese firms likely to have trouble using their personnel performance evaluation techniques in the United States? Cite two reasons. What do these firms need to realize to make the necessary adjustments in their approach? Are these changes possible, or will the Japanese firms continue to have trouble?

Internet Exercise: Looking at the Best

In Table 12-6 the most admired 25 global companies were listed. Each of these companies uses decision making and controlling to help ensure its success in the world market. Visit two of these company sites: British Airways and ABB Asea Brown Boveri. The addresses are http://www.british-airways.com and http://abb.com. Carefully examine what these firms are doing. For example, what markets are they targeting? What products and services are they offering? What new markets are they entering? Then, after you are as familiar with their operation as possible, answer these two questions: (1) What types of factors may influence future management decision making in these two companies? (2) What types of control criteria would you expect them to use in evaluating their operations and determining how well they are doing?

Spain

Spain, which covers 195,000 square miles, is located on the Iberian peninsula at the southwest corner of Europe; its southernmost tip is directly across from Morocco. The country has a population of approximately 40 million and a gross domestic product of about $570 billion ($14,250 per capita). Until the mid-1990s, Spain, known for its sunny climate, colorful bullfights, and storybook castles, was one of the most underdeveloped countries in Western Europe. Now, it is an industrialized country whose economy relies heavily on trade, manufacturing, and agriculture. Many of the old Spanish customs, such as taking a siesta (nap or rest) after lunch, are less common. The democratic government uses a constitutional monarchy, which was adopted in 1978, in which the king is head of state and commander-in-chief of the armed forces, but the legislative power rests in a bicameral parliament consisting of a Congress of Deputies and a Senate.

Investors Limited, a partnership based in Hong Kong and headed by Stanley Wong, owns 17 medium and large hotels throughout Asia and a total of 9 others throughout the United Kingdom, France, and Germany. The group now plans on buying a large hotel in Madrid. This hotel was built at the turn of the century but was completely refurbished in 1990 at a cost of $20 million. The current owners have since decided that the return on investment, which has been averaging 5.2 percent annually, is too small to justify continuing the operation. They have offered the hotel to the Wong group for $60 million. One-half is payable immediately, and the rest will be paid in equal annual installments over 5 years.

Stanley Wong believes that this is a good investment and has suggested to his partners they accept the offer.

"Europe is going to boom during the new millennium," he told them, "and Spain is going to be an excellent investment. This hotel is one of the finest in Madrid, and we are going to more than triple our investment by the end of the decade."

In the past, the partnership has handled all hotel investments in the same way. A handful of company-appointed managers are sent in to oversee general operations and monitor financial performance, and all other matters continue to be handled by those personnel who have been with the hotel before acquisition. The investment group intends to handle the Madrid operation in the same way. "The most important thing," Stanley noted recently, "is that we keep control of key areas of performance such as costs and return on investment. If we do that and continue to offer the best possible service, we'll come out just fine."
www.docuweb.ca/sispain

Questions

1. What are some current issues facing Spain? What is the climate for doing business in Spain today?

2. Do you think the Wong group, in running the hotel, should use centralized or decentralized decision making?

3. What types of direct controls might the Wong group use? What types of indirect control might be employed?

4. What are some likely differences between the control measures that the Wong group would use and those that typically are used in countries such as Spain?

Expansion Plans

Kranden & Associates is a very successful porcelain-manufacturing firm based in San Diego. The company has six world-renowned artists who design fine-crafted porcelain statues and plates that are widely regarded as collectibles. Each year, the company offers a limited edition of new statues and plates. Last year, the company made 30 new offerings. On average, 2,500 of each line are produced, and they usually are sold within 6 months. The company does not produce more than this number to avoid reducing the value of the line to collectors; however, the firm does believe that additional statues and plates could be sold in some areas of the world without affecting the price in North America. In particular, the firm is thinking about setting up production facilities in Rio de Janeiro, Brazil, and Paris, France.

The production process requires skilled personnel, but there are people in both Rio de Janeiro and Paris who can do this work. The basic methods can be taught to these people by trainers from the U.S. plant, because the production process will be identical.

The company intends to send three managers to each of its overseas units to handle setup operation and get the production process off the ground. This should take 12 to 18 months. Once this is done, one person will be left in charge, and the other two will return home.

The company believes that it will be able to sell just as much of the product line in Europe as it does in the United States. The South American market is estimated to be one-half that of the United States. Over the last 5 years, Kranden has had a return on investment of 55 percent. The company charges premium prices for its porcelain but still has strong demand for its products because of the high regard collectors and investors have for the Kranden line. The quality of its statues and plates is highly regarded, and the firm has won three national and two international awards for creativity and quality in design and production over the past 18 months. Over the last 10 years, the firm has won 27 such awards.

Questions

1. In managing its international operations, should the firm use centralized or decentralized decision making?

2. Would direct or indirect controls be preferable in managing these operations?

3. What kinds of performance measures should the company use in controlling these international operations?

Integrative Case 1

KNP, N.V.

Koninklijke Nederlandse Paperfabrieken, N.V. (KNP), or Royal Dutch Papermills, produces and sells paper and board products to printing and packaging industries throughout the world. The firm originated in 1850 as a small papermill in Maastricht, the Netherlands. One of the firm's three papermaking mills operates in the city today. Another papermill is located across the Maas River in Belgium. The firm also produces packaging materials at various European locations and has investments in paper merchant operations in a number of countries.

The company's headquarters are in a modern office building in a newer section of the ancient and historic city of Maastricht. It is here that Wilmer Zetteler, the commercial director of KNP België, ponders the emerging international business strategy of KNP and the decisions that will be necessary to meet the challenges faced by the firm.

KNP and the World Paper Industry

The evolution of the papermaking industry and the emergence of the modern European economic system have shaped KNP. In the year following World War II, the relatively undamaged but depreciated plant at Maastricht produced only 10,000 tons of paper. By 1950 the firm was pioneering the production of coated paper. KNP was the first European producer of such papers to use technology obtained under a license from the Consolidated Paper Company in the United States. A companion plant that produces top grade coated paper for brochures, art books, and catalogs is located at Nijmegen on the Waal River. Another mill at Meerssen, a town outside Maastricht, produces colored and watermarked paper.

The oil price shock of 1973 led the firm to reconsider its fundamental strategy and further specialize in the production of high-grade coated papers to gain prominence in international markets. The firm was already well known for this specialty, but managed to expand its position. A mill was constructed at Lanaken, across the Maas in Belgium, just north of the Albert Canal, to produce more lightweight coated paper. This paper is used for magazines, brochures, catalogs, and promotional material.

A separate packaging division of KNP has nine plants that produce various forms of carton board for the packaging industry and other industrial applications. These products include solid, folding, corrugated, and other board products for making boxes. In addition, the plants at Oude Pekela and Sappemeer produce a greyboard for jigsaw puzzles, books and various types of deluxe packaging.

The plant at Oude Pekela in the Netherlands also produces solid board that is used in making boxes for shipping flowers, vegetables, fruits and various exports. This board product is manufactured on machines similar to those that make paper, but the board machines at KNP use wastepaper rather than virgin pulp as a raw material in the manufacturing process. The firm owns and operates eight wastepaper collection firms that handle 250,000 tons of raw material a year. Some 30,000 tons of capacity were added in 1986 when two more firms were purchased.

A factory in the Dutch town of Eerbeek produces folding box board. The pharmaceutical and food industries use this product, which also is manufactured from wastepaper. Overall, KNP processes 500,000 tons of wastepaper a year.

KNP acquired in 1986 the German firm of Herzberger Papierfabrik Ludwig Osthushenrich GmbH and Co. KG, which manufactures boxes in four locations in western Germany. The Oberstot plant, gained in the Herzberger acquisition, also produces liner and corrugated board used in boxes and other packaging applications. The Herzberg and Oberau plants that were acquired also produce the corrugated materials used in box converting operations. These acquisitions increased the capacity of the packaging division of KNP by 60 percent.

In addition to the four German packaging plants, KNP owns box-making operations in the Netherlands, Italy, and Spain. Each is supplied with board stock manufactured by other divisions of the firm. KNP also has a joint venture with Buhrman-Tetterode, nv in operating a mill that can produce 350,000 tons of paper for the manufacture of corrugated board. With the addition of a fourth machine at the mill in 1986, this joint venture has become one of the principal suppliers of packaging paper of the European market.

KNP began a series of acquisitions of paper merchants beginning in the late 1970s. Each acquisition was a defensive strategy to prevent competitors from capturing existing channels of distribution of KNP products. KNP has paper merchant operations in Belgium, France, and the United Kingdom. The firm also owns a 35 percent interest in Proost en Brandt, one of the two largest paper merchants in the Netherlands, and a 51 percent share in Scaldia Papier B.V. in Nijmegen.

Exhibit 1 displays the group structure of KNP, while Exhibits 2 and 3 summarize the plant capacity of the principal divisions of the company. Exhibit 4 shows the location of facilities in the Netherlands.

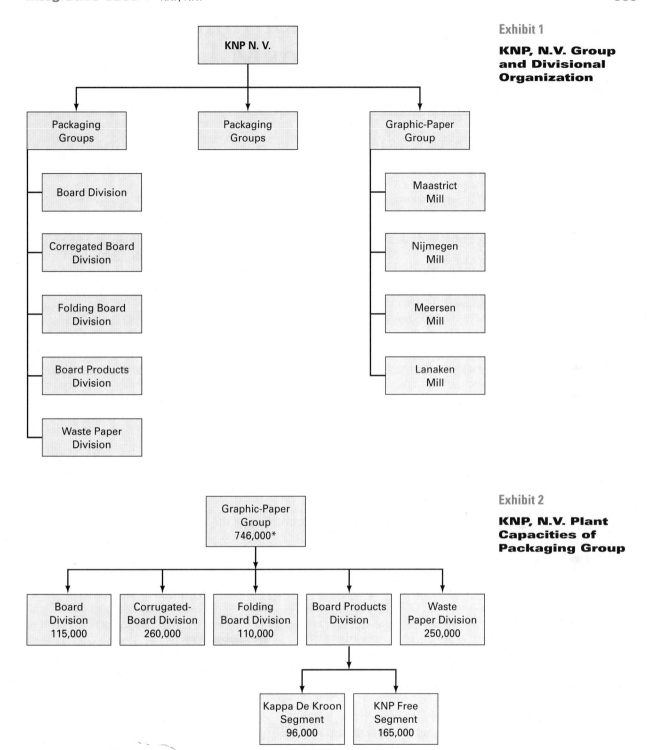

Exhibit 1

**KNP, N.V. Group
and Divisional
Organization**

Exhibit 2

**KNP, N.V. Plant
Capacities of
Packaging Group**

* Tons per annum

Internationalizing of the Firm

KNP's activity outside the Netherlands is not surprising. As with most Dutch manufacturers, the firm has always been an exporter and maintained an international perspective. The market for paper in the Netherlands is insufficient to support a plant. Europe is KNP's principal market. In 1986, 75 percent of its paper and 45 percent of its packaging materials were sold outside the Netherlands.

The modern, manufacture of paper products depends upon machines that produce large volumes. KNP has state-of-the-art technology that can produce such volumes.

The Netherlands has a population of 15 million, not nearly enough people to support a single modern paper

Exhibit 3

KNP, N.V. Plant Capacities of Graphic Paper Group

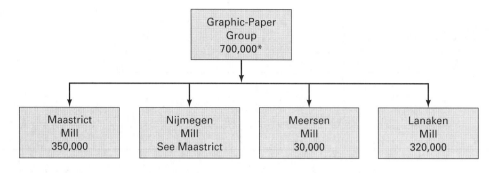

* Tons per annum

manufacturing plant. On the other hand, the European Community has a population of about 275 million and a modern economy that can easily support a number of competing paper firms.

In most European countries, paper is traditionally marketed through paper merchants who distribute products to converters and printers. These merchants serve national or sub-national markets.

Yet sometimes market development is not straightforward. When the demand for lightweight machine-coated paper emerged in the United States, KNP had a paper merchant on each coast for other products of the firm. But the lightweight coated product requires a more direct approach to the printing customer. KNP skirted traditional distributors and developed an exclusive relationship with the Wilcox-Walter-Furlong Paper Company, a paper merchant in Philadelphia that stocked KNP's product in the eastern United States. In the western United States, the firm marketed its product through the offices of MacMillan Bloedel, a firm with a 30 percent stock interest in KNP.

KNP's foreign activities can be divided into two segments and two stages. Part of the first stage has existed since the firm began exporting to adjacent nations in the early 19th century.

The second stage began with the development of the European Community, which was an important factor in the growth of KNP. The development of the company after World War II was typical of other manufacturers in Europe. Management knowledge and skill was necessary to seize the opportunity provided by the reconstruction of the European economy.

The European Community is designed to break down barriers that prevent economic activity. As the community emerged, paper firms and other businesses use skilled sales agents who were proficient in dealing with the new market. Firms succeeded in extending their markets by meeting the needs of each nation.

Language was not a barrier at KNP, where executives typically speak a number of European languages. Cultural differences also were not a factor.

Outside Europe, KNP initially exported specialized products to Africa and the Middle East. In the early 1980s,

the company began exporting to Australia and the Far East and began testing markets in the United States and Canada. No special cultural and language barriers emerged because of the company's previous experience in exporting to European nations.

KNP penetrated the United Kingdom market by working through a sales agent with contacts in the printing trades. Later, the company solidified its position in the United Kingdom by hiring an English paper merchant, Contract Papers Limited, to distribute its products. KNP now owns 45 percent interest in the company.

KNP today is one of Europe's largest exporters of coated paper and a leading producer of board. According to KNP's 1986 annual report, 31 percent of sales were in the Netherlands, 55 percent elsewhere in the European Community, and 14 percent elsewhere in the world.

Globalization of the Firm

KNP cannot be considered a fully globalized company because it does not manufacture products in the markets it serves.

While the specialized paper products of KNP are global products, their manufacture does not fit the global integrated strategy as described by Yves Doz and other theorists of international business. Therefore, KNP would be best described as following a multi-focal international business strategy.

The paper industries of Europe and North America have different configurations. American firms tend to be more fully integrated vertically and horizontally in respect to the full range of forest products. European firms, with the exception of the Scandinavians, have little opportunity to buy extensive woodlands in their home countries. Because North American firms have woodlands and a large domestic market, it is difficult for European firms to become established in the market. The Swedes and Finns, on the other hand, have forest resources, but they are handicapped by poor markets for finished paper in their countries.

KNP has acquired foreign paper merchants with connections in various world markets. KNP owns Papetries

Exhibit 4

KNP Plant Locations

Libert S.A. in Paris. The firm has a 51 percent holding in Saldiaa Papier, N.V. in Wilrijk, Belgium, and a 45 percent stake in Contract Papers (Holdings) Ltd. in London. In the Netherlands, KNP has a 35 percent interest in Proost en Brandt, N.V. in Amsterdam, and a 51 percent interest in Scaldia Papier B.V. in Nijmegen.

These acquisition were made in 1978 and 1979 as a defensive move against competitors in the European Community. Competitors had begun acquiring paper merchants that sold KNP products and threatened to use them to promote their own products. Meanwhile, the paper merchants acquired by KNP continue to stock a full range of goods, including those produced by competitors.

No distinct figures are available on KNP's foreign revenues. Overall, distribution provided 2 percent of operating results, while the paper group provided 62.9 percent of operating revenues and 71.7 percent of operating results. The packaging group produced 29.2 percent of operating revenue and 26.3 percent of operating results. These figures ignore the influence of internal transfers, which made up 8.2 percent of the total operating activity of the firm.

Other Aspects of Globalization

In many respects, the creation of KNP België, N.V. in Lanaken is a prime example of the establishment of a greenfield manufacturing operation in a foreign country. The Lanaken paper manufacturing operation was established at the point when the business strategy of the firm shifted toward the production of special grades of coated paper for the printing trades. This decision, just before the energy crisis in the early 1970's, enabled the firm to exploit those grades of specialty paper that had a higher value added in manufacture. The creation of the greenfield operation at Lanaken supported an offensive European niche strategy, while the acquisition of paper merchants in France, Belgium and the United Kingdom was a defensive maneuver to prevent erosion of existing channels of distribution that supported the more extensive range of products produced by KNP.

The plant that was finally constructed at Lanaken had to be located somewhere in the heavy industrial triangle of northwest Europe to minimize transportation costs to key European markets. The Liege-Limburg-Aachen area is close to the heart of this triangle and has the necessary infrastructure for paper production. The nearby Albert Canal provides direct access to the facilities of the port of Antwerp and pulp shipments from worldwide sources.

The situation is somewhat different at the packaging materials operations of KNP in Germany, Italy, and Spain. Raw materials are shipped from KNP operations in the Netherlands and Germany. These location are strategically situated to minimize transportation costs.

Future Globalization

A more important question is whether KNP would ever consider harvesting forest resources, given the limited opportunity to manufacture pulp in the Netherlands. In contrast, some American and Japanese firms have been enticed by less developed nations to develop and harvest forests so that they have sure sources of pulp. This is one example of globalization. Another example is shipping antiquated paper machines or converting equipment to less developed countries where labor and energy costs are lower.

Future Strategic Developments

The top management team at KNP is aware of these developments in the world paper industry. Zetteler will take these features into account as he helps plan KNP's future, as marketing and production strategies in the industry are already showing signs of change. For example, the firm in early 1987 started a 70,000 ton capacity chemi-thermomechanical pulp line in at the Lanaken mill. This is KNP's first integrated production operation that uses softwood drawn from the Ardennes, instead of the chemical pulp purchased in the international commodity markets. The firm is considering doubling this integrated capacity with a second pulp line in the next few years.

The emergence of KNP and other firms of integrated European producers of special papers would enhance competition in various world markets. The U.S. market has already been penetrated because of the declining value of the dollar and the superior quality of certain European paper products. Any firm that entered the U.S. market, however, would have to consider transportation costs and the advantages of U.S. producers that have forest resources.

1. In formulating its strategy for the next decade, what are the first steps that KNP should undertake?

2. What type of organizational arrangement does the firm use currently? If it expanded operations into North America, what type of structure would you recommend it use? What other organizational changes would you recommend?

3. In controlling operations, on what types of performance should KNP be focusing its attention? If the firm were to expand operations into South America and Asia, how would this impact on the way it would need to control operations? Explain.

By Alan Bauerschmidt, Professor of Management, University of South Carolina, and Daniel Sullivan, Professor of Management, Tulane University. Used with permission.

Cultural Differences Doom a Seemingly Perfect Alliance between Corning and Vitro

Vitro is a Mexican glass manufacturer located in Monterrey, Mexico. Vitro's product line concentrates on drinkware but includes dozens of products, from automobile windshields to washing machines. Vitro has a long history of successful joint ventures and is globally oriented.

Corning, Inc., is most famous for its oven-ready glass wear; however, Corning has diversified into fiberoptics, environmental products, and laboratory services. Like Vitro, Corning has a long history of successful joint ventures and globalization. Vitro and Corning share similar corporate cultures and customer-oriented philosophies.

After realizing such similarities and looking to capitalize on NAFTA by accessing the Mexican market, Corning, Inc., entered into a joint venture with Vitro in the fall of 1992. The similarities in history, philosophy, culture, goals, and objectives of both companies would lead to the logical conclusion that this alliance should be an instant success. However, as Francisco Chevez, an analyst with Smith Barney Shearson in New York, said, "The cultures did not match . . . it was a marriage made in hell." As history reveals, Corning and Vitro dissolved the joint venture 25 months after the agreement. Both companies still have an interest in maintaining the relationship and continue to distribute each other's products.

A further look at the strategic history of Corning and the joint venture between Corning and Vitro will lead to a better understanding of the difficulties that are involved in creating and maintaining foreign alliances. A more in-depth investigation also will reveal the impact of culture on business transactions.

The Strategic History of Corning

Corning, Inc., has been an innovative leader in foreign alliances for over 73 years. One of the company's first successes was an alliance with St. Gobain, a French glass maker, to produce Pyrex cookware in Europe during the 1920s. Corning has formed approximately 50 ventures over the years. Only 9 have failed, which is a phenomenal number considering one recent study found that over one-half of foreign and national alliances do not succeed. Over the last 5 years, Corning's sales from joint ventures were over $3 billion, which contributed more than $500 million to its net income.

Corning enters into joint ventures for two primary reasons, which are best explained through examples of its past ventures. The first is to gain access to markets that it cannot penetrate quickly enough to obtain a competitive advantage. Corning currently has multiple ventures that exemplify market penetration. Samsung-Corning is an alliance in which Corning provided its distinctive competency of television tube production while Samsung provided expansion into the television market. Corning was able to achieve a strong market share in the Asian market, with sales in excess of $500 million.

The second reason is to bring its technology to market. For example, the strategic alliance of Corning with Mitsubishi led to the creation of Cometec, Inc. Corning produces the ceramic substrates in automotive catalytic converters. The venture employs coating technology developed by Mitsubishi that extends Corning's business into stationary pollution control. Corning reports that the venture is quite successful.

Corning's CEO, James R. Houghton, summarizes the major criteria for deciding whether an equity venture is likely to succeed as follows:

1. You need a solid business opportunity.
2. The two partners should make comparable contributions to the new enterprise.
3. The new enterprise should have a well-defined scope and no major conflicts with either parent company.
4. The management of each parent firm should have the vision and confidence to support the venture through its inevitable rough spots.
5. An autonomous operating team should be formed.
6. Responsibility cannot be delegated.

Houghton also emphasizes that the most important dimension of a successful joint venture is trust between the partners.

Corning's track record indicates that it has been able to establish and run a large number of joint ventures successfully. What went wrong with the recent Vitro venture?

Vitro and Corning seemed to have similar operating procedures, and Vitro's product line complemented Corning's consumer business. Therefore, how could a seemingly perfect alliance fail so miserably? Probing deeper into the Corning–Vitro joint venture reveals the important role that culture may play in international alliances.

Background on the Corning-Vitro Joint Venture

The Corning–Vitro venture seemed to be ideal. However, a strong Mexican peso, increased overseas competition, and strong cultural differences spelled trouble for the alliance. The economic problems are understandable, but the cultural differences should have been given more attention before the alliance was entered.

Although both companies appeared so similar on the surface, they really were quite different. Cultural clashes erupted from the very beginning of the venture because of differing approaches to work. One example was in the marketing area. Vitro's sales approach was less aggressive than the Americans at Corning thought necessary; the slower, deliberate approach to sales in Mexico was a result of the previously highly controlled economy. Corning's sales approach, on the other hand, was more quick-action oriented and aggressive, which had developed from decades of competition.

Once in the venture, the Mexicans thought the Americans were too forward, and the Americans believed that their Mexican partners wasted time being too polite. The Americans perceived the Mexican characteristics to include an unwillingness to acknowledge problems and faults. With respect to speed, the Mexicans thought Corning moved too quickly, while the Americans thought Vitro moved too slowly.

Another obvious cultural difference was the conflicting styles and time allotment for decision making. Vitro is bureaucratic and hierarchical, and loyalty is to family members and patrons in the ranks of the company. Decisions often are left either to a member of the controlling family or to top executives, while middle-level managers seldom are asked to contribute their opinions, let alone to make important decisions. Mr. Loose (Corning's chief executive of the joint venture) observed, "If we were looking at a distribution decision, or a customer decision, we would have a group of people in a room, they would do an assessment, figure alternatives and make a decision, and I as chief executive would never know about it. My experience on the Mexican side is that someone in the organization would have a solution in mind, but then the decision had to be kicked up a few levels."

These examples indicate that culture was an especially sensitive issue between Corning and Vitro, and the alliance was not able to overcome these problems. Corning felt that the cross-cultural differences were depriving both companies of the flexibility to take the fast management action that is necessary in the dynamic business climate of both countries. Vitro basically agreed. Corning gave Vitro back its $130 million investment, and the joint venture was called off. The companies still recognize the opportunity to continue business with each other, however. They have changed their relationship into a mutual distribution of each other's products.

The Aftermath of the Breakup

Vitro and Corning each responded publicly to the dissolution of their alliance, and each indicated the strong differences in culture. Corning wanted to discuss the problems and learn from them, while Vitro was hesitant to criticize anyone, especially a visible U.S. partner like Corning. The Mexicans preferred to concentrate on continuation of the marketing arrangement between the companies. Houghton, the Corning CEO, openly spoke of the alliance as one that stopped making sense. He stated that cross-cultural differences inhibited the potential of the alliance. Corning's chief executive of the venture, Mr. Loose, openly acknowledged the different decision-making styles between the two cultures. Vitro executives were defensive and disappointed that Mr. Loose had expressed his views so frankly in public. "It is unfortunate that he made those comments," said an anonymous Vitro executive. The president of Vitro, Eduardo Martens, flatly denied that the cultural differences were any greater than in other alliances. In an interview with the Harvard Business Review, however, he admitted, "Business in Mexico is done on a consensus basis, very genteel and sometimes slow by U.S. standards."

Corning feels they learned a lesson in the failed Vitro alliance; both foreign and domestic alliances require additional skills and more management time. CEO Houghton says that alliances carry a lot of risk and misunderstandings, but they can be significantly beneficial to the operations of a company if they are done carefully and selectively. Corning continues to analyze why the cultural differences with Vitro were too strong to overcome.

1. Identify and discuss Corning's strategic predisposition toward a joint venture with Vitro.
2. Cultural clashes among partners in joint ventures are not a new issue. Discuss why an MNC, and specifically Corning, would be interested in fully understanding the culture of a potential partner before deciding on an alliance.

3. If Corning and Vitro had decided to remain in the alliance, how could they have overcome their differences to make the partnership a success?

4. Discuss why both companies would continue to distribute each other's products after the joint venture failed. What impact might the public statements about the failure have on this relationship?

Source: This case was written specially for this book by Cara Okleshen, University of Nebraska.

Integrative Case 3

Questionable Strategy at the Pebble Beach Golf Links: An International Investor Goes Off Course

To dedicated golfers, the Pebble Beach Golf Links on California's beautiful Monterey Peninsula is "hallowed ground." The chance to play Pebble Beach is considered a once-in-a-lifetime thrill. Pebble Beach has attained its celebrated status for a variety of reasons. First, it truly is one of the most gorgeous, natural settings in golf. Second, several important golf tournaments are televised from Pebble Beach each year, and many members of the golfing public feel they personally "know" the course. Moreover, Pebble Beach has been the site of several memorable U.S. Open Golf Championships, most recently in 1992. Finally, Pebble Beach is distinctive in that average golfers *do* have the opportunity—albeit an expensive one, with the cost of a single round of golf ranging between $150 and $200—to play Pebble Beach. Although privately owned, Pebble Beach has been open to the general public for its entire history. Thus, while actually playing Pebble Beach likely will remain a distant dream for most golfers, a unique combination of circumstances has resulted in considerable public interested in its welfare.

Pebble Beach as a real estate commodity also has evoked a great deal of interest from a diverse group of investors. In fact, the history of investment in Pebble Beach mirrors the changing nature of the global economy over the past century. Initially purchased and developed by a group of U.S. railroad barons in 1880, Pebble Beach over the years has been owned by an early environmentalist, who managed to protect most of the area's natural beauty in the early years; a sand-mining firm, which ruined parts of the peninsula; a Hollywood film company; a cunning Denver oil billionaire; and most recently, and reflective of the evolution of international economic power, two dissimilar groups of Japanese investors.

A brief overview of the investment history of Pebble Beach provides a context for understanding the curious nature of transactions in a global economy and, specifically, the unique problems and opportunities faced by international investors.

Pebble Beach Yesterday and Today

The original owners (a group of railroad barons) purchased several thousand acres of undeveloped land on the Monterey Peninsula for approximately $35,000 in 1880. These develops built a resort and golf course (the first of four) to attract members of San Francisco's high society. In

1915, they hired Samuel F. B. Morse to manage the resort. Morse, who eventually would purchase the course in 1919, is credited with preventing the overcommercialization of the area, developing a second golf course—Pebble Beach—on the stretch of coastline originally earmarked for houses. Ironically, Morse was not much of a golfer, and perhaps not much of an environmentalist, because his main goal in developing the course was not to protect the coastline but primarily to enhance the value of the real estate. Morse ran the resort complex until his death in 1969. From 1969 to 1979, the complex was rather benignly owned by a sand-mining firm called Wedron Silica Company, which would later change its name to the Pebble Beach Corporation.

In 1979, flush with cash from its successful film *Star Wars,* 20th Century Fox purchased the Pebble Beach Corporation for $72 million and held it until 1981. Then, Marvin Davis, a shrewd billionaire from Denver, Colorado, purchased 20th Century Fox and all its holdings for $722 million. The Pebble Beach property alone was valued at $150 million when purchased by Davis and would be worth approximately $300 million 4 years later. By that time, because of completion of a new inn and golf course, the Pebble Beach Corporation consisted of four golf courses, two hotels, a scenic $6-per-car toll road, and a 5,300-acre forest potentially open to additional lucrative development.

The value of the property continued to grow and attracted considerable interest from a variety of investors from several countries. By 1988, Davis had set a price of $900 million for Pebble Beach, although neutral appraisers suggested its true value was closer to $550 million. The high price did discourage most potential investors, and Davis was without a buyer for 2 years. In September 1990, however, a Japanese businessman named Moritsu Isutani agreed to purchase Pebble Beach for approximately $841 million (the price has been estimated to be even $100 million higher by some sources). Although the purchase involved a U.S. landmark and a significant amount of money, Isutani's purchase was relatively small compared with many other overvalued real estate properties acquired by the Japanese during this time period. There was not the U.S. public uproar, for example, that accompanied the Mitsubishi Estate Corporation's purchase of Rockefeller Center in New York the previous year. Indeed, Isutani's purchase probably would have attracted little attention had his plan to recoup his purchase price been successful.

Unfortunately, Isutani's plan did encounter several major obstacles. In combination with a declining Japanese stock market, rising interest rates, a growing worldwide recession, and the developing crisis in the Persian Gulf, Isutani's apparently less-than-ideal strategy forced him to relinquish ownership of Pebble Beach. The current owners (also Japanese)—the Sumitomo Credit Service Corporation, and the Taiheyo Club, Inc.—purchased Pebble Beach from Isutani in January 1992 for $574 million. The saga of Moritsu Isutani provides an interesting glimpse into the complicated world of international management.

Isutani and the Pebble Beach Strategy

Moritsu Isutani was no stranger to high finance, golf courses, or international investment. Isutani, an avid and very competent golfer, was a secretive figure in both Japan and the United States. In fact, some business observers described him as a "stealth" investor. It was known that he owned at least 9 golf courses in Japan, however, and as many as 17 around the world. In addition, at the time of his purchase of Pebble Beach, he was involved in at least three other major golf course development efforts within the United States: a planned $30 million golf course (opposed by environmentalists) on a flood plain in the San Fernando Valley in California; a $200 million golf course—casino complex outside Las Vegas; and a $357 million golf and hotel complex along Hawaii's Kona Coast. In other words, Isutani was familiar with investment and development in the United States and should have been well prepared to garner a profit from a venture such as Pebble Beach in spite of its inflated purchase price. Indeed, Isutani attempted to implement a strategy that apparently had been successful in past—although lesser—development efforts.

Isutani's plan was to sell golf course memberships at very high prices to anyone who could afford them. This is a regular practice in Japan, where it is not unusual to pay more than $1 million to secure a "lifetime" of tee times. It was rumored that Isutani believed he could sell more than 700 memberships for over $700,000 apiece, potentially generating more than $500 million and defraying a considerable portion of Isutani's debt.

Importantly, however, was that to implement his membership plan, Isutani had to obtain the approval of the local county board of supervisors and the California Coastal Commission. Both groups regulate land use along California's coastline. This approval process also brought the plans of the mysterious new owner of Pebble Beach to the attention of the previously unconcerned local public.

Local Reaction

A local environmentalist first suggested that the expensive membership plan would effectively privatize the Pebble Beach golf course, limiting access to the course—and subsequently the coastline—to the very wealthy. The California Coastal Act of 1976, which requires that any new coastal development guarantee public access to the coastline, was employed to block, or at least slow, Isutani's development efforts. Because Isutani had borrowed almost the entire purchase price, he could ill afford to wait any length of time before beginning to pay off his enormous debt.

Noting, and eventually sharing, the environmentalist concern with privatization, local golfers also became incensed, envisioning wave after wave of rich Japanese golfers swarming over Pebble Beach, denying locals the opportunity to ever play "their" course again. Isutani's representatives insisted this would never be allowed to happen, but their pleas fell on disbelieving ears. This lack of trust may have been exacerbated by Isutani's secretive nature. During the entire time he owned the course, he seldom visited or made public appearances. He made no effort to get to know local politicians, civic leaders, the press, or even golfers. Because of his perceived secretive nature, local citizens were inclined to believe largely unsubstantiated rumors about Isutani's involvement in a variety of shady deals—for example, overselling memberships in his Japanese golf courses—and even his possible ties to the *yakuza,* Japan's mafia.

In November 1991, stating that their decision was based on a continuing concern with the impact of privatization, the Coastal Commission vetoed the last of a series of revised membership plans. Because he was unable to make payment on his debt, cash flow became a problem for Isutani. On December 12, Monterey County declared that the Pebble Beach Corporation was $3 million behind in property taxes.

Isutani finally granted a local interview in late December and portrayed himself as a victim of increasing interest rates and plunging property values in Japan, as misunderstood by the U.S. press and public, and as originally misled by Marvin Davis to believe that his private membership plan would be acceptable to local authorities. Not unaccustomed to disgruntled buyers, Davis, who incidentally once referred to Pebble Beach as a mere "pimple" on his total assets, denied the charge. In spite of these difficulties, by the end of 1991 Isutani still did not believe he would be required to sell Pebble Beach.

National and International Reaction

To compound Isutani's local problems, the U.S. Open—the premier annual golfing event in the United States—was scheduled to be played on the Pebble Beach Golf Links in June 1992, only 6 months away. U.S. Golf Association officials began to worry if a potentially bankrupt Pebble Beach would be able to host such an event. Contingency plans were made to shift the event to another site. Interestingly, while the fate of the Open was of considerable concern to U.S. golfers, the Japanese business establishment apparently was even more disturbed. Relations between the United

States and Japan already were less than ideal, and Isutani's Pebble Beach—U.S. Open difficulties were seen by the Japanese business community as a potential source of great embarrassment in the eyes of the U.S. public. If disruption in scheduling the U.S. Open on a classic U.S. golf course were attributed to a Japanese businessman, the image of Japanese investors in the United States could only suffer more damage.

Under considerable pressure from the Japanese business establishment, Isutani sold Pebble Beach to Japan's Sumitomo Credit Service Corporation and Taiheyo Club, Inc., for approximately $574 million. In other words, 18 months after purchasing Pebble Beach, Isutani sustained losses approaching $270 million. He later would be quoted as saying that he bought the property with 50 percent of his business mind and 50 percent of his golf mind because that was his dream, but he learned a very severe lesson from this transaction.

The New Owners

The new owners quickly moved to remove any lingering doubts about Japanese ownership of Pebble Beach. The famous public relations firm of Hill and Knowlton—known for its handling of controversial issues—was retained to improve public perception and acceptance of its new clients. The new owners were encouraged to be visible and available to the public and to assure locals that plans to privatize Pebble Beach were now a dead issue. The new owners explained that unlike Isutani, they were influenced by Japanese pride, as well as profit, in their acquisition. They wished to provide quality ownership, appreciating Pebble Beach as more than just a piece of real estate.

The Sumitomo Credit Service Corporation and Taiheyo Club, Inc., apparently have provided that type of owner-ship. The 1992 U.S. Open was played without difficulty, and the right of public golfers willing to pay $200 per round to play Pebble Beach has been safeguarded. The new owners also have been careful to avoid Isutani's mistakes. In addition to increasing their local visibility, they changed the name of the corporation (at the suggestion of Hill and Knowlton) to the very California-sounding Lone Cypress Corporation. Interest in a partnership with U.S. investors has been expressed, and a joint board of Americans and Japanese for Pebble Beach has been suggested by the Japanese multinational corporation. It appears a complicated and expensive lesson in international management has been learned, and a new course of action has put Pebble Beach back on course.

1. Identify and discuss Moritsu Isutani's strategic predisposition toward the purchase and management of Pebble Beach. Suggest and defend alternatives.

2. Identify and discuss strategy implementation issues pertinent to this case, particularly in regard to ownership, locale, and functional implementation.

3. Political risk is the likelihood that a business's foreign investment will be constrained by a host government's policies. Discuss how a macro and micro analysis of political risk might have provided Isutani valuable strategic information before his purchase.

4. The new Japanese owners of Pebble Beach have suggested several options regarding local participation in the management of Pebble Beach. Identify and discuss those options most likely to encourage managerial success in the current environment.

Source: This case was written specially for this book by Rex Karsten, the University of Northern Iowa.

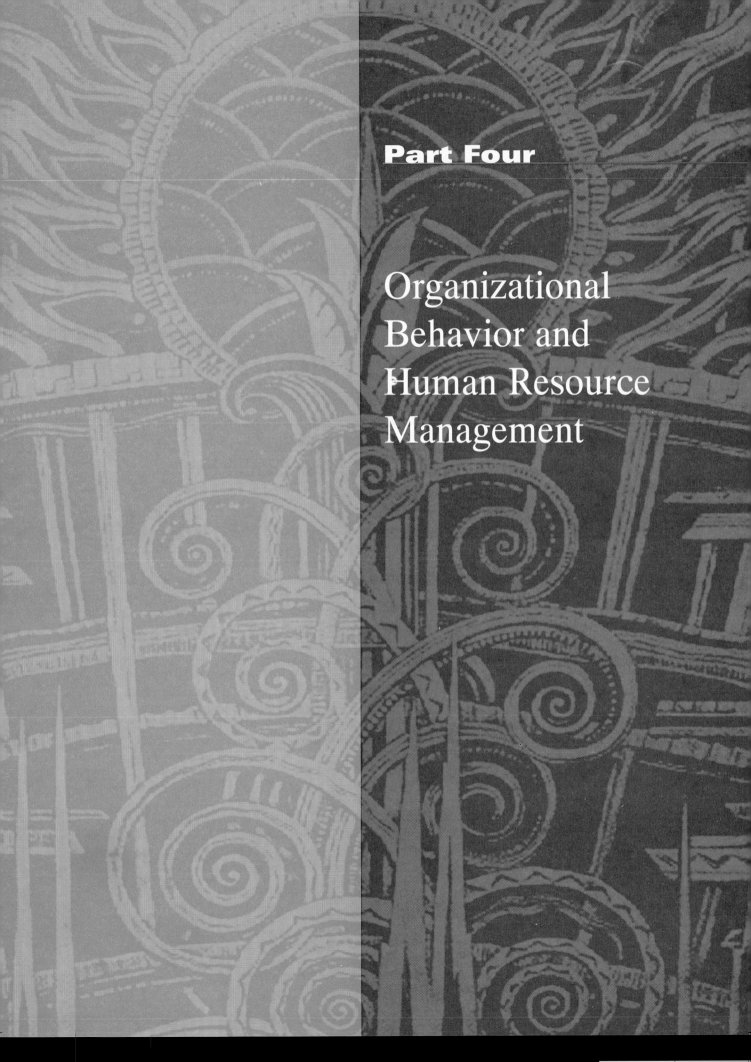

Part Four

Organizational
Behavior and
Human Resource
Management

Chapter 13

Motivation across Cultures

Objectives of the Chapter

Motivation is closely related to the performance of human resources in modern organizations. When motivation is applied to international management, it must be remembered that although the motivation process may be the same across cultures, the content of what motivates people often is culturally based. What motivates employees in the United States may only be moderately effective in Japan, France, or Nigeria. Therefore, although motivation is the concept of choice for analyzing employee performance, an international context requires country-by-country, or at least regional, examination of differences in motivation.

This chapter examines motivation as a psychological process and how motivation can be used in understanding and improving employee performance. It also identifies and describes internationally researched work motivation theories and discusses their relevance for international human resource management. The specific objectives of this chapter are:

1.   DEFINE "motivation," and explain it as a psychological process.

2.   EXAMINE the hierarchy-of-needs motivation theory, and assess its value to international human resource management.

3.   DISCUSS the two-factor theory of motivation and how an understanding of employee satisfaction can be useful in human resource management throughout the world.

4.   DESCRIBE achievement motivation theory, and illustrate how this type of motivation can help to motivate employees in the international arena.

5.   RELATE the importance of job design and work centrality in understanding how to motivate employees in an international context.

BusinessWeek

The World of Business Week:

Bosses under Fire

Christian Strenger, an unassuming 55-year-old, hardly looks like a guy who could send tremors down CEOs; spines. But as chief executive of DWS, Deutsche Bank's mutual-fund arm, he controls assets of nearly $95 billion. Since the early 1990s, he has quietly prodded companies to boost shareholder returns, and lately he has made real headway. In just the past two weeks, three pillars of Germany Inc.—conglomerate Siemens, retailer Metro, and most recently, chemical maker Hoechst—have launched or sped up long-awaited restructurings, partly thanks to Strenger's persistence.

After years of struggling behind the scenes to influence corporate behavior, shareholders across Europe are starting to achieve results. In recent months, they have fired CEOs and dismissed entire boards. They have blocked plans to relocate corporate headquarters and forced companies into greater disclosure. And they have banded together a prod corporate laggards into restructurings and mergers.

The rise of shareholder activism comes just as Europe's CEOs are under pressure from powerful global forces to improve performance. For one thing the ongoing crises in Asia and Russia are hurting their bottom lines. Perhaps more important, the advent of the single currency is changing the way equity investors approach Europe. Stocks in all European Monetary Union nations are priced in euros. So institutions and individuals alike are increasingly looking

outside their national borders for higher returns. "Investors will make their comparisons on a pan-European basis," says Michael Tory, a managing director at Morgan Stanley Dean Witter in London.

Tattered Strategy

Even some of Europe's most seemingly impregnable corporate fortresses are under fire. The CEOs of these companies may blame their problems on economic tumult, but investors aren't accepting any excuses. Take British Airways, which bills itself as "The World's Favourite Airline." With the unraveling of its long-planned alliance with American Airlines, the company's international strategy is in tatters and its stock price has halved since the start of the year. CEO Bob Ayling is feeling the heat, as some of BA's biggest investors start to question his leadership. Says one: "Two-and-a-half years after announcing the merger, you have to ask whether this could have been done differently."

Publicly voicing doubts about a corporate chieftain marks a dramatic shift for European fund managers. Until now, their performance was largely measured against that of other managers in the same country. Now that they must compete internationally for investment capital, they are far more eager to wring the most out of their assets. "There has been a sea change in the willingness of institutional investors to flex their muscles," says Stewart Bell, research director for Pension & Investment Research Consultants, Ltd., which has about 55 pension funds as clients.

Strenger has long agitated for faster change at chemical giant Hoechst, which is trying to focus itself on life sciences. Partly in response to Strenger and other investors, the $26 billion giant on Nov. 17 announced that it would break itself up into a drug company and Celanese, a separately listed chemical concern. "We see the pressure. We are facing it. We are prepared," says CEO Jürgen Dormann.

There could be more showdowns as American institutions partner with Europeans to turn up the heat on complacent managers. California Public Employees' Retirement System (CalPERS), with assets of more than $126 billion, is on the verge of announcing alliances with local investors in Britain, France, Germany, and Japan. CalPERS has nearly doubled its international equity holdings since 1995, to $22.8 billion in 1998. So it wants to participate in efforts to boost shareholder value in the biggest foreign markets where it has holdings.

In January, CalPERS announced that it would invest $200 million in London-based Active Value Capital, a small fund that targets underperforming companies and aims to shake them up. Active Value Capital has successfully taken on such British companies as footwear maker Scholl, whose chairman was ousted and whose stock price has since risen steeply.

Companies that have raised money in the United States or merged with an American company are quickly getting in line with Anglo-American practices. DaimlerChrysler is setting up a performance-related pay scheme unlike anything seen in Europe before. And a new generation of European managers recognize that unless they make shareholder value a priority, raising capital will be tough for them in the future. Plenty of European companies still don't get it. But the cozy world in which European managers could shrug off investors; concerns without feeling the consequences is fast disappearing.

Source: **Reprinted from November 30, 1998, pp. 52–54 issue of** *Business Week* **by special permission, copyright © 1998 by McGraw-Hill Companies, Inc.**

This opening news story examines an area that is now beginning to emerge as one of the most important challenges for multinational managers—keeping the stockholders happy. More and more executives are now having to face the question: What motivates the owners of the company and what are we going to have to do to satisfy the growing appetite of these investors? The answers to this question permeate all levels of the MNC from top level executives to hourly employees. Simply put, investors want the management team to motivate the personnel and to generate profits and higher stock market values. If they can do this, the management team will find that the investors are pleased. If they cannot, however, they will find that investors demand that management be replaced and put in individuals who can generate the desired performance.

The Nature of Motivation

Motivation

A psychological process through which unsatisfied wants or needs lead to drives that are aimed at goals or incentives.

Motivation is a psychological process through which unsatisfied wants or needs lead to drives that are aimed at goals or incentives. Figure 13-1 shows this motivation process. The three basic elements in the process are needs, drives, and goal-attainment. A person with an unsatisfied need will undertake goal-directed behavior to satisfy the need. A simple example is a person working to earn money so that she or he can put a down payment on a house. This individual will be motivated or driven to earn this money as quickly as possible and might look for overtime work or a second job to supplement her or his regular salary. Once the down payment is made, the person then might drop the overtime or second job and not be as driven as before. The individual also might have another goal, such as a new car, and the process would begin anew.

Motivation is an important topic in international human resource management, because many MNC managers assume they can motivate their overseas personnel with the same approaches that are used in the home country. Is this true, or do major differences require tailor-made, country-by-country motivation programs? As described in earlier chapters (especially Chapter 5), there obviously are some motivational differences caused by culture. The major question is: Are these differences highly significant, or can an overall theory of work motivation apply throughout the world? Considerable research on motivating human resources has looked at motivation in a large number of countries; however, before reviewing these findings, two generally agreed-on starting assumptions about work motivation in the international arena should be made.

The Universalist Assumption

The first assumption is that the motivation *process* (not content) is universal. All people are motivated to pursue goals they value—what the work-motivation theorists call goals with "high valence" or "preference." Although the process is universal, however, the specific content and goals that are pursued will be influenced by culture. For example, one recent analysis suggests that the key incentive for many U.S. workers is money; for Japanese employees, it may be respect and power; and for Latin American workers, it may be an array of factors, including family considerations, respect, job status, and a good personal life. Similarly, the primary interest of the U.S. worker is him- or herself; for the

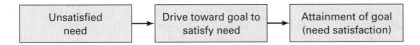

Figure 13–1

**The Basic
Motivation
Process**

Japanese, it is group interest; and for the Latin American employee, it is the interest of the employer.[1] Simply put, motivation differs across cultures. Adler sums up the case against universality of motivation as follows:

> Unfortunately, American as well as non-American managers have tended to treat American theories as the best or only way to understand motivation. They are neither. American motivation theories, although assumed to be universal, have failed to provide consistently useful explanations outside the United States. Managers must therefore guard against imposing domestic American theories on their multinational business practices.[2]

In the United States, personal achievement is an important need, and individual success through promotions and more money may be an important goal. In China, however, group affiliation is an important need, and harmony becomes an important goal. Therefore, the ways to motivate U.S. employees may be quite different from those used with Chinese workers. The motivational process is the same, but the needs and goals are different because of differences between the two cultures. This conclusion was demonstrated in a study by Welsh, Luthans, and Sommer that examined the value of extrinsic rewards, behavioral management, and participative techniques among Russian factory workers. The first two motivational approaches worked well to increase worker performance, but the third did not. The researchers noted that

> this study provides at least beginning evidence that U.S.-based behavioral theories and techniques may be helpful in meeting the performance challenges facing human resources management in rapidly changing and different cultural environments. We found that two behavioral techniques—administering desirable extrinsic rewards to employees contingent upon improved performance, and providing social reinforcement and feedback for functional behaviors and corrective feedback for dysfunctional behaviors—significantly improved Russian factory workers' performance. By the same token, the study also points out the danger of making universalist assumptions about U.S.-based theories and techniques. In particular, the failure of the participative intervention does not indicate so much that this approach just won't work across cultures, as that historical and cultural values and norms need to be recognized and overcome for such a relatively sophisticated theory and technique to work effectively.[3]

At the same time, however, it is important to remember that as a growing number of countries begin moving toward free market economies and new opportunities for economic rewards emerge, the ways in which individuals in these nations are motivated will change. Commenting on the management of Chinese personnel, for example, Sergeant and Frenkel have pointed out that new labor laws now allow both state enterprises and foreign-invested Chinese enterprises to set their own wage and salary levels. However, the companies have to be careful about believing that they can simply go into the marketplace, pay high wages, and recruit highly motivated personnel. In particular, the researchers note that:

> Devising reward packages for Chinese employees has been difficult because of the range and complexity of nonwage benefits expected by workers as a legacy of the "iron rice bowl" tradition. However, health and accident insurance, pensions, unemployment and other benefits are increasingly being taken over by the state. There are two cultural impediments to introducing greater differentials in pay among workers of similar status: importance accorded to interpersonal harmony which would be disrupted by variations in earnings; and distrust of performance appraisals because in state enterprises evaluations are based on ideological principles and *guanxi*.[4]

So some of what foreign MNCs would suspect about how to motivate Chinese employees is accurate, but not all. The same is true, for example, about Japanese employees. Many people believe that all Japanese firms guarantee lifetime employment and this practice, in turn, is motivational and results in a strong bond between employer and employee. In truth, much of this is a myth. Actually, less than 30 percent (and decreasing) of the workforce has any such guarantee, and in recent years a growing number of Japanese employees have been finding that their firms may do the best they can to ensure jobs for them—but they will not guarantee this if the company begins to face critical times. As in the West, when a Japanese firm has a crisis, people are often let go. This has been clearly seen in recent years as the Japanese economy has remained stalled and the country's joblessness rate as hit new highs.[5]

The Assumption of Content and Process

Content theories
Theories that explain work motivation in terms of what arouses, energizes, or initiates employee behavior.

Process theories
Theories that explain work motivation by how employee behavior is initiated, redirected, and halted.

The second starting assumption is that work-motivation theories can be broken down into two general categories: content, and process. **Content theories** explain work motivation in terms of what arouses, energizes, or initiates employee behavior. **Process theories** of worker motivation explain how employee behavior is initiated, redirected, and halted.[6] Most research in international human resource management has been content-oriented, because these theories examine motivation in more general terms and are more useful in creating a composite picture of employee motivation in a particular country or region. Process theories are more sophisticated and tend to focus on individual behavior in specific settings. Thus, they have less value to the study of employee motivation in international settings, although there has been some research in this area as well. By far, the majority of research in the international arena has been content driven, and this chapter focuses on those findings.

The following sections examine work motivation in an international setting by focusing on three content theories that have received the greatest amount of attention: the hierarchy-of-needs theory, the two-factor motivation theory, and the achievement motivation theory. Each offers important insights regarding international human resource management.

The Hierarchy-of-Needs Theory

The hierarchy-of-needs theory is based primarily on work by Abraham Maslow, a well-known U.S. psychologist how deceased.[7] Maslow's hierarchy of needs has received a great deal of attention from international management researchers, who have attempted to identify its value in understanding employee motivation throughout the world.[8]

The Maslow Theory

Maslow postulated that everyone has five basic needs, which constitute a need hierarchy. In ascending order, beginning with the most basic, they are physiological, safety, social, esteem, and self-actualization needs. Figure 13-2 illustrates this hierarchy.

Figure 13–2

Maslow's Need Hierarchy

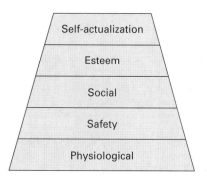

Physiological needs consist of food, clothing, shelter, and other basic physical needs. Maslow contended that if someone were deprived of all need satisfaction, the individual's drive to satisfy these physiological needs would be greater than the drive to satisfy any other need. Applied to work motivation, these physiological needs often are satisfied through the wages and salaries paid by the organization.

Safety needs include the desire for security, stability, and absence of pain. Organization typically help personnel to satisfy these needs through safety programs and equipment and by providing security through medical insurance, unemployment and retirement plans, and similar benefits.[9]

Social needs include the need to interact and affiliate with others and the need to feel wanted by others. This desire for "belongingness" often is satisfied on the job through social interaction within the work group, in which people give and receive friendship. Besides the formally assigned work group, the formation of informal groups and acquaintanceships also is typical.

Esteem needs involve the needs for power and status. These result in individuals' needing to feel important and receive recognition from others. Promotions, awards, and feedback from the boss lead to feelings of self-confidence, prestige, and self-importance.

Self-actualization needs are desires to reach one's full potential by becoming everything that one is capable of becoming. Although less is known about this highest-level need, most closely associated would be the ideas concerning human potential. In the organization, this may not be a promotion but instead may involve mastering one's environment as well as setting and achieving attainable goals.[10]

Maslow's theory, translated over the years, includes a number of basic assumptions. One is that lower-level needs must be satisfied before higher-level needs become motivators. A second is that once a need is satisfied, it no longer serves as a motivator. A third is that there are more ways to satisfy higher-level than lower-level needs. Some of these assumptions came from Maslow's original work, some from others' work, and some have been modified by Maslow. These assumptions have driven much of the international research on the theory.

International Findings on Maslow's Theory

Do people throughout the world have needs that are similar to those described in Maslow's need hierarchy? Research generally shows that they do. For example, in a classic study undertaken by Haire, Ghiselli, and Porter, a sample of 3,641 managers from 14 countries was surveyed. This study is quite dated but still the most comprehensive and relevant for showing the different cultural impacts on employee motivation. Countries in this survey included the United States, Argentina, Belgium, Chile, Denmark, England, France, Germany, India, Italy, Japan, Norway, Spain, and Sweden.[11] With some minor modification, the researchers examined the need satisfaction and need importance of the four highest-level needs in the Maslow hierarchy. The esteem need was divided into two groups: esteem and autonomy. The first examined the importance of self-esteem and prestige; the second examined the importance of authority and the opportunity for independent thought and action.

The results of this study showed that all these needs were important to the respondents across cultures. It should be remembered, however, that the subjects in this huge international study were managers, not rank-and-file employees. Upper-level needs were of particular importance to these managers. These findings, for select country clusters (Latin Europe, United States/United Kingdom, and Nordic Europe), show that autonomy and self-actualization were the most important needs for the respondents. Interestingly, these same managers also reported that these needs were those with which they were *least* satisfied, which led Haire and his associates to conclude:

> It appears obvious, from an organizational point of view, that business firms, no matter what country, will have to be concerned with the satisfaction of these needs for their managers and executives. Both types of needs were regarded as relatively quite important by managers, but, at the present time at least, the degree to which they were fulfilled did not live up to their expectations.[12]

Physiological needs
Food, clothing, shelter, and other basic, physical needs.

Safety needs
In Maslow's hierarchy of needs, the desire for security, stability, and the absence of pain.

Social needs
The need to interact and affiliate with others and the need to feel wanted by others.

Esteem needs
The needs for power and status.

Self-actualization needs
In Maslow's hierarchy of needs, the desire to reach one's full potential by becoming everything one is capable of becoming.

Since this classic study, a number of others have examined management groups from other countries. One follow-up study surveyed managers in eight East Asian countries and found that autonomy and self-actualization in most cases ranked high; however, the degree of satisfaction/dissatisfaction varied much more widely than that reported by Haire and his associates. Some East Asian managers apparently are quite dissatisfied with their ability to satisfy autonomy and self-actualization needs.

Both research studies indicate the value of examining motivation of human resources (in this case, managers) in terms of country or geographic clusters. Each country or geographic region appears to have its own need-satisfaction profile. In using this information to motivate managers, MNCs would be wise to consider the individual country's or region's profile and adjust their approach accordingly.

Some researchers even have suggested modifying Maslow's hierarchy by reranking the order of needs. Nevis believes that the Maslow hierarchy reflects a culture that is Western-oriented and focused on the inner needs of individuals.[13] Obviously, not all cultures function this way. Eastern cultures emphasize the needs of society. As a result, Nevis suggested that the Chinese hierarchy of needs has four levels, which from lowest to highest are: (1) belonging (social); (2) physiological; (3) safety; and (4) self-actualization in the service of society. If this is true, MNCs attempting to do business in China must consider this revised hierarchy and determine how they can modify their compensation and job-design programs to accommodate the requisite motivational needs. In any event, Nevis's idea is worth considering, because it forces the multinational firm to address work motivation based on those cultural factors that are unique to it.

The discussion so far indicates that even though it is culturally specific, the need-hierarchy concept is a useful way to study and apply work motivation internationally. Others such as the well-known Dutch researcher Geert Hofstede, however, have suggested that need-satisfaction profiles are *not* a very useful way of addressing motivation, because there often are so many different subcultures within any given country that it may be difficult or impossible to determine which culture variables are at work in any particular work setting. The Haire and follow-up studies dealt only with managers, but Hofstede has found that job categories are a more effective way of examining motivation. He reported a linkage between job types and levels and the need hierarchy. Based on survey results from over 60,000 people in more than 50 countries who were asked to rank a series of 19 work goals (see Tables 13-1 and 13-2), he found that:

- Professionals ranked all four top goals corresponding to "high" Maslow needs.
- Clerks ranked all four top goals corresponding to "middle" Maslow needs.
- Unskilled workers ranked all four top goals corresponding to "low" Maslow needs.
- Managers and technicians showed a mixed picture—with at least one goal in the "high" Maslow category.[14]

The tables from Hofstede's research show that self-actualization and esteem needs rank highest for professionals and managers. Conversely, security, earnings, benefits, and physical working conditions are most important to low-level, unskilled workers. These findings illustrate that job categories and levels may have a dramatic effect on motivation and may well offset cultural considerations. As Hofstede noted, "There are greater differences between job categories than there are between countries when it comes to employee motivation."[15]

In deciding how to motivate human resources in different countries or help them to attain need satisfaction, researchers such as Hofstede recommend that MNCs focus most heavily on giving physical rewards to lower-level personnel and on creating a climate in which there is challenge, autonomy, the ability to use one's skills, and cooperation for the middle- and upper-level personnel. Of course, this does not mean that executives are unmotivated by largely compensation packages or that new employees are not looking for flexible compensation. As seen in "International Management in Action: Rethinking the Motivation Equation," compensation packages for the personnel in Japan is beginning to change.

	Table 13–1
	Top-Ranking Goals for Professional Technical Personnel from a Large Variety of Countries

Rank	Goal	Questionnaire Wording
1	Training	Have training opportunities (to improve your present skills or learn new skills)
2	Challenge	Have challenging work to do—work from which you can get a personal sense of accomplishment
3	Autonomy	Have considerable freedom to adopt your own approach to the job
4	Up-to-dateness	Keep up-to-date with the technical developments relating to your job
5	Use of skills	Fully use your skills and abilities on the job
6	Advancement	Have an opportunity for advancement to higher-level job
7	Recognition	Get the recognition you deserve when you do a good job
8	Earnings	Have an opportunity for high earnings
9	Cooperation	Work with people who cooperate well with one another
10	Manager	Have a good working relationship with your manager
11	Personal time	Have a job which leaves you sufficient time for your personal or family life
12	Friendly department	Work in a congenial and friendly atmosphere
13	Company contribution	Have a job which allows you to make a real contribution to the success of your company
14	Efficient department	Work in a department which is run efficiently
15	Security	Have the security that you will be able to work for your company as long as you want to
16	Desirable area	Live in an area desirable to you and your family
17	Benefits	Have good fringe benefits
18	Physical conditions	Have good physical working conditions (good ventilation and lighting, adequate work space, etc.)
19	Successful company	Work in a company which is regarded in your country as successful

Source: Geert H. Hofstede, "The Colors of Collars," *Columbia Journal of World Business,* September 1972, p. 74. Used with permission.

Overall, there seems to be little doubt that need-hierarchy theory is useful in helping to identify motivational factors for international human resource management. This theory alone is not sufficient, however. Other content theories, such as the two-factor theory, add further understanding and effective practical application for motivating personnel.

The Two-Factor Theory of Motivation

The two-factor theory was formulated by well-known work-motivation theorist Frederick Herzberg and his colleagues. Similar to Maslow's theory, Herzberg's has been a focus of attention in international human resource management research over the years. This two-factor theory is closely linked to the need hierarchy.

The Herzberg Theory

The **two-factor theory of motivation** holds that two sets of factors influence job satisfaction: hygiene factors and motivators. The data from which the theory was developed were collected through a critical incident methodology that asked the respondents to answer two basic types of questions: (1) When did you feel particularly good about your job? and (2) When did you feel exceptionally bad about your job? Responses to the first question generally related to job content and included factors such as achievement, recognition, responsibility, advancement, and the work itself. Herzberg called these job-content factors **motivators.** Responses to the second question related to job context and included factors such as salary, interpersonal relations, technical supervision, working conditions, and company

Two-factor theory of motivation
A theory that holds there are two sets of factors that influence job satisfaction: hygiene factors and motivators.

Motivators
In the two-factor motivation theory, the job content factors which include achievement, recognition, responsibility, advancement, and the work itself.

Table 13-2
The Four Most Important Goals Ranked by Occupational Group and Related to the Need Hierarchy

Goals Ranked in "Need Hierarchy"	Professionals (Research Laboratories)	Professionals (Branch Offices)	Managers	Technicians (Branch Offices)	Technicians (Manufacturing Plants)	Clerical Workers (Branch Offices)	Unskilled Workers (Manufacturing Plants)
High—Self-actualization and esteem needs:							
Challenge	1	2	1	3	3		
Training		1		1			
Autonomy	3	3	2				
Up-to-dateness	2						
Use of skills	4	4		4			
Middle—Social needs:							
Cooperation			3/4			1	
Manager			3/4			2	
Friendly department					4	3	
Efficient department						4	
Low—Security and physiological needs:							
Security				2	1		2
Earnings					2		3
Benefits							4
Physical conditions							1

Source: Geert H. Hofstede, "The Colors of Collars," *Columbia Journal of World Business*, September 1972, p. 78. Used with permission.

For many years Japanese firms have used a traditional approach to motivating their personnel. Twice a year workers would be paid a bonus, and when they retired they would receive an additional lump sum payment that was tied to their salary and length of time with the company. Additionally, there was a package of perquisites that the company would provide for those who were going to be staying with the firm for their entire career. Today, however, this traditional approach is undergoing radical change.[16] A growing number of companies, Matsushita being a good example, are starting to offer their personnel a more flexible benefits package—and a growing number of employees are beginning to take it.

One reason for the change is that Japanese companies are coming to realize that their standard benefits package may not be the best for all of their people. In particular, a growing number of personnel are now changing jobs and moving to other firms. In 1995, for example, approximately 80 percent of all workers in Japan were still with the same company with which they had begun their careers. By 1998 this percentage had dropped to 70 percent and by the year 2010 traditional lifetime employment in many Japanese companies will be a thing of the past.

Since many people will not be staying with their firm in the future, a growing number of companies are now offering more flexible options. For example, in some enterprises an employee who has special skills but does not intend to stay with the firm for a long time can command higher pay and is allowed to take advances on his or her pension. In turn, of course, the individual agrees to give up some benefits. And for those who want even more flexibility, there is the option of putting one's pension payments into savings plans rather than simply having the company provide a lump sum amount upon retirement.

One reason for the change in the traditional approach is that many firms now believe that they must do business a different way. Rather than giving people lifetime employment, they want to be able to hire new recruits who have skills and abilities not possessed by current personnel; and rather than having to keep the older personnel as well, they can move them out. In addition, companies such as Matsushita are now moving from a seniority-based management reward system to a merit-based one. In fact, Matsushita is now negotiating with its union over a performance-based plan that will scrap much of the old seniority system and apply the new system to all 80,000 nonmanagerial workers!

Will this new approach prove motivational? Many young Japanese believe that it will because it offers them more control over their retirement option and it is based on a pay-for-performance philosophy. Older Japanese workers are not sure. However, one thing is certain: A growing number of major Japanese corporations are rethinking the motivation equation and looking for a different approach to motivating their people and maintaining world-class organizations in the face of growing worldwide hypercompetition.

---

policies and administration. Herzberg called these job-context variables **hygiene factors**. Table 13-3 lists both groups of factors; a close look at the two lists shows that the motivators are heavily psychological and relate to Maslow's upper-level needs but that hygiene factors are environmental in nature and relate more to Maslow's lower-level needs. Table 13-4 illustrates this linkage.

The two-factor theory also holds that these two sets of factors relate to employee satisfaction. This relationship is more complex than the traditional view that employees are either satisfied or dissatisfied; according to the two-factor theory, if hygiene factors are not taken care of or are deficient, there will be dissatisfaction (see Figure 13-3). Importantly, however, if hygiene factors are taken care of, there may be no dissatisfaction, but there also may not be satisfaction. Only by providing the motivators will there be satisfaction. In short, hygiene factors help to prevent dissatisfaction (thus the term "hygiene," as it is used in the health field), but only motivators lead to satisfaction. Therefore, according to this theory, motivating human resources must include recognition, a chance to achieve and grow, advancement, and interesting work.

Before examining the two-factor theory in the international arena, it is important to note that Herzberg's theory has been criticized by some organizational-behavior academics. One criticism surrounds the classification of money as a hygiene factor and not as a

Hygiene factors
In the two-factor motivation theory, job context variables that include salary, interpersonal relations, technical supervision, working conditions, and company policies and administration.

Table 13–3
Herzberg's Two-Factor Theory

Hygiene Factors	Motivators
Salary	Achievement
Technical supervision	Recognition
Company policies and administration	Responsibility
Interpersonal relations	Advancement
Working conditions	The work itself

Table 13–4
The Relationship between Maslow's Need Hierarchy and Herzberg's Two-Factor Theory

Maslow's Need Hierarchy	Herzberg's Two-Factor Theory
Self-actualization	Motivators
	Achievement
	Recognition
	Responsibility
Esteem	Advancement
	The work itself
Social	Hygiene factors
	Salary
	Technical supervision
Safety	Company policies and administration
	Interpersonal relations
Physiological	Working conditions

Figure 13–3

Views of Satisfaction/ Dissatisfaction

Traditional View

Satisfaction ——————————————— Dissatisfaction

Two-Factor View
(hygiene factors)

Absent ——————————————— Present
(dissatisfaction)   (no dissatisfaction)

(motivators)

Absent ——————————————— Present
(no satisfaction)   (dissatisfaction)

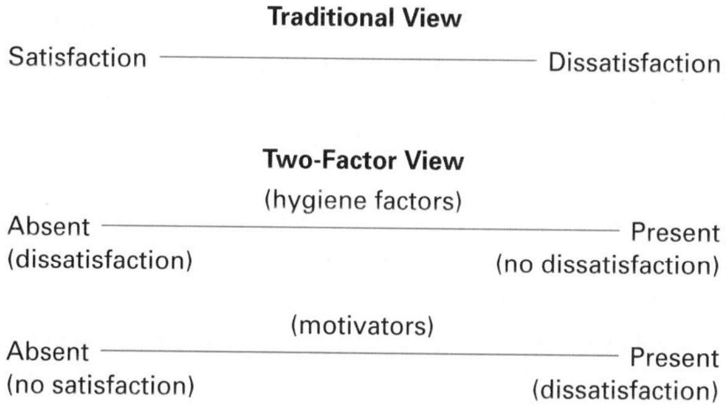

motivator. There is no universal agreement on this point, and some researchers report that salary is a motivator for some groups, such as blue-collar workers, or those for whom money is important for psychological reasons, such as a score-keeping method for their power and achievement needs.

A second line of criticism is whether Herzberg has developed a total theory of motivation. Some argue that his findings actually support a theory of job satisfaction. In other words, if a company gives its people motivators, they will be satisfied; if it denies them motivators, they will not be satisfied; and if the hygiene factors are deficient, they may well be dissatisfied. Much of the international research on the two-factor theory discussed next is directed toward the satisfaction/dissatisfaction concerns rather than complex motivational needs, drives, and goals.

International Findings on Herzberg's Theory

International findings related to the two-factor theory fall into two categories. One consists of replications of Herzberg's research in a particular country; that is, do managers in country X give answers similar to those in Herzberg's original studies? The other consists of cross-cultural studies that focus on job satisfaction; that is, what factors cause job satisfaction and how do these responses differ from country to country? The latter studies are not a direct extension of the two-factor theory, but they do offer insights regarding the importance of job satisfaction in international human resource management.

Two-Factor Replications A number of research efforts have been undertaken to replicate the two-factor theory, and in the main, they support Herzberg's findings. George Hines, for example, surveyed 218 middle managers and 196 salaried employees in New Zealand using ratings of 12 job factors and overall job satisfaction. Based on these findings, he concluded that "the Herzberg model appears to have validity across occupational levels."[17]

Another similar study was conducted among 178 managers in Greece who were Greek nationals. Overall, this study found that Herzberg's two-factor theory of job satisfaction generally held true for these managers. The researchers summarized their findings as follows:

> As far as job dissatisfaction was concerned, no motivator was found to be a source of dissatisfaction. Only categories traditionally designated as hygiene factors were reported to be sources of dissatisfaction for participating Greek managers. . . . Moreover . . . motivators . . . were more important contributors to job satisfaction than to dissatisfaction . . . (66.8% of the traditional motivator items . . . were related to satisfaction and 31.1% were related to dissatisfaction). Traditional hygiene factors, as a group, were more important contributors to job dissatisfaction than to job satisfaction (64% of the responses were related to dissatisfaction and 36% were related to satisfaction).[18]

Another study tested the Herzberg theory in an Israeli kibbutz. Motivators there tended to be sources of satisfaction and hygiene factors sources of dissatisfaction, although interpersonal relations (a hygiene factor) were regarded more as a source of satisfaction than of dissatisfaction. The researcher was careful to explain this finding as a result of the unique nature of a kibbutz, however, where interpersonal relations of a work and nonwork nature are not clearly defined, thus making difficult the separation of this factor on a motivator/hygiene basis. Commenting on the results, the researcher noted, "the findings of this study support Herzberg's two-factor hypothesis: Satisfactions arise from the nature of the work itself, while dissatisfactions have to do with the conditions surrounding the work."[19]

Similar results on the Herzberg theory have been obtained by research studies in developing countries. For example, one study examined work motivations in Zambia, employing a variety of motivational variables, and work motivation was a result of six factors: work nature, growth and advancement, material and physical provisions, relations with others, fairness/unfairness in organizational practices, and personal problems. These variables are presented in Figure 13-4. They illustrate that in general, the two-factor theory of motivation was supported in this African country.[20]

Cross-Cultural Job-Satisfaction Studies A number of cross-cultural studies related to job satisfaction also have been conducted in recent years. These comparisons show that Herzberg-type motivators tend to be of more importance to job satisfaction than hygiene factors. For example, one study administered the Job Orientation Inventory (JOI) to MBA candidates from four countries.[21] As seen in Table 13-5, the relative ranking placed hygiene factors at the bottom of the list and motivators at the top. What also is significant is that although Singapore students do not fit into the same cultural cluster as the other three groups in the study, their responses were similar. These findings provide evidence that job-satisfaction-related factors may not be culturally bounded.[22]

Another, more comprehensive study of managerial job attitudes investigated the types of job outcomes that are desired by managers in different cultures. Data were gathered from

Figure 13–4

Motivation Factors in Zambia

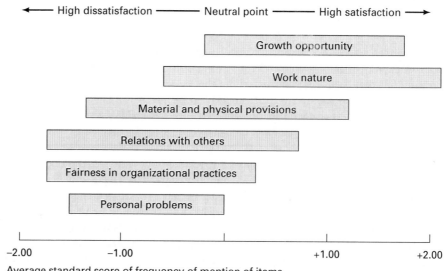

Source: Adapted from Peter D. Machungwa and Neal Schmitt, "Work Motivation in a Developing Country," *Journal of Applied Psychology,* February 1983, p. 41. Used with permission.

Table 13–5
The Results of Administering the JOI to Four Cross-Cultural Groups

	Relative Rankings			
	United States (*n*=49)	**Australia** (*n*=58)	**Canada** (*n*=25)	**Singapore** (*n*=33)
Achievement	2	2	2	2
Responsibility	3	3	3	3
Growth	1	1	1	1
Recognition	10	10	8	9
Job status	7	7	7	7
Relationships	5	5	10	6
Pay	8	8	6	8
Security	9	9	9	10
Family	6	6	7	5
Hobby	4	4	4	4

Source: G. E. Popp, H. J. Davis, and T. T. Herbert, "An International Study of Intrinsic Motivation Composition," *Management International Review,* vol. 26, no. 3, 1986, p. 31. Used with permission.

lower- and middle-management personnel who were attending management development courses in Canada, the United Kingdom, France, and Japan.[23] The researchers sought to identify the importance of 15 job-related outcomes and how satisfied the respondents were with each other.

The results indicated that job content is more important than job context. Organizationally controlled factors (**job context factors**, such as conditions, hours, earnings, security, benefits, and promotions) for the most part did not receive as high a ranking as internally mediated factors (**job content factors**, such as responsibility, achievement, and the work itself). The data also show that managers from the four countries differ significantly regarding both the perceived importance of job outcomes and the level of satisfaction experienced on the job with respect to these outcomes. These differences are useful in shedding light on what motivates managers in these countries and, in the case of MNCs, in developing country-specific human resource management approaches. The most striking contrasts were between the French and the British. Commenting on the applicability of this

Job context factors
In work motivation, those factors controlled by the organization, such as conditions, hours, earnings, security, benefits, and promotions.

Job content factors
In work motivation, those factors internally controlled, such as responsibility, achievement, and the work itself.

research to the formulation of motivational strategies for effective human resource management, the researchers noted the following:

> The results suggest . . . that efforts to improve managerial performance in the UK should focus on job content rather than on job context. Changes in the nature of the work itself are likely to be more valued than changes in organizational or interpersonal factors. Job enrichment programs which help individuals design their own goals and tasks, and which downplay formal rules and structure, are more likely to improve performance in an intrinsically oriented society such as Britain, where satisfaction tends to be derived from the job itself, than in France, where job context factors such as security and fringe benefits are more highly valued. The results suggest that French managers may be more effectively motivated by changing job situation factors, as long as such changes are explicitly linked to performance.[24]

In summary, Herzberg's two-factor theory appears to reinforce Maslow's need hierarchy through its research support in the international arena. As with the application of Maslow's theory, however, MNCs would be wise to apply motivation–hygiene theory on a country-by-country or a regional basis. Although there are exceptions, such as France, there seems to be little doubt that job content factors are more important than job context factors in motivating not only managers but also lower-level employees around the world, as Hofstede pointed out.

Achievement Motivation Theory

Besides the need-hierarchy and two-factor theories of work motivation, the achievement motivation theory has been given a relatively great amount of attention in the international arena. Achievement theory actually has been more applied to the actual practice of management than the others, and it has been the focus of some interesting international research.

The Background of Achievement Motivation Theory

Achievement motivation theory holds that individuals can have a need to get ahead, to attain success, and to reach objectives. Note that like the upper-level needs in Maslow's hierarchy or like Herzberg's motivators, the need for achievement is learned. Therefore, applied to the international scene, in the United States, where entrepreneurial effort is encouraged and individual success promoted, the probability is higher that there would be more people with high needs for achievement than, for example, in China, Russia, or other Eastern European countries,[25] where cultural values have not traditionally supported individual, entrepreneurial efforts.

Researchers such as the well-known Harvard psychologist David McClelland have identified a characteristic profile of high achievers.[26] First, they like situations in which they take personal responsibility for finding solutions to problems. They want to win based on their own efforts and not on luck or chance. Second, they tend to be moderate risk-takers rather than high or low risk-takers. If a decision-making situation appears to be too risky, they will learn as much as they can about the environment and try to reduce the probability of failure. In this way, they turn a high-risk situation into a moderate-risk situation. If the situation is too low-risk, however, there usually is an accompanying low reward, and they tend to avoid these situations with insufficient incentive.

Third, high achievers want concrete feedback on their performance. They like to know how well they are doing, and they use this information to modify their actions. High achievers tend to gravitate into vocations such as sales, which provide them with immediate, objective feedback of how they are doing. Finally, and this has considerable implications for human resource management, these high achievers tend to be loners. They genuinely do not like or get along well with other people. They do not form warm, close relationships, and they have little empathy for others' problems. This last characteristic may distract from their effectiveness as managers of people.

Achievement motivation theory
A theory which holds that individuals can have a need to get ahead to attain success and to reach objectives.

Researchers have discovered a number of ways to develop high achievement needs in people. These involve teaching the individual to do the following: (1) obtain feedback on performance, and use this information to channel one's efforts in areas where success likely will be achieved; (2) emulate people who have been successful achievers; (3) develop an internal desire for success and challenge; and (4) daydream in positive terms by picturing oneself as successful in the pursuit of important objectives.[27] In other words, this suggests that the need for achievement can be taught and learned.

International Findings on Achievement Motivation Theory

A number of international researchers have investigated the role and importance of high achievement needs in human resource management.[28] One study, discussed under the two-factor theory, used the JOI scale and found that achievement or a sense of accomplishment ranked as the second most important work-reward factor.[29] Remember, however, that these results were obtained with MBA students from various countries who were studying in the United States. It should not be surprising that these respondents who came to the United States for advanced study of business, regardless of their home country, would have a high need for achievement. The question remains as to what degree people throughout the world have this need.

Early research among Polish industrialists found that many of them were high achievers.[30] The average high-achievement score was 6.58, which was quite close to that of the U.S. managers' score of 6.74. This led some to conclude there is evidence that managers in countries as diverse as the United States and those of Eastern European have high needs for achievement.[31] More recently, however, researchers have *not* found a high need for achievement in Eastern European countries. One study, for example, surveyed Czech industrial managers and found that the average high-achievement score was 3.32, considerably lower than that of U.S. managers.[32] Because the need for achievement is learned, differences in these samples can be attributed to cultural differences. By the same token, given the dramatic, revolutionary changes that occurred in Eastern Europe at the end of the 1980s, one could argue that the achievement needs of Eastern Europeans, once they are allowed to be freely expressed, may well be high today.[33] The important point, however, is that because achievement is a learned need and thus largely determined by the prevailing culture, it is not universal and may change over time.

China is a good example of a country where a high need for achievement has largely been absent. In recent years, however, a growing segment of the population, especially younger people, such as those who demonstrated at Tiananmen Square, seem to have this need. In high-achieving societies, work goals such as autonomy, challenge, promotions, and earnings are valued. The need for affiliation and safety rank far down the list; the high achiever is not very interested in these. In China, achievement-oriented goals traditionally have not ranked very high, although recent government-sponsored economic programs may be changing this.[34] Table 13-6 reports standardized scores on work goals for four East Asian countries.[35] Note that there are five variables to which high achievers would tend to give high scores: autonomy, challenge, earnings, recognition, and promotion. The managers from the People's Republic of China gave high scores to only one of these: autonomy. On the other four high-achievement responses, two were the lowest and the other two second lowest. Conversely, high achievers would not give high scores to affiliation or security-related goals such as cooperation with coworkers, security, benefits, physical working conditions, and time for nonwork activities. Yet most of these are rated relatively high for the Chinese sample.

On the other hand, as China's economy continues to grow and the government allows more market-based efforts, the achievement motivation drive likely will increase among the general population. This finding has been reinforced by a recent study of Chinese and U.S. businesses that found Chinese employees were economically oriented and favored reward systems giving more to some individuals than to others. Conversely, U.S. employees were more humanistically oriented and preferred a more equal distribu-

Table 13–6
Standardized Scores on Work Goals for Managers from Four Countries

Variables	People's Republic of China	Hong Kong	Taiwan	Singapore
Making a contribution	671	—	—	—
Coworkers who cooperate	635	579	571	624
Autonomy	603	512	480	532
Training	583	596	657	611
Efficiency	578	—	—	—
Skills	—	555	577	536
Challenge	515	548	548	571
Working relationship with manager	483	522	524	551
Earnings	454	567	442	552
Security	450	452	506	437
Recognition	446	487	487	442
Benefits	439	323	363	439
Area	—	477	438	362
Favorable physical conditions	433	436	407	432
Promotion	364	640	630	593
Time for nonwork activities	345	307	372	348

Note: Data, except those for the People's Republic, are from Geert Hofstede's book *Culture's Consequences: International Differences in Work-Related Values* (Beverly Hills: Sage, 1980). For the variabilities of the People's Republic, included are the skills goals in the training goal; the area goal is irrelevant in the context of the People's Republic.

Source: Oded Shenkar and Simcha Ronen, "Structure and Importance of Work Goals among Managers in the People's Republic of China," *Academy of Management Journal,* September 1987, p. 571. Used with permission.

tion of material rewards. Among other things, the study concluded that, "The Chinese differential preferences . . . are consistent with efforts to encourage individual responsibility and to link reward to performance . . ."[36] So, the seeds of the achievement motivation drive now appear to be taking root in China.

One of the other countries in Table 13-6, Singapore, had fairly high achievement scores and more recent research reports that indeed this is one of the reasons why the country has done so well. Lee and Chan, for example, recently examined high achievement drive among second-generation Singaporean Chinese businesspeople and found that many of them had the same characteristics that were described by McClelland: a desire for autonomy, individualism, a willingness to take risks, a willingness to actively search the environment for opportunities, initiative, and ambition. This led the researchers to conclude that "second-generation Chinese entrepreneurs in Singapore possess numerous characteristics which are highly consistent with . . . major related research studies on entrepreneurial characteristics."[37] This may well be one of the reasons why, despite a downturn in the Southeast Asian economy, Singapore has continued to be relatively economically successful.[38]

These examples show there is considerable cultural impact on achievement motivation theory. The ideal profile for high-achieving societies can be described in terms of the cultural dimensions examined in Chapter 5. In particular, two basic cultural dimensions identified by Hofstede in Chapter 5 best describe high-achieving societies. First, these societies tend to have the cultural dimension of low uncertainty avoidance. Those in high-achieving societies are not afraid to take at least moderate risks or to live with ambiguity. Second, they tend to have the cultural dimension of moderate to high masculinity (Hofstede's term), as measured by the high importance assigned to the acquisition of money and other physical assets and the low value given to caring for others and quality of work life. This combination is found almost exclusively in Anglo countries or in nations that have been closely associated with them through colonization or treaty, such as India, Singapore, and Hong Kong (countries that have been associated with Great Britain) and the Philippines (which has been associated with the United States).

Countries that fall into one of the other three quadrants in Figure 13-5 will not be very supportive of the high need for achievement. MNCs in these geographic regions would be wise to formulate a human resource management strategy for either changing the situation or adjusting to it. If they decide to change the situation, they must design jobs to fit the needs of their people or put people through an achievement motivation training program to create high-achieving managers and entrepreneurs.

A number of years ago, McClelland was able to demonstrate the success of such achievement motivation training programs with underdeveloped countries. For example, in India, he conducted such a program with considerable success. In following up these Indian trainees over the subsequent 6 to 10 months, he found that two-thirds were unusually active in achievement-oriented activities. They had started new businesses, investigated new product lines, increased profits, or expanded their present organizations. For example, the owner of a small radio store opened a paint and varnish factory after completing the program. McClelland concluded that this training appeared to have doubled the natural rate of unusual achievement-oriented activity in the group studied.[39]

If international human resource managers cannot change the situation or train the participants, then they must adjust to the specific conditions of the country and formulate a motivation strategy that is based on those conditions. In many cases, this requires consideration of a need-hierarchy approach blended with an achievement approach. Hofstede offers such advice in dealing with the countries in the various quadrants of Figure 13-5.

> The countries on the feminine side . . . distinguish themselves by focusing on quality of life rather than on performance and on relationships between people rather than on money and things. This means *social motivation:* quality of life plus security and quality of life plus risk.[40]

In the case of countries that are attempting to introduce changes that incorporate values from one of the other quadrants in Figure 13-5, the challenge can be even greater.

In summary, achievement motivation theory provides additional insights into the motivation of personnel around the world. Like the need-hierarchy and two-factor theories, however, achievement motivation theory must be modified to meet the specific needs

Figure 13-5

Selected Countries on the Uncertainty Avoidance and Masculinity Scales

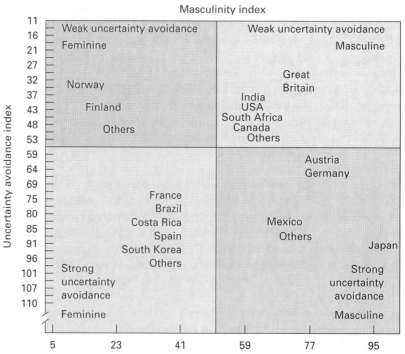

Source: Adapted from Geert Hofstede, "The Cultural Relativity of Organizational Practices and Theories," *Journal of International Business Studies,* Fall 1983, p. 86. Used with permission.

of the local culture. The culture of many countries does not support high achievement. However, the cultures of Anglo countries and those that reward entrepreneurial effort would support achievement motivation, and their human resources would be managed accordingly.

Motivation Applied: Job Design and Work Centrality

Although content theories provided important insights into how to motivate human resources in international management, two areas of application that have received a great deal of recent attention are job design and the role of work in people's lives, or what is called "work centrality."

Job Design

Job design consists of a job's content, the methods that are used on the job, and the way in which the job relates to others in the organization. The job design typically is a function of the work to be done and the way in which management wants the job to be carried out. These factors help to explain why the same type of work may have a different impact on the motivation of human resources in various parts of the world and result in different quality of work life.

Job design
A job's content, the methods that are used on the job, and the way the job relates to others in the organization.

Quality of Work Life: The Impact of Culture

Quality of work life (QWL) is not the same throughout the world. For example, assembly line employees in Japan will work at a rapid pace for hours and have very little control over their work activities. In Sweden, assembly line employees work at a more relaxed pace and have a great deal of control over their work activities. U.S. assembly line employees are somewhere in between; they typically work at a pace that is less demanding than that in Japan but more structured than that in Sweden.

What accounts for these differences? One answer is found in the culture of the country. QWL is directly related to culture. Table 13-7 compares the three industrialized nations mentioned earlier using the four cultural dimensions described in Chapter 5. A brief look shows that each country has a different cultural profile, helping to explain why similar jobs may be designed quite differently from country to country. Assembly line work is a good comparative example.

In Japan, there is strong uncertainty avoidance. The Japanese like to structure tasks so there is no doubt regarding what is to be done and how it is to be done. Individualism is low, so there is strong emphasis on security and individual risk-taking is discouraged.

Table 13–7
Cultural Dimensions in Japan, Sweden, and the United States

Cultural Dimension	Degree of Dimension				
	High/Strong X ←		Moderate X —		Low/Weak → X
Uncertainty avoidance	J			USA	S
Individualism	USA	S		J	
Power distance			J	USA	S
Masculinity	J		USA		S

Source: Adapted from Geert Hofstede, "The Cultural Relativity of the Quality of Life Concept," *Academy of Management Review*, July 1984, pp. 391, 393. Used with permission.

The power distance index is high, so Japanese workers are accustomed to taking orders from those above them. The masculinity index for the Japanese is high, which shows that they put a great deal of importance on money and other material symbols of success. In designing jobs, the Japanese structure tasks so that the work is performed within these cultural confines. Japanese managers work their employees extremely hard. Although Japanese workers contribute many ideas through the extensive use of quality circles, Japanese managers give them very little say in what actually goes on in the organization (in contrast to the erroneous picture often portrayed by the media, which presents Japanese firms as highly democratic and managed from the bottom up[41]) and depend heavily on monetary rewards, as reflected by the fact that the Japanese rate money as an important motivator more than the workers in any other industrialized country do.

In Sweden, however, uncertainty avoidance is low, so job descriptions, policy manuals, and similar work-related materials are more open-ended or general as opposed to the detailed procedural materials developed by the Japanese. In addition, Swedish workers are encouraged to make decisions and take risks. Swedes exhibit a moderate to high degree of individualism, which is reflected in their emphasis on individual decision making (in contrast to the collective or group decision making of the Japanese). They have a weak power distance index, which means that Swedish managers use participative approaches in leading their people. Swedes score low on masculinity, which means that interpersonal relations and the ability to interact with other workers and discuss job-related matters are important. These cultural dimensions result in job designs that are markedly different from those in Japan.

Cultural dimensions in the United States are closer to those of Sweden than to those of Japan. In addition, except for individualism, the U.S. profile is between that of Sweden and Japan (again see Table 13-7). This means that job design in U.S. assembly plants tend to be more flexible or unstructured than that of the Japanese but more rigid than that of the Swedes.

This same pattern holds for many other jobs in these countries. All job designs tend to reflect the cultural values of the country. The challenge for MNCs is to adjust job design to meet the needs of the host country's culture. For example, when Japanese firms enter the United States, they often are surprised to learn that people resent close control. In fact, there is evidence that the most profitable Japanese-owned companies in the United States are those that delegate a high degree of authority to their U.S. managers.[42] Similarly, Japanese firms operating in Sweden find that quality of work life is a central concern for the personnel and that a less structured, highly participative management style is needed for success. Some of the best examples are provided by sociotechnical job designs.

Sociotechnical Job Designs

Sociotechnical designs
Job designs that blend the personnel and the technology.

Sociotechnical designs are job designs that blend personnel and technology. The objective of these designs is to integrate new technology into the workplace so that workers accept and use these developments to increase overall productivity. Because technology often requires people to learn new methods and, in some cases, work faster, employee resistance is typical. Effective sociotechnical design can overcome these problems. There are a number of good examples, and perhaps the most famous is that of Volvo, the Swedish automaker. Sociotechnologic changes that were reflective of the cultural values of the workers were introduced at the firm's Kalmar plant. Autonomous work groups were formed and given the authority to elect their own supervisors as well as to schedule, assign, and inspect their own work. Each group was allowed to work at its own pace, although there was an overall output objective for the week and each group was expected to attain this goal.[43] The outcome was very positive and resulted in Volvo's building another plant that employs even more sophisticated sociotechnical job design concepts. More recently, however, Volvo's plant layout has not prevented the firm from having some problems. Both Japanese and North American automakers have been able to produce cars in far less time, putting Volvo at a cost disadvantage. As a result, the economic downturn in Asia, coupled with weakening demand for its product lines in both Europe and the United States, has resulted in the firm beginning to lay off workers and take steps to increase its efficiency.[44]

Without sacrificing efficiency, a number of other firms have introduced sociotechnical designs for better blending of their personnel and technology. A well-known U.S. example is General Foods, which set up autonomous groups at its Topeka, Kansas, plant to produce Gaines pet food. Patterned after the Volvo example, the General Foods project allowed workers to share responsibility and work in a highly democratic environment. Other U.S. firms also have opted for a self-managed team approach. In fact, recent research reports that the concept of multifunctional teams with autonomy for generating successful product innovation is more widely used by successful U.S., Japanese, and European firms than any other form of teamwork concept.[45] Its use must be tempered by the cultural situation, however. And even the widely publicized General Foods project at Topeka in the United States had some problems. Some former employees there indicate that the approach has steadily eroded and that some managers were openly hostile because it undermined their power, authority, and decision-making flexibility. The most effective job design will be a result of both the job to be done and the cultural values that support a particular approach.[46] For MNCs, the challenge will be to make the fit between the design and the culture.

At the same time, it is important to realize that functional job descriptions now are being phased out in many MNCs and replaced by more of a process approach. This new approach is explained as follows:

> Process management differs from managing a function in three ways. First, it uses external objectives. Old-line manufacturing departments, for example, tend to be measured on unit costs, an intradepartmental number that can lead to overlong production runs and stacks of unsold goods. By contrast, an integrated manufacturing and shipping process might be rated by how often it turns over its inventory—a process-wide measurement that reveals how all are working together to keep costs down. Second, in process management, employees with different skills are grouped to accomplish a complete piece of work. . . . Third, information moves straight to where it's needed, unfiltered by a hierarchy. If you have a problem with people upstream from you, you deal with them directly, rather than asking your boss to talk to theirs.[47]

The result is a more horizontal network that relies on communication and teamwork.[48] This approach also is useful in helping to create and sustain partnerships with other firms.[49]

Work Centrality

Work centrality, which can be defined as the importance of work in an individual's life relative to his or her other areas of interest (family, church, leisure), provides important insights into how to motivate human resources in different cultures.[50] After conducting a review of the literature, Bhagat and associates found that Japan has the highest level of work centrality, followed by moderately high levels for the former Yugoslavia and Israel, average levels for the United States and Belgium, moderately low levels for the Netherlands and Germany, and low levels for Britain.[51] In other words, these findings would indicate that successful multinationals in Japan must realize that although work is an integral part of the Japanese lifestyle, work in the United States must be more balanced with a concern for other interests. Unfortunately, this is likely to become increasingly more difficult for Japanese firms because the low birthrate in Japan is creating a shortage of personnel. As a result, a growing number of firms are now trying to push the mandatory retirement age to 65 from 60.[52]

Additional areas also could be evaluated in terms of helping to determine the role of work in the scheme of things. For example, in the United States there recently has been a pronounced increase in the number of hours worked annually, while the number in Japan has shrunk considerably.[53] The average American now is adding 9 hours annually to the time that he or she spends on the job.[54] Work is becoming a greater part of the U.S. employee's life and a lesser part among Japanese workers.[55] Moreover, this is occurring at a time when according to the Japanese Ministry of Labor, U.S. productivity per hour is running 62 percent higher than that of Japan when adjusted for purchasing power parity.[56]

Work centrality
The importance of work in an individual's life relative to other areas of interest.

Value of Work   Although work is an important part of the lifestyles of most people, there still are a large number of misconceptions. For example, one reason that Japanese work such long hours is that the cost of living is very high and hourly employees cannot afford to pass up the opportunity for extra money. Among salaried employees who are not paid extra, most Japanese managers expect their subordinates to stay late at work, and this has become a requirement of the job. Moreover, there is recent evidence that Japanese workers may do far less work in a business day than outsiders would suspect.[57] On the other hand, it is equally true that many Japanese do accept work as an integral part of their lifestyle, and in some cases, this is resulting in serious physical maladies. A survey by the Japanese prime minister's office found that 63 percent of those who were surveyed complained of being chronically tired, and 53 percent felt emotionally stressed. Additionally, only 26 percent said they were very healthy, compared with 48 percent in 1979.[58] In fact, as seen in the accompanying sidebar, "*Karoshi*, or Stressed Out in Japan," the effects of overwork are beginning to be recognized as a problem in Japan. At the same time, some Japanese traditionally have had lifetime employment and thus feel committed to their firm because of everything that it has done for them. Most Japanese were never given lifetime employment, however, and with the downturn in the Japanese economy, those who are ensured of continued employment feel that they are special and, in turn, respond with dedication and fervor. Quite simply, they value work as an integral part of their existence.[59]

Job Satisfaction   In addition to the implications that value of work has for motivating human resources across cultures, another interesting contrast is job satisfaction. For example, one current study has revealed that Japanese office workers may be much less satisfied with their jobs than their U.S., Canadian, and EU counterparts are. The Americans, who reported the highest level of satisfaction in this study, were pleased with job challenges, opportunities for teamwork, and ability to make a significant contribution at work. Japanese workers, however, were least pleased with these three factors.[60] Similar findings also were found in an earlier study by the coauthor (Luthans and colleagues) of this text, who reported that U.S. employees had higher organizational commitment than Japanese or Korean workers in this cross-cultural study. What makes these findings particularly interesting is that a large percentage of the Japanese and Korean workers were supervisory employees, who could be expected to be more committed to their organization than nonsupervisory employees, and a significant percentage of these employees also had lifetime guarantees.[61] This study also showed that findings related to job satisfaction in the international arena often are different than expected.[62]

Conventional wisdom not always being substantiated was reinforced recently by research in cross-cultural studies that found Japanese workers who already were highly paid compared with their colleagues, and who then received even higher wages, experienced decreased job satisfaction, morale, commitment, and intention to remain with the firm. This contrasts sharply with U.S. workers, who did not experience these negative feelings.[63] These findings show that the motivation approaches used in one culture may have limited value in another.[64]

Research by Kakabadse and Myers also has brought to light findings that are contradictory to commonly accepted beliefs. These researchers surveyed managers from several European countries such as the United Kingdom, France, Belgium, Sweden, and Finland and, among other things, examined job satisfaction among managerial levels. It has long been assumed that satisfaction is highest at the upper levels of organizations; however, this study found varying degrees of satisfaction among managers, depending on the country. The researchers reported that

> senior managers from France and Finland display greater job dissatisfaction than the managers from the remaining countries. In terms of satisfaction with and commitment to the organization, British, German and Swedish managers display highest levels of commitment. Equally, British and German managers highlight that they feel stretched in their job, but senior managers from French organizations suggest that their jobs lack sufficient challenge and stimulus. In keeping with the job related views displayed by French managers, they equally indicate their desire to leave their job because of their unsatisfactory work-related circumstances.[65]

International Management in Action

Karoshi, or Stressed Out in Japan   www.jbc.gol.com/index.html

Doing business in Japan can be a real killer. Overwork, or **karoshi**, as it is called in Japan, claims 10,000 lives annually in this hard-driving, competitive economic society according to Hiroshi Kawahito, a lawyer who has founded the National Defense Council for Victims of Karoshi.

One of the latest cases is Jun Ishii of Mitsui & Company. Ishii was one of the firm's only speakers of Russian. In the year before his death, Ishii made 10 trips to Russia, totaling 115 days. No sooner would he arrive home from one trip than the company would send him out again. The grueling pace took its toll. While on a trip, Ishii collapsed and died of a heart attack. His widow filed a lawsuit against Mitsui & Company, charging that her husband had been worked to death. Tokyo labor regulators ruled that Ishii had indeed died of *karoshi*, and the government now is paying annual worker's compensation to the widow. The company also cooperated and agreed to make a one-time payment of $240,000.

The reason that the case received so much publicity is that this is one of the few instances in which the government has ruled that a person died from overwork. Now regulators are expanding *karoshi* compensation to salaried as well as hourly workers. This development is receiving the attention of the top management of many Japanese multinationals, and some Japanese MNCs are beginning to take steps to prevent the likelihood of overwork. For example, Mitsui & Company is assessing its managers based on how well they set overtime hours, keep subordinates healthy, and encourage workers to take vacations. Matsushita Electric is extending vacations from 16 days annually to 23 days and is requiring all workers to take this time off. One branch of Nippon Telegraph & Telephone has found that stress is making some workers irritable and ill, so the company is initiating periods of silent meditation. Other companies are following suit, although there still are many Japanese who work well over 2,500 hours a year and feel both frustrated and burned out by job demands.

Fortunately, the Ishii case likely will bring about some improvements in working conditions for many Japanese employees. Experts admit, however, that it is difficult to determine if *karoshi* is caused by work demands or by private, late-night socializing that may be work-related. Other possible causes include high stress, lack of exercise, and fatty diets, but whatever the cause, one thing is clear: More and more Japanese families no longer are willing to accept the belief that *karoshi* is a risk that all employees must accept. Work may be a killer, but this outcome can be prevented through more carefully implemented job designs and work processes.

On the other hand, research also reveals that some of the conditions that help to create organizational commitment among U.S. workers also have value in other cultures. For example, a recent, large study of Korean employees ($n = 1192$ in 27 companies in eight major industries) found that consistent with U.S. studies, Korean employees' position in the hierarchy, tenure in their current position, and age all related significantly to organizational commitment. Also, like previous studies in the United States, as the size of the Korean organizations increased, commitment decreased, and the more positive the climate perceptions, the more the commitment.[66] In other words, there is at least beginning evidence that the theoretic constructs predicting organizational commitment may hold across cultures.

Karoshi
Overwork or job burnout, in Japanese.

Also related to motivation are job attitudes toward quality of work life. Recent research reports that EU workers see a strong relationship between how well they do their jobs and the ability to get what they want out of life. U.S. workers were not as supportive of this relationship, and Japanese workers were least likely to see any connection.

This finding raises an interesting motivation-related issue regarding how well, for example, American, European, and Japanese employees can work together effectively. Some researchers have recently raised the question of how Japanese firms will be able to have effective strategic alliances with American and European companies, if the work values of the partners are so different. Tornvall, after conducting a detailed examination of the work practices of five companies—Fuji-Kiku, a spare parts firm in Japan, Toyota Motor Ltd. of Japan, Volvo Automobile AB of Sweden, SAAB Automobile AB, Sweden, and the General Motors plant in Saginaw, Michigan—concluded that there were benefits from the approaches used by each. This led him to recommend what he calls a "balance in the synergy" between the partners.[67] Some of his suggestions included the following:

Moving away from	Moving toward
Logical and reason-centered, individualistic thinking.	A more holistic, idealistic, and group thinking approach to problem solving.
Viewing work as a necessary burden.	Viewing work as a challenging and development activity.
The avoidance of risk-taking and the feeling of distrust of others.	An emphasis on cooperation, trust, and personal concern for others.
The habit of analyzing things in such great depth that it results in "paralysis through analysis."	Cooperation built on intuition and pragmatism.
An emphasis on control.	An emphasis on flexibility.

In large degree, these changes will require all three groups—American, Europeans, and Japanese—to make changes in the way they approach work.

In conclusion, it should be remembered that work is important in every society. The extent of importance will vary, however, and much of what is "known" about work as a motivator often is culture-specific. The lesson to be learned for international management is that although the process of motivation may be the same, the content may change from one culture to another.

Motivation and Culture

Finally, it is critical to keep in mind that effective motivation is also grounded in a sound understanding of culture. The way in which a manager motivates employees in one culture is often different from that which will be used in another culture. One of the clearest contrasts is provided by Trompenaars' affective and neutral cultures covered in Chapter 5. In affective cultures, such as the United States, people exhibit their emotions. In neutral cultures such as Japan, people do not show their emotions. Moreover, in some cultures people are taught to exhibit their emotions but not let it affect their making rational decisions, while in other cultures the two are intertwined.

> Americans tend to exhibit emotion, yet separate it from "objective" and "rational" decisions. Italians and south European nations in general tend to exhibit and not separate. Dutch and Swedes tend not to exhibit and to separate . . . there is nothing "good" or "bad" about these differences. You can argue that emotions held in check will twist your judgments despite all efforts to be "rational." Or you can argue that pouring forth emotions makes it harder for anyone present to think straight. Similarly, you can scoff at the "walls" separating reasons from emotions, or argue that because of the leakage that so often occurs, these should be thicker and stronger.[68]

Researchers have also found that the way in which managers speak to people can motivate or influence the outcome. For example, in some situations it is common to wait until the other person has finished speaking before saying anything. Anglo Saxon and Asian cultures are good examples. This is in contrast to Latin cultures where it is very common to speak at the same time as the other person. Similarly, in Anglo Saxon cultures it is common for managers to raise their voice in order to emphasize a point. In Asian cultures managers generally speak at the same level throughout their communication, using a form of self-control that shows respect for the other person. Latin managers, meanwhile, vary their tone of voice continually, and this form of exaggeration is viewed by them as showing that they are very interested in what they are saying and committed to their point of view. Knowing how to communicate can greatly influence how effectively one motivates. Here is an example:

> A British manager posted to Nigeria found that it was very effective to raise his voice for important issues. His Nigerian subordinates viewed that unexpected explosion by a normally self-controlled manager as a sign of extra concern. After success in Nigeria he was posted to Malaysia. Shouting there was a sign of loss of face; his colleagues did not take him seriously and he was transferred.[69]

The key to successfully using communication to motivate personnel is that of determining what works best in a given culture and adapting to these needs. In the case of affective and neutral cultures, for example, Trompenaars and Hampden-Turner have offered the tips provided in Table 13-8.

The World of Business Week Revisited

The opening news story examined some of the key motivations that help explain how and why today's managers do things. A great deal of the emphasis in this chapter was placed on the worker level and careful consideration was given to whether there can be a universal approach to motivating human resources across cultures or

Table 13–8
Motivation Tips for Doing Business in Affective and Neutral Cultures

When Managing or Being Managed in

Affective Cultures	Neutral Cultures
Avoid a detached, ambiguous, and cool demeanor because this will be interpreted as negative behavior.	Avoid warm, expressive, or enthusiastic behaviors because these will be interpreted as a lack of personal control over one's feelings and be viewed as inconsistent with one's high status.
Find out whose work and enthusiasm is being directed into which projects, so you are able to appreciate the vigor and commitment they have for these efforts.	Extensively prepare the things you have to do and then stick tenaciously to the issues.
Let people be emotional without personally becoming intimidated or coerced by their behavior.	Look for cues regarding whether people are pleased or angry and then amplify their importance.

When Doing Business with Individuals in

Affective Cultures (for Those from Neutral Cultures)	Neutral Cultures (for Those from Affective Cultures)
Do not be put off stride when others create scenes and get histrionic; take time-outs for sober reflection and hard assessments.	Ask for time-outs from meetings and negotiations where you can patch each other up and rest between games of poker with the "impassive ones."
When others are expressing goodwill, respond warmly.	Put down as much as you can on paper before beginning the negotiation.
Remember that the other person's enthusiasm and readiness to agree or disagree does not mean that the individual has made up his or her mind.	Remember that the other person's lack of emotional tone does not mean that the individual is disinterested or bored, only that the person does not like to show his or her hand.
Keep in mind that the entire negotiation is typically focused on you as a person and not so much on the object or proposition that is being discussed.	Keep in mind that the entire negotiation is typically focused on the object or proposition that is being discussed and not on you as a person.

Recognize the Way in Which People Behave in

Affective Cultures	Neutral Cultures
They reveal their thoughts and feelings both verbally and nonverbally.	They often do not reveal what they are thinking or feeling.
Emotions flow easily, vehemently, and without inhibition.	Emotions are often dammed up, although they may occasionally explode.
Heated, vital, and animated expressions are admired.	Cool and self-possessed conduct is admired.
Touching, gesturing, and strong facial expressions are common.	Physical contact, gesturing, or strong facial expressions are not used.
Statements are made fluently and dramatically.	Statements are often read out in a monotone voice.

Source: Adapted from Fons Trompenaars and Charles Hampden-Turner, *Riding the Waves of Culture: Understanding Diversity in Global Business,* 2nd ed. (New York: McGraw-Hill, 1998), pp. 80–82.

whether the approach must vary by culture. The general conclusion was that cultures are different and what works in one country will often not work in another.

However, this news story transcended culture barriers to some degree and focused on a more universal concern: investor demand for performance. In considering what is happening in this area, answer these three questions: (1) What are some of the motivation steps that managers need to take in order to increase worker productivity and ensure that their operations remain world class? (2) Are the approaches that need to be taken, for example, by German managers the same as those by North American managers or are these approaches culturally driven? (3) Regardless of your answer to the previous question, how will investors decide whether or not the management of these firms is properly motivating the personnel?

Summary of Key Points

1. Two basic types of theories explain motivation: content and process. Content motivation theories have been given much more attention in international management research, because they provide the opportunity to create a composite picture for motivation of human resources in a particular country or region of the world. In addition, content theories apply more directly to providing ways for managers to improve the performance of their human resources.

2. Maslow's hierarchy-of-needs theory has been studied in a number of different countries. Researchers have found that regardless of country, managers have to be concerned with the satisfaction of these needs for their human resources.

3. Some researchers have suggested that satisfaction profiles are not very useful for studying motivation in an international setting, because there are so many different subcultures within any country or even at different levels of a given organization. These researchers have suggested that job categories are more effective for examining motivation, because job level (managers versus operating employees) and the need hierarchy have an established relationship.

4. Like Maslow's theory, Herzberg's two-factor theory has received considerable attention in the international arena, and his original findings from the United States have been replicated in other countries. Cross-cultural studies related to job satisfaction also have been conducted. The data show that job content is more important than job context to job satisfaction.

5. The third content motivation theory that has received a great amount of attention in the international arena

is the need for achievement. Some current findings show that this need is not as widely held across cultures as was previously believed. In some parts of the world, however, such as Anglo countries, cultural values support people to be high achievers. In particular, Dutch researcher Geert Hofstede has suggested that an analysis of two cultural dimensions, uncertainty avoidance and masculinity, helps to identify high-achieving societies. Once again, it can be concluded that different cultures will support different motivational needs, and that international managers developing strategies to motivate their human resources for improved performance must recognize cultural differences.

6. Although content theories provide important insights into the motivation of human resources, two additional areas that have received a great deal of recent attention in the application of motivation are job design and the role of work in people's lives, or work centrality. Job design is influenced by culture as well as the specific methods that are used to bring together the people and the work. Work centrality helps to explain the importance of work in an individual's life relative to other areas of interest. Research reveals that in recent years, work has become a relatively greater part of the average U.S. employee's life and perhaps less a part of the average Japanese worker's life. Recent evidence also indicates that Japanese office workers may be much less satisfied with their jobs than U.S., Canadian, and EU workers are. These findings suggest that MNCs should design motivation packages that address the specific needs of different cultures.

Key Terms

achievement motivation theory
content theories
esteem needs
hygiene factors
job content factors
job context factors

job design
karoshi
motivation
motivators
physiological needs
process theories

safety needs
self-actualization needs
social needs
sociotechnical designs
two-factor theory of motivation
work centrality

Review and Discussion Questions

1. Do people throughout the world have needs similar to those described in Maslow's need hierarchy? What does your answer reveal about using universal assumptions regarding motivation?

2. Is Herzberg's two-factor theory universally applicable to human resource management, or is its value limited to Anglo countries?

3. What are the dominant characteristics of high achievers? Using Figure 13-5 as your point of reference, determine which countries likely will have the greatest percentage of high achievers. Why is this so? Of what value is your answer to the study of international management?

4. A U.S. manufacturer is planning to open a plant in Sweden. What should this firm know about the quality of work life in Sweden that would have a direct effect on job design in the plant? Give an example.

5. What does a U.S. firm setting up operations in Japan need to know about work centrality in that country? How would this information be of value to the multinational? Conversely, what would a Japanese firm need to know about work centrality in the United States? Explain.

Internet Exercise: Making Things Work at Bankers Trust and the Deutsche Bank

The Deutsche Bank of Frankfurt recently acquired Bankers Trust, a major American financial institution. The purpose of the acquisition is to establish a global platform for the profitable growth of both enterprises. However, as in many recent acquisitions, there is concern about the compensation packages that are being offered. European executives feel that these packages are too lucrative. Go to the Bankers Trust web site at **www.bankerstrust.com** and download the latest annual report for the company. Then carefully read the stock options section. Then go to the Deutsche Bank web site at **public.deutsche-bank.de/index.htm** and look over its latest financial statements. Next, visit the profile and current issues materials that are offered at both sites and find out what is going on with regard to making the merger work. Finally, access *Business Week* on-line at **www.businessweek.com** or another current news source and find out how things might be working out between the two companies. Based on your information, then formulate your answers to these three questions: (1) What type of motivational needs do stock options meet? (2) Why do you think the Germans might feel that the American's compensation package is too lucrative? (3) What potential problems does this perception present for the success of the merged firms?

Singapore

Singapore is an island city-state that is located at the southern tip of the Malay Peninsula. The small country covers 239 square miles and is connected by train across the Johore Strait to West Malaysia in the north. The Straigt of Malacca to the south separates Singapore from the Indonesian island of Sumatra. There are approximately 3.5 million people in Singapore, resulting in a population density per square mile of almost 15,000 people. About three-fourths of Singaporeans are of Chinese descent, 15 percent are Malays, and the remainder are Indian and European. The gross national product of this thriving country is over $65 billion, and per-capita GNP is around $23,000. One of the so-called newly industrialized countries or Four Tigers (along with Korea, Taiwan, and Hong Kong), Singapore in recent years has been affected by the economic crisis in Southeast Asia, but the currency and prices have remained relatively stable. The very clean and modern city remains as the major commercial and shipping center of Southeast Asia. The government of this former British colony consists of a cabinet headed by Prime Minister Goh Chok Tong and a parliament of 81 members, who are elected by universal suffrage.

For the last 6 months, the Madruga Corporation of Cleveland has been producing small electronic toys in Singapore. The small factory has been operated by local managers, but Madruga now wants to expand the Singapore facilities as well as integrate more expatriate managers into the operation. The CEO explained: "We do not want to run this plant as if it were a foreign subsidiary under the direct control of local managers. It is our plant and we want an on-site presence. Over the last year we have been staffing our Canadian and European operations with headquarters personnel, and we are now ready to turn attention to our Singapore operation." Before doing so, however, the company intends to conduct some on-site research to learn the most effective way of managing the Singapore personnel. In particular, the Madruga management team is concerned with how to motivate the Singaporeans and make them more productive. One survey has already been conducted among the Singapore personnel; this study found a great deal of similarity with the workers at the U.S. facilities. Both the Singapore and U.S. employees expressed a preference for job content factors such as the chance for growth, achievement, and increased responsibility, and they listed money and job security toward the bottom of the list of things they looked for in a job.

Madruga management is intrigued by these findings and believes that it might be possible to use some of the same motivation approaches in Singapore as it does in the United States. Moreover, one of the researchers sent the CEO a copy of an article showing that people in Singapore have weak uncertainty avoidance and a general cultural profile that is fairly similar to that of the United States. The CEO is not sure what all this means, but she does know that motivating workers in Singapore apparently is not as "foreign" a process as she thought it would be. **www.sg**

Questions

1. What are some current issues facing Singapore? What is the climate for doing business in Singapore today?

2. Based on the information in this case, determine the specific things that seem to motivate human resources in Singapore.

3. Would a knowledge of the achievement motive be of any value to the expatriate managers who are assigned to the Singapore operation?

4. If you were using Figure 13-5 to help explain how to motivate Singapore human resources effectively, what conclusions could you draw that would help provide guidelines for the Madruga management team?

Motivation Is the Key

Over the last 5 years, Corkley & Finn, a regional investment brokerage house, has been extremely profitable. Some of its largest deals have involved cooperation with investment brokers in other countries. Realizing that the world economy is likely to grow vigorously over the next 25 years, the company has decided to expand its operations and open overseas branches. In the beginning, the company intends to work in cooperation with other local brokerages; however, the company believes that within 5 years, it will have garnered enough business to break away and operate independently. For the time being, the firm intends to set up a small office in London and another in Tokyo.

The firm plans on sending four people to each of these offices and recruiting the remainder of the personnel from the local market. These new branch employees will have to spend time meeting potential clients and building trust. This will be followed by the opportunity to put together small financial deals and, it is hoped, much larger ones over time.

The company is prepared to invest whatever time or money is needed to make these two branches successful. "What we have to do," the president noted, "is establish an international presence and then build from there. We will need to hire people who are intensely loyal to us and use them as a cadre for expanding operations and becoming a major player in the international financial arena. One of our most important challenges will be to hire the right people and motivate them to do the type of job we want and stay with us. After all, if we bring in people and train them how to do their jobs well and then they don't perform or they leave, all we've done is spend a lot of money for nothing and provide on-the-job training for our competitors. In this business, our people are the most important asset, and clients most often are swayed toward doing business with an investment broker with whom they think they can have a positive working relationship. The reputation of the firm is important, but it is always a function of the people who work there. Effective motivation of our people is the key to our ultimate success in these new branches."

Questions

1. In motivating the personnel in London and Tokyo, would the company find that the basic hierarchical needs of the workers were the same? Why or why not?

2. How could an understanding of the two-factor theory of motivation be of value in motivating the personnel at both of these locations? Would hygiene factors be more important to one of these groups than to the other? Would there be any difference in terms of the importance of motivators?

3. Using Figure 13-5 as a point of reference, what recommendation would you make regarding how to motivate the personnel in London? In Tokyo? Are there any significant differences between the two? If so, what are they? If not, why not?

Chapter 14

Leadership across Cultures

Objectives of the Chapter

Leadership often is credited for the success or failure of international operations. Note that like the other topics discussed so far, effective leadership styles and practices in one culture are not necessarily effective in others. For example, the leadership approach used by effective U.S. managers would not necessarily be the same as that employed in other parts of the world. Even within the same country, effective leadership tends to be very situation-specific; however, also like the other areas studied in international management, certain leadership styles and practices transcend international boundaries. This chapter examines these leadership differences and similarities.

First the basic foundation for the study of leadership is reviewed. Next, leadership in various parts of the world, including Europe, East Asia, the Middle East, and developing countries, is examined. The specific objectives of this chapter are:

1. DESCRIBE the basic philosophic foundation and styles of managerial leadership.

2. EXAMINE the attitudes of European managers toward leadership practices.

3. COMPARE and CONTRAST leadership styles in Japan with those in the United States.

4. COMPARE and CONTRAST leadership approaches in Middle Eastern and developing countries with those in the economic powers of the world.

BusinessWeek

The World of Business Week:

Can Valeo's Driver Keep Up His Winning Streak?

In corporate suites from New York to Hong Kong, chief executives view the coming years with foreboding. Between banking collapse in Japan, depression in Asia, recession in Latin America, and a U.S. slowdown, they find few bright spots. But Noël Goutard, chief executive of $7.4 billion French auto supplier Valeo, sees opportunities where others see danger. "You can transform a company faster in recession than when the market is booming," he says.

Goutard's recent $1.7 billion takeover of ITT Industries Co.'s automotive unit will give him a chance to prove it. His new acquisition needs a total efficiency overhaul. Meanwhile, he must keep slashing costs at Valeo as global growth stagnates. So Goutard has a three-pronged plan. He will retool production, juice up growth with high-tech innovations, and offset the risks of a strong single European currency by investing more outside the euro zone. Valeo will keep moving low-tech operations out of Western Europe and the United States to lower-cost Mexico and Central Europe.

In October, Goutard introduced a program to speed up the restructuring of Valeo's and ITT's plants around the world—especially then 71 plants in the euro zone, where Goutard has made more than a dozen acquisitions or joint ventures over the past two years. The goal is to boost capacity utilization to 95%, improve return on assets by 10%, and reduce fixed assets by $277 million over the next 18 months. Division man-

agers will have to rethink production and submit pro-posals before they turn in their budgets.

Meanwhile, Valeo will continue using technology to stay ahead of the competitoin . . . Its latest inve-tion: rain sensors that flip on the windshield wipers if they detect moisture and adjust to the proper speed automatically.

Visionary

Goutard is counting on more innovations. Engineers now represent 15% of Valeo's total workforce, up from 5% a decade ago. And Valeo ranks among the leading companies for patent applications in Europe, with 550 filed in 1997. Goutard was also an early adopter of advanced computer-aided design systems to link virtual design teams with suppliers, a move that helped Valeo pioneer big cost savings at Chrysler Corp. "[Goutard] was among the first to understand the strategic aspect of virtual design," says Bernard Charles, CEO of Dassault Systems.

The 67-year-old, Casablanca-born Goutard has developed a knack for making the most of difficult situations. Since he took the reins of ailing, Paris-based Valeo in 1987, he has nearly quadrupled sales and transformed a loss-making regional player into a global champion. Valeo now boasts above-average operating margins exceeding 7%—a challenge in a cutthroat industry where purchasing managers at such giants as Volkswagen and General Motors Corp. continually pressure their supplies to come in with ever lower prices. "Goutard has the right

vision," says Otto Jetter, executive director for worldwide electrical parts purchasing at GM. "He sees where the competition is weak, and he moves."

But to meet his goals of 10%-plus growth and ris-ing margins, Goutard will have to get even more cre-ative. Big competitors, including GM subsidiary Delphi, Ford's Visteon, and Denso in Japan, are accelerating their drives to grab market share in Europe following the Daimler-Chrysler merger. General Motors has announced plans to spin off its in-house supplier Delphi next year, and market experts believe Ford will do the same with Visteon. "Delphi will go after Valeo's traditional customer base," predicts Marc Santucci, president of consult-ant ELM International, based in East Lansing, Mich.

An early career on Wall Street as a commodities trader, followed by international stints with U.S. com-panies, fostered an eclectic management philosophy in Goutard. He became obsessed with speed, innova-tion, and customer service. But he also makes use of European practices, including a more collaborative relationship with labor, motivating his 50,000 employ-ees through a steady dialogue with management.

He'll need all of his people skills to fix the ITT unit. That will involve plant closings, a reorganiza-tion, and streamlining at corporate headquarters. ITT underinvested in plants and R&D and its margins trail those of Valeo. Already, Goutard has reassigned 1,400 headquarters administrators to operating units and set about flattening what he calls an "incredible management pyramid."

Goutard lives simply, driving an Audi 6 that he has been told is too small for a French chief executive. But even such modesty is strategic, analysts say. Flashing his wealth might encourage executives at GM and Chrysler to ask him for bigger discounts. And having taken the company this far, Goutard is not about to give anything away.

www.hoovers.com/capsules/92020.html

Source: **Reprinted from November 9, 1998, pp. 70E6, 8 issue of *Business Week* by special permission, copyright © 1998 by McGraw-Hill Companies, Inc.**

This opening news story provides an interesting view of international leadership. Noel Goutard's company has worldwide operations and the key decisions that he makes will affect all of the personnel. In particular, notice how he is trying to balance a concern for costs with a need for continuing innovation. So as a leader, he will need to keep the focus on efficiency and work-related areas, but at the same time he cannot crack down too much or he may stifle the ingenuity and morale on employees. In short, he must be concerned with both the work and the people, without giving either one too much emphasis at the expense of the other. Moreover, with the expected competition that is likely to be generated by GM's Delphi subsidiary, Ford's Visteon, and Denso in Japan, Goutard is going to have his leadership skills tested within the next few years. In particular, he will not only be encountering stiff international competition but will have to lead a diverse, multicultural workforce in a unified effort that focuses on providing customers better and better products at continually lower costs and maintain morale and cohesiveness throughout the ranks. The next five years are going to be interesting ones for the leader of this MNC.

Foundation for Leadership

Leadership
The process of influencing people to direct their efforts toward the achievement of some particular goal or goals.

When one realizes that much of history, political science, and the behavioral sciences is either directly or indirectly concerned with leadership, the statement that more concern and research has focused on leadership than on any other topic becomes believable. With all this attention over the years, however, there still is no generally agreed-on definition, let alone firm answers to which approach is more effective than others in the international arena. For present purposes, however, **leadership** can be defined as the process of influencing people to direct their efforts toward achievement of some particular goal or goals.[1] Leadership is widely recognized as being very important in the study of international management, but relatively little effort has gone to systematically studying and comparing leadership approaches throughout the world.[2] Most international research efforts on leadership have been directed toward a specific country or geographic area.

The following two comparative areas provide a foundation for understanding leadership in the international arena: (1) the philosophic grounding of how leaders view their subordinates; and (2) leadership approaches as reflected through use of autocratic-participative characteristics and behaviors of leaders. The philosophies and approaches used in the United States often are quite different from those employed by leaders in overseas organizations, although these differences often are not as pronounced as is commonly believed.

Philosophical Background: Theories X and Y

One primary reason that leaders behave as they do is their philosophy or beliefs regarding how to direct their subordinates most effectively. Managers who believe their people are naturally lazy and work only for money will use a leadership style that is different from those who believe their people are self-starters and enjoy challenge and increased responsibility. Douglas McGregor, the pioneering leadership theorist, labeled these two sets of philosophic assumptions with the terms "Theory X" and "Theory Y."

A **Theory X manager** believes that people are basically lazy and that coercion and threats of punishment must be used to get them to work. The specific philosophic assumptions that Theory X leaders feel are most descriptive of their subordinates are:

1. By their very nature, people do not like to work and will avoid it whenever possible.
2. Workers have little ambition, try to avoid responsibility, and like to be directed.
3. The primary need of employees is job security.
4. To get people to attain organizational objectives, it is necessary to use coercion, control, and threats of punishment.[3]

A **Theory Y manager** believes that under the right conditions, people not only will work hard but seek increased responsibility and challenge. In addition, a great deal of creative potential basically goes untapped, and if these abilities can be tapped, workers will provide much higher quantity and quality of output. The specific philosophic assumptions that Theory Y leaders feel are most descriptive of their subordinates are:

1. The expenditure of physical and mental effort at work is as natural to people as resting or playing.
2. External control and threats of punishment are not the only ways of getting people to work toward organizational objectives. If people are committed to the goals, they will exercise self-direction and self-control.
3. Commitment to objectives is determined by the rewards that are associated with their achievement.
4. Under proper conditions, the average human being learns not only to accept but to seek responsibility.
5. The capacity to exercise a relatively high degree of imagination, ingenuity, and creativity in the solution of organizational problems is widely distributed throughout the population.
6. Under conditions of modern industrial life, the intellectual potential of the average human being is only partially tapped.[4]

Theory X manager
A manager who believes that people are basically lazy and that coercion and threats of punishment often are necessary to get them to work.

Theory Y manager
A manager who believes that under the right conditions people not only will work hard but will seek increased responsibility and challenge.

The reason behind these beliefs, however, will vary by culture. U.S. managers believe that to motivate workers, it is necessary to satisfy their higher-order needs. This is done best through a Theory Y leadership approach. In China, Theory Y managers act similarly—but for different reasons. After the 1949 revolution, two types of managers emerged: Experts and Reds. The Experts focused on technical skills and primarily were Theory X advocates. The Reds, skilled in the management of people and possessing political and ideologic expertise, were Theory Y advocates. The Reds also believed that the philosophy of Chairman Mao support their thinking (i.e., all employees had to rise together both economically and culturally). Therefore, both U.S. and Chinese managers support Theory Y, but for very different reasons.[5]

The same is true in the case of Russian managers. In a survey recently conducted by Puffer, McCarthy, and Naumov, 292 Russian managers were asked about their beliefs regarding work.[6] Table 14-1 shows the six different groupings of the responses. The results, reported in Table 14-2, clearly indicates that some Russian managers endorsed certain beliefs about work more than others. In particular, top-level executives scored higher on organizational beliefs and lower on both participation and Marxist-related beliefs than did other managers. Additionally, managers 40 years of age or older had stronger agreement than those in their twenties and thirties regarding work ethic beliefs and the importance of leisure. Also, as shown in Table 14-2, women more strongly endorsed humanistic, participative, leisure, and Marxist-related beliefs than did men.

Table 14–1

Russian Managerial Beliefs about Work

A. **Humanistic Beliefs**
Work can be made meaningful.
One's job should give one a chance to try out new ideas.
The workplace can be humanized.
Work can be made satisfying.
Work should allow for the use of human capabilities.
Work can be a means of self-expression.
Work should enable one to learn new things.
Work can be organized to allow for human fulfillment.
Work can be made interesting rather than boring.
The job should be a source of new experiences.

B. **Organizational Beliefs**
Survival of the group is very important in an organization.
Working with a group is better than working alone.
It is best to have a job as part of an organization where all work together even if
   you don't get individual credit.
One should take an active part in all group affairs.
The group is the most important entity in any organization.
One's contribution to the group is the most important thing about one's work.
Work is a means to foster group interests.

C. **Work Ethic**
Only those who depend on themselves get ahead in life.
To be superior a person must stand alone.
A person can learn better on the job by striking out boldly on his own than by
   following the advice of others.
One must avoid dependence on other persons whenever possible.
One should live one's life independent of others as much as possible.

D. **Beliefs about Participation in Managerial Decisions**
The working classes should have more say in running society.
Factories would be better run if workers had more of a say in management.
Workers should be more active in making decisions about products, financing,
   and capital investment.
Workers should be represented on the board of directors of companies.

E. **Leisure Ethic**
The trend towards more leisure is not a good thing. (R)
More leisure time is good for people.
Increased leisure time is bad for society. (R)
Leisure time activities are more interesting than work.
The present trend towards a shorter workweek is to be encouraged.

F. **Marxist-Related Beliefs**
The free enterprise system mainly benefits the rich and powerful.
The rich do not make much of a contribution to society.
Workers get their fair share of the economic rewards of society. (R)
The work of the laboring classes is exploited by the rich for their own benefit.
Wealthy people carry their fair share of the burdens of life in this country. (R)
The most important work is done by the laboring classes.

Notes: 1. The survey is from Buchholz (1977).
2. Response scales ranged from 1 (strongly disagree) to 5 (strongly agree).
3. (R) denotes reverse-scoring items.
4. The 45-individual items contained in the 6 belief clusters were presented to respondents in a mixed fashion, rather than categorized by cluster as shown above.
5. Participation was a subset of Marxist-related values in Buchholz's original study, but was made a separate cluster in his later work.

Source: Adapted from Sheila M. Putter, Daniel J. McCarthy, and Alexander I. Naumov, "Russian Managers' Beliefs about Work: Beyond the Stereotypes," *Journal of World Business,* vol. 32, no. 3, 1997, p. 262.

Table 14–2
Russian Beliefs about Work by Managerial Level, Age, and Gender

Managerial Groups	Humanistic	Organi-zational	Work Ethic	Participation	Leisure	Marxist-Related
Total sample (*n*=292)	4.71	3.81	3.70	3.20	3.18	2.99
Managerial Levels						
Executives (*n*=110)	4.71	**3.95**	3.70	**3.03**	3.16	**2.91**
Other managers (*n*=177)	4.72	**3.73**	3.71	**3.26**	3.18	**3.05**
Age groups						
20–29 (*n*=106)	4.71	**3.67**	**3.68**	3.18	**3.04**	2.92
30–39 (*n*=87)	4.69	**3.73**	**3.61**	3.05	**3.18**	3.00
40+ (*n*=92)	4.75	**4.05**	**3.83**	3.33	**3.35**	3.09
Gender						
Men (*n*=171)	**4.67**	3.82	3.71	**3.08**	**3.12**	**2.90**
Women (*n*=116)	**4.77**	3.79	3.71	**3.34**	**3.26**	**3.12**

Notes: 1. Numbers in bold denote statistically significant differences within subgroups for a specific work value, as found in t-tests and analyses of variance. For example, executives rated organizational beliefs higher than did lower-level managers, while the latter group rated participation and Marxist-related beliefs higher. Significant differences were at the .05 level. Exceptions were Marxist-related beliefs for managerial level, and leisure ethic for gender, which were significant at the .10 level.

2. Standard deviations and alpha reliability coefficients for the total sample are: humanistic (.34 SD, .64 alpha), organizational (.66, .72), work ethic (.58, .43), participation (.90, .58), leisure ethic (.70, .66), and Marxist (.61, .45).

3. In addition to the above findings, analyses of variance found a significant 3-way interaction for participation, such that women over age 40 in nonexecutive managerial positions were the strongest reporters of worker participation in decision making.

Source: Adapted from Sheila M. Puffer, Daniel J. McCarthy, and Alexander I. Naumov, "Russian Managers' Beliefs about Work: Beyond the Stereotypes," *Journal of World Business,* vol. 32, no. 3, 1997, p. 263.

Drawing together the findings of the study, the researchers have pointed out the importance of Westerners going beyond the stereotypes of Russian managers and learning more about the latters' beliefs, so that it is possible to be more effective in working with them as both employees as well as joint venture partners. Quite obviously, assuming that Russian managers are strict adherents of Theory X may be a common assumption, but it may also be an erroneous one.

These philosophic assumptions of both the Chinese and Russian managers help to dictate the leadership approach that is used. They most easily are seen in behaviors used by managers, such as giving orders, getting and giving feedback, and creating an overall climate within which the work will be done.

Leadership Behaviors and Styles

Leader behaviors can be translated into three commonly recognized styles: (1) authoritarian; (2) paternalistic; and (3) participative. **Authoritarian leadership** is the use of work-centered behavior that is designed to ensure task accomplishment. As shown in Figure 14-1, this leader behavior typically involves the use of one-way communication from manager to subordinate. The focus of attention usually is on work progress, work procedures, and roadblocks that are preventing goal attainment. Although this leadership style often is effective in handling crises, some leaders employ it as their primary style regardless of the situation. It also is widely used by Theory X managers, who believe that a continued focus on the task is compatible with the kind of people they are dealing with.

Authoritarian leadership
The use of work-centered behavior designed to ensure task accomplishment.

Figure 14–1

**Leader-
Subordinate
Interactions**

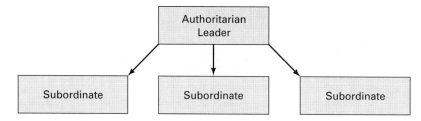

One-way downward flow of information and influence from authoritarian leader
to subordinates.

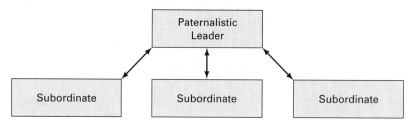

Continual interaction and exchange of information and influence between leader
and subordinates.

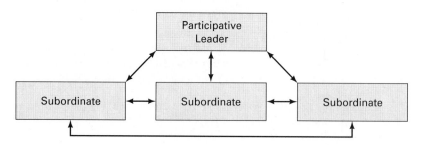

Continual interaction and exchange of information and influence between leader
and subordinates.
Source: Adapted from Richard M. Hodgetts, *Modern Human Relations at Work,*
7th ed. (Hinsdale, IL: Dryden, 1999), p. 264.

Paternalistic leadership
The use of work-centered
behavior coupled with a protective employee-centered
concern.

Participative leadership
The use of both a work- or
task-centered and people-
centered approach to leading
subordinates.

   Paternalistic leadership uses work-centered behavior coupled with a protective
employee-centered concern. This leadership style can be best summarized by the statement, "work hard and the company will take care of you." This approach was described
in Figure 13-5 and perhaps is best supported by cultures such as those found in Japan.
Paternalistic leaders expect everyone to work hard; in turn, the employees will be guaranteed employment and given security benefits such as medical and retirement programs.
Paternalistic leaders often are referred to as "soft" Theory X leaders because of their
strong emphasis on strictly controlling their employees coupled with concern for their
welfare. They often treat their employees as strict but caring parents would their children.
   One way of contrasting authoritative and paternalistic leaders is in terms of Likert's
management systems or leadership styles, as presented in Table 14-3. As shown, an
authoritarian leader is characterized by Likert's system 1, and a paternalistic leader is
characterized by system 2.
   Participative leadership is the use of both a work-centered and people-centered
approach. Participative leaders typically encourage their people to play an active role in
assuming control of their work, and authority commonly is highly decentralized. In terms
of Likert's four systems shown in Table 14-3, participative leaders are characterized by
system 3. (Likert's system 4 leaders are fully democratic and go beyond the participative

Table 14-3
Likert's Systems or Styles of Leadership

Leadership Characteristic	System 1 (Exploitive Autocratic)	System 2 (Benevolent Autocratic)	System 3 (Participative)	System 4 (Democratic)
Leadership processes used (extent to which superiors have confidence and trust in subordinates)	Have no confidence and trust in subordinates	Have condescending confidence and trust, such as master has in servant	Substantial but not complete confidence and trust, still wish to keep control of decisions	Complete confidence and trust in all matters
Character of motivational forces (underlying motives tapped)	Physical security, economic needs, and some use of the desire for status	Economic needs and moderate use of ego motives (e.g., desire for status, affiliation, and achievement)	Economic needs and considerable use of ego and other major motives (e.g., desire for new experiences)	Full use of economic, ego, and other major motives such as motivational forces arising from group goals
Character of communication process (amount of interaction and communication aimed at achieving organization's objectives)	Very little	Little	Quite a bit	Much, with both individuals and groups
Character of interaction influence process (amount and character of interaction)	Little interaction and always with fear and distrust	Little interaction and usually with some condescension by superiors; fear and caution by subordinates	Moderate interaction, often with fair amount of confidence and trust	Extensive friendly interaction with high degree of confidence and trust
Character of decision-making process (at what level in organization are decisions formally made)	Bulk of decisions at top of organization	Policy at top; many decisions with prescribed framework made at lower levels but usually checked with top before action is taken	Broad policy decision at top; more specific decisions of lower levels	Decision making widely done throughout organization, although well integrated through linking process provided by overlapping groups
Character of goal setting or ordering (manner in which usually done)	Orders issued	Orders issued, opportunity to comment may exist	Goals are set or orders issued after discussion with subordinates of problems and planned action	Except in emergencies, goals are usually established by group participation

Source: Adapted from Rensie Likert, *The Human Organization* (New York: McGraw-Hill, 1967). Used with permission.

International Management in Action

Welch Leads the Way

When Jack Welch became chief executive officer of General Electric in 1981 the company had a market value of $12 billion. By 1999 this value had increased to $300 billion making him, in the words of one of today's leading management writers, "the greatest corporate leader of the century." And this accolade is based not just on Welch's success in increasing stockholder value but also on of the way he has helped establish a new, contemporary paradigm for the corporation that is the model for the twenty-first century. What makes Welch so effective in leading an international firm that has almost $100 billion in sales and 276,000 employees in more than 100 countries? People who have studied his approach believe he does a series of critical things well—and these result in outstanding success for this outstanding MNC year after year.[7]

First, Welch believes that effective leaders keep their customers happy. This means doing whatever is necessary to meet client needs. As a result of this emphasis, GE has significantly reduced its bureaucracy and streamlined operations. In the process, the firm has created an "informal" enterprise in which communications flow in an unfettered manner and departments and units cooperate in an almost "boundaryless" enterprise. Result: worldwide teamwork.

Second, closely coupled with the emphasis on customers is consideration of employee satisfaction and cash flow. Welch contends that a leader needs to focus on just three areas of information: customer feedback, employee feedback, and cash flow. If the customers like the goods and services they are receiving, the employees are pleased with their work environment, and there is enough money to keep the doors open—the leader is doing a good job.

Another of Welch's leadership beliefs is that managers have to focus on developing three things in their followers: speed, simplicity, and self-confidence. People have to work faster because speed is critical to worldwide success. Employees also have to learn how to do their job simply and correctly, so that greater speed is possible. Finally, employees have to be confident of their own abilities because this is the ultimate key to success.

In getting his managers to do these things, Welch sets himself up as the model and those who work for him emulate his style and approach. In turn, their subordinates do the same, so that there is consistency of leadership throughout the organization. This also includes the way managers reward their personnel. Welch believes strongly in differentiated pay. People who do the best job should get the biggest rewards. Gone are the days when everyone who did their job well would get a 5 percent raise. As a result:

> Although GE set an overall 4% salary increase as a target last year, base salaries can rise by as much as 25% in a year without a promotion. Cash bonuses can increase as much as 150% in a year, to between 20% and 70% of base pay. Stock options, once reserved for the most senior officers at GE, have been broadly expanded under Welch. Now, some 27,000 employees get them, nearly a third of GE's professional employees. More than 1,200 employees, including over 800 below the level of senior management, have received options that are now worth over $1 million.[8]

Many observers believe that what makes Welch most successful is that his ideas transcend national boundaries. Bureaucracy-bashing is as useful to operations in Toledo, Ohio as they are in Toledo, Spain. Leaders who are successful in achieving high customer and employee satisfaction ratings in Paris, France are as effective as those who do this in Paris, Texas. The criteria by which effective leaders must be measured remains the same and, as a result, Welch's ideas work just as well in Athens, Georgia as they do in Athens, Greece.

style.) Another way of characterizing participative leaders is in terms of the managerial grid, which is a traditional, well-known method of identifying leadership style. As shown in Figure 14-2, participative leaders are on the 9,9 position of the grid. This is in contrast to paternalistic leaders, who tend to be about 9,5 and autocratic leaders, who are more of a 9,1 position on the grid. Participative leadership is very popular in many technologically advanced countries. Such leadership has been widely espoused in the United States, England, and other Anglo countries, and it currently is very popular in Scandinavian countries as well. For example, at General Electric, managers are encouraged to use a participative style that delivers on commitment and shares the values of the firm, which is an

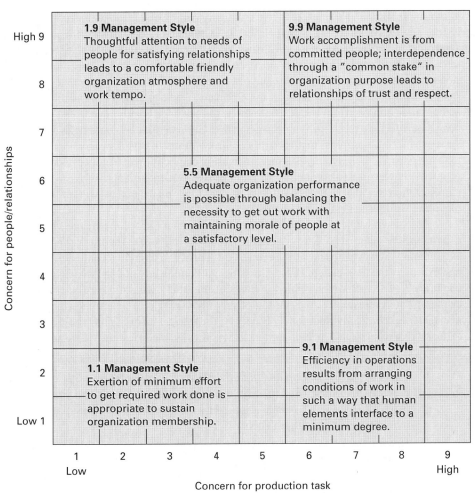

Figure 14–2

The Managerial Grid

Source: Adapted from Robert S. Blake and Jane S. Mouton, "Managerial Facades," *Advanced Management Journal,* July 1966, p. 31.

approach that also is common in these other nations. The accompanying box, "International Management in Action: Welch Leads the Way," provides some additional insights regarding how CEO Jack Welch has put his own brand of leadership on General Electric. The remainder of the chapter gives more details and research results relating leadership styles by country and area of the world.

Leadership in the International Context

How do leaders in other countries attempt to direct or influence their subordinates? Are their approaches similar to those used in the United States? Research shows that there are both similarities and differences, which in many cases are a result of culture.[9] Most international research on leadership has focused on Europe, East Asia, the Middle East, and on developing countries such as India, Peru, Chile, and Argentina.

Attitudes of European Managers toward Leadership Practices

In recent years, much research has been directed at leadership approaches in Europe. Most effort has concentrated on related areas, such as decision making, risk-taking, strategic planning, and organization design, that have been covered in previous chapters. Some of this previous discussion is relevant to an understanding of leadership practices in Europe.

For example, British managers tend to use a highly participative leadership approach. This is true for two reasons: (1) the political background of the country favors such an approach; and (2) because most top British managers are not highly involved in the day-to-day affairs of the business, they prefer to delegate authority and let much of the decision making be handled by middle- and lower-level managers. This preference contrasts sharply with that of the French and the Germans,[10] who prefer a more work-centered, authoritarian approach. In fact, if labor unions did not have legally mandated seats on the boards of directors, participative management in Germany likely would be even less pervasive than it is, a problem that currently confronts firms like Volkswagen that are trying to reduce sharply their overhead to meet increasing competition in Europe.[11] Scandinavian countries, however, make wide use of participative leadership approaches, with worker representation on the boards of directors and high management–worker interaction regarding workplace design and changes.

As a general statement, most evidence indicates that European managers tend to use a participative approach. They do not entirely subscribe to Theory Y philosophical assumptions, however, because an element of Theory X thinking continues. This was made clear by the now-classic Haire, Ghiselli, and Porter study of 3641 managers from 14 countries.[12] (The motivation-related findings of this study were reported in the previous chapter.) The leadership-related portion of this study sought to determine whether these managers were basically traditional (Theory X, or system 1/2) or democratic-participative (Theory Y, or system 3/4) in their approach. Specifically, the researchers investigated four areas relevant to leadership:

1. *Capacity for leadership and initiative.* Does the leader believe that employees prefer to be directed and have little ambition (Theory X), or that characteristics such as initiative can be acquired by most people regardless of their inborn traits and abilities (Theory Y)?

2. *Sharing information and objectives.* Does the leader believe that detailed, complete instructions should be given to subordinates and that subordinates need only this information to do their jobs, or does the leader believe that general directions are sufficient and that subordinates can use their initiative in working out the details?

3. *Participation.* Does the leader support participative leadership practices?

4. *Internal control.* Does the leader believe that the most effective way to control employees is through rewards and punishment or that employees respond best to internally generated control?

Overall Results of Research on Attitudes of European Managers   Responses by managers to the four areas covered in the Haire, Ghiselli, and Porter study, as noted in the last chapter, are quite dated, but these responses still are the most comprehensive available and are relevant to the current discussion of leadership similarities and differences across cultures. The specifics by country may have changed somewhat over the years, but the leadership processes revealed should not be out of date. The clusters of countries studied by these researchers are shown in Table 14-4. Results indicate that none of the leaders from various parts of the world, on average, were very supportive of the belief that individuals have a capacity for leadership and initiative. The researchers put it this way: "In each country, in each group of countries, in all of the countries taken together, there is a relatively low opinion of the capabilities of the average person, coupled with a relatively positive belief in the necessity for democratic-type supervisory practices."[13]

An analysis of standard scores compared each cluster of countries against the others, and it revealed that Anglo leaders tend to have more faith in the capacity of their people for leadership and initiative than do the other clusters. They also believe that sharing information and objectives is important; however, when it comes to participation and internal control, the Anglo group tends to give relatively more autocratic responses than all the other clusters except developing countries. Interestingly, Anglo leaders reported a much stronger belief in the value of external rewards (pay, promotion, etc.) than did any

Table 14–4
Clusters of Countries in the Haire, Ghiselli, and Porter Study

NORDIC-EUROPEAN COUNTRIES	ANGLO-AMERICAN COUNTRIES
Denmark	England
Germany	United States
Norway	
Sweden	DEVELOPING COUNTRIES
	Argentina
	Chile
LATIN-EUROPEAN COUNTRIES	India
Belgium	
France	
Italy	JAPAN
Spain	

of the clusters except that of the developing countries. These findings clearly illustrate that attitudes toward leadership practices tend to be quite different in various parts of the world.

The Role of Level, Size, and Age on European Managers' Attitudes toward Leadership The research of Haire and associates provided important additional details within each cluster of European countries. These findings indicated that in some countries, higher-level managers tended to express more democratic values than lower-level managers; however, in other countries, the opposite was true. For example, in England, higher-level managers responded with more democratic attitudes on all four leadership dimensions, whereas in the United States, lower-level managers gave more democratically oriented responses on all four. In the Scandinavian countries, higher-level managers tended to respond more democratically; in Germany, lower-level managers tended to have more democratic attitudes.

Company size also tended to influence the degree of participative-autocratic attitudes. There was more support among managers in small firms than in large ones regarding the belief that individuals have a capacity for leadership and initiative; however, respondents from large firms were more supportive of sharing information and objectives, participation, and use of internal control. Those from large U.S. companies were most supportive of the first three attitudes, and those from small firms were more supportive of internal control.

There were findings that age also had some influence on participative attitudes. Younger managers were more likely to have democratic values when it came to capacity for leadership and initiative and to sharing information and objectives, although on the other two dimensions of leadership practices older and younger managers differed little. In terms of specific countries, however, some important differences were found. For example, younger managers in both the United States and Sweden espoused more democratic values than their older counterparts; in Belgium, just the opposite was true.

Conclusion about European Leadership Practices Although now quite dated, as already mentioned, data from this classic Haire and associates study do nevertheless show differences in the attitudes toward leadership practices between European managers. In most cases, these leaders tend to reflect more participative and democratic attitudes, but not in every country. In addition, organizational level, company size, and age seem to greatly influence attitudes toward leadership. Because many of the young people in this study now are middle-aged, European managers in general are highly likely to be more participative than their older counterparts of the 1960s and 1970s; however, no empirical evidence proves that each generation of European managers is becoming more participative than the previous one. Also, just because they express favorable attitudes toward participative leadership does not mean that they actually practice this approach, although it is certainly true that boards of directors of U.S. multinationals operating in Europe are becoming more international and that this multicultural mix may indeed promote participative management. More research that actually observes today's European managers' style in their day-to-day jobs is needed before any definitive conclusions can be drawn.

Japanese Leadership Approaches

Japan is well known for its paternalistic approach to leadership. As noted in the previous chapter's Figure 13-5, Japanese culture promotes a high safety or security need, which is present among home country–based employees as well as MNC expatriates. For example, one study examined the cultural orientations of 522 employees of 28 Japanese-owned firms in the United States and found that the native Japanese employees were more likely to value paternalistic company behavior than their U.S. counterparts.[14] Another study found that Koreans also value such paternalism.[15] However, major differences appear in leadership approaches used by the Japanese and those in other locales.

For example, the comprehensive Haire, Ghiselli, and Porter study found that Japanese managers have much greater belief in the capacity of subordinates for leadership and initiative than do managers in most other countries.[16] In fact, in the study, only managers in Anglo-American countries had stronger feelings in this area. The Japanese also expressed attitudes toward the use of participation to a greater degree than others. In the other two leadership dimensions, sharing information and objectives and using internal control, the Japanese respondents were above average but not distinctive. Overall, however, this classic study found that the Japanese respondents scored highest on the four areas of leadership combined. In other words, although these findings are quite dated, they do provide evidence that Japanese leaders have considerable confidence in the overall ability of their subordinates and use a style that allows their subordinates to actively participate in decisions.

In addition, the leadership process used by Japanese managers places a strong emphasis on ambiguous goals. Subordinates are typically unsure of what their manager wants them to do. As a result, they spend a great deal of time overpreparing their assignments. Some observers believe that this leadership approach is time-consuming and wasteful. However, it has a number of important benefits. One is that the leader is able to maintain stronger control of the followers because the latter do not know with certainty what is expected of them. So they prepare themselves for every eventuality. Second, by placing the subordinates in a position where they must examine a great deal of information, the manager ensures that the personnel are well prepared to deal with the situation and all of its ramifications. Third, the approach helps the leader maintain order and provide guidance, even when the leader is not as knowledgeable as the followers.

Two experts on the behavior of Japanese management have noted that salarymen (middle managers) survive in the organization by anticipating contingencies and being prepared to deal with them. So when the manager asks a question and the salaryman shows that he has done the research needed to answer the question, the middle manager also shows himself to be a reliable person. The leader does not have to tell the salaryman to be prepared; the individual knows what is expected of him.

> Japanese managers operate this way because they usually have less expertise in a division's day-to-day business than their subordinates do. It is the manager's job to maintain harmony, not to be a technical expert. Consequently, a senior manager doesn't necessarily realize that E, F, G, and H are important to know. He gives ambiguous directions to his subordinates so they can use their superior expertise to go beyond A, B, C, and D. One salaryman explained it this way: "When my boss asks me to write a report, I infer what he wants to know and what he needs to know without being told what he wants." Another interviewee added that subordinates who receive high performance evaluations are those who know what the boss wants without needing to be told. What frustrates Japanese managers about non-Japanese employees

is the feeling that, if they tell such a person they want A through D, they will never extract E through H; instead, they'll get exactly what they asked for. Inferring what the boss would have wanted had he only known to ask is a tough game, but it is the one salarymen must play.[17]

Differences between Japanese and U.S. Leadership Styles

In a number of ways, Japanese leadership styles differ from those in the United States. For example, the Haire and associates study found that except for internal control, large U.S. firms tend to be more democratic than small ones, whereas in Japan, the profile is quite different.[18] A second difference is that younger U.S. managers appear to express more democratic attitudes than their older counterparts on all four leadership dimensions, but younger Japanese fall into this category only for sharing information and objectives and in the use of internal control.[19] Simply put, evidence points to some similarities between U.S. and Japanese leadership styles, but major differences also exist.[20]

A number of reasons have been cited for these differences. One of the most common is that Japanese and U.S. managers have a basically different philosophy of managing people. Table 14-5 provides a comparison of seven key characteristics that come from the work of William Ouchi, author of the widely recognized *Theory Z*, which combines Japanese and U.S. assumptions and approaches. Note in the table that the Japanese leadership approach is heavily group-oriented, paternalistic, and concerned with the employee's work and personal life. The U.S. leadership approach is almost the opposite.[21]

Another difference between Japanese and U.S. leadership styles is how senior-level managers process information and learn. Japanese executives are taught and tend to use **variety amplification**, which is the creation of uncertainty and the analysis of many alternatives regarding future action. By contrast, U.S. executives are taught and tend to use **variety reduction**, which is the limiting of uncertainty and the focusing of action on a limited number of alternatives.[22] Some specific characteristics of these two approaches are shown in Table 14-6.

When this study of processing information and learning examined the leadership styles used by Japanese and U.S. senior managers, it found that the Japanese focused very heavily on problems while the U.S. managers focused on opportunities.[23] The Japanese were more willing to allow poor performance to continue for a time so that those who were involved would learn from their mistakes, but the Americans worked to stop poor performance as quickly as possible. Finally, the Japanese sought creative approaches to

Variety amplification
The creation of uncertainty and the analysis of many alternatives regarding future action.

Variety reduction
The limiting of uncertainty and the focusing of action on a limited number of alternatives.

Table 14–5
Japanese vs. U.S. Leadership Styles

Philosophical Dimension	Japanese Approach	U.S. Approach
Employment	Often for life; layoffs are rare	Usually short-term; layoffs are common
Evaluation and promotion	Very slow; big promotions may not come for the first 10 years	Very fast: those not quickly promoted often seek employment elsewhere
Career paths	Very general; people rotate from one area to another and become familiar with all areas of operations	Very specialized; people tend to stay in one area (accounting, sales, etc.) for their entire careers
Decision making	Carried out via group decision making	Carried out by the individual manager
Control mechanism	Very implicit and informal; people rely heavily on trust and goodwill	Very explicit; people know exactly what to control and how to do it
Responsibility	Shared collectively	Assigned to individuals
Concern for employees	Management's concern extends to the whole life, business and social, of the worker	Management concerned basically with the individual's work life only

Source: Adapted from William Ouchi, *Theory Z: How American Business Can Meet the Japanese Challenge* (Reading, MA: Addison-Wesley, 1981).

Table 14–6

Japanese and U.S. Senior Management Approaches to Processing Information

Japanese Senior Management Approach (Variety Amplification)	U.S. Senior Management Approach (Variety Reduction)
State a policy that all phenomena are relevant	State a policy that focuses only on relevant issues and sources of information
Require all employees to be identifiers of corporate problems and opportunities	Identify specific employees who will identify problems and opportunities
Seek a large quantity of information from the environment	Seek only high-quality information from the environment
State a desire for the firm to attain an idea—a dream	State a desire for the firm to attain a realistic level—a goal
Focus on creating challenges—barriers to hurdle and problems to solve	Focus on taking advantage of opportunities—holes in the barrier to crawl through
Vitalize people	Direct people

Source: Adapted from Jeremiah J. Sullivan and Ikujiro Nonaka, "The Application of Organizational Learning Theory to Japanese and American Management," *Journal of International Business Studies,* Fall 1986, pp. 130–131. Used with permission.

managing projects and tried to avoid relying on experience, but the Americans sought to build on their experiences.[24]

Still another major reason accounting for differences in leadership styles is that the Japanese tend to be more ethnocentric than their U.S. counterparts. The Japanese think of themselves as Japanese managers who are operating overseas; most do not view themselves as international managers. As a result, even if they do adapt their leadership approach on the surface to that of the country in which they are operating, they still believe in the Japanese way of doing things and are reluctant to abandon it.

Similarities between Japanese and U.S. Leadership Styles

Although differences exist and get considerable attention in both research and the popular media, important similarities in leadership approaches also exist between the Japanese and the Americans. For example, a somewhat dated, but still relevant, study examined the ways in which leadership style could be used to influence the achievement motivation of Japanese subjects.[25] Achievement motivation was measured among a series of participants, and two major groups were created: one consisted of Japanese high achievers, the other of Japanese low achievers. Four smaller groups of high-achieving participants and four more of low-achieving participants then were created. Each high-achieving group was assigned a supervisor who used a different leadership style. The same pattern was used with the low-achieving groups.

In each of the two major clusters (high achievers and low achievers), one group was assigned a leader who focused on performance (called "P supervision" in the study). The supervisor used a 9,1 (high on task, low on people) type of style on the managerial grid (see Figure 14-2, which identifies all the styles on the grid). This supervisor was work-centered, took the initiative in solving problems that impeded performance, and ensured that all rules were followed, exhorting the workers to "hurry up," "work more quickly," and "don't fool around; get to work." The supervisor also compared this group with the others, related how far behind they were, and pressed them to catch up.

In a second group within each major cluster, the supervisor's leadership style focused on maintaining and strengthening the group (called "M supervision" in the study). The individual used a 1,9 (low on task, high on people) leadership style on the managerial grid. The supervisor was open to suggestions, never pushed personal opinions on the workers, and encouraged a warm, friendly environment. This supervisor often said, "Let's be pleasant and cheerful," and "Let's be more friendly." The supervisor also was sympathetic when things did not go well and worked to improve interpersonal relations by reducing tensions and increasing the sociability of the environment.

In a third group within each major cluster, the supervisor focused on both performance and maintenance (called "PM supervision" in the study). This supervisor put pressure on the workers to do their work but, at the same time, offered encouragement and support to the workers. In other words, this supervisor used a 9,9 leadership style from the managerial grid.

In the fourth group within each major cluster, the supervisor focused on neither performance nor maintenance (called "pm supervision" in the study). This supervisor simply did not get very involved in either the task or the people side of the group being led. In other words, the supervisor used a 1,1 leadership style on the grid.

The results of these four leadership styles among the high-achieving and low-achieving groups are reported in Figures 14-3 and 14-4. In the high-achieving groups, the PM (or 9,9) leadership style that emphasized both the task and human dimension was the most effective throughout the entire experiment, and the pm (or 1,1) leadership style was consistently ineffective. The P (or 9,1 [high on task, low on people]) leadership style was the second most effective during the early and middle phases of the study, but it was supplanted by the M (or 1,9 [low on task, high on people]) leadership style in the later phases. Among the low-achieving groups, the P (or 9,1) supervision was most effective. The M (or 1,9) leadership style was the second most effective during the early sessions, but it soon tapered off and produced negative results in later sessions. The PM (or 9,9) style was moderately ineffective during the first three sessions but improved rapidly and was the second most effective by the end of the seventh session. The pm (or 1,1) leadership style was consistently effective until the fifth session, then productivity began to level off.

The results of this study are similar to those that would be expected among high- and low-achieving groups of U.S. managers. In addition, the study showed that high-achieving groups of Japanese tend to be more productive than low-achieving groups.

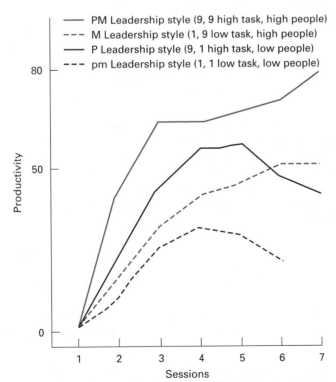

Figure 14–3

Productivity of Japanese Groups with High-Achievement Motivation under Different Leadership Styles

Source: Adapted from Jyuji Misumi and Fumiyasu Seki, "Effects of Achievement Motivation on the Effectiveness of Leadership Patterns," *Administrative Science Quarterly,* March 1971, p. 57. Used with permission.

Figure 14–4

Productivity of Japanese Groups with Low-Achievement Motivation under Different Leadership Styles

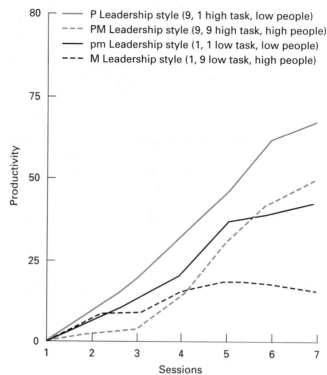

P Leadership style (9, 1 high task, low people)
PM Leadership style (9, 9 high task, high people)
pm Leadership style (1, 1 low task, low people)
M Leadership style (1, 9 low task, high people)

Source: Adapted from Jyuji Misumi and Fumiyasu Seki, "Effects of Achievement Motivation on the Effectiveness of Leadership Patterns, *Administrative Science Quarterly,* March 1971, p. 57. Used with permission.

Thus, this study shows some degree of convergence or similarity between Japanese and U.S. managers regarding the most effective types of leadership styles given the achievement motivation of the group members.

Recent findings support these conclusions and suggest they can be extended to other countries as well. For example, in the United States the Saturn recently has proved to be one of General Motors' most successful new auto offerings. The approach used in managing workers in the Saturn plant is quite different from that employed in other GM plants. Strong attention is given to allowing workers a voice in all management decisions, and pay is linked to quality, productivity, and profitability.[26] Japanese firms such as Sony use a similar approach, encouraging personnel to assume authority, use initiative, and work as a team.[27] Major emphasis also is given to developing communication links between management and the employees[28] and to encouraging people to do their best.[29] Korean firms also are relying more heavily on a 9,9 leadership style. Sang Lee and associates recently reported that among Korea's largest firms, a series of personality criteria are used in screening employees, and many of these directly relate to 9,9 leadership: harmonious relationships with others, creativeness, motivation to achieve, future orientation, and a sense of duty.[30] For example, at the big Korean MNC LG Electronics (formerly Lucky Goldstar), more and more authority now is being delegated down the line to the middle-management ranks.

Another common trend is the movement toward team orientation and away from individualism. The accompanying sidebar, "Global Teams," illustrates this point.

Leadership in the Middle East

Research also has been conducted on Middle East countries to determine the similarities and differences in managerial attitudes toward leadership practices. For example, in a follow-up study to that of Haire and associates, mid-level managers from Arab countries

---

International Management in Action

Global Teams

International leaders now put increasing focus on developing global teams that are capable of overcoming cultural barriers and working together in an efficient, harmonious manner. At Dallas-based Maxus Energy (a wholly owned subsidiary of YPF, the largest Argentinean corporation in the world), teams consist of Americans, Dutch, British, and Indonesians who have been brought together to pursue a common goal: maximize oil and gas production. Capitalizing on the technical expertise of the members and their willingness to work together, the team helped the company to achieve its objective and add oil reserves to its stockpiles—an almost unprecedented achievement. This story is only one of many that help to illustrate the way in which global teams are being created and used to achieve difficult international objectives.

In developing effective global teams, companies are finding there are four phases in the process. In phase one, the team members come together with their own expectations, culture, and values. In phase two, members go through a self-awareness period, during which they learn to respect the cultures of the other team members. Phase three is characterized by a developing trust among members, and in phase four, the team begins working in a collaborative way. How are MNCs able to create the environment that is needed for this metamorphosis? Several specific steps are implemented by management, including:

1. The objectives of the group are carefully identified and communicated to the members.

2. Team members are carefully chosen so that the group has the necessary skills and personnel to reinforce and complement each other.

3. Each person learns what he or she is to contribute to the group, thus promoting a feeling of self-importance and interdependency.

4. Cultural differences between the members are discussed so that members can achieve a better understanding of how they may work together effectively.

5. Measurable outcomes are identified so that the team can chart its progress and determine how well it is doing. Management also continually stresses the team's purpose and its measurable outcomes so that the group does not lose sight of its goals.

6. Specially designed training programs are used to help the team members develop interpersonal, intercultural skills.

7. Lines of communication are spelled out so that everyone understands how they can communicate with the other members of the group.

8. Members are continually praised and rewarded for innovative ideas and actions.

MNCs now find that global teams are critical to their ability to compete successfully in the world market. As a result, leaders who are able to create and lead these interdisciplinary, culturally diverse groups are finding themselves in increasing demand by MNCs.

---

were surveyed and found to have higher attitude scores for capacity for leadership and initiative than those from any of the other countries or clusters reported in Table 14-4.[31] The Arab managers' scores for sharing information and objectives, participation, and internal control, however, all were significantly lower than those of managers in the other countries and clusters reported in Table 14-4. The researcher concluded that his results were accounted for by the culture of the Middle East region. Table 14-7 summarizes not only the leadership differences between Middle Eastern and Western managers but also other areas of organization and management. The researcher noted that

> management should recognize the Middle Eastern executive's desire to have the opportunity to become more of an integral part of the management team. His democratic attitude towards individual's capacity for leadership and, yet, classical attitude towards other management practices (participation, sharing information and internal control) are largely a function of his cultural values, and to a much lesser degree, of western influence in education and work setting and their countries' stage of economic development.[32]

More recent research provides some evidence that there may be much greater similarity between Middle Eastern leadership styles and those of Western countries.[33] In

Table 14–7

Differences in Middle Eastern and Western Management

Management Dimensions	Middle Eastern Management	Western Management
Leadership	Highly authoritarian tone, rigid instructions. Too many management directives.	Less emphasis on leader's personality, considerable weight on leader's style and performance.
Organizational structures	Highly bureaucratic, over centralized, with power and authority at the top. Vague relationships. Ambiguous and unpredictable organization environments.	Less bureaucratic, more delegation of authority. Relatively decentralized structure.
Decision making	Ad hoc planning, decisions made at the highest level of management. Unwillingness to take high risk inherent in decision making.	Sophisticated planning techniques, modern tools of decision making, elaborate management information systems.
Performance evaluation and control	Informal control mechanisms, routine checks on performance. Lack of vigorous performance evaluation systems.	Fairly advanced control systems focusing on cost reduction and organizational effectiveness.
Personnel policies	Heavy reliance on personal contacts and getting individuals from the "right social origin" to fill major positions.	Sound personnel management policies. Candidates' qualification are usually the basis for selection decisions.
Communication	The tone depends on the communicants. Social position, power, and family influence are ever-present factors. Chain of command must be followed rigidly. People relate to each other tightly and specifically. Friendships are intense and binding.	Stress usually on equality and a minimization of difference. People relate to each other loosely and generally. Friendships not intense and binding.

Source: Adapted from M. K. Badawy, "Styles of Mid-Eastern Managers," *California Management Review,* Spring 1980, p. 57. Copyright 1980 by the Regents of the University of California. Reprinted by permission of the Regents.

particular, the observation was made that Western management practices are very evident in the Arabian Gulf region because of the close business ties between the West and this oil-rich geographic area.

This study used a questionnaire survey among 381 managers in the two top levels of 10 multinational organizations that were engaged in either production or marketing in the Persian Gulf region.[34] The questionnaire was designed to determine which of Likert's leadership styles or systems these Middle Eastern managers were using. (See Table 14-3 for Likert's systems or styles.) Organization climate characteristics that were measured included communication flows, decision-making practices, concern for employees, influence on departments, and motivation of employees. The findings showed that almost all managers were operating in a system 3 (participative) style, the same approach that was used by their U.S. counterparts.[35] These findings indicate more similarity between leadership styles of Middle Eastern and Western managers than previously thought. Once again, we see the danger of generalizations and stereotypes in international management.

Leadership Approaches in Developing Countries

Some research has focused on leadership styles in developing countries such as India, Peru, Chile, and Argentina. These studies have examined leadership in terms of Likert's systems or styles (see Table 14-3) and the managerial attitudes toward the four dimensions of leadership practice from the Haire, Ghiselli, and Porter study.

Because of India's long affiliation with Great Britain, leadership styles in India would seem more likely to be participative than those in the Middle East or other developing countries. Haire and associates found some degree of similarity between leadership styles in India and Anglo-American countries, but it was not significant. The study found Indians to be similar to the Anglo-Americans in terms of managerial attitudes toward capacity for leadership and initiative, participation, and internal control. The difference is in sharing information and objectives. The Indian managers' responses tend to be quite similar to those of managers in other developing countries.[36]

Other early research on leadership styles in India found that a highly controlling superior had a positive effect on subordinates' job satisfaction.[37] Other research that focused more on Indian industrial firms, however, indicates that the most effective leadership style used by Indian managers often is a more participative one. One study, for example, found that the job satisfaction of Indian employees increases as leadership style becomes more participative.[38] Still another study reached similar conclusions based on interviews and surveys conducted with managers in a cross-section of industries in northern and western India using a questionnaire that identified Likert systems or styles of leadership.[39] Of the 120 respondents, 14 percent classified their organization as operating under exploitive autocratic leadership (system 1), 63 percent as benevolent autocratic (system 2), and 23 percent as consultative participative (system 3). None viewed their firm as operating under fully democratic leadership (system 4). In addition, this study found that the more autocratic the leadership style (systems 1 and 2), the lower the level of job satisfaction.[40]

These findings from India show that participative leadership style may be more common and more effective in developing countries than has been reported previously. Over time, developing countries (as also shown in the case of the Persian Gulf nations) may be moving toward a more participative leadership style.[41]

A similar situation exists in Peru. There is little reason to believe that managerial attitudes toward leadership practices would have been any different from those reported by Haire and associates for other South American countries, such as Argentina or Chile. The results from the Haire and associates study for those two developing countries were similar to those for India.[42] More recent research, however, has found that leadership styles in Peru may be much closer to those in the United States than was previously assumed.

Stephens conducted research among three large textile plants in an urban area in Peru.[43] These three Peruvian plants were matched with three U.S. plants of similar size in urban settings in the southwest United States. Because these Peruvian and U.S. firms all were in the same industry and faced similar competitive pressures, this study was an excellent opportunity to compare intercultural leadership profiles and identify any significant differences. Using the same four dimensions of leadership practice that were used in the Haire and associates study, Stephens found that the leadership profiles of the Peruvian and U.S. managers were similar. Commenting on the results, he noted that

> there is little reason to conclude that leader styles are much different in Peru than in the U.S. Absolutely, U.S. leaders appear to perceive workers as having more initiative, being more internally motivated, and therefore more capable of meaningful participation. However, the differences for initiative and locus of control were not statistically significant and differences for sharing of information and objectives showed Peruvians to be statistically more inclined to share than U.S. managers. Taken in total, this does not suggest a more participative, democratic leader style in the U.S. and an authoritarian, external control oriented style in Peru.[44]

As in the case of Middle Eastern managers, these findings in South America indicate there indeed may be more similarities in international leadership styles than previously assumed. As countries become more economically advanced, participative styles may well gain in importance. Of course, this does not mean that MNCs can use the same leadership styles in their various locations around the world. There still must be careful contingency application of leadership styles (different styles for different situations); however, many of the more enlightened participative leadership styles used in the United States and other economically advanced countries, such as Japan, also may have value in managing international operations even in developing countries as well as the emerging Eastern European countries.[45]

New Findings Regarding Universalism in Leadership

In recent years researchers have begun raising the question of universality of leadership behavior. Do effective leaders, regardless of their country culture or job, act similarly? A second, and somewhat linked, research inquiry has focused on the question: Are there a host of specific behaviors, attitudes, and values that leaders in the twenty-first century will need in order to be successful? Thus far the findings have been mixed. Some investigators have found that there is a trend toward universalism for leadership; others have concluded that culture continues to be a determining factor and an effective leader, for example, in Sweden will not be as effective in Italy if he or she employs the same approach. One of the most interesting recent efforts has been conducted by Bass and his associates and has focused on the universality and effectiveness of both transformation and transactional leadership.

Transformational leaders
Leaders who are visionary agents with a sense of mission and who are capable of motivating their followers to accept new goals and new ways of doing things.

Transactional leaders
Individuals who exchange rewards for effort and performance and work on a "something for something" basis.

Transformational and Transactional Leadership   **Transformational leaders** are visionary agents with a sense of mission who are capable of motivating their followers to accept new goals and new ways of doing things. **Transactional leaders** are individuals who exchange rewards for effort and performance and work on a "something for something" basis.[46] Do these types of leaders exist worldwide and is their effectiveness consistent in terms of performance? Bass, drawing on an analysis of studies conducted in Canada, India, Italy, Japan, New Zealand, Singapore, and Sweden, as well as the United States, discovered that very little of the variance in leadership behavior could be attributed to culture. In fact, in many cases he found that national differences accounted for less than 10 percent of the results. This led him to create a model of leadership and conclude that "although this model . . . may require adjustments and fine-tuning as we move across cultures, particularly into non-Western cultures, overall, it holds up as having considerable universal potential."[47]

Simply stated, Bass discovered that there was far more universalism in leadership than had been believed previously. Additionally, after studying thousands of international cases, he found that the most effective managers were transformational leaders and they were characterized by four interrelated factors. For convenience, the factors are referred to as the "4 I's" and they can be described this way:

1. *Idealized influence.* Transformational leaders are a source of charisma and enjoy the admiration of their followers. They enhance pride, loyalty, and confidence in their people and they align these followers by providing a common purpose or vision which the latter willingly accept.

2. *Inspirational motivation.* These leaders are extremely effective in articulating their vision, mission, and beliefs in clear-cut ways, thus providing an easy-to-understand sense of purpose regarding what needs to be done.

3. *Intellectual stimulation.* Transformational leaders are able to get their followers to question old paradigms and to accept new views of the world regarding how things now need to be done.

4. *Individualized consideration.* These leaders are able to diagnose and elevate the needs of each of their followers through individualized consideration, thus furthering the development of these people.[48]

Bass also discovered that there were four other types of leaders. All of these are less effective than the transformational leader, although the degree of their effectiveness (or ineffectiveness) will vary. The most effective of the remaining four types was labeled the contingent reward (CR) leader by Bass. This leader clarifies what needs to be done and provides both psychic and material rewards to those who comply with his or her directives. The next most effective manager is the active management-by-exception (MBE-A) leader. This individual monitors follower performance and takes corrective action when deviations from standards occurs. The next manager in terms of effectiveness is the passive management-by-exception (MBE-P) leader. This leader takes action or intervenes in situations only when standards are not met. Finally, there is the laissez-faire (LF) leader. This person avoids intervening or accepting responsibility for follower actions.

Bass has found that through the use of higher-order factor analysis it is possible to develop a leadership model that illustrates the effectiveness of all five types of leaders: I's (transformational), CR, MBE-A, MBE-P, and LF. Figure 14-5 presents this model. The higher the box in the figure and the farther to right on the shaded base area, the more effective and active the leader. Notice that the 4 I's box is taller than any of the others in the figure and it is located more to the right than any of the others. The CR box is second tallest and second closest to the right, on down to the LF box which is the shortest and farthest from the right margin.

Bass also found that the 4 I's were positively correlated with each other, but less so with contingent reward. Moreover, there was a near zero correlation between the 4 I's and management-by-exception styles, and there was an inverse correlation between these four factors and the laissez-faire leadership style.

Does this mean that effective leader behaviors are the same regardless of country? Bass has concluded that this statement is not quite true—but there is far more universalism than people have believed previously. In putting his findings in perspective, he has concluded that there certainly would be differences in leadership behavior from country to country.[49] For example, he has noted that transformational leaders in Honduras would have to be more directive than their counterparts in Norway. Moreover, culture can create some problems in using universal leadership concepts in countries such as Japan, where the use of contingent reward systems is not as widely used as in the west. These reward systems can also become meaningless in Arab and Turkish cultures where there is a great belief that things will happen "if God wills" and not because a leader has decided to carry them out. Yet, even after taking these differences into consideration, Bass contends that universal leadership behavior is far more common than many people realize.[50]

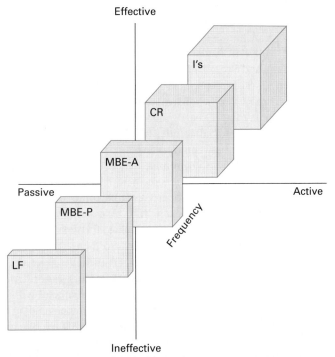

Figure 14–5

An Optimal Profile of Universal Leadership Behaviors

Source: Adapted from Bernard M. Bass, "Is There Universality in the Full Range Model of Leadership?" *International Journal of Public Administration,* 1996, vol. 16, no. 6, p. 738.

I cannot and do not want to dismiss the evidence of systematic differences in beliefs, values, implicit theories, traits associated with leadership, decision styles, paternalism, trait and institutional historical and legal differences that shape leader-subordinate relations. Nevertheless, although the model of transformational or transactional leadership may have needs for adjustments and fine-tuning as we move across cultures, particularly into non-Western, overall, it holds up as having a lot of universal potential. Generally speaking, transformation leadership is more effective than managing-by-exception and managing-by-exception is more effective than laissez-faire leadership. Secondly, transformation leadership augments transactional leadership, it does not replace it. Thirdly, the ideals and implicit leadership theories of leadership people carry around in their heads are more transformational than transactional.[51]

Qualities for Successful Leaders   Another recent research approach that has been used to address the issue of international leadership is that of examining the characteristics that companies are looking for in their new executive hires. Are all firms seeking the same types of behaviors or qualities or, for example, are companies in Sweden looking for executives with qualities that are quite different from those being sought by Italian firms? The answer to this type of question can help shed light on international leadership because it helps focus attention on the behaviors that organizations believe are important in their managerial workforce. It also helps examine the impact, if any, of culture on leadership style.

Tollgerdt-Andersson recently examined thousands of advertisements for executives in the European Union (EU). She began by studying ads in Swedish newspapers and journals, noting the qualities, characteristics, and behaviors that were being sought. She then expanded her focus to publications in other European countries including Denmark, Norway, Germany, Great Britain, France, Italy, and Spain. The results are reported in Table 14-8. Based on this analysis, she concluded that:

> Generally, there seem to be great differences between the European countries regarding their leadership requirements. Different characteristics are stressed in the various countries. There are also differences concerning how frequently various characteristics are demanded in each country. Some kind of personal or social quality is mentioned much more often in the Scandinavian countries than in the other European countries. In the Scandinavian advertisements, you often see many qualities mentioned in a single advertisement. This can be seen in other European countries too, but it is much more rare. Generally, the characteristics mentioned in a single advertisement do not exceed three and fairly often, especially in Mediterranean countries (in 46–48% of the advertisements) no personal or social characteristics are mentioned at all.[52]

At the same time, Tollgerdt-Andersson did find that there were similarities between nations. For example, Italy and Spain had common patterns regarding desirable leadership characteristics. Between 52–54 percent of the ads she reviewed in these two countries stated specific personal and social abilities that were needed by the job applicant. The same pattern was true for Germany and Great Britain where 64–68 percent of the advertisements set forth the personal and social abilities required for the job. In the Scandinavian countries the percentages ranged between 80–85.

Admittedly, it may be difficult to determine the degree of similarity between ads in different countries (or cultural clusters) because there may be implied meanings in the messages or it may be the custom in that country not to mention certain abilities but simply to assume that applicants know that these will be assessed in making the final hiring decision. Additionally, Tollgerdt-Andersson did find that all countries expected executive applicants to have good social and personal qualities. So there was some degree of universalism uncovered in terms of leadership behaviors. On the other hand, the requirements differed from country to country, showing that effective leaders in northern Europe may not be able to transfer their skills to the southern part of the continent with equal results. This led Tollgerdt-Andersson to conclude that multicultural understanding will continue to be a requirement for effective leadership in the twenty-first century. She put it this way: "If tomorrow's leaders possess international competence and understanding of other cultures it will, hopefully, result in the increased competitive cooperation which is essential if European commerce and industry is to compete with, for example, the USA and Asia."[53]

Table 14–8
Qualities Most Demanded in Advertisements for European Executives

Quality	Sweden (N=225)	Denmark (N=175)	Norway (N=173)	Germany (N=190)
Ability to cooperate (interpersonal ability)	25	42	32	16
Independence	22	22	25	9
Leadership ability	22		16	17
Ability to take initiatives	22	12	16	
Aim and result orientation	19	10	42	
Ability to motivate and inspire others	16	11		
Business orientation	12			
Age	10	25		13
Extrovert personality/contact ability	10	8	12	11
Creativity	9	10	9	9
Customer ability	9			
Analytic ability		10		
Ability to communicate		12	15	
High level of energy/drive			12	
Enthusiasm and involvement			14	14
Organization skills				7
Team builder				
Self-motivated				
Flexibility				
Precision				
Dynamic personality				
Responsibility				

Quality	Great Britain (N=163)	France (N=164)	Italy (N=132)	Spain (N=182)
Ability to cooperate (interpersonal ability)	7	9	32	18
Independence			16	4
Leadership ability	10		22	16
Ability to take initiatives			10	8
Aim and result orientation	5			2
Ability to motivate and inspire others		9	26	20
Business orientation				8
Age		12	46	34
Extrovert personality/contact ability				
Creativity	5			4
Customer ability				2
Analytic ability			10	
Ability to communicate	23			8
High level of energy/drive	8			20
Enthusiasm and involvement				
Organization skills		6	12	12
Team builder	10	5		
Self-motivated	10			
Flexibility				2
Precision		7		
Dynamic personality		6		6
Responsibility				10

Note: The qualities most demanded in Swedish, Danish, Norwegian, German, British, French, Italian, and Spanish advertisements for executives are expressed in percentage terms. N = total number of advertisements analyzed in each country. Each entry represents the percentage of the total advertisements requesting by each quality.

Source: Adapted from Ingrid Tollgerdt-Andersson, "Attitudes, Values and Demands on Leadership—A Cultural Comparison among Some European Countries," in Pat Joynt and Malcolm Warner (eds.), *Managing across Cultures* (London: International Thomson Business Press, 1996), p. 173.

The World of Business Week Revisited

As seen in the opening news story, the leadership challenges facing Noel Goutard of the French-based MNC are many and diverse. He is going to have to coordinate the activities of the auto supply operations from Europe to North America to Asia and do so in an efficient and effective manner. At the same time, the material presented in this chapter can indeed be of value in his role as a leader. In particular, he will need to adjust his style to meet the demands of different worldwide managers with whom he interacts. In linking the chapter material to Goutard's challenges, begin by briefly reviewing the opening story and the major chapter concepts. Then answer these question: Using the managerial grid in Figure 14-2 as the point of reference, what type of leadership style will Goutard need to use to effectively meet the competition? Will he have to be a transformational leader if he hopes to succeed in these efforts or can he accomplish his objectives while using one of the other leadership styles illustrated in Figure 14-5? Why or why not? Finally, what types of behaviors, qualities, and characteristics do you think Goutard will need to have in his senior level staff, if the company is to be successful? Is his style going to be similar from country to country or will it be significantly influenced by each nation's culture?

Summary of Key Points

1. Leadership is a complex and controversial process that can be defined as influencing people to direct their efforts toward the achievement of some particular goal or goals. Two areas warrant attention as a foundation for the study of leadership in an international setting; philosophical assumptions about people in general, and leadership styles. The philosophical foundation is heavily grounded in Douglas McGregor's Theories X and Y. Leadership styles relate to how managers treat their subordinates and incorporate authoritarian, paternalistic, and participative approaches. These styles can be summarized in terms of Likert's management systems or styles (systems 1 through 4) and the managerial grid (1,1 through 9,9).

2. The attitudes of European managers toward dimensions of leadership practice, such as the capacity for leadership and initiative, sharing information and objectives, participation, and internal control, were examined in a classic study by Haire, Ghiselli, and Porter. They found that Europeans, as a composite, had a relatively low opinion of the capabilities of the average person coupled with a relatively positive belief in the necessity for participative leadership styles. The study also found that these European managers' attitudes were affected by hierarchical level, company size, and age. Overall, however, European managers espouse a participative leadership style.

3. The Japanese managers in the Haire and associates study had a much greater belief in the capacity of subordinates for leadership and initiative than managers in most other countries. The Japanese managers

also expressed a more favorable attitude toward a participative leadership style. In terms of sharing information and objectives and using internal control, the Japanese responded above average but were not distinctive. In a number of ways, Japanese leadership styles differed from those of U.S. managers. Company size and age of the managers are two factors that seem to affect these differences. Other reasons include the basic philosophy of managing people, how information is processed, and the high degree of ethnocentrism by the Japanese. However, some often overlooked similarities are important, such as how effective Japanese leaders manage high-achieving and low-achieving subordinates.

4. Leadership research in the Middle East traditionally has stressed the basic differences between Middle Eastern and Western management styles. More recent research, however, shows that many managers in multinational organizations in the Persian Gulf region operate in a Western-oriented Likert system 3 (participative) style. Such findings indicate that there may be more similarities of leadership styles between Western and Middle Eastern parts of the world than has previously been assumed.

5. Leadership research also has been conducted among managers in developing countries, such as India, Peru, Chile, and Argentina. These studies show that Likert's system 3 (participative) leadership styles are more in evidence than traditionally has been assumed. Although there always will be important differences in styles of leadership between various parts of the world, participative leadership styles may

become more prevalent as countries develop and become more economically advanced.

6. In recent years there have been research efforts that focused on the topic of universalism in the leadership process. Bass has found that there is a great deal of similarity from culture to culture and transformational leaders, regardless of culture, tend to be the most effective. At the same time, however, he has found

that culture continues to be a mitigating factor. This same conclusion has been reached by research focused on the qualities needed in new managers. The qualities that are demanded by companies in Scandinavia, for example, are not the same as those required by firms in Italy. So, at least for the time being, research indicates that effective leader behaviors are less universal and more culturally driven.

Key Terms

authoritarian leadership
leadership
participative leadership
paternalistic leadership

Theory X manager
Theory Y manager
transactional leader

transformational leader
variety amplification
variety reduction

Review and Discussion Questions

1. Using the results of the classic Haire and associates study as a basis for your answer, compare and contrast managers' attitudes toward leadership practices in Nordic-European and Latin-European countries. (The countries in these clusters are identified in Table 14-4.)

2. Is there any relationship between company size and the attitude toward participative leadership styles by European managers?

3. Using the Haire and associates study results and other supporting data, determine what Japanese managers believe about their subordinates. How are these beliefs similar to those of U.S. and European managers? How are these beliefs different?

4. A U.S. firm is going to be opening a subsidiary in Japan within the next 6 months. What type of leadership style does research show to be most effective when leading high-achieving Japanese? Low-achieving Japanese? How are these results likely to affect the way that U.S. expatriates should lead their Japanese employees?

5. A British firm is in the process of setting up operations in the Middle East Gulf States. What Likert system or style of leadership do managers in this region seem to use? Is this similar to that used by Western managers?

6. What do U.S. managers need to know about leading in the international arena? Identify and describe three important guidelines that can be of practical value.

7. Is effective leadership behavior universal or does it vary from culture to culture? Explain.

Internet Exercise: Taking a Closer Look

Over the last decade, one of the most successful global firms has been General Electric. In the International Management in Action box in this chapter, some of the basic leadership ideas of the company's CEO, Jack Welch, were described. Now we are going to take a closer look at the firm and the role of leadership in its success. Go to the company's web site at **www.ge.com** and review its latest annual report. Pay close attention to the MNC's international operations and to its product lines. Also read about the new members on the board of directors and look through the information on the company's six sigma program. Then, aware of what GE is doing worldwide as well as in regard to its quality efforts, answer these questions: On how many continents does the company currently do business? Based on this answer, is there one leadership style that will work best for the company or is it going to have to choose managers on a country-by-country basis? Additionally, if there is no one universal style that is best, how can Jack Welch effectively lead so diverse a group of worldwide managers? In what way would an understanding of the managerial grid be useful in explaining leadership behaviors at GE? Finally, if GE were advertising for new managers in England, Italy, and Japan, what qualities would you expect them to be seeking in these managers? Would there be a universal list or would it be different on a country-by-country basis?

Germany

A unified Germany has become a major event of modern times. Although problems remain, Germany remains a major economic power in the world. The single Germany is big but still only about the size of the state of Nevada in the United States, and with a population of about 84 million, Germany has about three times the population of California. In addition, the one Germany still is only 50 percent of the economic size of Japan and 20 percent that of the United States. Because Germany has rebuilt almost from the ground up since World War II, however, many feel that Germany, along with Japan, is an economic miracle of modern times. Unified Germany's GDP is behind that of both the United States and Japan, but Germany exports more than Japan, its gross investment as a percent of GDP is higher than that of the United States, and its average compensation with benefits to workers is higher than that of the United States or Japan. It is estimated that Germany has direct control of about one-fourth of Western Europe's economy, which gives it considerable power in Europe. The German people are known for being thrifty, hardworking, and obedient to authority. They love music, dancing, good food and beer, and fellowship. The government is a parliamentary democracy headed by a chancellor.

For the last 13 years the Wiscomb Company has held a majority interest in a large retail store in Bonn. The store has been very successful and also has proved to be an excellent training ground for managers whom the company wanted to prepare for other overseas assignments. First, the managers would be posted to the Bonn store and, then, after 3 or 4 months of international seasoning, they would be sent on to other stores in Europe. Wiscomb has holdings in the Netherlands, Luxembourg, and Austria. The Bonn store has been the primary training ground because it was the first one the company had in Europe, and the training program was created with this store in mind.

A few months ago, the Wiscomb management and its German partners decided to try a new approach to selling. The plan called for some young U.S. managers to be posted to the Bonn store for a 3-year tour while some young German managers were sent stateside. Both companies hoped that this program would provide important training and experience for their people; however, things have not worked out as hoped. The U.S. managers have reported great difficult in supervising their German subordinates. Three of their main concerns are: (1) their subordinates do not seem to like to participate in decision making, preferring to be told what to do; (2) the German nationals in the store rely much more heavily on a Theory X approach to supervising than the Americans are accustomed to using, and they are encouraging their U.S. counterparts to follow their example; and (3) some of the German managers have suggested to the young Americans that they not share as much information with their own subordinates. Overall, the Americans believe that the German style of management is not as effective as their own, but they feel equally ill at ease raising this issue with their hosts. They have asked if someone from headquarters could come over from the United States and help to resolve their problem. A human resources executive is scheduled to arrive next week and meet with the U.S. contingent.

www.userpage.chemie.fu-berlin.de/addressen/ brd.html

Questions

1. What are some current issues facing Germany? What is the climate for doing business in Germany today?

2. Are the leadership styles used by the German managers really much different from those used by the Americans?

3. Do you think the German managers are really more Theory X–oriented than their U.S. counterparts? Why, or why not?

4. Are the German managers who have come to the United States likely to be having the same types of problems?

An Offer from Down Under

The Gandriff Corporation is a successful retail chain in the U.S. Midwest. The St. Louis-based company has had average annual growth of 17 percent over the last 10 years and would like to expand to other sections of the country. Last month, however, it was made a very interesting offer by a group of investors from Australia. The group is willing to put up $100 million to help Gandriff set up operations Down Under. The Australian investors believe that Gandriff's management and retailing expertise could provide it with a turnkey operation. The stores would be built to Gandriff's specifications, and the entire operation would be run by Gandriff. The investors would receive 75 percent of all profits until they recovered their $100 million plus an annual return of 10 percent. At this point the division of profits will then became 50–50.

Gandriff management likes the idea but feels there is a better chance for higher profit if they were to set up operations in Europe. The growth rate in European countries, it is felt, will be much better than that in Australia. The investors, all of whom are Australian, are sympathetic and have promised Gandriff that they will invest another $100 million in Europe, specifically England, France, and Germany, within 3 years if Gandriff agrees to first set up

and get an Australian operation running. The U.S. firm believes this would be a wise move but is delaying a final decision, because it still is concerned about the ease with which it can implement its current approach in foreign markets. In particular, the management is concerned as to whether the leadership style used in the United States will be successful in Australia and in European countries. Before making a final decision, management has decided to hire a consultant specializing in leadership to look into the matter.

Questions

1. Will the leadership style used in the United States be successful in Australia, or will the Australians respond better to another?

2. If the retailer goes into Europe, in which country will it have the least problem using its U.S.-based leadership style? Why?

3. If the company goes into Europe, what changes might it have to make in accommodating its leadership approach to the local environment? Use Germany as an example.

Chapter 15

Human Resource Selection and Repatriation

Objectives of the Chapter

MNCs annually select thousands of people to staff not only their home-country facilities but also their subsidiaries around the world. Who should be selected for a foreign assignment, and how are they handled when they get back? Chapter 15 focuses on potential human resources that can be used for overseas assignments, criteria that are used in the selection process, and how MNCs handle repatriation of the managers back to their country of origin (in most cases, home-country managers are returning to headquarters or to local operations). The specific objectives of this chapter are:

1. IDENTIFY the three basic sources that MNCs can tap in filling management vacancies in overseas operations.

2. SET FORTH some of the most common selection criteria used in identifying the best people for overseas assignments.

3. DESCRIBE the selection procedures used in making the final decisions on the part of both the organization and the individual manager.

4. DISCUSS the reasons for people's returning from overseas assignments and present some of the strategies used in ensuring a smooth transition back into the local operation.

BusinessWeek

The World of Business Week:

It's Gonna Get Ugly

The emerging-markets crisis has settled in for an extended stay. Around the world, markets are drying up, prices are contracting, and economic development is slowing. And with the major industrialized nations still putting together a rescue plan, there is no sign of improvement on the horizon.

Much of the U.S. economy remains unscathed, but the deepening crisis has become an immense challenge for American business. "The world economic crisis is front and center of what we're thinking about," says General Motors Chairman and Chief Executive John F. Smith Jr.

Radical Moves

What are U.S. companies doing to cope? Surprisingly few of them are pulling back from foreign markets. Three or four years from now, overseas markets will again provide the best growth potential, executives say. In the meantime, they are trying to preserve profits—using measures usually reserved for domestic recessions, including layoffs and reductions in capital spending.

A prime example is 3M. For years, it counted on global markets to produce double-digit earnings growth. But 3M's sales, whacked by softness in Asia and the strong dollar, fell 1% in the first half, while profits declined 5%. So on Aug. 27, Chief Executive Livo D. DeSimone launched 3M's most radical

restructuring in two decades. The company is laying off 6% of its workforce, exiting marginal businesses, and taking a pretax charge of up to $500 million.

Similarly, on Sept. 22, Crown Cork & Seal Co. said it would slash 7% of its workforce, cut capital spending, and buy back shares. And the pain is spreading to financial services: Citicorp and Travelers Group Inc. will cut jobs after their planned merger, which won U.S. regulatory approval Sept. 23. Wall Street is bracing for other layoffs as traders tally emerging-markets losses. Already, corporate layoffs are 37% ahead of 1997, say outplacement specialists Challenger, Gray & Christmas Inc.

To be sure, not every industry is scaling back—or needs to. "We're having the best year in 20 years," says David Seiders, chief economist for the National Association of Homebuilders. Interest rates are low, and the Asian crisis has reduced lumber prices, he notes.

And virtually everyone still sees enormous opportunities in emerging markets long-term. Short-term, some companies are trimming their sails. On Aug. 20, Federal Express Corp. announced that it would put its Asian expansion plans on hold. And Polaroid Corp. recently stopped all of its shipments to Russia.

Still, retreat is the exception. At Corning Inc., the Asian recession and the weak yen have cut prices for the company's core product by 30%, says CEO Robert G. Ackerman. "But we're not backing down," he says. "Our strategy is to fight like hell." To cut costs, Ackerman has instead reduced Corning's

salaried head count by some 600, or 10%. Indeed, some multinationals, such as Wal-Mart Stores Inc., see this as an ideal opportunity. Wal-Mart remains "committed to being more of a presence in [Latin] markets," says CEO David Glass. "What we are learning is how to operate in volatile economies."

Indeed, the crisis is teaching executives to view globalization more warily. "Many U.S. executives were too naive," says Harvard business school professor Rosa-beth Moss Kanter. "Asia and China were really overhyped." Going forward, companies will have to be far more realistic about the promise—and peril—of emerging markets.

www.macweb.acs.usm.maine.edu/ economics/intl_pagehtml

The opening news story points out the economic problems that have plagued emerging economies in recent years. In this crisis environment, many MNCs such as 3M, Crown Cork & Seal, Citicorp and Travelers Group mentioned in the article are cutting back on their workforces—they are downsizing because of the downturn in their Asian markets. This chapter is on human resource selection of expatriates and repatriation when they return. In a downsizing environment, there are repercussions for both selection and repatriation.

Specially, if people are being laid off because of a downturn in overseas markets, this will also directly affect the needs to send over expats to these countries. However, those that are selected may feel grateful to have a job at all and thus it will be easier to recruit existing employees for overseas assignments. On the repatriation side, those currently on an overseas assignment will be hearing about the cutbacks back home and experience even more apprehension than usual about their future. In other words, both selection and repatriation are complicated by the changing environment such as depicted in the *Business Week* article. This chapter will provide the background for dealing with these international human resource challenges.

Sources of Human Resources

There are four basic sources that MNCs can tap for positions: (1) home-country nationals; (2) host-country nationals; (3) third-country nationals; and (4) inpatriates. The following sections analyze each of these major sources.

Home-Country Nationals

Home-country nationals
Expatriate managers who are citizens of the country where the multinational corporation is headquartered.

Expatriates
Those who live and work away from their home country. They are citizens of the country where the multinational corporation is headquartered.

Home-country nationals are managers who are citizens of the country where the MNC is headquartered. In fact, sometimes the term "headquarters nationals" is used. These managers commonly are called **expatriates**, or simply "expats," which refers to those who live and work away from their home country. Historically, MNCs have staffed key positions in their foreign affiliates with home-country nationals or expatriates.[1] Based on research in U.S., European, and Japanese firms, Rosalie Tung found that U.S. and European firms used home-country nationals in less-developed regions but preferred host-country nationals in developed nations. The Japanese, however, made considerably more use of home-country personnel in all geographic areas, especially at the middle- and upper-level ranks.[2]

There are a variety of reasons for using home-country nationals.[3] Tung found that the most common reason for using home-country nationals (given by 70 percent of the respondents) was to start up operations. MNCs prefer to have their own people launch a new venture. The second most common reason (cited by 68 percent of the respondents) was that the home-country people had the necessary technical expertise. Other reasons for using home-country nationals include

> the desire to provide the company's more promising managers with international experience to equip them better for more responsible positions; the need to maintain and facilitate organizational coordination and control; the unavailability of managerial talent in the host country; the company's view of the foreign operation as short lived; the host country's multiracial population, which might mean that selecting a manager of either race would result in political or social problems; the company's conviction that it must maintain a foreign image in the host country; and the belief of some companies that a home country manager is the best person for the job.[4]

In recent years, however, there has been a trend away from using home-country nationals. This is true even among Japanese firms, which long preferred to employ expats and were reluctant to allow local nationals a significant role in subsidiary management. Beamish and Inkpen recently conducted an analysis of over 3,200 Japanese subsidiaries and found that the percentage of expats in larger units has been declining steadily over the last four decades.[5] Table 15-1 shows the precise breakdown. What has caused this? Four reasons for the declining use of Japanese expats have been cited. First, as the number of Japanese subsidiaries worldwide have increased, it has become more difficult to find the requisite number of qualified expats to handle these assignments. Second, there are a growing number of effective local managers that make it no longer necessary to rely as heavily on expats. Third, the high cost of keeping expats overseas is having a strong negative effect on company profits. Fourth, Japanese human resource management policies

Table 15–1						
Number of Japanese Expatriates per Subsidiary by Subsidiary Entry Date						
	Number of Japanese Expatriate Managers					
When Subsidiary Was Started	**0**	**1–2**	**3–5**	**6–10**	**over 10**	**Number of Subsidiaries**
pre-1960	5 10.6%	9 19.1%	8 17.0%	8 17.0%	17 36.2%	47
1961–1965	11 13.4%	18 22.0%	18 22.0%	19 23.2%	16 19.5%	82
1966–1970	42 19.1%	59 26.8%	49 22.3%	39 17.7%	31 14.1%	220
1971–1975	83 14.1%	164 28.3%	142 24.5%	111 19.1%	80 13.8%	580
1976–1980	53 12.6%	143 34.1%	122 29.1%	60 14.3%	41 9.8%	419
1981–1985	87 17.6%	156 31.6%	109 22.1%	90 18.2%	52 10.5%	494
1986–1990	148 12.4%	406 33.9%	346 28.9%	184 15.4%	113 9.4%	1,197
1991–1993	35 15.6%	85 37.9%	66 29.5%	25 11.2%	13 5.8%	224
All Subsidiaries	**464 14.2%**	**1,040 31.9%**	**860 26.4%**	**536 16.4%**	**363 11.1%**	**3,263**

Note: The first number in each cell is the number of subsidiaries; the second number is the row percentage.

Source: Adapted from Paul W. Beamish and Andrew C. Inkpen, "Japanese Firms and the Decline of the Japanese Expatriate," *Journal of World Business,* vol. 33, no. 1, 1998, p. 40.

are changing and the old "rice paper ceiling" which prevented non-Japanese from being promoted into the upper management ranks of subsidiaries is now beginning to disappear. This latter development, in the United States in particular, is a result of Japanese firms realizing that their American subsidiaries have not been able to compete effectively. Japanese expat managers have been outflanked by their American counterparts. In particular, Japanese managers have not known how to fine-tune products for the U.S. market; did not understand how to tailor market approaches to different customer segments; and were unable to develop the speed, flexibility, and responsiveness needed to compete with the Americans.[6] It is highly likely that MNCs from other countries besides Japan are also following this trend of using local managers in lieu of expats.

Host-Country Nationals

Host-country nationals are local managers who are hired by the MNC. For a number of reasons, many multinationals use host-country managers at the middle- and lower-level ranks: Many countries expect the MNC to hire local talent, and this is a good way to meet this expectation.[7] Also, even if it wanted to staff all management positions with home-country personnel, the MNC is unlikely to have this many available managers, and the cost of transferring and maintaining them in the host country would be prohibitive.

Host-country nationals Local managers who are hired by the MNC.

Although top management positions typically are filled by home-country personnel, this is not always the case. For example, many U.S. MNCs use home-country managers to get the operation started; then they turn things over to host-country managers. However, there are exceptions even to this pattern. An early study found that U.S. managers often were put in charge of subsidiaries in MNCs that were in the process of marketing a product worldwide.[8] As the product was introduced into each new country, however, the local manager was replaced by a home-country manager. Then, when the international effort was completed, host-country managers were again put in charge.[9]

This traditional pattern of managerial positions filled by home- and host-country personnel illustrates why it is so difficult to generalize about staffing patterns in an international setting.[10] An exception would be in those cases where government regulations dictate selection practices and mandate at least some degree of "nativization." In Brazil, for example, two-thirds of the employees in any foreign subsidiary traditionally had to be Brazilian nationals. In addition, many countries exert real and subtle pressures to staff the upper-management ranks with nationals. In the past, these pressures by host countries have led companies such as Standard Oil to change their approach to selecting managers.

In European countries, home-country managers who are assigned to a foreign subsidiary or affiliate often stay in this position for the remainder of their career. Europeans are not transferred back to headquarters or to some other subsidiary, as is traditionally done by U.S. firms. Another approach, although least common, is always to use a home-country manager to run the operation.

U.S. firms tend to rely fairly heavily on host-country managers. Tung has identified four reasons that U.S. firms tend to use host-country managers: (1) these individuals are familiar with the culture; (2) they know the language; (3) they are less expensive than home-country personnel; and (4) hiring them is good public relations. European firms who use host-country managers gave the two major reasons of familiarization with the culture and knowledge of the language, whereas Japanese firms gave the reason that the host-country national was the best-qualified individual for the job.[11] The accompanying box, "International Management in Action: Important Tips on Working for Foreigners," gives examples of how Americans can better adapt to foreign bosses.[12]

Third-Country Nationals

Third-country nationals
Managers who are citizens of countries other than the one in which the MNC is head-quartered or the one in which the managers are assigned to work by the MNC.

Third-country nationals are managers who are citizens of countries other than the one in which the MNC is headquartered or the one in which they are assigned to work by the MNC. Available data on third-country nationals are not as extensive as those on home- or host-country nationals. Tung found that the two most important reasons that U.S. MNCs use third-country nationals were that these people had the necessary expertise or were judged to be the best ones for the job. European firms gave only one answer: The individuals were the best ones for the job.[13]

Phatak reports that U.S. MNCs use third-country nationals only from highly developed countries, and this is the ultimate promotion for this person.[14] Unlike U.S. managers, who commonly are put in a foreign position to gain experience before being routed back to headquarters, the third-country national assigned to head a foreign subsidiary or affiliate will tend to remain there indefinitely.

Third-country nationals (TCNs) more typically are found in MNCs that have progressed through the initial and middle stages of internationalization and now are in the more advanced stages.[15] Figure 15-1 shows that the number of third-country subsidiary managers in the U.S. companies studied was greatest during the stable growth period and into the stage characterized by political and competitive threat. Among European firms, a somewhat different pattern was found. Beginning with the initial manufacturing stage, these European MNCs began using third-country managers and continued to do so until political and competitive threats were faced (stage 6). At this point, as for the U.S. firms, use of third-country managers began to decline; they were replaced by host-country nationals.

A number of advantages have been cited for using TCNs. One is that the salary and benefit package usually is less than that of a home-country national, although in recent years, the salary gap between the two has begun to diminish. A second reason is that the TCN may have a very good working knowledge of the region and/or speak the same language as the local people. This helps to explain why many U.S. MNCs have hired English or Scottish managers for the top positions at subsidiaries in former British colonies such as Jamaica, India, the West Indies, and Kenya. It also explains why successful multinationals such as Gillette, Coca-Cola, and IBM recruit local managers and train them to run overseas subsidiaries.[16] Other cited benefits of using TCNs include:

As the Japanese, South Koreans, and Europeans continue to expand their economic horizons, increased employment opportunities will be available worldwide. Is it a good idea to work for foreigners? Those who have done so have learned that there are both rewards and penalties associated with this career choice. Here are some useful tips that have been drawn from the experiences of those who have worked for foreign MNCs.

First, although most U.S. managers are taught to make fast decisions, most foreign managers take more time and view rapid decision making as unnecessary and sometimes bad. In the United States, we hear the cliché that "the effective manager is right 51 percent of the time." In Europe, this percentage is perceived as much too low, which helps to explain why European managers analyze situations in much more depth than most U.S. managers do. Americans working for foreign-owned firms have to focus on making slower and more accurate decisions.

Second, most Americans are taught to operate without much direction. In Latin countries, managers are accustomed to giving a great deal of direction, and in East Asian firms, there is little structure and direction. Americans have to learn to adjust to the decision-making process of the particular company.

Third, most Americans go home around 5 p.m. If there is more paperwork to do, they take it with them. Japanese managers, on the other hand, stay late at the office and often view those who leave early as being lazy. Americans have to either adapt or convince the manager that they are working as hard as their peers but in a different physical location.

Fourth, many international firms say that their official language is English. However, important conversations always are carried out in the home-country's language, so it is important to learn that language.

Fifth, many foreign MNCs make use of fear to motivate their people. This is particularly true in manufacturing work, where personnel are under continuous pressure to maintain high output and quality. For instance, those who do not like to work under intense conditions would have a very difficult time succeeding in Japanese auto assembly plants. Americans have to understand that humanistic climates of work may be the exception rather than the rule.

Finally, despite the fact that discrimination in employment is outlawed in the United States, it is practiced by many MNCs, including those operating in the United States. Women seldom are given the same opportunities as men, and top-level jobs almost always are reserved for home-office personnel. In many cases, Americans have accepted this ethnocentric (nationalistic) approach, but as Chapter 4 discussed, ethics and social responsibilities are a major issue in the international arena and these challenges must be met now and in the future.

1. In terms of control, these TCN managers, particularly those who have had assignments in the headquarters country, can often achieve corporate objectives more effectively than expatriates or local nationals. In particular, they frequently have a deep understanding of the corporation's policies from the perspective of a foreigner and can communicate and implement those policies more effectively to others than can expats.

2. During periods of rapid expansion, TCNs cannot only substitute for expatriates in new and growing operations, but they offer different perspectives that can complement and expand on the sometimes narrowly focused viewpoints of both local nationals and headquarters personnel.

3. In joint ventures, TCNs can demonstrate a global or transnational image and bring unique cross-cultural skills to the relationship.[17]

Inpatriates

In recent years a new term has emerged in international management—inpatriates. An **inpatriate** is an individual from a host country or a third-country national who is assigned to work in the home country. Even Japanese MNCs are now beginning to rely on inpatriates to help them meet their international challenges. Harvey and Buckley recently reported that:

Inpatriate
An individual from a host country or a third-country national who is assigned to work in the home country.

Figure 15–1

MNC Internationalization

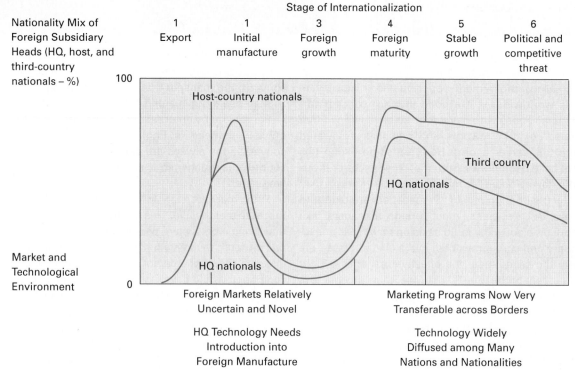

Source: Lawrence G. Franco, "Who Manages Multinational Enterprises?" *California Management Review,* Summer 1973, p. 33. Copyright © 1973 by the Regents of the University of California. Reprinted by permission of the Regents.

The Japanese are reducing their unicultural orientation in their global businesses. Yoichi Morishita, president of Matsushita, has ordered that top management must reflect the cultural diversity of the countries where Matsushita does business. Sony sells 80 percent of its products overseas and recently recognized the need to become multicultural. It has appointed two foreigners to its board of directors and has plans to hire host-country nationals who are to be integrated into the top management of the parent organization. At the same time, the Chairman of Sony has stated that in five years the board-of-directors of Sony will reflect the diversity of countries that are important to the future of the company. Similarly, Toshiba plans to have a more representative top management and board of directors to facilitate long-run global strategies.[18]

This growing use of inpats is helping MNCs better develop their global core competencies. As a result, today a new breed of multilingual, multiexperienced, so called global managers or transnational managers is truly emerging.

These new managers are part of a growing group of international executives who can manage across borders and do not fit the traditional third-country nationals mold. With a unified Europe and other such developments in North America and Asia, these global managers are in great demand. Additionally, with labor shortages developing in certain regions of the world, there is a wave of migration from regions with an abundance of personnel to those where the demand is strongest.[19]

Selection Criteria for International Assignments

International selection criteria
Factors used to choose personnel for international assignments.

Making an effective selection decision for an overseas assignment can prove to be a major problem.[20] Typically, this decision is based on **international selection criteria**, which are factors used to choose international managers.[21] These selections are influenced by the MNC's experience and often are culturally based. For example, Hoecklin has noted that in

Anglo-Saxon cultures, what is generally tested is how much the individual can contribute to the tasks of the organization. In these cultures, assessment centers, intelligence tests and measurements of competencies are the norm. In Germanic cultures, the emphasis is more on the quality of education in a particular function. The recruitment process in Latin and Far Eastern cultures is very often characterized by ascertaining how well the person "fits in" with the larger group. This is determined in part by the elitism of higher educational institutions, such as the *grandes ecoles* in France or the University of Tokyo in Japan, and in part by their interpersonal style and ability to network internally. If there are tests in Latin cultures, they will tend to be more about personality, communication and social skills than about the Anglo-Saxon notion of "intelligence."[22]

Sometimes as many as a dozen criteria are used, although most MNCs give serious consideration to only five or six.[23] Table 15-2 reports the importance of some of these criteria as ranked by Australian, expatriate, and Asian managers from 60 leading Australian, New Zealand, British, and U.S. MNCs with operations in South Asia.

General Criteria

Some selection criteria are given a great deal of weight; others receive, at best, only lip service. A company sending people overseas for the first time often will have a much longer list of criteria than will an experienced MNC that has developed a "short list." For example, in one study, Tung found that personnel sent overseas by MNCs could be grouped into four categories—chief executive officer, functional head, troubleshooter, and operative—and each category had its own criteria for selection.[24] Chief executive officers had to be good communicators, and they had to have management talent, maturity, emotional stability, and the ability to adapt to new environmental settings. Functional heads had to be mature and have emotional stability and technical knowledge about their job. Troubleshooters had to have technical knowledge of their business and be able to exercise initiative and creativity. Operatives had to be mature, emotionally stable, and respectful of the laws and people in the host country. In short, the nature of the job determined the selection factors.

Typically, both technical and human criteria are considered. Firms that fail to consider both often find that their rate of failure is quite high. For example, Tung investigated both U.S. and Japanese companies and found that many U.S. firms had poor success in

Table 15–2
Rank of Criteria in Expatriate Selection

	Australian Managers *n*=47	Expatriate Managers[a] *n*=52	Asian Managers *n*=15
1. Ability to adapt	1	1	2
2. Technical competence	2	3	1
3. Spouse and family adaptability	3	2	4
4. Human relations skill	4	4	3
5. Desire to serve overseas	5	5	5
6. Previous overseas experience	6	7	7
7. Understanding of host country culture	7	6	6
8. Academic qualifications	8	8	8
9. Knowledge of language of country	9	9	9
10. Understanding of home country culture	10	10	10

Note: [a]U.S., British, Canadian, French, New Zealand, or Australian managers working for an MNC outside their home countries.

Source: Raymond J. Stone, "Expatriate Selection and Failure," *Human Resource Planning*, vol. 14, no. 1, 1991, p. 10. Used with permission.

choosing people for overseas assignments; meanwhile, the Japanese firms were quite successful. The primary difference between the two was that the Americans tended to focus most heavily on technical considerations, whereas the Japanese also considered behavioral or relational skills, such as the ability of the managers to deal with clients, customers, superiors, peers, and subordinates.[25] The following sections examine more specific commonly used criteria in choosing overseas managers.

Adaptability to Cultural Change

Overseas managers must be able to adapt to change. They also need a degree of cultural toughness. Research shows that many managers are exhilarated at the beginning of their overseas assignment. After a few months, however, a form of culture shock creeps in, and they begin to encounter frustration and feel confused in their new environment. One analysis noted that many of the most effective international managers suffer this cultural shock.[26] This may be a good sign, because it shows that the expatriate manager is becoming involved in the new culture and not just isolating himself or herself from the environment. Here is an example provided by a North American who was assigned to the Middle East:

> My third day in Israel, accompanied by a queasy stomach, I ventured forth into the corner market to buy something light and easy to digest. As yet unable to read Hebrew, I decided to pick up what looked like a small yogurt container that was sitting near the cheese. Not being one hundred percent sure it contained yogurt, I peered inside; to my delight, it held a thick white yogurt-looking substance. I purchased my "yogurt" and went home to eat—soap, liquid soap. How was I to know that soap came in packages resembling yogurt containers, or that market items in Israel were not neatly divided into edible and inedible sections, as I remembered them in the United States. My now "clean" stomach became a bit more fragile and my confidence waned.[27]

As this initial and trying period comes to an end, an expatriate's satisfaction with conditions tends to increase. In fact, as seen in Figure 15-2, after the first 2 years, most people become more satisfied with their overseas assignment than when they first arrived. Research also shows that men tend to adjust a little faster than women, although both sexes

Figure 15–2

Development of Satisfaction in Host Country Over Time

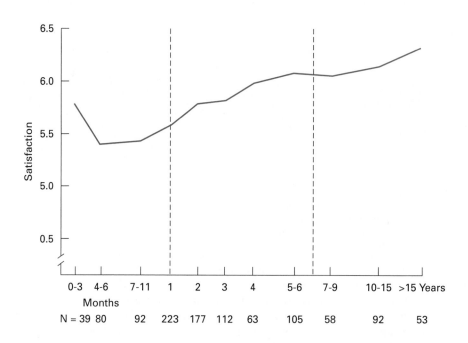

Note: Satisfaction scale: 1 = extremely low; 7 = extremely high.
Source: Ingemar Torbiorn, *Living Abroad* (New York: John Wiley & Sons, 1982), p. 98. Copyright 1982 by John Wiley & Sons. Used with permission.

exhibit a great deal of similarity in terms of their degree of satisfaction with overseas assignments. In addition, people over 35 years of age tend to have slightly higher levels of satisfaction after the first year, but managers under 35 have higher satisfaction during the next 3 to 4 years. In all cases, however, these differences are not statistically significant.[28]

Organizations examine a number of characteristics in determining whether an individual is sufficiently adaptable. Examples include work experiences with cultures other than one's own, previous overseas travel, a knowledge of foreign languages (fluency generally is not necessary), and recent immigration background or heritage. Others include: (1) the ability to integrate with different people, cultures, and types of business organizations; (2) the ability to sense developments in the host country and accurately evaluate them; (3) the ability to solve problems within different frameworks and from different perspectives; (4) sensitivity to the fine print of differences of culture, politics, religion, and ethics, in addition to individual differences; and (5) flexibility in managing operations on a continuous basis despite lack of assistance and gaps in information.

Independence and Self-Reliance

In many overseas assignments, managers must carry out responsibilities and functions at levels higher than those to which they are accustomed. At the same time, managers have fewer people to call on for assistance and guidance. At company headquarters, a large staff of technical advisors may be available to provide assistance and guidance. In foreign assignments, managers often must be more self-reliant. One analysis reported that some of the determinants of independence and self-reliance include prior field experience (domestic or foreign), special project or task force experience, a hobby or avocation that requires a high degree of self-reliance, and a record of extracurricular college activities or community service activities.[29]

Physical and Emotional Health

Most organizations require that their overseas managers have good physical and emotional health. Some examples are fairly obvious. An employee with a heart condition would be rejected for overseas assignment; likewise, an individual with a nervous disorder would not be considered.

The psychological ability of individuals to withstand culture shock also would be considered, as would the current marital status as it affects the individual's ability to cope in a foreign environment. For example, one U.S. oil company operating in the Middle East considers middle-aged men with grown children to be the best able to cope with cultural shock, and for some locations in the desert, people from Texas or southern California make better risks than those from New England.

Age, Experience, and Education

Most MNCs strive for a balance between age and experience. There is evidence that younger managers are more eager for international assignments. These managers tend to be more "worldly" and have a greater appreciation of other cultures than older managers do. By the same token, young people often are the least developed in terms of management experience and technical skills; they lack real-world experience. To gain the desired balance, many firms send both young and seasoned personnel to the same overseas post. As Blue and Haynes put it, "Ideally, that team should be selected for both its youth and its experience, taking into consideration reporting relationships, specific responsibilities, authority and professional judgment as the determinants of whether youth or experience is best suited to a specific job."[30]

Many companies consider an academic degree, preferably a graduate degree, to be of critical importance to an international executive; however, universal agreement regarding the ideal type of degree is nonexistent. As one expert observed:

Companies with highly technical products tend to prefer science degrees. Other firms feel that successful management requires depth, drive, imagination, creativity, and character—and that the type of person exemplified by these traits is more likely to be produced by a liberal arts education. But the overall prize-winning combination seems to be an undergraduate degree combined with a graduate business degree from a recognized business school.[31]

MNCs, of course, use formal education only as a point of departure for their own training and development efforts. For example, Siemens of Germany gives its international management team specific training designed to help them deal more effectively with the types of problems they will face on the job.

Language Training

One recognized weakness of many MNCs is that they do not give sufficient attention to the importance of language training. English is the primary language of international business, and most expatriates from all countries can converse in English. Those who can speak only English are at a distinct disadvantage when doing business in non-English-speaking countries, however. One study asked 1,100 Swedish expatriates how satisfied they were with knowledge of the local language. These Swedish managers expressed particular dissatisfaction with their understanding of Japanese and Middle Eastern languages.[32] In other words, language can be a very critical factor, and international experts have referred to it as "a most effective indirect method of learning about a country . . . as well as the value systems and customs of its people."[33]

Traditionally, U.S. managers have done very poorly in the language area. For example, a recent survey of 1,500 top managers worldwide faulted U.S. expatriates for minimizing the value of learning foreign languages. Executives in Japan, Western Europe, and South America, however, placed a high priority on speaking more than one language. The report concludes that "these results provide a poignant indication of national differences that promise to influence profoundly the success of American corporations."[34]

Motivation for a Foreign Assignment

Although individuals being sent overseas should have a desire to work abroad, this usually is not sufficient motivation. International management experts contend that the candidate also must believe in the importance of the job and even have something of an element of idealism or a sense of mission. Applicants who are unhappy with their current situation at home and are looking to get away seldom make effective overseas managers.

Some experts believe that a desire for adventure or a pioneering spirit is an acceptable reason for wanting to go overseas. Other motivators that often are cited include the desire to increase one's chances for promotion and the opportunity to improve one's economic status. For example, many U.S. MNCs regard international experience as being critical for promotion to the upper ranks. In addition, thanks to the supplemental wage and benefit package, U.S. managers sometimes find that they can make, and especially save, more money than if they remained stateside.

Spouses and Dependents or Work-Family Issues

Spouses and dependents are another important consideration when a person is to be chosen for an overseas assignment. If the family is not happy, the manager often performs poorly. In a survey of 80 U.S. MNCs assessing the reasons for expatriate failure, the number-one reason was the inability of the manager's spouse to adjust to a different physical or cultural environment.[35] For this reason, some firms interview both the spouse and the manager before deciding whether to approve the assignment. This can be a very important decision on the part of the firm because it focuses on the importance of family as an issue. In fact, in a recent survey that she conducted of over 400 expats, Tung found that people had very firm views in this area regarding what they would and would not do. Here is how expats responded to select work-family issues on a scale that ranged from 1 (strongly disagree) to 5 (strongly agree).[36]

I am willing to forgo an important function at home if it conflicts with an important job-related function.	3.37
I would accept an international assignment even if it means that my spouse/partner has to make career sacrifices.	3.07
I place my career above my family.	2.21
I would accept an international assignment even if my family objected to the assignment.	1.83
I would accept an international assignment even if my family will not be able to relocate with me.	1.69

One popular approach in appraising the family's suitability for an overseas assignment is called **adaptability screening**. This process evaluates how well the family is likely to stand up to the rigors and stress of overseas life. The company will look for a number of things in this screening, including how closely knit the family is, how well it can withstand stress, and how well it can adjust to a new culture and climate. The reason this family criterion receives so much attention is that MNCs have learned that an unhappy executive will be unproductive on the job and the individual will want to transfer home long before the tour of duty is complete. These findings have been recently affirmed and extended by Borstorff and her associates, who examined the factors associated with employee willingness to work overseas and concluded that:

Adaptability screening
The process of evaluating how well a family is likely to stand up to the stress of overseas life.

1. Unmarried employees are more willing than any other group to accept expat assignments.

2. Married couples without children at home or those with non-teenage children are probably the most willing to move.

3. Prior international experience appears associated with willingness to work as an expatriate.

4. Individuals most committed to their professional careers and to their employing organizations are prone to be more willing to work as expatriates.

5. Careers and attitudes of spouses will likely have a significant impact on employee willingness to move overseas.

6. Employee and spouse perceptions of organizational support for expatriates are critical to employee willingness to work overseas.[37]

These findings indicate that organizations cannot afford to overlook the role of the spouse in the expat selection decision process. What, in particular, can be done to address their concerns?[38] Table 15-3 provides some insights regarding this answer. Additionally, the table adds a factor that is often overlooked in this process—situations in which the wife is being assigned overseas and the husband is the "other" spouse. While many of the concerns of the male spouse are similar to those of spouses in general, a close look at Table 15-3 shows that some of the concerns of the males are different in terms of their rank ordering.

Leadership Ability

The ability to influence people to act in a particular way, commonly called "leadership," is another important criterion in selecting managers for an international assignment. Determining whether a person who is an effective leader in the home country will be equally effective in an overseas environment can be difficult, however. In determining whether an applicant has the desired leadership ability, many firms look for specific characteristics, such as maturity, emotional stability, the ability to communicate well, independence, initiative, creativity, and good health. If these characteristics are present and the person has been an effective leader in the home country, MNCs assume that the individual also will do well overseas.

Table 15–3

**Activities that Are Important for Expatriate Spouses
(scale: 1–5, 5 = very important)**

Mean Score	Activity
Average	From all respondents:
4.33	Company help in obtaining necessary paperwork (permits, etc.) for spouse
4.28	Adequate notice of relocation
4.24	Predeparture training for spouse and children
4.23	Counseling for spouse regarding work/activity opportunities in foreign location
4.05	Employment networks coordinated with other international networks
3.97	Help with spouse's reentry into home country
3.93	Financial support for education
3.76	Compensation for spouse's lost wages and/or benefits
3.71	Creation of a job for spouse
3.58	Development of support groups for spouses
3.24	Administrative support (office space, secretarial services, etc.) for spouse
3.11	Financial support for research
3.01	Financial support for volunteer activities
2.90	Financial support for creative activities
Average	From male spouses:
4.86	Employment networks coordinated with other international organizations
4.71	Help with spouse's reentry into home country
4.71	Administrative support (office space, secretarial services, etc.) for spouse
4.57	Compensation for spouse's lost wages and/or benefits
4.29	Adequate notice of relocation
4.29	Counseling for spouse regarding work/activity opportunities in foreign location
3.86	Predeparture training for spouse and children
3.71	Creation of a job for spouse
3.71	Financial support for volunteer activities
3.43	Financial support for education
3.14	Financial support for research
3.14	Financial support for creative activities
3.00	Development of support groups for spouses

Source: Adapted from Betty Jane Punnett, "Towards Effective Management of Expatriate Spouses," *Journal of World Business,* vol. 33, no. 3, 1997, p. 249.

Other Considerations

Applicants also can take certain steps to prepare themselves better for international assignments. Tu and Sullivan have suggested the applicant can carry out a number of different phases.[39] In phase one, they suggest focusing on self-evaluation and general awareness. This includes answering the question: Is an international assignment really for me? Other questions in the first phase include finding out if one's spouse and family support the decision to go international and collecting general information on the available job opportunities.

Phase two is characterized by a concentration on activities that should be completed before being selected. Some of these include: (1) conducting a technical skills match to ensure that one's skills are in line with those that are required for the job; (2) starting to learn the language, customs, and etiquette of the region where one will be posted; (3) developing an awareness of the culture and value systems of this geographic area; and (4) making one's superior aware of this interest in an international assignment.

The third phase consists of activities to be completed after being selected for an overseas assignment. Some of these include: (1) attending training sessions provided by the company; (2) conferring with colleagues who have had experience in the assigned region; (3) speaking with expatriates and foreign nationals about the assigned country; and (4) if possible, visiting the host country with one's spouse before the formally scheduled departure.[40]

International Human Resource Selection Procedures

Besides considering the selection criteria discussed so far, MNCs use a number of selection procedures. The two most common are tests and interviews. Some international firms use one; a smaller percentage employ both. Recently, theoretical models containing the variables that are important for adjusting to an overseas assignment have been developed. These adjustment models can help contribute to more effective selection of expatriates. The following sections examine traditional testing and interviewing procedures, then present an adjustment model.

Testing Procedures

Some evidence suggests that although testing is used by some firms, it is not extremely popular. For example, an early study found that almost 80 percent of the 127 foreign operations managers who were surveyed reported that their companies used no tests in the selection process.[41] This contrasts with the more widespread testing these firms use when selecting domestic managers. A number of comments were offered regarding why testing was not used. Here is a sampling of the reasons:

> Tests are too expensive and you have to be a mathematical and psychological wizard to construct and interpret them. What you get for your money and effort is not worth it.

> Testing and predicting success are inseparable partners. We know this and selectors in other firms know this. However, measuring managerial performance in overseas operations is something that is taking time to pinpoint. Thus, until we make progress in measuring success it is our belief that there is no reason why we should become involved in constructing tests for overseas managerial candidates.

> We have used tests in the past and found that they did not improve the selection process. If something does not pay its own way we discard it. Testing did not pay and had to be eliminated as a screening device. We now use the candidate's domestic record and our personal opinions about his adaptability potential. We think that our overseas experience enables us to be excellent judges about a candidate's probability of succeeding abroad.[42]

More recently Tung uncovered similar findings.[43] Only a small percentage of the U.S., Japanese, and Western European MNCs that she surveyed used tests to determine a candidate's technical competence. Things were not much better when it came to relational abilities—only 5 percent of the U.S. firms and 21 percent of the German firms used testing for this purpose, and none of the Japanese firms did. The U.S. firms used a combination of approaches when testing, but the Germans relied most heavily on psychological testing.

Interviewing Procedures

Many firms use interviews to screen people for overseas assignments. One expert notes: "It is generally agreed that extensive interviews of candidates (and their spouses) by senior executives still ultimately provide the best method of selection."[44] Tung's research supports these comments. For example, 52 percent of the U.S. MNCs she surveyed reported that in the case of managerial candidates, MNCs conducted interviews with both the manager and his or her spouse, and 47 percent conducted interviews with the candidate alone. For technically oriented position, 40 percent of the firms interviewed both the candidate and the spouse, and 59 percent conducted interviews with the candidate alone. German MNCs follow a pattern similar to that of U.S. companies. In the case of management positions, 41 percent interviewed both the candidate and the spouse, and 59 percent interviewed the candidate only. For technically oriented positions, these percentages were 62 and 39, respectively. Concerning these findings, Tung concluded:

> These figures suggest that in management-type positions which involve more extensive contact with the local community, as compared to technically oriented positions, the adaptability of the spouse to living in a foreign environment was perceived as important for successful performance

abroad. However, even for technically oriented positions, a sizable proportion of the firms did conduct interviews with both candidate and spouse. This lends support to the contention of other researchers that MNCs are becoming increasingly cognizant of the importance of this factor to effective performance abroad.[45]

An Adjustment Model

In recent years, international human resource management scholars have developed theoretical models that help to explain the factors involved in effectively adjusting to overseas assignments.[46] These adjustment models help to identify the theoretical underpinnings of effective selection of expatriates. Figure 15-3 provides an example of one such adjustment model.

As shown, there are two major types of adjustments that an expatriate must make when going on an overseas assignment. One is the anticipatory adjustment. This is carried out before the expat leaves for the assignment. The other is the in-country adjustment, which takes place on-site.

The anticipatory adjustment is influenced by a number of important factors. One individual factor is the predeparture training that is provided. This often takes the form of cross-cultural seminars or workshops, and it is designed to acquaint expats with the culture and work life of the country to which they will be posted. Another individual factor affecting anticipatory adjustment is the previous experience the expat may have had with the assigned country or those with similar cultures. These two individual factors, training and previous experience, help to determine the accuracy of the expat's expectations.

The organizational input into anticipatory adjustment is most directly related and concerned with the selection process. Traditionally, MNCs relied on only one important selection criteria for overseas assignments: technical competence. Obviously, technical competence is important, but it is only one of a number of skills that will be needed. If the

Figure 15–3   **A Theoretic Model for Explaining International Adjustment of Expatriates**

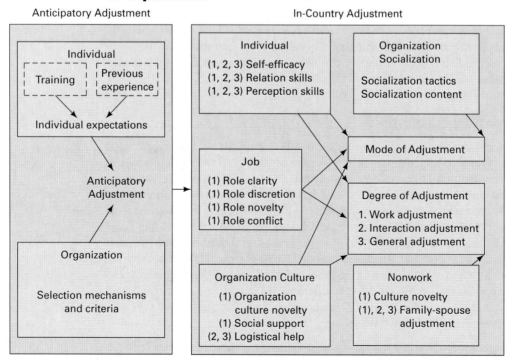

Source: J. Stewart Black, Mark Mendenhall, and Gary Oddou, "Toward a Comprehensive Model of International Adjustment: An Integration of Multiple Theoretical Perspectives," *Academy of Management Review,* April 1991, p. 303. Used with permission.

MNC concentrates only on technical competence as a selection criterion, then it is not properly preparing the expatriate managers for successful adjustment in overseas assignments. Expats are going to go abroad believing that they are prepared to deal with the challenges awaiting them, and they will be wrong.

Once the expatriate is on-site, a number of factors will influence his or her ability to adjust effectively. One factor includes the expat's ability to maintain a positive outlook in the face of a high-pressure situation, to interact well with host nationals, and to perceive and evaluate the host country's cultural values and norms correctly. A second factor is the job itself, as reflected by the clarity of the role the expat plays in the host management team, the authority the expat has to make decisions, the newness of the work-related challenges, and the amount of role conflict that exists. A third factor is the organizational culture and how easily the expat can adjust to it. A fourth input is nonwork factors, such as the toughness with which the expatriate faces a whole new cultural experience and how well his or her family can adjust to the rigors of the new assignment. A fifth and final factor identified in the adjustment model is the expat's ability to develop effective socialization tactics and to understand "what's what" and "who's who" in the host organization.

These anticipatory and in-country factors will influence the expatriate's mode and degree of adjustment to an overseas assignment. As identified in Figure 15-3, these factors cover a wide continuum of considerations. They can help to explain why effective selection of expatriates is multifaceted and can be very difficult and challenging. On the other hand, if all works out well the individual can become a very important part of the organization's overseas operations. McCormick and Chapman recently illustrated this by showing the changes that an expat goes through as he or she seeks to adjust to the new assignment.[47] As seen in Figure 15-4 early enthusiasm often gives way to cold reality and the expat typically ends up in a search to balance personal and work demands with the new environment. In many cases, fortunately, everything works out well. Additionally, one of the ways that MNCs often try to put potential expats at ease about their new assignment is by presenting an attractive compensation package.

Figure 15–4   **The Relocation Transition Curve**

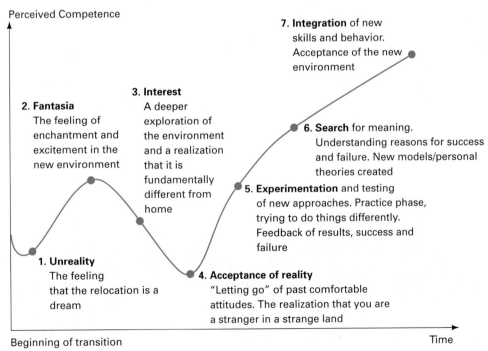

Source: Adapted from Iain McCormick and Tony Chapman, "Executive Relocation: Personal and Organizational Tactics," in Pat Joynt and Malcolm Warner (eds.), *Managing across Cultures: Issues and Perspectives* (London: International Thomson Business Press, 1996), p. 368.

The Compensation Issue

One of the reasons why there has been a decline in the number of expats in recent years is that MNCs have found that the expense can be prohibitive. Reynolds has estimated that, on average, "expats cost employers two to five times as much as home-country counterparts and frequently ten or more times as much as local nationals in the country to which they are assigned."[48] As seen in Figure 15-5, the cost of living in some of the major cities is extremely high and these expenses must be included somewhere in the compensation package.

Common Elements of Compensation Packages

The overall compensation package often will vary from country to country. As Bailey has noted:

> Compensation programs implemented in global organization will not mirror an organization's domestic plan because of differences in legally mandated benefits, tax laws, cultures, and employee expectation based on local practices. The additional challenge in compensation design is the requirement that excessive costs be avoided and at the same time employee morale be maintained at high levels.[49]

There are, however, five common elements in the typical expatriate compensation package. These include base salary, benefits, allowances, incentives, and taxes.

Base Salary Base salary is the amount of money that an expatriate normally receives in the home country. In the United States this was around $175,000 for upper-middle managers in the late 1990s, and this rate was similar to that paid to managers in both Japan and Germany. The exchange rates, of course, also affect the real wages.

Expatriate salaries typically are set according to the base pay of the home countries. Therefore, a German manager working for a U.S. MNC and assigned to Spain would have a base salary that reflects the salary structure in Germany. U.S. expatriates have salaries tied to U.S. levels. The salaries usually are paid in home currency, local currency, or a combination of the two. The base pay also serves as the benchmark against which bonuses and benefits are calculated.

Benefits Approximately one-third of compensation for regular employees is benefits. These benefits compose a similar, or even larger, portion of expat compensation. A number of thorny issues surround compensation for expatriates, however. These include:

Figure 15–5   **Cost of Living in Select Cities**

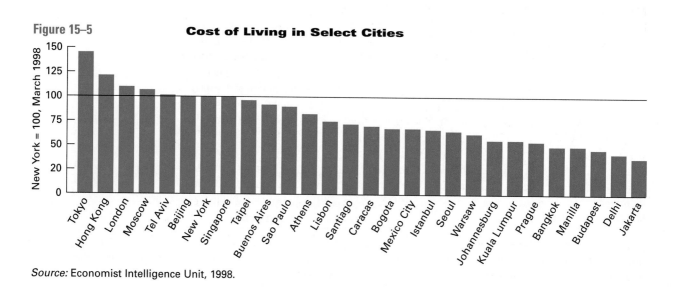

Source: Economist Intelligence Unit, 1998.

1. whether MNCs should maintain expatriates in home-country benefit programs, particularly if these programs are not tax-deductible;

2. whether MNCs have the option of enrolling expatriates in host-country benefit programs and/or making up any difference in coverage;

3. whether host-country legislation regarding termination of employment affects employee benefits entitlements;

4. whether the home or host country is responsible for the expatriates' social security benefits;

5. whether benefits should be subject to the requirements of the home or host country;

6. which country should pay for the benefits;

7. whether other benefits should be used to offset any shortfall in coverage; and

8. whether home-country benefits programs should be available to local nationals.[50]

Most U.S.-based MNCs include expatriate managers in their home-office benefits program at no additional cost to the expats. If the host country requires expats to contribute to their social security program, the MNC typically picks up the tab. Fortunately, several international agreements between countries recently have eliminated such dual coverage and expenses.

Additionally, MNCs often provide expatriates with extra vacation and with special leaves. The MNC typically will pay the airfare for expats and their families to make an annual visit home, for emergency leave, and for expenses when a relative in the home country is ill or dies.

Allowances   Allowances are an expensive feature of expatriate compensation packages. One of the most common parts is a cost-of-living allowance—a payment for differences between the home country and the overseas assignment. This allowance is designed to provide the expat with the same standard of living that he or she enjoyed in the home country, and it may cover a variety of expenses, including relocation, housing, education, and hardship.

Relocation expenses typically involve moving, shipping, and storage charges that are associated with personal furniture, clothing, and other items that the expatriate and his or her family are (or are not) taking to the new assignment. Related expenses also may include cars and club memberships in the host country, although these perks commonly are provided only to senior-level expats.

Housing allowances cover a wide range. Some firms provide the expat with a residence during the assignment and pay all associated expenses. Others give a predetermined housing allotment each month and let expats choose their own residence. Additionally, some MNCs help those going on assignment with the sale or lease of the house they are leaving behind; if the house is sold, the company usually pays closing costs and other associated expenses. Firms such as General Motors encourage their people to retain ownership and rent their houses. In these cases, it is common to find the MNC paying all rental management fees and reimbursing the employees for up to 6 months of rent if the houses are unoccupied.

Education allowances for the expat's children are another integral part of the compensation package. These expenses cover costs such as tuition, enrollment fees, books, supplies, transportation, room, board, and school uniforms. In some cases, expenses to attend postsecondary schools also are provided.

Hardship allowances are designed to induce expats to work in hazardous areas or an area with a poor quality of life. Those who are assigned to Eastern Europe, China, and some Middle Eastern countries sometimes are granted a hardship premium. These payments may be in the form of a lump sum ($10,000 to $50,000) or a percentage (15% to 50%) of the expat's base compensation.

Incentives   In recent years some MNCs have also been designing special incentive programs for keeping expats motivated. In the process a growing number of firms have dropped the ongoing premium for overseas assignments and replaced it with a one-time, lump-sum premium. For example, in the early 1990s over 60 percent of MNCs gave ongoing premiums to their expats. Today that percentage is under 50 percent and continuing to decline.

The lump sum payment has a number of benefits. One is that expats realize that they will be given this payment just once—when they move to the international locale. So the payment tends to retain its value as an incentive. A second is that the costs to the company are less because there is only one payment and no future financial commitment. A third is that because it is a separate payment, distinguishable from regular pay, it is more readily available for saving or spending.

The specific incentive program that is used will vary, and expats like this. Researchers, for example, have found that some of the factors that influence the type and amount of incentive include whether the person is moving within or between continents and where the person is being stationed. Table 15-4 provides some of the latest survey information related to worldwide employer incentive practices.

Finally, it is important to recognize that a growing number of MNCs are beginning to phase out incentive premiums. Instead, they are focusing on creating a cadre of expats who are motivated by nonfinancial incentives.

> More companies are starting to take an entirely different approach, paying *no* premiums to expatriates regardless of where they send them. According to this philosophy, an assignment itself is its own reward. It's an opportunity for an employee to achieve personal and career growth. In some organizations, succession planning for senior-level positions requires international experience. Others view expatriate assignments as a step toward achieving globalization. Companies that subscribe to the philosophy of paying no premiums only consider cost-of-living issues, not motivational rewards, when designing pay packages.[51]

Taxes The other major component of expatriate compensation is tax equalization. For example, an expat may have two tax bills, one from the host country and one from the U.S. Internal Revenue Service, for the same pay. IRS Code Section 911 permits a deduction of up to $70,000 on foreign-earned income. Top-level expats often earn far more than this, however; thus, they may pay two tax bills for the amount by which their pay exceeds $70,000.

Usually, MNCs pay the extra tax burden. The most common way is by determining the base salary and other extras (e.g., bonuses) that the expat would make if based in the home country. Taxes on this income then are computed and compared with the taxes due on the expat's income. Any taxes that exceed what would have been imposed in the home country are paid by the MNC, and any windfall is kept by the expat as a reward for taking the assignment.[52]

Table 15–4
Employer Incentive Practices around the World

MNCs Paying for Moves within Continents				
	Asia	**Europe**	**North America**	**Total**
Type of premium				
Ongoing	62%	46%	29%	42%
Lump sum	21	20	25	23
None	16	27	42	32
MNCs Paying for Moves between Continents				
	Asia	**Europe**	**North America**	**Total**
Type of premium				
Ongoing	63%	54%	39%	49%
Lump sum	24	18	30	26
None	13	21	27	22

Source: Derived from Geofferey W. Latta, "Expatriate Incentives: Beyond Tradition," *HR Focus,* March 1998, p. S4.

Tailoring the Package

Working within the five common elements just described, MNCs will tailor-make compensation packages to fit the specific situation. For example, senior-level managers in Japan are paid only around four times as much as junior staff members. This is in sharp contrast to the United States, where the multiple is much higher.[53] A similar situation exists in Europe, where many senior-level managers make far less than their U.S. counterparts and stockholders, politicians, and the general public oppose U.S.-style affluence. For example, when Daimler-Benz bought Chrysler there was controversy regarding the differences in the executive pay packages. German managers believe that executive pay should be closer to that of the average employee. American companies, on the other hand, reward executives with bonuses and stock options. Here is a contrast between the compensation packages of the chairman and chief executive at both companies at the time of the merger.[54]

	Chrysler Chairman and CEO	Daimler-Benz Chairman and CEO
Salary	$1,612,500	$1,137,300
Bonus	3,000,000	—
Other annual payments (dividends, tax reimbursement)	218,903	—
Other programs (matching payment to savings plan)	77,400	—
Performance shares	1,209,701	—
Options granted (estimate of value)	4,753,000	796,100
Options exercised (granted in previous years)	5,259,600	—
Total	$16,131,104	$1,933,400

These data help pinpoint a thorny problem: Can a senior-level U.S. expat be paid a salary that is significantly higher than local senior-level managers in the overseas subsidiary, or will this create morale problems? This is a difficult question to answer and must be given careful consideration. One solution is to link pay and performance to attract and retain outstanding personnel. For example, at Salomon Brothers, the U.S. investment bank, employees are well paid if they do well and penalized if they do poorly—and this system is acceptable to all concerned. One report noted:

> The result is that in exceptionally good years Salomon's new system appears to offer its employees exceptional returns, but it will be less generous than at present when times are hard. The firm's aim is to make staff behave as if they own the business, rather than merely work for it. It is a big gamble. Some of the firm's most profitable traders may be tempted away by fatter bonuses elsewhere. Alan Howard, one of its top traders in London, left Salomon after the pay deal was confirmed, moving to Japan's Tokai Bank for a two-year package reputedly worth a guaranteed [$7.5 million].[55]

In formulating the compensation package, a number of approaches can be used. The most common is the **balance sheet approach**, which involves ensuring that the expat is "made whole" and does not lose money by taking the assignment. A second, and often complementary approach, is negotiation, which involves working out a special, ad hoc arrangement that is acceptable to both the company and the expat. A third approach is called **localization** and involves paying the expat a salary that is comparable to those of local nationals. This approach most commonly is used with individuals early in their careers and who are being given long-term overseas assignment. A fourth approach is the **lump sum method**, which involves giving the expat a predetermined amount of money and letting the individual make his or her own decisions regarding how to spend it. A fifth is the **cafeteria approach**, which entails giving expats a series of options and then letting them decide how to spend the available funds. For example, if expats have children, they may opt for private schooling; if expats have no children, they may

Balance sheet approach
An approach to developing an expatriate compensation package that is based on ensuring the expat is "made whole" and does not lose money by taking the assignment.

Localization
An approach to developing an expatriate compensation package that involves paying the expat a salary comparable to that of local nationals.

Lump sum method
An approach to developing an expatriate compensation package that involves giving the expat a predetermined amount of money and letting the individual make his or her own decisions regarding how to spend it.

Cafeteria approach
An approach to developing an expatriate compensation package that entails giving the individual a series of options and letting the person decide how to spend the available funds.

Regional system
An approach to developing an expatriate compensation package that involves setting a compensation system for all expats who are assigned to a particular region and paying everyone in accord with that system.

choose a chauffeur-driven car or an upscale apartment. A sixth method is the **regional system**, under which the MNC sets a compensation system for all expats who are assigned to a particular region. Therefore, everyone going to Europe falls under one particular system, and everyone being assigned to South America is covered by a different system.[56]

The most important thing to remember about global compensation is that the package must be cost effective and fair. If it meets these two characteristics, it likely will be acceptable to all parties.[57]

Individual and Host-Country Viewpoints

Until now, we have examined the selection process mostly from the standpoint of the MNC: What will be best for the company? However, two additional perspectives for selection warrant consideration: (1) that of the individual who is being selected; and (2) that of the country to which the candidate will be sent. Research shows that each has specific desires and motivations regarding the expatriate selection process.

Candidate Motivations

Why do individuals accept foreign assignments? One answer is a greater demand for their talents abroad than at home. For example, a growing number of senior U.S. managers have moved to Mexico because of Mexico's growing need for experienced executives. In another case, a U.S. engineering professor quit his job and moved to Japan to learn Japanese and to work in a Fujitsu manufacturing plant, learning how the company operates. Today, he has been promoted into the management ranks and is helping to run a plant back in the United States.[58]

A number of researchers have investigated overall candidate motivations. One early study administered an opinion questionnaire to 13,000 employees of a large electrical equipment manufacturing firm with operations in 46 countries. There were 200 multiple-choice items in the questionnaire, and the instrument was translated into 12 foreign languages to accommodate all groups of people.[59] Fourteen goals were found to have varying degrees of importance. These extended from a desire for training to the need to work for a successful company. Table 15-5 presents a brief description of the 10 most important goals.

Table 15–5
Goal Ranking among Overseas Personnel

Rank	Goal	Questionnaire Wording
1	Training	Have training opportunities (to improve your present skills or learn new skills)
2	Challenge	Have challenging work to do—work that gives you a personal sense of accomplishment
3	Autonomy	Have considerable freedom to adopt your own approach to the job
4	Earnings	Have opportunity for high earnings
5	Advancement	Have an opportunity for advancement to higher-level jobs
6	Recognition	Get the recognition you deserve for doing a good job
7	Security	Have job security (steady work)
8	Friendly department	Work in a department where the people are congenial and friendly to one another
9	Personal time	Have a job which leaves you sufficient time for your personal and/or family life
10	Company contribution	Have a job which allows you to make a real contribution to your company's success

Source: Adapted from David Sirota and J. Michael Greenwood, "Understand Your Overseas Workforce," *Harvard Business Review,* January–February 1971, p. 55.

This study found that the importance of each goal was somewhat influenced by the individual's occupation. Table 15-6 shows this breakdown. The most important objectives related to achievement; the least important related to what the organization gives to its employees.

In drawing together their findings, these researchers grouped the participating countries into clusters: Anglo (Australia, Austria, Canada, India, New Zealand, South Africa, Switzerland, United Kingdom, and United States); Northern European (Denmark, Finland, Norway); French (Belgium and France); northern South American (Colombia, Mexico, and Peru); southern South American (Argentina and Chile); and Independent (Brazil, Germany, Israel, Japan, Sweden, and Venezuela). Based on these groupings, they were able to identify major motivational differences. Some of their findings included:

1. The Anglo cluster was more interested in individual achievement and less interested in the desire for security than any other cluster.

2. The French cluster was similar to the Anglo cluster, except that less importance was given to individual achievement and more to security.

3. Countries in the Northern European cluster were more oriented to job accomplishment and less to getting ahead; considerable importance was assigned to jobs not interfering with personal lives.

4. In South American clusters, individual achievement goals were less important than in most other clusters. Fringe benefits were particularly important to South American groups.

5. Germans were similar to those in the South American clusters, except that they placed a great emphasis on advancement and earnings.

6. The Japanese were unique in their mix of desires. They placed high value on earnings opportunities but low value on advancement. They were high on challenge but low on autonomy. At the same time, they placed strong emphasis on working in a friendly, efficient department and having good physical working conditions.[60]

Another study investigated the reasons why personnel accept overseas positions.[61] The study sampled 135 U.S. xpatriate managers at the upper-middle ranks of three foreign subsidiaries of three major U.S. MNCs. Four major sets of variables explained why people go overseas. The most important reason was the enhancement of one's international business career. This included things such as increased promotion potential, the opportunity to

Table 15–6
Goal Ranking by Occupation

Goal	Average Rank		
	Salespeople	Technical Personnel	Service Personnel
Training	2	1	1
Challenge	1	2	2.5
Autonomy	3	3	7
Earnings	4	4.5	4
Advancement	5	6	5
Recognition	6	4.5	9
Security	10	11	2.5
Friendly department	9	8	8
Personal time	11	7	6
Company contribution	7.5	9.5	10

Source: Adapted from David Sirota and J. Michael Greenwood, "Understand Your Overseas Workforce," *Harvard Business Review,* January–February 1971, p. 56.

improve career mobility, and the opportunity for greater responsibility. The second most important reason was the attraction to overseas assignments. This included the opportunity to go overseas, the desire to live in a particular locale, and encouragement from one's family to take the assignment. The third most important reason was technical competence. The individual had knowledge of the particular job to be done and/or had proven performance or capability in this area of work. The fourth was that the assignment was viewed as necessary for one's career. For example, some candidates felt that all managers who wanted to reach the upper ranks had to have international experience and/or these jobs were necessary in gathering knowledge and experience for future assignments.

Another interesting focus of attention has been on those countries that expatriates like best. The Torbiorn study cited earlier found that the 1,100 Swedish expatriates surveyed were at least fairly well satisfied with their host country, and in some cases were very satisfied. Figure 15-6 reports these findings. In particular, the expatriates were more satisfied in countries that had the same general living standard or level of industrial development as their own. Similar language and religion also were important factors.[62]

Host-Country Desires

Although many MNCs try to choose people who fit in well, little attention has been paid to the host country's point of view. Whom would it like to see put in managerial positions? One study surveyed over 100 host-country organizations (HCOs) in five countries: Germany ($n=38$), England ($n=33$), France ($n=16$), Holland ($n=16$), and Belgium ($n=8$). The respondents were either chief executive officers of the HCO or heads of departments that interacted extensively with expatriate managers heading the subsidiary. Data were collected via a questionnaire survey and a comprehensive interview. The 200-item questionnaire was designed to determine both present and desired personnel policies and patterns of managerial behavior.[63] The findings are presented in Table 15-7.

The results showed that in the main, accommodating the wishes of HCOs can be very difficult. They are highly ethnocentric in orientation. They want local managers to head the subsidiaries; and they set such high levels of expectation regarding the desired characteristics of expatriates that anyone sent by the MNC is unlikely to measure up. These findings help to explain why many MNCs welcome input from their host-country nations regarding staffing decisions but do not let themselves be totally swayed by these opinions. Quite obviously, many MNCs are as guilty of ethnocentric behavior as their host-country counterparts. The accompanying sidebar, "Recruiting Managers in Japan," provides a detailed example of Japanese ethnocentricity.

Repatriation of Expatriates

Repatriation

The return to one's home country from an overseas management assignment.

For most overseas managers, **repatriation**, or the return to one's home country, occurs within 5 years of the time they leave.[64] Few expatriates remain overseas for the duration of their stay with the firm. When they return, these expatriates often find themselves facing readjustment problems, and some MNCs now are trying to deal with these problems through use of transition strategies.

Reasons for Returning

The most common reason that expatriates return home from overseas assignments is that their formally agreed-on tour of duty is over. Before they left, they were told that they would be posted overseas for a predetermined period, often 2 to 3 years, and now are returning as planned. A second common reason is that expatriates want their children educated in a home-country school, and the longer they are away, the less likely this will happen.[65]

A third reason that expatriates return is because they are not happy in their overseas assignment. Managers with families who return home early often do so because the spouse

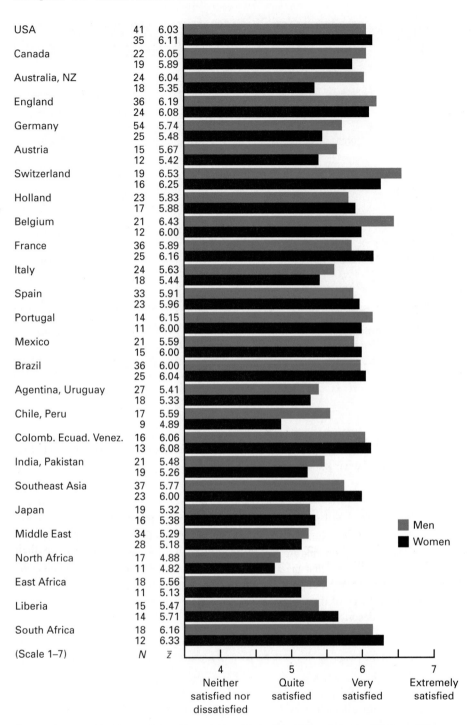

(Scale 1–7)	N	z̄
USA	41	6.03
	35	6.11
Canada	22	6.05
	19	5.89
Australia, NZ	24	6.04
	18	5.35
England	36	6.19
	24	6.08
Germany	54	5.74
	25	5.48
Austria	15	5.67
	12	5.42
Switzerland	19	6.53
	16	6.25
Holland	23	5.83
	17	5.88
Belgium	21	6.43
	12	6.00
France	36	5.89
	25	6.16
Italy	24	5.63
	18	5.44
Spain	33	5.91
	23	5.96
Portugal	14	6.15
	11	6.00
Mexico	21	5.59
	15	6.00
Brazil	36	6.00
	25	6.04
Agentina, Uruguay	27	5.41
	18	5.33
Chile, Peru	17	5.59
	9	4.89
Colomb. Ecuad. Venez.	16	6.06
	13	6.08
India, Pakistan	21	5.48
	19	5.26
Southeast Asia	37	5.77
	23	6.00
Japan	19	5.32
	16	5.38
Middle East	34	5.29
	28	5.18
North Africa	17	4.88
	11	4.82
East Africa	18	5.56
	11	5.13
Liberia	15	5.47
	14	5.71
South Africa	18	6.16
	12	6.33

Men

Women

4	5	6	7
Neither satisfied nor dissatisfied	Quite satisfied	Very satisfied	Extremely satisfied

Figure 15–6

Expatriate Satisfaction in Various Host Countries

Source: Ingemar Torbiorn, *Living Abroad* (New York: John Wiley & Sons, 1982), p. 125. Copyright 1982 by John Wiley & Sons. Used with permission.

or children do not want to stay, and the company feels that the loss in managerial productivity is too great to be offset by short-term personal unhappiness. Therefore, the individual is allowed to come back even though typically the cost is quite high.[66]

A fourth reason that people return is failure to do a good job. Such failure often spells trouble for the manager. As a director of employee relations of a large U.S. MNC put it: "If a person flunks out overseas . . . we bring him home. . . . He's penalized indirectly because

Table 15–7
Beliefs of Home-Country Organization Expats

Beliefs	Percentage of Respondents Who Agree				
	Holland	England	Germany	Belgium	France
All top managers of foreign subsidiaries should be host-country nationals.	87.5	78.0	35.1	42.9	81.3
Expatriate managers should be of West European ethnic origin.	90.0	95.0	96.3	100.0	58.3
Expatriate managers should be thoroughly familiar with the culture of the host country.	93.8	90.3	78.9	100.0	81.3
Expatriate managers should adhere to local managerial patterns of behavior.	87.5	96.9	73.7	100.0	93.3
Expatriate managers should be proficient in the host-country language.	100.0	100.0	100.0	100.0	100.0
Expatriate managers should have a working knowledge of the host country's social characteristics.	93.3	96.9	84.2	100.0	100.0
Expatriate managers should be thoroughly familiar with the history of the host country.	93.3	83.9	81.6	100.0	100.0

Source: Adapted from Y. Zeira and M. Banai, "Attitudes of Host-Country Organizations toward MNCs' Staffing Policies: A Cross-Country and Cross-Industry Analysis," *Management International Review,* vol. 21, no. 2, 1981, p. 42. Used with permission.

the odds are that if he flunked out over there, he's in trouble over here. But we bring him back and, generally, he has a tough row to hoe."[67]

Readjustment Problems

After returning to the home country, some expatriates have readjustment problems. In fact, on occasion, the reentry problems are greater than the adjustment problems faced overseas. Sometimes, expatriates feel that their international experience is not highly regarded by the company. For some, their current job has less responsibility and is boring when compared with the challenge of their overseas position. Here are some representative expatriate comments that describe these frustrations:

> My colleagues react indifferently to my international assignment. . . . They view me as doing a job I did in the past; they don't see me as having gained anything while overseas.

> I had no specific reentry job to return to. I wanted to leave international and return to domestic. Working abroad magnifies problems while isolating effects. You deal with more problems, but the home office doesn't know the details of the good or bad effects. Managerially, I'm out of touch.

> I'm bored at work. . . . I run upstairs to see what [another returning colleague] is doing. He says, "Nothing." Me, too.[68]

A study by Tung found that in general, the longer the duration of an off-shore assignment, the more problem the expatriate has being reabsorbed into the home office. Here are the major reasons:

1. The "out of sight, out of mind" syndrome is common.
2. Organizational changes made during the time the individual was abroad may make his or her position in the parent headquarters redundant or peripheral.

International Management in Action

Recruiting Managers in Japan

Recruiting managers in host countries can be a very difficult chore. For example, small U.S. firms in Japan report that local managers often do not want to work for them because they are unfamiliar with the company and do not want to run the risk of joining a business that may be around for only a short time. Larger, highly visible MNCs, such as IBM, Coca-Cola, and Ford Motor, do not have this problem, but there are other recruiting challenges for human resources management in Japan that are just as formidable.

One of these challenges facing an MNC in Japan is the significant amount of time it takes to recruit a Japanese manager. In the United States, when an MNC wants to hire an identified manager from another company, it will either have a headhunter contact the individual or have someone from the MNC do it. In either case, the MNC doing recruiting in the United States will quickly find out if the person is interested in changing jobs. If the answer is yes, a tentative offer will be made, and negotiations will begin. Quite often, the entire process will take only two or three meetings spread over a few weeks. Managers are recruited quite differently in Japan. There, the recruitment process is very slow and very deliberate, often taking 6 months to a year. The extended time is necessary, because there are a number of rules of business etiquette that must be followed.

A multinational doing recruiting in Japan typically goes through the following steps. A top manager from the multinational that is seeking to hire a manager away from a Japanese firm will first meet with that person's manager, and perhaps even the person's family, and request permission to negotiate with the individual. The MNC will have to provide assurances regarding this person's future position, security, and opportunities. Only then will meetings and negotiations with the manager begin. Moreover, the higher up the organization the recruited manager is located, the more delicate and slow-moving the process tends to be. There is little that the multinational can do, however, because it needs to recruit the top local talent.

The primary reason why it is so important for MNCs doing business in Japan to have local managers is because the Japanese are extremely ethnocentric. Japanese consumers and firms prefer to buy from Japanese businesses. They prefer local products to imports. In selecting people, MNCs in Japan typically put a Japanese national in charge of the subsidiary or make the individual the number-two person. They also recruit a large percentage of the managerial work force from the local market and do everything they can to give their subsidiary a "local look." In fact, in many Japanese subsidiaries of MNCs, there are no visible foreign managers.

One of the most important things that MNCs have learned about doing business in Japan is that they must be regarded as a local firm if they hope to succeed. MNCs such as IBM have done this so well that they are regarded as "Japanese" by the locals. As a result, many of the barriers that prevent other multinationals from doing business in Japan do not exist for companies such as IBM, which clearly understands the value of recruiting managers in Japan.

3. Technological advances in the parent headquarters may render the individual's existing skills and knowledge obsolete.[69]

Still another problem is adjusting to the new job back home. It sometimes takes from 6 months to 1 year before managers are operating at full effectiveness. Figure 15-7 provides an illustration.

Other readjustment problems are more personal in nature. Many expatriates find that the salary and fringe benefits to which they have become accustomed in the foreign assignment now are lost, and adjusting to this lower standard of living is difficult. In addition, those who sold their houses and now must buy new ones find that the monthly cost often is much higher than when they left. The children often are placed in public schools, where classes are much larger than in the overseas private schools. Many also miss the cultural lifestyles, as in the case of an executive who is transferred from Paris, France, to a medium-sized city in the United States, or from any developed country to an underdeveloped country.

Figure 15–7

Effectiveness of Returning Expatriates

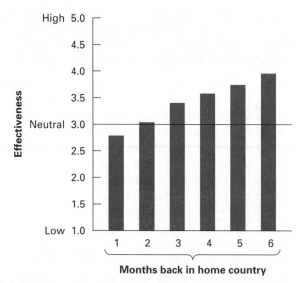

Source: Nancy J. Adler, *International Dimensions of Organizational Behavior,* 2nd ed. (Boston: PWS-Kent, 1991), p. 238. Copyright © 1991 by Wadsworth, Inc. Reprinted by permission of PWS-Kent Publishing Company, a division of Wadsworth, Inc.

Recent research supports the findings noted here and offers operative recommendations for action. Based on questionnaires completed by 174 respondents who recently had been repatriated from four large U.S. MNCs, Black found the following:

1. With few exceptions, individuals whose expectations were met had the most positive levels of repatriation adjustment and job performance.

2. In the case of high-level managers in particular, expatriates whose job demands were greater, rather than less, than expected reported high levels of repatriation adjustment and job performance. Those having greater job demands may have put in more effort and had better adjustment and performance.

3. Job performance and repatriation adjustment were greater for individuals whose job constraint expectations were undermet than for those individuals whose expectations were overmet. In other words, job constraints were viewed as an undesirable aspect of the job and having them turn out to be less than expected was a pleasant surprise that helped adjustment and performance.

4. When living and housing conditions turned out to be better than expected, general repatriation adjustment and job performance were better.

5. Individuals whose general expectations were met or overmet had job evaluations that placed them 10 percent higher than those whose general expectations were unmet.[70]

Transition strategies
Strategies used to help smooth the adjustment from an overseas to a stateside assignment.

Repatriation agreements
Agreements whereby the firm tells the individuals how long she or he will be posted overseas and promises to give the individual, on return, a job that is mutually acceptable.

Transition Strategies

To help smooth the adjustment from an overseas to a stateside assignment, some MNCs have developed **transition strategies**, which can take a number of different forms. One is the use of **repatriation agreements**, whereby the firm tells the individual how long she or he will be posted overseas and promises to give the individual, on return, a job that is mutually acceptable. This agreement typically does not promise a specific position or salary, but the agreement may state that the person will be given a job that is equal to, if not better than, the one held before leaving.

Some firms also rent or otherwise maintain expatriates' homes until they return. The Aluminum Company of America and Union Carbide both have such plans for managers going overseas. This plan helps to reduce the financial shock that often accompanies home shopping by returning expatriates.

A third strategy is to use senior executives as sponsors of managers abroad, as described here:

> It is the responsibility of a sponsor to monitor the performance, compensation, and career paths of expatriate managers who are under their wings, and to plan for their return. Sponsors begin scouting anywhere from six months to a year prior to an expatriate's return for a suitable position that he or she can come back to. Union Carbide and IBM are two companies who make use of such sponsors, but there are others as well.[71]

Still another approach is to keep expatriate managers apprised of what is going on at corporate headquarters and to plug these managers into projects at the home office whenever they are on leave in the home country. This helps maintain the person's visibility and ensures the individual is looked on as a regular member of the management staff.

In the final analysis, a proactive strategy that provides an effective support system to allay expatriate concerns about career issues while serving abroad may work best. Tung found that the successful U.S., European, Japanese, and Australian MNCs that she studied had: (1) mentor programs (one-on-one pairing of an expatriate with a member of home-office senior management); (2) a separate organization unit with primary responsibility for the specific needs of expatriates; and/or (3) maintenance of constant contacts between the home office and the expatriate.[72]

Recent research supports and expands these findings. One study surveyed 99 employees and managers with international experience in 21 corporations.[73] The reactions of the respondents to statements regarding the repatriation experience are provided in Table 15-8. The findings reveal that cultural re-entry, financial implications, and the nature of job assignments are three major areas of expatriate concern. In particular, some of the main problems of repatriation identified in this study include: (1) adjusting to life back home; (2) facing a financial package that is not as good as that overseas; (3) having less autonomy in the stateside job than in the overseas position; and (4) not receiving any career counseling from the company. To the extent that the MNC can address these types of problems and others presented in Table 15-8, the transition will be smooth, and the expatriate's performance effectiveness once home will increase quickly. Some additional steps suggested by experts in this area include:

1. Arrange an event to welcome and recognize the employee and family, either formally or informally.
2. Establish support to facilitate family reintegration.
3. Offer repatriation counseling or workshops to ease the adjustment.
4. Assist the spouse with job counseling, resume writing, and interviewing techniques.
5. Provide educational counseling for the children.
6. Provide the employee with a thorough debriefing by a facilitator to identify new knowledge, insights, and skills and to provide a forum to showcase new competencies.
7. Offer international outplacement to the employee and reentry counseling to the entire family if no positions are possible.
8. Arrange a postassigned interview with the expatriate and spouse to review their view of the assignment and address any repatriation issues.[74]

Hammer and his associates echo these types of recommendations. Based on recent research they conducted in two multinational corporations among expats and their spouses, they concluded that:

> The findings from the present study suggest that one of the key transitional activities for returning expatriates and their spouses from a corporate context should involve targeted

Table 15–8
Assessment of Repatriate Experience

Survey Categories	Mean Score[a]
Cultural Reentry	
1. The transition back to the American lifestyle was very easy.	3.71
2. I do not miss the people I worked with in the overseas assignment.	5.27
3. I felt comfortable giving up the friendships that I had developed overseas.	4.69
4. *If my spouse and/or children joined me overseas,* their transition back to the American lifestyle was very easy.	4.10
5. My family and friends back in the U.S. were interested in hearing about my experiences living overseas.	3.93
6. *If my spouse and/or children joined me overseas,* their friends in the U.S. were interested in hearing about the overseas experience.	4.23
7. Life back in the States seems exciting in comparison with the cultural experience I had during my overseas assignment.	4.95
8. My company provided me with help regarding relocation problems like housing and transportation.	3.44
Financial Implications	
1. The total financial package that I received in my new U.S. job assignment was better than my total financial package overseas.	5.42
2. The salary offer in the U.S. job assignment was better than my salary overseas.	4.20
3. The fringe benefits in the new U.S. job assignment were better than when I was working overseas.	5.65
4. *If you did not own your house or apartment in the U.S. while working overseas,* the cost of buying one upon returning from overseas was very reasonable.	5.87
5. My personal finances since returning from overseas are in better shape than was true *before* I left for the overseas assignment.	3.23
6. My company provided me bridge loans or other interim financial assistance when I returned from overseas.	5.31
7. My company provided me with considerable accounting advice/financial planning upon my return from overseas.	5.40
Nature of Job Assignment	
1. It was clear to me what permanent job I would have when I first returned from overseas.	3.42
2. I experienced more autonomy in my new job than had been the case in my overseas assignment.	5.37
3. My job status is less in my new job than had been the case in my overseas assignment.	4.54
4. I have less political influence in the company in my new job than had been the case in my overseas assignment.	4.69
5. *If it applies,* my mentor was helpful in apprising me of company developments when I first returned from overseas.	4.92
6. *If it applies,* my mentor helped in finding a good job assignment for me when I returned from overseas.	4.50
7. The present job is less challenging than the one I held overseas.	4.38
8. I consider that the company was fair with me in terms of identifying a suitable job assignment for me when I returned from overseas.	3.68
9. I view my present job assignment as very permanent.	3.96
10. I feel a high sense of job (employment) security with my present company.	3.02
11. Looking back at it, I consider that the overseas assignment benefitted me in terms of career opportunities in the company.	3.41
12. Overall, the managerial skills I gained overseas are being utilized by my employer now that I am working back in the U.S.	4.20
13. I was placed in a "holding pattern" when I first returned from the overseas assignment.	2.76
14. My company was helpful in providing me with career counseling when I returned from overseas.	5.88
15. My company provided my spouse with considerable help with career counseling when I returned from overseas.	6.51

[a]1 = strongly agree; 7 = strongly disagree.

Source: Nancy K. Napier and Richard B. Peterson, "Expatriate Re-entry: What Do Expatriates Have to Say?" *Human Resource Planning,* vol. 14, no. 1, 1991, pp. 26–27. Used with permission.

communication from the home environment concerning the expectations of the home office toward the return of the repatriate executive and his/her family (role relationships). Further, reentry training should focus primarily on helping the repatriate manager and spouse align their expectations with the actual situation that will be encountered upon arrival in the home culture both within the organizational context as well as more broadly within the social milieu. To the degree that corporate communication and reentry training activities help the returning executive and spouse in expectation alignment, the executive's level of reentry satisfaction should be higher and the degree of reentry difficulties less.[75]

Additionally, in recent years many MNCs have begun using inpatriates to supplement their home-office staff.

The World of Business Week Revisited

The *Business Week* story that opened this chapter presented a number of human resource management challenges. Having read this chapter, you are now aware that the selection of the best people for international assignments is critical. This is particularly true in the case of MNCs doing business in Asia because that is where things are turning down the fastest. How can multinationals address this challenge? One way is by applying the very same approaches to HRM that we have been studying here. In linking HRM with the challenge of making headway in the emerging markets of Asia, answer these questions: (1) In choosing people for overseas assignments in locales where the economies remain weak, how much reliance should MNCs be putting on expats? Host-country nationals? Third-country nationals? Inpats? (2) What criteria do you think would be important in screening people for jobs in Asia? What is the reasoning behind your choices? (3) What type of compensation program do you think MNCs should be looking at in order to motivate managers to take jobs in their Asian operation? Will this program be different from the one you would expect them to offer to managers in their European operations? (4) Will the repatriation strategy that is used for American managers returning to the states from overseas assignments be the same as the one that should be used with inpats who are leaving the states and returning to their home country?

Summary of Key Points

1. MNCs can use four basic sources for filling overseas positions: home-country nationals (expatriates), host-country nationals, third-country nationals, and inpatriates. The most common reason for using home-country nationals, or expatriates, is to get the overseas operation under way. Once this is done, many MNCs turn the top management job over to a host-country national who is familiar with the culture and language and who often commands a lower salary than the home-country national. The primary reason for using third-country nationals is that these people have the necessary expertise for the job. The use of inpatriates (a host-country or third-country national assigned to the home office) recognizes the need for diversity at the home office. This movement builds a transnational core competency for MNCs.

2. Many criteria are used in selecting managers for overseas assignments. Some of these include adaptability, independence, self-reliance, physical and emotional health, age, experience, education, knowledge of the local language, motivation, the support of spouse and children, and leadership.

3. Those who meet selection criteria then are given some form of screening. Some firms use psychological testing, but this approach has lost popularity in recent years. More commonly, candidates are given interviews. A recent development, theoretic models that identify important anticipatory and in-country dimensions of adjustment, offers help in effective selection.

4. Compensating expatriates can be a difficult problem, because there are many variables to consider. However, most compensation packages are designed around four common elements: base salary, benefits, allowances, and taxes. Working within these elements, the MNC will tailor-make the package to fit the specific situation. In doing so, there are six different approaches that can be used, including the balance

sheet approach, the complementary approach, localization, lump sum method, the cafeteria approach, and the regional method. Whichever one (or combination) is used, the package must be both cost-effective and fair.

5. A manager might be willing to take an international assignment for a number of reasons, including: increased pay, promotion potential, the opportunity for greater responsibility, the chance to travel, and the ability to use his or her talents and skills. Research shows that most home countries prefer that the individual who is selected to head the affiliate or subsidiary be a local manager, even though this often does not occur.

6. At some time, most expatriates return home, usually when the predetermined tour is over. Sometimes, managers return because they want to leave early; other times, they return because of poor performance on their part. In any event, readjustment problems can happen back home, and the longer the managers have been gone, the bigger the problems usually are. Some firms now are developing transition strategies to help expatriates adjust to their new environments.

Key Terms

adaptability screening
balance sheet approach
cafeteria approach
expatriates
home-country nationals

host-country nationals
inpatriates
international selection criteria
localization
lump sum method

regional system
repatriation
repatriation agreements
third-country nationals
transition strategies

Review and Discussion Questions

1. A New York-based MNC is in the process of staffing a subsidiary in New Delhi, India. Why would it consider using expatriate managers in the unit? Local managers? Third-country managers?

2. What selection criteria are most important in choosing people for an overseas assignment? Identify and describe the four that you judge to be of most universal importance, and defend your choice.

3. Building on your answer to the question above, discuss some theoretical dimensions that may affect anticipatory and in-country adjustment of expats. How can these be turned into selection criteria?

4. What are the major common elements in an expat's compensation package? Besides base pay, which would be most important to you? Why?

5. Why are individuals motivated to accept international assignments? Which of these motivations would you rank as positive reasons? Which would you regard as negative reasons?

6. Why do expatriates return early? What can MNCs do to prevent this from happening? Identify and discuss three steps they can take.

7. What kinds of problems do expatriates face when returning home? Identify and describe four of the most important. What can MNCs do to deal with these repatriation problems effectively?

Internet Exercise: A Global Auto Merger

As seen in this chapter, one of the most recent, and important, international mergers has been that of Daimler-Benz of Germany and Chrysler of the United States, creating the Daimler-Chrysler Corporation. There are many aspects of this merger that are attractive to investors, who feel certain that Chrysler will help Daimler become a major player in the North American market and, in turn, Daimler will help Chrysler exploit the European auto market. At the same time, however, there are a number of problems that the two companies are going to have to work out. One of these is the executive salary schedules which, in the minds of the Daimler management, are too lucrative and need to be brought into line with those of the German executives. Another is the potential difficulty that is posed by having managers from two different national cultures now working together as a team. At the same time, of course, the merger has

opened up a host of opportunities for both firms and they will certainly want to exploit these. Visit the web site for Daimler-Chrysler at **www1.daimlerchrysler.com** and review some of the latest developments that are taking place in the company. In particular, look at the corporate information and news section and investigate the careers section regarding jobs at the firm's European locations. Then answer these four questions: (1) From what you have learned from this material, what types of training and experience would you need to be hired by Daimler-Chrysler for its European operations? (2) What types of career opportunities does the firm offer? (3) Since the web page is offered in both English and German, do you think a working knowledge of German would be helpful to you if you took a job with this company? (4) If you were posted to Europe, what type of financial package would you expect the company to provide for you?

Russia

Russia is by far the largest republic in the former Soviet Union. Russia stretches from Eastern Europe across northern Asia and to the Pacific Ocean. The 150 million people consist of 83 percent Russians, 4 percent Tarters, and a scattering of others. The largest city and capital is Moscow, with about 9 million people. At present, there is both social and economic turmoil in Russia. As of 1999 the economy still was poor. Although prices no longer are controlled and privatization has begun, the GDP and the value of the ruble both have deteriorated. At the same time, the country has been scurrying to meet payments to its international creditors and faces political uncertainty.

Despite poor economic conditions and the difficulty of attracting foreign investors, Russia still is considered to be an attractive place to do business by some MNCs. One that has been extremely interested in the country is Earth, Inc. (EI), a farm-implement company that is headquartered in Birmingham, Alabama. EI recently entered into an agreement with the government of Russia to set up operations near Moscow in a factory that was operating at about one-half of capacity. The factory will produce farm implements for the newly emerging Eastern European market. EI will supply the technical know-how and product design as well as assume responsibility for marketing the products. The Russian plant will build the equipment and package it for shipping.

The management of the plant operation will be handled on a joint basis. EI will send a team of five management and technical personnel from the United States to the Russian factory site for a period of 12 to 18 months. After this time, EI hopes to send three of them home, and the two who remain would continue to provide ongoing assistance. At the same time, EI intends to hire four middle-level managers and eight first-level supervisors from Italy and Germany, because the operation will need Europeans who are more familiar with doing manufacturing in this part of the world. Very few locals have inspired EI with confidence that they can get the job done. However, over a 2-year period, EI intends to replace the third-country nationals with trained local managers. "We need to staff the management ranks with knowledgeable, experienced people," the CEO explained, "at least until we get the operation up and running successfully with our own people. Then we can turn more and more of the operation over to local management, and run the plant with just a handful of headquarters people on site."

This arrangement has been agreed to by the Russian government, and EI currently is identifying and recruiting managers both in the United States and Europe. Initially, the firm thought that this would be a fairly simple process, but screening and selecting is taking much longer than anticipated. Nevertheless, EI hopes to have the plant operating within 12 months.

Questions

1. What are some current issues facing Russia? What is the climate for doing business in Russia today?

2. What are some of the benefits of using home-country nationals in overseas operations? What are some of the benefits of using host-country nationals?

3. Why would a multinational such as EI be interested in bringing in third-country nationals?

4. What criteria should EI use in selecting personnel for the overseas assignment in Russia?

A Selection Decision

The Star Corporation is a Hong Kong manufacturing firm that is going to do business in mainland China. The company's contract with the Chinese government calls for it to supply technical know-how and machinery for producing consumer electronics. These products are not state-of-the-art, but they will be more than adequate for the needs of the Chinese consumers. Star has agreed to sell the Chinese its plant, which was being closed because it no longer was competitive.

The Chinese will pay to move all the machinery and equipment to the mainland and install it in a factory that currently is being modified for this purpose. The two then will become partners in the venture. Star will provide the management and technical expertise to run the plant, and the Chinese government will provide the workers and be responsible for paying for all output. Star will receive an annual fee of $3 million and 5 percent of all sales.

The Star management is very pleased with the arrangement. Although they are of Chinese descent, they have lived in Hong Kong all their lives and know relatively little about doing business either with or in mainland China. To provide Star with the necessary information and assistance, a native of Beijing, educated there but living in Hong Kong the past 5 years, was brought in. The individual told the company the following facts about mainland China:

- Chinese managers do not plan. They usually are told what to do and they do it. Planning is handled by others and simply passed on to them.
- Chinese managers are not concerned with profit or loss. They simply do their jobs and let the government worry about whether the operation is making money.
- No rewards are given to workers who perform well; everyone is treated the same. If there is no work, the workers are still paid, although they may not be required to come to the factory.
- There is a basic aversion to individual decision making; most decisions are collective efforts.
- The current government of China would like its managers to learn how to run a profit-oriented operation and eventually eliminate the need for forcing managerial assistance.
- When outsiders tell the Chinese how to do things, they have to be careful not to insult or offend the Chinese, who often are sensitive about the way they are treated.

Questions

1. What selection criteria would you recommend to Star when deciding whom to send to mainland China?
2. What procedures should the company use in making the final selection?
3. What type of repatriation agreement would you recommend the firm use? Be specific regarding some things you would suggest be contained in the agreement.

Chapter 16

Human Resource Development across Cultures

Objectives of the Chapter

Firms conducting international business need to be particularly concerned with training and organization development to better prepare their personnel for overseas assignments.[1] This chapter examines how successful multinational organizations prepare personnel to go overseas. A specific focus is the reasons for training and development and the various types of training that commonly are offered. Training by use of cultural assimilators is discussed, and their value in providing effective acculturation is analyzed. Broader-based organization development also is considered—how it works as well as its value in helping to resolve human problems in an international setting. The specific objectives of this chapter are:

1. **IDENTIFY** the training process as used in international management, and note that people from different cultures often have different learning styles.

2. **DISCUSS** the most common reasons for training and the types of training that often are provided.

3. **EXPLAIN** how cultural assimilators work and why they are so highly regarded.

4. **IDENTIFY** the term "organization development," and discuss its use in international management.

BusinessWeek

The World of Business Week:

Marks & Sparks Isn't Throwing off Any

Aside from British Broadcasting Corp. and the monarchy, there's probably no other institution as much a part of British daily life as Marks & Spencer. The $13.7 billion retailer sells one out of four men's suits bought in the country. Former Prime Minister Margaret Thatcher buys her underclothes there, along with 40% of British women. Chances are nearly everyone on a British street is wearing something from Marks & Sparks, as it is affectionately nicknamed.

But venerable M&S is coming under fire. On Nov. 3, the retailer stunned investors by announcing a 23% drop in midyear profits. The bad news sent its stock skidding to a three-year low, prompted analysts to slash their full-year earnings estimates, and rocked London's stock market. The earnings slump also casts doubt on M&S's quest to become a global retailer and raises questions about the future of chief executive Sir Richard Greenbury.

Slow Uptake

M&S is suffering from bad timing. It has been hit with poor sales in Britain, North America, Continental Europe, and Asia just as it embarks on the most ambitious expansion push in its 114-year history—adding 3 million square feet of new selling space to its 683 existing stores and opening new

sites. The sales slump partly reflects mistakes in merchandising, inventory control, and pricing. But analysts say M&S was slower to react to a tough environment than many rivals. And flagging economic growth worldwide means things will get even tougher for M&S.

Greenbury passionately defends M&S's performance. He blames a downturn in consumer confidence and a strong pound for most of its woes. But investors and analysts don't buy it. "The majority of M&S's problems have to do with M&S, not with the retail environment," insists Nathan Cockrell, an analyst at BT Alex Brown, Inc. in London. M&S shares have underperformed those of other British retailers by 25% over the past year, and its market share has been slipping.

Growth Hit

Other British retailers are also running fall sales. But few of M&S's rivals are expanding as fast. Last year, the company paid $321 million in cash to buy 19 stores from Littlewoods, a rival department-store chain. Now, it has slashed its budget for adding nearly a quarter more retail space by 2000 from $3.7 billion to $3.2 billion.

Such problems at home could derail M&S's critical global initiative. With 85% of sales and 94% of profits coming from Britain, the company needs to diversify. "Overseas expansion is absolutely crucial to us long-term," says Greenbury. Yet to cut costs, M&S is slowing its aggressive expansion plans on the Continent. It had hoped to have 60 stores in Continental Europe by 2000. Now, it's aiming for 44. Likewise, the company is reviewing the growth plans of its North American stores, which include the revived Brooks Brothers chain and the upscale Kings Super Markets Inc., and slowing expansion in Asia.

Amid the missteps, scrutiny of Greenbury has intensified. The 62-year-old executive, who plans to retire in 2001, is under pressure from some institutional investors to name a sucessor and divide his roles as chairman and CEO. There's even talk of a boardroom power struggle in which Peter Salsbury, one of three joint managing directors who works for Greenbury, might unseat Deputy Chairman J. Keith Oates as heir apparent. If sales over the crucial holiday season don't show more sparkle, Greenbury's 10-year reign at M&S could end ignobly.

Source: **Reprinted from November 16, 1998, p. 64 issue of** *Business Week* **by special permission, copyright © 1998 by McGraw-Hill Companies Inc.**

This opening international management news story shows clearly that Marks & Spencer (M&S) is having problems. Not only are sales at home in a slump, but international expansion is not proceeding as rapidly as planned. Obviously there are many things that M&S must do to increase its competitiveness including pushing harder in North America and tempering growth in Asia. Much of the material presented thus far in this book would be of value in meeting the challenges. However, so can the information in this chapter which focuses on human resource development across cultures. Remember, M&S is in the retail business—it is a labor-intensive service enterprise. As a result, employee training and development, and in turn, customer service is the most critical and distinguishing factor between those MNCs that succeed and those that do not. Many of the concepts and techniques that are discussed in this chapter can be of value to M&S in their development and leadership transformation efforts. How well the company is able to do this needed development, especially across cultures, may well determine overall success in its effort to become a world-class retail firm.

Training in International Management

Training

The process of altering employee behavior and attitudes in a way that increases the probability of goal attainment.

Training is the process of altering employee behavior and attitudes in a way that increases the probability of goal attainment. This training process is particularly important in preparing employees for overseas assignments.[2] For example, most expatriates (defined in Chapter 15 as those who live and work away from their home country and who are citizens of the country in which the MNC is headquartered) are unfamiliar with the customs, cultures, and work habits of the local people. As a result, they often make critical mistakes. Here is such a blunder:

> An American company eager to do business in Saudi Arabia sent over a sales manager to "get something going." The salesman began calling contacts soon after his arrival on Monday. . . . After many disappointing appointments, the salesman ran into an old buddy who gave him an introduction to some basic rules of Saudi etiquette and how to do business with the Arabs. The salesman learned that he had repeatedly insulted his contacts by his impatience, refusal of coffee, the "all business talk" attitude and aggressive selling. Even incidental acts such as handing people papers with his left hand and exposing the side of his shoe while sitting on the floor were improper Saudi customs.[3]

The simplest training, in terms of preparation time, is to place a cultural integrator in each foreign operation. This individual is responsible for ensuring that the operation's business systems are in accord with those of the local culture. The integrator advises, guides, and recommends actions needed to ensure this synchronization.[4] The "International Management in Action: The Cultural Integrator," accompanying box, describes in detail the use of such a person.

Unfortunately, although using an integrator can help, it is seldom sufficient.[5] Recent experience clearly reveals that in creating an effective global team, the MNC must assemble individuals who collectively understand the local language, have grown up in diverse cultures or neighborhoods, have open, flexible minds, and who will be able to deal with high degrees of stress.[6] In those cases where potential candidates do not yet possess all of these requisite skills or abilities, MNCs need a well-designed training program that is administered before the individuals leave for their overseas assignment (and, in some cases, also on-site) and then evaluated later to determine its overall effectiveness. One review of 228 MNCs found that cross-cultural training, which can take many forms, is becoming increasingly popular. Some of these findings included the following:

1. Of organizations with cultural programs, 58 percent offer training only to some expatriates, while 42 percent offer it to all of them.
2. Ninety-one percent offer cultural orientation programs to spouses, and 75 percent offer them to dependent children.
3. The average duration of the cultural training programs is 3 days.
4. Cultural training is continued after arrival in the assignment location 32 percent of the time.
5. Thirty percent offer formal cultural training programs.
6. Of those without formal cultural programs, 37 percent plan to add such training.[7]

The most common topics covered in cultural training include social etiquette, customs, economics, history, politics, and business etiquette. However, the MNC's overall philosophy of international management and the demands of the specific cultural situation are the starting

International Management in Action

The Cultural Integrator

In recent years, some international management experts have suggested that firms use a cultural integrator to deal with the cultural differences they face overseas. The basic concept of integration is not new; MNCs long have tested their products in foreign markets to ensure that any necessary modifications are made before full-scale selling begins. Similarly, many of these firms have trained and developed their people before sending them to foreign assignments. In most cases, however, the personnel are not totally prepared to deal with the day-to-day cultural challenges, because they lack field experience. This is where the cultural integrator enters the picture.

The integrator is responsible for helping handle problems between the subsidiary and host cultures. Among other things, the person advises management about the consequences of those actions that can negatively affect its position in the host country and market, and he or she works with management in developing an appropriate response.

Some companies send the cultural integrator from the home office. Many choose a host-country national who has intimate knowledge of the multinational's culture and can view operations from both

sides. Quite often, the individual holds a staff position and can only advise and recommend courses of action; the person has no authority to demand implementation of such actions. For this reason, the integrator needs proficiency in both conceptual and human relations skills. He or she must be able to envision the relationships between the MNC and host country that will result in the best "fit" for both. At the same time, the individual must be able to persuade the managers to accept her or his point of view.

Will the coming years see greater use of cultural integrators? This trend appears to be very likely.

As more corporations expand internationally, there is a greater need to integrate their operations into foreign societies. It cannot be expected that an international manager can function effectively in all host societies. Nor can it be expected that a manager will remain in a society long enough to gain the cultural familiarity necessary to function effectively there, since one of the competitive advantages of an international firm is its managerial mobility. The cultural integrator offers a clear resolution to this dilemma, allowing international organizations to achieve their full potential.

point. This is because countries tend to have distinctive human resource management (HRM) practices that differentiate them from other countries. For example, the HRM practices that are prevalent in the United States are quite different from those in France and Argentina. This has been clearly illustrated by Sparrow and Budhwar, who compared data from 13 different countries on the basis of HRM factors. Five of these factors included the following:

1. Structural empowerment that is characterized by flat organization designs, wide spans of control, the use of flexible cross-functional teams, and the rewarding of individuals for productivity gains.

2. Accelerated resource development that is characterized by the early identification of high potential employees, the establishment of both multiple and parallel career paths, the rewarding of personnel for enhancing their skills and knowledge, and the offering of continuous training and development education.

3. Employee welfare emphasis that is characterized by firms offering personal family assistance, encouraging and rewarding external volunteer activities, and promoting cultures that emphasize equality in the workplace.

4. An efficiency emphasis in which employees are encouraged to monitor their own work and to continually improve their performance.

5. Long termism that stresses long-term results such as innovation and creativity rather than just weekly and monthly short-term productivity.[8]

When Sparrow and Budhwar used these HRM approaches on a comparative country-by-country basis, they found that there were worldwide differences in human resource management practices. Table 16-1 shows the comparative results, after each of the 13 countries was categorized as being either high or low on the respective factors.

Table 16–1
Human Resource Management Practices in Select Countries

	Structural Empowerment		Accelerated Resource Development		Employee Welfare Emphasis		Efficiency Emphasis		Long-Termism	
	High	Low	High	Low	High	Low	High	Low	High	Low
United States	X		X		X		X			X
Canada	X		X		X			X		X
United Kingdom	X		X			X		X		X
Italy		X	X			X		X		X
Japan		X	X		X		X		X	
India		X	X		X			X	X	
Australia	X			X		X	X		X	
Brazil	X		X		X			X	X	
Mexico	X		X		X			X		X
Argentina		X	X		X			X		X
Germany		X	X			X		X	X	
Korea		X	X			X	X		X	
France		X	X			X	X			X

Source: Adapted from Paul R. Sparrow and Pawan S. Budhwar, "Competition and Change: Mapping the Indian HRM Recipe Against Worldwide Patterns," *Journal of World Business,* vol. 32, no. 3, 1997, p. 233.

These findings reveal that countries are unique in their approach to human resources management. What works well in the United States may have limited value in France. In fact, a close analysis of Table 16-1 shows that none of the 13 countries had the same profile; each was different. This was even true in the case of Anglo nations such as the United States, Canada, Australia, and the United Kingdom where differences in employee welfare emphasis, accelerated resource development, long efficiency orientation, and long termism resulted in unique HRM profiles for each. Similarly, Japan and Korea differed on two of the factors, as did Germany and France; and India, which many people might feel would be more similar to an Anglo culture, because of the British influence, than to an Asian one, differed on two of factors with Canada, on three of the factors with both the United States and the United Kingdom, and on four factors with Australia.

These findings point to the fact that MNCs in the new millennium will have to focus increasingly on HRM programs designed to meet the needs of local personnel. A good example is provided in the former communist countries of Europe where international managers are discovering that in order to effectively recruit college graduates their firms must provide training programs that give these new employees opportunities to work with a variety of tasks and to help them specialize in their particular fields of interest. At the same time the MNCs are discovering that these recruits are looking for companies that offer a good social working environment. A recent survey of over 1,000 business and engineering students from Poland, the Czech Republic, and Hungary found that almost two-thirds of the respondents said that they wanted their boss to be receptive to their ideas; 37 percent wanted to work for managers who had strong industry experience; and 34 percent wanted a boss who was a good rational decision maker. These findings indicate that multinational human resource management is now becoming much more of a two-way street: both employees and managers need to continually adjust to emerging demands.[9]

The Impact of Overall Management Philosophy on Training

The type of training that is required of expatriates is influenced by the firm's overall philosophy of international management.[10] For example, some companies prefer to send their own people to staff an overseas operation; others prefer to use locals whenever possible.[11]

Briefly, four basic philosophic positions of multinational corporations (MNCs) can influence the training program:

1. An **ethnocentric MNC** puts home-office people in charge of key international management positions. The MNC headquarters group and the affiliated world company managers all have the same basic experiences, attitudes, and beliefs about how to manage operations. Many Japanese firms follow this practice.

2. A **polycentric MNC** places local nationals in key positions and allows these managers to appoint and develop their own people. MNC headquarters gives the subsidiary managers authority to manage their operations just as long as these operations are sufficiently profitable. Some MNCs use this approach in East Asia, Australia, and other markets that are deemed too expensive to staff with expatriates.

3. A **regiocentric MNC** relies on local managers from a particular geographic region to handle operations in and around that area. For example, production facilities in France would be used to produce goods for all EU countries. Similarly, advertising managers from subsidiaries in Italy, Germany, France, and Spain would come together and formulate a "European" advertising campaign for the company's products. A regiocentric approach often relies on regional group cooperation of local managers. The Gillette MNC uses a regiocentric approach.

4. A **geocentric MNC** seeks to integrate diverse regions of the world through a global approach to decision making. Assignments are made based on qualifications, and all subsidiary managers throughout the structure are regarded as equal to those at headquarters. IBM is an excellent example of an MNC that attempts to use a geocentric approach.

All four of these philosophical positions can be found in the multinational arena, and each puts a different type of training demand on the MNC.[12] For example, ethnocentric MNCs will do all training at headquarters, but polycentric MNCs will rely on local managers to assume responsibility for seeing that the training function is carried out.

Ethnocentric MNC
An MNC that stresses nationalism and often puts home-office people in charge of key international management positions.

Polycentric MNC
An MNC that places local nationals in key positions and allows these managers to appoint and develop their own people.

Regiocentric MNC
An MNC that relies on local managers from a particular geographic region to handle operations in and around that area.

Geocentric MNC
An MNC that seeks to integrate diverse regions of the world through a global approach to decision making.

The Impact of Different Learning Styles on Training and Development

Another important area of consideration for development is learning styles. **Learning** is the acquisition of skills, knowledge, and abilities that results in a relatively permanent change in behavior.[13] Over the last decade a growing number of multinationals have tried to become a "learning organization" (discussed in Chapter 3), which is typified by a continual focus on activities such as training and development. In the new millennium this learning focus applied to human resource development may go beyond learning organizations to "teaching organizations." For example, Tichy and Cohen, after conducting an analysis of world-class companies such as General Electric, PepsiCo, AlliedSignal, and Coca-Cola, found that teaching organizations are even more relevant than learning organizations because they go beyond the belief that everyone must continually acquire new knowledge and skills and focus on ensuring that everyone in the organization, especially the top management personnel, pass their learning on to others. Here are their conclusions:

Learning
The acquisition of skills, knowledge, and abilities that results in a relatively permanent change in behavior.

> In teaching organizations, leaders see it as their responsibility to teach. They do that because they understand that it's the best, if not only, way to develop throughout a company people who can come up with and carry out smart ideas about the business. Because people in teaching organizations see teaching as critical to the success of their business, they find ways to do it every day. Teaching every day about critical business issues avoids the fuzzy focus that has plagued some learning organization efforts, which have sometimes become a throwback to the 1960s- and 1970s-style self-exportation and human relations training.[14]

There are many examples of how successful leaders are doing this teaching. One of the best is Jack Welch of General Electric, who spends close to 30 percent of his own time teaching and developing. Moreover, Welch insists that all other GE leaders also teach. Larry Bossidy of AlliedSignal follows a similar approach. When he began transforming the company, he started by teaching his senior-level people about strategy and spent hundreds of days each year with other managers throughout the company. In his first year on the job, he personally met and worked with over 15,000 employees. As a result, Bossidy began to show his people how to create a mindset for growing a business that was operating in a mature market. This learning helped the firm become the best performing company on the Dow Jones Industrial Average within five years.[15]

Of course, the way in which training takes place can be extremely important. A great deal of research has been conducted on the various types and theories of learning.[16] However, the application of these ideas in an international context often can be quite challenging because cultural differences can affect the learning and teaching.

As one group of researchers has noted, "Two countries may be very similar in ecology and climate and, for example, through a common legacy of colonialism, have a similar language and legal, educational and governmental infrastructure but may be markedly different in terms of beliefs, attitudes and values."[17] Moreover, research shows that people with different learning styles prefer different learning environments, and if there is a mismatch between the preferred learning style and the work environment, dissatisfaction and poor performance can result.[18]

One study investigated learning styles by giving a learning style questionnaire to British middle managers, Indian midcareer managers, and East African midcareer managers. Two dimensions of learning style were measured: analysis and action. The analysis dimension measures the extent to which the learner adopts a theory-building and test approach as opposed to using an intuitive approach. The action dimension measures the extent to which the learner uses a trial-and-error approach as opposed to employing a contemplative or reflective approach.[19] The researchers found important differences in learning style between the three cultures. Indian managers were much higher on analysis than the other two groups. British managers were much higher on action. East African managers were the lowest on both analysis and action scores. The results were summarized as follows:

> The results of this study advance the argument . . . and raise questions about not only the aims and content of management development activities in different cultures but also about the nature of the learning process and the design of learning environments employed. . . . It may well be that the kind of learning environments and activities which promote effective learning in some cultures may not promote the same outcomes in other cultures where different learning styles predominate. This could have important implications for the design of learning environments, the composition of training groups and the location of training (in host country, regional center or home country) undertaken by transnational organizations.[20]

In addition to these conclusions, those responsible for training programs must remember that even if learning does occur, the new behaviors will not be used if they are not reinforced.[21] For example, if the head of a foreign subsidiary is highly ethnocentric and believes that things should be done the way they are in the home country, new managers with intercultural training likely will find little reward or reinforcement for using their ideas. This cultural complexity also extends to the way in which the training is conducted.[22] A corporate trainer and specialist for Esso Production Malaysia recently offered the following advice for training in cross-cultural settings:

> Start with a problem-oriented approach—avoid using complicated theories and definitions. Focus on here and now and "how to's." For teaching in cross-cultural settings, start with affirming the values of the participants, especially those which are part of their cultural heritage and are the basis of their shared practices. Once these values are identified, begin to look for gaps in performance and create an awareness of what is needed. The trainer will then focus on the steps to be taken to develop the new skills repertoire. A word of caution—if the skills have to do with interpersonal skills, it is better to have some contribution from the local participants. In this instance the trainer's task is to inform not to instruct.[23]

Reasons for Training

Training programs are useful in preparing people for overseas assignments for many reasons. These reasons can be put into two general categories: organizational and personal.

Organizational Reasons Organizational reasons for training relate to the enterprise at large and its efforts to manage overseas operations more effectively.[24] One primary reason is to help overcome **ethnocentrism**, the belief that one's way of doing things is superior to that of others. Ethnocentrism is common in many large MNCs where managers believe that the home office's approach to doing business can be exported intact to all other countries, because this approach is superior to anything at the local level. Training can help home-office managers to understand the values and customs of other countries so that when they are transferred overseas, they have a better understanding of how to interact with local personnel. This training also can help managers to overcome the common belief among many personnel that expatriates are not as effective as host-country managers. This is particularly important given that an increasing number of managerial positions now are held by foreign managers in U.S. MNCs.[25]

Ethnocentrism
The belief that one's own way of doing things is superior to that of others.

Another organizational reason for training is to improve the flow of communication between the home office and the international subsidiaries and branches. Quite often, overseas managers find that they are not adequately informed regarding what is expected of them while the home office places close controls on their operating authority. This is particularly true when the overseas manager is from the host country. Effective communication can help to minimize these problems.

Finally, another organizational reason for training is to increase overall efficiency and profitability. Research shows organizations that closely tie their training and human resource management strategy to their business strategy tend to outperform those that do not.[26] Stroh and Caligiuri recently conducted research on 60 of the world's major multinationals and found that effective HRM programs pay dividends in the form of higher profits. Additionally, their data showed that the most successful MNCs recognized the importance of having top managers with a global orientation. One of the ways in which almost all of these organizations did this was by giving their managers global assignments that not only filled technical and managerial needs but also provided developmental experiences for the personnel—and this assignment strategy included managers from every geographic region where the firms were doing business. Drawing together the lessons to be learned from this approach, Stroh and Caligiuri noted that:

> The development of global leadership skills should not stop with home country nationals. Global HR should also be involved in developing a global orientation among host country nationals as well. This means, for example, sending not only home-country managers on global assignments but host national talent to the corporate office and to other divisions around the world. Many of the managers at the successful MNCs talked about how their companies develop talent in this way. In addition, they described a "desired state" for human resources, including the ability to source talent within the company from around the world. Victor Guerra, an executive at Prudential, commented: *We need to continually recognize that there are bright, articulate people who do not live in the home country. U.S. multinationals are especially guilty of this shortsightedness.* Acknowledging that talent exists and using the talent appropriately are two different issues—one idealist, the other strategic.[27]

Personal Reasons Although there is overall organizational justification, the primary reason for training overseas managers is to improve their ability to interact effectively with local people in general and their personnel in particular.[28] One early study that surveyed 75 countries in England, Holland, Belgium, and Germany found that some of the biggest complaints about managers by their personnel revolved around personal shortcomings in areas such as politeness, punctuality, tactfulness, orderliness, sensitivity, reliability, tolerance, and empathy.[29] As a result, an increasing number of training programs now address social topics such as how to take a client to dinner, effectively apologize to a customer, appropriately address one's overseas colleagues, communicate formally and politely with others, and learn how to help others "save face."[30] These programs also focus on dispelling myths and stereotypes by replacing them with facts about the culture. For example, in helping expatriates better understand Arab executives, the following guidelines are offered:

1. There is a close relationship between the Arab executive and his environment. The Arab executive is looked on as a community and family leader, and there are numerous social pressures on him because of this role. He is consulted on all types of problems, even those far removed from his position.

2. With regard to decision making, the Arab executive likely will consult with his subordinates, but he will take responsibility for his decision himself rather than arriving at it through consensus.

3. The Arab executive likely will try to avoid conflict. If there is an issue that he favors but is opposed by his subordinates, he tends to impose his authority. If it is an issue favored by the subordinates but opposed by the executive, he will likely let the matter drop without taking action.

4. The Arab executive's style is very personal. He values loyalty over efficiency. Although some executives find that the open-door tradition consumes a great deal of time, they do not feel that the situation can be changed. Many executives tend to look on their employees as family and will allow them to bypass the hierarchy to meet them.

5. The Arab executive, contrary to popular beliefs, puts considerable value on the use of time. One thing he admires most about Western or expatriate executives is the use of their time, and he would like to encourage his own employees to make more productive use of time.[31]

Another growing problem is the belief that foreign language skills are not really essential to doing business overseas. Effective training programs can help to minimize these personal problems.

A particularly big personal problem that managers have in an overseas assignment is arrogance. This is the so-called Ugly American problem that U.S. expatriates have been known to have. Many expatriate managers find that their power and prestige are much greater than they were in their job in the home country. This often results in improper behavior, especially among managers at the upper and lower positions of overseas subsidiaries. This arrogance takes a number of different forms, including rudeness to personnel and inaccessibility to clients. Zeira and Harari made the following observations:

> Another manifestation of expatriate managers' arrogance is their widespread tendency to ignore invitations to become participant observers in HCOs [host-country organizations]. The underlying idea behind these invitations involves rotating expatriate managers in various HCO departments to enable them to observe patterns of organizational behavior at various hierarchical levels. The purpose of this observation is to familiarize expatriate managers, especially those new in their jobs or about to begin to assume them, with the goals, policies, procedures, formal and informal norms, and expectations of HCOs regarding expatriate managers and their respective subsidiaries.[32]

Another common problem is expatriate managers' overruling of decisions, often seen at lower levels of the hierarchy. When a decision is made by a superior who is from the host country and the expatriate does not agree with it, the expatriate may appeal to higher authority in the subsidiary. Host-country managers obviously resent this behavior, because it implies that they are incompetent and can be second-guessed by expatriate subordinates.

Still another common problem is the open criticizing by expatriate managers of their own country or the host country. Many expatriates believe that this form of criticism is regarded as constructive and shows them to have an open mind. Experience has found, however, that most host-country personnel view such behavior negatively and feel that the manager should refrain from such unconstructive criticism. It just creates bad feelings and lack of loyalty.

In addition to helping deal with these types of personal problems, training can be useful in improving overall management style.[33] Research shows that many host-country nationals would like to see changes in some of the styles of expatriate managers, including their leadership, decision making, communication, and group work. In terms of leadership, the locals would like to see their expatriate managers be more friendly, accessible, receptive to subordinate suggestions, and encouraging to subordinates to make their best efforts. In decision making, they would like to see clearer definition of goals, more involvement in the process by those employees who will be affected by the decision, and greater use of group meetings to help make decisions. In communication, they would like to see more exchange of opinions and ideas between subordinates and managers. In group work, they would like to see more group problem solving and teamwork. When Harari and Zeira researched the attitudes in six subsidiaries of non-Japanese MNCs, three in Japan and three from outside (United States, France, and Israel), they found that all host-country nationals wanted to see the use of more behavioral management techniques.[34]

The specific training approach used must reflect both the industrial and the cultural environment. For example, there is some evidence that Japanese students who come to the United States to earn an MBA degree often find this education of no real value back home. One graduate noted that when he tactfully suggested putting to use a skill he had learned during his U.S. MBA program, he got nowhere. An analysis of Japanese getting an outside education concluded:

> Part of the problem is the reason that most Japanese workers are sent to business schools. Whatever ticket the MBA degree promises—or appears to promise—Americans, the diploma has little meaning within most Japanese companies. Rather, companies send students abroad under the life-time employment system to ensure that there will be more English speakers who are familiar with Western business practices. Some managers regard business schools as a kind of high-level English language school, returning students say, or consider the two years as more or less a paid vacation.[35]

However, very recently, as the Japanese economy continues to have problems, American-style business education is beginning to receive attention and respect. In the 1980s American managers went to Japan to learn; now Japanese managers are going to the United States in increasing numbers to see what they can pick up to help them better compete.

Types of Training Programs

There are many different types of multinational management training programs.[36] Some last only a few hours; others last for months. Some are fairly superficial; others are extensive in coverage. Figure 16-1 shows some of the key considerations that influence development of these programs. As shown, there are nine phases. In the first phase the overall objective of the program to increase the effectiveness of expats and/or repatriated executives is emphasized. The second phase focuses on recognition of the problems that must be dealt with in order to reach the overall objective. The third phase is the identification of the developmental objectives. The fourth phase consists of determining the amount of development that will be needed regarding each of these objectives. The fifth phase entails choosing the specific methods to be used in the development process from types or predeparture training to language instruction to reentry training. The sixth phase is an intermediate evaluation of how well things are going and the institution of any needed midstream corrections. The seventh phase is an evaluation of how well the expat managers are doing, thus providing evaluation feedback of the developmental process. The eighth phase is devoted to reentry training for returning expats. The ninth, and final, phase is an evaluation of the effectiveness of the executives after they have returned. By carefully laying out this type of planning model, MNCs ensure that their development training programs are both realistic and productive. In this process they often rely on both standardized and tailor-made training and development approaches.

Figure 16–1   **A Model for the Development of Multinational Managers**

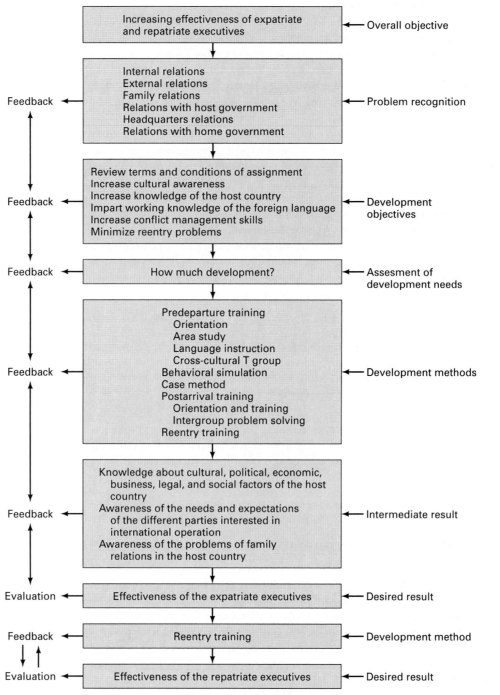

Internal relations
External relations
Family relations
Relations with host government
Headquarters relations
Relations with home government

Review terms and conditions of assignment
Increase cultural awareness
Increase knowledge of the host country
Impart working knowledge of the foreign language
Increase conflict management skills
Minimize reentry problems

How much development?

Predeparture training
  Orientation
  Area study
  Language instruction
  Cross-cultural T group
Behavioral simulation
Case method
Postarrival training
  Orientation and training
  Intergroup problem solving
Reentry training

Knowledge about cultural, political, economic,
  business, legal, and social factors of the host
  country
Awareness of the needs and expectations
  of the different parties interested in
  international operation
Awareness of the problems of family
  relations in the host country

Source: "A Model for Developing Key Expatriate Executives," by A. Rahim, © April 1983. Reprinted with permission of PER-SONNEL JOURNAL, ACC Communications, Inc., Costa Mesa, CA. All rights reserved.

Standardized vs. Tailor-Made

Some management training is standard, or generic. For example, participants often are taught how to use specific decision-making tools, such as quantitative analysis, and regardless of where the managers are sent in the world, the application is the same. These tools do not have to be culturally specific. For example, successful Japanese MNCs tend to provide all their personnel with a common training and development program.[37] Similarly, basic behaviorally oriented concepts such as communication, motivation, and leadership often initially are taught within a generic program, then a tailor-made program is created so that the material can be made country- or region-specific. Research shows that small firms usually rely on standard training programs and larger MNCs design their own. Some of the larger MNCs are increasingly turning to specially designed video and power-point programs for their training and development needs.

Tailor-made training programs are created for the specific needs of the participants. Input for these offerings usually is obtained from managers who currently are working (or have worked) in the country to which the participants will be sent as well as from local managers and personnel who are citizens of that country. These programs often are designed to provide a new set of skills for a new culture. Quite often, the offerings are provided before the individuals leave for their overseas assignment; however, there also are postdeparture training programs that are conducted on-site. These often take the form of systematically familiarizing the individual with the country through steps such as meeting with government officials and other key personnel in the community; becoming acquainted with managers and employees in the organization; learning the host-country nationals' work methods, problems, and expectations; and taking on-site language training.[38]

A good example is provided by Underwriters Laboratories, Inc., which has developed a 2-day, in-house training program for professional members of its staff who travel to Japan to work with clients on projects and for staff members who deal extensively with Japanese clients in the United States.[39] The program is designed around a series of minilectures that cover topics ranging from how to handle introductions to the proper way to exchange gifts to the correct way of interpreting Japanese social and business behavior. The 2-day program consists of lectures, case studies, role plays, language practice, and a short test on cultural terminology; it concludes with a 90-minute question-and-answer period. At the end of the program, participants have a fundamental understanding of how to communicate with the Japanese. More importantly, they know the types of information they lack and how to go about learning more on becoming more effective intercultural communicators.

One of the most common types of training in both standard and tailor-made packages is that of self-evaluation. Participants in such training are provided personal insights about their behaviors. For example, managers will be given tests to determine if their managerial style is basically factual, intuitive, analytical, or normative. A **factual manager** looks at the available information and makes decisions based on the data. An **intuitive manager** is imaginative, innovative, and can jump from one idea to another. An **analytical manager** is systematic, logical, and carefully weighs alternatives to problems. A **normative manager** is idealistic and concerned with how things should be done. Every manager will be some combination of all four types, but by learning their individual preferences, participants gain insights into their own approach to dealing with people.

Table 16-2 shows how these managerial styles will influence the way that an individual plans, appraises performance, makes decisions, and coaches. For example, a factual manager will focus on how things are done here-and-now, while an intuitive manager will focus more on the future. Similarly, an analytical manager will integrate consideration of the past, present, and future into his or her planning activities, while a normative manager will focus heavily on reviewing what has happened in the past and use this to determine new directions. Simply put, different managers use different styles in doing their jobs. This is an important finding because it shows that when these managers are being trained, the trainer must keep in mind the trainees' personal orientations. Some people learn best with factual styles, others do better with intuitive, analytical, or normative styles.

Table 16-3 illustrates this in more depth by showing how each of the management styles will differ based on the cultural background of the trainees. A close look at the table, for example, shows that a factual management style applied in European cultures would need to emphasize theoretical as opposed to factual information, while in North America a much more pragmatic approach would be required if the training were to be effective. Similarly, when using an intuitive management style, North American trainees tend to look for ideas which can be applied, while in African cultures perceptions are often given much

Factual manager
A manager who looks at the available information and makes decisions based on that data.

Intuitive manager
A manager who is imaginative, innovative, and able to jump from one idea to another.

Analytical manager
A manager who is systematic and logical and carefully weighs alternatives to problems.

Normative manager
A manager who is idealistic and concerned with how things should be done.

Table 16–2
Cultural Characteristics of Managerial Styles and Activities

Activity	Factual Style	Intuitive Style	Analytical Style	Normative Style
Planning	Focus on the present, on the here-and-now. The manager clarifies the existing situation, what is.	Focus on the future. The manager sets up objectives.	Relate past, present, and future. The manager works on strategies and tactics.	Focus on the past. The manager reviews and assesses what has been done to direct new action.
Performance appraisal	Deal with skills. (Register the facts.)	Concentrate on potential. (Look for possibilities.)	Assess performance according to several factors. (The individual, the situation, the manager, the environment.)	Insist on the perform-ance appraisal process, the relationship, the sharing of perceptions. (To understand each other is the aim.)
Decision making	Decision are based on facts and on thorough investigations; they are always well docu-mented.	Decision are related to hunches, imagination, guesses, trial and error, risk-taking.	Decisions are the result of a systematic way to iden-tify options, alternatives and weigh them accord-ing to a set of well-analyzed pros and cons.	Decisions are closely linked to the value sys-tems which exist in the team, organization, or culture concerned.
Coaching	Each individual has to find his or her own way. The manager can only facilitate the process by clarifying the facts.	The manager moti-vates the employee in describing a "could be" situation appealing to him or her.	Coaching is systematically organized, in a kind of step-by-step approach: "This is what has to be done to change what is into what should be."	The basic assumption that underlines the evaluative approach toward coaching is that weaknesses and strengths should be fairly evaluated and taken care of.

Source: This information is found in Pierre Casse, *Training for the Multicultural Manager* (Washington, DC: Society for Intercultural Education, Training and Research, 1982), p. 41.

greater importance than basic facts, and in South American cultures the intuitive style often results in a great deal of excitement and emotion regarding how the information can be used—in sharp contrast to the more subdued approach used by North Americans. Additionally, when an analytical style is used in European cultures, the focus is often on get-ting things done through a hierarchical, bureaucratic design, while North Americans tend to process analytical information in terms of how it can be used in a decentralized, empowered structure. Both of these approaches are quite different, for example, from those of African cultures where the analytical style would focus on the process used to get things done, and from Asian cultures where ambiguity is widely accepted and the training participants would not feel that there was only one right way to do things. In South American cultures, mean-while, the analytical approach is more problematic because of the belief that many times things should just be allowed to take their own course and not be overly controlled through analysis. Finally, a normative approach will also have to be modified to meet the needs of the participant's culture. Europeans place a great deal of attention on quality of work life and are often overly critical of how things are done. North Americans are far less critical and put their focus on getting things done and achieving self-esteem for their professional accom-plishments. In contrast, African cultures value interpersonal relations and the training must reflect these needs. Meanwhile, Asians like to avoid conflict and prize simplicity and humil-ity, so many of the ideas that might get active discussion in European and North American training sessions receive very little, if any, attention. Finally, in South American cultures dig-nity and personal relations are important and normative ideas are dealt with accordingly.

A close evaluation of the material in Table 16-3 shows that the training approaches that are successful in one geographic region of the world may need to be heavily modified if they are to be as effective elsewhere. This finding has been echoed by Sergeant and Frenkel who recently conducted interviews with expatriate managers with extensive experience in China.[40] Their objective was to identify HRM issues and the ways in which they need to be addressed

Table 16–3
Management Styles Applied to Five Cultures

Management Style	European Cultures	North American Cultures	African Cultures	Asian Cultures	South American Cultures
Factual	•Meanings are in individuals •Theoretic as opposed to practical •Inconsistent	•Individuals rely on the spoken words •Professional experiences are perceived as important •Pragmatic	•Meanings come from the environment •Time is viewed as flexible; it is not rigid •"Things" are alive	•Meanings are everywhere; in people, things •No clear-cut separation between the internal and external worlds •Sensing is an illusion	•Touching is an important part of the communication process •Sensual •Attracted to poetry, art, literature
Intuitive	•Like to play with ideas •Creative and imaginative •Enjoy exploring new avenues	•Look for ideas which can be used •Enjoy learning •Can be perceived as "naive" at times (simplistic ideas)	•Superstitious •Ideas come from group interactions •What is perceived is at least as important as what is	•Highly "spiritual" •A great sense of unity is shared by many people •Metaphysical	•Enjoy disagreements on principles, ideas; the stimulation of an exchange of opinions •Jump from one idea to another •Emotional when talking about possibilities and opportunities
Analytical	•Deductive •Rigid organizational structures •Centralized decision-making process	•Inductive •Flexible organization cultures •Decentralized decision-making process	•Are process oriented •Thinking is highly internalized (visual thinking) •Thinking is assimilated to "feeling"	•Accept ambiguity •Open to many options (there is not just "one way") •Integrate polarities and contradictions	•A certain fatalism (faith is valued) •*Mañana* concept •Disorganized and highly centralized
Normative	•Overcritical •Quality of life is highly valued •Conflicts are enjoyable	•Getting the job done is the priority •People like to be liked at the same time that they "push" people around •Self-esteem is based largely on professional accomplishments	•The concept of kinship is highly valued •Friendship comes before business and is lasting •Interpersonal relationships are based on sincerity	•Simplicity and humility are highly valued •Peacefulness is what counts above all •Enjoy flowing with situational forces	•*Machismo* (conservative) •*Dignita* •*Personalismo*

Source: This information is found in Pierre Casse, *Training for the Multicultural Manager* (Washington, DC: Society for Intercultural Education, Training and Research, 1982), p. 43.

by MNCs going into China. As seen in Table 16-4, many of the human resource management approaches that are employed are different from those used in the United States or other developed countries because of the nature of both the Chinese culture and its economy.

In the final analysis, the specific training program to be used will depend on the needs of the individual. Tung, after surveying managers in Europe, Japan, and the United States, has found that there are six major types of cross-cultural training programs:

1. Environmental briefings used to provide information about things such as geography, climate, housing, and schools
2. Cultural orientation designed to familiarize the individual with cultural institutions and value systems of the host country

Table 16–4
Human Resources Management Challenges Facing MNCs in China

Human Resource Management Function	Comments/Recommendations
Employee recruitment	The market for skilled manual and white-collar employees is very tight and characterized by rapidly rising wages and high turnover rates. Nepotism and overhiring remain a major problem where Chinese partners strongly influence HR policies; and transferring employees from state enterprises to joint ventures can be difficult because it requires approval from the employee's old work unit.
Reward system	New labor laws allow most companies to set their own wage and salary levels. As a result, there is a wide wage disparity between semiskilled and skilled workers. However, these disparities must be balanced with the negative effect they can have on workers' interpersonal relations.
Employee retention	It can be difficult to retain good employees because of poaching by competitive organizations. In response, many American joint-venture managers are learning to take greater control of compensation programs in order to retain high-performing Chinese managers and skilled workers.
Work performance and employee management	Local managers are not used to taking the initiative and are rarely provided with performance feedback in their Chinese enterprises. As a result, they tend to be risk-averse and are often unwilling to innovate. In turn, the workers are not driven to get things done quickly and they often give little emphasis to the quality of output. At the same time, it is difficult to dismiss people.
Labor relations	Joint-venture regulations give workers the right to establish a trade union to protect employee rights and to organize. These unions are less adversarial than in the West and tend to facilitate operational efficiency. However, there is concern that with the changes taking place in labor laws and the possibility of collective bargaining, unions may become more adversarial in the future.
Expatriate relations	Many firms have provided little cross-training to their people and family, education, and health issues limit the attractiveness of a China assignment. Some of the major repatriation problems include limited continuity in international assignments and difficulties of adjusting to more specialized and less autonomous positions at home, lack of career prospects, and undervaluation of international experience. Management succession and the balancing of local and international staff at Chinese firms are also problematic.

Source: Adapted from Andrew Sergeant and Stephen Frenkel, "Managing People in China: Perceptions of Expatriate Managers," *Journal of World Business,* vol. 33, no. 1, 1998, p. 21.

3. Cultural assimilators using programmed learning approaches designed to provide the participants with intercultural encounters

4. Language training

5. Sensitivity training designed to develop attitudinal flexibility

6. Field experience, which sends the participant to the country of assignment to undergo some of the emotional stress of living and working with people from a different culture[41]

Surprisingly, Tung found that only 32 percent of the U.S. firms she surveyed had formal training programs to prepare individuals for foreign assignments. This contrasted sharply with the 57 percent of Japanese firms and 69 percent of European companies that had formal programs. Table 16-5 reports the findings based on type of program and functional task. She concludes the following:

Results indicate that for both the U.S. and West European samples, most of the firms that had training programs recognized the need for more rigorous training for the CEOs and functional heads than for trouble-shooters and operatives. In contrast, the Japanese firms that sponsored training programs appear to provide slightly more rigorous training for operatives. This could arise from the fact that since CEOs have more extensive records of overseas work experience, the need to subject them to the more rigorous programs was perceived as less important.[42]

Table 16–5
Frequency of Training Programs in U.S., European, and Japanese Samples (percent)

Training Programs	Job Category											
	CEO			Functional Head			Troubleshooter			Operating Personnel		
	U.S.	Eur.	Japan.	U.S.	Eur.	Japan.	U.S.	Eur.	Japan.	U.S.	Eur.	Japan.
Environmental briefing	52	57	67	54	52	57	44	38	52	31	38	67
Cultural orientation	42	55	14	41	52	14	31	31	19	24	28	24
Culture assimilator	10	21	14	10	17	14	7	10	14	9	14	19
Language training	60	76	52	59	72	57	36	41	52	24	48	76
Sensitivity training	3	3	0	1	3	0	1	3	5	0	3	5
Field experience	6	28	14	6	24	10	4	3	10	1	7	24

Source: Rosalie L. Tung, "Selection and Training Procedures of U.S., European, and Japanese Multinationals," *California Management Review,* Fall 1982, p. 66. © 1982 by the Regents of the University of California. Reprinted from the *California Management Review,* vol. 25, no. 1. By permission of the Regents.

Some organization now have extended this idea to include cross-cultural training of family members, especially children who will be accompanying the parents. The accompanying sidebar, "U.S.-Style Training for Expats and Their Teenagers," explains how this approach to cultural assimilation is carried out.

In addition to training expats and their families, effective MNCs also are developing carefully crafted programs for training personnel from other cultures who are coming into their culture. These programs, among other things, have materials that are specially designed for the target audience. Some of the specific steps that well-designed cultural training programs follow include:

1. Local instructors and a translator, typically someone who is bicultural, observe the pilot training program and/or examine written training materials.

2. The educational designer then debriefs the observation with the translator, curriculum writer, and local instructors.

3. Together, the group examines the structure and sequence, ice breaker, and other materials that will be used in the training.

4. The group then collectively identifies stories, metaphors, experiences, and examples in the culture that will fit into the new training program.

5. The educational designer and curriculum writer make the necessary changes in the training materials.

6. The local instructors are trained to use the newly developed materials.

7. After the designer, translator, and native-language trainers are satisfied, the materials are printed.

8. The language and content of the training materials are tested with a pilot group.[43]

In developing the instructional materials, culturally specific guidelines are carefully followed so that the training does not lose any of its effectiveness. For example, inappropriate pictures or scenarios that might prove to be offensive to the audience must be screened out. Handouts and other instructional materials that are designed to enhance the learning process are provided for all participants. If the trainees are learning a second language, generous use of visuals and live demonstrations will be employed. Despite all of these

International Management in Action

U.S.-Style Training for Expats and Their Teenagers

One of the major reasons why expatriates have trouble with overseas assignments is that their teenage children are unable to adapt to the new culture, and this has an impact on the expat's performance. To deal with this acculturation problem, many U.S. MNCs now are developing special programs for helping teenagers assimilate into new cultures and adjust to new school environments. A good example is provided by General Electric Medical Systems Group (GEMS), a Milwaukee-based firm that has expatriates in France, Japan, and Singapore. As soon as GEMS designates an individual for an overseas assignment, this expat and his or her family are matched up with those who have recently returned from this country. If the family going overseas has teenage children, the company will team them up with a family that had teenagers during its stay abroad. Both groups then discuss the challenges and problems that must be faced. In the case of teenagers, they are able to talk about their concerns with others who already have encountered these issues, and the latter can provide important information regarding how to make friends, learn the language, get around town, and turn the time abroad into a pleasant experience. Coca-Cola uses a similar approach. As soon as someone is designated for an overseas assignment, the company helps initiate cross-cultural discussions with experienced personnel. Coke also provides formal training through use of external cross-cultural consulting firms who are experienced in working with all family members.

A typical concern of teenagers going abroad is that they will have to go away to boarding school. In Saudi Arabia, for example, national law forbids expatriate children's attending school past the ninth grade, so most expatriate families will look for European institutions for these children. GEMS addresses these types of problems with a specially developed education program. Tutors, schools, curricula, home-country requirements, and host-country requirements are examined, and a plan and specific program of study are developed for each school-age child before he or she leaves.

Before the departure of the family, some MNCs will subscribe to local magazines about teen fashions, music, and other sports or social activities in the host country, so that the children know what to expect when they get there. Before the return of the family to the United States, these MNCs provide similar information about what is going on in the United States, so that when the children return for a visit or come back to stay, they are able to quickly fit into their home-country environment once again.

An increasing number of MNCs now give teenagers much of the same cultural training they give their own managers; however, there is one area in which formal assistance often is not as critical for teens as for adults: language training. While most expatriates find it difficult and spend a good deal of time trying to master the local language, many teens find that they can pick it up quite easily. They speak it at school, in their social groups, and out on the street. As a result, they learn not only the formal language but also clichés and slang that help them communicate more easily. In fact, sometimes their accent is so good that they are mistaken for local kids. Simply put: The facility of teens to learn a language often is greatly underrated. A Coca-Cola manager recently drove home this point when he declared: "One girl we sent insisted that, although she would move, she wasn't going to learn the language. Within two months she was practically fluent."

A major educational benefit of this emphasis on teenagers is that it leads to an experienced, bicultural person. So when the young person completes college and begins looking for work, the parent's MNC often is interested in this young adult as a future manager. The person has a working knowledge of the MNC, speaks a second language, and has had overseas experience in a country where the multinational does business. This type of logic is leading some U.S. MNCs to realize that effective cross-cultural training can be of benefit for their workforces of tomorrow as well as today.

efforts, however, errors sometimes occur.[44] One consultant, whose team was working with Japanese trainers and managers, reported the following story:

> We assumed that the Japanese trainers would be extemporaneous. But we found that they expected to "blend" into a rigorous manual and follow it to the letter. They also expected to follow an exact time schedule and work through all of the material without veering too far from the lesson plan, even to respond to trainees' questions. What's more, we American trainers were

criticized for our behavior in the training sessions. We thought we were being professional. But, to the Japanese trainers, anything that wasn't in the manual was considered "out of form." From the Japanese perspective, harmony in training comes from conforming. But our trainers from the United States felt as if the Japanese expected them to be robots. In the Japanese culture, if a trainer's behavior and activities lack form, trainees may view the trainer as irresponsible.[45]

Cultural Assimilators

The cultural assimilator has become one of the most effective approaches to cross-cultural training. A **cultural assimilator** is a programmed learning technique that is designed to expose members of one culture to some of the basic concepts, attitudes, role perceptions, customs, and values of another.[46] These assimilators are developed for each pair of cultures. For example, if an MNC is going to send three U.S. managers from Chicago to Caracas, a cultural assimilator would be developed to familiarize the three Americans with Venezuelan customs and cultures. If three Venezuelan managers from Caracas were to be transferred to Singapore, another assimilator would be developed to familiarize the managers with Singapore customs and cultures.

In most cases, these assimilators require the trainee to read a short episode of a cultural encounter and choose an interpretation of what has happened and why. If the trainee's choice is correct, he or she goes on to the next episode. If the response is incorrect, the trainee is asked to reread the episode and choose another response. Table 16-6 provides an example.

Cultural assimilator
A programmed learning technique designed to expose members of one culture to some of the basic concepts, attitudes, role perceptions, customs, and values of another culture.

Choice of Content of the Assimilators
One of the major problems in constructing an effective cultural assimilator is deciding what is important enough to include. Some assimilators use critical incidents that are identified as being important. To be classified as a critical incident, a situation must meet at least one of the following conditions:

1. An expatriate and a host national interact in the situation.
2. The situation is puzzling or likely to be misinterpreted by the expatriate.
3. The situation can be interpreted accurately if sufficient knowledge about the culture is available.
4. The situation is relevant to the expatriate's task or mission requirements.[47]

These incidents typically are obtained by asking expatriates and host nationals with whom they come in contact to describe specific intercultural occurrences or events that made a major difference in their attitudes or behavior toward members of the other culture. These incidents can be pleasant, unpleasant, or simply nonunderstandable occurrences.

Validation of the Assimilator
The term **validity** refers to the quality of being effective, of producing the desired results. It means that an instrument—in this case, the cultural assimilator—measures what it is intended to measure. After the cultural assimilator's critical incidents are constructed and the alternative responses are written, the process is validated. Making sure that the assimilator is valid is the crux of its effectiveness. One way to test an assimilator is to draw a sample from the target culture and ask these people to read the scenarios that have been written and choose the alternative they feel is most appropriate. If a large percentage of the group agrees that one of the alternatives is preferable, this scenario is used in the assimilator. If more than one of the four alternatives receives strong support, however, either the scenario and/or the alternatives are revised until there is general agreement or the scenario is dropped.

A second validation step is to ask the sample group to rate how important each episode is. This helps to identify those incidents that should be included and those that are of only marginal value and can be omitted.

After the final incidents are chosen, they are sequenced in the assimilator booklet. Similar cultural concepts are placed together and presented, beginning with simple situations and progressing to more complex ones. Most cultural assimilator programs start out with 150 to 200 incidents, of which 75 to 100 eventually are included in the final product.

Validity
The quality of being effective, of producing the desired results. A valid test or selection technique measures what it is intended to measure.

Table 16–6

A Cultural Assimilator Situation

Sharon Hatfield, a school teacher in Athens, was amazed at the questions that were asked of her by Greeks whom she considered to be only casual acquaintances. When she entered or left her apartment, people would ask her where she was going or where she had been. If she stopped to talk, she was asked questions like, 'How much do you make a month?" or "Where did you get that dress you are wearing?" She thought the Greeks were very rude.

                                                                                                          Page X-2
Why did the Greeks ask Sharon such "personal" questions?

1. The casual acquaintances were acting like friends do in Greece, although Sharon did not realize it.

                                                                                                  Go to page X-3

2. The Greeks asked Sharon the questions in order to determine whether she belonged to the Greek Orthodox Church.

                                                                                                  Go to page X-4

3. The Greeks were unhappy about the way in which she lived and they were trying to get Sharon to change her habits.

                                                                                                  Go to page X-5

4. In Greece such questions are perfectly proper when asked of women, but improper when asked of men.

                                                                                                  Go to page X-6

                                                                                                          Page X-3
You selected 1: The casual acquaintances were acting like friends do in Greece, although Sharon did not realize it.

Correct. It is not improper for in-group members to ask these questions of one another. Furthermore, these questions reflect the fact that friendships (even "casual" ones) tend to be more intimate in Greece than in America. As a result, friends are generally free to ask questions which would seem too personal in America.

                                                                                                  Go to page X-1

                                                                                                          Page X-4
You selected 2: The Greeks asked Sharon the questions in order to determine whether she belonged to the Greek Orthodox Church.

No. This is not why the Greeks asked Sharon such questions. Remember, whether or not some information is "personal" depends upon the culture. In this case, the Greeks did not consider these questions too "personal." Why? Try again.

                                                                                                  Go to page X-1

                                                                                                          Page X-5
You selected 3: The Greeks were unhappy about the way in which she lived and they were trying to get Sharon to change her habits.

No. There was no information given to lead you to believe that the Greeks were unhappy with Sharon's way of living. The episode states that the Greeks were acquaintances of Sharon.

                                                                                                  Go to page X-1

                                                                                                          Page X-6
You selected 4: In Greece such questions are perfectly proper when asked of women, but improper when asked of men.

No. Such questions are indeed proper under certain situations. However, sex has nothing to do with it. When are these questions proper? Try to apply what you have learned about proper behavior between friends in Greece. Was Sharon regarded as a friend by these Greeks?

                                                                                                  Go to page X-1

Source: Adapted from Fred E. Fiedler, Terence Mitchell, and Harry C. Triandis, "The Culture Assimilator: An Approach to Cross-Cultural Training," *Journal of Applied Psychology*, April 1971, pp. 97–98.

The Cost-Benefit Analysis of Assimilators The assimilar approach to training can be quite expensive. A typical 75- to 100-incident program often requires approximately 800 hours to develop. Assuming that a training specialist is costing the company $50 an hour including benefits, the cost is around $40,000 per assimilator. This cost can be spread over many trainees, however, and the program may not need to be changed every year. An MNC that sends 40 people a year to a foreign country for which an assimilator has been constructed is paying only $200 per person for this programmed training. In the long run, the costs often are more than justified. In addition, the concept can be applied to virtually all cultures. Many different assimilators have been constructed, including Arab, Thai, Honduran, and Greek, to name but four. Most importantly, research shows that these assimilators improve the effectiveness and satisfaction of those being trained as compared with other training methods.

Other Approaches

In addition to assimilators, a variety of other approaches are used in preparing managers for international assignments. These include visits to the host country, briefings by host-country managers, in-house management programs, and training in local negotiation techniques.[48]

The best "mix" of training often is determined by the individual's length of stay. The longer that a person will be assigned to an international locale, the greater the depth and intensity of the training should be. Figure 16-2 illustrates this idea. Using the model in this figure, if the expected level of interaction is low and the degree of similarity between the individual's culture and the host culture is high, the length of the training should be less than a week, and methods such as area and cultural briefings should be used. Conversely, if the level of interaction is going to be high and the individual will be gone for 1 to 3 years, use of assessment centers, field experiences, and simulations should be considered. The degree, type, and length of training is a result of expected integration and length of stay. Simply put, today's MNCs use a contingency approach in developing their training strategy.

Organization Development

Organization development (OD) has been broadly defined as the deliberate and reasoned introduction, establishment, reinforcement, and spread of change for the purpose of improving an organization's effectiveness and health. The OD process has been widely used in the United States and Western Europe to help organizations identify problems that are associated with change and to formulate effective solutions.

Nature of OD

A basic purpose of OD is to reconcile individual-group-organization differences. Two of the most common reasons for this reconciliation are: (1) individual or group conflicts in the organization are resulting in a loss of overall effectiveness; and (2) the organization is introducing changes, such as new technology, and efforts must be made to gain acceptance by the personnel.

Most OD efforts are led by an individual who is skilled in the behavioral sciences and knows how to guide and facilitate the introduction and implementation of change effectively. This OD change agent typically will use one or more OD interventions. **OD intervention** is a catchall term used to describe the structured activity in which targeted individuals, groups, or units engage in accomplishing task goals that relate to organization development. There are many examples of OD interventions. Some are fairly simple and designed to improve individual or interpersonal behavioral skills. Others are more sophisticated and involve large groups or even the entire organization. Some of the most common interventions include the following:

- **Team building.** An extension of classic T-groups (training groups) and sensitivity training, which were designed to help the participants better understand themselves and each other, team building is geared more to improving organizational effectiveness through cooperation and a "team" effort by key personnel.
- **Management by objectives (MBO).** A management system for the joint setting of subordinate goals, coaching and counseling the personnel, and providing feedback on their performance.

Organization development (OD)
The deliberate and reasoned introduction, establishment, reinforcement, and spread of change for the purpose of improving an organization's effectiveness.

OD intervention
The structured activity in which targeted individuals, groups, or units engage in accomplishing task goals that are related to organization development.

Team building
An extension of classic T-groups (training groups) and sensitivity training that is geared to enhancing organizational effectiveness through cooperation and a "team" effort of key personnel.

Management by objectives (MBO)
A management system for the joint setting of subordinate goals, coaching and counseling personnel, and providing feedback on their performance.

Figure 16-2   **A Contingency Approach to Cross-Cultural Training**

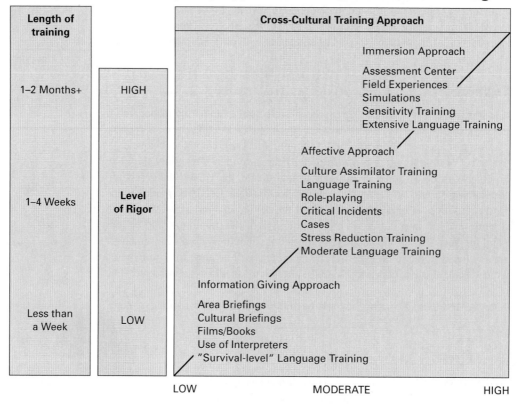

Source: M. E. Mendenhall, E. Dunbar, and G. R. Oddou, "Expatriate Selection, Training and Career-Pathing: A Review and Critique," *Human Resource Management,* Fall 1987, p. 338. Used with permission. © 1987. Reprinted by permission of John Wiley & Sons, Inc.

Confrontation meetings
The gathering and analysis of information related to intra- and intergroup conflict followed by the formulation of a plan of action by the participants for the purpose of resolving these problems.

Third-party peacemaking
The diagnosis of group conflict followed by the use of an outside party (usually the OD change agent) to facilitate a constructive resolution of a problem.

Survey feedback
An OD intervention that involves the gathering and analysis of information related to group behavior and problems and the feeding back of this information to develop effective action plans.

- **Confrontation meetings.** The gathering and analysis of information related to intra- or intergroup conflict, followed by formulation of a plan of action by the participants to resolve these problems.

- **Third-party peacemaking.** The diagnosis of group conflict followed by use of an outside party (usually the OD change agent) to facilitate a constructive resolution of the situation.

- **Survey feedback.** Often more detailed and long-range than the confrontation meeting, this intervention involves the gathering and analysis of information related to group behavior and problems and the feeding back of this information to develop effective action plans.

These interventions can focus on the individual, groups of two or three people, large groups, intergroup relations, or the total organization. The OD intervention that is used will be determined by the particular problems that are uncovered after an OD change agent analyzes the situation.

Research shows that in most cases, success of an OD intervention depends on a number of important conditions. These include:

1. Use of an outside OD consultant who will collect the data, determine how best to deal with the problem, and lead the intervention.

2. Support for the effort from all levels of management.

3. Proper implementation of the OD intervention.

4. Follow-up to ensure that once things are improved, they do not slip back.

OD in International Settings

Can OD techniques be applied successfully in international settings? Researchers have found that although OD interventions can be useful, some limitations are caused by cultural barriers. Bourgeois and Boltvinik, for example, note that in South America, egalitarian social principles do not attract as much support as in the United States. This results in a lack of democratic management, communication, and trust among the personnel and personal willingness to participate in decision making. They observe:

> Authoritarian management styles are not only accepted, but practically demanded by both Latin American workers and subordinate managers. Recent research has confirmed that, at least among Mexican managers, the perceived need to share information and objectives with subordinates is less than it typically is among American managers; there is also less belief in participative management styles. Any offer made to a Latin American subordinate to participate in decision making would not only be met with bewilderment but would result in a lowering of respect for the superior. With the acceptance of autocratic style comes complete faith in the superior's competence and wisdom. Any request for subordinate input would erode this faith and be perceived as a sign of weakness.[49]

Another major problem is language. Some of the words and concepts that are used in OD do not translate into Spanish. For example, although there in concept, the actual word *compromise* does not exist in Spanish. As a result, there may be confusion and many of the conditions critical to the success of OD change efforts are missing. Thus, many OD techniques will not work well in South American cultures.

There also are problems in applying OD in regions such as Europe, Asia, and Australia. As noted in Chapter 5, four cultural dimensions are given major attention. Two of these are power distance and uncertainty avoidance. In a typical OD intervention, participants are asked to share information, be open and honest in their communications, listen to what is being said by others, and work as a team to identify and resolve problems. This process requires the individuals to let down their guard and take the chance that they will be embarrassed or have their egos bruised. Participants who do these things must have low power distance. They must be willing to treat everyone else as an equal and not allow hierarchical rank or status to affect their interaction with the other individuals.

At the same time, participants must have low uncertainty avoidance. They must be able to live with ambiguity. Hofstede's research shows that few countries have these two dimensions of low power distance and low uncertainty avoidance. He found the four countries that best fit this cultural pattern are Denmark, Sweden, Ireland, and Great Britain. Jamaica also is a good candidate because of its low uncertainty avoidance, although it does have moderately high power distance. The United States, Canada, Australia, and others in that cluster also are good candidates for OD, although not as good as the Denmark cluster.[50] The overall conclusion is fairly obvious: OD interventions in many cases do not work well overseas, because the culture does not lend itself to these techniques. This is particularly true of unstructured interventions such as team building.[51]

Even management by objectives, which is so popular in the United States, has not been widely accepted. Comparing its success in the United States with that in Germany and France, Jaeger has noted that

> in Germany, which scores quite a bit higher on uncertainty avoidance, MBO has become management by joint goal setting, mitigating some of the risk and emphasizing the team approach, which is in line also with the lower individualism present in the German culture.
>
> In France, MBO has generally run into problems. . . . The original DPO (Director par Objectifs) became DPPO (Direction Participative par Objectifs) after the 1968 student revolts: "anything that fostered participation and decentralization was welcomed." Nevertheless, the high power distance to which the French are accustomed from childhood ultimately has thwarted the successful utilization of MBO as a truly participative process. Trepo notes that

the problem is not necessarily with MBO per se but its implementation by French managers. He describes examples of managers who are unaware that they are trying to exert control through the implementation of the objectives of MBO almost by fiat.[52]

Similarly, the confrontation meeting, with its strong emphasis on low uncertainty avoidance and power distance, is particularly inappropriate in areas such as South America, the Mediterranean, Japan, Pakistan, Iran, Thailand, and Taiwan. However, some OD interventions do seem to have value. Third-party peacemaking is particularly compatible in many cultures, and if handled correctly, survey feedback could be used in countries with high uncertainty avoidance and power distance. Jaeger comments:

> Survey feedback generates data that at first may be looked at in a dispassionate way, without generating uncertainty or raising questions that would overstep the boundaries of hierarchy. Thus, an evaluation of the data can proceed slowly and not reach sensitive issues very quickly, if at all. With survey feedback one also has some control over the type of data generated, as the consultant can decide which questions are asked. A culturally sensitive consultant can therefore put together a questionnaire that generates data in such a way that a problem can be defined and discussed without upsetting the power relationships present. Hence, survey feedback could be an appropriate intervention even in those countries . . . that have high uncertainty avoidance and high power distance.[53]

In addition, OD practitioners can improve the chances of effectively using these techniques by accepting that cross-cultural OD interventions must be adapted to local conditions. Joint efforts with local practitioners can be of particular value. OD practitioners also need to learn the language of the country where the intervention is used to facilitate the exchange of information between participants and the OD change agent. The change agent can gain participant assistance in modifying the intervention for local use. As Bourgeois and Boltvinik have noted: "The straightforward transfer of American organizational development technologies to an alien cultural setting could have deleterious consequences for both the focal organization and the individuals in it if a concerted effort is not made to recognize and compensate for the potential conflicts inherent in applying its value-laden techniques in foreign organizations."[54]

Organizational Behavior Modification

Attention was briefly given to organizational behavior modifications or O.B. Mod. research in Chapters 6 and 13, where it was noted that in motivating and leading international personnel, U.S.-based theories and techniques often need to be modified. At the same time, however, recent research reveals that a behavioral management approach, if applied properly, can prove to be very valuable in improving performance across cultures. The basic O.B. Mod. application model is presented in Figure 16-3. As shown, the five major steps include:

1. *Identification of performance behaviors.* The first step of the O.B. Mod. application model is to identify the critical, observable, performance-related behaviors. In this way high-impact behaviors that may account for most of the performance outcomes are targeted for primary consideration.

2. *Measurement of the behavior.* The next step is to measure the baseline frequencies of the behaviors that were identified in Step 1. This is typically done through approaches such as direct observation, time sampling, and the gathering and analysis of existing records.

3. *Functional analysis of the behavior.* The next step consists of a functional analysis of the antecedents—behavior—contingent consequences of the behavior. Antecedents are identified in order to determine those factors that cue or set the occasion for the behavior to be carried out. Behaviors are the actions that follow from the antecedents. Contingent consequences are what determine the subsequent behavior and give power to the antecedent cues; these are reinforcers and punishers.

Figure 16–3   **The Organizational Behavior Modification Model**

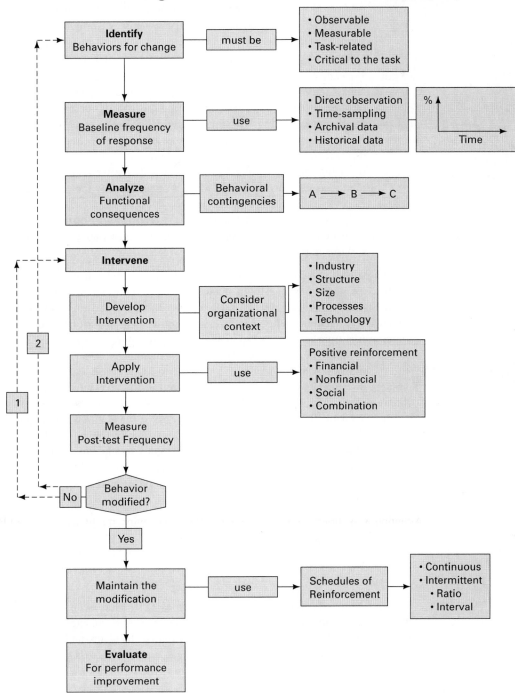

Source: Fred Luthans, Alex Stajkovic, Brett C. Luthans, and Kyle W. Luthans, "Applying Behavioral Management in Eastern Europe," *European Management Journal,* vol. 16, no. 4, 1998, p. 469. This model was originally formulated in Fred Luthans and Robert Kreitner, *Organizational Behavior Modification* (Glenview, IL: Scott, Foresman, 1975) and refined by Alex Stajkovic and Fred Luthans, "A Meta-Analysis of the Effects of Organizational Behavior Modification, 1975–1995," *Academy of Management Journal,* vol. 40, 1997, pp. 1122–1141.

4. *Develop and implement an intervention strategy.* This action step accelerates and strengthens the identified functional behaviors that are increasing performance, while weakening the dysfunctional ones. The main intervention strategy is to use positive reinforcement to increase desirable, functional behaviors. Corrective feedback is used to decrease undesirable, dysfunctional behaviors,

followed by positive reinforcement of the desired alternative behaviors. While positive reinforcers can be anything that increases performance behavior, they typically take forms such as monetary rewards, performance feedback, and social attention and recognition. Moreover, the performance feedback uses the guideline of being positive, immediate, graphic, and specific.

5. *Evaluate to ensure performance improvement.* The last step in the O.B. Mod. behavioral management approach is to systematically evaluate the effectiveness in improving performance. During this phase four levels of evaluation are encouraged: reaction, learning, behavioral change, and performance improvement. Reaction is measured to assess whether the process was well-liked and well-received by those involved in the program because the better the reaction the better the chance of the process being used effectively. Learning is measured to assess how well O.B. Mod. is understood by the participants. Behavioral change is assessed in order to see if there has been any change from the baseline measures obtained in Step 2. Performance improvement is measured to assess outcomes such as the quantity and quality of goods and services that are being produced.

Research by Stajkovic and Luthans found that O.B. Mod. had a very positive impact on employee performance in both manufacturing and service settings primarily in the United States.[55] A meta-analysis of 19 studies that employed the O.B. Mod. approach found that it resulted in a 17 percent average improvement in performance. This was higher than results from meta-analysis on such widely recognized approaches as goal setting. Yet, can O.B. Mod. be of value in the international arena?

As briefly noted in Chapter 13, research on O.B. Mod. by Welsh, Luthans, and Sommers was conducted in the largest textile mill in Russia. The purpose of this investigation was to examine the value of transferring organizational behavior/HRM techniques in a Russian factory. Using a field experimental design, the researchers tested whether both a participative and an O.B. Mod. approach (independent variables) would have a positive impact on Russian workers' productivity (dependent variable). It was found that the participative technique did not work, but the O.B. Mod. approach, using both extrinsic and social reward interventions, did lead to highly significant increases in the performance of the Russian workers.

> Both administration of desired extrinsic rewards and the trained supervisors deliberately providing attention, recognition and feedback contingent upon the workers exhibiting the impact behaviors identified in step one of the O.B. Mod. led to highly significant increases in performance. Importantly, since this was a field experimental research design, we can confidently conclude that the O.B. Mod. was indeed the cause for the performance to significantly improve.[56]

So, if properly applied, techniques such as O.B. Mod. seem to hold promise for MNCs seeking to improve their international human resource management programs. O.B. Mod. and other HRM techniques such as multisource feedback and self-managed teams are needed to develop the human resource core competency across cultures.[57]

Global Leadership Development

Another current trend of human resource development is to focus on leadership. Tichy has noted that a number of leadership training approaches can be used.[58] As shown in Figure 16-4, these range from awareness to cognitive and conceptual understanding to the development of skills and then on to new problem-solving approaches and, ultimately, fundamental change. In this process, management development becomes deeper, involves greater risk, incorporates a longer-term time horizon, and focuses on organization (rather than just individual) change.

At the same time, effective MNCs now encourage strong leadership in the areas of both hard and soft organizational issues. Examples of hard issues include the budget, manufacturing, marketing, distribution, and finance; soft issues address values, culture, vision,

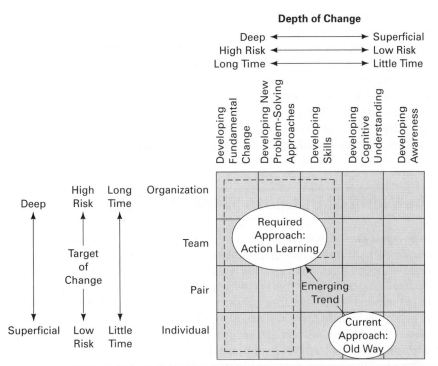

Figure 16–4

The Tichy Development Matrix

Source: Reported in Noel M. Tichy, "Global Development," in Vladimir Pucik, Noel M. Tichy, and Carole K. Barnett (eds.), *Globalizing Management* (New York: John Wiley, 1993), pp. 206–224.

leadership style, and innovative behavior. In exercising strong leadership on hard organizational issues, attention is focused on becoming a low-cost provider of goods and services. In exercising strong leadership on soft organizational issues, the emphasis is on developing and maintaining innovativeness.

GLP Program   One of the best examples of the emerging leadership development programs used by MNCs is the Global Leadership Program (GLP), which is a consortium of leading U.S., European, and Japanese firms, global faculty, and participating host countries. Here is how the GLP has been described:

> The companies are part of an ongoing partnership started in 1988 jointly committed to research and development on issues of globalization. The program design, facilities, and support staff are directed by core faculty from universities in the United States, Europe, and Japan. The members of the consortium participate in a research partnership and in an intensive 5-week Global Leadership Program designed for senior executives with CEO potential.[59]

The GLP is designed to provide participants with an intensive international experience to develop a global mindset, instill cross-cultural competency, and provide the opportunity for global networking. The program is 5 weeks in duration, but before attending, each person is given specially prepared briefing materials about the country that he or she will visit. At the beginning, participants are asked to complete the survey instruments that are designed to assess the individual's perceptions regarding the characteristics of a global organization, dimensions of global leadership, and the way that managers carry out their global responsibilities.

The core of the program is a 2-week, on-site, country assessment carried out by cross-cultural teams. Each group of trainees is required to use information from the assessment to produce investment opportunities and entry strategy recommendations as well as video documentaries as part of their country assessment. Among other things, each team of trainees spends 2 weeks preparing for the country assessment by working on its personal global leadership capabilities and its global mindset and team skills. Preparation also includes a weekend at an Outward Bound school and a 2-day assessment in Washington, DC.

The GLP is designed to blend rigorous intellectual development of global leaders, beginning with each individual's map of his or her own personal global mindset. Then, these are shared with the members of each team, who then are responsible for creating an analytical framework to guide its assessment of a major geopolitical region of the world. By the second week of the program, the teams have started on their country assessment. During the third and fourth weeks, the participants split up and travel to their respective countries. During the fifth and last week of the program, the individuals write their reports and make their video documentaries and presentations. Because of its strong emphasis on involvement and action learning, the GLP has become one of the best recognized development programs for training global leaders for MNCs.

The World of Business Week Revisited

As seen in the *Business Week* article that opened this chapter, M&S faces a host of problems. Some of these can be addressed through a careful review of its human resource development strategies. This is particularly true in the case of those related to upper-level leadership for this is where the critics feel the company is weakest. As noted in the news story, investors question whether the head of M&S is wearing too many hats and needs to name a successor and divide his roles as chairman and CEO. Of course, this concern for human resource development must trickle down through the whole organization. As M&S continues to go international, both the training and organization development discussed in this chapter becomes relevant.

In linking this chapter to the current news, briefly review the opening article and the major concepts that were presented in the chapter. Then answer the following three questions: (1) Using Table 16-1 as your guide, how would the training and development programs that M&S uses in Great Britain be different from those employed in France, Italy, and the United States? What types of differences would there be? (2) How could the new head of M&S turn the company into a "teaching" organization? What are some practical guidelines that would be of value? (3) How could the firm profit from the creation of a global leadership development program? If it chose to do this, what would you expect to be included in the program?

Summary of Key Points

1. Training is the process of altering employee behavior and attitudes to increase the probability of goal attainment. Many expatriates need training before (as well as during) their overseas stay. A number of factors will influence a company's approach to training. One is the basic type of MNC: ethnocentric, polycentric, regiocentric, or geocentric. Another factor is the learning style of the trainees.

2. There are two primary reasons for training: organizational and personal. Organizational reasons include overcoming ethnocentrism, improving communication, and validating the effectiveness of training programs. Personal reasons include improving the ability of expatriates to interact locally and increasing the effectiveness of leadership styles. There are two types of training programs: standard and tailor-made. Research shows that small firms usually rely on standard programs and larger MNCs tailor their training. The six major types of training include environmental briefings, cultural orientation, cultural assimilators, language training, sensitivity training, and field experience.

3. A cultural assimilator is a programmed learning approach that is designed to expose members of one culture to some of the basic concepts, attitudes, role perceptions, customs, and values of another. Assimilators have been developed for many different cultures. Their validity has resulted in the improved effectiveness and satisfaction of those being trained as compared with other training methods.

4. Organization development (OD) is the deliberate and reasoned introduction, establishment, reinforcement, and spread of change for the purpose of improving an organization's effectiveness. The basic purpose of OD is to reconcile individual-group-organization differences, often accomplished through the use of OD interventions such as team building, MBO, confrontation meetings, third-party peacemaking, and survey feedback.

5. Research shows that OD interventions often are less effective in international settings. One primary reason is that many cultures do not have low power distance or low uncertainty avoidance, which are two key dimensions for successful OD efforts. This is why team building has not worked well and MBO has been greatly modified. On the other hand, third-party peacemaking and survey feedback have been successful, because they can be adapted to the two cultural dimensions of power distance and uncertainty avoidance. Also, proven techniques such as O.B. Mod. have been shown to hold considerable potential for improving employee performance across cultures.

Key Terms

analytical manager	intuitive manager	regiocentric MNC
confrontation meetings	learning	survey feedback
cultural assimilator	management by objectives (MBO)	team building
ethnocentric MNC	normative manager	third-party peacemaking
ethnocentrism	OD intervention	training
factual manager	organization development (OD)	validity
geocentric MNC	polycentric MNC	

Review and Discussion Questions

1. How do the following types of MNCs differ: ethnocentric, polycentric, regiocentric, and geocentric? Which most likely would provide international management training to its people? Which would least likely provide international management training to its people?

2. IBM is planning on sending three managers to its Zurich office, two to Madrid, and two to Tokyo. None of these individuals has any international experience. Would you expect the company to use a standard training program or a tailor-made program for each group?

3. Ford Motor now is in the process of training managers for overseas assignments. Why might this MNC want to learn the managerial styles (factual, intuitive, analytical, and normative) of each person?

Of what value would this be in the training process? Give two examples.

4. Zygen, Inc., a medium-sized manufacturing firm, is planning to enter into a joint venture in China. Would training be of any value to those managers who will be part of this venture? If so, what types of training would you recommend?

5. Hofstadt & Hoerr, a German-based insurance firm, is planning on expanding out of the EU and opening offices in Chicago and Buenos Aires. How would a cultural assimilator be of value in training the MNC's expatriates? Is the assimilator a valid training tool?

6. Why would an MNC be interested in using OD techniques? What are their benefits? What are their limitations? On balance, how useful are they?

Internet Exercise: Searching On-Line for Excellence

This chapter focused on human resource management approaches that are used by MNCs to develop their international workforce as well as to better prepare their home-office personnel to meet the international challenge. Three of the firms that were mentioned in the chapter are leaders in creating training programs to meet this challenge: Coca-Cola, PepsiCo, and AlliedSignal. Visit the web sites of these three firms at: **www.cocacola.com**, **www.pepsico.com**, and **www.alliedsignal.com**. In each case, look carefully at the firm's current operations and international expansion activities. In most cases the organization's current annual report will provide you with much of this information, but also look at special product lines and new develop-

ments that are taking place. Then tie your findings to the chapter material by answering these four questions: (1) In what areas of the world is each firm beginning to focus more of its attention? (2) What types of training and development programs do you believe will be of value to each company in these efforts? Be specific and describe the tools and techniques that you would expect the firms to use. (3) What challenges do you think each will face in creating these programs and what are some steps that will be of value in minimizing these challenges? (4) Do you think a global leadership program such as the one discussed at the end of this chapter and used by General Electric would have value to any of these three firms in developing their leadership programs? Why or why not?

Argentina

Argentina occupies most of the southern part of South America. The country covers a triangular area of approximately 1.1 million square miles. It is bordered on the west by Chile, on the north by Bolivia and Paraguay, and on the east by Uruguay and the Atlantic Ocean. There are approximately 36 million people in the country (in South America, only Brazil is larger and has more people). People from many European countries settled Argentina, but most came from Spain and Italy. The urban Argentines thus have European customs and continue to draw from them in terms of fashion, art, literature, and architecture. Much of the country's wealth comes from the land (Argentina exports more beef than any other country). The economy during the past decade had many problems, but in recent years, it has been improving. Both GDP and capital investments are increasing, and the inflation rate has gone from an unbelievable 3103 percent in 1989 to single digits today. As noted in one recent report, Argentine shopkeepers now dare to label prices in ink. The economic outlook for the future remains risky, but hopeful.

For the last 2 years Warren Worthy's U.S.-based company has been operating two shopping malls in Buenos Aires and one in Cordoba. The operations have not been as profitable as the company would like, but they are making money, unlike most of the rest of the retail industry in the country.

Earlier this year, Warren sent one of his senior-level management people, Paul Flexner, to look over the mall operations and see if there were any changes that might be made. Paul was met at the airport by one of the eight U.S. managers who held the top jobs in the Buenos Aires and Cordoba operations. Paul was accompanied by an interpreter. During his stay, Paul had an opportunity to look over the operations of the shopping malls and talk to many relevant parties. Paul was able to put together a number of recommendations that he was convinced could be useful. Overall, the major problem he felt was that the Americans

being sent down from the United States did not have enough training or orientation to Argentinean culture and language. When Paul asked one of the expatriate managers about this, he was tersely told, "Oh, we pick up things as we go along. If there's something I don't understand, I ask my interpreter. These guys are worth their weight in gold down here."

Paul also noticed that the U.S. managers remained aloof in terms of involvement. Their style was to give orders and then depend on the Argentineans who worked for them to implement the decisions. Paul believes that the reason for this approach is that the Americans are not really sure of how to do things, so they prefer not to get too involved. On his return to the United States, Paul is going to recommend that a detailed training program be put together and that no one be sent to Argentina until he or she has successfully completed this course. In particular, Paul wants to see major emphasis given to culture and language training. Before leaving, he mentioned some of his ideas to one of the U.S. managers, but the expatriate did not seem very receptive. "Oh, it's not necessary to go through all of that trouble," he told Paul. "We're doing just fine by relying on interpreters."

www.invertir.com

Questions

1. What are some current issues facing Argentina? What is the climate for doing business in Argentina today?

2. Do you agree with Paul that language training is needed?

3. Should the firm develop a standardized or a tailor-made training program?

4. What are some things that Americans need to know about management styles in South America? In your answer, incorporate data from Table 16-2.

A Southern Expansion

A small but rapidly growing U.S. irrigation equipment company is thinking about expanding its operation into the South American market. Founded 8 years ago, the firm has annual sales of $25 million and is growing at a 25 percent annually compounded rate. Most of these sales are in the United States, although the company has been trying to penetrate the Indian market and had sales of $1 million there last year.

The company sells a patented piece of irrigation equipment that has proven performance capabilities. The biggest problem for the firm is that many buyers prefer better-known companies' products, so it has to compete vigorously based on price. Thus, the board of directors is considering entering markets that are not as competitive. "There is very little irrigation equipment selling in South America," the chair of the board recently told top management. "Why don't we look into this market and see if we can develop a foothold. Admittedly, the agricultural community down there won't be as knowledgeable as they are in the states, but we could end up getting in on the ground floor."

Following up this suggestion, the company sent three representatives to South America to investigate the market. These individuals all agreed that there is a large, untapped potential in the region that could be the base for a very profitable foreign venture. As a result, the company has drafted a preliminary plan of action for doing business in Argentina, Brazil, Chile, and Colombia. If sales are suf-ficient in these four countries, the firm will then expand to other South American locations. The company wants to enter into a business arrangement with foreign partners whereby the firm provides the equipment and the partners handle the selling activities. Each country would have a central sales office that would serve as the link between the firm and its local foreign-run outlets. The head of this sales office would be a U.S. American appointed by company headquarters' senior management. This individual would be responsible for providing assistance to the local outlets and keeping headquarters' senior management informed about developments in the region. The sales office head would have a small staff consisting of two expatriates and three locals.

Initial plans call for setting up the first unit in each country within the next 18 months and, if things go according to plan, expanding coverage to an average of three outlets per country within the first 3 years. In each case, the company will set up the initial units in the country's agricultural centers and then slowly expand into other areas.

Questions

1. What type of training would you recommend for the expatriate managers?

2. Would you recommend the use of cultural assimilators? If no, why not? If yes, for whom?

3. If there are operating problems, would it be possible to use OD techniques to resolve them?

Chapter 17

Labor Relations and Industrial Democracy

Objectives of the Chapter

Besides personnel selection and repatriation (Chapter 15) as well as training and organization development (Chapter 16), another critical part of managing human resources in the international arena is how the MNC handles its labor relations. How domestic firms deal with their labor relations and determine union contracts can differ significantly from country to country. A second challenge, especially for those MNCs operating in Europe and Asia, is industrial democracy, which is much more prevalent there than in other parts of the world. A third challenge is the need to coordinate worldwide efforts through formulation of an effective labor relations strategy.

This chapter addresses these challenges. Initially, it examines labor relations in the international arena using the United States as the point of comparison. Next, the internationalism of labor unions is explored. The chapter then looks at the various approaches to industrial democracy that are employed in Europe and Asia. Finally, how MNCs attempt to integrate industrial relations into their overall strategy is reviewed. The specific objectives of this chapter are:

1. DEFINE "labor relations," and examine the approaches used in the United States and other countries.

2. REVIEW the international structure of labor unions.

3. EXAMINE the nature of industrial democracy, and note some of the major differences that exist throughout the world.

4. DESCRIBE the philosophical views and strategic approaches that are used by MNCs in managing international industrial relations and future strategies.

BusinessWeek

The World of Business Week:

The German Worker Is Making a Sacrifice

Hans-Gunter Eidtner felt like the first officer on a jet that was losing altitude with sickening speed. Head of the works council at the Hamburg factory of struggling Daimler Benz Aerospace (DASA), Eidtner faced the ugly prospect of 800 fellow workers losing their jobs. But the 60-year-old labor boss last month averted disaster, persuading the powerful IG Metall union to O.K. concessions, such as axing overtime pay. "We had a big fight" to push through the givebacks, says Eidtner.

Such a deal would have been unthinkable a few short years ago. Historically, Germany's big unions forced companies to accept nationwide "pattern" contracts, a practice that gave them enormous power. Ailing steelmakers in the north had to give workers the same cushy contracts as thriving carmakers in the south. But now, with a near-record 4.3 million people out of work and jobs fleeing the country, workers suddenly are eager to compromise. What began as a trickle of reform at stumbling mid-size companies in eastern states quickly has spread to Germany's biggest companies. "The German worker is making a sacrifice," says Hubertus von Grünberg, chief executive of tiremaker Continental.

But German business, on a campaign to boost profits and shareholder value, is pushing ever harder to restructure. Increasingly, companies are cutting

deals with workers that improve productivity and flexibility. Most negotiate concessions with the works councils at individual factories or subsidiaries, then gain reluctant approval from national unions. Some even sever all union links and deal directly with workers. At DASA's Hamburg plant, which assembles Airbus 319 and 321 jets, some employees will shift to a 40-hour workweek, up from 35 now. All 7,000 workers agreed to up to 100 hours of overtime a year without extra pay, in return for free time when demand slackens.

Such deals are most common in eastern Germany. That's because, ironically, unions have less clout in the former communist zone. Moreover, companies there, unable to compete in a market economy, have scrambled to slash labor costs. In Saxony, for instance, only about 8% of companies in the electrical and metalworking industries are bound by pattern contracts, says Dietmar Voigt, an official at the regional employers federation in Dresden. The rest have cut their own deals—either with or without the consent of IG Metall, Germany's largest union.

In the west, small and midsize companies were first to jump on the bandwagon. At Gustav Selter Ltd., a knitting-needle maker near Dortmund that employs 40 people, workers have agreed to flexible working hours and pay cuts totaling 16% since 1994. In return, they now receive a share of profits. Sales are growing 15% a year, vs. just 5% before the concessions were implemented, and profits should jump nearly 50% in 1997, says owner Thomas Selter. "At the grass roots, major change is under way."

It's trickling up, too. One German union has decided to support the trend toward company-tailored contracts. IG Chemie-Papier-Keramik, the nation's third-largest labor group with 725,000 members, in June struck a ground-breaking, industrywide deal. It allows hard-pressed companies to reduce pay by as much as 10% in return for job security and commitments for further investment in German operations. Although the contract doesn't go into effect until January, about 50 companies already are negotiating to take advantage of the new provisions.

Will workers reap the rewards of their newly accommodating spirit? Unfortunately, even over the medium term, most of Germany's new labor agreements aren't likely to boost employment. That's because most simply give companies greater ability to meet increased demand without hiring new staff. It's a huge benefit for employers, since layoffs are so difficult and costly under German law. And some companies will continue to trim payrolls by attrition. But workers are facing the fact that concession now could forestall another bout of radical surgery. Says DASA's Eidtner: "Each one of us knows that in three or four years, when the [aircraft] boom is over, we'd have exactly the same problem as before."

Indeed, until Germany undertakes far more sweeping structural reform of its labor market and regulatory system, companies will have to struggle to stay globally competitive. Even with the mark hitting a six-year low against the dollar, 1.79 on July 15, Germany's wage costs are still the world's highest.

And social security taxes are headed toward 42%, in part because of the added costs brought on by high unemployment.

But business has long since stopped waiting for Bonn to get moving on tax and regulatory reform. Companies continue to shift some labor-intensive operations to lower-cost locations. And in their relentless pursuit of efficiency, they are finding that with workers back home, they have more leverage than ever before.

Source: **Reprinted from July 28, 1997, pp. 46–47 issue of *Business Week* by special permission, copyright © 1997 by McGraw-Hill Companies, Inc.**

This opening news story discusses a development that is beginning to change the face of labor relations in Europe. German unions, with the highest paid members in the world, are beginning to accept the fact that their industries and businesses cannot remain competitive unless they, the unions, agree to change. Wage guarantees of the past must be reviewed in light of current market conditions because businesses throughout the EU are being hurt in competitive battles by high labor costs. So if union wages are too high in Germany, MNCs will look for less expensive sources of labor in Portugal, Spain, and locations outside of Europe. In short, globalization is forcing German unions to think much more strategically and to be increasingly prepared to accommodate changing conditions or they will price themselves out of jobs. In this chapter we will examine the nature and trends in labor relations and industrial democracy in Germany and selected other countries around the world.

Labor Relations in the International Arena

Labor relations
The process through which management and workers identify and determine the job relations that will be in effect at the workplace.

The term **labor relations** can be defined as the process through which management and workers identify and determine the job relationships that will be in effect at the workplace. These relationships often are communicated verbally, but in some cases, they also are written in the form of a contract, particularly when workers are represented by a union and a management-labor contract is negotiated and agreed to by both parties. The percentage of workers who are union members varies widely by country. In Sweden, in recent years over 85 percent of employees have been unionized, while in France and the United States, only 12 percent are unionized.[1] Therefore, depending on the countries where it does business, an MNC will face varying degrees of organized labor challenges.

As in other areas of international human resource management, the specific approaches to labor relations will vary from country to country. Some nations employ a labor negotiation process similar to that in the United States, in which both sides have power; others are characterized by either a strong management group or a highly powerful union. This is true in terms of the way that labor agreements are negotiated and enforced as well as the way industrial conflicts are resolved. Using the U.S. approach to labor relations as a benchmark, the following sections discuss how the labor relations process is carried out in selected countries around the globe.

The U.S. Approach to Labor Relations

Collective bargaining
The process whereby formal labor agreements are reached by union and management representatives; it involves the negotiation of wages, hours, and conditions of employment and the administration of the labor contract.

Union
An organization that represents the workers and in collective bargaining has the legal authority to negotiate with the employer and administrator the labor contract.

In the United States, formal labor agreements result from **collective bargaining**, in which union and management representatives negotiate wages, hours, and conditions of employment and administer the labor contract. A **union** is an organization that represents the workers and, in collective bargaining, has the legal authority to negotiate with the employer and to administer the labor contract. How collective bargaining is carried out in the United States often differs from how it is done in other countries because of the nature of U.S. labor laws.

For a work group to unionize in the United States, 30 percent of the workers must first sign authorization cards requesting that a specific union represent them in bargaining with the employer. If this percentage is met, the union can petition the National Labor Relations Board (NLRB) to hold an election. When this is done, it will be certified as the bargaining agent if the union receives more than 50 percent of the workers' votes. The two sides then will meet and hammer out a labor contract. This agreement typically remains in effect for 2 to 3 years. When it expires, a new agreement is negotiated, and assuming that the union continues to represent the workers, the cycle continues anew. If the workers are dissatisfied with their representation, they can vote out the union and go back to things the way they were before.

Note that if the workers support the union but that union is unable to negotiate a labor agreement that is acceptable to them, the workers may go on strike to pressure management to agree to their terms. Management, however, can bring sanctions of its own, including locking out employees or hiring strike breakers (called "scabs" by union members) to fill the positions of those who refuse to work. Such a lockout occurred by the owners in the National Basketball Association strike in the 1998–1999 season. Unlike those in most other countries, however, labor strikes in the United States, such as the NBA, almost always are confined to periods when the contract is being renegotiated. Strikes seldom are used in the middle of the labor contract agreement, because mechanisms such as a grievance procedure can be employed.

Steps of a Grievance Procedure   A **grievance** is a complaint brought by an employee who feels that he or she has been treated improperly under the terms of the labor agreement. In the United States, efforts are made to solve these problems at the lowest level of the hierarchy and as quickly as possible. The contract will spell out the specific steps in the grievance procedure. The first step usually involves a meeting of the union representative at the operating level (commonly called the "shop steward") and the supervisor, who attempt to agree on how to solve the grievance. If it is not solved at this level, the grievance may go to the next steps, involving union officials and higher-level management representatives. These conciliatory approaches usually solve the grievance to the satisfaction of both parties. Sometimes, however, the matter ends up in the hands of a mediator or an arbitrator.[2]

Mediation and Arbitration   A **mediator** brings both sides together and helps them to reach a settlement that is mutually acceptable. An **arbitrator** provides a solution to a grievance that both sides have been unable to resolve themselves and that both sides agree to accept. A number of arbitration approaches typically are used. In resolving wage-related issues, for example, three of the most common include: (1) splitting the difference between the demands of the two parties; (2) using an either–or approach, in which one side's position is fully supported and the other side's rejected; and (3) determining a fair wage based on market conditions.

Importance of Positive Labor Relations   Labor relations are important, because they directly determine labor costs, productivity, and eventually, even profits. The accompanying box, "International Management in Action: They're Leading the Pack," gives details on some of the benefits from healthy labor relations. If the union and management do not have good relations, the organization's cost of doing business likely will be higher than it otherwise would be. In fact, in recent years, many MNCs entering the United States have been looking for sites where they can set up nonunion plants. They are convinced that unions make them less competitive. This conviction certainly is debatable (e.g., highly successful Southwest Airlines is highly unionized), although some MNCs have been effective by keeping out unions. One example is the productive Japanese Nissan plant in Smyrna, Tennessee, which continually defeats union efforts.

Labor Relations in Other Countries

Because labor relations strategies vary greatly from country to country, MNCs find that the strategy used in one country sometimes is irrelevant or of limited value in another. A number of factors can account for this. One is the economic development of the country, given

Grievance
A complaint brought by an employee who feels that he or she has been treated improperly under the terms of the labor agreement.

Mediator
A person who brings both sides (union and management representatives) together and helps them to reach a settlement that is mutually acceptable.

Arbitrator
An individual who provides a solution to a grievance that both sides (union and management representatives) have been unable to resolve themselves and that both sides agree to accept.

International Management in Action

They're Leading the Pack   www2.ford.com

Many believe that MNCs are attracted to lesser developed countries because of labor relations policies that are conducive to cooperation, low wages, and productivity. In truth, the United States is still proving to be one of the most attractive locations for international firms. Although the power of U.S. labor unions is declining, the labor relations climate is conducive to rising productivity. Today, the United States is not only the most productive nation in the world, its overall productivity is increasing faster than that of the other major industrial powers, such as Japan, Germany, and France. The Japanese economy has been having trouble since the early 1990s, and the surging value of the yen has reduced its international competitiveness. Despite having some of the most successful MNCs in the world (e.g., Hitachi, Mitsubishi, Sony, and Toyota), Japan is experiencing some difficulties. The same is true in Europe. Many MNCs on the continent now are engaged in painful restructuring that is designed to make them more efficient and competitive in world markets. Their governments fight such downsizing, however, because of the negative impact on employment. As a result, firms such as Volkswagen in Germany and Alcatel Alsthom in France continue to face the challenge of becoming more efficient on the one hand and accommodating government directives to hire more people on the other. These are problems that U.S. MNCs do not yet face, and it helps them to maintain high productivity. There also are other reasons why U.S. productivity is doing so well relative to the rest of the world.

One is that the U.S. work ethic seems to be stronger than ever. For example, U.S. workers now are working more hours per week than they did 20 years ago. Other major economic powers such as Germany and Japan are finding just the opposite; their people are working shorter workweeks than at any time in the past. In Japan, for example, the average manufacturing worker today puts in approximately 20 percent fewer hours than in 1960, and this downward trend likely will continue. A couple of reasons are that many Japanese feel they already make enough money to take care of their needs, and many claim that they are fed up with hard work. Even Japanese union members oppose lengthening the workweek, despite efforts from their leadership to cooperate with the companies and put in more hours. Part of this opposition is a belief among the rank-and-file Japanese workers that the union represents the company's interests rather than their interests.

A second factor is that labor costs in the United States actually are lower in recent years than in most other major industrial countries. Thanks to union-management cooperation, U.S. companies have been able to introduce high-tech, efficient machinery. As a result, firms such as Ford now can manufacture cars at lower prices than foreign competitors can. Moreover, as Ford continues closing outmoded plants and running others at close to capacity, costs per car should decline even further. Much of this outcome is a result of effective labor relations strategies and shows that U.S. manufacturers not only are back in the ballgame but, in many cases, may be leading the pack.

that general labor relations strategies often change as a country's economic situation changes. In addition, entry strategies often must be modified as the firm begins to settle in. Changes in the political environment also must be taken into consideration. For example, under the Thatcher government, British labor unions had a difficult time; in fact, prounion recognition provisions that were legislated in the mid-1970s were repealed in the 1980s. With the landslide election of Tony Blair as the British prime minister, the Labor Party now dominates, although its policies are decidedly more middle-of-the-road than that of previous Labor governments.

Still another factor is strike activity. Unions in many countries often call strikes in the middle of a contract period. These strike decisions often catch the company unprepared and result in lost productivity and profit as the firm tries to negotiate with the union and/or transfer work to other geographic locales and minimize the economic effect.

Other differences are more regional in nature. For example, labor relations throughout Europe are somewhat similar, but they differ sharply from those in the United States. Some of these differences in European labor relations include:

1. In Europe, firms typically negotiate their agreements with unions at the national level, through employer associations representing their particular industries, even when there also is local, within-company negotiations. This national agreement establishes certain minimum conditions of employment that frequently are augmented through bargaining with the union at the firm or the local level.

2. Unions in many European countries have more political power than those in the United States, so when employers deal with their union(s), they in effect often are dealing directly or indirectly with the government. Unions often are allied with a particular political party—generally referred to as the labor party, although in some countries these alliances are more complex, such as a number of different political parties, each supported and primarily identified with a particular union or set of unions.

3. There is a greater tendency in Europe for salaried employees, including those at managerial levels, to be unionized, often in a union of their own.

4. Unions in most European countries have existed longer than those in the United States. Consequently, they occupy a more accepted position in society and are less concerned about gaining approval.[3]

The following sections examine industrial relations approaches in a number of selected countries.

Great Britain In contrast to the situation in the United States, the labor agreement in Great Britain is not a legally binding contract. It is merely an "understanding" among the parties that sets forth the terms and conditions of employment that are acceptable at present. Violations of the agreement by the union or management carry no legal penalties, because the contract cannot be enforced in court. Additionally, while unions are relatively powerful and strikes are more prevalent than in the United States, British union membership has declined in recent years.[4]

Labor agreements in Great Britain typically are less extensive than those in the United States. These understandings usually contain provisions that define the structure of the relationships among the parties and set forth procedures for handling complaints. Typically, however, there is no provision for arbitration of disagreements or grievances, although both mediation and arbitration on occasion are used.

Germany Traditionally, unions and management in Germany have had a more cooperative relationship than those in the United States, where an adversarial relationship often has existed. While some observers believed that the unification of West and East Germany would increase labor conflict, this has not happened. In fact, as integration continues, labor harmony seems to be improving. Certainly, on an overall basis, there is a spirit of cooperation between German management and labor brought about by, among other things, the use of industrial democracy, in which workers serve on the board of directors and ensure that the rank and file are treated fairly. A detailed discussion of industrial democracy is given toward the end of this chapter.

Union power in Germany is still quite strong. Although union membership is voluntary, there generally is one union in each major industry. This powerful industry union will negotiate a contract with the employers' federation for the industry, and the contract will cover all major issues, including wages and terms of employment. All firms that are members of the employers' federation then will pay the agreed-on wages. Firms that are not members of the federation typically will use the contract as a guide to what they should pay their people. Although a minority of the labor force is organized, unions set the pay scale for about 90 percent of the country's workers, with wages determined by job classifications. If an individual is replaced because of automation or laid off because of declining business, the workers' wage settlement also is handled according to the previously determined agreement. Still other agreements are hammered out to cover general working conditions, work hours, overtime pay, personal leave, and vacations.

If there is a conflict over interpretation or enforcement of the agreement, the situation typically is negotiated between the company and the worker with participation of a union representative and/or work council. If an impasse is reached, the situation can be referred to a German labor court for final settlement.

By the mid-1990s, some German unions became more adversarial. For example, IG Metall union began adopting an approach in dealing with employers that was more like that used in the United States. However, more recent economic developments (see the opening *Business Week* article) have resulted in a softening of this union position. In fact, the labor relations climate in Germany traditionally is much more serene than in the United States, and most unions lack the firepower to engage in prolonged strikes. One reason is that the rights of workers are addressed more carefully by management. A second is that even though they are covered by a labor contract, individual workers are free to negotiate either individually or collectively with management to secure wages and benefits that are superior to those in the agreement.

Japan   Unions and management have a cooperative relationship in Japan. One reason is social custom, which dictates nonconfrontational union–management behavior. The provisions in Japanese labor agreements usually are general and vague, although they are legally enforceable. Disputes regarding the agreement often are settled in an amicable manner. Sometimes, they are resolved by third-party mediators or arbitrators. Labor commissions have been established by law, and these groups, as well as the courts, can help to resolve negotiations impasses.

Japanese unions are most active during the spring and again at the end of the year, because these are the two periods during which bonuses are negotiated. Recently, Japanese unions, like the German unions, have been trying to extend wage bargaining to cover all firms in a particular industry. This would provide the union with greater negotiating power over the individual firms within the industry. Their success in this industrywide bargaining strategy would have particular impact on MNCs operating in Japan. Compared with those of most other industrialized countries, however, Japanese unions remain relatively weak.

How Industrial Conflict Is Handled around the World

When the union and management reach an impasse in contract negotiations or over some issue, conflict results. The union may call for a strike, or management may have a lockout. A **strike** is a collective refusal to work to pressure management to grant union demands. In recent years, strikes have been less common in most countries; however, when measured in terms of working days lost per 1,000 employees, strikes are still a powerful weapon in dealing with industrial conflict. A **lockout** is the company's refusal to allow workers to enter the facility. Other typical union strategies resulting from conflict include slowdowns, sabotage, sit-ins, and boycotts. The following sections show how these approaches are handled around the world.

Strike
A collective refusal to work to pressure management to grant union demands.

Lockout
A company's refusal to allow workers to enter the facility during a labor dispute.

United States   Most U.S. labor contracts have a specific provision that outlaws strikes; thus, sudden or unauthorized strikes (commonly called "wildcat strikes") are uncommon. If either party to the contract feels that the other is not acting in good faith or living up to the terms, the grievance procedure is used to resolve the matter peacefully. However, once the contract period is over and if a new one is not successfully negotiated, the workers may strike or continue to work without a contract while threatening to walk out. On the other side, management also may lock out the workers, although this is much more rare. The modern position of more and more U.S. unions is that a philosophy of "us against them" is not as conducive to the long-range welfare of the union as is a strategy of working together to find common ground. In this regard, U.S. unions are moving closer to the approach that is used by many unions in other countries.

Great Britain   In Great Britain, labor unions are relatively powerful (although this power has been eroded in recent years), and strikes are more prevalent than in the United

States. Labor agreements typically do not prohibit strikes, and the general public is more used to and tolerant of them. Strikes in Britain often are brief, however, and do not involve a large number of people, although British miners have had prolonged strikes.

Some labor experts believe that industrial conflict in Britain results in more problems than in the United States, because the system is not geared toward the efficient resolution of problems. For example, many in the British general public as well as the workers believe that it is management's job to look after workers, and failure to do so is a breach of management's social responsibility. This climate often results in hard feelings and impedes rapid solutions. In addition, the procedure for handling grievances, in contrast to that used in the United States, often is informal, cumbersome, and sometimes results in fragmented efforts with the outcome costly in terms of both time and money. Sometimes, management uses the lockout to vent its frustration over the bureaucratic delays in resolving labor-related problems. Although things have been changing for the better in recent years, the British in general still appear willing to accept conflict with resulting strikes and lockouts as the price of protecting the rights of the workers.

Germany   A number of similarities exist between the United States and Germany in terms of managing labor conflicts. As in the United States, strikes and lockouts are prohibited in Germany during the period when a labor agreement is in effect. A strike is legal, however, when the contract has run out and a new one has not yet been ratified by the workers. Although German unions tend to be industrywide, quite often several agreements are in force in a particular company, and these agreements do not have the same termination dates. Therefore, one group of workers may be striking or working out a contract while another is working under contract. In addition, different terms and conditions of employment exist for different groups of workers, just as in the United States. Similarly, there sometimes are strikes in the middle of a contract period in clear violation of the labor agreement, indicating that the German preference for orderly and well-defined work relationships is not always present. Overall, however, there tends to be a fair amount of cooperation between management and labor because of the way labor relations are legally structured.

Japan   Strikes and lockouts in Japan are very rare. Following World War II, there was a period of severe labor unrest coupled with massive, and sometimes crippling, labor strikes. Today, however, strikes are of short duration and used only to drive home a particular, minor point, not to cripple an industry or inconvenience the public. One knowledgeable observer has explained it this way:

> Since threats are generally unnecessary, a strike in Japan is merely a way to embarrass management, and thus may last from a couple of hours to a couple of days, with those of a week or more considered very long. But an equally important reason for strikes' being so short is the strong social pressure to keep the conflict quiet and resolve it quickly and quietly without having to resort to the law. In Japan the law is regarded as the instrument with which the state imposes its will. Hence, the Japanese do not like the law and will try to stay as far away from it as possible.[5]

Sometimes, strikes occur when a Japanese union is negotiating with management during industrywide negotiations. These strikes are aimed at showing that the workers support their union and are not designed to indicate any particular grievance or complaint with management. This is understood by both sides. The issues over which both sides might disagree are fairly limited. This is true for two reasons: (1) An individual's term of employment never exceeds those provided for in the labor contract, because this would indicate that this worker was more important than the other members of the work group; and (2) the law establishes standards for minimum wages, hours, overtime, rest periods, vacations, sick leaves, sanitary conditions, and discharge. Therefore, individual needs or desires are not given a great deal of attention by the union; however, Japanese unions still try to gain benefits for their people, as seen in recent efforts to win wage increases and cuts in working hours.

An insight into Japanese labor relations is provided by the cultural value of *Wa*, which implies that individuals should subordinate their interests and identities to those of the group. This cultural value helps to account for a great deal of the harmony that exists between management and labor in Japan.

International Structure of Unions

So far, this discussion has centered on the international implications of labor relations, but the structure of unions themselves also has important implications. Most labor unions are locally or nationally based, but some are internationally active.[6] Union internalization has been achieved in three basic ways: (1) through use of intergovernmental organizations; (2) through use of transnational union affiliations; and (3) through extension of domestic contracts.

Intergovernmental Organizations

International Labour Office (ILO)
A United Nations affiliate, consisting of government, industry, and union representatives, that works to promote fair labor standards regarding health and safety, working conditions, and freedom of association for workers.

There are two important intergovernmental organizations. The **International Labour Office (ILO)** is a United Nations affiliate that consists of government, industry, and union representations. The ILO has worked to define and promote fair labor standards regarding health and safety, working conditions, and freedom of association for workers throughout the world. A number of years ago, the ILO published a study of social policy implications of MNCs. Some topics in that study included investment concentration by area and industry, capital and technology transfers, international trade, workforce efforts, working conditions, and industrial relations effects. The study concluded by noting the different views and concerns of employers and workers, and it recommended that the social problems and benefits specific to MNCs be identified and studied further.

The ILO has also conducted a series of industry-specific studies on MNCs in Western Europe, and country studies on the employment effects of MNCs, including jobs lost and gained as a result of MNCs as well as the quality of jobs within MNCs. Some of its important conclusions were: (1) jobs were growing faster in MNCs than in non-MNCs; (2) white-collar positions were increasing at the expense of blue-collar jobs; and (3) one key reason for this employment growth was the R&D intensity of MNCs.

Organization for Economic Cooperation and Development (OECD)
A government, industry, and union group founded in 1976 that has established a voluntary set of guidelines for MNCs.

The **Organization for Economic Cooperation and Development (OECD)** is a government, industry, and union group that was founded in 1976 and that has established a voluntary set of guidelines for MNCs. These guidelines include MNCs' obligation to respect the laws and regulations of foreign countries, and in turn, these foreign countries are obliged to provide national treatments to MNCs within their borders. In recent years, these guidelines have been used to help countries regulate the operations of MNCs within their national boundaries.

Transnational Union Affiliations

Global international trade affiliations
Trade relationships that cut across regional and industrial groups and are heavily concerned with political activities.

International Confederation of Free Trade Unions (ICFTU)
The most global international trade union confederation.

There are four basic types of international trade affiliations: global, regional, specialized, and industrial operations. **Global international trade affiliations** cut across regional and industrial groups and are heavily concerned with political activities. The **International Confederation of Free Trade Unions (ICFTU)** is the most important global international for MNCs. Most of the **regional internationals** are subdivisions of the globals, and the regionals' activities are application of the globals' activities. **Specialized internationals**, such as the ILO, the Trade Union Advisory Committee in the OECD, and the European Trade Union Congress, which represents workers' interests at the European Union level, function as components of intergovernment agencies and lobby within these agencies. The **industrial internationals** also are affiliates of the global internationals. In the ICFTU, they are called International Trade Secretaries (ITS), and there is an individual ITS for each major industry group.

Also of transnational interest are worldwide company councils that have been formed under the auspices of the International Trade Secretaries (ITS). For example, there is a General Motors Council, which consists of union representatives from GM plants throughout the world. This council meets periodically to share information about collective bargaining, working conditions, and other developments that can be valuable to unions in gaining comparable treatment for their people in country-level bargaining.

The international structure of the ITS provides a union vehicle that is parallel to the international structure of an MNC. On occasion, an ITS representative has sought to intervene at the global headquarters of an MNC on behalf of a member union having difficulty in its dealings with a subsidiary of the MNC at the national level. Some labor relations experts believed that when worldwide company councils were developing during the 1970s, they would become vehicles for transnational collective bargaining with MNCs; however, the diverse legal and cultural environments of the various countries have been a major barrier to this development.

Regional internationals
Subdivisions of the global affiliation; regional applications of the global's activities.

Specialized internationals
Trade union associations that function as components of intergovernmental agencies and lobby within these agencies.

Industrial internationals
Affiliates of the global international trade groups that focus on a particular industry.

Extensions of Domestic Contracts

Some U.S. unions have sought to deal with MNCs by bargaining with them on a global basis. The International Union of Electrical (IUE) workers, for example, invited union representatives from General Electric's overseas plants to participate in its collective bargaining. These foreign representatives were only observers, however, because U.S. labor law limits collective bargaining to matters that relate to the U.S. labor unit. In another action, the IUE contended that GE was transferring work overseas and charged that this was an unfair labor practice under the provisions of the collective bargaining agreements; however, the general counsel for the National Labor Relations Board rejected the charge and held that the union had not substantiated its claim. Overall, unions have been unsuccessful in attempting to prevent companies from transferring work overseas, although this certainly will continue to be a major focal point in the years ahead.

Industry Democracy

Industrial democracy involves the rights of employees to participate in significant management decisions. This participation by labor includes areas such as wage rates, bonuses, profit sharing, vacations and holiday leaves, work rules, dismissals, and plant expansions and closings. Industrial democracy is not widely used in the United States, where management typically refuses to relinquish or share its authority (commonly called "managerial prerogatives") to make major decisions. In many other countries, however, and especially in Europe, the right of industrial democracy is guaranteed by national law. This right can take a number of different forms.

Industrial democracy
The rights that employees have to participate in significant management decisions.

Common Forms of Industrial Democracy

As the EU consolidates its goal of unification, the head of the European Commission has stated that a primary objective is to obtain a minimum threshold of social rights for workers, to be negotiated between a "European union" and employers. At present, several forms of industrial democracy exist in European countries and elsewhere. In some countries, one form may be more prevalent than others, but it is common to find a number of these forms existing simultaneously.

Codetermination Codetermination, which was discussed briefly in Chapter 12, involves the participation of workers on boards of directors. The idea began right after World War II in Germany to prevent the re-emergence of Nazism in the coal and steel industries. By the mid-1970s, European countries besides Germany, such as Austria,

Denmark, the Netherlands and Sweden, all had legally mandated codetermination. In most cases, boards of directors had to consist of one-third worker representatives. In the late 1970s, Germany increased this to 50 percent for private companies with 2,000 or more employees. Despite such efforts, some researchers report that the workers are not greatly impressed with codetermination; many regard such participation on boards as merely a cosmetic attempt to address the substantive issue of true industrial democracy.

Work Councils   To varying degrees, work councils exist in all European countries. These councils are a result of either national legislation or collective bargaining at the company–union level. Their basic function is to improve company performance, working conditions, and job security. In some firms, these councils are worker- or union-run, whereas in others, members of management chair the group. Workers typically are elected to serve on the council, and management representatives are appointed by the company. The amount of council power will vary. In England, France, and Scandinavia, the groups tend not to be as powerful as in Germany, the Netherlands, and Italy.

Shop Floor Participation   A wide number of approaches are used to achieve shop floor participation. Some of the most common include worker involvement programs, quality circles, and other forms of participative management discussed in earlier chapters. QWL (quality of work life) programs such as those used in the Scandinavian countries and currently very popular in manufacturing and assembly plants throughout Europe and the United States are excellent examples.

Financial Participation   Financial participation takes a number of forms. One of the most common is profit sharing between management and workers. In some cases, productivity or gain sharing plans are used, whereby management shares productivity gains in a predetermined ratio, such as 50-50, with the workers. This motivates workers to recommend efficiency measures and develop shortcuts to doing their jobs in return for a share of the increased profits. Overall, financial participation has not been widely adopted overseas, although it has gained a foothold in a number of U.S. firms, especially those using gain sharing as a team incentive for performance improvement.

Collective Bargaining   If no specific forms of industrial democracy are in effect, collective bargaining itself can become the mechanism to obtain industrial democracy for workers. As noted previously, the ability of unions to bargain collectively is legally restricted in some countries (e.g., a majority vote of the bargaining unit is required in the United States) and is not widely used in others. However, some nations, such as Sweden, require collective bargaining and allow many matters that in the United States are considered to be managerial prerogatives and not applicable to bargaining, such as work rules and production standards, to be open for negotiation with the workers.

Industrial Democracy in Selected Countries

Industrial democracy takes a number of different forms depending on the country. For example, the approach used in the United States differs from those used in Europe and Asia. The following discussion briefly highlights some of these differences.

United States   In the United States, the most common form of industrial democracy is collective bargaining, whose guidelines are spelled out by law. A union that is certified by the NLRB becomes the exclusive bargaining agent for employees in the unit and is authorized to represent workers in the negotiation and administration of a labor–management contract. During the last decade, other forms of industrial democracy have gained ground, most notably employee participation in the form of problem-solving teams, special purpose teams, and self-management teams.

Problem-solving teams
Employee groups that discuss ways of improving quality, efficiency, and the overall work environment.

Problem-solving teams meet weekly to discuss ways of improving quality, efficiency, and the overall work environment. While they generally are not empowered to implement their ideas, their suggestions often result in more efficient operations. These teams have begun to gain widespread support as managers turn to employees for help in improving performance.

Special purpose teams design and introduce work reforms and new technology. In unionized firms, both management and labor will collaborate on operational decisions at all levels. This involvement often creates the necessary environment for both quality and productivity improvements. These teams are continuing to gain popularity, especially in unionized operations.

Self-managing teams consist of individuals who learn all the tasks of all group members, which allows them to rotate from job to job. These teams also take over supervisory duties such as scheduling work, ordering materials, and determining vacation times. These teams have been so effective that in some cases, productivity has increased and quality has risen dramatically. In recent years, these teams have become increasingly popular, and the future will apparently see even greater use of them.

The three types of industrial democracy described here represent a radical departure from the way that U.S. firms traditionally have been managed. The old approach of a top-down management holding on to all the authority now is being replaced with an industrial democracy philosophy of sharing power with the workers. Spurred on more by creative human resource management and the total quality movement, the currently popular empowerment of employees, defined in Chapter 3 as the process of giving employees the resources, information, and authority needed to carry out their jobs effectively, is bringing U.S. firms more into step with the industrial democracy approach taken by firms in other countries over the years.

Great Britain   Industrial democracy is not new to England. Self-governing workshops (worker cooperatives) existed as early as the 1820s; however, Great Britain has not become the hub of industrial democracy in the twentieth century. For example, unlike many workers in Germany and Scandinavia, British workers are not legally mandated to have seats on the board of directors. During the mid-1970s, it appeared that this would happen, but by the early 1990s, indications were that it would not occur in the near future, if at all. As in the United States, however, there is industrial democracy in Great Britain in the form of collective bargaining and worker representation through the use of teams.

Work groups within a British company or plant will elect a chief spokesperson or steward from their ranks to act as their interface with management. If the employees are unionized, a union council will represent them. These councils help to ensure that workers are treated fairly by management. Unfortunately, this sometimes creates a problem, because spokespersons or stewards in the firm may not agree with the union councils.

During the coming years, British firms likely will begin relying more heavily on participative approaches such as those used in the empowerment process in the United States and Northern Europe. The primary reason is that competitive nations have been able to show that shop floor democracy is a key element in reducing production costs and increasing product quality. However, even with the Labor government now in power, legally mandated industrial democracy measures are unlikely in Great Britain any time in the near future.

Germany   Industrial democracy and codetermination are very strong in Germany, especially in the steel and auto industries. Although the union is charged with handling the collective bargaining, internal boards have been established by law for ensuring codeterminism in the workplace. As noted earlier, the full impact of unifying with East Germany is yet to be determined, but all firms with 2,000 or more employees (1,000 or more in the steel industry) presently must have boards composed of workers. One supervisory board is made up of an equal number of representatives who are elected by both the shareholders and the employees, and of one additional, neutral person. This supervisory board in German companies is similar to the board of directors in U.S. firms. The other type of board in German firms is the management board, which is responsible for daily operation. Employees in each plant also elect a plant work council; if it is a multiplant company, members of the plant work council serve on a company work council as well.

Special purpose teams
Employee groups that design and introduce work reforms and new technology.

Self-managing teams
Employee groups that take over supervisory duties and manage themselves; teams consist of individuals who learn all the tasks of all the group members, allowing team members to rotate jobs.

Work councils perform a number of important functions, including negotiating wage rates above the contractually established minimums, negotiating benefits, setting wage rates for new jobs, and re-evaluating pay when workers are transferred between jobs. In multiplant operations, these councils sometimes have difficulty finding out what is happening at the shop floor, so they rely heavily on meetings with employees and communication with shop stewards. As a result, German workers have two groups working for them: the union, which is bargaining collectively with management; and the work council, which is negotiating employment issues relating to that particular plant.

Because of the strong degree of codeterminism, some German managers have argued that the process undermines their ability to operate efficiently. They contend that the legally established industrial democracy hampers their efforts; however, research does not support such a position. For example, School conducted a study of both managers and work councils to determine whether codetermination results in more complex, and thus slower, decision making.[7] He focused on decisions that related to both investment and personnel matters. In general, the study found that the ability of German firms to make decisions is not hampered by codeterminism. However, German businesses must continue to push for changes that make them more competitive worldwide. For example, Daimler-Benz is beginning to develop labor strategies similar to those used by their merger partner Chrysler. A number of reasons help account for this including the fact that over half of the company's shareholders are Americans and the firm sells two-thirds of its cars and light tracks in the U.S. market. So as Daimler begins to absorb Chrysler, it is also likely to be very influenced by the way the latter does business. In addition, noted one observer recently:

> Daimler-Chrysler could also help bring down German wage costs and ease work rules without any policy changes from Bonn. The merged company will continue to include a works council in its decision making—a structure mandated by German law. That means Daimler-Chrysler's labor representatives, too, will be more attentive to U.S. attitudes. Watch for more contract talks allowing flexible labor rules, and changes in the tone of industrywide collective bargaining in Germany.

> Daimler won't be all-American, of course. Key elements of German corporate culture will remain, including the two-tiered system of a supervisory and a management board. But Corporate Germany and [the government] had better keep their eyes on Stuttgart. It may turn out that what's good for Daimler-Chrysler is good for Germany.[8]

Denmark   Industrial democracy ensures that Danish workers participate in the management of their firms both directly and indirectly. The direct form includes use of semiautonomous work groups that provide ideas on enhancing productivity and quality and on scheduling the work. The indirect form includes use of shop stewards on the work floor, representation on boards of directors, cooperation committees consisting of worker and manager representatives, safety groups made up of a supervisor and an elected employee representative, and participation on safety committees that are headed by a manger. Figure 17-1 provides an organizational illustration of these employee participation and industrial democracy arrangements.

Unlike the situation in Germany, where the participation of workers on boards of directors is perceived as cosmetic, cooperation committees of firms in Denmark seem particularly important in ensuring a true feeling of industrial democracy on the part of Danish workers. For example, one study found that most Danish workers felt the cooperation committees contributed heavily to openness, coordination of effort, and a feeling of importance.

Sweden   Industrial democracy in Sweden is directed very heavily toward ensuring quality of work life (QWL) and worker participation in the operation of the enterprise. QWL efforts are closely associated with Sweden's Volvo approach. The creation of semiautonomous work teams and development of a cooperative spirit between management and workers are key elements in Volvo and the Swedish approach to industrial democracy. In addition, councils and committees encourage employee involvement in identifying and implementing changes, which lead to improved QWL, which helps to sustain high

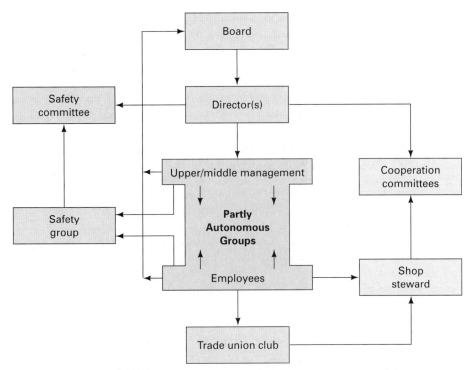

Source: Adapted from Reinhard Lund, "Industrial Democracy in Denmark," *International Studies of Management & Organization,* Summer 1987, p. 18. Used with permission.

Figure 17-1

Employee Participation in All Levels of Danish Firms

morale and positive attitudes of workers and to improve productivity and quality of products and services. There is some evidence, however, that the early, glowing reports from Volvo may have been overstated, and that instead of returning dignity to the workers, the assembly lines are just more efficient but not really reaching the standards that are required for world-class competition.

Swedish firms also have workers who are members of the board of directors. To ensure that these worker board participants are competent in handling their tasks, they typically are given formal training and spend time with other workers on the board in learning how to do things such as analyze and evaluate financial statements, read reports, and focus on both long-range and short-range issues.

China China has the largest work force in the world, but even now, little is known to outsiders about how industrial democracy really works there. Similar to the situation in Eastern Europe, many changes have occurred in China. Unlike what has happened in Eastern Europe, many of the reforms and Westernized policies and practices in China, including the nature of industrial democracy, are closely related to the current political climate.

Chinese enterprises traditionally had two policy-making committees; one contained Communist party leaders and members, and the other included managers and worker representatives. Which committee had more power depended on the political climate, but after reforms in the 1980s, the workers (not the party members) represented industrial democracy in communist countries; however, worker participation in management decision making is less open than Westerners may expect. One study of a variety of enterprises in Beijing found that the number of employees who participate in management decisions is not very high but that the scope was quite broad and important (sales and business plans, production operations decisions, wages and bonuses, employee benefits, housing allocations, transfer of funds, and termination of problem employees).[9] Only time will tell what course industrial democracy will take in China.

Japan Unlike the situation in Europe and China, industrial democracy in Japan is not closely tied to political philosophy. Like in the United States, Japan is oriented more to the operating philosophy of enhancing worker performance. The best example is quality circles, in which Japanese workers are encouraged to identify and help solve job-related problems that are associated with quality and flow of work. Management is particularly receptive to workers' ideas that will produce bottom-line results. Except for a few unusual cases, however, such as the Tokyo-based consulting and advertising firm of ODS— where all workers have a say in everything from office smoking, hours, and tardiness rules to the approval of board members, salaries of managers, and allocation of profits—Japan has very little industrial democracy in the European sense. This is reflected by the basic nature of Japanese union–management relations.

Enterprise unions
Unions that represent both the hourly and salaried employees of a particular company.

There are over 70,000 unions in Japan, and most of them are **enterprise unions**, which means that they represent both the hourly and salaried employees of the particular company. Including salaried employees is a marked departure from labor unions in other countries. Employees join the union because they are members of the firm and union membership is expected; however, they do not expect the union to negotiate and win big salary increases for them. A major reason that Japanese unions are relatively weak is because many are company-dominated, a practice that is outlawed in the United States. In the large firms such as Toyota, for example, the president of the union typically is a middle-level manager who has been nominated by the company and elected by the membership. This arrangement ensures that the unions act in harmony with the company's wishes and undermines European-style industrial democracy.

Although there sometimes are labor strikes in Japan, as noted earlier, they usually are short-lived and have little effect on company operations. In fact, these strikes often are just ceremonial in nature and designed to encourage the workers to think of themselves as union employees. In truth, most workers think of themselves as company employees who are simply associated with the union. Moreover, it is not uncommon to find a union strike in a company with two or three work shifts and no loss of work output. This is because when the strikers are done picketing or marching, they go to work and the group coming out of the factory takes up the strike activity. In a factory with three shifts, a line employee will work a full shift, picket for a while, go home to eat and sleep, and then return to the factory for her or his shift.

Of all the industrialized nations, Japan faces the greatest challenge from industrial democracy during the years ahead. Japanese MNCs in Europe, and to a growing degree in the United States, will find that they must relinquish more control over operations to the workers if they hope to achieve the same productivity results they have at home. Conversely, MNCs in Japan report that Japanese white-collar workers are too used to working in a disciplined, corporate environment and fail to make decisions and take initiative. Therefore, changes are needed at home as well.

Strategic Management of International Labor Relations

The strategic management of international labor relations will be a major challenge facing MNCs in the years ahead, because so many different approaches can be taken. The approach used in U.S. firms may not be the same as that employed in other countries, including Anglo nations. In Great Britain, as noted earlier, unions do not have the power they once had. In many other European countries, such as Germany, however, unions continue to be quite strong, and especially as the Eastern European traditions of industrial democracy become infused in the EU, the workers will continue to have a great deal of authority in determining what the firm will do. It also is important to realize that those strategies benefitting unions in one country may have no value in others. This sometimes can be a conflict between international unions. For example, when Ford Motor felt that the labor climate in Britain was unfavorable to further investing, the company was approached by a group of Dutch businesspeople and urged to consider the Netherlands for future investment. Despite the strong criticism of British unions, the leadership of the Dutch trade unions did not object to these suggestions that investment funds be transferred to their country.[10]

The Philosophical Backdrop

As noted in earlier chapters, MNCs can use a number of philosophies as a starting point for their approach to management functions, including labor relations. For instance, under an ethnocentric philosophy, the MNC will take an approach to labor relations in other countries that is identical to its approach at home. Cultural, legal, and economic factors of the host country will not be considered in industrial relations efforts. This approach, quite obviously, generally is not effective and can even have disastrous results; as companies begin going international, they soon abandon such an approach.

A second approach is to use a polycentric philosophy in managing international industrial relations. Under this philosophy, the MNC will evaluate each country or geographic region as a separate entity. The MNC's international industrial relations strategy will be a series of different approaches depending on the country.

A third approach is a geocentric philosophy that is characterized by an effort to understand the interrelationships between the various geographic locations and a strategy to link them with a unifying thread and a composite industrial relations approach. The primary difference between a polycentric and a geocentric philosophy is that the latter considers the interrelationships between the various groups. Here are some examples of how industrial relations in one country can affect those in others:

1. Opel (General Motors' German subsidiary) negotiates an *increase* in the basic workweek hours with Belgian unions as it adds a second shift at its Belgian assembly plant. The intent of management is to keep the costs of production there competitive with those at a similar Opel plant in Germany. The intent of the Belgian workers is to expand employment and enhance job security.

2. A U.S. electronics firm cuts back its U.S. manufacturing output by 10 percent through laying off a like percentage of its U.S. workers. Its French subsidiary picks up the resulting product market slack. By cutting back employment in the United States, the firm avoids the large payments to workers that French law would have required if the cutback had been made by the French subsidiary.

3. Workers at a German company's British subsidiary go out on strike to support their demand for improved wages. Operations at the company's German plants continue, providing substantial cash inflows (revenues) to the entire system. The British workers completely forgo their cash inflows—their wages—during the strike. The company is less severely pressed financially than these workers are and can sustain a long strike if need be.

4. Ford of Europe integrates production among several European subsidiaries. For certain models of cars, the engines are British-made, the power train and some stampings are German-made, the wheels and other stampings are Belgian-made, and so on. A strike by workers in Belgium could shut down plants in Britain, Germany, and elsewhere. This gives the Belgian workers operational leverage vis-à-vis management and enhances their power in collective bargaining.[11]

The Japanese also make an interesting case study of the need for a geocentric philosophy toward industrial relations. Japanese auto firms long have realized that auto capacity is outstripping demand both in North America and Europe. As Japan continues to increase its foothold in North America, it will have to pay greater attention to its industrial relations approaches and modify them to meet the local labor market. Japan also will need to coordinate its worldwide holdings with a carefully formulated geocentric strategy toward labor relations.

Labor Costs

Another major area of consideration in formulating an international labor relations strategy is labor costs. Wages that are paid in one country offer differ considerably from those in other countries for the same job. In manufacturing, for example, hourly rates in

Germany have been substantially higher than those paid elsewhere. Some of the latest data,[12] complemented by the average weekly hours worked in manufacturing, reveal the following:

Country	Average Total Hourly Compensation in U.S. Dollars for Production Workers	Average Weekly Hours Worked
Germany	$31.87	29.0
France	19.34	31.7
Italy	18.08	35.0
United States	17.74	37.9
Great Britain	14.19	35.6

A close analysis of this information shows, in the main, that there is an inverse relationship between hourly compensation and hours worked. By holding down weekly hours, unions have been able to increase the hourly pay of their members. At the same time, however, while real wages have increased, research shows that a growing number of high paid workers have found themselves priced out of the market. Businesses are finding it easier to transfer work to other geographic locales than to pay these high prices. Figure 17-2 shows some of the most current data related to the real wages of low-paid employees in North America, Australia, and Europe. The average annual percentage change in the United States, Canada, and Australia during this time period was negative compared, for example, to Norway, Italy, Sweden, and Germany, where it was over 1.5 percent. Clearly, something had to be done to make the labor rates in the European countries more reasonable, to make them more competitive. The Dutch provide a good example of some of the latest changes that are being implemented. These changes combine the flexibility found in America with the security that is so common in Germany. In particular, the Dutch:

> have made part-time work easier by permitting part-timers to be paid less than full-timers for the same job. This has helped Dutch companies to adjust their workforce to the demand for labour and has helped unemployed people get back into work. At the same time, centralised wage bargaining has helped build a consensus in favour of wage restraint. Dutch wages in manufacturing have been moderate, compared with Germany and France, where bargaining occurs sector by sector. Finally, the Dutch have tried to provide incentives to work, because sickness benefits were busting the social security-budget. As long ago as 1985 the value of both unemployment insurance and disability insurance was cut to 70% of final pay from 80%. In 1991 and 1995 the government made it harder to qualify for unemployment; in 1995 it removed the coverage for those who chose to become unemployed. The system has also gradually shifted the burden of supporting the sick on to companies. In 1996, for example, firms became responsible for the benefits paid during the first year of illness.[13]

Figure 17-2

Real Wages of Low-Paid Workers*

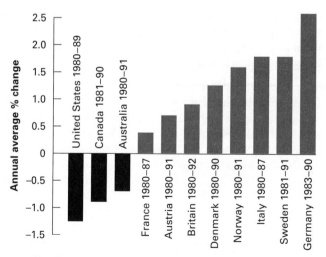

Note: *Tenth percentile of earnings for men (both sexes for Norway and Denmark) deflated by consumer-price inflation.
Source: Organization for Economic Cooperation and Development, 1997.

New Labor Force Trends

In recent years there have been pronounced new labor force trends in the international arena. As discussed above, this is particularly true in Europe, and to a lesser degree in Asia, where companies are trying to regain some of the competitiveness they lost through high labor costs. In the process, many of these firms are going through the same approach that their counterparts did in the United States a decade ago: The workforce is being down-sized, and a strong focus is being placed on providing higher quality output at lower costs.

Some of these recent changes are being fought by the unions, but a growing number of informed observers seem to agree that during the first decade of the new millennium workers are going to have to realize that when national values collide with the realities of global competition, the latter is likely to win. Renault offers a good example. In the 1990s the French auto firm tried to strike a deal with Volvo to build trucks. However, the agreement collapsed when it became clear that Renault would have to cut its own workforce and close some inefficient production operations. This was not something the firm was prepared to do. Since then, however, faced with competitive reality, Renault has cut 25 percent of its workforce and is continuing to make cost-related changes—and the unions are finding that they must accommodate these new decisions or face the fact that work will be moved elsewhere and members will lose their jobs. This is a strategy that has been employed by other European automakers such as Volkswagen and Fiat, which have set up new factories in Latin America, Asia, and Europe in recent years. Additionally, companies that fail to proactively revise their labor agreements and become more competitive are going to find competition seeking them out. In France, for example, the Japanese market share for autos had been in the range of 7 percent for many years, much of this caused by the country's high barriers to non-European imports. Now those barriers are being removed and Asian manufacturers are beginning to more aggressively enter the market. Toyota, for example, is building a $1.6 billion factory in the northern part of France with an annual capacity of 200,000 cars.[14]

European firms are beginning to respond to global competition in a number of ways. One is with flexible working arrangements that help contain costs and better link work demands with the employees. Four of the most prominent of these flexible arrangements include the use of part-time workers, greater reliance on shift work, the introduction of temporary contracts, and increased reliance on subcontracting.

Part-Time Work Part-time work is the most widely used form of flexibility in Europe. Today one in seven people in the EU is a part-time worker; and during the last few years this form of employment accounted for more new jobs than did any other. The OECD has estimated that during the years 1983–1996 the percentage of part-time workers in the labor force increased substantially in many European countries. In Ireland, for example, it rose from 6.7 percent of the workforce up to 11.6 percent; in France it increased from 9.6 percent up to 16 percent; in Germany it went from approximately 12 percent of the labor force up to 16 percent; and in the Netherlands it zoomed from 21 percent of the labor force up to 36.5 percent.[15] Moreover, far more employers are now increasing their use of part-time workers than reducing them with the greatest increase occurring in northern Europe.[16]

Shiftwork Shiftwork has become very popular in Europe. In particular, it is wide-ly used in newspaper production, public transportation, utilities, food production, delivery services, hospitals, emergency services, telephone sales, and banking. Additionally, it is very popular with employers in Italy, Sweden, Belgium, England, France, and Germany.

Nonpermanent Employment Nonpermanent employment refers to any form of employment other than permanent open-ended contracts. Typical examples include temporary and fixed-term contractual agreements. In recent years nonpermanent employment has been popular in southern European countries such as Greece, Portugal, and Spain, where it accounts for over 15 percent of the workforce. It is far less popular in countries such as Luxembourg, Belgium, and Italy, where only 5 percent of the employees have nonpermanent employment contracts. As would be expected, all of these workers would like to see the arrangements changed and permanent jobs assigned to them. However, many managers feel there are too many benefits to be derived from the use of nonpermanent employment. These benefits include:

1. Many managers know that work needs to be done, but they do not know how long the demand will last or whether further work will accrue. Nonpermanent employment allows them to hedge on the conservative side. A good example is provided by Rank Xerox, which transformed its United Kingdom copier and printer business in the face of Asian competition. Because Rank Xerox did not know whether it could sustain the growth, the firm chose to use only temporary employees until things became clearer.

2. Employers know that some jobs will require only a limited period of time. A typical example is seasonal work As a result, they opt for nonpermanent employment arrangements as in the case of American Express which relies heavily on temporary workers.

3. Organizations believe that short-term recruitment is a cost-effective human resources approach because very little money needs to be spent on the selection of these individuals. The process can be simple and inexpensive. Additionally, these temporary employees do not get benefits, one of the largest factors in wage rates. These are some of the reasons that British Telecom has chosen to use temporary workers.

4. Enterprises are convinced that short-term recruiting is an excellent way to deal with situations where special skills are needed and the firm does not have the time, nor want to invest the money, to develop these skills internally. Additionally, when these workers are no longer needed, it is easy to terminate them.

5. Managers feel that short-term employment is a good way to determine if someone will "fit in" on a permanent basis. British Air and Lufthansa, for example, hire new employees as temporary workers and then, after evaluating their performance, decide those who will be offered full-time jobs.[17]

Subcontracting   Subcontracting involves replacing employment contracts with commercial contracts. This approach is widely used in construction where workers simply move from one contract to another or are laid off until the contractor lands a new client. Subcontracting in Europe is also very popular in public sector organizations, as well as in private organizations that prefer to focus on their core business and to subcontract the other activities. Research shows that in recent years there has been an increase in subcontracting in all major western European countries. Based on their international survey research, Brewster, Mayne, and Tregaskis have found that in recent years subcontracting has increased among half of the organizations in West Germany and the Netherlands and among one-third or more in enterprises in Finland, France, Ireland, Spain, Switzerland, and the United Kingdom.[18]

Many of the subcontracting approaches that are being used are quite creative. For example, a Swedish businessman who used to run Saab's human resources department realized that sometimes the company would need to quickly hire more employees to meet increasing work demands and at other times it would have more people than it needed. He then formulated a plan of action.

> If area manufacturers got together and formed a labor pool, they could pluck workers out of it whenever they needed them and give them back when they didn't. [He] took his plan to 10 big companies, including Saab, ABB and Ericsson. Within a few months, he left Saab to start Industrie Competens, a sort of temp agency for engineers, skilled technicians and assembly-line workers. One of the agency's temps is Niclas Arkstal . . . a technician who has assembled air conditioners for NAF AB and telephones for Ericsson. At both, he says, he became bored after a while. Joining Industrie Kompetens was the perfect tonic. "It's so flexible," he says, "I don't worry about boredom anymore."[19]

The discussion in this section shows that flexible work arrangements are now becoming much more common in Europe, a situation that has existed in the United States for quite some time. However, the *specific* approach that is used tends to vary based on country. Here is a summary observation of the current situation:

> The evidence shows a clear and widespread trend to increase flexibility across Europe. However, the trend is starting from markedly different bases. The form, extent and nature of flexible working that employers are most likely to use is different in the different countries. . . . Interestingly, despite this national variability, flexibility is not determined by employment legislation per se. The North/South divide on the use of part-time and nonpermanent work, which emerges from much of the data, indicates that there is a complex set of factors involved in the use of particular forms of flexibility. Both high-regulated and low-regulated countries use considerable amounts of flexibility and in many cases show very similar levels of increase . . . employers are facing the same pressures to use their human resources in the most cost-effective manner. The national context is a more powerful predictor of the use of flexibility by employers than size of organization or sector, although within the national boundaries these variables may also be important.[20]

When analyzed in terms of total labor costs, recent statistics show that during most of the past decade countries have faced rising costs for two major reasons: higher local wages (rates expressed in local currency) and higher costs in terms of U.S. dollars (when local currencies are converted to reflect prices in dollars). Figure 17-3 shows these changes from 1990–1997. The data reveal that unit labor costs among Japanese manufacturing firms were almost unchanged when measured in yen (the local currency). The 0.1 percent annual increase only marginally outpaced productivity gains. However, when measured in dollar terms, the yen had strengthened considerably against the dollar during these years. As a result, the total cost of labor required to produce a unit of output in Japanese manufacturing rose in dollar terms by 2.8 percent annually during these years. This is in marked contrast, for example, to the United States where unit labor costs fell by 0.1 percent a year in dollar terms, thus making the U.S. manufacturing more competitive in labor costs than that of Japan's. The accompanying sidebar "Unions Become More Flexible—and Do Better" shows some of the ways in which unions are now beginning to address this problem.

Figure 17-3

Manufacturing Labor Costs (per unit of output, annual average percentage change: 1990–1997)

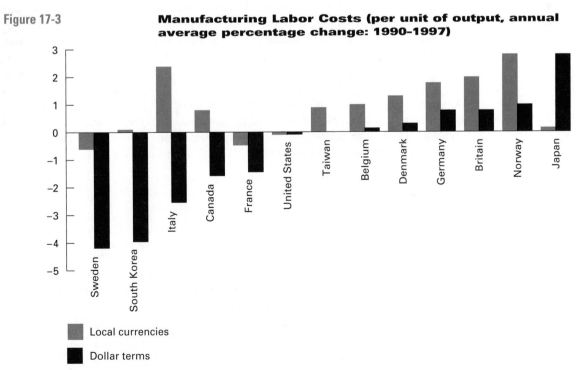

Source: U.S. Bureau of Labor Statistics, 1998.

International Management in Action

German Unions Become More Flexible—and Do Better

In recent years, unions in countries such as Germany have become less confrontational with management and, as a result, are becoming more successful in persuading companies not to send work elsewhere. This is a turnaround from just a few years ago when German wage levels were not just the highest, but were increasing more quickly than those of other nations. What has led to this new flexibility? One answer is that German unions are finding that with high unemployment throughout the country, especially in the East, there is less room for negotiating. They have to accommodate the needs of German firms or risk losing membership through layoffs and plant closings. Moreover, many union workers now seem more willing to adjust their job schedules and accept lower wages in return for continued employment. As a result, in the eastern part of Germany union employees now earn much less than their counterparts in the western part of the country (approximately $32 hourly including benefits). In fact, recent statistics show that hourly rates in the east are very competitive vis-à-vis other parts of the continent including the Netherlands ($22 hourly) and Italy ($18 hourly).

There are a growing number of German companies that are winning concessions from their unions. One is CED Informationstechnik GmbH, a small firm that assembles personal computers. The company's union contract allows it to cut back the workforce when orders are weak. And since CED focuses on delivery of computers within 24 hours of receiving an order, it has no need to build inventory. So the workforce size is tied directly to the amount of orders on hand, thus allowing CED to operate with a basic crew of only 200 people. In turn, another group of approximately 40 workers has contracts guaranteeing them at least 1,000 hours of work annually, so these people can count on approximately 20 hours a week on average—although this is all tied to work orders. The remaining 300 employees at CED work as needed and can find after a month or two of large orders that things dry up and they have no work for the next couple of months. It is a chance they have to take.

While all of this is a big change from the days when the unions used to dictate terms, it is one that is accepted by both the workers and the CED's worker council. The head of the council explained it this way, "You can only keep your job when the company does well. These agreements have to be adopted everywhere if we're going to protect jobs." This attitude is reflective of a growing number of German unions. For example, the IG Chemie chemical workers union recently signed a milestone agreement that conditionally allows troubled employers to cut wages in return for job security. The contract, which covers approximately 1,700 companies, is designed to trade wages and other financial benefits for job security. In turn, the newfound flexibility offers the promise of making German industry more competitive than it has been in a long time.

Organizing International Industrial Relations

In organizing international industrial relations, a number of factors help to explain the relative degree of centralized and decentralized control and employment flexibility that is exercised. The following compares the organizational dimensions of U.S. and European MNCs that are critical to labor relations:

1. A number of studies have shown that compared with European MNCs, U.S. firms tend to concentrate authority at corporate headquarters, with greater emphasis on formal management controls and a close reporting system (particularly within the area of financial control) to ensure that planning targets are met.

2. European MNCs tend to deal with labor unions at the industry level (frequently via employer association) rather than the company level. The opposite is more typical for U.S. firms. In the United States, employer associations have not played a key role in the industrial relations system, and company-based labor relations policies are the norm.

3. A final factor is the extent of the home product market. If domestic sales are large relative to overseas operations (as in the case with many U.S. companies), it is more likely that overseas operations will be regarded by the parent

company as an extension of domestic operations. This is not the case for many European MNCs, whose international operations represent the major part of their business.[21]

In addition, when compared with British firms, U.S. MNCs are much more likely to be involved in collective bargaining and strike settlement issues of their overseas subsidiaries. British firms tend to adopt a more "hands off" approach and confine themselves to giving advice and guidance to their subsidiaries, allowing local management to deal with day-to-day industrial relations matters.[22] These examples point out that industrial relations practices differ from country to country, and MNCs need to be concerned with coordinating these activities.

A number of alternative approaches can be used in managing labor relations in different cultures. For example, one study found that labor relations often is delegated to the local management, except in the case of pension issues, which are handled by the MNC headquarters.[23] The foreign subsidiary is not totally on its own when it comes to labor relations, however. A great deal of guidance and advice still comes from the home office, and hiring and staffing policies also ensure that headquarters plays a role in industrial relations. In addition, many expatriate subsidiary managers use the same industrial relations approach, or a modified version of the approach, that they used back home.

The linkage between the subsidiary and headquarters often is handled by a home-based industrial relations staff, which provides advice and assistance. This industrial relations staff typically gathers information related to wages, benefits, and working conditions around the world as well as at the location of the particular subsidiary. This helps local managers to determine the labor contract that should be negotiated or, in the case of nonunionized operations, the level of wages and benefits that should be paid.

The MNC industrial relations staff also provides assistance in dealing with labor disputes and grievances. The staff can provide information as to how similar problems have been handled in other locales and can be of particular importance to the subsidiary. Many local managers may be unaware of the variety of approaches that can be used in negotiating labor agreements and resolving related problems.

Information provided by the MNC headquarters industrial relations staff can be used by upper-level management in determining when and where to make changes in production work worldwide as well. For example, if wage rates in France go up 10 percent next year, will this reduce the MNC's competitiveness in that market? If it will, what costs are associated with moving some of this work to the MNC's plant in Barcelona? The industrial relations staff at headquarters can help to answer this question in terms of wages, salaries, and benefits. When this information is coupled with that provided by the staffs in manufacturing, marketing, and legal, the MNC then is in a position to make a final decision regarding the wisdom of transferring the work to another locale.

A Final Word

In this book, a great deal has been said about how to effectively manage international operations. In closing, two points merit consideration: the inevitability of joint partnering, and the need for ongoing research and learning.

Joint Partnering

Current trends leave no doubt that the world of international management will be one of joint partnerships and agreements. Transnationals will be boundaryless companies in the twenty-first century, because this is the only way that they will be able to survive. Sometimes called a **virtual corporation**, defined as a network of companies that come together to exploit fast-changing opportunities and share costs, skills, and access to global markets,[24] good examples would be IBM, Toshiba, and Siemens. These MNCs created

Virtual corporation
A network of companies that come together to exploit fast-changing opportunities and share costs, skills, and access to global markets.

a joint venture to develop state-of-the-art, "benchmark" (best in the world) memory chips. These chips will be able to store 256 million bits of data each, which is equivalent to 10,000 pages of typed text. Large-capacity chips will make it much easier for businesses in the twenty-first century to store information as well as open the door for computer scientists to achieve breakthroughs in areas such as computer speech recognition, machine vision, and computer reasoning.

One main reason for this joint venture is to help control the expenses of research and production. In the early 1990s, it cost approximately $500 million to build a manufacturing plant capable of producing the most advanced chips, which at one time could store 16 million bits of information. By the end of the decade, the cost of these high-tech plants had risen sharply and was now in the neighborhood of $1 billion. No computer firm could afford to take such a large risk, hence the need for a joint venture. These types of arrangements will become increasingly prevalent in the next century. Here is what Rosabeth Kantor, a widely recognized management of change expert, has to say about such partnering and collaborating:

> To gain strength to compete in more demanding global markets, companies collaborate—e.g., to achieve speed and quality through closer integration with suppliers and customers, to attain scale through alliances, or to redefine an industry. At Polaroid, purchasing has become "global supply chain management." Yellow Springs Instruments lists its strategic partners next to the balance sheet in its annual report. Software companies, for whom ties with independent developers, venture partners, and customers are a critical asset, dedicate senior executives and large departments solely to the management of alliances and partnerships. Companies like Disney that once licensed rights to others and stepped away now want to get more value from those arrangements, using them to gain ideas for innovation or intelligence about new country markets—or to push more Disney-branded product through those channels, with more influence over partners' businesses.[25]

She also notes that this collaboration in a way follows the well-established Japanese *keiretsus*, Korean *chaebols*, or the interlocking companies in Southeast Asian conglomerates. However, the emerging arrangement of MNC collaboration tend to be looser, with a wider range of partners and fewer permanent, contractual commitments.

Another reason for partnering is that the success of MNCs depends heavily on a strong worldwide economy, a genuine commitment to helping nations improve the well-being of their citizens, and a willingness to share success with other businesses, MNCs and local firms alike. Akio Morita, the late chairman of Sony and a leading proponent of worldwide partnering, suggested that Japanese MNCs take the following steps:

- Manufacture more products locally in the United States—reducing exports from Japan and creating high-quality jobs for U.S. workers.
- Discover and develop more parts and components suppliers among U.S. firms in the United States.
- Augment U.S. "human capital" by training workers in the most advanced aspects of Japanese production processes, and do advanced R&D locally.
- Build business partnerships, including technology exchanges and transfers, with like-minded U.S. corporations.
- Practice "borderless" policies within Japanese corporations—internationalizing management as much as possible and offering equal training and promotional opportunities to all employees.
- Participate fully as "corporate citizens" in community activities and philanthropic endeavors in the United States, with special attention to supporting education, skills training, and scientific research.
- Work to reduce trade-related imbalances by identifying high-quality companies and products in the United States that can be introduced to the Japanese market.[26]

Such suggestions clearly reinforce the need for cooperation and joint partnering as well as key mergers and acquisitions.[27] They also illustrate that the international environment now is, and in the century ahead will be, markedly different from that of the past.

Continued Research and Learning

A great many theories have relevance to the study of international management. Many have been discussed in this book, but all must be continually subjected to review, analysis, and reformulation. A good example is the theory of lifetime employment in Japan. For many years, international management experts have argued that lifetime employment creates a highly motivated workforce and that Western organization should emulate this approach. More recent research, however, reveals that lifetime employment is less useful as a motivator than as a control tool for ensuring worker loyalty and performance. In return for guaranteed employment, the personnel stay with the firm for their entire career, work hard, and are compliant to management's wishes. Based on an analysis of empirical data collected on this topic, two researchers concluded: "Lifetime employment is offered within a . . . context of loyalty and benevolence based on cultural values. Its impact, however, is to increase the control of Japanese employees by managers."[28] Moreover, these researchers found that lifetime employment was not widely used by firms in tight labor markets, because it was not possible to control the workers, who could easily find jobs with other companies and derived little motivation from such guarantees.

International management research also is important because it generates new hypotheses for testing.[29] For example, as workers in large companies with guaranteed lifetime employment near retirement (55 to 65 years of age), will management replace them with younger people who are not given such guarantees? As the competitive environment increases, will MNCs stop offering these guarantees because they reduce the firms' flexibility in responding to changing conditions? Will young workers entering the Japanese workforce during this decade be motivated by such guarantees, or will they turn them down because they are unwilling to commit their career to one firm in return for job security?[30] These types of questions must be focal points for international management research and learning, because changing economic, cultural, and social environments are creating new conditions in which MNCs must compete. Research can help to shed light on the effect of these changes. A recent summary of research on Japanese management practices concluded the following:

1. The cultural underpinnings of Japanese society are shifting toward Western values, although this shift is not uniform across culture and is not rapid in all sectors.

2. Industrial organization in Japan, especially the *keiretsu*, will continue to provide competitive advantages and is being extended internationally.

3. Long-range planning is becoming more formal and moving toward a Western style, although it will retain a more visionary perspective.

4. Manufacturing productivity per employee in the United States is rapidly approaching or exceeding parity with Japan. Advantages for Japanese companies appear in certain areas such as R&D and product design, but these appear to be heavily supported by governmental and vertical alliances.

5. The Japanese possess some advantages in the management of quality processes; however, the gap between Japanese and U.S. quality management is closing, though perhaps more slowly than the productivity gap.

6. In neutral countries, the quality image of Japanese products continues to slightly exceed those of the United States, largely because of distribution, promotion, and service advantages.

7. The Japanese will continue to invest more heavily in R&D than U.S. firms and to introduce new products both faster and more economically than the United States by using superior organizational, communicative, and integrative arrangements, discriminatory patent protection, superior governmental funding, and exceptional support by *keiretsus*. These advantages will be aggressively protected and enhanced in the future.

8. Traditional Japanese human resource management practices, including lifetime employment, seniority-based systems, and company unions, are rapidly disappearing and cannot be relied on to produce future competitive advantage. Transplanted Japanese organizations have had limited success in implementing these practices and will make fewer attempts to do so in the future.

9. Because of the rapidly converging parity of U.S. and Japanese productivity and quality, as well as diminishing human resource management advantages, future competitive advantages of the Japanese, if they persist, will derive largely from managerial and organization learning excellence, strengthened by structural systems that promote information amplification, and bolstered by even greater reliance on the *keiretsu* and the Ministry of International Trade and Industry.[31]

Only time will tell how accurate these predictions prove to be, but such information is valuable to the field of international management.

Research also will play an increasing role in helping to uncover how and why multinationals succeed. In particular, greater attention must be given to research designed to explain why some MNCs do better than others and how the strategies are changing.[32] For example, traditional international business strategy gave strong support to the concept of **strategic fit**, in which an organization must align its resources in such a way as to mesh with the environment. Auto firms had to design and build cars that were in demand, and this might mean a variety of models and accessories depending on the number of markets being served. Analogously, electronics firms had to maintain state-of-the-art technology to meet consumer demands for new, high-quality, high-performance products. Today, successful multinationals do much more than attempt to attain a strategic fit. The rapid pace of competitive change requires linkages between all segments of the business, from manufacturing on down to point-of-purchase selling, in the supply chain and in every phase of operation, there must be attention to value-added concepts.[33]

Recently, the concept of strategic fit is being supplemented by the concept of **strategic stretch**, which is the creative use of resources to achieve ever more challenging goals.[34] It is important for MNCs to employ strategic stretch, because without it, they find that what is immediately feasible drives out what is ultimately desirable. Without strategic stretch, Percy Barnevik never would have been able to build ABB into a global giant, and Ted Turner never would have dared to dream of creating CNN. Those multinationals with the greatest amount of resources today will not be the leaders in tomorrow's international arena if they fail to use the creative judgement that is fundamental to strategic stretch. Scarcity of resources can be offset by creativity and risk-taking, and this can make all the difference in besting competitors whose primary strength is an abundance of resources. Commenting on this, Hamel and Prahalad have noted:

> We believe that companies like NEC, Charles Schwab, CNN, Sony, Glaxo, Canon, and Honda were united more by the unreasonableness of their ambition and the creativity exhibited in getting the most from the least than they were by a common cultural or institutional heritage. If further evidence is needed, consider the less-than-sterling performance of Japan's largest banks and brokerages in world markets. Almost unique among Japan's multinationals, these firms possessed immense resource advantages where they entered world markets. Yet material advantages have proved to be a poor substitute for the strategic creativity engendered by resource scarcity.[35]

Of course, it is unlikely there will ever be agreement on all aspects of international management strategy, if only because the specific environmental demands made on one company or industry will require a response different from that needed in another. However, there will continue to be efforts to find overriding strategic principles that have broad value and can be used by most transnationals. A good example was provided by Sullivan and Bauerschmidt, who surveyed managers of large multinationals in an effort to discover those international management strategy principles that were of most value. They found that three were of critical importance to large MNCs: (1) the ability to optimize efficiency; (2) rapid response to environmental changes; and (3) the ability to develop distinct,

Strategic fit
An approach to strategically managing an organization that involves aligning resources in such a way as to mesh with the environment.

Strategic stretch
The creative use of resources to achieve ever more challenging goals.

proprietary advantages.[36] In the case of small firms, major emphasis was needed on innovation, because this helps to make up for the companies' lack of expertise in international manufacturing and marketing.[37]

Another good example is provided by Kanter, whose research shows that the successful MNC of the twenty-first century will empower its people and leverage relationships, both inside and outside its boundaries. As a result, successful MNCs will be able to reach further and faster to both gain and spread knowledge. In this process, it will:

1. Connect its people and partners globally, using horizontal networks to take advantage of all of the resources in the entire extended enterprise of business units, suppliers, customers, and alliances to create value for end users;

2. Craft global strategies and standards but encourage and learn from local customization and innovation, neither commanding everything from the center nor letting each unit or territory act on its own;

3. Use collaborative methods—networks, cross-boundary teams, supply chain partnerships, strategic alliances—to support innovation and then spread knowledge from local innovations everywhere quickly; and

4. Shape a shared culture of unity that appreciates and derives strength from diversity, and develop common tools and measurements to put everyone "on the same page," while also encouraging everyone to "break the mold."[38]

In other words, successful twenty-first century MNCs will be connected, innovative, and build strength and competitive advantage from their diversity.

The World of Business Week Revisited

As seen in the *Business Week* article which opened this chapter, international labor relations is undergoing rapid change. This is particularly true in Europe, where the EU is creating a giant market in which resources are able to move unimpeded. As a result, companies are now more efficient in finding the most labor value for their money and unions are learning that they must accommodate these new developments or lose jobs. Review the material in this chapter and then use it to revisit this news story answering the following questions: (1) How are labor relations developments in Germany likely to affect labor conditions throughout the EU? (2) Is the empowerment movement popular in the United States likely to be adopted by other countries? (3) Which of the forms of industrial democracy used in Europe and Asia would have value in the United States? (4) During the next five years, which of the emerging new labor force trends in Europe will gain in popularity? Which are likely to decline? (5) When comparing emerging labor relations in Europe with those currently being used in the United States, are labor developments in the EU beginning to more closely resemble those in the United States? Explain.

Summary of Key Points

1. Labor relations is the process through which management and workers identify and determine the job relationships that will be in effect at the workplace. In the United States, these agreements result from negotiation at the union–management bargaining table. In other countries, the approach is different. For example, the labor agreement in Great Britain is not a binding contract. In Germany, however, it is binding, and the unions are particularly influential in determining wages, salaries, and working conditions.

In Japan, labor agreements usually are general and vague, although they are legally enforceable.

2. From time to time, industrial conflicts result from disagreements between management and the union. In the United States, these often are solved through use of a grievance procedure, the steps of which are spelled out in the union contract. In Great Britain, the conflict resolution process often is fragmented and costly, because the system is not designed to deal with such problems. The approach in Germany is similar to that in the

United States. In Japan, industrial conflict is minimal because of the way that unions are formed and led.

3. Unions have attempted to become internationally active in three basic ways. One is through use of intergovernmental organizations such as the ILO (International Labour Office) and the OECD (Organization for Economic Cooperation and Development). Another is through transnational union affiliations. A third is by extending domestic contracts into the international arena.

4. Industrial democracy is the rights that employees have to participate in significant management decisions. Such decisions include wage rates, bonuses, profit sharing, vacations and holiday leaves, work rules, dismissals, and plant expansions and closings. Except for the recent emphasis given to empowerment in total quality and human resource management, traditionally defined industrial democracy is not as widespread in the United States as it is in other countries, especially in Germany and the Scandinavian countries. Some of the most common forms of industrial democracy include codetermination, work councils, shop floor participation, financial participation, and collective bargaining.

5. In formulating a strategy and managing international industrial relations, MNCs can draw on a number of philosophies. The most effective tends to be a geocentric philosophy that is characterized by an effort to understand the interrelationships between the various geographic locations and a strategy to link them with a composite unifying theme. This approach to labor relations can be helpful in dealing with compensation policy issues as well as in providing assistance to the worldwide subsidiaries on labor issues or challenges that they face.

6. In recent years a growing number of unions, especially in Europe, have been adopting flexible work contracts. These contracts allow companies to adjust their staffing levels to meet work demands by using non-full-time workers. Four of the most prominent of these flexible work arrangements include use of part-time workers, greater reliance on shift work, the introduction of temporary contracts, and increased reliance on subcontracting.

7. Trends for the future point to the inevitability of joint partnering and the need for ongoing research and learning. Collaboration will become a way for MNCs to compete effectively in the global economy, and continued international research is needed to learn and to innovate for future success.

Key Terms

arbitrator	labor relations	specialized internationals
collective bargaining	lockout	special purpose teams
enterprise unions	mediator	strategic fit
global international trade affiliations	Organization for Economic Cooperation and Development (OECD)	strategic stretch
industrial democracy		strike
industrial internationals		union
International Confederation of Free Trade Unions (ICFTU)	problem-solving teams	union grievance
	regional internationals	virtual corporation
International Labour Office (ILO)	self-managing teams	

Review and Discussion Questions

1. What are three major differences between the way that labor–management agreements are reached in the United States and in Great Britain? Germany? Japan? Compare and contrast the process in all four countries.

2. How are industrial conflicts handled in the United States? Great Britain? Germany? Japan? Compare and contrast the process in all four countries.

3. A U.S. MNC is considering opening a plant in Germany. What are three labor relations and industrial democracy developments that this firm needs to know about? Identify and describe each.

4. A French firm is talking to state officials in Indiana about setting up a new plant in Terre Haute. What types of labor relations issues should the company be investigating so that it can have the most efficient and effective operation?

5. How would each of the following philosophical views affect the formulation of strategy and the management of international industrial relations: ethnocentric, polycentric, and geocentric?

6. A Japanese MNC is considering setting up a manufacturing plant east of Los Angeles. How is the firm likely to organize and control the industrial relations strategies and practices of this overseas subsidiary? Are there any particular problems the home office is likely to confront? Be complete in your answer.

Internet Exercise: Challenges of a New World Auto Industry

Labor relations is a critical area for multinationals, especially among those firms that are expanding their worldwide operations. A good example is provided by the major auto firms headquartered in North America, Europe, and Asia, which are now pushing into emerging markets as well as setting up factories in current market locales. Visit four of these firms—General Motors, Volvo, Toyota, and Honda—and find out what they have been up to in the last year. Their web site addresses are the following: **www.gm.com**, **www.volvo.com**, **www.toyota.com**, and **www.honda.com**. At the General Motors site, look closely at some of the new developments that are occurring in the company, review its annual reports, and examine the information on global supplier networks. In the case of

Volvo, look at new developments in the company. In the case of Toyota, focus on both its manufacturing efforts and its community service. At the Honda site, concentrate your attention on recent community press releases and what the company is doing in the area of research and development. When you have finished this assignment, answer these three questions: (1) What recent changes have been taking place in these major auto firms in the manufacturing area? (2) How do you think these changes will impact the firms' labor relations policies and practices? (3) What changes would you expect to take place in the way these companies manage their labor forces during the millennium?

Denmark

Denmark is a small country in Northern Europe that is surrounded by water except for a 42-mile border shared with Germany to the south. The country is approximately 17,000 square miles of small green farms, blue lakes, and white coastal beaches. The population is 5.2 million, one-fourth of whom live in Copenhagen. Although poor in natural resources, the Danes are famous for their dairy products, processed foods, and beautifully designed manufactured goods, including furniture and silverware. Since the time of the Vikings, the Danes have been a seafaring people. Denmark maintains large shipping and fishing industries. The prosperous Danes have a high standard of living, and the economy is fairly stable and moderately strong. A fairly rich country, per capita income is around $22,500. Denmark has been a constitutional monarchy for over 130 years. Legislative power is in the hands of a parliament whose members are elected for 4-year terms, and a prime minister heads the government.

Two months ago, a medium-sized, high-tech firm based in Seattle, called Seattle Tech, Inc. (STI), entered into a joint venture with a Danish electronics manufacturing firm. STI is going to invest $1.4 million and give its Danish partner the right to use its patents to manufacture a portable facsimile machine. The Danish company is going to renovate one wing of its factory and devote this area to the production of these machines.

There are two reasons that STI wanted to enter into this agreement: One is that the arrangement provides it entry into the EU. A second is an analysis that indicated overall costs for producing the fax machines in Denmark would be about 25 percent less than if they were made in the United States and shipped over. Cost is a very important factor in STI's decision. Control also is important. STI insists that the units be produced according to the master blueprint that is being provided. "Quality is a key factor in the success of these machines," the vice president of production noted, "and this means that we must produce them to a strict manufacturing tolerance. We can't have anyone making arbitrary changes in the process."

Everything appeared to be going well until earlier this week, when the CEO of STI was talking to the top management of the Danish company in Copenhagen. There, for the first time, he learned that the board of directors consists of seven members of management and six members of the union. Moreover, to his surprise, he learned that Danish workers often get involved in shop floor decision making and make recommendations regarding how to change production flows and techniques to increase productivity and quality. The president is happy to learn that the workers are so interested in trying to improve output and quality, but he is concerned that any tinkering with the production process for the facsimile machines could result in major quality problems. He explained these concerns to his counterpart in the Danish firm, but he feels that his points were not well received. "We may have made a major mistake," the CEO of STI told his assistant when they returned from their meeting in Copenhagen. "It may be necessary for us to back out of this venture and look for a different partner."

www.geocities.com/thetropics/4597

Questions

1. What are some current issues facing Denmark? What is the climate for doing business in Denmark today?

2. Do the workers have to be included on the board of directors? Can the company force them off?

3. How important is worker participation in decision making in Denmark?

4. What would you recommend that STI do at this point?

They're Back

During the 1970s, Volkswagen was the leading U.S. foreign car importer. By 1979 the German firm was selling 300,000 cars and had 2.8 percent of the total U.S. market. The next year saw sales slip to 275,000 units, but because of the general decline of industry sales as a whole, Volkswagen's share of the U.S. market rose to 3 percent, and the next year it did slightly better. However, this was the company's zenith. By 1982 sales had fallen to 160,000, and market share was down to 1.8 percent. The firm was being overrun by Japanese imports and revitalized German lines such as Mercedes and BMW. In an effort to cut costs, the company closed its U.S. manufacturing plant in Pennsylvania in 1988, eventually moving production to Mexico. Despite this decision, the United States has remained a major key market for the company, as explained by one industry observer, who noted:

> Because Volkswagen builds more than three million cars and trucks a year worldwide, its financial performance in [the U.S.] constitutes a small fraction of its overall results. But with increased competition [in] Europe . . . and Japanese rivals poised to intensify their threat, the company sees the American market as an important battleground in a larger struggle that includes Europe and South America. VW believes a return to mass-market strategy in the United States will help it gird for fierce battles on its home turf.

In more recent years, Volkswagen has made a stunning comeback in America. Perhaps its biggest success story is the New Beetle which was introduced in March 1998. By the end of the year the company had sold 55,842 units including 7,516 in December. Its Jetta line that year led the list with total sales of 89,311, the third best in the model's 19-year history. The Volkswagen Passat model posted all-time record sales of 39,272 units, an increase of 164 percent over 1997's mark of 14,868; and another record was set by the Volkswagen Cabrio with sales of 15,230 units, a 59.7 increase over 1997 and the best in the model's 18-year history. In all, Volkswagen sold 219,679 cars in the U.S. market, an increase of 59.3 percent over 1997 and the best showing since 1981 when it sold 278,513. As a result, the firm's 1998 share of the American car market stood at 3.4 percent—the highest ever. Of course, part of this success is accounted for by the fact that cars account for only around 53 percent of new vehicle sales. The other major group is light trucks where Ford, General Motors, and Chrysler hold 80 percent of the market. Moreover, in the case of Ford and Chrysler, sales of light trucks are significantly greater than those of automobiles. Yet this growth market has not gone unnoticed by Volkswagen, which recently introduced its EuroVan into the United States. The van is built in Hannover, Germany, and comes with a V6 engine and a host of standard equipment and safety features. If this new entry does as well as predicted, it will combine with the New Beetle to sharply increase the firm's U.S. market share. Yet it is the Beetle that holds the greatest promise. In addition to brisk sales the first year, the auto was selected as the 1999 North American Car of the Year by an independent jury of 48 journalists who cover the auto industry for daily newspaper, magazines, television, radio, and on the Internet. The award is a comprehensive evaluation of the year's most outstanding new car based on consumer appeal, quality, and driving characteristics. Each jury member is allowed to allot 25 votes to a small selection of finalist cars. The New Beetle garnered 292 votes, more than double the second place finisher, the Honda Odyssey, with 142 votes, and well ahead of the third place car, the Chrysler 300M, with 124 votes. Indeed, Volkswagen is back!

Questions

1. What was the logic behind Volkswagen's decision to close its U.S. plant?

2. How critical will labor relations be in helping Volkswagen further increase its market share in the United States? Defend your answer.

3. What would you recommend that Volkswagen do in coordinating its worldwide labor operations so as to produce the lowest-price car and thus further increase its competitiveness?

Chiba International, Inc.

Ken Morikawa, the general manager for administration of a Japanese manufacturing plant under construction in rural Georgia, was troubled. Earlier that morning, his American personnel manager, John Sinclair, had walked eagerly across the temporary, open-plan office and announced, "I've found a professor of Japanese at Georgia State University who is willing to help translate our corporate philosophy. I'd like to hire him for the job." He felt pressured. In his mind, Sinclair, like many Americans, was expecting too much of Japanese companies. The company philosophy that he, Ken, had learned to live by in Tokyo would continue to guide him, but he did not feel that Americans would welcome or even understand a Japanese company philosophy.

Ken had a very large task in supervising the building of a plant that might one day provide jobs for up to 2,000 employees, in a region where very few workers had any industrial experience. He wanted to show them that his company cared about the welfare of its workers and their job security and could be trusted to treat them fairly and not to lay them off. He believed that such a philosophy, if it could be properly explained to workers and carefully implemented, would help build a high morale among the employees. And that would improve productivity.

Ken also wanted to ensure that high morale be maintained while the workforce expanded to full capacity. Aside from issues of ease of transportation and distribution, the characteristics of the local workforce—mainly their "Japanese" work ethic—had been one of the primary reasons for establishing the plant here. He believed that the training costs involved in transforming very "green" workers were well worth it. With training, you could avoid people who had picked up "bad habits" or had had their morale lowered in prior industrial jobs. In Japan, Ken knew, teaching company philosophy was an important part of the company's introductory training program. But would it work in rural Georgia?

Ken wondered if his new administrative duties were lowering his concern for personnel matters. Ever since he'd read Alfred Sloan's *My Years with General Motors* during the company training program and had written a review that focused on human resource issues, he had held positions in HR. Even though he had majored in mathematical economics in college, his first assignment had been in the personnel "design center," which controlled training and salary administration for white-collar employees. After two years, he was sent to a district office as a salesman. He returned after 13 months to the employee welfare selection of the personnel department at the head office, administering such programs as house loans and recreational activities. Eight years with the company had passed by the time he was sent to an American college to study personnel related subjects and improve his English.

After receiving his MBA, he returned to the head office. His most recent assignment before coming to Georgia was in personnel development research, planning new wages systems. In this new job in Georgia, it was expected that he would eventually hand the reins over to an American general manager and remain only in an advisory capacity. However, at this vital stage he felt that the corporation depended on his human relations expertise to set the scene for future success. Was he neglecting an area in which he had been trained to be sensitive?

He brought the subject up at lunch with John Sinclair. "Let me tell you something, John. I have a hunch why the Japanese are more successful in achieving high quality and productivity than Americans have been recently. It has to do with application, rather than ideas. Many great ideas have come from the United States, but the Japanese concentrate on applying them very carefully. Americans emphasize creating something new and then moving on. The Japanese meticulously analyze a problem from all angles and see how a solution might be implemented. However, John, as they say, Rome wasn't built in a day. I'm not sure our American workers will understand what it really means to have a company philosophy. Let's take it slowly and see what kind of people we hire and then see what best meets their needs."

John, who had worked at a rather traditional U.S. company for 11 years and had become increasingly interested in how Japanese companies managed their U.S. employees, had been eager to join a Japanese company. He wanted to see in action such "Japanese" strategies as long-term employment, the expression of a company philosophy, and careful attention to integrating the employees into the company. He answered comfortingly, "Ken, I know you hate conflict. But you also think it's important to gather information. One of our purchasing agents, Billy, told me about a Japanese company he recently visited, Chiba International. Apparently, they have already fully implemented their company philosophy, and I understand that they're doing very well with it. Why don't we go out to California and talk with their management and try and understand how and why they concentrated on communicating their philosophy to their American workforce."

"And soak up some sun, too," beamed Ken. "You're on!"

The Company

Chiba International, Inc. in San Jose, California, makes high-precision, sophisticated electronics parts used in the final assembly of customized and semicustomized integrated circuits, particularly the expensive memory chips used in computers and military hardware. In such products, reliability is everything (price is a lesser consideration). The similar, but cheaper, parts that manufacturers use once a product reaches high volume are left for others to make.

Chiba International is a subsidiary of Chiba Electronics Company. *Nihon Keizai Shimbun*, Japan's preeminent business paper, recently ranked Chiba Electronics as one of the foremost companies in Japan on the basis of its management earnings stability and performance, ahead of such better-known giants as Sony, Matsushita Electric, and Toyota Motor. Chiba Electronics has 70 percent of the $350 million-a-year world market for its products. Chiba International likewise has a 70 percent share of the $250 million-a-year U.S. market.

Chiba International started with a small sales office in the United States 12 years ago. A manufacturing plant that had been losing $100,000 to $200,000 a month was acquired from an American competitor. The American management was replaced by a team of Japanese headed by a Canadian-born Japan-reared executive. They succeeded in turning it around in two years.

Today, 14 out of the 24 top executives and 65 out of 70 salesmen at Chiba are Americans. All the employees in other categories are also American.

Chiba's Philosophy

> As the sun rises brilliantly in the sky,
> Revealing the size of the mountain, the market,
> Oh this is our goal.
> With the highest decree of mission in our heart we serve our industry
> Meeting the strictest decree of customer requirement.
> We are the leader in this industry and our future path
> Is ever so bright and satisfying.

"That's a translation of our company song," said a high-ranking Japanese executive, one of the group of Japanese and American managers who had agreed to meet with Ken and John. "But we haven't introduced it to our employees yet. That's typical of the way we brought the company philosophy to our employees—slowly and carefully. Every line worker gets a leaflet explaining our company philosophy when he or she starts work. We don't have a specific training session on it and we don't force them to swallow it. It's up to them to digest and understand it."

"What about when you acquire a company, as you have done over the past few years?" asked John.

"The same thing: It's very gradual. If we force it, it causes nothing but indigestion. Here it has been easy: The work is very labor intensive, repetitive, tedious assembly.

In other places, the soil is different. At one, for example, almost all the employees are salaried. They understand the philosophy, but won't necessarily go by it. Engineers and technical people also seem to be less receptive than people in sales, personnel and administration. In other sites, though, where the technology is more similar to this one, we have had no problems at all."

One of the other managers present in the group, an American, interrupted to show Ken and John a copy of the leaflet. It was quite rhetorical in tone and a few paragraphs struck them as particularly interesting.

The Leaflet

Management philosophy: Our goal is to strive toward both the material and spiritual fulfillment of all employees in the Company, and through this successful fulfillment, serve mankind in its progress and prosperity.

Management policy: Our purpose is to fully satisfy the needs of our customers and in return gain a just profit for ourselves. We are a family united in common bonds and singular goals. One of these bonds is the respect and support we feel for our fellow family coworkers.

Other exhortations: When there is a need, we all rally to meet it and consider no task too menial or demeaning; all that matters is that it should be done! We are all ready to sweep floors, sort parts, take inventory, clean machines, inspect parts, load trucks, carry boxes, wash windows, file papers, run furnaces, and do just about anything that has to be done.

Meetings

"Daily meetings at the beginning of each shift are held in the courtyard," explained a manager. "All the workers stand in lines (indicated by metal dots in the asphalt). Each day, a different member of management speaks for about five minutes. On Mondays, executives speak; on Tuesdays, personnel and administration are represented. Wednesdays are about safety concerns and on Thursdays and Fridays, members of production and sales speak. They are all free to say whatever they like. The shift workers tend to develop favorites, especially among the more extroverted sales managers.

"Then a personnel coordinator delivers news about sports events and so on, and perhaps a motivational message, and goes on to lead the group in exercises for one minute. These calisthenics are voluntary, but most of the employees join in. After that, the large group breaks up for brief departmental meetings.

"Again, in the departmental meetings, a speaker is chosen for the day and speaks for about five minutes. Even people at the lowest exempt ('salaried') level speak. Then the department manager discusses yesterday's performance, today's schedule and any other messages such as that housekeeping is inadequate or that certain raw materials are in short supply.

"Once a month, there is an announcement of total company performance versus plans. This is important, as all company employees share at the same rate in the annual company bonus, which is based on profitability and usually equals about one month's salary or wages."

Another Japanese manager continued: "Years ago, there were complaints about having so many meetings, but I haven't heard any for a long time now. The employees like to hear important announcements and even less important ones, such as who is selling theater tickets, bowling league reports, and tennis match dates."

The American personnel manager chimed in. "I was the one who came up with the idea of exercises. I saw it on my visit to Japan. They are just a part of the rituals and symbols that you need in order to get better mutual understanding. The atmosphere was right and the timing was good. Even so, because they weren't mandatory, it took about one-and-a-half years until everyone joined in. Now most people understand the meaning behind it. If we were to stop it now, we'd get complaints.

"Besides the morning meeting, we have served other meetings. On Mondays, we have a very large liaison meeting for information sharing. All the executives attend: sales managers and staff managers, the plant manager and the assistant plant manager. On Tuesdays, we have a production meeting attended by the production managers and any staff involved with their problems. On Monday at four o'clock every second week we have a supervisors' meeting, mainly for one-way communication to them. On the alternating weeks, we have a training meeting. The whole personnel department also meets every week.

"Less formally, we have many sales meetings about, for example, new products. We have combination sales and production meetings, which are called on as an as-needed basis. Team meetings on the production lines are also called whenever needed.

"All these formal meetings are supplemented by many company-sponsored activities. We have a company bowling league, tennis matches, softball, fishing, and skiing. We often organize discount tickets. We're planning the Christmas party. Each employee can bring a guest, so it costs us about $40,000. Our company picnic costs $29,000."

"It sounds very well-worked out for the non-exempts," said John. "What about for the exempts?"

Sales Force

The company started with the largely American sales force. "They're a very different species. They have tremendous professional pride. Most of the American sales engineers have a very arrogant take-it-or-leave-it attitude. Our attitude is almost the complete opposite. We try to serve our customer's needs. Almost like a geisha girl, who makes her customer feel that he is the only one served by her," explained one of the Chiba managers.

"We try to communicate the following motto to them:

S	incerity
A	bility
L	ove
E	nergy
S	ervice

"Sincerity is the basic attitude you have to have as well as the ability to convince the customer. You must love the products that you sell, or you can't convince the customer. You must have energy because, at the end of the day, it's always the case that you could have done one more thing or made one more sales call. Finally, the mentality of serving the customer is the most important.

"We communicate that to our sales force and they like it, especially when they don't have to tell white lies to customers or put up with harassment from customers. We also want them to be honest with us, even about their mistakes. Quite often, we depend on input from the salespeople for our understanding of customers, so an objective daily report by telex or phone is very important to us.

"No one in our company works on a commission basis, not even salesmen. We would lose market share for products that are difficult to promote. Also, the nature of different sales territories would make commissions unfair.

"Although we pay on straight salary only, we don't just have a unilateral sales quota. The salespeople discuss targets with their boss. They are purposely set high, so good performance against goals is grounds for a merit increase the next year.

"We don't really have a marketing department. We feel that it is an expensive luxury. We have a vice president in charge of marketing, but this is almost a corporate sales staff function."

U.S. Management

John was curious about how American line managers reacted to working in a Japanese company. A Japanese manager explained. "When Americans join us, they expect the usual great deal of internal politicking. They scan people in meetings, looking for those with real power; looking, to use our expression, for whose apple they should polish. It takes time for them to realize that it's unnecessary.

"When we interview American executives for a job, we do it collectively, so five to ten interviews are present. That usually puzzles the interviewees. They wonder whom they will report to. We reply that they will be hired by the *company*, although they may report to one individual. As in

Japan, the company will take care of them, so it does not depend on their loyalty to one individual."

"What about your company criteria for hiring managers?" asked John.

"We focus on a manager's way of thinking, not necessarily on ability. Although a Harvard MBA is welcomed, it is not essential. In fact no one here has one. We don't provide an elegant fit to his or her social elite. There are no private offices. Salary and benefits are up to par for the location (and industry), but not especially high. We work long hours.

"We're looking for devotion and dedication as well as an aggressive attitude. We conduct two or three long interviews for an important position. We ask questions like 'what is your main shortcoming?' We're interested not in the answer itself but in the kind of thinking behind it. We do make mistakes sometimes, but our batting average is good.

"Sometimes there's a very deep communication gap between Japanese management and U.S. management because we believe in dedication and devotion to the company. They do too, but only up to a certain point. We often tell them that the joy of working for the company can be identical to personal happiness with the family. I ask my wife for her understanding of that, and I work six days a week from seven o'clock to ten o'clock. Their wives place demands on them to come home at six o'clock. U.S. executives put personal and family happiness first. I'm not telling you which is right. But it is second nature for me to think about the future of the company. So long as I have challenging assignments and job opportunities, I will put the company before my personal happiness."

"What do American interviewees feel about all this?" inquired John.

"One problem is that they ask, 'What's my real future? Can I be considered for president?' There's no real answer because it probably will be a Japanese. However, we don't like to close those doors to a really capable American.

"The issue of communication between Japanese and Americans is still a problem. After the Americans go home, the Japanese get together at seven or eight o'clock and talk in Japanese about problems and make decisions without the Americans present. Naturally, this makes the Americans feel very apprehensive. We're trying to rectify it by asking the Japanese managers not to make decisions alone and by asking the Americans to stay as late as possible.

"More important, if we could really have our philosophy permeate the American managers, we Japanese could all go back to Japan and not worry about it. Our mission is to expedite that day by education and training.

"So far, however, there is a gap. Americans are more interested in individual accomplishment, remuneration, and power. When they are given more responsibility, they don't feel its heavy weight, rather they feel that it extends their sovereign area so that they have more of a whip. That creates power conflicts among U.S. managers."

"Let me tell you, though," summarized the American personnel manager. "I like it. I was recruited by a headhunter. Now, I've been with the company five years and the difference from my former employer is astounding. I don't have to get out there and be two-faced, fudging to keep the union out, hedging for the buck. In general, it's hard to find an American employer that really, sincerely cares for the welfare of the low-level employee. This company went almost too far in the opposite direction at first. They wanted to do too much for the employees too quickly, without their earning it. That way, you don't get their respect."

Financial Principles

"Our financial people throughout the company are proud because of our impressive company performance," said one of Chiba team. "Only 20 percent of our financing is through debt, in contrast to many Japanese companies. We also have a rather unique way of treating some of our raw materials internally. We try to expense everything out. It's derived from our founder's very conservative management. We ask the question: 'If we closed down tomorrow, what would our liquid assets be?' In line with that, for example, internally we put our inventory at zero.

"We follow the 'noodle peddler theory.' The noodle peddler is an entrepreneur. He has to borrow his cart, his serving dishes and his pan to make ramen. He has to be a good marketer to know where to sell. He has to be a good purchasing director and not overbuy noodles, in case it rains. He could buy a fridge, but he would need a lot of capital, the taste of the noodles would deteriorate, and he would need additional manpower to keep an inventory of the contents of the fridge. The successful noodle peddler puts dollars aside at the end of the day for depreciation and raw materials for tomorrow. Only then does he count profits. That's also why we don't have a marketing department. The successful peddler doesn't have time to examine opportunities in the next town.

"This is the way a division manager has to operate. In order to maximize output with minimum expenditure, every effort is made to keep track on a daily basis of sales, returns, net shipment costs, and expenses."

Open Communication

"I understand all that you've said so far," mused John, "but how exactly do you take all these abstract philosophical ideas and make them real?"

"Oh, open communications is the key. We have a fairly homogeneous workforce. Most are intelligent, some are even college graduates. Most are also very stable types with dependents or elderly parents they send money to.

"We're lucky, but of course, it's not as homogeneous as in Japan, where everyone has experienced one culture. So here, the philosophy has to be backed up by a great deal of communication.

"We mentioned the meetings. We also have a suggestion box, and we answer all the suggestions in print in the company newspaper. Also, one person from personnel tours the plant all day, for all three shifts, once a week, just chatting and getting in touch with any potential problems as they arise. It's kind of a secondary grievance systems. We're not unionized and I guess we'd rather stay that way as it helps us so much with flexibility and job changes among our workforce.

"In the fall, when work is slow, we have many *kompas*. You may not know about this, John. A *kompa* is a small gathering off-premises after work. Eight to eighteen people participate, and the company pays for their time and for refreshments. They're rarely social: They have an objective. For example, if two departments don't get along and yet they need to work together, they might hold a *kompa*. A *kompa* can take place at all levels of the company. Those groups that do it more frequently tend to move on from talking about production problems to more philosophical issues."

Appraisal and Reward Systems

"It all sounds great," sighed Ken, "just as good as Japan. But tell me, how does it tie with wages and salaries, because people here are used to such different systems?"

"Well, we don't have lifetime employment, but we do have an explicit no-layoff commitment. We are responsible for our employees. This means that employees also have to take responsibility and have broad job categories, so we don't have to redo paperwork all the time. We have tried to reduce the number of job classifications to the raw minimum, so we have two pay grades covering 700 workers. At the higher levels, we have three pay grades for craftsmen and two for technicians."

John ventured: "I guess an example of your job flexibility in action is the mechanic you mentioned when we toured the plant."

"Yes, the person you spoke with was a dry press mechanic. He's doing menial labor this week, but his pay hasn't been cut and he knows he wouldn't be taken off his job if it weren't important."

"We don't hire outside, if we can avoid it," added the personnel manager, "only if the skill is not available in-house. The bulk of our training is on the job. We don't utilize job postings. We promote when a person's skills are ripe or when there is a need.

"The job of a 'lead' or team leader is the stepping-stone to supervisor. It's not a separate job status within our system, but the lead is given a few cents an hour extra and wears a pink, not a yellow, smock. Leads are carefully groomed for their position, and although a lead might be demoted because a specific need for them no longer existed, a lead would rarely be demoted for lack of skills or leadership ability.

"Rewards are for service and performance. Plant workers, unskilled and semiskilled, are reviewed every six months. The lead completes the evaluation form [see Exhibit 1]. This is checked or confirmed by the supervisor, and the overall point score translates into cents per hour. There are two copies, one for the supervisor and one for the employee. Depending on the supervisor, some employees get a copy, some don't.

"The office clerical staff are all reviewed on April 1st and October 1st. The review form for managers [see Exhibit 2] is used to determine overall letter scores. All the scores are posted on a spread sheet and compared across departments, through numerous meetings of managers and personnel people, until the scores are consistent with one another. Then the scores are tied to dollars. Some managers provide feedback, some don't.

"Salaried staff are reviewed on April 1st and, as a separate process, the spread procedure just outlined is carried out. At least two managers review any exempt employee, but feedback is usually minimal. The reason is that we encourage feedback all year. If there are no surprises for your subordinate at review time, then you've managed well.

"Agreements on reviews for exempt personnel take place in many meetings at various levels. The process is very thorough and exceptionally fair, and contributes to the levels of performance we get."

Quality and Service

A question from John as to how Chiba International was doing as a result of all this elicited much pride.

"Turnover is 2-1/2 percent a month, which is very satisfactory for our kind of labor, given a transient society. We rarely have to advertise for new employees now. The community knows about it. But we do select carefully. The personnel department does the initial screening and then the production managers and supervisors get together and interview people.

"The lack of available, technically trained people used to be a big problem, but over the years, we've developed the expertise internally. Our productivity is now almost as high as in Japan."

Ken and John asked what other aspects of the company they had not yet discussed. They were told that quality, and hence customer service, was another central part of the philosophy. "Our founder, Mr. Amano, firmly believes in zero defect theory. Doctor Deming taught us the concept of quality control. Unfortunately, many American companies did not emphasize this. During World War II, the concept of acceptable quality level was developed in the United States. The idea was that, with mass production, there will be some defects. Rather than paying for more inspectors on the production line, real problems, for example, with cars, could be identified by the consumer in the field and repaired in the field.

"We don't allow that. We have 100 percent visual inspection of all our tiny parts, which only cost $50 per

Exhibit 1   **Semiannual Performance Review**

Employee's name	Clock no.	Dept.	Shift	Over last six-month period			
				Days absences	Number tardies	Number early exits	Work days leave of absence
Employee's job title	Anniversary						

Rate on factors below	Numerical score			
	L	S	M	F
1. Loyalty/Dedication: Faithful to the company cause, ideals, philosophy, and customers; devoting or setting aside, time for company purposes.				
2. Spirit/Zeal: Amount of interest and enthusiasm shown in work; full of energy, animation, and courage; eagerness and ardent interest in the pursuit of company goals.				
3. Cooperation: A willingness and ability to work with leaders and fellow employees toward company goals.				
4. Quantity of work: Volume of work regularly produced; speed and consistency of output.				
5. Quality of work: Extent to which work produced meets quality requirements of accuracy, thoroughness, and effectiveness.				
6. Job knowledge: The fact or condition of knowing the job with familiarity gained through experience, association and training.				
7. Safety attitude: The willingness and ability to perform work safely.				
8. Creativeness: The ability to produce through imaginative skill.				
9. Attendence: Includes all types of absence (excused or unexcused), tardies, early exits, LOAs from scheduled work.				
10. Leadership: The ability to provide direction, guidance, and training to others.				
Overall evaluation of employee performance:				

Supervisor's approval	Manager's approval	Personnel dept. approval

Do not write below this line – for human resource department use only

---

1,000 units. We inspect every finished package under a microscope, so we have 130 inspectors, which is about one sixth of our production staff.

"Mr. Amano, has said to us, 'We try to develop every item our customers want. Being latecomers, we never say no, we never say we can't.' Older manufacturers would evaluate a proposal on a cost basis and say no. Yet we have been profitable from the start."

As the interview drew to a close, one Japanese manager reflected, "Mr. Amano has a saying:

Ability × philosophy × zeal = performance.

"If the philosophy is negative, performance is negative because it's a multiplicative relationship.

"But in our company, which now numbers 2,000, we must also start to have different kinds of thinking. The Japanese sword is strong because it is made of all different kinds of steel wrapped around one another. The

Chinese sword is also very strong, but because it's all one material, it's vulnerable to a certain kind of shock. We must bear that in mind so that we have differences within a shared philosophy.

"We're thinking of writing a book on our philosophy, addressing such issues as what loyalty is, by piecing together events and stories from our company history. This would be a book that would assist us in training."

Ken and John walked out into the parking lot. "Whew!" sighed John. "It's more complicated than I thought."

"Oh yes! You need a great deal of patience," responded Ken paternally.

"So we'd better get started quickly," said John, enthusiastic. "Where shall we begin? Perhaps I should call the translator."

Ken wasn't sure what his answer should be.

Exhibit 2   **Example of Completed Performance Review**

Values

Below average					Aver-age	Above average						DOE, John
Unsatisfactory	Fair				Good			Very good			Excellent	
E–	E	D–	D–	D+	C–	C	C+	B–	B	B+	A–	A
1	2	3	4	5	6	7	8	9	10	11	12	13

Factors

1. Loyalty/Dedication:	Faithful to the company cause, ideals, philosophy, and customers; devoting or setting aside, time for company purposes.	B+	11
2. Spirit/Zeal:	Amount of interest and enthusiasm shown in work; full of energy, animation, and ardent interest in the pursuit of company goals.	C	7
3. Consultation:	The ability to consult and listen to subordinates, fellow employees, superiors in an effort to arrive at the best possible direction.	C–	6
4. Communications:	The ability to communicate effectively with subordinates, fellow employees, superiors and business associates.	C+	8
5. Philosophy:	The willingness to learn and practice company philosophy; the ability to train others regarding company philosophy.	B–	9
6. Method of thinking:	The ability, good sense and judgement to discern inner qualities and relationships to determine the best course of action.	D	4
7. Cooperation:	A willingness and ability to work with leaders and fellow employees toward company goals.	A	13
8. Job knowledge:	The fact or condition of knowing the job with familiarity gained through experience, association and training.	B–	9
9. Attendance:	This factor includes reliability, dependability and puntualness; one's ability to be "on-the-job."	A–	12
10. Results:	The efforts which have brought about a beneficial effect in line with company goals.	E	2

Overall comment | C+ | $\frac{81}{10} = 8.1$

1. Of all the information that Ken and John have learned at Chiba International, what human resources ideas do you think were the most important? Why?

2. What will be the greatest challenges in implementing what they have learned at Chiba back at their manufacturing plant?

3. If you were in charge of operations at the manufacturing plan, which of the ideas from chiba would you implement first? Choose three and give your reasoning.

Source: This case was written by Professors Vladimir Pucik (IMD) and Nina Hatvany (formerly of Columbia University) as a basis for class discussion rather than to illustrate either effective or ineffective handling of a business situation. Copyright © 1998 by IMD— International Institute for Management Development, Lausanne, Switzerland. Not to be used or reproduced without written permission directly from IMD. Reprinted with permission.

Integrative Case 2

The Road to Hell

John Baker, chief engineer of the Caribbean Bauxite Company of Barracania in the West Indies, was making his final preparations to leave the island. His promotion to production manager of Keso Mining Corporation near Winnipeg—one of Continental Ore's fast-expanding Canadian enterprises—had been announced a month before, and now everything had been tidied up except the last vital interview with his successor, the able young Barracanian, Matthew Rennalls. It was crucial that this interview be successful and that Rennalls leave his office uplifted and encouraged to face the challenge of a new job. A touch on the bell would have brought Rennalls walking into the room, but Baker delayed the moment and gazed thoughtfully through the window, considering just exactly what he was going to say and, more particularly, how he was going to say it.

John Baker, an English expatriate, was 45 years old and had served 23 years with Continental Ore in East Asia, several African countries, Europe, and for the last 2 years, the West Indies. He hadn't cared much for his previous assignment in Hamburg and was delighted when the West Indian appointment came through Climate was not the only attraction. Baker had always preferred working overseas (in what were termed "the developing countries"), because he felt he had an innate knack—better than most other expatriates working for Continental Ore—of knowing just how to get along with the regional staff. After 24 hours in Barracania, however, he realized that he would need all this "innate knack" to deal effectively with the problems that awaited him in this field.

At his first interview with Hutchins, the production manager, the problem of Rennalls and his future was discussed. There and then it was made quite clear to Baker that one of his most important tasks would be "grooming" Rennalls as his successor. Hutchins had pointed out that not only was Rennalls one of the brightest Barracanian prospects on the staff of Caribbean Bauxite—at London University he had taken first-class honors in the BSc engineering degree—but being the son of the minister of finance and economic planning, he also had no small political pull.

The company had been particularly pleased when Rennalls decided to work for it rather than the government in which his father had such a prominent post. The company ascribed his action to the effect of its vigorous and liberal regionalization program, which since World War II had produced 18 Barracanians at mid-management level and given Caribbean Bauxite a good lead in this respect over all other international concerns operating in Barracania. The success of this timely regionalization policy led to excellent relations with the government.

This relationship was given an added importance when Barracania, 3 years later, became independent—an occasion that encouraged a critical and challenging attitude toward the role that foreign interests would play in the new Barracania. Therefore, Hutchins had little difficulty in convincing Baker that the successful career development of Rennalls was of primary importance.

The interview with Hutchins was now 2 years old, and Baker, leaning back in his office chair, reviewed his success in grooming Rennalls. What aspects of the latter's character had helped and what had hindered? What about his own personality? How had that helped or hindered? The first item to go on the credit side would, without question, be the ability of Rennalls to master the technical aspects of the job. From the start, he had shown keenness and enthusiasm and often impressed Baker with his ability in tackling new assignments as well as the constructive comments he invariably made in departmental discussions. He was popular with all ranks of Barracanian staff and had an ease of manner that placed him in good stead when dealing with his expatriate seniors. These were all assets, but what about the debit side?

First and foremost, there was his racial consciousness. His 4 years at London University had accentuated this feeling and made him sensitive to any sign of condescension on the part of expatriates. It may have been to give expression to this sentiment that as soon as he returned from London, he threw himself into politics on behalf of the United Action Party, which later won the preindependence elections and provided the country with its first prime minister.

The ambitions of Rennalls—and he certainly was ambitious—did not lie in politics, because staunch nationalist that he was, he saw that he could serve himself and his country best—for bauxite was responsible for nearly half the value of Barracania's export trade—by putting his engineering talent to the best use possible. On this account, Hutchins found that he had an unexpectedly easy task in persuading Rennalls to give up his political work before entering the production department as an assistant engineer.

Baker knew that it was Rennalls' well-repressed sense of race consciousness that had prevented their relationship from being as close as it should have been. On the surface, nothing could have seemed more agreeable. Formality between the two men was at a minimum. Baker was delighted to find that his assistant shared his own

527

peculiar "shaggy dog" sense of humor so that jokes were continually being exchanged; they entertained each other at their houses and often played tennis together—and yet the barrier remained invisible, indefinable, but ever present. The existence of this "screen" between them was a constant source of frustration to Baker, because it indicated a weakness that he was loath to accept. If he was successful with all other nationalities, why not with Rennalls?

At least he had managed to "break through" to Rennalls more successfully than any other expatriate. In fact, it was the young Barracanian's attitude—sometimes overbearing, sometimes cynical—toward other company expatriates that had been one of the subjects Baker had raised last year when he discussed Rennalls' staff report with him. He knew, too, that he would have to raise the same subject again in the forthcoming interview, because Jackson, the senior draftsperson, had complained only yesterday about the rudeness of Rennalls. With this thought in mind, Baker leaned forward and spoke into the intercom, "Would you come in, Matt, please? I'd like a word with you." As Rennalls entered the room, Baker said, "Do sit down," and offered a cigarette. He paused while he held out his lighter, then went on.

"As you know, Matt, I'll be off to Canada in a few days' time, and before I go, I thought it would be useful if we could have a final chat together. It is indeed with some deference that I suggest I can be of help. You will shortly be sitting in this chair doing the job I am now doing, but I, on the other hand, am 10 years older, so perhaps you can accept the idea that I may be able to give you the benefit of my longer experience."

Baker saw Rennalls stiffen slightly in his chair as he made this point. Consequently, he added in explanation, "You and I have attended enough company courses to remember those repeated requests by the personnel manager to tell people how they are getting on as often as the convenient moment arises and not just the automatic 'once a year' when, by regulation, staff reports have to be discussed."

Rennalls nodded his agreement, and Baker went on. "I shall always remember the last job performance discussion I had with my previous boss back in Germany. He used what he called the 'plus and minus' technique. His firm belief was that when a senior, by discussion, seeks to improve the work performance of his staff, his prime objective should be to make sure that the latter leaves the interview encouraged and inspired to improve. Any criticism must, therefore, be constructive and helpful. He said that one very good way to encourage a person—and I fully agree with him—is to tell him about his good points—the plus factors—as well as his weak ones—the minus factors. I thought, Matt, it would be a good idea to run our discussion along these lines."

Rennalls offered no comment, so Baker continued. "Let me say, therefore, right away, that, as far as your own work performance is concerned, the plus far outweighs the minus. I have been most impressed, for instance, with the way you have adapted your considerable theoretic knowledge to master the practical techniques of your job—that

ingenious method you used to get air down to the fifth-shaft level is a sufficient case in point—and at departmental meetings I have invariably found your comments well-taken and helpful. In fact, you will be interested to know that only last week I reported to Mr. Hutchins that, from the technical point of view, he could not wish for a more able man to succeed to the position of chief engineer."

"That's very good indeed of you, John," cut in Rennalls with a smile of thanks. "My only worry now is how to live up to such a high recommendation."

"Of that I am quite sure," returned Baker, "especially if you can overcome the minus factor which I would like now to discuss with you. It is one that I have talked about before, so I'll come straight to the point. I have noticed that you are more friendly and get on better with your fellow Barracanians than you do with Europeans. In point of fact, I had a complaint only yesterday from Mr. Jackson, who said you had been rude to him—and not for the first time either.

"There is, Matt, I am sure, no need for me to tell you how necessary it will be for you to get on well with expatriates, because until the company has trained sufficient people of your calibre, Europeans are bound to occupy senior positions here in Barracania. All this is vital to your future interests, so can I help you in any way?"

While Baker was speaking on this theme, Rennalls sat tensed in his chair, and it was some seconds before he replied. "It is quite extraordinary, isn't it, how one can convey an impression to others so at variance with what one intends? I can only assure you once again that my disputes with Jackson—and you may remember also, Godson—have had nothing at all to do with the color of their skins. I promise you that if a Barracanian had behaved in an equally peremptory manner I would have reacted in precisely the same way. And again, if I may say it within these four walls, I am sure I am not the only one who has found Jackson and Godson difficult. I could mention the names of several expatriates who have felt the same. However, I am really sorry to have created this impression of not being able to get along with Europeans—it is an entirely false one—and I quite realize that I must do all I can to correct it as quickly as possible. On your last point, regarding Europeans holding senior positions in the company for some time to come, I quite accept the situation. I know that Caribbean Bauxite—as it has been doing for many years now—will promote Barracanians as soon as their experience warrants it. And, finally, I would like to assure you, John—and my father thinks the same too—that I am very happy in my work here and hope to stay with the company for many years to come."

Rennalls had spoken earnestly. Although not convinced by what he heard, Baker did not think he could pursue the matter further except to say, "All right, Matt, my impression *may* be wrong, but I would like to remind you about the truth of that old saying, 'What is important is not what is true but what is believed.' Let it rest at that."

But suddenly Baker knew he didn't want to "let it rest at that." He was disappointed once again at not being able to break through to Rennalls and having yet again to listen to his bland denial that there was any racial prejudice in his makeup. Baker, who had intended to end the interview at this point, decided to try another tactic.

"To return for a moment to the 'plus and minus technique' I was telling you about just now, there is another plus factor I forgot to mention. I would like to congratulate you not only on the calibre of your work but also on the ability you have shown in overcoming a challenge which I, as a European, have never had to meet. Continental Ore is, as you know, a typical commercial enterprise—admittedly a big one—which is a product of the economic and social environment of the United States and Western Europe. My ancestors have all been brought up in this environment for the past 200 or 300 years, and I have, therefore, been able to live in a world in which commerce (as we know it today) has been part and parcel of my being. It has not been something revolutionary and new that has suddenly entered my life." Baker went on, "In your case, the situation is different, because you and your forebears have had only some 50 or 60 years in this commercial environment. You have had to face the challenge of bridging the gap between 50 and 200 or 300 years. Again, Matt, let me congratulate you—and people like you—once again on having so successfully overcome this particular hurdle. It is for this very reason that I think the outlook for Barracania—and particularly Caribbean Bauxite—is so bright."

There was a pause, and for a moment, Baker thought hopefully that he was about to achieve his long-awaited breakthrough, but Rennalls merely smiled back. The barrier remained unbreached. There remained some 5 minutes of cheerful conversation about the contrast between the Caribbean and Canadian climate and whether the West Indies had any hope of beating England in the Fifth Test before Baker drew the interview to a close. Although he was as far as ever from knowing the real Rennalls, he nevertheless was glad that the interview had run along in this friendly manner and, particularly, that it had ended on such a cheerful note.

This feeling, however, lasted only until the following morning. Baker had some farewells to make, so he arrived at the office considerably later than usual. He had no sooner sat down at his desk than his secretary walked into the room with a worried frown on her face. Her words came fast, "When I arrived this morning, I found Mr. Rennalls already waiting at my door. He seemed very angry and told me in quite a peremptory manner that he had a vital letter to dictate that must be sent off without any delay. He was so worked up that he couldn't keep still and kept pacing about the room, which is most unlike him. He wouldn't even wait to read what he had dictated. Just signed the page where he thought the letter would end. It has been distributed, and your copy is in your tray."

Puzzled and feeling vaguely uneasy, Baker opened the confidential envelope and read the following letter:

From: Assistant Engineer

To: Chief Engineer,
Caribbean Bauxite Limited

14 August

Assessment of Interview between Baker and Rennalls

It has always been my practice to respect the advice given me by seniors, so after our interview, I decided to give careful thought once again to its main points and so make sure that I had understood all that had been said. As I promised you at the time, I had every intention of putting your advice to the best effect.

It was not, therefore, until I had sat down quietly in my home yesterday evening to consider the interview objectively that its main purport became clear. Only then did the full enormity of what you said dawn on me. The more I thought about it, the more convinced I was that I had hit upon the real truth—and the more furious I became. With a facility in the English language which I, a poor Barracanian, cannot hope to match, you had the audacity to insult me (and through me every Barracanian worth his salt) by claiming that our knowledge of modern living is only a paltry 50 years old whereas yours goes back 200 or 300 years. As if your materialistic commercial environment could possibly be compared with the spiritual values of our culture. I'll have you know that if much of what I saw in London is representative of your most boasted culture, I hope fervently that it will never come to Barracania. By what right do you have the effrontery to condescend to us? At heart, all you Europeans think us barbarians; as you say amongst yourselves, we are "just down from the trees."

Far into the night I discussed this matter with my father, and he is as disgusted as I. He agrees with me that any company whose senior staff think as you do is no place for any Barracanian proud of his culture and race—so much for all the company "clap-trap" and specious propaganda about regionalization and Barracania for the Barracanians.

I feel ashamed and betrayed. Please accept this letter as my resignation, which I wish to become effective immediately.

cc: Production Manager
Managing Director

1. What mistake did John Baker make? Why did he not realize this mistake when it occurred?

2. What would you recommend that Baker do now? Explain.

3. What does this case illustrate about human resource management in the international enviornment? Be complete in your answer.

Source: This case was prepared by Gareth Evans and is used with permission.

Gillette's Prescription for International Business Success: In-House Training and Expat Experience

Alfred Zeien, Chairperson and CEO of internationally prominent Gillette, recently was quoted as saying, "It takes at least 25 years to build an international management corps that possesses the skills, experience and abilities to take a global organization from one level of success to the next." With this philosophy as the foundation, Gillette is committed to following two key strategies for building its worldwide management corps. The first is the firm's in-house International Trainee Program; the second is development through expatriate experience, hiring and assigning foreign nationals to staff operations not only in their home countries but around the world.

Background on Gillette

Gillette has four main divisions and subsidiaries: the North Atlantic Group, the Diversified Group, the Stationary Products Group, and the International Group. The International Group makes and markets Gillette's personal-care, shaving, and stationery products and staffs operation throughout the world (excluding North America and Western Europe). The International Group is made up of three geographic groups: (1) Africa, Latin America, and the Middle East; (2) Eastern Europe; and (3) the Asian Pacific. The Latin American and International headquarters are in Boston; the Asian Pacific headquarters are in Singapore; and the headquarters for the Middle East, Africa, Russia, and Eastern Europe are in London. By 1993, Gillette had 57 manufacturing facilities in 28 countries. More than three-fourths of the company's employees work outside the United States. As indicated by this organizational structure, Gillette is a globally involved consumer-products company. The firm now has more than 90 years of experience in the international marketplace, and it competes in three major consumer businesses: personal grooming products for men and women, small electrical appliances, and stationery products. Widely recognized brand names such as Liquid Paper, Paper Mate, Oral-B, Braun, and Jafra are among this MNC's products, which are distributed through retailers, wholesalers, and agents in more than 200 countries and territories around the world.

A good example of Gillette's international efforts was the launch of the SensorExcel razor a few years ago. Using a global communications strategy, the SensorExcel was announced simultaneously in 19 countries. A comprehen-sive guidelines manual was developed and served as the "blueprint" for the public relations launch. This manual put forth a strategic framework for the program, communicated Gillette's overall business goals, and provided country-by-country guidelines for the new product launch. The company combined a global integration and local differentiation strategy by ensuring consistency of the messages on product quality across the market area, but the nature of the message delivery was left to local discretion. This differentiation recognized that each culture and clientele was unique.

The International Trainee Program

Besides the strategic marketing emphasis, the Gillette Company made a significant recruitment and management-development decision during the mid-1980s. Already bringing in high-priced executives on a "just-in-time" basis to provide the needed talent for Gillette's global operations, the company also decided to develop managers internally. The International Trainee Program (ITP) was launched in 1983 by Gillette's international human resources department.

When the ITP began, students from countries outside the United States were hired by Gillette to come to Boston as interns. At that time, the company's reasons were purely philanthropic. A few years later, the vice-president of human resources for Gillette International realized that the internship program could be turned into an in-house management training program. In the words of top management, the objective was "to bring recent graduates to Boston specifically to groom them for Gillette jobs in their home countries." After a few years, responsibility for identifying foreign students was moved from an outside international student-exchange program to the human resources director and general manager for each of Gillette's worldwide operations. Each manager was responsible for identifying the top business students in prestigious universities internationally, who were to be recruited into the program.

The approach taken by the ITP is representative of Gillette's regiocentric approach to international management. In international operations, Gillette relies on managers from a particular geographic region to handle things in and around that location. The regiocentric approach also guides the manner in which training is set up. On entering Gillette's program, junior trainees typically work for 6 months at the Gillette subsidiary in their home country. Gillette corporate management then may choose to transfer them to one of the company's three international headquarters: Boston, London, or Singapore. These assignments usually last for 18 months and depend on which world region their subsidiaries fall into. The trainee program basically is the same in each location; however, Boston (where the program originated) has more trainees than either London or Singapore.

Gillette's international trainee program and on-site training programs both have personal and organizational objectives. At a personal level, Gillette provides the training and direct experience to improve the management trainee's ability to interact effectively with the local people at foreign operations and, in particular, with their own direct reports. Such training not only enhances the individual's competitiveness and marketability within Gillette but also with other companies. Gillette generally extends permanent job offers to nine of every ten trainees who go through the ITP. Eight of the nine usually accept, and six of these stay with the firm longer than a year after returning to their home countries. Although graduates often receive other job offers at higher salaries, Gillette has been successful in keeping its graduates. In the first 10 years, 113 trainees went through the program, and over one-half are still with the company.

Besides the personal benefits from the training, the company also clearly benefits. For example, trainees note that they are much more willing to communicate with headquarters and other operations, because they know people at the home office and understand how things work at other facilities around the world. The trainees also gain an appreciation for different ways of doing things during their training. Most enter the program having only limited experience with people and customs from cultures other than their own. After living and working for a year and a half with people from different cultures, the trainees naturally emerge as more open-minded managers and take this with them wherever they go on their permanent assignment.

The international-trainee program costs Gillette $20,000 to $25,000 per trainee per year. However, expatriates sent to overseas assignments can end up costing much more. In Boston alone, the total trainee-program budget is about $1 million per year; however, the firm estimates that only three expatriates could be hired for that amount. The head of international human resources feels that the cost of the ITP is worth it to Gillette even though it may take longer to develop managers this way. He states, "This is the core of our international recruiting. All of our efforts and resources are directed toward this program."

After completing their 18-month terms, trainees return to their home countries to take entry-level manager positions. If they show continued success, they usually will move on to assignments in other countries, ultimately returning to their home countries as general managers or senior operating managers. For example, many ITP graduates of several years ago now hold mid- to senior-level management positions. Gillette looks to ITP graduates beyond expatriate assignments; they are slated to be this MNC's future senior international leaders.

Development through Expatriate Experience

Besides the in-house ITP, Gillette also provides expatriate experience to its managers. For example, about 80 percent of the 40 top executives have had at least one foreign assignment, and more than 50 percent have worked in at least three countries. In 1993 alone, 269 Gillette employees were on expatriate assignments, representing 38 home countries and 47 host countries.

A very large majority of Gillette's expatriates come from one of the other 27 countries in which the company has operations. Most of the time, Gillette hires foreign nationals to staff management positions in countries other than the United States. Often, these individuals are first identified while studying at U.S. universities for their MBAs. On a training track similar to those in the company's international trainee program, these new hires typically work for a year at Gillette's Boston headquarters and then return to a Gillette subsidiary in their home country. Then, after working in their home countries for approximately 4 years, these managers usually are moved to other countries and assignments. A major side benefit of Gillette managers gaining such broad international experience is that as they do so, they teach and develop other potential managers within the organization.

Managers with international experience often are prime candidates for positions that open when Gillette enters joint ventures or new markets. A good example is the joint venture that Gillette undertook with a company in China. Gillette began planning this alliance more than 4 years before it solidified and actually occurred. Importantly, Gillette began identifying individual managers who would be right for assignments in the China business early in the process. Gillette knew that managers who had Chinese experience had to be pulled from other countries, such as Australia, England, and France, but also that others in the company with relevant experience would then have to move into the positions these people left behind.

Chairman and CEO Zeien recently told his shareholders: "I contend that the transferability of management is the glue that holds the various parts of the company together." And Dieu Eng Seng, area vice-president of Oral-B, Asia Pacific, echoed this philosophy and that of his Gillette management colleagues in saying, "One of my key objectives is to identify, recruit and develop competent managers. I'm confident that these good people will generate a flow of business growth and profits for the future."

1. How does Gillette's overall management philosophy and strategy influence its training and development program?

2. What are some benefits of training home-country nationals at one of Gillette's international headquarters?

3. What does Gillette feel that graduates of the international trainee program offer the company?

Source: This case was written specially for this book. The assistance of Jill Ormesher is acknowledged, as well as the following references: Jennifer J. Laabs, "Building a Global Management Team," *Personnel Journal,* August 1993, p. 75; Jennifer J. Laabs, "How Gillette Grooms Global Talent," *Personnel Journal,* August 1993, pp. 65–68, 71, 73, 76; and "Gillette: Cooperation Between Client and Firm Yields Successful 19-Country Product Launch," *Public Relations Journal,* August 1993, p. 24.

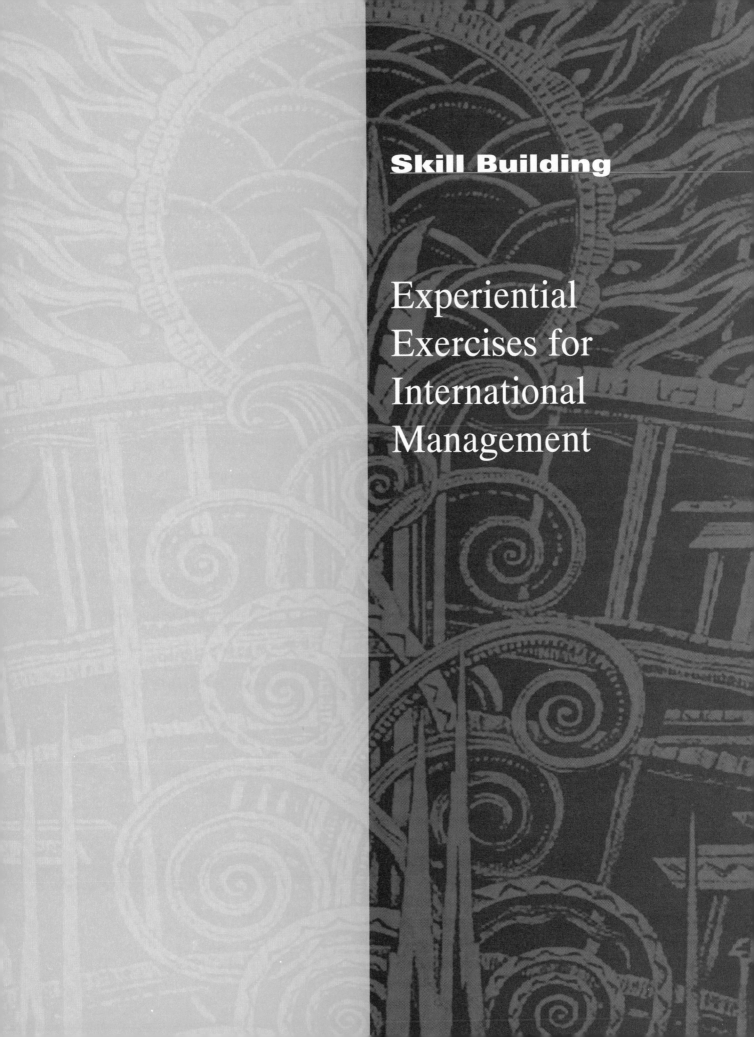

Skill Building

Experiential Exercises for International Management

The Culture Quiz

Objectives

- **To stimulate awareness of cultural differences**

- **To promote consideration of the impact of cultural differences in a global economy**

- **To stimulate dialogue between domestic and international students**

- **To explore issues raised by culturally diverse workforces**

Background

Few, if any, traditions and values are universally held. Many business dealings having succeeded or failed because of a manager's awareness or lack of understanding of the traditions and values of his/her foreign counterparts. With the world business community so closely intertwined and interdependent, it is critical that managers today become increasingly aware of the differences that exist.

How culturally aware are you? Try the question below.

Instructions

Working alone or with a small group, answer the questions (without peeking at the answers). When you do look at the answers, be sure to read the explanations. If you are taking the quiz with students from other countries than your own, explore what the answer might be in your country and theirs.

1. In Japan, loudly slurping your soup is considered to be
   - *a.* rude and obnoxious.
   - *b.* a sign that you like the soup.
   - *c.* okay at home but not in public.
   - *d.* something only foreigners do.

2. In Korea, business leaders tend to
   - *a.* encourage strong commitment to teamwork and cooperation.

   - *b.* encourage competition among subordinates.
   - *c.* discourage subordinates from reporting directly, preferring information to come through well-defined channels.
   - *d.* encourage close relationships with their subordinates.

3. In Japan, virtually every kind of drink is sold in public vending machines except for
   - *a.* beer
   - *b.* diet drinks with saccharin.
   - *c.* already sweetened coffee.
   - *d.* soft drinks from U.S. companies.

4. In Latin America, managers
   - *a.* are most likely to hire members of their own families.
   - *b.* consider hiring members of their own families to be inappropriate.
   - *c.* stress the importance of hiring members of minority groups.
   - *d.* usually hire more people than are actually needed to do a job.

5. In Ethiopia, when a woman opens the front door of her home, it means
   - *a.* she is ready to receive guests for a meal.
   - *b.* only family members may enter.
   - *c.* religious spirits may move freely in and out of the home.
   - *d.* she has agreed to have sex with any man who enters.

6. In Latin America, businesspeople
   - *a.* consider it impolite to make eye contact while talking to one another.
   - *b.* always wait until the other person is finished speaking before starting to speak.
   - *c.* touch each other more than North Americans do under similar circumstances.
   - *d.* avoiding touching one another as it is considered an invasion of privacy.

7. The principal religion in Malaysia is
   - *a.* Buddhism.
   - *b.* Judaism.
   - *c.* Christianity.
   - *d.* Islam.

8. In Thailand
   a. it is common to see men walking along holding hands.
   b. it is common to see a man and a woman holding hands in public.
   c. it is rude for men and women to walk together.
   d. men and women traditionally kiss each other on meeting in the street.

9. When eating in India, it is appropriate to
   a. take food with your right hand and eat with your left.
   b. take food with your left hand and eat with your right.
   c. take food and eat it with your left hand.
   d. take food and eat it with your right hand.

10. Pointing your toes at someone in Thailand is
   a. a symbol of respect, much like the Japanese bow.
   b. considering rude even if it is done by accident.
   c. an invitation to dance.
   d. the standard public greeting.

11. American managers tend to base the performance appraisals of their subordinates on performance, while in Iran, managers are more likely to base their performance appraisals on
   a. religion.
   b. seniority.
   c. friendship.
   d. ability.

12. In China, the status of every business negotiation is
   a. reported daily in the press.
   b. private, and details are not discussed publicly.
   c. subjected to scrutiny by a public tribunal on a regular basis.
   d. directed by the elders of every commune.

13. When rewarding an Hispanic worker for a job well done, it is best not to
   a. praise him or her publicly.
   b. say "thank you."
   c. offer a raise.
   d. offer a promotion.

14. In some South American countries, it is considered normal and acceptable to show up for a social appointment
   a. ten to fifteen minutes early.
   b. ten to fifteen minutes late.
   c. fifteen minutes to an hour late.
   d. one to two hours late.

15. In France, when friends talk to one another
   a. they generally stand about three feet apart.
   b. it is typical to shout.

   c. they stand closer to one another than Americans do.
   d. it is always with a third party present.

16. When giving flowers as gifts in Western Europe, be careful not to give
   a. tulips and jonquils.
   b. daisies and lilacs.
   c. chrysanthemums and calla lilies.
   d. lilacs and apple blossoms.

17. The appropriate gift-giving protocol for a male executive doing business in Saudi Arabia is to
   a. give a man a gift from you to his wife.
   b. present gifts to the wife or wives in person.
   c. give gifts only to the eldest wife.
   d. not give a gift to the wife at all.

18. If you want to give a necktie or a scarf to a Latin American, it is best to avoid the color
   a. red.
   b. purple.
   c. green.
   d. black.

19. The doors in German offices and homes are generally kept
   a. wide open to symbolize an acceptance and welcome of friends and strangers.
   b. slightly ajar to suggest that people should knock before entering.
   c. half-opened suggesting that some people are welcome and others are not.
   d. tightly shut to preserve privacy and personal space.

20. In the area that was formerly West Germany, leaders who display charisma are
   a. not among the most desired.
   b. the ones most respected and sought after.
   c. invited frequently to serve on boards of cultural organizations.
   d. pushed to get involved in political activities.

21. American managers running business in Mexico have found that by increasing the salaries of Mexican workers, they
   a. increased the numbers of hours the workers were willing to work.
   b. enticed more workers to work night shifts.
   c. decreased the number of hours workers would agree to work.
   d. decreased production rates.

22. Chinese culture teaches people
   a. to seek psychiatric help for personal problems.

b.   to avoid conflict and internalize personal problems.

c.   to deal with conflict with immediate confrontation.

d.   to seek help from authorities whenever conflict arises.

23.   One wedding gift that should not be given to a Chinese couple would be

a.   a jade bowl.

b.   a clock.

c.   a basket of oranges.

d.   shifts embroidered with dragon patterns.

24.   In Venezuela, New Year's Eve is generally spent

a.   in quiet family gatherings.

b.   at wild neighborhood street parties.

c.   in restaurants with horns, hats, and live music and dancing.

d.   at pig roasts on the beach.

25.   If you order "bubble and squeak" in a London pub, you will get

a.   two goldfish fried in olive oil.

b.   a very cold beer in a chilled glass, rather than the usual warm beer.

c.   Alka Seltzer® and a glass of water.

d.   chopped cabbage and mashed potatoes fried together.

26.   When a stranger in India wants to know what you do for a living and how much you earn, he will

a.   ask your guide.

b.   invite you to his home and, after getting to know you, will ask.

c.   come over and ask you directly, without introduction.

d.   respect your privacy above all.

27.   When you feel you are being taken advantage of in a business exchange in Vietnam, it is important to

a.   let the anger show in your face but not in your words.

b.   say that you are angry, but keep your facial expression neutral.

c.   not show any anger in any way.

d.   end the business dealings immediately, and walk away.

28.   When a taxi driver in India shakes his head from side to side, it probably means

a.   he thinks your price is too high.

b.   he isn't going in your direction.

c.   he will take you where you want to go.

d.   he doesn't understand what you're asking.

29.   In England, holding your index and middle fingers up in a vee with the back of your hand facing

another person is seen as:

a.   a gesture of peace.

b.   a gesture of victory.

c.   a signal that you want two of something.

d.   a vulgar gesture.

Answers to the Culture Quiz

1.   *b.* Slurping your soup or noodles in Japan is good manners in both public and private. It indicates enjoyment and appreciation of the quality. (Source: Eiji Kanno and Constance O'Keefe, *New Japan Solo.* Japan National Tourist Organization: Tokyo, 1990, p. 20.)

2.   *b.* Korean managers use a "divide-and-rule" method of leadership that encourages competition among subordinates. They do this to ensure that they can exercise maximum control. In addition, they stay informed by having individuals report directly to them. This way, they can know more than anyone else. (Source: Richard M. Castaldi and Tjipyanto Soerjanto, "Contrasts in East Asian Management Practices." *The Journal of Management in Practice*, 2:1, 1990, pp. 25–27.)

3.   *b.* Saccharine-sweetened drinks may not be sold in Japan by law. On the other hand, beer, a wide variety of Japanese and international soft drinks, and so forth, are widely available from vending machines along the streets and in buildings. You're supposed to be at least 18 to buy the alcoholic ones, however. (Source: Eiji Kanno and Constance O'Keefe, *New Japan Solo.* Japan National Tourist Organization: Tokyo, 1990, p. 20.)

4.   *a.* Family is considered to be very important in Latin America, so managers are likely to hire their relatives more quickly than hiring strangers. (Source: Nancy J. Adler, *International Dimensions of Organizational Behavior*, 2nd ed., PWS-Kent: Boston, 1991.)

5.   *d.* The act, by a woman, of opening the front door, signifies that she has agreed to have sex with any man who enters. (Source: Adam Pertman, "Wandering No More," *Boston Globe Magazine*, June 30, 1991, p. 10 ff.)

6.   *c.* Touching one another during business negotiations is common practice. (Source: Nancy J. Adler, *International Dimensions of Organizational Behavior*, 2nd ed., PWS-Kent: Boston, 1991.)

7.   *d.* Approximately 45 percent of the people in Malaysia follow Islam, the country's "official" religion. (Source: Hans Johannes Hoefer, ed., *Malaysia.* Prentice-Hall: Englewood Cliffs, NJ, 1984.)

8.   *a.* Men holding hands is considered a sign of friendship. Public displays of affection between

men and women, however, are unacceptable. (Source: William Warren, Star Black, and M.R. Priya Rangsit, eds., *Thailand.* Prentice-Hall: Englewood Cliffs, NJ, 1985.)

9. *d.* In India, as in many Asian countries, toilet paper is not used. Instead, water and the left hand are used, after which the left hand is thoroughly cleaned. Still, the left hand is considered to be polluted and therefore inappropriate for use during eating or touching another person. (Source: Gitanjali Kolanad, *Culture Shock! India.* Graphic Arts Center Publishing Company: Portland, Oregon, 1996, p. 117.)

10. *b.* This is especially an insult if it is done deliberately, since the feet are the lowest part of the body. (Source: William Warren, Star Black, and M.R. Priya Rangsit, eds., *Thailand.* Prentice-Hall: Englewood Cliffs, NJ, 1985.)

11. *c.* Adler suggests that friendship is valued over task competence in Iran. (Source: Nancy J. Adler, *International Dimensions of Organizational Behavior.* 2nd ed., PWS-Kent: Boston, 1991.)

12. *b.* Public discussion of business dealings is considered inappropriate. Kaplan, et al. report that, "the Chinese may even have used a premature announcement to extract better terms from executives," who were too embarrassed to admit that there was never really a contract. (Source: Frederic Kaplan, Julian Sobin, Arne de Keijzer, *The China Guidebook.* Houghton Mifflin: Boston, 1987.)

13. *a.* Public praise for Hispanics and Asians is generally embarrassing because modesty is an important cultural value. (Source: Jim Braham, "No, You Don't Manage Everyone the Same," *Industry Week*, February 6, 1989.) In Japan, being singled out for praise is also an embarrassment. A common saying in that country is, "The nail that sticks up gets hammered down."

14. *d.* Though being late is frowned upon in the United States, being late is not only accepted but expected in some South American countries. (Source: Lloyd S. Baird, James E. Post, and John F. Mahon, *Management: Functions and Responsibilities.* Harper & Row: New York, 1990.)

15. *c.* Personal space in most European countries is much smaller than in the United States. Americans generally like at least two feet of space around themselves, while it is not unusual for Europeans to be virtually touching. (Source: Lloyd S. Baird, James E. Post, and John F. Mahon, *Management: Functions and Responsibilities.* Harper & Row: New York, 1990.)

16. *c.* Chrysanthemums and calla lilies are both associated with funerals. (Source: Theodore Fischer, *Pinnacle: International Issue.* March–April 1991, p. 4.)

17. *d.* In Arab cultures, it is considered inappropriate for wives to accept gifts or even attention from other men. (Source: Theodore Fischer, *Pinnacle: International Issue.* March–April 1991, p. 4.)

18. *b.* In Argentina and other Latin American countries, purple is associated with the serious fasting period of Lent. (Source: Theodore Fischer, *Pinnacle: International Issue.* March–April 1991, p. 4.)

19. *d.* Private space is considered so important in Germany that partitions are erected to separate people from one another. Privacy screens and walled gardens are the norm. (Source: Julius Fast, *Subtext: Making Body Language Work.* Viking Penguin Books: New York, 1991, p. 207.)

20. *a.* Though political leaders in the United States are increasingly selected on their ability to inspire, charisma is a suspect trait in what was West Germany, where Hitler's charisma is still associated with evil intent and harmful outcomes. (Source: Nancy J. Adler, *International Dimensions of Organizational Behavior.* 2nd ed., PWS-Kent: Boston, 1991, p. 149.)

21. *c.* Paying Mexican workers more means, in the eyes of the workers, that they can make the same amount of money in fewer hours and thus have more time for enjoying life. (Source: Nancy J. Adler, *International Dimensions of Organizational Behavior.* 2nd ed., PWS-Kent: Boston, 1991, pp. 30 and 159.)

22. *b.* Psychological therapy is not an accepted concept in China. In addition, communism has kept most Chinese from expressing opinions openly. (Source: James McGregor, "Burma Road Heroin Breeds Addicts, AIDS Along China's Border." *Wall Street Journal*, September 29, 1992, p. 1.)

23. *b.* The Chinese regard a clock as a bad omen because the word for clock, pronounced *zhong*, is phonetically similar to another Chinese word that means the end. Jade is highly valued as symbolizing superior virtues, and oranges and dragon patterns are also auspicious symbols. (Source: Dr. Evelyn Lip, "Culture and Customs." *Silver Kris*, February 1994, p. 84.)

24. *a.* Venezuelans do the reverse of what most people in other countries do on Christmas and New Years. On Christmas, they socialize. While fireworks are shot off on both nights, most restaurants are closed, and the streets are quiet. (Source: Tony Perrottet, ed., *Venezuela.* Houghton Mifflin: Boston, 1994, p. 97.)

25. *d.* Other popular pub food includes Bangers and Mash (sausages and mashed potatoes), Ploughman's lunch (bread, cheese, and pickled onions), and Cottage pie (baked minced meat with onions and topped with mashed potatoes). (Source: Ravi Desai, ed., *Let's Go: The Budget Guide to Britain and Ireland.* Pan Books: London, 1990, p. 83.)

26. c. Indians are generally uninhibited about staring at strangers and asking them about personal details in their lives. Social distance and personal privacy are not common social conventions in India. (Source: Frank Kusy, *India.* The Globe Pequo Press: Chester, Conn., 1989, p. 27.)

27. *c.* Vernon Weitzel of the Australian National University advises never to show anger when dealing with Vietnamese officials or businesspeople. Showing anger causes you to lose face and is considered rude. Weitzel also recommends always smiling, not complaining or criticizing anyone, and not being inquisitive about personal matters. (Source: Daniel Robinson and Joe Cummings, *Vietnam, Laos & Cambodia.* Lonely Planet Publications: Australia, 1991, p. 96.)

28. *c.* What looks to Westerners like a refusal is really an Indian way of saying "yes." It can also express general agreement with what you're saying or suggest that an individual is interested in what you have to say. (Source: Gitanjali Kolanad, *Culture Shock! India:* Graphic Arts Center Publishing Company: Portland, Oregon, 1996, p. 114.)

29. *d.* In England, this simple hand gesture is considered vulgar and obscene. In a report to *The Boston Globe*, an American who had been working in London wrote, "I wish someone had told me before I emphatically explained to one of the draftsmen at work why I needed two complete sets of drawings." (Source: "Finger Gestures Can Spell Trouble," *The Berkshire Eagle:* January 26, 1997, p. E5.)

Using Gung Ho to Understand Cultural Differences

Background

There is no avoiding the increasing globalization of management. Few, if any, current students of business can expect to pursue a successful career without some encounter of an international nature. Gaining early and realistic exposure to the challenges of cross-cultural dynamics will greatly aid any student of business.

The Pacific Rim will continue to play a dominant role in North American transnational organization and global markets. The opening doors to China offer an unprecedented market opportunity. Korea, Singapore, and Taiwan continue to be unsung partners in mutually beneficial trading relationships. And, of course, Japan will always be a dominant player in the international arena.

An important aspect of cross-cultural awareness is understanding actual differences in interpersonal style and cultural expectations, and separating this from incorrect assumptions. Many embellished stereotypes have flourished as we extend our focus and attention abroad. Unfortunately, many of these myths have become quite pervasive, in spite of their lack of foundation. Thus, North American managers frequently and confidently err in their cross-cultural interactions. This may be particularly common in our interactions with the Japanese. For example, lifetime employment has long been touted as exemplifying the superior practices of Japanese management. In reality, only one-third of Japanese *male* employees enjoy this benefit, and in 1993, many Japanese firms actually laid off workers for the first time. Also, Japan is promoted as a collectivist culture founded on consensus, teamwork, and employee involvement. Yet Japan is at the same time one of the most competitive societies, especially when reviewing how students are selected for educational and occupational placement.

Films can provide an entertaining yet potent medium for studying such complex issues. Such experiential learning is most effective when realistic and identifiable with one's own likely experiences. Case studies can be too sterile. Role plays tend to be contrived and void of depth. Both lack a sense of background to help one "buy into" the situation. Films on the other hand can promote a rich and familiar presentation that promotes personal involvement. This exercise seeks to capitalize on this phenomenon to explore cross-cultural demands.

Procedure

Step I. (110 minutes). Watch the film *Gung Ho*. (This film can be obtained at any video store.)

Step II. (30 minutes). Use one of the following four formats to address the discussion topics.

Option A Address each issue in an open class forum. This option is particularly appropriate for moderate class sizes (40 students) or for sections that do not normally engage in group work.

Option B Divide the class into groups of four to seven to discuss the assigned topics. This is a better approach for larger classes (60 or more students). This approach might also be used to assign the exercise as an extracurricular activity if scheduled class time is too brief.

Option C Assign one group to adopt the American perspective and another group to take the Japanese perspective. Using a confrontation meeting approach (Walton, 1987), have each side describe its perception and expected difficulties in collaborating with each other. Then, have the two sides break into small mixed groups to discuss methods to bridge the gap (or avoid its extreme escalation as portrayed in the film). Ideas should extend beyond those cited in the movie. Present these separate discussions to the class as a whole.

Option D Assign students to groups of four to seven to watch the film and write a six-page analysis addressing one or more of the discussion topics.

Discussion Topics

1. In the opening Scenes, Hunt observes Kaz being berated in a Japanese "management development center." According to at least one expert, this is a close representation of Japanese disciplinary practices. Would such an approach be possible in an American firm? How does this scene illustrate the different perspectives and approaches to motivation? To reinforcement? To feedback?

Source: Steven M. Sommer, University of Nebraska, Lincoln. Used with permission.

2. The concepts of multiculturalism and diversity are emerging issues in modern management environments. The importance of recognizing and responding to racial, ethnic, and other demographic factors has been widely debated in the popular press. What does *Gung Ho* offer to the discussion (both within and across the two groups)? How does each culture respond to different races, genders, cultures?

3. Individualism and collectivism represent two endpoints on a continuum used to analyze different cultural orientations. Individualism refers to a sense of personal focus, autonomy, and compensation. Collectivism describes a group focus, self-subjugation, obligation, and sharing of rewards. How do you see American and Japanese workers differing on this dimension? You might compare the reactions of the Japanese manager whose wife was about to give birth with those of the American worker who had planned to take his child to a doctor's appointment.

4. How does the softball game illuminate cultural differences (and even similarities)? You might consider this question in reference to topic 3; to approaches to work habits; to have "fun"; to behavioral norms of pride, honor, sportsmanship.

5. On several occasion we see George Wendt's openly antagonistic responses to the exercise of authority by Japanese managers. Discuss the concept of authority as seen in both cultures. Discuss expectations of compliance. How might George's actions be interpreted differently by each culture? Indeed, would they be seen as different by an American manager as compared with a Japanese manager?

6. Throughout the film, one gains an impression of how Americans and the Japanese might differ in their approach to resolving conflict. Separately describe how each culture tends to approach conflict, and how the cultures might be different from each other.

7. Experienced conflict between work and family demands has also gained attention as an important managerial issue. How do both cultures approach the role of work in one's life? The role of family? How does each approach balance competing demands between the two? Have these expectations changed over time (from twenty years ago, forty years ago, sixty years ago)? How might they change as we enter the twenty-first century?

8. In reality, Japanese managers would be "shamed" if one of their subordinates was seriously injured on the job (the scene where the American worker's hand is caught in the assembly line belt). Taking this into account, what other issues in the film might be used to illustrate differences or similarities between American and Japanese management and work practices?

"When in Bogotá . . ."*

As Jim Reynolds looked out the small window of the Boeing 757, he saw the glimmer of lights in the distance. After a five-hour flight, he arrived in Bogotá, Colombia at 9:35 P.M. on a clear Friday evening. It had been nearly five years since Jim had seen his best friend, Rodrigo Cardozo. The two had met in college and kept in touch over the years. During their school years, Rodrigo would often accompany Jim when he went home to Chicago for the holidays.

Entering the main terminal, Jim found himself in what looked like a recently bombed building. Piles of debris were everywhere. Lights hung from the ceiling by exposed electrical wires, and the walls and floors were rough, unfinished concrete. "Certainly, aesthetics are not a major concern at the Bogotá International Airport," Jim thought.

As he came to the end of the long, dimly lit corridor, an expressionless customs official reached out his hand and gestured for Jim's travel documents.

"Passaporte, por favor. Bienvenidos a Bogotá, Señor Reynolds. Estás en vacacciones?"

"Sí," Jim replied.

After a few routine questions, Jim was allowed to pass through customs feeling relatively unscathed.

"Loquillo! Loquillo! Estamos quií! Jim, Jim," a voice shouted.

Trying to find the origin of the voice among the dense crowd, Jim finally spotted Rodrigo. "Hey, man. How've you been? You look great!"

"Jim, it's so good to see you. How've you been? I would like you to meet my wife, Eva. Eva, this is my best friend, Jim. He's the one in all those pictures I've shown you."

Late Night Begins the Day

Close to an hour later, Jim, Rodrigo, and Eva arrived at Rodrigo's parents' house on the other side of Bogotá from the airport. As Jim was aware, it is customary for couples to live with their parents for a number of years after their marriage, and Rodrigo and Eva were part of that custom.

Darío, Rodrigo's father, owned an import/export business in Bogotá. He was a knowledgeable and educated man and, from what Jim knew, a master of business negotiations. Over the years, Darío had conducted business with people in nearly every country in Central and South America, the United States, Europe, Hong Kong, and some parts of Africa. Jim had first met Darío with Rodrigo in Boston in 1989.

"Jim, welcome to my house," Darío boomed effusively as the group walked in. "I am so pleased that you're finally in Bogotá. Would you like something to drink-whiskey, bourbon, Aguardiente?"

"Aguardiente!" Rodrigo urged.

"Yes, Jim would like some Aguardiente. I understand you're going to Bahía tonight," Darío added.

"Where?" Jim asked, looking around. "I didn't know we were going anywhere tonight."

"Don't worry, Jim, todo bien, todo bien," Rodrigo assured him. "We're going dancing, so get dressed. Let's go."

The reality of being in Colombia hit Jim at about 11:15 that night when he and his friends entered Bahía, a Bogotá nightclub. The rhythms of salsa and merangue filled the club. Jim's mind flashed back to the Latin dance parties he and Rodrigo had had in Boston with their friends from Central and South America.

"Jim, this is my cousin, Diana. She'll be your partner tonight," Rodrigo said. "You'll get to practice your Spanish too; she doesn't speak a word of English. Have fun."

For the next six hours, they danced and drank. This is the Colombian way. At 5:30 the next morning, Rodrigo decided it was time to leave to get something to eat. On the drive home, they stopped at an outdoor grill in the mountains where many people had congregated for the same reason. Everyone was eating arepas con queso and mazorca, and drinking Aguardiente.

Next, they continued to an outdoor party just down the street. Here, they danced and drank until the sun crested over the mountains of Bogotá. It was about 7:00 A.M. when they decided to conclude the celebration-for now.

Saturday was spent recovering from the previous evening and also touring some local spots in the country. However, Saturday night was a repeat of Friday. After being in Colombia for three days, Jim had slept a total of about four hours. Fortunately, Monday was a national holiday.

Business before Pleasure before Business?

Although Jim was having a great time, he had also scheduled a series of business meetings with directors of business schools at various Bogotá universities for the week to

---

*Copyright 1994 by Matthew B. Shull. Used with permission.

come. Jim worked as an acquisitions editor for Academia Press, a major publisher of college-level business textbooks. The purpose of the meetings was to establish business contacts in the Colombian market. It was hoped that these initial contacts would lead to others in Latin America.

At Academia Press headquarters in New York, Jim and Caroline Evans, his boss, had discussed the opportunities in Latin America. Although Academia Press routinely published international editions of its texts, total international sales never represented more than 15 percent of their gross. Consequently, international markets had never been pursued aggressively. Caroline, however, saw the Latin American markets as having a lot of potential within the next three to five years. She envisioned this market alone could, in time, represent 15 to 20 percent of gross sales. Moreover, she felt that within the next ten years, international sales could reach 40 percent if developed properly. With numbers like that, it was evident to Jim that this deal was important, not only to the company but to his career as well. If Jim was able to open these markets, he might receive a promotion and be able to continue to work in Central and South America.

Jim's first meeting was scheduled for 11:00 A.M. on Tuesday, the second on Wednesday at 11:00 A.M., and the third on Friday at 3:00 P.M. At precisely 11:00 A.M. on Tuesday, Jim arrived at Javeriana University where he was to meet with Professors Emilio Muñoz, Diana Espitia, and Enrique Ronderos. When he arrived, Professor Muñoz was waiting for him in the conference room.

"Señor Reynolds, I am delighted to meet you. How was your flight?"

"Wonderful," Jim replied.

"And how do you like Bogotá so far? Have you been able to sightsee?"

"No, I haven't had the chance to get around the city yet. I hop to see some things later in the week."

"Well, before you leave, you must visit *El Museo de Oro*. It is the finest collection of gold artifacts from the various indigenous Indian tribes in Colombia. Although much of the gold was stolen by the Spanish, many pieces have survived." For the next thirty minutes, Professor Muñoz spoke of everything from the upcoming presidential elections to world cup soccer.

Jim looked at his watch, concerned about the other professors who had not yet arrived and about the meeting for which he had prepared.

"Is there something wrong, Señor Reynolds?"

"No, no, I was just wondering about the others; it's 11:30."

"Don't worry. They'll be here shortly. Traffic in Bogotá at this hour is terrible. They're probably caught in a traffic jam."

Just then, Professors Espitia and Ronderos walked in.

"Muy buenas, Señor Reynolds," Professor Espitia said warmly. "Please forgive us for the delay. Traffic is simply

awful at this time of day."

"Oh, that's not necessary. I understand. Traffic in New York can be absolutely horrendous as well," Jim replied. "Sometimes it takes two hours to get from one end of the city to the other."

"Have you had lunch yet, Señor Reynolds?" asked Professor Ronderos.

Jim shook his head.

"Why don't we go to lunch, and we can talk there?" Professor Ronderos suggested.

After discussing the restaurants in the area, the professors decided on El Club Ejecutivo. It was nearly 12:30 P.M. when they arrived.

"It's been an hour and a half, and we haven't discussed anything," Jim thought. He was concerned that the Colombians were not very interested in what he had to offer. Throughout lunch, Jim grew increasingly concerned that the professors were more interested in his trying typical Colombian dishes and visiting the sights in Bogotá than in Academia's textbooks. They were fascinated that Jim knew how to dance salsa and merangue and impressed that he spoke Spanish with a slight Colombian accent; Señorita Espitia said she found it amusing. That seemed much more important than his knowledge of business textbooks and publishing in general.

By the end of lunch, Jim was nearly beside himself. It was now after 2:30 P.M., and nothing had been accomplished.

"Why don't we all go to Monserate tomorrow? It's absolutely beautiful up there, Señor Reynolds," Professor Ronderos suggested, going on to describe the mountain that overlooks Bogotá and the myths and traditions that surround it.

"That's a wonderful idea," Professor Espitia added.

"Monserate it is then. Jim, it has been a pleasure. I look forward to our meeting tomorrow," Professor Ronderos said with a slight bow.

"Señor Reynolds, would you like a ride home?" Professor Muñoz asked.

"Yes, if it's not too much trouble."

On the way home, Jim was relatively quiet.

"Do you feel okay?"

"It must be jet lag catching up to me. I'm sure it's nothing," Jim responded. Concerned about the way the meeting had gone, Jim realized that he had never even had a chance to mention Academia Press's various titles and how these texts could be used to create a new curriculum or supplement an existing curriculum at the professors' business school.

When in Bogotá

On arriving at the house, Jim went upstairs and sat in the living room glumly sipping a cup of aguapanela. "I just don't get it," he thought. "The Colombians couldn't have been happier with the way the meeting turned out, but we didn't do anything. We didn't even talk about one book. I just don't understand what went wrong."

In a short time, Darío arrived. "Muy buenas, Jim. How did your meetings go today with the directors?" he asked.

"I don't know. I don't know what to think. We didn't do anything. We didn't talk about business at all. We talked more about the sights I should see and the places I should visit before I leave Colombia. I'm supposed to call my boss this afternoon and tell her how the initial meeting went. What am I going to tell her. `Sorry, we just decided to plan my vacation in Colombia instead of discussing business.' I can't afford to have this deal fall through."

Darío laughed.

"Señor, I'm serious."

"Jim, I understand. Believe me. Tell me about your meeting today."

Jim recounted every detail of the meeting to Darío, who smiled and nodded his head as he listened.

"Jim, you have to understand one thing before you continue negotiating with the directors."

"What's that?"

"You're in Colombia now," Darío said simply.

Jim stared at him with a puzzled look. "And?"

"And what, Jim?"

"Is there something else I should know?"

"That's where you need to start. You let the directors set the tone of the meeting. It's obvious they felt very comfortable with you, or they wouldn't have invited you to Monserate. Here in Colombia, Jim, we do business dif-

ferently. Right now, you're building friendship. You're building their trust in you. This is very important in doing business in all of Latin America."

"Jim," Darío continued, "would you rather do business with a friend or someone you hardly know?"

As Darío went on to analyze the meeting, Jim realized that his perception of the situation had been formed by his experiences in the United States. "When in Bogotá," he thought, "I guess I had better think like the Colombians."

"Jim, you've gained the respect and the trust of the directors. In my opinion, your first meeting was a complete success."

"What should I expect in the meetings to come?" Jim asked.

"Don't worry," he responded. "Just let the directors worry about that. You'll come to an agreement before the end of the week. I guarantee it."

Questions for Discussion

1. What differences does Jim notice between life in the United States and life in Colombia?

2. What differences does Jim notice between doing business in the United States and doing business in Colombia? How might these same factors differ in other countries?

3. What advice would you give Jim for closing his deals? Why?

The International Cola Alliances

Objectives

- **To introduce some of the complexities involved in doing business across international borders**

- **To examine what happens when countries seek to do business with one another without the benefit of a common language and customs**

Background

Even with a common language, communication can break down, and interpretations of words and actions often can confound understanding and incur negative attributions of purpose. Add to this the differences of personal needs that exist from individual to individual, as well as national and cultural needs that exist from country to country. These limitless variables make cooperation across borders even that much more complex.

The Story

You are a delegation from a country that would like to enter into a large cooperative effort with a number of other countries for the production and distribution of a popular soft drink produced by the American company International Cola. In the past, countries in your region of the world have been resistant to allowing foreign soft drinks into their markets, despite consumer demands. However, recent thinking is that the advantages of allowing this competition outweigh the disadvantages.

International Cola has expressed an interest in setting up a bottling plant, a regional corporate headquarters, and four distribution depots. Their goal, of course, is to do this in the most economically efficient way possible to maximize profits. However, because the executives at International Cola believe this area to be a rich new market with outstanding potential and are therefore eager to get in, they have ceded to the demands of the various governments in the proposed alliance. These require International Cola to allow for local control of the facilities; to maintain only 49 percent interest in the facilities with local partners holding 51 percent ownership; and to allow the participating governments to work out among themselves the details of where the facilities will be located.

For the countries involved, having one or more of these facilities located within their borders will bring jobs, revenue, and a certain amount of prestige. (It is possible for a single country to have all six of the facilities: regional headquarters, bottling plant, distribution depots.)

Each of the countries involved shares at least two borders with the other countries. This has not always been the most peaceful area. Border skirmishes are frequent, most stemming from minor misunderstandings that became inflated by vast cultural and religious differences.

These distinct cultural differences between your country and your neighbors will likely become even more evident as you pursue the negotiation. It will be up to you to decide how to respond to them. While it is important for you to retain your own cultural integrity—for example, when you first meet a delegate from another country you will likely greet him or her in the cultural style of your country—you understand the importance of being sensitive to one another. If you understand, for example, that the cultural style of another country is to bow on meeting, whereas you shake hands, you may wish to bow instead.

Since you are negotiating the venture across borders, and each country has a different primary language, you have agreed to negotiate in English, but none of you is entirely fluent. Therefore, a few phrases will creep in from your own languages.

Wear your country's flag in a visible place at all times.

Instructions

Step 1 (*30–40 minutes—may be done before class*)
Working in small groups (5–7), develop a profile of your country and its people based on profile sheets 1 and 2.

You will also be given a third profile sheet that details cultural norms within your country. Information given will include the ways in which people in your country deal with areas such as time, personal physical space, gender, social mores, and oral communication.

After you have completed profile sheets 1 and 2 and everyone in your group has read profile sheet 3, briefly discuss them to be sure there is mutual understanding of what the group's behavior and negotiating stance are to be during the negotiation.

Step 2 (*20 minutes—may be done before class*)
Based on the profile sheets, decide which International Cola facilities you believe you should have in your country and why you believe they should be in your country

rather than one of the others that will be represented. For example, if you have a highly educated population, you may argue that you should be the home of the regional corporate headquarters; be aware, however, that another country might argue that you should not have bottling and distribution facilities because these do not require a highly educated or skilled labor force.

On the negotiation sheet, make a list of the facilities you believe your country should have and some notes as to what your arguments will be for having them. Also, make some notes on what you believe the other countries' counter-arguments will be and how you expect to respond to them.

Step 3 *(30–45 minutes—in class)*

Everyone in your group should pin a copy of your country's flag and motto on himself or herself in a visible place. One to three representatives from your group (delegation) should negotiate the arrangements for International Cola's facilities with the representatives from the other delegations. Be sure to use the cultural norms of your country during the negotiation, but *do not tell* the others what your social norms are.

Representatives should introduce themselves to one another on an individual basis. After personal introductions, representatives should form a circle in the center of the room with their delegations behind them, briefly describe their countries, state their positions, and begin negotiations. During negotiations, representatives should make an effort to use their new language at least three times. They should not use English for any of the six phrases listed.

Delegation representatives and the other members of their groups may communicate with one another at any point during the negotiation, but only in writing. Group members may also communicate among themselves, but only in writing during the negotiation.

Any group or representative may ask for a side meeting with one or more of the other groups during the negotiation. Side meetings may not last more than five minutes.

At any time in the negotiation, the delegation may change its representative. When such a change is made, the new representative and the other delegates must reintroduce themselves and greet one another.

Those members of each delegation who are not directly negotiating should be active observers. Use the observer sheet to record situations in which other groups insulted them, shamed them, or were otherwise offensive.

At the end of 45 minutes, the negotiation should be concluded whether or not an agreement has been reached.

Step 4 *(open-ended)*

Class discussion. Each group should begin by reading their profile sheet 3 aloud. A reporter should note some of the events in which members of other delegations caused them shame, embarrassment, and so forth. Open discussion of the meaning of what took place should follow.

Question for Discussion

1. What role did cultural differences play in the various phases of the negotiation process? Be careful not to overlook the introductory phase. Was the negotiation frustrating? Satisfying? Other? Why?

2. At any time, did delegations recognize the cultural differences between themselves and the others? If so, was any attempt made to try to adapt to another country's norms? Why? Why not? Would there have been a benefit in doing so? Why?

3. What role did language differences play during the negotiation? What was the effect of lack of understanding or miscommunication on the process?

4. Did the delegations from various countries attempt to find mutual goals and interests despite their differences? In what ways were the best interests of the overall plan subjugated to the individual interests of each country? What rhetoric was used to justify the personal interests?

5. To what degree did groups construct their countries to best justify their position? In situation where this happened, did it work? Why? Why not?

Profile Sheet 1

1. Select a name for your country:

   _____

Be sure that the name of your country appears on or around the flag (see below).

2. In the space below, design your country's flag or emblem. Make enough copies so that each member of your group has one to wear.

3. Write a slogan for your country that best embodies your country's ideals and goals. Include the slogan on or around the flag.

   _____

   _____

   _____

4. Make up a partial language with a vocabulary of up to twenty-five (25) words into which you should translate the following phrases for use during negotiations:

   Phrase   *Translation*

   I agree. _____

   I disagree._____

   This is unacceptable. _____

   I don't understand your point._____

   _____

   You have insulted me. _____

   Please repeat that. _____

5. Briefly describe how people in your country react when they have been insulted.

_____

_____

_____

_____

_____

_____

Profile Sheet 2

Describe your country by selecting one element from each of the following lists. After you have made your selections, list the elements that make up your country's description on a separate piece of paper and add any additional elements you wish.

Population Density

_____ high density with overpopulation a problem
_____ moderate density-high end
_____ moderate density-average
_____ moderate density-low end
_____ low density

Average Educational Level

_____ less than 3 years-large percent totally illiterate
_____ 3–6 years-widespread functional illiteracy
_____ 6–9 years-functional illiteracy a problem in scattered areas
_____ 9–12 years-most read and write at functional levels
_____ 12+ years-a highly educated and functioning population

Per Capita Income

_____ under $1,000 per year
_____ $1,000–5,000 per year
_____ $5,000–10,000 per year
_____ $10,000–20,000 per year
_____ $20,000–30,000 per year
_____ $30,000–40,000 per year
_____ $40,000+ per year

Climate

_____ tropical
_____ arctic
_____ mixed in different areas
_____ runs range from season to season

Form of Government

_____ socialist
_____ democratic
_____ communist
_____ monarchy
_____ dictatorship
_____ other (specify)

Dominant Racial-Ethnic Group

_____ Asian
_____ black
_____ white
_____ other (specify)

Dominant Religion

_____ animist
_____ atheist/agnostic
_____ Buddhist
_____ Catholic
_____ Hindu
_____ Jewish
_____ Mormon
_____ Protestant (specify)
_____ other (specify)

Negotiation Sheet

1. What facilities do you believe your country should have?

_____

_____

_____

2. What facilities of those listed above are you willing to relinquish to reach agreement?

_____

_____

_____

3. On what bases will you justify your need or desire for having the facilities you have listed?

_____

_____

_____

_____

_____

_____

_____

Observer Sheet

1. List actions taken by members of other delegations that were insulting, created shame for you and your delegation, or were otherwise offensive based on your country's norms. Include notes on the context in which the actions were taken.

_____

_____

_____

_____

_____

_____

_____

_____

_____

2. Based on the above list, what happened to your interest in forming an alliance and your belief that a mutual agreement could be reached?

_____

_____

_____

Who to Hire?

Objectives

- **To explore participants' cultural biases and expectations**

- **To examine cultural differences**

- **To consider the impact culture has on hiring decisions**

Instructions

Step 1 *(10–15 minutes)*
Read the background information and descriptions of each of the applicants. Consider the job and the cultures within which the individual to be hired will be operating. Rank the candidates from 1 to 5, with 1 being your first choice, and enter your rankings on the ranking sheet in the column marked "My Ranking." Briefly, list the reasons for each of your rankings.

Do not discuss your rankings with your classmates until told to do so.

Step 2 *(30–40 minutes)*
Working with three to four of your classmates, discuss the applicants, and rank them in the order of group preference. Do not vote.

Rank the candidates from 1 to 5, with 1 being the group's first choice, and enter your group rankings on the ranking sheet in the column marked "Group Ranking." Briefly list the reasons for each of the group's rankings.

If your group represents more than one culture, explore the ways in which each person's cultural background may have influenced his or her individual decisions.

Step 3 *(open-ended)*
Report your rankings to the class, and discuss the areas of difference that emerged within your group while you were trying to reach consensus.

Question for Discussion

1. Was your group able to explore openly any culturally based biases that came up-for example, feelings about homosexuality, religion, personality traits, politics?

2. Did you make any comments or observations that you feel would have been fully acceptable in your own culture but were not accepted by the group? Explain.

3. If the answer to number 2 was yes, how did the reaction of the group make you feel about your membership in it? How did you handle the situation?

4. What implications do you believe these cultural differences would have in business dealings?

Background

You are a member of the management committee of a multinational company that does business in 23 countries. While your company's headquarters are in Holland, your offices are scattered fairly evenly throughout the four hemispheres. Primary markets have been in Europe and North America; the strongest emerging market is the Pacific Rim. Company executives would like to develop what they see as a powerful potential market in the Middle East. Sales in all areas except the Pacific Rim have shown slow growth over the past two years.

At present, your company is seeking to restructure and revitalize its worldwide marketing efforts. To accomplish this, you have determined that you need to hire a key marketing person to introduce fresh ideas and a new perspective. There is no one currently in your company who is qualified to do this, and so you have decided to look outside. The job title is "vice-president for international marketing"; it carries with it a salary well into six figures (US\$), plus elaborate benefits, an unlimited expense account, a car, and the use of the corporate jet. The person you hire will be based at the company's headquarters and will travel frequently.

A lengthy search has turned up five people with good potential. It is now up to you to decide whom to hire. Although all the applicants have expressed a sincere interest in the position, it is possible that they may change their minds once the job is offered. Therefore, you must rank them in order of preference so that if your first choice declines the position, you can go on to the second, and so on.

Applicants
Park L, age 41, Married with Three Children

Park L. is currently senior vice president for marketing at a major Korean high technology firm. You have been told by the head of your Seoul office that his reputation as an expert in international marketing is outstanding. The market share of his company's products has consistently increased since he joined the company just over fifteen years ago. His company's market share is now well ahead of that of competing producers in the Pacific Rim.

Mr. Park started with his present company immediately after his graduation from the University of Seoul and has worked his way up through the ranks. He does not have a graduate degree. You sense that Mr. Park has a keen understanding of organizational politics and knows how to play them. He recognizes that because the company he works for now is family controlled, it is unlikely that he will ever move much higher than his present situation. Mr. Park has told you that he is interested in the growth potential offered at your company.

In addition to his native tongue, Mr. Park is able to carry on a reasonably fluent conversation in English and has a minimal working knowledge of German and French. His wife, who appears quiet and quite traditional, and his children speak only Korean.

Kiran K., age 50, Widow with One Adult Child

Kiran K. is a Sikh woman living in Malaysia. She began her teaching career while finishing her DBA (doctorate in business administration) at the Harvard Business School and published her first book on international marketing 10 months after graduation. Her doctoral dissertation was based on the international marketing of pharmaceuticals, but she has also done research and published on other areas of international marketing.

Two months after the publication of her book, Kiran went to work in the international marketing department of a Fortune 500 company, where she stayed for the next 10 years. She returned to teaching when Maura University offered her a full professorship with tenure, and she has been there since that time. her academic position has allowed her to pursue a number of research interests and to write authoritative books and papers in her field. At present, she is well published and internationally recognized as an expert on international marketing. In addition, she has an active consulting practice throughout Southeast Asia.

You have learned through your office in Kuala Lumpur that Kiran's only child, a 23-year-old son, is severely mentally and physically disabled. You sense that part of her interest in the job with your company is to have the income to guarantee his care should anything happen to her. Her son would go with her to Holland, should she be given the job, where he will need to be enrolled in special support programs.

In addition to fluency in Malay, English, and Hindi, Kiran speaks and writes German and Spanish and is able to converse in Japanese and Mandarin.

Peter V., age 44, Single

Peter is a white South African. He had worked in a key position in the international marketing division of an American Fortune 100 company until the company pulled out of his country eight months ago. While the company wanted to keep him on, offering to move him from Johannesburg to its New York headquarters, Peter decided that it was time to look elsewhere. He had begun to feel somewhat dead-ended in his position and apparently sees the position at your company as an opportunity to try out new territory. Like your other candidates for the position, Peter has a long list of accomplishments and is widely recognized as outstanding in his field. People in your company who have had contacts with him say that Peter is creative, hard working, and loyal. In addition, you have been told that Peter is a top-flight manager of people who is able to push his employees to the highest levels of performance. And, you are told, he is very organized.

Peter has a PhD in computer science from a leading South African university and an MBA from Purdue's Krannert School of Business.

Peter had been a vehement opponent of apartheid and is still very much a social activist. His high political visibility within South Africa had made his life there difficult, and even now, with the end of apartheid, he would like to get out. His constant male companion, P. K. Kahn, would be coming with him to Holland, and Peter would like your personnel office to help P. K. find an appropriate position.

Peter speaks and reads English, Dutch, Afrikaans, and Swahili and can converse in German.

Tex P., age 36, Divorced with One Child

Tex is currently job hunting. His former job as head of marketing for a single-product high-technology firm—highly specialized work stations for sophisticated artificial intelligence applications—ended when the company was bought out by Texas Instruments. Tex had been with his previous company virtually from the time the company was started six years earlier. Having to leave his job was an irony to Tex as it was largely due to the success of his efforts that the company was bought out. You sense that he is a little bitter, and he tells you that jobs offered to him by TI were beneath him and not worthy of consideration.

Tex has both his undergraduate and MBA degrees from Stanford University. In addition, he was a Rhodes Scholar and won a Fulbright scholarship, which he used to support himself while he undertook a two-year research project on the marketing of high-technology equipment to Third World countries.

You have learned through your New York office that Tex has a reputation for being aggressive and hard driving. Apparently he is a workaholic who has been known to work eighteen to twenty hours a day, seven days a week. He seems to have little time for his personal life.

In addition to his native English, Tex has a minimal command of French—which he admits he hasn't used since his college days.

Zvi C., age 40, Married with Five Children

Zvi began his career after receiving his MBA from the Sloan School of Management at the Massachusetts Institute of Technology (MIT). His first job was as marketing manager for a German company doing business in Israel.

Zvi's phenomenal success with this company led to his being hired away by an international office equipment company in England. Again, he proved to be outstanding, boosting the company's market share beyond all expectations within two years. After five years, Zvi was offered a chance to go back to Israel, this time to oversee and coordinate all the international marketing programs for an industrial park of fourteen companies run as an adjunct to Israel's leading scientific research institution. It has been his responsibility to interface the research component with product development and sales as well as to manage the vast marketing department. Again, he has shown himself to be a master.

You have learned through your Haifa office that Zvi is highly respected and has extensive contacts in the scientific and high-tech worlds. He is exceptionally creative in his approach to marketing, often trying bold strategies that most of his peers would dismiss as too risky. Zvi, however, has made them work and work well.

Zvi is a religious man who must leave work by noon on Friday. He will not work Saturdays nor any of his religion's major and minor holidays—about eighteen a year. He will, however, work on Sundays.

In addition to his native language, Dutch (Zvi and his family moved to Israel form Holland when Zvi was six), he speaks and writes fluent Hebrew, English, German, and Arabic.

Ranking Sheet

Rank candidates from one to five with one as your first choice.

Applicant		Reasons	Group Ranking	Reasons
Park L.				
Kiran K.				
Peter V.				
Tex P.				
Zvi C.				

Using the Internet for International Management Research

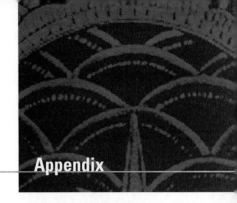

The world of international management is in a continual state of flux. Acquisitions, mergers, joint ventures, new government regulations, and changing social and economic conditions all impact the way business is done. Keeping up with these developments can be very challenging. Fortunately, however, the Internet allows easy access to many of the sources needed to remain on the cutting edge of international developments. The purpose of this appendix is to introduce the Internet and provide sources that can be of value in conducting international management research.

The Internet

The Internet is a network of thousands of computers that allows you to access information stored on computers around the world. As a result, it is possible to gather data from governmental agencies, newspapers, journals, and business organizations without ever leaving your computer screen. There are a number of ways that this Internet information can be accessed. Four of the most common include the World Wide Web, gopher, FTP, and Telnet.

World Wide Web (WWW)

The World Wide Web is the most popular and fastest growing part of the Internet. It is easy to use and has excellent graphics, image, and sound capabilities. This is one reason why corporations use it to promote their products. For example, if you would like to obtain information on Kodak, well-known for its cameras and film, you could go to the company's home page at www.kodak.com. Here you could obtain information about their products, recent company developments, and even job opportunities. This same approach could be used in researching any large, and in many cases small as well, company.

Gopher

Gopher is a navigational tool that has been developed at the University of Minnesota and that uses a simple menu system to move among various sites on the Internet. Gophers are easy to use and are accessible through the Web.

FTP

File Transfer Protocol (FTP) allows you to send and receive data and program files that are stored on other computers. You can use FTP to get copies of software documents that are available to the public. Generally, you need access privileges to do this, although some sites will allow you to use "anonymous" as your user name and "guest" or your e-mail name as the password.

Telnet

Telnet lets your computer connect to host computers on the Internet and to act as though you were directly connected. For example, if you want to browse the University of Texas's computerized library catalog from home, you can connect to it through Telnet. Although you need permission to access the remote computer, as in the case of FTP, some sites are available to the public.

Browsers

Browsers are software programs that let you move from site to site within a site. Two of the most popular browsers are Netscape and Explorer. With a browser you can move forward to new documents or retrace your steps by pressing the "Back" button. Netscape and other browsers also allow you to create "bookmarks" which let you store the addresses of favorite sites to which you expect to return.

Search Engines

Unless you know the Uniform Resource Locator (URL) of the site you want to view or have a directory of URLs such as the one that follows this section, you have little chance of finding what you want on the Web unless you are using a search engine. A search engine can be extremely useful in locating sources of information, but there is no one search engine that does everything. Quite often it is necessary to use two or three in looking for information because one of these will provide you leads or data that you were not able to locate with the others. After you have gained some familiarity with search engines and learn what each does best, you can pick the one that best meets your particular search needs. Ten of the most popular search engines are the following:

1. Alta Vista
2. HotBot
3. Yahoo
4. Excite

5. Infoseek
6. Lycos
7. Magellan
8. Open Text
9. WebCrawler
10. WWWWorm

The editors of *PC Magazine* have reported that HotBot, Excite, and Yahoo used together lead to more Internet content, more of the time, than any other combination. However, depending on the specific search, any of the above 10 (individually or in combination) can provide the needed information. The important thing is to learn about the language of the specific search engine you are using because this will help you improve your efficiency in working with it.

Some Helpful Suggestions

Here are half a dozen suggestions that can help you in your Internet international management research.

1. Be prepared for constant change on the Web. There are additions and deletions of sites on a daily basis, and addresses sometimes change.

2. If you receive an error message saying, "There was no response. Server could be down. Try later." this may be because there are too many people trying to reach the site at the same time. Try a second time, and then 30 minutes later. You will often find that you will eventually be able to log on to the site.

3. Sometimes when you enter a long URL you will receive a response that it does not exist. In this case, enter the address but omit some of the last part. For example, the address for the Organization of American States student intern program is **www.oas.org./EN/PINEFO/HR/jobstudy.htm**. If this address is rejected, enter it again, but eliminate the information to the right of the last slash. If this does not work, enter only up to the slash before this. Then, once you are connected to the OAS, you can enter the rest of the information and learn about the student intern program.

4. To save time entering site addresses on the Web, omit the http://. It is not necessary. Begin instead with www. If the URL begins with www and ends with com, type only the part in the middle between www and com. However, when you enter Gopher, FTP, and Telnet, you need to begin with gopher, ftp, or telnet, respectively.

5. If you get a message saying that "there are no pages to print" when you try to print a page from the screen, hit the "Print" button again. Usually it works the second time.

6. Keep a list of the search words you use that produce good results.

References

CHAPTER 1

Privatization in Great Britain John Moore, "British Privatization—Taking Capitalism to the People," *Harvard Business Review*, January–February 1992, pp. 115–124; Paula Dwyer and Wendy Zellner, "This Splice Could be Golden," *Business Week*, February 8, 1993, pp. 36–37; Robert Neff, "Japan Airlines Cinches Its Seat Belt," *Business Week*, February 1, 1993, p. 42; "A Great Train Crash," *Economist*, January 5, 1995, p. 20; and Nicholas Bray, "Britain's Labor, Miming Tories, Unveils 3-Year Privatizing Plan," *Wall Street Journal*, June 12, 1998, p. A9.

International Management in Action: Separating Myths from Reality Stanley J. Modic, "Myths about Japanese Management," *Industry Week*, October 5, 1987, pp. 49–53; Richard M. Hodgetts and Fred Luthans, "Japanese HR Management Practices: Separating Fact From Fiction," *Personnel*, April 1989, pp. 42–45; and Jon Wonoroff, *The Japanese Management Mystique* (Chicago: Probus Publishing, 1992).

In the International Spotlight: India Anthony Spaeth, "India Beckons—and Frustrates," *Wall Street Journal*, September 22, 1989, p. R23; Subrata N. Chakravarty, "Getting the Elephant to Dance," *Forbes*, July 20, 1992, p. 130–139; Rahual Jacob, "India Is Now Open for Business," *Fortune*, November 16, 1992, pp. 128–130; John F. Burns, "India Now Winning U.S. Investment," *New York Times*, February 6, 1995, pp. C-1, C-5; "The Trouble With Democracy, Part 2," *Economist*, December 17, 1994, pp. 17–18; and Rahual Jacob, "India Gets Moving," *Fortune*, September 5, 1994, pp. 101–102.

CHAPTER 2

The U.S. Goes to the Mat Robert Neff, Brian Bremner, and Edith Updike, "The Japanese Have a New Thirst for Imports," *Business Week*, June 5, 1995, pp. 52, 54; Gabriella Stern and Nichole M. Christian, "GM Plans to Sell Saturn Line in Japan in Network of Stand-Alone Dealerships," *Wall Street Journal*, June 2, 1995, p. A4; Keith Bradsher, "U.S. Called Ready to Compromise on Date for Japan Trade Talks," *New York Times*, June 1, 1995, pp. C1, C15; and Bhushan Bahree, "Auto Talks by U.S., Japan Seem Set for Geneva in June," *Wall Street Journal*, June 1, 1995, p. A11.

In the International Spotlight: Vietnam Mary Ann Von Glinow and Linda Clarke, "Vietnam: Tiger or Kitten?" *Academy of Management Executive*, November 1995, pp. 35–47; Amy Borrus and Michael Collins, "What's Keeping U.S. Companies out of Vietnam? The U.S.," *Business Week*, April 17, 1995, p. 60; Pete Engardio and Bruce Einhorn, "Rising from the Ashes," *Business Week*, May 23, 1994, pp. 44–48; and Joyce Barnathan et al., "Destination, Vietnam," *Business Week*, February 14, 1994, pp. 26–27.

CHAPTER 3

International Management in Action: Where's the Quality Service in Deutschland? Greg Steinmetz, "Customer-Service Era Is Reaching Germany Late, Hurting Business," *Wall Street Journal*, June 1, 1995, pp. A1, A8; G. Pascal Zachary, "Service Productivity Is Rising Fast—and So Is the Fear of Lost Jobs," *Wall Street Journal*, June 8, 1995, pp. A1, A10; and Richard M. Hodgetts, *TQM in Small and Medium-Sized Organizations* (New York: Amacom, 1996), Chapters 2–3.

International Management in Action: Bit Players Bite the Dust Amy Borrus, Edith Hill, and Keith Naughton, "This Trade Gap Ain't What It Used to Be," *Business Week*, March 18, 1996, p. 50; Brian Bemner and Steven Brull, "At Last—Sayonara to the Blahs," *Business Week*, January 22, 1996; and Andrew Pollack, "Japan Inc.'s Dying Bit Players," *New York Times*, May 27, 1995, pp. 17–18.

In the International Spotlight: France Stewart Toy, Linda Bernier, and Bill Javetski, "Now, the Whirlwind," *Business Week*, May 22, 1995, p. 59; Stewart Toy et al., "Can Anyone Fix This Country?" *Business Week*, May 8, 1995, pp. 56–58; and Philip R. Harris and Robert T. Moran, *Managing Cultural Differences*, 3rd ed. (Houston: Gulf Publishing, 1991), pp. 464–471.

CHAPTER 4

Getting Tough . . . Or Else Amy Borrus, Dexter Roberts, and Joyce Barnathan, "Counterfeit Disks, Suspect Enforcement," *Business Week*, September 18, 1995, p. 68; Pete Engardio and Joyce Barnathan, "China: Strife at the Top May Spark a War on Corruption," *Business Week*, March 6, 1995, p. 53; Seth Faison, "Razors, Soap, Cornflakes: Pirating in China Balloons," *New York Times*, February 17, 1995, pp. A1, C2; and "Copy to Come," *Economist*, January 7, 1995, pp. 51–52.

CHAPTER 5

Business Customs in Japan William Morrow, "Speaking the Japanese Business Language," *European Business*, Winter 1974, pp. 45–46; Ted Holden and Suzanne Wolley, "The Delicate Art of Doing Business in Japan," *Business Week*, October 2, 1989, p. 120; and Roger E. Axtell, *Dos and Taboos around the World*, 2nd ed. (New York: Wiley, 1990), pp. 33, 90.

International Management in Action: Common Personal Values George W. England, "Managers and Their Value Systems: A Five-Country Comparative Study," *Columbia Journal of World Business*, Summer 1978, pp. 35–44; Geert Hofstede, *Culture's Consequences: International Differences in Work-Related Values* (Beverly Hills, CA: Sage Publishing, 1980); and Geert Hofstede, *Cultures and Organizations: Software of the Mind* (London: McGraw-Hill U.K., Ltd., 1991).

In the International Spotlight: Taiwan Dori Jones Yang, "Taiwan Isn't Just for Cloning Anymore," *Business Week*, September 25, 1989, pp. 208–212; *The World Almanac* (New York: Pharos Books, 1993), p. 803; Michael J. Marquardt and Dean W. Engel, *Global Human Resource Development* (Englewood Cliffs, NJ: Prentice-Hall, 1993), pp. 183–186; and "China (Taiwan)," *Europa World Year Book 1995*, vol. 1 (London: Europa Publications, 1995), pp. 833–842.

CHAPTER 6

International Management in Action: Ten Key Factors for MNC Success James F. Bolt, "Global Competitors: Some Criteria for Success," *Business Horizons*, January–February 1988, pp. 34–41; Tom Peters, *Liberation Management* (New York: Knopf, 1992); and Alan S. Rugman and Richard M. Hodgetts, *International Business* (New York: McGraw-Hill, 1995), Chapter 1.

Managing in Hong Kong J. Stewart Black and Lyman W. Porter, "Managerial Behaviors and Job Performance: A Successful Manager in Los Angeles May Not Succeed in Hong Kong," *Journal of International Business Studies*, First Quarter 1991, pp. 99–112; Geert Hofstede, *Cultures and Organizations: Software of the Mind* (London: McGraw-Hill U.K., Ltd., 1991), Chapters 4–6; and Michael J. Marquardt and Dean W. Engel, *Global Human Resource Development* (Englewood Cliffs, NJ: Prentice-Hall, 1993), pp. 187–188.

In the International Spotlight: Mexico   David Wessel, Paul B. Carroll, and Thomas T. Vogel, Jr., "How Mexico's Crisis Ambushed Top Minds in Officialdom, Finance," *Wall Street Journal*, July 6, 1995, pp. A1, A4; Craig Torres and Paul B. Carroll, "Mexico's Mantra for Salvation: Export, Export, Export," *Wall Street Journal*, March 17, 1995, p. A6; and "Mexico," *Europa* (London: Europa Publications, 1995), pp. 429–444.

CHAPTER 7

International Management in Action: Matsushita Goes Global   P. Christopher Earley and Harbir Singh, "International and Intercultural Management Research: What's Next," *Academy of Management Journal*, June 1995, pp. 327–340; Karen Lowry MIller, "Siemens Shapes Up," *Business Week* May 1, 1995, pp. 52–53; Christine M. Riordan and Robert J. Vandenberg, "A Central Question in Cross-Cultural Research: Do Employees of Different Cultures Interpret Work-Related Measures in an Equivalent Manner?" *Journal of Management*, vol. 20, no. 3., 1994, pp. 643–671; and Brenton R. Schlender, "Matsushita Shows How To Go Global," *Fortune*, July 11, 1994, pp. 159–166.

CHAPTER 8

International Management in Action: Doing It Right the First Time   http://www.jetro.go.jp/JETROINFO/DOING/4.html; Alan M. Rugman and Richard M. Hodgetts, *International Business* (New York: McGraw Hill Book Company, 1995); and Phil R. Harris and Robert T. Moran, *Managing Cultural Differences*, 3rd ed. (Houston: Gulf Publishing, 1991), pp. 393–406.

Communicating in Europe   Karen Matthes, "Mind Your Manners When Doing Business in Europe," *Personnel*, January 1992, p. 19; Philip R. Harris and Robert T. Moran, *Managing Cultural Differences: High-Performance Strategies for a New World of Business*, 4th ed. (Houston: Gulf Publishing, 1994), Chapter 13; and Alan Rugman and Richard M. Hodgetts, *International Business* (New York: McGraw-Hill, 1995), Chapter 16.

You Be the International Consultant: Foreign or Domestic?   The auto sales data can be found in Doron P. Levin, "In Autos, U.S. Makes Strides," *New York Times*, March 24, 1989, pp. 23, 25.

CHAPTER 9

International Management in Action: Point/Counterpoint   Wendy Bonds, "Fuji, Accused by Kodak of Hogging Markets, Spits Back: 'You Too,'" *Wall Street Journal*, July 31, 1995, pp. A1, A5; "Photo Wars: Shuttered," *Economist*, August 5, 1995, pp. 59–60; and Mark Maremont, "Next a Flap Over Film," *Business Week*, July 10, 1995, p. 34.

Joint Venturing in Russia   Keith A. Rosten, "Soviet-U.S. Joint Ventures: Pioneers on a New Frontier," *California Management Review*, Winter 1991, pp. 88–108; Steven Greenhouse, "Chevron to Spend $10 Billion to Seek Oil in Kazakhstan," *New York Times*, May 19, 1992, pp. A1, C9; Louis Uchitelle, "Givebacks by Chevron in Oil Deal," *New York Times*, May 23, 1992, pp. 17, 29; Craig Mellow, "Russia: Making Cash from Chaos," *Fortune*, April 17, 1995, pp. 145–151; and Daniel J. McCarthy and Sheila M. Puffer, "Strategic Investment Flexibility for MNE Success in Russia," *Journal of World Business*, vol. 32, no. 4, 1997, pp. 293–318.

You Be the International Consultant: Go East, Young People, Go East   Amy Borrus et al., "The Asians Are Bracing for a Trade Shoot-Out," *Business Week*, May 1, 1989, pp. 40–41; John W. Verity, "If It Looks Like a Slump and Crawls Like a Slump . . .," *Business Week*, May 1, 1989, p. 27; and Geoff Lewis, "Is the Computer Business Maturing?" *Business Week*, March 6, 1989, pp. 68–78.

CHAPTER 10

International Management in Action: Sometimes It's All Politics   John Stackhouse, "India Sours on Foreign Investment," *Globand Mail*, August 10, 1995, Sec. 2, pp. 1–2; Peter Galuszka and Susan Chandler, "A Plague of Disjointed Ventures," *Business Week*, May 1, 1995, p. 55;

and Marcus W. Brauchli, "Politics Threaten Power Project in India," *Wall Street Journal*, July 3, 1995, p. A14.

Negotiating with the Japanese   Rosalie J. Tung, "How to Negotiate with the Japanese," *California Management Review*, Summer 1984, pp. 62–77; Carla Rapoport, "You Can Make Money in Japan," *Fortune*, February 12, 1990, pp. 85–92; Margaret A. Neale and Max. H. Bazerman, "Negotiating Rationally," *Academy of Management Executive*, August 1992, pp. 42–51.

CHAPTER 11

Organizing in Germany   Hermann Simon, "Lessons from Germany's Midsize Giants," *Harvard Business Review*, March–April 1992, pp. 115–123; Carla Rapoport, "Europe's Slump Won't End Soon," *Fortune*, May 3, 1993, pp. 82–87; and Robert Neff and Douglas Harbrecht, "Germany's Mighty Unions Are Being Forced to Bend," *Business Week*, March 1, 1993, pp. 52–56.

You Be the International Consultant: Getting In on the Ground Floor   Some of the data in this case were reported in Thane Peterson and Mark Maremont, "Adding Hustle to Europe's Muscle," *Business Week*, 1989 special edition, pp. 32–33.

CHAPTER 12

International Management in Action: Kodak Goes Digital   Wendy Bonds, "Fuji, Accused by Kodak of Hogging Markets, Spits Back: 'You Too,'" *Wall Street Journal*, July 31, 1995, pp. A1, A5; Peter Nulty, "Digital Imaging Had Better Boom Before Kodak Film Busts," *Fortune*, May 1, 1995, pp. 80–83; and Mark Maremont, "Kodak's New Focus," *Business Week*, January 30, 1995, p. 62.

How the Japanese Do Things Differently   Ford S. Worthy, "Japan's Smart Secret Weapon," *Fortune*, August 12, 1991, pp. 72–75; Brenton R. Schlender, "Hard Times for High Tech," *Fortune*, March 22, 1993, p. 98; Ronald Henkoff, "Companies that Train Best," *Fortune*, March 22, 1993; and Jim Carlton, "Sega Leaps Ahead by Shipping New Player Early," *Wall Street Journal*, May 11, 1995, pp. B1, B3.

CHAPTER 13

***Karoshi*, or Stressed Out in Japan**   William S. Brown, Rebecca E. Lubove, and James Kwalwasser, "*Karoshi:* Alternative Perspectives of Japanese Management Styles," *Business Horizons*, March–April 1994, pp. 58–60; Karen Lowry Miller, "Now, Japan Is Admitting It: Work Kills Executives," *Business Week*, August 3, 1992, p. 35; and Philip R. Harris and Robert T. Moran, *Managing Cultural Differences: High-Performance Strategies for a New World of Business*, 3rd ed. (Houston: Gulf Publishing, 1991), pp. 393–408.

CHAPTER 14

Global Teams   Charlene Marmer Solomon, "Global Teams: The Ultimate Collaboration," *Personnel Journal*, September 1995, pp. 49–58; Andrew Kakabdse and Andrew Myers, "Qualities of Top Management: Comparison of European Manufacturers," *Journal of Management Development*, vol. 14, no. 1, 1995, pp. 5–15; and Noel M. Tichy, Michael I. Brimm, Ram Chran, and Hiroraka Takeuchi, "Leadership Development as a Lever for Global Transformation," in Vladimir Pucik, Noel M. Tichy, and Carole K. Barnett, (eds.), *Globalizing Management: Creating and Leading the Competitive Organization* (New York: John Wiley & Sons, 1993), pp. 47–60.

In the International Spotlight: Germany   The statistics on unified Germany come from Bill Javetski and John Templeman, "One Germany," *Business Week*, April 2, 1990, pp. 47–49; "Putting on Weight," *Time*, March 28, 1990, p. 36.

CHAPTER 15

International Management in Action: Important Tips on Working for Foreigners   Faye Rice, "Should You Work for a Foreigner?' *Fortune*, August 1, 1988, pp. 123–124; John Holusha, "No Utopia But to Workers It's a Job," *New York Times*, January 29, 1989, Sec. 3, pp. 1, 10; and Roger E. Axtell (ed.), *Do's and Taboos around the World* (New York: Wiley, 1990).

Recruiting Managers in Japan   James C. Morgan and J. Jeffrey Morgan, *Cracking the Japanese Market* (New York: Free Press, 1991); Richard M. Hodgetts and Fred Luthans, "U.S. Multinationals' Expatriate Compensation Strategies," *Compensation & Benefits Review*, January–February 1993, p. 61; Philip R. Harris and Robert T. Moran, *Managing and Cultural Differences: High-Performance Strategies for a New World of Business*, 3rd ed. (Houston: Gulf Publishing, 1991), p. 393; and Alan M. Rugman and Richard M. Hodgetts, *International Business* (New York: McGraw-Hill, 1995), pp. 498–499.

You Be the International Consultant: A Selection Decision   William H. Davidson, "Creating and Managing Joint Ventures in China," *California Management Review*, Summer 1987, pp. 77–94; Denis Fred Simon, "After Tiananmen: What Is the Future for Foreign Business in China?" *California Management Review*, Winter 1990, p. 106; and S. Gordon Redding, *The Spirit of Chinese Capitalism* (New York: Walter de Gruyter, 1990).

CHAPTER 16

International Management in Action: The Cultural Integrator
Robert C. Maddox and Douglas Short, "The Cultural Integrator," *Business Horizons*, November–December 1988, pp. 57–59; Peter J. Dowling and Randall S. Schuler, *International Dimensions of Human Resource Management* (Boston: PWS-Kent, 1990); and Michael J. Marquardt and Dean W. Engel, *Global Human Resource Development* (Englewood Cliffs, NJ: Prentice-Hall, 1993).

U.S. Style Training for Expats and Their Teenagers   Dawn Anfuso, "HR Unites the World of Coca-Cola," *Personnel Journal*, November 1994, pp. 112–121; Karen Dawn Stuart, "Teens Play a Role in Moves Overseas," *Personnel Journal*, March 1992, pp. 72–78; Richard M. Hodgetts and Fred Luthans, "U.S. Multinationals' Expatriate Compensation Strategies," *Compensation & Benefits Review*, January–February 1993, p. 61; and Philip R. Harris and Robert T. Moran, *Managing Cultural Differences: High-Performance Strategies for a New World of Business*, 3rd ed. (Houston: Gulf Publishing, 1991), Chapter 9.

CHAPTER 17

International Management in Action: They're Leading the Pack
Steven R. Weisman, "More Japanese Workers Demanding Shorter Hours and Less Hectic Work," *New York Times*, March 3, 1992, p. A6; Germany's Mighty Unions Are Being Forced to Bend," *Business Week*, March 1, 1993, p. 52; and Christopher Farrell and Michael J. Mandel, "Riding High," *Business Week*, October 9, 1995, pp. 134–146.

Unions Become More Flexible—and Do Better   Edmund L. Andrews, "German Union Gives Opening for Wage Cuts," *New York Times*, June 5, 1997, pp. A1, C5; Greg Steinmetz, "One Union Accepts Reality, Breaking with Inflexible Past," *Wall Street Journal*, June 12, 1997, p. A14; Greg Steinmetz, "Under Pressure, Germany's Unions Bend," *Wall Street Journal*, July 29, 1997, p. A10; and Edmund L. Andrews, "Germans Cut Labor Costs with a Harsh Export: Jobs," *New York Times*, March 21, 1998, pp. A1, 3.

You Be the International Consultant: They're Back   Doron P. Levin, "For VW, the Future Is Its Past," *New York Times*, August 8, 1989, pp. 25, 41; John Templeman, "A Hard U-Turn at VW," *Business Week*, March 15, 1993, p. 47; and "Kohl Prods the Giant," *Business Week*, January 25, 1993, p. 52.

Endnotes

Chapter 1 Endnotes

1. Seth Faison, "G.M. To Expand Investment in Building Trucks in China," *New York Times,* June 23, 1998, p. C3.

2. Thomas Kamm, Brian Coleman, and Cacilie Rohwedder, "EU Takes First Steps Toward Single Currency," *The Wall Street Journal,* May 4, 1998, p. A17; Nicholas Bray, "Euro Is Expected to Level Exchange-Rate Playing Field," *The Wall Street Journal,* May 8, 1998, p. A13; and Craig R. Whitney, "Europeans Accept a Single Currency Despite Late Snag," *New York Times,* May 3, 1998, pp. A1, 10.

3. "No End of Woe at the WTO?" *Economist,* February 4, 1995, p. 59; "The WTO: A Rocky Start," *Economist,* March 25, 1995, pp. 82–83.

4. Nathaniel C. Nash, "Coke's Great Romanian Adventure." *New York Times,* February 26, 1995, Section 3, pp. 1, 10.

5. Alan M. Rugman and Richard M. Hodgetts, *International Business* (New York: McGraw-Hill, 1995), p. 532.

6. Sharon Moshavi et al., "India Shakes Off Its Shackles," *Business Week,* January 30, 1995, pp. 48–49; Rahul Jacob, "India Gets Moving," *Fortune,* September 5, 1994, pp. 100–104.

7. Matt Murray, "GE Capital Goes Bargain Hunting in Troubled Asia," *The Wall Street Journal,* March 12, 1998, p. B4.

8. "Trade Gap Biggest in History," *Omaha World Herald,* February 20, 1999, p. 9.

9. Rugman and Hodgetts, *International Business,* p. 527.

10. Andrew Kupfer, "Ma Bell and the Seven Babies Go Global," *Fortune,* November 4, 1994, pp. 118–128.

11. Fred R. Bleakley, "Foreign Investment in U.S. Surged in 1994," *The Wall Street Journal,* March 15, 1995, p. A2.

12. Milt Freudenheim, "Hoechst to Pay $7.1 Billion for Dow Unit," *New York Times,* May 5, 1995, pp. C21, C5.

13. Bleakley, "Foreign Investment."

14. Larry Holyoke, William Spindle, and Neil Gross, "Doing the Unthinkable," *Business Week,* January 10, 1994, pp. 52–53.

15. Stratford Sherman, "Bronfman's Buying Binge Isn't Finished." *Fortune,* May 1, 1995, p. 77.

16. Johnnie L. Roberts, "He Owns the Songs," *Newsweek,* June 1, 1998, pp. 52–53.

17. "Putting Mexico Together Again," *Economist,* February 4, 1995, pp. 65–67.

18. Geri Smith et al., "Mexico: Can It Cope?" *Business Week,* January 16, 1995, pp. 42–46.

19. Jerry Flint, "We Do What Mexicans Do," *Forbes,* September 2, 1991, p. 80.

20. Elizabeth Malkin, "Holding Off Asia's Assault," *Business Week,* April 13, 1998, pp. 44–45.

21. Joel Millman, "Mexico Is Becoming Auto-Making Hot Spot," *The Wall Street Journal,* June 23, 1998, p. A17.

22. James Brooke, "U.S. Investors Stampede Into Brazil," *New York Times,* April 17, 1995, p. C10.

23. "Emerging Market Indicators," *Economist,* March 7, 1998, p. 114.

24. Helene Cooper and Jose de Cordoba, "Chile Is Invited to Join NAFTA as U.S. Pledges Free-Trade Zone for Americans," *The Wall Street Journal,* December 12, 1994, p. A23.

25. Gianluigi Guido, "Implementing a Pan European Marketing Strategy," *Long-Range Planning,* October 1991, p. 30.

26. Rugman and Hodgetts, *International Business,* p. 470.

27. Jonathan Sapsford, Norihiko Shirouzu, and David P. Hamilton, "IMF Sets $22.6 Billion Loan Accord with Russia," *The Wall Street Journal,* July 14, 1998, pp. A12, 14.

28. Also see Neela Banerjee, "Russia Taking Privatization to the Bank," *The Wall Street Journal,* April 20, 1995, p. A8.

29. Fred Luthans, Richard R. Patrick, and Brett C. Luthans, "Doing Business in Central and Eastern Europe: Political, Economic, and Cultural Diversity," *Business Horizons,* September–October 1995, pp. 9–16.

30. "Transition Economics, *Economist,* March 25, 1995, p. 116.

31. See Tina Rosenberg, *The Haunted Land* (New York: Random House, 1995).

32. Fred Luthans and Sang Lee, "There Are Lessons to Be Learned as Albania Undergoes a Paradigm Shift," *International Journal of Organizational Analysis,* January 1994, p. 12.

33. Fred Luthans and Laura T. Riolli, "Albania and the Bora Company: Lessons Learned Before the Recent Chaos," *Academy of Management Executive,* August 1997, pp. 61–72.

34. Stephanie Strom, "Japanese Majority Owner Forces Bankruptcy of Rockefeller Center," *New York Times,* May 12, 1995, pp. A1, C4; Mitchell Pacelle and Steven Lipin, "Japanese Firm Turns to Laws on Bankruptcy," *The Wall Street Journal,* May 15, 1995, p. A4.

35. "Will Tokyo Finally Clean House?" *Economist,* June 27, 1998, p. 71.

36. For more on this see Andrew Pollack, "Japanese Banks Cutting Back on U.S. Presence," *New York Times,* July 10, 1998, pp. C1–2; and Mortimer B. Zuckerman, "Land of the Sinking Sun?" *U.S. News & World Report,* July 13, 1998, p. 64.

37. James Cox, "China's Leaders Face 'Grim Reality' of Skidding Economy," *USA Today,* August 19, 1998, p. 5B.

38. Seth Faison, "Razors, Soap, Cornflakes: Pirating in China Balloons," *New York Times,* Beburary 17, 1995, pp. A1, C1; Seth Faison, "Fighting Piracy and Frustration in China," *New York Times,* May 17, 1995, pp. C1, C8.

39. Louis Kraar, "The Risks Are Rising in China," *Fortune,* March 6, 1995, pp. 179–180.

40. Craig R. Smith and Marcus W. Brauchli, "To Invest Successfully in China, Foreigners Find Patience Crucial" *The Wall Street Journal,* February 23, 1995, p. 1.

41. Jim Rohwer, "Asia's Meltdown," *Fortune,* February 16, 1998, p. 88.

42. "South Korea Announces Plans for Privatizing Its Industries," *New York Times,* July 4, 1998, p. B5.

43. Moon Ihlwan and Brian Bremner, "The Crisis At Samsung," *Business Week,* March 23, 1998, pp. 46–47.

44. Mary Ann Von Glinow and Linda Clarke, "Vietnam: Tiger or Kitten," *Academy of Management Executive,* November 1995, pp.

35–47. "Vietnam Beats China at its Own Game," *Economist,* November 5, 1994, pp. 31–32; and Joyce Barnathan, Alex McKinnon, and Doug Harbrecht, "Destination, Vietnam," *Business Week,* February 14, 1994, pp. 26–27.

45. Sharon Moshavi et al., "India Shakes Off Its Shackles," *Business Week,* January 30, 1995, pp. 48–49.

46. Also see "Saudi Arabia's Future: The Cracks in the Kingdom *Economist,* March 18, 1995, pp. 21–23.

47. For more on Israel see "Israel At 50," *Economist,* April 25, 1998, pp. 3–18.

Chapter 2 Endnotes

1. Joyce Barnathan et al., "Can China Avert Crisis?" *Business Week,* March 16, 1998, p. 47.

2. G. Bruce Knecht, "Asia Shudders at 'Normal' Growth," *The Wall Street Journal,* December 5, 1997, p. A13; and Ian Johnson, "China's Growth Slows to 7.2%, Below Key Goal," *The Wall Street Journal,* April 23, 1998, p. A16.

3. Ian Johnson, "China's Jiang Outlines Privatization Steps," *The Wall Street Journal,* July 31, 1997, p. A14.

4. "Can China Reform Its Economy?" *Business Week,* September 29, 1997, p. 120.

5. William Safire, "China's 'Four Fears,'" *New York Times,* May 22, 1995, p. A11.

6. Seth Faison, "Fighting Piracy and Frustration in China," *New York Times,* May 17, 1995, pp. C1, C8.

7. Pete Engardio, Dexter Roberts, and Bruce Einhorn, "China's New Elite," *Business Week,* June 5, 1995, pp. 48–49.

8. "Europe's Diminished Leaders," *Economist,* January 21, 1995, pp. 51–53.

9. Helene Cooper, "All of Europe Watches as Britain's Tony Blair Hacks Away at Welfare," *The Wall Street Journal,* June 25, 1998, p. A18.

10. Craig W. Whitney, "Chirac Assures Kohl on Europe's Monetary Policy," *New York Times,* May 22, 1995, p. A3.

11. Also see Craig R. Whitney, "French Annoyance at the U.S. Comes in Several Courses," *New York Times,* June 4, 1995, p. E6.

12. "Can Russia Fight Back?" *Economist,* June 6, 1998, pp. 47–48.

13. "The Endless Winter of Russian Reform," *Economist,* July 12, 1997, p. 6.

14. Ibid., p. 5.

15. "The Battle of Russia's Capitalism," *Economist,* August 9, 1997, p. 14.

16. "Solidarity v Solidarity," *Economist,* April 25, 1998, p. 51.

17. "Is Central Europe, Along with Hungary, Turning Right?" *Economist,* May 30, 1998, pp. 49–50.

18. Robert Frank, "Czech Republic Is Free, Fun to Visit and Rich, but Only Superficially," *The Wall Street Journal,* July 15, 1997, pp. A1, 8.

19. Abbass F. Alkhafaji, *Competitive Global Management: Principles and Strategies* (Delray Beach, FL: St. Lucie Press, 1995), p. 382.

20. More details on these principles can be found in Anant K. Sundaram and J. Stewart Black, *The International Business Environment: Text and Cases* (Englewood Cliffs, NJ: Prentice-Hall, 1995), pp. 120–122.

21. Kate Gillespie, "Middle East Response to the U.S. Foreign Corrupt Practices Act," *California Management Review,* Summer 1987, p. 9.

22. John Graham, "Foreign Corruption Practices Act: A Manager's Guide," *California Management Review,* Summer 1987, p. 9.

23. Gillespie, "Middle East Response," p. 28.

24. Also see Nicholas D. Kristof, "Dutchman Strikes Chord in a Less Confident Japan," *New York Times,* June 4, 1995, p. Y40.

25. "The Next Target in Japan," *Economist,* February 18, 1995, pp. 29–30.

26. David E. Sanger, "Japan's Bad Debt Is Now Estimated Near $1 Trillion," *New York Times,* July 30, 1998, pp. A1, C5.

27. Bay Fing, "Will China's Army Get Out of Business?" *U.S. News & World Report,* August 3, 1998, p. 43.

28. "Let the Party Begin," *Economist,* April 26, 1997, pp. 57–59.

29. Seth Schiesel, "Brazil Sells Most of State Phone Utility," *New York Times,* July 30, 1998, pp. C1, 4.

30. *Economist,* February 21, 1998, p. 108.

31. "Online Subscribers Booming Among Non-English Speakers," *Management Review,* June 1998, p. 7.

32. "So Much for the Cashless Society," *Economist,* November 26, 1994, pp. 21–22.

33. See Kelley Holland and Amy Cortese, "The Future of Money," *Business Week,* June 12, 1995, pp. 66–78.

34. Ibid., p. 23.

35. Also see Timothy A. Lavery, "Cross-Border Payments Hold Promise For Expediting International Payroll," *HRM Magazine,* March 1998, pp. 30–39.

36. See "In Peru, A Cellular Revolution," *Miami Herald,* May 22, 1995, p. 6A.

37. "Private Numbers," *Economist,* February 4, 1995, p. 60.

38. Ibid.

39. Jan Syfert, "Up There with the Best," *Productivity SA,* November/December 1998, p. 49.

Chapter 3 Endnotes

1. William M. Carley, "GE Implements $200 Million Program to Slash Number of Defects per Product," *The Wall Street Journal,* April 25, 1996, p. A6.

2. Neil Gross and Peter Coy, "The Technology Paradox," *Business Week,* March 6, 1995, p. 77.

3. Ibid.

4. Ibid., p. 78.

5. Dean Takahashi, "How the Competition Got Ahead of Intel in Making Cheap Chips," *The Wall Street Journal,* February 12, 1998, pp. A1, 11.

6. Quentin Hardy, "Motorola, Broadsided by the Digital Era, Struggles for a Footing," *The Wall Street Journal,* April 22, 1998, pp. A1, 14.

7. Michael E. Porter, *Competitive Advantages of Nations* (New York: Free Press, 1990).

8. "The Mass Production of Ideas, and Other Impossibilities," *Economist,* March 18, 1995, p. 72.

9. "Producer Power," *Economist,* March 4, 1995, p. 70.

10. Bart Ziegler, "Gerstner Slashed R&D by $1 Billion; for IBM It May Be a Good Thing," *The Wall Street Journal,* October 6, 1997, pp. A1, 10.

11. Also see Larry Dignan, "Why German Auto Makers Are Humming," *New York Times,* August 24, 1997, Section F, p. 5; and "Measuring Up," *The Wall Street Journal,* August 19, 1997, p. A5.

12. Frederic M. Biddle, "Boeing Is Placing Its Bets on Smaller, Cheaper Airlines," *The Wall Street Journal,* July 6, 1998, p. A22.

13. Charles Goldsmith, "After Trailing Boeing for Year, Airbus Aims for 50% of the Market," *The Wall Street Journal,* March 16, 1998, pp. A1, 8; and Frederic M. Biddle and John Helyar, "Behind Boeing's Woes: Clunky Assembly Line, Price War with Airbus," *The Wall Street Journal,* April 24, 1998, pp. A1, 16.

14. "Silicon Valley, PRC," *Economist,* June 27, 1998, pp. 64–65.

15. "Asia, At Your Service," *Economist,* February 11, 1995, p. 54.

16. Peter M. Senge, *The Fifth Dimension* (New York: Doubleday, 1990).

17. Michael E. McGill, John W. Slocum, Jr., and David Lei, "Management Practices in Learning Organizations," *Organizational Dynamics,* Summer 1992, pp. 10–16. For additional insights to learning organizations, see J. Bernard Keys, Robert A. Wells, and L. Trey Denton, "Japanese Managerial and Organizational Learning," *Thunderbird International Business Review,* March/April 1998, pp. 119–139.

18. Also see Fred Luthans, Michael Rubach, and Paul Marsnik, "Going Beyond Total Quality: The Characteristics, Techniques and Measures of Learning Organizations," *International Journal of Organizational Analysis,* January 1995, pp. 24–44.

19. Ibid., p. 11.

20. Albert Bandura, *Social Foundations of Thought and Action* (Englewood Cliffs, NJ: Prentice-Hall, 1986); Albert Bandura, *Self-Efficacy: The Exercise of Control* (New York: W. H. Freeman and Company, 1997).

21. Alexander D. Stajkovic and Fred Luthans, "Social Cognitive Theory and Self-Efficacy: Going Beyond Traditional Motivational and Behavioral Approaches," *Organizational Dynamics,* Spring 1998, p. 66.

22. Alexander D. Stajkovic and Fred Luthans, "Self-Efficacy and Work-Related Performance," *Psychological Bulletin,* September 1998, in press.

23. Bandura, *Self-Efficacy*; and Stajkovic and Luthans, "Social Cognitive Theory and Self-Efficacy."

24. See Richard M. Hodgetts, *Measures of Quality and High Performance* (New York: American Management Association, 1998), pp. 146–149; and Stephane Brutus, John W. Fleenor and Manuel London, "Does 360-Degree Feedback Work in Different Industries," *Journal of Management Development,* vol. 17, no. 3, 1998, pp. 177–190.

25. Bill Gates, "Compete, Don't Delete," *The Economist,* June 13, 1998, p. 20.

26. John J. Keller, "AT&T Bypasses Normal Suppliers in Local-Phone Race," *The Wall Street Journal,* March 20, 1997, p. B4.

27. Michael E. Porter, *Competitive Advantage of Nations,* p. 103.

28. Jonathan Friedland, "VW Puts Suppliers on Production Line," *The Wall Street Journal,* February 15, 1996, p. A11.

29. Jeffrey Pfeffer, *The Human Equation* (Boston: Harvard Business School Press, 1998), p. xv–xvi.

30. Ibid., p. xvi.

31. Richard M. Hodgetts, *Implementing TQM in Small- and Medium-Sized Organizations* (New York: American Management Association, 1996), Chapter 7.

32. "Stores of Value," *Economist,* March 4, 1995, p. 6.

Chapter 4 Endnotes

1. Dinah Payne, Cecily Raiborn, and Jorn Askvik, "A Global Code of Business Ethics," *Journal of Business Ethics,* December 1997, pp. 1727–1735.

2. Georges Enderle, "A Worldwide Survey of Business Ethics in the 1990s," *Journal of Business Ethics,* December 1997, pp. 1475–1483.

3. See Iwao Taka, "Business Ethics In Japan," *Journal of Business Ethics,* October 1997, pp. 1499–1508.

4. For some insights into the Recruit scandal, see Susan Chira, "Another Top Official in Japan Loses Post in Wake of Scandal," *New York Times,* January 25, 1989, pp. 1, 5; "Bribery Trial to Challenge Japanese Ways," *Omaha World Herald,* November 24, 1989, p. 4; and "Remember the Recruit Scandal? Well . . . ," *Business Week,* January 8, 1990, p. 52.

5. Greg Wiegand, "Arrests Put Focus on Ethics in Japan," *USA Today,* January 20, 1998, p. 2B.

6. Sheryl WuDunn, "Japan's Corruption Fighter Is Shunted Aside," *New York Times,* August 14, 1998, p. C4.

7. See also "Never Mind the Quality," *Economist,* June 28, 1997, p. 15.

8. Steven R. Weisman, "Landmark Harassment Case in Japan," *New York Times,* April 17, 1992, p. A3.

9. Andrew Pollack, "In Japan, It's See No Evil; Have No Harassment," *New York Times,* May 7, 1996, p. C5.

10. Peter Elstrom and Steven V. Brull, "Mitsubishi's Morass," *Business Week,* June 3, 1996, p. 35; and "Mitsubishi Settles with Women in Sexual Harassment Lawsuit," *New York Times,* August 29, 1997, p. A9.

11. Also see Urban C. Lehner and Masayoshi Kanabayashi, "Politicians' Anti-U.S. Remarks Greeted with Silent Approval by Many Japanese," *The Wall Street Journal,* January 23, 1992, p. A12.

12. James B. Treece, "What the Japanese Must Learn about Racial Tolerance," *Business Week,* September 5, 1988, p. 41.

13. Robert E. Cole and Donald R. Deskins, Jr., "Racial Factors in Site Location and Employment Patterns of Japanese Auto Firms in America," *California Management Review,* Fall 1988, pp. 17–18.

14. Richard E. Wokutch, "Corporate Social Responsibility Japanese Style," *Academy of Management Executive,* May 1990, pp. 56–74.

15. Pat Choate, *Agents of Influence* (New York: Knopf, 1991).

16. See, for example, Richard C. Morais, "People in Glass Houses Throwing Stones," *Forbes,* May 25, 1992, pp. 84–93.

17. Helmut Becker and David J. Fritzsche, "A Comparison of the Ethical Behavior of American, French, and German Managers," *Columbia Journal of World Business,* Winter 1987, pp. 87–95.

18. Ibid.

19. Ibid., p. 90.

20. Ibid., p. 94.

21. Ibid.

22. Evelyne Serdjenian, "Women Managers in France," in Nancy J. Adler and Dafna N. Izraeli (eds.), *Competitive Frontiers: Women Managers in a Global Economy* (Cambridge, MA: Blackwell Publishing, 1994), p. 199.

23. Ibid., pp. 199–200.

24. Ibid., p. 204.

25. Ariane Berthoin Antal and Camilla Krebsbach-Gnath, "Women in Management in Germany: East, West, and Reunited," in Nancy J. Adler and Dafna N. Izraeli (eds.), *Competitive Frontiers: Women Managers in a Global Economy* (Cambridge, MA: Blackwell Publishing, 1994), pp. 210–211.

26. Valerie Hammond and Viki Holton, "The Scenario for Women Managers in Britain in the 1990s," in Nancy J. Adler and Dafna N. Izraeli (eds.), *Competitive Frontiers: Women Managers in a Global Economy* (Cambridge, MA: Blackwell Publishing, 1994), p. 230.

27. Ibid., p. 241.

28. Dinal Lee et al., "China's Ugly Export Secret: Prison Labor," *Business Week,* April 22, 1991, pp. 42–46.

29. Pete Engardio, "The Wild, Wild East," *Business Week,* December 28, 1992, pp. 50–51.

30. See "Making War on China's Pirates," *Economist,* February 11, 1995, p. 33.

31. Edward A. Robinson, "China's Spies Target Corporate America." *Fortune,* March 30, 1998, p. 119.

32. Seth Faison, "China Appears to Crack Down on CD Pirating," *New York Times,* April 7, 1997, pp. A1, 6; and Seth Faison, "U.S. and China Agree on Pact to Fight Piracy," *New York Times,* June 18, 1996, pp. A1, 8.

33. "Better Than the Real Thing," *Economist,* January 24, 1998, pp. 65–66.

34. Dexter Roberts, Christopher Power, and Stephanie Anderson Forest, "Cheated in China?" *Business Week,* October 6, 1997, p. 142.

35. Also see Lu Xiaohe, "Business Ethics in China," *Journal of Business Ethics,* October 1997, pp. 1509–1518.

36. Karen Korabik, "Managerial Women in the People's Republic of China: The Long March Continues," in Nancy J. Adler and Dafna N. Izraeli (eds.), *Competitive Frontiers: Women Managers in a Global Economy* (Cambridge, MA: Blackwell Publishers, 1994), p. 118.

37. Ibid., p. 124.

38. Clyde H. Farnsworth, "Proposal on Foreign Investors," *New York Times,* July 15, 1989, p. 20.

39. For example, see Matt Moffett, "U.S. Child-Labor Law Sparks a Trade Debate over Brazilian Oranges," *The Wall Street Journal,* September 9, 1998, pp. A1, A9.

40. Amy Borrus and Mark Maremont, "The Japanese Go Globe-Trotting, but the Yen Stays Home," *Business Week,* October 17, 1988, pp. 45–46.

41. John Graham, "Foreign Corruption Practices Act: A Manager's Guide," *Columbia Journal of World Business,* Fall 1983, p. 93.

42. Robert S. Greenberger, "Foreigners Use Bribes to Beat U.S. Rivals in Many Deals, New Report Concludes," *The Wall Street Journal,* October 12, 1995, pp. A3, A17.

43. James Bennet, "4 Former Honda Employees Sentenced in Kickback Case," *New York Times,* August 26, 1995, p. 19.

44. Greg Steinmetz, "U.S. Firms Are Among Least Likely to Pay Bribes Abroad, Survey Finds," *The Wall Street Journal,* August 25, 1997, p. 5.

45. Edmund L. Andrews, "29 Nations Agree to Outlaw Bribing Foreign Officials," *New York Times,* November 21, 1997, p. C2.

46. Amy Borrus et al., "Japan Digs Deep to Win the Hearts and Minds of America," *Business Week,* July 11, 1988, p. 75.

Chapter 5 Endnotes

1. Pat Joynt and Malcolm Warner, "Introduction: Cross-Cultural Perspectives," in Pat Joynt and Malcolm Warner (eds.) *Managing across Cultures: Issues and Perspectives* (London: International Thomson Business Press, 1996), p. 3.

2. For additional insights see Gerry Darlington, "Culture—A Theoretical Review," *Managing across Cultures: Issues and Perspectives,* pp. 33–55.

3. Fred Luthans, *Organizational Behavior,* 7th ed. (New York: McGraw-Hill, 1995), pp. 534–535; J. P. Spradley, *The Ethnographic Interview* (New York: Holt, 1979).

4. Gary Bonvillian and William A. Nowlin, "Cultural Awareness: An Essential Element of Doing Business Abroad," *Business Horizons,* November-December 1994, pp. 44–54.

5. Srilata Zaheer, "Overcoming the Liability of Foreignness," *Academy of Management Journal,* June 1995, pp. 341–363.

6. Roger E. Axtell (ed.), *Dos and Taboos around the World,* 2nd ed. (New York: Wiley, 1990), p. 3.

7. "Teaching Asia to Stay Asia," *Economist,* October 8, 1994, p. 39.

8. Lillian H. Chaney and Jeanette S. Martin, *Intercultural Business Communication* (Englewood Cliffs, NJ: Prentice-Hall, 1995), p. 115.

9. Fons Trompenaars and Charles Hampden-Turner, *Riding the Waves of Culture: Understanding Diversity in Global Business,* 2nd ed. (New York: McGraw-Hill, 1998), p. 23.

10. Christopher Orpen, "The Work Values of Western and Tribal Black Employees," *Journal of Cross-Cultural Psychology,* March 1978, pp. 99–111.

11. William Whitely and George W. England, "Variability in Common Dimensions of Managerial Values due to Value Orientation and Country Differences," *Personnel Psychology,* Spring 1980, pp. 77–89.

12. Ibid., p. 87.

13. George W. England and Raymond Lee, "The Relationship between Managerial Values and Managerial Success in the United States, Japan, India, and Australia," *Journal of Applied Psychology,* August 1974, pp. 418–419.

14. George W. England, "Managers and Their Value Systems: A Five-Country Comparative Study," *Columbia Journal of World Business,* Summer 1978, p. 39.

15. A. Reichel and D. M. Flynn, "Values in Transition: An Empirical Study of Japanese Managers in the U.S.," *Management International Review,* vol. 23, no. 4, 1984, pp. 69–70.

16. Hermann F. Schwind and Richard B. Peterson, "Shifting Personal Values in the Japanese Management System," *International Studies of Management & Organization,* Summer 1985, pp. 60–74.

17. Ibid., p. 72.

18. Geert Hofstede, *Culture's Consequences: International Differences in Work-Related Values* (Beverly Hills: Sage Publications, 1980).

19. Geert Hofstede, *Cultures and Organizations: Software of the Mind* (London: McGraw-Hill U.K., Ltd., 1991), pp. 251–252.

20. Geert Hofstede and Michael Bond, "The Need for Synergy among Cross-Cultural Studies," *Journal of Cross-Cultural Psychology,* December 1984, p. 419.

21. A. R. Negandhi and S. B. Prasad, *Comparative Management* (New York: Appleton-Century-Crofts, 1971), p. 128.

22. For additional insights, see Mark F. Peterson et al., "Role Conflict, Ambiguity, and Overload: A 21-Nation Study," *Academy of Management Journal,* June 1995, pp. 429–452.

23. Hofstede, *Culture's Consequences.*

24. Ibid.

25. Ibid.

26. Also see Chao C. Chen, Xiao-Ping Chen, and James R. Meindl, "How Can Cooperation Be Fostered? The Cultural Effects of Individualism–Collectivism," *Academy of Management Review,* vol. 23, no. 2, 1998, pp. 285–304.

27. Hofstede, *Culture's Consequences,* pp. 419–420.

28. Ibid., p. 420.

29. Simcha Ronen and Allen I. Kraut, "Similarities among Countries Based on Employee Work Values and Attitudes," *Columbia Journal of World Business,* Summer 1977, p. 90.

30. Ibid., p. 95.

31. Simcha Ronen and Oded Shenkar, "Clustering Countries on Attitudinal Dimensions: A Review and Synthesis," *Academy of Management Journal,* September 1985, pp. 435–454.

32. Ibid., p. 452.

33. Fons Trompenaars, *Riding the Waves of Culture* (New York: Irwin, 1994), p. 10.

34. Talcott Parsons, *The Social System* (New York: Free Press, 1951).

35. Also see Lisa Hoecklin, *Managing Cultural Differences* (Workingham, England: Addison-Wesley Publishing, 1995).

36. Charles M. Hampden-Turner and Fons Trompenaars, "A World Turned Upside Down: Doing Business in Asia," in Pat Joynt and Malcolm Warner (eds.) *Managing across Cultures: Issues and*

Perspectives (London: International Thomson Business Press, 1996), p. 279.

37. Ibid., p. 288.

38. Trompenaars, *Riding the Waves of Culture*, p. 131.

39. Ibid., p. 140.

Chapter 6 Endnotes

1. Nancy J. Adler, *International Dimensions of Organizational Behavior*, 3rd ed. (Cincinnati, OH: Southwestern, 1997).

2. See Clifford C. Clarke and Douglas Lipp, "Contrasting Cultures," *Training & Development Journal*, February 1998, pp. 21–31.

3. For more on this topic, see Paul Klebnikov, "The Powerhouse," *Forbes*, September 2, 1991, pp. 46–49.

4. William Taylor, "The Logic of Global Business: An Interview with ABB's Percy Barnevik," *Harvard Business Review*, March–April 1991, p. 92.

5. Fons Trompenaars and Charles Hampden-Turner, *Riding the Waves of Culture: Understanding Diversity in Global Business*, 2nd ed. (New York: McGraw-Hill, 1998), p. 188.

6. For a more detailed analysis, see Allen J. Morrison, David A. Ricks, and Kendall Roth, "Globalization versus Regionalization: Which Way for the Multinational?" *Organizational Dynamics*, Winter 1991, pp. 17–28.

7. Lisa Hoecklin, *Managing Cultural Differences* (Workingham, England: Addison-Wesley, 1995), pp. 98–99.

8. "The Personal Touch: Making McDonald's and Coca-Cola Less American," *Economist*, May 15, 1998, p. 5.

9. Linda M. Randall and Lori A. Coakley, "Building a Successful Partnership in Russia and Belarus: The Impact of Culture on Strategy," *Business Horizons*, March–April 1998, pp. 15–22.

10. Ibid., p. 21.

11. Trompenaars and Hampden-Turner, p. 202.

12. Adapted from Richard Mead, *International Management* (Cambridge, MA: Blackwell, 1994), pp. 57–59.

13. Fred Luthans, Richard M. Hodgetts, and Stuart A. Rosenkrantz, *Real Managers* (Cambridge, MA: Ballinger Publishing, 1988).

14. Fred Luthans, Dianne H. B. Welsh, and Stuart A. Rosenkrantz, "What Do Russian Managers Really Do? An Observational Study with Comparisons to U.S. Managers," *Journal of International Business Studies*, Fourth Quarter 1993, pp. 741–761.

15. Diane H. B. Welsh, Fred Luthans, and Steven M. Sommer, "Organizational Behavior Modification Goes to Russia: Replicating an Experimental Analysis across Cultures and Tasks," *Journal of Organizational Behavior Management*, vol. 13, no. 2, 1993, pp. 15–35; Diane H. B. Welsh, Fred Luthans, and Steven M. Sommer, "Managing Russian Factory Workers: The Impact of U.S.-Based Behavioral and Participative Techniques," *Academy of Management Journal*, February 1993, pp. 58–79.

16. Welsh, Luthans, and Sommer, "Organizational Behavior Modification," p. 31.

17. Steven M. Sommer, Seung-Hyun Bae, and Fred Luthans, "The Structure-Climate Relationship in Korean Organizations," *Asia Pacific Journal of Management*, vol. 12, no. 2, 1995, pp. 23–36. Also see Steven Sommer, Seung-Hyun Bae, and Fred Luthans, "Organizational Commitment across Cultures," *Human Relations*, vol. 49 (in press).

18. Sommer, Bae, and Luthans, "The Structure-Climate Relationship."

19. Trompenaars and Hampden-Turner, p. 196.

20. Shari Caudron, "Lessons for HR Overseas," *Personnel Journal*, February 1995, p. 92.

21. Richard M. Hodgetts and Fred Luthans, "U.S. Multinationals' Compensation Strategies for Local Management: Cross-Cultural Implications," *Compensation & Benefits Review*, March–April 1993, pp. 42–48.

22. Also see Randall S. Schuler and Nikolai Rogovsky, "Understanding Compensation Practice Variations across Firms: The Impact of National Culture," *Journal of International Business Studies*, First Quarter 1998, pp. 159–177.

23. Tara Parker-Pope, "Culture Clash," *The Wall Street Journal*, April 12, 1995, p. R7.

24. Rochelle Kopp, "International Human Resource Policies and Practices in Japanese, European, and United States Multinationals," *Human Resource Management*, Winter 1994, p. 590.

25. Philip M. Rosenzweig and Nitin Nohria, "Influences on Human Resource Management Practices in Multinational Corporations," *Journal of International Business Studies*, Second Quarter 1994, pp. 229–251.

26. Miki Tanikawa, "In Japan, Some Shun Lifetime Jobs to Chase Dreams," *New York Times*, June 25, 1995, p. F11.

27. Also see Richard W. Wright, "Trends in International Business Research: Twenty-Five Years Later," *Journal of International Business Studies*, Fourth Quarter 1994, pp. 687–701; Schon Beechler and John Zhuang Yang, "The Transfer of Japanese-Style Management to American Subsidiaries: Contingencies, Constraints, and Competencies," *Journal of International Business Studies*, Third Quarter 1994, pp. 467–491.

28. Eric W. K. Tsang, "Can *Guanxi* Be a Source of Sustained Competitive Advantage for Doing Business in China?" *Academy of Management Executive*, vol. 12, no. 2, 1998, p. 64.

29. Rosalie L. Tung, "Managing in Asia: Cross-Cultural Dimensions," in Pat Joynt and Malcolm Warner (eds.) *Managing across Cultures: Issues and Perspectives* (London: International Thomson Business Press, 1996), p. 239.

30. For more on this topic, see Philip R. Harris and Robert T. Moran, *Managing Cultural Differences*, 3rd ed. (Houston: Gulf Publishing, 1991), pp. 410–411.

31. William B. Snavely, Serguel Miassaoedov, and Kevin McNeilly, "Cross-Cultural Peculiarities of the Russian Entrepreneur: Adapting to the New Russians," *Business Horizons*, March–April 1998, pp. 10–13.

32. Ibid.

33. Ibid., p. 13.

34. John F. Burns, "Indian Politics Derail A Big Power Supply," *New York Times*, July 5, 1995, pp. C1, C4.

35. Adapted from Harris and Moran, *Managing Cultural Differences*, p. 447.

36. Jean-Louis Barsoux and Peter Lawrence, "The Making of a French Manager," *Harvard Business Review*, July–August 1991, pp. 58–67.

37. Adapted from Harris and Moran, *Managing Cultural Differences*, p. 471.

38. Changiz Pezeshkpur, "Challenges to Management in the Arab World," *Business Horizons*, August 1978, p. 50.

39. Adapted from Harris and Moran, *Managing Cultural Differences*, p. 503.

Chapter 7 Endnotes

1. Lisa Hoecklin, *Managing Cultural Differences* (Workingham, England: Addison-Wesley, 1995), p. 146.

2. Edgar Schein, *Organizational Culture and Leadership* (San Francisco: Jossey Bass, 1985), p. 9.

3. Fred Luthans, *Organizational Behavior*, 7th ed. (New York: McGraw-Hill, 1995), pp. 497–498.

4. In addition see W. Mathew Jeuchter, Caroline Fisher, and Randall J. Alford, "Five Conditions for High-Performance Cultures," *Training & Development Journal*, May 1998, pp. 63–67.

5. Greg Steinmetz and Matt Marshall, "How a Chemical Giant Goes about Becoming a Lot Less German," *The Wall Street Journal,* February 18, 1997, p. A18.

6. Hoecklin, *Managing Cultural Differences,* p. 145.

7. Andre Laurent, "The Cultural Diversity of Western Conceptions of Management," *International Studies of Management and Organization,* Spring–Summer 1983, pp. 75–96.

8. Nancy J. Adler, *International Dimensions of Organizational Behavior,* 2nd ed. (Boston: PWS-Kent Publishing, 1991), pp. 58–59.

9. Robert Frank and Thomas M. Burton, "Cross-Border Merger Results in Headaches for a Drug Company," *The Wall Street Journal,* February 4, 1997, p. A1.

10. Hoecklin, *Managing Cultural Differences,* p. 151.

11. Carla Rapoport and Justin Martin, "Retailers Go Global," *Fortune,* February 20, 1995, pp. 102–108.

12. Rita A. Numeroff and Michael N. Abrams, "Integrating Corporate Culture from International M&As," *HR Focus,* June 1998, p. 12.

13. See Maddy Janssens, Jeanne M. Brett, and Frank J. Smith, "Confirmatory Cross-Cultural Research: Testing the Viability of a Corporation-Wide Safety Policy," *Academy of Management Journal,* June 1995, pp. 364–382.

14. Richard Gibson and Matt Moffett, "Why You Won't Find any Egg McMuffins for Breakfast in Brazil," *The Wall Street Journal,* October 23, 1997, pp. A1, 8.

15. Ibid.

16. Fons Trompenaars, *Riding the Waves of Culture: Understanding Diversity in Global Business* (Burr Ridge, IL: Irwin, 1994), p. 156.

17. Ibid., p. 164.

18. Ibid., p. 167.

19. Ibid., p. 172.

20. Fons Trompenaars and Charles Hampden-Turner, *Riding the Waves of Culture: Understanding Diversity in Global Business,* 2nd ed. (New York: McGraw-Hill, 1998), p. 182.

21. Adler, *International Dimensions of Organizational Behavior,* p. 121.

22. Noboru Yoshimura and Philip Anderson, *Inside the Kaisha* (Boston: Harvard Business School Press, 1997).

23. Edmund L. Andrews, "Meet the Maverick of Japan, Inc." *New York Times,* October 12, 1995, pp. C1, 4.

24. Sheryl WuDunn, "Incubators of Creativity," *New York Times,* October 9, 1997, pp. C1, 21.

25. Adler, *International Dimensions of Organizational Behavior,* p. 132.

26. Adler, *International Dimensions of Organizational Behavior,* p. 137.

27. Wellford W. Wilms, Alan J. Hardcastle, and Deone M. Zell, "Cultural Transformation at NUMMI," *Sloan Management Review,* Fall 1994, p. 103.

28. Ibid., p. 111.

Chapter 8 Endnotes

1. See Lillian H. Chaney and Jeanette S. Martin, *Intercultural Business Communication* (Englewood Cliffs, NJ: Prentice-Hall, 1995), p. 102.

2. Paul R. Lawrence and Charalambos A. Vlachoutsicos, *Behind the Factory Walls: Decision Making in Soviet and U.S. Enterprises* (Cambridge, MA: Harvard University Press, 1990), p. 282. Also see James E. McLauchlin, "Communicating to a Diverse Europe," *Business Horizons,* January–February 1993, pp. 54–56.

3. See Fred Luthans, Dianne H. B. Welsh, and Stuart A. Rosenkrantz, "What Do Russian Managers Really Do? An Observational Study with Comparisons to U.S. Managers," *Journal of International Business Studies* 4th Quarter, 1993, pp. 741–761.; Fred Luthans, Richard Hodgetts, and Stuart A. Rosenkrantz, *Real Managers* (Cambridge, MA: Ballinger, 1988).

4. Richard Tanner Pascale, "Communication and Decision Making across Cultures: Japanese and American Comparisons," *Administration Science Quarterly,* March 1978, pp. 91–110.

5. Ibid., p. 103.

6. E. T. Hall and E. Hall, "How Cultures Collide," in G. R. Weaver (ed.) *Culture, Communication, and Conflict: Readings in Intercultural Relations* (Needham Heights, MA: Ginn Press, 1994).

7. Noboru Yoshimura and Philip Anderson, *Inside the Kaisha: Demystifying Japanese Business Behavior* (Boston: Harvard Business School Press, 1997), p. 59.

8. William C. Byham and George Dixon, "Through Japanese Eyes," *Training and Development Journal,* March 1993, pp. 33–36; Linda S. Dillon, "West Meets East," *Training and Development Journal,* March 1993, pp. 39–43.

9. Fons Trompenaars and Charles Hampden-Turner, *Riding the Waves of Culture: Understanding Diversity in Global Business,* 2nd ed. (New York: McGraw-Hill, 1998), p. 204.

10. Nancy J. Adler, *International Dimensions of Organizational Behavior,* 2nd ed. (Boston: PWS-Kent Publishing, 1991), pp. 75–76.

11. Giorgio Inzerilli, "The Legitimacy of Managerial Authority—A Comparative Study," *National Academy of Management Proceedings,* Detroit, 1980, pp. 58–62.

12. Ibid., p. 62.

13. Philip R. Harris and Robert T. Moran, *Managing Cultural Differences,* 3rd ed. (Houston: Gulf Publishing, 1996), pp. 36–37.

14. Richard Tanner Pascale and Anthony G. Athos, *The Art of Japanese Management* (New York: Warner Books, 1981) pp. 82–83.

15. Naoki Kameda, "Englishes' in Cross-Cultural Business Communication," *The Bulletin,* March 1992, p. 3.

16. See "Double or Quits," *Economist,* February 25, 1995, pp. 84–85.

17. Brock Stout, "Interviewing in Japan," *HR Magazine,* June 199, p. 73.

18. Ibid., p. 75.

19. H. W. Hildebrandt, "Communication Barriers between German Subsidiaries and Parent American Companies," *Michigan Business Review,* July 1973, p. 9.

20. John R. Schermerhorn, Jr., "Language Effects in Cross-Cultural Management Research: An Empirical Study and a Word of Caution," *National Academy of Management Proceedings,* 1987, p. 103.

21. Brenda R. Sims and Stephen Guice, "Differences between Business Letters from Native and Non-Native Speakers of English," *Journal of Business Communication,* Winter 1991, p. 37.

22. James Calvert Scott and Diana J. Green, "British Perspectives on Organizing Bad-News Letters: Organizational Patterns Used by Major U.K. Companies," *The Bulletin,* March 1992, p. 17.

23. Ibid., pp. 18–19.

24. Mi Young Park, W. Tracy Dillon, and Kenneth L. Mitchell, "Korean Business Letters: Strategies for Effective Complaints in Cross-Cultural Communication," *Journal of Business Communication,* July 1998, pp. 328–345.

25. Robert S. Greenberger, Bob Davis, and Kathy Chen, "Misperceptions Divide U.S. and China," *The Wall Street Journal,* July 14, 1995, p. A8.

26. Joseph Kahn, "Fraying U.S.-Sino Ties Threaten Business," *The Wall Street Journal,* July 7, 1995, p. A6; Nathaniel C. Nash, "China Gives Big Van Deal to Mercedes," *New York Times,* July 13, 1995, pp. C1, C5; and Seth Faison, "China Times a Business Deal to Make a Point to America," *New York Times,* July 16, 1995, pp. 1, 6.

27. David A. Ricks, *Big Business Blunders: Mistakes in Multinational Marketing* (Homewood, IL: Dow Jones-Irwin, 1983), p. 39.

28. Ibid., p. 55.

29. Edwin Miller, Bhal Bhatt, Raymond Hill, and Julian Cattaneo, "Leadership Attitudes of American and German Expatriate Managers in Europe and Latin America," *National Academy of Management Proceedings,* Detroit, 1980, pp. 53–57.

30. Abdul Rahim A. Al-Meer, "Attitudes Towards Women as Managers: A Comparison of Asians, Saudis and Westerners," *Arab Journal of the Social Sciences,* April 1988, pp. 139–149.

31. Sheryl WuDunn, "In Japan, Still Getting Tea and No Sympathy," *New York Times,* August 27, 1995, Section E, p. 3.

32. Fathi S. Yousef, "Cross-Cultural Communication: Aspects of the Contrastive Social Values between North Americans and Middle Easterners," *Human Organization,* Winter 1974, p. 385.

33. Ibid., p. 383.

34. See Roger E. Axtell (ed.), *Dos and Taboos around the World* (New York: Wiley, 1990), Chapter 2.

35. Jane Whitney Gibson, Richard M. Hodgetts, and Charles W. Blackwell, "Cultural Variations in Nonverbal Communication," *55th Annual Business Communication Proceedings,* San Antonio, November 8–10, 1990, pp. 211–229.

36. For more on proxemics, see Jane Whitney Gibson and Richard M. Hodgetts, *Organizational Communication: A Managerial Perspective,* 2nd ed. (New York: HarperCollins, 1991), pp. 124–129.

37. William K. Brandt and James M. Hulbert, "Patterns of Communications in the Multinational Corporation: An Empirical Study," *Journal of International Business Studies,* Spring 1976, pp. 57–64.

38. Hildebrandt, "Communication Barriers," pp. 13–14.

39. Ibid., p. 9.

40. Also see Linda Beamer, "Bridging Business Cultures," *China Business Review,* May/June 1998, pp. 54–58.

41. Kenichi Ohmae, "The Global Logic of Strategic Alliances," *Harvard Business Review,* March–April 1989, p. 154.

Chapter 9 Endnotes

1. Alex Taylor III, "How Toyota Defies Gravity," *Fortune,* December 9, 1997, p. 100.

2. Ibid., p. 106.

3. Trevor Merriden, "U.S. Investments in Europe," *Management Review,* July/August 1998, p. 26.

4. Fara Warner, "Ford Uses Aggressive Marketing Approach in Thailand," *The Wall Street Journal,* June 3, 1998, p. B4.

5. G. Bruce Knecht, "Bertelsmann Breaks through a Great Wall with Its Book Clubs," *The Wall Street Journal,* September 18, 1998, pp. A1, 6.

6. Gregory L. White, "Chrysler Makes Manufacturing Inroads at Plant in Brazil," *The Wall Street Journal,* August 13, 1998, p. B4.

7. Christopher Rhoades, "Low-Key GE Capital Expands in Europe," *The Wall Street Journal,* September 17, 1998, p. A18.

8. Anant R. Negandhi, *International Management* (Boston: Allyn & Bacon, 1987), p. 230.

9. James M. Hulbert and William K. Brandt, *Managing the Multinational Subsidiary* (New York: Holt, Rinehart and Winston, 1980), pp. 35–64.

10. Noel Capon, Chris Christodoulou, John U. Farley, and James Hulbert, "A Comparison of Corporate Planning Practice in American and Australian Manufacturing Companies," *Journal of International Business Studies,* Fall 1984, pp. 41–45.

11. Negandhi, *International Management,* pp. 235–236.

12. Martin K. Welge, "Planning in German Multinational Corporations," *International Studies of Management and Organization,* Spring 1982, pp. 6–37.

13. Martin K. Welge and Michael E. Kenter, "Impact of Planning on Control Effectiveness and Company Performance," *Management International Review,* vol. 20, no. 2, 1988, pp. 4–15.

14. See Rosalie L. Tung, "Strategic Management Thought in Eastern Asia," *Organizational Dynamics,* Spring 1994, pp. 55–65.

15. See for example Masaaki Kotabe, "Global Sourcing Strategy in the Pacific: American and Japanese Multinational Companies," in Michael R. Czinkota and Masaaki Kotabe (eds.) *Trends in International Business: Critical Perspectives* (Malden, MA: Blackwell Publishing, 1998), pp. 237–256.

16. Joan Magretta, "Fast, Global, and Entrepreneurial: Supply Chain Management, Hong Kong Style," *Harvard Business Review,* September–October 1998, p. 108.

17. Nikhil Deogun, "For Coke in India, Thums Up Is the Real Thing," *The Wall Street Journal,* April 29, 1998, pp. B1, 6.

18. Richard M. Hodgetts, *Measures of Quality and High Performance* (New York: American Management Association, 1998).

19. For more on this topic, see Richard J. Schonberger, "Total Quality Management Cuts a Broad Swath—Through Manufacturing and Beyond," *Organizational Dynamics,* Spring 1992, pp. 16–28.

20. Sang M. Lee, Fred Luthans, and Richard M. Hodgetts, "Total Quality Management: Implications for Central and Eastern Europe," *Organizational Dynamics,* Spring 1992, pp. 44–45.

21. Erik Calonius, "Smart Moves by Quality Champs," *Fortune,* Special Edition 1991, pp. 24–25.

22. Emily Tornton and Kathleen Kerwin, "Nissan Is Back in the Mud," *Business Week,* November 2, 1998, p. 56.

23. Quentin Hardy, "Motorola, Broadsided by the Digital Era, Struggles for a Footing," *The Wall Street Journal,* April 22, 1998, p. A1, 14.

24. Jonathan Friedland and Louise Lee, "The Wal-Mart Way Sometimes Gets Lost in Translation Overseas," *The Wall Street Journal,* October 8, 1997, p. A12.

25. Also see Stephen J. Kobrin, "Is There a Relationship Between a Geographic Mind-Set and Multinational Strategy?" *Journal of International Business Studies,* Third Quarter 1994, pp. 493–511.

26. For insights to global strategy, see George S. Yip, *Total Global Strategy* (Englewood Cliffs, NJ: Prentice-Hall, 1995), Chapter 1.

27. John Templeman et al., "How Mercedes Trumped Chrysler in China," *Business Week,* July 31, 1995, pp. 50–51.

28. Sea Jin Chang, "International Expansion Strategy of Japanese Firms: Capacity Building Through Sequential Entry," *Academy of Management Journal,* April 1995, p. 402.

29. David A. Andelman, "Merging across Borders," *Management Review,* June 1998, p. 45.

30. Jathon Sapsford, "Real-Estate Buyers Circle Japan," *The Wall Street Journal,* March 11, 1998, p. B10.

31. Craig Torres, "Foreigners Snap Up Mexican Companies: Impact Is Enormous," *The Wall Street Journal,* September 30, 1997, p. A1.

32. Peter Waldman, "India Seeks to Open Huge Phone Market," *The Wall Street Journal,* July 25, 1995, p. A9.

33. Miriam Jordan, "Indian Nationalists Pick the Next Targets," *The Wall Street Journal,* August 22, 1995, p. A7.

34. John Garland and Richard N. Farmer, *International Dimensions of Business Policy and Strategy* (Boston: Kent Publishing, 1986), pp. 62–63.

35. See Mariah E. de Forest, "Thinking of a Plant in Mexico?" *Academy of Management Executive,* February 1994, pp. 33–40.

36. Harry I. Chernotsky, "Selecting U.S. Sites: A Case Study of German and Japanese Firms," *Management International Review,* vol., 23, no. 2, 1983, pp. 45–55.

37. Ian Johnson, "China's Venture Ban Could Cost Foreign Firms," *The Wall Street Journal,* September 23, 1998, p. A14; and

Elisabeth Rosenthal, "U.S. Trade Official Says China Market Is Closed Tighter," *New York Times,* September 23, 1998, p. C2.

38. Youssef M. Ibrahim, "British Petroleum Is Buying Amoco in $48.2 Billion Deal," *New York Times,* August 12, 1998, pp. A1, C5; and Charles Goldsmith and Steven Lipin, "BP to Acquire Amoco in a Huge Deal Spurred by Falling Oil Prices," *The Wall Street Journal,* August 12, 1998, pp. A1, 8.

39. Keith Bradsher, "Industry's Giants Are Carving Up the World's Market," *New York Times,* May 8, 1998, pp. C1, 4; and Robyn Meredith, "A Joining of Opposites Could Help Customers," *New York Times,* May 8, 1998, p. C4.

40. Harry G. Barkema and Freek Vermeulen, "International Expansion through Start-up or Acquisition: A Learning Perspective," *Academy of Management Journal,* February 1998, pp. 7–26.

41. For additional insights to joint ventures see William Newburry and Yoram Zeira, "General Differences between Equity International Joint Ventures (EIJVs), International Acquisitions (IAs) and International Greenfield Investments (IGIs): Implications for Parent Companies," *Journal of World Business,* vol. 32, no. 2, 1997, pp. 87–102.

42. Also see David Lei, Robert A. Pitts, and John W. Slocum, Jr., "Building Cooperative Advantage: Managing Strategic Alliances to Promote Organizational Learning," *Journal of World Business,* vol. 32, no. 3, 1997, pp. 203–222.

43. For more on this see Ana Valdes Llaneza and Esteban Garcia-Canal, "Distinctive Features of Domestic and International Joint Ventures," *Management International Review,* vol. 38, no. 1, 1998, pp. 49–66.

44. David P. Hamilton, "Japanese Chip Makers May Team to Develop Production Methods," *The Wall Street Journal,* July 11, 1995, p. A12.

45. M. Tina Dacin, Edward Levitas, and Michael A. Hitt, "Selecting Partners for Successful International Alliances: Examination of U.S. and Korean Firms," *Journal of World Business,* vol. 32, no. 1, 1997, pp. 14–15.

46. Edith Hill Updike, "When in Japan, Do as the Germans Do," *Business Week,* July 3, 1995, p. 43.

Chapter 10 Endnotes

1. "Declining Passion," *Economist,* October 17, 1998, pp. 47–48.

2. Seth Faison, "China Applies Brakes on Move toward Market Economy," *New York Times,* September 30, 1998, p. C3.

3. Elisabeth Rosenthal, "U.S. Trade Official Says China Market Is Closed Tighter," *New York Times,* September 23, 1998, p. C2.

4. Betsy McKay, "Russia Considers Limiting Access to Foreign Currency," *The Wall Street Journal,* October 2, 1998, p. A12.

5. Jonathan Karp, "Indian's Legal System Bedevils Foreigners," *The Wall Street Journal,* July 11, 1997, p. A10.

6. Mark Landler, "Back to Vietnam, This Time to Build," *New York Times,* September 13, 1998, section 3, pp. 1, 11.

7. Dana Milbank and Marcus W. Brauchli, "How U.S. Concerns Compete in Countries Where Bribes Flourish," *The Wall Street Journal,* September 29, 1995, p. A1.

8. David E. Sanger, "U.S. Settles Trade Dispute, Averting Billions of Tariffs on Japanese Luxury Autos," *New York Times,* June 29, 1995, pp. A1, C4.

9. John Tagliabue, "For Japan Auto Makers, It's Tougher in Europe," *New York Times,* June 28, 1995, p. C4.

10. Chris Adams, "Ailing Steel Industry Launches a Battle against Imports," *The Wall Street Journal,* October 1, 1998, p. B4; and Chris Adams, "U.S. Steelmakers to File Trade Complaint," *The Wall Street Journal,* September 29, 1998, p. A2.

11. Joel Millman, "Club Medellin," *Forbes,* January 4, 1993, pp. 44–45.

12. David A. Schmidt, "Analyzing Political Risk," *Business Horizons,* July–August 1986, pp. 43–50.

13. Matthew Brzezinski, "Russia Kills Huge Oil Deal with Exxon," *The Wall Street Journal,* August 28, 1997, p. A2.

14. For more, see Thomas A. Pointer, "Political Risk: Managing Government Intervention," in Paul W. Beamish, J. Peter Killing, Donald J. LeCraw, and Harold Crookell (eds.), *International Management: Text and Cases* (Homewood, IL: Irwin, 1991), pp. 119–133.

15. Ann Gregory, "Firm Characteristics and Political Risk Reduction in Overseas Ventures," *National Academy of Management Proceedings,* 1982, pp. 73–77.

16. For more, see Richard Mead, *International Management: Cross-Cultural Dimensions* (Cambridge, MA: Blackwell Publishing, 1994), Chapter 10; Gary Bonvillian and William A. Nowlin, "Cultural Awareness: An Essential Element of Doing Business Abroad," *Business Horizons,* November–December 1994, pp. 44–50.

17. David K. Tse, June Francis, and Ian Walls, "Cultural Differences in Conducting Intra- and Inter-Cultural Negotiations: A Sino-Canadian Comparison," *Journal of International Business Studies,* Third Quarter 1994, pp. 537–555.

18. Also see Lillian H. Chaney and Jeanette S. Martin, *International Business Communication* (Englewood Cliffs, NJ: Prentice-Hall, 1995), pp. 203–204.

19. Nancy J. Adler, *International Dimensions of Organizational Behavior,* 2nd ed. (Boston: PWS-Kent Publishing, 1991), p. 197.

20. For more, see Kathleen Kelly Reardon and Robert E. Spekman, "Starting Out Right: Negotiation Lessons for Domestic and Cultural Business Alliances," *Business Horizons,* December 1994, pp. 71–79.

21. Arvind V. Phatak and Mohammed M. Habib, "The Dynamics of International Business Negotiations," *Business Horizons,* May–June, pp. 30–38.

22. Jeanne M. Brett, Debra L. Shapiro, and Anne L. Lytle, "Breaking the Bonds of Reciprocity in Negotiations," *Academy of Management Journal,* August 1998, pp. 410–424.

23. Stephen E. Weiss, "Negotiating with 'Romans'—Part 1," *Sloan Management Review,* Winter 1994, pp. 51–61.

24. Stephen E. Weiss, "Negotiating with 'Romans'—Part 2," *Sloan Management Review,* Spring 1994, p. 89.

25. Fons Trompenaars and Charles Hampden-Turner, *Riding the Waves of Culture: Understanding Diversity in Global Business,* 2nd ed. (New York: McGraw-Hill, 1998), p. 112.

26. For an interesting comparison of negotiating tactics in the Far East, see Rosalie L. Tung, "Handshakes across the Sea: Cross-Cultural Negotiating for Business Success," *Organizational Dynamics,* Winter 1991, pp. 30–40.

27. John L. Graham, "Brazilian, Japanese, and American Business Negotiations," *Journal of International Business Studies,* Spring/Summer 1983, pp. 47–61; John L. Graham, "The Influence of Culture on the Process of Business Negotiations in an Exploratory Study," *Journal of International Business Studies,* Spring 1983, pp. 81–96.

28. For more, see Adler, *Organizational Behavior,* pp. 204–209.

29. Graham, "Influence on Culture," pp. 84, 88.

Chapter 11 Endnotes

1. Christopher Rhoads, "A Contrarian Motorola Picks Germany," *The Wall Street Journal,* October 10, 1997, p. A18.

2. Craig S. Smith, "Motorola Expands Operations in China," *The Wall Street Journal,* June 12, 1998, p. A9

3. Quentin Hardy, "Motorola Readies Major Restructuring," *The Wall Street Journal,* March 31, 1998, pp. A3, 14.

4. Raju Narisetti, "Xerox to Cut 9,000 Jobs over Two Years," *The Wall Street Journal,* April 8, 1998, p. A3.

5. Joan Magretta, "Fast, Global, and Entrepreneurial: Supply Chain Management, Hong Kong Style," *Harvard Business Review,* September–October 1998, p. 106.

6. See George S. Yip, *Total Global Strategy* (Englewood Cliffs, NJ: Prentice-Hall, 1995), Chapter 8.

7. James Bennet, "Eurocars: On the Road Again," *New York Times,* August 20, 1995, Section 3, pp. 1, 10.

8. See Karen Lowry Miller, "Siemens Shapes Up," *Business Week,* May 1, 1995, pp. 52–53.

9. Valerie Reitman and Gabriella Stern, "Adapting a U.S. Car to Japanese Tastes," *The Wall Street Journal,* June 26, 1995, pp. B1, B6.

10. A. V. Phatak, *International Dimensions of Management* 2nd ed. (Boston: PWS-Kent, 1989), pp. 92–93.

11. Alan M. Rugman and Richard M. Hodgetts, *International Business* (New York: McGraw-Hill, 1995), p. 79.

12. Reported in Peter J. Dowling, Randall S. Schuler, and Denice E. Welch, *International Dimensions of Human Resource Management,* 2nd ed. (Belmont, CA: Wadsworth Publishing, 1994), p. 33.

13. "The Biggest Yet," *New York Times,* August 12, 1998, p. C5.

14. Thane Peterson, "A Breakthrough in Bavaria," *Business Week,* August 4, 1997, p. 54.

15. Milt Freudenheim, "Hoechst to Pay $7.1 Billion for Dow Unit," *New York Times,* May 5, 1995, pp. C1, C5.

16. Laxmi Nakarmi, Richard A. Melcher, and Edith Updike, "Will Lucky Goldstar Reach Its Peak with Zenith?" *Business Week,* August 7, 1995, p. 40.

17. Also see Andrew C. Inkpen and Adva Dinur, "Knowledge Management Processes and International Joint Ventures," *Organization Science,* July–August 1998, pp. 454–468.

18. Laxmi Nakarmi, Kevin Kelly, and Larry Armstrong, "Look Out World—Samsung Is Coming," *Business Week,* August 7, 1995, p. 53.

19. Seth Faison, "Morgan Stanley Establishes a Joint Venture in China," *New York Times,* August 12, 1995, p. 18.

20. For some insights regarding the importance of networking, see "The Battle for Ukraine," *Economist,* February 11, 1995, p. 56.

21. For an example of a venture in disarray, see Peter Galuszka and Susan Chandler, "A Plague of Disjointed Ventures," *Business Week,* May 1, 1995, p. 55.

22. Thomas W. Malone and Robert J. Laubacher, "The Dawn of the E-Lance Economy," *Harvard Business Review,* September–October 1998, p. 148.

23. For more on this see Michael Goold and Andrew Campbell, "Desperately Seeking Synergy," *Harvard Business Review,* September–October 1998, p. 133.

24. Ibid., p. 134.

25. Durward K. Sobek, II, Jeffrey K. Liker, and Allen C. Ward, "Another Look at How Toyota Integrates Product Development," *Harvard Business Review,* July–August 1998, p. 49.

26. For more on this see M. Bensaou and Michael Earl, "The Right Mind-set for Managing Information Technology," *Harvard Business Review,* September–October 1998, pp. 119–128.

27. Steven M. Sommers, Seung-Hyun Bae, and Fred Luthans, "The Structure-Climate Relationship in Korean Organizations," *Asia Pacific Journal of Management,* vol. 12, no. 2, 1995, pp. 23–36.

28. James R. Lincoln, Mitsuyo Hanada, and Kerry McBride, "Organizational Structures in Japanese and U.S. Manufacturing," *Administrative Science Quarterly,* September 1986, p. 356.

29. Rhy-song Yeh and Tagi Sagafi-nejad, "Organizational Characteristics of American and Japanese Firms in Taiwan," *National Academy of Management Proceedings,* 1987, pp. 111–115.

30. Ibid., p. 113.

31. Abbass F. Alkhafaji, *Competitive Global Management: Principles and Strategies* (Delray Beach, FL: St. Lucie Press, 1995), pp. 390–391.

32. Michael Yoshino and N. S. Rangan, *Strategic Alliances* (Boston: Harvard Business School Press, 1995), p. 195.

33. For additional insights, see Anant K. Sundaram and J. Stewart Black, *The International Business Environment: Text and Cases* (Englewood Cliffs, NJ: Prentice-Hall, 1995), pp. 314–315.

34. Lincoln, Hanada, and McBride, "Organizational Structures," p. 349.

35. Lincoln, Hanada, and McBride, "Organizational Structures," p. 355.

36. Masumi Tsuda, "The Future of the Organization and the Individual to Japanese Management," *International Studies of Management & Organization,* Fall–Winter 1985, pp. 89–125.

37. Yeh and Sagafi-nejad, "Organizational Characteristics," p. 113.

38. Also see Valerie Reitman, "Toyota Names a New Chief Likely to Shake Up Global Auto Business," *The Wall Street Journal,* August 11, 1995, pp. A1, A4.

39. Tsuda, "The Future of the Organization," p. 114.

Chapter 12 Endnotes

1. Joel Millman, "Mexico's Cemex Moves to Expand in Asia," *The Wall Street Journal,* September 29, 1997, p. A19.

2. Kathy Chen and Hilary Stout, "Boeing, GM Obtain China Agreements," *The Wall Street Journal,* March 25, 1997, p. A3.

3. Raghu Nath, *Comparative Management: A Regional View* (Cambridge, MA: Ballinger Publishing, 1988), p. 126.

4. Ibid., pp. 74–75.

5. Noboru Yoshimura and Philip Anderson, *Inside the* Kaisha (Boston: Harvard Business School Press, 1997), p. 44.

6. Anant R. Negandhi, *International Management* (Boston: Allyn & Bacon, 1987), p. 193.

7. Karen Lowrey Miller, "The *Mittelstand* Takes a Stand," *Business Week,* April 10, 1995, pp. 94–95.

8. Sang M. Lee, Fred Luthans, and Richard M. Hodgetts, "Total Quality Management: Implications for Central and Eastern Europe," *Organizational Dynamics,* Spring 1992, p. 45.

9. For additional insights into this area, see Jerry Flint, "The Myth of U.S. Manufacturing's Decline," *Forbes,* January 18, 1993, pp. 40–42.

10. Jerry Bowles, "Is American Management Really Committed to Quality?" *Management Review,* April 1992, pp. 44–45.

11. For more on this topic, see Richard J. Schonberger, "Total Quality Management Cuts a Broad Swath—through Manufacturing and Beyond," *Organizational Dynamics,* Winter 1992, p. 23.

12. Emily Thornton, "Mazda Learns to Like those intruders," *Business Week,* September 14, 1998, p. 172.

13. Joanne Lee-Young, "Starbucks' Expansion in China Is Slated," *The Wall Street Journal,* October 5, 1998, p. A27C.

14. "Vietnam Branch Status for Two U.S. Banks," *Financial Times,* November 11, 1994, p. 5.

15. Robyn Meredith, "The Brave New World of General Motors," *New York Times,* section 3, October 26, 1997, p. 1 and Brandon Mitchener, "GM Takes a Gamble on Eastern Europe," *The Wall Street Journal,* June 23, 1997, p. A10.

16. Rebecca Blumstein, "Cadillac Has Designs on Europe's Luxury Car Buyers," *The Wall Street Journal,* September 9, 1997, p. B1.

17. Peter Elstrom, "For Lucent, Hunting Season Is About to Begin," *Business Week,* September 21, 1998, p. 42.

18. Robert L. Simison, "New Dana Illustrates Reshaping of Auto Parts Business," *The Wall Street Journal,* September 2, 1997, p. B4.

19. For more on this system see Saul Hansell, "Is This the Factory of the Future?" *New York Times,* July 26, 1998, section 3, pp. 1, 12–13.

20. Fons Trompenaars and Charles Hampden-Turner, *Riding the Waves of Culture: Understanding Diversity in Global Business,* 2nd ed. (New York: McGraw-Hill, 1998), pp. 157–159.

21. Yves Doz and C. K. Prahalad, "Patterns of Strategic Control within Multinational Corporations," *Journal of International Studies,* Fall 1984, p. 55.

22. John D. Daniels and Jeffrey Arpan, "Comparative Home Country Influences on Management Practices Abroad," *Academy of Management Journal,* September 1972, p. 310. Also see Magoroh Maruyama, "Some Management Considerations in the Economic Reorganization of Eastern Europe," *Academy of Management Journal,* May 1990, pp. 90–91.

23. Jacques H. Horovitz, "Management Control in France, Great Britain and Germany," *Columbia Journal of World Business,* Summer 1978, pp. 17–18.

24. Ibid., p. 18.

25. William G. Egelhoff, "Patterns of Control in U.S., U.K., and European Multinational Corporations," *Journal of International Business Studies,* Fall 1984, p. 81.

26. Ibid., pp. 81–82.

27. M. Kreder and M. Zeller, "Control in German and U.S. Companies," *Management International Review,* vol. 28, no. 3, 1988, pp. 64–65.

28. Lane Daley, James Jiambalvo, Gary L. Sundem, and Yasumasa Kondo, "Attitudes toward Financial Control Systems in the United States and Japan," *Journal of International Business Studies,* Fall 1985, pp. 91–110.

29. Yoshimura and Anderson, *Inside the* Kaisha, p. 55.

30. Phatak, *International Dimensions of Management,* p. 154.

31. David A. Garvin, "Japanese Quality Management," *Columbia Journal of World Business,* Fall 1984, pp. 3–12.

32. Ibid., p. 6.

33. Cited in John Holusha, "Improving Quality, the Japanese Way," *New York Times,* July 20, 1988, p. 25.

34. "Key To Success: People, People, People," *Fortune,* October 27, 1997, p. 232.

35. Golpira Eshgi, "Nationality Bias and Performance Evaluations in Multinational Corporations," *National Academy of Management Proceedings,* 1985, p. 95.

36. Jeremiah Sullivan, Terukiho Suzuki, and Yasumasa Kondo, "Managerial Theories and the Performance Control Process in Japanese and American Work Groups," *National Academy of Management Proceedings,* 1985, pp. 98–102.

37. Ibid.

Chapter 13 Endnotes

1. Abbass F. Alkhafaji, *Competitive Global Management* (Delray Beach, FL: St. Lucie Press, 1995), p. 118.

2. Nancy L. Adler, *International Dimensions of Organizational Behavior,* 2nd ed. (Boston: PWS-Kent, 1991), p. 160.

3. Dianne H. B. Welsh, Fred Luthans, and Steven Sommer, "Managing Russian Factory Workers: The Impact of U.S.-Based Behavioral and Participative Techniques," *Academy of Management Journal,* February 1993, p. 75.

4. Andrew Sergeant and Stephen Frenkel, "Managing People in China: Perceptions of Expatriate Managers," *Journal of World Business,* vol. 33, no. 1., 1998, p. 21.

5. Stephanie Strom, "A Surprising Jump in Japanese Joblessness," *New York Times,* April 29, 1998, p. C3.

6. For a more detailed discussion, see Fred Luthans, *Organizational Behavior,* 8th ed. (Boston: Irwin/McGraw-Hill, 1998), Chapter 6.

7. A. H. Maslow, "A Theory of Human Motivation," *Psychological Review,* July 1943, pp. 390–396.

8. For more information on this topic, see Richard Mead, *International Management Cross-Cultural Dimensions* (Cambridge, MA: Blackwell Publishers, 1994), pp. 209–212.

9. See "In Europe, Cash Eases the Pain of Getting Fired," *Business Week,* March 16, 1992, p. 26; Stewart Toy et al., "Europe Gets in Shape by Pushing Out Pink Slips," *Business Week,* March 2, 1992, pp. 52–54; and Alan S. Blinder, "How Japan Puts the `Human' in Human Capital," *Business Week,* November 11, 1991, p. 22.

10. See Richard M. Hodgetts, *Modern Human Relations at Work,* 7th ed. (Hinsdale, IL: Dryden press, 1999), Chapter 2; and John Dobbs, "The Empowerment Environment," *Training and Development Journal,* March 1993, pp. 55–57.

11. Mason Haire, Edwin E. Ghiselli, and Lyman W. Porter, *Managerial Thinking: An International Study* (New York: John Wiley & Sons, 1966).

12. Ibid., p. 75.

13. Edwin C. Nevis, "Cultural Assumption and Productivity: The United States and China," *Sloan Management Review,* Spring 1983, pp. 17–29.

14. Geert H. Hofstede, "The Colors of Collars," *Columbia Journal of World Business,* September 1972, pp. 72–78.

15. Ibid., p. 72.

16. See Stephanie Strom, "Japan's New `Temp' Workers," *New York Times,* June 17, 1998, pp. 1–4.

17. George H. Hines, "Cross-Cultural Differences in Two-Factor Motivation Theory," *Journal of Applied Psychology,* December 1973, p. 376.

18. Donald D. White and Julio Leon, "The Two-Factor Theory: New Questions, New Answers," *National Academy of Management Proceedings,* 1976, p. 358.

19. D. Macarov, "Work Patterns and Satisfactions in an Israeli Kibbutz: A Test of the Herzberg Hypothesis," *Personnel Psychology,* Autumn 1972, p. 492.

20. Peter D. Machungwa and Neal Schmitt, "Work Motivation in a Developing Country," *Journal of Applied Psychology,* February 1983, pp. 31–42.

21. G. E. Popp, H. J. Davis, and T. T. Herbert, "An International Study of Intrinsic Motivation Composition," *Management International Review,* vol. 26, no. 3, 1986, pp. 28–35.

22. Also see Rabi S. Bhagat et al., "Cross-Cultural Issues in Organizational Psychology: Emergent Trends and Directions for Research in the 1990s," in C. L. Cooper and I. Robertson (eds.), *International Review of Industrial and Organizational Psychology* (New York: John Wiley & Sons, 1990), p. 76.

23. Rabindra N. Kanungo and Richard W. Wright, "A Cross-Cultural Comparative Study of Managerial Job Attitudes," *Journal of International Business Studies,* Fall 1983, pp. 115–129.

24. Ibid., pp. 127–128.

25. Fred Luthans, "A Paradigm Shift in Eastern Europe: Some Helpful Management Development Techniques," *Journal of Management Development,* vol. 12, no. 8, 1993, pp. 53–60.

26. For more information on the characteristics of high achievers, see David C. McClelland, "Business Drive and National Achievement," *Harvard Business Review,* July–August 1962, pp. 99–112.

27. For more detail on the achievement motive, see Luthans, *Organizational Behavior,* pp. 165–167.

28. Fred Luthans, Brooke R. Envick, and Mary F. Sully, "Characteristics of Successful Entrepreneurs: Do They Fit the Cultures of Developing Countries?" *Proceeding of the Pan Pacific Conference,* 1995, pp. 25–27.

29. For an earlier example of similar findings using sample groups of male Australian MBA candidates and University of California-Berkeley MBA candidates, see Theodore T. Herbert, Gary E. Popp, and Herbert J. Davis, "Australian Work-Reward Preferences," *National Academy of Management Proceedings,* 1979, pp. 289–292.

30. These data were reported in David C. McClelland, *The Achieving Society* (Princeton, NJ: Van Nostrand, 1961), p. 294.

31. E. J. Murray, *Motivation and Emotion* (Englewood Cliffs, NJ: Prentice-Hall, 1964), p. 101.

32. David J. Krus and Jane A. Rysberg, "Industrial Managers and N ach: Comparable and Compatible?" *Journal of Cross-Cultural Psychology,* December 1976, pp. 491–496.

33. For example, see Henry Grunwald, "New Challenges to Capitalism," *Fortune,* May 7, 1990, pp. 138–144; Shawn Tully, "What Eastern Europe Offers," *Fortune,* March 12, 1990, pp. 52–55.

34. See James McGregor, "China Wants Urban Workers to Purchase Their Homes, Abandoning Mao's Vision of Nearly Cost-Free Shelter," *The Wall Street Journal,* January 23, 1992, p. A13.

35. Oded Shenkar and Simcha Ronen, "Structure and Importance of Work Goals among Managers in the People's Republic of China," *Academy of Management Journal,* September 1987, pp. 564–576.

36. Chao C. Chen, "New Trends in Rewards Allocation Preferences: A Sino-U.S. Comparison," *Academy of Management Journal,* April 1995, p. 425.

37. Jean Lee and Havihn Chan, "Chinese Entrepreneurship: A Study in Singapore," *Journal of Management Development,* vol. 17, no. 2, 1998, p. 139.

38. Erik Guyot, Christina Mungan, and Richard Borsuk, "Streamlined Singapore Gives Hong Kong a Run for the Big Money," *The Wall Street Journal,* November 19, 1998, p. A19.

39. David C. McClelland, "Achievement Motivation Can Be Developed," *Harvard Business Review,* November–December 1965, p. 20.

40. Geert Hofstede, "Motivation, Leadership, and Organization: Do American Theories Apply Abroad?" *Organizational Dynamics,* Summer 1980, pp. 55–56.

41. For a systematic analysis of this and other myths of Japanese management, see Richard M. Hodgetts and Fred Luthans, "Japanese HR Management Practices," *Personnel,* April 1989, pp. 42–45.

42. "Japanese Employers Are 'Locking Out' Their U.S. Managers," *Business Week,* May 7, 1990, p. 24.

43. For more on this topic, see Noel M. Tichy and Thore Sandstrom, "Organizational Innovations in Sweden," *Columbia Journal of World Business,* Summer 1974, pp. 18–28; Fred Luthans, *Organizational Behavior,* 5th ed. (New York: McGraw-Hill, 1989), pp. 273–274.

44. Almar Latour, "Volvo Plans to Lay Off Workers," *The Wall Street Journal,* November 18, 1998, p. A17.

45. "Product Innovation Gains Worldwide Importance," *HR Focus,* March 1992, p. 12.

46. Eric Sundstrom, Kenneth P. DeMeuse, and David Futrell, "Work Teams: Application and Effectiveness," *American Psychologist,* February 1990, pp. 120–133.

47. Thomas A. Stewart, "The Search for the Organization of Tomorrow," *Fortune,* May 18, 1992, p. 95.

48. For some interesting insights on horizontal networking, see Larry Hirschhorn and Thomas Gilmore, "The New Boundaries of the 'Boundaryless' Company," *Harvard Business Review,* May–June 1992, pp. 104–115.

49. See, for example, Akio Morita, "Partnering for Competitiveness: The Role of Japanese Business," *Harvard Business Review,* May–June 1992, pp. 76–83.

50. See Lillian H. Chaney and Jeanette S. Martin, *Intercultural Business Communication* (Englewood Cliffs, NJ: Prentice-Hall, 1995), pp. 46–47.

51. Bhagat et al., "Cross-Cultural Issues," p. 72.

52. Stephanie Strom, "Japan's New 'Temp' Workers," *New York Times,* June 17, 1998, p. 4.

53. Tim W. Ferguson, "Japan's Buffeted Banks—and U.S. Opportunity: Long on Jobs," *The Wall Street Journal,* February 25, 1992, p. A15.

54. John Conston, "More Work, Less Play Is the Rule of the Day," *The Wall Street Journal,* February 14, 1992, p. A9.

55. Also see Christopher J. Chipello, "Japan's Quality of Life," *The Wall Street Journal,* January 28, 1992, p. A9.

56. Andrew Tanzer and Gale Eisenstodt, "Rich Country, Poor Japanese," *Forbes,* May 25, 1992, p. 45.

57. Urban C. Lehner, "Is It Any Surprise the Japanese Make Excellent Loafers?" *The Wall Street Journal,* February 28, 1992, pp. A1, A10.

58. "Stress Takes Toll on Japanese," *The Wall Street Journal,* February 4, 1992, p. A11.

59. Eamonn Fingleton, "Jobs for Life: Why Japan Won't Give Them Up," *Fortune,* March 20, 1995, pp. 119–125.

60. "Satisfaction in the USA, Unhappiness in Japanese Offices," *Personnel,* January 1992, p. 8.

61. Fred Luthans, Harriette S. McCaul, and Nancy G. Dodd, "Organizational Commitment: A Comparison of American, Japanese, and Korean Employees," *Academy of Management Journal,* March 1985, pp. 213–219.

62. For additional insights, see Abdul Rahim A. Al-Meer, "Organizational Commitment: A Comparison of Westerners, Asians, and Saudis," *International Studies of Management and Organization,* Summer 1989, pp. 74–84.

63. David I. Levine, "What Do Wages Buy?" *Administrative Science Quarterly,* September 1993, pp. 462–483.

64. David Heming, "What Wages Buy in the U.S. and Japan," *Academy of Management Executive,* November 1994, pp. 88–89.

65. Andrew Kakabadse and Andrew Myers, "Qualities of Top Management: Comparisons of European Manufacturers," *Journal of Management Development,* vol. 14, no. 1, 1995, p. 6.

66. Steven M. Sommer, Seung-Hyun Bae, and Fred Luthans, "Organizational Commitment across Cultures: The Impact of Antecedents on Korean Employees," *Human Relations,* 1996, vol. 49, no. 7, pp. 977–993.

67. Anders Tornvall, "Work-Values in Japan: Work and Work Motivation in a Comparative Setting," in Pat Joynt and Malcolm Warner, eds., *Managing across Cultures: Issues and Perspectives* (London: International Thomson Business Press, 1996), p. 256.

68. Fons Trompenaars and Charles Hampden-Turner, *Riding the Waves of Culture: Understanding Diversity in Global Business,* 2nd ed. (New York: McGraw-Hill, 1998), p. 74.

69. Ibid., p. 77.

Chapter 14 Endnotes

1. Richard M. Hodgetts, *Modern Human Relations at Work,* 7th ed. (Hinsdale, IL: Dryden Press, 1999), p. 255. Also see Daniel Goleman, "What Makes a Leader?" *Harvard Business Review* November–December 1998, pp. 93–102.

2. See Nancy J. Adler, *International Dimensions of Organizational Behavior,* 2nd ed. (Boston: PWS-Kent, 1991), pp. 147–152.

3. Douglas McGregor, *The Human Side of Enterprise* (New York: McGraw-Hill, 1960), pp. 33–34.

4. Ibid., pp. 47–48.

5. Adler, *International Dimensions of Organizational Behavior,* p. 150.

6. Sheila M. Puffer, Daniel J. McCarthy, and Alexander I. Naumov, "Russian Managers' Beliefs about Work: Beyond the Stereotypes," *Journal of World Business,* vol. 32, no. 3, 1997, pp. 258–276.

7. See John A. Byrne, "Jack: A Close-up Look at How America's #1 Manager Runs GE," *Business Week,* June 8, 1998, pp. 91–111.

8. Ibid.

9. See Rosemary Stewart, Jean-Louis Barsoux, Alfred Kieser, Hans-Dieter Ganter, and Peter Walgenbach, "A Comparison of British and German Managerial Roles, Perceptions, and Behaviour," in Pat Joynt and Malcolm Warner (eds.), *Managing across Cultures* (London: International Thomson Business Press, 1996), pp. 202–211; and Geert Hofstede, "Cultural Constraints in Management Theories," paper presented at the National Academy of Management, August 1992.

10. Karen Lowry Miller, "The Toughest Job in Europe," *Business Week,* October 9, 1995, pp. 52–53.

11. Ferdinand Protzman, "New Leadership for Volkswagen," *New York Times,* March 30, 1992, pp. C1–2. John Templeman, "A Hard U-Turn at VW," *Business Week,* March 15, 1993, p. 47.

12. Mason Haire, Edwin E. Ghiselli, and Lyman W. Porter, *Managerial Thinking: An International Study* (New York: John Wiley & Sons, 1996).

13. Ibid., p. 21.

14. James R. Lincoln, Mitsuyo Hanada, and Jon Olson, "Cultural Orientation and Individual Reactions to Organizations: A Study of Employees of Japanese-Owned Firms," *Administrative Science Quarterly,* March 1981, pp. 93–115; also see Karen Lowry Miller, "Land of the Rising Jobless," *Business Week,* January 11, 1993, p. 47.

15. Sangjin Yoo and Sang M. Lee, "Management Style and Practice of Korean Chaebols," *California Management Review,* Summer 1987, pp. 95–110.

16. Haire, Ghiselli, and Porter, *Managerial Thinking,* p. 29.

17. Noboru Yoshimura and Philip Anderson, *Inside the* Kaisha (Boston: Harvard University Press, 1997), p. 167.

18. Haire Ghiselli, and Porter, *Managerial Thinking,* p. 140.

19. Ibid., p. 157.

20. Also see "The Trouble with Excellence," *Economist,* July 4, 1998, p. 68.

21. For more on this topic, see Edgar H. Schein, "SMR Forum: Does Japanese Management Style Have a Message for American Managers?" *Sloan Management Review,* Fall 1981, p. 55–68.

22. Jeremiah J. Sullivan and Ikujiro Nonaka, "The Application of Organizational Learning Theory to Japanese and American Management," *Journal of International Business Studies,* Fall 1986, pp. 127–147.

23. Ibid., pp. 130–131.

24. Ibid. Also see Emily Thornton, "Japan's Struggle to Be Creative," *Fortune,* April 19, 1993, pp. 129–134.

25. Iyuji Misumi and Fumiyasu Seki, "Effects of Achievement Motivation on the Effectiveness of Leadership Patterns," *Administrative Science Quarterly,* March 1971, pp. 51–59.

26. David Woodruff et al., "Saturn," *Business Week,* August 17, 1992, pp. 88–89.

27. Brenton R. Schlender, "How Sony Keeps the Magic Going," *Fortune,* February 24, 1992, pp. 75–84, Rabi S. Bhagat et al., "Cross-Cultural Issues in Organizational Psychology: Emergent Trends and Directions for Research in the 1990s," in C. L. Cooper and I. Robertson (eds.), *International Review of Industrial and Organizational Psychology* (New York: John Wiley & Sons, 1990), p. 83.

28. Robert Neff and William J. Holstein, "The Harvard Man in Mitsubishi's Corner Office," *Business Week,* March 23, 1992, p. 50.

29. See Gary Hatzenstein, "Japanese Management Style beyond the Hype: What to Try, What to Toss," *Working Woman,* February 1991, pp. 49, 98–101.

30. Sang M. Lee, Sangjin Yoo, and Tosca M. Lee, "Korean Chaebols: Corporate Values and Strategies," *Organizational Dynamics,* Spring 1991, p. 41.

31. M. K. Badawy, "Managerial Attitudes and Need Orientations of Mid-Eastern Executives: An Empirical Cross-Cultural Analysis," *National Academy of Management Proceedings,* 1979, pp. 293–297.

32. Ibid., p. 297.

33. Abdulrahman, Al-Jafary and A. T. Hollingsworth, "An Exploratory Study of Management Practices in the Arabian Gulf Region," *Journal of International Business Studies,* Fall 1983, pp. 143–152.

34. Ibid.

35. Ibid., p. 146.

36. Haire, Ghiselli, and Porter, *Managerial Thinking,* p. 22.

37. Robert D. Meade, "An Experimental Study of Leadership in India," *Journal of Social Psychology,* June 1967, pp. 35–43.

38. Sudhir Kakar, "Authority Patterns and Subordinate Behavior in Indian Organizations," *Administrative Science Quarterly,* September 1971, pp. 298–307.

39. Bikki Jaggi, "Job Satisfaction and Leadership Style in Developing Countries: The Case of India," *International Journal of Contemporary Sociology,* October 1977, pp. 230–236.

40. Ibid., p. 233.

41. For more information on this topic, see Jai B. P. Sinha, "A Model of Effective Leadership Styles in India," *International Studies of Management & Organization,* Summer–Fall 1984, pp. 86–98.

42. Haire, Ghiselli, and Porter, *Managerial Thinking,* p. 22.

43. D. B. Stephens, "Cultural Variations in Leadership Style: A Methodological Experiment in Comparing Managers in the U.S. and Peruvian Textile Industries," *Management International Review,* vol. 21, no. 3, 1981, pp. 47–55.

44. Ibid., p. 54.

45. See Pete Engardio, Dexter Roberts, and Bruce Einhorne, "China's New Elite," *Business Week,* June 5, 1995, pp. 48–51.

46. Hodgetts, *Modern Human Relations at Work,* p. 276.

47. Bernard M. Bass, "Is There Universality in the Full Range Model of Leadership?" *International Journal of Public Administration,* vol. 16, no. 6, 1996, p. 731.

48. Ibid., pp. 741–742.

49. Ibid., p. 731.

50. For additional insights to recent research by Bass and his associates, see Bruce J. Avolio and Bernard M. Bass, "You Can Drag a Horse to Water but You Can't Make It Drink Unless It Is Thirsty," *Journal of Leadership Studies,* Winter 1998, pp. 4–17.

51. Bass, "Is There Universality in the Full Range Model of Leadership?" pp. 754–755.

52. Ingrid Tollgertd-Andersson, "Attitudes, Values and Demands on Leadership—A Cultural Comparison Among Some European Countries," in Pat Joynt and Malcolm Warner (eds.), *Managing*

across Cultures (London: International Thomson Business Press, 1996), p. 172.

53.   Ibid., p. 176.

Chapter 15 Endnotes

1.   Also see Kenneth Groh and Mark Allen, "Global Staffing: Are Expatriates the Only Answer?" *HR Focus,* March 1998, pp. S1–2.

2.   Rosalie L. Tung, "Selection and Training Procedures of U.S., European and Japanese Multinationals," *California Management Review,* Fall 1982, p. 59.

3.   Ingemar Torbiorn, "Operative and Strategic Use of Expatriates in New Organizations and Market Structures," *International Studies of Management & Organization,* vol. 24, no. 3, 1994, pp. 5–17.

4.   Arvind V. Phatak, *International Dimensions of Management,* 2nd ed. (Boston: PWS-Kent Publishing, 1989), p. 106.

5.   Paul W. Beamish and Andrew C. Inkpen, "Japanese Firms and the Decline of the Japanese Expatriate," *Journal of World Business,* vol. 33, no. 1, 1998, pp. 35–50.

6.   Ibid., pp. 44–45.

7.   Also see Jan Selmer, Inn-Lee Kang, and Robert P. Wright, "Managerial Behavior of Expatriate versus Local Bosses," *International Studies of Management & Organization,* vol. 24, no. 3, 1994, pp. 48–63.

8.   Lawrence G. Franco, "Who Manages Multinational Enterprises?" *Columbia Journal of World Business,* Summer 1973, pp. 30–42.

9.   See Charles M. Vance and Peter Smith Ring, "Preparing the Host Country Workforce for Expatriate Managers: The Neglected Other Side of the Coin," *Human Resource Development Quarterly,* Winter 1994, pp. 337–352.

10.   H. Scullion, "Strategic Recruitment and Development of the 'International Manager,'" *Human Resource Management Journal,* vol. 3, no. 1, 1992, pp. 57–69.

11.   Tung, "Selection and Training Procedures," pp. 61–62.

12.   See Oded Shenkar and Mee-Kau Nyaw, "The Interplay of Human Resources in Chinese-Foreign Ventures," in Oded Shenkar, *Global Perspectives of Human Resource Management* (Englewood Cliffs, NJ: Prentice-Hall, 1995), pp. 280–285.

13.   Tung, "Selection and Training Procedures," pp. 61–62.

14.   Phatak, *International Dimension of Management,* p. 107.

15.   Franco, "Who Manages Multinational Enterprises?" p. 33.

16.   Jennifer J. Laabs, "The Global Talent Search," *Personnel Journal,* August 1991, pp. 38–40; Richard M. Hodgetts and Fred Luthans, "U.S. Multinationals' Expatriate Compensation Strategies," *Compensation and Benefits Review,* January–February 1993, pp. 57–62.

17.   Calvin Reynolds, "Strategic Employment of Third Country Nationals," *HR Planning,* vol. 20, no. 1, 1997, p. 38.

18.   Michael G. Harvey and M. Ronald Buckley, "Managing Inpatriates: Building a Global Core Competency," *Journal of World Business,* vol. 32, no. 1, 1997, p. 36.

19.   Jennifer Smith, "Southeast Asia's Search for Managers," *Management Review,* March 1998, p. 9.

20.   Michael Selz, "For Many Small Firms, Going Abroad Is No Vacation," *The Wall Street Journal,* February 27, 1992, p. B2; David C. Bangert and Jozsef Poor," Human Resource Management in Foreign Affiliates in Hungary," in Oded Shenkar (ed.), *Global Perspectives of Human Resource Management* (Englewood Cliffs, NJ: Prentice-Hall, 1995), pp. 258–266.

21.   A. Haslberger and L. K. Strok, "Development and Selection of Multinational Expatriates," *Human Resource Development Quarterly,* Autumn 1992, pp. 287–293.

22.   Lisa Hoecklin, *Managing Cultural Differences* (Workingham, England: Addison-Wesley, 1994), p. 124.

23.   Winfred Arthur, Jr. and Winston Bennett, Jr., "The International Assignee: The Relative Importance of Factors Perceived to Contribute to Success," *Personnel Psychology,* Spring 1995, pp. 99–114.

24.   Rosalie L. Tung, "U.S. Multinationals: A Study of Their Selection and Training Procedures for Overseas Assignments," *National Academy of Management Proceedings,* Atlanta, 1979, pp. 298–299.

25.   Rosalie L. Tung, "Human Resource Planning in Japanese Multinationals: A Model for U.S. Firms?" *Journal of International Business Studies,* Fall 1984, p. 141.

26.   Indrei Ratiu, "Thinking Internationally: A Comparison of How International Executives Learn," *International Studies of Management & Organization,* Spring–Summer 1983, pp. 139–150.

27.   Nancy J. Adler, *International Dimensions of Organizational Behavior,* 2nd ed. (Boston: PWS-Kent Publishing, 1991), pp. 228–229.

28.   Ingemar Torbiorn, *Living Abroad* (New York: John Wiley, 1982), pp. 100–101.

29.   Jeffrey L. Blue and Ulric Haynes, Jr., "Preparation for the Overseas Assignment," *Business Horizons,* June 1977, p. 63.

30.   Ibid., p. 65.

31.   Jean E. Heller, "Criteria for Selecting an International Manager," *Personnel,* May–June 1980, p. 50.

32.   Torbiorn, *Living Abroad,* p. 128.

33.   Blue and Haynes, "Preparation for the Overseas Assignment," p. 64.

34.   The survey was conducted by executive recruiters for Korn-Ferry International and the Columbia Business School. Excerpts were reported in "Report: Shortage of Executives Will Hurt U.S.," *Omaha World Herald,* June 25, 1989, p. 1G.

35.   Rosalie L. Tung, "Expatriate Assignments: Enhancing Success and Minimizing Failure," *Academy of Management Executive,* May 1987, p. 117.

36.   Rosalie Tung, "A Study of the Expatriation/Repatriation Process," A report prepared under the auspices of Arthur Andersen, 1997, p. 6.

37.   Patricia C. Borstorff, Stanley G. Harris, Hubert S. Field, and William F. Giles, "Who'll Go? A Review of Factors Associated with Employee Willingness to Work Overseas," *Human Resource Planning,* vol. 20, no. 3, 1997, p. 38.

38.   See Betty Jane Punnett, "Towards Effective Management of Expatriate Spouses," *Journal of World Business,* vol. 33, no. 3, 1997, pp. 243–256.

39.   Howard Tu and Sherry E. Sullivan, "Preparing Yourself for an International Assignment," *Business Horizons,* January–February 1994, p. 68.

40.   Ibid.

41.   James C. Baker and John M. Ivancevich, "The Assignment of American Executives Abroad: Systematic, Haphazard or Chaotic?" *California Management Review,* Spring 1971, p. 41.

42.   Ibid.

43.   Tung, "Selection and Training Procedures," p. 64.

44.   Heller, "Criteria for Selecting an International Manager," p. 53.

45.   Tung, "Selection and Training Procedures," p. 65.

46.   This section is based on J. Stewart Black, Mark Mendenhall, and Gary Oddou, "Toward a Comprehensive Model of International Adjustment: An Integration of Multiple Theoretical Perspectives," *Academy of Management Review,* April 1991, pp. 291–317.

47.   Iain McCormick and Tony Chapman, "Executive Relocation: Personal and Organizational Tactics," in Pat Joynt and Malcolm Warner (eds.), *Managing across Cultures: Issues and Perspectives* (London: International Thomson Business Press, 1996), pp. 326–337.

48. Calvin Reynolds, "Expatriate Compensation in Historical Perspective," *Journal of World Business,* vol. 32, no. 2, 1997, p. 127.

49. Elaine K. Bailey, "International Compensation," in Oded Shenkar (ed.), *Global Perspectives of Human Resource* (Englewood Cliffs, NJ: Prentice-Hall, 1995), p. 148.

50. See Hodgetts and Luthans, *Compensation & Benefits Review,* pp. 58–59.

51. Geoffrey W. Latta, "Expatriate Incentives: Beyond Tradition," *HR Focus,* March 1998, p. S4.

52. Also see "Income Tax, 1998," *Economist,* April 4, 1998, p. 113.

53. Eamonn Fingleton, "Jobs For Life: Why Japan Won't Give Them Up," *Fortune,* March 20, 1995, p. 122.

54. Greg Steinmetz and Gregory L. White, "Chrysler Pay Draws Fire Overseas," *The Wall Street Journal,* May 26, 1998, p. B1.

55. "Bonus Points," *Economist,* April 15, 1995, pp. 71–72.

56. See Dennis R. Briscoe, *International Human Resource Management* (Englewood Cliffs, NJ: Prentice-Hall, 1995), pp. 111-120.

57. Charlene Marmer Solomon, "Global Compensation: Learn the ABCs," *Personnel Journal,* July 1995, pp. 70–76.

58. Jacob M. Schlesinger, "A U.S. Professor Takes an Unusual Course-In a Japanese Factory," *The Wall Street Journal,* March 30, 1992, pp. A1, 5.

59. David Sirota and J. Michael Greenwood, "Understand Your Overseas Workforce," *Harvard Business Review,* January–February 1971, pp. 53–60.

60. Ibid., pp. 59–60.

61. Edwin L. Miller and Joseph L. C. Cheng, "Circumstances That Influenced the Decision to Accept an Overseas Assignment," *National Academy of Management Proceedings,* Kansas City, 1976, pp. 336–429; Edwin L. Miller and Joseph L. C. Cheng, "A Closer Look at the Decision to Accept an Overseas Position," *Management International Review,* vol. 18, no. 3, 1978, pp. 25–33.

62. Torbiorn, *Living Abroad,* p. 127.

63. Y. Zeira and M. Banai, "Attitudes of Host-Country Organization toward MNCs' Staffing Policies: A Cross-Country and Cross-Industry Analysis," *Management International Review,* vol. 21, no. 2, 1981, pp. 38–47.

64. Also see Anders Edstrom and Jay Galbraith, "Alternatives Policies for International Transfers of Managers," *Management International Review,* vol. 34, Special Issue, 1994, pp. 71–82.

65. Torbiorn, *Living Abroad,* p. 41.

66. Zeira and Banai, "Selection of Expatriate Managers," p. 34.

67. John S. McClenahan, "The Overseas Manager: Not Actually a World Away," *Industry Week,* November 1, 1976, p. 53.

68. Adler, *International Dimensions of Organizational Behavior,* p. 236.

69. Rosalie L. Tung, "Career Issues in International Assignments," *The Academy of Management Executive,* August 1988, p. 242.

70. J. Stewart Black, "Coming Home: The Relationship of Expatriate Expectations with Repatriate Adjustment and Job Performance," *Human Relations,* vol. 45, no. 2, 1992, p. 188.

71. Phatak, *International Dimensions of Management,* p. 126.

72. Tung, "Career Issues in International Assignments," p. 243.

73. Nancy K. Napier and Richard B. Peterson, "Expatriate Reentry: What Do Expatriates Have to Say?" *Human Resource Planning,* vol. 14, no. 1, 1991, pp. 19–28.

74. Charlene Marmer Solomon, "Repatriation: Up, Down or Out?" *Personnel Journal,* January 1995, p. 32.

75. Mitchell R. Hammer, William Hart, and Randall Rogan, "Can You Go Home Again? An Analysis of the Repatriation of Corporate Managers and Spouses," *Management International Review,* vol. 38, no. 1, 1998, p. 81.

Chapter 16 Endnotes

1. Karen Roberts, Ellen Ernst Kossek, and Cynthia Ozeki, "Managing the Global Workforce: Challenges and Strategies," *Academy of Management Executive,* November 1998, pp. 93–106.

2. See Barbara Kres Beach, "The Canadians Are Training, The Canadians Are Training," *Training and Development Journal,* February 1998, pp. 38–39.

3. Lennie Copeland, "Making Costs Count in International Travel," *Personnel Administrator,* July 1984, p. 47.

4. Robert C. Maddox and Douglas Short, "The Cultural Integrator," *Business Horizons,* November–December 1988, pp. 57–59.

5. Kerr Inkson, Michael B. Arthur, Judith Pringle, and Sean Barry, "Expatriate Assignment Versus Overseas Experience: Contrasting Models of International Human Resource Development," *Journal of World Business,* vol. 32, no. 4, 1997, pp. 351–368.

6. Michael Hickins, "Creating a Global Team," *Management Review,* September 1998, p. 6.

7. Charlene Marmer Solomon, "Global Operations Demand that HR Rethink Diversity," *Personnel Journal,* July 1994, p. 50.

8. Paul R. Sparrow and Pawan S. Budhwar, "Competition and Change: Mapping the Indian HRM Recipe Against Worldwide Patterns," *Journal of World Business,* vol. 32, no. 3, 1997, p. 231.

9. Bodil Jones, "What Future European Recruits Want," *Management Review,* January 1998, p. 6.

10. See Paul R. Sparrow and Jean-Marie Hiltrop, "Redefining the Field of European Human Resource Management: A Battle between National Mindsets and Forces of Business Transition," *Human Resource Management,* Summer 1997, pp. 201–219.

11. Filiz Tabak, Janet Stern Solomon, and Christine Nielsen, "Managerial Success: A Profile of Future Managers in China," *SAM Advanced Management Journal,* Autumn 1998, pp. 18–26.

12. Also see Allan Bird, Sully Taylor, and Schon Beechler, "A Typology of International Human Resource Management in Japanese Multinational Corporations: Organizational Implications," *Human Resource Management,* Summer 1998, pp. 159–176.

13. Fred Luthans, *Organizational Behavior,* 8th ed. (New York: McGraw-Hill, 1998), Chapter 8.

14. Noel M. Tichy and Eli Cohen, "The Teaching Organization," *Training and Development Journal,* July 1998, p. 27.

15. Ibid., p. 28.

16. Fred Luthans, Alex Stajkovic, Brett C. Luthans, and Kyle W. Luthans, "Applying Behavior Management in Eastern Europe," *European Management Journal,* vol. 16, no. 4, 1998, pp. 466–475.

17. J. Hayes and C. W. Allinson, "Cultural Differences in the Learning Styles of Managers," *Management International Review,* vol. 28, no. 3, 1988. p. 76.

18. Ibid., p. 79.

19. Ibid., pp. 75–80.

20. Ibid., p. 79.

21. Also see Joel Cutcher-Gershenfeld et al., "Japanese Team-Based Work Systems in North America: Explaining the Diversity," *California Management Review,* Fall 1994, pp. 42–64.

22. See Kalburgi M. Srinivas, "Globalization of Business and the Third World," *Journal of Management Development,* vol. 14, no. 3, 1995, pp. 44–46; Donna L. Wiley, "Developing Managers in the Former Soviet Union," *International Studies of Management & Organization,* vol. 24, no. 4, 1994, pp. 64–82.

23. John R. Schermerhorn, "Intercultural Management Training: An Interview with Asma Abdullah," *Journal of Management Development,* vol. 13, no. 3, 1994, pp. 60–61.

24. See for example, Jennifer Smith, "Southeast Asia's Search for Managers," *Management Review,* June 1998, p. 9.

25. Also see Schon Beechler and John Zhuang Yang, "The Transfer of Japanese-Style Management to American Subsidiaries: Contingencies, Constraints, and Competencies," *Journal of International Business Studies,* Third Quarter 1994, pp. 467–491.

26. Allan Bird and Schon Beechler, "Links Between Business Strategy and Human Resource Management Strategy in U.S.-Based Japanese Subsidiaries: An Empirical Investigation," *Journal of International Business Studies,* First Quarter 1995, p. 40.

27. Linda K. Stroh and Paula M. Caligiuri, "Increasing Global Competitiveness through Effective People Management," *Journal of World Business,* vol. 33, no. 1, 1998, p. 10.

28. Phillip C. Wright, "The Expatriate Family Firm and Cross-Cultural Management Training: A Conceptual Framework," *Human Resource Development Quarterly,* vol. 5, no. 2, 1994, pp. 153–167.

29. Yoram Zeira and Ehud Harari, "Host-Country Organizations and Expatriate Managers in Europe," *California Management Review,* Spring 1979, p. 42.

30. For more on this, see Tomoko Yoshida and Richard W. Breslin, "Intercultural Skills and Recommended Behaviors," in Oded Shenkar (ed.), *Global Perspectives of Human Resource Management* (Englewood Cliffs, NJ: Prentice-Hall, 1995), pp. 112–131.

31. Alan M. Barrett, "Training and Development of Expatriates and Home Country Nationals," in Oded Shenkar, *Global Perspectives of Human Resource Management* (Englewood Cliffs, NJ: Prentice-Hall, 1995), p. 135.

32. Zeira and Harari, "Host-Country Organizations," p. 43.

33. Also see Clinton O. Longenecker and Serguei Popovski, "Managerial Trials of Privatization: Retooling Russian Managers," *Business Horizons,* November–December 1994, pp. 35–43.

34. For more on this topic, see Ehud Harari and Yoram Zeira, "Training Expatriates for Managerial Assignments in Japan," *California Management Review,* Summer 1978, pp. 56–62.

35. Yukimo Ono, "Japanese Firms Don't Let Masters Rule," *The Wall Street Journal,* May 4, 1992, p. B1.

36. See also Stalislav Shekshnia, "Western Multinationals' Human Resource Practices in Russia," *European Management Journal,* August 1998, pp. 460–465.

37. Karen J. Lindberg, "The Intricacies of Training and Development in Japan," *Human Resource Development Quarterly,* vol. 2, no. 2, 1991, pp. 101–114; Sam Stern, "Invited Reaction: Training and Development in Japan—the Basis for Relationships," *Human Resource Development Quarterly,* vol. 2, no. 2, 1991, pp. 115–120.

38. Also see C. B. Derr and G. Oddou, "Internationalizing Managers: Speeding Up the Process," *European Management Journal,* December 1993, pp. 435–441.

39. Robert Cyr, "Client Relations in Japan," *Training and Development Journal,* September 1990, pp. 83–85.

40. See Andrew Sergeant and Stephen Frenkel, "Managing People in China: Perceptions of Expatriate Managers," *Journal of World Business,* vol. 33, no. 1, 1998, pp. 17–34.

41. Rosalie L. Tung, "Selection and Training Procedures of U.S., European, and Japanese Multinationals," *California Management Review,* Fall 1982, p. 65.

42. Ibid., pp. 66–67.

43. Michael J. Marquardt and Dean W. Engel, *Global Human Resource Management* (Englewood Cliffs, NJ: Prentice-Hall, 1995), p. 44.

44. Ibid.

45. Cynthia L. Kemper, "Global Training's Critical Success Factors," *Training and Development Journal,* February 1998, p. 37.

46. Fred E. Fiedler, Terence Mitchell, and Harry C. Triandis, "The Culture Assimilator: An Approach to Cross-Cultural Training," *Journal of Applied Psychology,* April 1971, p. 95.

47. Ibid., p. 97.

48. Peter J. Dowling, Randall S. Schuler, and Denice E. Welch, *Human Resource Management,* 2nd ed. (Belmont, CA: Wadsworth Publishing Company, 1994), p. 134.

49. L. J. Bourgeois III and Manuel Boltvinik, "OD in Cross-Cultural Settings: Latin America," *California Management Review,* Spring 1981, p. 77.

50. Geert Hofstede, "The Cultural Relativity of Organizational Practices and Theories," *Journal of International Business Studies,* Fall 1983, p. 84.

51. Alfred M. Jaeger, "The Applicability of Organization Development Overseas: Reality or Myth?" *National Academy of Management Proceedings,* Boston, August 12–15, 1984, p. 95–104.

52. Alfred M. Jaeger, "Organization Development and National Culture: Where's the Fit?" *Academy of Management Review,* January 1986, p. 185.

53. Alfred M. Jaeger, "The Appropriateness of Organization Development outside North America," *International Studies of Management & Organization,* Spring 1984, p. 32.

54. Bourgeois and Boltvinik, "OD in Cross-Cultural Settings," p. 80.

55. A. D. Stajkovic and F. Luthans, "A Meta-Analysis of the Effects of Organizational Behavior Modification on Task Performance, 1975–1995," *Academy of Management Journal,* vol. 40, 1997, pp. 1122–1141.

56. Dianne H. B. Welsh, Fred Luthans, and Steven Sommer, "Managing Russian Factory Workers: The Impact of U.S.-Based Behavioral and Participative Techniques," *Academy of Management Journal,* February 1993, p. 74.

57. Fred Luthans, Richard M. Hodgetts, and Brett C. Luthans, "The Role of HRM in Sustaining Competitive Advantage into the 21st Century," *National Productivity Review,* Winter 1997, pp. 73–81.

58. Noel M. Tichy, "Global Development," in Vladimir Pucik, Noel M. Tichy, and Carole K. Barnett (eds.), *Globalizing Management* (New York: John Wiley, 1993), pp. 206–224.

59. Ibid., p. 219.

Chapter 17 Endnotes

1. See "Getting Their Dues," *Economist,* March 25, 1995, pp. 68, 73.

2. See Fred Luthans and Richard M. Hodgetts, *Business Today: Functions and Challenges* (Houston, TX: Dame Publishing, 1995), p. 218.

3. Dennis R. Briscoe, *International Human Resource Management* (Englewood Cliffs, NJ: Prentice-Hall, 1995), p. 159.

4. Jeffrey P. Kotz and Stanley W. Elsea, "A Framework for Assessing International Labor Relations: What Every Human Resource Manager Needs to Know," *Human Resource Planning,* 1997, vol. 20, no. 4, p. 22.

5. Keith Atkinson, "State of the Unions," *Personnel Administrator,* September 1986, p. 58.

6. Andreas Breitnerfellner, "Global Unionism: A Potential Player," *International Labor Review,* Winter 1997, pp. 531–555.

7. Wolfgang Scholl, "Codetermination and the Ability of Firms to Act in the Federal Republic of Germany," *International Studies of Management & Organization,* Summer 1987, pp. 27–37.

8. Karen Lowry Miller, "A Secret Weapon for German Reform," *Business Week,* October 12, 1998, p. 138.

9. See Irene Hall-Siu Chow and Oded Shenkar, "HR Practices in the People's Republic of China," *Personnel,* December 1989, pp. 41–47.

10. Peter J. Dowling, Randall S. Schuler, and Denise E. Welch, *International Dimensions of Human Resource Management,* 2nd ed. (Belmont, CA: Wadsworth, 1994), pp. 198.

11. Robert Grosse and Duane Kujawa, *International Business: Theory and Managerial Applications* (Homewood, IL: Irwin, 1988), p. 447.

12. For more on this see John Tagliabue, "Buona Notte, Guten Tag: Europe's New Workdays," *New York Times,* November 12, 1997, section C, pp. 1, 6.

13. "Europe Hits a Brick Wall," *Economist,* April 5, 1997, p. 22.

14. For more on this see John Tagliabue, "Continental Divide," *New York Times,* April 10, 1997, section C, pp. 1, 28.

15. Edmund L. Andrews, "Only Employment for Many in Europe Is Part-Time Work," *New York Times,* September 1, 1997, pp. A1, B7.

16. Chris Brewster, Lesley Mayne, and Olga Tregaskis, "Flexible Working in Europe," *Journal of World Business,* vol. 32, no. 2, 1997, p. 138.

17. Ibid., pp. 141–142.

18. Ibid., pp. 133–151.

19. Helene Cooper and Thomas Kamm, "Much of Europe Eases Its Rigid Labor Laws, and Temps Proliferate," *The Wall Street Journal,* June 4, 1998, p. A6.

20. Brewster, Mayne, and Tregaskis, pp. 143–144.

21. Reported in Dowling, Schuler, and Welch, *International Dimensions,* p. 188.

22. Malcolm Warner and Riccardo Peccei, "Worker-Participation and Multinational Companies," *Management International Review,* Special Issue 1994, p. 84.

23. Grosse and Kujawa, *International Business,* pp. 463–464.

24. Also see "Global Risk," *Business Week,* October 12, 1998, pp. 113–125.

25. Rosabeth Moss Kanter, "Change Is Everyone's Business: Managing the Extended Enterprise in a Globally Connected World," *Organizational Dynamics,* Summer 1999, in press.

26. Akio Morita, "Partnering for Competitiveness: The Role of Japanese Business," *Harvard Business Review,* May–June 1992, p. 78.

27. See "The Auto Baron," *Business Week,* November 16, 1998, pp. 82–90.

28. Jeremiah J. Sullivan and Richard B. Peterson, "A Test of Theories Underlying the Japanese Lifetime Employment System," *Journal of International Business Studies,* First Quarter 1991, p. 79.

29. See for example, "America vs. The New Europe," *Fortune,* December 21, 1998, pp. 149–156.

30. Robert Neff, "Fixing Japan," *Business Week,* March 29, 1993, pp. 68–74.

31. J. Bernard Keys, Luther Trey Denton, and Thomas R. Miller, "The Japanese Management Theory Jungle—Revisited," *Journal of Management,* vol. 20, no. 2, 1994, pp. 373–402.

32. For some interesting insights see "The Top 25 Top Executives of the Year," *Business Week,* January 11, 1999, pp. 58–84.

33. See Thomson A. Stewart, "Toward the Century of Quality: A Conversation with Joseph Juran," *Fortune,* January 11, 1999, pp. 168, 170.

34. Gary Hamel and C. K. Prahalad, *Competing for the Future* (Boston: Harvard Business School Press, 1994), p. 23.

35. Ibid., p. 156.

36. Daniel Sullivan and Alan Bauerschmidt, "The 'Basic Concepts' of International Business Strategy: A Review and Reconsideration," *Management International Review,* Special Issue 1991, pp. 111–124.

37. Also see B. Joseph Pine II and James H. Gilmore, "Welcome to the Experience Economy," *Harvard Business Review,* July–August 1998, pp. 97–105.

38. Kanter, "Change Is Everyone's Business," in press.

39. Also see Richard W. Wright and David A. Ricks, "Trends in International Business Research: Twenty-Five Years Later," *Journal of International Business Studies,* Fourth Quarter 1994, pp. 687–701.

Glossary

Achievement culture   A culture in which people are accorded status based on how well they perform their functions.

Achievement motivation theory   A theory which holds that individuals can have a need to get ahead to attain success and to reach objectives.

Act of state doctrine   A jurisdictional principle of international law which holds that all acts of other governments are considered to be valid by U.S. courts, even if such acts are illegal or inappropriate under U.S. law.

Adaptability screening   The process of evaluating how well a family is likely to stand up to the stress of overseas life.

Adaptive organizations   Organizations that are characterized by reaction to required changes but failure to anticipate them and stay on or ahead of the cutting edge.

Administrative coordination   Strategic formulation and implementation in which the MNC makes strategic decisions based on the merits of the individual situation rather than using a predetermined economically or politically driven strategy.

Analytical manager   A manager who is systematic and logical and carefully weighs alternatives to problems.

Arbitrator   An individual who provides a solution to a grievance that both sides (union and management representatives) have been unable to resolve themselves and that both sides agree to accept.

Ascription culture   A culture in which status is attributed based on who or what a person is.

Assessment center   An evaluation tool used to identify individuals with potential to be selected or promoted to higher-level positions.

Authoritarian leadership   The use of work-centered behavior designed to ensure task accomplishment.

Balance sheet approach   An approach to developing an expatriate compensation package that is based on ensuring the expat is "made whole" and does not lose money by taking the assignment.

Benchmarking   The process of identifying what leading-edge competitors are doing and then using this information to produce improved products or services.

Bicultural group   A group in which two or more members represent each of two distinct cultures, such as four Mexicans and four Taiwanese who have formed a team to investigate the possibility of investing in a venture.

Cafeteria approach   An approach to developing an expatriate compensation package that entails giving the individual a series of options and letting the person decide how to spend the available funds.

Centralization   A management system under which important decision are made at the top.

Chaebols   In South Korea, very large, family-held conglomerates, including internationally known firms, in which many key managers have attended school in the West and use this education to help formulate successful international strategies for their firms. *Chaebols* have considerable political and economic power in Korea.

Chromatics   The use of color to communicate messages.

Chronemics   The way in which time is used in a culture.

Civil or code law   Law that is derived from Roman law and is found in the non-Islamic and nonsocialist countries.

Codetermination   A legal system that requires workers and their managers to discuss major decisions.

Collective bargaining   The process whereby formal labor agreements are reached by union and management representatives; it involves the negotiation of wages, hours, and conditions of employment and the administration of the labor contract.

Collectivism   A culture in which people tend to belong to groups or collectives and to look after each other in exchange for loyalty.

Common law   Law that derives from English law and is the foundation of legislation in the United States, Canada, and England, among other nations.

Communication   The process of transferring meanings from sender to receiver.

Communitarianism   Refers to people regarding themselves as part of a group.

Confrontation meetings   The gathering and analysis of information related to intra- and intergroup conflict followed by the formulation of a plan of action by the participants for the purpose of resolving these problems.

Conglomerate investment   A type of high-risk investment in which goods or services produced are not similar to those produced at home.

Content theories   Theories that explain work motivation in terms of what arouses, energizes, or initiates employee behavior.

Context   Information that surrounds a communication and helps to convey the message.

Controlling   The process of evaluating results in relation to plans or objectives and deciding what action, if any, to take.

Cross-cultural school of management thought   An approach to international management holding that effective managerial behavior is a function of the specific culture: A successful manager in one location may not be effective in another location around the world.

Cultural assimilator   A programmed learning technique designed to expose members of one culture to some of the basic concepts, attitudes, role perceptions, customs, and values of another culture.

Culture The acquired knowledge that people use to interpret experience and to generate social behavior. This knowledge forms values, creates attitudes, and influences behavior.

Decentralization Pushing decision making down the line and getting the lower-level personnel involved.

Decision making The process of choosing a course of action among alternatives.

Delayed differentiation A manufacturing strategy in which all products are manufactured in the same way for all countries or regions until as late in the assembly process as possible, with differentiation of features or components introduced in the final stages of production.

Diffuse culture A culture in which both public and private space are similar in size and individuals guard their public space carefully, because entry into public space also affords entry into private space as well.

Direct controls The use of face-to-face or personal meetings for the purpose of monitoring operations.

Doctrine of comity A jurisdictional principle of international law which holds that there must be mutual respect for the laws, institutions, and government of other countries in the matter of jurisdiction over their own citizens.

Downward communication The transmission of information from superior to subordinate.

Economic imperative A worldwide strategy based on cost leadership, differentiation, and segmentation.

Eiffel Tower culture A culture that is characterized by a strong emphasis on hierarchy and orientation to the task.

Emotional culture A culture in which emotions are expressed openly and naturally.

Empowerment The process of giving individuals and teams the resources, information, and authority they need to develop ideas and effectively implement them.

Enterprise unions Unions that represent both the hourly and salaried employees of a particular company.

Environmental scanning The process of providing management with accurate forecasts of trends related to external changes in geographic areas where the firm currently is doing business and/or is considering setting up operations.

Esteem needs The needs for power and status.

Ethics The study of morality and standards of conduct.

Ethnocentric MNC An MNC that stresses nationalism and often puts home office people in charge of key international management positions.

Ethnocentric predisposition A nationalistic philosophy of management whereby the values and interests of the parent company guide the strategic decisions.

Ethnocentrism The belief that one's own way of doing things is superior to that of others.

European Research Cooperation Agency (Eureka) An agency that funds projects in the fields of energy, medical technology, biotechnology, communications, and the like, with the objective of making Europe more productive and competitive in the world market.

Expatriates Those who live and work away from their home country. They are citizens of the country where the multinational corporation is headquartered.

Expropriation The seizure of businesses by a host country with little, if any, compensation to the owners.

Factual manager A manager who looks at the available information and makes decisions based on that data.

Family culture A culture that is characterized by a strong emphasis on hierarchy and orientation to the person.

Femininity A situation in which the dominant values in society are caring for others and quality of life.

Foreign Corrupt Practices Act (FCPA) Made into U.S. law in 1977 because of concerns over bribes in the international business arena, this act makes it illegal to influence foreign officials through personal payment or political contributions.

Formalization The use of defined structures and systems in decision making, communicating, and controlling.

Franchise A business arrangement under which one party (the franchisor) allows another (the franchisee) to operate an enterprise using its trademark, logo, product line, and methods of operation in return for a fee.

Geocentric MNC An MNC that seeks to integrate diverse regions of the world through a global approach to decision making.

Geocentric predisposition A philosophy of management whereby the company tries to integrate a global systems approach to decision making.

Global area division A structure under which global operation are organized on a geographic rather than a product basis.

Global functional division A structure which organizes worldwide operations primarily based on function and secondarily on product.

Global international trade affiliations Trade relationships that cut across regional and industrial groups and are heavily concerned with political activities.

Globalization The production and distribution of products and services of a homogeneous type and quality on a worldwide basis.

Globalization imperative A belief that one worldwide approach to doing business is the key to both efficiency and effectiveness.

Global product division A structural arrangement in which domestic divisions are given worldwide responsibility for product groups.

Global sourcing The use of worldwide suppliers, regardless of where they are located geographically, who are best able to provide the needed output.

Grievance A complaint brought by an employee who feels that he or she has been treated improperly under the terms of the labor agreement.

Groupthink Social conformity and pressures on individual members of a group to conform and reach consensus.

Guanxi In China means good connections.

Guided missile culture A culture that is characterized by a strong emphasis on equality in the workplace and orientation to the task.

Haptics Communicating through the use of bodily contact.

Home-country nationals Expatriate managers who are citizens of the country where the multinational corporation is headquartered.

Homogeneous group   A group that is characterized by members who share similar backgrounds and generally perceive, interpret, and evaluate events in similar ways.

Honne   A Japanese term which means "what one really wants to do."

Horizontal investment   An MNC investment in foreign operations to produce the same goods or services as those produced at home.

Horizontal specialization   The assignment of jobs so that individuals are given a particular function to perform and tend to stay within the confines of this area.

Host-country nationals   Local managers who are hired by the MNC.

Hygiene factors   In the two-factor motivation theory, job context variables that include salary, interpersonal relations, technical supervision, working conditions, and company policies and administration.

Incubator culture   A culture that is characterized by a strong emphasis on equality and orientation to the person.

Indigenization laws   Laws that require that nationals hold a majority interest in the operation.

Indirect controls   The use of reports and other written forms of communication to control operations.

Individualism   A culture in which people tend to look after themselves and their immediate family only.

Industrial democracy   The rights that employees have to participate in significant management decisions.

Industrial internationals   Affiliates of the global international trade groups that focus on a particular industry.

Inpatriate   An individual from a host country or a third-country national who is assigned to work in the home country.

Integrative techniques   Techniques that help the overseas operation become a part of the host country's infrastructure.

International Confederation of Free Trade Unions (ICFTU)   The most important global international trade union confederation.

International division structure   A structural arrangement that handles all international operations out of a division created for this purpose.

International joint ventures (IJVs)   Formal arrangements with foreign partners who typically, although not always, are located in the country where the business will be conducted.

International Labour Office (ILO)   A United Nations affiliate, consisting of government, industry, and union representatives, that works to promote fair labor standards regarding health and safety, working conditions, and freedom of association for workers.

International management   The process of applying management concepts and techniques in a multinational, multicultural environment.

International selection criteria   Factors used to choose personnel for international assignments.

Intimate distance   Distance between people that is used for very confidential communications.

Intuitive manager   A manager who is imaginative, innovative, and able to jump from one idea to another.

Islamic law   Law that is derived from interpretation of the *Qur'an* and the teachings of the Prophet Mohammed and is found in most Islamic countries.

Job content factors   In work motivation, those factors internally controlled, such as responsibility, achievement, and the work itself.

Job context factors   In work motivation, those factors controlled by the organization, such as conditions, hours, earnings, security, benefits, and promotions.

Job design   A job's content, the methods that are used on the job, and the way the job relates to others in the organization.

Joint venture   An agreement in which two or more partners own and control an overseas business.

Kaizen   A Japanese term that means continuous improvement.

Karoshi   Overwork or job burnout, in Japanese.

Keiretsu   In Japan, a newly emerging organizational arrangement in which a large, often vertically integrated group of companies cooperate and work closely with each other to provide goods and services to end users; core members may be bound together by cross-ownership, long-term business dealings, interlocking directorates, and social ties.

Key factor for success (KFS)   A factor necessary for a firm to effectively compete in a market niche.

Kinesics   The study of communication through body movement and facial expressions.

Labor relations   The process through which management and workers identify and determine the job relations that will be in effect at the workplace.

Leadership   The process of influencing people to direct their efforts toward the achievement of some particular goal or goals.

Learning   The acquisition of skills, knowledge, and abilities that results in a relatively permanent change in behavior.

Learning organizations   Organization that are able to transform themselves by anticipating change and discovering new ways of creating products and services; they have learned how to learn.

License   An agreement that allows one party to use an industrial property right in exchange for payment to the other party.

Localization   An approach to developing an expatriate compensation package that involves paying the expat a salary comparable to that of local nationals.

Lockout   A company's refusal to allow workers to enter the facility during a labor dispute.

Lump sum method   An approach to developing an expatriate compensation package that involves giving the expat a predetermined amount of money and letting the individual make his or her own decisions regarding how to spend it.

Macro political risk analysis   Analysis that reviews major political decisions likely to affect all enterprises in the country.

Management by objectives (MBO)   A management system for the joint setting of subordinate goals, coaching and counseling personnel, and providing feedback on their performance.

Maquiladora industry   An arrangement created by the Mexican government that permits foreign manufacturers to send materials to their Mexican-based plants, process or assemble products, and ship them back out of Mexico with only the value added being taxed.

Masculinity A culture in which the dominant values are success, money, and things.

Mass customization Tailor-making mass-production products to meet the expectations of the customers.

Mediator A person who brings both sides (union and management representatives) together and helps them to reach a settlement that is mutually acceptable.

Micro political risk analysis Analysis directed toward government policies and actions that influence selected sectors of the economy or specific foreign businesses in the country.

Ministry of International Trade and Industry (MITI) A governmental agency in Japan that identifies and ranks national commercial pursuits and guides the distribution of national resources to meet these goals.

Mixed organization structure A structure that is a combination of a global product, area, or functional arrangement.

Monochronic time schedule A time schedule in which things are done in a linear fashion.

Motivation A psychologic process through which unsatisfied wants or needs lead to drives that are aimed at goals or incentives.

Motivators In the two-factor motivation theory, the job content factors which include achievement, recognition, responsibility, advancement, and the work itself.

Multicultural group A group in which there are individuals from three or more different ethnic backgrounds, such as three U.S., three German, three Uruguayan, and three Chinese managers who are looking into mining operations in South Africa.

Multidomestic A firm that operates production plants in different countries but makes no attempt to integrate overall operations.

National responsiveness The need to understand the different consumer tastes in segmented regional markets and respond to different national standards and regulations imposed by autonomous governments and agencies.

Nationality principle A jurisdictional principle of international law which holds that every country has jurisdiction over its citizens no matter where they are located.

Negotiation The process of bargaining with one or more parties for the purpose of arriving at a solution that is acceptable to all.

Neutral culture A culture in which emotions are held in check.

Nonreciprocal trade partners Nations that sell (export) goods to other countries but do not buy (import) from them.

Nonverbal communication The transfer of meaning through means such as body language and the use of physical space.

Normative manager A manager who is idealistic and concerned with how things should be done.

North American Free Trade Agreement (NAFTA) A free trade agreement, including the United States, Canada, and Mexico, that will effectively eliminate trade barriers between the three countries.

Oculesics The areas of communication that deal with conveying messages through the use of eye contact and gaze.

OD intervention The structured activity in which targeted individuals, groups, or units engage in accomplishing task goals that are related to organization development.

Operational risks Government policies and procedures that directly constrain management and performance of local operations.

Organization development (OD) The deliberate and reasoned introduction, establishment, reinforcement, and spread of change for the purpose of improving an organization's effectiveness.

Organization for Economic Cooperation and Development (OECD) A government, industry, and union group founded in 1976 that has established a voluntary set of guidelines for MNCs.

Organizational culture A pattern of basic assumptions that are developed by a group as it learns to cope with problems of external adaptation and internal integration and that are taught to new members as the correct way to perceive, think, and feel in relation to these problems.

Ownership-control risks Government policies or actions that inhibit ownership or control of local operations.

Paradox A statement that appears to be contradictory but is not, such as "increases in product quality often result in a decline of the cost of producing the goods."

Parochialism The tendency to view the world through one's own eyes and perspectives.

Participative leadership The use of both a work- or task-centered and people-centered approach to leading subordinates.

Particularism The belief that circumstances dictate how ideas and practices should be applied and something cannot be done the same everywhere.

Paternalistic leadership The use of work-centered behavior coupled with a protective employee-centered concern.

Perception A person's view of reality.

Personal distance In communicating, the physical distance used for talking with family and close friends.

Physiologic needs Food, clothing, shelter, and other basic, physical needs.

Political imperative Strategic formulation and implementation utilizing strategies that are country responsive and designed to protect local market niches.

Political risk The likelihood that a business's foreign investment will be constrained by a host government's policies.

Polycentric MNC An MNC that places local nationals in key positions and allows these managers to appoint and develop their own people.

Polycentric predisposition A philosophy of management whereby strategic decisions are tailored to suit the cultures of the countries where the MNC operations.

Polychronic time schedule A time schedule in which people tend to do several things at the same time and place higher value on personal involvement than on getting things done on time.

Power distance The extent to which less powerful members of institutions and organizations accept that power is distributed unequally.

Practical school of management thought A traditional approach to international management, which holds that effective managerial behavior is universal: a successful manager in one location will be effective in any other location around the world.

Principle of sovereignty   An international principle of law which holds that governments have the right to rule themselves as they see fit.

Problem-solving teams   Employee groups that discuss ways of improving quality, efficiency, and the overall work environment.

Process theories   Theories that explain work motivation by how employee behavior is initiated, redirected, and halted.

Product proliferation   The creation of a wide array of products that the competition cannot copy quickly enough.

Profit   The amount remaining after all expenses are deducted from total revenues.

Protective and defensive techniques   Techniques that discourage the host government from interfering in operations.

Protective principle   A jurisdictional principle of international law which holds that every country has jurisdiction over behavior that adversely affects its national security, even if the conduct occurred outside that country.

Proxemics   The study of the way people use physical space to convey messages.

Public distance   In communicating, the distance used when calling across the room or giving a talk to a group.

Quality control circle (QCC)   A group of workers who meet on a regular basis to discuss ways of improving the quality of work.

Quality imperative   Strategic formulation and implementation utilizing strategies of total quality management to meet or exceed customers' expectations and continuously improve products and/or services.

Regiocentric MNC   An MNC that relies on local managers from a particular geographic region to handle operations in and around that area.

Regiocentric predisposition   A philosophy of management whereby the firm tries to blend its own interests with those of its subsidiaries on a regional basis.

Regional internationals   Subdivisions of the global affiliation; regional applications of the global's activities.

Regional system   An approach to developing an expatriate compensation package that involves setting a compensation system for all expats who are assigned to a particular region and paying everyone in accord with that system.

Repatriation   The return to one's home country from an overseas management assignment.

Repatriation agreements   Agreements whereby the firm tells the individual how long she or he will be posted overseas and promises to give the individual, on return, a job that is mutually acceptable.

Return on investment   Return measured by dividing profit by assets.

Ringisei   From Japan, decision making by consensus.

Safety needs   In Maslow's hierarchy of needs, the desire for security, stability, and the absence of pain.

Self-actualization needs   In Maslow's hierarchy of needs, the desire to reach one's full potential by becoming everything one is capable of becoming.

Self-efficacy   A person's belief or confidence in his or her abilities to marshal the motivation, resources, and courses of action needed to successfully accomplish a specific task.

Self-management teams   Employee groups that take over supervisory duties and manage themselves; teams consist of individuals who learn all the tasks of all the group members, allowing team members to rotate jobs.

Simplification   The process of exhibiting the same orientation toward different culture groups.

Smallest space analysis (SSA)   A nonparametric multivariate analysis. This mathematic tool maps the relationship among the countries by showing the distance between each. By looking at this two-dimensional map, it is possible to see those countries that are similar to each other and those that are not.

Social distance   In communicating, the distance used to handle most business transactions.

Social needs   The need to interact and affiliate with others and the need to feel wanted by others.

Socialist law   Law that comes from the Marxist socialist system and continues to influence regulations in countries formerly associated with the Soviet Union as well as China.

Sociotechnical designs   Job designs that blend the personnel and the technology.

Special purpose teams   Employee groups that design and introduce work reforms and new technology.

Specialization   An organizational characteristic that assigns individuals to specific, well-defined tasks.

Specialized internationals   Trade union associations that function as components of intergovernmental agencies and lobby within these agencies.

Specific culture   A culture in which individuals have a large public space they readily share with others and a small private space they guard and share only with close friends and associates.

Strategic fit   An approach to strategically managing an organization that involves aligning resources in such a way as to mesh with the environment.

Strategic planning   The process of determining an organization's basic mission and long-term objectives, then implementing a plan of action for attaining these goals.

Strategic stretch   The creative use of resources to achieve ever more challenging goals.

Strategy implementation   The process of providing goods and services in accord with a plan of action.

Strike   A collective refusal to work to pressure management to grant union demands.

Subsidiary board of directors   A board that overseas and monitors the operations of a foreign subsidiary.

Survey feedback   An OD intervention that involves the gathering and analysis of information related to group behavior and problems and the feeding back of this information to develop effective action plans.

Tatemae   A Japanese term which means "doing the right thing" according to normal models of decision making.

Team building   An extension of classic T-groups (training groups) and sensitivity training that is geared to enhancing organizational effectiveness through cooperation and a "team" effort of key personnel.

Technology paradox   (Also see **Paradox**) That high-tech businesses can thrive at the very moment that their prices are falling the fastest.

Territoriality principle A jurisdictional principle of international law which holds that every nation has the right of jurisdiction within its legal territory.

Theory X manager A manager who believes that people are basically lazy and that coercion and threats of punishment often are necessary to get them to work.

Theory Y manager A manager who believes that under the right conditions people not only will work hard but will seek increased responsibility and challenge.

Third-country nationals Managers who are citizens of countries other than the one in which the MNC is headquartered or the one in which the managers are assigned to work by the MNC.

Third-party peacemaking The diagnosis of group conflict followed by the use of an outside party (usually the OD change agent) to facilitate a constructive resolution of a problem.

Token group A group in which all members but one have the same background, such as a group of Japanese retailers and a British attorney.

Total quality management (TQM) An organizational strategy and the accompanying techniques that result in the delivery of high-quality products and/or services to customers.

Training The process of altering employee behavior and attitudes in a way that increases the probability of goal attainment.

Transactional leaders Individuals who exchange rewards for effort and performance and work on a "something for something" basis.

Transfer risks Government policies that limit the transfer of capital, payments, production, people, and technology in and out of the country.

Transformational leaders Leaders who are visionary agents with a sense of mission and who are capable of motivating their followers to accept new goals and new ways of doing things.

Transition strategies Strategies used to help smooth the adjustment from an overseas to a stateside assignment.

Transnational corporations (TNCs) Multinational corporations that view the world as one giant market.

Transnational network structure A multinational structural arrangement that combines elements of function, product, and geographic designs, while relying on a network arrangement to link worldwide subsidiaries.

Two-factor theory of motivation A theory that holds there are two sets of factors that influence job satisfaction: hygiene factors and motivators.

Uncertainty avoidance The extent to which people feel threatened by ambiguous situations and have created beliefs and institutions that try to avoid these.

Union An organization that represents the workers and in collective bargaining has the legal authority to negotiate with the employer and administer the labor contract.

Universalism The belief that ideas and practices can be applied everywhere in the world without modification.

Upward communication The transfer of meaning from subordinate to superior.

Validity The quality of being effective, of producing the desired results. A valid test or selection technique measures what it is intended to measure.

Values Basic convictions that people have regarding what is right and wrong, good and bad, and important or unimportant.

Variety amplification The creation of uncertainty and the analysis of many alternatives regarding future action.

Variety reduction The limiting of uncertainty and the focusing of action on a limited number of alternatives.

Vertical investment The production of raw materials or intermediate goods that are to be processed into final products.

Vertical specialization The assignment of work to groups or departments where individuals are collectively responsible for performance.

Virtual corporation A network of companies that come together to exploit fast-changing opportunities and share costs, skills, and access to global markets.

Virtual organization An organization that is able to conduct business as if it were a very large enterprise when, in fact, it is much smaller, made up of core business competencies and the rest outsourced.

Wholly owned subsidiary An overseas operation that is totally owned and controlled by an MNC.

Work centrality The importance of work in an individual's life relative to other areas of interest.

World-class organization (WCOs) Enterprises that are able to compete with anybody, anywhere, anytime.

World Trade Organization (WTO) Started in 1995 to replace GATT, the WTO has power to enforce rulings in trade disputes and monitor trade policies.

Name and Organization Index

Subject Index

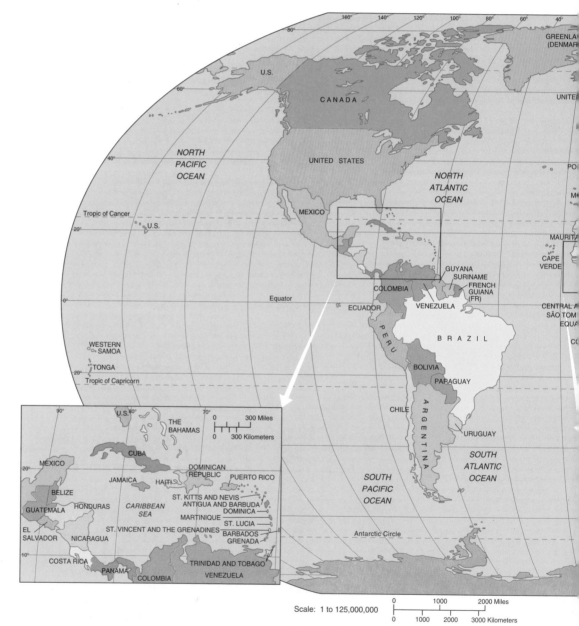

160° 140° 120° 100° 80° 60° 40°

80°

GREENLA
(DENMAR

U.S.

60°

CANADA

UNITE

NORTH
PACIFIC
OCEAN

UNITED STATES

NORTH
ATLANTIC
OCEAN

PO

40°

M

MEXICO

Tropic of Cancer

20°

MAURITA

U.S.

CAPE
VERDE

GUYANA
SURINAME
FRENCH
GUIANA
(FR)

COLOMBIA

VENEZUELA

CENTRAL A
SÃO TOM
EQUA

Equator

0°

ECUADOR

CO

P
E
R
U

B R A Z I L

WESTERN
SAMOA

BOLIVIA

TONGA

20°

PARAGUAY

Tropic of Capricorn

CHILE

A
R
G
E
N
T
I
N
A

URUGUAY

SOUTH
ATLANTIC
OCEAN

SOUTH
PACIFIC
OCEAN

Antarctic Circle

Scale: 1 to 125,000,000

0   1000   2000 Miles

0   1000   2000   3000 Kilometers

Note: All world maps are Robinson projection.

90° U.S. 80° 70°

THE
BAHAMAS

0   300 Miles

0   300 Kilometers

CUBA

MEXICO

20°

DOMINICAN
REPUBLIC

PUERTO RICO

JAMAICA

HAITI

BELIZE

ST. KITTS AND NEVIS
ANTIGUA AND BARBUDA

GUATEMALA

HONDURAS

CARIBBEAN
SEA

DOMINICA

MARTINIQUE

ST. LUCIA

EL
SALVADOR

NICARAGUA

ST. VINCENT AND THE GRENADINES

BARBADOS
GRENADA

10°

COSTA RICA

PANAMA

COLOMBIA

TRINIDAD AND TOBAGO

VENEZUELA